THE GREAT WAR

VOLUME 5

This Volume Combines Volume 5 & Volume 6
of an Original 13 Volume Set.

Reprinted 1999 from the 1916 editions
TRIDENT PRESS INTERNATIONAL
Copyright 1999

ISBN 1-582790-27-2 Standard Edition

Printed in Croatia

Frontispiece to Vol. V "THE GREAT WAR."

Specially painted by C. M. SHELDON.

Charging Through the German Trenches at Loos, September 25th 1915.

THE GREAT WAR

THE STANDARD HISTORY
OF THE ALL-EUROPE CONFLICT

EDITED BY

H. W. WILSON

Author of "With the Flag to Pretoria"
"Japan's Fight for Freedom" etc.

and

J. A. HAMMERTON

Editor "Harmsworth History of the World"

PROFUSELY ILLUSTRATED

VOLUME 5

LONDON
THE AMALGAMATED PRESS LIMITED
1916

CONTENTS OF VOLUME 5

SPECIAL PHOTOGRAVURE PLATES

THE GREAT WAR

THE STANDARD HISTORY OF THE ALL-EUROPE CONFLICT

VOLUME 5

CHAPTER LXXXIV.
INTRIGUE AND TREACHERY IN THE BALKANS.
By Robert Machray.

How the Situation in the Balkans Favoured the Entente when 1915 Opened—More in Seeming than in Reality—Factors at Work Below the Surface—The Balkans a Geographical and Historical Tragedy—Bitter Racial and Ecclesiastical Animosities Prevent Union of Balkan States—Yet Union their Only Strength—One Effort at Union—The Three Men who Made It—The Balkan League's Success in First Balkan War—How Discord Arose over Macedonia—Increased by Treaty of London—Bulgaria's Anger Exploited by Austria—How Bulgaria Fought Serbia and Greece, Rumania Intervened, and Turkey Recovered Lost Ground—Discomfiture of Bulgaria—Sinister Character of Ferdinand of Bulgaria—Entente Negotiations for Union of the Balkan States against Germany—Opposition of Germany—Demands of Bulgaria—How the Entente Tried to Meet Them—Struggle between Venizelos and the King of Greece—Fall of Venizelos—"The Terror of the Danube"—The Secret Treaty Between Bulgaria and Germany—Bulgaria Drops the Mask—Greece Mobilises—Sir Edward Grey's Warning—Russia's Ultimatum—Fresh Quarrel between Venizelos and Greek King—Venizelos Again Resigns—French and British Troops Land at Salonika—The Secret Treaty Revealed—Serbia Invaded

A**T the beginning of 1915 the situation in the Balkans appeared to be distinctly favourable to the Entente Powers. To the surprise of the whole world, the third invasion of Serbia by Austria had in the end been disastrously defeated by the heroic mountaineers, their astonishing victories culminating in one of the most dramatic episodes of the war—the recapture on December 15th, 1914, of Belgrade, their capital, after it had been in the hands of their arrogant enemy for no longer a period than a fortnight.

Bitterly humiliated, but on that account all the more determined to destroy her small but unexpectedly formidable opponent, Austria soon concentrated on the Danube another large and powerful army. In January, however, her attention was diverted from Serbia by successful Russian offensives in Bukovina and in the Carpathians, which placed Hungary in danger, and led her to withdraw the bulk of her forces from the Balkan frontier and mass them in her

MR. HUGH O'BEIRNE, C.B., C.V.O.
Succeeded Sir H. G. O. Bax-Ironside, K.C.M.G., as British Minister in Sofia, a few weeks before the British declaration of war against Bulgaria.

[Kate Pragnell

threatened territory—with the result that the little kingdom was given a respite from serious attack.

Serbia was the pivot on which the war turned in South-Eastern Europe, and her signal defeat of the big bully who had planned to compass her ruin was of vital service to the Entente Powers, as it prevented the Austro-Germans from carrying out then their cherished project of linking up with their ally Turkey.

The striking triumph of Serbia had naturally a marked effect on the other Balkan States, who, as the new year opened, were still further impressed by the débâcle of the Turks which Russia brought about in the Caucasus and, later, by the Russian operations against Austria. Greece, allied by treaty with Serbia and inalienably hostile to Turkey, rejoiced, the great majority of her people showing openly their strong animosity to the Germanic league. Popular feeling was deeply stirred in Rumania, whose contiguity to Bukovina made the Russian occupation of that province of peculiarly intimate interest, and whose

in spite of Russian and Serbian victories. Well might the Balkans be called the witches' cauldron of Europe!

The geography of the Near Eastern region was an embodied tragedy. In some period not geologically far distant a vast subsidence of the earth's crust took place in that quarter—the Balkan countries, the Ægean Islands, and Asia Minor—the highlands of the submerged continent remaining above the invading waters. Of these survivals the area to which the ranges of the Balkans have given their name was a veritable maze of mountains, broken only by small rivers, and devoid of valleys or plains suitable for large communities. Within the peninsula there was no natural centre around which, as a nucleus, a really great State could **Geographical and** form and grow. This meant **historical tragedy** that amongst the inhabitants of the land intense rivalries were sure to develop. From north to south there was but one highway —or rather defile, for it was not unobstructed— the road from the Danube at the modern Belgrade to Salonika on the sea. It had been the avenue along which many armies had passed, and nothing was more significant of the terror it inspired than the fact that, with the exception of a few cities, the towns and villages hid themselves away from it in the hills. There were two other natural highways, both branching from the north-to-south road; one went south-east to the Bosphorus—another blood-stained passage—and the other struck west to the Adriatic; both were difficult, being defiles rather than roads.

History is the child of geography, and the story

KING CONSTANTINE AND M. VENIZELOS.
The King of the Hellenes chatting with his Prime Minister prior to the latter's resignation in October, 1915.

hopes of union with her blood-brethren in Transylvania flamed high because of the terrible reverses Austria had sustained. M. Take Jonescu, one of Rumania's leading statesmen, declared emphatically that his country would cast in her lot with Great Britain, France and Russia, and said he was confident that Bulgaria, of whose probable course he professed himself to be well informed, would act in a similar manner.

But if the aspect of affairs in the Balkans thus looked roseate for the Powers of the Entente, there were factors in the situation which, on close scrutiny, **Treachery beneath** inevitably suggested that beneath the **the surface** smiling surface lay treacherous, perilous depths. These factors were based on geography and racialism, and rooted in history and religion. They included the aspirations and ambitions, the passions and the prejudices, the struggles and the bitternesses of hundreds of years all centred, as by a burning glass, in the war. In no other portion of the globe, or within so comparatively small a part of its extent, could there be found such a welter of human beings, such differences of character, disposition and outlook, as in the Balkans. And over all towered the colossal form of the Central Powers, whose "Drang nach Osten" was a constant menace to their independence, if not their very existence, long before the war began, and still was a force to be reckoned with

M. ELEUTHEROS VENIZELOS. *[Barnett.*
Greek patriot and statesman. Retired from his position as Premier on King Constantine refusing to support his policy.

of the Balkans but accentuated the tragedy which Nature had imposed. In modern times that story revolved round the slow, painful deliverance from the Turks of the races they had conquered centuries before, and the establishment of these races in the kingdoms of Greece, Serbia, Rumania, and Bulgaria. Montenegro, of close kin to Serbia, never had been entirely subdued, and Albania, though it had been made into a principality, was not much more than a mere name. At the outset of the war, Greece,

Serbia, Montenegro, Rumania, and Bulgaria were known collectively as the Balkan States; but, except between Serbia and Montenegro, and more loosely between Serbia and Greece, genuine cohesion did not exist. Neither in race nor in religion did they find a bond of union. The Serbians and the Bulgarians hated each other, though they came of Slav stock, and racially neither had anything in common with the Greeks, nor with the Rumanians, who were of Latin origin, and whose territory, properly speaking, lay outside the Balkans, yet was brought within their orbit by the force of circumstances. Furthermore, of the monarchs who occupied the Balkan thrones only the

BRITISH TROOPS DISEMBARKING AT SALONIKA.
When, in October, 1915, Bulgaria threw in her lot with Austria, Germany, and Turkey, British and French troops were landed at Salonika to aid Serbia, Greece making only a purely formal protest.

ARRIVAL OF BRITISH TRANSPORT AT SALONIKA.
The landings at Salonika proceeded in perfect order. It was reported that some enemy submarines tried to cause trouble, but without any success.

At various times in their history one Balkan State or another had invoked and received the assistance of one or the other of these Great Powers, and hence the policy of individual States had a definite leaning towards Austria or Russia.

It might be thought that at least in one direction the Balkan States would have presented a united front — that is, against Turkey; but the only union of the States against her did not include them all, and eventually led to further divisions, which seriously complicated the whole Balkan situation. This union produced the First Balkan War, and it looked at its outset as if the world were in sight of

Kings of Serbia and Montenegro were natives. The faith professed by the bulk of the Balkan peoples was that of the Eastern or Greek Church, but the religious organisation of each country was independent of that of the others, and all were at variance.

Yet it was in union, and only in union, that the Balkan States could be really strong. Separately each was weak; but together their population approximated to twenty millions, and, having universal and compulsory service, they would have been able to put into the field very nearly two million of men—a formidable army which not even a Great Power could despise. Mutual **Balkans' strength in union** interests in commerce and industries did not suffice to unite them. Outside pressure might conceivably have welded them into one; outside pressure there was, but it was divided, and instead of leading to a confederation of the States, had the effect of making it impossible. They were overshadowed by Austria and Russia, both of whom showed the deepest concern with their affairs; but as these mighty empires were rivals, the one more or less offset the other.

the achievement of what had been held impossible—the formation of a veritable Balkan League, which was the title given **Balkan League's deceptive promise** to the allied States who declared war on Turkey at the close of September, 1912. Rumania stood aloof; her interest, however, in the struggle was less direct than that of the others. On the other hand, her very aloofness from it made her position decisive in the conflict which came afterwards. In spite of the fact that Bulgaria and Serbia had not been friends, and had tried conclusions on the battlefield of Slivnitza with disaster to the Serbians, they were the first members of the League. Greece joined them a little later, and with Serbia went Montenegro. This union of four of the States was in the main the work of three remarkable men, natives of the country, Pasich the Serbian, Gueshoff the Bulgarian, and Venizelos the Greek, each of them being at the time Prime Minister of his State.

The story of Eleutheros Venizelos was one of the romances of modern politics. When he was no more than fifteen he shouldered a rifle in Crete, which then belonged to Turkey, and fought bravely with other insurgents to bring about

BRITISH STRETCHER-BEARERS PASSING FRENCH INFANTRY ON THEIR WAY FROM SALONIKA TO CAMP.

While the Allies were landing troops at Salonika in the early part of October, 1915, gallant little Serbia was being attacked from the north by Austro-German forces under Generals von Mackensen, von Gallwitz and von Koevess, and from the east by the Bulgarians. While the Teutonic forces occupied Belgrade, the Bulgarians attacked the Salonika-Nish railway near Vrania. It was announced that the French General Sarrail was in full command of the allied operations. The British troops were met on their arrival by Brigadier-General A. B. Hamilton.

4

the cession of the island to Greece. For long this was his chief aim in life. His honesty caused him to protest against the arbitrary rule of Prince George of Greece, to whom, as High Commissioner, the Powers had entrusted the government of Crete on its being handed over by the Turks, and he was instrumental in procuring that prince's recall. He came to have a great reputation in Greece, and 1910 brought him his opportunity there. In the previous year, as the result of a peaceful revolution headed by

DR. DANEFF.
The Bulgarian patriot, one of the most enthusiastic followers of Karaveloff, the founder of the party which arose in opposition to the anti-Russian propaganda of the notorious Stambuloff.

certain Army officers, Greece was governed for some months by "The Military League," but finding the situation getting beyond control, the League appealed to Venizelos, then Prime Minister of Crete, for help. Within three weeks he brought order out of chaos by obtaining the consent of all parties, including the King, who had thought of abdicating, to the creation of a National Assembly to revise the constitution. Shortly afterwards he became Prime Minister of Greece, and immediately set about reorganising the administration and reconstructing the Army and Navy. Simple in life and unaffected in manners, he had the gift of persuasive eloquence, a cool judgment joined to the power of rapid decision, and executive ability of the highest kind.

M. Pasich, the Premier of Serbia, was by profession an engineer, but soon turned his attention to politics, in which he achieved marked success. He was not always on the winning side, for during the reign of King Milan he stoutly

Workers for Balkan unity opposed the pro-Austrian policy of that sovereign, was arrested, and thrown into prison. Easily the best and most progressive politician in Serbia, he was a strenuous advocate of the unification of Serbia, Montenegro, Bosnia, Herzegovina, Dalmatia, Croatia, Slavonia, and the Slovene districts of Austria in one mighty confederation of the Southern Slavs.

Of M. Gueshoff, the third of the Balkan leaders, not so much was known, but he was a statesman of the first rank, a far-sighted patriot, and a man in whom the majority of

the Bulgarians had every confidence. Behind him, however, stood the sinister figure of Ferdinand, the King, a crafty, intriguing prince with ideas of his own, one of which was to make himself not only Autocrat of Bulgaria but of All the Balkans.

The Balkan League had for its object the freeing of Macedonia and Albania from the Turks, and the division among its members of the land thus acquired. The chief preoccupation of Bulgaria was to get Macedonia; of Serbia, to obtain an outlet to the sea through Northern Albania (of which Montenegro also desired a share); and of Greece, to add to herself Epirus, in Southern Albania, Crete, and some at least of the Ægean Islands.

War broke out on September 30th, 1912, and its issue was a wonderful triumph for the League. The Bulgarians were victorious at Lule Burgas,

M. P. HADJIMISCHEFF.
Bulgarian Minister in London from December, 1914, to October, 1915.

and the Serbians at Kumanovo, while the Greeks drove their old enemy to and then from Salonika. Adrianople was occupied, and Constantinople threatened. The Serbians reached Durazzo on the Adriatic, and the Montenegrins took Scutari. Turkey, hopelessly beaten, sued for peace, which was arranged by the Treaty of London, May 30th, 1913.

The very success of the Leaguers, however, opened up grave disputes among them, and one of the Great Powers that overshadowed the Balkans, and had hoped that

SIR FRANCIS E. H. ELLIOT.
British Minister to Greece. He went to Athens in 1903, after being Consul-General at Sofia from 1895 to 1903.

SIR GEORGE H. BARCLAY.
British Minister to Rumania. He went to Bukarest in 1912. In 1906 he was at the British Embassy in Constantinople.

SIR CHARLES LOUIS DES GRAZ.
British Minister to Serbia. He was appointed in 1913, having been formerly attached to the Legations at Teheran, Athens, and Rome.

MAP OF THE BALKANS BEFORE THE FIRST BALKAN WAR
OF 1912-13.

without her there could have been no League, and that Turkey could not have been conquered, she yet obtained less under the Treaty of London than either Serbia or Greece.

Macedonia, or rather " the Macedonian Question," as it was termed, had for years been one of the open sores both of the Balkans and of Europe. Bounded on the north by the Kara Range and Bulgaria, on the east by the Mesta, on the south by the Ægean and Greece, and on the west by the Shar, Grammus, and Pindus chains, the province derived its importance mainly from containing the valley of the Vardar, the southern part of the great natural highway across the Balkans, the gate of which in the north was Belgrade and in the south **" The Macedonian** Salonika. A railway connected the two **Question "** cities, crossed the Danube, and linked up with Central Europe. The vast majority of the population, which was over two million, was Christian, Greek or Bulgar ; Salonika, a city of 160,000 souls, was largely Jewish.

Bulgaria, after being subjected to atrocities which shocked the world, was rescued from Turkey by Russia, aided by Rumania, in 1877-78, after a desperate and pro-tracted struggle. By the Treaty of San Stefano, March 3rd, 1878, all Macedonia, except Salonika and the Chalcidic Peninsula, was included in Bulgaria, but this was set aside by the Treaty of Berlin, July 13th, 1878, which gave Macedonia back to the Turks who, however, covenanted to reform their administration of it, according the Powers the right of seeing this bargain carried out.

Turkey, taking advantage of the rivalries of the Powers, introduced few reforms, and the general condition of the province gradually became worse instead of better. When the revolution brought about by the Young Turks suc-ceeded, and the restoration of the Turkish Constitution

the war, through the defeat of the League, would lead to her own profit, persistently busied herself in adding fuel to the flames. This Great Power was Austria. Had she acted differently, there would have been no Second Balkan War ; but she hated Serbia, and already was resolved on her destruction.

Largely because of the determined attitude of Austria, who had the support of Germany in the London Conference, Albania was made an independent principality, Serbia was denied its coveted outlet, and Greece was deprived of Epirus, while Montenegro had to give up Scutari. Both Serbia and Greece had conquered parts of Macedonia during the war, nor would they yield to Bulgaria those portions which she had earmarked for herself.

The Treaty of   Macedonia was the rock on which the
London   League went to pieces. The Treaty of London confirmed Serbia and Greece in the possession of the portion of the province from which they had ousted the Turks, and no more than a month passed when Bulgaria, deeply resentful, particularly with Serbia, and secretly egged on by Austria, plunged the Balkans into war again.

Feeling between the two little Slav nations was most bitter ; their immemorial mutual hatred was stirred to the lowest depths. Both had a case. Serbia maintained that at the London Conference Bulgaria failed to back up her claim to a port in Albania, and, therefore, that she was entitled to compensation in Macedonia ; but Bulgaria retorted that the treaty between herself and Serbia, which had been entered into before the war and was the founda-tion of the League, definitely assigned to her that part of Macedonia which Serbia had taken, and further, that this territory was inhabited by Bulgarians, who desired to unite themselves with her and not with Serbia. Bul-garia undoubtedly had a certain amount of justice on her side, and it was unquestionably the fact that, although

MAP SHOWING THE NEW BALKAN FRONTIERS, AS SETTLED
BY THE TREATY OF BUKAREST IN 1913, AT THE CLOSE OF
THE SECOND BALKAN WAR.

RUMANIAN INFANTRY ON THE MARCH.
The Rumanian infantry was armed with the Mannlicher magazine rifle (calibre '256).

MOUNTED BATTERY OF THE RUMANIAN ARTILLERY.
Both horse and field batteries of the Rumanian artillery were armed with the 75 mm. Krupp quick-firer.

of 1876 was proclaimed, the Powers, looking for a change in the state of Macedonia, desisted from urging reforms; but there was no improvement under the Young Turks. The Bulgars of Macedonia turned their eyes to Bulgaria, and it was to deliver them that she allied herself with Serbia against Turkey. The Treaty of London, however, placed them under Serbia.

Rankling under what she considered an intolerable wrong, and incited by Austria, her evil genius, who was playing a deep game of her own, Bulgaria suddenly began the Second Balkan War, on June 29th, 1913, but was defeated—to her great surprise and the profound disappointment of Austria, who had anticipated an opposite issue. Within a fortnight Rumania intervened with such

The Second Balkan War decisive effect that the conflict was at an end, and on August 10th of the same year, the terms of peace were settled by the Treaty of Bukarest, the upshot being that Bulgaria was left in a much worse position than that existing after the first war. She had to give a slice of her own territory to Rumania, and return a portion of Thrace, including Adrianople, to the Turks, who had taken advantage of her reverses to regain some of the ground which they had lost to her shortly before. Serbia kept South-East Macedonia, and Greece both Salonika and Kavala, the latter the natural economic outlet of Bulgaria on the Ægean. Bulgaria retained as a port on that sea the poor roadstead of Dedeagach, but as some miles of the railway by which it was reached passed through Turkish territory, the operation of the line was dependent on the goodwill of Turkey.

Naturally, the Bulgarians were wroth with Serbia, Greece, and Rumania, but it was against the first that their anger burned hottest; many of them were furious with their King, and threatening notices were displayed on his palace walls. Expecting a successful issue from the Balkan Wars and the realisation of his grand dreams of becoming Autocrat of All the Balkans, King Ferdinand had ordered, it was reported, a magnificent diamond crown to be made for him in Paris for his coronation in Constantinople; but here, at any rate for a time, was an end to his dreams.

Ferdinand of Bulgaria was in some respects the most striking figure among the Balkan sovereigns; if for nothing else, his inordinate ambition placed him in a separate class. Of mixed German and French blood, he was connected with some of the highest families of Europe, and he had inherited from his mother, a daughter of Louis Philippe, immense wealth. His mind and talents, which were not inconsiderable, were bent on securing a great position for himself. Elected Prince of Bulgaria in 1877, when the country was still under the suzerainty of Turkey, he strove in all manner of ways, some of them devious enough, to add to his dignity and importance. He was ill-content with the little principality, but he had the satisfaction of declaring it independent of Turkey in 1908, and of being recognised by the Powers as "King of the Bulgarians"—he preferred to style himself Tsar. Before going to Bulgaria he had been an officer of the Austrian Army, he had vast estates in Hungary, and his sympathies were markedly pro-Austrian, whereas the bulk of his people regarded with reverence Russia, who had freed them from Turkish tyranny. Russia did not look on him with much favour, and to please her, as well as the Bulgarians, he had his son Boris baptised into the Orthodox Church. In spite of his mental powers, he was personally a coward, and always kept well in the rear of the fighting-line. In the **Character of King Ferdinand** First Balkan War he was fortunate in having in his service two military men of eminence, General Savoff and General Radko Dimitrieff, and it was owing to them, and more especially to the leadership of the latter, that Bulgaria was successful in that conflict. He put the blame for the Second Balkan War on General Savoff, but it was well known that he himself was the culprit.

When the European War broke out in 1914, Bulgaria declared herself neutral, but Ferdinand kept an eager eye for some congenial opening. He must have been terribly disappointed with the splendid victories the Serbians won over the Austrians, but he bided his time.

Of the other Balkan monarchs, King Peter of Serbia was old, infirm, and ill, but he had shown the fine fibre

SERBIAN GUNNERS DEFENDING THEIR NORTHERN FRONTIER AGAINST THE AUSTRO-GERMAN INVADERS.

Though with the aid of their heavy guns the Austro-German forces soon drove the Serbians out of Belgrade and pierced Serbian territory south and south-west of the capital, the passage of the Danube and the conquest of the hills behind Semendria were only achieved after a desperate resistance on the part of the heroic Serbs. The Serbian artillery, in particular, made a brilliant and memorable stand.

PANORAMIC VIEW OF THE TOWN OF STRUMNITZA.
Strumnitza (or Strumitza) is a Macedonian town just inside the Bulgarian frontier, about sixty miles north-west of Salonika, and about twelve miles from the Serbian railway-station of the same name.

The treaty which existed between Greece and Serbia against Bulgaria contained a provision for the lease to Serbia for fifty years of a small tract of land at Salonika, and for running powers over the Greek portion of the railway from that city to the north. It was in this way that Serbia was remunitioned by the French and the British in November and December, 1914, and was enabled to defeat the third Austrian invasion.

King Nicholas of Montenegro identified himself and his tiny State with Serbia throughout. He it was who commenced the

of which he was made by appearing in the trenches when the plight of his country seemed desperate during the third Austrian invasion, and, by telling his soldiers that they might, if they pleased, return to their homes, but that he and his sons would die where they stood, so inspired them with enthusiasm that they fought as never had they fought before. He had retired from the active government of his kingdom, his second son, Prince Alexander, having been appointed Regent.

King Ferdinand of Rumania came to the throne on October 11th, 1914, in succession to his uncle King Carol, and was an unknown quantity. The Second Balkan War had given the leadership in the Balkans to Rumania. King Carol was a Hohenzollern, and Rumania, who did not easily forgive Russia for the loss of Bessarabia in 1878, was for many years pro-German, and had, it was said, a treaty with Germany of a defensive character, perhaps similar to that which subsisted between Italy and Austria-Germany. Latterly, however, the Rumanians had leaned somewhat to Russia, chiefly because of their desire for union with the four millions of their kin in Transylvania—a union which they could not hope to consummate through Austria. Besides, they were sincerely friendly to France, and were on excellent terms with Italy.

Rumania and Greece

Rumania was in no hurry to make up her mind. She enjoyed a very profitable trade with Austria and Germany, and powerful vested interests were hostile to action. There was also the problem of the Dardanelles, a favourable solution of which was most important to her, as, apart from the Black Sea, she had access to the Mediterranean only by land routes through other countries which could be closed against her. Her position was a difficult one, and she remained neutral, as did Greece.

King Constantine had ascended the throne of Greece on March 18th, 1913, after the assassination of his father, King George, by a lunatic at Salonika; but he was married to the Princess Sophia of Prussia, the only sister of the Kaiser William, by whom he was made a German field-marshal, and strong German influence was brought to bear upon him. In the earlier part of his career he had been extremely unpopular with the Greeks; but his success in the Balkan Wars completely altered their attitude towards him and made him a favourite—he was the idol of the Greek Army. Venizelos had been his father's staunch friend and trusted adviser, and he continued him in the Premiership. But Venizelos, like most of his countrymen, was anti-German, and thus there was the probability of sharp differences between him and the King.

THE ANCIENT AND PICTURESQUE SEAPORT OF ENOS
On the south side of the gulf of the same name, twelve miles east-south-east of the Bulgarian port of Dedeagach. Serious damage was inflicted upon the harbour works, railway-station, and shipping at Dedeagach by the allied bombardment on October 21st, 1915.

attack on the Turks in the First Balkan War, and when Austria declared war on Serbia in July, 1914, he took up arms in support of the bigger-brother Slav nation. He and his people were pro-Russian in their sympathies.

Although apparently favourable to the Entente Powers, the general situation in January, 1915, in the Balkan States, apart from Serbia and Montenegro, was thus in reality confused and doubtful. If in Rumania, in Greece, and even in Bulgaria there were pro-Entente elements, there also were elements which were distinctly pro-German; in Bulgaria opinion was biased by hatred of Serbia, and in a less degree of Greece and Rumania, and the Austrian predilections of the King materially affected the whole attitude of the country.

Beginning of the crisis

The best hope for the Balkan States themselves lay in

BULGARIAN ARTILLERY INSIDE THE CHATALJA
BATTERIES.

THE BULGARIAN GENERAL SAVOFF.
This distinguished soldier (seen on the right) was falsely blamed by
King Ferdinand for the Second Balkan War.

BULGARIAN FIELD TELEGRAPH AT WORK.

their union, and as this union also was manifestly to the disadvantage of Germany, the Powers of the Entente worked assiduously to bring it about. The principal effort of the Entente was directed to the reconciliation of Bulgaria with the other States, who, she maintained, had "robbed" her of territory, though it was obvious that she had lost it in consequence of being defeated in a war which she herself had sprung on her former friends.

To placate Bulgaria meant concessions from the others, and the next eight months—until well into September—were chiefly concerned with the endeavours of the Entente to secure such concessions, and, having succeeded in their attempts, to get Bulgaria to accept them. But in this field, as in every other, the Entente Powers were faced with the persistent and unscrupulous opposition of Germany. It is now known that in January a secret agreement had been negotiated between Bulgaria and Germany. This was signed a little later by Prince Bülow and M. Rizoff at Rome.

Bulgaria's secret treaty

The respite given to Serbia by her great defeat of the third invasion by Austria proved to be a long one, as the attention of her enemy was almost entirely occupied for several months—first by the Austro-German campaign against Russia and, secondly, by defensive operations against Italy, who joined the Entente Powers on May 23rd, 1915.

It was not till the beginning of October, 1915, that Serbia was called on to meet another serious attack, the fighting which took place in the interval being comparatively unimportant; but during a considerable part of that time she had to encounter foes of a different and exceedingly formidable kind.

The Austrians, on being driven out of Valievo, had left behind them a dreadful legacy in the shape of typhus and other terrible maladies, and these diseases fastened themselves on the unfortunate Serbians, who succumbed in large numbers. The brave little country had suffered heavy losses in its conflicts with Austria, as well as in the First and Second Balkan Wars, and, utterly unprepared for fighting these new and more insidious enemies, which threatened the utter extermination of its people, it sent forth a cry for help, which was heard and responded to in

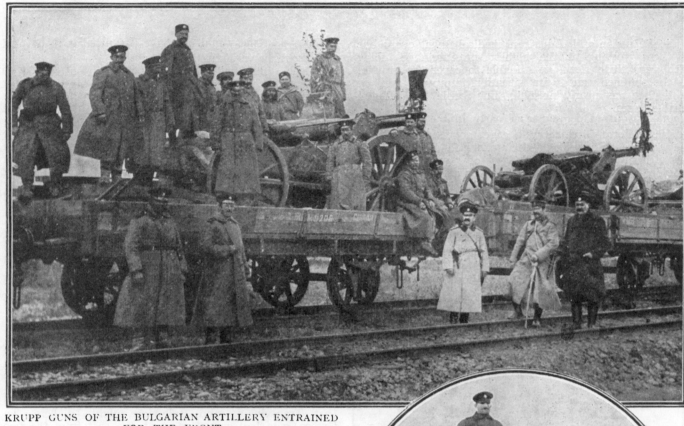

KRUPP GUNS OF THE BULGARIAN ARTILLERY ENTRAINED FOR THE FRONT.

Great Britain, France, Russia, the United States, and other lands. Organisations were formed for assisting Serbia in this extremity, and private persons also came forward with offers of money and service. The Red Cross bestirred itself actively, but, overwhelmed with demands elsewhere, was unable to do much. Sir Thomas Lipton took his yacht, the Erin, to Salonika with a supply of doctors, nurses, and medical stores. Lady Paget, Lady Wimborne, and other women of rank in England devoted their whole energies to the cause.

A society of women doctors, known as the Scottish Women's Hospitals, an organisation which was the offspring of the Scottish Federation of the National Union of Women's Suffrage Societies, did a noble work in Serbia. After sending two hospital units to France, the Scottish Women despatched the third they had raised and equipped to the Balkan State, which received it with the deepest gratitude, agreeing with enthusiasm to pay the salaries of its members and the cost of its maintenance. It was stationed at Kragujevatz, where it was given a hospital of two hundred and fifty beds.

Women's noble work in Serbia

There were thousands of desperate cases in the country—men, women, and children dying everywhere unattended and in the most distressing circumstances—and hardly had the unit arrived in the sorrowful land when, recognising the immensity of the effort required, it inundated the mother society with telegrams and letters appealing for more doctors and nurses. The tales these messages told were of the saddest and darkest kind. Owing to the virulent character of the fevers that ravaged every district, the mortality was frightful; in many localities fifty per cent. of the sufferers died.

With all possible speed funds for another hospital unit were invited. In memory of Miss Fraser, the woman golfer who had perished of typhus in Serbia, several well-known golfers sent in handsome contributions. Sufficient money was soon forthcoming, and the unit was got together and sent out; but the cry was for more and more medical assistance, and later a third unit followed the second. All the spring and summer of that year the need of Serbia was extreme. In July there were in that country four hundred and twenty British doctors, in addition to

BOMB-PROOF SHELTER IN THE BULGARIAN LINES.

BULGARIAN SIEGE-GUN IN POSITION, WITH ITS CREW.

11

French, Russian and American medical men, every one of them working at the highest pressure, and doing with very little sleep, yet unable to cover the ground. As the summer waned the situation improved, and by September was nearly normal; but Serbia had endured terrible losses.

Offers were made to Serbia early in the year by the Germanic Powers, which were eager to detach her from the Entente. She rejected their offers on receiving from the British Government pledges of "solid support," provided she reorganised her Army for a fresh campaign. She had not succeeded, unfortunately, in making good these pledges, and when her hour of desperate danger came the 500,000 allied troops needed to save her were not within easy reach.

Negotiations had been proceeding under the auspices

BROTHER-IN-LAW OF THE KAISER.
A remarkable photograph of King Constantine, who succeeded to the throne of Greece on the assassination of his father (George I.) on March 18th, 1913. He married the German Emperor's sister, Princess Sophia of Prussia, in 1889. His hesitation to support the cause of the Allies compelled M. Venizelos twice to resign the Premiership.

of the Entente in furtherance of the union of the Balkan States, and some progress was made, but from the beginning Bulgaria pursued a tortuous course. Rumania had earlier received financial assistance from Austria, but in January a change in the direction of her policy was indicated by her obtaining a loan from Great Britain **Rumania's loan** of several millions, most of which she **from Britain** applied to her Army, then partially mobilised.

On the other side of the account, Bulgaria got money from Berlin. Attempts were made at the time to explain away the political bearing of the transaction by representing the advance as an instalment of a loan the terms of which had been concluded long before the war, but the essential fact was that the cash came from Germany at

a time when she would not have permitted it to be paid out except for very substantial reasons.

In the same month Rumania tried to arrange with Bulgaria for common action by offering to restore to her part of the territory of which she had been deprived under the Treaty of Bukarest. Bulgaria coquetted with the proposal, but let it be understood that her price for joining in a union of the States which would support the Entente was the part of Macedonia allotted to her by the treaty of alliance between herself and Serbia prior to the First Balkan War, the Valley of the Struma including the port of Kavala, the southern Dobruja, the whole of the territory Rumania had annexed under the Treaty of Bukarest, and that area of Thrace which she herself had taken from the Turks in 1912.

Bulgaria asked a great deal. The Entente Powers took counsel with the other Balkan States, and in order to induce them to fall in, as far as possible, with the Bulgarian programme, suggested certain compensations for what they were asked to surrender. To Serbia, who at first was very averse from the idea of ceding the desiderated part of Macedonia to Bulgaria, they pointed out that she could find compensation in **Bulgaria's big** adding to her territory Bosnia, Herze- **price** govina, and other Slav provinces and districts of Austria—that, in fact, she would be able to realise that confederation of the Southern Slavs which had been the ideal of Pasich, her ablest statesman. To Rumania, who already was willing to meet Bulgaria half-way, they said that Transylvania and Bukovina might be hers. To Greece, who had gained more at less cost from the two Balkan Wars than the others, and so might be generous, they held out the prospect of obtaining a considerable area in Asia Minor, in which many thousands of people of her own race were domiciled. To Montenegro, who did not look for much, and who, in any case, might wish to attach herself to the projected confederation of the Southern Slavs under the headship of her friend Serbia, they stated that she could have Scutari and part of the Albanian coast. And as for Thrace, Turkey would have to yield not only the part of it Bulgaria wanted, but also a very large extent of her whole empire.

These suggestions of change and compensation were all dependent on the complete defeat of Germany, which the Entente Powers were confident was a certainty; but Bulgaria requested that at least some—and particularly one or two, such as Serbian Macedonia—of the proposed cessions should be actually made to her forthwith.

Here was a great stumbling-block in the negotiations. The other Balkan States considered that, admitting even that the result of the war would be absolutely in favour of the Entente, these cessions might very well wait till the war had come to an end. In principle they were inclined to agree with the proposals submitted by the Entente.

Venizelos, in a memorandum to the King of the Hellenes, wrote that on the part of Greece concessions were possible to Bulgaria in return for compensation in Asia Minor, the concessions he had in his mind being the Struma Valley with Kavala. But to the evident intention of Bulgaria to aggrandise herself at their expense, before any of the suggested compensations were in sight, the other States took exception. In February no real advance towards a settlement had been made, although a special French Mission, with General Pau at its head, visited the Balkan capitals and tried to expedite matters. But that month was signalised by an event—the bombardment of the Dardanelles by the warships of the Entente—which had a considerable influence in the Balkans, Greece in particular being greatly stirred by it. Venizelos stated, in an interview some weeks later, that he was privy to this action, and had proposed despatching 50,000 Greek soldiers to aid in the attack, this number being afterwards reduced to 15,000 owing to the objections of the Staff of the Greek Army. In the end not one Greek was sent, because King

Serbia's heir & Rear=Admiral Troubridge.

"The Entente in the trenches."

Getting a British gun into position in the vicinity of Belgrade.

British gunners helping in the defence of Serbia against invasion.

"Assembling" a big gun on the Serbian frontier.

Hauling a big gun over Serbia's muddy highways.

British aid for Serbia: Another big gun mounted.

Sighting a gun against the Austrian position at Semlin.

In hard pressed Serbia: Heavy gun en route to the firing line.

Rear Admiral Troubridge and Lt. Commander C. L. Kerr, D.S.O., on the Danube front.

Constantine could not see eye to eye with his great Minister, and because the Greek Staff was dissatisfied with the careless manner in which the Dardanelles operations were conducted. In the same interview Venizelos said that twice Greece had been requested by the Entente Powers to send men to help Serbia, but was compelled to decline through her fear of being set upon by Bulgaria.

In March the Balkans were convulsed by the sudden and unexpected resignation of Venizelos because of insurmountable differences of view with his sovereign, the points in dispute being connected with definite action by Greece on the side of the Entente, which was urged by the statesman, but vetoed by the King. On the morning of March 6th Venizelos called at the British Legation in Athens to say that he was unable to carry King Constantine with him ; and that night he resigned.

It was a singular situation. The man who had saved Greece from anarchy in 1910, met crisis after crisis in her affairs, and guided her through the two Balkan Wars, practically dismissed by the son of the monarch whose dynasty he had virtually kept on the throne ! The comment of the German Press was enlightening ; it spoke of the King as moved by "dynastic considerations" — the reference was to Queen Sophia, the King's consort and the German Kaiser's sister — and declared that if Greece sided with the Entente she had "much to lose and little to gain." The fall of Venizelos, which his organ, the "Patris," pointedly ascribed to German machinations, was a heavy disappointment to the Entente. He was succeeded by M. Gounaris, an ex-Finance Minister, who announced that his policy was, with respect to the war, neutrality, and, with regard to Serbia, the observance of treaty obligations. Venizelos left Greece, declaring in deep disgust that he intended to withdraw from public life.

Notably increased by the capture, from the Austrians by the Russians, of Przemysl on March 22nd, the agitation in Rumania continued in favour of action against Germany. This agitation was led by M. Jonescu, a former Minister and the head of the Conservative Democrats. M. Bratiano, the Prime Minister, whose party was that of the Liberals, also was friendly to the Entente. On the last day of March the Parliament of Bulgaria was closed after a statement by M. Radoslavoff, the Premier, and a creature of King Ferdinand, that Bulgaria would preserve her neutrality, though Gueshoff, now in opposition, maintained that the real interests of the State were with the Entente.

April opened with an occurrence that was pregnant with meaning. A feature of Macedonia under Turkish rule had been the activity of revolutionaries organised in komitajis, or armed bands of men, who kept up a guerilla warfare upon the Turks. These societies, which were composed of Bulgar Macedonians, did not disappear with the transference of the country to Serbia, but, instigated by Bulgaria, remained in being and evinced hostility to the new owner of the land. On April 2nd several of these bands made a raid in considerable force on the south-eastern frontier of Serbia, and after attacking with success outposts and block-houses in an attempt to

Guerilla raids on Serbia

cut the railway, were repelled only after severe fighting. Bulgaria loudly disavowed any participation in the affair, but Greece thought the occasion grave enough to demand a Note of protest, which she sent to Sofia a few days later. Bulgaria again affirmed that she had nothing to do with the matter. She was watching and waiting on events in the main theatres of the war. Though now bound to Germany, she did not mean to strike as yet. If the bombardment of the Dardanelles by the Entente had failed, the Russians were victorious in the Carpathian regions and menaced Hungary. It was well, therefore, to be circumspect, an attitude which the landing on Gallipoli of Entente troops on April 25th probably confirmed.

Bulgaria disclaims responsibility

After the overwhelming defeat of the Austrians in December only insignificant fighting took place between them and the Serbians, such fighting as there was being mostly in the nature of artillery actions, the trifling character of which was demonstrated by an arrangement between the two belligerents to the effect that if the Serbians would not bombard Semlin the Austrians would refrain

PRINCE ALEXANDER OF SERBIA INTERESTED IN RANGE-FINDING.
On the right of the photograph is Rear-Admiral E. C. T. Troubridge, C.B., C.M.G., M.V.O., who was in charge of the British artillery force sent to Belgrade in the spring of 1915. One of the members of this force, Lieut.-Commander Kerr, was awarded the D.S.O. for his effective torpedo work while in command of a small picket-boat, which came to be known as "The Terror of the Danube."

from shelling Belgrade. There was, however, some lively work on the river lying between these two towns. Belgrade was defended by a mixed force of Serbians, French, and British. The last had naval guns, and was at least in part drawn from the Navy.

For some time Austrian monitors and picket-boats armed with machine-guns had patrolled the Danube and annoyed the Serbians, but the Belgrade garrison, towards the end of April, put an end to the activities of these vessels, the naval guns being employed with great skill and good results. The British sailors also distinguished themselves by the feats they performed by means of a small picket-boat which, though armed with no more than a single machine-gun, inspired such fear among the Austrians that it came to be called "The Terror of the Danube." Commanded by Lieutenant-Commander Kerr, R.N., the terror poked its way on dark nights into creeks and passages of the river to the serious disturbance of the enemy, subjecting him to constant alarms and no little loss. One of its exploits was the decoying, by pretending to retreat

OFFICERS OF THE MONTENEGRIN GENERAL STAFF.
Reading from left to right, the photographs are of Major P. Lompar, Major Martinovitch (First A.D.C.), General Prince Petar (Commander-in-Chief), Lieut. Radonitch, Capt. Yovitchevitch, and Lieut. Giurkovitch (Second A.D.C.).

heavily for her. This was the success of the Austro-German campaign in Western Galicia, which resulted in driving the Russians from the Dunajec to the San, and in freeing Hungary from their menace, and was destined to bring about a colossal change in the whole aspect of the war.

On the Balkans, as was inevitable, this triumphant offensive had a tremendous effect; but as by the close of the month it was still in its first stages, **The Galician factor** that influence was not so manifest as it became later when further victories fell to the German arms in the eastern theatre. For one thing, Rumania saw any immediate prospect of seizing Transylvania vanish, and for another, Bulgaria became more and more pro-German. The Entente Powers, however, on May 29th, made proposals to Bulgaria which, by offering her concessions, the fruit of their negotiations with the other Balkan States, were considered to be likely to lead her to fall in with their views. On June 15th Radoslavoff presented in return a Note asking for further explanations. This meant delay, if nothing else.

M. ANDRE RADVITCH.
Ex-Prime Minister of Montenegro. Later prominent in the organisation of supplies.

Meanwhile M. Venizelos had determined to return to public life, and on June 11th he reappeared in Athens, where he received a warm welcome. Within a few days he resumed the leadership of the Greek Liberal Party, and at the general elections, which took place shortly afterwards, had a majority of over one hundred and twenty seats, notwithstanding the most determined efforts made by his opponents. The Greek Parliament had previously consisted of one hundred and eighty members, but by representation accorded to the districts annexed after the Balkan Wars, the number was brought up to three hundred

with all speed, of an Austrian monitor into a prepared mine-field—with disastrous consequences to the monitor. For this its commander was awarded the D.S.O., and its crew received the D.C.M.

May saw a fresh and momentous development of the war in the adhesion of Italy to the Entente, which henceforward was described as Quadruple. This action of Italy was greatly facilitated by a treaty, signed in the first week of the month, between her and Serbia, which defined their respective interests in Dalmatia and on the eastern shores of the Adriatic. All this told heavily against Germany, but May also saw a development of the war that told more

KING NICHOLAS OF MONTENEGRO AND HIS HARDY SOLDIERS.
King Nicholas receiving a report. At the outbreak of the Great War, when Montenegro took such a dramatic stand by the side of her neighbour Serbia, the gallant Army of the little Balkan State was estimated at about 30,000 men, who were armed very largely by Russia and Italy.

WITH THE MONTENEGRIN ARMY IN THE FIELD: AN OUTPOST PHOTOGRAPHED ON THE FRONTIER SOUTH-EAST OF PODGORITZA.

ANOTHER CAMERA-VIEW OF THE FORCES OF KING NICHOLAS: MONTENEGRIN MACHINE-GUN IN ACTION.

and sixteen.   The new constituencies were manipulated by the Government of Gounaris, who still was Prime Minister, in the most unscrupulous manner in order to defeat Venizelos, but all in vain, for he secured a great majority. Venizelos and his pro-Entente policy were emphatically endorsed by the vast bulk of his countrymen, who were well aware that he was the strong man of Greece, and that her fortunes were best committed to his hands. His victory at the polls was a blow to the King, the pro-Germans, and the Neutralists, but they could point to the taking of Przemysl and Lemberg by the Austro-Germans as confirming their opinions.

During July Serbia was once more approached by Germany with an offer of a separate peace, but M. Pasich, the Prime Minister, passionately declared that she would agree to nothing of the sort, and proclaimed her unshaken loyalty to the Entente.   On the 8th of that month Austria delivered a Note to Rumania offering rewards in territory for her neutrality and substantially larger rewards for her early entrance into the war in favour of Germany and her allies. In the latter eventuality Austria dangled a tempting bait before her eyes by promising to con- **Austro-German** quer Bessarabia from Russia **offers to Rumania** and transfer it to her as a permanent possession. In the meantime she was asked to permit at once the passage of munitions of war over her railways to Turkey, a permission which Rumania had steadfastly refused previously.

Just a week afterwards Prince Hohenlohe-Langenburg, whose wife was a sister of the wife of the King of Rumania—both were daughters of the Duke of Edinburgh, who became Duke of Saxe-Coburg-Gotha—arrived in Bukarest, and tried to induce his brother-in-law, King Ferdinand, to come to terms with Austria, or, at all events, to allow the transportation of munitions through the

AUSTRIAN INFANTRY ON THE MARCH IN SERBIA'S MOUNTAIN FASTNESSES.
When Germany decided on her great adventure in the Balkans, with a view to linking up Berlin with Bagdad, General von Mackensen, the organiser of the Grand Phalanx, was withdrawn from the eastern front to the chief Austro-German command on the Danube.   In the smaller view General von Mackensen is seen crossing a stream on a white horse.

THE WOULD-BE TSAR OF ALL THE BALKANS.
Elected Prince of Bulgaria in 1877, Ferdinand became King in
1908. A man of great mental ability and an ex-officer of the
Austrian Army, he was described as a coward personally. It
was his ambition to be known as the Tsar of All the Balkans.
In our photograph he is seen with his Staff.

country, as requested. The prince's visit to the
Rumanian capital had been preceded by a campaign
in the German Press with the object of intimidating
Rumania. But the King stood firm, and Prince
Hohenlohe-Langenburg moved on to Sofia, where he
met a more sympathetic soul in the other Balkan
Ferdinand, who, at that moment, was endeavouring
to get Turkey to conclude a treaty, for which
secret negotiations had been going on for a long
period, and by which Bulgaria was to obtain all the
Turkish land on the west side of the Maritza River,
and so free from Turkish interference the railway
to Dedeagach. King Ferdinand was successful,
and on July 23rd a convention was signed which
gave Bulgaria sole possession of the line.

So far as Bulgaria was concerned, things did
not look well for the Entente Powers, who could
not but perceive the drift of affairs, and they made
further efforts to procure her support. Early in
August they made a collective representation to
the Balkan States, and delivered to Bulgaria a
reply to her Note of June 14th; in
Turkish cession the one they spoke of the desirability
to Bulgaria of making further concessions to
Bulgaria, and in the other they stated
that it was probable that the causes of friction would be removed and a union of the States brought about. Bulgaria,
however, was not satisfied, and Radoslavoff, in an interview
with an American correspondent, said that she would
enter the war only on receiving absolute guarantees of
achieving her national ideals. It afterwards transpired
that a fortnight earlier she had completed her arrangements
with Germany, Austria, and Turkey. This final treaty,
which had been engineered by Prince Hohenlohe-
Langenburg, explained the cession of Turkish territory on the
Maritza, and promised Bulgaria a great deal more than the
realisation of her national ideals—Greek Macedonia being
offered besides Serbian Macedonia. Unaware then of the
existence of this or the earlier compact, the Entente brought
additional pressure to bear on the other Balkan States.

The lion in the path now appeared to be Serbia, and,
on behalf of the cause, she was again urged to surrender

"THE NERO OF THE BALKANS."
King Ferdinand of Bulgaria taking the air. After the victorious war
against Turkey in 1912-13 he turned upon his allies at the instigation of
Austria. In 1915, at the instigation of Germany, he turned against the
Power (Russia) to whom primarily he owed his throne.

to Bulgaria all South-East Macedonia. The sacrifice was
very great to her, but in a secret session of her Parliament,
held on August 24th, she nobly consented to make it.
Rumania had been ready to agree to the stipulated
concessions, and had advised Serbia and Greece to act
in a similar way. On the 16th the Greek Parliament
assembled, the Venizelosts were in a large majority, and
on the next day the Gounaris Govern-
ment resigned. On the 22nd M. Venizelos **Serbia's useless**
was once again Prime Minister of Greece, **sacrifice**
and the Entente Powers, who still were
ignorant of that fatal treaty, believed that the whole
situation in the Balkans had become much more hopeful,
from their point of view, than it had been for a long
time. They were soon to be undeceived.

Perhaps the presence of Duke John of Mecklenburg,
a relative of the Queen of Bulgaria, in Sofia, in the first

MAP OF THE BALKAN WAR AREA, INDICATING THE RESPECTIVE BOUNDARIES, THE RAILWAY
FROM VIENNA TO SALONIKA, DEDEAGACH AND CONSTANTINOPLE, AND THE TERRITORY CEDED
TO BULGARIA BY TURKEY.

and second weeks of September, passed unobserved or was deemed unimportant, and nothing may have been thought of his going on to Constantinople, but as he was accompanied by Dr. von Rosenberg, a high German diplomatist and a specialist in Balkan affairs, the Entente Powers might have been on their guard. Bulgaria, however, still kept up the mask, yet her action on September 10th in calling for Macedonian Bulgars and Bulgars from Thrace to come forward and embody themselves in a " Macedonian Division," might have been deemed significant of her real attitude.

By this date reports of the concentration on the Serbian frontier of considerable numbers of Austro-German troops, with heavy artillery, had become much more definite and circumstantial, and the belief was general throughout the Balkans that the fourth invasion of Serbia was imminent, and would be made in great strength.

Diplomacy's final efforts Like the rest of the world, the Balkan States were aware that during August and up till this time in September the Russians had suffered the most serious reverses and lost their best fortresses, while the British and the French had made no advance of importance in the west, and had failed of decisive victory in Gallipoli. It was of the utmost moment, therefore, for the Entente to bring to a favourable conclusion without further delay the negotiations between Bulgaria and her neighbours. On September 15th the Entente Powers presented a new Note to Bulgaria, setting forth the concessions they had induced Serbia, Greece, and Rumania to offer to her in the interests of the projected union, provided that she should unreservedly declare against Germany.

Bulgaria temporised, but the pro-German tendency of her policy was evident from the suppression, two days after she had received the Note of the Entente, of the " Preporetz," a Sofia journal, which had urged the Government to agree to the terms of the **King Ferdinand and** Note and come out without further **M. Stambuliski** hesitation against Germany. The whole State, at last aware of the manner in which things were shaping, was thrown into violent commotion. The Parliamentary Opposition, which was favourable to the Entente, and held Russia, who had freed their country from the Turks, in special regard, was greatly perturbed, and the leaders of the various parties comprised within it demanded an audience of King Ferdinand to place their views before him.

Ferdinand agreed to the interview, which lasted for several hours, and was of the stormiest. M. Malinoff, the leader of the Democrats, spoke his mind freely, and told the King that neutrality, or siding with Germany, meant the ruin of the country; even neutrality would not do, he said, for neutrality would result in Bulgaria becoming the Belgium of the Balkans and being ground to powder between the Germans invading Serbia and the Franco-British forces coming to assist Serbia. The leader

WHERE SERBS AND BULGARS FIRST EXCHANGED SHOTS.
Bulgarian troops in a typical mountain pass near Bielogradchik. According to the Bulgarian account, Serbian, soldiers, "without any cause," crossed the frontier on October 12th, 1915, in an attempt to occupy the heights west of Bielogradchik. "In reply to this foolish provocation," the Bulgarians captured, after a sharp conflict, the heights of Kitka, in Serbian territory. According to another report received in Bucharest from the frontier, the Bulgarians opened hostilities on the same date by bombarding a Serbian train conveying munitions.

of the Agrarian Party, M. Stambuliski, did not hesitate to tell his sovereign that if he, the King, led the country into a fresh catastrophe the people would hold him personally responsible, and that it would cost him his throne. Ferdinand was bluntly told that he was guilty of a premeditated crime. White with rage at the fearlessness of these men, he replied that he took note of their threats—four weeks later he had Stambuliski arrested, tried, and given a life-sentence—but on that very day, which was September 18th, he showed his hand by ordering certain military measures to be taken, and four days afterwards commanded the mobilisation of the Bulgarian Army.

In a moment the gaze of the whole world was dramatically diverted from all the theatres of the war to Bulgaria and the Balkans. German guns were already shelling Semendria, on the Danube, and it was evident that Germany was about to endeavour to realise her grandiose scheme of making a bridge across the Balkans into Turkey, who in any case was now short of munitions and in need of help. The question on the lips of everyone was: What would Bulgaria do? Outside of the Bulgarian Government there was doubt even among Bulgarians themselves as to the answer. M. Angeloff, the Bulgarian Consul-General in Great Britain, said at Manchester it was unthinkable that Bulgaria should support Germany, and that no

Greece begins mobilising

Bulgarian would take up arms against the British or the Russians. Bulgaria herself, by the mouth of Radoslavoff, declared that the mobilisation of her Army was self-defensive, connoted armed neutrality, and had no other meaning. In a Note to the Powers she stated that she had "not the slightest aggressive intention," and gave specific assurances to Serbia and Greece that she had no hostile designs.

Venizelos, however, was not to be hoodwinked. On September 23rd, Greece, to the surprise and disgust of Bulgaria and Germany, who was loud in her anger, began mobilising, took over the Salonika railways from the Austrians administering them, and summoned her Parliament to meet. Excitement grew

THE WAR IN THE AIR: BULGARIA PREPARING TO TAKE HER PART.

When Bulgaria took the field in October, 1915, little was generally known regarding her aerial resources. Above is a view of one of King Ferdinand's army biplanes making a practice flight, meanwhile an interested group of country folk looked on at its evolutions. The smaller photograph is of a Bulgarian observation balloon used for military purposes.

French infantry column advancing from Salonika. The Bay of Salonika and a portion of the port are dimly discernible behind the cypresses.

British troops on the march after the landing at Salonika.

French supply column en route from Salonika to the Serbian fighting-line.

CAMERA STUDIES OF THE LANDING OF THE ALLIED TROOPS AT SALONIKA.

more and more intense throughout the Balkans, anti-German riots occurred in Bukarest and elsewhere, eminent Russians appealed to the leaders of the Bulgarian Opposition to remember what Russia had done for their country, and reports spread that there were divisions in the Bulgarian Cabinet. As late as September 28th Bulgaria still maintained that she would not attack Serbia or Greece. The mask was not yet lowered.

Sir Edward Grey's warning In spite of Bulgaria's disclaimers, the Entente Powers, from whose eyes the scales at last were falling, issued a solemn warning to her through Sir Edward Grey. Speaking in the House of Commons on September 28th, the Foreign Secretary reviewed the whole Balkan situation, and said that in Great Britain not only was there no hostility to Bulgaria, but on the contrary there existed traditionally a warm feeling of sympathy for the Bulgarian people. There was no desire to disturb the friendly relations of the two countries, but, he went on to state, if Bulgaria assumed an aggressive attitude on the side of Great Britain's enemies, Great Britain, in concert with her Allies,

would give her friends in the Balkans all the support in her power.

Coinciding in point of time with a great success by the Franco-British forces in the west, and a fine rally of the Russians in the east, this statement might have had a good effect, but it came too late, as was manifest when on October 2nd Sir Edward Grey published a supplementary declaration of policy. In this it was pointed out that as German and Austrian officers had for several days been arriving in Bulgaria with a view to taking an active part in directing the Bulgarian Army, and as this action was precisely similar to that taken in Turkey, where German officers had forced Turkey to make an entirely unprovoked attack on Russia in 1914, a condition had arisen of the utmost gravity, since the Entente Powers were bound to support the States threatened by such proceedings.

Bulgaria made no satisfactory response, but continued her mobilisation, and concentrated two divisions of her troops on the Serbian frontier. Russia thereupon sent an ultimatum to Bulgaria, in which, after reciting the facts that indicated the latter's decision for Germany, she said that **Russia's ultimatum** Russia, who had liberated **to Bulgaria** Bulgaria from the Turkish yoke, could not sanction a fratricidal aggression against a Slav and allied people, and that the Russian Minister would be withdrawn if within twenty-four hours the Bulgarian Government did not openly break with the enemies of the Slav cause and of Russia, and dismiss the German and Austrian officers.

In the meantime the Greek Parliament had met. On September 29th M. Venizelos delivered a speech in which he justified the mobilisation of the Greek Army. Bulgaria, he said, had given pacific assurances, but as she made no secret of her intention not to respect the *status quo* which had been established by treaty between the Balkan States,

IN THE TERRITORY OF "FRIENDLY NEUTRALS": STRIKING SCENES IN THE LEVANT.
Above is an interesting photograph of British bluejackets and Greek soldiers fraternising, the men having exchanged headgear before posing themselves in front of the camera. Inset: Men of the British Army Service Corps riding their mules through Salonika.

The first regiment to land on the "Serbian Quay" at Salonika on October 5th, 1915, marching through the harbour precincts. We were told by eye-witnesses of the landing that the hearts of the Greek people "beat vigorously for the Allied cause."

Before the main body of the allied troops arrived at Salonika a company of French soldiers was sent ashore and the officers placed single and double sentries all along the streets to the camps. The above camera-picture shows French soldiers resting on their way to camp.

THE ADVANCE GUARD OF THE ALLIED LANDING AT SALONIKA.

it was necessary for Greece to take the precaution of mobilising. Gounaris, the former Prime Minister, and now leader of the Opposition, endorsed the action of the Government. Greece appeared to be united; there had been rumours of a disagreement between the Cabinet and the Crown, but the unanimous approval in Parliament of the Government's course seemed to disprove and dispel them. The German Press, however, expressed its opinion that this accord between King Constantine and Venizelos was unreal, and prophesied that Greece would not give armed support to the Entente. This forecast proved to be correct, for on October 5th Venizelos resigned, owing to the King's disagreement with his pro-Entente policy, although that policy, after a long and heated debate which lasted many hours, had been approved by a majority of over forty votes in the Greek Parliament that very morning.

Venizelos had declared that it was not only the duty of Greece in fulfilment of her treaty obligations, but also a matter of necessity for her self-preservation, that she should support Serbia by force against Germany as well as Bulgaria, but King Constantine told him that he did not take the same view. Next day a Coalition Ministry was formed, the Premier being M. Zaimis, Governor of the National Bank, the son of a former Prime Minister, and who himself had been Premier twice before. He was known to be friendly to the Entente Powers, and he announced that, while Greece would continue an armed neutrality, that neutrality towards them would be characterised by complete and sincere benevolence. The Entente, however, had already derived considerable advantage from the benevolence of Greece, for after making a formal protest, she had permitted the landing of French and British troops at Salonika in the first week of September in support of Serbia. Bulgaria had replied to the Russian ultimatum, but in so unsatisfactory a manner that Russia, who was acting as the representative of all the Entente Powers, broke off relations with her, the other Powers following suit.

Any lingering doubts that might still have been felt regarding the treacherous part Bulgaria had played were removed on October 8th when the British Minister at Athens revealed the existence of the secret treaty, a copy of which had come into his hands, between Germany, Austria, and Turkey on the one side and Bulgaria on the other, that had been signed on July 17th and provided for Bulgaria's aggrandisement at the expense of her neighbours, including Greece. Germany hastened to deny there was such a treaty, but in a powerful oration Venizelos told the Greek Parliament that if, as his opponents asserted, Germany was victorious, Bulgaria would be so enlarged as to render Greece's chances against her illusory. The Greek Government, however, was not to be moved, and on October 12th categorically refused Serbia's request for help in her hour of need. Serbia's need was bitter. Against Germans, Austrians, and Bulgarians she was able to muster scarcely 300,000 soldiers, who had to defend a line over three hundred miles in length.

GENERAL BAILLOUD AND SERBIAN OFFICERS.
The French General (right) is seen in conversation with two Serbian officers, entrusted with the duty of meeting the allied troops at Salonika.

SEA POWER: REMARKABLE CAMERA-PICTURE OF THE ALLIED FLEETS IN MUDROS HARBOUR, LEMNOS.

CHAPTER LXXXV.

THE BREAKING OF THE RUSSIAN FORTRESS LINE AND THE FAILURES OF MACKENSEN AND HINDENBURG.

The Kaiser's Anger at Russian Army's Escape—German Troops March Five Days Without Food—Alexeieff Checks Hindenburg's Swoop Over the Narew—Mackensen Held Up on Wieprz River—Masterly Manœuvring by Central Russian Forces—Hindenburg Loses 100,000 Men at Kovno—The Terrible Price of the Vistula Fortress—Osoviec the Russian Mafeking—The Vast Movement of Seven Germanic Armies on Brest Litovsk—Russia's Black Week of Misfortunes—Mackensen's Grand Phalanx Becomes Worn Out—Its Total Losses Exceed 1,000,000 Men—Evert Hangs Too Long on to Grodno Fortress—Hindenburg's Gigantic Scheme to Shatter Russia—The Battles on the Wings Preparatory to the Blow at the Centre—Russky Stands Firm at Riga and Ivanoff Withdraws in the South—Unexpected Return of Ivanoff in Great Strength—His Smashing Blows Against Four Austro-German Armies—Hindenburg Leaps at Evert—Russky Comes South to Vilna to Help Evert—Marvellous Stand by Russian Imperial Guard—Extraordinary Achievement of Great German Cavalry Force—Russky and Evert are Nearly Surrounded—Tremendous Battle of Four Weeks in the Vilna Salient—Russky's Deadly Subtlety Leads to Complete Defeat of Hindenburg's Plan.

AFTER the fall of Warsaw, on August 5th, 1915, Kaiser Wilhelm came to the bank of the Vistula with his engineers, and looked at the three bridges which the Russians had blown up in their retreat. The leading generals of the Bavarian army approached him, hoping for glowing congratulations on reaching the goal towards which Hindenburg had been struggling since his victory at Tannenberg in August, 1914. But the Kaiser remarked bitterly, "There will be no decorations for anybody on this occasion. We have paid too dearly for Warsaw. We have captured only the cage; the bird has flown. So long as the Russian Army is free, the problem of the campaign remains unsolved."

Under the personal impetus of the angry Emperor, all available German and Austrian troops were at once fiercely driven forward across the Vistula, with the aim of bringing off the grand coup. As in the cavalry raid in Belgium at the opening of the war, the advanced forces were flung out with such rapidity that no arrangements for feeding them were made. They were expected to live on the country, but as the Russians destroyed everything as they retired, after removing the civil population, the German vanguards starved. Moreover, the men were marched for five days and five nights, in spurts of three or five hours' length, each followed by twenty minutes' rest. The result was that when they came upon the Russian rearguards there was no fight left in them. All along the retiring Russian front in the great bend of the Bug River, from Novo Georgievsk to a point a few miles east of Cholm, the Teutonic troops nominally engaged in pursuing their enemy were so mishandled that some of them fell out with feet lacerated by incessant marching, and others gave themselves up as prisoners in order to get food. The Kaiser in a fit of bad temper had kicked his generals forward, and the generals, always too much inclined to treat their men as machines, had tasked them beyond the powers of human endurance. So

GENERAL NICKOLAUS JAUNSCHKEVITCH.
Appointed Deputy Viceroy of the Caucasus, September, 1915.

the amazing spectacle was seen of an apparently badly beaten Russian Army, bent only on retreating to a place of safety, being clogged in its movement of retirement by an increasing number of prisoners.

The fact was, of course, that General Alexeieff's forces were in no wise beaten. By this time every Russian soldier thoroughly understood it was only the **Alexeieff's grip on** heavy German and Austrian artillery **realities** which compelled the withdrawal into the interior of Russia. The hostile guns and howitzers could not be moved forward more than three miles a day at the most; on many important sectors the rate of movement of the enemy's guns was scarcely half a mile a day. The Russian infantry, therefore, remained in good heart and, instead of being demoralised, was fiercely eager for all opportunities of meeting the enemy on equal terms. The German scheme of sending out advanced troops by forced marches was merely one of the examples of paper strategy by which men were sacrificed without any concrete advantages.

General Alexeieff, on the other hand, fought with a splendid grip on the realities of the situation. His problem was to withdraw a quarter of a million men from Warsaw towards Brest Litovsk, a distance of one hundred and thirty miles, while Hindenburg was pressing on his right flank and Mackensen on his left flank, with the armies of Prince Leopold of Bavaria and General von Woyrsch assailing his retreating front. Mackensen, with the artillery of the Grand Phalanx, was the most dangerous assailant; so Alexeieff joined his left wing with Ivanoff's right wing, and between Ivangorod and Cholm the combined Russian forces made a surprise attack upon Mackensen's group of armies in a battle that lasted till August 9th. Mackensen's

left wing was held up along the Wieprz River, while his centre and right wing were severely handled along the Bug River, some twenty-five miles south of the town of Vlodava. There was a Russian railway running from Brest Litovsk through Vlodava towards Cholm, and it fed the Russian defending forces more quickly than Mackensen could be supplied by the light railway he had built to connect his rear with the Lemberg system. It was not until August 10th that the army of General von Woyrsch, advancing through the Ivangorod region, got into touch with the Austrian force forming the left wing of Mackensen's army group, and on that day Mackensen's centre was merely some eighteen miles north of the Lublin-Cholm railway, which he had reached on July 29th. It had taken him twelve days to advance nineteen miles with his 2,000 heavy pieces of ordnance and the ordinary artillery corps of a group of armies numbering originally close upon a million men. In other words, Mackensen's advance towards Brest Litovsk was so slow that the grandiose scheme of encircling the central Russian armies completely broke down on this section of the front through the magnificently combined efforts of Alexeieff and Ivanoff.

Hindenburg, however, who was working with another million men, from a point near Warsaw to a point near Riga, proved a very formidable opponent. His troops were fresher and less wasted than **Hindenburg** those of Mackensen, his siege artillery was **held up** less worn, and he had close behind him the double system of East Prussian railways, which had been extended by roughly-built lines across the frontier towards the Narew, Bobr, and Niemen battle-fronts. There were steam tramways for bringing up ammunition and food,

DEVASTATING EFFECT OF ARTILLERY FIRE ON A RUSSIAN VILLAGE.

Unique impression of a Russian village within the war zone after it had been subjected to continual bombardment. Save for a number of forlorn chimney-stacks, which had strangely escaped being struck, the village shared the same fate as many others on the eastern front—obliteration. German supply waggons are seen passing on their way to the new zone of operations.

RUSSIAN "DELICATESSEN" IN THE HANDS OF THE ENEMY.

Doubtless spirits ran high among the Germans who assisted in capturing the Russian convoy of eatables, some of which are seen in the above photograph in process of distribution. The whole of the supply was divided among the soldiers by their officers as a special favour. To even the best official liver-sausage and rye-bread available, a little caviare or other dainty from Petrograd might well have been a welcome change.

with asphalted roads and motor-tractors, and deep beds of concrete were laid from ten to thirteen miles distance from the great Russian fortress towns, in preparation for the great siege-howitzers.

In the open field fighting against Alexeieff's right wing, behind Warsaw, Hindenburg was not successful. He was held up between Lomza and Warsaw by struggles of a terrible kind in the forests and along the river-banks, and being violently impatient to carry out his part of the enveloping movement as punctually as Mackensen had done, he used his infantry without waiting for his siege ordnance. On August 7th, nine days after Mackensen had cut the Lublin-Cholm railway, Hindenburg made a series of superhuman efforts to storm the northern Russian front. Deep, dense columns of infantry were launched against the fortresses of Novo Georgievsk, Osoviec, and Kovno, after clouds of poison gas had been floated over the outer defences of the strongholds. But by this time the Russian troops were expert in meeting poison gas by means of lines of petrol fires, which, by the ascension of hot air, lifted the gas over the trenches. At Kovno the German infantry was smashed by the heavy fortress guns. At Osoviec the attacking column was destroyed on the highway between the marshlands. But it was at Novo Georgievsk that the old German Field-Marshal proved himself once more the most terrible waster of men in history. He tried to cut off the Vistula stronghold by driving in on the west, at the town of Sierok, where the Narew flows into the Bug River, and at the same time the proper German siege army, under General von Beseler, assailed the stronghold from the north along the Mlava railway.

On the north, the Russian fortress guns broke the enemy; but on the west, in the difficult river country, where the

Petrol fires v. poison gas

Russian field artillery was protected by a couple of broad streams from the longer-ranged German ordnance, the infantry battle was indescribable. The attacking columns were slaughtered like sheep. The Russians held the Narew River line only with weak rearguards.

These rearguards fell back immediately the pressure against them became severe. Every German commander—brigadier, divisional, army corps, and army general—misinterpreted the yielding movement of the troops opposed to him. Each thought it was a sign of weakness, and the sign of apparent weakness occurred on the day on which the Kaiser refused to decorate anybody for the Warsaw victory and commanded the pursuit to be carried out with extreme energy.

German commanders deceived

The German infantry was thrown in great masses across the Narew. The result was that the Russian gunners along the second river line of the Bug were able to use their shrapnel with wholesale murderous effect. Then, as they lifted on the German rear, the large main body of Russian infantry concealed in the riverside forests surged forward and recovered Sierok at the point of the bayonet. Hindenburg was also checked at Ostrov, to the north-west of Sierok, where he attempted a lightning stroke against the Warsaw-Petrograd railway line.

His northernmost forces operating in the Riga region were likewise violently handled, and driven out of their trenches near the Dwina River. The beginning of the second week in August was thus marked by a series of defeats all along the immense line controlled by Hindenburg. Every other German or Austrian commander had some success to show. Prince Leopold of Bavaria was cutting off the Russian army corps at Novo Georgievsk by a movement on Praga, north of Warsaw. General von

Woyrsch was at Garwolin, on the road to Brest Litovsk, and Mackensen was across the Wieprz River, and advancing in the same direction. Hindenburg alone with his army generals—Beseler, Gallwitz, Scholtz, Eichhorn, Below, and Lauenstein—could not make any progress whatever, though they had the largest and the best-armed forces. Hindenburg appears to have attributed his disastrous delay in closing down upon Alexeieff's army

TSAR AS PRIVATE.
The Tsar of Russia photographed in the uniform of an ordinary infantryman.

to the long time required for making the concrete beds of the 16½ in. howitzers needed to batter down the chain of Russian frontier fortresses. As a matter of fact, there was ample room for him to advance between Lomza and Sierok in the south; and in the north, between Lomza and Grodno, only the small bridgehead fort of Osoviec barred his way. He had, in fact, concentrated his main forces between Lomza and Sierok; but on this section of the front Alexeieff clean outfought him by means of the brilliant use of forest cover and river marshlands.

Hindenburg was no master of strategy. His early successes amid the Masurian Lakes, which had made him the hero of the German people, had been due largely to the treachery of certain highly-placed Russian officers, who had communicated to the German Staff plans of the Russian Staff.. Even at the headquarters of the Grand Duke Nicholas there were persons in the pay of the enemy, with means of communicating important plans of attack. But during the great retreat some of the principal traitors were discovered and hanged, their names having been strangely obtained from documents found upon dead German officers along the French front, and revealed to the Russian Staff by General Pau. Even if this did not entirely remove all the machinery of treachery at Russian headquarters, the nature of the operations of the retreat considerably disorganised the German spy system; for each army commander—Alexeieff, Ivanoff, Evert, and Russky—was largely thrown on his own

Where German spies failed

resources; and as the plans of the Russian headquarters altered day by day with the sudden change of circumstances, there was little time for the spy to reveal anything. The immediate fighting plan of each army commander was usually not within the range of knowledge of the spies at headquarters; and in particular Hindenburg and his generals, in their struggle against Alexeieff, a close-minded, reticent, hard-thinking man, bitterly suspicious of all German influences, had no help whatever from their intelligence agents, and were thrown back on their own intellectual powers of divination.

Secret Russian dispositions

These powers were very small. The consequence was that Alexeieff moved southwards through the narrow corridor between the Warsaw-Petrograd railway line and the Garwolin-Lukov front—a distance of from thirty-five to fifty miles—in as complete secrecy as aeroplane methods of reconnaissance would allow. He hid his armies in woodlands; he scattered his grey-coated reserves in the tall growth of harvest-fields; and when he had to send a column on the march in daylight, he did not mind if the ranks grew ragged and looked like a stream of fugitives. When night fell and veiled his dispositions, his main manœuvres for battle were conducted in the darkness. On August 9th he withdrew from Novo Georgievsk, leaving much less than an army corps in the fortress and only half the fortress guns, with orders to hold out till the main forts were stormed. The troops, sacrificed to win time, formed his chief rearguard, and their most important duty was to sink every vessel that came up the Vistula.

SPIRITED STUDY OF THE TSAR.
His Imperial Majesty in his uniform as the Commander-in-Chief of the Russian Army.

The enemy was using the river as his great line of communications, and bringing up cartridges, shells, and charges, by means of steam and motor tug boats. For as the railway bridges at Warsaw and Ivangorod were destroyed, and the rails for some miles in front of both towns needed relaying, the Vistula remained the only quick means of supplying the armies of Prince Leopold of Bavaria and General von Woyrsch. In these circumstances the

THE TSAREVITCH.
As Colonel of the 12th Regiment of Western Siberian Sharpshooters.

TRAPPED IN A FOREST OF BARBED-WIRE ENTANGLEMENTS.

Fighting with a strong spiritual conviction that his cause is just, and a fatalism which is characteristic of the Slav temperament, the Russian peasant makes one of the finest soldiers in Europe. Oblivious to personal danger, he is ever willing to sacrifice his life even in what would appear to be a forlorn assault, if it be for the subsequent good of Slavdom. This wonderful photograph shows how hapless Russian soldiers threw themselves against strong barbed-wire entanglements in an endeavour to break through to the German trenches. The attitude of the figure in the foreground is tragic to a degree. While still grasping his rifle, the man's body is seen suspended by the fatal wire.

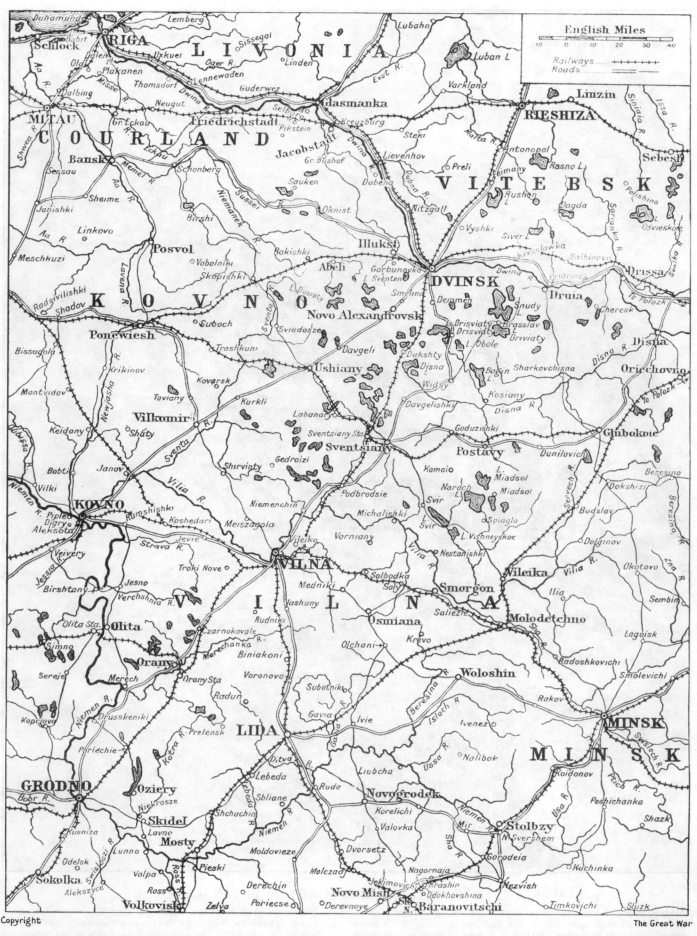

The Great War

MAP OF THE EASTERN BATTLE AREA SPECIALLY DRAWN TO ILLUSTRATE THE BREAKING
OF THE RUSSIAN FORTRESS LINE AND THE ESCAPE OF RUSSKY AND EVERT FROM
HINDENBURG'S GRANDIOSE PLAN OF ENVELOPMENT.

Russian commander thought it well worth while to sacrifice 25,000 men in Novo Georgievsk, in order to delay the supplies of ammunition and food for the central Austro-German forces.

All these stratagems of General Alexeieff increased the difficulties of his chief opponent, Hindenburg, and as the capture of Warsaw, Ivangorod, Lublin, and Cholm only served to bring out the impotence of the German left wing, Hindenburg lost all sense of measure in his mad efforts to carry out his part of the movement. He **German left wing's** was getting far behind the general time- **impotence** table. Instead of closing down on the Russians well within a fortnight, in co-operation with Mackensen, he was taking five weeks to advance over the critical distance of forty miles. Save on his old field of strategy at Tannenberg, the bull-necked, grim-faced old Field-Marshal had proved himself the most terrible waster of men in modern history ; but the troops he had wasted the previous autumn and winter, in front of Warsaw and Ivangorod, were a small drain on his country's resources compared with the numbers he now employed to retrieve his tactical mistakes on the northern front.

It will be remembered that the excuse which the Germans made for opening the Great War by an invasion of Belgium was that the German Staff reckoned it would cost a hundred thousand men to break through the frontier line of French fortresses. In order to avoid this loss they openly challenged the sea-power of Great Britain for the advantage of getting room for a large flanking movement on the Belgian plain. But twelve months after the invasion of Belgium, the most popular of all German generals was reduced to such straits, at a time when Germany seemed to have Russia at her mercy, that he was ready to lose a hundred thousand men in the capture of a single Russian frontier fortress. We have seen that Hindenburg tried to carry by sudden storm, on August 6th, Novo Georgievsk, Osoviec, and Kovno. He returned to the attack on Kovno and Novo Georgievsk on August 8th,

and for nearly two weeks his main forces maintained a tremendous struggle round these strongholds.

Some days passed before all the 16½ in. Krupp howitzers were fully brought into action against the steel domes and concrete walls of the Russian forts. In the meantime, the fortress guns and the mobile Russian batteries were able to fight on fairly equal terms against the besieging armies. But Hindenburg wanted a quick decision. It was necessary for him to break through the line of Russian fortresses, and get on the flank of Alexeieff's retiring troops. His first thrust at Ostrov, between the Narew and the Bug Rivers, had proved ineffectual. For at Ostrov the very slowly advancing German spearhead was not directed sufficiently far north to strike the flank of the withdrawing Russian army. By the time Hindenburg's subordinate, General von Gallwitz, broke through Lomza, he was fighting Alexeieff's front instead of his flank. Therefore, to get a grip round the retreating Russians, Hindenburg had to strike again farther northward ; and as the fortress of Grodno was covered by a very strong line of Cossack sharpshooters, fighting with the advantage of ground in the forests, swamps, and lakes west of the Niemen River, the fortified city of Kovno, on the northern bend of the Niemen, was the only possible point at which vast massed German forces could be quickly concentrated for a belated attempt to obtain a decision.

Kovno lies only fifty miles from the Prussian frontier, at the confluence of the Niemen, the Vilia, and some small brooks. Originally it had a girdle of eleven forts, extending about two and a **The costly attack** half miles from the old Lithuanian town. **on Kovno** In times of peace a railway connected Kovno with the Prussian frontier town of Eydtkuhnen, and though the line had been destroyed, the engineers of General von Eichhorn's army rebuilt the track, and along it brought up a great siege train, including some of the famous 16½ in. howitzers and many 11 in. and 12 in. pieces. The fortress could have been captured at a comparatively small expense of life by allowing the work to be slowly done by the siege

ON THE PICTURESQUE BORDER-LINE BETWEEN THE AUSTRIAN AND RUSSIAN EMPIRES.
Austrian artillery crossing the frontier.

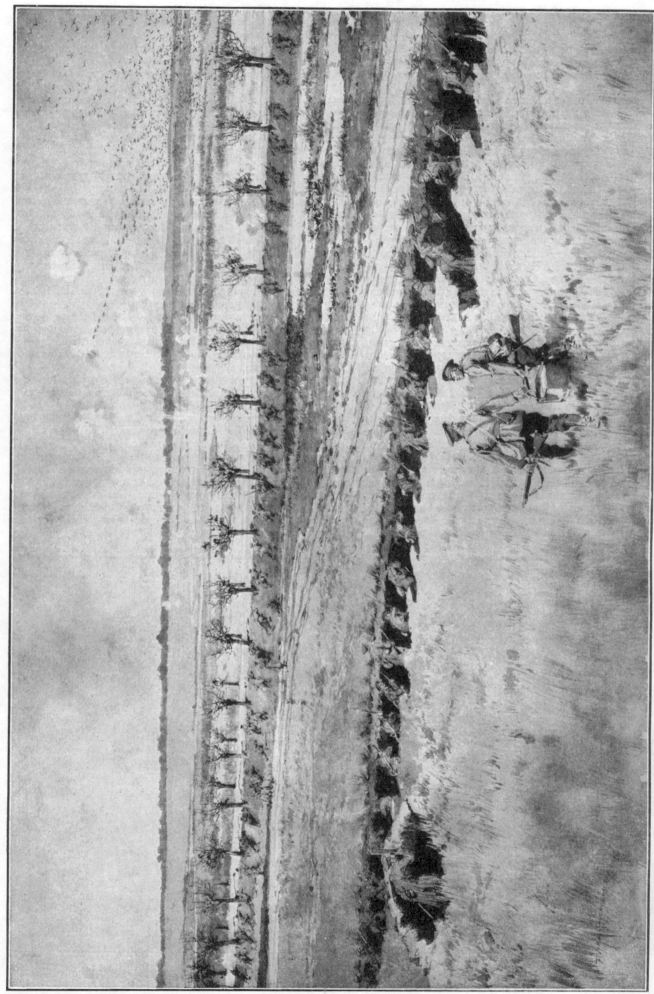

GREAT SLAV-TEUTON BATTLE WHICH RAGED OVER A GALICIAN LAGOON.

Striking panoramic study of a battle in Galicia during the great Mackensen onslaught of June, 1915, which culminated in the fall of Warsaw, Novo Georgievsk, and Brest Litovsk. The position illustrated was known as the Lagoon, and the Russian troops were strongly entrenched on the marshy ground. The shriek of German projectiles, which fell short of the Russian position and struck the water of the lake, disturbed flocks of water-fowl which flew over the conflicting lines in wild confusion, augmenting the din of battle with their raucous cries. In the foreground of the drawing two Russian soldiers are approaching the trench with a cauldron of water, while an officer is seen using a hyposcope in an observation pit on the extreme left.

train. But Eichhorn's assistant, General Litzmann, who directly controlled the operations at Kovno, was in as great a hurry as Emmich had been at Liège. He began the attack across the western forest section, extending from the Jessia brook to the village of Piple. His gunners opened fire at midnight with long-range ordnance, in order to draw the fire of the mobile batteries of defence and mark their points by the flames showing in the darkness. This is the manner in which a superior modern artillery always tries to annul the new advantage given in daylight to weaker opposing batteries by the invention of smokeless powder. After a hurricane fire of two hours, **German infantry thrown back** the German infantry threw out some skirmishing lines, and behind these came dense storming columns. But the wooded ground over which the assailers charged was full of land-mines and wolf-pits, and behind these devices were the Russian wire entanglements and trenches, concealed in a tangle of trees and bushes. The mobile Russian field-guns, which had reserved their fire during the hostile bombardment, now came fiercely into action, and the German columns were so terribly shattered by

A TWELVE-YEAR-OLD RUSSIAN BISON
This photograph, like that on the right of it, was taken in a Lithuanian forest The Russian bison—popularly, but erroneously, called aurochs—are the last survivors of their kind from an age when Europe was a savage wilderness.

shell fire, machine-gun, and rifle fire, that the Russian troops in the advanced trenches were able to make a daring bayonet charge into the enemy's front. By five o'clock in the morning the German infantry was thrown back into the ravines beyond the village.

The German gunners then tried to wipe out the Russian trenches with some hundreds of thousands of shells. The intense bombardment lasted all day on August 8th, and when night fell the enemy columns again charged up from the forest ravines across the flame-lit rim of woodland between the Jessia and the Niemen. After a struggle of

RUSSIAN BISON CHARGE THE GERMAN INVADERS.
Russian bison in his native haunt. In August, 1915, a company of some two hundred German soldiers was marching through the Bielovieska Forest when a bull at the head of a small herd of bison charged down on the invaders, and, taking them by surprise, trampled and gored nearly all of them to death.

two hours they broke into the advanced Russian trenches, only to be blasted out of them by high-explosive shell and hand-bombs. Then, just before dawn, Litzmann sent fresh masses forward, and the new columns managed to get a footing in a few trenches in front of the outer forts near Digry village.

All the force of the attack was concentrated against the western face of the fortress, but the outer defences were still resisting by August 12th, after six days and six nights of horrible slaughter. On Friday, August 13th, Litzmann managed to capture a **Besiegers' enormous** work in one of the Niemen woods, but his **losses** besieging army was broken by its enormous losses. Large forces had to be detached from the northernmost army under Below, to enable the siege operations to continue. There was a lull of some days in the infantry attacks on Kovno, during which the heavy German artillery, fed with shell by the Prussian railway, maintained an unceasing storm of fire on the Russian trenches, redoubts, and forts. Then on Monday, August 16th, the reinforced German infantry resumed its mass attacks. In the evening a small fort on the left bank of the Niemen, which had been put out of action by the enemy's incessant shell fire, was

E

captured, and in the intervening spaces between other forts on the western sector the German columns stormed over the trenches.

The Russian commander at first hoped to be able to close in on the German wedge and cut it off by a double counter-attack, based on the forts which still held out on either side of the section of shattered works. But this scissor-like movement had been foreseen by the director of the siege operations. He answered it by massing all his siege-guns on the works between which his troops were advancing. Fort after fort continued to fall under the overwhelming storm of heavy shell, while the mobile Russian field artillery operating in front of the forts was

also overwhelmed. The Russian engineers had designed their cupolas to resist 8 in. shells, but the extraordinary explosive power of the $16\frac{1}{2}$ in. Krupp projectiles battered down the armoured domes and put the machinery out of order.

The garrison withdrew over the Jessia brook, using its embankment as a last line of defence. For three days the struggle fiercely raged along the western bank of the Niemen and the Jessia brook. General Litzmann had two thousand pieces of ordnance; of these six hundred guns were ranged in an unbroken semicircle, several rows deep, and they were all massed on a single fort until the work was completely smashed. Then the blast of huge shells was directed upon another single fort. An air fleet of thirty aeroplanes and three large airships circled above the town, dropping bombs, and controlling the gun fire. The front of Kovno Cathedral was wrecked by a big shell, and much damage was done in both the new town and the old. Yet, though the garrison of the fortress was hammered out of the forts, these works, with their supporting field artillery, wrought a terrible amount of slaughter before the guns were put out of action; for General Litzmann was too eager to consummate his artillery victory, and continued to throw his infantry forward in repeated storming attacks. The result was that the Russian troops won many opportunities of meeting the German troops on fairly equal terms in hand-to-hand fighting, and as the defenders of the half-shattered wing of fortresses had the Vilna railway behind them, and large supplies of war material, they fought with exceeding stubbornness. According to an Austrian report, the German casualties at Kovno amounted to one hundred thousand men.

Since Hindenburg was ready to make this enormous sacrifice of life at a time when he possessed a terrific

The withdrawal from Kovno

GERMAN OFFICERS OVERLOOKING THE COUNTRY FROM AN OBSERVATION POST ON THE CASTLE TOWER AT VILNA.
The castle at Vilna, in Lithuania, formerly an archiepiscopal seat, had become the residence of the Governor-General. Vilna was evacuated by the Russians on September 21st, 1915. Above: Group of German officers at an al-fresco meal near Vilna.

IN A RUSSIAN TRENCH: OFFICERS STUDYING PLANS.

Fortresses had to be treated in the same way as temporary earthworks, and abandoned as soon as the maximum amount of loss had been inflicted on the advancing enemy. It is a matter of great credit to the Russian Staff that no fortress, however important, was held too long. But the effect upon the general mind of the Russian people, as stronghold after stronghold fell all along the line of invasion, was extremely disturbing. The week from August 17th to August 25th was the blackest in Russian history. Kovno practically fell on August 17th; Novo Georgievsk was occupied by the enemy on August 20th. The next day Bielsk was captured. Osoviec was abandoned on August 22nd; the Austrian cavalry entered Kovel on August 24th; and Brest Litovsk was occupied by the Germans and Austrians on August 25th. It was more like a game of ninepins than a contest between the still intact armies of the largest land empire in the world and the forces of the greatest race of technical experts.

Russia's black week

superiority in heavy artillery and shell supplies, the wonder is not that he captured Kovno, but that he failed to capture the garrison. The Russian troops, however, kept their line of retreat open at Janov, north-east of the town, and at Koshedari, eastward on the line to Vilna. Leaving only a rearguard in the last forts, they withdrew from Kovno on August 21st, on which day part of their forces were still fighting on the west bank of the Niemen. Undoubtedly the fall of Kovno was an extremely disagreeable surprise to the Russian Staff. It had been expected that this town, which was the chief frontier fortress of Russia, as Verdun was of France, would have resisted for several months, and formed a firm pivoting point for the field armies on either side of it, between Riga and Grodno. Had the Russian armies been fully supplied with ammunition and big guns, Kovno could have been held, as Verdun was, by means of the new system of earthworks, enveloping the forts at a distance of seven to ten miles from the town. But the supporting Russian field armies were still weak owing to the deficiency of munitions, and when the enemy concentrated against them and smashed up their trenches by hurricane high-explosive fire, they could only escape destruction by continuing their retreat.

Fortresses as death-traps

All the frontier fortresses upon which the Russian engineers had expended great treasure and labour became death-traps. The field armies could not hold them when the German siege trains came fully into action.

ANOTHER VIEW OF A RUSSIAN TRENCH: OBSERVATION OFFICERS AT WORK.

Apparently German technical science, on its warlike side, was absolutely triumphant over the grand human resources of the unprogressive peasant State of Russia. Appearances, however, are not always the same thing as realities.

The swift, smashing victories of the Teutons resembled those which the phalanx of the Greek King Pyrrhus won against the Romans. They were as expensive of life as great defeats would have been. The Germans and Austrians had the advantage of moving forward, which enabled them to recover in many cases the weapons of their dead, and capture many of the rifles of the dead and badly-wounded Russians. But the loss of life, especially on Hindenburg's front, told more heavily against the attacking troops than against the garrisons of the Russian forts and of the field armies behind them. The single wasted Russian army corps, locked up in Novo Georgievsk, took as terrible a toll of its victors as the garrison of Kovno; for Hindenburg could not wait for the Vistula fortress to be reduced by gun fire. His need for the command of the river communications was urgent. He was racing against time, and the check to the munition supplies impeded the advance of his two southern armies, under Gallwitz and Scholtz, between Warsaw and Grodno, besides interfering even more seriously with the fighting power of the group of armies under Prince Leopold and

COSSACK SCOUTS AND THE TELEPHONE.
On the eastern front Cossack scouts were sent on in advance of the Russian armies, and by means of the field telephones they fixed up, communicated to headquarters all the information they could glean relative to the movements of the enemy.

Marshal von Mackensen. Hindenburg, therefore, used two armies against Novo Georgievsk, the besieging army under General von Beseler being reinforced by another hundred thousand men.

Novo Georgievsk cut off Gallwitz cut off the fortress on August 9th by his thrust across the Narew River, while Beseler advanced along the Wkra River on the north, using artillery of double the calibre which the Russian forts were designed to resist. The comparatively small garrison had the odds of nearly eight to one against them in the matter of troops, and still more enormous odds against them in the matter of artillery power. But the German commanders lost all their advantages through using their infantry forces with too brutal a violence. As at Kovno, so at Novo Georgievsk,

rushing tactics by close-packed columns, vainly screened by lines of skirmishers, were employed within the range of the Russian fortress-guns. Night after night there was a hurricane bombardment, followed by a tremendous infantry attack. The Russians lost trench after trench of their outer defences, but the slaughter they wrought with their machine-guns before they fell back was appalling. It certainly appalled the German troops, and they had to be drugged in order to make them careless of their danger.

By August 14th the approach defences on the north-east sector were broken, and, pushing closer his siege ordnance, Beseler for sixty hours bombarded one of the chief forts and its two neighbouring smaller works. These were completely shattered and at last were carried by storm on August 18th, so as to enable the railway running down from Mlava to be reconstructed closer to the doomed fortress. The Russian troops with their field-guns withdrew across the Wkra River, and fought in the angle between that stream and the larger breadth of water formed by the confluence of the Bug and the Narew, with the still wider expanse of the Vistula protecting them on the south. The Russian wire entanglements were covered with German bodies on both the Narew and the Vistula sectors; for when the fortress guns had been put out of action, the heroic Russian **Heroic Russian** infantry fought on with machine-gun **infantry** and rifle against the German troops advancing to take the ruins. Beseler, however, brought his siege-guns round to the Vistula section on the night of August 18th, and by another hurricane bombardment, lasting two days, all the outer works were destroyed. After inflicting terrible losses on the hostile attacking columns at Zakroczym, near the Vistula, the remnant of the garrison withdrew on the night of August 19th to the old central forts surrounding the citadel. But, battering down two of the forts with shell fire on August 20th, the German commander again launched his infantry columns, and in a violent hand-to-hand combat Novo Georgievsk fell. As it seems to have cost the enemy nearly the effectives of three army corps to take it, the Russian engineers who built the fortress and the wasted Russian army corps that lost half its remaining men in defending it were well repaid for their labours and self-sacrifice.

After Kovno and Novo Georgievsk had fallen, the little marshland fortress of Osoviec was assailed. Osoviec was the Russian Mafeking. It consisted of a small system of earthworks, with some concealed concrete gun emplacements, lying on the causeway which connected the Prussian town of Lyck with the Russian town of Bielostok. It had been subjected to assault for nearly twelve months. The German Emperor had come to the neighbouring town of Grajevo to watch the storming of the little fort. Several 16½ in. Krupp howitzers were hauled up to blast away the defences of Osoviec, and altogether some two million shells were hurled upon the works. But the men of Osoviec held out when stronger Russian entrenched camps were battered down and stormed. This was due to the fact that no arc of hundreds of pieces of heavy artillery could be ranged against the little bridgehead. The fort was almost entirely surrounded by marshlands, and as the besieging army could only operate along the narrow causeway, the small garrison could hold the enemy back in the manner in which Horatius and his two comrades held the Tiber bridge against the Tuscans.

The garrison at Osoviec killed quite five times their number of German troops before they retired on Bielostok, and linked up with the Grodno army. It was reported that a gas attack of an unusual character at last drove them from the causeway on August 22nd. The Germans it is said, floated large balloons full of poison gas over the fortress, and exploded them. But we are inclined to believe that it was the progress of the German armies

Nurse Edith Cavell, a victim of German savagery.

This English lady, whose life had been devoted to works of mercy, was, by the order of Baron von Bissing, shot, after summary trial, at Brussels on October 11th, 1915, for helping British and Belgian fugitives across the Belgian frontier.

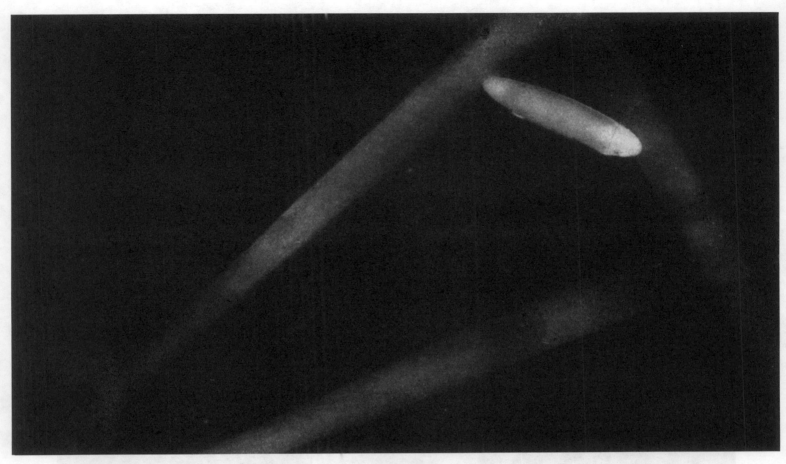

Raiding Zeppelin as it appeared to Londoners on the night of October 13th, 1915.

Untouched photograph of Zeppelin over Eastern Counties on September 8th, 1915.

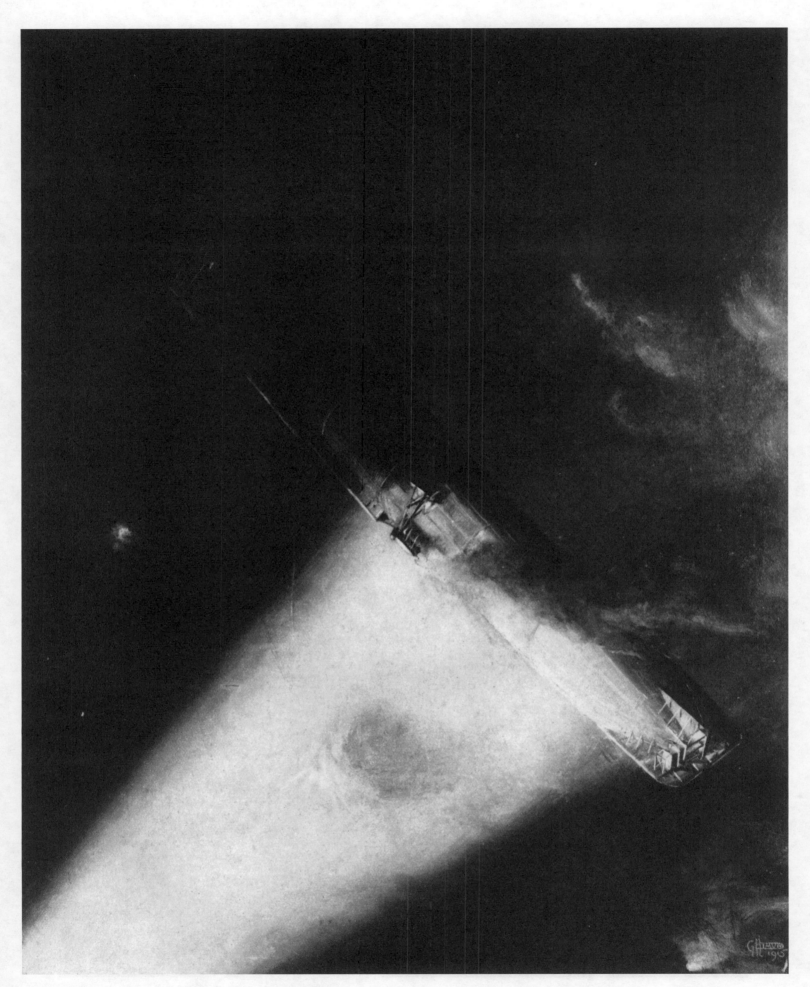

Zeppelin rising when attacked by anti-aircraft guns and caught by searchlight.

[Russell.

Admiral Sir Percy Scott, in charge of London's gunnery defences against enemy aircraft.

over the Narew front which compelled the Russians to evacuate Osoviec. On August 21st the army of General von Gallwitz had advanced to the town of Bielsk, some thirty miles south of Bielostok and more than sixty miles south of Osoviec. So it was high time for the garrison to retire. Moreover, some ninety miles south of Bielostok the main forces of the Teutonic Empires were then closing round the great Russian entrenched camp of Brest Litovsk. There were seven German and Austrian armies engaged in a vast sweeping movement in the bend of the Bug River and along the forested country between the Bug and Bielostok. These armies were all converging towards the edge of the immense Pripet Marshes, where Brest Litovsk stood, at the junction of the roads and railways leading to Kieff and Moscow.

So long as the Russians held Brest Litovsk, they could keep all their armies united for common action, with an intercommunicating system of railways behind them. But if the great junction fortress were lost, Ivanoff's army would lose touch with Alexeieff's army, and the two forces would be divided by the greatest stretch of difficult ground in Europe, the Pripet or Pinsk Marsh. The marsh formed a vast wedge with its point near Brest, and beyond Pinsk it broadened eastward to a width of more than two hundred miles of roadless bog, heath, and forest, quite impassable for an army. For centuries the Pripet Marsh had been one of the main defences of Russia. Russians had sheltered in it during the Mongolian invasions, and Peter the Great's grand manœuvre was to wait till the enemy reached the Pripet Marsh, and then drive him in and drown him. Since the age of Peter, some 8,000,000 acres of swamp had been reclaimed between Brest and Pinsk, and a single-line railway had been thrown across the morasses to connect the Moscow and Kieff trunk lines. But, despite the immense labour spent upon it, the primeval marsh, three hundred miles long and two hundred miles broad, broke into two distinct portions any forces advancing on it or retiring by it. Marshal von Mackensen expected that General Alexeieff and General Ivanoff would concentrate for a decisive stand round Brest, rather than allow the Russian front to be split by the immense natural obstacle. A grandiose scheme of attack had been planned soon after the fall of Warsaw, and though Hindenburg's southern wing, consisting of Gallwitz's and Scholtz's armies, did not move quickly enough, Mackensen's forces were able to sweep in a wide movement of envelopment round Brest Litovsk.

In the north, the army of Gallwitz slowly moved towards the Bielovieska Forest, which is one of the most remarkable tracts of primeval woodland in the Old World. Extending for three hundred and ninety-six square miles between Bielostok and Brest Litovsk, the forest contains—or did contain, towards the end of August, 1915—the last herd of wild European bison surviving from the age when Europe was a savage wilderness. The animals are popularly called aurochs, but they are really closely akin to the bison of North America, on which the Red Indians lived. It was not known at the time of writing if the great herd of the Bielovieska Forest had been made into meat by the armed missionaries of "Kultur," but if the last auroch has vanished we must praise the shaggy, humped picturesque bull for his final exploit. A company of some two hundred German soldiers was marching down one of the forest ways when a bull at the head of a small herd charged down on the invaders, and taking them by surprise, trampled and gored nearly all the company. It is said that only twenty of the German troops escaped without injury.

The army group under Prince Leopold of Bavaria, which included General von Woyrsch's forces, advanced from Warsaw and Ivangorod towards Siedlce, on the road to Brest Litovsk. But about midway it turned leftward and crossed the Bug towards Wysoko Litovsk, and

(margin note) **Invaders charged by bison**

there thrust out along the south side of the Bielovieska Forest. The forest was thus hemmed in on the northwest and the north by Gallwitz's troops, and enveloped south-west and south by Prince Leopold's armies. It was barely fifteen miles from the southernmost skirts of the great northern forest to the northern sector of the outer defences of Brest Litovsk. Consequently the mighty fortress was partly encircled near the main line of retreat open to the garrison. Mackensen in person operated with two armies, his own and that of the Archduke Joseph Ferdinand, on the western sector of the great entrenched camp. He also extended his forces northward towards the edge of the Bielovieska Forest, in order to combine with Prince Leopold along the Russian line of retreat. Immediately south of Brest, General von Linsingen, who was supposed to have been retired after his disasters on the

DENTISTRY IN THE FIELD.
Russian soldier having a tooth drawn by an Army doctor outside a field hospital.

Dniester front in Galicia, unexpectedly appeared with another large army. He advanced on the south-western edge of the Pripet Marsh near the town of Vijva, through which ran the railway connecting Brest with Rovno. Then about fifteen miles south-east of Vijva a large force of Teutonic and Hungarian cavalry, under General Puhallo, was fighting its way to Kovel, along one of the tributaries of the Pripet River.

(margin note) **Linsingen's unexpected appearance**

The general design was to do to the Russians what they had done to one of the Swedish armies in 1717. West of Wysoko Litovsk, and across the River Liesna, there was only a corridor of dry firm land between the morasses of the Bielovieska Forest and the vast stretch of the Pripet Marsh. By massing the main forces of both Mackensen's and Prince Leopold's groups of armies at the

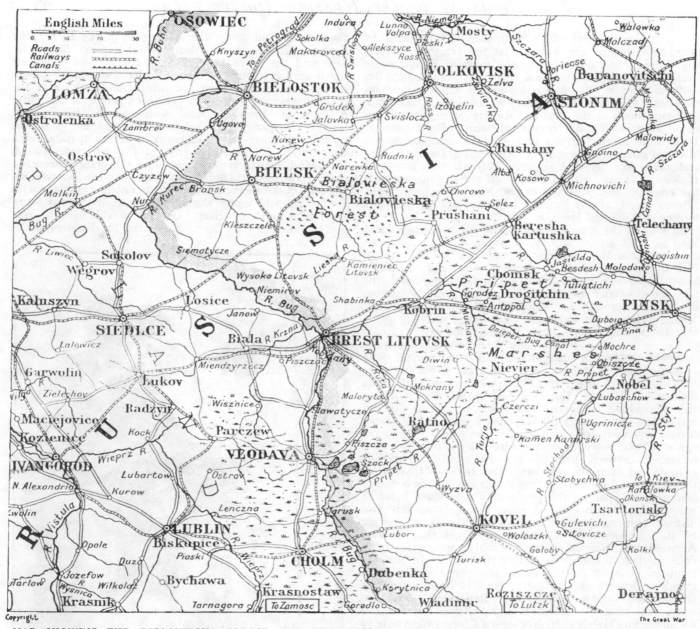

MAP SHOWING THE BIELOVIESKA FOREST AND THE PRIPET MARSH WHERE THE TREMENDOUS DRIVE OF SEVEN TEUTON ARMIES AGAINST THE RUSSIAN CENTRE ENDED.

entrance to the corridor and along the southern edge of the forest as far as Prushani, it was hoped to deliver a flank attack in overwhelming force on the Russian troops, just as their front was being broken at Brest Litovsk, and thus throw them into the marshes, where Linsingen's army and Puhallo's forces would press up from the south and complete the work of destruction.

In order to batter down quickly the defences of Brest Litovsk, the two thousand siege-guns of the Grand Phalanx were hauled up from Lublin on the rebuilt railway running through Lukov to Brest. For three weeks after the fall of Warsaw, fighting of a most furious, incessant, and general character went on in the hilly, water-threaded country stretching for ninety miles between Ivangorod and Brest Litovsk. It was largely owing to the remarkable stubbornness with which the wings of Ivanoff's and Alexeieff's forces contested every hill and stream, that the idea was confirmed that the Grand Duke Nicholas and his Staff were preparing to offer battle. At the beginning of the second week in August, Mackensen's artillery was hammering the Russian field army in front of Brest, while Prince Leopold's troops were making their surprising swerve far to the north of the fortress. But the Russian Staff was fully aware of the fact that Mackensen's giant howitzers, though worn by fifteen weeks' work in which they had discharged

The siege of Brest Litovsk

an unparalleled number of shells, were still well enough rifled to outrange and overpower the smaller, older guns of the fortress. The Russian Commander-in-Chief therefore treated Brest Litovsk as he had treated Kovno and Novo Georgievsk. The garrison removed about half the artillery, mainly pieces of 6 in. calibre that could be used in field warfare, and left about 20,000 infantry-men to hold out as long as they could in the spaces between the forts, while the gunners inflicted as much punishment as possible upon the attacking German and Austrian columns. Meanwhile the Russian field armies under Alexeieff withdrew northward, in answer to the formidable pressure along the decisive line of attack.

Feint and counter-feint

In this way the siege of the greatest of Russian fortresses became a mere incident in the contest of the opposing field armies. Each side tried to deceive the other by attacking and counter-attacking with the utmost violence along the south-western and western sectors of Brest. The German commander wished to force the Russian commander to throw more troops into Brest, so that they might be captured by the turning movement of Prince Leopold's armies. The Russian commander had also to make a brave show around Brest, to prevent Mackensen from abandoning the attempt to carry the stronghold by sudden storming attacks, and combining with Prince Leopold on the north in the far more dangerous turning movement. As in all great military movements of an intricate and far-reaching kind, the result depended almost entirely upon the play of mind of the opposing commanders, for the forces engaged were fairly equal. The Germans had the mechanical advantage of superior artillery; but the Russians, with the magnificent human material of the retreating armies from Cholm, Lublin, Ivangorod, and Warsaw, could balance, by the slaughter they wrought in infantry fighting, the losses they incurred in the bombardment. There was no question of holding on to Brest. Such a course would only have

Invaders appalled at Brest

given Mackensen his last great chance to make the best use of his heavier artillery and of his larger supply of shells. The problem was to continue the retreat along the railway to Minsk and the railway to Pinsk, while so misleading the enemy as to get full opportunity for two smashing blows against Gallwitz, Prince Leopold, and Woyrsch in the north, and Mackensen and the Archduke Joseph Ferdinand on the west and southern fronts.

This object was achieved by the evening of Wednesday, August 25th. Using the remaining guns of the fortress, the reduced garrison of Brest fought one of the most tremendous rearguards actions in the war, while the main Russian forces mowed down Prince Leopold's and Woyrsch's troops, and part of the northern wing of the Mackensen army group, in a battle in the open field by the Liesna River and the edge of the Bielovieska Forest. The army of General von Gallwitz was also met and checked on the north-western side of the same forest, along the narrowing, high-banked waters of the Upper Narew. At Brest the Russians fought until all their guns were put out of action by the enemy's siege ordnance, and so stubbornly did they hold out that when they retired in the darkness towards Pinsk, the victorious Austrian army corps under Field-Marshal von Arz, which first broke through the last line of defences, was appalled by what it saw.

Brest Litovsk had ceased to exist. Everything of value had been removed, excepting the heaviest fortress guns. These had been completely destroyed, and of the town there remained nothing but flaming or smoking ruins. Every bit of war material, food, useful metal, and household material of importance had been transported by road towards Kieff or Moscow. The Russian in the summer of 1915 met the invader with even more resolution than he had done in the summer of 1812. Moscow was not burned down until Napoleon

COMMANDER OF RUSSIA'S SECOND ARMY.
General Smirnoff, Commander of the Second Russian Army, on a station platform just prior to the evacuation of Warsaw. The General had been sharing his men's crude meal at the goods waggon.

A BONAPARTE FIGHTING FOR RUSSIA.
Prince Louis Bonaparte, brother of Prince Victor Napoleon. He was a General in the Russian Army, and Colonel-in-Chief of a Dragoon Regiment.

had entered the ancient capital; but Brest Litovsk, which the modern Russian regarded as the supreme rallying-point of the armies defending Kieff and Moscow, was entirely burnt down before the enemy reached it.

In the afternoon of August 25th the army corps of Marshal von Arz, the most brilliant of Austro-Hungarian commanders, stormed two forts on the south-west front of Brest, the Hungarian Landwehr leading the attack by the village of Kobylany. About the same time some of the new levies from Galicia and Silesia rushed a fort on the west front, and in a night attack Prussian regiments from Brandenburg captured the citadel near the railway bridge. The Hungarians and Austrians carried out the most terrible part of the work, advancing by daylight in the open in dense formations against the shattered forts, round which the Russian troops fought with field artillery, machine-guns, and rifles. When the defence had been broken down by the use of Austrian cannon fodder, the lordly Prussian troops were launched under cover of darkness to win the honour of actually taking the town. There was great exultation in the German Reichstag on August 26th over the news of the fall of Brest Litovsk. The President explained that the capture of the fortress was the crown of the almost incredible achievements of the German and Austrian armies. But it was noteworthy that no claim was made as to the capture of men and material.

Germans' premature joy

As a matter of fact, the proper garrison of the great Russian entrenched camp was 100,000 men. But only a division was left to hold the forts along the Bug River.

The small body of troops held out while the main army retired towards Pinsk. When this movement had been effected, all the fortifications and bridges were blown up, the large railway-station was set on fire, the citadel was destroyed, and the market-place burnt. A very small rearguard checked the Brandenburg regiment during the night attack, and enabled the garrisons of all the forts to rejoin the field army.

Thus ended the march of the Grand Phalanx, which had begun four months before on the river-line of the Dunajec and Biala, in Western Galicia. **Mackensen's artillery train useless** When Brest fell, Mackensen's enormous artillery train was found to be of no further use against the Russians. His heaviest piece was the famous 42 centimetre Krupp howitzer, which weighed eighty-nine tons, with a carriage of thirty-seven tons. It needed a crew of two hundred men, each shot cost £550, and carried thirteen miles. But for the transport of this gigantic siege-gun twelve railway waggons were required. The Skoda 12 in. gun also needed several railway waggons; and in the muddy soil of Poland

"THE OLD MAN OF THE LAKES."

Field-Marshal von Hindenburg. A photograph taken when he was Commander-in-Chief of all the German forces on the eastern front. Called by the Kaiser from the obscurity of his retirement before the war, Von Hindenburg became the popular idol of the German people. From being referred to contemptuously as " the Old Man of the Lakes," on account of his close study of the Masurian region, he came to be hailed by the Kaiser as " the saviour of Germany." Even though he was eventually superseded by General von Mackensen, this seems to have had but little effect on his popularity among his countrymen.

and Lithuania concrete beds had to be built to prevent the huge pieces of ordnance from burying themselves in their tremendous recoil. Therefore, when the line of battle moved eastward from the front of the fortresses into the dreary region of immense swamps and tumbled forest land, through which ran only woodland ways and unmetalled roads, the technical resources of Germany were exhausted. Even the great concrete construction trusts and asphalt-paving syndicates could not provide material and men for further road-making. So the Grand Phalanx was broken up. One thousand of the heaviest pieces of ordnance, all somewhat the worse for wear, were slowly hauled back to Warsaw, and thence sent through Berlin to the western front, where they arrived with the Prussian Guard Corps of the 1st and 2nd Divisions about the middle of September. A large number of the 12 in. Skoda howitzers were returned to Austria, and railed down to the Danube for use against

the Serbians. Then a part of the Archduke Ferdinand Joseph's army, comprising the troops under the command of General von Kövess, were placed in reserve to refit and rest, preparatory to the new campaign against Serbia, with the general direction of which Field-Marshal von Mackensen was entrusted.

The vast combined movement by Mackensen and Hindenburg had failed. The Russian armies had completely eluded the pair of pincers formed of two army groups, each containing about a million men, with 2,000 heavy siege-guns in addition to their full artillery corps. Hindenburg was mainly responsible for the failure to grip the retiring Russian forces. Yet Mackensen also, though he reached Brest Litovsk in accordance with the revised time-table, had likewise failed in another direction. He had misused his men. Not only was his casualty list enormous, but the men who remained were nearing a condition of utter physical exhaustion. They had been driven harder than they had driven the Russians, with the result that, though the condition of the Russian troops was such as to test these hardy peasants most severely, the state of the German and Austrian soldiers was still more miserable.

Between June 1st, 1915, and August 1st, 1915, the losses of the Austro-Hungarians are said to have exceeded a million men. The troops that suffered these appalling casualties, which we give on the authority of a Hungarian actuary, only formed part of the group of armies over which Field-Marshal von Mackensen exercised a general control. Linsingen's army, for instance, was mainly German, as was also the Grand Phalanx, of which the Prussian Guard was the spearhead, and German units were used in almost every division, from the Bielovieska Forest front to the Dniester front, in order to stiffen the weakening forces of the Southern Empire. Then, since the actuary's date of August 1st, there had been nearly four more weeks of exceedingly violent fighting between the Vistula and the Bug Rivers, during which the Austro-German forces only progressed slowly by terribly costly rushing tactics. In nearly every case the Russian troops were skilfully entrenched on a well-chosen line of positions of great natural strength; and instead of weakening under four months of incessant attack, they increased their force of resistance every week. In Galicia, Mackensen had progressed at the rate of three miles a day. But after the fall of Warsaw and Ivangorod his pace slackened to two miles a day, and ended at scarcely more than one mile a day. By the time he captured Brest Litovsk, and arrived on the edge of the Pripet Marsh, it was close on September, and wanted barely two weeks before the first fall of heavy autumn rain turned the earth-made roads into mud channels and the summer-dried surface of the marshes into yielding death-traps.

All this, of course, was not a happy accident of climate and soil which turned to the advantage of the Russians. Throughout the great retreat the Russian Staff had chiefly been fighting for time, with a view to using the marshes in autumn as a defence against the enemy's heavy artillery. The first design of the Russian Staff was to **Russky firm at Riga** employ the lakes and morasses round the Niemen against Hindenburg's howitzers, and place the Pripet Marsh in front of Mackensen's siege train, with the Bielovieska Forest as the central link between the two boggy fronts. But the unexpected suddenness of the fall of Kovno, the chief fortress of the Niemen, made the execution of this design impossible. In the north, the Petrograd army of defence under General Russky had to withdraw its left wing from Kovno, and make a fighting retreat to the intricate lake district between Vilna, Smorgon, and Dwinsk. Northward towards Riga, Russky's army still held to the river-line of the Dwina, with another immense stretch of lakeland behind it, which was being fortified by the peasantry of the Vitebsk and Pskov Governments, as the ultimate

Hungarian cavalrymen scouting near the river-bank beyond Warsaw. Unlike its infantry, the cavalry of the Austro-Hungarian Army proved extremely good, and maintained the reputation it had built up since the wars with Louis XIV. The Austro-Hungarian Army first formed and developed light cavalry regiments of hussars. But its admittedly splendid horsemen were unable to save the arms of Austria-Hungary from defeat.

Austrian division advancing towards Novo Georgievsk along a typical Polish road. Partly owing to the vast extent of Poland and partly to the sparse population, the roads were very badly kept. In summer they were buried in sand and dust; in winter, in mud. The armies that operated in Poland and Western Russia in 1915 had to contend with practically the same transport difficulties which beset Napoleon.

AUSTRO-HUNGARIAN SOLDIERS IN POLAND ADVANCING AGAINST THE RUSSIANS.

RUSSIANS RESTING AFTER THE EXODUS FROM WARSAW.
Russian troops halting in the square of a Polish village, about thirty miles from Warsaw, for a brief rest before continuing their march eastward.

REMOVAL OF GUNS DURING THE RETREAT.
Loading guns on the special trucks in which they were conveyed to Minsk, after the final struggle which preceded the withdrawal from Warsaw.

line of defence for Petrograd. General Russky regarded his position as impregnable. Riga he was ready to lose in case of dire necessity, as his main scheme of defence was based upon the lake district, the rains of autumn, and the frosts of winter. Meanwhile, he held on to Riga in spite of the fact that on September 1st, 1915, one of Eichhorn's group of armies, consisting of a very strong force under General von Lauenstein, had approached within fifteen miles of the famous seaport.

All the principal Russian generals, except one, were beginning to feel confident. Russky was gathering increased strength in the north, owing to the progress of

munition making in the Petrograd region. On the southern wing General Ivanoff, with his brilliant army leaders, Brussiloff and Lechitsky and Cherbachoff, was growing stronger as the Russian factories increased their output, and products of the munition works of Japan reached his troops. The central Russian army, working north of the Pripet Marsh and defending the Moscow line, was also growing stronger, after escaping at last from the siege trains of both Mackensen and Hindenburg. Its fine commander, General Alexeieff, was taking over the grand position of Chief of Staff, while the Tsar in person prepared to lead all his armies in the critical phase of the titanic struggle with the invaders. General Alexeieff left a man of well-tried genius in command of **Hindenburg's leap at Evert** the central army group, whose escape from the salients of the Vistula, Narew, and Bug constituted the most masterly feat in modern strategy.

But one principal Russian general still remained in a position of extreme difficulty. He was General Evert, the new commander of the Niemen army, which had been operating near the Prussian frontier, in the extension of the Masurian Lakes system, west of the Grodno fortress.

After the fall of Kovno and Brest Litovsk the lines held by General Evert's army formed another salient of great size on the Russian front. Hindenburg thereupon designed to concentrate in immense force against Evert with a view to retrieving his own mistakes and Mackensen's lack of decisive success. It was still the German aim to envelop and annihilate an entire Russian army, and thus force the Tsar to sue for peace. Hindenburg, however, had become quite a megalomaniac; the destruction of one Russian army did not content him, and with his brilliant but overreaching Chief of Staff, Ludendorff, he made a grandiose plan for the destruction of both Evert's and Alexeieff's armies. The main feature of the scheme was a vast cavalry raid on the railway junction of Molodetchno, between Vilna and Minsk, and the larger

Scheme for vast cavalry raid

part of the German and Austrian cavalry, numbering about 40,000 sabres, were collected for the purpose near Kovno, under General von Schmettau, with 600,000 German infantry behind them. It was foreseen that the thrust against the new Russian centre would be answered with a fierce counter-thrust by the northern Russian army under General Russky. The northern German wing, t h e r e f o r e, entrenched along a line of sandhills and stone-built farmhouses, turning the buildings into machine-gun redoubts, and bringing up more guns and shells to strengthen the fortified line.

While this work was proceeding, the German Staff made two skilful moves to weaken the Russian centre. It was expected that the Russian Staff would be well acquainted with the fact that Mackensen's chief forces had been redistributed after the fall of Brest

on Petrograd, while Böhm Ermolli, Bothmer, and Pflanzer would be reinforced in Galicia, with the object of an attack on Kieff. The idea, of course, was to induce the Russian Commander-in-Chief to strengthen both his wings at the expense of his centre, so that the great German central thrust towards Minsk and Moscow would meet with less resistance.

Undoubtedly, the great project was as well designed as Hindenburg, Ludendorff, and Falkenhayn, with their Staffs, could elaborate it. And the Russian commanders all along the front were at a serious disadvantage in regard

RUSSIAN DESTROYER BOMBARDING
A TURKISH POSITION.
The gun in action is a quick-firer, and the crew are seen about to place another shell in the breech.

to the modern method of reconnaissance, owing to the superior numbers and equipment of the hostile aircraft. The German aeroplane factories were as remarkable as the German ordnance works; in the matter of output and incessant technical improvements they were far superior to the Russian factories. Russia had some remarkable inventors such as Sykorsky, who built the famous gigantic aeroplane, but her manufacturing plant was very small compared with that of the Teutonic Empire. Everything the Germans learned on the western front by woeful experience, regarding the progress of aeroplane design in Britain and France, they rapidly applied in new machines used on the eastern front. The conse-

TURKISH CRAFT SET ON FIRE BY SHELLS FROM A RUSSIAN SQUADRON.
The Russian Navy in the Black Sea proved itself a formidable menace to Turkish coast positions and shipping, in spite of the augmentation of the Ottoman Fleet by the elusive German ships, the Goeben and the Breslau.

Litovsk, leaving the German centre weaker than the Russian. Naturally, the Russian Staff would want to know to what new use Mackensen's troops would be put. Hindenburg, therefore, arranged that it should seem as though the direct, straightforward method of reinforcing the two Austro-German wings was being followed. In other words, it was made to appear that General von Lauenstein and General von Morgon would be strengthened round Riga with the object of an attack

quence was that the Russian airmen were always outnumbered by the enemy, and generally outclassed in pace and climbing power. For nearly all practical purposes

German mastery of the air

the Germans seem to have temporarily won the mastery of the air during the great retreat, with the result that they could conduct in comparative secrecy their new concentrations of great striking forces.

They opened their misleading attack on the Russian

MAP OF THE GALICIAN AND VOLHYNIAN FIELD OF WAR.
Drawn to illustrate the victories of Ivanoff's generals, Brussiloff, Lechitsky,
and Cherbachoff against the Austro-German forces under Linsingen.

wings by a fierce attack on the fords of the Dwina, below
Riga, and by a sudden assault, at the end of August,
on the southernmost Russian positions along the Zlota
Lipa and the Dniester. The attacks on the Dwina fords,
near Kreuzburg, were repulsed, but the armies of Pflanzer
and Bothmer carried by storm the Zlota Lipa lines, and
forced the passage of the river, throwing Brussiloff's forces
eastward towards the Strypa River. At the same time
the army under Böhm Ermolli advanced on Zloczow, and
crossed the mountains where the Bug and Sereth Rivers
rise on the road to Dubno and Rovno. Then at Lutzk,
a few marches north of Dubno, Linsingen's army progressed
by fierce fighting along the southern edge
of the Pripet Marsh, in order to connect
with the Austrian armies and menace
Kieff. This series of sudden converging
strokes against Ivanoff's southern army was calculated
to perturb the Russian Staff. It was not effected by any
abrupt accession of courage in the troops or skill in their
commanders; the result was merely obtained by greatly
reinforcing the Austrian lines with Skoda guns from
Mackensen's command and reserve troops that were no
longer needed by the Archduke Joseph Ferdinand. A
division of the Prussian Guard was also railed up through
Lemberg for the movement of assault with another German

Ivanoff hard-pressed

division. Brussiloff's men, though strongly entrenched
along a deep, winding river-course, were unexpectedly
overwhelmed by a storm of shell fire from heavier artillery
than that against which they had hitherto been contending.
Their trenches were blown up by 8 in. and 12 in. shells,
but though they were forced to retire, they made a desperate
stand along a brook between the two rivers, and thus
won time to strengthen their second line on the Strypa.

Again they were attacked all along the front from the
Dniester to the southern fringe of the Pripet Marsh,
during the last two days in August and the first two days
in September. Lutzk was lost, and Brody and Dubno,
and the line of the Strypa River, and the enemy began
to press strongly against the Galician railway junction
of Tarnopol and the main Russian southern fortress of
Rovno. Had Tarnopol fallen, the Russians would have
completely lost their footing in Eastern Galicia, and their
chance of still connecting with Rumania along the Austro-
Rumanian frontier. Had Rovno fallen, the road to Kieff
and Odessa, the Black Sea, and Constan-
tinople would have been open. The   **Tarnopol and Rovno**
menace was thus a very serious one, and   **threatened**
it seems to have been backed by a large
part of the men and guns in Mackensen's group of armies,
The railway from Brest Litovsk to Lemberg had enabled
the central Austro-German forces to be rapidly moved
against Ivanoff's southern army group.

It is extremely probable that Mackensen delayed his
Serbian adventure in order to direct in person, with the
bulk of the new Danube army reinforcing Pflanzer's,
Bothmer's, Böhm Ermolli's, and Linsingen's forces, the
sudden and very violent movement against Ivanoff's
armies; for if Mackensen had succeeded in this drive
towards Kieff and Odessa, he would have been able to
exert a pressure on Rumania, on both sides of her frontier,
calculated to force King Ferdinand, the new Hohenzollern
ruler of the Rumanian nation, to resume the alliance
with the Central Empires into which his uncle, King
Carol, had entered. Then, with both Rumania and Bulgaria
fighting on the side of Germany and Austria, the pro-
German King of Greece, and his pro-German General Staff
and pro-German Government, would have been able to
quell the Venizelos movement, and swing Greece also
into the Teutonic camp.

Thus the violent attack on the southern Russian
armies was a campaign of as high importance as the
advance against the Serbians which followed it. The
march towards Kieff and the Black Sea ports promised
large results more speedily than the subsequent attempt
to burst through the Serbian mountains. Indeed, Serbia
was not seriously threatened until the greater movement
was fought to a standstill. Meanwhile, General Ivanoff
was not the kind of man to respond passively to hostile
pressure. For some months his forces in Galicia and
the Russian province of Volhynia had stood quietly on
the defensive, guarding Southern Russia, and drawing on
the local factories and troop depots for small quantities
of ammunition and small drafts. After the fall of Brest
Litovsk, the huge wedge of the Pripet Marsh practically
transformed Ivanoff's command into the independent
army of Southern Russia. Until end of August
Ivanoff's men lived on the resources of the Kieff and Odessa
regions, with the Volhynian triangle of fortresses—Lutzk,
Dubno, and Rovno—strengthening their flank near the
Pripet Marsh. But when Mackensen's guns and men
returned to Galicia and were allotted to the forces of
Linsingen, Böhm Ermolli, Bothmer, and Pflanzer, General
Ivanoff appealed to his Commander-in-Chief for heavy
artillery and more rifles and ammunition. A large part
of the supplies of munitions obtained from Japan
reached him by the beginning of September, 1915, soon
after the southern Teutonic forces had revealed their full
strength of attack.

When Ivanoff was in a position to strike back, he had

to skilfully select the most telling point for his counter-stroke. He chose Tarnopol. It was his railhead in Galicia, by which he was directly connected with Odessa and Kieff. Tarnopol was more important to him than Rovno. It was a source of political prestige, as it lay in Austrian territory, and it was a great military base, by reason of its direct railway communications with the chief cities of Southern Russia. There was also the advantage of quickness of movement from Tarnopol, as the fresh supply of munitions poured by railway directly into the town, and no delay in distribution was occasioned. So Ivanoff answered the unexpected, staggering blow by Mackensen, which had been delivered south-east of Lemberg at Brzezany, by an equally unexpected and still more staggering counter-blow delivered from the region of Tarnopol.

For the first time on the eastern theatre of war the German and Austrian troops were forced to submit to the inhuman ordeal which they had been for many months imposing on the Russian infantry. A fierce, intense,

Ivanoff turns the tables annihilating storm of heavy high-explosive shell swept the trenches and gun positions of the overconfident enemy. He was more than surprised; he was dumbfounded. His view of life was shattered, for he had come to regard it as the foundation of his national faith that only the countrymen of Krupp and Škoda were able to kill men in scores of thousands by using massed siege-guns in open field battles. Least of all did he dream of the unprogressive Slav soldiers dealing with him as he had dealt with them.

And the worst of it was that the Russian did not treat the German and Austrian as they had treated him. When the Russian gunner had obtained the famous hurricane fire effect, the Russian infantryman and Cossack horseman displayed a terrifying eagerness to use bayonet and sabre. They did not wait with Teutonic cautiousness to pick up the fragments of the front broken by the artillery. All they wanted was for their guns to break a path for their charge, and keep down the enemy's shrapnel fire, while they went to it with flashing steel and hand-bombs. Since the Dunajec and San **The foe at** River battles, Ivanoff's men had spent **a disadvantage** five months in wild, desperate longing for equal artillery conditions, enabling them to meet the enemy with bayoneted rifle, in a manly hand-to-hand struggle. Now they had their desire, and their furious joy of it was exalted to frenzy by the long, terrible ordeal of unequal combat with a decivilised foe.

To add to the difficulties of the enemy, the weather became very rainy at the beginning of September, with

WITH RUSSIAN AND ENEMY SUPPLY COLUMNS ON THE EASTERN FRONT.
Russian waggons, typical of those used by peasantry, which were requisitioned for military service, passing through a village to a new position. Above: A German supply column grinding along a road which had been reduced by heavy rains and much war traffic to a quagmire.

THE WARFARE ON THE RIVERS.
Russian military cutter used for patrol work on the Vistula and armed with a quick-firing gun.

the result that the rough country roads in Eastern Galicia were churned by the motor traffic into bottomless swamps. All the mechanical means of transport, on which the Germans relied for quickness of manœuvre, were put out of action. It needed six horses to drag one motor-vehicle, and the labour knocked up the ordinary army horses in a few days. Everywhere supply columns were stuck in hopeless mire, and the task of providing the troops with food and munitions was terribly difficult. The condition of the ground grew worse on the north of General Ivanoff's front, which extended into the Pripet Marsh along the lines of the Styr and Goryn Rivers, guarding the railway embankment running across the swamps and linking Pinsk with Rovno. There were many morasses

between the Styr and the Goryn, and the swamps were overtopped by hills, on which the Russian forces entrenched with field-guns. General Ivanoff did not rely upon the Volhynian triangle of fortresses—Lutzk, Dubno, and Rovno—but based his northern wing on the more northerly village of Derajno, from which branched three small lines of light railways, connecting with the munitioning centre of Rovno. With the light railways he was able to waste Linsingen's forces by constantly moving to and fro between the Styr and the Goryn; for with his three light railways he could concentrate rapidly on a wide marshy front, and destroy the German troops mired between the rivers. In their attacks the Russians seldom went in pursuit farther than Kolki on the Styr, which was about twelve miles from the central light railway-head. It was by this method that Rovno was defended and Lutzk for a time recaptured.

How Rovno was defended

Tarnopol, in Galicia, however, remained the grand striking point for the southern Russian army, and it was against Tarnopol that Mackensen directed his main effort. In the first week of September the German commander brought up hundreds of his heaviest siege-guns by the railway running from Lemberg to Zloczov, and thence to

RUSSIA'S DEFENSIVE DESTRUCTION.
Entrance hall of the Kovno railway-station as the enemy troops found it on entering the town.

Zborov towards Tarnopol. A division of the Prussian Guard —the 3rd Division—with the 48th Reserve Division, and an Austrian brigade, advanced from Zborov on the night of September 7th, for an assault on Tarnopol. Then, eighteen miles farther south, near the little riverside town of Trembovla, an Austrian army, with Skoda siege-guns, also advanced to break the Russian line on the Sereth, hoping thus to destroy entirely Ivanoff's forces in Galicia.

However, Ivanoff was not only a great general, but he had in his lieutenants, Brussiloff, Lechitsky, and Cherbachoff, three

THE ENEMY ADVANCE IN RUSSIAN POLAND.
Kalisz, Russian Poland, after its bombardment by the Austro-German forces; scarcely a building remained intact.

of the most skilful and deadly fighters in the modern world. These three local commanders observed the enemy's preparations for an attack in the Grand Phalanx style, and having fought the Grand Phalanx when it was at its full strength between the Dunajec and the Bug, Generals Lechitsky and Cherbachoff knew how to deal with it in its decline.

The two Russian armies moved out from their trenches in the darkness of the September night, followed by a strong force of Cossack cavalry, and the famous " Rushing Victories." The latter were merely a **The " Rushing Victories "** squadron of armoured motor-cars carrying Maxim guns; but they were used along the road from Tarnopol to Zloczov in a very adventurous and daring manner. When the German and Austrian siege-guns began the usual hurricane fire on the Russian trenches, these were empty. The troops were already breaking through the German and Austrian lines of advanced infantry, and groping for the columns behind the skirmishing screens, and massing machine-guns on their flanks. As soon as the infantry struggle so mixed the troops up that the artillery on either side could not fire into the field of carnage, the new heavy Russian guns, lifted on the enemy's arc of siege artillery, producing one

WOUNDED ON A RUSSIAN WATERWAY.
Removing wounded from a hospital barge at a Russian Red Cross base.

flight; but the arc of siege-guns was not reached by the Cossack cavalry until daylight on September 8th. Then, by massed shrapnel fire, the great guns and howitzers broke up the first charging squadrons of cavalry. The Cossacks, nevertheless, captured 14 siege-guns and 16 field-guns, with 200 officers and 8,000 men. At Trembovla, 3 guns and 36 machine-guns were taken, with 150 officers and 7,000 men. The enemy fled in a panic haste to the Strypa River. The Russians followed them up, and by September 12th the prisoners numbered 40,000 and the spoil included 14 siege-guns, 35 field-guns, and 70 machine-guns. In the following week 40,000 more prisoners, with 2 guns and 79 Maxims, were taken in the more northerly sector round Ltuzk.

WAIFS OF THE WAR.
Scene on a Russian railway siding, where peasant children, separated from their parents during the general hurried exodus before the German invader, were being cared for.

of the grand surprises of the war. The Russian infantry and cavalry, with their daring motor-car crews, then gave both the German army and the Austrian army a lesson in attacking tactics. The Austrian and Hungarian troops in the Tarnopol section surrendered; the German Reserve Division was half destroyed, and twenty thousand of the Prussian Guard, after trying to maintain their traditions by making a stand, were outflanked, ridden down, bayoneted, and knocked over in hundreds by the machine-guns. The German line was broken, and the troops put to

TSAR'S SOLDIERS AS GOOD SAMARITANS.
Women refugees of the Polish peasantry entertained by the good-natured soldiers of the Tsar at a military camp near to the zone of operations.

The total losses of the enemy, including prisoners, could not have been less than a quarter of a million, and were probably more—for 80,000 prisoners usually means 80,000 dead and 160,000 wounded. In, other words, the Russian armies on the Sereth line, when supplied with all the shell they needed, were able to put out of action fully half the effectives opposed to them. So shattering was their double blow that when Mackensen, in consequence of it, decided it would be easier to pierce through Serbia than to get round to the Black Sea, he had to delay his Danube adventure in order to obtain fresh forces therefor.

A considerable body of Austrian troops was available, as it was possible to detach Woyrsch's army from Prince Leopold of Bavaria's group, north of the Pripet Marsh. But the German Staff pointed out with extraordinary insolence, in an official communiqué relating to the actions at Tarnopol and Trembovla, that the enormous number of prisoners taken by the Russians were all Austrians and Hungarians, and the guns lost were also Austro-Hungarian. In an answering communiqué, the Russian Staff maliciously pretended to agree with the untrue German statement, for General Alexeieff, the new Chief of Staff to the Tsar, was not unwilling to accentuate the bitter feeling between the Teutonic allies. The plain meaning of the German communiqué was that it publicly condemned the Austrians as cowards, in spite of the probability that the large number of Austrians taken was due to the fact that the angry victorious Russian troops slew their cruellest foes out of hand, but spared Austrian and Hungarian regiments likely to contain Galician Poles and Russians, Catholic Serbs and Bohemians. Many of the guns, such as those taken from the Prussian Guard and Linsingen's troops, were clearly German.

In any case, Mackensen, after the Battle of the Sereth River, would not conduct a campaign against Serbia unless he had at least one army of German troops. **Mackensen's Danube adventure** As things stood on the eastern and western fronts, no German army was immediately available; and Mackensen had to wait until Hindenburg had completed his great coup against General Evert, which was expected to release one or two German armies. It seems to have been calculated in advance that fully two German armies would be released by the decisive victory near Vilna; and the Bulgars were therefore promised a co-operating force of about 400,000 troops for the combined attack against the Serbians. In the event, however, only General von Gallwitz's army was detached from Hindenburg's command; and for reasons that will soon be apparent to the reader, this solitary German force which was given to Mackensen arrived on the Danube in a sad condition of wastage. Meanwhile, the fact that Mackensen was left in the middle of September with no troops of his own is a telling instance of the grim expenditure of life during the five months' campaign of the Grand Phalanx and its supporting forces.

Even allowing for the fact that some divisions were at last sent, with a thousand heavy guns, to the western front, to prepare against the Franco-British offensive movement, the dissolution of Mackensen's huge army group was of grave significance. Something like a million men had been put out of action, and, after this fearful drain upon the resources of the Teutonic Empires, the armies of the Tsar, though severely shaken, were now beginning to increase in power as their supplies of munitions augmented. Never in his wildest and most sanguinary period had Napoleon I. expended the lives of trained men so recklessly as Mackensen and Hindenburg had done. All the military caste could show the populace, in return for a gigantic sacrifice of life without parallel in history, was a line of fallen Russian frontier fortresses and the occupation of Russian Poland.

Recapture of Grodno

After the comparative failure of Mackensen, who was undoubtedly the best of its commanders, the German Staff had one source of hope left; for Hindenburg promised at last to make good. The new Russian Army general, Evert, had hung too long on to the last great frontier fortress of Grodno. Grodno did not fall until the afternoon of September 3rd, 1915, when an amazing Russian rearguard recaptured the town, and then retired with a hundred and fifty German prisoners and eight machine-guns. General Evert stayed in Grodno till he had cleared it of everything and blown up all the works, bridges, railways, and buildings useful for military purposes. While he did so, the Vilna army with General Russky's southern wing held up a great German turning movement along the Vilia River, at a distance of nearly a hundred miles north-west of Grodno. But this far-stretched Russian operation of retirement was in the circumstances daring to the point of national peril. Had General Evert been fully aware that Hindenburg was holding in reserve for a terrible lightning stroke a force of 40,000 cavalry with a hundred and forty pieces of horse artillery, and a large supporting army of infantry, he would not have waited to strip Grodno of every gun and shell.

Evert's army was not harried in the first days of its retreat. A little pressure was exerted against it at Orany, where the great Trans-European railway line passed through the Grodno-Vilna section, on the route to Petrograd.

BOUND FOR THE POLISH FRONT: ONE OF HER BIG GUNS ON WHICH AUSTRIA PLACED SO MUCH RELIANCE.

GERMAN ENGINEERS REBUILDING A BRIDGE COMMUNICATION ON THE RUSSIAN FRONT.
Interesting camera picture of a German engineer corps engaged in reconstructing a bridge blown up by the Russians on the eastern front. With the powerful mechanical accessories of modern warfare, the strategic destruction of a bridge involved at the most only a temporary delay to an advancing army. The Germans soon repaired even the imposing bridges across the Vistula

It was, however, not at Evert's army that Hindenburg was immediately striking. For, as we have seen, the envelopment of the forces of a single Russian command did not content the old Field-Marshal. This was merely the sort of thing he had accomplished the year before at Tannenberg. What he now aimed at was a tremendous stroke, crashing right through Russia, the success of which would exalt him above the older Moltke and Napoleon I. and the strategists in the grand style. He designed to capture Evert's army by the way, making a double turning movement against the northern army under Russky and against the central army under Alexeieff's successor. His point of attack was an extraordinary one. It was the railway junction at Molodetchno, nearly one hundred and fifty miles in the rear of Grodno. He intended to reach it by breaking through Russky's southern wing in a hurricane of shell fire followed by the greatest cavalry charge in modern history. All this part of the work was to be done by Litzmann's army with Kovno as its base and Schmettau's cavalry as its advanced

Hindenburg's point of attack guard. On the Niemen front, facing the rearguards of Evert's army, was the army of Scholtz, whose southern wing curled round Grodno and linked with the army of Gallwitz, which was advancing north of the Bielovieska Forest towards the town of Lida. Still farther south, on the road to Slonim, was the army of Prince Leopold of Bavaria, connecting in turn southward with a large mixed force of Landsturm and Landwehr troops, operating very slowly along the Pripet Marsh. The southernmost inferior force did little more than hold the Russians by marsh entrenchments bristling with machine-guns. The hammer blow against Alexeieff's old army and the former Lublin and Cholm army was designed to fall on their northern flank, when Prince Leopold reached the railway junction of Baranovitschi. But all this part of the front was, for the time, of little importance.

The critical sector was that between Sventsiany, on the Petrograd railway, half-way from Vilna and Dvinsk, and Baranovitschi, the railway junction between Minsk and Pinsk. It was Russky who foresaw the extreme peril of the situation. He came down from the Riga-Dvinsk sector on September 1st, and hurried Evert out of **Russky foresees the peril**
Grodno. Evert worked downwards in a north-easternly direction towards Baranovitschi and Pinsk, to counter the upward thrust of Gallwitz's and Prince Leopold's armies. This part of the operation was just straightforward hard fighting and incessant manœuvring all along the northern curve of the huge salient, from Skidel, near Grodno, and thence along the Upper Niemen, past the towns of Lida, Slonim, and Novo Grodek to the critical railway junction at Baranovitschi. The northern wing of Alexeieff's former army group co-operated with Evert's retreating forces and greatly assisted in the defence of the southern dent in the salient. There was never any immediate danger at this point, for the German troops were held and violently punished.

All the desperate difficulties of the great Russian retreat from the last and most dangerous salient fell upon General Russky. Coming down from the north, with part of the Petrograd army of defence, he boldly threw a considerable portion of his forces into the salient, bringing up the number of troops enclosed in it to about 400,000. He reckoned that he would be half-encircled by 600,000 German troops, and his estimate was correct. But he does not seem to have been fully aware of the existence of the 40,000 horsemen, with 140 guns, under Schmettau, who

A TEMPORARY DELAY.
Wreck of a military train conveying munitions to part of the Russian front. A number of Polish civilians are seen contemplating the damage.

REDOUBTABLE COSSACKS IN A SYLVAN SETTING.
Reserves of Russian cavalry resting awhile in a wood, in anticipation of a call to action.

moved his men by night northward towards Sventsiany, as Russky pushed his men northwards towards Vilna.

There was a curious beginning to the grand German attempt to obtain a smashing decision against Russia by the envelopment of two or three army groups, followed by an advance to Smolensk. A throng of refugee farmers from the Niemen region came into Orany, on the Warsaw-Petrograd railway line, between Grodno and Vilna. They had their cattle, sheep, horses, and waggons piled with household stuff. But the Russian troops in the town remarked the absence of children in the procession of fugitives, and some of their officers stopped the carts. A fierce street fight at once broke out, for beneath a covering of ordinary articles, the farm waggons were filled with machine-guns and ammunition, and the peasants and their wives were all German soldiers. But the absence of children, who were the most characteristic feature of a genuine stream of fugitive farming folk, had made the Russians suspicious, and they were prepared for the fight that ensued. The Germans were badly beaten, and the survivors fled from Orany.

Discovery of bogus " refugees " This episode did not lead General Russky to alter his plan of operations. He fixed on the angle between the Sventa and Vilia Rivers, between Kovno and Vilna, as the region of the German turning movement.

On September 1st he placed two divisions of the Russian Imperial Guard on a hill, some seven hundred feet high. by the village of Meiszagola. The position was eighteen miles north-west of Vilna, on the road to Vilkomir. It completely barred the turning movement with infantry forces which General Litzmann, the conqueror of Kovno, had ordered to carry out, for the famous Imperial Guard, a body of 24,000 bayonets, with a considerable

number of field batteries, fought with magnificent skill and tenacity. " Even the ranks of Tuscany could scarce forebear to cheer." Indeed, German war correspondents, basing their remarks on the testimony of German officers, were eloquent in praise of the army corps of Russian Guardsmen.

Day and night the battle went on, and the assailing German forces, as the Germans themselves related, " melted away as in a September storm. Regiments dwindled into companies, and companies vanished." For ten days and ten nights the battle lasted in a narrow valley at the foot of the hill, below the trenches of the Guardsmen, whose well-designed earthworks became **Russian Guards'** afterwards the object of admiration of **great stand** German soldiers. " They learned something in trench-making from the Japanese," said the hostile officers. " The position, even when we stormed the hill above, remained almost impregnable." Three times the Guards retook the hill. The Germans had at last to haul up their siege-guns from Kovno, and after the trenches were flattened out by a storm of big shells on September 12th, the Guardsmen, reduced to the number of a single division, made a slow rearguard fight across the low, rolling hill country, trenching on every line of crests. Their machine-guns were terrible, and six days' more fighting had to be done before the enemy got into Vilna, on September 18th, and found the city emptied.

As a matter of fact, Litzmann's army was practically defeated. Unaided, it could not have entered Vilna, even with the aid of its siege ordnance. The Imperial Guard at last retired before the shattered German army, because of a startling event that happened some fifty miles farther north. Here, near the town of Sventsiany, on the night of September 14th, the great hostile cavalry force under General Schmettau found a gap in the overstretched line of Russky's armies.

It would be rash to say that Russky had been over-confident and negligent, for Russky was a man with a quiet, subtle, and far-reaching mind. The German cavalry had been seriously menacing him in the Riga region. It inconvenienced him there, and it was like him to have left a gap at the spot where he wanted to deal with it. He did somewhat the same thing with two army corps under Mackensen, near the Piontek Marshes, by Lodz, in the previous autumn. He left a gate open, let the enemy penetrate far towards his rear, and then pushed the gate to, and sent for Rennenkampf to close down behind the too adventurous German force. With anybody except Russky one would decide that he made a mistake of omission at Sventsiany and afterwards nobly retrieved it. But with Russky it is hazardous to make such a statement, unless and until the Russian Staff history of the war confirms it.

For Russky, the conqueror of Galicia and the destroyer of the first-line Austrian army, under General Auffenberg, in Poland, had become a passionate believer in the war of attrition. He was in a salient enclosing 400,000 men at the most, with the odds of three to two against him in men, and the odds of three or four to one against him in guns and shell supplies. His immediate problem was to reduce rapidly a force of 640,000 Germans to 300,000 effectives, or less. After that, he would rely on autumnal rains and winter frosts—the first frost being due in a month's time in the northern Russian climate—to accelerate further the exhaustion of the human material of Germany and Austria. It was more than two hundred miles to Smolensk, and even Smolensk was not Petrograd or Moscow. Therefore, with winter approaching and the Russian roads sticky with deep mud, he could afford to give ground to the enemy east of Vilna, if the enemy would pay his price. Hindenburg and his lieutenants—Eichhorn, Litzmann, Schmettau, Scholtz,

The open gate at Sventsiany

and Leopold of Bavaria—were ready to risk anything for a fighting chance of a great decisive victory. So General Russky had only to leave the gate open at Sventsiany, in order to get a vast, furious medley of battles between the Vilia and Upper Niemen Rivers and along the lake district from Dvinsk to Smorgon.

The mighty German cavalry raid through Sventsiany on to the Russian rear at Smorgon was marked by characteristic episodes. At a village near Sventsiany the German horsemen burnt a church and hanged the priest, because he would not—or could not—inform them the position of the Russian troops. The country people, taken by surprise, were terribly treated in places, but happily at the beginning of the eruptive movement the raiders were in a great hurry. They wanted to drive down strongly and swiftly

WELCOME RESPITE BEFORE GOING INTO ACTION.
Russian soldiers, prior to relieving their comrades in the firing-line, snatch a few hours' repose in the open. Using their baggage as pillows and their greatcoats as rugs, they managed to infuse a semblance of comfort into their bleak Polish environment. Above is seen a type of Russian armoured train halting at a wayside station.

"FLOWERS OF THE FOREST."
Russian Red Cross nurse in a woodland cemetery in Poland, where rough carven wooden crosses marked the resting-places of her country's dead.

There were few critics in the Quadruple Entente who were not anxious as to the position if Russky were shattered. If Russky's side of the salient were suddenly driven in near the base, Evert's side of the salient would be quickly subjected to a similar cutting thrust. Then, with both Russky and Evert's forces partly enveloped and partly outflanked, the position of the central Russian armies round Pinsk and the Pripet Marsh would also be disastrous. Russia would be in the same tragic situation as France was after the encircling operation at Sedan.

There was an incontestable majesty of design about Hindenburg's project. In Imperial manœuvres it might have won the author the rank of Chief of Staff.

Weather-lore in German strategy

Doubtless Falkenhayn had something to do with it. But its defect was that it had been prepared with Germanic thoroughness. For many years the aspirants to positions on the German General Staff and the Staff officers themselves had elaborated plans for a campaign against Russia. Both novices and masters in strategy began with the determination to avoid Napoleon's capital mistake in regard to the Russian weather. Never did meteorologists go into the problems of weather-lore with the energy of the German Russian campaign planners. They tabulated all the data concerning rainfall, frost, and thaw, and the effects thereof on the muddy Russian roads and swamps, and after the most scientific study arrived at the correct conclusion that September was the best month for operations in the Russian marsh regions. The full drying effect of the

to Smorgon, along the river line of the Vilia, entrench there, advance, with Smorgon as their base of operations, and cut the railways to Minsk and to Polozk and Petrograd at the junction of Molodetchno.

This they accomplished, in a movement of magnificent speed and force, by September 17th. They broke apart Russky's Dvinsk and Vilna wings and penetrated his centre at Molodetchno, which is sixty miles southeastwards of Vilna. And Vilna at the time had not been evacuated. The Imperial Guard was still defending the city, the earthwork defences of which were being bombarded uninterruptedly day and night. Meanwhile, south of the Vilia, a large German army was fighting on the Merechanka River, while still stronger hostile forces were making deeper turning movements south-eastward towards Lida and Slonim.

Fear of a Russian Sedan

To all appearance, the Russians had not been in so perilous a position since Radko Dimitrieff was broken between Tarnov and Gorlice, near the Carpathian line. Indeed, with 40,000 German horsemen sixty miles behind him, with one hundred and forty guns, and huge infantry supports coming to reinforce them, the situation of Russky seemed darkened by the shadow of impending doom.

GERMAN AIR-RAIDERS' RECKLESS WORK NEAR THE RUSSIAN FRONT.
Russian motor-ambulance outside a temporary hospital, near which a bomb had been dropped from a German Taube. The hole in the earth near the front wheel of the ambulance indicates how nearly the airman's fell purpose achieved its object.

August sun was necessary to make the lake morasses and the immense river swamps passable.

All this, however, was but a sound deduction from the law of averages. The summer of 1915 had been an exception to the general rule; for it was a wet summer, and instead of drying the Russian roads and bogs, it soaked them. But the Germans, with their reliance upon the knowledge they had patiently organised, did not allow fully for the new facts beneath their eyes. They used knowledge instead of thought. The result was that the raid of Schmettau's cavalry horde failed for want of infantry support. It was possible, in spite of the adverse weather conditions, for the raiders to operate according to the time-table, and by riding their horses to exhaustion they

The Tsar and Tsarevitch, happily restored to health, inspecting a regiment of Cossacks from the Caucasus.

The Tsar Commander-in-Chief and his heir, in Caucasian uniforms, posing before the camera with a group of Cossack officers.

TSAR NICHOLAS II. DIRECTS THE FORTUNES OF THE HOUSE OF ROMANOFF IN THE FIELD OF WAR.
This photograph of a divine service, showing the two great Romanoffs, bareheaded before an improvised altar erected in a wood on the eastern front, is indicative of the simplicity with which the Tsar carried out the work of Generalissimo of the Russian Army. The Emperor of All the Russias, in taking over supreme command, stimulated the spirit of his soldiers, and his presence among them went far to stop the German invasion of Russia and hold the enemy in check. The third snapshot on this page shows the Russian ruler conversing with an officer of h.s Staff.

FINDING THE RANGE.
Russian artillery officer, concealed by foliage, finding the range for his gun.

reached the railway junction, and tore up the line to Minsk and the line to Moscow. But the huge force of infantry, with many guns, limbers, and ammunition waggons, which was to follow the cavalry with the aim of occupying in great strength the line the horsemen won, was held up by mud and morass. Some 20,000 cavalry of the reserve were hurried forth to support Schmettau's raiders, bringing his forces up to 60,000 men. But these men were extended along a front of eighty miles, from Sventsiany to Molodetchno Junction, and many of them were needed to form a powerful advance guard at Widsy, below Dvinsk, to stave off a possible flank attack from Russky's Dwina troops. The raiding cavalry, therefore, had scarcely seven hundred men to the mile along the great line of their thrust. Owing to this weakness, which continually increased through the delay in the advance of the German infantry and artillery, Schmettau's menace to Russky was nothing so great as Russky's menace to Schmettau.

For the Russian Imperial Guard, with the sharpshooters of Pskov and other famous fighting corps, were retreating alongside the line of the Vilia River, which **Schmettau's raiders** the German cavalry had crossed. Instead **half enveloped** of the cavalry raiders getting a driving blow against the rear of the retreating Russian armies, the overstretched string of horsemen was half enveloped. The Russian troops, retreating from Vilna, held them firmly south of the Vilia River, while a sudden irruption of Russian cavalry forces, coming down the Polozk-Molodetchno railway line, struck them on the head and began to smash in their northern flank. There was a long and extremely violent struggle at the little town of Vileika on the railway line, and at Widsy, farther north. Both battles ended in a Russian victory and a German

rout, in which the enemy lost several batteries of light guns and field-howitzers, showing that his line had been completely penetrated. Nearly half the huge Teutonic cavalry force was destroyed before the German infantry succeeded in getting to Smorgon two weeks after the retreat from Vilna began.

After fighting for fourteen days in the salient, Russky preserved in his rear a passage eighty miles wide, from Molodetchno Junction to the **German siege-guns** Lebeda River between Grodno and Lida. **unavailable** It was a wide enough gate for the largest army to pass through; it had two main roads and two lines of railway. It was indeed so broad and secure that, instead of rapidly retreating through it, General Russky entrenched on a line of hills and streams from Lida to Molodetchno, with a little cross-country railway running immediately behind his line, and provisioning and

HANDIWORK OF THE INCENDIARY.
Russian mill on fire—the work of the Germans in their advance.

munitioning his army. The Germans in front of him had no railway communications, therefore they could not bring up their siege-guns, and even their light artillery was badly supplied, owing to the roads being waist-deep in mud. Yet the German commanders had to attack incessantly and with the utmost possible driving power.

For, according to their own plan, they were engaged in the greatest enveloping movement in history, and the desired decision was only to be obtained by speedy progress. As soon as the march-worn German infantry arrived near

EMERGENCY ENGINEERING ON THE EASTERN FRONT.
Bridge over a railway track in course of temporary reconstruction. The supports of the bridge were formed of rectangular piles of sleepers.

the Russian lines, it was flung forth in wide waves and packed columns, through the Russian curtains of shrapnel fire, against the Russian hill-trenches.

It is impossible to describe in detail the battles that went on, day and night, till the end of September on the gradually flattening curve of flame, thunder, and slaughter, stretching from a point near Slonim in the south to the lake region above Sventsiany in the north. The description will run into volumes in the great scientific Staff histories, and the pages will be full of long, outlandish names of Lithuanian hamlets which cannot be traced on any ordinary map. Russky's men were, like Ivanoff's, well provided with munitions, and the Russian machine-guns, hundreds of them captured from the enemy with cartridge supplies, were used with murderous effect. The Russian cannon, with few German siege-guns to beat them down, were able to open a way for those fierce

THE MEN WITH THE ROUBLES.
Russian paymaster and his assistants ready to distribute the soldiers' wages.

bayonet charges, in which the slow, sombre passion of the Russian peasant flames into terrible fury. Here and there a Russian regiment got into a tight corner. Some Cossacks were surrounded, but escaped by a stratagem, while another battalion cut its way out with the loss of half its men. But the act of heroism that most pleased the Russians themselves was that of an Army nurse, Myra Ivanova, who was attending to the wounded in the fighting-line on September 22nd. Her brother was the surgeon of the regiment, and she was serving as a Red Cross sister with his men. The battalion was suffering terribly from rifle and Maxim fire, and all the company officers were either killed or wounded, and the men began to retire. But Sister Ivanova saw that they would all be slaughtered if they tried to flee, and she collected them together and led the charge against the hostile trench, falling mortally wounded just as her men broke the defence of the German force.

By September 28th General Russky was still holding out, well inside the salient on the Smorgoni line, having fought Hindenburg to a standstill. The movement of envelopment had entirely failed after four weeks' fighting and a German loss of half a million men.

WAITING FOR THE LAST TRAIN AT GRODZISK.
Russian soldiers, including a number of wounded, about to retreat by rail from a shell-wrecked station on the eastern front. In circle: Scene at a junction on the eastern front. Wounded Russian and German soldiers were being hastily treated by the surgeons and sent to the rear.

CONTROLLING FOURTEEN HUNDRED SHELL FACTORIES: MR. LLOYD GEORGE, MINISTER OF MUNITIONS, AT WORK IN HIS OFFICE.

From the control of silver bullets to the supervision of the steel bullets to the steel harbingers of triumph was a momentous change; but so energetically did Mr. Lloyd George fill his unique position as temporary organiser and director of the Ministry of Munitions, inaugurated on May 25th, 1915, that as many as 1,400 establishments were under Government control within five months. All these shops were working full speed ahead in order, to use Mr. Lloyd George's own phrase, "to crash through to victory." Though the enemy started with a colossal advantage in respect of guns and shells, the tables were slowly but surely turned as the war, again to quote Mr. Lloyd George, "resolved itself into a conflict between the mechanics of Germany and Austria on the one hand, and the mechanics of Great Britain and France on the other."

CHAPTER LXXXVI.

THE NEW CABINET AND ITS WORK : POLITICS & MUNITIONS.

Lord Fisher Visits Mr. Asquith—Civilians and the War—Distrust of Experts—Trouble at the Admiralty—A National Government Arranged—Asquith Tells the Commons—Members of the New Cabinet—The Shuffling of Portfolios—Mr. Redmond and the National Government—Ministers and the Super-Tax—Their Real Reason :—What Was It ?—The Shortage of Munitions—Lloyd George and Kitchener Speak Out—New Powers for the Government—Lloyd George and Trade Union Restrictions—The Lure of Drink—A "Good, Strong Business Man" Secured—Mr. Asquith at Newcastle—Lloyd George Gives an Account of His Work —Fresh Restrictions on Drinking—Our Losses on the Aubers Ridge—A Ministry of Munitions Formed—Lloyd George Gets to Work—His Munitions Bill.

ON the afternoon of Saturday, May 15th, 1915, Mr. Asquith's motor-car was standing in front of 10, Downing Street, ready to take the Prime Minister into the country for the week-end. About 3.30 that statesman came out of his front door, entered the car, and was just about to give the word to the chauffeur when Lord Fisher walked across the street and spoke to him. Mr. Asquith alighted, and the two stood together for some time talking ; then the car was sent away and they entered the house. About an hour later Lord Fisher walked away, and after that the Prime Minister was driven off in his car.

At this time the Great War had been waged for nine and a half months, and no decisive success had been attained. The worst fears—the interruption of the British food supply and a German invasion—had, happily, not been realised ; but, on the other hand, the Germans were still in France and Belgium, and the campaign in Gallipoli was proving a very costly operation. There was nothing approaching panic among the people, but there was a feeling that the situation was graver, far graver, than had been hitherto believed.

During these nine months, the war—at least, as far as Great Britain was concerned—had been conducted, with one distinguished exception, by civilians and politicians, and worse than that, by politicians representing only one, and that the smaller, of the two great historic parties in the State. By concessions to two smaller groups these men

had secured control of the House of Commons in 1910, and they still held it when the Great War broke out. In France, at the beginning of September, 1914, a Committee of National Safety, representing all parties, took over the conduct of the war ; but for one reason or other Great Britain did not then follow this good example.

The fact that, with the exception of Lord Kitchener, these men were civilians did not matter much if only they were wise civilians. The best expert advice was at their disposal, and if they only followed this all would be well.

But, unfortunately, the nation, or a considerable part of it, had got into the way of distrusting the experts, and of thinking that because all men were equal in votes they were equal in wisdom ; and politicians had shared and encouraged this delusion. The nation had been told quite coolly that Lord Roberts, one of the greatest soldiers of all time, and the man who saved the Empire after the dark December of 1899, knew little or nothing about strategy ; while Lord Rothschild and other banking authorities were jeered at when, in 1910, they said that certain taxation proposals would injure our national credit. This spirit, a most astounding monument to the size of human folly, was certainly sobered by the outbreak of the Great War, but it was not destroyed, and we fear that it was not unrepresented in Mr. Asquith's Cabinet. It may perhaps have been possible to take risks when fighting the Boers, or tampering with a tried financial system, and yet to escape serious

THE SHELL MINISTERS.
Mr. Lloyd George and M. Thomas, the British and French Ministers of Munitions, photographed together on the occasion of the latter's visit to London in October, 1915.

disaster, but it was suicidal to do so when Germany was on the warpath.

The members of Mr. Asquith's Cabinet, Lord Kitchener excepted, were not only civilians, they were politicians. Mr. Asquith had shown himself loyal to the Empire by the firm stand which he took during the Boer War. He realised the gravity of the nation's task, and his quiet and authoritative manner, added to his luminous speech, was a useful asset ; but the fact cannot be disguised that his lack of power or inclination to control his headstrong colleagues might easily become a serious danger. But several members of his Cabinet deserved no word of praise whatever. They were party politicians of the narrowest kind, men whose highest ideal in life was a cheap score off a political opponent, and who could not wholly rid themselves of this spirit even in the presence of our greatest war. In August, 1914, they had it in their power to do their country one service, but they forbore. They could have retired into private life.

For some time previous to the interview between Mr. Asquith and Lord Fisher it had been rumoured that Mr. Winston Churchill, the First Lord of the Admiralty, and Lord Fisher, the First Sea Lord, were not working very harmoniously together, and some went as far as to say that the former had arranged the expedition to the Dardanelles against the desire of the latter. Whatever the truth was, there was certainly trouble at the Admiralty, and it did not need a seer to guess that Lord Fisher's visit to the Prime Minister had something to do with this.

Trouble at the Admiralty

On the Saturday of this interview, or the following Sunday, Mr. Asquith decided to take the step which some thought

CAMERA VIEWS OF THE GREAT SCHNEIDER WORKSHOPS AT LE CREUSOT, THE FRENCH WOOLWICH.

The town of Le Creusot, in the Department of Saone-et-Loire, is situated at the foot of lofty hills, in a district rich in coal and iron. Here, in 1837, were established the ironworks of Adolphe and Eugène Schneider, which developed into one of the greatest enterprises of the kind in the world.

From the Schneider factories huge quantities of war material were supplied to the French armies during the Crimean and the Franco-Prussian Wars. In the present war the guns and munitions of this great firm proved no mean rivals to the productions of Krupp and Skoda.

WOMEN MUNITION WORKERS IN THE SCHNEIDER
BRANCH WORKSHOPS, CHALON-SUR-SAONE.

he should have taken on the outbreak of war. He
decided to ask the leaders of the other political parties to
unite with him in forming a Coalition Government to carry
on the war. He did this, as by our unwritten Constitution
he was entitled to do, without consulting his colleagues as
a whole, although he may have talked the matter over with
one or two of his more intimate friends among them, and
to clear the way he asked them to place their resignations in
his hands. They did so, and the Liberal Government, which
had been in office since December, 1905, came to an end.

Mr. Asquith then wrote to Mr. Bonar Law, the Unionist
leader in the House of Commons, asking him and those
associated with him, " to join forces with us in a combined
administration," and telling him that he intended also
to ask the leaders of the Irish and Labour parties to participate. The Prime Minister gave his
reasons for taking this step in the following
words : " After long and careful consideration, I have definitely come to the con-
clusion that the conduct of the war to a successful and decisive
issue cannot be effectively carried on except by a Cabinet
which represents all parties of the State." Their common
action, he added, " should be exclusively directed to the
issues of the war."

The non-party
Cabinet

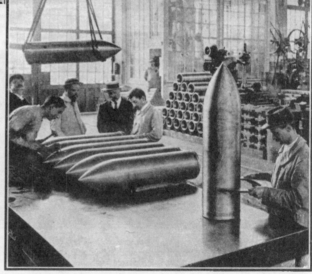

EXAMINING 11 IN. SHELLS IN ONE OF THE GREAT
SCHNEIDER FACTORIES.

Mr. Bonar Law accepted the invitation in the following
sentences : " The considerations to which you refer have for
some time been present to the mind of Lord Lansdowne and
myself. We have now communicated your views and your
invitation to our colleagues, and we shall be glad to co-operate
with you in your endeavour to form a National Government."

While these letters were passing, and the preliminaries
of the Coalition were being arranged, the public was
speculating, knowing little more than the stories of trouble
at the Admiralty. On Tuesday morning, May 18th, " The
Times " stated that Lord Fisher insisted on resigning
his post on account of his differences with Mr. Churchill,
and on the evening of that day " The Pall Mall Gazette "
said that a Coalition Government was being formed.

On the following day, Wednesday, May 19th, Mr.

FOR THE FAMOUS "75's": SHELL INSPECTION IN ONE
OF THE SCHNEIDER WORKSHOPS.

Asquith set all doubts at rest. Speaking in the House of Commons, he said :

I think it right, at the earliest possible moment, to say two or three words to the House in regard to the matters which have been the subject of public report and rumour. I cannot say more at the moment than that steps are in contemplation which involve the reconstruction of the Government on a broader personal and political basis. Nothing is yet definitely arranged, but to avoid any possible misapprehension, and as the House is about to adjourn, I wish here and now to make clear to everybody three

Mr. Asquith and reconstruction things. The first is that any change which takes place will not affect the offices of the head of the Government, or of the Secretary of State for Foreign Affairs. They will continue to be held as they are now. The second is that there is absolutely no change of any kind in contemplation in the policy of the country with regard to the continued prosecution of the war with every possible energy, and by means of every available resource.

The third and last point, one of great importance to my hon. friends behind me, and I have no doubt also to hon. gentlemen who sit behind the Leader of the Opposition, is this : Any reconstruction that will be made will be for the purposes of the war alone, and is not to be taken in any quarter as any reason for

THE TSAR IN A MUNITION FACTORY.
Photograph, taken by His Majesty's command, of the Tsar's visit to the Putiloff works at Petrograd.

indicating anything in the nature of surrender or compromise on the part of any person or body of persons of their several political purposes and ideals.

For a week the newspapers and the public were busy guessing at the names of the members of the new Government. One or two were certain, and several others practically so. Mr. Asquith, Lord Kitchener, and Sir Edward Grey would stay at their posts, and room would be found for Mr. Bonar Law, Mr. Balfour, Mr. Austen Chamberlain, and possibly Lords Lansdowne and Curzon. Mr. Lloyd George would remain a member of the Cabinet, and Mr. Arthur Henderson, the Leader of the Labour Party, would join it, but there was more uncertainty about the position of Mr. Winston Churchill and the attitude of Mr. John Redmond.

On May 26th the newspapers contained the names of the members of the new Cabinet. There were one or two surprises, but on the whole the forecasts had been tolerably accurate. The late Cabinet had consisted of twenty members—nineteen Liberals and Lord Kitchener—but the new one contained twenty-two. Twelve of these were

members of the retiring Cabinet—Mr. Asquith, Sir Edward Grey, Lord Kitchener, Lord Crewe, Mr. Lloyd George, Mr. McKenna, Mr. Harcourt, Mr. Birrell, Sir John Simon, Mr. Runciman, Mr. McKinnon Wood, and Mr. Winston Churchill. The eight who retired were Viscount Haldane, Lords Beauchamp, Lucas, and Emmott, Mr. Herbert Samuel, Mr. Hobhouse, Mr. J. A. Pease, and Mr. Montagu. Of these, two—Mr. Samuel and Mr. Montagu—received positions in the new Government, but outside the Cabinet. Mr. Samuel returned to his former position of Postmaster-General, and Mr. Montagu became again Financial Secretary to the Treasury.

Of the ten new-comers eight were Unionists, one was a Liberal, and one the Leader of the Labour Party. The Unionists were Lord Lansdowne, Mr. Bonar Law, Lord Curzon, Mr. Balfour, Mr. Austen Chamberlain, Mr. Walter Long, Lord Selborne, and Sir Edward Carson. The Liberal was Sir Stanley Buckmaster, afterwards Lord Buckmaster, who succeeded Viscount Haldane as Lord Chancellor.

There was a good deal of shuffling of positions to find suitable places for these gentlemen. Mr. Asquith, Sir Edward Grey, Lord Kitchener, Mr. Runciman (President of the Board of Trade), Mr. Birrell (Chief Secretary for Ireland), and Mr. McKinnon Wood (Secretary for Scotland) remained at their posts, but all the others were moved. Mr. Balfour took Mr. Churchill's place as First Lord of the Admiralty, but this did not surprise people so much as the appointment of Mr. McKenna to succeed Mr. Lloyd George as Chancellor of the Exchequer. Mr. Churchill became Chancellor of the Duchy of Lancaster, and Mr. Lloyd George Minister of Munitions, a new office which we shall deal with in a moment.

Important positions were reserved for Mr. Bonar Law and Mr. Austen Chamberlain, who became Secretary for the Colonies and Secretary for India respectively. Mr. Walter Long was made President of the Local Government Board, Lord Selborne President of the Board of Agriculture, while Lord Curzon succeeded Lord Crewe in the sinecure office of Lord Privy Seal. Sir John Simon became Home Secretary in place of Mr. McKenna, and Sir Edward Carson took the former's place as Attorney-General. Lord Crewe became Lord President of the Council instead of Secretary for India, and Mr. Harcourt First Commissioner of Works, a position he had formerly filled, instead of Colonial Secretary.

Lord Lansdowne entered the Cabinet without any particular office, a member "without portfolio," as he was styled. In the eighteenth and earlier part of the nineteenth centuries it was not unusual to have members of this kind in the Cabinet, but since then the custom had been dropped. Curiously enough, the last Minister previously to hold a position of this kind in this country was Lord Lansdowne's grandfather, in 1855. It remains to be said that Mr. Arthur Henderson, Labour's representative in the new Cabinet, became President of the Board of Education.

Little need be said about the appointments to offices outside the Cabinet. They were divided fairly evenly between Liberals and Unionists, with two representatives of Labour—Mr. William Brace, the **Offices outside** Under-Secretary for Home Affairs, and **the Cabinet** Mr. G. H. Roberts, a Junior Lord of the Treasury. Of the other appointments, perhaps the most interesting were those of Lord Robert Cecil to be Under-Secretary for Foreign Affairs, and of Mr. (now Sir) F. E. Smith to be Solicitor-General. Mr. John Redmond declined Mr. Asquith's invitation, and consequently the Irish Nationalists were unrepresented in the Coalition Government. The party, at a meeting held in Dublin on May 25th, supported Mr. Redmond in his refusal, but decided to give to the new

Munitions in the making : Oil=hardening a 12 in. gun tube.

The King in France, with President Poincaré and General Joffre on his left.

French infantry passing in review order before his Majesty and President Poincaré.

King George with the French troops: An earnest talk with General Joffre.

The King at the front : Greeting Canadian General Officers.

The Prince of Wales admires the Spahis.

Symbol of "La Belle Alliance," 1915.

In one of Britain's new munitions factories : Alloys being shot into molten steel to strengthen it.

Government the support they had hitherto accorded to the old one.

The change was for the better, but in certain important respects the new Cabinet was as unsatisfactory as the old one had been. It was all to the good that the leaders of the Unionist Party and the official head of the Labour Party should take a share of the responsibility of the war; but two main objections to the old Cabinet had not been removed by the advent of the new one.

Defects of the new Ministry As before, the Cabinet was too big and too civilian. Its membership, originally far too large, had actually been increased from twenty to twenty-two, and a body of this size cannot, in the very nature of things, conduct a war efficiently. Decisions cannot be taken promptly when twenty-two persons have to weigh and discuss the pros and cons, and much valuable time is lost in talking.

Again, with the solitary exception of Lord Kitchener, the Cabinet was still exclusively civilian,

COLONEL F. F. MINCHIN, [*Elliott & Fry.*]
Military adviser to the Ministry of Munitions.

[*Vandyk.*]
SIR FREDERICK DONALDSON, K.C.B.,
Chief Superintendent of Ordnance Factories. He acted as technical adviser to the Ministry of Munitions.

and several of these civilians were, by training and inclination, the last men in the world to take prompt action on any question whatsoever. They were essentially men of inaction, men of the " wait and see " type. Possibly they could, after long and anxious consideration, put in force a muzzling order for dogs, but to decide in five minutes what to do in a sudden emergency with the lives of thousands and perhaps the fate of the nation hanging in the balance, was altogether too much for them.

In those critical days the nation really needed a Committee of Public Safety, small in number and of extraordinary efficiency, in constant session and with absolute confidence in each other. For this ten men would have been ample, five or six probably sufficient. They should have consisted of a soldier, a sailor, a financier, a Foreign Minister, and one or two others, and armed with full powers they could have saved Britain millions of money and thousands of lives.

One rather curious matter may be mentioned here. As is known, the salaries of Cabinet Ministers vary very much, from the £10,000 a year paid to the Lord Chancellor to the £2,000 a year paid to the Presidents of the Boards of

Agriculture, Education, and one or two others. The members of the Coalition Cabinet, however, decided to equalise their salaries by pooling them, and this action was defended by Mr. Asquith in the House of Commons. The matter was arranged quite privately, and the exact details were not made known, but it was generally understood that each Cabinet Minister received something over £4,000 a year. This meant that the Lord Chancellor surrendered nearly £6,000 a year, the Attorney-General, the five principal Secretaries of State, the Presidents of the Board of Trade and the Local Government Board, and the Chancellor of the Exchequer, some hundreds a year each, while the salaries of the less important Ministers were about doubled.

In this arrangement two Ministers, Mr. Asquith and Lord Lansdowne, took no part. The former, as head of the Government, retained his full salary of £5,000 a year, while the latter had no salary to put into the pool. On the other hand, it was believed that Sir F. E. Smith **Effect of pooling salaries** brought the £6,000 a year which he received as Solicitor-General into the common stock.

Such, in brief, is the story of the formation of a National Government, " exclusively directed to the issues of the war," in May, 1915. What was the real reason of it all? The quarrel between Mr. Churchill and Lord Fisher was not the whole story. If this had been all it could have been arranged by the retirement of one or both of them, without involving the rest of their colleagues. There was more in it than met the eye, and an inkling of the truth was already getting about. *The Army was short of the munitions of war.* This was a simple fact, and the real reason for the crisis. As one writer has said : " Ministers are human, and so long as things seem to be going well they are anxious to keep the credit for themselves. It is only responsibility, when it looks as if it may be heavy, that they are ready to share."

It was one of Napoleon's maxims that victory goes to the big battalions, but the experience of the Great War has been that it goes rather to the big batteries. The need of all the armies was for an enormous supply of guns and ammunition, especially perhaps of machine-guns and

SMALL BRITISH AIR BOMB.
Small air bomb used by the British, containing a safety-bolt, drawn prior to dropping, by which the propeller was started.

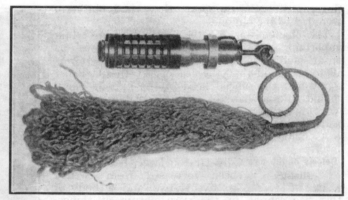

THE ROPE-HANDLE GRENADE.
Steel hand-grenade fastened to a rope handle, by which it was swung and thrown. Its weight was about twenty-three ounces, and it could be thrown about fifty yards.

high-explosive shells; an amount far greater than anyone had previously thought possible was required, and the Germans were the first to realise this new and pregnant fact in the art of war. They were first in the field with an overwhelming supply of munitions, as they had been, in August, 1914, with an overwhelming supply of men, and the result was the stoppage of the expected offensive in the west and the Russian retreat in the east.

In October, 1914, France grappled seriously with this question, but not so Great Britain. In September Mr. Asquith had appointed a Committee of the Cabinet, which included Lord Haldane and Mr. Lloyd George, to look into the matter, but in general everyone was content to leave it in the hands of Lord Kitchener, forgetting the gigantic tasks to which he was already committed.

So matters continued until well into 1915, when one or two hesitating steps were taken. On February 9th, for instance, it was announced that the President of the

RIFLE-GRENADE IN POSITION
Miniature shrapnel shell fitted to a rod, and fired from a rifle a distance of about three hundred yards.

Board of Trade had appointed Sir George Askwith, Sir Francis Hopwood, and Sir George Gibb to inquire into and report upon the best steps to secure that all the available productive power of the employees engaged in the engineering and shipbuilding establishments of the country should be utilised in the present emergency.

About this time, reasons for the shortage were being discussed. The failure to produce more munitions was ascribed to the prevalence of strikes and the temptations of drink. In a speech delivered at Bangor on February 28th, Mr. George referred to both of these, and Lord Kitchener did the same on March 15th in the House of Lords. Mr. Lloyd George said that "For one reason or another we are not getting all the assistance we have a right to expect from our works," and added: "I say here solemnly that it is

HEMP-BOUND AERIAL BOMB.
German incendiary bomb dropped in England, but extinguished with water.

GERMAN INCENDIARY BOMB DROPPED ON LONDON.
Burnt-out shell of a Zeppelin bomb dropped on London. Bound round with tarred rope, it contained a charge which developed terrific heat.

HAND-GRENADE ON STICK.
Another type of hand-grenade used for short-range trench warfare.

intolerable that the life of Britain should be imperilled for the matter of a farthing an hour." He spoke equally strongly about the lure of the drink, as he called it: "Drink is doing us more damage in the war than all the German submarines put together." Lord Kitchener mentioned the restrictions imposed by the trade unions as another

Photograph taken from a French first-line trench. The enemy's first-line trenches were in front of the belt of trees. A "Jack Johnson" shell was exploding in the air, thus illustrating inaccurate shooting on the part of the German gunners.

French shell that burst in the German trenches. This photograph was taken from a French first-line trench during an artillery duel that was the prelude to the infantry attack shown below.

Preceded by a curtain of shrapnel shells, the French infantrymen, after their artillery had bombarded the German trenches, began their advance. The men had left their trenches, and were seeking scanty cover behind rising ground, awaiting the order to charge.

FRENCH ARTILLERY BOMBARDMENT AS PRELUDE TO INFANTRY ATTACK.

reason for the inadequate output of munitions. In this matter of munitions Mr. Lloyd George was rapidly taking the leading place. On March 9th he introduced into Parliament a Bill, called the Defence of the Realm Amendment (No. 2) Bill, which gave the Government the power to take over the control of all works capable of being used for the production of the munitions of war.

Ministers and munitions

This meant that at any time a manufacturer might be told that his works were required and he must turn out—a drastic, but in the circumstances a necessary proceeding. In his speech, Mr. Lloyd George said : " It is vitally important that we should increase the output, and every facility for the output of munitions of war," and he remarked that he was arranging for a central committee to take charge of the scheme and was looking out for " a good, strong business man with some ' go ' in him, who will be able to push the thing through."

Six days later Lord Kitchener referred to the same subject. He mentioned the excellent response of the armament trades to the nation's need and the loyalty of the great majority of the employees, but added : " Not-

withstanding these efforts to meet our requirements, we have unfortunately found that the output is not only not equal to our necessities, but does not fulfil our expectations, for a very large number of our orders have not been completed by the dates on which they were promised." It was on this occasion that he said that " the supply of war material at the present moment and for the next two or three months is causing me very serious anxiety."

On March 17th Mr. George met the representatives of the trade unions and suggested to them that during the war all their rules and regulations restricting output should be suspended and that labour disputes should be arranged without any stoppage of work. The result was that a memorandum containing certain recommendations to workmen was signed by Mr. George and Mr. Runciman on behalf of the Government, and by Mr. Arthur Henderson and Mr. William Mosses on behalf of the workmen. Its chief points were as follows :

During the war period there shall in no case be any stoppage of work upon munitions and equipments of war.

All differences on wages or conditions of employment shall be the subject of conferences between the parties. In all cases of failure to reach a settlement of disputes by the parties directly concerned or their representatives, or under existing agreements, the matter in dispute shall be dealt with under any one of three alternatives as may be mutually agreed, or, in default of agreement, settled by the Board of Trade.

An Advisory Committee representative of the workers engaged in production for Government requirements shall be appointed by the Government.

During the war period, the relaxation of the present trade practices is imperative. Any departure from the practice ruling shall only be for the period of the war.

The relaxation of existing demarcation restrictions or admission of semi-skilled or female labour shall not affect adversely the rates customarily paid for the job.

On March 29th the Shipbuilding Employers' Federation sent a deputation to Mr. Lloyd George to advocate the closing of public-houses and clubs in areas where munitions of war were produced. They brought forward evidence that much of the increased wages earned by the workmen was spent in drink, and pointed out the obvious fact that this drinking was detrimental to good and regular work and had already caused serious delays. Mr. Lloyd George's reply should be given in some detail. Mr. George said :

Having gone into this matter a great deal more closely during the last few weeks, I must say that I have a growing conviction, based on accumulating evidence, that nothing but root and branch methods will be of the slightest avail in dealing with this evil. I believe that to be the general feeling. The feeling is that if we are to settle with German militarism we must first of all settle with drink. We are fighting Germany, Austria, and Drink ; and as far as I can see, the greatest of these three deadly foes is Drink. Success in the war is now purely a question of munitions ; I say that not on my own authority, but on the authority of our great General, Sir John French. He has made it quite clear what his conviction is on the subject. I think I can venture to say that that is also the conviction of the Secretary of State for War, and it is the conviction of all those who know anything about the military problem—that in order to enable us to win all we require is an increase, and an enormous increase, in the shells, rifles, and

FRENCHWOMEN'S SHARE IN MAKING MUNITIONS.
Frenchwomen testing shells in a French munitions factory. The women of France played a great part in providing our ally's soldiers with ammunition, being largely employed in the manufacture of shells.

all the other munitions and equipment which are necessary to carry through a great war. You have proved to us to-day quite clearly that the excessive drinking in the works connected with these operations is interfering seriously with that output. I can only promise you this at the present moment, that the words you have addressed to my colleagues and myself will be taken into the most careful consideration by my colleagues when we come to our final decision on this question.

In this speech Mr. George referred to the opinion of Sir John French, **Sir John French's** and in his de-**opinion** spatch of April 5th the Field-Marshal again mentioned this matter. "An almost unlimited supply of ammunition," he said, "is necessary, and a most liberal discretionary power as to its use must be given to the artillery commanders. I am confident that this is the only means by which great results can be obtained with a minimum of loss."

"PIOU-PIOUS'" PROFITABLE HOBBY.
During their hours of surcease from fighting, numbers of French soldiers made rings from aluminium taken from spent shells.

FRENCH SHELLS FOR THE "TERRIBLE TURK."
Truckloads of 9·2 in. shells, before they were sent to a French battery on Gallipoli, being guarded by a French Colonial sentry.

the output of munitions, promised to "deliver the goods," and "do their bit," and ended by inviting the Prime Minister to address them. Mr. Asquith accepted the invitation, and on April 20th spoke at Newcastle.

The speech was a cause of amazement. Mr. Asquith said: "I saw a statement the other day that the operations of war, not only of our Army but of our Allies, were being crippled, or, at any rate, hampered, by our failure to provide the necessary ammunition. There is not a word of truth in that statement." He declared that it was neither true nor fair to suggest that there had been anything in the nature of general slackness in **The Government's** the armaments industry on the part of **two voices** either employers or employed, and throughout took an entirely opposite line from that followed by Mr. George and, to a less extent, by Lord Kitchener.

If Mr. Asquith was right, then these two gentlemen had been unduly alarming the nation. The speech aroused a general sense of perplexity, which was the reverse of reassuring. It should be said, however, that the Prime Minister laid great stress upon the need for a large and rapid increase in the output of munitions, this being "one of the first necessities of the State."

On the following day Mr. George spoke on the question in the House of Commons. He gave some account of the work done in providing more munitions, being on the whole optimistic, but he said nothing by way of modifying his earlier warnings. He stated that the output of

Early in April Mr. George found his "good, strong business man" in Mr. G. M. Booth, of Liverpool, who became secretary of a new departmental committee of the War Office. Of this Lord Kitchener was chairman, and its business was "to give assistance in expediting and, if possible, accelerating the supply of munitions of war." In addition a larger committee was appointed to work with this War Office one. This was called the Munitions of War Committee, and its duties were "to ensure the promptest and most efficient application of all the available productive resources of the country to the manufacture and supply of munitions of war for the Army and Navy." Its chairman was Mr. Lloyd George, and among its members was Mr. Balfour.

Everything seemed going well when a bomb fell from a very unexpected quarter. The trade unionists of Newcastle-on-Tyne welcomed the new departure, which included the establishment of local committees for increasing

munitions had grown from 20, an arbitrary figure taken to represent the output in the month of September, to 90 for October and November, 156 for December, 186 for January, 256 for February, and 388 for March. In other words, the factories in March had turned out more than nineteen times the amount they produced in September. He added that the production of high explosives had been placed on a footing which relieved us of all anxiety and enabled us to supply our Allies.

On the liquor question Mr. George experienced a rebuff. In order to deal with " the lure of the drink," he brought in on April 29th a Bill giving the Government power, during the period of the war, to control or close all public-houses in areas where munitions were produced or transport was carried on, or troops were quartered, if they thought such action was desirable. Moreover, he proposed to double the tax on spirits and to put a heavy tax on beer and wine. There was a good deal of opposition to the new duties, and they were abandoned, for many, reassured by Mr. Asquith's speech, considered that such drastic remedies were hardly called for. However, as a substitute, the sale of spirits under three years of age was entirely prohibited. This, it was hoped, would put an end to the drinking of raw and fiery spirits. Shorn of these taxation proposals, the Bill became law, and the Government appointed a Central Control Board to deal with the drink problem in the munitions, transport, and camp areas. This set to work, its chairman being Lord

Peril of the drink lure D'Abernon, better known as Sir Edgar Vincent, and in a short time it had issued regulations closing public-houses earlier in certain industrial areas, notably those around Glasgow and Newcastle, and in general making it more difficult for workmen to procure drink.

On Sunday, May 9th, the British troops made an attack upon the Aubers Ridge which resulted in failure and heavy losses, revealed piecemeal in the long lists of casualties published in the papers. On May 14th " The Times " printed a telegram from its correspondent in Northern France, who said that the attack failed because of " the want of an unlimited supply of high explosive." Our men were unable to level the German parapets to the ground after the French practice, and, consequently, they came up against unbroken wire and undestroyed parapets. Five days later, " The Times," in a leading article, said : " Men died in heaps upon the Aubers Ridge ten days ago because the field-guns were short, and gravely short, of high-explosive shells."

A yell of anger broke from that section of the Press which had consistently opposed all measures for the defence of the country, whether on sea or on land ; but the statements in " The Times " were true, and Mr. Asquith had been misinformed when he spoke on April 20th. Such was the position when the quarrel at the Admiralty became serious, and the Prime Minister sought a way out of his difficulties by forming " a National Government."

The munitions crisis had an immediate effect on the formation of the new administration. When the arrangements for the new Coalition Government were being discussed, there was much talk about the need for a Minister to devote his whole   **A Ministry** time to the organisation of the supply   **of Munitions** of munitions, and so to relieve Lord Kitchener and the War Office, who were clearly over-burdened with work. In this connection the name of Mr. Lloyd George was freely mentioned, and when the members of the new Cabinet were announced, it was seen that that energetic gentleman had become Minister of Munitions. A Bill establishing the new Ministry became law on June 9th.

The new Minister had not waited for the passing of the Bill before getting to work. He took the first steps towards forming his Department, and then went on tour round the country. At Manchester, Liverpool, Bristol, and elsewhere he preached from the same text. The war was a war of munitions. We were short of munitions, and we could only hope for victory by turning out more, much more, of them. For this we required " all the industry, all the labour, and all the strength, power, and resource of everyone to the utmost."

On May 23rd Mr. George was back in Parliament, introducing his Bill for increasing the output of munitions. This, called the Munitions of War Act, provided " for furthering the efficient manufacture, transport, and supply of munitions for the present war and for purposes incidental thereto." The task involved was a big one.

HOW FRANCE MET THE DEMAND FOR MUNITIONS.
Pointing " 75 " shells in a French munitions factory. Our Allies divided their country into industrial districts and groups, each under a responsible metallurgist. To the left of the illustration an engineer officer is watching a shell being tested ; to the right is a hammer stamper.

Lieut. General Sir William R. Birdwood, K.C.S.I., K.C.M.G., D.S.O.

CHAPTER LXXXVII.

THE CONQUEST OF TOGOLAND AND CAMEROON.

Togoland Described—Its Products—Preparations for War—The Fighting—Surrender of the Germans—The German Acquisition of Cameroon—Its Boundaries, Size, and Population—A British Reverse—Naval Successes—Duala Captured—The Advance Into the Interior—A Fight for Jabassi—French Victory at Japona—The German Capital Taken—Assistance of the Belgians—Further Allied Successes—The Fight at Edea—Duala Open to Trade—The French in the Hinterland—Heroic Defence of Gurin—Garua Captured—Strength of the Place—Garua Fables—Climatic and Other Difficulties.

I N a famous passage in "The Decline and Fall," Gibbon remarks that a certain statement made by Seneca is a very just observation, and one "confirmed by history and experience." The statement is that "wheresoever the Roman conquers he inhabits."

This is undoubtedly a right principle for colonising nations, and, in general, Great Britain has followed it. Germany, on the other hand, has not. In this, as in other matters, she has forgotten or flouted lessons "confirmed by history and experience," and this is one reason why she has not ranked as a colonising nation. It also helps to explain the ease with which most of her colonies fell into British hands, although it is not the only, or even the main, reason for this. Germany's colonies fell mainly because the Navy of her foe swept the seas, because amid the northern mists Sir John Jellicoe and his men kept ceaseless watch and ward.

In West Africa, Germany, at the outbreak of the Great War, had two colonies, Togoland and Cameroon. Togoland is a country 33,700 square miles in extent, or about the size of Ireland, and it lies between Dahomey, belonging to France, and the Gold Coast Colony, a British possession. It became German in 1884, thirty years before the war, when the traveller Gustav Nachtigal landed at Lome from a gunboat, and by an arrangement with the local chiefs declared the land to be a German Protectorate. In shape it is not unlike a pyramid, tapering down to its coastline

[Elliott & Fry.
SIR FREDERICK DEALTRY LUGARD, G.C.M.G., C.B., D.S.O.
Governor-General of Nigeria.

on the Gulf of Guinea, where it is only thirty-two miles from end to end.

The capital of the colony is Lome, on the coast. Other stations are Bagida, also on the coast; Togo on Lake Togo, Misahöhe about a hundred miles inland, and Bismarckburg on the high lands at the back of the country. The population consists of about a million Hausas, and before the war there were less than four hundred white folk there. A railway runs along the coast from Little Popo to Lome and thence inland to Misahöhe, and there are about eight hundred miles of good roads.

Being a tropical country, Togoland produces palms, cocoa, rubber, and cotton, as well as maize, bananas, ginger, and a little tobacco. The products of the palm—oil and kernels—are the chief exports, others being rubber, cotton, and cocoa. In some parts the inhabitants rear horses, sheep, goats, pigs, and poultry, while others work at native industries, such as weaving, pottery-making, straw-plaiting, and wood-cutting.

On the evening of August 4th, 1914, war was declared by Great Britain on Germany, and in a few minutes the fateful news had been flashed across the ocean to the Acting-Governor of the Gold Coast and the French Governor of Dahomey. At once they arranged a joint plan of campaign, while British cruisers were ready with their assistance. In two or three days one of these appeared before Lome, and with its guns trained on the town, politely asked the Germans to surrender. They did so, but before the British came on shore their little army, consisting of about sixty

Europeans and four hundred natives, had retired inland towards Atakpame.

In the Gold Coast British officials were preparing to send a small expeditionary force against the Germans. This was composed of men of the Gold Coast Regiment, officered by Britons and commanded by Captain F. C. Bryant, R.A. On August 8th or 9th it crossed the frontier in motor-cars, and at the same time a French force entered Togoland from the other side. The German Governor made the naïve suggestion that the colony should remain neutral, but of this Bryant would not hear, and he pressed on with his troops. By the 10th the southern part of Togoland was in the hands of the Allies, and the united force then advanced towards Atakpame, near which, at Kamina, was one of Germany's chief wireless stations.

On the 25th, Bryant and his men crossed the River Monu, and there the only fighting of the campaign took place. The Allies had seventy-three casualties, two officers and twenty-one men being killed, but they drove the enemy from his entrenchments, occupied Atakpame, and seized the wireless station.

Surrender of Togoland

The Germans then offered to surrender, and on the 26th it was announced that they had done so unconditionally. When they did this they had an ample supply of arms and ammunition, and they handed over to Captain Bryant three Maxim guns, 1,000 rifles, and 320,000 rounds of ammunition. A reason for their feeble resistance was that many natives refused to take up arms against the British. Secret agents brought word that the sympathies of the natives were with us, though in some cases they had been forced to take up arms against us on penalty of instant death. The number of prisoners taken at this time was two hundred and six.

In this way Togoland fell to the Allies. Great Britain and France agreed to govern it between them, and officials

MAP OF TOGOLAND.
Showing the coast line and the boundaries of the Gold Coast Colony on the left and Dahomey on the right.

of each nationality were appointed to look after the part adjacent to their own possessions. Trade was resumed, private property was not interfered with, and there is no reason to suppose that the natives had any reason to regret the change of rulers.

Cameroon is a larger country than Togoland, from which it is separated by French Dahomey and British Nigeria, and its conquest was a bigger proposition. The name comes from a Portuguese word meaning prawns, and its coast was discovered by Fernando Po towards 1500. Either he or some other Portuguese navigator gave the name Rio dos Camaroes, or River of Prawns, to the big estuary there; and later, the interior was called Cameroon.

It was in 1884 that Germany, represented again by Nachtigal, took possession of the colony, calling it Kamerun, but it was not then as large as it is now. In 1911, after the trouble in Morocco, France and Germany made a new colonial agreement, and one of the clauses of this said that France should hand over to Germany about 100,000 square miles of land on the south and east of Cameroon, a piece taken from her Congo territories. This was accordingly done.

The Cameroon described

It is desirable to say something about the boundaries and nature of the country before attempting to describe the military operations therein. Cameroon has a sea coast of about two hundred miles on what is called the Bight of Biafra. To the north-east an arbitrary line divides it from the British Protectorate of Nigeria, and this stretches up to Lake Chad; part of the southern shore of this lake is in Cameroon. From Lake Chad southwards, another arbitrary line divides the colony from French Equatorial Africa, although in two places

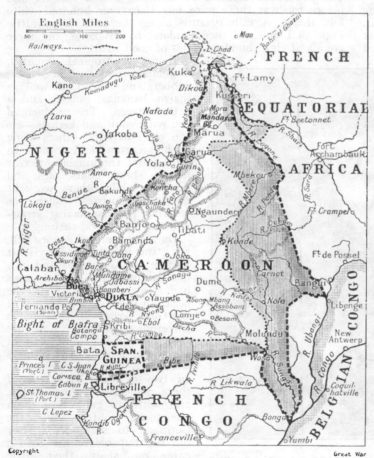

MAP OF THE CAMEROON.
Drawn to illustrate the account of the Allies' operations. The ruled portions indicate the territory ceded to Germany by France in 1911.

To render Garua, an important position in the interior of the German Cameroon, difficult of assault, barbed-wire and sand-bag defences were utilised to an extraordinary extent, and pits were dug round the forts to further strengthen them.

Impression of one of the German forts at Garua, which capitulated on June 10th, 1915, after being besieged and bombarded by a Franco-British force

Reading from left to right: Captain Cooke, Brigadier-General C——, and Major Wright in line before a fallen German fort at Garua. The Germans put up a hard fight in the Cameroon, but after the fall of Garua on June 10th, 1915, where the bulk of the enemy forces and ammunition was concentrated, their resistance proved comparatively weak. It will be recalled that after the Agadir crisis an agreement was entered into between France and Germany, whereby the latter extended her Cameroon borders at the expense of French territory, on the understanding that our ally's supremacy in Morocco should go unchallenged by the Pan-Germanists.

LEADERS WHO DIRECTED THE OPERATIONS AGAINST THE HUN IN EQUATORIAL AFRICA.

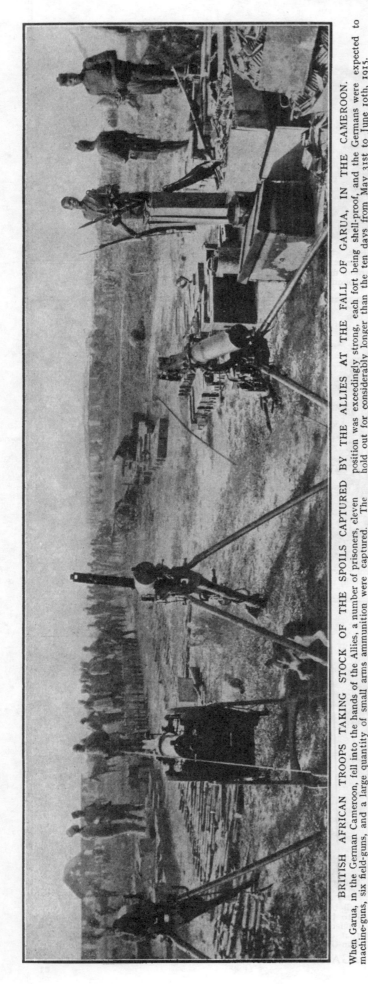

BRITISH AFRICAN TROOPS TAKING STOCK OF THE SPOILS CAPTURED BY THE ALLIES AT THE FALL OF GARUA, IN THE CAMEROON.
When Garua, in the German Cameroon, fell into the hands of the Allies, a number of prisoners, eleven machine-guns, six field-guns, and a large quantity of small arms ammunition were captured. The position was exceedingly strong, each fort being shell-proof, and the Germans were expected to hold out for considerably longer than the ten days from May 31st to June 10th, 1915.

spurs of land jut out and touch the Belgian Congo. On the south a straight line separates it from more French territory.

The transfer of 1911 had one curious result. It left, surrounded by German territory, a little Spanish colony called Rio Muni, or Spanish Guinea, a square of land which Bernhardi in his notorious book claimed for Germany.

The size of Cameroon is about 290,000 square miles, or about five times the size of England and Wales. Much of it is mountainous, and sloping down to the sea is the magnificent Cameroon Mountain, called by the natives the Mountain of Greatness. It is over 13,000 feet high, and is the highest point on the western side of Africa. It is a volcano, and not an extinct one, and from top to bottom it is covered with dense forests. On the **The transfer of 1911** rest of the coast there is a level strip of land, and at the back of the colony there is a good deal of low-lying country.

Cameroon has many rivers and several good harbours. Into the great Cameroon estuary, which is twenty miles across, flow the Rivers Wuri and Mungo, and through the centre of the colony the Sanaga runs to the sea. The hinterland is watered by the Logone and the Shari, which unite before they fall into Lake Chad, and the Sanga, a tributary of the Congo.

The population consists of about 2,500,000 negroes, mostly of the Bantu race, but some belonging to the Fula and the Hausa tribes live in the north. Before the war there were less than 2,000 whites in the colony. Buea, on the slopes of the Cameroon Mountain, is the official capital, but Duala on the Cameroon Estuary is the largest place, and a trading centre of some importance. Other considerable towns are Victoria, Batanga, and Campo on the coast, Garua on the Benue River, and near the Nigerian frontier, Ngaundere, the largest town in the interior, and Yaunde, about a hundred miles from the sea.

The soil is fertile, and produces rubber, cotton, cocoa, and coffee, as well as a great number of palms, the oil and kernels of which are exported in large quantities. Ivory and copra are also exported, and the land grows much excellent timber, notably ebony. Many cattle are raised, and in some parts the natives grow corn, maize, and rice. The Germans had built about one hundred and fifty miles of railway connecting the towns near the coast, and had made a certain number of good roads.

Such was the German colony which the British in Nigeria and the French on the Congo prepared to invade in August, 1914. For this purpose the British had the West African Regiment, stationed at Sierra Leone, and the West African Frontier Force, consisting of the several battalions of the Northern Nigeria and the Southern Nigeria Regiments. The French had their troops in Equatorial Africa, the whole being composed of natives officered by white men.

The first attempts were not conspicuously successful, doubtless because they were undertaken in the rainy season. On August 25th some mounted infantry belonging to the West African Frontier Force left Yola, in Nigeria, crossed the frontier and, after a fight in which two British officers were killed, seized Tepe, a German post on the Benue River. Lieut.-Colonel P. R. **A British disaster** Maclear commanded the detachment, and on the 29th he led it against the bigger station of Garua. One fort was captured, but on the 30th the Germans brought up a big force and totally defeated the British. Lieut.-Colonel Maclear and four other white officers were killed, while nearly half the native force was destroyed. The excellent work of the German Maxims was mainly responsible for this disaster, which ended in the retreat of the remainder of the Frontier Force to Nigeria.

Two more expeditionary forces, meanwhile, had entered Cameroon from Nigeria. One marched from Ikom to Nsanakong, a few miles from the border, which was occupied without trouble, and the other from Calabar seized

Archibong with equal ease. A week later, at the beginning of September, came the German counter-stroke. A large force marched against Nsanakong, where the British resisted until all their ammunition had gone, and then cut their way out with the bayonet. Three British officers and many native soldiers were killed, while a large number of the latter became prisoners of war; but the remainder, like those from Garua, managed, after some hardships in the bush, to get back to Nigeria. The force at Archibong did not give much trouble, and in return the Germans crossed the border and seized the Nigerian station of Okuri, not far from Calabar

As happens always when matters are not very prosperous with them, Britons turned to the Navy, and the Navy did not fail. Several German ships were in the Cameroon Estuary, and outside watching them were H.M.S. Cumberland and H.M.S. Dwarf, the former a cruiser and the latter a gunboat. On September 14th an attempt was made to wreck the Dwarf, which had made her way into the estuary, a missionary and an infernal machine playing the leading parts in this abortive enterprise, and a little later a merchantman, the Nachtigal, tried to ram

NIGERIAN MACHINE-GUN IN ACTION.

A CONQUEROR OF THE CAMEROON.
Typical soldier of the Nigerian Regiment. These coloured patriots fought splendidly for the Empire in the Cameroon Campaign.

the same vessel. On this occasion the Nachtigal was wrecked, and a further attempt, made by launches and spar-torpedoes, to destroy the Dwarf also failed. One report spoke of an attempt to wreck the Cumberland.

It was now the turn of the Allies to take the offensive. The Germans had sunk ten or twelve steamers in order to block up the channel leading to Duala, but the British cleared away some of the obstructions and swept up the mines for about three miles. Soon H.M.S. Challenger, escorting five troopships, arrived to join the Cumberland and the Dwarf, and on September 26th Duala was approached and bombarded. An attempt to get a small landing-party on shore was abandoned, but on the 27th the Germans intimated their wish to surrender the town. Brigadier-General C. M. Dobell, D.S.O., who was in command of the expedition, landed on the 30th and took it over, the surrender being unconditional, and at the same time a battalion was landed at Bonaberi, on the other side

Surrender of Duala

A CORNER OF THE CAMEROON, NOW A BRITISH "PLACE IN THE SUN."

As in South-West Africa, the transport of stores, guns, and equipment was one of the chief difficulties of the Cameroon campaign. Camels were utilised as being the most reliable beasts of burden in this tropical region. This photograph shows a heap of officers' baggage about to be put aboard the "ship of the desert." Native soldiers are seen at work in the background, while in front is a typical British officer.

of the river from Duala, which also capitulated after a little firing by both parties. The Germans had destroyed their wireless station at Duala and had withdrawn most of their troops, but several hundred prisoners were taken by the British. About the same time a French force, having come by sea from Libreville, in French Congo, under the escort of their warship Surpris, attacked Ukoko on Corisco Bay, in the south of Cameroon, while the Surpris sank two armed vessels, the Khios and the Itolo.

Lying in the river above Bonaberi, the British found nine merchant steamers belonging to the Woermann Line, of Hamburg, and the Hamburg-Amerika Line, which had, presumably, taken refuge there on the outbreak of war. A small party was sent to take possession of them, and in one of them were found about thirty British prisoners. All the ships were in good order, most of them containing general outward and homeward cargoes and considerable quantities of coal. The German gunboat Soden was also seized and commissioned for the British Navy, and attempts were made to raise the Herzogin Elisabeth and a floating dock which the Germans had sunk.

The Allies now controlled the coast, and the first stage of the campaign was over. The second, however, was still before them, and this was by far the more difficult of the two, for it meant warfare in a mountainous and almost roadless country, and under climatic conditions which are very unfavourable to white men.

French victory at Japona With Duala and Bonaberi as bases, a start was made. The Germans had retreated, as far as could be ascertained, by three routes—along the valley of the Wuri and by the two railways which run from Duala and Bonaberi inland, one, the shorter, towards the north, and the other towards the south-east. Along the southern railway a French column took its way, and on October 6th there was a fight at Japona, where the Germans had found a suitable defensive position on a river. However, the bridge was forced and they were compelled to continue their retreat.

Another party of Germans was followed by a British force, containing both naval and military contingents, under Colonel E. H. Gorges, D.S.O. With four field-guns this sailed up the Wuri in launches, and landed about four miles from Jabassi, where the enemy was entrenched. An accurate fire met our men as they advanced, and they did not get very far. A flank attack was equally unsuccessful, and the order was given to retire. This was on October 8th, and after a day's rest the force returned to Duala, the general having come up in person to arrange this.

On the 14th the Allies returned to the attack. Additional troops were employed, and lighters, specially constructed, carried two 6 in. guns, which soon silenced the German batteries. Then the infantry made for Jabassi, and this time they got there. After a sharp engagement the place **The Germans hard pressed** was occupied, and ten Europeans were made prisoners. A few days later, the column under Lieut. Colonel A. H. W. Haywood, R.A., which was pursuing the enemy along the northern railway, came up with him at Susa, and inflicted a defeat upon him. Far away, in the north-east, a detachment of the Nigerian Regiment entered the colony, and proceeded to occupy the region around Mora, in the neighbourhood of Lake Chad.

All the columns were pressing on the heels of the retiring Germans, and soon two further successes were announced. Aided by some British soldiers and sailors, the French detachment under Colonel Mayer, after its success at Japona, marched towards Edea; this is an important place, fifty-six miles from the coast, for it stands on the Sanaga River and also on the Duala railway. The road thereto led through dense forest, wherein snipers were cleverly concealed, and they paid special attention to officers. However, the force pressed on, as did another detachment which sailed up the Sanaga, and on October 26th Edea was occupied without resistance. About a fortnight later, Haywood's column, following up its success at Susa, took Mujuka, a station about fifty miles from Duala.

THE EMPIRE'S COLOURED TROOPS IN ACTION.
Men of the Nigerian Regiment fighting for the Empire behind stone barricades near Garua, in the German Cameroon.

AFRICAN NATIVE TROOPS ADVANCING THROUGH A RAILWAY CUTTING IN THE CAMEROON.

The difficulties of transport in Equatorial Africa were mainly responsible in prolonging the Cameroon Campaign. Two hundred miles of railways were commandeered by our troops. This photograph shows a body of native soldiers patrolling a section of cutting. Immediately after it was taken a severe fight took place in the vicinity.

By this time General Dobell was prepared with a plan for attacking the German capital Buea and its seaport Victoria. The French cruiser Bruix and the yacht Ivy, belonging to the Nigerian Government, bombarded the latter place, and then some Marines were landed. In a very short time it was in their possession, and on November 14th detachments advanced from different points up the hills which lead to Buea. Here the enemy, unable to offer any very serious resistance, was soon scattered in all directions.

The German offensive—for it must be said that wherever Germans were found they acted on the offensive—was directed against Nigeria. At various points small parties crossed the border line, and at Danare, twenty five miles from Ikom, there was a skirmish on November 8th, when the British leader, a colour-sergeant of the Royal Sussex, was killed. A little later, three hundred natives, led by eight Germans, made two additional attacks on a station in the same district, but were repulsed with some loss.

Meanwhile, the French were winning a very gratifying success in the hinterland. The authorities of the Belgian Congo lent them a steamer and one hundred and thirty men, and under General Aymerich the united force soon drove the Germans from the greater part of the territory given up to

COLONEL EDMUND HOWARD GORGES, D.S.O.

[Bassano.

Commandant of the West African Regiment. He was in charge of the naval and military force which successfully occupied Jabassi.

them in 1911, the so-called Congo-Ubanghi region. At the end of October, after fierce fighting, which lasted for two days, the German post at Numen was captured, and so was the post at Nola, where several officers, some guns, and ammunition were taken.

To return to the campaigns near the coast. In December the greatest success was the capture of the whole line of the northern railway. From Mujuka, Haywood's column marched to Lum, about twenty miles farther north, meeting with opposition almost at every step. At Lum there was a sharp skirmish, but on the 10th, Nkimgsamba, the railway terminus, was seized. There five locomotives, some rolling-stock, and two aeroplanes were captured, as well as about sixty white men. An advance was at once made to Bare, about six miles from the railhead; but beyond this point progress was not easy, owing to the rocky and mountainous nature of the country. Haywood's task had been helped by the operations of another force, moving along the valley of the Mungo, which had seized Mendawi, an important post, on November 21st.

Another little expeditionary force was also " doing its bit." This left Lagos on November 22nd, and sailed up the Cross River to Ikom. It marched to Nkami, on the boundary between Nigeria

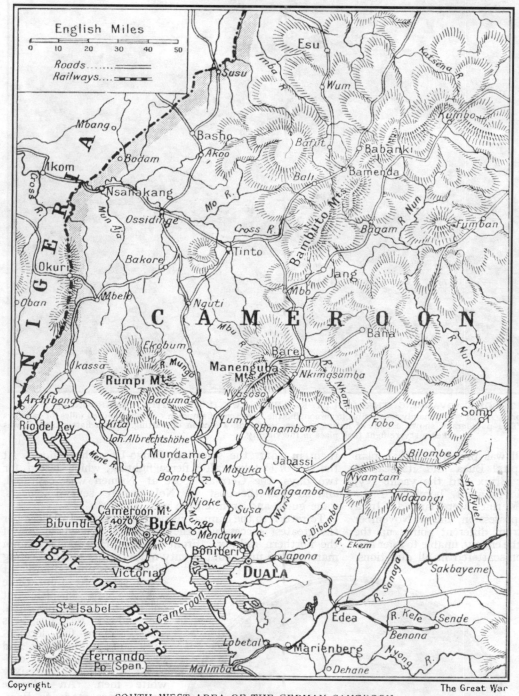

SOUTH WEST AREA OF THE GERMAN CAMEROON.
Map showing part of the German territory in West Africa, and the three rivers—Mungo, Wuri, and Sanaga—which were utilised to a great extent in the Allied campaign against the German Cameroon. The landing bases were at Duala and Victoria, the seaport of Buea.

but the work was well forward and the position of the Germans therein was not pleasant. Nothing whatever could reach them from the outside, and slowly, but surely, they were being driven off the railways and into the interior, while in the more inhospitable northern and eastern parts of the colony they were also being harried and chased. Their surrender or extermination was only a matter of time.

From the British point of view the position was so satisfactory that on December 21st the port of Duala was opened to trade, this being allowed only with those parts of the colony which were in the occupation of the Allies. For the time being the German tariff on imports was kept in force.

During the hot season little was done, but soon the allied columns were again on the move. Leaving Edea, Colonel Mayer and his troops fought two engagements and seized the post of Bersona. Following the railway, they forced their way across the River Kele in April, while a British force, marching somewhat to the north, seized with equal ease the bridge across the Ngwa. Their objective was Yaunde, which the Germans had made their headquarters. On May 11th the station of Escha was captured, and on the 29th the enemy was driven from a strong position at Njoke.

In the hinterland French columns were hard at work. On the Sanga they drove the enemy from place to place until he fell back on Monso, a fortified position. Thereafter a stiff struggle, the Germans were obliged to capitulate, and their guns and ammunition were captured. Besam and Assobam fell quickly to the French

and on June 25th they were in possession of the important post of Lomje. Their task was made easier by the conduct of the Germans in burning villages in their retreat and so exasperating the native population, and by a mutiny among the native troops in the German service. In these operations the Belgians gave some useful assistance. Their original contingent of one hundred and thirty men was increased to five hundred and eighty, and they took part in all the engagements just mentioned.

On the Nigerian frontier there was some sharp fighting in April and May. Just inside British territory is Gurin, a large native town on the River Faro, and this was attacked in April by Germans from Garua, who brought against it sixteen Europeans, three hundred and fifty natives, some

Natives mutiny against Germans

and Cameroon, crossing no less than twenty-three rivers, and then made its way towards Ossidinge, or Mamfe, a German post. When that place was reached, it was found that the Germans had evacuated it, but there was a little skirmishing with parties of them in the neighbourhood before its possession was quite assured.

At Edea the French were attacked on October 26th, when there was a somewhat sanguinary engagement. The Germans, having lost twenty whites and fifty-four natives, were repulsed; the victors had two officers and twenty-nine native soldiers killed. In the north an encounter was reported on November 17th between a British and a German patrol. The Germans continued their raids into Nigeria, but all these were repulsed, the skirmish near Bakundi being perhaps the most serious.

At the end of the year Cameroon was not conquered,

where the British had met with their reverse in the previous August, was perhaps the most notable event in this campaign. Its fortifications had been strengthened after that time, and its seizure was apparently a fairly tough proposition.

On May 31st Colonel Cunliffe opened the attack. At a range of 4,000, and then of 3,000 yards, heavy guns bombarded the four forts, three on the hills and one in the plain, while steady sapping, carried on only by night, took the British trenches nearer to their objective. In a few days smaller guns were got into concealed positions about 1,000 yards from the forts, and these added much to the vigour of the attack. All the time mounted infantry and French cavalry were patrolling the neighbourhood, watching especially the fords of the Benue in order to head off any attempt to escape.

This lasted until June 10th, when white flags were seen above the forts. The commandant and two or three other officers went forward and met a German who offered, on

THE ALLIED ADVANCE IN THE CAMEROON.
Naval gun section on the way to a station on the railway from Duala. Natives are drawing the truck, to which spare rails are lashed.

COLOURED SOLDIERS WHO BEAT THE GERMANS.
Outpost of native sentries of the Nigerian Regiment after they had been inspected by the British officer seen in the background.

NAVAL ARTILLERY IN THE CAMEROON.
British troops placing a naval gun in a well-screened position in the bush during the advance on Edea. Above: The French commissariat at the station of Piti.

mounted infantry, and four Maxims. Under two white men the garrison of forty native soldiers put up a sturdy resistance in a fort about three-quarters of a mile from the town, and although they lost their leader, Lieutenant Pawle, they continued the fight under the direction of a civilian. After seven hours the Germans retired. From Gurin two native soldiers managed to reach Yola in order to ask for help. Under Colonel F. H. G. Cunliffe, a detachment of the West African Frontier Force set out at once, and arrived there on the day following the siege.

Colonel Cunliffe, aided by a French detachment, then made his way towards Garua, and the capture of that place,

Another view of Nlohe Bridge, giving an idea of the wild Cameroon scenery. When the water is high the rocks seen in this photograph are completely covered. The tropical vegetation, so profuse in this part of the colony, added materially to the normal difficulties of military progress.

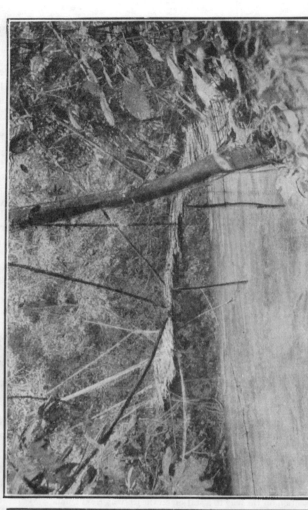

Native "Tie-tie" bridge near Nlohe, Cameroon. It was erected, with considerable ingenuity, entirely of short branches and undergrowth from the jungle. Though fragile, the structure proved strong enough for its temporary purpose.

Nlohe Bridge, Cameroon, the original structure of which was destroyed by the retreating German forces. After a short delay the communication was re-established, as seen above, the three piers in the centre being additional to the original German ones at each end.

The work of reconstructing Nlohe Bridge in progress. Lieutenant Nash (Gold Coast Railway) is seen in charge of the operations. The track was levelled by natives. In a few hours the structure was sufficiently complete for the British forces to advance.

CAMERA VIEWS OF BRITISH AND NATIVE ENGINEERING AT NLOHE, IN THE REMOTE CAMEROON.

THE FRENCH MARCH UP COUNTRY.
Senegalese Tirailleurs marching up country from Duala to Edea, Cameroon. Their light field-pieces are packed on mules.

FRENCH AND BRITISH OFFICERS IN THE CAMEROON.
A French doctor and a British officer, attached to the French service, on the railway between Duala and Edea.

accepted. On the next day (the 11th) the Allies entered Garua, hoisted the Union Jack and the Tricolour, and took over thirty-seven German and two hundred and seventy native prisoners. The booty included several field-guns and Maxims, many rifles, much ammunition, and a great quantity of stores of all kinds.

In a report on this siege forwarded to England by Sir Frederick Lugard, the Governor - General of Nigeria, it was mentioned that the melinite and lyddite shells completely destroyed the nerve of the defenders, and on the 9th they began to mutiny and desert. Those who got away were vigorously pursued by the mounted men, but not a single European escaped. The strength of the fortifications amazed those who inspected them, and they were told by the **How Garua was** Germans that 2,000 men **fortified** had been working on them for six months. The most extraordinary fact about this siege, however, is still to be told The Allies did not lose a single man.

From Garua the force moved along the Benue towards Ngaundere, an important town on the route between Duala and Lake Chad, and the capital of the Adamawa district. This was seized with very slight loss on June 29th. when the Germans there, followed by the Allies, retired in a south-westernly direction to Tibati, and then turning northwards reached Tingere, nearly 4,000 feet upon the plateau. This was captured by the Allies on July 12th, and a German attempt to retake it was repulsed eleven days later. Koncha and Gaschaka, sixty-five miles apart,

the part of the governor, to surrender the place. He asked, however, that the Germans should be allowed to march out with the honours of war and to join their comrades in the other parts of the colony. This was refused, unconditional surrender being requested, and the Germans were given two hours—they asked for two days—in which to decide. Within this time the envoys returned saying that the terms had been

fell to the British in August, and then the rains put a stop for a time to active operations.

Before this, however, the French had got still nearer Yaunde. After two small encounters they occupied the station of Dume, and so surprised the Germans that they quickly abandoned several fortified places and threw their transport into the river. **Fables for native consumption** They continued to hold the hill above the town of Dume, but this was soon captured, and a light column was sent forward to Abong-Mbong, which was seized on August 29th.

In this campaign the Germans, it must be admitted, put up a good fight, employing also those weapons of craft in which they so excel. Their appeals to the Mohammedans and their stories of British and French reverses in Europe were the most fantastic nonsense. One spoke of the capture of four English and three French towns, 10,000 English being killed in one of the former of these. Another told of Paris taken and Versailles in flames, and a third that the English wanted Constantinople to give it to the pagans. The feats of their Zeppelins were thus rendered into pidgin-English for the benefit of the natives :

The white men under the earth (i.e., the Germans) are fit to send plenty ships to fly for air over all English country. Each ship fit to throw down one " tiger " for chop every white man, and one gun as " dash " for every black man.

However, the Allies overcame these and other difficulties, the most serious being the climate and the country. A letter from an officer there gives a good description of the latter. He says :

It is very trying and difficult country to negotiate. The climate (with its intense heat, tropical downpours, and violent tornados), mangrove swamps, thick, dense jungle, transport, carriers, etc., etc., all combine to make progress anything but rapid. At M—— is a large palm-kernel factory, and soon after leaving this the character of the country changes completely, and one enters thick bush (so close and dense is it that it brushes against the trunks) varied by luxuriant palm groves and acres of flourishing bananas. Sometimes it is the low, thick bush of the Sierra Leone Protectorate, more often of the wild West African forest. There are great trees hung and festooned with creepers, lianes, and tendrils—a perfect orgy of luxuriant vegetation—but always with man-high undergrowth, varied by mauve convolvuli and large ferns. Birds of every hue, from brilliant blue and purple to shimmering yellow, apricot, and orange, fly from tree to tree and branch to branch, while insects of every description, from huge butterflies to " stinging-mangos," abound.

Equally graphic is an extract from another account :

We think out here that the fighting in Belgium must be an absolute picnic compared with our scrap here. In this country it is nearly impossible to march more than twenty or twenty-five miles per day, starting at 5.30 a.m. (dark), and going on until 6.30 in the evening (darkness). Most of the paths are only bush tracks in the everlasting forest. You go marching along in single file, never knowing when you are going to be shot at. The enemy may be only a few yards away, but you cannot see him—the bush is so thick. It is a bit nerve-racking when suddenly a shot rings out in the wonderful stillness—very often a signal for all your carriers (500 or more) to stampede with their loads. There is an eternal twilight in these thick forests, the trees meeting overhead and interlaced by creepers. It is a fine sight to see the column on the march ; it covers two or three miles of road, taking nearly an hour to pass a given spot, of course, in single file. And it is a very serious matter to defend this long line. And the heat ! Another chief difficulty is the transport, and the line of communication has to be guarded (one hundred and fifty miles).

Yet once again man prevailed over Nature, a more terrible foe—at least, in West Africa—than the German. At the end of August the enemy was hemmed in on all sides, and although he still held Yaunde and a certain district in the centre of the country, Cameroon was in no sense a German possession. **The enemy hemmed in** He had still some British prisoners, taken during the earlier stages of the war, who were interned in a camp between Yaunde and Dume, but happily in September these were reported to be in good health and spirits. Their captivity was clearly nearing its end.

NIGERIAN ARTILLERY'S NIGHT ATTACK ON MOUNTAIN HILL CAMP, CAMEROON.
Coming unexpectedly upon the German camp in the Bare-Jang district at night-time, the British force was subjected to a fierce fire. But after three hours of strenuous fighting, the enemy being aided by flare rockets, the Nigerian artillery drove the Germans from their camp.

CHAPTER LXXXVIII.

THE GREAT DRIVE IN THE WEST AND THE BATTLE OF LOOS.

Fall of Russian Fortresses Upsets Franco-British Plan—Germans Rail a Thousand Heavy Guns to Western Front—Race Between French and German Railways with Shell Supplies for the Great Bombardment—Lord Kitchener and Admiral Bacon Threaten a Landing Battle on the Belgian Coast—General Joffre Makes a Strong Demonstration Against the Alsatian German Wing—The Alsace Potash Mine and the Part it Played in the War—After Threatening Both Wings, the French and British Mass their Guns in Champagne and Artois—An Army of 600,000 Men Drives In at Lens—How a German Engineer Upset General Foch's Plan of Attack—The Creation of a New River-Swamp at Souchez Forces the French to Swerve Southward—A Dangerous Gap is Left Between the French and British Armies—Sir John French has to Hold Back His Reserve to Protect the Gap—The Artois Armies Fail to Get a Good Wind for their Clouds of Intoxicating Gas—General Foch Delays His Attack while the British Commander Launches Both His Armies—The Second Army Wins One of the Ridges East of Ypres and Captures the German First Line Round the Lille Plateau—The Heroism of the Berkshires, Lincolns, and Rifle Brigade—By Using Up His Local Reserves, the German Commander Throws Our Second Army Back—Great Difficulties of Our Generals and Staff Officers Due to the Blindness of the British People—Like the Ancient Romans, We Have to Learn by Hard Knocks How to Wear Down the Better-Trained Enemy—The Plan of Attack on Loos—Why Kitchener's Men and the London Territorials were Placed in the Van—The Magnificent Heroism of the Londoners and Highlanders—The Charge of the Guards and the Smashing of the German Counter-Attack.

AFTER the fall of Warsaw it was almost a matter of necessity for the western Allies to make a powerful movement against the German lines in France and Flanders. According to rumour, Sir John French, having obtained large supplies of munitions and an army of 600,000 men, was ready to attack and draw off pressure from the Russians in the middle of August, 1915. But the French armies were then only just completing their new armament of monster Creusot howitzers, which were named "The Conquerors." Many of these great pieces of siege artillery had been placed in position, but the labour of bringing up three or four million of shells, and transforming the larger part of the French railway system into a gun-feeding machine, required a long time. The British armies were readier to act by reason of the smallness of their front and the facility of their short sea-based lines of communications. The British front had been extended from the village of Boesinghe, north of Ypres, to the hamlet of Nœux les Mines, near Carency. But even this extension only set free two

[Lafayette.

MAJOR-GENERAL MICHAEL F. RIMINGTON, C.V.O., C.B.
Commanded the Indian Cavalry Corps at Doullens. In October, 1915, he was awarded the Cross of a Commander of the Legion of Honour.

French army corps, and the railway organisation of supplying the French guns remained an enormous affair.

No surprise attack on a grand scale was possible during the critical month of August when the principal forces of German artillery were completely occupied at Novo Georgievsk, Kovno, and Brest Litovsk. The German Staff was well aware of the danger it was running; but by its secret service men, it carefully watched the progress of French munitions, and the transport of shell supplies, and, meanwhile, urged Hindenburg and Mackensen to use up men in order to release quickly the heavy guns for service on the western front. This was the real reason why Hindenburg, for example, sacrificed a hundred thousand men for a rapid success at Kovno. The German Staff was afraid that the new Creusot howitzers would come fully into action before a considerable portion of its own new siege trains, with the larger part of the output of the German shell factories, was railed to the French front. One of the grounds why General Grigoreff, the Russian defender of Kovno, fell into disgrace and was court-martialled by General Russky was that he had enabled the

Germans to release one of their most important siege trains, through not making a more desperately stubborn defence of the entrenched camp at Kovno.

By the middle of September, 1915, the eastern German armies were able to send a thousand heavy howitzers through Berlin and Cologne to strengthen their lines in Flanders, France, and Alsace, and the factories which fed with shells this multitude of great pieces despatched their trucks westward instead of eastward. Thus the fall of Kovno was a blow to the French and British as well as to the Russians; and in conjunction with the

unexpectedly rapid destruction of Novo Georgievsk it added to the difficulties of Joffre and Sir John French, besides endangering the armies of Generals Russky and Evert. It is not extravagant to say that had the Russian line of fortresses held out a month, or even a fortnight, longer the German line in the west would have been broken by the new heavy ordnance of the French and British armies.

As it was, the result of the long-prepared campaign in France became largely dependent upon the race between the French and German railway organisations. We have seen that the heavy German batteries passed through the Friedrichstrasse Station in Berlin on September 15th. It was on this day that General Joffre issued the Army Order for a grand offensive, but though by this time the new Creusot guns were placed in position, the organisation of the French railways was not completed.

Shells by the million were about to be employed. The local underground magazines near the batteries were utterly inadequate as store places. Each main attacking army had to have some hundreds of trains in its service, bringing up a constant supply of ammunition, which had to be laboriously **A race between** carted to the batteries and placed **rival railways** in the magazines beyond the reach of the most powerful enemy projectile. The work of preparation was of an unparalleled vastness and difficulty. Nearly all the ordinary

BRITISH SOLDIERS CONSOLIDATING A NEWLY-WON POSITION ON THE WESTERN FRONT.

No sooner had the merest fraction of ground been gained on the western front than the work of defence went on in feverish haste. Barbed-wire entanglements were fixed up and trenches dug and consolidated. The above photograph shows some British outposts placing wire obstacles in advance of a new position. The smaller view is of a 155 mm. shell which fell into a British trench without exploding.

THE PRICE OF A VAIN ASSAULT.
Dead German soldiers in front of the British trenches just before the great advance on Loos and Hulluch. They remained thus for some days before our soldiers could commit their bodies to Mother Earth.

goods traffic had to be stopped. It was a railway war absolutely. The troops were ready, the guns and the shells were ready, and the event depended on whether the German railway managers could get their guns and shells into France in time to cope with a hostile bombardment of incomparable length and intensity.

Had the German airmen been as bold, strong, and adventurous as the German Staff constantly pretended they were, the railway organisation of the Franco-British offensive might have been very seriously disturbed by dashing and deadly bombing squadrons. But though the Germans had fine machines, and in some individual cases displayed a vehement lust for battle, the general spirit of their Flying Corps was not such as to make for victory. British and French airmen maintained that ascendancy in the air which the enemy tried to win by increasing his engine power, armour, and firing power. Not only did the Germans attempt with success no important attack on the French railway junctions, but **Franco-British aerial** the ordinary raids of reconnoitring aerial **ascendancy** observers were severely checked all along the allied lines. Throughout the daylight hours there was a very efficient aerial patrol system from the North Sea to the Alps, and when a German airman was seen coming over the allied front a squadron of battle-planes rose to meet him. Over the British lines alone there were more than a hundred combats in the air during the period of preparation, and in nearly every case our pilots had to seek the enemy behind his own lines, where he was assisted by the fire of his mobile anti-aircraft guns. The German pilot had to be outmanœuvred and, by continual threats, shepherded over our lines before the machine could be captured. This result, therefore, was achieved in only a few cases, and, as a rule, the wreckage tumbled into the German lines.

No matter, however, where the wreckage fell, the general command of the air along the front resided with the Allies; and, as the fruit of this command, their power of attack was greatly increased. When the bombardment began in the middle of September the German Staff had no definite knowledge of the section in which the great drive would take place; for the French train service by which the shell supplies were brought up was handled by General Joffre and his Staff in rapier-like fashion. Day after day the trucks moved to different parts of the line, producing

THE INVISIBLE EYE AT WORK.
Indian observer keeping watch on the enemy trenches with the aid of a periscope, which had been covered with twigs to give it the appearance of a small tree-trunk.

an intense bombardment from the batteries they served. Violent demonstrations were thus made at every point at which an important result might be achieved. The only light which the German Staff could obtain on the intentions of the Allies was derived from the study of the strategical situation, as viewed from a Franco-British standpoint. It was well known on both sides that the vast German salient, stretching from Ypres towards Noyon, and continuing along the Aisne and the Suippes Rivers to the Forest of the Argonne, would be best attacked at its bases. These **A Belgian landing** bases were — first, the Champagne **rumour** sector, between the Argonne Ridge and Rheims; and, secondly, the Lille sector between Ypres and Arras. The fact that 600,000 Britons and half a million Frenchmen were massed against the Lille sector was known to the German Staff; and the guns from the Russian front were, therefore, hurried towards this line of danger. The German Staff was also well aware that the most powerful French army, under General de Castenau, was collected in the Champagne sector, and was preparing to strike.

But these two main elements of the situation did not constitute a sufficient basis for the enemy's final dispositions of his defences. The German Staff had to reckon with

HOODED BRITISH TERRITORIALS CHARGING THE GERMAN TRENCHES AT LOOS, SEPTEMBER 25TH, 1915.

One of the most awe-inspiring charges during the whole of the war was that made by the London Territorials on the German trenches between the "Tower Bridge" of Loos and the great double slagheap opposite Grenay, known as the Double Crassier. The first line having been cleared, a number of fortified houses were rushed, and finally Loos Cemetery was taken. Under cover of gas, the Territorials, wearing their respirators, dashed forward with irresistible élan, and eventually emerged on to the front German line. The eerie effect produced by their Inquisition-like hoods struck terror into the hearts of the enemy. Sweeping with comparative ease over the German first-line trench, they encountered greater resistance at the sunken road and Lens Road junction at Valley Cross-roads, but this, too, was overcome, the enemy retiring to his third line of defence through Loos. The masked figure on the right is wearing the regulation belt filled with bombs. On the left three German machine-gunners are surrendering.

three other elements of at least equal importance. Working in direct collaboration with General Joffre, Lord Kitchener had assembled an army of great strength at Dover with sufficient troopships within call to transport half the force at least to the Belgian coast. A squadron of battleships and monitors, some of which mounted 14 in. weapons, bombarded the Belgian coast under the direction of Admiral Bacon doing great damage to Zeebrugge and to the German howitzer batteries along the sand-dunes. By way of giving a lead to the German spies in our country, a popular rumour spread that our Dover army was preparing to fight a landing battle on the Belgian coast, and take in the rear all the enemy forces between Ostend and Lille. The Germans were kept on tenter-hooks by the threatened attack of a landing force of a hundred thousand men, ready in transports for rapid disembarkation. This demonstration against the right flank of the German line is a classic example of the disconcerting scope of sea-power.

It disquieted the German commanders. All through the critical period of Prussian history the Prussian strategists had had no occasion to study the possibilities of sea-power; they had taken the work of our admirals as a matter of course, and **Disconcerting scope** had attributed to their own armies the **of sea-power** land victories that were in some degree derived from the British mastery of the sea. The French Fleet had not seriously troubled the Germans in 1870.

So when this direct, immediate, and violent threat was exerted against the German right flank, the two commanders immediately endangered thereby were seriously perturbed.

The Duke of Würtemberg held the line from the sea to Ypres, and the Crown Prince of Bavaria connected with him and covered Lille. Left to themselves, the Würtemberger and the Bavarian might have defeated our move by ignoring it. That is to say, they might, notwithstanding their anxiety, have blindly trusted in their coast batteries and covering troops, and have allowed our demonstration to proceed. Happily for us, there was a German admiral in command at Zeebrugge, and, like all German admirals, he had studied Mahan with Teutonic thoroughness, until he was inclined rather to exaggerate than minimise the reach of British sea-power. His judgment was furthermore strongly supported by the German Marine Staff, who, being professional, felt an intense admiration for the part played by the British Navy in the Gallipoli landing actions. In its view the British admiral was reckoned to be, like Voltaire's Habbakuk, capable of everything.

And it is not unlikely that the reports of the carefully spoon-fed German spies in our country helped to deepen its perturbation.

The upshot was a marked triumph for the British Navy. Two German army corps, badly needed in the fighting-line, were collected at Antwerp and other Flemish towns for use as a reserve against the Dover army. A considerable number of Mackensen's guns, which were urgently needed in both Galicia and France, were railed from Cologne to the Flemish coast in order to increase the resistance to our bombarding squadron and shrapnel our phantom troops while they were landing. Altogether, Admiral Bacon, in conjunction with Admiral Hood, who conducted the earlier bombardment, must have diverted the artillery force of a modern siege train and the infantry force of a very respectable army. All these guns and men were acting on the defensive; the most they could do was to try to strike back if and when they were struck.

They had to remain on the spot for fear of a surprise assault. All through the war our Navy had made the German Army pay a heavy price for the occupation of the Belgian coast, and the little additional submarine activity which the enemy displayed from Zeebrugge still left a large margin of wasted, inactive military force in the general balance against him. By reason of British sea-power the right flank of the German army was at a permanent disadvantage, and this disadvantage culminated in the effect which our bombarding squadron produced in September, 1915, on the dispositions made by the German Staff to meet the Franco-British offensive movement.

From the military point of view, the important fact about the naval demonstration against the enemy's right wing was that our feint there did not clog the action of our army; for no roads or **The threat** railways immediately behind the front **against Alsace** were occupied in bringing up munitions for a mere demonstration. It was otherwise in regard to the similar threat against the German left wing, which General Joffre directed while Admiral Bacon was menacing the right.

ONE OF THE HIDEOUS EFFECTS PRODUCED BY THE GERMAN POISON-GAS ATTACKS.

A close view of a British " trench helmet." Provided with respirators and protection for the eyes, these hideous but beneficent anti-gas masks recall old-world pictures of the Vehmgericht and the weird garb of the Ku-Klux-Klan which figured so prominently in the Southern States at the close of the American Civil War.

A large number of the new Creusot guns, with hundreds of thousands of shells, had to be withdrawn from the decisive fields of action and used to bombard the German forces in Alsace, in order to produce the impression that the Allies intended to drive in both enemy wings. There was a special reason for threatening Alsace. In the past all the potash resources in the world lay in Stassfurt, not far from Berlin.

Control of the Stassfurt mines enabled the Germans to withhold from the rest of mankind the chemicals and fertilisers worked up from crude potash. But it had recently been found that a much larger potash mine lay in Alsace, and German experts calculated that the wealth of it was so enormous as to be sufficient to pay the German expenses of the war. Being fully acquainted with all these facts, and knowing with what a reckless expense of life the German Government would defend the Alsace mine, General Joffre brought up his new Creusot guns towards the Vosges Heights, and kept his lines in a state of bustle, to make it appear that a grand attack was being prepared there. A large force of the new guns was also massed against the mountain route towards Strassburg, indicating that the attack on Alsace would be launched north and south, with a view to driving wedges between all the enemy's forces in the Mulhouse region.

A regular, intense, and dominating bombardment was

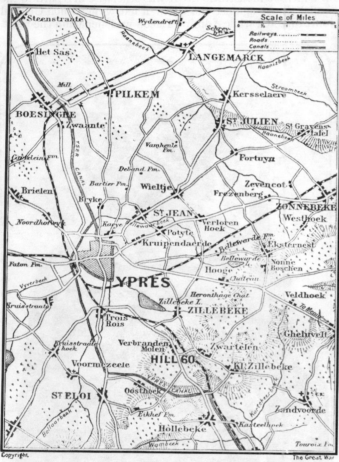

THE BRITISH FEINT AT YPRES.

Map showing the scene of the great Ypres demonstration which drew the enemy's reserves towards the ridges at Hooge and the wood south of Menin Road, and facilitated the capture of Loos.

thus directed upon four principal sections of the enemy's front—the right wing, the left wing, the Lille sector, and the Champagne sector. The tremendous gun fire went on day and night, forcing the Germans to engage in a heavy artillery duel against their wishes. The effect upon the hostile infantry may be judged from an order by a divisional commander, General von Ditfurth, which was afterwards picked up on the field of battle. Ditfurth stated that he had observed that his infantry limited its action simply to defensive firing, and even then fired little in order not to provoke a reply. When the allied bombardment opened on the German positions, the infantry officers in the trenches immediately called for artillery support, and their men manifested great satisfaction when the hostile attacks ceased.

Forcing the German artillery

General von Ditfurth emphatically condemned such conduct, as tending to kill the spirit of the offensive among German troops, and to convince the Allies of their superiority. Commanders of brigades and regiments were urged to make a great effort to maintain at the highest pitch an offensive activity all along the front. It was stated in the order that the artillery could only intervene in proportion to the quantity of munitions at its disposal, and that the infantry would very often have to work alone.

In regard to the Ditfurth Division, there was also obtained from officer prisoners an order showing that the German troops were fully prepared for the allied attack. The order ran as follows:

Five weeks' notice of attack

Ditfurth Division. For Officers Only.
I 221. Divisional Headquarters.
Secret August 15th, 1915.

Divisional Order.

According to the general situation, it is necessary to prepare for the possibility of a great French offensive. We do not yet know exactly in what sector it will come. But having regard to the prospect of a hostile offensive, it is indispensable that everyone should once more make sure that all positions have been placed in a perfect state of defence. Any observed points of weakness should be strengthened, and the greatest vigilance is recommended to the entire service of observation. Measures are being taken to bring back to the front without delay the officers and men who have been granted leave.

VON DITFURTH.

The enemy thus had more than five weeks' notice of the Franco-British attack, and knowing the excellent organisation of the German command, we cannot doubt that all possible measures were taken to strengthen the German lines in men, ammunition, and heavy artillery. And the remarkable thing was that General Joffre was well content that the enemy should be aware of the coming attack, for the principal object of this attack was to relieve the pressure on Russia and hamper as much as possible the intended Austro-German invasion of Serbia. Had it been possible to start the offensive on a date when General von Ditfurth expected it, the result would have been more decisive than it was later; but as General Joffre could not at the time attack with the advantage of all his heavy guns behind him, he contented himself with keeping the German Staff anxiously alert for a movement against the western front.

Little or nothing was lost by giving the enemy notice in the middle of August that an attack was preparing. This may have been accomplished by letting a few men be captured with a false order upon them. Feints of this sort, with a show of bustle behind them, formed one of the specialities of General Joffre. When his veritable attack began, there was no possible mistake as to his real intention.

The artillery duel had gone on along the Belgian coast and along the land front from the Yser to Delle from the second to the third week in September. Then abruptly on Thursday, September 23rd, 1915, the French Commander-in-Chief massed his guns and his trains near Arras, in Champagne, and in Lorraine and Alsace. Day and night the extraordinary hurricane of shell swept the German centre and the German left wing. The German commander moved guns and troops into the Strassburg sector, till, in many of the villages in the plain of Alsace, there were more troops than civilians.

About twenty hours after the French scheme of bombardment was being put violently into operation, General Foch and Sir John French opened fire along the Arras-Ypres sector, while Admiral Bacon increased the fury of his attack on the Belgian coast. The length of the bombardment seems to have been about seventy hours in the Champagne sector, and just a little less in the Strassburg sector, and about fifty hours on the Arras-Ypres front.

The gas cloud is seen starting from the left. Shells are bursting on the right. The British trenches and approaches can be traced by the chalk which has been excavated. Fosse 8 and Hohenzollern Redoubt are hidden by smoke and gas.

The British are out of their trenches, and are racing towards the Hohenzollern Redoubt on this side of Fosse 8, which can just be made out behind the cloud of smoke to the right.

British gas attack on the Hohenzollern Redoubt, captured October 13th, 1915.

New Army's first great success: The taking of the village o[f]

by one of the new British Divisions, September 25th, 1915.

German prisoners captured during the fighting in South-West Flanders being marched from Furnes to Ypres, thence to be transferred to an internment camp.

German prisoners in the hands of French Algerian troops.

Tens of thousands of German wounded soldiers were observed in Belgium, and the German Commander-in-Chief decided that infantry battles were about to follow along the four sectors where the bombardment was being conducted with increasing intensity. In this manner General Joffre, with the aid of Admiral Bacon, produced on both the hostile wings an important distraction of the enemy's forces at scarcely any expense in life to the allied troops. By some millions of pounds' expenditure in shell, artillery, and new model warships, the Allies produced as effectual

Army Corps, and the 10th Bavarian Division. There were elements of the 111th, 117th, and 123rd Divisions, the 1st Bavarian Corps, the 6th Bavarian Reserve Division, and the 2nd Reserve Division of the Prussian Guard. None of the army corps seems to have been up to establishment, and in some cases there was quite a medley of units working loosely in the old army corps framework. It is doubtful if the infantry holding the three German lines north of Arras consisted of more than 120,000 bayonets, the principal defensive strength of the enemy residing in the remarkable number and efficiency of his machine-guns. His artillery also was extremely powerful in comparison with his wasted infantry force. The German human power on the western front was at a low ebb. In soldiers the Allies had generally the odds of at least two to one in their favour. In the matter of heavy armament the attackers also had a superiority, which, however, was slight in regard to the actual number of pieces of ordnance. It was in the accumulation of high-explosive shells and in the remarkable organisation of the French train service that the allied ascendancy in gun fire resided.

German reliance on earthworks

During the attack on Russia the German Staff had overtaxed its munition factories, so that it could not keep its western front as well supplied with shell as the French and British batteries. The German Staff, as we have seen from Ditfurth's order to his troops, had come to rely in the western front on its extraordinary system of earthwork defences, magnificently designed and laboriously executed, strengthened by innumerable machine-gun redoubts and sunken steel-domed forts containing quick-firing guns. The dug-outs were thirty feet below the surface of the

WHERE THE CRICKETER-SOLDIER SCORED.
British soldiers practising bomb-throwing at a base in Northern France.

a double containing movement as though they had launched two great armies at both the German wings. The way was then left open for a plain, straightforward renewal of that attempt to break through in Artois and in Champagne, which had been checked in February, March, May, and June of the same year.

For practical purposes the armies under Sir John French and General Foch formed one vast force of over a million men attacking the flank of the central German salient. Against the German front in the critical sector of the twenty-mile stretch between the Argonne Forest and the Rheims hills was the largest French army, under General de Castelnau. Though in the event Castelnau's army achieved the more important result, the greater force under French and Foch was originally expected to drive in with a more immediately decisive effect.

According to the statement of a Swiss military writer, Colonel Feyler, the Crown Prince of Bavaria seems to have had only about thirty-six regiments at the beginning of the Artois battles. The troops chiefly belonged to the first-line 4th, 6th, 7th, and 19th Army Corps, the 2nd Bavarian

ONE OF THE WEAPONS THAT HELD BATTALIONS AT BAY.
British officers at machine-gun practice.

ground, and in many places there were tunnels through which the troops could move without danger from the heaviest high-explosive shell. In the rear of all the redoubts were great stores of hand-bombs, and for months the chief recreation of the troops seemed to have been matches between battalion and battalion, brigade and brigade, in the game of throwing dummy bombs of the proper weight the longest possible distance. According to the reports of some matches, found afterwards in the captured trenches, the Germans had eagerly taken to this useful kind of weight-putting contest, and had acquired at it a skill equal to that of our best men. Moreover, their machine-gun corps remained incomparable, and by working with the aerial torpedo-throwers and the small trench mortars, the machine-gun corps more than doubled the fire-power along the German front.

The German idea was to remain passive during an attack, and almost invite the French and British troops to take the first line. During the preliminary bombardment the defending troops scampered like rabbits into their gigantic warrens, where many of the underground chambers were lighted with electricity, boarded, **Traps for** and made remarkably comfort- **attacking forces** able. Their observing officers had only to watch through periscopes for the infantry advance, and then decide whether to evacuate the trench or beat back the attack with machine-gun fire. When the trench was deliberately evacuated, it was turned into a trap for the attacking forces. At an order through a telephone, the German batteries were carefully laid on it, and when it was filled with hostile troops, a storm of shells fell and battered it down, and the German troops advanced along

their communicating saps, and, drawing on their great store of hand-bombs, smashed out the remaining attackers.

It was impossible for attacking troops to bring up large quantities of hand-bombs, as the road between the opposing trenches was swept with shrapnel from the German batteries. And by reason also of this shrapnel curtain, it was impossible for the charging lines of infantry to bring

THE MARK OF THE MODERN VANDAL.
Beautiful carvings in a church near the British front shattered by German shell fire.

up with them a quarter, or even an eighth, of the number of machine-guns the defending troops possessed.

So heavy were the disadvantages of the Allies in attacking against hidden machine-guns and deeply-entrenched troops, provided with huge magazines of bombs, that there was only one means of overcoming the difficulties in the way of an infantry attack. This means was a gas cloud. If the Germans had not stooped to chemical weapons of torture during their second thrust at Ypres, their own position in the west would have remained stronger. But from April, 1915, they had continued to use asphyxiating and poison gases in so general a way that the Allies were at last compelled in self-defence to adopt a similar method. Nevertheless, the British and French com- **Germans use** manders were even then able **prussic-acid gas** to show the difference between the methods of neo-barbarism and those of the warlike forces of civilisation. The enemy at the time was using the deadliest poison that could be manufactured on a large scale—prussic-acid gas. But the French and the British chemists provided their armies with merely an intoxicating, stupefying mixture of heavy gases, which put the Germans out of action, and did not kill our own troops if the wind suddenly changed. As a matter of fact, there were cases of British soldiers being suddenly overcome by their own fumes. The result was only long sleep, an orange-coloured

A MISS-FIRE.
An unexploded German shell, obviously intended for the church in the background, discovered by British soldiers in a meadow.

A DEAD VILLAGE THAT WILL LIVE IN HISTORY.

A street in Loos after the British advance. The "Tower Bridge," or "Crystal Palace," which figured so prominently in the fighting in this section of the British line, is seen in the background. It was part of the Loos mining machinery.

face, and a little discomfort on awakening. There was an avoidance of that moral effect of making men afraid of their own chemical weapons, which had clearly been seen in the hesitating advances of the German infantry at Ypres in the previous April, and yet the direct aim of putting deeply-entrenched defending troops out of action was attained.

There was, however, one grave defect in the use of gases of any sort in a series of combined operations on a winding front. The army of Champagne faced **Grave defect in use** north, while the armies of Artois faced **of gases** east. Their attacks were fixed for the same hour—6.30 a.m. on Saturday, September 25th, 1915. It was extremely unlikely that the wind would be blowing northward in Champagne and eastward in Artois at the same time. As a matter of fact, the new weather-gage seems to have fallen to the Champagne army, enabling it to stupefy a large proportion of the German forces in the opposite trenches. But the gas engineers of Sir John French and General Foch could not get a direct, steady stream of air flowing over the enemy's position at Loos

AFTER THE BATTLE : THE APPALLING ASPECT OF A FIELD NEAR LOOS.

Impression of the German trench road to Loos. On either side, as far as eye could see, were shattered guns, limbers, automobiles, dead horses, etc. Nothing could live in the hurricane of fire to which this German position was subjected. The second photograph on this page is a near view of the memorable "Tower Bridge."

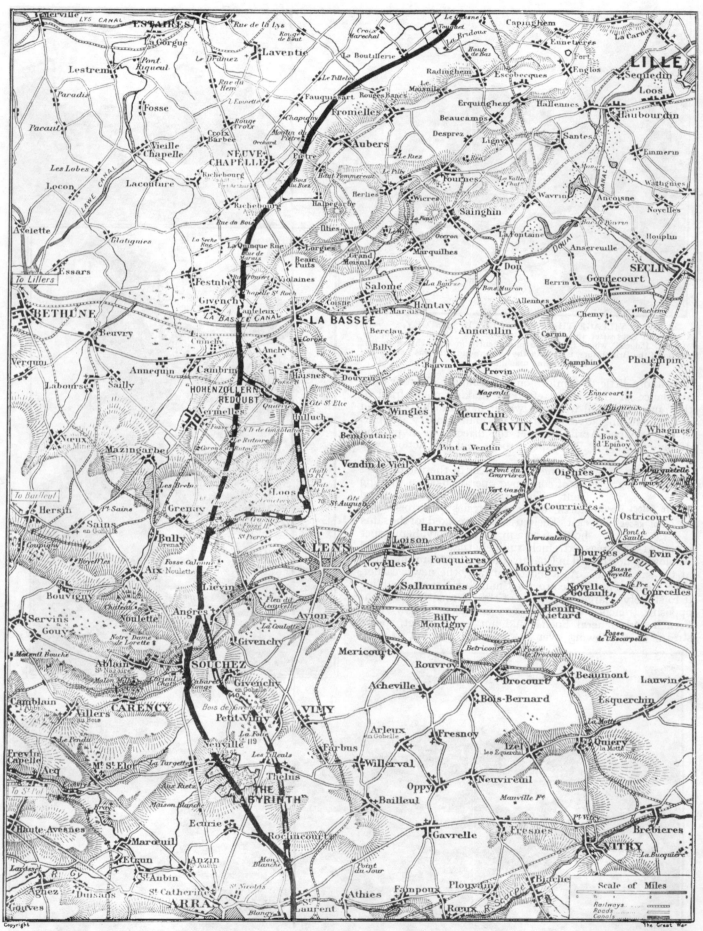

THE LINES OF VICTORY IN THE BRITISH AND FRENCH ARTOIS BATTLES.

The solid black line shows the position of the First British Army under Sir Douglas Haig and the Tenth French Army under General Foch at dawn on September 25th, 1915. The two great gains of ground north and south of Lens are shown by black and white lines.

and Souchez. This appears to have led to a serious disturbance in the combined operations of the Artois armies. The British troops did what they could by means of side-waftings of gas; and though, as has been remarked, they caught some of their own men, the grand infantry charges were punctually made with notable success. But the Tenth French Army delayed for some four hours to advance, waiting, perhaps, for a change of wind to enable them to bring their gas apparatus fully into action.

As misfortunes never come singly, General Foch suddenly found another difficulty in the way of his advance. Since the battles in the Carency region in May and June, 1915,

Feat of German engineering

there had been an important alteration in the geography of the country. With fine ingenuity the German engineers had turned the stream that used to flow through Carency, and had directed most of the water into a valley near Souchez, forming there a new and difficult bog. The existence of this bog was unknown to the French Staff, as the Germans held a line of posts in front of it, covering their main position of defence and protecting the new marsh-trap from reconnaissance by the French patrols working in the darkness of night. Even observing officers of the French Flying Corps could see nothing about the well-known patch of their own country calculated to arouse suspicion. The grass in the valley was very green, but there had been a good deal of rain all the summer, and hay crops everywhere were remarkably good. The stratagem therefore remained undiscovered until the French infantry forces attempted to advance and reach the new swamp. The German engineer who planned and carried out the diversion of the stream was then fully rewarded. It is scarcely too much to say that he saved the German armies on the western front, for not only did he check in a decisive manner the attack of the Tenth French Army, but he indirectly held up the more successful British advance on the north of Lens by robbing the British troops in the critical hour of the battle of the French support on which they were relying.

The swamp at Souchez, indeed, proved to be the key position in the Artois operations. According to the original plan of attack drawn up by Sir John French and General Foch, in consultation with General Joffre, General de Castelnau, and the French Staff, all the movements of the attacking armies of the Allies were arranged in clockwork order. In particular, the Artois operations, which were more vital than those of Champagne, were centred against the mining town of Lens, with the more easterly historic city of Douai as the great objective. The scheme was for Sir John to feint at Ypres and Lille, while driving in on Lens from the north, and for Foch to feint at the ridges looking over towards Cambrai, while closing in with his main force on Lens from the south. From the hills north and south of Lens all the Douai plain could be dominated, and the German troops defending the small mining town were known to be so inferior in number to the forces French and Foch intended to mass against them that the smashing, violent, encircling movement seemed in plan to be as perfect as man could make it. But the trouble with intricate clockwork schemes of converging attack of this sort is that if half the machinery is suddenly put out of order the other half usually fails of full effect.

This is what happened at Loos. The British force carried out its part of the combined operations with perfect punctuality. In fact, our troops reached Lens by a charging movement of such force and speed that the result was achieved an hour or more in front of the time-table. They were fighting in the outskirts of Lens while Foch's troops were still waiting in their own trenches for the order to advance. But our thrust at Lens was not completed by the French forces. What was still worse was that Sir John French was unable to support his own men with the great mass of reserve troops he had brought up for the purpose; for, owing to the skill of the Germans in turning

the Carency stream and making a marsh south of Lens, General Foch had to swerve away from Lens and concentrate against a ridge north-west of Arras. This swerving of the French forces away from the marsh left a gap between the French and British wings through which a very enterprising hostile commander would have struck. Sir John French was afraid that such a stroke would come. The peril was great and immediate, and it compelled him during the critical hours of the Loos conflict to refrain from reinforcing his thin, heroic line of attacking troops, and to hold his reserve divisions near his right flank, in case the enemy should thrust fiercely through the gap existing to the west of Lens.

All this, of course, throws no reflection whatever upon the genius of General Foch and the fighting power of his

"VIVE LE PRINCE DE GALLES!"

An unconventional snapshot of the Prince of Wales conversing with a Staff officer. The two French children, judging by their obvious interest, had apparently discovered the identity of his Royal Highness.

men. Had geographical conditions allowed it, the swamp-trap might have been formed in the line of the British advance, and have made it impossible for us to co-operate with our French comrades. In the former battle for Lille, on May 9th, 1915, it was the British part of the scheme that went awry on the Fromelles Ridge, and General Foch and his troops had to struggle on unaided

in the Carency region. In the later battle **"Foch's troubles, French's troubles"** it was the unlucky turn of the French army to be checked. In quality of genius

Foch and French were so equally matched that accident alone could make one seem greater than the other. The two men were strangely similar, even in the character of the temperament which animated the workings of their intellect —passionate feeling, impulse, and intuition, combined with much experience, wide study, and profound military learning, marked both the Irishman and the Lorrainer. Hard

WRECKAGE ON THE LINE OF THE BRITISH
ADVANCE.
British transport column driving through a shell-shattered
village near Ypres. The streets were deserted, and scarce
a house stood intact.

QUIET MOMENTS IN A BRITISH TRENCH NEAR YPRES.
British soldiers at rest in a first-line trench during a brief lull in the fighting. With their
loaded rifles ready to hand, they were smoking, and about to play cards, while one was
preparing food at a trench brazier.

would it be to find in history two men of different countries,
thrown by eventful chance side by side on the battlefield,
so united by mutual admiration and sympathy of temperament as Sir John French and General Foch ; and the fact
that the Souchez swamp prevented Foch from carrying
out his part of the operations round Lens was an inevitable
misfortune which only served to increase and strengthen
the genial bond connecting the two commanders—for in
quite a literal manner Foch's troubles were French's
troubles.

All this framework of preliminary matter is necessary to
the proper appreciation of the study of the most splendid
failure in British military history. For the Battle of
Hulluch and Loos cannot be understood if it is treated as a
mere conflict between the First British Army and part of

the German forces under the Crown Prince
of Bavaria. The British soldiers who took
the chief part in the action were not in a
position to understand why their magnificent
effort had failed of full effect. And when the
British public in October, 1915, began to
learn the broader details of the great fight,
they, too, were commonly misled into a
wrong idea of the British achievement,
through not understanding fully that the
British plan of battle was only one part of a
larger scheme of attack which had failed
through geographical difficulties.

Fate was dead against the Allies on
Saturday morning September 25th, 1915.
They might have said, like Cato :

'Tis not in mortals to command success,
But we'll do more, Sempronius, we'll deserve it !

By a long, careful, and well-designed national effort, they had
brought into the field more troops, more
guns, and more shells than the enemy had   **Fate against**
at hand. They had distracted him by   **the Allies**
successful feints at both his wings, and had
then overwhelmed him on two critical sectors by the most
terrific bombardment in mortal history. The bombardment
exceeded by a million shells at least the extraordinary
hurricane fire with which Mackensen and his Grand
Phalanx had broken the Russian line in Galicia. When
the decisive artillery action opened, on September 23rd,
the autumnal air was clear and bright, enabling the aerial
observers and the gunners to make the fullest use of their

superiority in artillery. But on September 25th, when the work of the guns was achieved and a path was cleared for the infantry advance, the weather changed to the advantage of the enemy. In Champagne there was a heavy fall of rain which made the chalky clay ground a thing to slip and slither and stick in. It was such heavy going that General de Castelnau reckoned that, in an attack in which speed was essential to victory, his troops were robbed by the rain and the mud of fifty per cent. of the results they deserved.

Fighting against the elements

In the Artois sector the rain at first was not a source of difficulty, but the artillery, the Staff officers, and airmen were perplexed by a heavy mist that blanketed the scene of operations. The aerial observers and the artillery could not trace the movements of their own troops and watch the enemy reserves mass against them, and then drop tens of thousands of shells in front of the advanced British positions. The Staff officers, working between brigade and brigade and

division and division, could not always quickly judge against what point the enemy was concentrating his main forces of resistance. Altogether the mist was disastrous to the classic conduct of the battle as arranged by Sir Douglas Haig, the commander of the First Army, and controlled by Sir John French. And when in addition to the difficulty of the haze and the storm of rain that followed, the British reserves had to be held back to guard the gap left by the swerving movement of the French Army,

THE HUN IN ENGLAND: SOME OF THE ELEVEN HUNDRED GERMAN PRISONERS TAKEN AT LOOS.
A number of the enemy who were captured during the great Battle of Loos, round which centred the fierce fighting leading to the British and French advance of September, 1915, on the front from La Bassée to Lens. The captured Germans are seen marching through the streets of Southampton.

GERMAN NAVAL GUNNERS DEFENDING THE BELGIAN COAST AGAINST THE BRITISH MONITORS.
Although during the whole of 1915 the German Navy's part in the war was practically negligible, enemy sailors were employed in various maritime duties. For instance, a large number were installed on the Belgian coast to reply to any British naval attack. This camera study shows a large German gun in action against British monitors.

the struggle degenerated into an old-fashioned soldiers' battle, in which our men were left to slog against an enemy who was able to manœuvre freely and secretly under cover of a vast system of trenches.

The main attack was made by the First Corps and the Fourth Corps between the La Bassée Canal on the north and the German trenches opposite the village of Grenay, on the south. There were thus only 48,000 British bayonets engaged in the principal operation. The first brunt of the fighting fell on a London Territorial Division (the 47th), and on a Scottish Division of the New Army (the 15th). Acting with these two divisions was the Immortal Division

LOCATING GERMAN COAST BATTERIES.
An artillery-spotting balloon used in co-operation with British monitors bombarding the Belgian coast. The gas-bag was a special type of stationary observation craft in use by all belligerents.

—the 7th—and the 9th Division. Sir John French, however, did not expect Kitchener's men and the London Territorials to perform miracles. He reckoned they would take the first or second German lines, but when this part of their work was done, he arranged to launch another large force forward to continue the breaking movement and complete the decisive attack.

With this object he held in reserve the 21st and 24th Divisions, and the flower of all his infantry—the Guards Division. It is easy to see what was in the mind of Sir Douglas Haig and his Commander-in-Chief. They were pleased with the appearance of the men of the New Army and of the London Territorials. But they could not feel the same trust in the newly-trained national troops as they felt in the well-tried regular corps. **The New Army** They therefore reverted to the method **in action** by which Hannibal, on the battlefield of Zama, endeavoured to use with safety a mass of new recruits of second-rate quality. They sent the new men forward to do their best in weakening the enemy and tiring him out, and reserved their veteran regiments to follow up whatever success the recruits obtained, and fall with fresh vigour upon the more fatigued Germans.

There is nothing striking in this disposition of forces. As has been remarked, it is as old as Hannibal, and the German Commander-in-Chief himself adopted it in the first Ypres battle, when he used up a quarter of a million new recruits in order to wear our men down preparatory to the grand charge of the Prussian Guard. Sir John French did not even feel secure when he had supported the London Territorials and the New Army Division with the 7th Division, the 9th Division, the 21st Division, the 24th Division, and the Guards. But just before the battle opened he wired to the commander of the Second Army to draw the 28th Division to the town of Bailleul, from which it could move to reinforce the Loos front. In all, therefore, eight British Divisions were to co-operate in the attack upon two weak German army corps entrenched between La Bassée and Lens. In actual numbers, the odds in men against the Germans must have been more than three to one; and in artillery, if we reckon not in guns but in the amount of shell actually fired, the odds against the enemy must have been still heavier. In some places our batteries were massed so densely that there was scarcely more than ten yards between gun and gun. And the gunners worked with intense energy in an effort prolonged beyond anything known to our forefathers. Many of them were stripped to the waist like the gunners at Trafalgar; for, despite the chillness of the early autumn morning, they sweated like lascars in a stokehold by reason of their violent labours. For fifty hours and more they worked their guns, and it is difficult to see how the men who took a spell of rest managed to get any sleep. The use of ear-shields and a change from the acrid air round the batteries to the more pleasant atmosphere of a deep dug-out could scarcely have soothed the battered senses of the men who worked the guns.

From Ypres to Lens the iron mouths of a mightier Britain roared at the enemy day and night. In daylight and darkness there were thirty miles of flame

Britain's new monster howitzers and thunder from the British lines, and thirty miles of earthquake and explosion along the German trenches. Neuve Chapelle was nothing to it. The number of heavy high-explosive shells pitched into the German lines in autumn must have been a hundred times greater than the number used in the previous spring, for the British soldier now had at his back new monster howitzers, which were as powerful as anything the Germans used in a general way. We had been long in climbing to the enemy's level in the matter of siege artillery. Two batteries of 6 in. siege-howitzers had reached Sir John French on the Aisne. Then, after the first Ypres battle, "Mother" had begun to arrive in considerable quantities, with her 9·2 in. mouth. Last of all "Granny" had come, enormous yet handy in her

work, numerous and well-provided with an inexhaustible progeny of huge shells, as befitted the grandmother of a million soldiers drawn from the race which had created the modern industrial movement and had invented the principal sources of mechanical power on which our civilisation rests.

The expansion of our comparatively small regular Army into a force of over two million men was largely a matter of patriotism, good drill, and the careful selection of instructors. But the arming of the new troops, the re-arming and the strengthening of the artillery in the old formations, and the equipment of factories for an increasing

BRITISH NAVAL BOMBARDMENT OF THE BELGIAN COAST-LINE.
British monitor in action off the Belgian coast. The men are watching a German aeroplane which was the target of an anti-aircraft gun aboard a sister ship. In circle: Machine-gun in operation. A petty-officer is seen finding the range.

supply of all kinds of ammunition, were tasks which taxed Great Britain's plant and energy to the utmost; and while they were being accomplished, our steel-making works and ammunition works were also employed in augmenting our naval power, inventing new kinds of warships, and giving us a Fleet with which, had we had so mad an ambition, we might even have stood out on the seas against the world.

Our artillery fire at first swept the whole German front with equal intensity. The Lille ridges were very heavily shelled from end to end in order to induce the enemy to believe that we intended to renew our attack on the

portance. In any case it was necessary to hold the enemy all along the line while making the great thrust. So all our army rose and charged, as the guns suddenly lifted soon after daybreak on Saturday morning. At Ypres the 3rd and 14th Divisions of the Fifth Corps attacked at 6 a.m., and by a magnificent effort stormed the great part of the enemy's front line. The German commander, Duke Albrecht of Würtemberg, was alarmed both by the violence of our artillery fire on the Ypres section and by the force of our infantry advance. He possessed a large part of the heavy pieces hurriedly **Duke of Wurtemberg** transported from the eastern front, and   **alarmed** these, with the

siege ordnance he already employed, enabled him to develop a shell fire almost as destructive as ours had been. He might have checked our advance with his artillery and infantry, and at least have prevented his front from being completely broken. But his infantry was terribly shaken by our preliminary bombardment, and it had been, moreover, severely handled in the previous actions at Hooge, the last of which occurred on August 9th, 1915. The upshot was that the Duke of Würtemberg made an urgent request for reinforcements about the time when our principal attack was developing thirty miles to the south. Most of the German reserves immediately

HANDYMEN OF THE AIR SERVICE.
In addition to flying and armoured-car fighting, the Royal Naval Air Service undertook engineering work at the front, and were able to build their own bridges for transport operations

Rouges Bancs-Aubers line. The object, of course, was to induce the Crown Prince of Bavaria to put most of his men in a position in which they would not be wanted urgently. It was only with the closing burst of fire at dawn on Saturday morning that the direction of the coming British infantry thrusts could be discerned; for the Germans could then tell by their sufferings that most of our batteries were collected on our wings at Ypres and in front of Loos and Hulluch. Sir John French seems to have had two plans of attack. He intended first to attempt to break the German line in two places —in the north at Menin, and in the south at Lens. He **British commander's** would then be able to destroy the entire **two plans** Bavarian army by thrusting around its right flank at Menin and its left flank at Lens. The result would be a gap of thirty miles in the German front, through which forces could be poured which would probably free Belgium and Northern France.

But while preparing this grand scheme, with Sir Herbert Plumer at Ypres and Sir Douglas Haig at Lens working together, the British Commander-in-Chief contemplated the failure of the movement from Ypres, and devoted most of his energy to assuring the success of the smaller scheme of the Lens attack which, in co-operation with the advance of General Foch's armies, would still be of decisive im-

AN ACTIVE SERVICE PICNIC.
Members of the Royal Naval Air Service enjoying a rough-and-ready meal at their camp behind the firing-line in France.

available round Lille were sent towards Ypres, where a fierce bombing battle raged all day long round the enemy's first line.

Our advance on August 6th had given us the mine crater north of the Menin Road, but the Germans still held part of the Hooge manor-house and the Bellewaarde Lake. Then south of the Menin Road they had a deadly redoubt in the corner of Sanctuary Wood, from which they had directed an enfilading fire against our right wing in the August action. We opened the new battle by exploding a mine south of the Menin Road, while our infantrymen were crawling forward with fixed bayonets towards the hillside under cover of our last intense bombardment. The men

One of the stone quarries near Hulluch which, by reason of its strong natural fortifications, the Germans imagined to be an impregnable position. However, in the memorable allied advance of September, 1915, our troops stormed the quarry and captured it at the point of the bayonet.

Another view of the "impregnable" German position near Hulluch, captured by British troops even after artillery bombardments had been practically ineffective, and in face of the enemy machine-guns which lined the quarry. The Germans recaptured the quarries, but the British won them again on the following day.

GERMAN STRONGHOLD WHICH FELL BEFORE THE BRITISH WAVE OF STEEL.

rose to charge at six o'clock on Saturday morning. Our artillery had worked havoc in the German trenches; and when our men sprang out in the pouring rain many of the defending troops fled helter-skelter to the second line, some three hundred yards to the rear. The remaining Germans were cleared out in a few minutes by hand-to-hand fighting.

The first German reinforcements came up at seven o'clock, and in some places our men retired, while the enemy bombarded his own trenches, and then charged and took them. In turn the new garrison of German reserves was being battered by our artillery and charged by our infantry, who again stormed the first enemy line. Both sides then settled down to a steady, fierce struggle, with all the guns curtaining off the scene of combat, and hammering at the supporting troops and the reinforcements. But our men not only regained the first German trench before the morning was out, but drove farther into the German position, and captured one of the ridges and some one hundred and forty prisoners. The great arc of heavy German artillery round Ypres was, however, exceptionally well provided with ammunition; and as the Fifth Army Corps had fulfilled the main part of its work in drawing the enemy's reserves, Sir John French was disinclined to pursue further a secondary line of attack that could not be quickly pushed to a decision. So at nightfall our troops in the Ypres sector returned to their own trenches, giving up all the ground they had won, with the exception of a few hundred yards of hostile trench by the Menin Road which had a high tactical value.

A chain of similar events marked the movements of the Second Army along its southern front. All the German trenches between Armentières and La Bassée were assailed. The right wing of our First Army took a notable part in this forceful demonstration. Our Third Army Corps resumed the attack on the **Attack on the Lille ridges** Lille ridges at the hamlet of Le Bridoux, a little to the north of Rouges Bancs and Fromelles. The Indian Army Corps, co-operating in the Neuve Chapelle region, assailed Pietre Mill and the Aubers section of the great low horse-shoe plateau, while a part of the First Army Corps charged the German trenches at Givenchy, immediately in front of La Bassée. These attacks were at first successful all along the line, and it looked as if our heavy failure against the Lille Plateau in May would at last be redeemed by a victory. The fighting power shown by our men was magnificent. The Lincolns' attack on Bridoux Fort, a very strong point in the German system of defence, was an heroic affair. The Lincolns took eighty prisoners, after killing hundreds of foes in the fighting round the stronghold. A middle-aged company cook, whose proper place was far in the rear, became so excited by the din of battle that he left his work and ran into the captured German trench. There he seized a rifle and sniped every German who came across his line of sight, crying as he did so, "There's another of the devils!"

The Berkshires had a still more difficult task before them, as they had to carry a formidable work known as the Lozenge. After storming it, they found that it was lined with deep dug-outs in which the garrison could safely shelter from everything but the heaviest howitzer fire. The Lozenge protected the main German first line, and its machine-guns did terrible work among the gallant Berkshires. But the Englishmen fought on with wonderful bravery. One private, noticing that the Germans were collecting behind a traverse, waited at the bend of the trench with a bayonet, and drove it in turn into seven of the enemy, while a comrade behind him hurled bombs into the mass of grey figures beyond. The Rifle Brigade also finely distinguished itself, by both its skill and its tenacity, in the holding battle of the ridges. The riflemen rushed to the assault, headed by a strong force of bombers The bombers at once began to extend to the right and left, and in less than an hour and a half both the first and the second German lines were captured, and our gunners lifted on the third **Rifle Brigade's** line, north-west of Lille and close to **fine work** the suburbs of the city.

The Germans, however, retained a wedge in the centre that checked connection with the battalion on the left of the Rifle Brigade. Both ends of the position captured by the riflemen were blocked with earth and sandbags. The enemy thus had time to recover from the first shock, and his reserves came up with a large supply of bombs; and by ten o'clock in the morning the men of the Rifle Brigade were compelled to abandon their conquest of the second line. But they held on to the first German line, and there repulsed with heavy losses another strong hostile attack. One officer, suddenly meeting a German bomber, and having no weapon with which to defend himself, knocked his enemy over with a blow on the chin. The same officer had previously shot two Germans at point-blank range, and knocked out two others.

In the afternoon, however, all the captured positions had to be abandoned along the curve of the Lille Plateau, owing to the fact that the German commander hurried up powerful reinforcements, who were able to draw upon their main bomb magazines and move up their supplies under cover of deep communicating trenches and tunnels. The enemy's first line had been deliberately held with comparatively weak forces, in order to escape huge losses from our prolonged and terrible artillery fire. The German machine-guns had largely been withdrawn to the second line, while the bomb magazines had been removed still farther back. The feeble front line was rather in the nature of a trap, in which it was hoped our men would mass, so that the German batteries could bombard them at an exactly known range, and prepare the way for the bombing parties advancing down the communication gaps. The organisation of the ridge defences had been much improved since the Neuve Chapelle and Rouges Bancs battles. The enemy had used the whole resources of the mining district south of Lille to establish large electric generating stations from which power was transmitted to the front. This immediate, handy, and flexible supply of motive power had enabled the German engineers to tunnel, excavate, and generally fortify in a marvellous way the German positions on the plateau.

BRITISH OFFICER'S QUARTERS IN THE ATTIC OF A FRENCH FARM-HOUSE BEHIND THE FIRING-LINE

HEROES FROM LOOS AT SHEFFIELD.
The King telling the wounded of their country's pride and gratitude. Corporal Fuller, V.C., is seen at the right of the front row.

With men like Rathenau, the chief electrical magnate of the world, in a position of authority at the German War Office, we can be sure that all the fine young brains of the inventive nation which had produced the gas-engine and the Diesel engine were completely at the service of the German Army. The result was such a display of solid, ant-like industry, directed by widely-trained and versatile intellects, as had never before been seen in war. When Germany stood on the defensive, with her vast machinery of industrial expansion at her back, the spectacle was more impressive than the first great German offensive movement, which had been engineered only by the German armament firms and the German Staff. Between Ypres and La Bassée we lost about 20,000 men, without obtaining more than a slight transient grip on part of the enemy's second line. The demonstration, of course, had to be made, or the resistance to our main thrust towards Lens would have been greatly strengthened. But the fact that our movement from our centre and our right wing absolutely failed, though we had used hundreds of thousands of high-explosive shells and had occupied two German army corps by a feint at the German coast, may be taken as a triumph for the German business man.

It was his brain, his experience, his technical knowledge, that were mainly responsible for the incomparable system of defensive work which held up our Second Army and part of our First Army. It must be remembered that the young German business man was, as a rule, also a conscript soldier, who even in peace time possessed sufficient practical knowledge as an officer of the reserve to enable him quickly to combine his industrial and military ideas. When the first-line German Army, with its professional

VICE-ADMIRAL R. H. S. BACON, C.V.O., D.S.O.,
who rendered valuable service in the bombardment of Zeebrugge and Ostend. He is seen in a captain's uniform.

officers, was half shattered at the end of October, 1914, and the young German business man, of a type similar to our Territorial lieutenant, was largely employed to fill the gaps in the officering of the battalions, the extraordinary ingenuity of the German defensive system became marked. There was then little need for an Office of Military Inventions in Berlin of the red-tape kind that too often worked so indifferently in London. The greater part of the inventive intellect of Germany was already in the trenches.

The ideas of the inventors were submitted by one man on the spot to another man on the spot, and put into practice with no delay. In London, on the other hand, inventions were at first sifted by men without first-hand knowledge of the latest forms of trench warfare—men with no experience later than that of the South African War. It was not, for instance, sufficient for an inventor, in the winter of 1914, to submit to our War Office the design of a handy, cheap bomb, capable of being quickly manufactured by the million, and to offer his design, for what it was worth, as a free gift to the country. The examiners of inventions would not send the design to Woolwich for approval, or better still, forward it to some ordnance authority at the front. The inventor was asked first to manufacture some specimen bombs, and, in the case which we have in mind, his free gift of the design was rejected, and he was informed that if the bomb were found to be what was needed he would receive the usual royalty. Months passed before the bombs were at last made by the inventor himself, who had grown weary of the whole business. Yet he was a man who had already made a name and a fortune by his improvements in one of the most ingenious pieces of mechanism

African War, were rather hostile than favourable to Lord Fisher's programme of naval construction, and at times interfered with it mischievously. King Edward VII., representing merely the old-fashioned monarchical principle, was the principal supporter of Lord Fisher. Mainly through the happy accident that King Edward discovered in Lord Fisher a greater and more inventive mind than Kaiser Wilhelm found in Grand Admiral von Tirpitz, Britain had surpassed Germany in the race for sea-power and in the development of naval weapons.

In regard to our military prepara- **Democracy's fatal** tions, Lord Roberts was ready to give **obstinacy** us an Army adequate to our political scope, in order to form the needed powerful adjunct to our Navy. But the British democracy would not submit to the sacrifice necessary to obtain a military force capable of assuring the safety of Belgium and the peace of the world. Mr. Balfour, while he was leader of the Unionist party, in every way discountenanced Lord Roberts's programme. We had created in our new Navy a force capable of prevailing against Germany in a purely naval duel between Britain and Germany. Therewith, all our politicians of every school rested content. They would not create such an Army as our policy required—the military force needed to help in keeping the Germans out of Antwerp and out of France, in accordance with our vital interests as expressed in our guarantee of Belgian independence, and our understanding with France and Russia. Therefore the German Emperor, believing that we were too weak and distracted to fight on land, turned on Russia, France, and Belgium in order to isolate us for a later conflict in which we were to be destroyed, and for which our democracy and its elected

Russell.]
MAJOR-GEN. G. H. THESIGER,
C.B., C.M.G., A.D.C.
Killed in action in France while gallantly endeavouring to consolidate gained ground, on September 27th, 1915.

in the modern industrial world. It is not likely that Germany treated her inventors in this manner. Whether the design were good or bad, it would have been tried and accepted or rejected in a week or two, especially in a critical stage of the war, when the bomb was coming into general use.

By nature nearly all first-rate fighting men are inveterate conservatives. They have a passionate dislike for new weapons, for the reason that untried methods may lead to unforeseen disasters. In the eighteenth century the British Navy was at first far behind its principal rival in regard to scientific ship construction. Our sailors had to supply by their surprising prowess and their skill as fighting gunners the deficiencies of our unprogressive, uninventive warship designers, and capture superb examples of enemy ships of the line to serve as models in our building yards.

A happy accident Even in recent years our extraordinary pre-eminence in every important branch of naval construction was due to this accident—that a man of unusual inventive genius, Lord Fisher, the first designer of armoured trains, had created our modern Navy on lines heartily disapproved of by almost every admiral of the old school. The work of Lord Fisher was furthermore facilitated by the existence of several important private warship building firms in our country, who had been induced by the force of international competition in armament design to develop the inventive talents of their principal men.

It was due to no general virtue residing in our democratic institutions that our Navy of the Dreadnought era was created. Manhood suffrage had as little to do with it as votes for women. Indeed, the chief representatives of our democracy, the leaders of the Liberal Government, who came into power soon after the close of the South

'Gale & Polden.

[Histed.
TWO DISTINGUISHED LEADERS WHO FELL NEAR LOOS.
The centre portrait: Major-General F. D. V. Wing, C.B. Above: Major-General Sir Thompson Capper, K.C.M.G., C.B., D.S.O., who was severely wounded on September 26th, 1915, and succumbed to his wounds the following day.

leaders had lacked the courage, as he supposed, to prepare.

This was the reason why our soldiers were unable to display little or none of the alert, inventive force that distinguished the work of our sailors. Sailor and soldier were fellow-countrymen of equal gifts, starting from the same level of intellect and character. But circumstances favoured the sailor and made his mind more progressive and wider in scope than that of the soldier. All that our best generals could do was to elaborate little plans for handling some 150,000 British soldiers, forming a small part of the wing of great French national armies, during a fierce and probably short campaign either in Belgium or France. The grand modern military problems, arising from the presence of all the fighting strength of the Empire on a Continental field of battle, were matters of idle speculation to British generals. They were not allowed to take practical steps to study the instruments and methods of gigantic national warfare, in which men clashed in millions together.

Our Staff officers were utterly unexercised in manœuvres on a grand scale. They had no opportunity of learning to overcome the intricate difficulties of team work between half a million men in furious, confused conflict along an immense front. The British commanders and their Staff had to learn in quick, decisive, actual experience the grand technique of modern national warfare which German, French, and Russian generals and Staff officers had been practising for forty years. It was as though a small band of sailors, used only to handling a destroyer flotilla with a couple of light cruisers, were given in the heat of battle the command of an armada of several battleship squadrons and battle-cruiser squadrons, with a swarm of smaller

Difficulties of our staff

vessels. To add to the difficulties of Sir John French and his Army, army corps, divisional, and brigade generals, they were forced by the enemy to undertake constantly the most delicate and hazardous operation—the offensive —against positions of immense strength. Their new-made machinery of control of their new-made armies was put to the severest test; for it is in movements of advance against highly developed defensive works, backed by heavy artillery, that the efficiency of the finer organisation of an army is manifest. For several months the jibing criticism of the German generals on the western front was that, though the British forces had such strength of character and such good marksmanship as to make them terrible in defensive actions, their Staff work was too slow, clumsy, and unalert to achieve a victorious attack on a large, decisive scale.

The test of control

Probably the explanation was that, having to undertake a vaster work than they were accustomed to, our military men had to learn by experience. After all, the ancient Romans were faced by a similar problem when Hannibal swept through Italy; they won through by a force of character which enabled them to survive blow after blow, and learn to win from each stroke that failed to fell them. Neuve Chapelle and Rouges Bancs had been severe checks to our armies. And as our French comrades in Champagne and Artois in February, May, and June were equally unsuccessful in their attempts to shatter and pierce the hostile front, the Germans had concluded that their own lines were impregnable.

As a matter of fact, the prophecies of M. Bloch, the brilliant, thoughtful Jewish banker, had been realised to a considerable extent. Owing to the introduction of siege artillery in the heaviest form and in large quantities into

BRITISH STORMING A GERMAN TRENCH NEAR LOOS.

Between September 25th and 27th, 1915, the Allies made a combined advance in Artois, in the course of which there was some exceptionally heavy fighting, resulting in tremendous loss to the enemy and the capture of the important village of Loos. After a terrific preliminary bombard-ment by our artillery, the infantry rushed the trenches, racing their officers, one of whom was heard to call out : " Faster, boys ! Give them hell ! " There was some rapid bayonet work, which brought the Germans to their knees screaming for mercy, and an immense number were taken prisoners.

open field warfare, and to the development of deep-dug earthwork defences, with numerous machine-gun redoubts and hand-bomb depots, the power of defending troops had become greater than the power of attacking troops. Even the poorly munitioned Russian armies, when nearly overwhelmed by a great hostile force possessing a gigantic artillery and shell supply, succeeded in retiring in order and remaining intact, by entrenching every three or five miles in their retreat and smiting from cover the attacking infantry advancing across the open field.

According to Bloch, this condition of things would lead to aggressive warfare becoming so costly in life as to be im-

Why gas was used — practicable. The Germans endeavoured to recover the advantage of the offensive by employing immense clouds of poison gas. But our men at Ypres learnt to avoid being asphyxiated. The German chemist then invented a less deadly but distressing weapon in the form of a weeping gas, which temporarily blinded soldiers by irritating their eyes and producing tears. The French troops in the fire trenches were transformed into monstrous apparitions by the masks with goggles and respirators, which protected

WOUNDED AND MUD-STAINED, BUT HAPPY.
Some of our men who took part in the advance of Loos photographed at a railway-station where a halt was made for refreshments during their journey home.

their faces from chlorine, ammonia, and other fumes. But the indefatigable Germans again changed their methods of gassing their opponents, and filled the air with a curious almond-like scent. This odour indicated prussic-acid gas. The contest between the gas-maker and the mask-maker resembled the older struggle between the gun-maker and the armour-plate maker. But up to the autumn of 1915 victory rested with the instrument of defence.

Judging from the number of prisoners taken in the British advance on Loos, our long-delayed gas attack was not a very decisive success. Apparently it had taken our chemists nearly five months to provide our Army with a weapon similar in operation to that employed by the enemy in April, 1915. No doubt, the new intoxicating fumes were reserved as an element of surprise for the great general offensive by the allied forces; but, as we have suggested, the wind, which had been blowing from a favourable quarter when the bombardment opened on September 23rd, appears to have veered at the critical moment on the morning of September 25th. A gas attack is a wind attack; it requires not only a current of air

flowing in a regular movement from the advancing force to the defending force, but the current must be of a nice quality, neither too strong, or it will disperse the gas before the effect is obtained, nor too gentle, or it may not carry the cloud of heavy fumes quickly and far enough.

Our available wind at daybreak on Saturday seemed to have been too gentle and too aslant of the enemy's main positions. Our infantry had chiefly to rely upon the terrifying destructive work of their massed batteries and the swiftness of their own charge. It is, however, cheering to find that our commanders had worked out in practice an old English idea to facilitate infantry attacks. Towards the end of the nineteenth century, Mr. Sutherland had pointed out in his work, "Twentieth Century Inventions," that the terrible defensive power of troops armed with rapid-fire rifles and guns might be overcome by blanketing their field of fire with vast thick smoke-clouds, through which the attacking infantry could advance with comparative safety, and drive in with the bayonet. Some brilliant officer or military chemist had given effect to Mr. Sutherland's smoke-screen form of bayonet attack, and it was by means of it that Loos, Hulluch, Hill 70, and the outskirts of Lens were captured.

Just before the guns lifted and the smoke clouds were formed, our expectant men could safely catch through the haze glimpses of the bleak, ugly stretch of country which they were set to win. It was a poor, chalky ground, overgrown with long grass and rolling in two low, rounded swells of chalk towards Hill 70 near Lens. Hill 70 was more than two hundred and ten feet above sea-level; but as all the land was a low chalk plateau, the summit of the hill was barely thirty feet above the neighbouring hollow in which Loos village spread in desolation. There was coal under the plateau, and what had been a hundred years ago as pleasant, lonely, and rural a countryside as the chalk edge of the Weald of Kent, had been transformed into a hideous tract of Black Country. Rows of mean miners' cottages extended near the gear of the pit-heads; there were great dark pyramids of slag, a church-tower or two, and crowning the open dismal scene were two high pit-shafts connected into a massive construction by a framework of girders. In shape it resembled the Tower Bridge, which was the name our soldiers gave it. Being some three hundred feet high, it formed an incomparable fire-control station for the enemy; and, by reason of its strong steel open-work construction, our heaviest artillery could not seriously damage it, even by a prolonged bombardment. For tactical reasons, the possession of "Tower Bridge" was a matter of high **Importance of the** importance to both contending armies. **"Tower Bridge"** It formed one of the most perfect of observing stations, with a field of vision of forty miles in clear weather, and artillery officers working on it, in telephonic communication with their batteries, had the whip-hand of all enemy guns and howitzers in this sector of the front.

On Loos and its "Tower Bridge," therefore, Sir Douglas Haig concentrated his forces of attack. The "Tower Bridge" was only about two and a half miles north-west of Lens, so that by the capture of it all our guns would be able to mass against the mining city and its important railway junction. Our artillery observers would also be able to reach the enemy batteries at Angers and Lievin, lying to the south-east and impeding the French advance on Souchez and the Vimy Ridge.

Our trenches, when the struggle opened, ran from a point near Cuinchy on the La Bassée Canal, and curved round the formidable enemy position of Auchy-La Bassée to the village of Vermelles, continuing south, past mine-pits, with a railway line and blocks of miners' cottages, to the villages of Grenay and Bully les Mines, which were opposite to Lens. There was about one to five hundred yards of No Man's Land between our brown parapets and the wall of dull grey sand-bags that formed the first German lines.

Wounded returning to dressing-station after an attack. (An official photograph of which the Crown reserves the copyright.)

Another official photograph of wounded on their way to receive treatment. In the smaller view are shown some virile types of the young men who fought so grandly at Loos and Hulluch.

NOTABLE CAMERA RECORDS OF SCENES BEHIND THE FIRING-LINE AT LOOS AND HULLUCH.

On the first crest of the low downs rose a great German fortification some five hundred yards in diameter, built around the path from Vermelles to Loos, and dominating with its machine-guns and its sunken quick-firing turrets of steel armour the bare, grassy hollows through which our men had to advance. There were three lines of barbed-wire to get through, machine-gun positions sheltering behind slag-heaps to storm, and rows and large blocks of colliers' cottages—called, in French, corons—to master by desperate hand-to-hand fighting. Great redoubts also extended along the second low swell of chalk, such as the Hohenzollern Redoubt and the Kaiser Wilhelm Redoubt, which defended

A HOLIDAY TASK IN FLANDERS.
Canadians sent back from the front-line trenches employing their time of rest by filling sand-bags for the construction of other trenches.

the southern approaches to La Bassée and enfiladed any body of troops advancing on Hulluch. Then, like two deadly horns tipping this triple crescent of fortified swells of chalk, were the batteries of La Bassée and Auchy in the north, and the batteries of Angres, Lievin, and the Lens suburbs in the south. The main German batteries were ranged behind the centre of the triple crescent, with the heaviest and longest range ordnance in a stretch of woodland near Pont-à-Vendin. Pont-à-Vendin was a vital railway junction from which four tracks radiated, and through it the defending troops were supplied with munitions.

All this land was less a countryside than one vast, straggling, grimed, and miserable city of industry. The open spaces, blistered with slag-heaps and sprinkled with hovels, were uglier than the patches of building land in the lowest suburbs of London. The general result was that all the fighting between the fortified chalk swells, the corons, and villages was practically street fighting combined with the most difficult kind of trench warfare. There was no room for a battle of manœuvres of the open field order, and the advance had to be made by the sheer weight and swiftness of the thrusting force. Swiftness, indeed, was the essence of victory, for the enemy's front could only be

Swiftness the essence of victory

smashed by a sudden drive that should take effect before the two German army corps in Belgium could arrive to save the situation.

After the failure of some of the men of the New Army in Suvla Bay, Sir John French and Sir Douglas Haig might have been anxious about the driving power of their new formations. But the event at Loos was to show that the new citizen armies of Britain, when well directed, were a striking force of the highest quality. The attack was made by the Scotsmen of the 15th Division in the centre, the Londoners of the 47th Territorial Division on the right wing, and the veterans and new drafts of the famous 1st Division on the left wing. The 1st Division was held up on the enemy's second line, and the check enabled the Germans to collect local reserves along the rampart of chalk. The 1st Brigade, however, found a gap, and its gallant brigadier showed extraordinary courage. Leaving his flank dangerously exposed, he pushed his troops ahead, and after capturing some gun positions and taking five hundred prisoners, he won the outskirts of the village of Hulluch.

How the attack began

The achievement of the London Territorials was of even greater importance. Swinging out from Bully and Grenay, the Londoners were met by wild artillery fire which did but little damage, and they steadily advanced over the shrapnel-swept fields to the immense slag-heaps known as the Double Crassier. Here they stormed the

UNDER FIRE OF GUNS AND CAMERAS.
Canadians at the front taking cover behind a ruined house. They would appear to be less interested in the approaching shells than in the attentions of the photographer.

German machine-gun positions which had been sheltered from our artillery fire by the mounds of rubbish. Pushing on from the Double Crassier, the Londoners reached the western cemetery at Loos, where the fighting became terrific. The Germans had specialised in cemetery fighting at Souchez and Neuve Chapelle, and among the lowly tombs at Loos their machine-gun parties had constructed a formidable fortress. They dug a trench at the upper end of the cemetery, and placed their machine-guns behind the burial mounds, using the tombstones as additional cover, and raising parapets among the graves. The Londoners who flung themselves on this disturbed resting-place of the dead rapidly added to the number of corpses in the cemetery. Leaping from one parapet to the other bombing and bayoneting as they went, they lost many men, but the Germans lost more. Yet so furious was the struggle that it was fifty minutes before the cemetery was cleared of living Germans. By that time the number of bodies outstretched among the fallen crosses and trampled wreaths greatly exceeded the number of coffined figures lying below the ground.

But the hand-to-hand fighting round the slag-heaps and colliers' cottages and cemetery was almost a pleasure for fighting men compared with other features of the advance. It was the enemy's artillery that made the charging movements so costly of life. As soon as our batteries, at 6.30 in the morning, lifted over the gas and smoke screens on to the enemy's reserve positions, every German gunner worked with furious intensity to maintain a curtain of fire between the British and German lines. A combination of high-explosive and shrapnel shell was principally used. It burst in thick black eddies of smoke over the advancing lines, and our men fell in thousands before they came into action. The enemy really possessed, in conjunction with his great number of machine-guns, sufficient artillery power to annihilate our infantry while it moved for two to three miles on a wide front, stopping on the way in order to clear the slag-heaps and trenches from the gas in its path.

It is quite likely that the low-hanging mist was not wholly a misfortune for the First British Army. No

Furious German cannonade

doubt it checked the work of our gunners and airmen, but after all they had carried out the principal part of their task by the great bombardment. By way of ample compensation, the hostile artillery observers could not mark through the haze the general movement of our troops. In the mist the German gunners had only local telephone reports to guide them, and the number of these reports diminished as trench after trench was taken. The best that the commanders of the German batteries could do was to maintain walls of fire all along the broken front lines, with a view to interrupting the movement of our reinforcements and punishing the men engaged in bringing up ammunition. Our smoke-screen, with the mist and the curtains of rain, gave us most of the advantages of a night attack with the bayonet. A veil was thrown over the general operations, which no searchlights, flares, and star-shells

TROPHIES OF THE BRITISH VICTORY AT LOOS.
General view of the Horse Guards Parade, London, with some of the guns taken from the Germans at Loos on exhibition. Below: A trench mortar captured by the Somerset Light Infantry. Above: Viscount Churchill examining a trench mortar.

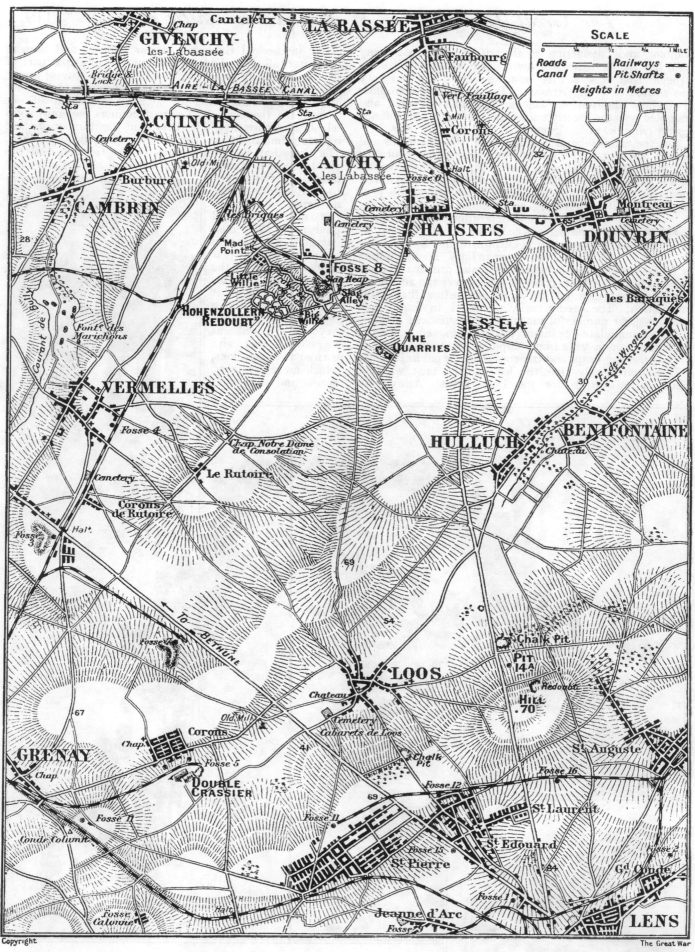

SCALE
0   ¼   ½   ¾   1 MILE

Roads ═══ Railways ═══
Canal ▬▬▬ Pit Shafts ⊙
Heights in Metres

Canteleux   LA BASSÉE
GIVENCHY-
les-Labassée   Chap
                                    le Faubourg
Bridge &
Lock   AIRE-LA BASSÉE CANAL   Vert Fauillage
Sta.   Mill
CUINCHY   Sta.   Sta.   Corons
                                                              Halt   32
              Cemetery   Fosse 0
Burbure   AUCHY
                                    les Labassée
CAMBRIN   Cemetery   Sta.   Montreau
                                                                                        Cemetery
28   les Briques   Cemetery   HAISNES   DOUVRIN
              Mad
              Point   FOSSE 8
"Little   Slag Heap   les Baraques
Willie"   Slag
Alley   St Elie
HOHENZOLLERN   "Big
REDOUBT   Willie"   THE
Fonte des   QUARRIES
Marichons   30   F. de Wingles
VERMELLES
                                                            HULLUCH   BENIFONTAINE
Fosse 4   Château
              Chap. Notre Dame
              de Consolation
Cemetery   Le Rutoire
Corons
de Rutoire
Fosse   69
3   Halt
                                                            54
                                                                        Chalk Pit
                                                                        PIT
                        To Béthune   14A
                                                                        Redoubt
              Fosse 7   HILL
                                                            LOOS   .70
67   Château
              Old M.   Cemetery   St Auguste
              Corons   Cabarets de Loos
GRENAY   Chalk   Fosse 16
Chap.   44   Pit
              Fosse 5   Fosse 12
Chap.   Fosse 84
              DOUBLE   St Laurent
              CRASSIER   69
Fosse 11   Fosse 11   St Edouard
Fosse   Fosse
Coule Column   St Pierre   84   Gd Conde
              Fosse 13
Halt   Fosse 1
Fosse   Jeanne d'Arc
Calonne   Fosse 29   LENS

Copyright   The Great War

LARGE SCALE MAP OF THE COUNTRY BETWEEN LA BASSEE AND LENS, SHOWING IN DETAIL
THE GROUND COVERED BY THE BATTLES OF LOOS AND HULLUCH.

could pierce. In these circumstances, which made Staff work difficult, not only did the London Territorial troops show great personal fighting power, but their officers displayed a skill in leading that provoked the admiration of Sir John French. In addition to getting hold of the cemetery, the division seized the chalk-pits south of Loos, and, by strongly linking these gains with their conquest of the Double Crassier, they formed a firm defensive flank running from Loos to Bully and Grenay. In this manner they repaired the gap which had suddenly been produced between the French and British lines, when the marsh at Souchez caused General Foch's men to swerve southward. Sir John French in his despatch states that the success of the London Territorial Division removed his fear of a German thrust from Lens, and enabled him at last to release his reserve and throw it into the fighting-line. Every Territorial soldier must take a high pride in this glorious achievement of the London Division of former amateur volunteer soldiers.

Glorious Territorials ! In the greatest of all ordeals, with a weakened flank through which the enemy might have divided the allied armies, they exhibited the most valuable kind of fighting talent. Theirs was a great strategical victory, and not merely an admirable tactical success. They enabled their Commander-in-Chief to bring into action at the critical point four more Divisions of infantry.

Meanwhile, the Highlanders of the New Army, the glorious 15th Division, were making their wonderful charge through Loos and over Hill 70 to the Cité St. Auguste, a northern suburb of Lens. This fierce and rapid spring, across four miles of fortified ground, is probably the finest thing the Highlanders of Scotland have done throughout their splendid history. The thing was accomplished, moreover, by men who knew little or nothing of warfare till the fateful month of August, 1914. They had volunteered for service and had begun their training when our little Regular Army was tramping from Mons to the Marne, and from the Marne to the Aisne. It was scarcely to be expected that Lord Kitchener could, in a single year, turn civilians into soldiers of the very finest class. Yet such were the Highlanders.

We have already observed that the British commander used his new recruits in the Hannibal manner, by placing them in the forefront of battle and relying on the strong reserve of veterans to maintain the attack and guard his own lines against any unexpected disaster. As a matter of fact, this arrangement of our freshly-trained troops brought out all that was best in the men of the New Army, as well as conformed with the sound old rule of war. The new men were impassioned volunteers who had worked with a will for a year, in stern, yet quiet desire to meet the German conscript on something like equal terms. They had trenched like navvies; they had tramped like athletes; and, though they were willing to settle down to the wearing monotony of a parallel siege battle, their minds were filled with a lust for the heroic ardour of the charge. The tall sinewy Highlanders especially, with their kindling Celtic temperament, had the instinct of the charge in their blood—something that came down to them from the days of Finn and Ossian, and survives, with a quality of flame, in our ancient Gaelic poetry. A very imaginative man with Celtic sympathies might have foreseen what would happen; but though Sir Douglas Haig was a Scotsman, it is clear that he did not expect from his newly-trained Highlanders a stroke so swift and violent as they gave. The new Division outraced, when they were released for the charge, all the elaborately timed battle plans of their commanders.

Many of the new soldiers have told us in letters what they felt. Like all sound, healthy men they had no love of death and little passion for the terrible scientific warfare of our times. Many of them wondered how they would behave, when their comrades began to drop around

MORE NERVE-RACKING THAN THE MAINMAST.

An incident, popularly called "treeing a linesman," somewhere behind the western front. Three members of the Signal Service were detailed off to repair an old "civil," not "military" wire. While one was up aloft a shell came straight at the pole. His two comrades, hearing the shriek of the projectile, took cover in a ditch. When the danger had passed, they looked up to see if the linesman was intact, but he had disappeared. "Poor fellow, he's gone," said one; but a grunt drew their attention to the foot of the pole, where the climber had subsided, regardless of consequences, which were a few bruises.

them, and were detachedly curious about themselves. The modern introspective mind does not, at first analysis, seem to make for a heroic strength of spirit. We rather like to turn our feelings inside out, and rely less on instinct than an intellectualised emotion. Shakespeare began this strange game in "Hamlet," and in the course of three centuries this apparent malady of the mind had spread deep into the nation. Everything that increased the power of education among the people increased the introspective habit. We inclined, in moods of frank self-judgment, to regard ourselves as inferior in downright courage to our fighting forefathers. They were Fortinbras, we were Hamlet; and, meanwhile, all the machinery for human slaughter had been developed in a terrifying manner.

Introspection and Heroism

It was no wonder, therefore, that the men of the New Army were rather apprehensive; but the event proved that the men of the Highland Division, in circumstances which would have dazed and staggered the clansmen of Bannockburn, were inspired, rather than daunted, by their introspective study of themselves. Almost to the last minute, the anxious subalterns were lecturing their platoons—a thing they had been doing at nearly every

ACT.-SERGT. J. C. RAYNES, V.C., "A" Battery, 71st Brigade R.F.A. Under intense fire from gas-shells carried Sergt. Ayres to shelter, gave him his own gas-helmet and returned, though gassed, to his gun.

LT. G. A. MALING, V.C., M.B., R.A.M.C. Treated three hundred men under heavy fire near Fauquissart; was twice flung down by shells, but continued his work.

PTE. A. VICKERS, V.C., 2nd Royal Warwickshires. Advanced before his company at Hulluch under heavy fire and cut the wires holding up the battalion.

CAPT. A. M. READ, V.C., 1st Northamptonshires. Killed near Hulluch. Though partially gassed, he rallied disorganised units, and was mortally wounded while encouraging them under a withering fire.

opportunity since the day for action had been fixed. But the men needed no haranguing, and though they did not take the battle as light-heartedly as the London Irish on their left, who played a football into the German trenches under a hurricane of shrapnel, the Gaels of Scotland **Scotland and Ireland** charged with extraordinary pace, strength, and judgment.

At ten minutes to six on the historic Saturday morning the heavy cloud of white-yellowish gas slowly rolled from our trenches, and still more slowly floated onward. The launchers of a battleship could not be more anxious than were the British troops over the result of their first important gas attack. But

MAJ. A. F. DOUGLAS-HAMILTON, V.C., 6th Q.O. Cameron Highlanders. Killed on Hill 70. His untiring energy and leadership checked the enemy's advance at this point.

unfortunately, the great cloud was carried too far northward, with the result that the enemy's second line was not overpowered by the stupefying fumes. At half-past six two brigades of the Highland Division swept out towards the "Tower Bridge." It was arranged that one brigade should make a direct attack on the Loos front, while the second **A marvellous achievement** brigade executed an enveloping movement to the north, bending round towards Loos and Hill 70. The third brigade was held in reserve, to be used as occasion required in either direction. There were thus only two bodies of newly trained troops, numbering each under four thousand bayonets, engaged in the

SECOND-LIEUT. A. J. T. FLEMING-SANDES, V.C., 2nd East Surreys. Seeing his men wavering at Hohenzollern Redoubt, he sprang to the parapet and, flinging bombs at twenty yards' range, saved the situation.

SEC.-LIEUT. (TEMP. CAPT.) C. G. VICKERS, V.C., 1/7th Sherwood Foresters. Though wounded and almost alone, held a barrier for some hours until a second barrier could be completed.

SECOND-LIEUTENANT A. B. TURNER, V.C., 3rd Royal Berkshires. At Vermelles, practically single-handed, drove the enemy back with bombs till reserves came up. Died of wounds since.

TEMP. SECOND-LIEUTENANT R. P. HALLOWES, V.C., 4th Middlesex. At Hooge set a magnificent example, throwing bombs and making daring reconnaissances. When mortally wounded, continued to cheer his men.

SOME OF THE V.C.'s WON IN THE BRITISH ADVANCE AT LOOS.

A CASE OF INSTRUMENTS.
Canadian officer within reach of the enemy, with his bombs and hand-grenades ready for instant use.

main attack on Lens. The achievement of this small force was marvellous. The first two brigades advanced in line against the first German position on the low downs. Going forward by short, swift rushes through a perfect tempest of shrapnel intensified by streams of bullets from machine-guns and rifles, the Highlanders took the whole of the first line in about half an hour. Then leaving some of their bombers to clear out the dug-outs, they smashed their way along the communicating trenches, or advanced in open order through the long grass, and quickly won a series of footholds in the German second line in front of Loos. Spreading out in furious fighting from each breach they had made, the Highlanders conquered the advanced defences of Loos as easily as they had stormed the first swell of chalk. The enemy was surprised by the speed and violence of the assault, and in less than an hour after the two brigades left their trenches they were fighting round the "Tower Bridge" and the outskirts of Loos. The fleeing Germans had crowded towards the village, where their officers got them well in hand and put up a stern rearguard fight.

But owing to the Scotsmen's plan of attack, which then came fully into operation, the enemy's stand at Loos did not greatly benefit him; for the brigade on the right began to work well north of Loos, where the enemy's resistance had weakened, and after getting without much difficulty well behind the village, the advanced brigade suddenly turned and stormed through some fir plantations to the summit of Hill 70. As the men charged they came under a terrible fire from a strong German position on their left flank at Pit 14-A, just between the chalk quarries and the hill. At the same time their right flank, as they climbed the down, was swept by German machine-gun fire from the eastern houses at Loos. But instead of stopping and seeking for cover, the furious Highlanders, under the lash of death, increased their pace till their brigadier-general lost control of them. He was a youngish man, with an agile habit of body, but when he arrived near Loos all that he could see was his men vanishing in the distance over

Under the lash of death

the hill. The brigade crossed the road from La Bassée to Lens, captured the German third line on the opposite slope; and at twenty minutes past nine the survivors of the four battalions stormed Cité St. Auguste, a pitmen's village forming the north-western suburb of Lens.

Four thousand Scotsmen had broken clean through the German front—through three fortified lines placed on dominating heights, and strengthened by strong redoubts, containing cannon as well as machine-guns. It was a finer feat than even the first tremendous drive by the men of Anzac in the landing battle beneath Sari Bair. In both cases fresh, untried troops displayed a vehemence of attack unparalleled elsewhere along the front. It is doubtful if the men of our Regular Army would have gone so fast and so far; for the regular soldier fought with more caution. The brigade of Highlanders was too impetuous, and, owing to the extraordinary speed of its advance, no other body of troops was able to co-operate with it. By half-past nine the brigade had turned at right angles, and had got into the suburbs of Lens. It seemed as though the base of the northern plain were about to be opened. The

The Anzacs eclipsed

left flank of the Scotsmen was exposed to a counter-attack, but the German commander had no men left to make the movement. On the other hand, the brigade had lost touch on the north with the 1st Division, which had been badly checked near Vermelles. The converging advances of the French Army in the south of Lens and the British forces at Loos either did not take place, or were slow in progress. But the French troops had scarcely moved, and when they did they swerved away from Lens. Only the London Territorial Division, battling

THE BOMBER'S CORNER.
Canadian grenade company's lieutenant sitting beside his varied stock of missiles.

in Loos Cemetery, and the other two brigades of the Highland Division, engaged in fighting desperately in Loos, were within call.

Meanwhile, the Germans hastily brought up machine-guns along the railway embankment north-east of Lens, and continued to concentrate on the adventurous brigade a wasting fire from all points of the compass. There was machine-gun and musketry fire from Cité St. Auguste in the north, from the outskirts of Loos in the west, from Lens

THROWING IT IN.
A Canadian officer in the act of hurling a hand-grenade. The broad streamers attached to the bombs in his belt served to steady their course through the air.

ATTENDING TO THE NERVES OF THE ARMY.
French telephone men linking up the trenches in Artois and testing the wires.

of the men undertook the difficult job of capturing the place by house-to-house fighting, with machine-guns playing on them from the first-story windows, and splutters of musketry fire from the doors. By this time the Germans were squeezed badly on both sides of the village, with the London Territorials hammering them at the western cemetery, and the Highland Brigade working round from the north and driving through the High Street. This street cuts the village in half from east to west, being lined with poor shops and cafés, and leading to the cemetery. In the centre of Loos stands the ancient parish church, with the core of a once **The village** pleasant, old-fashioned village around it, **of Loos** from which spread rows of two-story pitmen's cottages of a cheap and shabby quality. The cellars were packed with field-grey figures, and our bombing parties went down the side streets searching for these underground shelters, and marking their progress by explosions.

There were trenches in the street, showing that the enemy had intended to fight for every house, and as the Scotsmen and Londoners worked forward, there was a good deal of sniping from the broken windows of the cafés and cottages. Some of the Germans had a strange notion of the conventions of modern warfare. They would fire away furiously, killing and wounding our men in considerable numbers, and then when they were caught at a disadvantage by a bomber or a bayoneter, they would throw up their hands and cry " Kamerad ! " The Bavarians especially seemed to think that their surrender would be accepted after they had gone on slaying till the last possible moment. The Briton may be chivalrous, but he is not an utter fool. One man was deliberately sniping from a window as our troops passed. He held up his hands in

in the south, and from Pit 14-A and a row of pit-men's cottages in the east. In this circle of death the unsupported, half-shattered brigade checked its headlong charge, and, sowing the ground with dead and wounded, withdrew in good order on Hill 70, and there entrenched just below the crest to get cover from the enemy's eastern line of fire. The Germans reoccupied the redoubt they had abandoned on the summit, but the Highlanders held on to the hill. After four hours of wonderful fighting the brigade, in spite of its check at Lens, had achieved one of the great things of the war. It held most of the hill which dominated the country. With the help of two more battalions it could have retaken the redoubt on the summit, and with proper ordinary support it could have got back into Lens by noon, and have opened that gate into the plain which was the objective of all the million men under Foch and French. As a French observer remarked : " The Highland Division was by this time exhausted, but if fresh troops had come up and a fresh attack had **Deficiency of** been delivered upon the Germans, who **reserves** were gathering all their men in the Douai region, the enemy's front would have been pierced as though it were of cardboard. The brigade had made a path. Had reinforcements arrived without delay, the path would have become a high-road leading to the entire Douai Plain. But the day wore on and behind us there were no signs of reserves. It was only at nightfall that they were reported. It is plain that, on this first day of the attack, advantage was not taken of the results achieved."

Meanwhile, the Division which had attacked Loos in front received the support of its 3rd Brigade. The village was partly surrounded by two battalions, while the rest

FROM ONE FORM OF CAPTIVITY TO ANOTHER.
German prisoners being escorted to the rear along their own communication trenches by their French captors.

Mediæval aspect of modern French infantrymen wearing the invaluable steel casque.

French bomber leaving his shelter fully equipped for action.
Off on his perilous errand.

German trench in Champagne which was captured by the French.   The posi
Inside a well=arranged Ger

French soldier loading trench cannon with bombs.
Primitive but practical.

In the background is seen a cavalry patrol
A column of the splendid

...ngly fortified, even to the steel revolving gun-turret seen in the photograph.
...ch when the Huns had gone.

The knife and revolver as substitutes for the bayonet and rifle.
French soldier ready for the charge.

...s scouting in advance of their foot comrades.
...infantry moving into action.

Heavy ordnance being drawn on to "caterpillar" tyre.
With the Belgian artillery.

Great French attack in Champagne: Reserves waiting in the trenches while their comrades advance.

FORTS ON WHEELS.
A German mobile steel-turret gun captured by the French

token of surrender, but as a British soldier walked towards him, he again raised his rifle and fired. His cartridge did not explode. So down went his rifle and up went his hands once more, and he cried " Kamerad ! " He got comrade-ship at the point of the bayonet.

There was, however, one German hero in Loos. While the street fighting was raging furiously, a battalion com-mander found a fairly intact house near the centre of the village, and decided to fix his headquarters there. The signallers came up with their flags, the sappers followed, and started their business of unpacking field telephones and laying wires. Amid all this work of preparation there
fell a thunderbolt. For no apparent
One German   reason, the house became the target for
hero   great German howitzer shells. The first
exploded near the doorstep, the second
burst in the back garden. Colonel, signallers, and engineers scattered in search of cover ; and some of the men who went to the cellar found a German officer there seated by an underground telephone, directing the German battery to fire upon himself and his foes. The German knew his shelter had become the battalion headquarters, and, in Samson-like fashion, he desired to bury himself with his enemies.

Loos had suffered severely from our bombardment. The village church was almost levelled to the ground, not even the shell remaining. Of the 12,000 inhabitants only about three hundred men, women, and children remained. Six women and a child came out amid our troops, but most of the unhappy people took refuge in their cellars. Yet in Loos there was one girl of extraordinary courage—a pretty maid of seventeen, named Emilienne Moreau. She left the shelter of the house and began to pick up and tend wounded Highlanders, though the battle was raging round

her. Then, when some Germans came up from their cellars to assail the Scotsmen, beautiful Emilienne acted like a countrywoman of Jeanne d'Arc. Seizing the grenades of the wounded men and taking a revolver, she attacked the brutal oppressors of her people and killed five of them.

Two or three snipers were brought down from the " Tower Bridge," and some of the London Territorials, who had worked round to a chalk-pit, south-west of Loos, climbed a slag-heap commanding a sunken road running to Hill 70. The Territorials brought up machine-guns and linked forces with the Highlanders who had cleared the village, and when the Germans tried to return down the sunken road they were shattered by machine-gun fire and shells from a trench mortar which the " Terriers " had also brought forward. The London Irish, who had led
the Territorial Division which closed the   **London Irish**
gap west of Lens, seem to have had a good   **on the ball**
share in the taking of Loos. After these
extraordinary footballers had kicked their leather into the German trenches, crying " Goal ! " and had captured three German lines, another regiment came up to relieve them. The Irishmen of London had done their work, and the taking of Loos was not their job ; but, swept on by the enthusiasm of battle, they worked away all the rest of the day, clearing house after house, or rather, what was left of the houses after the bombardment, and stabbing, shooting, and bombing until they felt ready to drop dead themselves. The 23rd Silesian Regiment was wiped out by them in a scene of horrible slaughter.

All this was only the preliminary work of the London Irish and the splendid Territorial Division to which they belonged. The far-extended and exhausted Highland

FORTS ON RAILS.
French armoured train which could be moved on light railways laid to any point with great rapidity.

Division, which had pierced to Lens and then held on to Hill 70, was relieved on Saturday night. But the bayonets of London, whose losses were not so heavy, were set to hold the line they had won against the enemy's grand counter-attack. The Germans began by a bombardment, lasting days and nights, and of extraordinary intensity.

The factor of race The Territorials of London were cut off from their army for three days by a wall of mingled shrapnel and high-explosive fire. Even water could not be brought up to them, and as most of their water-bottles were smashed in the fighting, the men learned what thirst was. The weather was very bad, raining on and off for the four days they held the line. Some of the troops hung out their muddy ground-sheets, and drank the water which collected in the waterproofs. Happily the new trenches, constituting the third German line, with the sand-bag parapets moved sack by sack to the other side, had been fairly well consolidated after the first victory, and by admirable foresight large quantities of supplies had been moved up. The men had food and ammunition, though they lacked water

THE EFFECT OF SHELL FIRE ON LANDSCAPE.
A wood in Champagne, the scene of a French success, reduced to a collection of charred stumps, with a huge crater in the foreground caused by a mine explosion.

and sleep. For the rest, the strength of the resisting line was a matter of racial character and individual power of endurance.

The troops holding the advanced trenches, which ran almost into the enemy's position, were continually attacked on both sides. When the German infantry held off, the German guns played on them in an almost incessant sweep of fire. All the ground held by the Division was plastered with shells, and the men wondered whether they would be blown to atoms or buried in one of the human waves that kept surging against them. The strain on the nerves of these new soldiers was terrible. The soaked, miserable figures could at last hardly stand from fatigue, but still they fought on almost blindly. It was an incessant " Stand to arms ! " for the entire Division. The men could not afterwards tell how they kept themselves up. The dawn broke on Sunday in a green, hazy atmosphere, pierced with flashes of light from rifles and machine-guns. The men battled all day, and went out in shifts at night to the shell-holes to act as listening patrols. It was most necessary to guard against surprise in this way, as there was no barbed-wire available for putting up until the third night. In the darkness, some of our men obtained fresh bread

from the packs of the Germans they had slain in front of the hard-fought line. In spite of the absence of wire entanglements, none of the German charges got nearer than a dozen yards of the "Terriers'" trenches. This was the distance at which the strongest German wave of infantry broke round the wedge of Londoners.

Sunday passed in a tumult of bombardments and broken bayonet attacks, and no relief came. Monday went by like a nightmare. Yet on this day, when things were at their worst, the marvellous "Terriers" not only threw back the enemy, but bombed their way into the vital German position in the wood south of the chalk-pit. This extraordinary advance against the German reinforcements saved the situation. Then at daybreak on Tuesday our guns were again so strongly massed and so well supplied with shells as to overpower the reinforced German batteries. Under cover of another great British bombardment, which broke down the German wall of fire, new troops were pushed forward, and the London Division was relieved.

It is said that some of the men were so overwrought that when they went back to their billets they cried like children. It was the effect of absolute physical fatigue, combined with the long nerve-racking strain of the continual hostile bombardment. Other men wildly sought for pencils and postcards to let their relatives know that they had done something fine, and had returned unhurt from one of the fiercest furnaces of the war. The Territorials were much cheered, their fresher comrades running to carry their kit and rifles, knowing how tired out they must be. The men were afterwards addressed by the general. " Not only am I proud to have had the honour of being in command of such a regiment as yours, lads," he said to one, " but the whole Empire will be proud whenever in after years the story of the Battle of Loos comes to be written. For I can tell you that it was the London Irish who helped to save a whole British army corps. You have done one of the greatest acts of the war." And these remarks may be applied to every battalion of the London Territorial Division. First of all, it closed the gap between the French and British armies. Then, after helping to clear Loos, it protected the right flank of the British force, and enabled the Guards Division to force back the German line and assure our hold on the new position. The new Highland Division and the Territorial Division fairly won the chief honour of the war.

We have seen that the veterans of the 1st Division were held up, near Vermelles, in their advance between Loos and Hulluch. And, unfortunately, the check occurred to the brigade on the right, which should have connected with the Highland Brigade that took Hill 70. Had our connecting Staffs been more expert, the vehe- **An unfortunate check** ment movement of the Highland Division might have been controlled and arrested at Hill 70, and touch maintained with the wing of the 1st Division which had been thrown back at Hill 69. The Scotsmen should not have been allowed to drive into the suburbs of Lens; they could have done more important work by stopping at Hill 70, and using what surplus energy they possessed in an advance along the German trenches northward, and thus weakening the resistance to the right brigade of the 1st Division

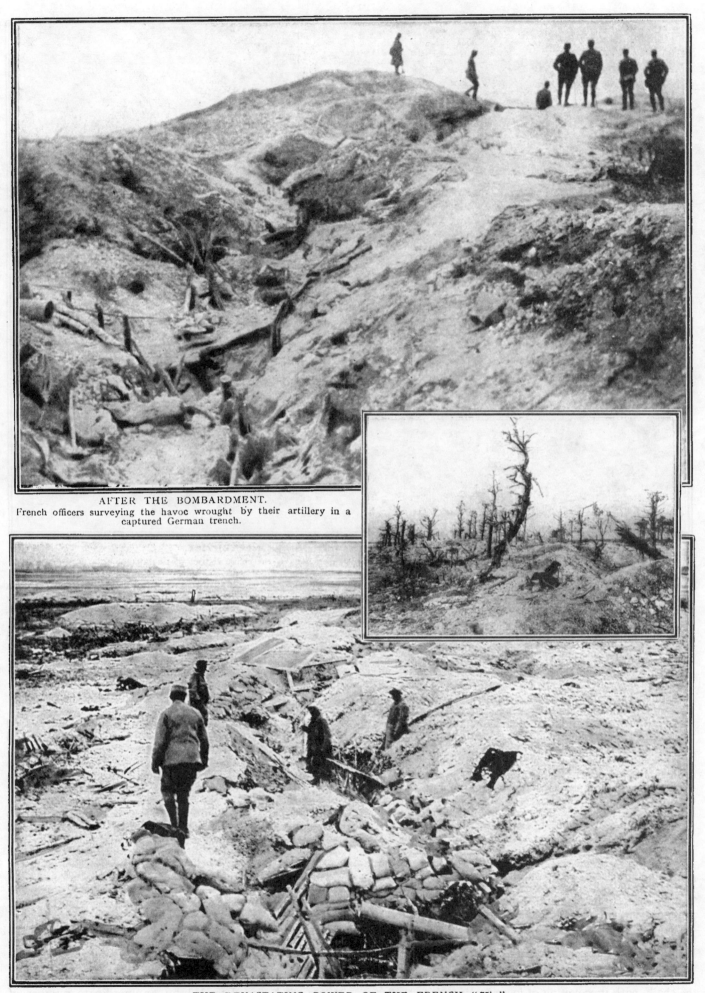

AFTER THE BOMBARDMENT.
French officers surveying the havoc wrought by their artillery in a
captured German trench.

THE DEVASTATING POWER OF THE FRENCH "75's."
A first-line German trench in Champagne captured by the French after a preliminary bombardment which almost obliterated it. In
centre: View of the Sabot Woods, with every tree destroyed and the ground rent and torn.

QUAINT HABITATIONS OF MEN ON ACTIVE SERVICE.
Bungalows, lean-tos and dug-outs made by German soldiers in the chalk district of Champagne.

The left brigade of this Division, as has already been described, had made a daring advance to the outskirts of Hulluch, and at ten o'clock on the morning of September 25th there was only a narrow wedge of German forces dividing the advancing British Divisions between Loos and Hulluch.

And immediately north of the 1st Division there was another scene of victory. The 7th Division, reduced to little more than 2,000 strong in the first Ypres battle, then filled out with drafts from the New Army, and again wasted by ten months of trench warfare, and brought up to establishment by more of the new men, went forward to another great triumph. The Immortal Division combined the inspiration of a glorious tradition with the impetuosity of attack of the New Army. It was directed against the quarries, lying north of the road between Vermelles and Hulluch and defending the mining hamlet of Cité St. Elie, that straggled down the highway from La Bassée to Lens. St. Elie was practically the centre of the German position. The pitmen's houses had been transformed into a modern fortress by increasing the protection afforded by the cellars and placing the machine-guns and quick-firers behind slag-heaps where only a howitzer shell, falling almost vertically, could strike them. The quarries were furnished with deep, narrow trenches, profound dug-outs, easily excavated from the chalk, and barbed cable entanglements. Further westward, on the line of low downs between the Quarries and the Vermelles Road, another network of underground ways was dug in the chalk, forming in the dry porous ground the most perfect form of entrenchments of the modern kind. For the chalk, with its covering of loose earth and its tendency

Perfect entrench-
ments at St. Elie

to break easily, was better shelter than hard rock in a modern artillery battle, and the ease with which the chalk could be cut and tunnelled gave the German engineers full opportunity of showing their skill.

But the men of the 7th Division took the ridge and all its machine-gun redoubts with terrible swiftness ; and, after trying to help the 1st Division, they swerved away from Hulluch, and, storming the western edge of the quarries reaching the La Bassée Road, broke into Cité St. Elie in fierce house-to-house fighting. Then from this pitmen's hamlet the leading brigade, headed by the 8th Gordon Highlanders, turned northward and smashed its way through a great German earthwork fortress to the village of Haisnes. At Haisnes, where a company of the Gordons, under Lieutenant Adamson, broke through three lines of wire and held on from 8 a.m. to 5 p.m., fighting in the village, the enveloping movement of the 7th Division should have been supported by the 9th Division in a frontal attack. But this latter Division, with its two leading brigades—the 26th and the 28th—was checked by one of the most formidable fortresses in the world. On the first swell of chalk, running alongside the Vermelles-La Bassée Road, the German sappers had constructed northward, between the coal-mine Fosse 8 and the artillery position at Auchy, a masterpiece of fortification known as the Hohenzollern Redoubt.

This strong work was thrust out nearly five hundred yards in front of the German lines, so that its fire-trench was close to our parapets. The work was shaped like a bean, with its broadest end pointing north-west. The whole position was on a gentle rise, giving a wide field of fire, and was defended by an inordinate number of

The immortal
Seventh Division

machine-guns. They were so placed as to be almost safe from shell fire, and so arranged that their streams of bullets could converge all along the front and sweep their own fire-trenches. The dug-outs in which the garrison sheltered were thirty feet underground—the depth of a three-story house—and, being so massively roofed with chalk, they were beyond the power of penetration of the heaviest shell. No steel cupolas and slabs of concrete were employed ; these mechanical aids to defensive strength would only have weakened the work.

The Hohenzollern Redoubt The more yielding chalk, used in sufficient thickness, was the best resisting material ; and, as constructed, the Hohenzollern Redoubt was comparable in strength with the terrible Labyrinth against which General Foch's army had broken in the spring of the year.

Only a direct gas attack, carried out with a fair wind and maintained with full intensity for an hour, could have incapacitated the defenders of the Hohenzollern work. But, as we have observed in the Loos advance, on the morning of September 25th the wind was too southerly for a successful attack of this kind. When the cloud of smoke and fumes rolled from our position near Vermelles, it did not spread and thicken eastward, but floated rather towards the north, interfering in places with the movement of our own infantry. The troops garrisoning the Hohenzollern Redoubt were able to resist the attack upon them ; for, though they lost some of their trenches in the fierce charge by the British troops, they won part of the position back by Saturday evening by means of their bomb magazine and machine-guns. Mean-

while, the gallant 26th Brigade managed, by terrific fighting around the big slag-heap and pithead buildings of Fosse 8, to capture this mine from which three communicating trenches ran into the Hohenzollern Redoubt. Our hold on the mine, however, remained weak, as the position was dominated by the guns and strong defences of the German troops at Auchy, on the west. The 26th Brigade, struggling with desperate courage against an enemy possessing larger and more accessible supplies of grenades, and having a cross-fire of artillery from the north-west at Auchy, the north-east at La Bassée, and the east at Douvrin, stood against continual counter-attacks on Saturday night, Sunday, and Sunday night. But when day broke on Monday the 4,000 British infantrymen, weakened by heavy losses and worn out by attacks delivered from three sides, slowly gave ground and fell back to the eastern part of the Hohenzollern Redoubt. They seem to have needed more bomb-throwers and a larger supply of bombs, but as the enemy's batteries flung a **Why bombs ran** terrible curtain of shell fire between the **short** newly-won ground and our bomb depots, it was practically impossible to bring forward abundant quantities of the special ammunition needed for the hand-to-hand struggle in the eight-foot-deep trenches. All the open field between the chalk rise and our original position was swept clean by the Hohenzollern machine-guns, and rows of miners' cottages ran along the neighbouring roads, affording excellent observation posts for the German artillery officers and emplacements for the lighter guns.

Using the heavy, wooden-handled grenades that can rip the sides out of a chalk trench, and cause blindness by

ELABORATION OF TRENCH CONSTRUCTION NECESSITATED BY MODERN ARTILLERY.
A corner in one of the first-line French trenches in Champagne massively constructed of blocks of stone and heavy timbers, and made in three tiers or storys.

OPEN-AIR WORKSHOP IN FRANCE.
French soldiers making barbed - wire entanglements for the defence of the trenches.

MAKING NETS TO CATCH THE HUNS.
Another open-air industrial centre, somewhere in France, where men were actively engaged in the manufacture of barbed-wire netting for the front.

exhausted, our new line between Cuinchy and Hill 70 was an intricate affair. The enemy retained a wedge in it between Loos and Hulluch, and the position round Fosse 8 and Haisnes was a maze of battle. The London Territorial Division, the Highland Division, and the 7th Division had made three piercing thrusts that each reached to the third German line. The 1st Division had also touched the enemy's final position of defence at Hulluch.

All these great results, however, had practically been achieved by eleven o'clock in the morning. The German commander did not bring up his principal reserves until two hours later—at 1 p.m. on Saturday. In the Loos and

their mere concussion, the Germans bombed us out of the trenches connecting with Fosse 8, and it was with marvellous heroism that the half-shattered brigade managed to stick to some part of the redoubt until fresh troops arrived. But as will afterwards be seen, the Hohenzollern work was to remain a place of contention between Briton and German for some considerable time, even as the Labyrinth for months was a scene of struggle between the French and the German. It was in the Hohenzollern trenches that our tacticians clearly learnt the lesson that all modern infantrymen needed to be as highly trained in bomb-throwing as in musketry ; the hand-bomb was

Every infantryman a grenadier more important than the bayonet, in a parallel trench battle, at least. It was wasting a decisive force at the critical moment to have it divided into bayonets and bombers. Every man was needed in grenade work, and grenades were required by tens of thousands when a combat went on for forty-eight hours in deep, narrow, underground passages, with sand-bag barricades separating the groups in every trench, and protecting them from practically everything but hand-bombs and aerial torpedoes.

The Hohenzollern position might have been turned by a combined attack north and south. This, indeed, had been planned, our northern advance coming from Givenchy. But the troops at Givenchy—the 2nd South Staffs, 1st Liverpool Regiment, 1st King's Royal Rifles, and 1st Berkshires—were held up by unbroken wire and terribly smitten from the strongly fortified German work thrusting into our lines. The complete failures of the Givenchy attack and the Vermelles attack seriously limited our advance.

When night fell on Saturday evening, September 25th, and all the advantages of our long prepared attack were

Lens sector especially, where the enemy was thrown out of his third line by 9.30 a.m., and in the Fosse 8 and Haisnes sector, where the 8th Gordons reached the village by 8 a.m., there was ample time for British supports to advance ; for the 24th Division was waiting close at hand at Noeux-les-Mines, and the 21st Division at Beuvry, east of Bethune. The Guards Division was preparing to march from Lillers to Noeux-les-Mines, and the 28th Division was advancing south from Bailleul.

The delay in bringing this powerful additional force into action against the retreating and badly shaken Germans was, of course, partly due to the check to the Tenth French Army. The French were not able to move until one o'clock on Saturday afternoon, and then, as previously mentioned, they swerved away from the prearranged Franco-British direction of attack. Nevertheless, this grave accident to the allied plan of operation does not fully explain the fateful slowness in the movement of the British reserves. Sir John French states in his despatch that the success of the London Territorial Division convinced him at 9.30 a.m. that there was no danger of a German rush between the **Fateful slowness of reserves**

British and French forces. He at once placed the 21st and 24th Divisions at the disposal of Sir Douglas Haig. Some of the brigades marched past the British commander at Noeux-les-Mines and Bethune. At 11.30 the heads of the two columns of 24,000 bayonets were both within three miles of our original trench-line. There were barely more than five miles to the decisive new positions which the Highlanders were holding at Hill 70, the men of the 1st Division at Hulluch, and the troops of the 7th Division at the quarries and along the La Bassée-Lens road. Twenty-four thousand fresh British infantrymen, with their artillery and bomb supplies, thrown at once into the struggle against a half-beaten, outnumbered enemy, should have won a decision before the hostile reserve forces came fully into action.

Something like a local disaster

At half-past eleven on Saturday the distance between the leading troops of the 24th Division and the sorely-pressed brigade of Highlanders holding the western slope of Hill 70 was scarcely more than four and a half miles. Allowing for the mist and the rain and disorder of the newly-won ground, a couple of brigades could have come up with ammunition in two hours, arriving at 1.30 p.m. But no reserves arrived at the critical spot until nightfall, by which time the enemy had grown too strong to be broken. Sir John French gave all these details, adding that the Guards Division reached Noeux-les-Mines by 6 p.m. on Saturday. He does not state why the 40,000 men he sent forward to strengthen the attack and deal the great sledge-hammer stroke did not arrive in time in the firing-line.

After the long delay, the men were at last launched on Sunday, September 26th, along the line between Hulluch and Hill 70 won by the Fourth Corps. But the German commander, after more than twenty-four hours' grace, had been able to gather large forces, and by organising a strong offensive east of the La Bassée-Lens road, he anticipated the British advance and threw back the foremost brigades of the 21st and 24th Divisions. Something like a local disaster seemed to have taken place, but Sir John French remarked in his despatch that " reports regarding this portion of the action are very conflicting, and it is not possible to form an entirely just appreciation of what occurred in this part of the field." At the time of writing the affair is in process of being thoroughly examined at the War Office, so it would be premature to attempt to pass judgment upon it. But it may be said the rumour runs that the troops were over-marched and unfed.

Sunday, September 26th, was a day of misfortune. One of the very finest of our younger generals, Sir Thompson Capper, who had commanded the 7th Division at the time of its great retreat from Ghent to Ypres, in October, 1914, was wounded during a terrific fight round the quarries, and died of his wounds. He was one of the greatest fighting men of Britain, adventurous and yet wary, magnificent in resistance, and also a grand thruster. The 9th Division, which was fighting near the 7th, round Fosse 8, at the eastern end of the Hohenzollern Redoubt, also lost its commander. Major-General G. H. Thesiger, on the day Sir Thompson Capper died ; and a third most able and distinguished general of division, Major-General F. D. V. Wing, commanding the 12th Division, fell soon afterwards by the Hohenzollern Redoubt.

A day of misfortune

By Sunday evening the enemy's pressure against our new line became very severe. The Germans continually counter-attacked, and the German gunners, using shells

AFTER THE VICTORY: RETURN TO QUARTERS OF A FRENCH REGIMENT SPECIALLY MENTIONED IN ARMY ORDERS FOR ITS HEROISM AT THE TAKING OF SOUCHEZ.

Preparatory to a great offensive, a mine-crater was converted into a strong French position close to the German first-line. Sacks of earth were massed on the top of the cavity, and gabions and barbed-wire were erected in lavish profusion. Behind this rude but ingenious and effective stronghold a large number of troops were concentrated.

Apart from a continuous bombardment of the German positions, our ally resorted to an elaborate system of mining the enemy trenches, and making strenuous efforts to capture the mine-craters, after the explosions in order to turn them into miniature forts, or magazine and artillery storehouses. This photograph shows the interior of one of these captured mine-craters. A light railway for the transport of munitions is at work. With the tree-trunks shelters are being built.

FRENCH SOLDIERS TURNING A MINE-CRATER IN CHAMPAGNE INTO A MINIATURE FORT.

containing torture gas and prussic-acid gas, tried to fill their lost trenches with poison fumes. But our men held on to the western slope of Hill 70, and the road from Loos to La Bassée as far as the western cottages of Hulluch. By dawn on Monday morning our hold on Fosse 8 was lost, and the enemy prepared to make a grand attempt to win back all his lost positions. It was then that the Guards Division, under Lord Cavan, made one of the most famous charges in the history of the Guards.

The men were at last fully representative of the Motherland of the British Isles. The ancient Coldstreams were the sole inheritors of the traditions of the new model army of Oliver Cromwell; their comrades the Grenadiers dated from the former age of hand-bomb warfare, and were first formed of exiled Royalists who returned when Cromwell died; the Scots Guards were raised soon after the Restoration; their organisation was at last completed by the Irish Guards, formed after the South African War, and the

New glory of the Guards Welsh Guards, created during the present conflict. Their numbers had increased from a Brigade to a Division of 12,000 bayonets; and by a happy chance there was a Division of the Prussian Guard fighting in the Loos salient. It is only fair to our county regiments to state that though our Guards were a splendid body of fighting men, they were not unequalled in valour and skill. The Worcesters, the West Kents, and a number of other regiments in France, Flanders, Gallipoli, and Mesopotamia, had proved themselves peers of the victors of Landrecies. Our Guards were fine representatives of Anglo-Celtic races; they did not pretend, like the Prussian Guard, to stand on a pedestal above the other troops.

The Division had only been formed in August, 1915, when the Guards Brigade separated from the 2nd Division, and began to train as a complete divisional unit. The new Division came into the Battle of Loos with a high resolve to make a name for itself, so that it combined the vehement spirit of a new formation with the hard-earned experience of war and noble traditions of veterans. On the morning of September 27th the Guardsmen held the captured German trenches from the north end of Loos to a point five hundred yards south of Hulluch. The 1st Brigade stretched towards Hulluch, the 2nd Brigade extended from Loos, and the 3rd Brigade was held in reserve. The general scheme of Lord Cavan's attack was for the 1st Brigade to hold on to their trenches and form a pivot for the movement, while the 2nd Brigade attacked the chalk-pit near the La Bassée-Lens road, and stormed the Mine-pit 14-A, south of the chalk-pit. Then it was arranged that the 3rd Brigade should march through Loos, and attack Hill 70 when the more northerly positions had been won.

From their trenches the Guards could clearly see across the valley the points they were about to attack. There was the white gash of the chalk-pit, with two ruined red cottages beside it, and a long narrow spinney running in a south-westerly direction in front of the pit. Southward, a little distance from the spinney, was the coal-mine Pit 14-A, crowned by a tall chimney rising from a large ugly building. Close to this building and between it and the Lens Road, were a small red house and a German machine-gun redoubt, with a sand-bagged house and a network of deep trenches. This was known as the Keep, and eastward of it across the Lens road, near the north-eastern slope of Hill 70, was a wood—Bois Hugo—full of entrenched machine-gun parties, whose terrible enfilading field of fire greatly strengthened the defences of the mine and the Keep.

At four o'clock in the afternoon of September 27th the Irish Guards, the leaders of the 2nd Brigade, leapt from their trenches and advanced in open order from the spinney. Capturing the lower part of this wood, they rapidly extended southward. This was done in order to help the Scots Guards in their attack on the mine-pit. The Scotsmen

doubled down the hill, and with the German batteries raking them with heavy shrapnel fire, they went on swiftly, and reached the road running from Loos to Hulluch. Then, climbing up the next rise, they linked on with the right flank of the Irish Guards, and the Gaels of Erin and Caledonia then swept down together towards the mine-pit and the Keep. A London regiment, holding the flank-line south of Loos, watched this extraordinary charge with deep admiration. One non-commissioned officer wrote: "While we sat and dodged the shells and bullets, the grandest scene I have ever seen in my life occurred— the Guards advancing in artillery formation over about three-quarters of a mile, completely in the open in broad daylight. At last the German gunners got news of it, and the shells they sent over came in a stream. The whistles and explosions were incessant, and the air must have been black with flying shells, if they had been visible through the thick smoke. Only half a dozen were touched. How we cheered them when they slowly, and in perfect order, crossed over us, and passed on! They were the grand

WHERE SHATTERED TREE-TRUNKS MARKED THE PASSAGE OF THE STORM.
Corner of a battlefield over which the French advanced. The limbs of the tree in the foreground bear witness to the effect of the German shells.

fellows who were in reserve to us at Givenchy, and now we were in reserve to them. Can you imagine the ordinary battle-pictures of troops advancing under hell's own shell fire? I thought such a thing was impossible. Now I not only know it is true, but saw it all."

The losses of the Guards from artillery fire were fairly light. Apparently the charge was made so swiftly and unexpectedly that the German gunners did not get on the target, and, misjudging the operation, made a curtain of fire along the Lens road, while our men were massing against the mine-pit and Keep at a point a quarter of a mile away from the road. But the German machine-guns in Bois Hugo were terribly effective. **Enfiladed from** When the Scots Guards charged south- **Bois Hugo** ward from the spinney their lines were riddled by fire from the mine-pit buildings and the Keep redoubt, and mowed down by sidelong streams of bullets from Bois Hugo. The colonel was wounded, and eleven other officers were killed or disabled; but the Scots Guards, though reduced to a remnant, charged onward. One party under Captain Cuthbert fought into the houses round the mine, while a platoon under Lieutenant Ayres reached the mine and the Keep. Lieutenant Ritchie was a subaltern of the Grenadier Guards, who had come up two companies strong to support the Scotsmen. The enemy's enfilading machine-gun fire from the wood swept most of the Grenadiers away, and prevented any further support from arriving. Lieutenant Ritchie was severely wounded in the right arm, but when his captain fell, and his company was checked, he reorganised the men and **Officers' magnificent** led them again to the assault. With the **gallantry** help of a corporal he bombed and destroyed a German machine-gun and its team on the second floor of the Keep ; and with Captain Cuthbert gallantly held on to the mine until the two of them were almost the only survivors. When the position became untenable, Lieutenant Ritchie told his men to withdraw, but he went forward under heavy fire and reconnoitred the enemy's defences, making some valuable discoveries. For six hours the young officer worked in great pain before

he retired to a dressing station. Meanwhile the Scots and Grenadier Guards had dug themselves in on a line running from the south end of the spinney towards Loos. The Irish Guards were on the east side of the spinney, and the Coldstream Guards, supporting the Irishmen on the left, had seized the north-east outskirts of the chalk-pit. The general result of the first charge by the 2nd Brigade was a failure ; but the way in which two companies of the Scots and one company of the Grenadiers retired under a cross-fire from the wood was magnificent. The men marched as coolly and steadily as if it were a movement on parade.

On the following day the attack on the mine-pit was resumed by the Coldstream Guards, who advanced from the south of the chalk-pit, while the Irish Guards tried to keep down the enfilading fire from Bois Hugo. Lieutenant Riley, by a superb effort, managed to reach the works around the mine ; but again the enemy's cross-fire prevented supports being moved up, and after heavy losses the Coldstreams fell back. It was while the attack on the mine was proceeding **Welsh Guards'** that Lord Cavan brought up his reserve **baptism of fire** —the 3rd Brigade—for a stroke against Hill 70. As the 2nd Brigade could not hold the mine, they were used to protect the flank of the charging troops. There was a gap left in our line between the spinney and the hill, but machine-guns were arranged to sweep the open space, should the enemy attempt to thrust through it. The 3rd Brigade was made up of battalions of the Grenadier, Scots, and Welsh Guards, the last of whom received their baptism of fire in this famous action. As the brigade reached the crest of the ridge running north-west of Loos, their silhouetted figures were perceived by the enemy and swept by a tornado of shrapnel fire. But the men went steadily on ; the leading battalion of the Grenadier Guards entered Loos on the north-west, a Welsh battalion

EXAMPLES OF FRENCH INGENUITY IN TRENCH WORK AND PLAY.
French soldiers at a barricade at Craonnelle at the moment of an alarm ; in the foreground a "spider," a portable wire entanglement which, being light, could be thrown in any direction whence attack might come. Above : A mechanical toy made in the trenches.

ROOMY, BUT WELL PROTECTED: OFFICIAL FRENCH CAMERA PICTURE OF A NOVEL FORM OF FIRST-LINE TRENCH IN CHAMPAGNE.

entered on the west, and the Scots Guards followed the Grenadiers on the north-west. As they came out of the communication trenches the German batteries rained so tremendous a fire of gas-shells upon them that they had to halt and put on smoke-helmets. The colonel of the Grenadiers was badly gassed, and had to leave the command to Major Ponsonby. The main work of the attack was entrusted to the Welsh Guards with part of the Grenadier Guards in support. The charging lines were first met with a comparatively slight rifle fire as they moved over the dead ground. But when they reached the crest of Hill 70, and their figures were thrown out against the sky-line, the short-range fire of the enemy caused heavy losses.

It had been thought, from information given by the troops who had fought on the hill, that the German trenches and machine-gun redoubts were constructed on the north slope of the rise. The rushing attack of the Guards had been designed to storm such a position. But the German line was really situated over **On the crest of** the summit and down the reverse slope. **Hill 70** Night was falling as the terrible struggle on the crest began, and the Welshmen held on for a time with grim courage. Captain Rhys Williams, commanding the machine-guns, was wounded; but after having his wound dressed he returned to his guns, and controlled them till midnight, having all the time to lie on his back by reason of his severe injuries. Private Grant, of the Welsh Guards, also distinguished himself by making two attempts to bring forward ammunition to the firing-line under heavy and continuous shelling. By his success in his second attempt he enabled his comrades, fighting close to the German trenches, to keep off their enemies. Private Grant also made two

endeavours to carry in a wounded officer, and after having one helper shot by his side, he rescued his countryman. He carried messages under a heavy artillery bombardment, and at last was himself badly wounded while taking a wounded man on his back towards the dressing station. Under cover of darkness the Welsh Guards were relieved by the Scots; and as the relieving troops found they could not hope to cling to the farthest line reached by the Welsh, they withdrew behind the crest of the hill, and there firmly established their **Every man** position. Then under a continuous bom- **a hero** bardment the Brigades held on to the western slope of Hill 70, the spinney, and the chalk-pit. At the pit the 1st Coldstream Guards had essayed to work round to Bois Hugo. But the whole ground in front of the chalk-pit was covered by the enemy's machine-guns, and in trying to rescue our wounded near the wood, Sergeant Hopkins was sniped, and had in turn to be rescued by Lance-Corporal Printer, who had brought in the first wounded man.

The charges of the Guards Division almost restored the line we had lost on September 26th, when the 21st and 24th Divisions fell back. Moreover, the London Territorial Division, after capturing a wood on the right of the Guards, on September 27th, made another gallant advance from our southern flank the next day, and gained more ground, taking a field-gun and several machine-guns. By this time however, the enemy had fully recovered from our first onrush, and the difficulties in the way of any immediate farther British advance were enormous. Loos was a smoke-pit, smothered in poison gases from the enemy's shells, and excavated by great howitzer projectiles. The Germans had placed mines under the church-tower, and wished to reach them with high-explosive shells and wreck the town.   But Captain Edward Blogg, a London Territorial engineer, found and unloaded the mines, and, working under a terrific shell fire, saved the position.

Sir John French again became anxious about his right flank, for the salient he had made in the enemy's line from the Double Crassier to Hill 70 and Hulluch, and back to the Hohenzollern Redoubt, necessitated a great extension of his forces.   The Tenth French Army south of Lens had been so strongly opposed that its movement did not assist and support our main line of thrust, still held by the Territorials of London.   In these circumstances, the British commander put the matter before General Joffre, who asked General Foch, commanding the northern group of French armies, to render assistance. The upshot was that the Ninth French Army Corps arranged to take over the ground extending from the French left through the village of Loos to the western slope of Hill 70.   The relief was begun on September 30th and completed on the two following nights.   There was afterwards considerable dispute over our position on Hill 70. The facts appear to be that after the Highland brigade was bombed from the crest on September 25th the hill was lost, and partly recovered by the Welsh and Grenadier Guards on September 27th, and our new position on the western slope was taken over by the Ninth French Army Corps and afterwards lost by them.   Our military authorities hesitated to explain the situation for the sound reason that Hill 70 had ceased to be their affair, and it would not have become them to discuss a matter of purely French interest.   There was, moreover, an objection to giving the enemy information about the part played by the Ninth French Army in taking over part of the Loos salient, and enabling our troops to concentrate **Intervention of the** in greater strength for the defence of the **French army** line running from the spinney and the chalk-pit and along the Lens-La Bassée road towards Hulluch, and there turning eastward to the Hohenzollern Redoubt, and thence back towards Vermelles.

During the last days of September the Hohenzollern Redoubt was the scene of fierce and continuous fighting. The enemy, indeed, attacked all along the salient.   But the loss of part of the redoubt galled him most, and his efforts to recover it were of extraordinary violence and persistence.   Among the British troops that greatly distinguished themselves in the Hohenzollern work were the 7th Seaforths, the 8th Gordon Highlanders, and the 8th Royal Highlanders, who fought from September 25th

to September 27th.   Towards the end of September and the beginning of October the 2nd East Surreys, the 1st Welsh Regiment, and the Yorkshire Light Infantry gallantly maintained the defence of the main work and of the trench known as "Little Willie."

Here and there the hostile bombers gained a little ground, but every German attack in force broke down with heavy loss under the fire of our guns, Maxims, and rifles.   All along the front our troops laboured with sustained energy to consolidate and strengthen the ground they had conquered.   It was known that the German commander was gathering troops in great numbers for a supreme counter-attack.   Five army corps were being moved from the Russian front for an effort to retrieve the defeats at Loos and in Champagne; Belgium was being almost stripped of its garrisons in order to get overwhelming concentrations of infantry against the two new salients made by the British and   **German efforts to** French armies.   More artillery from the   **retrieve defeat** siege-trains brought from Russia was got into position, and some hundreds of trainloads of large shells were brought behind the western front.

The German Staff had three courses open—first, to attack the new British salient; second, to attack the new French salient in Champagne; and third, to make strong simultaneous attacks against both of the new allied positions.   The first course was adopted.   It was resolved to attack only the First British Army and the French corps reinforcing it on the Loos-Hulluch-Hohenzollern front.   By selecting only one objective, the German Staff was able to strike with all possible energy at the nation which was most to be feared; for Britain was still engaged in organising her armies, and the military result of a severe set-back to Sir John French's men was, so the enemy calculated, likely to have moral and perhaps political consequences.   So General de Castelnau's army in Champagne was only held by a reinforced line of bombers, while the great new German mass of infantry was brought up to Lens, Hill 70, the eastern part of Hulluch, and the northern part of the Hohenzollern Redoubt.

Happily, the great movement of German troops was observed by our airmen; who were at last able to discover that the concentration was taking place close to our lines. One of our scouting patrols also heard in the darkness the click of weapons, and the distant tramp of feet.   It was therefore clear that the enemy intended to deliver an overwhelming frontal attack in an endeavour to break through by sheer weight of numbers.

A FEW OF THE MANY FRENCH TROPHIES WON IN CHAMPAGNE.
A group of the formidable German "77's" outclassed by the still more formidable French "75's."   These guns were taken by the French after heavy fighting in Champagne.

FRENCH WOMEN IN THE LINE OF FIRE.
Quite one of the most remarkable features of the war was the apathy of civilians caught in the zone of operations. Many preferred to remain in their homes to swelling the bands of refugees. This photograph shows two French women running for shelter during a violent bombardment.

In the patches of woods east of the Lens-LaBassée road, beginning with the Bois Hugo and continuing along the spinneys extending towards Hulluch, our airmen reckoned that there were four German Divisions massed against the trenches held by our troops.

The battle that followed was really a triumph for our airmen; for it was won decisively and with exceeding little cost on the information they had obtained by their daring reconnoitring swoops through the mist and rain. From their information Sir Douglas Haig, commanding our First Army, prepared to surprise the men who were preparing to surprise him. Our guns were massed less than ten yards apart, as though we intended another intense bombardment to clear the way for another great infantry attack. The French Army assisted us with many of their wonderful 3 in. quick-firers, capable of breaking up advancing infantry attack by a semi-automatic movement. But our own infantry, instead of getting their ladders ready and packing their ammunition for quick transport, deepened their bomb-proof shelters, strengthened their parapets, put networks of wire over weak parts of their trenches to keep out hand-bombs, and extended their magazines of hand-grenades. Our observing artillery officers carefully studied all objects by which the ranges of every enemy movement could instantly be calculated, and then very quietly, on the morning of October 8th, the First British Army calmly awaited the grand German counter-stroke.

But the German plan went

WINGED INSTRUMENT OF DEATH.
Type of aerial torpedo used with deadly effect by the men in the French trenches.

wrong; for it was our guns that suddenly opened the hurricane fire. In the afternoon a ranging shot from behind our lines went over the wood beyond the Lens-La Bassée road. A branch rose in the air, showing the range had been found. Then gun after gun, battery after battery, opened fire and began to smash up the trenches in which some eighty thousand grey figures were expectantly packed. The wood was destroyed by our fire, and the surrounding German trenches, clear white streaks and glittering zigzags shining from the green slopes, were marks that no gunner could miss; for the distance from the British to the German lines was only three to four hundred yards.

The German batteries tried to assist the plan of attack by beating down our terrific fire and breaking up our front trenches. But the difference between the effect of our shells on the tightly-packed German lines and the effect of the German shells on our lightly-manned ditches told on the mind of the hostile commander.

The Germans were suffering horribly. There was no time to withdraw them; they had to be launched with the utmost speed to prevent them perishing where they stood. They came out in four thick lines, shoulder to shoulder — the old massed formation of the German infantry attack. Through our batteries rang the order "Gunfire!" — meaning that every piece of artillery was to fire as it liked at the utmost possible speed. In the trenches our officers did not try to direct their men; they each took a rifle and pelted lead into the nearest grey multitude.

TROOPERS AT AN ALFRESCO LUNCH.
Members of a cavalry regiment enjoying a hurried meal behind the lines prior to going into action in the neighbourhood of Ypres.

NOW SILENT IN THE CAUSE OF THE FATHERLAND.
Captured Krupp gun which excited the interest of British and French soldiers at a railway-siding in Northern France.

the long-service men of the regular British battalions could break, by rapid musketry fire, any frontal attack, the German leaders fancied that the new British troops would not stand so steady and shoot so straight and quick as the "Old Contemptibles" had done. Herein the German Staff made a great mistake. To all our new troops, entering on their musketry course, the tradition of the "mad minute" had been a fierce inspiration. They had striven their utmost to work up to the proper number of aimed rounds a minute, and had nursed their rifles in barracks practising the famous trigger play that makes a musket almost equal to a machine-gun.

Some connoisseurs of German mass infantry tactics did not think much of the Loos affair; even the Guards, who lost for a minute a part of their

Mass tactics at Loos

No leadership was necessary; the targets were so immense and so near that the soldiers of the New Army were loosened for the first time for the "mad minute" of rapid fire. Almost a year had passed since the new German formations at Ypres had given the men of the Regular Army an opportunity of showing what could be done with the Lee-Enfield rifle, with one cartridge in the breech and ten cartridges in the magazine. Since then the "mad minute" had faded into the legend of the British Army, and though all the new recruits had been carefully trained in rapid fire tactics, it was scarcely expected that a large occasion for this kind of musketry would arise again. In fact it was commonly thought the German commanders had fully learnt the lesson that the British soldier could stop a mass infantry attack at fifty yards from his trenches. Field-Marshal von Heeringen had observed to a neutral war correspondent that this was the great new fact in the war.

Inspiration of the "mad minute"

Apparently the German Staff underestimated the marksmanship of our New Army. While allowing that

trenches, did not praise their enemies. The general opinion of the "Old Contemptibles" was that the German had lost pace and power since his charges at Mons and round the Marne and above the Aisne. He came on slower, and did not get so near our trenches as a rule. When struck down he took longer to rally, and in his second assault he was easier to hammer to a standstill. But it must be remembered that our troops in the old days had always had the odds in artillery power heavy against them. Never before had we been able to hound the enemy into desperate battle by means of our gun fire. The counter-attack at Loos was the first occasion in which a German commander used mass infantry tactics against a British line backed by an artillery power equal to his.

It is very unlikely that a German commander will use again such tactics in similar circumstances. Our men hitched themselves on the parapets to get a good field of fire, and they flung out lead until their rifles grew almost too hot to hold. The machine-gunners had as targets solid blocks at three hundred yards and less distance. The

THE MILITARY KITCHEN: A POPULAR RENDEZVOUS.
British soldiers lining up for their rations. The neighbourhood of the camp was turned into a quagmire through inclement weather.

gunners of the light field artillery made the paint on their pieces bubble, blister, and flake off by their rate of fire, and the men were half deaf for days after. The four Divisions charged in four lines—south-west, south-east, and north-east of Loos.

Before the eyes of our men was a long smoke cloud from our bombardment which had broken the enemy up in the woods. Then, emerging from the fog was a grey wall of men, looming onward, falling back, coming forward again, and finally melting into blotches on the grass. " This

Getting their own back

pays for the ninth of May," said one British soldier, in an interval between the ebb and resurgence of the grey masses. " Getting a bit of our own back at last," remarked another. As a matter of fact, we had had altogether some 50,000 casualties in our advance on Loos and Hulluch and in our checks at Vermelles, Cuinchy, Fosse 8, and the upper part of the Hohenzollern Redoubt. We captured at this time 26 guns, 3 mine-throwers, 40 machine-guns, and 3,000 men and officers. In an ordinary way, 3,000 prisoners would

" NECESSITY IS THE MOTHER OF INVENTION."
Jolly Britons working a light railway which they constructed in connection with their camp to facilitate transport. In circle: Two British officers in an observation pit.

mean in addition 3,000 dead Germans and 9,000 wounded, making the enemy's total casualties 15,000. But the house-to-house fighting was very fierce, and the combats round the slag-heaps and in the deep mazes of trenches were extremely violent. In many places the Germans fought on to the last moment, and only offered to surrender when they had done all the killing they possibly could. Therefore their dead probably much outnumbered their surrendering men, and their casualties were heavily increased by the terrific preliminary bombardment, in which something like a million shells were flung from our guns. It is likely that the total German losses in the first week of the battle were at least half ours. Ours were 20,000 for the Ypres-Givenchy front, and 50,000 for the Cuinchy-Loos front. So we can provisionally put the German losses in the first phase of the battle at 35,000.

But in the great, vain counter-attack of October 8th there were left before the British and French trenches from nine to ten thousand dead Germans. There were probably two thousand more German dead in the woods, and of wounded men there were over twenty-five thousand. The

SUBLIME INDIFFERENCE TO DANGER.
To show so much as a finger above a trench was to invite death. Yet, in a spirit of superb self-sacrifice, soldiers were found, like the courageous Belgian in this photograph, who were not only willing but eager to crawl along the parapet to discover the meaning of any suspicious movement on the part of the enemy.

total enemy losses exceeded ours. Though the casualty lists on both sides were in the end about equal, the Germans had a larger proportion of dead, while we had a very remarkable multitude of men suffering only from slight shrapnel wounds. In other words, our men, who were mostly civilians when the war opened, and who later were checked in their musketry training by our lack of a large national magazine of rifles, took two or three of the most formidably entrenched lines in the world, and ultimately inflicted upon the enemy heavier losses than they themselves sustained. And only some defect in the handling of the two reinforcing Divisions—the 21st and **British disadvantages** 24th—saved the enemy's front from being **at Lens** broken during the first phase of the attack. Our Army, moreover, laboured under the heavy disadvantages of being unsupported in the drive on Lens by the Tenth French Army and of having a dangerous gap to guard between Bully les Mines and Notre Dame de Lorette.

It may fairly be said that, despite the mischances and mistakes which made a grand decisive success impossible,

the First British Army, in the battle in which Kitchener's men were for the first time fully engaged, showed itself animated by the qualities that make for final victory. Having regard to the fact that we had suddenly to improvise our military power on a modern Continental scale, and build up a framework for two million men at a time when our regular forces were wasted by thirteen months' conflict, we could not expect to manifest at once the perfection of movement attained in huge national armies with a generation or **Our school** more of training. We had to learn on **the battlefield** the battlefield, and, like the Romans of old, look forward to purchasing by hard experience the means of winning the final victory

During the repulse of the German counter-attack, which was especially fierce round the chalk-pit north of Hill 70, our troops, after throwing the enemy back, captured a German trench between the quarries and the hamlet of Cité St. Elie. The enemy only succeeded in penetrating our front line at one point in the southern communicating trench of the Hohenzollern Redoubt, and here he was promptly driven out by our bombers. The 2nd and 3rd Battalions of the Coldstream Guards had an exciting time of it. Some men of the 2nd Battalion held a sap-head in St. Elie Avenue, and practically the whole of this sap-head was smashed up by the German guns, leaving only the barricade standing Then when the German infantry attacked and reached the barricade and got on our parapet, our supply of hand-grenades ran out. Private J. W. Chisholm, Private F. Moore, and Sergeant R. J. Vale obtained more bombs, and, charging over the open ground, where the enemy bombed them as they ran, the three heroic Guardsmen smashed the Germans from the sap-head, and held the position under heavy bomb and rifle fire, while their officer, Lieutenant Henry C. Loyd, directed them with great skill and courage. Private Chisholm was wounded, but he fought on, and by his bravery and resource helped to save what might have been a very critical situation.

These three Guardsmen were awarded the Distinguished Conduct Medal, which was also won by six privates of the 3rd Battalion of the Coldstreams—E. Anderson, A. Chillingworth, H. Londesbrough, H. A. Teesdale, H. Smith, and W. White. The enemy took the trench on the left of that occupied by the six Guardsmen, and some sixty German bombers came pouring into our position, smashing their way down our line by their rain of high-explosives. The condition of things was very dangerous, but the six Guardsmen rushed forward towards the enemy, and by the skill and the rapidity with which they used their hand-grenades they outfought at least ten times their number, and bombed the German bombers foot by foot down the trench, and then captured the whole of it.

It would be impossible in our space to describe all the deeds of bravery of the First Army, in the conflicts on the Loos front ; but we may attempt roughly to group some of the regiments that won marks of distinction in the long and furious battle. On Hill 70 the 7th Battalion of the King's Own Scottish Borderers produced an officer of great gallantry in Captain Dennis, who, though wounded in the trenches before the assault, led his men until, being

WOUNDED FRIEND AND FOE FIND SANCTUARY IN A FRENCH CHURCH.

This little village church in Northern France was used by the French Red Cross workers to shelter wounded soldiers. Comrades and enemies— yet all of the tragic fraternity of suffering—lay in rows on piles of straw down both sides of the church. Here, under the richly-carved pulpit and images of the saints and martyrs, they found sanctuary, though the danger zone of withering fire was only a few yards from the porch.

IN A BELGIAN TRENCH NEAR YPRES.
Some Belgian officers who faced the camera as cheerily as they faced the enemy attacks in their indomitably defended part of the line near the coast.

IN READINESS FOR THE ENEMY'S EXPECTED ATTACK.
Machine-gun concealed behind a pile of earth sacks. Two Belgian soldiers are seen waiting for the enemy to attack. Sir John French reported that the part taken by the Belgian troops " was very effective in holding the enemy in front of them to his position."

again wounded, he was carried back to the dressing-station, from which he disappeared. He caught up with his company on the hill, and was wounded a third time when leading them on. The 8th Battalion Seaforth Highlanders, which took part in the first great charge on Hill 70, had a man of noble character—Private Holligan.

Some deeds of bravery After having one arm shattered by a bullet, Holligan attended to other wounded men until, after refusing to leave his post, he at last collapsed, having both his legs wounded as well as his arm.

The 10th Gordon Highlanders had a very remarkable officer in Temporary Second-Lieutenant John Bruce Wood. This hero began to attract attention in the attack on Loos, where he took the extraordinary number of two hundred and seventy-five prisoners. After marching them back under heavy fire, he returned with ammunition to the

men in the firing-line, and assisted in its distribution. He went forward with his company in the marvellous swoop on Lens, and when the check occurred he was the only officer left. He rallied the remnant of his company on the western slope of Hill 70, and by fine bravery and resourcefulness he held the position until relief came. The 13th Battalion of the Royal Scots also produced a very remarkable man in Temporary Second-Lieutenant Alexander Linton. This gallant subaltern, with only a few men, held the hill at midnight on September 26th, when practically everyone else had withdrawn. The enemy's gun and machine-gun fire was terrible, and the British position was **Lothian subaltern's heroism** veiled in drifts of poison gas, through which at intervals the German infantry charged expecting to find the British position evacuated. But Lieutenant Linton continually rallied the handful of Lothians and held on to his ground.

Sergeant F. McAlear and Lance-Corporal G. McEvoy, also of the Lothian Regiment, showed great coolness and fearlessness at Hill 70 on September 26th, when our trenches had been abandoned owing to the violence of the German counter-attack. Another Scottish Battalion that won fame on Hill 70 was the 10th Cameronians. They also produced a hero in Temporary Second-Lieutenant Leonard Cecil Paton, who had done fine work in training the brigade bombers. On the night of September 25th, when other troops were compelled to withdraw from the enemy's redoubt on the eastern slopes of Hill 70, Lieutenant Paton remained at his post with five wounds, including one arm broken and a gunshot wound, inflicted at point-blank range (twenty yards); in his thigh. His superior officer had to order him to retire. Another Scotsman of the great Highland Division who was averse from retiring was Captain Walter William Macgregor, attached to the 9th Gordon Highlanders. During the action round Loos on September 26th, when the Germans were trying to turn our flank, Captain Macgregor received an order to retreat. He withdrew to the enemy's first line; but as this position did not seem to him right, he called on two companies and led them back through Loos, and

Gallant Gordon's refusal to retire reached his advance defensive position, close to the enemy. There he held on until reinforcements arrived; and throwing these into the fight, he beat off all the enemy's attempts to turn our flank, holding on to his line until daylight.

Meanwhile, the famous 15th Highland Division, with its leading brigade at Hill 70, was reinforced by the 9th Battalion of the Yorkshire Light Infantry, the 10th Yorkshires, the 12th Northumberland Fusiliers, and the 8th Somerset Light Infantry. All four Battalions produced fighting men of distinction. Temporary-Lieutenant Arthur Beach Hatt, of the 8th Somerset Light Infantry, equalled the achievement of the Lothians' Lieutenant Linton, by holding on to Hill 70 on the night of September 25th with only a sergeant and six men until he and his little handful were left alone against the enemy. Lance-Corporal McKelvey, of the 9th Yorks Light Infantry, led his men up the hill until he was wounded. He then went forward until he received a second wound, and again, with wonderful coolness and bravery he led his men and encouraged them until a third wound completely disabled him. Private H. Rendall, of the 12th Northumberland Fusiliers, remained on the hill during the terrible night of September 25th, when his comrades on either side of him were killed. Working at his machine-gun till daybreak, under heavy and continuous fire, he greatly helped our army to retain its hold on the important slope. Corporal G. Stubbs, of the 10th Yorkshires, also distinguished himself by his utter contempt for death on the historic Saturday night on Hill 70 by conveying messages through the enemy's tornado of shell and shrapnel, thus main-

NEW TYPE OF FRENCH MORTAR.
Formidable type of French mortar after being discharged. Centre: Gunner in charge testing the level.

taining communications between our headquarters and the extreme point of the British wedge.

Among the London Territorial Division holding the flank from Grenay to the wood and chalk-pit south of Loos, near Hill 70, Major Adrian Charles Gordon, of the 6th London Brigade of the Royal Field Artillery, was conspicuous. He reconnoitred the German lines on September 25th, and although under a heavy fire, he captured twelve of the enemy at the point of his revolver, after shooting one man. Second-Lieutenant Carr, of the

APPALLING ENGINE OF DESTRUCTION USED IN A SEVENTY-HOUR BOMBARDMENT.
This weapon had a calibre of 22 cm. (about 9 inches), and was an appalling engine of destruction. Mortars of this type were used in the terrific seventy-hour bombardment at the great Champagne battle. Left: Loading and fixing the range. Right: Firing the gun.

FEEDING DEATH IN CHAMPAGNE.
Zouaves working a machine-gun during the great advance in Champagne made by the French Army, in which they more than maintained their fighting fame.

24th London Regiment, was the first of the London Territorial Division to win distinction. Before his Battalion moved out to attack from Les Brebis hamlet, he was directing the removal of the grenades of the division. Seeing that the fuse of a bomb had become ignited, he picked it up and carried it from the dug-out; but before

At the Double Crassier he could get cover, it exploded and wounded him in the face. But he saved a great explosion which would have killed many men, and by destroying the divisional bomb reserve, would have seriously weakened the London Territorials.

At the slag-heap of the Double Crassier, the first important position captured by the "Terriers," Sergeant Christey, of the Civil Service Rifles, moved across the open with his battery of trench mortars, and with fine skill and imperturbable valour worked his gun in close support of the infantry brigade, smashing up the enemy's machine-guns, and then helping to make the captured position impregnable against all German counter-attacks. When the London "Terriers" entered Loos through the cemetery, Sergeant Taylor, of the 7th City of London Battalion, who with three men had beaten the Germans back with bombs at the Double Crassier, further displayed his genius for leadership by cutting off and capturing a troop of Germans. It was in the "Terrier" attack on the south-west of Loos that Private A. Gray, of the St. Pancras Battalion, carried his machine-gun forward under the enemy's fire to a position he selected with quick judgment. Then, with only two men of his team left, he brought such a sweeping fire against the enemy that he saved his Battalion from extremely heavy casualties. In the fight in the chalk-pit south of Loos, Private F. Hill, of the Blackheath and Woolwich Battalion, made a series of splendid attacks with hand-bombs. Though wounded several times, he

refused to retire, and continued his bombing work until the position was won. Another man of the same Battalion, Private C. H. I. Stewart, was wounded when carrying in a wounded man; but he refused to go to the base hospital, and fought on for four more days with extreme gallantry. When the Division was most severely pressed, on September 27th, one of the subalterns of the St. Pancras Battalion, Second-Lieutenant Pusch, collected some of the Grenadier Guards, and launched them in a bomb attack from the chalk-pit against the wood, and brought about the capture of the position. Lieutenant Pusch may be regarded as the flower of London chivalry, for on September 25th he first showed

FRENCH COLONIAL TROOPS AFTER THE VICTORY IN CHAMPAGNE.
Moroccan troops returning after the fighting, tired but elated, and more formidable than ever.

great ability and resource in the southern drive at Loos; then in the advance through the town he led a party of bombers, and going alone into a house, he was badly shot in the face by a German; but he fought on single-handed and captured seven of the enemy. It was two days afterwards, with his face half shattered, that he relieved the pressure on the British flank by thrusting into the enemy's lines and capturing the wood beyond the chalk-pit. Our readers will observe that this officer's name is of German origin. Lieutenant Pusch showed that there were descendants of the men who fled to England from Prussian oppression who were eager to fight heroically for the land in which they had been **Flowers of Chivalry** born and bred in liberty. We may be sure that there are many men of the stamp of Lieutenant Pusch in the United States, and though their voices may at times be drowned in the clamour of plotters linked with Berlin, they will make a stand, if need be, for the cause of freedom for which their fathers endured exile.

Round Hulluch and the quarries, near the Lens-La Bassée road, Captain Hugh Alexander Ross, after his commanding officer had fallen, led the 2nd Gordon Highlanders against the enemy's unbroken wire entanglements near Hulluch. The captain was himself badly gassed, and in great pain , but he held on all day to an advanced and exposed position, though his battalion was badly cut up. When relief arrived, he went back with his men into support, and had to be then ordered to go to hospital. Private C. Craig, of the 2nd Gordons, also assisted Captain Ross

Invincible non-com's

by bringing up ammunition and taking messages. The London Scottish were also hung up by wire near Hulluch, and the company under Captain Claud John Low was caught on both flanks by machine-guns. Nevertheless, Captain Low and his men hung on to the ground they had won, and it was largely due to them that the Germans were compelled to surrender. The London Scottish then advanced and occupied the German third line. One of their sergeants, K. S. Bowron, showed great skill and daring in leading his platoon towards Lone Tree. From this point the sergeant crawled out alone to reconnoitre, and was shot ; but he went on with his work, and obtained

ON THE "QUI VIVE."
French soldiers at a listening-post, with rifles at the ready, and a few spare cartridges by their side.

information which led to important results.

The 8th Berkshires were gassed at the beginning of the assault ; but Regimental Sergeant-Major Lainsbury, rallying about sixty men, fought his way through to Hulluch, organising as he advanced parties for the supply of ammunition. Then, on September 26th, when the supplies were running out, the invincible sergeant-major crawled out of the trenches under heavy fire, and collected ammunition from the dead and wounded. Captain Tosetti, after being badly wounded in the leg, led his Berkshire company close up to Hulluch, captured a trench there, and beat off all counter-attacks till compelled to seek medical aid. Another hero of the 8th

Berkshires was Temporary Second-Lieutenant T. B. Lawrence, who rallied the machine-gun teams near Hulluch, and bringing the guns into action, captured two German field-pieces. In the same scene of conflict, Captain James Dawson, 6th Territorial Battalion of the Gordon Highlanders, showed fine skill in organising the wedge his men had driven into the German lines, and when his commanding officer was killed, he took command of the battalion and hung on to the position all day and night. Captain F. R. Kearsley, commanding the 1st Welsh Fusiliers, in a similar position near Hulluch, was badly wounded during the assault ; but it was not until he was knocked out by seven wounds that he relinquished his command. Before being totally disabled, he captured several lines of German trenches under a hail of musketry and Maxim fire.

The 8th Devonshires, who had very heavy losses, greatly distinguished themselves at Hulluch. By 7.15 a.m. all the officers of the battalion were killed or wounded except Temporary-Captain Gwynne and one subaltern.

"No officers left"

Captain Gwynne led his men on and captured four German guns, and held on to the ground he had won until he, too, was wounded. Sergeant-Major Bryant then assumed command, the subaltern having also been put out of action, and when the Germans, after dark, got round the flank of the position, the sergeant-major withdrew the remnant of the battalion to a trench two hundred yards away, and then drove forward again and smashed up the enemy. At last Sergeant-Major Bryant was stunned by a bomb while trying to save one of his sergeants. The battalion was nobly helped by another of its non-commissioned officers — Sergeant Holland. He was wounded

PREPARING A SURPRISE FOR THE "BOCHES."
In a section of a French trench taken from the Germans a group of infantrymen are seen crouching in anticipation of a counter-attack. Entrance to the bomb-proof dug-out in the background.

in the thigh in the first charge, but followed his Battalion, and ran out a telephone-wire five hundred yards forward to a position near the quarries, and so kept his front line in communication all day with brigade headquarters. The 1st South Staffords produced a hero in Private Edwards, who walked in the open field near Hulluch, attending to the wounded when he himself had been badly hurt. In the frontal attack on Hulluch, Lieutenant Pringle, of the 1st Cameron Highlanders, was remarkable for his skill and determination. When all the company officers were slain or disabled, Lieutenant Pringle organised the shattered ranks of the Highlanders and carried on the attack, and it was largely due to his fine leadership that the advanced position by the village was taken and consolidated on September 25th. Then on September 27th the Territorial Battalion of the Camerons was sent forward to hold the Hulluch front. A British bombing-party was temporarily withdrawn from our barricade in the communication trench during a hurricane of shell fire, and by suddenly stopping the guns and launching an infantry attack, the German commander captured the barricade. Lance-Corporal McDonell, one of the Cameron "Terriers," collected a few men and bombed the enemy back to the barricade, and, there recapturing one of our bomb depots, he pursued the Germans farther and chased them over their own barricade, killing them as he went forward.

knocked out one of his guns, but he coolly remounted it, and kept it in action, steadying all the men around him by his marvellous fearlessness under a terrible tornado of high-explosive projectiles. The 2nd Royal Scots Fusiliers produced a great fighting man in Sergeant Hogg. In the action near Hulluch Sergeant Hogg took charge of the Battalion machine-guns after his officers had been wounded, and fought them for some days and nights with unusual ability. But on September 30th, as he was using a machine-gun on the extreme left of the gun trench, the enemy attacked him in front from a communication trench, after breaking through our line on the left. The sergeant was bombed front and back; but he killed ten of the enemy, and when **The K.R.R.C. hard hit** he had thus won a little time, he dragged his gun towards the right, and there he made a fierce and impregnable stand throughout the night operations.

The 2nd King's Royal Rifle Corps lost most of their officers early in the attack on the German position near Hulluch on September 25th, when the battalion was somewhat severely gassed. Temporary-Captain Currie, though affected by the gas, reorganised the men and led them forward to the farthest line reached. Second-Lieutenant Reid, of the King's Royal Rifles, was also badly gassed with all his section at the beginning of the attack. Yet when the battalion was held up by the enemy's wire, he collected some troops, went forward with a machine-gun,

STEEL TUNNELS WHICH TOOK THE PLACE OF DUG-OUTS.
A distinct advance, in point of comfort, on the dug-out was the erection in part of the French lines of steel shelters, which served the double purpose of workshops and refuges from German grenades. The above shows some of our allies constructing barbed-wire defences in these steel huts.

On the front at Hulluch on September 30th the 2nd Bedfordshires produced a fine leader in Company Sergeant-Major Stringer, who handled a group of bomb-throwers with great skill, won back the famous gun trench, and broke up several violent counter-attacks.

In the earlier fighting near Hulluch and round the quarries, the 2nd Sussex d.d some fine work. There was, for instance, Corporal Tilling, who was wounded in the first assault and was stretched out all day close to the German wire. But when the last and successful charge was made, the badly injured corporal joined in it; and as most of the machine-gunners were killed, he took charge of an abandoned Maxim, dug an emplacement for it in the second German line, and charged with **Fine work of 2nd Sussex** the Battalion in the forest. He was a disobedient man, for he was ordered to the dressing-station when he was seen digging a hole for his machine-gun; but he would not leave the quarries until September 26th. The 2nd Sussex were among the Battalions badly gassed at the opening of the attack, but another gallant sergeant of theirs, W. R. Smethurst, got his men well in hand, and captured the position at Le Rutoire.

Corporal Walker, of the 1st Royal Highlanders, was another hero of Hulluch. He first brought in wounded under very heavy shell fire, then took charge of two machine-guns which the enemy was shelling. The Germans

and found a gap in the entanglements, through which he kept down the enemy's fire and helped the battalion out of a difficult situation. But all his own men were at last killed or wounded, and he then got all his injured men to the dressing-station, and came back himself with his machine-gun, and fought on until he was wounded.

The 10th Gloucesters deserve a place of honour in the story of the frontal attack on Hulluch. The Battalion was held up by heavy uncut wire entanglements, but it produced in Private W. Ingles a man who could cope with the terrible situation. Ingles rushed alone to the German parapet, and by his swift and furious marksmanship as a bomb-thrower he kept the German troops well down in their chalk warren, and prevented them from bombing or firing upon the Gloucesters as they struggled through the uncut wire. Great was the saving of life among his comrades that Private Ingles effected.

But deeds of this sort in an army numbering six Divisions were too common to be fully told. At the beginning of the advance there were 72,000 British bayonets struggling to advance between Cuinchy and Grenay. Our tale of Loos is already very long, yet we have not related the details of the struggle in the Hohenzollern Redoubt, and around Fosse 8, and at Haisnes village, Cuinchy, and Vermelles. The fighting near Vermelles, where our men were held up and slaughtered from September 25th to October 1st, was a tragedy of heroism. Among the regiments near

"THE PLACE DE L'OPERA," CHAMPAGNE.

Save for the bicycles, the above might almost be a picture of some scene in mediæval warfare. It is an official photograph of a stoutly-constructed rest camp behind the French lines, which was familiarly known as "The Place de l'Opéra." In oval: French soldiers illustrating the difficulty of passing through barbed-wire entanglements, even in the absence of enemy machine-guns.

Vermelles who won awards for their stubborn valour were the 2nd Warwicks, the 2nd Wiltshires, the 3rd Royal Fusiliers, the 3rd Berkshire Regiment, the 2nd East Kents, the 2nd East Yorkshires, the 2nd Worcesters, the 1st York and Lancasters (who lost all their company officers, had both their flanks endangered, and won out by superhuman courage), the 3rd York and Lancasters (who ran out of bombs and recovered a trench by bayonet work), the 3rd Middlesex, the 1st Suffolk, the 1st Welsh, and the 2nd Cheshires (one company of which fought until Private W. H. Nixon was the only man left of two hundred and fifty, after a bomb struggle of twenty-four hours).

In conclusion, we may remark that the twenty-six guns taken round Loos and exhibited in London, are marked as being captured by the 2nd Border Regiment, the 2nd Gordon Highlanders, a Territorial Battalion of the Gordon Highlanders, the 8th Devonshires, the 9th Devonshires, the St. Pancras Battalion of the London Territorial Division, the 1st Welsh Guards, and the 46th Brigade. The remainder of the guns, with the exception of one taken by the 9th Division, are stated to have been captured by the Immortal Division—the 7th. But Mr. John Redmond, M.P., justly remarked that, of the Territorial Division, the London Irish should be credited with five captured guns. All were captured on September 25th, except that taken by the Welsh Guards on the 27th of that month. The 39th Garhwal Rifles took a trench mortar; another was taken by the 1st Somerset Light Infantry and the 1st Rifle Brigade.

FRENCH BATTERY AT WORK IN THE MASSIGES SECTOR OF THE CHAMPAGNE BATTLEFIELD.
The guns, well screened save from enemy airmen, were trained on the second-line trenches of the Germans.

CHAPTER LXXXIX.

THE GREAT FRENCH OFFENSIVE IN CHAMPAGNE AND ARTOIS.

The Extraordinary German Fortress in Champagne—Four Hundred Miles of Trenches, Caverns, and Tunnels Served by Two Light Railways on a Front of only Fifteen Miles—Seven German Army Corps Mass for Victory, and German War Correspondents are Invited to the Triumph—The Kettle-drums of Death Roll over the Germans—The Blue Waves of France Break upon the Five Great Fortressed Downs—One French Battalion Reaches the Last German Line—The Battle of the Hand of Massiges and the Struggle in Earhole Down—The Butte of Mesnil Resists and Breaks up the French Attack—But the Column Swerves Towards another Fortress and the Bretons and Arabs Win a Great Victory—Trou Bricot with its Chain of Redoubts and Ten Thousand Prisoners is Strangely Captured—How Marchand of Fashoda Led the French Colonials to Victory through the Punch-bowl of Souain—The Fortress of Bois Sabot and the Heroic Death of the Foreign Legion—The Terrible Struggle at L'Epine—Fog Falls on the Battlefield and Interrupts the Work of the French Gunners and Airmen—The Army of Champagne Breaks Through the Last German Line at Tahure Down, and is then Checked—The Germans Counter-Attack till their Losses Balance the French —General Foch Fails to Advance in Artois—A Footing is Gained on the Great Ridge, but the Main Operation does not Succeed—The Position of the Allies at the End of the Battles of Champagne and Artois.

THERE is an ancient Roman road running from Rheims to the Argonne Forest. About twenty miles east of Rheims this Roman way crosses the Suippes River near the small town of Auberive; thence it runs for about fifteen miles to the outskirts of the forest, some distance south of the hamlet of Massiges. The country through which the old road runs is a barren tableland of chalk, that continually swells into low, rounded hills, many of which have been planted with pine-trees. The land is part of the Champagne district, but to mark it from the fertile region of famous vineyards the French themselves call the unfruitful waste of chalk Lousy Champagne. This coarse term is indeed quite an official geographical expression among our frank-spoken allies. The small stream of La Tourbe flows in front of the old German position at Massiges. Then north of the hand-shaped down at Massiges is another stream, the Dormoise River. On the western side of this section of the front several streams flow into the Suippes River, the most important of these tributaries being the Py.

Immediately south of the Roman road is a vast circle of earthworks, known as the Camp de Chalons. Old tradition has it that the earthworks were made by Attila, king of the Huns, whose forces were

for the first time broken in a great battle on the plateau, whereby Paris was saved and the Huns chased from France. A few miles due west of Attila's camp is the hamlet of Valmy, where the Army of the French Revolution won its first victory over the Royal forces of Prussia and Austria, and thereby founded the democratic movement in modern Europe. For these reasons all the poor, mean country was holy ground to the French soldier, and despite the previous checks to the Army of Champagne, the general opinion in France was that over the stretch of chalk between the Argonne and Rheims the decisive advance against the German host would at last take place; for it was at this position that the breaking of the German front would be most disastrous to the enemy. All the invaders' lines, from Zeebrugge and the Yser to the northern heights of the Aisne, and the hills round Rheims would be taken in flank and the rear, and menaced by a cutting of all the lines of communication, if a French army crossed the Dormoise and Py streams. But the Germans proudly boasted that their lines in Champagne were absolutely impregnable, and General von Kluck remarked to a German-American war correspondent that the position was that, if he could not take Paris, neither could the French capture Vouziers. The town of Vouziers, on

AFTER THE KNOCK-OUT BLOW.
German 105 mm. gun shattered by accurate French fire. Shells and their cases were strewed around in wild confusion.

An eyrie in France: British observation officer and sniper overlooking enemy trenches.

News from the trenches: British despatch-rider arrives at headquarters in an old French chateau with reports from the front.

"From war, pestilence and famine. Good Lord deliver us." Modern Crusaders at prayer in a ruined fane in France.

French engineers towing a long pontoon bridge into position.

the northern edge of the Argonne Forest, and well to the north of the Py River, was one of the principal German headquarters.

Between Vouziers and the French front there were four fortified lines, each a mile or more apart. All the downs, on and between these lines, were deeply excavated and transformed into underground fortresses, armed with quick-firing batteries, mortars for aerial torpedoes, piping for the emission of poison gas clouds, and thousands of machine-guns. Of all their military engineering works the Germans most prided themselves upon their Champagne defences. These defences had been greatly strengthened and extended since the French made their first great thrust in February, 1915. The French had then captured the first German line, running close to the Roman road by the hamlet of Perthes. But the loss of this line had put the German engineers on their mettle, and in the intervening months they had brought up hundreds more guns and thousands more Maxims; they had fitted many of the sunken invisible forts with domes of armoured steel, and had driven a series of tunnels through the chalk, to allow of supports being moved to the fire trenches safely through the heaviest storm of shrapnel and melinite shell.

We have already seen that the allied offensive movement was expected in the middle of August, 1915. It was then that the Germans began to reinforce both the Champagne and the Lille-Lens sectors. The German Staff, after the battle, had the lying impudence to state that their fifteen-mile front between Auberive and Massiges had only been held by a single division of infantry. This would have given less than one man to every two yards, which is a disposition of troops so extremely feeble as to invite a shattering defeat. As a matter of fact, the German Staff was quite competent in its work, and was in possession of all the necessary resources in trained men. At least fifty-six regiments of infantry were placed in that section of the front which the French attacked. Usually a German regiment consists of three battalions, so that at full strength the fifty-six regiments would have amounted to 168,000 bayonets, or seven army corps. The German formations, however, were much wasted by war, and many of the brigades were a medley of broken units, newly and roughly soldered together.

Confused German brigades The army corps most fully represented were the Eighth, Twelfth, and Eighteenth Reserve Corps, and the Fourth, Fifth, Sixth, and Seventh Reserve Corps. Then there were fragments of the Third, Fifth, Ninth, Tenth, Twelfth, Thirteenth, Fourteenth, and Sixteenth Active Army Corps. This extraordinary mixture of units is interesting, not merely by its extent, but by the proof it furnishes of the hurry with which the German Staff was obliged to transport men from many other parts of the front in order to prepare against this urgent peril. The regiments of the Tenth Corps arrived in hot haste from the Russian front in an outworn and wretched condition, and these fatigued, ragged, ill-fed men were among those that did very badly.

Yet, despite the confused haste with which this large medley of forces was assembled, the German commander on the Champagne front, General von Einem, had so absolute an assurance of victory that on the eve of the struggle he invited German war correspondents to come and watch the spectacle of his triumph. It was from one of these correspondents, Dr. Max Osborn of the "Vossische Zeitung," that we obtained the best description of the French bombardment. After telling how the French heavy artillery swept the German rear, seeking to explode hand-bomb depots and other magazines of ammunition, the German with the English **Kettle-drums of Death** name said: "The violence of the bombardment then reached its zenith. At first it had been a raging, searching fire; now it became a mad drumming, beyond all power of imagination. It is impossible to give any idea of the savagery of this hurricane of shells. Never has this old planet heard such an uproar. An officer who had witnessed in the summer the horrors of the Souchez and the Lorette heights, told me they could not in any way be compared with this inconceivably appalling artillery onslaught. Night and day for fifty hours, and in some places

NOVEL FORM OF RAILWAY SPECIAL: WATER TRAIN TO THE TRENCHES.
Curious locomotive and trucks used in the French Army railways for the transport of water to the trenches. This service once again demonstrated the marvellous capacity of our ally to adapt herself to every condition of war.

for seventy hours, the French guns vomited death and destruction against the German troops and the German batteries. Our strongly-built trenches were filled in, and ground to powder; their parapets and fire platforms were razed and turned into dust-heaps; and the men in them were buried, crushed, and suffocated. One of our privates, a high-school young man who survived, amused himself by counting the shells that fell in his limited field of vision. He calculated that nearly a hundred thousand projectiles fell around him in fifty hours."

Another German war correspondent says that from the height on which he stood the southern sky-line looked like a vast volcanic eruption, and the unending roll of the French artillery sounded like the kettle-drums of death. French artillery of every calibre was used, from the light mountain "75's" to the latest mammoth howitzers from the Creusot and Bourges foundries, named by the workmen who made them, "The Conquerors." For a full week the French troops in the trenches in Champagne had been expectantly awaiting the order to charge; for the bombardment opened on September 18th, and each night, as darkness fell, loads of strange, long steel cylinders were brought into the fire-trenches and placed in the underground store-chambers. Some of the African troops—Arabs, Moors,

"A LA BAIONETTE."
French soldiers springing over the parapet of a trench to assault the German position with cold steel and the fiery enthusiasm so formidable in the Latin temperament when on the offensive.

EVENTIDE SOMEWHERE IN CHAMPAGNE, 1915.
Part of the German first-line trenches in Champagne recaptured by the French. The natural scenery hereabouts is very beautiful. The autumnal calm of the countryside but tended to emphasise the frightfulness of war.

and negroes from Senegal—wondered what was in the steel tubes; but the men of the Foreign Legion and the Colonial and home regiments knew what the cylinders meant, and smiled grimly. After a long wait of six months, France had come to the conclusion that her brutal, de-civilised enemy must be taught the lesson that two could play at the game of gas attacking. But for reasons of sound policy, which happily chimed with the desire not to degrade warfare to the conditions of the cannibal period of the old Stone Age, the French chemists had prepared a gas that stupefied instead of killed.

The stupefaction lasted long enough to enable the stricken men to be captured. Though no doubt it would have produced a more terrorising effect upon the German troops if they had been slain by poison fumes, and thus put permanently out of action whether the French infantry advance reached them or not, this method of frightfulness was not adopted. From some points of view it would have been well worth while to use a gas of a deadly nature, such as the prussic-acid mixture which the Germans employed. The German had all the weakness of the born bully; and if men in his third line had been affected by poison gas those who remained unaffected would have fled. On the other hand, the advantage of the use of

Stupefaction instead of death

a stupefying gas is that the troops employing it do not fear their own weapon when the wind seems about to change, and when it may be necessary to charge through the gas cloud. At Loos we might have killed a considerable part of our own army had we employed poison gas.

By September 24th the bombardment reached its sustained level of intensity, and a trifling event that happened in the evening told the soldiers that the advance was about to be made. They were given an extra ration of wine. They tried to sleep, with the kettle-drums of death roaring close behind them, and when réveillé sounded at half-past five on Saturday morning, September 25th, the men drank their coffee, and as the guns made talk impossible, they squatted in their shelters, as far out of the rain as they could get, and smoked their pipes.

Meanwhile the British advance on Loos was taking place and drawing off the northern reserves of the enemy. Just when our new Highland Brigade made its swoop into the suburbs of Lens, General Joffre's order was read for the last time before action. This order has been misrepresented in the British Press. As read to the soldiers by their battalion commanders, it ran as follows:

Soldiers of the Republic,—After months of waiting, which have enabled us to strengthen our forces and resources while our adversary has been wasting his, the hour has come to attack and conquer, and add fresh glories to those of the Marne and Flanders, the Vosges and Arras. Behind the tempest of iron fire, unloosened by the toil in all our workshops, where our brothers are labouring for us night and day, you will go to the assault all together, along the whole front, in close union with the armies of our allies. Your driving force will be irresistible. It will carry you, in one effort, as far as the adversary's batteries, beyond the fortified lines which face you. You will give him neither rest nor respite until victory is achieved. Go to it with all your heart, for the deliverance of our country, for the triumph of right and freedom.   J. JOFFRE.

General Joffre's order

The men answered this appeal with the battle-cry of "Victory or Death!"; and at a quarter past nine, as the rain was falling more heavily, a long line of strange figures

STEEL-CAPPED SOLDIERS IN AN ARMOURED FRENCH TRENCH: SURPRISING DEVELOPMENTS OF SIEGE WARFARE.
After about twelve months of siege warfare on the western front, the French provided their troops with steel helmets to protect them from head wounds, and, to a great extent, armoured their trenches, developing the old-style defences of heaped-up earth and sand-bags into steel-plated, metal-shielded redoubts, with heavy overhead works of timber and earth. The revolving steel cupola shown in the above scene had been captured from the Germans, and was being used against them by the French who, in their armoured trench, were under a heavy artillery fire. One man is holding a metal shield in front of the entrance to his dug-out, while others are seeking shelter in the cupola.

leaped from the fire-trenches, and charged across the grassy slopes, over which the gas cloud had rolled. Clad in their new invisible blue uniforms, with steel helmets to protect them from shrapnel, the infantry looked more like mediæval warriors than like modern soldiers. Their bayoneted rifles resembled the ancient spears, and the most novel weapon they carried, the hand-bomb, was but a deadlier form of the old-fashioned grenade. Most of the battalions seem to have been divided into two sections, bombers and bayoneters. On reaching the first German trenches, the men with the bayonets crossed them and charged farther into the German lines, while the men with the bombs stayed in the captured position until they had smashed the Germans out of it.

The average distance an infantry attack can cover in the open against modern artillery is three hundred yards. This was the average distance that the French charge covered. Where the distance was greater, as in the Punch-bowl of Souain, and where the gallant Colonial Division under General Marchand had to cross some 1,000 yards of open grassland, the French sappers ran out **Opening of** a system of trenches close to the enemy's **the assault** lines, from which the assault debouched. Near the French fire-trenches round Souain there had been constructed very large earthworks, in some of which a battalion could stroll about as safely as in a barrack-square, yet within shouting distance of the enemy. These strongholds enabled the French generals to concentrate great numbers of men on a single point.

The first waves of the assault broke over the entire German front, from Auberive to the Argonne Forest, for a length of fifteen miles. But this was only meant to test the general strength of the enemy and pin his men down to every yard of the Champagne position. The main series of thrusts were then delivered at four points, the men advancing in narrow but very long and loose masses which spread out behind the first hostile line of downs. On the extreme left, at the village of Auberive,

where the Germans held most of the fortified houses and the French were deeply entrenched along the southern outskirts, little progress could be made. Here the force of our allies' attack was skilfully directed north-westward up the long slopes leading to the hamlet of L'Epine de Vedegrange. Another strong attacking force was directed from Souain through the Punch-bowl northward and against a line of fortified heights known as Hill 185, on which Navarin Farm lay, the Butte of Souain, and Tree Hill. Eastward of Tree Hill was the formidable height of Tahure Butte, with the village of Tahure south of it, and in the triangle of Tahure, Souain, and Perthes villages was the immense German **German** fortress called the Trou Bricot, and nick- **defensive system** named the Hollow of Death. East of this hollow was the fortressed escarpment of the Butte of Mesnil. Eastward of Mesnil was Bastion Crest, with the group of houses called Maisons de Champagne behind it, and still farther eastward, near the edge of the Argonne Forest, was a large, hand-shaped down, known as the Hand of Massiges, with south of it a quarried hill, called from its curious appearance the Earhole.

To sum up, the heights of (1) L'Epine, (2) Navarin Hill, Souain Butte, and Tree Hill, (3) Tahure Butte, (4) Mesnil Butte, and (5) Bastion Crest and the Hand of Massiges, formed five systems of defensive works against which the French Army of Champagne worked forward. It was expected that some of the positions would prove too strong to be carried by storm, and it was arranged that in this case the most formidable fortresses should be left awhile unattacked, and then approached by a double flanking movement from behind. This is how Mesnil Butte, a down with a high, steep face thrusting into the French line, was dealt with. It remained for some days a quiet salient in the French front, while the tumult of battle sounded on both sides of it.

General de Castelnau's main scheme was to penetrate between each principal German hill position, and then turn

FIRST-LINE GERMAN TRENCHES TAKEN BY THE FRENCH.
Group of French infantry filing into the captured German first-line trenches in Champagne. The whole country-side was devastated by "75" shells. A casual observer might have imagined himself to be in desert territory; not a blade of grass was visible, and every tree was blasted.

A SOUVENIR OF VICTORY.
French infantryman choosing a " pickelhaube " from a motley collection of " Boche " helmets gathered together after a Champagne attack.

and encircle it with two flanking columns. But before this could be done, the first German line had to be captured, the strength of each hostile fortress tested, and then the columns had to advance along the valleys and the slopes with terrible enfilading fires sweeping them on both sides. It was afterwards calculated by observers of the conquered ground that along this front of fifteen miles, with a depth of two and a half miles, the German engineers had constructed nearly four hundred miles of trenches. And, despite the extraordinary duration and intensity of the French bombardment, in which millions **General de Castelnau's** of shells were used, this enormous system **scheme** of human warrens was only damaged badly on the front slopes and in the southernmost hollows between the downs The high ramparts of chalk protected from destruction far the greater part of the vast earthworks. The new French howitzers threw to a height of 12,000 feet a very heavy shell that descended almost vertically. Yet this wonderful projectile could not destroy the sheltered caverns and trenches in the

downs on which the German sappers had been labouring for twelve months.

The German had first taught the Allies that no ordinary concrete and armour-plate fortress could resist his monster howitzers. Then, when forced himself to remain on the defensive, the German had invented a new kind of underground fortress, with mobile defence guns, against which monster howitzers were of little direct use. There were lines of railways of narrow gauge spreading through the German works and connecting with the French railway running from Challerange to St. Souplet. In the Trou Bricot there were even two railway tracks for bringing up supplies and moving heavy guns. Imagine a system of sewers, half as large as those of London but more densely grouped, **Underground fortress** connected by tunnels of chalk as long **of Champagne** as the London Tubes, served by light railways, screened by a line of downs nearly six hundred feet above sea-level, and lighted by electricity and comfortably furnished. Such was the German fortress of Champagne. No wonder General von Kluck proudly proclaimed it impregnable.

But the vehemence of attack of the French troops carried them in one hour through this fortress at two important points. At Massiges a Colonial Division, formed largely of Frenchmen born and bred in North Africa, reached in their first charge the Maisons de Champagne, a farm north of the Hand of Massiges Down. At Souain another French Colonial Division swept through the Punch-bowl and captured Navarin Hill. Between these two Colonial Divisions a column of Bretons and Vendeans, advancing from Perthes, reached the western slopes of the Butte of Tahure, while on the other side of this Butte an African Division of Arab, Berber, Moorish, and Senegal troops took the eastern slopes, and there connected with the men of Savoy and Dauphiné in a flanking movement between the Butte of Tahure and Tree Hill. From 10 to 10.30 o'clock on Saturday morning, September 25th, 1915, the situation on the battlefield of Champagne was similar to that obtaining at the same hour on the battlefield of Lens.

Both the French and British leading Divisions had made advances of a miraculous kind. In particular, the position of the Colonial troops at Maisons de Champagne resembled that of the Highland Brigade at the Cité St. Auguste at Lens. Pouring with sweat, the men had stormed through machine-gun fire, wire entanglements, rows of trenches, and gun positions, and after a rush of three miles they reached the last crest of chalk from which

Miraculous advances

the valley of the Dormoise and the village of Ripont were dominated. Had supports quickly arrived, the road to Vouziers, Namur, and Liège would have been won. But, apparently, the single battalion that reached the Maisons, having lost all its officers and being commanded by a sergeant, had moved too quickly. The French Staff could not get more men up in time, and the half-shattered battalion, caught between two flanking fires from Massiges and Beauséjour, and attacked in front from Ripont, had to leave the heavy German and Austrian batteries it had captured on the crest, and fall back at two o'clock on Saturday afternoon. There was another battalion also in a still more advanced position at the entrenchments north-west

of the Maisons, known as the Work of the Defeat. The men had held the hill for three and a half hours without help arriving, and it was only at the end of this time that the Germans at Ripont were able to re-form and return to the attack. As a matter of fact, the two wings at the height of the Hand of Massiges and at the Butte of Mesnil could not get forward as quickly as the centre had done. There had been a com-

A check at Mesnil

plete check at Mesnil, and this had thrown the operation out of gear. In the same way our check at Vermelles interfered with the success of our Highland Brigade beyond Hill 70. In both cases the local commanders, Sir Douglas Haig and General de Langle de Cary, seemed not to have cared for a Napoleonic gamble, such as General Foch risked near the Marne, when he instantly poured his reserves through

FRENCH STRONGHOLDS MADE BY GERMAN SHELLS.
Huge crater of a German mine in Champagne that was converted by the French into a strongly-defended position. Having captured the shell-torn ground, the French quickly built up the sides of the crater with stones and timber, so that it formed a deep and solid trench. Above : Shell-wrecked house turned to military advantage by French soldiers. The cellars were used as dug-outs for a commandant and his Staff.

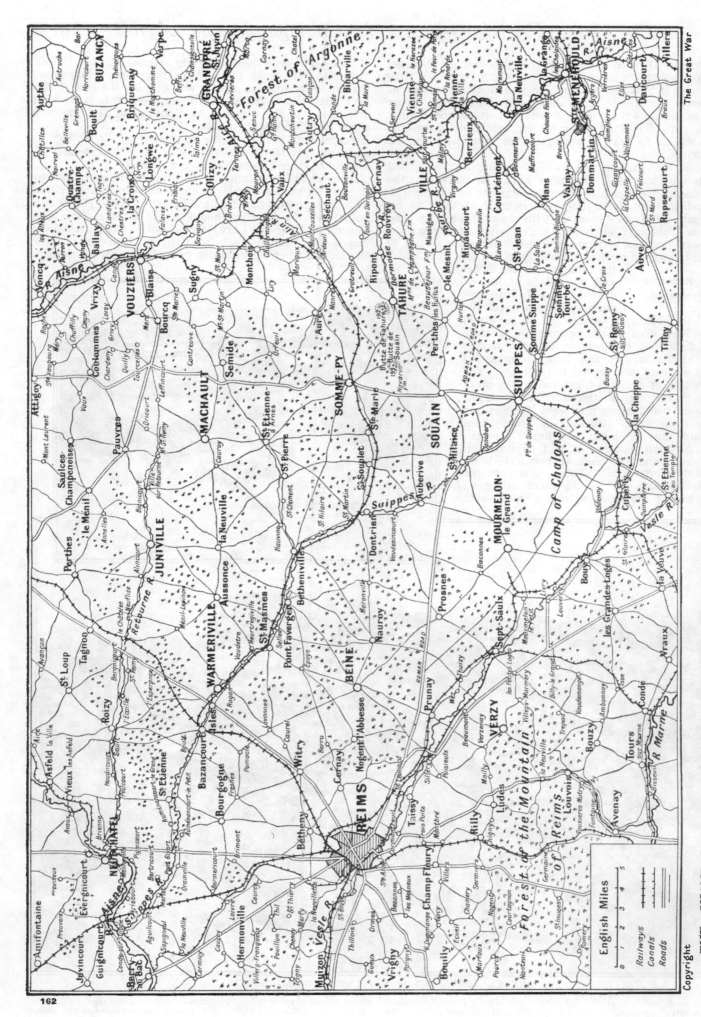

162

The Great War

THE CHAMPAGNE BATTLEFIELDS, SHOWING THE FORTRESSED DOWNLAND BETWEEN AUBERIVE AND VILLE-SUR-TOURBE.

The main French Army, under General de Castelnau, attacked on September 25th, 1915, the line of hills of which Tahure Down is the centre. The first and second German lines, which contained 400 miles of trenches behind a 15-mile front, were captured, and 150 guns were taken and 25,000 prisoners. One French battalion reached the last German line, but the enemy's front was not completely broken.

a small breach by the marshes of St. Gond made between the Prussian Guard and Bülow's army. The commanders on either side had become very cautious, and wanted to feel that both their feet were firmly planted before making another step forward. The machine guns were the factor that made them anxious to consolidate their ground ere they thrust out on the decisive attack.

The Germans at Massiges had a saying that Earhole Down, or Hill 191, rising south of the Hand, could be held by two washerwomen with two machine-guns; for this trenched, caverned, wired, and tunnelled lump of chalk dominated the plain on which the French were camped. But in twenty-two minutes a Colonial Brigade, with the general charging, in the gallant fashion of the French, at the head of his men, reached the quarry that formed the Earhole. The German regiments holding the hill had been too confident in the mechanical strength of their fortress. Many of their machine-guns, being worked from bomb-proof shelters, had escaped the French howitzer fire, but the speed of the infantry attack disconcerted and surprised the garrison. Several of the running, panting, roaring Frenchmen carried light telephones on their backs, and the result was that, when the German machine-guns lifted above the damaged parapets and began to fire, the French batteries of mountain artillery came again swiftly into action, and flung a storm of 3 in. melinite shells a few yards in front of the first wave of light-blue figures.

The French mountain-gun, first issued in small numbers to the Chasseurs in the mountains had become the supreme weapon for nearly all battlefields. It was a variation of the "75," lighter and shorter of range, but with a higher angle of fire. It was used close behind the troops, almost like a machine-gun, but while a machine-gun could not hit men behind a hill, the mountain-gun could shell or shrapnel enemy troops sheltering in a hollow or on the reverse slopes of a down. Under the cover of a bombardment of this kind the French bombers rushed to the German hill trenches, and flung in grenades, forcing the Germans to retreat. The hill was close to the Argonne, where the Crown Prince was fighting with a newly-reinforced army, directed by General von Mudra. In answer to telephone calls for help, Mudra sent some of his best troops to the Earhole, where they

Desperate courage of the Germans arrived quickly and safely by means of the deep communication trenches that ran from the sea to the Alps.

The new German supports fought well, refusing to surrender. The colonel of a French Colonial regiment climbed with his grenadiers within thirty yards of a German position. "Surrender, you are surrounded!" he cried to them. A German lieutenant flung a bomb at the colonel, but missed, and the angry French privates then charged and killed the lieutenant and all his men. In the end there were so many field-grey figures piled in the trenches of Earhole Down that at some important points the conquered works were choked by them, and in order to get forward the victorious French troops had to climb out in the open ground of the hill, under a hail of shrapnel from the enemy's batteries. Fighting went on day and night till September 30th; for long after the original garrison was destroyed, fresh troops poured into the northern works from the village of Rouvroy, coming

from the Crown Prince's army a few miles to the east. Towards the north the French Colonials reached Mont Tetu, overlooking the plateau; then, hour by hour, they pressed down eastward in the direction of the town of Ville-sur-Tourbe. The Germans were encircled in little groups in the trenches in the eastern valleys until a thousand prisoners were taken. The capture of a German bomb depot and three thousand grenades greatly facilitated the operations on the Hand of Massiges and the Earhole.

There seem to have been three Divisions employed round Massiges. The first Division captured Earhole Down; the second Division stormed the middle finger and ring-finger of the Hand of Massiges; the third Division took the height known as Bastion Crest, between the Hand of Massiges and the Butte of Mesnil. In all, five waves of French infantry swept up and over the heights and **French troops round Massiges** along the downland valley, which had been transformed into a maze of trenches and dug-outs. The enemy's gun-positions were reached and the French cavalry were thrown into the action. But the condition of the slippery, muddy ground

QUEUE OF GERMANS CAPTURED IN CHAMPAGNE.
Some of the German prisoners captured by the French during their advance in Champagne on September 25th, 1915. At this time the French held some sixteen thousand German prisoners in this district.

prevented the horsemen from charging up the slopes where the guns and machine-guns were sited; so most of the men dismounted and fought on foot as supports to the infantry. Had it only been dry weather, the cavalry would, in all probability, have reached the Dormoise River, and sabred the last line of German artillery there.

From September 25th to the 30th, the Germans round Massiges continually counter-attacked, with a view to winning back their lost line. It was then that they suffered quite as heavy losses as the French had done in their attacks. The last of the German counter-attacks came from Cernay, in the north-east. The troops deployed at the foot of the slopes of the little rounded down known as La Justice. But the French light guns shattered this counter-attack before it got under way, and the troops round La Justice broke and fled in a panic. This was quite an extraordinary feature of the conflict, for hitherto the German soldiers had fought with remarkable tenacity, and when defeated had either surrendered or been killed. The spectacle of a large body of veteran enemy troops breaking and fleeing in panic under shell fire was regarded by the French command as highly significant.

Westward, beyond the Butte of Mesnil, the French

MOMENTS OF EASE.
French soldiers resting awhile in the course of their strenuous offensive against the enemy positions in Champagne.

MOMENTS OF ANGUISH.
Wounded soldiers from a Champagne battlefield waiting their turn to be conveyed to a hospital. They were temporarily resting at a farm some distance behind the zone of operations. Some captured members of the German Red Cross are seen at work.

attack was directed on Perthes towards Tahure and the down north of the village known as the Butte of Tahure. The German guns and machine-guns on this butte crossed fires with the guns and Maxims on Tree Hill, lying to the south-west The road to the railway town of Somme Py ran in a long upward slope between the two fortified downs. The road was a death-trap, even when the village of Tahure had been captured ; and it was necessary first to storm or mask one of the two heights before a decisive advance could be made. The French commander decided to attack Tree Hill, but instead of making a frontal assault on this formidable position, he launched at it two flanking movements. The Breton and Vendean troops advanced towards Tahure from the east, while the African troops set out westward from Souain, and reached the junction of the roads from Souain to Tahure and Perthes to Somme Py.

In practically every case the tactics of General de Castelnau consisted in bringing two French forces against a single German force. Nearly every German main position was assailed, on two or three sides, by some 12,000 French

French attack on Tree Hill

soldiers on one flank and another 12,000 on the other. When, as in the case of the Butte of Mesnil, the enemy's flank defences proved too strong to be stormed by a swift movement, the troops veered as much as possible to the north-east and north-west, with a view to cutting the rear communications of the fortress.

At Perthes the Germans had a salient in a wood west of the village, the position being known to the French as the Pocket. It was attacked on two sides by the regiments of Savoy and Dauphine, who captured it in seventeen minutes. The place was a labyrinth of trenches, caverns, and entanglements, but the Frenchmen went over it at the double, and captured in the wood the guns that should have been playing on them as they charged. Two German officers were caught in bed! Then north of Perthes there was a large punch-bowl between the downs, and across this hollow the Germans had driven two lines of trenches. The Rhine Trench was in front, and about five furlongs behind it was the support line known as the Yorck Trench. When the French column attacked the Punch-bowl, it skilfully threw out battalions along its wings to mask the wooded slopes on the right and left. The troops on the left wing had little to do but to dig themselves in, get good cover, and wait; for when the main Breton force of attack from Perthes linked up with the African troops coming from Souain, all the Germans in the western woods were completely encircled, driven in from the rear, and captured. East of the Punch-bowl, however, the process of encirclement was slower; for it was here that the great German fortress on the Butte of Mesnil dominated the field of conflict. There was an extraordinary series of redoubts on this long down. On its southern face was the Trapeze Works, and going northward toward Tahure was the Toothbrush Works, with a network of trenches and caverns connecting them.

From the Perthes side the Mesnil Butte seemed as

Encircling the "Punch-bowl"

impregnable as Gibraltar; for all the slope was very steep, and the Germans in the trenches above swept the incline with machine-gun fire, or broke up every attacking line with hand-bombs. So skilfully were the works constructed that the long, intense, preliminary bombardment had not injured them; and though the French brought up their light guns, and, placing them in the opposite wood across the Punch-bowl, maintained a storm of shell a few yards in front of their charging infantry, the German garrisons above the steep survived the hurricane, and rose above their parapets in time to bomb back the wave of assault. It was not until October 6th that the Butte of Mesnil fell, after the Trapeze and the Toothbrush Redoubts had been slowly reduced.

Meanwhile the main Breton force pushed along over the Punch-bowl to the outskirts of the village of Tahure, and there a portion of them advanced with part of the African troops towards the two downs that crossed their fires over the road to Somme Py. All along this region, towards the Butte of Souain on the west and the Butte of Mesnil on the east, the third and last German line was approached. But progress was very slow in this decisive field of battle.

PRIMITIVE WELL IN THE AISNE DISTRICT.
As was to be expected in the circumstances, "bucket" and "pitcher" were more serviceable than ornamental.

Slow progress towards last line The wire entanglements had not been reached by the French artillery, and behind the wire were numerous machine-gun positions which were but slightly injured by gun fire. The French gunners were pulling their pieces out of the pits which had been built in the spring, and their horses were being taken out of their underground stables and whipped across the holed and slippery slopes of chalk to positions between the first and second German lines. There, in the open field in the pouring rain, the Frenchmen worked their guns against the last chain of the Champagne downs. But in the thick weather their aerial observers could not mark the enemy batteries, especially those eastward, which enfiladed on the right flank the columns of attacking French infantry. The infantry were thus held up by three forces of the defence—wire entanglements, machine-guns, and artillery. Heavy, overwhelming, and exact howitzer fire was needed between the Butte of Tahure, Tree Hill, and the Butte of Souain. So the troops dug themselves in, and waited for clearer weather.

CAMERA PICTURE OF A FRENCH FIRST-LINE TRENCH IN THE AISNE DISTRICT.
Another example of the elaboration of modern trench warfare. The trench shown in this official French photograph had the characteristics of a miniature fort. The stretcher seen on the right tells of the care taken for the prompt treatment of the wounded. In circle: Operating a land mine in Northern France. (A German photograph.)

and some of the lines on the reverse slopes were entirely intact. Even the officers' log-houses had not been struck by a single shell. But fifty yards farther away, where the crest gave no protection, the work of destruction was terrible. Spandau Wood was not merely woodless, but transformed into a chalk quarry by some thousands of shells.

Trou Bricot, seen first on the photographs taken by the reconnoitring French airmen, formed three round, pale blots, connected by a long white streak—the communication trench. Then there were six more whitish rounds, strung along the white line like balls on a string. It was on the white line that the French gunners began their work, and their heaviest shells fell in hundreds, at a range **Awful slaughter at Trou Bricot** of five miles, on the main communication trench, cutting the telephone wires, destroying the shrapnel-proof passages, and choking the outlet. Then, at a signal from the watching airmen, a hurricane of shells fell on Trou Bricot and on the great Elberfeldt Camp behind it, and turned the gigantic fortress into a slaughter-house. The German divisions that garrisoned the extraordinary fortress were so staggered and dazed by the bombardment that a single division of French African troops sweeping up the road from Souain to Tahure cut them off in the rear from Tree Hill and the position of Baraque, where the Breton Division, advancing

PRUSSIAN TROPHY AT NAPOLEON'S SHRINE.
Captured German 155 mm. gun on view in the courtyard of the Invalides, Paris, taken from the Germans in Champagne.

Work of great importance, however, went on south of this last line of downs. North-west of Perthes was a farm known as Trou Bricot, connected with Souain by a rough country road. Here the enemy had built the most formidable of his underground fortresses. Two light railways ran through the position connecting with the main line near Somme Py. There were four cross tracks between the two parallel lines of light railway in the Trou Bricot salient. Thus munitions and supporting troops could rapidly be circulated through the fortress, one of whose lines connected with the Toothbrush Redoubt on the wooded Butte de Mesnil, and with the fortifications in the Bois Sabot towards the north west. A fold of chalk ran from Trou Bricot to the Bois Sabot, passing by numerous systems of defence, some of whose picturesque names were—the Satyr's Trench, Gretchen Trench, Kiao - Chau Wood, Elberfeldt Camp, and Von der Goltz Works. The fold of chalk formed a magnificent protection against the heavy French guns,

JOY-DAY FOR PARIS: INSPECTING SPOILS OF WAR AT THE INVALIDES.
The joyous, though discreet, enthusiasm of the Paris crowd which flocked to see the captured German guns after the Champagne victory can well be imagined from this photograph. Ranged in a long row, these weapons presented an inspiring sight, and paid a potent tribute to the skill of "Père Joffre."

A valuable " bag." Large body of Prussian officers of the Crown Prince's Command marching into captivity under a French escort.

Types of German prisoners, captured near Souain, on their way to enjoy the hospitality of their enemies till the end of the war. On the right : Wounded German prisoners at Souain about to be conducted to the rear. They were all duly ticketed.

Another batch of prisoners whose expressions bear unmistakable signs of modern German " Kultur."

ALL SORTS AND CONDITIONS OF THE UNSPEAKABLE HUN IN CAPTIVITY AFTER THE CHAMPAGNE ADVANCE, SEPTEMBER, 1915.

from the other side of the work, connected and formed a great net with the Savoy troops working forward from the Pocket in front.

The net of Arabs, negroes, Bretons, and Vendeans moved backward over Trou Bricot, and taking all the Germans in the rear, where only the low parados topped the trenches, they bombed and bayoneted the encircled enemy until the Germans surrendered in one great multitude of ten thousand prisoners. The taking of Trou Bricot, with its many guns and machine-guns and its great garrison, holding one of the most important subterranean fortresses in the world, may justly be ranked among the finest feats in the war. And it is worthy of note that the conquest was made more by generalship than by the courage of the troops; for brave as the African and Breton Divisions were, and magnificent as had been the work of their supporting artillery, the immense stronghold, with its underground railways and caverns, could not have been taken by a frontal attack. It was by demonstrating against the Butte de Mesnil, attacking the frontal Pocket, and throwing out a line of troops to keep the defenders of the eastward down occupied, that the French general, by a sudden swerve westward, linked with the African Division and gained the incomparable advantage of being able to attack the woodland fortress along its undefended rear.

While the African Division was slanting off eastward from Souain towards the pine-woods round Trou Bricot, a famous Colonial Division, commanded by the hero of Fashoda, General Marchand, made a straight, swift leap northward up the road to Somme Py, **Marchand's leap on** midway along which was the down on **Navarin Farm** which rose Navarin Farm. According to a French custom in war, which might well be changed in this era of scientific warfare, General Marchand did not remain behind his division and watch its movements, and reinforce the leading brigades when they were checked. Instead, he advanced at the head of his 12,000 bayonets and, pipe in mouth and cane in hand, led them to the attack. Marchand had already told his army commander, General de Langle de Cary: " Mon General, when the attack opens, we shall carry Navarin Farm in an hour." Though Marchand fell early in the attack, with a bad shell-wound in his spine just as his men reached the first German trench the fall of their leader only made the troops more resolute to reach their objective.

There were two miles of German trenches and fortifications between the town of Souain and the hill-farm of Navarin. In fierce, desperate spurts, the Colonial Division, with the Foreign Legion in support and a Zouave Brigade and Moroccan Division acting with it, worked through the Punch-bowl of Souain, where the enemy had built underground fortresses known as the Palatinate and Magdeburg Works. The last trench before Navarin Farm was taken by the Colonial Division in the time stated. But then all progress eastward was stopped by the earthworks in Bois Sabot. The absence of the directing mind of General Marchand must have been sorely felt during this check.

The Bois Sabot was a horse-shoe shaped fortress, surrounding a pine-wood on the right of Navarin Farm. The work spread along the foot and sides of a gently-sloping hill, and it was laid out with such skill by the German engineers that they regarded   **Check at** it as one of the strongest points in their   **Bois Sabot** entire line of defence. The heavy bombardment had done little damage to its network of wire entanglements and deep subterranean lines; and in the evening of September 25th the French troops could only lie flat on their stomachs near this work, with the rain pouring on them and asphyxiating shells from the German batteries along the Py River blinding and strangling them. It was then that the Foreign Legion advanced through a curtain of shrapnel and flung themselves down by the Colonials. The Colonials were relieved in the night by the Zouaves and Moroccan troops, and the Legion crawled the following day into a stretch of woods to prepare for an attack. But the weather was so foggy that the French guns on September 26th and September 27th could not do any useful work, and, much to the disadvantage of the Allies, the fighting had to be temporarily suspended, so that the enemy won forty-eight hours in which to rail down reinforcements, guns, and ammunition to the Champagne front.

At last, at half-past three in the afternoon of September 28th, the air cleared sufficiently for the attack to be launched. The Legion had lost more than half its force in the great drive on the Vimy Heights in Artois in the spring, when it penetrated farther than any French troops. But two thousand more foreign lovers of France had since joined the Legion, and brought it up to full strength.

GOING INTO ACTION: SCENE ON THE WAY TO THE FRENCH FIRST LINE.
French infantry filing down a road to the trenches, in open order and exposed to enemy fire, in the neighbourhood of Navarin. Each man is fully equipped for his duty in the first line, even to the steel helmet which was eventually generally used in the French Army as an effective protection from shrapnel.

"HANDS UP": GERMAN SOLDIERS SURRENDERING AT THE END OF THE BATTLE OF CHAMPAGNE.
After the battle was over long files of German soldiers came in, holding up their hands in token of surrender to the grim figures that stood watching them in silence.

In the advance from Souain, in the pine-wood near Navarin Farm, the Legionaries had again lost nearly a quarter of their men from shell and shrapnel before firing a shot. This made them very angry. They always disliked being in reserve when a charge was made, and they asked their colonel, in the evening of September 27th, to beg the general at Souain to let the Legion, as a special favour, lead the grand charge against the enemy's last line.

The request was allowed, and the famous corps, which has figured in so many romantic novels since Ouida wrote "Under Two Flags," went out to die. Every Legionary knew that he was doomed; for the plan of attack was that the Legion should fling itself straight on the front of the fortress of Bois Sabot, and there engage the enemy with such fury that 12,000 other men—Zouaves, Moors, and Colonials—could make a surprise attack on both flanks. The Legion gathered in the wood in two columns, and then, amid the cheers of the French troops occupying the trenches in front of them, they leapt across these trenches, over the heads of their comrades, and charged across the zone of death into the mouth of the Horse-shoe. First a rain of shrapnel smote them: then the stream of bullets from machine-guns and rifles caught them in the front and raked them on both sides. With a dense curtain of shrapnel behind it and torrents of lead pouring on its front and flanks, the Legion was mowed down as by a gigantic scythe. Platoons fell to a man, but the regiment went forward. At some points in the line the stream of lead was so thick that falling men were turned over and over, the dead bodies being rolled along the ground by more bullets, as withered leaves roll in the winds of autumn. Yet some men of the leading battalion lived through it, and, reaching

the wire entanglements, pounded them aside with the butts of their rifles. But of that battalion only one man got through the wires, and he fell headlong into the first German trench with a bullet through his knee. Then the second battalion followed, and a few men lived to get into the first trench and began to clear it out. But the last battalions of the Legion came forward in a tiger spring and bombed and bayoneted their way into the fortress.

There, in the maze of trenches, amid the shattered pine-wood, the Legion fought to the last man, and when the other troops closed on the flanks there were very few Germans alive in Bois Sabot. The Foreign Legion had also perished; only a small handful of its men remained. But in its great death-struggle the regiment had done one of the most amazing things in war. And when the noise of its achievement spread through France and echoed over the earth, thousands of volunteers from neutral countries came to Paris to enlist. Thus out of its glorious ashes the most famous of all corps in the modern world was born again from the inspiration given by the men who died on Vimy Ridge in Artois and the slopes of Bois Sabot in Champagne. Such is the power of the heroism of the dead upon the minds of living men who have scarcely any call to fight; for it was the Swiss, the American, the Scandinavian, and the Spaniard and Portuguese who travelled at their own expense to France to join the new Foreign Legion. The heroism of the Legion firmly established the Army of Champagne in the region of Navarin Farm. Then west of the farm was a great stretch of downland, dappled with pinewoods, reaching to the town of Auberive. Midway between the farm and town a road cut

SOME OF THE TWENTY THOUSAND PRISONERS.
When the Germans moved along their trenches for the last time, after their capture by the French, they did so with empty hands uplifted and anxious eyes fixed on their conquerors.

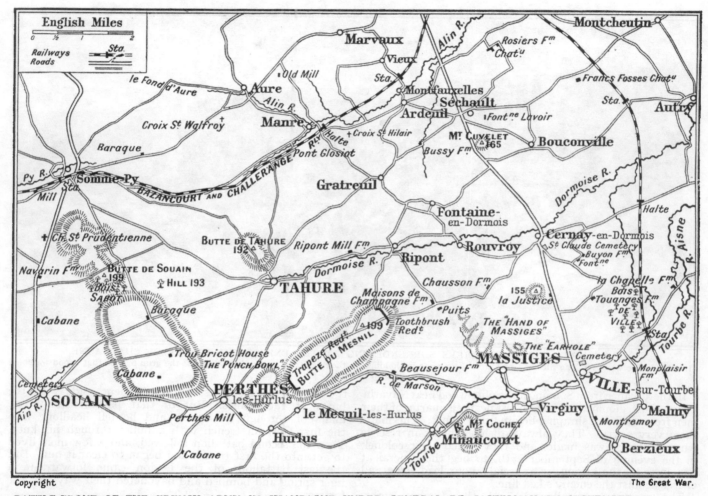

BATTLE-FRONT OF THE FRENCH ARMY IN CHAMPAGNE UNDER GENERAL DE CASTELNAU ON SEPTEMBER 25TH, 1915.
The main attack was delivered on the Hand of Massiges, but the French were held up by the Butte of Mesnil, to the north of which they advanced and captured Tahure. In the great fortress of Trou Bricot ten thousand German prisoners were taken.

across the down country, running from the village of St. Hilaire to the town of St. Souplet, on the Py River. Half-way along this road were the farm-buildings of Epnie de Vedegrange, close to Hill 150. In this part of the field General de Castelnau's design seems to have been to carry Auberive by storm, and then attack Epine and the hill by two flanking columns, which should go on with their supports and light artillery, and break the last German position at St. Souplet. But Auberive proved to be impregnable. In the previous Battle of Champagne the French had reached the outskirts of the town, and had afterwards sapped close up to the enemy's position. But later the ingenious German engineers had transformed Auberive into a subterranean city.

Auberive impregnable

Hundreds of thousands of shells fell on the buildings of the town during the great bombardment, but the ground-floors were heaped with sand-bags, and the cellars beneath were so strengthened with concrete that the troops in the chalk caverns beneath the cellars suffered little from the heaviest projectiles. A few observing officers sat among sand-bags in the attics, watching the French lines through periscopes and telephoning to their own batteries and to the various caverned headquarters. The only way in which Auberive could have been taken was by a grand attack in which a hundred thousand men would have been lost, or by a dense and immense gas-cloud, floating down gently on a steady, favourable wind. It needed, however, a direct south wind to carry the stupefying fumes over the town; but, as we have already seen at Loos, the wind on the morning of September 25th blew from the south-west. It enabled our allies to clear the entrance of some of the valleys in the Champagne region, but it did not affect the hill defences, and it slanted away from Auberive. The consequence was that the frontal attack on this position at once became an affair of house-to-house fighting with

hand-bombs against both bombs and machine-guns, in which the French troops made only very slow progress; for north of the town the Germans had powerful groups of artillery which formed a fire curtain along the front and rear trenches of our allies and checked the movement of their supporting troops.

In these circumstances, the principal French forces paused in the attack on Auberive, and swerved to the right towards the wooded slopes leading to Epine. At the same time the division operating from St. Hilaire, in a direct northward movement, also approached the crest. Only the first line of German defences in the Epine area had been destroyed by the French guns. The second line was erected on the northern slope of a ridge of chalk, and it was practically intact and defended by Würtemberg and Hanoverian troops. There were eight lines of barbed-wire bound to the trunks of the pine-trees, with old-fashioned rows of sharp wooden stakes strengthening the great obstacle. Behind the wire and the stakes were machine-guns, so placed as to sweep with their fire all the slope fifty yards wide, running up to the crest.

When the French arrived their figures were thrown out against the grey sky above the ridge and the German riflemen and machine-gunners had targets they could not miss. All the first line went down, but with a savage cry the blue-clad helmeted sons of **Savage charge on** France surged, wave after wave, up to the **German second line** crest, and then charged down with such speed that the Germans could not kill them quickly enough. How they got through the stakes and lines of barbed-wire no one remembered. Some made a path with the butt-ends of their rifles, others crawled under or cut the steel cables, while their bombers stood upright and pelted every German head within sight. After the battle it was seen that large stretches of wire still remained intact before the chief

German machine-gun positions; but there were gaps through which the German parapet was reached by the grenadiers, and the infantrymen pulled down the sand-bags, and, jumping to the trench, worked along it with dagger and revolver.

Meanwhile, when a series of footings had been won in this line, the succeeding waves of French infantry, leaving their predecessors to finish cleaning out the works, dashed into the pine-wood behind it and descended into

Epine valley of death

the long chalky bottom. There, some five hundred yards from the line below the crest, was a third system of German works with more unbroken wire entanglements, machine-guns, and light field-guns. Then on the opposite slope of the long valley was another pine-wood through which a road ran to Epine. Here there was a fourth German line with all the usual defences and a larger number of light field-guns, and the first heavy German howitzers which were placed in armoured casemates. The width of the valley was about a mile and a quarter, and when the French infantry appeared on the crest all the howitzers, guns, and machine-guns on both sides of the chalk hollow were worked at top speed against the charging blue lines. The German gunners had the range of every yard of the ground, and when the French were checked by the entanglements the storm of fire directed on them from the three German lines was of an appalling intensity.

The French won through chiefly by the skill and courage of their machine-gunners and their telephone signallers.

The men of both these sections followed close upon the first lines of attacking infantry, though the burden they had to carry was heavier than that of their comrades. The French machine-guns were placed close to the German trenches to keep down the enemy's fire while the wire was being cut. The field telephones were even more quickly brought into action, and the French artillery officers worked out the ranges with great speed, and telephoned to their batteries far away over the ridge. The result was that, as soon as the German guns in the valley began to fire, a hurricane of shells in turn fell upon them. Never has the French artillery officer shone to better advantage than he did in this valley of death, with three strongly-fortified German lines blazing at him in a way calculated to shake the nerve of any man; for the instant precision of the answering French bombardment was of a terrifying kind. The French gunnery officers by their telephones made their calculations with a swiftness and an exactness that must be acclaimed incomparable. The third and fourth German lines were completely smashed; and it was only the second line, just below the crest where the French soldiers were struggling within ten yards of the enemy, that gave very serious trouble. This barrier ex-

Incomparable French gunners

tended all below the crest of the long valley, and the fighting was so close that the distant French howitzer batteries could not safely intervene. But, as we have seen, the Frenchmen worked through, some crawling under the wires, some blanketing them with their coats and then rolling over,

WINTER FASHIONS IN A FRENCH FRONT-LINE TRENCH.
Warmth, and not smartness, was what the troops required in respect of their winter dress. Balaclava helmets worn under their service caps, fur-lined, fur-trimmed overcoats, and blankets worn cloak-wise, protected them against the low temperature, and warming food kept them cheerful.

NO NEW THING UNDER THE SUN.

Modern warfare reintroduced many ancient military weapons and devices. The old grenade and the older catapult were combined, and the resultant hybrid engine bore a curious resemblance to the crossbow of our forefathers.

and others working away with wire-cutter and butt. A wounded Zouave, returning on September 27th by the Wacques Farm, from the Epine position, stared at the two and a half miles of casemated batteries, sunken mazes, and entanglements through which he had stormed. "However did we get through all this?" he said in wonder.

The main second line of the enemy extended far along the crest eastwards, past Navarin Farm and Bois Sabot, to the fortresses of Tree Hill and Tahure Down; and after the troops on the Auberive-St. Hilaire section broke through the ridge entanglements, the general movement was still held up by the enemy's resistance at Bois Sabot, Spandau Wood, and Cameroon Trench, north of Souain. In the meantime, Tree Hill, which was the key to the central German position, was masked by some of the Africans and

Enemy resistance north of Souain Bretons who had met at La Baraque, and the Bretons and Vendeans also hung on to the slopes near Tahure Down.

The French position near Tahure rested on Hill 170, south-west of the village, along the road from Perthes. Immediately in front of the men from Normandy, Brittany, and Vendée was Tahure Down, which was some ninety-six feet higher than Hill 171. From the dominating height the German batteries and machine-guns poured so terrible a fire on the advanced French troops, in the afternoon of September 25th, that the position seemed hopeless. Happily, several French batteries galloped down the Perthes road, through the curtain of fire by which the Germans were trying to keep off the opposing reserves. The French gunners unlimbered and worked their pieces in the open, and at close range beat down the covered German guns and howitzers on the high down northward, and so slackened the enemy's fire that the French infantry were able to lie out all night on the ground they had won,

wet through with the rain, cheerless and hungry, and yet indomitable.

Throughout the night more guns and more supports were moved through the conquered German lines, and at dawn on September 26th the attack upon the works stretching from the Butte of Souain to the Butte of Tahure was begun. The resistance offered by the Germans, however, was very formidable. They had the French in a great horse-shoe of heights, of which Souain Butte, Tree Hill, and Tahure Butte formed the centre. The attacking forces were overlapped by two unconquered downs, nicknamed the Deux Mamelles, and by the long line of the Mesnil Down. Most of the German trenches in this protected stretch of downland had escaped the devastating effects of the French bombardment. The ground had been divided into compartments by the German engineers, and the systems of wire-fenced earthworks were so arranged that enfilading fire could be used by the defending forces at every important point. In some places the French troops in their first vehement movement had captured parts of the fire-trenches around this great horse-shoe. Some troops were struggling to maintain a hold on the steep western side of Mesnil Down, but they had to be withdrawn in the night of September 25th, and some time passed before the

The Horse-shoe Heights

WHEN THE NERVES WERE HIGHLY STRUNG.

Waiting for the signal that the guns were about to lift and that the charge was to be made. This was the moment when every man was at fullest tension, for British and French alike well knew how the Germans feared to meet them with the cold steel.

two points of the Horse-shoe, Deux Mamelles and Mesnil Down, were definitely conquered.

The great Horse-shoe had originally formed the enemy's third and last line. But when his first line was captured in the spring of 1915, he not only strengthened his second line, which was lost on September 25th, but extended his third down-land line, of which the Horse-shoe formed part, and then built a fourth line on the heights beyond the Py River. There seems also to have been a fifth reserve line south of Vouziers. The immediate objective of General de Castelnau was the old cross-country railway, running along the Py River, and connecting the army of the Crown Prince and the army of Metz with the army of Field-Marshal von Heeringen, fighting in front of Rheims and along the Aisne. This railway was already under the fire of the heavy French howitzers, but the gunners could only work from wireless signals received from aerial observers.

Attack on the Butte of Tahure When the country was covered with fog, as happened on September 26th and September 27th, the heavy French batteries could merely fire at random at the railway, hoping there would be something on the line worth hitting. What they needed was an artillery observation post on a down overlooking the railway. The Butte of Tahure, one hundred and ninety-nine metres high, with a summit only about a mile and a quarter from the railway line, overlooking some lower heights, was an admirable station for the French artillery officers. The Butte therefore became the chief object of the French attack.

But the trouble was that all the German positions on the heights of the Horse-shoe were situated on the northern slopes. There was nothing in view that could be attacked by direct fire. The systems of parallel trenches with their wire entanglements were hidden behind the ridges. Only a few observing officers, sheltered in dug-outs and using periscopes, faced the attacking French forces. A little way behind them were a few machine-gun posts, widely spaced to escape destruction, and situated so as to command the slopes up which the French battalions must climb. Everything else was hidden below the crests. In these circumstances, General de Castelnau held back his troops for some days. He had some small successes on September 28th and September 29th, when a fine Norman regiment took part of the Vistula Trench, west of the Butte of Tahure, and part of the position west of Navarin Farm near Chevron Wood was captured. In the last place the breach made in the enemy's lines was four hundred yards wide; but the French commander would not attempt to push his troops through it, for he knew that the heavy German batteries would come into play all round the Horse-shoe, and destroy his advanced battalions. So very little was done for eleven days.

In the meantime the French army was labouring with

HOW GENERAL JOFFRE'S "NIBBLES" GREW INTO "BITES."

"Laissez-moi faire. Je les grignotte." ("Leave me alone. I nibble them".) So said General Joffre when asked, early in the war, how things were going. In the great Champagne advance the "nibbles" grew into "bites," and the above official photograph of French infantry advancing into action under cover of artillery fire was taken during one of the "bites." Above: Dummy gun to deceive the hovering Taube.

A SCHOOL FOR GRENADE-THROWING AT THE FRONT: FRENCH GRENADIERS LEARNING THE ART.

The experiences of trench warfare proved the importance of bomb-throwing, and the British and French Armies both established training schools for bombers. This photograph shows a specially-constructed French trench near the firing-line, used as a school for grenadiers. The soldier making a practice throw stood in the farther rectangular trench surrounded with parapets and linked by a passage-way with the trenches behind. In the event of a learner accidentally dropping a primed grenade, he had time to escape through the passage-way to the rear trench before the explosion. This passage circled a shelter, behind which instructors stood, watching the results of the bomb-throwing through periscopes.

TEST OF GERMAN TEAR-PROVOKING FUMES.
Explosion of a tin of German " weeping-gas." The dense, tear-provoking fumes had a smell of ether, and the cans containing the gas were exploded by being flung to the ground.

MASKED FRENCHMAN IN " WEEPING-GAS " CLOUD.
French soldier, wearing his anti-gas mask, amidst the fumes of German " weeping-gas." The cans containing the gas were exploded by the French as a test.

extraordinary energy. The French infantry turned to the navvy work of constructing a new front line on the ground they had conquered, driving communication saps down the valleys to connect with their old positions, while most of the French guns moved to new pits, new subterranean shelters, and stables close to the fortressed hills behind which the enemy was massing. The idea of General de Castelnau was that he could afford to waste time in order to save the lives of his men. His great howitzers had rather a short range —five miles it is said—the length of their throw having been deliberately lessened in order to get a heavier projectile and a more vertical fall. They could destroy anything if they were brought close enough, but on widely-spaced lines such as the German they made the advance something of a crawl.

But at last, on the night of October 6th, the great new

Waiting for larger guns

Creusot pieces were ready in their fresh positions, and all the smaller guns were thrown out well in front of them, close to the enemy's hill-line. A few days of clear weather had enabled the French airmen to photograph the wire entanglements and parallels behind the ridges ; and all the French gunners used their pieces in howitzer fashion so as to get indirect fire effects. Even the ordinary light field-gun—the " 75 "—had a device which enabled it to be used somewhat in the fashion of a howitzer, so that it could throw shells high into the sky to an altitude at which they would fall behind an intervening hill-top. The arc of fire of a " 75 " was not as great as that of a howitzer ; nevertheless, it was extremely useful in all this downland fighting. It was a great gun the " 75."

The second great French bombardment shattered the German defences around Tahure, and the great down of Tahure commanding the railway was captured by a

TROPHIES OF GERMAN TRENCH WARFARE.
German trophies captured by the French in Champagne. Miscellaneous collection of hand-grenades, bombs, and gas-cans, with a trench-mortar shell and a land-mine.

FRENCH SOLDIER WITH GERMAN GAS-CANS.
French soldier posing with cans of poisonous and " weeping-gas," captured from the enemy. The Germans carried these cans attached to their belts in the manner illustrated in the above photograph.

Picardy Division, which took some hundreds of prisoners. There was also a very fierce struggle among the downs north of Navarin Farm where the Moroccan troops tried to thrust into Somme Py town. They took some of the heights along the road to Souain and Somme Py, but could not reach the river line. Yet they broke up a regiment of the Tenth German Army, which had been brought from the Russian front. The French guns curtained this force off from the Py River, so that the men had no water for four days, and lived on their "iron ration." Then the Moors burst among them, and the survivors of the 4,000—four hundred and eighty-two men and ten officers—surrendered.

This attack by the Moorish troops was more in the nature of a strong demonstration, designed to weaken the defences around Tahure, and in this respect it succeeded; for at Tahure the French drove strongly within a mile and a quarter of the enemy's supply railway. Meanwhile the great German counter-attack had been launched on the British front at Loos, ending in one of the most complete disasters in the western theatre of war. The French army in Champagne profited by this weakening of the enemy, and the Breton and Vendean troops, having taken the Toothbrush Redoubt at Mesnil, closed round the Trapeze Redoubt on three sides, and blasted their way into it by aerial torpedoes and mines. In one of their mines they used more than twenty tons of high-explosive, which shattered two hundred and fifty feet of German trenches. Then day and night the French guns played on the position, until at last the surviving German garrison fled into their underground passages, and when the Breton infantry charged they met with scarcely any resistance.

In all some 26,000 German prisoners were taken in Champagne, besides three hundred and fifty officers and one hundred and fifty cannon. And as the enemy suffered terribly in his counter-attacks, the chief of which was launched on October 18th between Auberive and Rheims, the total French losses were at least balanced by those of Einem's, Heeringen's, and the Crown Prince's troops. It is calculated that the killed, wounded, and captured among the Germans were equivalent to the infantry of six army corps, or about 150,000 men. Fully twelve German army corps were shattered, and had to withdraw for large drafts. The general result of the French thrust in Champagne and the British thrust in Artois was that the enemy's entire strength was so diminished that the pressure against the Russian armies was greatly relaxed. This was the principal achievement of the western Allies. They obtained breathing space for Russia.

What the Allies achieved

The action of the Tenth French Army in Artois, under the command of General d'Urbal, with General Foch as director of all the north-western front, was not a marked success. As we have already related, the creation by German engineers of a great new valley marsh near Souchez checked at the outset the advance of the Tenth French Army and prevented it from co-operating with the First British Army in the drive on Lens. Then on the reverse slope of the Vimy Ridge, protected from French shell fire, the enemy had built a vast underground system of enormous strength. It was not until September 26th that the French forces in Artois were able to find a weak place in the German lines, and they were then held up on the north at Angres and Lieven, as we had been at Auchy and La Bassée, and the main strength of their movement was directed against the Vimy Ridge.

The French Army in Artois

On this occasion every yard of ground had to be won by desperate fighting; for on the south, above Arras, the Germans still held some communication trenches of the Labyrinth, and in the north they retained powerful gun positions from which the French troops were enfiladed. In all these adverse circumstances, and with the chalk country slippery with rain, and the air thick with mist, General d'Urbal's troops pressed on in an effort of magnificent endurance, and captured Souchez, La Folie, and a footing on Hill 140, the highest hump of Vimy Ridge. For the most part the fighting consisted of ferocious hand-bombing work, in which ground was slowly won, trench by trench, until the enemy's reserves were brought up in sufficient force to immobilise the French army. What General d'Urbal aimed at was to facilitate the advance of the First British Army, immediately on his left, by pressing the common foe strongly and forcing him to spread his army in full strength southward. When the charge of our Guards' Division and the advance of our other reserve divisions did not produce any further marked deflection of the enemy's lines, the Tenth French Army relieved its British comrades in a more direct manner by taking over the Double Crassier, Loos, and Hill 70 trenches, and there beating back the left wing of the great German counter-attacking army on October 8th. It was just the fortunes of war that, on September 25th, 1915, Sir John French and Sir Douglas Haig should have achieved a considerable local success, while General Foch and General d'Urbal made no important advance. On May 9th of the same year the positions had been reversed. It is these accidents that test to the uttermost the loyalty of allied commanders, and if they meet the tests fully, their common trials deepen their bonds of comradeship and co-operation.

SMILING FRENCH SOLDIERS AT THE END OF THE BATTLE OF CHAMPAGNE.
Proudly and happily conscious of their splendid victory, the French soldiers piled their arms and flung themselves down to rest, or gathered in groups for animated conversation about the events of the great day.

WOMEN'S SUPREME WORK IN THE WAR.

WORK OF THE NURSING ASSOCIATION : Women Doctors—Nurses Sent to Our Allies—Belgian Refugees—Socks and Mufflers—Families of Soldiers and Sailors—Care of Child Life—Substitution of Female for Male Labour—Royal Examples. NURSING THE WOUNDED : Services of British Nurses—Death of Edith Cavell—Conditions of the Nursing Service—British Nurses to the Front—Their Work in Belgium—Last Days in Antwerp—British Nurses in Serbia—A Soldier's Egg—The Hospitals at Home—Japanese Nurses at Netley—Regular Army Nurses—Territorial Nurses—Red Cross Nurses—The French Red Cross—Les Dames Infirmières—A Heroine at Rheims—Russian Nurses. THE V.A.D. AT WORK : Its War Organisation—Surplus Workers—Assistance Sent to the Front—A Personal Experience—A Storehouse of Gifts. WOMEN DOCTORS IN THE FIELD : Demand for Their Services— Dr. Garrett Anderson's Hospitals—Dr. Alice Hutchison's Work—Notable Women Doctors. WORK FOR OUR ALLIES : Dr. Haden Guest's Hospital—The Gift of Anæsthetics—Work of Quaker Women—The Abbaye de Royaumont Described—Hospitals at Troyes and Salonika—Terrible Conditions in Serbia—This Fact Illustrated. CARE OF BELGIAN REFUGEES : The First Rush—Sorting Out the Arrivals—The Refugees from Antwerp—Varied Work Done—Some Figures and Facts. COMFORTS FOR THE SOLDIERS : The Whole Country Divided into Districts—The Winter of 1914-15—A Badge of Membership—The New Scheme at Work—A Chance for Women. WOUNDED AND MISSING : An Inquiry Bureau—Prisoners and Dead Traced—Parcels for Prisoners. THE S. AND S. F. A. : Methods of Work—Liverpool Branch—Forms of Help—A Useful Society. THE NEW GENERATION : Work Done by the French—Misery in Britain in August, 1914—League of Rights—Hospital at Bromley. WOMEN AND INDUSTRIAL LIFE : In Munition Factories—Heavy Work Done by Women—Their Industrial Capacity Proved—Women in Agriculture—In Manufacturing Employments—In Railway Stations and on 'Buses—In Clerical Occupations and Shops—The War Register.

THE statue of Florence Nightingale in Waterloo Place reminds the passer-by of the supreme work which women, and women alone, can do in time of war. The care of the wounded, who are brought back from our modern battlefields in unprecedented numbers, is the great war work of women, and happily they have proved themselves fully equal to the task. Their service is, although not in the sense that Cromwell used the words, " the crowning mercy."

The handful of nurses who constitute the Army Nursing Service and the Territorial Forces Nursing Association are far too few for times of war, but they form a nucleus round which an augmented service can gather. Their chief reinforcement comes from the great amalgamation of the British Red Cross Society and the Order of St. John of Jerusalem, which has sent thousands of trained volunteers to staff its hospitals in the war zone and elsewhere. Behind these are other thousands, the members of the Voluntary Aid Detachments, commonly called the V.A.D., who look after hundreds of hospitals scattered all over the country, and also send

LADY RALPH PAGET.

As a Red Cross nurse, Lady Paget worked incessantly for the Serbians. Refusing to leave her post, she was taken prisoner by the Bulgarians when Uskub fell, but was allowed to continue her noble calling.

women to the front for various purposes. This, however, is not all. Since the Crimean War women have become emancipated, and have begun to enter professional life. Some of them have taken up the study of medicine, and women doctors are now among us everywhere. By the side of their male colleagues, some of these women have placed their skill and knowledge at the service of the wounded, and among the most successful and up-to-date hospitals in France were several staffed entirely by women.

When ample provision had been made for the great work of tending the sick and wounded, there were a vast number of women left in this country who wanted to have some little share in beating back the new barbarism, for they realised, although perhaps unconsciously, that the Great War was not a struggle of soldiers only, or even of men only, but of whole nations, and that Britain's women were as surely pitted against Germany's women as their sons and brothers in the trenches were against each other. Fortunately there was plenty of useful work which they could do, and some prominence may be given to one or two of these spheres of activity.

Britain did not wage the Great War alone, and she had certain duties to her Allies, especially to the weaker among them. In succouring the wounded, British women know no distinctions of race, and their services were given as freely to the French, even to the enemy, as they were to their own countrymen. Some went to the aid of the Russians and the Serbians, who were specially in need of assistance of this kind.

With regard to one ally, there was a special problem. The invasion and devastation of Belgium had rendered thousands of women and children homeless, and the best, almost the only asylum for them, was the island home of their big ally. To Britain they came in

Special problem of Belgium

thousands, penniless, poor in every sense of the word, and the burden of finding for them food, shelter, and clothing for an indefinite time taxed the industry and the resources of an army of voluntary women workers. However, they were equal to it, and soon every town and many villages had each its colony of Belgians, looked after by the women of the locality.

Again, our soldiers in the field were, on the whole, well-fed and well-clothed, it is true, but still they were on active service, and this meant at the best much hardship and privation. Private effort set to work to do something

and by training and environment many of these women were unfitted to grapple with the difficulties of a novel situation. Happily there was little actual distress, so they needed, not charity, but a little advice given tactfully and in due season, and in certain cases temporary aid. Many capable women devoted their energies to this question, and much useful work was done by the Soldiers' and Sailors' Families Association.

Here may be mentioned a matter of the utmost importance to the nation, and one with which women alone can deal successfully. This is the care of child life. Even in times of peace this is most important and necessary work, but it is much more so in times of war, when thousands of our best and bravest are dying in the very prime of life. The nation must take thought for the citizens of to-morrow, and must make renewed efforts to reduce materially the rate of infant mortality. Women cannot do their country a greater service than this, and early in the war many of them were alive to its importance.

All these activities were left mainly and by common consent to women, but the Great War opened up an entirely new field for them, one of which no one even dreamed in the past. As long as Britain only required for her wars an

An industrial revolution

Army of, at the most, a few hundred thousand men, there was no need to replace male labour by female to any extent, but when millions were needed, the whole position was changed. To take them away from their regular employment would derange industry entirely, unless substitutes could be found, and apart from a small reserve of boys and older men, the only possible substitutes were women. This substitution may be called the industrial revolution of 1915, for it was nothing less. Not only did women swarm into

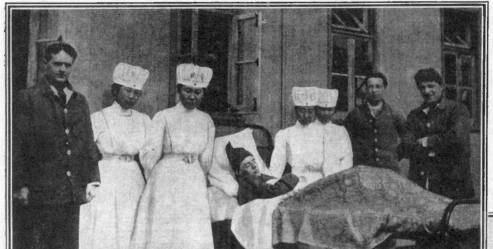

THE ALLIANCE OF EAST AND WEST.
Some of the Japanese Red Cross nurses with their wounded British charges.

to mitigate their sufferings, and by providing the troops with certain comforts, such as socks and mufflers, many valuable lives were probably saved. Everywhere —as the popular alliterative refrain about Sister Susie reminded us—women were knitting for the soldiers and huge parcels were sent to the front. At first some of this work was ill-directed, and not a little of it was well-nigh useless, but very soon there was a signal improvement, and under the able direction of Sir Edward Ward this particular form of war energy was turned to excellent account.

Another class, British prisoners in the hands of the enemy, was in direr need than even the combatants. A further useful channel for voluntary effort was not neglected. Our soldiers left behind them wives and children,

THE QUEEN-MOTHER INSPECTING THE JAPANESE RED CROSS CONTINGENT.
Queen Alexandra conversing with a member of the staff of our Far Eastern Allies' Ambulance at Netley, who came to England to assist in the care of British wounded.

NURSES FROM UNDER THE SOUTHERN CROSS WEARING THE RED CROSS OF COURAGE.
Group of Australian nurses in charge of a number of convalescent wounded Australians photographed at Hampton Court, prior to the former's departure to the Dardanelles.

commercial occupations into which they had begun to make their way before the war, but they took to novel employments, such as driving vans, punching tickets, delivering letters, and, above all, making munitions of war. In this way they made possible the addition of many thousands of men to our Army.

To these activities no one can place a limit, and certainly a single chapter of this history cannot indicate a tithe of them. A walk through a busy street, a glance at the daily life of friends and neighbours, revealed something of the nature and extent of the war work done by women. The example was set in high places. The Queen and Queen Alexandra were constantly employed in practical works of charity; the Queen of the Belgians was continually seen in the hospitals of Flanders; and the Tsaritza and her daughters wore the uniform and did the work of Sisters of Charity. The pages of this number give some slight indication of the extent to which British women of all classes took up their share of the burden of the war.

NURSING THE WOUNDED.
By A. W. Holland.

Very little in the way of public honour falls to the lot of the nursing sisters, who fulfil the oldest and most honoured of the war activities of women. From time to time one and another is mentioned in despatches, or there is a separate paragraph in the Roll of Honour allotted to nurses, but for the most part the service rendered by them is given silently and without recognition. Yet this work forms one of the noblest chapters of the war. British women, trained in the great London and provincial hospitals, have gone to the aid of the British wounded in France, in Malta, and in Egypt, and on the hospital ships;

Noble work on the Continent

they have gone, too, to Belgium, to France, to Serbia, to Montenegro, and to Russia, to the aid of our Allies, none of whom possessed an organised service such as ours.

The tale of the life and martyrdom of Edith Cavell stirred the deepest emotion in this country. She lived and died faithful to the ideals of her profession. It was fitting that in the memorial service held in her honour at St. Paul's, in October, 1915, the nursing services of the Regular Army, of the Territorial Force, of the Royal Navy, and of the Red Cross should be officially represented. In the minds of many who listened to the solemn words of the service there were thoughts of friends and colleagues, sisters

Edith Cavell's martyrdom

in the same profession, who had laid down their lives in the execution of their duty since the war began. Many of those uniformed women who sat under the dome on that historic occasion had served their country and their fellow-men with a skill and devotion that is not yet adequately realised.

From the rank and file of the profession there are demanded endurance, submission to a necessarily strict discipline, and a conscientious observance of the details of highly complicated and skilled work. In the higher ranks there is necessary a business and organising ability that is rare in either sex. If one set out to prove that women may be great administrators, no better example could be found than in the ranks of the matrons who ruled in the nursing world under the stress and strain of the Great War.

In the first terrible days of August, 1914, contingents of British nurses left London in answer to the urgent call for help from Brussels, Antwerp, Charleroi, and elsewhere. Some of them had hardly reached Brussels before the German advance, rapid beyond all expectation, overwhelmed the city. Isolated parties of British nurses in different parts of Belgium continued to tend Belgian and French wounded until their patients were taken from them by the Germans.

Some found themselves impressed into the service of the enemy wounded. When they were required to serve the desperately wounded they made no complaint, for to the nurse every man in that case is a patient and no more, but when they were commanded to tend the feet of footsore Germans, so that they might the sooner be able to resume the field against the nurses' fellow-countrymen, it was a different matter.

Nurses in enemy hands Yet the nurses who found themselves in the enemy's hands were able to render some service to our own soldiers. They were only in a few cases permitted to nurse them, but they were able in the early days to attend at the railway-stations and to take the names and addresses of the wounded prisoners, so that they might send word of their condition to their friends at home. The British nurses stranded at Charleroi contrived, after some thrilling adventures, to escape over the frontier into Holland. Those in Brussels were eventually given passports, not,

HEROIC SCIONS OF A TRAGIC MONARCH.
Princess Helena, King Peter's only daughter, who worked as strenuously for her unhappy subjects in the ward as did her father on the field. Prince Alexander, her brother, is seen facing the camera.

however, by the direct route through Holland, but by a weary round-about journey through North Germany to Copenhagen. A small group of them made their way to Petrograd to join the Russian Red Cross when the rest of the party returned to England.

In Antwerp the British nurses remained to the last with their patients. When the bombardment began on October 7th a shell pitched into the garden of Mrs. St. Clair Stobart's hospital. Within twenty-five minutes the nurses, women orderlies, and doctors had got all their patients downstairs into the cellar. Next day, as the bombardment proceeded, they discharged those wounded men who were able to walk, and those who could not be otherwise provided for were put on a motor-lorry and taken to Ostend. The women orderlies deserve a share of the honours.

The tale of one young girl who accompanied a motor-ambulance into the Belgian firing-line in Flanders,

and helped to remove the wounded under heavy fire, has been made public. She was not the only one who rendered this dangerous service in the field.

Those who answered the call to Serbia in the New Year of 1915 had, perhaps, the hardest task of all. The earliest contingents had to cope with conditions which were indescribably bad. They went to hospitals where the wounded and the fever patients lay huddled together on filthy mattresses, or on the floor, swarming with vermin. Gradually, by dint of hard and ceaseless toil, they brought order and cleanliness out of chaos and filth. The fever patients were separated from the wounded, and the typhus epidemic was got under, but not before it had taken its toll of the nurses' lives.

The Red Cross nurse in Serbia found it necessary to adopt a novel costume to suit the conditions of her work. She wore a combination garment with the trousers tucked safely away into high boots, with an overall for appearance sake, a cap which entirely covered the hair, with anklets and wristlets soaked in camphor oil. Some of the nurses, in their anxiety to fit themselves for their task, even learned Serbian, and they accommodated themselves with extraordinary success to an environment which lay quite outside their experiences at home. There is a story of a Serbian patient who was invariably in possession of a new-laid egg. No one knew how this came about until it was discovered that the obedient hen laid it in the soldier's bed! The nurse who made this discovery had travelled a long way from the ordered cleanliness of a great London hospital. Adaptability was an essential for the volunteer for work in the Balkans, where comedy and tragedy were both found.

A less exciting lot fell to the share of the women who worked in the hospitals at home, out of sound of the guns and away from the more horrible sights of the war. The nurse serving in a military hospital in France had the interest that always attaches to foreign service. But the great majority of our nurses did their work in the great hospitals at home. These home-staying sisters deserve honour as high as that paid to the nurses whose fortune took them abroad. Their work was hard and unceasing, and the very large numbers of admissions (no civil hospital ever had so large a number of new cases at once as our military hospitals had when the Red Cross train came in) made great demands on the organising capacity of matrons and sisters.

The nurses serving in the hospitals belonged to nearly as many groups as the soldiers. The Army sister's grey cape with its scarlet band was to be seen with that of the Red Cross nurse with her distinctive badge. Then there was the St. John's, with the black cross on the white ground, the smart military dress of the Canadian, and now and again the Australian or the New Zealand uniform. At the British Red Cross Hospital at Netley there were some twenty or thirty Japanese sisters, and the white uniform with the little red cross on the cap was a picturesque feature of the place. The Japanese sisters came for six months, but their stay was extended for another half year. Most of them understood very little English, but they were most popular with their patients, and kept excellent discipline.

The terms of service of the nurses differ. The Army nurses (Queen Alexandra's Imperial Nursing Service), who staff the regular military hospitals, are employed in **Terms of nursing service** peace time at the large military establishments at Millbank, Woolwich, Netley, Aldershot, and on the foreign stations. They are on the Army List, and they are entitled to a pension when they retire at fifty-five. The service is under a Matron-in-Chief, who is a War Office official. After the outbreak of war the service was largely increased.

The Territorial Nursing Force is also directed from the War Office, the present Matron-in-Chief being Miss Sidney Browne. It is a comparatively new organisation, dating only from 1908. In peace time qualified nurses enrol themselves

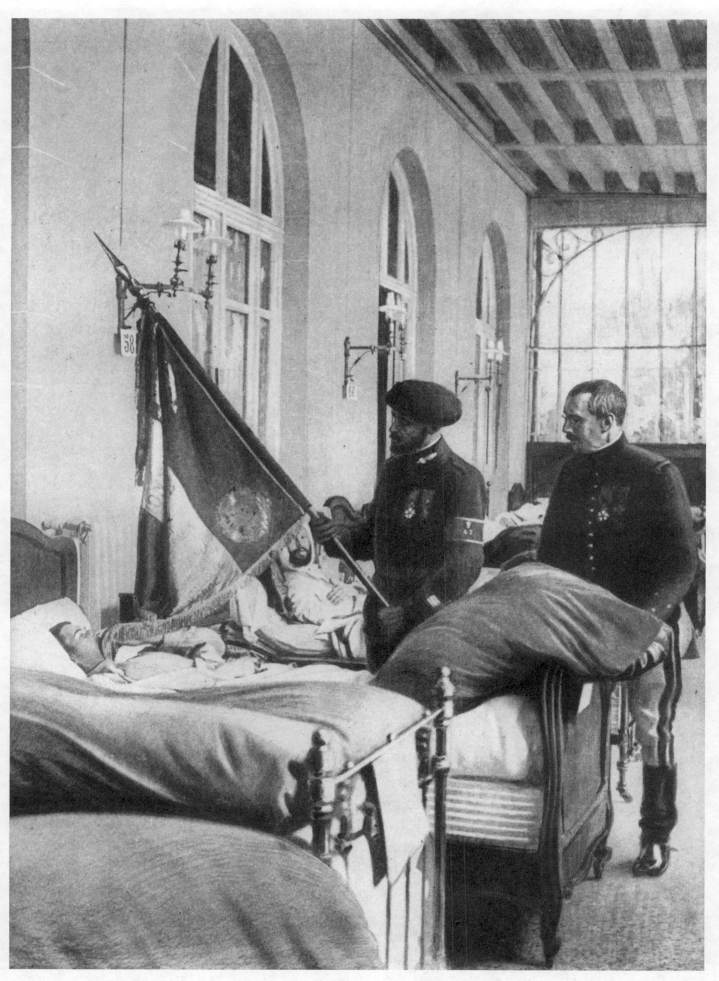

Touching ceremony in a French hospital. Wounded Chasseur kisses the beloved Tricolour.

Her Majesty the Queen, who founded Queen Mary's Needlework Guild.

Her Majesty Queen Alexandra, President of the British Red Cross Society.

Missioners of mercy at the convent portico. Night scene at the R.A.M.C. headquarters behind the firing-line in France.

LADY RALPH PAGET BIDDING GOOD-BYE TO FRIENDS LEAVING USKUB, IN ANTICIPATION OF THE CITY'S FALL.
When the Bulgarians captured Uskub, Lady Paget decided to remain behind with her wounded Serbian patients and staff of nurses. She is here seen, wearing the Serbian decorations conferred on her by King Peter, in front of General Popovitch and another Serbian officer.

in the Territorial Nursing Force, but like the Territorials themselves they pursue their ordinary civil duties. As they are, however, nurses in full practice, they are ready when the call of mobilisation comes. The Territorial hospitals do not exist in peace time, but the buildings are earmarked, and at the outbreak of war they were immediately requisitioned. At Birmingham, for instance, the Territorial Hospital was housed in the University, and an excellent hospital it made. The hospitals staffed by the T.F.N.S., like the regular military hospitals, have greatly increased their borders since 1914, and the Territorial Hospital at Manchester alone had 4,000 beds in September, 1915.

The Red Cross nurse was a volunteer serving under the Joint War Committee of the British Red Cross Society and the Order of St. John of Jerusalem. The Nursing Department of the Joint War Committee was placed under a Board of Matrons, with Miss Swift as Matron-in-Chief, by whom the qualifications of the nurses were examined before they were posted to hospitals at home or abroad.

The Naval Nursing Service is a separate service. The naval sisters are engaged in peace time in the naval hospitals at Haslar, Chatham, and Plymouth, and on the principal foreign stations.

But whether the war nurse serves under the War Office in a Regular or Territorial hospital, or serves in a Red Cross hospital, she must have her full nursing certificate. In the military hospitals she had R.A.M.C. orderlies under her as assistants in the wards, but these **Women hospital** men were rapidly replaced by women **orderlies** probationers or Voluntary Aid Workers, so that the trained R.A.M.C. men might be released for service in the field. In the Red Cross hospitals the orderly work was for the most part in the hands of women from the beginning.

The ward of a military or Red Cross hospital on visiting days unfortunately soon became familiar to many, and there is no one who had friend or relative lying there who has not cause to be grateful to the nurses who gave their strength and energy to the work of restoring the sick and wounded to health, or mitigating their sufferings by all the means that nursing science could command.

Under the French Croix Rouge, there are three societies which exist to care for the sick and wounded : The Société

de Secours aux Blessés Militaires (which includes both men and women), the Association of French Ladies, and the Union of French Women. These three form the French Red Cross, and establish auxiliary hospitals for the care of wounded soldiers and sailors. At the outbreak of war the French Red Cross put at the disposal of the Government 16,125 beds, and 4,000 dames infirmières and infirmières surveillantes, with medical staffs, trained women clerks, and storekeepers.

The training of the dame infirmière is quite different from that of our trained **Training of the** nurse or V.A.D. worker. She obtains her **dames infirmieres** training in peace time in the dispensaries maintained by the Red Cross Society for the assistance of the poor. There her instruction is limited, but is, as far as it goes, very thorough, especially in the matter of the application of rigid cleanliness to the treatment of wounds. The course lasts four months, at the end of which the student obtains her diploma if she passes successfully the prescribed oral and written examination. To obtain a superior diploma the student must give a good deal of time and study for two years more, concluding with four months' service in the mornings at a military or civil hospital. Thus though our French allies have not the advantage of a great body of trained nurses such as we have in England, they have a great number of women who have had a limited training, and who have been fully recognised by the Government.

Frenchwomen showed abundant heroism in nursing the sick. Who can forget the calm and heroic courage with which Sœur Julie defended her wounded when the Germans broke into Gerbéviller in the first flush of their victory in Lorraine ? Many others displayed equal calmness and presence of mind in the face of the enemy. There was the heroine of Rheims, Madame Mazuechi, Spanish by birth, who with her husband left her chateau outside Rheims, not to seek safety in some distant place, but for a cellar in the city, which they made a centre for the help and relief of the wounded when the first bombardment by the Germans began. Out of 2,900 cases treated in Rheims in one fortnight, half were attended to by Mme. Mazuechi herself. Perhaps no woman worked harder under shell fire than this devoted woman.

The Russian Red Cross sisters followed the armies in

185

HELPLESS VICTIMS OF THE "FUROR TEUTONICUS."
Group of picturesque Serbian women and children at a home and hospital for orphaned Serbs founded by Mme. Grovitch, wife of the Serbian Under-Secretary for Foreign Affairs, who is seen with an infant patient.

A PLEASANT CHAT OFF DUTY.
Miss Sandes, one of the British nurses who worked consistently in Serbia throughout the war, conversing with the Director of the Fourth Reserve Hospital at Valjevo, situated a few miles to the south of Belgrade.

the field. We get a glimpse of their contempt of danger and death in the pages of Miss Violetta Thurstan's book. Russian women were not, in fact, content with the service of the wounded, but in many cases took their places as combatants in the firing-line beside their husbands and brothers.

THE V.A.D. AT WORK.
Vital Service to Army Organisation.

The official world in this country is slow to recognise voluntary effort, and in the early months of the war it looked as if there was to be little use made of the patriotism of the members of Voluntary Aid Detachments, who had been at pains to prepare themselves in peace for the duties that would devolve upon them in war. The organisation of the Voluntary Aid movement approximates to that of the Territorial Force in that it is local. The idea underlying the original scheme was that in case of invasion there should be complete local arrangements for the care of the wounded, and for the assistance of the old and the weak. The local detachment was prepared at a moment's notice to equip a hospital, to provide its personnel, and the necessary stretcher-bearers and transport. Its members qualified by passing the First Aid and Nursing examinations of the St. John Ambulance Association.

The V.A.D. hospitals, of which there were some seven hundred and fifty in Great Britain, served as auxiliaries to the military hospitals. The expenses of doctors and nurses were met from the funds of the Red Cross and St. John's Societies. Much of the provisioning was met by local subscriptions, as the War Office allowance of two shillings to three shillings per day per bed occupied was not over generous, and in many cases no grant at all

Development of V.A.D. system

SCOTLAND'S QUOTA TO ALLAY SUFFERING IN SERBIA.
A few of the many Scottish nurses, who volunteered for work in Serbia, where their skill and devotion were taxed to the uttermost. Many of these Spartan women endured hardships in the cause of humanity comparable only to the suffering of the soldiers on the field. In addition to the horrors of war, epidemics of typhus swept through the civilian population, filling all the available hospitals with contagious cases.

was asked for. The cooking and cleaning were done without payment by the members of the detachment.

But it was soon found that the V.A.D. hospitals did not absorb the energies of the 100,000 voluntary workers who had fitted themselves, as far as opportunity allowed, for the service of the sick and wounded. The military and the hospital authorities maintained that the wounded must be in the hands of trained nurses, and took an optimistic view of the resources of the country in this matter. But the supply of hospital trained nurses is limited ; the needs of the civil population do not cease with the outbreak of war, and gradually it came to be recognised that the nurses must rely for the work of the wards partly on willing recruits. Then gradually a new system was developed.

The Voluntary Aid worker sent in her application for general service through her county director to the head-

WOMEN'S WORK ON A SERBIAN BATTLEFIELD.
Curious scene in a field near Kragujevatz, where a little Serbian girl was undergoing open-air treatment for typhus. She was a patient of Mrs. St. Clair Stobart, who was adored by the Serbians for her devotion to the sick and wounded of this ill-fated kingdom.

quarters at Devonshire House, where the Commandant-in Chief, Mrs. Furse, established a complete organisation to send Voluntary Aid workers where they were needed. She was given facilities for a brief experience of hospital life, and then, if she showed aptitude for the work, was drafted into a military hospital, where very much the same kind of work was allotted to her as would be given to an ordinary probationer in a civil hospital. Her services were in request, not only in the military hospital at home, but in France, in Egypt and at Malta.

For V.A.D. members who were qualified, not for nursing but for other work, there was a special service scheme under which women were drafted into the hospitals as storekeepers, clerks, and cooks, and so released trained R.A.M.C. orderlies for service at the front. So the V.A.D. members rendered a real and vital service to Army organisation.

They filled many rôles. A very vivid picture of one side of their work is given in the report, dated October, 1915, of a year's work in France, by Miss Rachel Crowdy, Principal Commandant in France, which is kindly placed at our disposal by headquarters.

It is just a year (writes Miss Crowdy) since the first V.A.D. Rest Station was formed in France. This first station, under Mrs. Furse, dealt with the big rush of October and November, when hundreds of wounded men were pouring down. Through the great Aisne battle, and later, through the week of Neuve Chapelle, and later still, when the wounded from Hill 60 were hourly coming down to the base, the V.A.D. members at this station worked ceaselessly, feeding the men with **A year's work in France** coffee, tea, cocoa, sandwiches, bread and butter, etc., and doing any dressings off the improvised trains which were urgently needed.

In the long periods of quiet between the rushes, the time was filled by doing laundry work for the sisters on the trains, running lending libraries for the orderlies and stretcher-bearers, making sand-bags, swabs, etc., for the hospitals, tracing misdirected letters for the soldiers, or doing whatever work seemed most needed.

Gradually other stations were formed at other points on the lines of communication, but it has needed this last week to show what work the V.A.D. members could do in real stress. Twenty-four hours after the fighting (i.e., at Loos) had begun, one Rest Station was in full swing, three improvised trains with 1,000 men in each were standing in the station. The men swarming round the big boilers of cocoa were getting hot drinks, and in the long wooden sheds by the side of the lines, where the V.A.D. Rest Station is, dressings were being done. Nurses waiting for their ambulance train, doctors from the trains waiting in the station, were all pressed into the service, the V.A.D. members waiting on them and helping with the dressings.

Then the wounded began to arrive at another of the Rest Stations, and there a trained nurse was added, and more dressings were done for the wounded from the trains. At one Rest Station I saw many wounded Germans being dressed and fed, a proof of that true international spirit of help to all sick and wounded. Another station at a base was dealing with a different kind of work, feeding

MRS. ST. CLAIR STOBART AND HER REFUGEE PATIENTS.
Mrs. St. Clair Stobart, in riding habit, in company with a group of refugee Serbians retreating from the danger zone. The figure on the extreme left is a rare type of Serbian beauty, which recalls some of the striking portraits by Mistrovic, the powerful Croat sculptor, whose inspiring work is so symbolical of the heroism of Serbia.

.the men evacuated from the hospital to make room for those worse than themselves, and giving hot drinks to the stretcher-bearers who have to work so ceaselessly in a great rush.

These stations are often formed at very short notice. One, asked for last week, was established within eight hours, and was prepared to deal with the feeding and dressing of men ; within twenty-four hours it had fed its first thousand.

Two small hospitals run by V.A.D. members for men from the Army Veterinary Camp have been doing good work for many months, and the Red Cross Hospitals in France have V.A.D. members in every capacity working for them. The kitchen of one big hospital is staffed entirely by V.A.D. members. Hostels for the nurses are run by them, and in one place a V.A.D. dispenser is responsible under the medical officer for all the drugs issued in that hospital.

Over four hundred members are working in military hospitals as probationers, but these sign a contract under the War Office, and come entirely under the control of the military authorities.

Many additional services helped to alleviate the lot of the sick soldier. If the man's condition was not too serious, he found the hospital a cheerful place, where he had many luxuries and much kindness. As an example of these auxiliary services, we may quote the great gifts stores of the Compassionate Fund in the vast hospital which grew up opposite Waterloo Station, in the building designed for the use of his Majesty's Stationery Department, but transformed into the King George V. Hospital. It was a miniature emporium, from which a man might procure, without coin of the realm, pipes, matches, cigarettes, tobacco, and a hundred other of the things that brighten life.

Gifts to cheer the wounded

At Netley the stores had a great run on woolwork materials, for many a wounded man proved handy with his needle, and passed the long hours of enforced rest in embroidering his regimental colours, or in doing wonderful floral patterns on canvas. At the store he could have these things, games, and homely treasures, as well as the more orthodox "comforts." So the women who could not help in the ward, or the kitchen, or the office, found ways of brightening the hours before the soldier was called back to the firing-line.

WOMEN DOCTORS IN THE FIELD.

Records of Devotion in France and Serbia.

Women doctors were in request in civil life to do the work of men who had gone to the front. There never was so much work for women medical practitioners as there was during the Great War. Anyone who is acquainted with the work of the women doctors at an institution like the Women's Hospital for Children, in the Harrow Road, knows how admirable the work of women doctors is in the business — more important than ever at a moment when the blood of men was being poured out on

battle-fronts stretching over hundreds of miles — of reserving the child life of the community.

The skill of women doctors and surgeons was increasingly urgent for the sick and wounded fighting men. The case of the Wimereux Hospital, directed by Dr. Louisa Garrett Anderson, was a striking example. This hospital was under the jurisdiction of the British military authorities in France, who were so impressed by its excellence that Dr. Garrett Anderson was asked to organise a military hospital at home which should be entirely staffed by women doctors, nurses, and orderlies. The result was the military hospital in Endell Street, in charge of Dr. Garrett Anderson and Dr. Flora Murray, where the British wounded were entirely under the care of women.

This chapter contains a brief account of the Scottish Women's Hospitals in France, working under the French military authorities. It is impossible to chronicle here all that women doctors accomplished in the war zone, but some examples may be given. Dr. Alice Hutchison had a good deal of war experience before the outbreak of the present conflict, for she was attached to the Bulgarian Army in the Balkan Campaign, and was present at the Battle of Kirk Kilisse. In the winter of 1914-15 she was asked by the great Belgian surgeon, Dr. Depage, to take charge of the typhoid hospital at Calais. Then in April she left for Serbia, to join the Scottish Women's unit at Valjevo. On her way she was detained for some time at Malta, and worked among the first arrivals of British wounded from the Dardanelles.

English women and Scottish women won the gratitude of the Serbs for the great efforts made in that country. A distinguished bacteriologist, Dr. Helen Porter, gave her skill and knowledge of research work to the problem of stamping out the epidemic of typhus in Serbia. Dr. Eleanor Soltau, who was chief medical officer of the Scottish Women's Hospital at Kragujevatz, was decorated by the Serbian Government. Dr. Elsie Inglis, not content with organising two fresh hospitals for the same organisation in Serbia, managed a Serbian field hospital in addition. These are only some of the women who, having made their mark in the profession in peace, afterwards practised their art in the military hospitals.

Some of the leaders

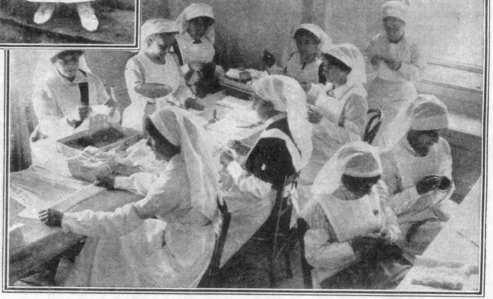

GREAT METROPOLITAN CENTRE FOR WOMEN'S WAR WORK.
Interior scene in Lady Parsons' Streatham Common War Supply Depot, where a staff of ladies is seen busily preparing surgical dressings which were despatched to Red Cross hospitals at home and abroad. This establishment was the second largest in the kingdom, employing seven hundred to eight hundred voluntary workers, each of whom contributed one shilling a week to the general fund. The smaller portrait is of Lady Herbert Parsons, one of the chief organisers of the Streatham Common War Supply Depot.

"GREEN CROSS" CORPS ON THE MARCH.
Members of the Women's Reserve Ambulance, known as the Green Cross Corps, and recognised by the War Office, marching to St. James's Church, Piccadilly, having been reviewed by Colonel Dundonald Cochrane, C.B.

WORK FOR OUR ALLIES.

The Hospital in the old Abbaye de Royaumont.

British women have worked hard among our wounded allies. There were a large number of Anglo-French hospitals in France, notably the two great establishments at Nevers and Limoges, which owed much to the efforts of Dr. and Mrs. Haden Guest. The Anglo-French hospitals were partly staffed by British nurses, sent out by the British Red Cross and the Order of St. John, though fewer nurses served there after the home need increased. Millicent

Women's devotion and good sense Duchess of Sutherland founded the hospital at Dunkirk, and when the unit was driven out of that place by shell fire, the work was carried on at Boulogne.

Englishwomen, with sisters from the British Dominions beyond the seas, worked side by side with Belgian Red Cross workers in the Belgian hospitals. In Serbia the devoted women, who came to the aid of that valiant country in its struggle against disease in the spring of 1915, stood by her in her still direr need, staying at their posts when the enemy threatened from the north and the east.

In their gifts for the service of the wounded, those who remained at home showed insight and good sense. The French War Emergency Fund, closely connected with the St. John Ambulance Association, sent large quantities of sorely needed things to the French hospitals. The work arose out of the personal experience of a lady who had worked in the French hospitals, and knew how hard put to it the authorities were to supply the men's needs. When she returned to England, she sent bales of clothing, cases of drugs, etc., to the hospitals of Normandy and Brittany, and gradually the work was extended.

The readers of "The Englishwoman" had the happy thought of providing anæsthetics for the French wounded—ether and chloroform for major operations, ethyl chloride for use in field-ambulances, and morphia for use in the field. Women members of the Society of Friends worked with the Friends' Committee behind the lines for the assistance of the French civilian population, and tried to build up the shattered homes, and to supply the means for the resumption of normal life. The Quaker women in Flanders supplied milk for nursing mothers and for babies, clothing for the destitute, and orphanages where children

STANDARD BEARERS OF THE GREEN CROSS.
Banners were presented to the W.R.A.C. by Colonel Cochrane. Our photograph shows members of the corps carrying their new banners to St. James's Church, where the colours were blessed.

could be placed in safety outside the war zone. The Wounded Allies Relief Committee maintained and managed two hospitals, at Dieppe and Limoges, which had between two hundred and three hundred French patients.

Any one of these efforts deserves a separate chapter, and if we select for more detailed description the hospital for French wounded at the Abbaye de Royaumont, it is because one instance must serve, and this one is particularly suited to the present chapter, because it was not only entirely staffed by British women, but was supported, like the other units of the Scottish Women's Hospitals in France and Serbia, by **One typical effort described** a women's organisation—the National Union of Women's Suffrage Societies.

The hospital was a beautiful old French abbey, standing in lovely grounds, about seven miles from Chantilly, and about twelve miles from Creil, a French Red Cross distributing station. Over 1,400 French wounded have passed through this hospital, which was a recognised auxiliary under the French military authorities. Its staff consisted of eight women doctors and surgeons, under Dr. Frances Ivens, a well-known Harley Street radiographer, Dr. Agnes Forbes Savill, a bacteriologist, thirty nurses, nearly as many orderlies, with men and women chauffeurs, women

MAKING GAS FOR PEACEFUL PURPOSES.

At Chew Magna, near Bristol, Mrs. Summers and her daughter under-took the laborious task of making the gas for the village. Under the supervision of a male manager, they did all the strenuous work involved.

cooks, and clerks. Both on the medical and surgical sides the Abbaye de Royaumont, with its splendid, airy rooms and its beautiful terrace, was a great success; it received generous praise from the French Army Medical Staff, and from General Joffre himself.

In all military hospitals, especially in improvised ones, there is much hard work besides the nursing and the medical attendance. The clerks of the clothing depart-ment at Royaumont had their work cut out for them. Miss Vera Collum has described this side of the work.

Picture (she says) the weary men arriving after twelve miles' drive in our ambulances, and, after being refreshed with hot soup and cigarettes in the hall, being conducted to a great vaulted ward with church windows, into any one of which we might stow away a little English village church quite comfortably. During their passage through the hall we seize upon their baggage and accoutre-ments, and label them—and the French soldier carries enough stuff on his back to clothe a regiment. Sometimes

Washing and mending

he has lost it all before he reaches us; but he is wonderfully tenacious, the citizen soldier of France, and, as a rule, the pile of baggage is enormous. As the men are bathed and put to bed, their uniforms and under-clothing are placed in numbered sacks and hauled up by a block-pulley to the fifth story, where our vast attics are. Time was when they went up on my back. The next morning we sort out the sacks, mark and send the soiled linen to the wash, collect the men's treasures (pipes, tobacco, love-letters, war trophies, and the like), into little parcels, put out the torn things for our mending heap, and store the sacks in numbered order in one of what Royaumont calls "garrets." We could put a row of our modern villas into our big store-room. The men's outdoor clothes go into a separate attic, where they hang from the good old rafters in a current of fresh air, and everything is numbered and entered up in our alphabetical record—grown from a penny notebook into a full-blooded card index. The next stage is the mending. A wonderful Frenchwoman, Madame Fox, the wife of a British resident in our village (Asnières-sur-Oise), undertakes the mending of the washed linen. Most of her helpers are volunteers, but the head of the local rubber toy manufactory has reinforced her working party by the loan of two of his women operatives for the entire afternoon every day of the week. We ourselves tackle the uniforms, with the noble assistance of Mrs. Hacon, an N.U. worker well-known in the Shetlands, through whose ingenuity I have seen the "veste" of an artilleryman, minus half a sleeve, made into a wondrous garment with warm woollen cuffs—all because there was nothing in the world to mend it with but a pair of navy blue bed-socks and an old scarlet sock to repair a breach made by shrapnel in a pair of infantryman's trousers.

Indeed, we are earning a good name for this women's hospital for turning out our men not only mended in body but repaired in

equipment. They say the men from Royaumont are recognisable by their healthy red cheeks and their clean, good clothes. It is a real pleasure to see the wounded man's face when he sees his kit, washed and renovated, folded ready for him to wear.

A striking tribute to the effi-ciency of the Scottish Women was the urgent request made by the French military authorities that they should establish a second hospital at Troyes. This hospital differed from Royaumont and from any other French hos-pital, in that the French wounded were, for the first time, being nursed under canvas. The Administrator at Troyes was Sir John French's sister Mrs. Harley. This unit, which was directly under the French military authorities, was afterwards ordered to

LEARNING TO READ THE GAS-METER.

Reading the gauge in order to check the amount of gas required. In the technical part of the business of gas manufacture the women were assisted by the superintendent.

Marseilles, to proceed to Salonika, and to be attached to the French army in the Balkans. Very few voluntary hospitals were so highly honoured as to be invited to follow the army in the field, and its medical head, Dr. Louise McCroy, received the grade of médecin-en-chef in the French Army.

In Serbia the need was most urgent, and here again, in spite of the language difficulty, in spite of distance and the all but insuperable difficulties of transport, Englishwomen went to stand by the side of **Appalling conditions** our ally. From the offices of the Serbian **in Serbia** Relief Fund there went out clothing, medi-cal stores of all kinds, money, and aid of every kind. British Red Cross nurses and voluntary workers gave their lives for Serbia, and the units of the Scottish Women's Hospitals in Serbia, organised and worked by women, stemmed the tide of disease.

Serbian doctors had coped with the wounded from the first Austrian invasion in August, 1914, but the second invasion in the autumn left them with so many wounded men that it was impossible to care for all. Men died in the streets, and many were left on the floors of cafés without help until their limbs were past saving. The Austrians left behind them in their retreat a terrible enemy, typhus, which threatened to destroy the nation itself. These were the appalling conditions by which the first British helpers were faced. It was a case for the sanitary expert and for the hospital orderly, quite as much as for the nurse and the doctor. The earliest Englishwomen to arrive were those who accompanied Madame Grouitch, then Lady Paget's unit, followed by the Scottish **In a big fever** Women, the Wounded Allies Relief, and **hospital** units sent by the British Red Cross. A letter from one of the early arrivals in Serbia will show the state of things which had to be tackled.

The most terrible sight I have seen here is the big fever hospital— a huge barracks where there are said to be 1,500 cases of fever, mostly enteric, typhus, and recurrent. Among their patients the acknowledged death rate is ten a day—the fill of our hospital in a fortnight ! With a fellow-member of the unit I went over the typhus wards one day. You really cannot imagine what it was like. There were only a few doctors for their hundreds of cases, and otherwise only orderlies who are terrified for their own safety—poor wretches— and just crowd in corners, doing nothing unless driven to it. All the windows were shut, and the place literally smelt like a sewer. All along the corridors patients were packed together, and one of the corridors was so dark one could not see the patients' faces at first. The wards, as regards hopeless dirt and squalor, were worse than the worst slum dwellings I have ever seen. The patients lay on mattresses on the floor ; often three lay shivering on two mattresses on the floor. Their clothing and bedding were filthy and alive with vermin, and helpless cases are simply left to become filthier and filthier.

All this was changed. The Serbian hospitals were revolutionised, and the revolution was due in no small part to the devotion of the two or three hundred British women attached to the various Serbian hospitals, and they bravely faced the new and menacing situation when Serbia was attacked in overwhelming force in October, 1915. Among the noble women who laid down their lives in this service of glory was the gifted playwright and authoress, Mrs. Dearmer.

CARE OF BELGIAN REFUGEES.
By the Hon. Mrs. Alfred Lyttleton.

In August, 1914, a few days after the war began and the Germans marched across Belgium, the rumours of a possible flight of refugees into England were heard. Lady Lugard, to whom eternal honour is due for her initiative in the matter, had word that a ship holding 2,000 women and children rescued from burning villages would arrive in three days. This information was, fortunately, not correct, as no preparations to receive them had been made, but it spurred on the few people who were already aware that a great effort would be asked of England. We began at once to prepare for the rush which was fortunately delayed for several days.

Hostels were opened in London and also in Dulwich, Clapham, and other London suburbs. The pause enabled us to organise these with the help notably of the V.A.D. We arranged also for the **Immensity of the** registration of each refugee. But it would **task** have taken many weeks to reduce to order the mass of letters offering hospitality and personal service, under which we were suffocated. The confusion at first was terrible. Not only did thousands of letters arrive daily, but people rushed personally to the little rooms in General Buildings, Aldwych, to offer their help in one form or another. When the stream of fugitives began to arrive

DUTCH CONCENTRATION CAMP FOR BELGIAN REFUGEES.
At Bergen-op-Zoom the Dutch authorities provided a large concentration camp for Belgian civilians who escaped from their country during its occupation by the hated Prussians. The camp was under military supervision, and was crowded with women and children.

LOOKING AFTER SOLDIERS' WIVES.
Making garments for wives of soldiers at the front at the Hammersmith branch of the " Tipperary Homes."

OLD GLOVES FOR NEW WAISTCOATS.
Trying on waistcoats made of old gloves. The Ladies' Territorial Committee, at the cost of a shilling apiece, made hundreds of these garments.

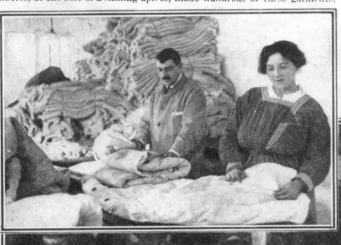

NO ONE TOO YOUNG OR TOO POOR TO HELP SOMEHOW.
Girls of the Rockingham Street Schools knitting for the sailors on H.M.S. Drake. Above : Examining sleeping-bags before despatch.

numbers of volunteers devoted themselves to the task of meeting the trains, sorting out the poor bewildered people as they arrived, and escorting them to the various temporary shelters which had been equipped.

A committee had by then been formed, with Lord Hugh Cecil as its chairman, and Lord Gladstone as its treasurer, and to this committee the General Omnibus Company lent the services of Mr. Campbell, who undertook the huge task of organising the transport of the refugees all over the British Isles.

Roughly, the scheme of the committee was to billet the refugees in homes provided by private hosts. Tens of thousands of hosts came generously forward and offered to house and feed the fugitives, who had just been driven from their homes and had in most cases lost everything they possessed. The difficulty of classifying and registering the thousands of offers, the fitting of the guests to the hosts in batches of twos and threes, the temporary housing, the final despatch of the refugees to the country districts, all involved an immense labour.

It was very soon realised that assistance from the Government was an absolute necessity. Mr. Samuel had publicly in the House of Commons offered the hospitality of the nation to the Belgian refugees, and the Local Government Board opened various **The rush from** camps and wards under the management **Antwerp** of the Metropolitan Asylums Board. At first accommodation was provided in some of the large workhouses—Marylebone, Endell Street, Edmonton, and so on—and later Alexandra Palace was furnished, as was Earl's Court. Just when it seemed as if a certain order and routine had been established and a system devised for dealing with thousands of individuals in detail, Antwerp fell. I shall never forget the day, when working quietly in the office at General Buildings, a message came up from a temporary waiting-room, which had been hired at the skating rink next door, for someone to come down immediately. I went, little thinking that for a full year I should be working in the great ramshackle building through which thousands of refugees have passed.

The rush was difficult to deal with. Four or five thousand people a day would arrive ; all had to be seen, talked to, and helped. People came eagerly from every part of the country and took away the refugees in batches of sixty and seventy. Local committees were formed, and there were soon 2,000 large committees in existence, without whose devoted work the whole enterprise would have been impossible. Glasgow, Bradford, Dublin, Cardiff, to mention only a few of the big towns which sheltered many hundreds ; smaller places, such as Blackpool, Exeter, Swindon, and Carnarvon ; villages and private people all sent representatives up to Aldwych to pick out the Belgians best suited to the hospitality they had to offer.

The Belgian Consulate early in the war, in conjunction with the War Refugees Committee, opened a special office in General Buildings, and here, too, helped by a band of volunteer workers, the people who had come from rich and sheltered lives were specially cared for.

Gradually the stream slackened, but the work of caring for our guests remained. The War Refugees Committee was like the government of a small country ; it had to legislate for the community ; it had to house, clothe, feed, doctor, nurse, marry, christen, bury, punish, fine, employ, educate, and pension something like 300,000 people. Many mistakes were made, and at first there was much confusion ; but Lord Gladstone, and the able Honorary General Secretary, Mr. A. Maudslay, gradually produced order out of chaos, and the whole organi- sation ran easily and smoothly. Some idea of its size and scope may be given by a few facts. Three hundred and seventy people were working in General Buildings alone. There were 2,000 local committees who cared for anything from twenty to 5,000 refugees each. About 30,000 private people gave hospitality. Thousands and thousands of pounds passed through the Committee's hands, more than half a million garments were given away, and tons of foodstuffs generously sent by the Colonies were distributed through the agency of the National Food Fund.

Some facts and figures

The War Refugees Committee doctored 5,684 people in its private dispensary, doctors and nurses giving their services voluntarily. Many workshops for the refugees were opened, and employment of all kinds was found for them. A considerable number worked in munition factories, others tilled the ground ; many who could not fight from various causes got places as correspondence clerks in business houses, as shop assistants, motor mechanics, etc.

COMFORTS FOR THE SOLDIERS.

By Mrs. Massey Lyon.

The Government scheme for the organisation of voluntary work for the troops was the most important development in that branch of war work which, when all is said and done, is the one which can absorb the greatest amount of the energy of women-kind.

As most people know, the organisation was after a time placed under Col. Sir Edward Ward, Bart., K.C.B., K.C.V.O., who was appointed Director-General of Voluntary Organisa- tions, or, as he was known in Army parlance, the D.G.V.O. Sir Edward Ward's reputation as an organiser was as well known as the charm of his personality, and both played no inconspicuous part in the work which was to co-ordinate voluntary effort all over the country.

Under the scheme, complete in its simplicity, the whole country was divided into districts under the Lords-Lieutenant, Lord Provosts, Lord Mayors, Mayors, and Provosts. They, in their turn, divided their districts into centres under responsible heads, who again had the right of redivision into any number of groups rendered necessary by the size or circumstances of their districts. Each group was responsible immediately to the one above it, both for the quality of the work produced and the carrying out of orders given to its workers ; so that, by the time the Lord-Lieutenant, or whoever might be the official head of the main district, was reached, a vast amount of guaranteed work was accumulated. This was at the disposal of the D.G.V.O. to meet demands which he received direct from the Army authorities, and by this means certainty was assured that whatever was needed by a particular unit at a particular time reached that unit.

Devolution of responsibility

WOMEN COAL-HEAVERS IN SCOTLAND.
Owing to the shortage of male labour, women were engaged by several Scottish coal merchants. All had been used to heavy farm-work, and they proved most efficient in their new employment. At the top : Weigh- ing out coal in hundredweights into bags from the railway trucks. In the centre : In the depot, filling bags for delivery At the bottom : Bringing in vans to the depot after delivering a load.

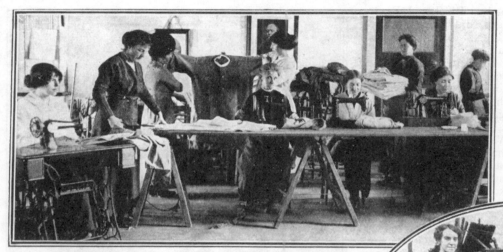

WOMEN'S WORK IN GALLANT LITTLE WALES.
Inside a women's war-work club at Swansea, where members were engaged in making shirts for soldiers at the front. The women of the Principality worked as loyally as the men fought gallantly.

it was a small one, in the great machine by which alone victory could be brought to our arms. For every one who supplied a definite purpose in that machine played a definite part in the whole.

In recognition of this truth, the Army Council provided each worker under the scheme who had proved her mettle with a special badge. This was only given to those who had worked in an approved manner for three

By this means the overlapping and waste which occurred in the winter of 1914-15 was prevented. Emergencies are notoriously extravagant, and the outbreak of war was a very big emergency indeed. It is not surprising, therefore, that some regiments were, as they expressed it "snowed up" in comforts, while others were left out in the cold—in a very literal sense of the words.

The new organisation also enabled the Army authorities to make use of voluntary work, and this is
Army Council recognition an important point, for unless they could count upon a definite number of definite things at the time they were wanted, all the "comforts" contributed (and incidentally blocking up transport already strained to the utmost) were of no use to them. The provision of warm things cannot be left to chance, or at any rate should not be. And this aspect had its own importance to sensible women, for it not only gave gratifying recognition to their work, but enabled them to play their own distinct part, none the less important because

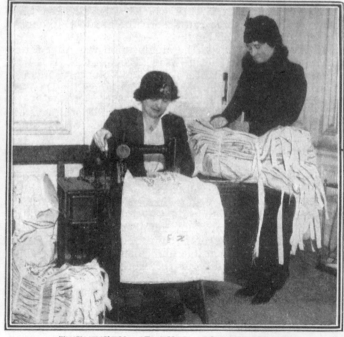

IN ONE OF THE BORDER MILLS.
Weaving tartan for soldiers' uniforms in one of the Border Tweed Mills. A large number of women were employed in these mills, keeping the armies of Britain and her Allies supplied with the universal khaki.

months, and was forfeited unless the due conditions were complied with, so that it was no mere form, but a tangible proof of recognised work

Work under the scheme divided itself naturally into two sections—for the men on active service and those in hospital. So one had one's choice as to which one

"FOR THOSE IN PERIL."
At the headquarters of the British and Foreign Sailors' Society, which successfully undertook the arduous work of supplying men of the Navy with thick jerseys and socks.

TWENTIETH CENTURY POWDER-HORNS.
Making ammunition bags for the Fleet. Wives of officers and men of the senior Service found occupation at Bo'ness, Scotland, converting red raw silk into pockets to hold powder and shells.

worked for. A scheduled list of articles required for each was provided by the D.G.V.O. for the guidance of each centre, each article being made according to the design passed by experts at headquarters. This immediately stopped the waste which had been caused by the making of garments, etc., on unpractical lines.

A certain amount of dismay was expressed at the announcement of the scheme, lest it should damp the ardour of the many societies and groups of workers all over the country. But very little consideration served to prove that the reverse must be the case, for every such body could "come in" under the central council, thus receiving Government recognition of its work and the right to the description "approved by the War Office."

Co-operation with headquarters — The big societies, whose work has become a household word amongst us—such as the Red Cross, the Order of St. John, Queen Mary's Needlework Guild, the Cavendish Square Hospital Depot, and so forth—soon received this imprimatur.

Of course, there were many tangible advantages to those co-operating in this way with headquarters; for instance, free carriage was given, and arrangements made in many cases where individual workers could have the advantage of the reduction in cost of materials bought in bulk. But more potent than such things to patriotic Englishwomen was the knowledge that they were playing their real part in the great work of the war, and, from the practical standpoint, that whatever they did, whether the knitting of a sock or the making of a simple bandage, went directly and inevitably to supply an immediate need. No more

would there be any uncertainty as to what was wanted; no more the lingering fear that the expenditure of time and money—both commodities of increasing value amongst us—might be wasted; no more should we hear horrid rumours of bales of garments, each representing no little time and trouble, and often of sacrifice too, lying about in some forsaken district, or of mufflers being used to polish harness, and so on.

This was doubly important in 1915; for, on the one hand, there was less money to spare, and on the other, the number of women who were ready to sew and knit

ITALIAN WOUNDED UNDER THE ARMS OF THE RED CROSS.
A most striking photograph showing the Italian Red Cross actually at work on the field of battle. The kind-faced sister and the capable Red Cross men were as unconscious of the presence of the photographer as the wounded soldiers whom they were tending. In circle: Princess Lætitia with three wounded Italians at the military hospital established at the Royal Castle of Moncalieri under the auspices of the princess.

had been considerably reduced ; for the months of war had provided numberless outlets for energy and devotion, and innumerable women, who previously found no outlets for their energies save in this way, were by then engaged in canteens, in nursing, and a hundred other directions. Many and many a woman with home duties which must come first, or denied the gifts of youth or of health, had been feeling just a little envious of the opportunities so gladly seized by those unhampered by such considerations to do something definite for England. Well, here was their chance, too ; and it was one which would be gladly welcomed and made the most of by all who realised that even the knitting of a muffler or the making of a shirt, provided it was the right muffler and the right shirt, made in the right way and at the right time, was part of the great work of securing a victory for our arms.

"WOUNDED AND MISSING."
By A. W. Holland.

The above legend brought a dark shadow into many homes. Inquiries were made, differing according to the circumstances of the inquirers, for the poor had little idea how to set about the business. Presently, one of the missing man's comrades might be home on leave, but his opinion, eagerly sought, did not necessarily dispel uncertainty. Happily, there was a department of the Red Cross given up to inquiries for prisoners of war. It had eyes and ears behind the lines in France, in the hospitals, in the neutral headquarters of the Red Cross in Geneva, and it was in regular, close touch with the War Office and the Record Office. It was not long before even into the obscurest villages of the kingdom, the knowledge penetrated that there was a place in London where an anxious mother or wife might go in search of news of one she loved.

The agony of suspense

RUSSIAN HONOUR FOR AN ENGLISH SOLDIER.

Corporal Fuller, V.C., of the Grenadier Guards, was under treatment at the No. 3 Base Hospital, Sheffield, when the King visited it, and his Majesty took advantage of the opportunity personally to pin on his breast the Cross of the Order of St. George (third class) which had been conferred upon the gallant soldier by H.I.M. the Tsar. Above : During his tour of inspection in the North, the King paid a visit to the No. 3 Base Hospital, Sheffield, and spoke to many of the wounded. His solicitude for his men was touching in its sincerity, and was gratefully appreciated.

GIRLS MAKING BOXES TO HOLD THE SHELLS THAT OTHER GIRLS HAD MADE.

At first it was supposed that much of the work in the munition factories would be too heavy and arduous for women, but in fact they proved themselves able to engage in every process connected with the manufacture and despatch to the front of even the heaviest shells. This photograph shows a group of girls making ammunition boxes and placing in them the rests that support the shells.

Sometimes there was definite news that the soldier was a prisoner in Germany, in which case there was the satisfaction of knowing where the man was, and of being able to write to him, and to send him parcels of necessaries and small luxuries. The German lists of prisoners were sometimes delayed. Wounded prisoners had no opportunity of writing home if they were delayed in a hospital on the lines of communication, and it was not until they were finally settled in a hospital or an internment camp in Germany that there was any likelihood of news. Sometimes all the consolation the Red Cross Inquiry Department could give was news of how son, lover, or husband died. Details are a consolation in these circumstances, and the Red Cross inquirer obtained them from comrades, or from doctors or nurses. Occasionally the answer was that the man was dead, but even then there was a small lightening of sorrow to learn from the Red Cross that the grave, "somewhere in France," was carefully tended. "I am glad to know," wrote a private's mother in answer to a description of her son's grave, "that he lies comfortable."

News of prisoners of war

HOW BRISTOL WOMEN HELPED THE "ADVENTURERS."
True to her long tradition of service to England, Bristol sent many "adventurers" into the Navy and Army. The women of the old town flocked into the munition works, this one a converted motor-cycle works, to release their men for military duty.

came to the Red Cross in London from the German Red Cross, transmitted through Geneva. The department had news from German camps and hospitals, and was kept posted about the movements of prisoners from one camp to another. We know now how hard was the lot of our countrymen who were prisoners of war. An agency that helped us to know where *our* prisoner of war was, and told us of his movements, was indeed blessed.

Another department of the Red Cross was one at Devonshire House, where Lady Dodds and her workers undertook to send parcels to prisoners in Germany. Each parcel cost five shillings, and was sent free of charge by the Post Office. It contained currant bread, jam, tinned meat, tea, milk, sugar, cheese, dripping, soap, and tobacco, and was packed by experienced hands, so that it was sure to arrive in good condition.

There is no space to tell here of other good work of a similar kind for "all prisoners and captives," but inquiries for Belgian prisoners in Germany were carried out by the Wounded Allies Relief Committee, and there were kindly people who undertook to advise and help in the composition and the safe tying-up of parcels for prisoners in Germany. The bread must be of a kind that would stand keeping, and the experienced sender of parcels learned just what was most acceptable.

THE WORK OF THE S.S.F.A.
By Eleanor Rathbone, C.C.
Hon. Secretary Liverpool Branch.

In distributing public funds in a number of small weekly grants three methods are possible—payment through the post, at pay stations, and through home visitors. The S.S.F.A. has always preferred the last-named system, because it saves the recipient the trouble and fatigue of attendance at a pay station, renders investigation of circumstances and detection of imposture much easier, and, above all, makes possible a personal relationship between visitor and visited. The vast majority of those assisted by the Association are women and children, although aged or invalid fathers also find their way on to its lists. It is natural, therefore, that most of the visitors should

READY TO START AT A MINUTE'S NOTICE.
Members of a Canadian nursing unit photographed near the headquarters, the Thackeray Hotel, when their unit was in hourly expectation of being ordered to the front.

and in this one branch alone it is estimated that well over a quarter of a million visits were made, in the course of a year of war, to the homes of our soldiers and sailors.

When it is stated that a large proportion of these visits were paid in the very poorest quarters, and that in some streets we had as many, or more, "cases" on our books as there were houses in the street, it will be realised that this great system of war relief visitation represented an opportunity for constructive social work which it would be difficult to overestimate. Into problems of housing, of

NURSE, ORGANISER, AND ADMINISTRATOR.
Miss Amy Nunn, Matron of Roehampton House, Queen Mary's Convalescent Auxiliary Hospital for soldiers and sailors who had lost their limbs in the war.

be women. In fact, there is probably no other national association in England, engaged in spending a great national fund, which is staffed so largely by women. Some of the large provincial cities have male officers and committees, but the county associations appear to have usually women office-bearers.

The branch of the Association with which the writer is best acquainted owes much to the work of its men helpers in its treasurer's office, its regimental correspondence department, and its index room; but the work of visitation is carried out mainly, though not entirely, by women,

PHYSICAL DRILL AT THE BELGIAN NURSES' TRAINING COLLEGE.
Dr. Jacob originated the idea of training temporarily exiled Belgian girls as auxiliary nurses to aid the Belgian Military Hospitals at the front. Premises were taken in Russell Square, and, at a minimum cost of £10 each, numbers of girls were trained under Nurse Owen.

THE NEW GENERATION.
By Mrs. Despard.

In the fine work that has been done by organised women during the war for hospitals, not only in Great Britain, but in France, Belgium, and Serbia, certain other work of fully as much value to the nation must not be forgotten.

In France, where there is a conscript Army, and where, consequently, the allowances made to the wives and children of the fighters are much less

FARM WORK FOR FARMERS' WIVES AND DAUGHTERS.
Country women recovered much of their old-time usefulness in farm life as a result of the shortage of male hands. Besides the more obvious dairywork, they undertook much of the labour into which machinery enters, and drove and managed harvesters with skill and self-possession.

sanitation, of child care, of temperance or intemperance, our visitors gained an insight which they had never had before, and an opportunity for improving conditions and exercising influence which it would have been a crime to neglect. At the same time, they were instructed always to remember that the Association was not a charitable institution, and that acceptance of assistance from it should not expose the recipient to interference into her private affairs.

But, without patronage or officiousness, a tactful visitor could usually do much to help those she visited in innumerable small ways which found no record on case papers. It must be remembered that many wives of soldiers and sailors, like the soldiers and sailors themselves, were very young, and were going through a time of great anxiety, and sometimes of great loneliness. Some of them were financially better off than before the war, and this was a state of things that had its temptations. Others were feeling the pinch of the high cost of living, and even with the aid of the grant made them from the Association's funds, found it not easy to make both ends meet without lowering the standard of family life. Most well-worked branches of the Association soon evolved a complex machinery for meeting both of these types of difficulty—clubs for education and recreation, thrift schemes, sub-committees for dealing with every kind of special need. The grants in aid of separation allowance made by most branches took the form of a rent allowance in cases where the rental of the house was over four shillings a week; others adopted a slightly different basis of assistance. All made provision for emergency help in cases of special need, such as convalescent change for invalids, milk for delicate children, free medicine and medical advice for those who could not afford to pay. Even where no material help was needed, however, the system of occasional visits was still kept up, and relations of real friendship often grew up between the visitor and the visited. In the poorest districts the Association tended perhaps to be even too much relied on. In the better class or more self-respecting districts its help had to be pressed upon the recipient rather than safeguarded from her. Its functions as the helper, friend, adviser, and last, but certainly not least, the confidential private secretary of the soldier's wife or mother in her often complicated transactions with the paymaster, were increasingly recognised, not only among the women, but among the soldiers and sailors themselves.

Complex machinery required

COUNTRY LIFE IN THE HEART OF THE TOWN.
Novel scenes were witnessed at Carlton House Terrace, London, in the course of the exhibition of farm work available for women. Hardly anyone would imagine that this pretty pastoral scene could have been photographed, as it was, within a quarter of a mile of Charing Cross.

NOVEL CLASSES IN CAMP COOKING.
At the King's College for Women, London, special classes were started to teach nurses leaving for the front how to cook out of doors. The classes were well attended and greatly enjoyed, the novelty of the course appealing to the nurses as much as its practical utility.

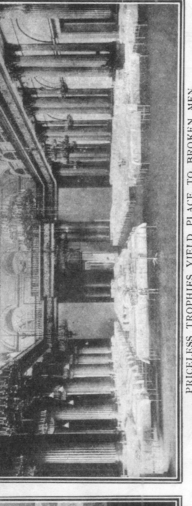

PRICELESS TROPHIES YIELD PLACE TO BROKEN MEN.

Another superb gallery of the Winter Palace, the Relic Hall, cleared of its trophies and furnished as a ward where wounded soldiers were tended and many priceless lives were saved. The name "Little Father" must have acquired a more personal meaning for the broken men welcomed into his home.

AMBULANCE TRAMS FOR HOSPITAL TRANSPORT.

A practical and comfortable way of conveying badly wounded men from the railway-stations to the various hospitals was adopted in Petrograd, where the trams were fitted with ambulance stretchers. The smooth running of these vehicles saved the patients much pain and fatigue.

THE "LITTLE FATHER'S" CARE FOR HIS CHILDREN.

The Tsar had his famous Winter Palace at Petrograd converted into a military hospital to which he gave the name Tsarevitch Alexis Hospital, after his only son. The Nicholas Hall, shown above, formed what was probably the most magnificent and luxurious hospital ward in the world.

GREAT LADIES ORGANISED FOR UNREMITTING SERVICE.

Russian nobles have been represented as the most haughty class in the world, and the most indifferent to the sufferings of others. But the entire nobility of Petrograd was organised for voluntary work to help the Army. This photograph shows one depot where ladies worked tirelessly making bandages and respirators.

than in this country, women of leisure and many engaged in keeping family businesses going organised themselves for the purpose of supplementing the meagre allowances, by giving out work and finding outdoor employment for those women who were able to undertake it.

In Paris they formed and kept up, principally by voluntary work, a bureau whose object it was to bring together families the members of which were separated through the war in Belgium and the North of France. The work was onerous. When the writer was in Paris, no less than 4,000 applications had come from English mayors about lost Belgian refugees ; sixty women clerks, all voluntary, were employed, and then, in the month of February, 1915, success had just begun to crown their long and patient efforts.

In our own country no one in touch with those living in the poorer districts of our great towns will ever forget the horror and bewilderment of the early days in August, 1914. It must be remembered that many who enlisted at that time were casual workers, living with their families from hand to mouth, and often out of work. Mothers of small children found themselves in many cases absolutely destitute. Moreover, they were ignorant as to their rights, and did not know where to apply for information.

An appalling situation The Soldiers' and Sailors' Families Association did what they could to grapple with the situation ; but in many places the work was far too heavy for them, and the relief they gave pending settlement was quite inadequate.

It was very well that this appalling situation found women organised. Had it not been so their efforts would have been ineffective. As it was, those who had banded themselves together to work for Women's Freedom were able, with but little difficulty, to throw much of their energy into the task of making life possible for the women and children whose husbands and fathers were in the Navy or at the front.

It would take volumes to record the numbers of help-centres, clubs for babies, welcomes, hospitals for women and children, cheap and good restaurants, maternity centres, that were started and carried through by women, and principally for women, during the months of war. As specially touching on the families of soldiers and sailors, the writer would refer to an admirable association formed in 1915, "The League of Rights for Soldiers' and Sailors' Dependents."

The committees of the branches of this League—and, in many cases, the officers—were soldiers' and sailors' relatives. To the committees were brought cases

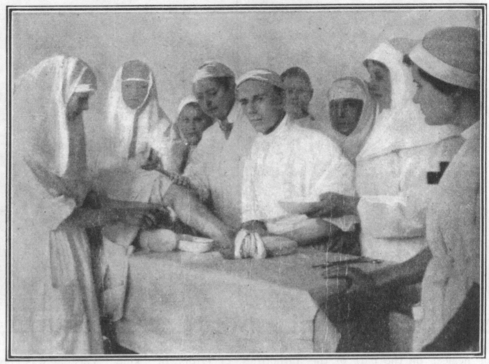

RUSSIAN GRAND DUCHESS AS A NURSE.
The Russian Royal Family worked strenuously throughout the period of the war as nurses in the hospitals of Petrograd. This photograph shows the beautiful Grand Duchess Tatiana tending the wounds of a Russian soldier.

THE RUSSIAN EMPRESS AND HER DAUGHTERS AT A HOSPITAL FOR THE WOUNDED.
Interior scene of a ward in the hospital at Tsarsköe Selo. The Grand Duchess Olga is seen on the extreme left, and in the background immediately in front of the closed door are the Grand Duchess Tatiana and the Tsaritza. The centre photograph shows Lady Sybil Grey, who acted with the Red Cross Commission at Petrograd.

ACTUAL WAR SERVICE FOR OUTDOOR WOMEN.

Work of a kind very congenial to healthy women fond of outdoor exercise was provided by the Forage Purchasing Department of the A.S.C., which engaged them to supervise the despatch of hay and straw from farms and stations. Two of them are shown on the right. They had O.H.M.S. badges on their coats and cycles, being engaged in actual war service. On the left: Four Nottingham girl window-cleaners, ready for work.

of neglect on the part of the authorities, of errors, of injustice, often arising from mistake. The recipients of allowances were made to realise, not only their rights, but their responsibilities; they met and discussed their affairs as women of business who, through their children at home and their men on the battlefields, had a heavy stake in the country; and the effect, as many of us believed, was salutary.

As more general in its objects, but as having helped women and children belonging to the Army and Navy, the hospital at Bracken Hill, Bromley, Kent, ought to be mentioned. There, in a fine house, surrounded by a beautiful garden, women who from lack of beds must leave the hospitals before they were cured, children, and expectant mothers, many of whom had husbands at the front, found a comfortable and happy resting-place during their time of trouble. Doubtless there were other homes of the same kind. This one was known to the writer. The conception and carrying out of the scheme came from one woman, and women have been her assistants right through. This hospital was started in November, 1914.

There can be no doubt that many of these institutions, such as the women's hospitals, the babies' welcomes, and the maternity centres, which in many parts of the country have done extraordinarily valuable work for the whole community, and which owe their origin to the war, have come to stay. It is to be hoped that they will expand and increase.

WOMEN AND INDUSTRIAL LIFE.
By Margaret Bryant.

There is no new thing under the sun. In an " Illustrated London News," dating from the Crimean War, there is a

AN ESSEX WOMAN WHO TOOK HER SONS' PLACE IN A VILLAGE SMITHY.

Mr. Saunders, village blacksmith of Aldbro Hatch, Essex, was assisted by his two sons until they joined the Army early in the war. One of them was killed subsequently at the Dardanelles. After their departure, Mrs. Saunders gave her husband active and efficient help in his business, and learned to shoe a horse as satisfactorily as she could mend a fire. On the left: At the forge. On the right: Filing the cap of a new shoe.

picture of our early Victorian grandmothers engaged in the making of cartridges. As a matter of fact, certain processes in armament factories have long been carried out by women, and in the months before the war there were over a thousand women employed in small arms factories. The chainmakers of Cradley Heath proved long ago that women could carry out heavy work in the metal trades, and even before the war over 25,000 women were engaged in the iron and steel works of England and Wales. But after the formation of the Ministry of Munitions there was a great extension of the labour of women in the making of war material, and where women munition makers had been counted by hundreds they were counted by thousands. Some of these women went to factory work for the first time, from purely patriotic motives, but by far the greater number were transferred from other industries, and were already inured to factory life.

Women munition workers were engaged for the most part on automatic or semi-automatic processes. But this was by no means always the case, and in instances where pains were taken to give expert training to the women, they were found to turn out excellent skilled work. There were factories where women carried out the whole work of shell-making from start to finish, involving twenty-one separate

"WOUNDED FIRST!": THE MOST BEAUTIFUL STORY OF THE WAR.
Touching scene of womanly heroism and devotion on board the hospital ship Anglia. When the vessel was sinking as the result of collision with a mine, the nurses insisted on all the wounded leaving the ship first, tying lifebelts round them and assisting them into the boats. Remaining to the last, several of these noble women perished, in addition to about eighty badly-wounded soldiers and members of the crew.

operations in the case of 18 in. high-explosive shells. In a certain munitions factory where three hundred women were employed in making shells, labourers were originally provided to lift the heavier pieces of metal, but the girls decided that they could do this themselves, and so they handled the material in all stages through all the processes.

The "Report on Women's Work" presented to the British Association, at Manchester, in 1915, quoted an engineering expert in a technical journal on the capacity of the woman munition worker. Higher tribute to her utility could hardly be forthcoming. "It may be safely said," he wrote, "that women can

SURVIVORS OF BATTLE AND SHIPWRECK.
Some of the wounded soldiers from the hospital ship Anglia, which was sunk by a mine in the Channel, on November 17th, 1915. After their terrible experience they were sent to the County of London War Hospital, where this group was taken.

THE HAPPY SMILE OF ANZAC.
Wounded Australians in charge of an escort of feminine admirers off for a picnic in the woods near Harefield, Sussex. The second photograph shows Lady Coglan (left) and Lady Talbot photographed by the bedside of a wounded Anzac, on the occasion of a garden-party in the grounds of Harefield Park, under the auspices of the New South Wales Clothing Distribution.

great service in the delicate work involved in the manufacture of the wings of aeroplanes. The previous experience of women workers was turned to account in other departments. Women who had been employed on photographic apparatus were very successful in the making of clinometers for artillery, and other instances might be adduced.

So women actually helped in the technical business of war. They put on the workmen's overalls, and showed themselves capable of hard physical toil; and they brought to their work a concentrated zeal and enthusiasm which went far to make them efficient craftswomen.

The woman industrial worker and the business woman helped

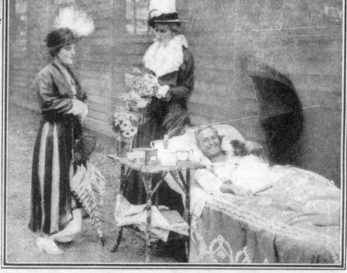

successfully handle very much heavier pieces of metal than had previously been dreamed of. Moreover, they have shown themselves capable of successfully carrying out arduous processes, such as forging, etc., which hitherto have only been performed by men, and of managing machine tools of a very different nature and requiring a very much higher standard of intellect than do automatic and semi-automatic tools.

Doing the work of men
In fact, it can be stated with absolute truth that, with the possible exception of the heaviest tools—and their inability to work even these has yet to be established—women have shown themselves perfectly capable of performing operations which have hitherto been exclusively carried out by men." In the making of fuses they excel, and some women, highly skilled in other trades, rendered

indirectly by setting free large numbers of men to join the Colours. In rural England, in spite of the farmer's deep-seated prejudice against the labour of women except as fruit pickers and possibly milkers, strong girls could be seen handling big cart-horses. The milkmaid began to return to her old province, which had been largely usurped by the cowman, and women began to take a hand in all the processes of a farm. There was on the whole more success in placing women on farms in the south - western counties than elsewhere. Certain counties gave special facilities for the training of women for agriculture, with the result that an increasing number became really skilled workers in a complicated art. The Central Committee for Women's Employment, which accomplished so much good work in the training of women for industrial occupations during the war, carried out an interesting agricultural experiment at

LOOKING AFTER THE LAND.
Lady Petre, in deep mourning for her husband (Lieutenant Lord Petre, who fell in action), with some juvenile pupils of her dairy-farm school at Thorndon Hall, Essex, whose work proved an admirable substitute for farm-hands on active service.

Radlett, in Hertfordshire. Mr. R. C. Phillimore gave the committee the use of thirty acres of land for a training scheme. There were about thirty girls, chiefly London factory girls, working there, chiefly at fruit growing, who were in due course well qualified for rural life.

The same committee enabled girls to qualify themselves for work in the more skilled branches of the leather trade at Bethnal Green. At Hammersmith the embroidery industry was revived, and in many other trades women acquired skill under the care of the committee. As the organisation was in close touch with Government departments, there was a certainty that plenty of work would be forthcoming for the women as they were trained.

Women's share in industry was, temporarily at all events, enormously increased. When the Queen's Work for Women Fund was started the problem before it was to cope with the distress among the many women thrown out of work at the outbreak of war. Later the tables were turned, and the business before the committee was to supply enough trained women to meet the demands of the industries with which it was concerned.

In every detail of daily life women workers were more and more in evidence. The morning milk was left by a girl, and a girl delivered the morning paper; at the station a girl booking-clerk handed out the ticket, another clipped it at the barrier, and though the male conductor or the guard was still at his post, the chances **Every industry** are that the railway-carriage had been **represented** cleaned out in the early hours of the morning by a woman. A woman called to inspect the gas-meter, or to rectify a defect in the geyser.

The first week in November, 1915, saw women conductors, clad in a suitable and becoming costume, on one at least of the London 'bus routes. In this instance, as was often the case on the railways, preference was given to the near relations of the man who was released to serve with the Colours. In France the tram was apt to stop at a certain point to allow the woman conductor to embrace her baby. "Allez donc! C'est mon bébé!" she cried. On the French farm ploughing, seedtime and harvest, found the fermière at her husband's post in the fields. English women did not fill the occupations of their men at the front to the same extent as in France, but we moved

rapidly in that direction. It was clearly in that development that economic safety lay, as our armies increased. For the war was one of money as well as guns, and women were compelled to bear an increasing part in the work of the nation. In clerical work, where there has always been a large field for women, they replaced men to a very large extent, and in some businesses like banking, which had hitherto been reserved for men, they were employed in considerable numbers.

The Government Departments employed many temporary women clerks. For the most part the State employed its temporary women assistants in the lower grades, but there were brilliant excep- **In the Diplomatic** tions. At the end of October, 1915, it was **Service** announced that a woman, Miss Pressley Smith, well known for her work in Edinburgh, had been appointed Secretary of the British Legation at Christiania. The Diplomatic Service is the most carefully guarded of all, but Sir Edward Grey is a staunch champion of feminism.

The war service of by far the greatest number of women, however, was in industry, especially in the clothing and tailoring trades. When they were engaged on piece work the problem of securing that the influx of female labour should not depress the standard of wages was simplified. When they were paid at time rates it was more difficult to say whether the difference between theirs and the men's wages was justified by the difference in skill and strength.

Mrs. Philip Martineau wrote in the "Englishwoman" that "The wives and sisters of the men who have enlisted have yet to see that they can take their share in saving England, just as the women of France are saving their land for their men who are fighting." They did come to realise their share more and more.

The response to the War Register opened at the Labour Exchanges showed their eagerness to do their part; what was needed was better organisation and extended opportunity, so that every woman might know exactly what her share in the service of her country was. The high hopes of those who placed their names on the War Register were hardly fulfilled. It was hoped that the call for more women workers, which was the necessary corollary of Lord Derby's, or any other scheme, for a larger army in the field, might offer the women more definite instruction and guidance.

ON THE UNDERGROUND.
The Tube liftwoman, a novel feature of London railways towards the end of 1915.

NOVEL SIGHT IN CONSERVATIVE BRITAIN.
Instruction in tram driving. Women learning the mechanism of electric-car control in the Corporation School, Albert Road, Cross Hill, Glasgow. Women in France and Germany were taught to control the traffic.

TICKET COLLECTORS
at the Caledonian Station, Edinburgh, wearing special badges pending the arrival of uniforms.
AA

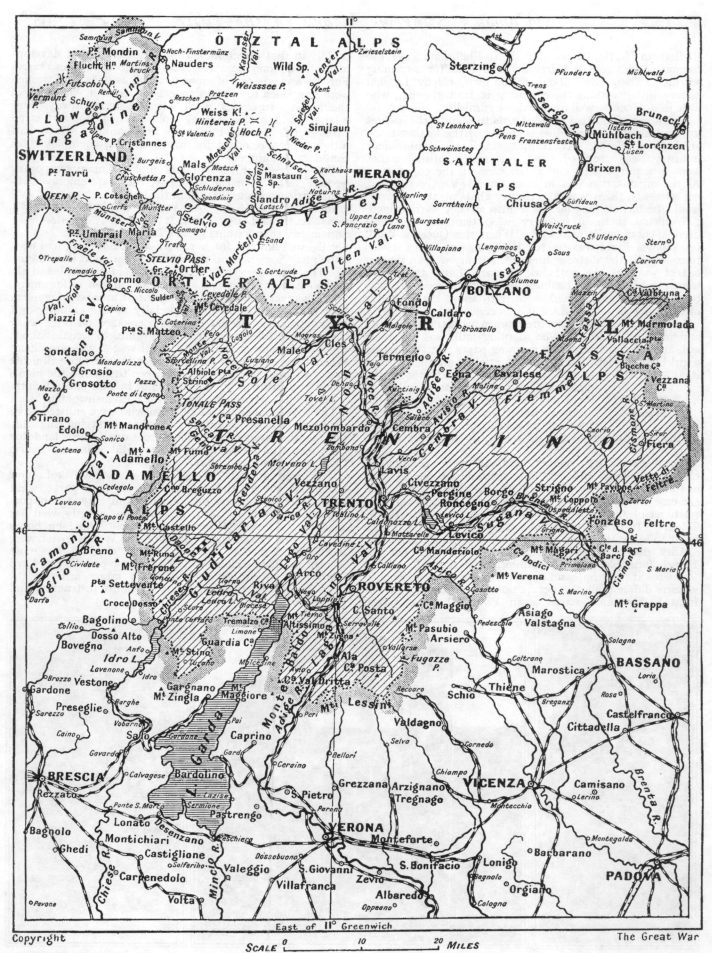

THE TRENTINO AND TYROL FRONT, SHOWING THE AUSTRIAN SYSTEM OF RAILWAYS FOR INVADING THE LOMBARDY PLAIN, AND THE MOUNTAIN PASSES WHICH THE ITALIANS CONQUERED BY A SUDDEN SWOOP ALL ROUND THE GREAT ENEMY SALIENT.

CHAPTER XCI.

THE MOUNTAIN BATTLES FOR "ITALIA IRREDENTA."

How Giolitti Upset the Plan of Attack by General Cadorna—The Enemy Gains Three Weeks in Which to Garrison His Alpine Fortresses —But Through Under-Estimating Her New Opponent Austria Loses All The Mountain-Passes—Part Played by the Alpine Clubs in Saving Italy from Invasion—Bull-Charge Against the Wire Entanglements on Korada Mountain—General Cantore's Lightning Dash to Ala—Wild Fighting on the Alps of Carinthia—How the Alpine Troops Dropped from the Glaciers into the Paradise of Cortina—Great Battle for the Dolomite Road—Advance-Guard of the Third Army Clears the Venetian Plain—Land Around the Isonzo is Flooded by Austrian Sappers—But the Italian Engineers Throw a Bridge Over the Flood—Monfalcone, With its Warship Building-Yards, is Captured—Italian Infantry of the Line Wait for their Heavy Guns—The Strategy of General Cadorna, and the Political Reasons for It—Bavaria Comes to the Help of Austria-Hungary—Violent Counter-Attacks all Along the Front— Terrific Struggle on the Carso Table-Land—the Siege of Gorizia and Tarvis—Closing the Gateways of Invasion in the Carnic Alps—Austrian Alpinists Arrive, and the Mountain Battles Grow Fiercer—Garibaldi at the Col di Lana—The Army of Cadore Presses Towards the Enemy's Vital Railway—The Italian Achievement in the First Phase of the War—It Compares Favourably With the Results of the Parallel Battles in France and Flanders.

 IN a previous chapter we related, as fully as was possible at the time, the stirring story of the renaissance of popular aspirations which flung Italy into the war. Some matters, however, had to be left diplomatically in the shadow while the patriotic directors of Italian policy were still engaged in educating their public opinion. Not until the Ancona was sunk, amid circumstances of extreme barbarity, by a German submarine flying the Austrian flag, was it possible to discuss frankly all the aspects of the Italian campaign.

For the first six months of this campaign King Victor Emmanuel and his generals were only able to fight for their unredeemed territories —*Italia irredenta*—in a very cautious manner, and with part only of their national strength. For there were mighty pro-German and pro-Austrian forces still working throughout the fabric of Italian society, and awaiting an opportunity for swinging the people back into a condition of servitude to Teutonic interests. In both politics and strategy Italy had still to temporise with her foes after the Austrian batteries on the Carnic Alps opened war at 7 p.m. on Saturday, May 23rd, 1915. In particular, General Cadorna never could seek for a sudden

AUTOGRAPH PORTRAIT OF GENERAL CADORNA.
This admirable portrait of General Count Luigi Cadorna was sent specially for insertion in our pages by the wife of the Italian Commander-in-Chief, whose act of courtesy testifies to the interest taken in THE GREAT WAR by our gallant allies.

decision at the cost of losing a hundred thousand men in a victorious thrust towards Trieste. He had to be very economical in expending the human resources of the most prolific of modern nations, for fear of Teutonic political influences.

It was these influences that defeated the great plan of attack which he, the son of one of the victorious generals in the 1866 war, had been elaborating for years. His father, General Cadorna senior, had routed the Austrians in 1866 in Friuli and captured the town of Gradisca ; but the enemy had won back this town in the treaty of peace, together with practically every other strategical position along the frontier. From the Stelvio Pass, near the Engadine edge of Switzerland, to the river line of the Isonzo on the Adriatic, the Austrians in 1866 had retained every dominating position over Italy. No mountain pass through which Italian troops could move was left in Italian hands. B i s m a r c k, having used Italy against Austria, betrayed his ally in order to win Austria over to the Teutonic cause, and keep her quiet during the attack on France, which he was preparing. Moreover, by giving the Austrians all the passes by which Lombardy and the Venetian plain could be invaded, Bismarck was able to force Italy into an alliance with the Teutonic Powers. General Cadorna the younger, therefore, had to open his campaign with everything against him. Every valley road along the front of three hundred and twenty miles was dominated by Austrian forts, many of which had recently been reconstructed and enlarged. In fact, since 1910, Austria had greatly increased the number of mountain fortresses, and in the ten months preceding the outbreak of hostilities new entrenched camps of enormous size had been built and gunned with 12 in. howitzers in order to intimidate the Italian people. In these circumstances, General Cadorna planned a great surprise assault on the Austrian line of fortified mountains. The Premier, Signor Salandra, and the Foreign Minister, Baron Sonnino, worked with the Commander-in-Chief, and if they had been men of the type which the old Florentine, Niccolo Machiavelli, admired, they would have abruptly declared war, in order

THE WATCH ON A MOUNTAIN BATTLEFIELD.
A lonely Italian outpost keeping watch among the rocks on the summit of the Dolomites, where " The hum of either army stilly sounds."

to enable their armies to use to the full the advantage of a surprise attack. But the modern Italian laboured under the same defects of character as the modern Frenchman and the modern Briton. He was so civilised that he thought of even making war in an honourable way, and the Italian Government gave the enemy full warning by denouncing the Triple Alliance on May 4th, 1915. It was expected that Germany and Austria would reply by breaking off diplomatic relations, and thus bringing about a rupture leading at once to a declaration of war. This was the real reason why King Victor Emmanuel decided to forgo attending the inauguration of the monument to the Thousand of Garibaldi on May 6th, at which he had promised to listen to the great speech of the poet Gabriele D'Annunzio in favour of war. For he expected that his armies would be moving to battle while the poet was speaking. But, as has

already been related, Signor Giolitti intervened and overthrew the War Cabinet, and hostilities were delayed for nineteen days.

By this means Signor Giolitti, the chief representative of Teutonism in Italy, saved Austria from a swift attack and immediate disaster. Giolitti, it must be understood, was only in a position similar to that of the boss of an American party. He was an agent, and not a first-hand force. He was, so to speak, the mechanic at the head of the commercial, financial and political machinery which the Germans had constructed in Italy. Immediately behind him were Italian men of business, working either in partnership with German magnates, or bound to Germany by business interests or financial obligations. The ruling men of this class, as in all modern plutocratic Governments, **Puppets of plutocracy** working under the cover of democratic institutions, did not get themselves elected into Parliament, but appointed lawyers and other professional politicians to act as their marionettes in the national assembly. Giolitti was merely the principal marionette in this commonplace tragi-comedy of a plutocracy which had corrupted everything in national and municipal politics, in order to increase its powers of money-making and establish its control over the working classes. As in Germany, so in Italy, the professed leaders of the working people—the Socialist deputies—were obscurely attached to the grand interests of the plutocratic party, and though it may not have been true in Italy that strikes were usually arranged to give vent to working-class discontent in as harmless a manner as possible, it was patent that the anti-national policy of the Socialist party largely agreed with the policy of the machine that Giolitti handled.

On the other hand, it must be admitted that the Italian plutocracy as a whole was not, like the Italian noble families that dominated the Cardinals' College, bitterly anti-national. Most of its members were moved by the same motives as the plutocracy which governs the United States through its bosses and elected marionettes. They esteemed neutrality as a means of making money out of the belligerent nations. This was a process which also had the advantage of possessing a colour of patriotism, in that it promised to augment the national wealth and leave the country in a position of great financial strength when the belligerent nations had almost exhausted each other. But though this may have been the view of the directors of the most powerful political machine in Italy, yet the nominal head of the machine, Signor Giolitti, through thwarted ambition or want of political insight, struck a blow at his country from which it took long to recover.

All the principal mountain fortresses could easily have been forced at the end of the first week in May, if the war had opened in accordance with the plans of General Cadorna, King Victor Emmanuel, and his Ministers; for both Austria and Germany had been taken unawares by the denunciation of the **What delay cost** Triple Alliance. The mountain forts were **Italy** held by only a few thousand troops, Austria's forces being employed against the Russians in the great Galician offensive, or massed along the Serbian front. But during the three weeks which Signor Giolitti won for his old friends, the mobilisation against Italy was carried out at high speed. The cemented trenches, the gun emplacements, the armour-plated casemates and strategic roads had long been ready; but the men to use them were mainly provided between May 4th and May 23rd. Every man who could be spared from Hungary and the Southern Austrian provinces was railed to the Italian front, until, by May 23rd, more than 300,000 men had been got into position. They were mostly Tyrolese and Hungarian Territorial troops, supported by first-line regiments in positions of importance. Against them General Cadorna brought up 700,000 first-line soldiers; but as his plan of a

Over Alpine heights: Italy's famous mountain soldiers on the march.

Heavy Italian howitzers in position on the slopes of Cadore.

The Austro-Italian Campaign: Italian howitzer battery in action.

Man-hauling a heavy gun into position on the Italian front.

Austrian artillery position: Giant ordnance screened amidst the mountain pines.

Italian motor-transport resting after a perilous descent from a mountain height.

211

The fight for Gorizia: Italian field=gun in action in the Carso.

great surprise attack had been defeated by Giolitti, the campaign opened badly for the Italians.

The fact that they had somewhat more than two men to the enemy's one was not of much importance. What counted was guns, and especially heavy siege-guns. The Austrians had their heavy artillery placed with precise science on every dominating height, fed by railways, defended by machine-gun redoubts on the mountain sides, with light quick-firers sheltered in caves or galleries hewed from the rock. The Italian guns were on railway lines in the plain, or being hauled up distant valley roads by oxen teams. The Italians had to set about build-

Comparison with Gallipoli ing mountain fortresses, from which their guns could work; and before they could build these fortresses they had first to conquer the mountains. The Italian position was similar to that of the Franco-British position in Gallipoli. But on the Austrian mountain line the peaks were higher and steeper; the front was enormously larger, giving the enemy room for grand manœuvres; and on the fortresses on the mountain heights millions of pounds had been spent, and the labour of ten years crowned by the recent work of thousands of engineers, with full and exact personal knowledge of all the recent developments in artillery fire and modern earthwork fortifications.

Had General Cadorna only retained his opportunity for surprise, he would have launched by night some hundreds of thousands of men, with Maxims and 3 in. mountain guns, to attack the Austrian forces in the rear before they were fully garrisoned. But after the long delay imposed by Signor Giolitti, the Italian commander, at midnight on May 23rd, only sent out battalions of Alpine troops to seize any ridges not held in strength by the Austrians near their main position. There was no surprise whatever about this movement, for the Austrian batteries had begun to fire on Italian redoubts five hours before hostilities were declared to be opened. The Austrian Chief of Staff, General von Höfer, was amply prepared for every manœuvre by his opponent. At least, he considered himself amply prepared. He, however, made the mistake of despising the men brought up against him.

This was the main reason why the Italian troops started the campaign with an uninterrupted series of brilliant successes. It was an article of faith in Austria-Hungary that the Italian soldier was a figure from romantic opera, who could sing better than he could fight. This tradition had come down from the eighteenth century, when the Austrian Court drew on Italy for her musicians and poets, and regarded the subject and oppressed people as an effete but still decorative race of artists. The fact that Italy had recovered her independence in the latter half of the nineteenth century by the help of other Powers, left the Austrians and Hungarians with their old pride of conquerors still unbroken. They regarded modern Italy as a flimsy structure with a stucco façade that could be shattered in a single battle; and they were blindly confident that, whatever happened in other fields of war, they could beat the Italian nation into the dust with but

New type of Italian little effort. It is only fair to the German to say he had a suspicion that the modern Italian might be formidable. Italian engineers, Italian mechanics, Italian navvies and labourers were well known in Germany and esteemed there. German engineers were aware that in skill, versatility, and solid knowledge, the fertile, virile race beyond the Alps was one of the great forces in European industry. But the Austrian nobleman and the Hungarian magnate, who disdained industrial affairs and held themselves above any person who lived by designing tools, remained ignorant of the fact that the Italian of the modern type had developed into as masterful and knowledgeable a character as the best men of Florence, Venice, and Genoa in the age of the warlike republican city States. They did not know that, as the French writer Stendhal pointed out a hundred years ago,

the human plant grows more strongly in Italy than anywhere else, and that fifty years of liberty and development had produced a hard-headed, cautious, and yet enterprising and tenacious type of Italian, who could hold his own in all ways with Briton, American, and German.

Thus it befell that the Archduke Eugene, with General von Höfer as his Chief of Staff, and Dankl as army commander in the Tyrol, made the mistake of holding the first line on the Austrian frontier with a ridiculously small number of troops. The Alpini and the Bersaglieri, with some battalions of the line and some gendarmes, crossed the frontier soon after midnight at all the strategical points, and by a hundred swift, fierce little skirmishes, began to reverse the positions of Austria and Italy. Among the points occupied at a singularly small loss of life to the victors were the Montozzo Pass, 8,585 feet high, and the Tonale Pass, 6,180 feet high, leading into the Western

ITALY'S FAMOUS GREEN-PLUMED WARRIORS.
Bersaglieri cyclists on their way to the front. Each Bersagliero is a picked, highly-trained athlete. The infantry invariably march at a quick trot. The cyclists' machines are so made that they can be quickly packed on the soldiers' backs.

Tyrol, and Ponte Caffaro, running into South-Western Trentino; the ridge of Monte Baldo, extending northward for fifteen miles towards Arco and Rovereto in the Southern Trentino; some of the heights giving westward towards Trento; all the valleys in the labyrinth of the Dolomite Alps, and several footholds on the Alps of Carinthia.

It was nearly all done by bayonet fighting, after splendid mountaineering feats. The cyclist sharpshooters advanced in a straightforward manner up the mountain paths till they were greeted with musketry fire. They then sought more carefully for cover, pushing forward from rock and tree with their wings extending up the mountain sides, and there engaging any enemy skirmishers. Meanwhile

while the Alpine troops were climbing the mountain, by ways only known to themselves through many mountaineering excursions undertaken by their leaders in summer holidays. The officers led the men over the trackless screes and rocky falls, over glaciers and snowdrifts, and then descended the opposite slopes at some distance behind the enemy vanguards skirmishing near the entrance to the path. It was the day of glory for many members of the C.A.I., the S.A.T., and S.A.F.—these letters standing for the Club Alpino Italiano, the Societa degli Alpinisti Tridentini, and the Societa Alpina Friulana. Englishmen had formed the first Alpine Club purely for the furtherance of their sport; but German and Austrian Alpinists had been encouraged by their Governments to create a variety of Alpine Clubs; and

Military use of Alpine Clubs

the Italian Government had seen the meaning of this manœuvre, and had also encouraged the pastime of climbing the Alps. For years the great game had gone on, in which all the more adventurous spirits worked over the snow and ice with ropes, crampons, and ice-axes, rejoicing in each discovery of a new practicable route, which was not always published in the Club's journal. The Swiss Alpinists entered into the game with as much zest as the Austrians, Germans, and Italians; and of all the nations of Alpine climbers only the British, who made a good many important discoveries, thought nothing of the possible warlike value of their explorations.

In recent years the Italian Alpinists drew up to the level of the British climbers, and in some cases surpassed our men. It was intense patriotism as well as sheer joy in mountain adventure that made many a young Italian lieutenant a peer of Freshfield and Whymper. But, unlike the Englishmen, the young Italian climber seldom published any of the results of his holiday sports. In fact, he was often more anxious to conceal his achievement than to talk about it, and he preferred, if possible, to strike an old well-known route, when he was descending, in order to make it appear as if he had come across the mountain in a commonplace way. He kept his special knowledge for the day after the declaration of war, when by means of it he was able to help to place his country at once in the position of which Austria had robbed her in

1866. By the evening of May 25th, all the passes of the Dolomite Alps were won, and good breaches were made at Tonale Pass along the north-west and in the Carnic and Julian Alps along the north-east front.

The gun trains began to move more rapidly towards the holes made in the great mountain rampart, and tens of thousands of Italian engineers went up by train and motor-vehicles, and started building trenches and making gun emplacements. Meanwhile, the main Italian infantry force, consisting of the Third Army, moved with great speed across the Friuli Plain through Udine, Palmanova, and St. Georgio, where two railway lines ran into the Isonzo Valley and the Torre Valley. Here the covering troops had moved forward over the frontier at midnight on May 24th, and in a single day they captured nearly all the towns and villages between the frontier and the Isonzo River, from Caporetto, nestling in the north below the precipices of Monte Nero, to the hamlet of

FRENCH GENERALISSIMO ON THE ISONZO FRONT.
During the two days that General Joffre spent at the Italian front in the autumn of 1915 he was taken to various important points, and was able to discuss the plans of the campaign with the King of Italy and his generals. In this photograph the French Commander-in-Chief is seen near the River Isonzo with the King and a group of Italian leaders.

General Joffre, King Victor (on the right), and two Italian generals on a mountain road at Plezzo. The French leader's short visit to Italy was kept secret until his return to France.

General Tassoni describing the Austrian defences of Tolmino to General Joffre. On the first day of his visit the Generalissimo inspected the Italian position near Doberdo.

From left to right: Generals Joffre, Porro, and Cadorna, the Italian Commander-in-Chief. The Grand Cross of the Military Order of Savoy was conferred on General Joffre by King Victor.

The Duke of Aosta (left), who entertained General Joffre during the visit. In his farewell message to General Cadorna, General Joffre praised highly the Italian Army, calling the men "superb troops."

GENERAL JOFFRE'S VISIT TO ITALY: HISTORIC MEETING OF THE ALLIED LEADERS.

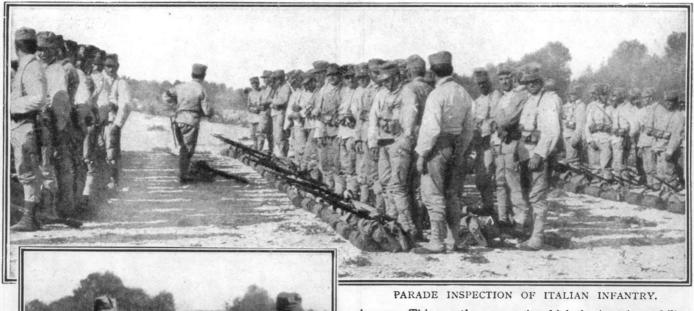

PARADE INSPECTION OF ITALIAN INFANTRY.

ITALIAN OUTPOST FORDING A RIVER.

Belvedere southward on the Gulf of Trieste. In this region the Italians had a strong fortress town, Palmanova, lying about fourteen miles west of the great Austrian fortress town of Gorizia, to guard against any irruption into the Venetian Plain. But General von Höfer had abandoned the direct attack through Gorizia, and had made a more subtle scheme of campaign. All he did was to place a strong force on the mountain of Korada between the Isonzo River and the Judrio. The mountain dominated the middle course of the Isonzo, and was transformed into a fortress with a network of deep trenches protected by wide wire entanglements. It was reckoned that by the time the Italians brought their heavy artillery into play on the trenches and began to cut up the wire with their field-guns, supports could easily be moved forward across the Isonzo.

But the Italian brigadier-general had looked at the wire-entanglements some time before the war broke out, and he now brought up a herd of very savage bulls and held them in a hollow, while his field and mountain artillery played upon the hostile trenches. The bulls were violently disturbed with the racket of the guns, and, just before they grew quite unmanageable, they were loosed and driven up the mountain. In their mad charge they broke through the obstacle, and before the last of them could be shot by the enemy the bayonets of Italy followed in their wake through the broken wires and captured the position. All the frontier skirmishes ended in successes of high strategical importance for the Italian troops, and the perturbed Austrians and Hungarians could then find nothing better to do than to attempt to terrorise the Italian people by dropping bombs on Venice and sending a battleship or two to bombard the open town of

Charge of the bulls

Ancona. This was the manner in which the Austrian nobility, which had never been remarkable for its fighting qualities, protested against the sudden, disagreeable revelation of the strength of the Italian democracy.

The skirmishing along the mountain frontier continued till the end of May. By this time, the forces attacking the Trentino southward had crossed the Lessini Mountains north of Verona, and, penetrating nearly ten miles into Austrian territory, had taken the town of Ala and brought forward heavy guns against the Rovereto forts. Further advances were also made in Southern Trentino along the Giudicaria Valley towards the towns at the head of Lake Garda and along the Sugana Valley towards Trent. All these actions, however, formed only a holding movement, like the operations in the Tyrol through the Stelvio, Montozzo, and Tonale Passes.

It will be seen on the map that the Austrian railway system spreads like the five fingers of a hand southward down the Trentino. These five railway lines were never designed for ordinary traffic. Though the valleys are beautiful and fertile, with silvery-white olive orchards, vineyards, orange groves and thickly-wooded slopes of chestnut and oak, forming, with the cloud-like peaks of white snow and the radiant waters of the lakes the loveliest landscape on earth, the network of modern railways was not built for the summer tourists or the picturesque old-fashioned peasantry. The lines were intended to transport and supply a large Austro-Hungarian army, and this army was to leap on Verona and all the rich, busy cities of Lombardy, thus beheading Italy by cutting off her chief centres of industry. Such was the plan of Conrad von Hötzendorf, who was the military mind of the Dual Monarchy. Then, according to his scheme, the Italians were to be allowed to approach the Isonzo line on the way to Trieste. But when they had become involved in this operation and the two railway lines running from Venice were choked with their supplies, another large Austro-Hungarian army was to advance through the passes of the Carnic Alps and through the Julian Alps from the entrenched camp of Tarvis, and by a quick southward swoop take in the flank the Italian forces on the Isonzo line.

Von Hotzendorf's scheme

All this was well-known to General Cadorna. It was indeed the reason for his drives at all the mountain passes, for each pass was a Thermopylæ where a battalion with a couple of quick-firing guns and half a dozen Maxims could hold back an army corps for days. Behind each out-flung battalion was a large reserve of Italian troops, ready to reinforce their comrades at any hard-pressed point. The Italian Commander-in-Chief, having conquered practically all the enemy's first line along a front of three hundred miles, waited to see in what sector the

Austrian pressure would be most strongly felt. The answering counter-thrust of the enemy came at Monte Croce Pass, in the Carnic Alps, on May 29th. It was a foggy day, and under cover of the mist the enemy massed a strong force through the railway from Villach and brought them to Mauthen, from which they made five stubborn attempts to regain the pass. The Alpini and Bersaglieri swept away each wave of assault by musketry and machine-gun fire at almost point-blank range; then, leaping up after the last attack, they drove the enemy down the valley at the point of the bayonet.

This was only the beginning of the Battle of Monte Croce. Each side had large forces within call, and fed the troops up the valleys as the fighting-lines wasted. So the struggle continued day and night, while **Battle of Monte Croce** the Italian commander pushed over the neighbouring passes and strengthened himself for the great counter-attack. The height known as Freikofel, commanding the Plöcken Plateau, near Monte Croce Pass, was stormed on June 8th, and the Pass of Valentina and the Pass of Oregione, 7,590 feet high, overlooking the thickly-wooded Gail Valley, were taken. The last pass was won by the Alpini climbing over the white mass of Paralba and fighting their way down to the high saddle. The Austrians brought up another army corps, and on the night of June 14th made a great attempt to break through the rampart of Italian valour and turn the Carnic Alps, according to design, into the gateway for a flank attack on the main Italian army. Oregione's saddle, the snowfields of Paralba, and all the peaks and wild ravines extending to Monte Croce and Freikofel, were dappled with groups of fighting men, some shooting from rocky cover, others trying to get home with a bayonet charge delivered at close quarters from some fold in the limestone. On Paralba, some 8,840 feet high, the Austrian troops were on Italian territory; but they were soon caught on the flank and threatened towards the rear, and scattered towards the Steinwand, a limestone mountain towering above the Gail Valley.

In this area of war the Austrians had the advantage of possessing a railway running through the Drave Valley, and approaching closer to the frontier rampart than the Italian railway system did. They could therefore bring up fresh troops with more speed. In the Gail Valley they had a wide, long region in which they could mass without being seen; they had a good road to the mountains from Mauthen, while the Italians had only rough valley tracks. Nevertheless, the Italians kept the gateway to Venice firmly closed, while they attacked the enemy force on both flanks. These flanks consisted of the Tarvis system of fortresses on the right, lying round the Predil Pass, by which Napoleon had invaded Austria, and the Cortina d'Ampezzo Pass on the left, running towards the Austrian railway at Toblach.

The beautiful village of Cortina, lying 4,000 feet high amid the most superb scenery in Europe, was captured by the Cadore army on May 30th. The far-famed road, winding through the spired and towered maze of the Dolomites, **On to Falzarego** was barricaded and trenched by the enemy, who had mountain guns behind his advanced garrison. But the Alpini worked over the mountain ranges, by the glaciers of Sorapis, and the tarns of Croda da Lago, and dropped into Cortina on either side. Then, holding the enemy on the east, they advanced into the Tyrol westward along the new Dolomite road to Falzarego. In this profound ravine, with impracticable but picturesque walls of green-hung limestone, an Austrian had built some years before an hotel which was very difficult of approach. Tourists thought the man did not know his business, because he put an hotel where it was not wanted. The building, however, did not cost him much, because he received a Government subsidy. When war broke out, sand-bags, machine-guns, and quick-firers were hauled up to the eyrie, and in a few hours

ITALIAN GUN OF HEAVY CALIBRE COMING INTO ACTION.
One of the most inspiring sights on the Italian front was the hauling into almost inaccessible positions of pieces of field artillery. As many as a hundred men would drag a weighty piece of ordnance up a slope. Frequently this was the only reliable means of haulage in the mountains.

A PEASANT PATRIOT.
An Italian leading his ox-drawn waggon to a military depot, where he received a receipt in exchange for his oxen and goods.

the hotel became a splendid fort, with quarters for a large garrison, and guns dominating the far-famed ravine. But the Alpini were led by men with ingenious minds and minute knowledge of the ground. Most of the fighting took place on the great northern mountain height, crowned by the glaciers and snow-fields of Tofana, and

On the glaciers of Tofana

around the Cinque Torri, a line of apparently inaccessible peaks. The most difficult is called the English Tower. Loose stones and an infinite number of fissures, holes, and ravines, sculptured in the grey - white, weathered rock, made the mountain skirmishes in the thin, cold air a test of climbing skill and ingenuity in manœuvring.

It was mainly sharpshooters' work, in which combination tactics had to be used, and the more dashing spirits had to be kept well in hand to prevent the force being too much scattered when intricate and well-timed team-work was necessary. And as the struggle went on for more than a week, there was the further task of keeping the men well supplied with food and ammunition, and relieving them before they became exhausted by the day and night

struggle at heights going up to 10,000 feet. But by their powers of endurance and their vehement and yet tricky way of fighting, the Alpini cleared the mountains above the ravine road, and then dropped on the hotel. By June 9th Falzarego Pass was won, and in the closing battle, in which the enemy lost a gun, a footing was obtained on a very important strategical position, three miles beyond the pass, on the Sasso d'Istria, close to the point at which the Dolomite road bends southward through its ravine and goes in two tunnels under the mountains.

It was this great and rapid success that disturbed the enemy commander, and

Western Tyrol threatened

made him anxious about the western defences of the Tyrol; for at Falzarego and Sasso d'Istria the Italian troops were approaching the rear of the Col di Lana, and its neighbouring mountain masses on which the fortresses defending Cordevole Valley were constructed. By a double flanking movement along the Cordevole River and the Dolomite road, the Cadore army had begun to extend in a pincer-like formation around one of the main Austrian

"VIVA ITALIA!" SOLDIERS IN BILLETS, BOYS IN TRAINING.
Italian soldiers comfortably billeted in a railway-station at a captured Austrian position. In oval: The ubiquitous Boy Scout in Italy. There, as in other Allied countries, this splendid organisation trained boys to useful war-time work.

systems of defence. General Dankl had to pour more troops and light artillery on to the Cadore front; for the Italian thrust up the Cordevole Valley was the most dangerous threat to Southern Austria. At the end of the valley, across another range of mountains, was the wrist of the Austrian hand-like railway system that fed and munitioned both the Trentino forces and the forces in the Southern Tyrol. If the wrist were cut by the army of Cadore all the lands between Switzerland and the Carnic Alps would be lost. The fortresses, field-batteries, and infantry divisions would not be able to resist for very long if their supply-line were cut behind them. It will be seen from the map that the Southern Tyrol and the Trentino form a great mountain wedge thrust into the Italian plain. For thousands of years this tortuous highland maze, with its hardy, mountaineering races, had been the principal menace to the peace of Italy. But General Cadorna rightly decided that, in the new era of railway warfare, a thrust at the eastern base of the salient towards the only trunk line feeding the army of General Dankl would make the enemy so alarmed about his own safety that he would not think of erupting into the plain.

General Cadorna, having both the gift of strategy and ample fighting troops of fine quality, was able to impose his will on his adversary. The Austrians had only to advance some twenty miles across their Trentino frontier to reach Verona, that city of old romance still **Strategy of** fragrant with the memories of **Cadorna** Romeo and Juliet. Brescia was still nearer, with all the fertile, busy plain of Lombardy extending around. The conquest of Verona was largely a matter of heavy siege-guns, and the new 12 in. Skoda howitzers, would have been instruments of great power. But it was General Cadorna who chiefly decided where most of these great hostile weapons should be used. Many of them were placed with great labour on the Cadore front, because the Italian pressure there was very severe. Many of them were also sited behind the Carnic and Julian Alps, especially in the corner near Predil Pass, by which Napoleon invaded Austria; then the Isonzo front, between Tolmino and the Adriatic, needed more heavy guns for its defence. In the end none remained for any movement into Italy.

This was very important, because for a considerable time the Italian artilleryman fought at a disadvantage. To say that his guns and mortars were unequal to those of his opponent is to understate the case; for the Austrians' heavy gun—the big Skoda—was the finest in the world. It had done much of the work of fortress smashing in Belgium and Russia, and the fact that the Austrians were in a position to lend heavy **Peerless Skoda** artillery to their allies for use on the **guns** western front is an indication of the wealth of big-gun power in Austria. And after ten months of war, when the great howitzers were being employed by the thousand in Galicia and along the Danube, the Skoda works could still produce an armament superior to that of Italy.

Besides the 12 in. Skoda, with its extraordinary handiness,

ITALY'S STURDY INFANTRYMEN IN ACTION AGAINST THEIR COUNTRY'S HEREDITARY FOES.
Italian infantrymen skirmishing at an outpost position near the Austrian lines. Above: Typical Italian scouts making their way to an advanced observation-post, under cover of long grass, during the summer operations of 1915.

due to its consisting of two separate parts easily hauled along and its magnificent force and precision, there were great and still increasing numbers of the new 6 in. steel-built Skoda, designed at first, in the summer of 1914, for mountain warfare in the Carpathians. Krupp had one larger, clumsier howitzer, slow in firing and intricate to handle, but he had nothing so fine as the new products of Skoda of Pilsen, an armament firm which the Germans despised before the war with more sincerity than they despised Schneider of Creusot.

The level-headed Italians did not make the mistake of underestimating the efficiency of the weapons of their enemy. Indeed, it was because they recognised that their old artillery was much inferior to the hurricane firing batteries of Austria-Hungary that they maintained for ten months so philosophic an attitude of neutrality. Meanwhile they created, at utmost speed, a new armament. They took as their field-gun the French 75 mm. quick-firer, as newly improved by its inventor, Colonel Déport, and they built 6 in. and 12 in. howitzers for attacking the Austrian forts. But an army of a million men needs 4,000 guns, and the twenty-five Italian army corps required also several siege trains of great power. This ordnance could not be turned out in a year, even with help from other countries. Every gun-maker in the world was overwhelmed with urgent orders, and Italy, being without coalfields, was not a steel-making nation.

Italian Army's disadvantage

So in spite of all the speeding up of the production of artillery of the finest type, the Italian armies entered on the war at a disadvantage. Their great peril was that an enormous quantity of heavy Austrian artillery might be released in the eastern theatre of war, by a decision against the Russians, and brought up against them.

This must be well borne in mind when studying the operations of General Cadorna and his assistant commander General Porro. All that happened in Galicia, Russian Poland, Lithuania, and Courland, directly influenced their plans. The Russian reverses, on the one side, and the checks to all Franco-British attempts at breaking the German line on the other side, made the Italian Commander-in-Chief very cautious. He had always to reckon with the possibility that an immense Austro-German host, with an incomparable artillery equipment, might be launched against his army before it was amply provided with new guns and shell supplies on the vast new scale.

Interdependence of Allies

We have also seen that, for political reasons, General Cadorna could not afford to sacrifice his men in offensive movements costing 50,000 or 70,000 men a day. Even with a view to reaching Trieste he could not do this. Much less could he contemplate doing it in order to attain some key position in the mountain ramparts. That is to say, he could not think of eking out his artillery forces by a tremendous use of his infantry. His problem was to conserve his forces for a possible, and sometimes probable, defensive campaign against mighty Teutonic forces, and meanwhile win victories and keep his casualty lists short,

ITALIAN STAFF OFFICER'S AUTOMOBILE CROSSES THE ISONZO.
The steep cliffs in the background, partly covered by mountain vegetation, give some idea of the locality and conditions of Italy's struggle for the Trentino. The Isonzo played as great a part in this hereditary feud against Teutonism as did the Vistula on the eastern front, the Danube in Central Europe, and the Marne in the west

LEADERS OF THE ITALIAN ARMY IN THE FIELD.

From the beginning of the war King Victor Emmanuel personally directed the fortunes of his armies in the field, sharing the hardships and perils of his men. Ever solicitous of their welfare, this most democratic of European monarchs worked as hard as the most enthusiastic subaltern. His Majesty is the second seated figure from the right, next to the Duke of Aosta, while General Zupelli is sitting, with his legs crossed.

while fighting heavy howitzers with light mountain guns and 3 in. quick-firers.

It was a very difficult programme to carry out, but the Italian commander at least equalled the achievement of General Joffre and Sir John French under the similar conditions of a parallel battle. The forces opposed to him were smaller than those entrenched against the French and British troops. The Austrians, Hungarians and Bavarians on the Italian front seem to have numbered 300,000, at first, increasing towards the autumn to 700,000. But on a line of three hundred miles, walled in everywhere by great mountains, entrenched hill camps, and fortressed plateaux, like the Carso, the actual fighting density of the enemy troops was not much less at last than that of the Germans on the Franco-Flemish front ; in fact, the points of incessant conflict in Italy may in the end have been more crowded.

Striking Italian achievement

Yet, in this modern kind of parallel battle, in which siege-guns were an important factor of success, and on which all the Allies entered under a disadvantage in regard to heavy armament, the Italians did quite as well as any. They broke farther into the fortified Alps, and the limestone tableland west of Trieste, than we did into the fortressed hill positions in Gallipoli, or into the low horse-shoe ridge in the Lille area ; the length of their thrusts exceeded those of the French advances in Artois and Champagne, and they were as successful amid the ice-crowned and snow-mantled peaks of Carinthia and the Tyrol as the Russians were amid the swamps and rivers of Courland and the Rovno region.

And all the first striking successes by General Cadorna, between the last week in May, 1915, and the third week in August, 1915, were accomplished with a total casualty list of less than 30,000 names. The Austro-Hungarian losses in the same period on the same front were 18,000 dead, 54,000 wounded, and 18,000 prisoners.

This is a very striking result, especially having regard to the fact that the Italian troops were continually attacking fortified mountain positions at a time when only part of their new artillery was available. General Cadorna told his men that they won their successes because they fought in a more scientific manner than their foes. And this was no inspiriting flattery.

The Italian soldier had learnt as much in the Libyan campaign as the British soldier did in the South African War. He had acquired a cooler, deadlier skill, and a gift for improvising stratagems which sadly surprised his enemy.

For the Austrians and Hungarians, being tempered by both defeat and victory in the great struggle with the Russians, and coming in veteran strength from the conflicts on the Carpathians and in the Serbian mountains, expected to find the Italians an easy prey. At first they felt for the Italians the scorn that Napoleon felt for Wellington when the forces of the two commanders first clashed in Portugal and Spain. Napoleon's view was founded on the fact that Wellington had been used only to fighting Indian armies, poorly trained and badly led, and he expected that, faced by large forces of experienced European troops handled in a scientific way, the Irish general would be defeated before he recognised he was so. In the same way, the Italians were regarded by their enemies as troops of the modern Continental school, originally poor in quality, and further

Austrians expect an easy prey

221

IN ACCORDANCE WITH THE LAWS OF CIVILISED WARFARE.
Striking photograph of an Italian patrol entering an Austrian village. The orderly conduct of this body of cavalrymen will interest those who hold that warfare and civilisation are incompatible. The village, being unfortified, bore no sign of destruction or the ravages of war, and the civil inhabitants were in no way molested by the conquerors.

themselves temptingly to a double side attack. The wings closed behind the creeping attacking force, waited silently until the enemy's frontal assaults failed, and then completely annihilated the trapped battalion, as it would not surrender.

All the long series of small but highly important frontier victories were won by light Italian troops, composed mostly of Alpini, cavalry, cyclists, the Bersaglieri, and batteries of horse artillery. On the Venetian Plain, by the Lower Isonzo, a few thousand men in two days conquered with little loss all the territory which Prince von Bülow had offered the Italian nation as the grudged price of her permanent neutrality. But the light troops that so swiftly moved to the enemy's second line were trained to great feats of skill and endurance. Many of the cavalrymen could climb, on horseback, mountain steeps up which an ordinary man of athletic habit would not care to clamber on all fours. The Alpine troops were known, by the results of competitive marches against the records of other crack European corps, to be able to outwalk all other light infantry.

After these troops had swiftly won the first round in the Austro-Italian struggle, there was an apparent relaxation of effort while the infantry of the line waited for their heavy siege artillery to come into action. This was mainly a matter of engineering, especially on the Isonzo front, where the river was in high summer flood owing to the melting of the snow on the mountain-tops. Bridging skill of an unusual kind was needed to get the new siege-guns across the floods, at the places where small bodies of the advanced troops were furiously holding bridge-heads on the enemy's side of the swollen waters. Along the Isonzo the retreating Austrians had broken down the high embankment used to carry off the snow-water, and had thereby inundated the plain in the manner of the Belgian Yser defences.

spoilt for European warfare by loose, easy fighting with the Arabs of Tripoli.

But what happened when the Italian and the Hungarian met was afterwards revealed with fine candour by the well-known Magyar novelist, Francis Molnar. Molnar wrote from Austrian Headquarters. He said that in the early fighting round Monte Nero, the 3rd Battalion of the 7th Honveds was ordered to attack the Italian position. The Hungarian Territorials, famous for their valour, moved forward by the method learned on the Carpathians. They crept up the mountain slopes, under the cover of the thick vegetation. Reaching the trench of the Alpini, they closed, poured in rapid fire and then charged with the bayonet. But they were beaten back, and as they turned to retreat they found themselves ambushed. The Alpini had seen them coming, and had flung out both wings high up the valley of approach. The two outflanking bodies did not fire when the Hungarians passed and exposed

The gallant Italian sappers, working under a plunging fire from the enemy's batteries on the mountains, foothills, and Carso tableland, had rapidly thrown some light pontoon bridges over the flood. Along these frail temporary structures the first Italian contingents crossed in the darkness, took the first line of Austrian trenches near the waterside, and broke up the light artillery positions close to the river. But this was the utmost that could be done to prepare the way for the attack on the enemy's last systems of hill and mountain fortifications. And it was accomplished by the first week in June, 1915.

Gallant Italian sappers

But though the enemy's main positions could not be assailed until the infantry of the line advanced with heavy guns, those troops on the Lower Isonzo made a happy stroke in a south-westerly direction on June 9th.

HEAVY ITALIAN ARTILLERY FIRING ACROSS AN ALPINE PLATEAU.
Field-howitzer in action against an Austrian position. The gunners are holding their ears, as the shriek of this weapon was truly deafening. The whole campaign between Italy and Austria resolved itself into an incessant artillery duel by reason of the geographical conditions.

POWERFUL INSTRUMENT OF DESTRUCTION CONCEALED IN AN ALPINE GROTTO.
Placing an 8·2 in. siege-mortar in position. The weapon has a special emplacement and is fixed to iron rails, along which it recoils. After continuous bombardment with these howitzers many of the Austrian mountain forts hitherto considered impregnable were reduced to fragments.

By the edge of the sea, just below a dominating height on the Carso tableland, was the seaport of Monfalcone, belonging to Venice, but stolen from her by the Austrians in the Napoleonic era. Monfalcone had become the third most important port in Austria-Hungary, and at its yards, Cantiere Navale, warships were still being built for the Dual Monarchy. Monfalcone was only sixteen miles from Trieste, and though the road and railway tracks by the sea were impracticable for an advance in force, Monfalcone itself was well worth taking. It had been bombarded by the Italian fleet on May 30th, when a large chemical factory, in which asphyxiating gases were being made, was destroyed.

The bombardment was continued by light cruiser squadrons on June 7th. Then the Castle of Duino, the magnificent residence of the Hohenlohe family, standing on the edge of the sea, nearer Trieste, and defended by three batteries of artillery, was shattered and set on fire, in order apparently to prepare for operations against Monfalcone from the south-western side in the Gulf of Panzano. The design was to threaten an advance on Trieste by the sea-road leading down through the famous pleasure palace of Miramar. The destruction of Prince Hohenlohe's Castle of Duino—the Prince had been the chief oppressor of the Italian subjects of Austria—was calculated to make the Archduke Eugene anxious about the probable line of Italian advance. Some of his troops were therefore collected hastily, but in strong force, above Duino, in preparation against an Italian landing-battle, but not an Italian landed. It was all a feint.

The attack on Monfalcone was launched from the opposite quarter, in a straightforward direction across the Isonzo, on June 8th. Only the light troops—Bersaglieri, cyclists' corps, and grenadiers—were employed, but they

How Monfalcone was won broke the enemy's river-line at a point where it was considered impregnable. Then, as the over-confident enemy had prepared no line of retirement between the river and the plateau, Monfalcone was won in a rapid running fight through the villages around the Isonzo delta. The most famous of these villages, Aquileia, had already been won by the advance guard. Great was their joy in winning it, though it was only a miserable hamlet with a few hundred poor people, mostly mendicants; for Aquileia was as

romantic a spot as Pompeii. It had been one of the greatest of Roman cities, and its sorry condition was the work of the ancient Attila, who levelled it to the ground after his defeat between the Aisne and the Marne in France. Like the modern Attila, the ancient leader of the Huns had intended to destroy and enslave France; and, next, to terrorise and subjugate Italy. But he died soon after he had treated Aquileia as the modern Germans have treated Ypres and Arras. To the Italians, with their historic memories, there was a deep source of inspiration in **An inspiriting victory** the swift capture of the little seaside hamlet, from which antique works of art and curiosities had been obtained in large quantities by the Austrian oppressors of the dominions of Venice.

Close to the hamlet the passage of the Isonzo was forced by a smashing bayonet attack, and the Italian troops, headed by motor-cyclists with machine-guns, cycling scouts, and aeroplane observers, flowed in two arms around every position at which the Austrians tried to make a stand. By this continual threat of an encircling movement they forced the Austrians into Monfalcone. The enemy then for the first time displayed a telling ingenuity in warfare. Like the Turk in the Suvla Bay battles, he set fire to some of the slopes which the Italians were attacking. But while the pine-wood near Monfalcone flared to the skies, the quick-manœuvring Italians, headed by a grenadier battalion, broke into the open town and occupied it, after storming the Rocca promontory. But as the seaport reposed at the foot of the Carso plateau, with two large clumps of limestone, rising a thousand feet above the streets on the northern side, the enemy's heavy artillery on the heights had the power of turning the town into another Aquileia.

But the Bersaglieri, grenadiers, and sharpshooters were not disposed to see the famous city they had captured ruined by 6 in. high-explosive shell. Moreover there were some warships lying in the shipyards in various stages of construction, and the Italians wanted to complete and gun these ships, and employ them against the men who had designed them for use against Italy. So the conquest of Monfalcone was completed by the brigade of light troops climbing up the limestone cliffs and hauling their 3 in. guns after them. With these they induced the enemy to drag his howitzers farther away from the seashore.

TREACHEROUS AUSTRIAN FOES CAPTURED BY BERSAGLIERI.
Dramatic scene on the Italian front. After eluding the vigilance of Italian scouts for many weeks, an Austrian sniper and spy were eventually tracked to their hiding-place. This document was recorded immediately after the arrest of the culprits in a mountain cottage. The little daughter of the sniper, anxious for the fate of her father, is crying.

ITALY'S EFFECTIVE ORDNANCE IN THE MOUNTAIN WAR.

One of Italy's heavy field howitzers on the Trentino front. From the angle of the gun it will be seen that the shell had to be fired completely over the mountain. The difficulties of transporting heavy ordnance in the Trentino were enormous, and this photograph gives a typical idea of the country.

The loss of Monfalcone stung the Austro-Hungarian Government very deeply, for the seaport had been one of the parts of old Italian territory which Austria had refused to relinquish, even under the threats and cajoleries of Prince von Bülow. Yet it had cost Italy only about a hundred dead and wounded men to capture the fourth most important seaport in the Dual Monarchy. All this happened at a time when the Austro - Hungarian army in Galicia had continually to be saved from destruction and helped forward by the Grand Phalanx under Mackensen. But though Ivanoff was killing the Austrians at the rate of a division a day, this loss was regarded as slight in comparison with the couple of thousand men who were put out of action at Monfalcone. The German jeered publicly at the Austrian over Monfalcone, especially in a violent and bitter satire, published in an important newspaper, the "Frankfürter Zeitung."

The "Frankfürter Zeitung" put its views of Austria in the form of fable: "There was a dog of noble birth, with the finest pedigree in the world. And this dog, knowing that purest blood was the source of the highest courage, resolved to go wolf-hunting.

AN ITALIAN GUN THAT BEAT AUSTRIA'S BEST.

An Italian heavy gun in position. One of the main features of the campaign along the Alpine frontiers was the superiority of the Italian artillery matched against the Austrian.

But, although the dog was extremely noble, it was also very old. It had lost its teeth and all its strength of muscle, and the result was that when it tried to tackle the wolf it was very badly mauled. Seeing what had happened, the master of the hunt called to a strong mastiff, whose fighting power was more striking than its pedigree, and thus the feeble, toothless dog of noble breed was saved from destruction. When the wolf was killed by the mastiff, the old dog wanted to lick up all the blood and claim the victory. But the master of the hunt gave it two severe kicks and saw to it that the mastiff had all the profit and the glory."

There is scarcely any need to point out that the master of the hunt was the Hohenzollern Emperor, and that Prussianised Germany was the mastiff. But the fact that an article of this sort was published in one of the most important papers in the Central Empires, a paper which indeed was the organ of international German-Jewish finance, was a clear indication of the condition of things between Germany and Austria. If the Italian successes had not been so important, Austria, who still served Germany well in the

AUSTRIAN VANDALISM AT VENICE.
Irreparable damage was caused by a bomb dropped by an Austrian airman, on October 24th, 1915, on the Church of Santa Maria degli Scalzi in Venice, primarily famed for its wonderful ceiling decoration by Tiepolo.

authorities let their men go over to another country and practically desert in army corps. The Italians themselves continually expected that Germany would regularise the situation by a declaration of war. But months elapsed and the declaration was not made.

Even when the latest and largest types of German submarines operating in the Mediterranean went over to the side of Austria and flew the Austrian flag, Germany did not declare war. Instead, she sent Prince von Bülow to Switzerland to get again into personal touch with certain Italian ecclesiastics and Italian politicians. **—and Prussian money-bags** The fact was that the German banks had more than £100,000,000 sunk in Italian industries, and the principal German financiers nursed the hope that the lucrative properties they wholly or partly possessed in Lombardy would be returned to them when the war was over. Naturally, the King of Italy and his Ministers were well aware of all the details of this manœuvre. Their knowledge enabled them to control their own pro-German party, which still watched over the industries of Teutonic capital and Teutonic Catholicism.

While thus lightly flourishing the whip against Giolitti and the Teutonic forces round the Vatican, the Italian Government continued the most vital matter of siege artillery, might have escaped from the intrigues of the Hungarian magnates and the nets of the German-Jewish financiers, and have remained to some extent an independent nation. But the blow from Italy, following on the blows from Russia and Serbia, reduced the governing class in Austria to a condition of decorative impotence. And the Prussian boa-constrictor, having swallowed and digested all the German States, offered to give Poland to Austria, on condition that the Austrians should allow themselves to be absorbed like the Bavarians.

Prussian arrogance—

In the meantime, a considerable force of Bavarian troops was railed south towards the Italian frontier. Several Austrian and Hungarian commanders on the Italian front were dismissed, and the struggle was resumed, with Prussian officers acting nominally as advisers, but actually as the directors of the campaign. Germany was afraid that, without her help, the great Austrian entrenched camps, such as Tarvis, would go the way of the Przemysl forts. With a view, however, to avoiding a state of open war between Italy and Germany, all the German soldiers brought up against the Italians were supposed to have volunteered for this service in an irregular, individual manner. No attempt was made to explain why the German military

TIEPOLO'S FAMOUS FRESCO BEFORE ITS DESTRUCTION.
Giovanni Battista Tiepolo was one of the greatest artists of the eighteenth century, and this beautiful ceiling decoration in the Church of Santa Maria degli Scalzi, on the Grand Canal, was perhaps his most famous piece of work. It was utterly destroyed by a high-explosive bomb.

work of educating the Italian middle-classes and the *haute bourgeoisie* in regard to the permanent interests of the country. It must always be remembered that it was the King, the populace, and a minority Parliamentary party that launched Italy into the war, at a period when the breaking of the Russian line in Galicia and the checks to the British and French advances on the western fronts made the fortunes of the Triple Entente look sombre and even doubtful. At any time between the Russian retreat and the disasters to the Allies in the Balkans a severe reverse to Italian arms might have stirred to violent action all the agents of Teutonism in Italy.

General Cadorna on land and the Duke of the Abruzzi at sea had to be conservative in their use of their principal forces, and in particular to avoid all attempts at brilliant strokes of decision, in which large risks were run. In short, they had to settle down like General Joffre to a rather slow, patient, scientific sort of chess-play, in which all their main pieces were covered by a well-arranged formation of pawns. Towards the middle of June, 1915, General Cadorna showed himself a fine statesman as well as a great soldier by issuing a statement in which the Italian people were clearly warned that the important series of preliminary successes, which had made good the strategical defects of their frontier, would be followed by a long stage of gradual approaches against the enemy's second line, during which the attrition of the Austro-Hungarian forces would be carried on by means of long-range artillery, sappers' work, and local trench warfare with hand-grenades.

ITALY'S SOLDIER-MOUNTAINEERS SCALING HEIGHTS IN THE TYROL.
The Italian Alpini, picked men, born in the mountains, and specially trained for their perilous work, were conspicuously successful in meeting Austrian attacks in the Alps. To approach and engage the enemy, the Alpini had to scale mountain crests high above the perpetual snow-line. This picture illustrates the Alpini's method of climbing a mountain face with ropes and ice axes.

In point of fact, General Cadorna and General Porro seem to have been the first leaders of the allied nations to work out fully the proper system of closely-combined strategy against the Central Powers. We have seen that General Pau first attempted to establish a well-linked Continental movement against the Teutonic Empires, but his scheme broke down when the Russians were compelled to retire from the Carpathians. General Porro then took up the matter and stayed for a considerable time on the French front, consulting with the Staffs of the Western Allies. It is, moreover, an open secret that the Italian Commander-in-Chief refused to divert any of his forces to the secondary theatre of war in the Dardanelles. His was the close logical mind of the Latin race, and he was even less susceptible to considerations of sentiment and prestige than was General Joffre. The possible danger to the new Italian dominion of Tripoli could not move him from his policy of maintaining a single concentrated effort in the field where the final decision was to be obtained. And later, when the Teutonic and Bulgarian advance towards Salonika and Asia Minor disturbed the French Cabinet, General Cadorna was personally inclined to answer this diversion by the simple and direct method of putting more pressure against the enemy's vital line.

But the enemy's line in the North of Italy was of incomparable strength; and after the first surprise attack, by which the Alpine passes were won, General Cadorna had to increase his troops in the field to a million men in order to withstand the enemy's counter-attacks; for the Austrian, Hungarian, and German forces were continually reinforced until they numbered more than double the troops which the Austrian Chief of Staff had first considered necessary on his south-western front. There can be little doubt that the Italians would have broken through the mountain rampart in one month, if the Austrian and German reserves could have been retained in combat by the Russians. As it was, the task of the Italian armies became more difficult than had been contemplated. All went well during the week following the capture of Monfalcone. General Cadorna had the keen joy of recapturing the Isonzo town of Gradisca, which his father had won from the same foe forty-nine years before.

Capture of Gradisca

The capture of Gradisca on June 9th completed the Italian control of the Lower Isonzo, and the general attack on all the fortresses guarding Trieste was then prepared. Of these fortresses four were of supreme importance. On the south was the Carso tableland, immediately defending Trieste. Between this tableland and the foothills

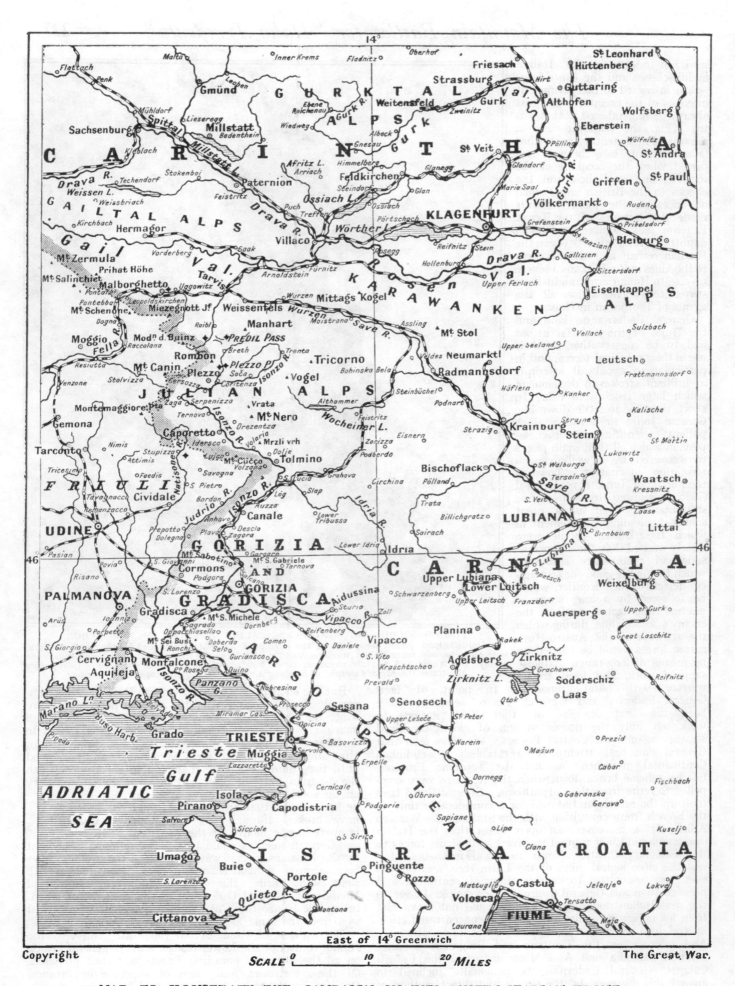

East of 14° Greenwich

SCALE 0   10   20 MILES

MAP TO ILLUSTRATE THE CAMPAIGN ON THE AUSTRO-ITALIAN FRONT.

of the Julian Alps was the river-valley of the Vipacco, barring which was the fortress system of the cathedral city of Gorizia. Then north of Gorizia was a fortified system of heights round the Isonzo town of Tolmino, and above Tolmino was the vast entrenched camp of Tarvis, that extended to Malborghetto and other Alps of Carinthia.

It was useless to mass an army against any one of these fortress systems. Had an attempt been made to win Trieste across the Carso tableland, the advancing forces would have been cut on the northern flank from the Gorizia area. It was also useless to attack merely the Carso and Gorizia. A well-defended advance towards Trieste could only be undertaken by using another large force in thrusting at Tolmino and the

An Alpine Gibraltar Tarvis fortresses, by which ran the road to Vienna. Ever since Napoleon overthrew Austria by clambering over the Carnic and Julian Alps, the Austrian engineers had turned this corner in the Alpine chain into a Gibraltar. The first important system of earthwork fortresses was built after the Napoleonic wars. The system was strengthened after Napoleon III. overthrew the Austrians in 1859 in the battles that freed Lombardy. And when the Italian kingdom was fully established by the war of 1866, the mountain roads to Vienna and to Trieste were again fortified in a more formidable manner. Another great reconstruction followed the Siege of Port Arthur, which was the first important test of the power which fortresses had of resisting high-explosive shells. Then, in 1910, when the German and Austrian Staffs made the great discovery that their new 11 and 12 in. howitzers rendered all armoured and concrete works practically useless, the Alpine fortresses were remodelled, and positions were selected on the plateaux for earthwork systems of defence in which mobile siege-guns could be used.

In the centre of this long fortress-line was the railway town of Plava, lying on the eastern bank of the Isonzo, beneath the wooded heights of Ternovane Forest. Plava, with its tunnels and entrenched heights, moated by the flooded river, formed the point of the middle Austrian salient. In short, it was a key position, and the general Italian offensive began by a night attack on Plava, from Mount Korada on the other side of the river. The Italian sappers, with great coolness and skill, built a pontoon bridge in the darkness; and the infantry crossed the water on June 17th, and by a violent bayonet attack carried the town and the surrounding heights. The fighting was similar to that of our First Army Corps on the Aisne; and it was only by the most stubborn valour that the Italian troops overcame the tremendous difficulties of the position, and won a further foothold on the thickly-wooded heights.

The Battle of Plava The Austrians returned with strong reinforcements, for their commander saw, as clearly as General Cadorna, the importance of the position. On the other hand, the Italian general, having breached the enemy's second line in this place, poured strong forces into the gap, and a great battle took place on the edge of the forested highland. The local conditions were in favour of the Austrian army, for its forces could be massed amid the screen of trees where no Italian airmen could spy them. On the other hand, the Italian heavy artillery across the river on Mount Korada was able to send a plunging fire on the lower tableland, and with this help the dashing Italian troops won the battle and drove the enemy back.

At the same time, the Hill of Podgora, directly covering Gorizia, and forming the barbican of the defence system of the city, was assailed, and a strong reconnoitring force advanced towards Mount Fortin. Then, with five hundred guns massed against the defences of Gorizia, the first great Italian offensive move was made. It was, however, more in the nature of a reconnaissance in force than a sustained attempt to break through the great entrenched camp.

General Cadorna wanted to discover exactly the enemy's new lines of defence and the new position of his heavy mobile artillery. The Italian infantry of the line charged with superb intrepidity, and penetrated both the northern and the southern entrenchments. These extended over a front of more than ten miles from San Gabriele Mount, below Plava, to San Michele Mount on the Carso tableland. The trenches were built in the latest German style, with concrete more than a yard in thickness and armour plate cover, so that not only was shrapnel futile, but even ordinary sized high-explosive shell did little or no damage. Bayonet and rifle also were of no avail in an assault; the lines had to be won and retained by hand-bombs and short knives. The Italian attack would have been a complete check,

PATRIOTS OF THE HOUSE OF SAVOY.
The Duchess Elena of Aosta, whose husband is cousin to King Victor of Italy, with her eldest son, Prince Amedeo, who served as a corporal in an Italian artillery regiment.

if the enemy had been content with having repulsed the four army corps operating under the Duke of Aosta, between Gorizia and the sea. But the comparative ease with which the assault had been beaten back led the Archduke Eugène and his lieutenant, General Boroevics, to take the offensive in turn. They thought the Third Italian Army would be so discouraged that it could be driven over the Isonzo and broken. Therefore, as soon as the Italian attacking forces slackened, the main Austrian army advanced in full force across the Carso Plateau.

Thus began the first grand open field battle between the Italians and the Austrians. It began on June 22nd, and it did not end on July 6th. Although there was a short breathing-space at the end of the first week in July, the Austrians brought up more army corps, and renewed their attack, and it was not until the last days of July that the battle drew to a close. In this long and terrible conflict in the open field, the theatre of which included all

WAR'S ERUPTION AMID THE ETERNAL SNOWS.
General Segato with his Staff in a trench in the Alps during an Italian bombardment of the Austrian positions.

few larger ravines, that resemble the picturesque limestone valleys of the Peak district in Derbyshire. Owing to the action of ·rain on the limestone the plateau is pitted with funnel-shaped holes, which form natural machine-gun redoubts. Then there are innumerable caves from which quick-firing guns could be worked, and labyrinths of crags and scattered rocks, and foliage-hung cliffs behind which large reserves could safely be sheltered.

But General Boroevics lost all the tremendous natural advantages of this immense natural fortress when he sent his divisions charging across the open ground against the lines to which the Italians were clinging ; for though the Italians only held on to the rim of the tableland, in positions somewhat like the Anzacs' under Sari Bair, with a flooded river a third of a mile broad beneath them, yet their well-built sand-bag trenches gave them excellent cover against the enemy's artillery. He seems to have had at first only a few 12 in. howitzers, the greater number of these heavy pieces having been diverted to the Carnic Alps line and the Tyrol and Trentino salients. And though his 6 in. pieces were numerous, the heavier Italian guns across the river could search out the batteries, for the Austrians, in a renewed outburst of over-confidence,

Variety of Austrian formation

the Carso front, the Vipacco River valley, and the southern part of the Ternovane Forest, the enemy suffered such heavy losses that his army was half shattered.

Yet his position had been found impregnable by the forces of the Italian commander, for the five hundred guns which the Italian general employed were quite inadequate. The ground was unassailable. The Carso is a tableland of broken rock rising in places to a thousand feet, and almost uninhabited in peace time. It is planted with trees, seamed with deep, narrow, winding gullies, with a

frequently tried the effect of nocturnal bombardments, followed by night assaults with the bayonet. Their troops were used in every possible variety of formation. They were sent forward in line, in artillery order, in the case of first-rate veteran troops brought from the Russian or Serbian fronts ; or a single fighting-line was established, consisting of a mixture of riflemen and bomb-throwers, and this line was fed, as it advanced and wasted, with files of supports creeping up under cover of the rocks. Then, as neither of these methods of infantry attack prevailed against the solidly - established Italian positions, the old Prussian method of mass attack in columns was employed.

By the second week in July, however, none of the conquered ground was wrested from the Italian army. And as soon as the enemy relaxed his efforts, the Italians began to work up the fortified hills overlooking Gorizia by means of sharp, dashing attacks with bayonet and bomb. In the cultivated ground the siege method of sapping forward could be practised ; but on the bare rock dynamite was needed to excavate a trench, and the charging soldiers had to carry sand-bags to make temporary cover from machine-gun fire. This extraordinary kind of trench-

GRANDSON OF GARIBALDI AS AN ALPINE FIGHTER.
Italian artillerymen hauling a field-gun over boulder-strewn ground during the Alpine fighting. Above: Captain Beppino Garibaldi (left), of the Alpini Brigade, a grandson of the great Italian patriot.

THE RIVER OF CONTENTION BETWEEN ITALY AND AUSTRIA: ENEMY ARTIST'S IMPRESSION OF A BATTLE NEAR THE ISONZO.
The mouth of the River Isonzo and the Isonzo Valley during heavy fighting between Italian and Austrian troops. The Isonzo, rising near Mount Terglon, at the junction of the Julian and Carnic Alps, flows tortuously southward for about seventy-five miles, entering the Gulf of Trieste five miles from Monfalcone, seen in the background and to the right of this picture. In the foreground is the celebrated old Castle of Duino.

making was indeed the general feature of warfare along the three hundred miles of mountain front, for though the rocky masses changed from limestone to granite, gneiss, and other kinds of hard stone, the depth of loose earth was usually small, and sand-bags had to serve as a defence until the engineering corps bored and blasted channels and galleries up and down the steep slopes. All this added greatly to the difficulties of the Italian advance.

The first phase of the Battle of Gorizia ended in the repulse of the Austrian counter-attack in the middle of July. General Cadorna then delivered a fiercer assault, based on the knowledge he had obtained by his first reconnaissance in force. For three days and nights— July 18th, 19th, and 20th—the troops of the Italian Second and Third Armies leaped forward with heroic energy all along the zone of the Isonzo, and broke through the wire entanglements and the armoured trenches, taking 3,500 prisoners. As a rule, the Italians attacked by day, and then resisted in their newly-won positions the nocturnal counter-attacks by the enemy. Owing to the fine work of their engineers, they retained all the ground they had won, and began to deliver night attacks themselves on July 20th.

Both sides reinforced

But the next morning General Cadorna stayed the forward movement of the Duke of Aosta, and bringing reinforcements, ordered every man to help the engineers in strengthening and extending the trenches; for the commander, either through his aerial observers or his secret agents, had obtained knowledge that the enemy was about to make his supreme effort. July 21st passed quietly; then, on July 22nd, a mightier concentration of heavy Austrian artillery opened a hurricane fire on the Italian lines. A large number of German gunners had been sent to the Carso by the Crown Prince of Bavaria, and the

railways from Trieste and Laibach were used to their utmost capacity in bringing up shells.

The main infantry attack was delivered towards Gradisca, where the Italians had built their chief bridges across the Isonzo. The design, of course, was to cut the Italian line of communications, interrupt their supplies of ammunition, and destroy or capture their forces on the tableland. Under cover of the bombardment the infantry advanced in close formation, after massing behind the neighbouring hills. The first line of Italian troops could not kill the close-packed lines quickly enough, and **Supreme Austrian effort** it seemed as though the position would be lost. But the Italian gunnery officers, watching the operation from their observing-posts, had the situation well in hand, and at the critical moment a storm of shrapnel from five hundred guns and howitzers fell on the large target in front of the first Italian line, and made such holes in it that the garrison of the fire-trench beat back the remnant of the attacking masses with little difficulty; and soon after they had stopped the great charge, they received, owing to the excellence of the Italian Staff work, a strong reinforcement. The old and the new troops then charged the shattered ranks of the enemy, captured the lines from which they had delivered the assault, and took two thousand of them prisoners.

The next day General Boroevics, pressed by the Archduke Eugène and his Headquarters Staff, launched another strong attack on the Italian positions near the sea-edge of the Carso tableland. This was an attempt to recover Monfalcone, but it failed completely, though the rough ground did not permit the Italians to make another fierce pursuit. Finally two Austrian divisions, which advanced from the heights of San Michele and San Martino to storm Sagrado, were so smashed up that, on July 25th, the Italian troops were able to carry some of the entrenched slopes of San Martino, and to storm the hill of Sei Busi. Monte Sei Busi, with its seven caverns, was the scene of one of the most violent contests on the whole front, for in a single day it was won, and lost, and won again, each strong opposing army throwing reinforcements up the height, after breaking up all the ground with direct and indirect shell fire.

The crest of San Michele was very important, as it dominated a large part of the tableland, and the main tide of battle surged around and over it for many days. At last the Italian infantry, on July 27th, tearing forward with passionate ardour, bombed and bayoneted their way to the summit, along which they then tried to establish themselves. They also sand-bagged part of the lower slope facing the enemy; but under the torrent of high-explosive

and asphyxiating shell the crest and the exposed slopes beneath it could not be garrisoned. The men had to retire to the sheltered side below the crest, where they were beyond the reach of the enemy's guns and hard to find by his howitzers. The British reader will understand the position by recollecting the struggles of his fighting country-men on Hill 70 at Loos. It is practically impossible to hold a hill-slope facing the enemy's artillery. The best that can be done is to entrench on the reverse slope, and, if possible, keep an observer, with a telephone and a peri-scope, in a dug-out near the summit. This was the method by which the Germans held their downland front in Cham-pagne, and it was the method by which the Austrians held the Carso. **Archduke Eugene's refined cruelty**

All the fighting was an affair of artillery, with thousands of machine-guns serving as secondary armament. In the defence, especially, the infantry was a force only of the third order, and the commanding Austrian, Archduke Eugène, with the refined cruelty of a decadent race of subtle intriguers, employed on the Isonzo front some hundreds of thousands of Slav and Italian troops, natives of the ancient Venetian territories which Italy was fighting to recover. The Italian, Old Serbian, and Croatian regiments were so placed that they had either to fight or be slain by the machine-guns and artillery behind them. All men up to the age of fifty were impressed in all the unredeemed territories, from the Trentino to the Dalmatian coast, and instead of being sent against the Russians, they were forced

SPIKED DEFENCES AND A MASKED MORTAR ON THE ITALIAN FRONT.
An elaborate trench defence built on the Italian front. Above the stone barricade, loopholed for rifle fire, the Italians erected formidable iron railings with spiked tops, sharply pointed. Above: A heavy mortar in position on the Italian front. The timber framework was later covered with brushwood as a mask.

to fight the armies which were struggling to free them.

Two ends were aimed at in this diabolical scheme. The first end was to set the women of the country against the army of liberation by alleging that their men would not have been called up for military service if the terms of neutrality arranged between Prince von Bülow and Signor Giolitti had been accepted. The second end was to depopulate the lands in dispute, so that if Italy won them their value would be lessened by the wholesale destruction of boys, able-bodied men, and middle-aged men. It was also calculated that by pitting the independent Italians against the oppressed peoples they were trying to liberate, the Italians' ardour for battle would be diminished.

In the battles with the Russians and Serbs, considerable bodies of Slav troops in the Austro-Hungarian armies had succeeded in surrendering to their fellow-Slavs.

But since then the Teutonic and Magyar officers had worked out stricter methods of maintaining the power of death over the men of oppressed subject races, whom they set in the front lines. German and Hungarian non-commissioned officers, both of an over-bearing, brutal temperament, were set over the discontented infantry, and this infantry was **Teuton way with** used only as a screen to a chain of **malcontents** machine-gun positions, whose fire swept the entire front. When the infantry charged under cover of an artillery bombardment, the guns were always ready to shatter the men if they tried to go over to the Italians.

It was these unfortunate, tragic, enslaved infantrymen of Latin and Southern Slav origin who were used up by the hundred thousand around Gorizia and around Trento in the first four months of the war. Then the Tyrolese, Austrian, Hungarian, and Bavarian troops had to be employed in larger numbers, as the steady pressure of the Italian offensive increased; for General Cadorna not only brought up continually more men from his resources of three million trained troops, but as progress in the great scheme of re-armament was accelerated by the gospel of munition work, which spread from Britain to all allied countries, the power of Italian artillery, in both the number of pieces and the supply of shells, augmented in a formidable, menacing manner. The Italians were compelled to refuse to take any part in the Dardanelles adventure, because they had no guns to spare on a side issue, and afterwards they were still unable, for the same reason, to send an expedition to Serbia in October, 1915. They had not,

ITALIAN ARTILLERY IN THE CARSO.
An Italian big gun the moment after it was fired. In the foreground is the beginning of a sand-bag barricade.

ALPINI TAKING COVER FROM THE ENEMY'S GUN FIRE.
Next to the Bersaglieri, the finest Italian troops are the Alpini, specially trained mountaineers. In this photograph some Alpini are seeking cover after firing their gun and while being bombarded by the enemy. Above: A patrol of Italian soldiers on the alert.

DD

TEN THOUSAND FEET ABOVE THE SNOW-LINE: ITALIAN SOLDIERS ENTRENCHING AT THE FOOT OF A GLACIER ON THE AUSTRIAN ALPS

Italian soldiers digging trenches and preparing breastworks at the foot of a glacier near a mountain which had to be-surmounted were tremendous. The trenches which the Italians were digging when crest, ten thousand feet above the snow-line of the Austrian Alps. At various points along the Italian this photograph was taken commanded the valley below. Nearer the great glacier was a row of battle-front fighting took place at many thousands of feet above the snow-line, so that the difficulties dug-outs, protected by sand-bags, while in the background a gun-platform was being prepared.

in fact, sufficient first-rate artillery for their own front, and it was not until the deep snows of midwinter increased their blockade of the Alpine passes that they could consider entering any third theatre of war besides the Austrian front and Tripoli.

All that General Cadorna could immediately do, when Austria, Hungary, Germany, and Bulgaria closed round Serbia in October, was to follow the early example of General Joffre and Sir John French. The French and British commanders had helped the Russians in May, June, and September, 1915, by launching great offensives in Artois and Champagne, which compelled the German Staff to rail quickly large forces from the eastern to the western front. In the same way General Cadorna had continually co-operated in the helping movements for Russia, by fierce, sustained thrusts at the Austrian lines, which forced the Austrian Staff to divert troops from Russia towards Italy. And in October, **Cadorna's** 1915, he employed all his power to draw **co-operation** off some of the Teutonic and Magyar pressure against Serbia, by launching a third great assault against the hostile positions along the Isonzo.

Like the grand drive of the Franco-British forces at Massiges and Loos, the Italian offensive on the Gorizia fortress chain failed to break the enemy's resistance. Yet, as in Artois and Champagne, so on the Isonzo, the heroism, endurance, and violence of effort of the attacking forces were tremendous. Of this there is a most striking proof, for the enemy commander on the Isonzo line, General Boroevics, was so moved by the superb courage of the Italian troops as to praise them to his own countrymen. In an interview published in a Hungarian newspaper soon after the battle, the general explained :

The third Italian offensive developed out of a stationary struggle that had lasted for months. The Battle of the Isonzo, from the Italian point of view, was nothing else but an unsuccessful Gorlice, and on our part it was a defensive effort of the greatest magnitude, which could be compared only to that of the German defensive of a few weeks ago on the western front. General Joffre visited the Italian front a month ago, and gave the Italians the benefit of his experiences.

The Third Italian Army, under the command of the Duke of Aosta, attacked the Doberdo Plateau. Part of the Second Italian Army was directed against Gorizia. Twenty-four divisions and two Alpine brigades were in action. Over three hundred thousand rifles and one thousand five hundred guns were directed against the defenders of the Isonzo. The first signs of an offensive were clearly evident in the middle of October, when an artillery cannonade was feeling its way all along the front. The first heavy shells fell on October 15th, and the first infantry hand-to-hand battle was fought on October 18th. On this day it was already clear that the Italians meant business. The first attack was delivered against the northern part of the front—Monte Nero and the bridge-head of Tolmino were the objectives. At the same time the battle began to rage on the Doberdo as well. This was the introduction.

The real battle began on October 20th, when the first important infantry action was fought. On the 20th and 21st the Italian artillery worked with such vigour that our men had to seek refuge in caves. The most strongly-fortified positions **Boroevics' praise** became quite unsafe, and the observers left **of the Italians** there to watch the movements of the enemy, and changed every half an hour, were invariably found to be killed by the time the reliefs arrived. Guns of all calibre were used, and the bombardment lasted for fully fifty hours. Most of our positions were demolished, and the nerves of the men shattered also, and when the Italians believed that the rocks had melted away and every human being had been destroyed in our lines, the infantry attack began. They took some of our positions, but they achieved no substantial success, and the battle raged throughout the day and the night following. There were gallant deeds on both sides, and, if I praise my own men, I likewise cannot deny a tribute to an enemy who fought with the courage of lions.

Instead of subsiding, the battle grew in vehemence, and reached its height on October 24th. On this day the attacks against the Doberdo ceased, only to begin against the Monte San Michele and the San Martino. On October 26th it seemed for a moment that the struggle was coming to an end. The Italians expended less ammunition and used fewer men ; they threw their reserves into the battle with more caution and much more slowly. But on October 28th the titanic struggle assumed a still more desperate character than before, towards the northern part of the front.

This time the bridge-head of Tolmino bore the brunt of the attack for fully three days. At this juncture the battle again took another turn, and the assaults were made on the southern sector of the front.

In the first days of November the bridge-head of Gorizia was the goal of Italian endeavour, not only because its capture would be a visible symbol of Italian success, but also because it is of first-rate importance from a strategical point of view, as it forms a gap between the mountainous region and the sea, and on a front of almost twenty miles contains six excellent roads leading from Italy into Austria. It is, therefore, the best starting-point for an invasion of the Monarchy, and the attacks delivered here were the most furious, and the losses inflicted on the enemy and by the enemy were the greatest. On October 28th the Italian attack was repulsed by the defending forces, yet a few days later, on November 1st, new Italian reserves appeared, two brigades being withdrawn from the Dolomite front. This time they succeeded in taking some advanced positions, and on November 2nd and 3rd more reserves appeared, and superhuman efforts followed, but with no result.

Podgora Hill, which dominates the town of Gorizia, was defended by the 23rd Dalmatian Landwehr Regiment, which on the afternoon of November 2nd repulsed six storming attacks, with the 52nd Hungarian Regiment as its reserve. The battlefield had three distinct areas—the Doberdo Plateau, the bridge-head of

THE CHALLENGE : ITALIAN SENTRIES ON GUARD.
An Italian patrol photographed at the moment they challenged the photographer, who was under the bridge they were guarding, near the Italian lines.

Gorizia, and the bridge-head of Tolmino. At the same time it raged in three distinct periods—first, from October 18th to the 22nd, which period was characterised by fierce assaults delivered on the whole of the front ; from the 22nd to the 26th, when the attacks were delivered only on the northern sector of the front ; and the period from the 26th, in which attacks were made solely on the bridge-head of Gorizia and the neighbouring heights, and which is still undecided. Yet there was one point where, from October 15th up to the present day, the battle did not cease for a moment, and that was the northern part of the Doberdo Plateau.

Although the enemy's efforts did not succeed, I cannot refrain from saying that the bravery of the Italian troops was almost incredible, for even if certain regiments lost all their officers, this did not deter the men from advancing with the greatest contempt for death.

It will be remarked that General Boroevics admits, with gallant frankness, that he lost various positions, and that the number of his men put out of action was great. It will also be noticed that the commander states that the Landwehr of Dalmatia (Italian and Old Serbian troops) were placed in the very forefront of the battle at Podgora

Hill, with an Hungarian force behind them. But the main feature of this extraordinary statement by the opposing army commander is his repeated references to the "incredible bravery" of the Italian soldiers. Not thus did any man in Austria-Hungary or Germany talk of the Italians in the last week of May, 1915. Vicious and base as was the abuse first poured upon our own Territorials and New Army men by the Germans, before Neuve Chapelle and Loos, this contemptuous invective was mild in comparison with Austro-Hungarian insults on Italian valour in the days when the struggle for "Italia Irredenta" was opening. We can fairly judge, from the change of tone in their traditional enemies, of what stuff are made the men of that fine creative race whom the best English minds have loved through all changes of history, from the age of Chaucer, the age of Shakespeare and Milton, the age of Byron and Shelley, and Swinburne and Browning. From the Italian of old we received the torch of poetry, art, and science, and it is pleasant to us to see him now compel his bitterest foe to praise him.

In spite of the exact work of the Italian gunners, in whose school at Turin the Serb and Bulgar artillery officers

AUSTRIAN DEVICE THAT RECALLS HANNIBAL'S PASSAGE OF THE ALPS.
Another instance of primitive weapons surviving to the days of 15 in. guns and high explosive shells. Like the ancient mountain tribesmen, the Austrians, during the Alpine campaign, utilised Nature's "munitions," hurling rocks on to the advancing Italians.

had been trained to the victories of the Balkan War, practically all the victories on the Isonzo line had to be won by hand-to-hand fighting; for though the Italians were terribly exact in handling their new artillery, as the Austrian army commander admits, the general damage they did was slight. The natural and artificial defences, behind which the Austrians fought, protected them from the Italian guns. Shells burst against the rocks and the cemented trenches without reaching the enemy. It was only in the counter-attacks that the effec-

Hand-to-hand on the Isonzo — tives of the Austro-Hungarian-German forces were slaughtered by thousands and tens of thousands. On the other hand, in order to provoke these counter-attacks, the Italian troops had continually to thrust forward. Thus there was produced on the heights overlooking Gradisca and the Gorizia Plain a kind of pumping movement, in which the Third Italian Army continually made little advances and smaller withdrawals in the neighbourhood of the village of San Martino del Carso. There was seldom a week of quietude on the Gorizia front.

The great offensives and counter-offensives were quite as violent as the French, British, and German movements in Champagne and Artois. But in Italy, when the great drive and counter-drive had slackened, fighting went on day and night—somewhat in the fashion of the Hohenzollern Redoubt and Labyrinth combats, but on a larger scale and with much stronger pressure. What we might call the sand-bag brigades moved forward yard by yard, with now and then a happy leap, and when the ground they had won was consolidated, **The sand-bag** the engineers bored and blasted out the **brigades** rock, making permanent fortress works in the Gibraltar style, while the sand-bag brigades, with machine-guns, quick-firers, and howitzers, brought up close to their temporary lines, continued to work forward to the enemy's main system of works. This system was built upon the Doberdo Plateau, rising some three miles south of the village of San Martino, and about the same distance north of Monfalcone. This upland, which dominated the general tableland, was in turn overlooked by a rocky height, Hill 209, towering by the road to Gorizia; and behind it, at Resolica, was the still taller mass of Hill 376. These two hills had well-protected galleries, from which expert German artillery officers directed the fire of the heavy Austrian batteries against the Italian lines at San Michele, San Martino, and Monte Sei Busi. On the Italian side there was no dominating height which could be used for controlling the gun fire; and this work had to be carried out from observation balloons sent up across the Isonzo River.

When it is remembered that Gibraltar, with only a hundred guns, held out against the attacking forces of two kingdoms for more than three and a half years, it cannot be wondered that the Italian army found the great, peaked, rocky mass of the Carso a very difficult thing to conquer; for most of the advantages derived from the developments in modern artillery rested with the defending forces. In particular the Austrians had heavy mobile batteries, moving on newly-made railway tracks, and lighter motor-batteries working along many new branching roads. These could seldom be put out of action, and they came rapidly into the battlefield when a movement of the Italian infantry was signalled on the observation heights. All night the tableland was swept by searchlights, which quickly picked out any body of troops trying to steal an advance, and lighted them up for destruction by the artillery. All the wire entanglements were charged with deadly currents of electricity; and more formidable than all the guns, howitzers, poison-gas cylinders, aerial torpedoes, and flame-projectors which the enemy employed, was his ubiquitous and skilfully used secondary armament of machine-guns. The sea-mists, floating in from the Adriatic, often tempted the Italian sand-bag brigades to make a dash for an enemy trench, when the hostile artillery was blanketed with the fog. But even in these circumstances the remarkably complete organisation of the enemy enabled him to parry a stab through the fog. As soon as a trench was lost, telephone reports reached the German and Austrian gunners, and these, knowing to an inch the range of the lost, invisible position, battered it with

Italian 305 mm. gun bombarding an Austrian fort on a remote mountain peak.

Austrian armoured fort at Malborghetto, in the Carnic Alps, before bombardment.

238

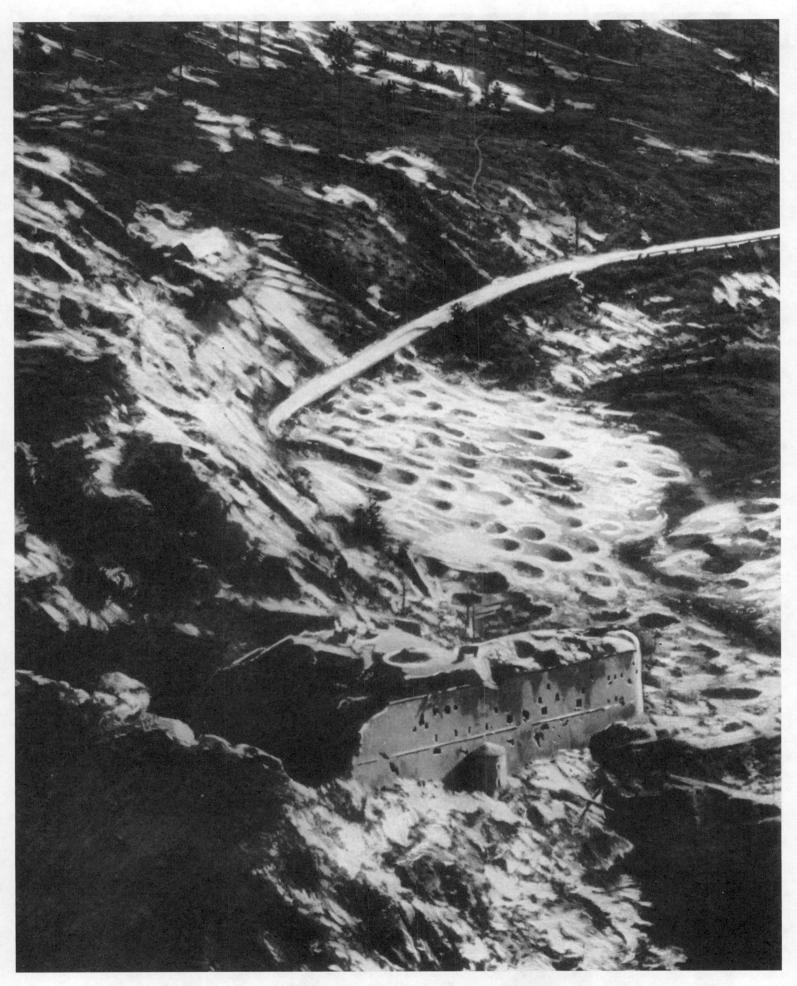

View of the same Malborghetto fort shattered by the Italian heavy guns.

Immense labour and great ingenuity were required to haul the monster Italian guns up the mountain steeps to their positions.

240

asphyxiating shell, by way of preparation for a strong counter-attack by their bombing parties. Such were the conditions under which the Third Italian Army wore down the opposing effectives, and very gradually yet continually worked forward to the Doberdo Plateau.

The deeds of heroism performed in this fortress war cannot be related even by the Italians themselves. For heroism became as common as at Anzac; and as the Italian army was much larger than the Australian and New Zealand Army Corps, and was fighting on a longer front, the adventures of men, battalions, brigades, and divisions were more numerous. There were some very remarkable points of resemblance between the soldiers of Italy and the men of Anzac. In both cases the troops began with a bayonet charge of a fierceness, passionateness, and prolonged fury that was amazing. There was not much science about either of these preliminary charges; but the desperate, deathless spirit of the men enabled them to conquer positions that should have been impregnable. When the Anzac men recovered from their Berserker raids, they showed an engineering skill superior to that of many British regular officers. In parcular, they thought out tricky, original ways of doing things which saved them during the campaign much trouble and many casualties. It was the same with the Italians. When they climbed the Carso, and, going at a run, got too far ahead of their guns and reserves, they fell back towards the edge of the steep, and there surprised their enemy by a speed in rock entrenching as great as their speed in a bayonet attack. They first penetrated into positions which they had to leave, and which afterwards took months for their main forces to approach; and their officers had very great difficulty in holding them back from certain and useless death. But General Cadorna knew his men, and the first extraordinary thrusts in which the troops were, so to speak, given their head, were part of a long-considered plan by the Italian commander. By using first the sheer vehemence in battle of the Italian race, he accomplished swiftly with a few thousand men more than he could have won with a great army by slow, scientific methods. Then when the need for siege-warfare tactics arose, he was still able to evoke at will the flaming spirit of his men, while keeping them firmer in hand and using their great technical ability in preliminary engineering works.

In order to illustrate our general remarks on the valour of the forces that stormed the Carso tableland, we must give one instance out of the hundred dramatic episodes of the war. The chief Austrian bridge-head south of Gorizia was the village of Sagrado. It rests beneath an overhanging hill, which forms a projection of the Carso Plateau, and the railway from Trieste to Gorizia runs under the cliff. Half a mile west of the railway is the Isonzo River, across which stretched an iron railway bridge. When the Austrians lost their advanced position at Gradisca, they tried to blow up the bridge, but only destroyed the centre, and two footbridges were left slightly damaged. In the third week in July some small detachments of Italian infantry crept out by night with sand-bags, and built

Italians and Anzacs

redoubts on the unbroken part of the bridge; and in the darkness their engineers repaired the footways across the broken central piers. Then in broad daylight an Italian field-gun rattled down the valley, horses and men running through the fire from the enemy's positions across the river, and halting by some trees near the bridge.

The gunners quickly got their gun on the target, and began to shell the tiers of Austrian trenches round Sagrado. They drew the fire of every rifle and machine-gun, while the infantry detachments sprinted across the bridge, and got home with the bayonet in the Austrian position. Meanwhile the distant Austrian batteries on the tableland, working by telephone through their observing officers at Sagrado, found the range of the single gun. The little group was soon wrapped in smoke; the men began to fall, and one wheel was shattered. Still the Italians served their gun, until an Austrian shell struck it full on the muzzle, and killed all the crew. But by this time the battalion was across the river, and fighting its way up the steep to the brink of the tableland. All the Austrian artillery curtained off this small force, smashed the bridge down again, and the Austrian troops were

HOW ITALIAN ARTILLERYMEN CARRIED GUNS OVER ROUGH COUNTRY.
The ease with which Italy's fine Alpini manipulated their guns when confronted with mountainous country or marshlands was similar to that of British naval men when operating ashore. When bad country rendered it impossible to drag the gun-carriages, the pieces were taken apart and different sections were carried by the men.

reinforced and flung round the cut-off battalion. But the Italians held out until night, and once more in the darkness their engineers repaired the bridge; an infantry brigade came over and, supporting the heroic battalion, captured a mile or so of the tableland, and there fought back every assault until there was room for an army corps to work forward towards the Doberdo Plateau.

By the middle of November, 1915, the situation on the Carso tableland resembled that in Champagne. The enemy had been driven back to his last line, and had been compelled to bring up half a million more troops.

A seeming stalemate

Having, however, won time to recover from the blow which he had received, General Boroevics constructed another system of lines behind the Doberdo Plateau, so that his position was practically as strong as it had been before. To all appearance the Italian army, like the Franco-British forces on the western front, was in a position of stalemate. It seemed as though only by gradual attrition could the enemy's power of resistance be worn down. But the

AN ITALIAN TRENCH ON A MOUNTAIN TOP.
Italian infantrymen amid the picturesque grandeur of the snow-covered Alpine heights. Alpini passing through a trench during the mountain fighting.

Alpinists clambered over the mountain in the darkness, killed the watchmen silently with the knife, and then dropped in the rear of the two sleeping companies and captured them. This is a good instance of those happy-go-lucky methods of the Austrian officer which excite the contempt of the more business-like and efficient German. In the present case it resulted in an alarming breach being made in the approaches to the entrenched camp of Tarvis.

The Italian siege-guns were able to use the peak of Monte Nero, which is a mountain in the form of a stump 7,370 feet high, as a fire-control station from which the 12 in. shells of their howitzers were pitched into the Tolmino forts, and the southern section of the Tarvis forts such as Flitsch, or Plezzo in Italian, a picturesque village only a few miles south of the famous Pass of Predil, and connecting with it by an easy highway. Plezzo valley, where the Austrians had a mobile battery, was surrounded by a series of brilliant infantry actions in the mountains.

Then at the western end of the great ring of fortified heights, barring the Predil Pass and the highway and railway running into the heart of Austria, was Malborghetto. The Malborghetto forts formed a mountain salient in Italian territory, and the chief works, such as Fort Hensel—a great white oblong of armoured concrete—could be plainly seen from the Italian mountains. The Italians quickly brought their heaviest howitzers against the Malborghetto system, and reduced Fort Hensel and other permanent works to the same condition as that to which the Skoda guns had reduced the Liège forts. When the Italian gunners had done with it, the bare Alpine valley looked in places like **Malborghetto Forts obliterated** a lunar photograph, by reason of the craters made by the 12 in. shells, while the long white fort, blown up at last by a projectile reaching the ammunition chamber, was an amazing spectacle of ruin.

This work of destruction, however, went on very slowly; for the high Alps, over which the shells had to be sent, were usually either veiled in mist or curtained by falling rain. Rare were the days when the air was clear, and the observation officers could watch every shot and telephone the gunners what allowance they had to make for the winds above the mountains. When the forts were destroyed the work of the Italian artillery became more difficult. The enemy brought up batteries of new 12 in. guns, which were hidden on what is properly known as an Alp, that is a stretch of pasture-land, well below the summit, and covered with snow in winter, but used for pasturing cattle in the short summer. The guns were placed in tufted pits and their muzzles concealed from reconnoitring airmen, while dummy wooden guns were partly displayed at a safe distance in order to draw the enemy's fire. The

Italian soldier, like the French and British soldier, did not believe that this state of things was permanent. He had clearly shown such a marked personal ascendancy over his foe that he confidently waited for more guns, more shells, and a large store of stupefying gas, so that he could balance the enemy's extraordinary machinery of warfare, and then engage in a decisive hand-to-hand struggle in the fortress from which the roads branched to Trieste and Vienna.

Meanwhile, the still more exciting, difficult, and wildly picturesque work of Alpine warfare went on in the Julian, Carnic, Dolomite, Trentino, and Tyrolean **A stroke of luck** mountains. In the Julian Alps the fighting mountaineers of Italy had a startling stroke of luck in the first phase of the struggle. From an order issued by the Austrian commander, General Rohr, it appears that two of his companies were set to guard a formidable rampart of rock between Tolmino and Monte Nero. The position was one which five hundred men, with Maxims and quick-firers, could easily have held against an army corps. But the strength of the cliff of rock was so apparent that the Austrian troops took their duties very lightly. Leaving a few men at the post of observation, both companies used to sleep at night. The

REVERTING TO PRIMEVAL WARFARE: AN AUSTRIAN TRAP IN THE ALPS.

A primitive ruse employed by the enemy during the Austro-Italian campaign in the Alps. The Austrians had lashed loose, heavy boulders to the edge of a precipice, and masked them with pine branches. According to this drawing, reproduced from an enemy journal, the Austrians cut the wires holding the avalanche of rocks in position, and so sent them hurtling on to a company of Italian soldiers passing along the mountain path below.

HALLOWED GROUND ON THE FIELD OF WAR.
Italian troops at Mass at a field altar in the Alps. The officer standing beside the priest was about to take the oath. The regimental colours are seen to the left of the altar, behind which are Staff officers.

CYCLIST SCOUTS OF THE BERSAGLIERI.
The cyclists attached to those world-famed regiments of green-plumed sharpshooters, the Bersaglieri, used specially-constructed machines which could be packed on their backs or as quickly unpacked for use.

heavy artillery on both sides could easily pitch a huge shell over the highest peak, and after a few trial shots hit a small target. But the Italians were undoubtedly the finer gunners. They made their calculations more quickly and more precisely, and got their shell home while their opponents were still ranging. This was seen all along the Carnic Alps from Malborghetto on the east to Landro and the grassy flat of Platz Wiese, near Monte Cristallo and Cortina. The Italian artillerymen, firing over glaciers and fields of eternal snow, were **Intricate** often able to report to their commander **artillery work** that they had silenced the enemy's great mobile guns which were invisible to them.

All this long artillery duel, with its weeks of waiting through cloudy weather, when the observing officers on the mountain-tops could not see through the clouds beneath their feet, and the fierce brief outbursts of thunder, when the clouds lifted from peak and glacier, was an involved and interesting affair. The 12 in. guns were not intended to fight each other. They were laboriously hauled up, by the hand-labour of brigades, to plateaux five or six thousand feet above sea-level, in order to outrange and destroy some hostile 6 in. batteries across the Alps. The 6 in. batteries had been brought up in order to overpower the opposing 3 in. mountain guns, some of which were worked by the Italians at the extraordinary height of

10,000 feet. These mountain guns were lifted with ropes, twined around pinnacles of rock, to a dominating position in order to smash up the enemy's machine-gun positions. And, lastly, the machine-guns were used in order to break up any charge by the Alpine troops. When both sides had a strong connecting chain between their 12 in. howitzers and their Alpine troops, the conditions of the duel were fairly regularised. If a 12 in. gun tried to smash up a 6 in. or 3 in. piece, a hostile 12 in. gun would intervene by a direct assault upon the big bully across the mountains. All the real work of advance consisted in winning the peak from which the enemy artillery officers were marking the target and correcting the fire of their heavy artillery.

The peak was not always the highest in the surrounding mountain masses. The strategical value of a height was determined by the direction of the views to be obtained from it, and the extent of the field of vision over hostile scenes of operation. Thus, when the Battle of the Alps became violent and continuous all along the line, **Freikofel and Cresta Verde** small summits, unmarked on ordinary maps and passed over by the happy summer climber in the days of peace, became world-famous through their frequent mention in the daily statements issued by the Austrian and Italian Staffs. Freikofel, as we have already seen, was one of the smaller peaks that stood out continually in the limelight of war. The Alpini captured it by a surprise attack with scarcely any loss, and then for months the Austrian commander sacrificed battalions and regiments, and even brigades, in vain attempts to recover the key-height in the central pass of the Carnic Alps. But the loss of Freikofel, though followed by the loss of Cresta Verde, near the Zellenkofel, on June 24th, did not quicken the minds of the Austrian officers; for in the first week in July the extremely important observation peak of Zellenkofel was lost by them. The enemy had a squad of forty men and some observation officers entrenched on the crest. Below them, on the reverse slope, was a battery of their mountain guns, with indirect fire to sweep the southern slopes of the heights. The battery was in telephonic communication with the observation-station, and the station could also speak by wire to more distant batteries of heavy howitzers, and to the large infantry reserves collected in the wooded valley.

But both the men and the officers on the peak were lulled into a blind sense of security by their extraordinary position; for, on the side on which they faced the Italians, there was not a slope, but an almost perpendicular precipice, with a fall of thousands of feet. In the darkness, twenty-nine Alpini, with an officer, crept up to the foot of the precipice with ropes and a machine-gun. The finest climbers—men who had made a special study of the Zellenkofel—pulled themselves up by jutting rocks, and then let down the ropes by which the other men ascended with a machine-gun. A clatter of falling stones would have alarmed the enemy, but the foot-holds and the rope-holds were so skilfully chosen that no detached pieces of rock were toppled over. Just at moonrise the Alpini squad reached the crest, shot down the sentries, and then killed the garrison of the observation-station by a bayonet charge.

Capture of the Zellenkofel There then followed a long and desperate fight with the mountain battery on the reverse slope. But by means of the machine-gun the Austrians were shattered in trying to make a charge, and their guns were captured just as day was breaking.

By the time the Austrian reserves arrived, the Italian Alpine troops had entrenched on the southern slopes, and with the captured battery protecting them and large reinforcements arriving, they were able to hold the mountain against all assaults, and to break the charging Austrian lines with gusts of Austrian shrapnel and shell, which formed part of the spoil of the Zellenkofel. That in the sixth week of the war the Austro-Hungarians should have let themselves be defeated at vital strategical points by forces of thirty men may, we think, be taken as a fair measure of comparison between the capabilities of the Italian soldier and the incapacity of his foes. The affair on the Zellenkofel also throws a light on the extraordinary series of grand victories which the southern Russian army won over the first-line armies of Austria-Hungary in September, 1914. The apparently formidable military power of the Dual Monarchy was a thing of parade—lath and plaster painted to look like iron. The Austro-Hungarian military caste, which had usurped political power in the manner of the Prussian caste on the ground that democratic government made for weakness in war, proved itself, when the test came, to be disastrously lacking in fighting skill. If the Prussian Staff, which was undoubtedly very efficient, had not reorganised and officered the Austro-Hungarian forces, Italy alone could have shattered the corrupt, spectacular, incompetent governing classes of the decadent Empire of the Hapsburgs. The fable published in the "Frankfürter Zeitung" stated only the brutal truth of the matter.

The present writer would not, however, rank the privates and non-commissioned officers of the Austrian Alpine troops below those of the Italian Alpine troops. Only a year before the war he made a climbing expedition in the Tyrol Alps, in company with a young Tyrolean Alpinist of the middle class. The knowledge, skill, and enterprising spirit of this friendly fellow-climber were remarkable. He was a perfect mountaineer, given to

OUTPOST SCENES ON RIVAL FRONTS DURING THE MOUNTAIN FIGHTING.
Alpini during the fighting in the Carso. A machine-gun section waiting for the approach of Austrians over a ridge of rock. Above: An Austrian outpost firing on Alpini from amid barren, snow-capped peaks in the Tyrol.

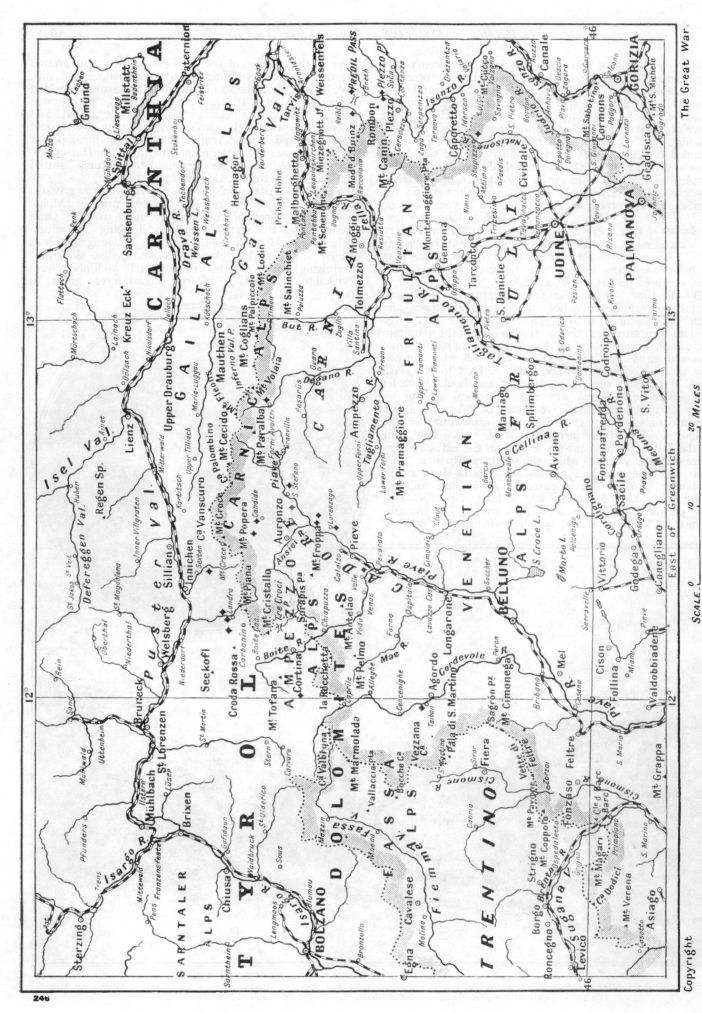

SCALE 0   10   20 MILES

MAP SHOWING THE CARNIC ALPS, THE CENTRE OF THE AUSTRO-ITALIAN FRONT.

The Great War.

exploring for new paths, but methodical and steady in his work. The fact is that the Tyrolean Mountain Corps were formed of excellent material, but they were badly officered. The Tyrolese Regiments had, unfortunately, the name of being the crack body of troops in Austria-Hungary. They therefore attracted from Vienna the kind of courtier officer who wanted to swagger, and who could rely on social and political influence to win for him promotion he could not earn by merit and hard work. Apparently the battles in the Carpathians had not eliminated officers of this kind from the Tyrolese Regiments, and in the first two months of the war they tarnished the bright fame which the bravest mountain race in Austria had won in the days of Andreas Hofer.

It was along the line of the Carnic and Julian Alps, where the Austrian Staff had most frequently conducted manœuvres in recent years, that its Alpine troops chiefly failed. And these troops came into action **Invasive threat** rich with knowledge that had been dearly **towards Lombardy** bought in the Carpathians, while the Italian Alpini were entirely lacking in experience of mountain warfare. It is almost with relief that we turn to the western edge of the rocky battle-front, and find that there the fighting mountaineers of Tyrol managed at last partly to redeem their reputation by a gallant and daring stroke.

Close above the Tonale Pass gleams one of the greatest glacier systems in Europe. The vast crown of ice extends from Alp to Alp for more than twenty miles, showing like a white, cloud-like crescent in the blue sky from Presanella to Care. The broadest part is that which stretches for some six miles to Monte Adamello, 11,640 feet high. There are several easy paths over or by the glaciers, and the Alpini had seized and fortified these, and drawn a retaining line over the system, most of which lay in Italian territory. But as they were watching the Austrian valleys

GENERAL COUNT PORRO.
Sub-Chief of General Staff of the Italian Army, who represented Italy at the Allies' War Councils.

eastward, while the infantry of the line hauled up big guns to dominate Western Trentino, a force of Tyrolean mountaineers, in mid-July, 1915, came over the glaciers by a new track, and penetrated a few miles into Italian territory. At the well-known Garibaldi Hut, belonging to the Italian Alpine Club, there was a battle just beneath the Adamello, and the Tyrolese were thrown back. They retained some peaks from which the Garibaldi Hut was afterwards shelled, but the intended threat of an invasive movement towards Lombardy was reduced to the shadow of a little Alpine skirmish.

Just north of the ice-capped Alps of the Adamello group was the upper part of the lovely Giudicaria Valley, that runs by the fruitful lands of Lake Garda. The Italian troops seized here one of the northern passes by a surprise attack and worked forward towards the forts defending Riva and Arco. All the **The attack on** country south of the Ledro Valley was **Pregasina** gradually won by fierce artillery actions amid the mountains and densely wooded slopes, the duels between the Austrian forts and the mobile Italian batteries being followed by infantry attacks. A striking victory, which had decisive consequence, was the attack on Pregasina, by the edge of Lake Garda, which was undertaken in bad weather in the second week in October, 1915. On the opposite side of the lovely waters the Italians had won Monte Altissimo early in the campaign. They now demonstrated against the town of Riva from this height, and drew the enemy's fire, while across the lake, in difficult mountain country, the western attacking force reached the enemy's entrenchments and cut the wires at Pregasina. Then, screened by a dense fog, the Italian troops charged and took the hill, and though the Riva guns massed their fire on the victors, and poured asphyxiating shells on them, the Italians took the town, and swept through it and conquered the northern hills dominating the Ledro Valley. Every day the force worked furiously forward, shattering

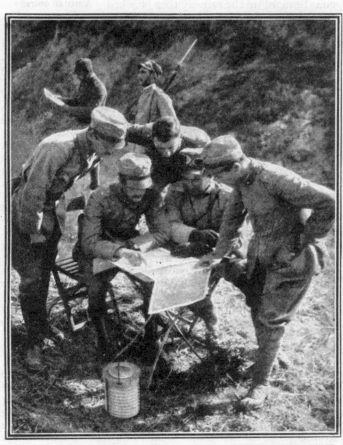

ITALIAN STRATEGISTS AT WORK TO OUTWIT AUSTRIANS.
Staff officers with the Italian forces in the field examining a map and deciding tactical problems.

ITALIAN PIECES, WHICH LORD KITCHENER PRAISED, SILHOUETTED AGAINST SNOW-CAPPED PEAKS.

Italian heavy artillery in position on the Alpine front. These huge, black muzzles, pointing up from the brushwood-covered earthworks, provide a strange contrast to the splendour of the snow-clad mountains against which they are silhouetted. "The achievements of the Italian artillery have been truly remarkable, and the manner in which heavy pieces have been hauled into almost inaccessible positions on lofty mountain peaks, and in spite of great difficulties, evokes universal admiration," declared Lord Kitchener in the House of Lords on September 15th, 1915.

hill forts with its guns, till at the end of October all the western side of Lake Garda, close to Riva, was the redeemed territory of the race that had peopled it.

A similar movement of advance went on at the same time along the eastern lands of Lake Garda and down the Lagarina Valley. As October closed, both forces on either side of the lake were pressing on Riva and battering its fortified heights and bombarding the defences of Rovereto, which barred the road to Trento. All this may appear informative, but unexciting to most of our readers. They would not be stirred, as by fine music, to learn that the village of Bezzecca, in the Ledro Valley, was captured on October 22nd, 1915. But to the Italian, Bezzecca, which Garibaldi had stormed in 1866, was a place of sacred memories, and all the orange groves, citron, myrtle, and pomegranate trees along Lake Garda were hallowed by the struggles of the great Liberator and his red-shirted heroes.

The joy of wresting this storied paradise from the ancient oppressors was felt by every Italian soldier. For months the men sang at their work, and this work of theirs was tremendous. An infantry charge was the rare, romantic thing in the war. Even an artillery duel was a holiday. The daily prose of the campaign was merely navvy work of a long, violent kind. Anything with any resemblance to a road along which a gun could be hauled was dominated by the enemy's forts. New roads had to be made up and down mountains. Round the site of the future road a line of infantry, with machine-guns and field and mountain guns, kept off the Austrians, while most of the Italian force was labouring at levelling the rock, blowing it to bits, shovelling the fragments aside, and making a surface along which 6 and 12 in. howitzers could be moved.

In some places the largest siege-guns were pulled to the tops of mountains by human force. Indeed, one steel monster was to be seen dangling over a precipice, **Incredible** where it was pulled up by ropes. The **engineering feats** Austrians, it is said, tried to do the same thing; but after getting a 12 in. Skoda gun half-way up a mountain they had to let it down again. Their engineers had not arranged the roping properly, or chosen the best scene of operations. Probably not since the Pyramids were built have human hands successfully tugged at such gigantic weights as the hardy peasantry of Italy, Sardinia, and Sicily lifted at need a mile above sea-level. The small guns were raised two miles above the sea by means of ropes, and by the same primitive method large stores of shells and provisions were hoisted above the clouds into the region of everlasting snow. Fuel was hauled up, and tools and dynamite for making caves in which to live in Eskimo fashion, when the valleys far below

were still sweltering in almost semi-tropical heat. This work went on in the Dolomite maze, north-west of the Lake Garda region. There, on the western front of the Trentino and the Tyrol, the Italian forces were thrusting against a series of vital points, along the Trento, Bozen, and Innsbruck railway line.

Trento was approached from the south by way of Riva, but the main advance against this historic town, with its cathedral, marble palaces and castles, rising in romantic beauty by the Adige River, was made along the Sugana Valley. The Italians had advanced very rapidly down this famous valley, till in a few weeks they were east of Roncogno, and barely twelve miles from Trento. But the forts of Cantangel and the mobile siege-guns brought up the railway then checked **Austrian outrage** the advance, and the Austrian gunners **near Roncogno** distinguished themselves by a diabolical act of cruelty. They shelled the alarmed Italian population of the village beyond Roncogno, when the people—old men, women, and children—tried to flee from the zone of death between the two forces and went westward towards the army of liberation.

The Bozen section of railway was menaced by the more northerly thrust along the Cordevole Valley and the connecting swoop from the Cortina region, the first striking incidents of which we have already described. When General Dankl was strongly reinforced from the Serbian and Russian fronts, the Austrians made a very gallant and adventurous attempt to outflank the advanced Italian position. A considerable force of Tyrolean mountaineers climbed over the enormous masses of Mount Tofana, and on a great line of bastion crags, rising two miles above sea-level, there was a long, fierce struggle between large detachments of Alpine troops. It was a more important affair than the battle on the Adamello glaciers, and for some months the conflict went on at this extraordinary altitude. But the Italian Alpini proved themselves the better fighters, and by their powers of endurance, as well as by their skill in shooting, learned in chamois hunting, they cleared the larger part of the Tofana range, threw the enemy back towards Bruneck, and built a line of block-houses to stall off any other surprise attack.

In these little forts men had somehow to live in winter, when even on the lower passes there was a depth of ten to twelve yards of snow. It was also in this region of mountain warfare, where the Italians were curving round their enemy by the new Dolomite road, that a most remarkable example of engineering warfare was seen. One of the grandsons of Garibaldi was colonel of a regiment which was trying to connect from the south with the forces advancing along the Dolomite road. One of the chief obstacles between the two tips of the Italian crescent was the rocky mass of the Col di Lana. This mountain, only 8,000 feet high, commanded a superb view. For this reason it had been a favourite climb with summer tourists, and for the same reason it was an object of desire to the fire-control officers of the contending armies. In their first dash the Italians had reached the western slopes; but the Austrian engineers redeemed the faults of their commander on the Dolomite front by making the Col di Lana a perfect work of military art. A system of trenches and galleries began on the eastern slopes and wound in a spiral up the height, so that the Italians at the western foot were completely mastered. If they tried to charge up the steep, an avalanche of rock would fall on them. This avalanching method of repelling an Alpine attack had been elaborated by both sides. Masses of rock were drilled, filled with sticks of dynamite and other explosives, with an electric detonator which an observation officer could fire when he thought the enemy were clustered sufficiently thickly on the lower slopes.

The hand-bomb and the heavy high-explosive shell were useless against the Austrian Col di Lana works, which had been excavated deeply in the solid rock.

Tunnelling extraordinary But Colonel Garibaldi met this marvellous system of defence with a still more marvellous system of attack. He engaged corps of skilled engineers, who had helped to drill and blast the great railway tunnels on the Swiss frontier. Under his direction, they tunnelled right through the mountain into the Austrian galleries low down on the reverse slope where a hostile battery was working. When the fumes of the last blast of dynamite cleared away, a strong force of bombers leaped from the jagged hole at the end of the tunnel, cleared all the neighbouring galleries, and then, constantly fed by supports, smashed their way up and down the mountain.

But towards the middle of September all this extraordinary Alpine warfare began to slacken, for winter was setting in, and veins of snow appeared on the bare rocks and broadened into white fields. Preparations for an Arctic campaign had been going on for months. Wire railways ran from the valley and caves on the summits; strong lowland torrents, that were known not to freeze, were harnessed to dynamos, and the currents were wired up to the heights to warm, light, and do cooking for the fur-clad garrisons of the peaks. Great stores of ordinary fuel and food were also hoisted up to the detachments likely to be cut off for weeks, or even for months, by the snow. Then in many places it was possible to arrange for snow-clearers to fight each fall of snow, and keep a practicable white ravine running to the mountain-top, by which frequent reliefs could be sent to the troops that lived and watched above the clouds. As on most mountains used for observation purposes the snow fell thickest on or near the summit, the garrisons had to work incessantly to prevent themselves from being buried in snowfalls; for no matter how well the direction of the prevailing winds was studied, practically nothing was known about the way in which the snow would drift and pile up. So the men had to be prepared to dig themselves out every morning, and maintain a sort of crater to the great snowfield. By November, 1915, the Alpine troops on both sides were more busy fighting against the terrible powers of Nature in her sombre moods than in trying to steal little tactical positions from each other. And so a halt was called until the spring.

Both sides fighting Nature

AN ITALIAN SIEGE-HOWITZER WELL SCREENED FROM ENEMY EYES.
Napoleon's scaling of the Alps falls into insignificance when compared with the gigantic task undertaken by Italy when she used her monster ordnance against the Austrians on the "roof" of Europe. By successfully transporting huge siege-howitzers into almost inaccessible positions among the Alpine heights and chasms, Italy proved herself a Hercules among the combatant nations in the Great War.

IN THE INTERNMENT CAMP
AT BADEN.

BRITISH PRISONERS LINED UP
FOR BATHING.

GERMAN INHUMANITY TO BRITISH PRISONERS.

By F. A. McKenzie.

The Hardships of Our Captured Soldiers—Brutal Tyranny of the German Guards—The American Ambassador Intervenes—The Official White Books Relating to Prisoners of War—Inhuman Treatment of Major Vandeleur—The Slaughter of Our Wounded—A Pleasing Contrast—A Canadian's Terrible Experience—British Herded in Cattle Trucks—German Women's Insults to British Prisoners—Pitiless German Red Cross Nurses—The Dum-Dum Bullet Charge—Wholesale Arrests of British Civilians in Germany—British Civilians Housed in Horse-Boxes and Stable-Lofts—" Coffee " of Burnt Barley—Horseflesh as Food for Interned British Civilians—Prisoner Organisation at Ruhleben—Clothing and Food Sent from England Stolen by the German Guards—Protest by Men of the West Kent Regiment at Sennelager—British Soldiers' Retorts to German Taunts—Daring Escapes from German Bondage—The Case of Private Lonsdale—An Outrageous Retrial—German Protests on Behalf of Lonsdale—Trench as a Hospital for Wounded Prisoners—Fruits of the American Ambassador's Representations—Prison Camps " Window-dressed " for Neutral Visitors.

BY the winter of 1915 there were over 32,000 British prisoners of war in Germany, confined in one hundred and eighty camps and one hundred hospitals. Some had been interned since August, 1914, sailors of merchantmen at German ports immediately before the declaration of war, and prisoners from Mons, wounded and left, or stragglers cut off during the great retreat. The British prisoners were scattered among French, Belgian, and Russian captives. A large number were kept in big prison camps such as Münster, Sennelager, Schneidemühl, Giessen, and Ohrdruf. Some of these camps held as many as 40,000 men. A few of the badly wounded were in semi-private hospitals in Belgium, where they received much kindness from the people. Others were imprisoned all over the German Empire ; in the suburbs of cities like Berlin and Hamburg, in the Harz Mountains, in Schleswig-Holstein, in Bavaria, in Mecklenburg, and in Westphalia.

Great indignation was aroused in Britain by the ill-usage of our captured soldiers. The Hague Convention, which Germany, in common with other great Powers, signed, laid down certain regulations for the protection of prisoners of war. These stipulated that prisoners must be humanely treated, that all their personal belongings, except arms, horses, and military papers, are to remain their property, and that their rations, quarters, and clothing are to be on the same footing as troops of the Government which captures them. These requirements, although strictly

observed by Great Britain in her provision for German prisoners, were ignored by Germany. Numbers of our men, particularly in the early days of the war, were stripped of their overcoats and coats, and were left in their shirt-sleeves to face the rigours of a North German winter.

In some cases, as in Schneidemühl Camp, even their boots were taken away and sabots substituted for them. Their housing accommodation was exceedingly bad. Men were left out in the fields for weeks during the wet autumn weather, sheltering themselves as best they could in holes in the ground. Later, they were transferred to circus tents, leaking badly, and forming no protection against wet weather. From these they were again transferred in due course to hastily erected wooden huts. In some camps the sanitary arrangements were so inadequate that typhus and cholera broke out. The guards were at first allowed to exercise the most brutal tyranny unchecked. The food was often bad, and was of a kind which even the hungriest of our men found it difficult to eat.

In the beginning little complaint was made from England about the treatment of the men.

It was feared that criticism and publicity might make the lot of the prisoners harder. Private representations were employed, and the good services of the American Ambassador at Berlin were enlisted to visit and inspect the camps and to help to relieve the most pressing wants of the prisoners.

Early in April, 1915, the British public were aroused by the issue of an official White

THE "ARMS" OF DÖBERITZ.
Mock coat of arms designed by British prisoner at Döberitz. The " canting heraldry " explains itself, but the brave motto only emphasises the bitterness of the joke.

Book containing correspondence with the United States Ambassador in London, relating to the treatment of prisoners of war and interned civilians. The facts given here left no doubt that our men were being treated, in many cases, with brutal cruelty, and that often the British prisoners were picked out for special severity. This was shown, for example, by the evidence of a Russian medical officer who had returned to Petrograd after three weeks' detention as a prisoner of war at Dän Hollam bei Stralsund. He said :

"The British officers are not as well treated as the Russian officers. They are placed among the less-educated Russians, so that they cannot talk. The Russians are allowed to buy books, but the British officers are not allowed to do so. The German lieutenant in charge is openly insulting and hostile towards the British prisoners." One British officer complained of his conduct, and expressed the opinion that the German officer was acting on his own feelings and that the German authorities were not aware of his conduct towards the British officers, but the doctor did not entirely share that view.

A Russian doctor's report

Sir Edward Grey sent to the American Ambassador in London a report by Major Vandeleur, of the 1st Cameronians, who escaped from Crefeld where he had been interned, on the treatment meted out to him and to other British officers and men after capture. Major Vandeleur was taken prisoner on October 13th, 1914, by the Prussian Guard Cavalry, close to La Bassée. The troops who captured him treated him well, giving him food and shelter, although they did not treat the other prisoners well. They evidently hoped to get some information out of the officer, for they bombarded him with numberless inquiries concerning the state of the British Army and our munitions.

Major Vandeleur, though wounded, was left on view at Douai, in the square in front of the Town Hall, where he was exposed to much abuse from the people. He and his fellow-prisoners were treated with the grossest inhumanity on their way to Germany to be interned. The officer declared that in his opinion this treatment was deliberately arranged for by superior authority "with the object of making us as miserable and despicable objects as possible." British officers were treated quite differently from the French. When they reached Crefeld the treatment improved. Major Vandeleur's complaints were supported by similar accounts from various other camps. They were afterwards amply confirmed by the stories told by helpless wounded exchanged prisoners of war on their return to this country.

There can be little doubt from the first-hand accounts of men present on the battlefield that in a number of cases the German troops in the first line of advance slaughtered some of our wounded men who were lying helpless on the field. They seemed to be worked up to a point where they were scarcely responsible for their actions, consumed with a blind lust for slaughter. It is only just to the

[Lafayette.

CAPT. A. STANLEY WILSON, M.P.,
Member for the Holderness Division of Yorkshire, who was taken prisoner, in December, 1915, from a Greek ship on the way to Messina, by an Austrian submarine commander.

MAJOR C. B. VANDELEUR,
1st Cameronians, who escaped, in December, 1914, from a prisoners' camp at Crefeld, and was honoured by an audience with King George, to whom he related details of his harrowing experience after his capture near La Bassée in the previous October.

[Lafayette.

Germans to say that this was not true in every case. Some prisoners have reported that they received great kindness from German Red Cross men. Thus one prisoner, telling of his capture in the opening attack at Mons on August 23rd, 1914, described how every man in his line was killed or wounded before the Germans pushed up :

One of the Red Cross men came up to me. Bullets were flying all around, but he took no notice of them. He spoke to me in English, and bandaged up my wound. He discovered that my other foot was wounded, and bandaged it also. He gave me a drink, two packets of cigarettes and some matches, covered my feet with straw, told me to lie still so that the bullets would not get me again, and moved on to other cases. He was all right, that Red Cross man was.

This, however, was an exception. In too many cases the wounded were treated with the greatest brutality. One of the most appalling stories was told by a Canadian prisoner who was in the deadly angle outside Ypres, where the Canadians held back the German advance in April, 1915. For two days his company held their ground amid the most terrible conditions. Then they were obliged to retire. They carried all the wounded back with them to a house somewhat in the rear, laid them in a cellar there, and after this was done set out to fight their way back through the Germans who were surrounding them. The man who told the story was one of the wounded left in the cellar. He related how :

We lost sight of our own men, and then the Germans rushed up to the house. There were two wounded officers among us who knew a little German. They called out that we were all wounded men under the Red Cross. The Germans took no notice. They poked their rifle barrels through the windows, and fired again and again among us. I expected every moment that a bomb would be hurled in the cellar, finishing us all at once. After a time the firing ceased and we were ordered out. We had to crawl or drag ourselves out, or help one another as best we could. Broken legs and wounded bodies didn't matter. We had to get out.

They made us parade in a row. There were no ambulances or stretchers. Some of them angrily asked us what Canadians were doing taking part in this war. They ordered us to make our way to the dressing station some distance back. They threatened us with the points of their bayonets, and forced us on. My leg was broken and badly splintered. Two other men who could walk let me put my arms round their necks, and I travelled in this fashion, dragging myself along while I hung on to them. It seemed to me that I went for a mile or a mile and a half.

Canadians' awful experience

You ask me how I did it? I do not know. You can do many things that seem impossible, when you have to. At last I reached a stage when nothing could force me another yard. The Germans then let me and some others, who were as bad as I was, lie on the grass, while they went on with the remainder, and said they would send an ambulance for us.

We were desperately thirsty. The only drink I had had for some time was water gathered from the pools formed by the rain, pools where the bodies of our dead lay, and where all the filth of the battle had run.

My mouth was like ashes. Water! A young fellow lying by me was in much the same state as myself.

Two German soldiers were passing. He called to them, "Water, water!" One of the Germans turned on him with a snarl on his face. "Wasser!" he said. "Wasser, Ja!" and he deliberately unslung his rifle, pointed it full at the young fellow, and shot him between the eyes.

Cold-blooded murder

Here is the story of another prisoner :

I fought with our regiment at Mons and at two other places, and then in the Aisne district I was captured. I felt sure that we would be shot, as they called us "English swine," poked us with bayonets, kicked us, and nearly knocked one poor fellow's eye out with the butt-end of a rifle. One or two other English prisoners joined us later on who had been knocked about badly with bottles.

We were put in a church one night, where one mad German devil struck one of our chaps in the mouth with his fist, loosening his teeth and cutting his mouth badly. Our chap looked like hitting him back, when the German brought his revolver out and several other Germans their bayonets. Of course, they knew we were unarmed, the cowards!

I may say that when we captured some Germans we gave them the last bite of food we had in our haversacks, also tobacco, and treated them well. I could swear before God that this is truth.

These stories, and others equally shocking, carry conviction by the dispassionateness with which they are told, and they were amply substantiated as time went on and new evidence became available.

BOXING MATCH IN THE CIVILIAN INTERNMENT CAMP AT RUHLEBEN.
At the outset, and throughout the first winter, conditions at Ruhleben were shocking, and many of the captives died of want and hardship. The survivors remained undaunted, and by organising every available means of mental and physical recreation they made their captivity just endurable.

BREAKFAST IN THE OPEN AIR AT TELTOW.

Breakfast in most of the German prison camps consisted only of " coffee " made from burnt barley, without milk or sugar, and any bread the man might have saved from the previous day.   The bread was made from rye and potatoes, without any wheat or flour, and was heavy and unpalatable.

The prisoners, often wounded and unwounded alike, were herded in cattle trucks and sent back to Germany for internment.   In some cases they were packed so tightly in the trucks that it was scarcely possible for a man to move.   There they were left, often for four days, moving slowly down the country, without food, save sometimes a few loaves of bread thrown in among them, without water, enduring untold torments.   People would come up to them at places, laugh at them, threaten them by pointing weapons at them, and call them every abusive name, of which " English swine " was the most common.   Even prisoners so badly wounded that they could only be carried back, were exposed to unspeakable brutality.   One man who was wounded in his back, his side, and his leg, described how after capture he was taken to a building in Courtrai, turned by the Germans into a temporary hospital.   The German doctors did little or nothing for the British prisoners, and as they lay there helpless and wounded, the Germans turned on them and abused them, calling them " swine," " pig-dogs," and the like.   The wounded were ordered next day to walk down two or three long streets to the station.   This was beyond the power of one of the wounded men, so a fellow-prisoner in the Royal Engineers carried him.

Unspeakable brutality—

I shall not soon forget that walk.   All the way along there were German soldiers who had come out to see the captured Englishmen.   They laughed at us, pointed at us, jeered at us, mocked us.   Some French women tried to reach us to give us water, fruit, or chocolate.   They pushed them back.   One Frenchwoman did succeed in reaching me.   They let her hand the fruit to me, and then a German soldier gave my hand a smart knock upwards, scattering it all !   Then they hustled the woman back again.

You must remember that we were the first British prisoners that these men had seen.   We were put in cattle trucks, and remained in them for three days, for most of the time without food or drink, on our way to Münster, our destination   At Brussels they handed us some bread, but it was so bad we could not eat it, much as we needed something.   When we reached Germany people came into our trucks to bait us.   Men would come with revolvers and hold them to our heads as we lay helpless, threatening to shoot

us.   Women were worse than men.   They knew a few words of English abuse, at any rate, and hurled them at us.   One of their tricks was to snap their umbrellas smartly open in our faces.

Another prisoner in Burg, Saxony, wrote :

At intervals throughout the journey we would stop at a station of some importance, where ladies (save the mark !) of the German Red Cross Society were in attendance with coffee, sandwiches, and cigars.   Not for the prisoners.   Do not think it !   No, for the escort—whose capacity, by the way, was fairly astounding.   Indeed, so far were these same ladies from understanding charity in our acceptance of the word, that at one station—Magdeburg—Davy heard one of them demand a solemn assurance that the coffee was not for the " Engländers," before she would hand a cup of the stimulating beverage to one of the escort.   It is gratifying to be able to record that the instant the " ministering angel's " back was turned, the escort, whose heart though Teutonic was not made of granite, handed the coffee to his thirsty charges.

When the first British prisoners of war reached German towns they were the victims of tremendous outbursts of indignation.   Great crowds waited for them.   They were put as it were on exhibition for a time, paraded round the streets of the cities in carts, and left under guard at the railway-stations.   The vilest stories had been spread abroad concerning them.   The favourite one was that our men gouged out the eyes of German wounded.   This tale was believed by great numbers of German people. The picks that are to be found in many British pocket-knives—picks really meant for extracting stones from horses' hoofs—were exhibited as the British weapons specially devised for taking out German eyes.   We were said to use dum-dum bullets.   The ordinary revolver bullet was declared by the Germans to be a dum-dum, and there is every reason to believe that a number of British prisoners, more particularly cavalry officers, were shot in cold blood after capture by the Germans for having these bullets on them.   The thing was a brutal outrage, contrary to every law of war and law of humanity.   But the Germans stuck at nothing.

--and vile misrepresentations

Besides the military prisoners, the Germans had from the first numbers of British civilians.   There were many

BRITISH OFFICERS SELECTED FOR REPRISALS BY THEIR
GERMAN CAPTORS.
Reading from left to right : Capt. the Hon. J. Coke, Scots Guards ; Capt.
H. Jump, Royal Dragoons ; Major S. Ashton, 2nd Life Guards ; Capt.
R. Stuart-Menzies, Scots Guards ; Lieut. K. Palmer, 2nd Life Guards ;
Sec.-Lieut. Schone, 60th Rifles ; Sec.-Lieut. Gage-Brown (Interpreter),
2nd Life Guards ; Sec.-Lieut. McNeile, Coldstream Guards ; Lieut. Lord
Garlies, Scots Guards ; Lieut. the Hon. R. Bingham, Royal Welsh
Fusiliers ; Capt. E. Trafford, Scots Guards ; Lieut. Wavell Paton, Cold-
stream Guards. These were some of the officers who, early in 1915, were
selected for reprisals following upon the announcement made by the
British Government that German submarine pirates would not be con-
sidered honourable prisoners of war, and would be treated as criminals.
This decision, however, was revoked.

INDIAN PRISONERS AT LILLE.
They are interested in a photographic negative of an engagement in
which they took part.

British people in Germany at the time of the outbreak of
war, people who had settled in Germany for business,
holiday-makers, tourists, people visiting health resorts,
and the like. There were many Germans in England.
The Germans in England were given time to leave. Our
Government gave them every facility for leaving, and
went so far as to permit large numbers of able-bodied
men of military age, Army reservists, to get back to
Germany from other lands in vessels that came under
the supervision of our Fleet. The Germans acted
very differently. British vessels in German ports were
prevented from leaving some days before the declaration
of war. British people, except under special circumstances,
were not allowed to leave Germany after war was declared.

Numbers of Englishmen, such as sailors at ports, and
visitors, were arrested as spies before the war broke out,
and were detained, often without trial. Others were kept
under semi-arrest. Even old men in the sixties and
seventies who had gone for heart treatment to Nauheim were not allowed to   Internment of
go back until some weeks after the   all Britons
outbreak of war ; and on November
6th, all Britons of whatever position were arrested
throughout Germany and placed in internment camps.

The main camp for civilian prisoners was at Ruhleben—
a race-course outside Berlin. The racing stables were
turned into prisons. The buildings were strong and
substantial, remarkably good for racing stables. On the
ground floor there were a number of loose-boxes, each
intended for one horse. These loose-boxes were made into
compartments for four, five, or more men. Those who were
housed in the loose-boxes were comparatively well off.

Above the loose-boxes were lofts about two hundred and
sixty feet long and thirty feet wide, with their roofs sloping
downwards on either side, from eight feet in the centre to
three feet high at the ends. The lofts were badly lit and
poorly ventilated. Two hundred men were placed in each
one of these ; there they had to live and sleep. A
description of life in these lofts, given by one returned
prisoner, speaks for itself :

These lofts, built for storing hay, have undergone no alteration
for the accommodation of men. The ventilators are four in number,
two on each side ; they measure each one foot square exactly, and
let the rain in when open. There are also four very small windows
on the sides ; but as they are only twenty inches off the ground, it
is impossible to open them during the night as men have to sleep
close against them. The wall in which these windows are set being

only three feet high, it will be seen at once that the loft is permanently dark, and that the inmates live in perpetual gloom, being unable to read either by day or by night. In the evening, after sundown, the lofts are illuminated by a half-dozen eight candle-power electric lights. This light is sufficient to move about by, but not for any other purpose.

Hot water is only in the pipes from five to eight o'clock, and for the rest of the time the cold is intense. On some days it is impossible to keep warm. The camp contains many rich people—quite a large number of Eton and Harrow men, and several

Cold and darkness at Ruhleben

well-known professional musicians being interned—and money has been offered to cover, and much more than cover, any necessary expense in having the extra fires; but no answer is returned to these requests. Such treatment gives the impression that a deliberate attempt is being made to punish these civilians for—well, for not being German.

For sleeping accommodation, it has been said in the papers that each man has a bed to himself. Yes, in the loose-boxes which the American Consul sees, but the large majority in the lofts have nothing of the kind. Here the prisoners have a cement floor. Each evening at eight o'clock they have to place two wooden blocks six feet apart. Each block is four inches thick, three inches high, and five feet six inches long, resembling the joists beneath the floor of a house. On these two supports a flat piece of wood resembling a table top is placed. This forms the bed, and on it, placed crosswise, are four sacks stuffed with hay, straw, and shavings. On these four sacks five persons have to sleep. This bed is only the size of an ordinary double bed in England. A thin cotton blanket is given to everybody, but the wealthy interned members have purchased good woollen blankets for everybody, in consequence of which these cotton ones have been taken away by the guards.

The food supplied to the men was the same as the food supplied in most of the German prison camps. Here and there there were slight improvements or variations according to the locality, but the general ration was as follows:

Early in the morning the men were served with a cup of coffee, the "coffee" being made from burnt barley (not coffee beans), without milk or sugar. During the morning the day's bread was issued, bread made from rye

and potatoes, dark, heavy, and unpalatable, and without any wheat or flour in it. The quantity of this bread was so inadequate that, as a prisoner said, one man could eat three men's daily portion at one meal. The noonday meal consisted of a dish of soup—bean soup, cabbage soup, barley soup—with a little piece of meat, usually horse-flesh, sometimes preserved pork. The amount of meat varied with the camp. In some camps every man obtained

CHEERFUL MEMBERS OF THE ALLIES' "COLONY" AT CREFELD PRISON CAMP.

From left to right, standing: Lieut. the Hon. R. Bingham, R.W.F.; Lieut. C. Norman, 9th Lancers; Lieut. R. E. Hindson, R.W.F.; Lieut. R. Bernier, French Artillery; Lieut. Firth, 18th Hussars; Capt. J. G. Smyth Osborne, R.W.F.; Lieut. E. Wodehouse, R.W.F.; Lieut. Michnevitch, Russian Sapper; Lieut. H. C. H. Poole, R.W.F.; Capt. G. Edwards, Sherwood Foresters; Sec.-Lieut. McNeile, Coldstream Guards; Capt. Jump, Royal Dragoons; Sec.-Lieut. C. Reynard, K.R.R.C.; Lieut. G. M. Evans, R.W.F.; Capt. Barrow, D.C.L.I. Sitting: Lieut. D. M. Barchard, R.W.F.; Lieut. C. G. H. Peppe, R.W.F.; Capt. C. C. Schneider, Sherwood Foresters. The first photograph on the page shows a group of French and British soldiers, including a Turco captured by the Germans. This was taken in Lille.

a small piece of meat ; in others the prisoners cheered when any man in their party had a piece in his soup, so few came their way. The great complaint about the soup was usually its bad quality. It took even hungry British prisoners a long time to be able to tackle the meat. The soup was sometimes putrid, sometimes full of maggots, and sometimes spoiled in preparation. In the evening the men would get either some coffee or similar dishes of soup. The conditions about food were at their worst at the beginning. Some improvement was made later on, but it was generally true that the prisoner who had nothing but his German rations to maintain life with lived in a state of semi-starvation.

Semi-starvation and punishment At Ruhleben the prisoners had at first to form up in each barracks every morning, and march along to the kitchens for their coffee, and wait there often in the rain or snow, maybe for two or three hours, before their turn came. Some were employed during the day with different work—in erecting sheds or barbed-wire fences, or cleaning out the camp. The guards placed over them had apparently unlimited powers of punishment, which they used very freely.

This great community of Englishmen of almost every class and almost every circumstance gradually began to evolve its own organisation. The lot of the sick in the camp was very pitiful, so one prisoner, a London coal merchant, asked the authorities to let him have a house that he could turn into a hospital. He organised this

TWO DISTINGUISHED CAPTIVES.
Lieut.-Col. Bolton and the Earl of Stair, both of the Scots Guards, who were among the British prisoners detained at Crefeld, where the shameful conditions of confinement were eventually improved.

SCARRED BY WAR AND RACKED BY PRISON.
Hapless Canadians who were incarcerated at a prisoners' camp in Germany. Each face bore signs of privation, and the motley condition of their attire is a further indictment of German inhumanity.

hospital with the utmost efficiency, and the comfort provided there undoubtedly saved the life of many a man. Another Englishman, Mr. Powell, was made captain of the camp, and after a time he took the entire charge of the food and of the camp organisation into his own hands, of course under the supreme control of the German authorities. He appointed different committees : a finance department, for the control of all camp funds and the distribution of money for relief ; a sanitation department ; an education department, for the control of schools, classes, lectures, etc. ; a recreation department, for sports, concerts, debates, and theatricals ; a health department, for care of the sick, the prevention of illness, and the distribution of relief in kind ; a watch and works **Organisation of** department, maintaining order in camp ; **prison life** a kitchen department, for all questions concerning prisoners' food ; and a canteen department, for the control of the camp canteens. Educational classes were opened. The prisoners started a monthly magazine. The poorer men tried to earn a little from the more prosperous by opening barbers' shops, by offering to clean shoes, by cobbling and the like.

The race-course at Ruhleben became the centre of a great community. But what a community ! Here were hundreds of men taken without warning, most of them, from their wives and families—professional men with their careers broken ; financiers, all of whose schemes had stopped ; working men whose wives and families had to do as best they could while the husbands were in prison. There

UNDER THE "EAGLE'S" WING.
Two wounded British soldiers as they appeared in their hospital garb at Döberitz. Both had their hair cropped short after the manner of German militarism.

was the mechanic who had been sent over to finish a job in Germany just before the outbreak of war; the photographer who had visited Germany to complete his collection, and who had narrowly escaped being shot as a spy; the man who had visited Germany for treatment for his eyes or his heart; the master who had just started his summer holiday with a long-anticipated tour down the Rhine; the son of English parents who had lived in Germany so long that he had come himself to look like a German—all were there.

While in some of the hospitals wounded prisoners were badly treated, this was not universally true. Many of the German doctors in the civilian hospitals to which wounded men were sent behaved with humanity and decency, and treated them as they would have done their own people.

Severity in military prisons In the numerous military camps the discipline was stricter and more severe than in the civilian camp at Ruhleben.

In some of them the conditions during the winter of 1914-15 were so bad that it would be difficult to paint them too darkly. Numbers of men had very little clothing, owing to their own having been stolen by their German captors. Their whereabouts were not immediately known to their friends in England, and consequently they had to rely almost wholly upon the German prison rations. Even when parcels began to be sent from England they were often stolen, or a large part of their contents taken away before they reached the man they were meant for. The discipline was brutal. The guards had

canes, which they freely used on the backs of the prisoners. Men were tied tightly to trees as a punishment, and left there for hours at a time, day after day. The guards would hit men over the head with their rifles, threaten them with their bayonets, and if they made the least show of resistance, would have them punished for attempted mutiny.

Thus at Schneidemühl on one occasion the British prisoners were deprived of breakfast because they were told there was not enough food in the camp for them. It was a rule at that time in this, as in many other camps, that when food was short the French and Russians were fed first and the British went without. One of the British prisoners lingered around the cook-house. The German guard told him **Injustice and cruelty** to hurry on, and struck him on the head with a rifle. The man raised his hands to his head to protect himself as the German was bringing down his rifle again. The guard thereupon reported the man for resisting authority. The British prisoners were paraded, and the man was brought out, tied over a barrel, and severely beaten with sticks by two of the guards. When this was finished he was tied to a tree. One English prisoner standing in the ranks whispered a word of protest to the man standing next to him. Thereupon one of the guards came up and struck him across the face with the stick he held in his hand.

We have only one blanket to keep us warm (one private in the Somerset Light Infantry wrote), and it has been freezing and snowing for a week. I had to buy a pair of boots out of the money you sent me and a guernsey to keep me warm, as when I was

MEN WHO "DID THEIR BIT."
Three more British captives posing for their photographs outside a German prison ward. All were wounded in the war.

wounded they took my boots from me and made me walk barefoot, and kicked us into the goods shed at Mons Station. But you must not worry about me, as I can stick all their games, and I am quite as hard as they are.

At first in many camps the British prisoners were not required to work, but very soon they were put to regular tasks around the camps, and then to all manner of labour in the mines, on farms, and elsewhere. The German authorities even tried to induce them to engage on munition work, or work for the manufacture of war material for the German Army. This they refused to do.

The result of the hardships and bad food, and the constant injustice, was to produce a feeling of deep resentment amongst the great masses of the British prisoners. On one occasion, at Sennelager, one of the large military camps, the prisoners belonging to the West Kent Regiment met together and demanded that they should see the commandant of the camp. "You're starving us," their spokesman told him. "If you want to kill us, why don't you line us up against the wall and shoot us? We're soldiers, and should understand that. But if you think **West Kents' proud protest** you will break our hearts by starvation, then you can't do it!" The commandant was not unnaturally very surprised to get this message from prisoners, and all he could say was "Dismiss the men." This story is told by a British doctor confined at the time at Sennelager, who afterwards returned.

"They can't down us," became a motto of the men. At Döberitz, where many of the Naval Brigade from Antwerp were interned, they made themselves a camp coat of arms with the motto "Always merry and bright." At Quedlinburg, which was supposed to be a camp for wounded

men, the gaolers one day, to annoy the prisoners, called them up at 2.40 in the morning, and marched them out road-making They were kept on without any food until five in the evening, and then were marched back. To show that they did not care, the prisoners began to sing "Tipperary" as they neared their camp. This camp boasted one prisoner, a man nicknamed "Little Tich." On one occasion the prisoners were paraded and kept standing in the sun for three hours as a punishment. After about an hour, however, **"Little Tich's" gay defiance** "Little Tich" sat down on the ground, despite orders. The guards at once seized him, and he was taken before the commandant and asked to explain. "I got so sick of looking at you blessed Germans for an hour that I could not stand any more of it." He was sentenced to five days of bread and water in the cells for impertinence. His offence was, of course, inexcusable from a military point of view, but he was a hero to his comrades from that day.

A German doctor went up to a British prisoner. "Well, what do you think of us now?" he asked, in English. "Damned little," the man replied. "The more I see you Germans the less I like you." He was punished for insubordination. The British prisoners could not be "downed." Their gaolers could starve them, take most of their clothes away, man-handle them, try, by false stories, torturing rumour, and cooked news to make them believe that the British cause was finished, and still Tommy would retain his cheerfulness and present a smiling face. The Germans could not understand this. They declared that: "From first to last the British had been the most discontented and insubordinate of all their prisoners, and had caused continuous trouble by their rebellious spirit."

A REPRESENTATIVE GROUP OF THE BRITISH PRISONERS AT DÖBERITZ WHO COULD NOT BE "DOWNED"

RECREATION TIME AT RUHLEBEN.
In whatever conditions Englishmen may be placed, they will find means to play cricket. The civilians interned at Ruhleben were no exception, and the nets attracted a great crowd.

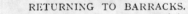

RETURNING TO BARRACKS.
The racing stables at Ruhleben were converted into prison barracks. They were strong buildings, with loose-boxes on the ground floor and large lofts above. As stables they were excellent, but they were quite unfit for human habitation, especially the lofts, which were hardly ventilated and almost dark.

The prisoners were always thinking of escape. Their camps were usually surrounded by barbed-wire, with armed sentries around, and with machine-guns mounted at either end, so that the whole place could be swept by fire in case of a riot. The punishment for attempts at escape varied. In some cases prisoners were shot, in others—probably partly depending on the commandant of the camp—they were let off with a comparatively light sentence. In December, 1914, one man, being taken to Aix-la-Chapelle, overcame his guard, seized his revolver, and fled. He was arrested later and shot. It was reported from Rotterdam in May, 1915, that ten British prisoners managed to escape when the backs of their guard were turned, while waiting on the platform at a railway-station at Louvain. They were recaptured shortly afterwards, and were promptly shot on the station approach. Some British prisoners at Osnabrück attempted to escape by excavating a tunnel under a wire entanglement around the camp. They were, however, caught.

Penalty for attempted escape

Gilbert H. Millar, a signalman of the R.N.V.R., an old Rugbeian, who was taken prisoner in the retreat from Antwerp in October, 1914, escaped from Döberitz, and walked to Warnemünde, a distance of one hundred and eighty miles. He travelled at night, avoiding the towns, and slept in the woods during the day. Reaching the coast, he walked several miles along the seashore, and at last secured a rowing-boat and set off, with some difficulty, for a point on the Danish coast twenty-two miles distant. He had to elude five German guard-ships that were cruising off the coast. When half-way across he was picked up by a Danish train ferry. He was kept for some time in quarantine in Denmark, and then was allowed to return to England. Two men, Sergeant Burley and Private Haworth, who were captured near Ypres in October, 1914, escaped from a prison camp in Westphalia. Six British soldiers reached Holland in May after a thrilling experience. They were cut off from their regiment in the retreat from Mons. They crept through the German lines, and for nine months they were fugitives in France and Belgium, living in the fields and dug-outs. Then a farmer gave them civilian

INDIAN PRISONERS WRESTLING AT WÜNSDORF.
Our Indian soldiers who had the ill-luck to become prisoners of war accepted everything with Oriental philosophy. Wrestling was a favourite form of recreation among them.

GERMAN GAOLERS AND BRITISH PRISONERS, CIVIL AND MILITARY.

The photograph on the left shows military prisoners of war, including a group of Royal Irish Rifles, at Limburgdahn. On the right: Baron Taube—decorated with a cross—who was Commandant of the Civil Camp at Ruhleben, where hundreds of Britons were interned.

"IN SWEET MUSIC IS SUCH ART: KILLING CARE AND GRIEF OF HEART."

At Quedlinburg an orchestra was formed of British, French, Belgians, and Russians, and provided solace for many weary hours. Döberitz, too, had its orchestra of British captives, and they are seen on the right at practice in their rude music-room.

The language of music is common to all nations.

clothes. They worked for some time for him, under the noses of the Germans, before they contrived to cross the frontier.

Other prisoners who did not easily submit to the harsh discipline of the German guards were in some cases tried before courts-martial, and given savage sentences. Thus John Bramwell, an old railway hand, was sentenced in the spring of 1915 to three years and three months' imprisonment for disrespect towards his superior in the presence of assembled troops and refusal to obey orders on two occasions. Two men at Sennelager, Eric Jennings and William Watts, were condemned, the one to eighteen months' and the other to fifteen months' imprisonment, for insubordination. The most severe case, however, was that of Private William Lonsdale, a former Leeds tramway conductor, who was sentenced to death, and whose sentence was subsequently revised to fifteen years' penal servitude.

On the morning of November 9th, 1914, several British prisoners at Döberitz refused to work, saying that they were ill. One of the German guards, a Landsturm man, aimed his revolver at an English prisoner and other soldiers drove the prisoners out of their hut with the butt-end of their rifles. Lonsdale squared up to the Landsturm man, who was making as though he would shoot one of the prisoners, struck him on the chest, and tried to hit him in the face. A German sergeant-major, who just then came upon the scene, drew his sword, and struck Lonsdale several blows on the back.

The English soldier was arrested, and was subsequently tried by court-martial, and sentenced to ten years' imprisonment. The president of the court, dissatisfied with this penalty, ordered that Lonsdale should be tried again, this time on a charge of aggravated assault. A fresh trial was held, and Lonsdale was sentenced to death. This outrageous retrial led to many protests, not only in England, but in Germany itself. Thus Dr. Edward David, the German Socialist deputy, declared : " I cannot maintain silence with regard to the death sentence passed upon the English prisoner of war at Döberitz Camp, and I hope that the great majority of German people share my feeling."

An appeal was made to a higher court against the sentence, and it was reduced to twenty years' imprisonment. And then came various trials and retrials, but in the end the sentence was fixed at fifteen years' penal servitude, and Lonsdale was sent to the fortress prison at Spandau.

Writing to his wife on one occasion, Lonsdale asked her to tell one of his soldier chums that he had better put a bullet through his brain than be taken prisoner. **Death better than a** "Death," he added, " is far preferable to **German prison** what I have gone through. If my time were to go over again, I would never be a prisoner of war—I would be with my comrades on the pit hills in Flanders. They have tried several ways to kill me. Now they are trying to starve me because I am English. I only get half as much to eat as the Russian prisoners." Later on he wrote from Spandau : " My fifteen years will soon pass away ; only another seven hundred and seventy Sundays. Not many. I only count the Sundays.

I have no time to trouble about the week-days—too busy working. Kiss my children for me, and never let them know that their father is such a bad man ; that he is doing fifteen years for striking a blow in self-defence."

One large camp was at Schneidemühl, where there was accommodation for 40,000 prisoners of war, most of these being Russians. Life here was very hard indeed during the first winter. The place **Russian prisoners at** was bitterly cold, and the accommodation **Schneidemuhl** exceedingly poor. The arrangement of the camp was so bad that epidemics of typhus and of cholera broke out in the spring. At first the dead were buried in blankets. Then the Russian prisoners cut down trees, made coffins, and blacked them over. There was a hospital, a deep trench cut in the ground, where the sick men were laid out in lines on straw to recover or die, as might be. There was no nursing, save by Russian orderlies. The German doctors evidently feared to come, and left the work to some Russian prisoner doctors, who did splendidly, but who were hampered by an almost total lack of medicines. The treatment of the sick in this camp would have been

HARD LABOUR—ON INSUFFICIENT FOOD.
British prisoners were put to regular tasks around the German prison camps and to all manner of labour in the mines, on farms, and elsewhere. They refused to undertake munition work, which their gaolers actually tried to induce them to do.

unworthy of the most barbaric tribe, and about 1,600 men died from the epidemics. After this, many improvements were made in the camp. Better commandants were put in. The severity of the rules at Schneidemühl may be gathered from two regulations passed for the prisoners, one that there must be no concerted singing—that is no singing together—and the other, that games were forbidden. After a time, however, both rules were ignored, in some of the lagers at least.

Six hundred members of the Royal Naval Volunteer Reserve and Naval Reservists were sent to the town of Döberitz, in October, 1914, to a camp formed there. And then others began to arrive, and by April the camp contained some 8,000 prisoners, 4,000 British, 3,000 Russians, and 1,000 French. These were first housed in tents, and afterwards lodged in wooden huts, each hut, about thirty-three yards long by thirteen yards wide, holding one hundred men. The camp proper was divided into four blocks, with forty barracks and ten tents. One American visitor questioned some of the British sailors, who had been

"IN DURANCE VILE."
Group of military and naval prisoners at Giessen, where from ten thousand to twelve thousand prisoners were confined.

captured at Antwerp. "How do they treat you here?" he asked. "Rotten, sir," said one. "Heaven knows what I would do if my folks at home did not send me food and money. It has saved me from starvation."

At Giessen, in Upper Hesse, from 10,000 to 12,000 prisoners were confined—Russians, French, Belgians, and British. The camp consisted of fifty barracks, with administrative buildings, and it was in many ways an improvement on some of the others. The British prisoners were, however, regarded here, as elsewhere, as the most hated of all. Thus one correspondent of the

"Beasts behind iron bars" "Giessener Anzeiger," in describing the various classes of the prisoners, after a visit to the camp, divided them as follows: "The French, who go their way with friendliness and politeness, fare the best. The Russians are regarded with a grateful feeling of superiority. 'Thank God we are not as they.' But the English receive something of the regard which is given to wild beasts behind iron bars. There is not much goodwill in the looks which examine their conceited, smooth-shaven faces."

As a result of the work and the visits of the American Ambassador at Berlin, and his representatives, improvements were made in a number of camps. The returned prisoners, coming back to England, had many stories to tell of the way the camps were "window-dressed" when visiting commissions arrived. On one occasion a body of Scandinavian investigators went around the camps. Their visits were all carefully prepared for. The British prisoners at one place were given good shirts on the morning of the arrival of the commission. Decent meals were served out to them that day, with some real meat. The camp was cleaned up, and the prisoners were given a football, and invited to show the visitors how Englishmen kept up their spirits under bad circumstances. "We all wished," said one returned prisoner, "that commissions would come and visit us once a week." In another case prisoners were housed

in leaking tents, and bedded on straw, which became soaked from the rain that penetrated through. One day—late in the evening—they were suddenly marched out from their tents into some newly-erected huts. They were given clean shirts, were afforded opportunities to wash, and had camp beds to lie on. The next day a distinguished visitor arrived, was taken round the camp by high officials, and expressed himself as fully satisfied by what he saw. He had scarcely left the grounds before the prisoners were ordered to take their shirts off, and were marched off to their tents again. Yet, despite subterfuges such as these, all were agreed that the investigations as a whole did good, and in some cases a great deal of good.

One German prison camp which had a very bad reputation was at Wittenberg. A number of British prisoners captured in the fighting around Mons were sent to this camp, and for months nothing was heard of them. No communication from them got through to England, and they received no letters. In the autumn of 1915 an attaché of the American Embassy at Berlin, Mr. Lithgow Osborne, visited the camp, and his report was so condemnatory that Mr. Gerard, the American Minister, decided to make a personal inspection.

"My whole impression of the camp authorities at Wittenberg was utterly unlike that which I have received in every other camp I have visited in Germany," Mr. Osborne reported. "Instead of regarding their charges as honourable prisoners of war, it appeared **American report on Wittenberg** to me the men were regarded as criminals, whom a régime of fear alone would keep in obedience. All evidence of kindly and human feeling between the authorities and the prisoners was lacking, and in no other camp have I found signs of fear on the part of the prisoners that what they might say to me would result in suffering for them afterwards."

Mr. Osborne went on to tell how, when he inquired among the prisoners who were drawn up in line, he was informed that practically no overcoats had been given

WITH THE INDIANS IN GERMANY.
Mohammedan Indian prisoners about to prepare dinner in accordance with the rites of their religion in the camp at Wünsdorf, near Zossen, in Brandenburg.

out by the authorities, and that ten overcoats which men had had sent from England had been taken from their owners and given to other British prisoners who were going to working camps.

"From many of the men I heard complaints," Mr. Osborne added, " that one of the watchmen had a large and fierce dog which he took inside the barracks, and which had attacked and torn the clothes of several of the prisoners. I suggested to the commandant that it was unnecessary to bring the dog inside the compound, particularly as I had never heard of it being done in other camps. He replied that he considered it necessary and that this could not be changed, as the prisoners were in the habit of remaining up late at night, keeping their lights burning, playing cards, etc. I had also heard several complaints regarding one of the German soldiers in the bathing-house, who had struck with his closed fist several of the prisoners, including one man with a crippled right arm, with whom I had spoken, for being slow in getting dressed. The commandant, however, did not wish to make any investigation in regard to the offender."

Reports from exchanged prisoners Shortly after the issue of this report a number of hopelessly wounded prisoners in Wittenberg camp were exchanged and sent back to England. Their accounts of the conditions that had existed there supplemented the American report, and surprised even those familiar with the treatment of British prisoners in Germany. When taken to Wittenberg in the autumn of 1914 they were subjected to the harshest treatment. The guards over them seemed to delight to inflict pain. Men told how the guards were accompanied in their rounds by police dogs, great brutes which they would occasionally set on the prisoners for their own amusement. They were armed not only with swords but with substantial lengths of solid rubber piping, which they used to beat men with. The food in the camp was shocking. The place was excessively dirty. There was scarcely any means of keeping clean, and for months the men had no soap. No parcels arrived and no communications went out. Ill-clothed, ill-fed, and man-handled on any excuse, it seemed as though the aim of the authorities was to provoke the Englishmen to revolt so that they might be shot down. One French prisoner, half delirious

Four British wounded prisoners who were sent back to England, being unfit for further service. One has a model of a boat made in his leisure time in prison.

"TAKE AND BREAK US: WE ARE YOURS, ENGLAND, MY OWN!"—*Henley.*

The great jubilation of the seventy-three British prisoners who were sent back to England after many months of privation and suffering in Germany is only faintly detected in these photographs. Nearly all of them arrived in a state of indescribable wretchedness, and some were still suffering from wounds a year old. The three photographs on this page were taken after they had been equipped in clean hospital dress.

SEA-POWER IN FETTERS.
Prisoner members of the Royal Naval Division, whose confinement at Döberitz must have proved even more irksome than that of their soldier compatriots.

A POLYGLOT PRISON PARTY
Group of allied prisoners, among whom were Scottish, French, Belgian, and Russian soldiers.

things were sufficiently bad, for the American Ambassador's horror at what he saw was evident in every line of his report. The result of Mr. Gerard's visit was to bring still further modifications in the harsh treatment of the men, but it would be a mistake to suppose that even the improvements effected were all that were necessary. The condition of the Wittenberg men when they arrived in England in their ragged garments sufficiently told their tale.

In December, 1915, a volume of correspondence between the Foreign Office and the American Ambassador concerning the treatment of British prisoners of war in Germany was published. One part of this correspondence which attracted special attention was a reply by the German military authorities to the report by Major C. B. Vandeleur, concerning his brutal treatment when a prisoner of war, which is referred to earlier in this chapter.

The German military authorities replied that Major Vandeleur's statements were partly untrue and in part immeasurably exaggerated. The Germans admitted that there was bitterness of feeling among the German troops against the British. "They respected the French on the whole as honourable and decent opponents, whereas the British mercenaries had in their eyes adopted a cunning method of warfare from the very beginning, and when taken prisoners bore themselves with an insolent and provocative mien."

Some other extracts from this reply show even better than the reports of the British prisoners themselves the hatred entertained for them by their captors:

"It is, with a few exceptions, untrue that British orderlies were afflicted with lice. Only three of them have suffered from scabies. The truth is, however, that the British private soldiers, like the Russians, but in distinction from the French and Belgians, always arrive in the internment camps filthy and lousy in the highest degree, and have to be freed from vermin with the greatest **Lying German reply** trouble. The British rank and file are sufficiently fed. None of them have been in a 'half-starved condition.'

"If it is a fact that British soldiers were especially employed on disagreeable work, the cause thereof is explained by the following facts: Prisoners of war are put to particular work in accordance with their particular training and ability. Most French and Russian soldiers have learned a handicraft or something of the sort, belonging as they do—as the result of universal military service—to some one or other civilian trade, and can therefore be

from his treatment, walked into another compound; the sentry there deliberately shot him. Floggings in the camp were so frequent that they almost passed unnoticed, save by their unhappy victims.

At the beginning of 1915 the filthy conditions of the camp brought on an epidemic of typhus. The bullying guards then showed what cowards they were. They fled from the inside of the camp, leaving the prisoners to themselves to do as best they could. The German sentries, with loaded rifles, guarded the outer lines. Food was sent over for the prisoners through a chute. It was left to them to fight the epidemic without medicines or any proper means of nursing or doctoring.

Six medical officers of the British R.A.M.C., prisoners in Germany, hearing of the deplorable condition of the camp, volunteered to go there to doctor the sick. Five of them were attacked with typhus almost as soon as they arrived, and three of these died. The sixth of the party did his best, and a splendid best it was. He asked for volunteers from among the other prisoners of war to nurse the sick. Volunteers gladly came, and nearly all of these volunteers at once took the disease, many of them dying. In the end the typhus was stamped out, but not before large numbers of men, Russian, French, and British, had succumbed; the number of British deaths being officially reported at fifty-nine.

When Mr. Gerard visited the camp, great improvements had been made as compared with the winter, but even then

Gen. Sir Charles C. Monro, K.C.B., British Commander=in=Chief in the Mediterranean.

Before the battle: French soldiers resting en route for the zone of operations near Strumnitza.

Imperial Britain in the field of classic combat: Mule=drawn artillery leaving Salonika for the hills

French infantry moving to the front from Salonika to the accompaniment of a Greek band.

La Belle Alliance in the Near East : British soldiers watching their French comrades marching by

General Sarrail, who commanded the French Army in the Balkans, going up to the firing front from Strummitza.

employed accordingly ; in their work they are mostly handy, willing, and industrious. The soldiers of the British standing paid Army, on the contrary, have usually learnt nothing, and are fit for no particular employ outside the care of horses and farm work ; they are besides frequently lazy, arrogant, and obstinate. Even those of them who know a little German pretend not to.

"British officer prisoners of war seem to find it disagreeable to be put together with Russian officers. The German Government see no reason whatever why any separation should be made among captured enemy officers in their quarters. Since England does not blush to use coloured troops of all races against Germany in the present war, British officers must not be surprised if they are brought into close contact in prison with their comrades-in-arms of other nationalities."

Organised aid for prisoners   When the lot of the prisoners in Germany became fully known, a number of organisations sprang up throughout Britain to aid them. Regiments raised funds for their men. Some counties took the work in hand for men born in their counties, and many philanthropic bodies did the same. The Canadian prisoners were cared for by a special branch of the Canadian Red Cross, and men from the Antipodes by their own special bodies. These various organisations were grouped together with a central body, the Prisoners of War Help Committee, with offices in Southampton Street, Strand, London, and did admirable and very practical work. The aim of many of the societies was to send a parcel of food to each of the prisoners weekly, the parcels consisting mainly of meat, biscuits, tea, and other solid foods. The British prisoners complained that they missed white bread as much as anything. Efforts were made to send white bread from England, but in consequence of the time taken for parcels to reach Germany—from two to three weeks—most of the bread sent from here arrived in a mouldy state. An international organisation in Berne then arranged for the regular despatch of bread from Switzerland to the prison camps, when paid for from England.

Bad as was the lot of our prisoners, there was universal agreement that the lot of the Russian prisoners of war was infinitely worse. The hundreds of thousands of these crowded into Germany were treated in many camps with the most incredible harshness. They were given a minimum of rations, and were reduced to such a state from sheer hunger that men would risk their lives for a mouthful of bread. Starved, beaten, ill-housed, their condition was an indelible disgrace to Germany. It must be remembered that in the conscript Russian Army there were not only peasants, but men of culture and education. British prisoners returned from Germany, describing what they saw, had terrible tales to tell of men they knew, able to speak several languages, men of refined tastes and good training, treated worse than wild beasts.

So vastly different was the treatment meted out to German prisoners of war and civilians interned in England, that popular indignation was aroused, for which it cannot be said there was not justification. Officers lived in conditions of luxury, which many of them had not known at home, and liberty to wander out of bounds was the only thing of which they were deprived. There was no question of "reprisals" being exacted ; it would have been alien to the national temper to commit iniquity in return for

BRITAIN'S DAY AT RUHLEBEN.
An anxious queue of interned civilians lined up at Ruhleben to receive parcels from home. The conditions of life at this camp, even for civilians, were such that a supply of food from England was very welcome, not to say an absolute necessity.

PRISONERS' PICK-A-BACK.
Two lonely but well-groomed British captives in Germany. Private A. R. Boulter, Coldstream Guards, and Private G. Slythe, Northumberland Fusiliers, at Döberitz.

iniquity ; but equal treatment of captives on both sides was another matter, and many people feared that the leniency of the British method was only misunderstood by the German prisoners as being due to some anxiety to conciliate them in case the war should take a course unfavourable to the Allies ; and further it was pointed out that the leniency was in the nature of a political blunder, since it tended to perpetuate the spirit of the Germans which had been a considerable factor in the deliberate provoking of the war. But no change was made, and the prisoners in this country continued to live in conditions for which "humane" was far too mild a term.

The difference in condition between the German prisoners of war confined in Great Britain and the British prisoners of war confined in Germany was never so strikingly shown as when the hopelessly wounded on either side were exchanged. The German prisoners from here, arriving in Holland, were well fed, well clothed, in whole, good garments, with sound boots on their feet, with complete suits, good underwear, and good caps. The British prisoners coming back from Germany into Holland were haggard wrecks, often clothed like scarecrows, with odd garments, rags of every kind, often with little or no underwear, men whose appearance excited pity in all who saw them. They were a vivid illustration of what the much-boasted "Kultur" of Germany means, and how it works out on helpless objects of German tyranny.

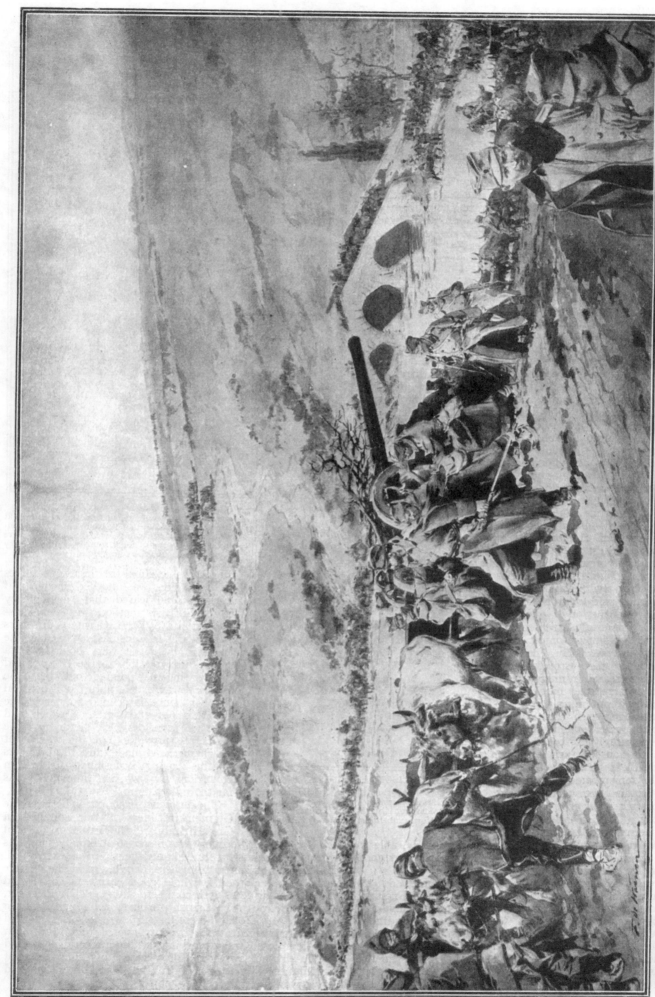

BATTERIES OF HEAVY SERBIAN ARTILLERY WITHDRAWING TO TAKE UP POSITIONS IN ANOTHER PART OF THE LINE DURING A RETREAT.

During a retreat—such as the great Russian retirement in the summer of 1915 and the Serbian withdrawal towards the end of the year—unquestionably the greatest difficulty is the transport of big guns. This spirited drawing shows the Serbians hauling their heavy guns out of the danger zone by bullocks, while lighter weapons on the heights are engaging the advancing enemy.

CHAPTER XCIII.

SERBIA'S GLORIOUS RESISTANCE AND THE FALL OF NISH.
By Robert Machray.

Fourth Invasion of Serbia begins by Germans Shelling Semendria—How Germany Prepared—Von Mackensen in Chief Command, with Von Gallwitz the German and Von Kövess the Austrian under him—Strength of the Austro-Germans and Serbians—Menace from Bulgaria—Serbia's Desire to Forestall It—Landing of the Allies at Salonika—King Peter's Pathetic Order of the Day—Serbia's Great Spirit—First Austro-German Efforts to Cross the Frontier Rivers Repulsed—Splendid Defence of Belgrade—Enemy Across the Danube—Belgrade Evacuated amid Terrible Scenes—Progress of the Invaders—Old Marshal Mishitch Wins a Battle—Von Mackensen's Advance up the Morava—Semendria and Pojarevatz Captured—Bulgaria Attacks Serbia without a Declaration of War—Serbian Forces on the East—Bulgarians Three to One—Heroic Serbian Resistance to Overwhelming Odds—Action by the Allies—Great Britain Offers Cyprus to Greece to Intervene, but Greece Declines—French Troops Moving up the Vardar—Desperate Effort of Serbians to Check Bulgarians—Bulgarians' Rapid Advance—The Railway Cut—Uskub Taken —Austro-Germans Pressing Slowly South—Serbian Policy of a Fighting Retreat—Exodus of Civil Population—Fall of Kragujevatz—A Victory for Gallant Shumadians—Bulgarians Take Frontier Towns on North-East—Navigation of Danube Open to Enemy—Magnificent Defence of the Serbian Passes—Allies Bombard Dedeagach and Varna—Pasich Appeals to Great Britain—Depressing Statement in British Parliament—France to the Rescue—Further Enemy Progress—Fall of Nish.

ALTHOUGH the portentous bearing of the fact was not generally perceived, *German* shells bursting on September 21st, 1915, over Semendria, the fortified town on the southern shore of the Danube which the Serbians call Smederivo, announced the beginning of the fourth invasion of Serbia, and marked the opening of a new and extremely important phase of the whole colossal world-conflict. Up to that date neither German guns nor German soldiers had taken part in the attacks on the little Slav kingdom, the first, second, and third invasions having been exclusively the work of Austria-Hungary—with disastrous consequences, as events had proved, to the Dual Monarchy. In the view of the German leaders the time had come for Germany herself to make a decisive appearance on the scene, and the rain of projectiles on Semendria, on that last day of the third week of September, was the earliest definite indication of what was in their mind.

With her usual foresightedness in military affairs, Germany had laid her plans well in advance, and she took good care to

GENERAL PUTNIK.

To General Putnik was mainly due Serbia's great resistance to the forces of the Dual Monarchy, but through illness he was compelled to resign at the commencement of the winter campaign of 1915.

conceal them until she was ready to strike and circumstances promised favourable developments. She thought the situation now was propitious. She felt safe in the western theatre of the war, because she believed that the French and the British were held by her strong defensive lines. The success of her great offensive in the eastern theatre had, she imagined, reduced the Russians to impotence and removed all danger in that quarter. Nor was she apprehensive with respect to the Dardanelles, for there her allies, the Turks, led by officers of her own, kept stationary the forces of the Entente. The Serbian field lay open and inviting; and Germany, having made certain of the active co-operation of Bulgaria and the non-intervention of Greece (as was related in Chapter LXXXIV.), commenced operations on a large scale.

Under cover of her tremendous campaign against Russia, Germany gradually, and in such a manner as to avoid attention, had railed considerable bodies of troops to Southern Hungary during the summer. Rumours were current later that she was assembling a formidable army north of the Danube with a view to the conquest of Serbia,

271

OFF TO ENGAGE THE BULGARIAN FRATRICIDES.
French soldiers from the base at Mudros, fully equipped for the Balkan front, waiting on the quay at Salonika for the train to convey them to the firing-line. The steel helmet was used almost universally in the French Army.

ROUGH WEATHER FOR ROUGH DAYS OF WAR.
In the early days of the allied occupation of Salonika heavy gales were prevalent, and these to some extent hampered military operations. This photograph shows the condition of the quay in December, 1915, with a transport waggon moving forward to the base.

but she effected the concentration of her forces, and those of the Austrians which were to be combined with her own, in that area practically in secret. The general in chief command was Marshal von Mackensen, who had shown conspicuous ability in Galicia and Poland, and one of the ways in which Germany hid her designs was to cause his name to be published in her official communiqués of actions on the Russian front weeks after his energies had been transferred to the new theatre. The Serbians themselves had got wind of the projected offensive, and as far back as July had begged the Entente Powers to despatch sufficient men to their aid, but for one reason or another their appeal then was made in vain. Help, when it was sent, arrived too late, and in any case was inadequate.

When the storm broke in full fury over the north of Serbia, and the dispositions of the hostile forces were disclosed, it was found that the Austro-Germans under

Mackensen were divided into two armies in close contact with each other. One army was commanded by General von Gallwitz, who had distinguished himself by forcing the passage of the Narew two months before, and its composition was wholly German. The other army was led by General von Kövess von Kövesshaza, an Austrian soldier, and was partly Austrian and partly German, the former predominating. Gallwitz covered the line of the Danube from Orsova on the east to a point opposite Semendria on the same river, where he joined up with Kövess, whose troops thence extended along the Save and part of the Drina. Farther up the Drina an Austrian army was in position near Vishegrad.

The three armies consisted of at least twenty divisions, and their total strength was well above 300,000 effectives. Ten divisions were German, mostly war-hardened men withdrawn from the other fronts. Remembering their previous bitter experiences at the hands of the Serbians, the Austrians put some of their best infantry into the field. Mackensen's famous drive through Galicia had been triumphant owing to the overwhelming power of his artillery, and he now had upwards of 2,000 guns, many of them pieces of large calibre. His intention was to beat down and smother the Serbian resistance by sheer weight of metal, and then to advance in force. His first great task was the crossing of the rivers, and he relied on his artillery for its accomplishment.

Ever since their superb repulse of the Austrians in December, 1914, the Serbians had anticipated a renewal of the attack on them, and Marshal Putnik and his Staff had taken all the measures that were possible in the circumstances to meet it. At the start of the fourth invasion their Army mustered some 310,000 combatants, the vast majority of whom were well seasoned in war, and they had guns and munitions proportionate to the size of their forces, except that they were short of heavy artillery such as the enemy possessed. If they had been called on to face only the Austro-Germans and Austro-German artillery they might, and probably would, have repeated the

A STUDY IN PHYSICAL ENERGY.
Serbian convoy passing through a snow-covered mountain pass. Laboriously the big guns were dragged along these bleak, muddy byways, principally by the aid of bullocks, supplemented by the physical strength of Serbian soldiers.

splendid victories of the Jadar, Matchkokanen, and the Suvobor Ridges, which respectively were the turning points of the other invasions. The force opposed to them was not too great in numbers, and if it had heavier guns this advantage was in a measure offset by the strong, natural defensive positions held by the Serbians. The entry of Bulgaria into the conflict made all the difference.

It was with the object of resisting assault on the north, the north-east, and the west that the Army of Serbia had been disposed and the Serbian fortifications constructed and organised ; the south-east—the Macedonian frontier and some distance north of it—was but little protected, and hence was easily vulnerable by any strong force. In other words, the position of Serbia, as a whole, was such that it could be turned, in military phrase, from the south-east. Unless this fact be grasped, it would be impossible to understand Serbia's desperate situation when Bulgaria joined the Austro-Germans in attacking her, or appreciate fully her glorious resistance of their combined efforts.

At the outset of the fourth invasion the line south of the Save and the Danube was held by three Serbian armies, comprising seven and a half divisions, or about 150,000 men—nearly half of the whole military strength of Serbia. On the west the First Serbian Army, of three divisions, which was commanded by the veteran Marshal Mishitch, occupied the angle between the Save and the Drina, with its headquarters at Shabatz. Next, eastward, came a force of a division and a half, under the leadership of General Zivkovitch, which was styled the Army for the Defence of Belgrade, a title that sufficiently indicated where it was placed. Farther east, and stretching towards the frontier of Rumania, lay the Third Serbian Army, of three divisions, with General Jourishitch at its head ; it was based on Pojarevatz, and the all-important Valley of the Morava was its special charge. To oppose the Austrians concentrated in the vicinity of Vishegrad, Serbia had the "Army of Ushitze," of less than two divisions, under General Goïkovitch, and the town of Ushitze was its centre.

It was upon these four armies, with some portion of the

Disposition of Serbia's armies

DURING THE GREAT SERBIAN RETREAT.
Unique dug-out used by Serbian snipers—a sentry keeping guard while some Serbian officers were finding the range for artillery.

"Army of the Timok," a force which was based on Zaichar, on the eastern frontier, some twenty miles from Vidin, in Bulgaria, operating along the Danube towards Orsova, that the Austro-German invaders fell, the odds in favour of the latter being more than three to two. The rest of the Serbian Army was deployed on the east facing Bulgaria, and had it not been for the menace from that country Serbia could have met her Germanic foes on fairly equal terms. As it was, Serbia felt compelled to keep more than 100,000 men to watch Bulgaria, with respect to whose aggressive intentions she had no illusions. It was something more than a coincidence when, at midnight of the day on which the Germans began shelling Semendria, King Ferdinand ordered the mobilisation of the Bulgarian Army.

For the ensuing fortnight the Austro-Germans were unable to show any real progress. They made several attempts at crossing the rivers—seven, it was reported, over the Danube alone—but every one was repulsed with

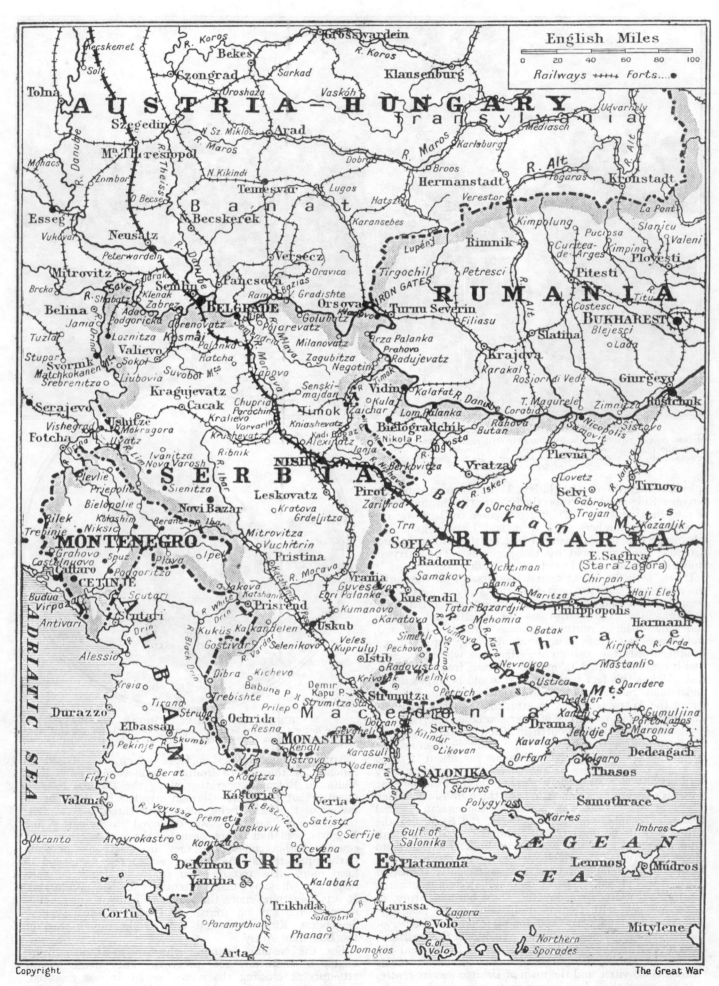

English Miles

Railways ┼┼┼┼┼ Forts.....●

MAP TO ILLUSTRATE THE AUSTRO-GERMAN AND BULGARIAN INVASION OF SERBIA.

heavy loss ; in an effort to gain the southern bank near Semendria a whole battalion was destroyed. Towards the end of September their aeroplanes flew daily over Serbia, reconnoitring the Serbian positions, and dropping bombs on Pojarevatz, Kragujevatz, and other places of importance ; one of their aeroplanes sailed round Nish, and then went on into Bulgaria. Meanwhile, Bulgarian troops were assembling on the frontier, and Serbia, knowing full well the desperate nature of the situation with which she would shortly be confronted, sought to forestall it, at any rate in part, by obtaining the consent of her Allies to attack the Bulgarians while their mobilisation was incomplete, but received an answer that led her to believe that the action contemplated was regarded with disfavour.

In all probability this was Serbia's last chance gone. When some weeks later this was understood, the subject was brought up in the House of Commons, and Lord Robert Cecil, speaking on behalf of Sir Edward

Diplomacy fetters strategy   Grey, admitted that the Serbian Government had expressed the opinion that the right military policy was to attack Bulgaria before her mobilisation was completed, but stated that the British Foreign Secretary had replied that all the political and diplomatic arguments were against this proceeding, and he felt unable to say whether strategic considerations should override them. Serbia, at all events, was under the impression that permission had been refused, and governed herself accordingly, with results that were most disastrous to herself, and extremely embarrassing, to say the least, to the Entente Powers.

On September 23rd, Greece, then still under the guiding hand of M. Venizelos, mobilised her Army as a precautionary measure in face of Bulgaria and in support of Serbia. At the request of the great Hellenic Minister, France and Britain agreed to send to Salonika 150,000 troops to make up for an equal number which, by the terms of the Serbo-Greek treaty for mutual defence against Bulgaria, Serbia would have provided had she been able to do so. This force began landing on October 5th, but on that very day Venizelos was compelled to resign because King Constantine disapproved of his pro-Entente policy. It was arranged, however, that under "protest" from Greece the troops of the Entente should continue to disembark with a view to assisting Serbia. The hopes of many Serbians ran high on hearing this, and Nish and several other Serbian towns made themselves gay with flags in honour of the coming of the Allies.

But the transference to Salonika of a powerful Franco-British army was an operation which required a considerable length of time, and this was precisely the intractable factor in the situation, with the Austro-Germans shelling the trenches along the frontier rivers of Serbia and the Bulgarians massing on her eastern boundary. The more intelligent Serbians must have known

Serbia solid on resistance   how matters stood, but the whole Serbian people, from the sovereign to the poorest peasant, had irrevocably resolved that, whether help came or not, they would resist to the uttermost. The determination of the nation found eloquent voice in the words of M. Pasich : "It was better to die in beauty than live in shame."

King Peter, on October 2nd, issued an Order of the Day which gave utterance to the feelings of himself and his subjects. He was well aware, he said, that every Serbian was ready to die for his country. As for himself, he lamented that old age prevented him from fighting in the ranks or leading his armies in this struggle for life or death. "I am an old man," he went on pathetically, "who can send only his blessing to his soldiers, to the people, to the women and children. . . If this fresh struggle should end in defeat, it will be a glorious death for us all."

It was in this spirit of absolute devotion that the Serbians defended their country against overwhelming odds, and the fight they made was one of the finest in all history.

For three days and nights prior to October 6th the Austro-Germans, seeking to reduce the Serbian entrenchments to dust, heavily bombarded the whole Serbian line on the Danube, the Save, and the Drina, and under cover of their fire made further and more persistent attempts to get across these rivers, but the Serbians drove them back at all points. Fighting raged most fiercely at Ram, Dubrovitza, and Semendria, on the Danube ; in and about Ciganlia, the "Island of the Gipsies," at Obrenovatz, Shabatz, and Jarak, on the Save ; and at Badovintse, on the Drina. Von Gallwitz directed a tremendous bombardment upon Ram and Semendria, the two fortress towns which guarded the approaches to the Morava Valley. On October 5th hundreds of shells were poured on this sector from the largest guns and howitzers of the enemy, yet the brave soldiers of Jourishitch, whose army was

"ARISTOCRATS OF THE BALKANS."

General Nisitch and his personal Staff, among whom will be seen, on the extreme left, Colonel Vositch. This snapshot was taken by a British nurse with the Serbian Red Cross.

composed for the most part of men of the second Serbian *ban*, held their ground, in spite of the fact that their own artillery was outclassed.

But Belgrade itself, which the Austrians burned to recapture after their ignominious expulsion from it ten months before, was the scene of the hottest of the struggle. Here the Army of the Defence of Belgrade, assisted by the Naval Missions of France, Britain, and Russia—in all, about five or six hundred men, with naval guns, who had been in the city for some months protecting the river front—offered the most strenuous resistance to the attacking forces of Von Kövess. For one whole day the British Naval Mission, which was commanded by Rear-Admiral Troubridge, swept with their guns the great lake-like expanse, formed by the junction of the Save and the Danube, on the northern side of the Serbian capital, and

MONTENEGRIN SHARPSHOOTERS ADVANCING TO COMBAT THE AUSTRIANS IN THE MOUNTAINS.
Following their emblem of liberty, this body of King Nicholas's soldiers were on their way to the zone of operations. Civilian members of this
Spartan race, among whom are a sprinkling of women and children, watched the fighters pass in silent admiration.

sunk every enemy craft, including two gunboats, that came in sight. On the afternoon of October 5th the Austro-Germans greatly augmented their fire in volume and destructiveness, employing several of the famous Austrian 16 in. howitzers. They were not content to shell the fortress of Belgrade and the neighbouring positions at Zamar, as was perfectly legitimate, but they threw large quantities of projectiles, including inflammatory bombs, upon the hospitals and on the open town, in which dwelt the civilian population.

It was a characteristic exhibition of German "frightfulness." In a semi-official communiqué the Serbians stated that the enemy, having been unable to demoralise by his fire their troops in their positions on the Danube and the Save at Belgrade, endeavoured to destroy the city systematically, and annihilate its inhabitants by pouring thousands of shells on the open town. They declared that the bombardment was carried out methodically with the object of killing as many persons as possible and of creating a panic, and that the Austro-Germans, to further their own diabolical ends, placed, before the shelling of the city began, a curtain of fire upon the suburbs and on the roads leading into the surrounding country, so that those who tried to flee might be destroyed or thrown back again. At Belgrade, as in other areas of the war, the enemy showed himself unendingly capable of any and every enormity.

Proud of their capital, the Serbians wished to preserve it from complete ruin, and, according to their own official statement, their troops for this reason evacuated it on October 8th. But on October 6th and 7th

Austro-Germans across the rivers the Austro-Germans, notwithstanding the valorous opposition of the Serbian armies, had effected the crossing of the rivers at several places, including Belgrade. After desperate fighting, the Serbians on the 6th threw back to the opposite bank of the Save the forces of Kövess which had got across at Jarak, Progorska Island, and Zabrez, but the enemy came on again and succeeded in making good his footing on the south side. On the same day he captured Gipsy Island in the Save, a short distance from Belgrade, and contrived to land under the Lower Fortress and on the Danube Quay in the city itself. All his men at the Lower Fortress were either captured or killed, but the Serbians

were unable to expel him from the quay. During that day the struggle was of the most determined and sanguinary character, and cost the enemy enormous losses.

Next day the Austro-Germans made further progress, their heavy guns playing havoc with the Serbian defences, and enabling them to overcome all opposition at more points on the rivers, among them being Ram, on the Danube. On October 8th the Austro-Hungarian troops of Kövess penetrated into the northern part of Belgrade, and took by storm the Citadel, an obsolete work in the same quarter of the town. Earlier in the morning the German soldiers attached to Kövess's command, who had landed west of the city and taken the heights in that district, fought their way to the Konak, the Royal palace, completed in 1894, which lay in the centre of the capital, captured it, and hoisted over it the flags of Germany and Austria-Hungary. Belgrade now lay at the mercy of the invaders, but their work was not yet finished.

Belgrade at their mercy

The Serbian troops had resisted magnificently, but the multitude of big guns had been too much for them. Their own gunners served their artillery until it was overwhelmed; the men of the French, British, and Russian Naval Missions fired until their pieces were destroyed by the heavier metal of the enemy. Everyone made a gallant, if ineffectual, stand. According to the testimony of the enemy, not a Serbian flinched, and correspondents of his newspapers admitted that the stubbornness of the resistance he encountered far exceeded his calculations. In the afternoon of the 8th, General Zikovitch, thinking to save from destruction what was left of the city, ordered his troops to retire upon the fortified positions lying immediately to the south.

But Belgrade was not yet in complete occupation by the Austro-Germans, and that night saw some of the grimmest and most terrible scenes of the war. Parties of stragglers who were unable to join in the withdrawal of the main body of the soldiers still fought on, preferring death to surrender. Large numbers of the citizens had made good their escape from the doomed town during the bombardment, but large numbers were left, and many of these joined the stragglers in their struggle against the foe. Men, women, and even children contested with the utmost desperation the possession of every street. All through the hours of that night the hopeless fight went on, raging from house to house, from terrace to terrace, the Serbians using bombs and any weapon that came to their hands to defend themselves and strike a blow for their beloved city and land. When morning came Belgrade was a charnel-house, and **Belgrade a charnel-house** much of it was in ruins, particularly in the outskirts, on which the bombardment had had the most devastating effect.

Belgrade was not, properly speaking, a fortified place, and was incapable of prolonged resistance. But its fall caused immense rejoicing in Berlin and Vienna, which were illuminated in celebration of the event, and Mackensen, as its conqueror, was extolled as a general only second to Hindenburg. This joy, however, was decidedly modified when it was learned that it had been captured at a great cost, and that the booty obtained in it was comparatively insignificant, the official list specifying nine naval guns, twenty-six unmounted field-guns—all of these pieces had been destroyed or rendered useless—ten officers, and " more than six hundred prisoners," who, no doubt, were wounded men. The Serbians at Nish, the war capital of their country, declared that its occupation by the enemy gave him no gain from the military point of view ; but, all the same, its possession by him had a high political significance which was not lost on the Balkans.

What happened at Belgrade was typical of the fighting all along the line of the three rivers. Everywhere the Austro-Germans were met with the most tenacious courage by the Serbian forces, who repulsed them, but in the end were compelled to give ground.

On the eastern riverine front the enemy, on October 7th and 8th, crossed the Danube between Gradishte and Semendria, near the village of Zatagna and the small fort of Kostolatz, but here he was held. He succeeded on the 8th in taking Ram, which he had been bombarding for days, and tried with his heavy guns to batter a way southward of it, without making any advance. After a " hurricane fire " he attacked in force the village of Petka, and was driven back with considerable losses. He endeavoured to cross near Semendria from the island of the same name lying opposite the mouth of the Morava. Believing that he had shelled the Serbian trenches and their defenders out of existence, he sent his troops forward in lighters holding fifty men apiece, but when they approached the bank the Serbians, who were very much alive, gave them such a hot reception that they speedily retired, many of the lighters being sunk and their occupants drowned.

On the western riverine front, on the same dates, the Austro-Germans were checked between Obrenovatz and the village of Kratinska on the Save, failed in three night attacks on the Serbian **Marshal Mishitch's fine work** positions near Zabrez, and were repulsed before Drenovatz, north-west of Shabatz. In this area the enemy was opposed by some of the finest soldiers of Serbia, the splendid Shumadia Division being amongst them, and their commander, able old Marshal Mishitch, who had won great fame for his generalship

THE WHITE SMOKE OF WAR IN THE BLACK MOUNTAINS.

Montenegrin gun in action against the Austrians. From the outbreak of the war the hardy soldiers of King Nicholas played no small part in the struggle with their hereditary foes. The whole Army was under Serbian officership. Is it to be wondered that the Montenegrins were able to battle against superior odds when one contemplates the natural condition of their country ?

GENERAL SARRAIL.

Commander of the Allied Forces in the Balkans leaving the flagship of Admiral de Bon to land at Salonika.

Kovess's left, and the plan was that together they should fight their way up the Morava, one taking its east bank and the other its west; but before they could make any progress the fortresses of Semendria and Pojarevatz had to be taken. For more than a fortnight the former had constantly been subjected to a severe bombardment, to which it replied with energy; but here again the Serbian guns were over-mastered. After being driven back near Ram, and repulsed on the sector between the Morava and the Mlava, a stream flowing a few miles east of the other, with a loss of four guns and four machine-guns, the Germans, under Gallwitz, had by October 10th made good their advance towards Semendria, which they occupied on the following day, the Serbians falling back on Pojarevatz. A desperate engagement took place at Lipe, near the fortress, which resulted in a victory for the invaders; but, thanks to Serbian bravery, at tremendous expense, the battlefield being thickly strewn with their dead. In no other encounter up to that time had the enemy suffered such terrible losses. On the 12th the Germans began attacking Pojarevatz, pounding it with their heavy guns, and two days later, having stormed the works on its south side, captured it, while the Serbians retired to the hills lying to the east. Mackensen had thus taken the first steps towards the accomplishment of his objective.

From Orsova west as far as Gradishte the left wing of Gallwitz made no advance, and attempted none, for a reason that presently appeared—it was waiting on a certain development—to wit, Bulgarian intervention. While the bitter struggle for the possession of the mouth of the Valley of the Morava had been going on, what Serbia had feared had already taken place. On the **Bulgaria declares war** day of the fall of Pojarevatz, Bulgaria declared war upon her; but, on the pretext that the Serbians had attacked her, she had begun operations on the 11th by assaulting Kadibogas, in the direction of Kniashevatz, north-west of Nish, and other Serbian positions on the eastern frontier. Serbia, with armies of about 200,000 men, had been holding on the north and west a line three hundred miles in length. Now she was called on to defend a line of equal extent on the east, and had not many more than 100,000 men available for the purpose. The task was beyond her.

On Serbia's eastern boundary Bulgaria had assembled two large armies, and at the same time had sent a third army to watch the frontier of Rumania, of whose intentions she was not sure. Of the two armies which were to operate against the Serbians, the First Army, under the command of General Bojadieff, had a strength of 200,000 combatants, and it was concentrated on the north from Vidin to Zaribrod, so as to threaten the Valley of the Timok and the part of the Belgrade-Sofia railway running through Pirot to Nish. The Second Army, which was led by General Teodoroff, was only half as large as the first, but it was designed to operate in Macedonia, a country many of whose inhabitants were Bulgarian or in sympathy with

during the third invasion, was the man to get the most and the best out of them. He also had charge of the defence of the Lower Drina, and opposite Badovintse several times repelled the Austrians with great slaughter.

Success attended Marshal Mishitch in a fierce battle at Zabrez on October 10th. In the afternoon the Austrians heavily bombarded the Serbian positions, using asphyxiating projectiles, in the expectation of throwing the Serbians into disorder, and then charged in masses. But the Serbians were not caught unprepared. Donning special masks, they hurried from their trenches to meet the advancing foe, whom they compelled to retire in confusion, some of the enemy's troops taking refuge in flight across the Save. The Austrians re-formed, and three hours later again came on under cover of a hail of gas-shells, but the Serbians once more were equal to the occasion, broke the Austrian ranks, and pursuing them for some distance captured many prisoners.

In spite of this and other Serbian victories in the region of the three rivers, the advantage, generally, lay with the invaders, for they had forced the crossing of the frontier. On October 11th Berlin Headquarters announced that on the front between Gradishte and Shabatz, **Serbian frontier forced** more than a hundred miles as the crow flies, the passage of the Danube and the Save had been completed. And at two or three points on the Drina the Austrians had reached its eastern side. In the meantime the enemy brought up large reinforcements, and continued a vigorous offensive east, south, and west of Belgrade, in a wide, sweeping movement along the whole front.

Mackensen concentrated his main effort on the east in securing possession of the Morava Valley and its railway. Near Semendria, Gallwitz's right wing was in touch with

LEADERS OF FRANCE IN THE LEVANT.
General Sarrail, in supreme command, leaving the camp at Salonika for the Serbian frontier.

Bulgarian ideals, a region, moreover, that was practically unfortified. Uskub was its chief objective, both on account of the strategic importance of that place as a railway centre, and as a point from which a wedge might be driven in between North and South Serbia. The main body of this force assembled at Kustendil, and its left wing extended down to Strumnitza (or Strumitza).

Serbia, well aware of these facts, appealed to the Allies for speedy assistance, and pending its arrival determined to make, as in December, 1914, a superhuman effort. But the dice were heavily loaded against her. From the start of the Austro-German invasion defensive warfare had been imposed upon her because of the menace from Bulgaria. "Let our Allies look after the Bulgarians," said a Serbian officer, "and we shall

Retreat imposed on Serbia go to battle singing." With the Bulgarians, however, on her hands, defensive fighting was more than ever necessary.

Serbia did not lose heart; on the contrary, she faced the situation with magnificent courage; but her Staff knew that a policy of retreat, with constant rearguard actions to delay the enemy's advance, had become essential until the arrival of the expected forces of her friends.

On the eastern frontier Serbia had three armies. On the north lay the "Army of the Timok," with Zaichar as its base, and it was commanded by General Zikovitch shortly after the fall of Belgrade, but it was strong neither in men nor artillery. South of it came the Second Serbian Army, of three divisions of the first *ban*, and attached to it was Serbia's division of cavalry. It was led by Marshal Stepanovitch, a soldier celebrated for victories won in

THE EVE OF THEIR NEW ADVENTURE.
French infantry disembarking from a transport to go ashore at Salonika. Never since the days of the Romans did Thessalonika, or Salonika, enjoy such world-prominence as it did during the twentieth-century upheaval.

earlier wars, and in whom his men had implicit confidence. This army was Serbia's second strongest force, numbering nearly 80,000 effectives. It was based on Pirot, and the defence of the trunk railway was in its hands. Lower down, the Serbians had a small force, known as the Detachment of the Southern Morava, with headquarters at Vrania.

LONG LINES OF LATINS FOR THE SERBIAN FRONT.
French forces breaking camp on the outskirts of Salonika, prior to moving up to support the Serbians. They looked a fine body of infantry, rather bigger than the usual run of French soldiers, and some figures in the line will be seen to stand out conspicuously tall.

In Macedonia, at Uskub, Veles, along the Vardur, and on to the Greek frontier there were bodies of troops stationed under General Bojovitch and Colonel Vassitch, their total strength being upwards of 25,000 men.

Serbia's cry to her Allies for help did not fall on deaf ears. On October 12th Greece had definitely declined to assist Serbia as against the Austro-Germans; but the Entente Powers still strove hard to get her to change her mind, Great Britain going so far as to offer Cyprus to her as a gift if she would cast in her lot with the Serbians. The Greek King, who, since the second dismissal of Venizelos, was in full, though unconstitutional, control of the destinies of his country, rejected the offer of Cyprus, and would listen to no entreaties or arguments, but persisted in declaring his intention not to depart from the attitude of "benevolent neutrality" which he had taken up. On October 15th France and Great Britain declared war on Bulgaria, and announced a blockade of the Bulgarian coast on the Ægean. For some days the Allies had been rushing troops by railway up the Vardar Valley beyond the Greek frontier, and on the day of the declaration of war French troops were attacked at Valandovo, by the Bulgarians, who were defeated and thrown back. The French, who were commanded by General Sarrail, gradually made their way northward along the railway as far as Krivolak and Gradsko, a few miles south of Veles, but their numbers were insufficient to make any change in the general situation of Serbia, daily becoming more critical, nor even to effect a junction with any of the Serbian forces.

Movement of the Allies

It was on the east particularly, as was natural in the circumstances, that the situation at this time developed most unfavourably. Conscious of their numerical superiority, and spurred on by feelings of hatred, jealousy, and revenge, the Bulgarians pursued their campaign with tremendous vigour and without mercy.

On the north-east, a difficult country of hills and valleys with indifferent roads or no roads at all, Bojadieff at the start, by bringing into action greatly superior forces, got across the Lower Timok, and dividing his army into two main groups sent one against Negotin, Zaichar, and Kniashevatz, and the other against Pirot, but his advance was stubbornly opposed. On October 15th the Serbians repulsed three strong Bulgarian attacks east and south-east of Zaichar, and many fierce encounters, with the fortune of war now on one side, now on the other, took place east of Kniashevatz, and in the St. Nicholas Pass. Next day there were great struggles around Svinski Vis, which changed hands several times, but north of Kniashevatz the Bulgarians made progress, and on the 19th lay before Negotin. Towards Pirot Bojadieff succeeded in moving forward, but slowly; after capturing Vraje on the frontier he was held up by the Serbians under Stepanovitch, who repulsed and counter-attacked him with the utmost energy, making him pay dearly for every step he took up the Nishava Valley.

Desperate Serbian defence

Dr. Momchiloff, President of the Bulgarian Parliament, who was present with the Bulgarian troops during these days, described the fighting between the Danube and Pirot as the most desperate in all Serbia, every yard of ground being contested with fury in savage hand-to-hand encounters in which quarter was neither asked nor given.

THE RED FLOWER OF TEUTONIC CULTURE: FIRE FOLLOWING THE SWORD THROUGH POJAREVATZ.

WITH THE MEN OF SIR BRYAN MAHON'S COMMAND IN THE BALKANS: CROSSING A RIVER NEAR DOIRAN, ON THE GRECO-SERBIAN BORDER.

Serbian civilians as well as soldiers took part; in the Serbian trenches women, children, and aged men fought the Bulgarians with bombs and grenades, using them like experts; in every Serbian village the inhabitants attacked the invaders with similar missiles, and every house and cottage was a miniature fort. According to this Bulgarian witness, the civilian population, urged by despair, showed themselves more stubborn foes than the Serbian regulars, and the fighting in all this area was far more terrible than any ever known in the most envenomed of former Balkan wars. But behind these statements lay the tragic fact that in this region the war on the Bulgarian side was one of extermination, ancient animosities being quenched in blood and fire.

On the south-east, in Macedonia, the Achilles' heel of Serbia, Teodoroff and the Second Bulgarian Army had much easier work, and achieved success with correspondingly less effort. In this district the Serbians had no armies large enough to withstand a Bulgarian advance in force, nor were its people Serbian in any great degree or genuinely friendly to them, the whole province being infested with Bulgar

comitajis, ready to turn on them at the first opportunity. Yet a large part of the vital railway from Belgrade to Salonika, via Nish and Uskub, passed through this section, several miles of it running close to the frontier. It was this portion of their country that the Serbians had expected the Greeks to defend, but the Greeks had failed them. Teodoroff's first business, of course, was to get astride the railway.

Detaching a strong force from his main body, he struck at the railway between Vrania and Zibeftcha, dominated the line with his guns, and cut it. The small number of Serbian troops, called the "Regiment of the Southern Morava," fought him stoutly, but could not prevent him from capturing Vrania on October 17th, 1915. On the same date Teodoroff took Egri Palanka, after having marched from the railhead of the Kustendil-Sofia railway, forced the pass on the frontier, and gained the highway en route for Kumanovo and Uskub. Farther south he penetrated the valley of the Bregalnitza in what the Bulgarians officially characterised as a lightning advance, capturing the important strategic point, Sultan Tepeh, and the town

A BLEAK OUTLOOK.
British sentry, wearing his winter coat, on duty at a corner of the Greco-Serbian frontier where the railway from Salonika turns eastward.

SERBIAN PRISONERS MEETING A GERMAN
SUPPLY COLUMN.
Of all the bitterness that war brought to the brave Serbians
the worst may well have been that tasted by the men
shown in this photograph as, captive and disarmed, they
passed over their own familiar mountains and watched their
conquerors march on to further triumphs.

ANKLE-DEEP MUD IN A SERBIAN VILLAGE.
Even in the populated districts the roads in Serbia were very bad. A German Red
Cross detachment passed through some villages ankle-deep in mud.

of Kotshana, taking twelve guns. Pressing on through
Ishtip, he occupied the portion of Veles, otherwise called
Kuprulu, lying on the east side of the Vardar, on October
20th, thus cutting the railway again, and checking the
advance of the French. Northward, he took Kumanovo
on the same day, and after a violent battle, in which the
Serbians under General Bojovitch performed miracles of
valour against an overwhelming superiority of the enemy,
captured Uskub on the 22nd. Bojovitch retired fighting
to the Katshanik Pass, north of Uskub, the prolonged
defence of which, together with the defence of the Babuna
Pass, south-west of Veles, was one of the most memorable
features of the struggle in Serbia, having the effect of
preventing for some time the complete cutting off from
each other of the Northern and Southern Serbian Armies
that had been Teodoroff's purpose.

While these grave events were taking place in the east
and south-east of Serbia, the Austro-Germans continued
their advance from the three rivers in the north, but it

was not rapid, because the hilly ground over
which they moved had been organised step by
step by the Serbians, one line of trenches
stretching behind another, and the Serbian
soldiers, instead of weakening as the enemy
anticipated, did not cease to defend their
positions with the most heroic endurance.
Austrian reports agreed that neither the Russians nor the Italians could be compared in
contempt of death and unflinching bravery
with the Serbians. Immediately after the
capture of Belgrade, Kövess attacked the heights south
of the capital, and after three days of intense fighting
took Mount Avala, an eminence over 1,600 feet high,
ten miles from the city, on October 18th. Farther to the
west, Obrenovatz fell into his hands on that day, and
Shabatz three days later, both important gains.

But the chief line of the enemy's advance southward lay
along the Morava, his other movements being co-ordinated
with it. Subsequently to the fall of
Semendria and Pojarevatz, he assaulted   **Von Gallwitz's**
the mountainous country of the Podun-   **costly advance**
avlie, and after heavy loss drove the
Serbians out of it. Gallwitz here had an exceedingly difficult task, the ground, rising in rocky step-like formation,
offering distinct advantages to the defence, but his heavy
artillery enabled him to progress, though very slowly. By
October 23rd he had reached the southern bank of the
Jasenitza, near Palanka, and had passed Rakinatz on the
road to Petrovatz on the Mlava. About the same time his

left wing, having shelled Tekia into ruins, crossed the Danube near Orsova, and took the heights overlooking the river. On the extreme west three Austrian battalions got across the Drina at Vishegrad. It thus might be said that the whole three-rivers' front of Serbia was in the enemy's possession, but it had been an expensive venture, his losses being put at from 70,000 to 80,000 men, of whom 25,000 had been killed, while the Serbian casualties were nothing like half so severe.

Marshal Putnik was steadily carrying out his policy of a stubborn fighting retreat, holding his ground as long as possible, causing the enemy everywhere the heaviest losses, and avoiding anything in the nature of a general engagement.

The Serbian exodus

But his plans were greatly impeded by the exodus of practically the whole population of the northern area. The flight southward of the civilian inhabitants began with the fall of Belgrade. Deep in the memories of the Serbian people had been cut the impression made by the horrible atrocities and indescribable outrages which the Austrians had perpetrated in the previous invasions, and their alarm naturally was poignant when the fourth invasion looked like entailing upon them a similar programme of horrors unspeakable.

Braving the merciless rain of shells, which the Germans wantonly threw around Belgrade, multitudes of its citizens managed to get away —a few by rail, others in ox-carts, or in some sort of conveyance, but the vast majority on foot. The weather was bad, rain fell heavily and incessantly, the roads were deep in mud, and the miserable plight of these poor creatures was most pitiful. As every man and boy who could fire a rifle or throw a bomb was in the fighting-line, these fugitives consisted of the aged of both sexes, of women with babies, and of young children. As the Austro-Germans moved forward, and the frontier towns with the neighbouring country fell into their hands, similar scenes occurred, until it seemed as if the whole population were travelling south. The

agony of Serbia, it might have been thought, had come full upon her, but it was to deepen with every day that passed. The world had never been the theatre of a darker, sadder tragedy.

Gallwitz and Kövess kept on with their slow but persistent advance from the north, the Serbians retiring in good order and with undiminished *moral*. During the fourth week of October Gallwitz stormed the commanding heights east of Banitzina, south of the Jasenitza, captured after severe fighting Livaditza and Zabari on the Morava Plain, and occupied the region south of Petrovatz. By the 28th he had gained Svilajnatz, beating down the Serbian resistance by sheer weight of men and guns, and on the 30th was within a day's march of Kragujevatz, the seat of Serbia's principal arsenal, and in former times the national capital. Situated on the Lepenitza, a tributary of the Morava, it lay about half-way between Belgrade and Nish, on a branch line of the main railway joining these two cities, and had about 19,000 inhabitants. It was a place well worth defending, but the Serbian Army, in accordance with the instructions of its Commander-in-Chief, on November 1st evacuated it, after destroying the arsenal and all its military stores.

The Serbians did not, however, withdraw from it without first giving the enemy a taste of their quality. The glorious

HURRYING TO THE HELP OF SERBIA: MEN AND HORSES ON THE QUAY AT SALONIKA.
Salonika was the scene of feverish activity when the Allies hurried to the help of Serbia. The harbour facilities were inadequate for rapid debarkation, and the quayside was congested every day. Above: British soldiers unloading baggage from a Greek Army transport cart.

PARTICIPANTS IN THE GREAT BOMBARDMENT OF BELGRADE.
Serbian artillery with masked guns in action against the Germans at Dedinje, west of Belgrade. In oval: An Austrian monitor which shelled the Serbian capital, and, later, was sunk by British guns.

Shumadia Division, which had been constantly engaged, now in one quarter of the field, and now in another, and which was recruited from this district, was entrenched on the hills to the north of the town, and, sick of constantly retreating, begged their commander to obtain permission to attack, which, to their delight, was granted. The day was wet, and through the clouds of mist which shrouded the hills, the gallant Shumadians, eager for the fray, fell with indescribable effect on the Germans, who, now accustomed to the purely defensive tactics of the Serbians, looked for nothing of the kind, and taken by surprise were thrown into disorder. Even when he sent up reinforcements to his reeling ranks, so that his strength presently was two divisions and a half, the men of Shumadia, though the ravages of war had by now materially reduced their numbers, were not to be denied. Fighting with irresistible fury they drove the Germans before them for a considerable distance, taking 3,000 prisoners and several guns, while the field was littered with hundreds of German dead. Then, having had this revenge, the Shumadians retired.

Fury of the Shumadians There is not the least doubt but that Serbia would have triumphed over her foes if she had had anything like a chance.

On the right of Gallwitz, Kövess had simultaneously advanced his forces, marching along the railways from Belgrade and Obrenovatz towards the Western Morava, and constantly in contact with the Germans in the Morava region itself. South of Belgrade the Serbians resolutely defended the Kosmai positions, but had to yield before the enemy's heavy fire. On October 25th Kövess reached Ratcha, south of Palanka, on the right side of the Morava, and after severe fighting arrived at Gran Milanovatz on the 30th, and at Cacak (Tsatsak) on November 1st, both

places being a few miles west of Kragujevatz. He had now struck the Western Morava and the railway passing along it eastward from Ushitze to the Belgrade-Nish railway. Farther west his cavalry, on October 26th, had occupied Valievo on the Upper Kolubara, and one of his divisions crossed the Maljen Ranges, which had been the scene of the Austrian rout in the previous year. Farther west, but more to the south, the Austrians, who had pushed on from Vishegrad, entered Ushitze on November 2nd, and soon joined up with Kövess. **Double attack on Nish**

In the beginning of November Mackensen could say that he was in possession of Northern Serbia, west of the Morava, and was holding for some distance the country on the east of the main river, almost in a straight line with that on the opposite side. But so far it had not been much more than a conquest of territory, for he had not brought the Serbians to a great battle, which might have been decisive, nor had he captured many prisoners and guns, while, on the other hand, the Serbian Army remained intact and full of fight, awaiting the assistance of the Allies, and hoping that all might still be well. Yet what had taken place on the north-eastern and south-eastern frontiers, in addition to the retreat before the Austro-Germans, might have filled it with dismay.

During this time Bojadieff, at the head of the First Bulgarian Army, was attacking with success the Serbians in two directions, one along the Timok against Kniashevatz, Zaichar, and Negotin, and the other along the Nishava against Pirot. Both efforts threatened Nish, but the more northerly had also the purpose of effecting a junction with the left wing of Gallwitz, which was advancing from Tekia, in the north-east corner of Serbia. This object was speedily

SERBIAN INFANTRY IN THEIR TRENCHES BEFORE THE GREAT RETREAT.
A Serbian first-line trench, screened from aircraft with branches, at Semendria. Above: A Serbian infantry position along the first-line by the Danube.

The Austrian troops when mustered after Divine service in the open air presented a most picturesque sight against the tree-clad, snow-powdered background that sloped upwards and away to the far mountain ranges.

" In Montenegro one does not ask how far, but how long," one of the British nurses said. The Austrians, as they rested on their marches over the mountains, must often have realised the point of the remark.

WITH THE FORCES OF FRANCIS JOSEPH IN MONTENEGRO.

A BRITISH HOSPITAL UNIT IN RETREAT.
One of the heroic British women of the Red Cross Mission in Serbia on the the road to Tutijne during the tragic retreat. The waggons were ramshackle and worn by constant hauling over rough country.

realised, for on October 23rd Bojadieff, here encountering very inferior numbers, took Negotin and Prahovo, the latter a port on the Danube, a few miles north of the former. This meant, when Kladovo was captured on the 25th, that the Serbian bank of the river, and the navigation of the Danube on that side, had passed to the enemy, who forthwith proceeded to utilise it, after clearing away mines, some of which were of Russian origin. Lower down, the Bulgarians, who were in overwhelming strength, occupied both Zaichar and Kniashevatz on October 28th, subsequent to many sanguinary and stubbornly contested battles, in which victory was often in doubt and fortified positions had to be stormed and stormed again several times.

It was much the same story of desperate resistance overcome by immensely larger forces in the Nishava Valley, though in this district the Serbians put up, if such a thing were possible, an even sterner and more stubborn fight. The fourth week in October opened well for them by their recapturing positions on the right bank of the river that had been lost on the previous day, and by their repelling hot assaults on the other bank. But on October 26th-27th they were compelled to abandon the commanding Drenova **Government removed** Glava height, fifteen miles north-west of **from Nish** Pirot, and on the 28th Pirot had to be evacuated, but not till after a battle of extraordinary intensity, in which they demonstrated their heroic quality to the full. With Pirot on the south and Kniashevatz on the north, both in the possession of the Bulgarians, the threat to Nish had become most direct and ominous, and the removal of the Serbian seat of Government from that city to Kralievo showed the gravity of the situation. King Peter, who had arrived in Nish on the 23rd, was present during some of the fighting in front of Pirot, and deploring his inability to take an active part, encouraged his brave soldiers, though they needed no spurring, to do their utmost.

In the south-eastern area, or Macedonia, the region which the Serbians called the "New Territories," the Second Bulgarian Army, under Teodoroff, was not so fortunate as the First, under Bojadieff, but it was able to retain the

THE WESTWARD FLIGHT FROM SERBIA TO THE ADRIATIC SEABOARD.
A section of the cavalcade of varied humanity—soldiers, British Red Cross workers, peasants, children—on the road between Kralievo and Rashka, and on the way to Podgoritza, in Montenegro. At foot: The arrival of French aeroplanes at Kralievo. The Serbian guns shown in the foreground were destroyed; nothing it was possible to render useless was left in a condition to be of service to the enemy.

ground which it had conquered earlier. After its occupation of Uskub, it advanced to the Katshanik Pass, and by violent attacks with great forces, drove the Serbians, under General Bojovitch, from some part of the defile on October 28th, but when, a little later, the Serbians received reinforcements in the shape of two regiments of the Morava Division and two of the Drina Division, Bojovitch counter-attacked, and by sheer dint of the hardest fighting, recovered and held the most important positions in the pass, continuing to hold them although the Bulgarians, who did not lack courage, came on again and again, all their efforts, day after day, being repulsed with great losses. Vassitch, a gallant soldier if ever there was one, meanwhile was fighting some miles to the south, with a considerable measure of success, which might have turned into something decisively favourable if the French had been able to co-operate with him more closely than they were. On October 22nd, after an extreme struggle, he recaptured Veles, which he retained for a week, steadily driving back all Bulgarian assaults. On the 29th, however, the conflict became too unequal, and he had to evacuate the town once more,

MAKING THE WAY LESS ROUGH FOR THE FEET OF THEIR FIGHTING MEN.
As every man and boy capable of bearing arms was fighting, the Montenegrin women repaired the roads for the passage of the Army.

Final evacuation of Veles

and withdraw to the Babuna Pass, the narrow defile, known as the Iron Gate, over which the highway went from Veles through Prilep to Monastir, the considerable city that he had wrested from the Turks in the First Balkan War. At the opening of November, 1915, the Serbians were still holding the pass, and still were preventing the driving in of the wedge that was to sunder the Southern from the Northern Armies of Serbia.

Although the Serbian main armies in the north were still intact, and the small Serbian forces in Macedonia were holding back the Bulgarians, it had been evident for days that Serbia was in danger, as the movements of her enemies on all sides threatened her with envelopment. She herself declared that she could go on resisting and delaying the enemy, but she appealed once more for instant assistance. On October 20th Italy declared war on Bulgaria, but beyond increasing the pressure in her own campaign against Austria, and in that way reducing the pressure elsewhere, she did not directly attempt to help the Serbians. The

SCENES IN THE TRAGEDY OF SERBIA'S FLIGHT BEFORE THE INVADER.
In their dreadful retreat from Serbia the British Mission ran out of all their own supplies of food, and practically nothing was procurable at the Albanian cafés. In circle: Serbian refugees mustered on the roadside. The determined spirit of the people can be seen in all these youthful faces.

LUXURY IN TRAVELLING
THROUGH SERBIA.
To ford a river in a cart was to make a luxurious crossing. On the retreat the British nurses had to wade through many streams, sometimes waist-deep in water.

other Allies, besides the landings at Salonika of additional troops, sent on as quickly as possible to the Franco-British front in the south-east corner of Serbia, instituted a bombardment of the Bulgarian coast on the Ægean on October 21st, in which British, French, and Russian ships took part. Dedeagach, on the Gulf of Enos, and a junction on the railway connecting Salonika with Constantinople, was shelled for some hours, and serious damage done to its harbour works, railway-station, and shipping, care being taken to avoid firing on non-military points.

There was a great panic in the town, and the soldiers in the barracks fled for their lives. On the 28th, Russian vessels, in spite of the danger they ran from submarines and mines, bombarded Varna, on Bulgaria's Black Sea coast, with notable effect. On land the French troops in Serbia routed a force of Bulgarians at Rabrovo on the 23rd, and pushed up to Krivolak, where the enemy attacked without success on the 30th. On November 2nd the French were at Gradsko, at the confluence of the Vardar and the Tserna, and began entrenching at Kavadar, with a view to getting into touch with Vassitch, at the Babuna Pass, or at some other place on the farther bank of the Tserna.

How Serbia was enduring the strain of these terrible days when her fate was trembling in the balance was shown in a telegram sent to London by M. Pasich, the Serbian Premier, in which he said:

"Serbia is making superhuman efforts to defend her existence, in response to the advice and the desire of her great ally. For this she is condemned to death by the Austro-Germans and Bulgarians. For twenty days our common enemies have tried to annihilate us. In spite of the heroism of our soldiers, our resistance cannot be expected to be maintained indefinitely. We beg you, the many friends of Serbia in England, to do all that you possibly can to ensure your troops reaching us that they may help our Army, and that we may defend together that common cause that is now so gravely menaced."

Throughout Great Britain these urgent words created a painful impression, which was not diminished when on October 27th, the day of their publication, the British public also saw in their papers a report of a speech Lord Lansdowne had delivered in the House of Lords the day before. In this he stated that the British, in answer to Serbia's cry for help, had landed at Salonika a force of only 13,000 men, but that a larger force, put under orders at the same time, might or might not, according to circumstances, go there, the circumstances at the moment being that the progress of the campaign in Northern Serbia had been such as to render it highly improbable that the Serbian Army would be able to withstand for any great length of time the attack to which it was exposed from the Austro-Germans in the north, added to the stab in the back it had received from

"O'ER MOOR AND FELL, O'ER CRAG AND TORRENT."
At Berane a bridge was washed away, and the river had to be crossed in a punt hauled by ropes. In circle: Exhausted Austrian prisoners resting by the roadside.

AN EVERYDAY SCENE DURING THE GREAT TEUTON OFFENSIVE IN THE BALKANS.
Unable to keep up with the retreating Serbian Army, these aged refugees fell into the hands of a patrol of Austrians, who conducted them to the enemy camp for interrogation.

Bulgaria. From these melancholy expressions, which were based on the considered opinion of the British General Staff, it could not but be gathered that effective assistance for Serbia—at all events, from the British—was unlikely. However, in the House of Commons next day Mr. Tennant, Under-Secretary of State for War, announced that the British troops in Serbia were co-operating with the French on the Greek frontier.

In France a very different view prevailed as to what should be done to help Serbia. Consequent on the resignation of M. Delcassé, who disapproved of the prosecution of the Serbian adventure, the members of the Cabinet of M. Viviani handed in their portfolios to the President, but M. Poincaré immediately found a new Prime Minister for France in M. Briand, the ex-Socialist and a former Prime Minister, whose strength of character had been conspicuously demonstrated by his handling of the great railway strike in Paris some years previously. Associating with himself M. Viviani and other ex-Ministers, M. Briand formed a Cabinet of exceptional distinction. This was on October 28th. On the following day General Joffre was in London, and it was said that he was in favour of vigorous action by the Allies on behalf of Serbia. His arguments may have been sufficiently convincing to induce a change of mind in the British Government. At all events, they forthwith resolved that large additional forces should be quickly despatched to Salonika, apparently having come to the conclusion that it was not yet too late to save the Serbians from subjugation.

While these and other reinforcements were being got ready and sent to the scene, attempts continued to be made by the Allies to get Greece to act in a manner more favourable to their purpose. Among other things they desired better facilities for the moving of troops by rail. But after the rejection of the offer of Cyprus, it came out that Greece had decided not to depart from what she called her benevolent neutrality in any way, unless

More troops sent to Salonika

and until the Entente Powers concentrated armies in strength sufficient to check the progress of the Austro-Germans, with whom otherwise she was determined at all costs to avoid an encounter. Her attitude, in fact, towards the Allies became stiff, if not positively hostile, and the Greek people, always and notoriously a fickle race, and now vastly impressed by the success of the enemy in Serbia, sympathised less and less with the Entente.

And all the time the invasion of Serbia was steadily running its course, with results which only too surely indicated how desperate the plight of the little country was becoming, notwithstanding the superhuman efforts of which M. Pasich had very truly spoken.

With scarcely a halt at Kragujevatz, where they were disappointed to find no large amount of booty, the Austro-Germans crossed the Cacak-Kragujevatz road, and

PRECIOUS STORES BEING CONVOYED TO THE REAR.
Kralievo was a point on the main line of retreat to Podgoritza, and incessant streams of Serbians and convoys of Serbian stores passed through its rough-paved streets.

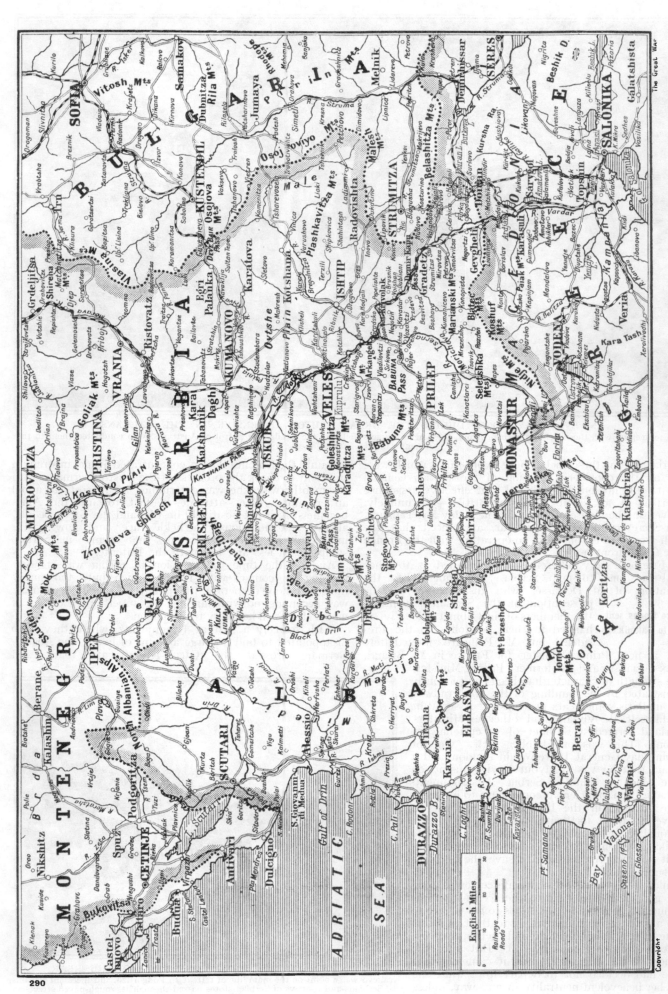

MAP TO ILLUSTRATE THE OPERATIONS IN THE BALKANS AFTER THE OCCUPATION OF SERBIA BY THE AUSTRO-GERMANS AND BULGARIANS.

The Great War

Copyright

THE IRON WAY IN THE ROCK-GIRT BALKANS.
Railway bridge on the Monastir line within a short distance of the city.
This photograph gives a graphic idea of the nature of the Balkan country,
in which ten nations were locked in deadly combat. Deep ravines,
rugged mountain passes, stunted vegetation—such was the scene of the
Near Eastern theatre of war.

marched south on both sides of the Morava. Kövess moved
over the Posetza, and the Germans entered Jagodina on
November 3rd. The passage of both banks of the Western
Morava was forced at Kralievo, and that town, from which
the Serbian Government had withdrawn in time, occupied
on the 5th, being captured by Brandenburg troops after
terrible fighting in the streets. Here the enemy laid
claim to his first big capture of guns—one hundred and
thirty, but most of the pieces were of obsolete pattern,
and the remainder had been rendered unserviceable. Next
day, or a day later, he was in Krushevatz, making prisoner,
according to his own account, 3,000 unwounded Serbian
soldiers, besides 1,500 wounded in the hospitals. The whole of the line of the
Western Morava was now in his possession. To the east of the Morava Gallwitz
pressed on, took the series of heights south of Lugotznir, by
storm, after the usual fierce struggle with Serbian rearguards,
and on November 4th seized Parachin, on the Belgrade-
Nish railway, from which a branch line extended through
the hills to Zaichar. He was now very near the Bulgarians,
who, as already narrated, had taken the last-named town,
and on November 5th their armies joined up at Krivivir,
a village lying midway between the two places. They were
then about thirty miles north of Nish. On the same day
German troops, by a surprise night assault, captured
Varvarin, on the main railway south of Parachin.

Other forces of Bojadieff, and these the most important
under him, continued their advance in the direction of
Nish, both southerly from Pirot and northerly along the
road from Kniashevatz. They had got within a short
distance of the Serbian war capital, and were in immense
strength as compared with the Serbians. On November
2nd, at the village of Svrlig and on the Kalafat Hill, six
miles from the city, a violent battle began, which Serbian
heroism caused to last for three days, marked by the
most determined and bitter fighting, the heaviest Bulgarian
attacks being repeatedly repulsed with frightful slaughter,
and many successful Serbian counter-attacks made. But
owing to the dominatingly larger number of the Bulgarians,
whose big guns wrecked the Serbian forts and trenches, and
damaged Nish itself, the end was inevitable. The Serbians
withdrew from the city on the 5th in good order, and
Bojadieff occupied it; and here he found, it was said, still
flying the flags to welcome the Allies who had never come,

Austro-Germans join Bulgarians

A TEMPLE OF MARS NEAR THE VARDAR.
Dominating Uskub and the Vardar Valley, these buildings were utilised
for barracks, hospitals, and various military purposes.

but discovered little plunder, the hundred guns he claimed
to have captured being of no value.

In some respects the loss of Nish was one of the worst
of the blows which a hard fate had dealt Serbia, for, if
the city was only of subsidiary military importance, its
fall had a decided political effect, coming second to that of
Belgrade. The German newspapers described its capture
as one of the greatest events of the war.

But the Bulgarians did not by any means have it all their
own way in every quarter of the field at this time, for while
Bojadieff was entering Nish in triumph, his colleague
Teodoroff in the south-east was not only making no progress
but was even suffering defeat. At the Pass of Katshanik,
by which entrance was effected from Uskub to the historic
Plain of Kossovo, the Serbians, under Bojovitch, with
dauntless courage daily rolled back every attack. But
it was in the Babuna Pass that Serbian heroism most fully
flowered. The sublime spirit in which this position was
defended was nobly expressed by Vassitch when he declared
that his soldiers would continue to fight desperately to the
end, and that all Serbians would await without desertion at
the foot of their cross the hour of their crucifixion, making
their sacrifice live as an example to future generations.

CHAPTER XCIV.

THE GLORIOUS AND TERRIBLE CAMPAIGN OF THE MESOPOTAMIAN ARMY.

Why Neither Turk nor Briton Ventured Far into Babylonia—A Region of Flies, Mosquitoes, and Deadly Tropical Diseases—Our Soldier-Sailors of the Bellum Brigade—Boating Infantry and Steaming Cavalry at the Battle of Norfolk Hill—Having Learned the Art of Navigation, our Army Sails to Amara and Captures It—The Unhappy Garrison of the Garden of Eden—Sandstorms, Bedouin Raids, and Desert Thirst—The Bedouin Chief, the Sheep's Tails, and a Little Dynamite—Disastrous Change in the British Plan of Campaign—Four Indo-British Brigades are Launched Against the Forces of the Ottoman Empire—Magnificent Skill, Heroism, and Endurance of General Townshend's Men—Splendid Deeds of the West Kents and Hants Territorials at the Battle of Nasiriyeh—The Victorious Column Returns to Kurna for the Tigris Campaign—General Townshend's Brilliant Strategy at the Opening of our Attack on Kut-el-Amara—Incomparable Marching Feat of General Houghton's Brigade—Fine Frontal Attack by Mahrattas and Dorsets—After Turning the Enemy's Flank, the British and Indian Column is Checked by Want of Water—Extraordinary Combat with a Turkish Brigade—Owing to Sufferings from Thirst, our Marching Wing Fails to Encircle the Enemy—Turks Retire towards Bagdad, and General Townshend Captures Azizie—The Terrible Battle of Ctesiphon—Want of Water again Forces our Troops to Retire, and they Fall Back with Heavy Losses on Kut-el-Amara.

T HERE is nothing of the romantic atmosphere of the "Arabian Nights' Entertainments" remaining in the region between Bagdad and the Persian Gulf. In ancient times, it is said, a cock could hop from house to house from Basra, the city of Sindbad, past Babylon and Seleucia, to the capital of Haroun Al-Raschid. But since the Mongol, the Turk, and the nomads of Arabia swept over the most fertile country on earth, the tract between the Tigris and the Euphrates has lapsed into desert sand and riverside jungles of cane-brakes, where the Mesopotamian lion ranges. Instead of being a land of vines, orange groves, and rose gardens, Babylonia has become one of the most desolate wastes in Asia, and the reason why neither the Turk at Mosul nor the Briton at Koweit succeeded in occupying the wilderness was apparent to our troops in the spring of 1915. In April the commander of the Indian Expeditionary Force, Sir Arthur Barrett, fell so seriously ill that Sir John Eccles Nixon had to take over his command. The following month many men of the British regiments began to feel unwell, and when the full heat of the summer smote the Indo-British force the sufferings of the white men were extreme. Among them were the 2nd West Kents, the 1st Oxford and Bucks, the 2nd

GENERAL SIR JOHN ECCLES NIXON, K.C.B., who took over the command of the Indo-British Expedition to Bagdad in April, 1915, when Sir Arthur Barrett fell seriously ill.

Norfolks, 2nd Dorsets, 1st Hants, the 1st Territorial Battalion Hants, the 1st Territorial Battalion of the Sussex Regiment, some of the 25th Royal Fusiliers (Frontiersmen), and the 4th Rifle Brigade, with others. Among the Indian troops were the 20th, 22nd, 24th, 66th, 67th, 76th, and 90th Punjabis, 120th Infantry, 104th Wellesley Rifles, 103rd Mahrattas, 110th Light Infantry, 117th Mahrattas, 7th and 11th Rajputs, and 1st and 2nd Battalions of the 7th Gurkhas. Among the mounted troops were the 7th Lancers, 16th, 26th, and 33rd Cavalry, and Royal Horse Artillery (S Battery), and others.

The heat was not much worse than that of the Punjab, yet the Indian troops suffered almost as much as the British troops. This was due to the fact that the steaming marshlands of the great rivers not only gave a trying, humid quality to the burning tropical sunlight, but also the vast stretches of stagnant water, full of rotting refuse, formed the breeding places of an absolutely incomparable swarm of mosquitoes, biting flies, and vermin. These biting and blood-sucking insects were the main defenders of the legendary site of Eden, of the river-lands of Ur, where Abraham pastured his cattle, and the desolate yellow mounds representing all that remained of the hanging gardens by the Euphrates, where Alexander the Great died. Alexander had been able to conquer

General Sir Bryan Thomas Mahon, D.S.O., commanding the British Force in Serbia.

King Peter, who accompanied his Army during the retreat, being lifted on to horseback when his car could go no farther.

King Peter rode until exhausted, when he exchanged the saddle for a stretcher. "I must stay till the end," he said.

A characteristic pass through the Serbian mountains to the west of Uskub.

all emperors, kings, and chieftains between the Mediterranean and the Indian Ocean, but at the height of his power and his glory he had been stung by a gnat, and infected with a deadly fever.

It was the insect-borne diseases of the immense river marshes which had for nearly three centuries stayed the march of both Turk and Briton. Only the Bedouin, after being naturally vaccinated for some thousands of years by the plague-insects of the swamps, was able to drag out a wretched existence amid the ruins of the earliest civilisation in the world. His children were infected with all the diseases of the region in infancy, but their inherited constitution had been so toughened that what killed stranger adults troubled

SINGULAR NATURAL FORMATION AT DAYIR, IN SOUTHERN PERSIA.
This curious structure, seemingly the product of some untutored sculptor's imagination, was built by Nature out of mud and salt.

eating flies. A piece of white bread became black before it reached one's mouth, and the inevitable result was some kind of dysentery. And such was the effect of the heat that a body of vigorous troops in the prime of life, marching at the top of their powers, seldom did more than eight miles a day. By this time they lost so much of the fluid of their blood that, though they emptied their water-flasks, they were tortured by thirst, and suffered like men in the last stages of kidney disease.

The campaign in East Africa was not exactly a picnic, but that in Mesopotamia was a nightmare. It would have been absolutely impossible for the Indian Expeditionary Force to have done more than hold on to Basra and guard the pipe-line of the Admiralty oil-fields in Persia but for the help given to our soldiers by our sailors. The men of the Royal Indian Marine, the Royal Navy, and the Royal Naval Reserve transformed the campaign into the most adventurous example of amphibious warfare in our history.

An amphibian army

Owing to their foresight, inventiveness, and resource, the army was practically transformed into a naval force that operated upon rivers, across stretches of flood-water, and through reed-grown marshes, haunted by the wild beasts of Babylonia. Every form of craft was employed, from the most primitive punt to the latest type of oil-driven vessels. There were three old sloops, which had been doomed by the Admiralty to destruction when the war broke out, but which were saved to perform great work in the river battles. There were flat-bottomed Irrawaddy paddle-steamers, in which Sir Harry Prendergast had conquered Burma, and which were brought across the ocean in their old age to bombard the Turkish trenches at Kut-el-Amara. Motor-boats, light-draught river-motors—which had seen service off Belgium, the Dardanelles, and German East Africa—sailed round the Garden of Eden by "Temptation Square" and "Serpent's Corner." Then there

TRACES OF EUROPEAN INFLUENCES IN AN ASIATIC TOWN.
The front at Bushire, which was occupied by the British as a protest against the failure of the Persian Government to punish the tribal chiefs whose rising was instigated by German agents. The ruins on the left are those of an old Portuguese fort, and the British Consulate is seen on the right.

them as lightly as chicken-pox does our children. In the same way the yellow fever of Central American ports only produces in native children a slight and passing disturbance. When, after some three hundred years of fairly friendly relations, the Briton and the Turk clashed at last in war round the Persian Gulf in the decisive struggle for the overland route to India, both of them suffered less from each other's weapons than from the deadly little pricks of the insect defenders of the land.

Insects v. man

The flies produced dysentery and typhoid, while the mosquitoes began by injecting the malaria germ; when this was kept down by means of quinine, they produced strange new kinds of tropical fever, which filled our base hospital with patients, who had to be taken to India to recover.

Many of our troops at last went through the campaign in a state of absolute nudity, protected by mosquito-nets, with mats of woven reeds over their heads, as a slight shade against the flame-like sunshine. But they could not get away from the flies; a man could not eat his food without

GENERAL VIEW OF BAGDAD, WITH THE TURKISH BARRACKS BELOW.
Like most Oriental cities, Bagdad, with its domes and minarets, its strong lights and shadows, and its palms and tamarisks, presents a picture that delights the artist. The building in the foreground of the upper picture is part of the Turkish barracks, of which the front elevation is shown in the lower photograph.

was an aeroplane which had flown at Singapore, and had afterwards shed its wings and become a launch with an aerial propeller, moving down the river with a series of detonations like a badly-firing motor-bicycle, and spreading dread among the Bedouins. There were tug-boats (mounting 4·7 in. guns), horse barges, and the Mesopotamian steamers belonging to the Lynch firm. But the foundation of our operations was the bellum—a native punt, which can carry ten armed men over a foot of water. A great flotilla of bellums often fought our strange infantry battles, while the steam-driven and motor-propelled vessels scouted in advance and acted like a cavalry division.

Sir John Nixon began his part of the campaign by turning his soldiers into sailors. For some weeks in the spring the whole brigade stationed at Kurna was engaged in learning the art of navigation in bellums. This type of boat has a length of about thirty-five feet and a beam of two and a half feet; it is propelled in shallow water by poles, and in deep water by paddles. Two men were required to work it, and as it was likely they would both be shot down when the action opened, all the men in the flat-bottomed craft had to learn how to punt and paddle, so as to be able to look after themselves if their boatmen fell. It was also at this time that a considerable part of our field artillery was put on the water, and, by great feats of carpentry and smith work, mounted on rafts, sailing-boats, tugs,

The Bellum Brigade

and launches. Machine-guns were also mounted in large numbers, and at dawn on May 31st the extraordinary new Indo-British navy moved out to attack.

In front of the hundreds of river-boats were the three sloops Clio, Odin, and Espiègle, each with six 4 in. guns, and the Royal Indian Marine steamer Lawrence, with the rafts and boats containing field-guns. This remarkable squadron had to steam through something that was neither land nor water, but a tract of mud thinning into a liquid form, while retaining the appearance of land by reason of the reeds growing out of it. The progress of the boats was much impeded by the reeds, and the Turks, with their Kurdish levies and German officers, entrenched on the low hills to the north, had a magnificent target. But their 6 in. field-guns used only the old segment shells, sold by our Government to the Ottoman Empire soon after the South African War. These shells made a noise, but did very little damage. What was more important, the Turks had no machine-guns, and their musketry fire was not good. After our steamer squadron had bombarded the enemy trenches, the newly-made sailor-soldiers of the bellum brigade—2nd Norfolks, 110th Mahratta Light Infantry, and 120th Rajputana Infantry—beached their boats among the reeds, then squelched through the marsh and charged with the bayonet up the high, dry ground. The entrenched Turks, on the hill now known as Norfolk Hill, put up a good fight, but they were rushed and shattered, and the enemy troops in the other six positions fled in disorder up the Tigris to Amara.

Battle of Norfolk Hill

Some of them were cut off in the marshes, but the main force could not be pursued; for an ingenious German engineer, who had been working on the river when war broke out, blocked the stream by sinking a line of large barges, and laying mines around them. It took our men two days to clear away the mines and the wrecks. On the evening of June 1st our steamers worked through the obstruction and puffed away in pursuit of the enemy. It was expected that the Turks would make another stand at Amara, which lies 87 miles above Kurna. Amara has a population of ten thousand, and is the most important place between Bagdad (which is 370 miles up-stream) and Basra (which is 130 miles down-stream). The Turks, however, were too deeply alarmed by our amazing boating army and its gun-rafts and machine-gunned bellums. We were exercising all the extraordinary advantages of sea-power in the heart of a desert, hundreds of miles from the sea. Had the enemy made a stand at Amara we could have sailed by him, have landed well in his rear, and have cut his line of communications. It was necessary for him to counter the naval tactics of our army by constructing a miniature system of Dardanelles forts on both banks of the river, with some powerful long-range guns capable of sinking the largest ship we could bring up-stream. The Turkish commander, Nuredin Pasha, therefore kept his men on the march until they reached Kut-el-Amara, near Bagdad, where the great cross-desert canal, Shat-el-Hai, runs from the Tigris to the Euphrates at Nasiriyeh. Here he built a formidable system of fortifications which Sir John Nixon's men afterwards found very useful.

Capture of Amara

With the advance to Amara, the original plan of our Persian Gulf campaign was concluded. We had safeguarded our Admiralty oil supply, and had swept the enemy far back from our sphere of influence along the Gulf. We had, moreover, captured the port of Mesopotamia, Basra, and had put a complete end to the river commerce of Bagdad, Mosul, and other towns. So far as India was concerned, the danger of any Turkish movement was restricted to Kurdish raids across the mountains to the north. These raids led into the northern provinces of Persia, which were under Russian influence; and the Russian army in the Caucasus, possessing quick and easy transport across the Caspian Sea, was excellently situated to meet any menace. So when the very hot weather came our Indian Expeditionary Force merely stood fast on the ground it had won, and consolidated the newly-conquered territory. With the capture of Amara, we had 136 miles of river communications to maintain between that town and Basra. And though the Turks had been pushed back, there were large numbers of armed Arabs scattered about the country. Some of them were friendly to us, for the simple reason that they wished to be on the winning side—and we looked like winning—but many of them had helped the Turks, and, under the influence of their priests, they continued to snipe our advanced detachments and raid our stores.

Transformation of Basra

At Basra things settled down so quietly that the British engineers began to transform the city of Sindbad the Sailor. Dikes were cut to control the flood-water, the creeks were bridged, and roads made through the pathless marshes.

Then a large scheme of town-planning was put into execution, in preparation for the day when Sir William Willcocks would dam the Tigris and Euphrates, and, by a vast system of irrigation, transform Babylonia into one of the great wheat-fields of the world. A beginning was made in establishing law, order, and industry by taking considerable tracts of land from the local owners. Much to the surprise of these Arab merchants, their land was bought from them at a fair price, instead of being seized by force, according to the immemorial custom of all other conquerors. Customs were established, and trade encouraged in every way; and what with the institution of

WHERE ROADS WERE BAD AND TELEGRAPH WIRES WERE NON-EXISTENT.
Mahailahs (a kind of wherry) passing Kumait Fort with supplies for Kut. The Mahailahs are towed by men by means of ropes attached to the mast-head. Above: Indian signallers using the heliograph during the fighting near Bagdad.

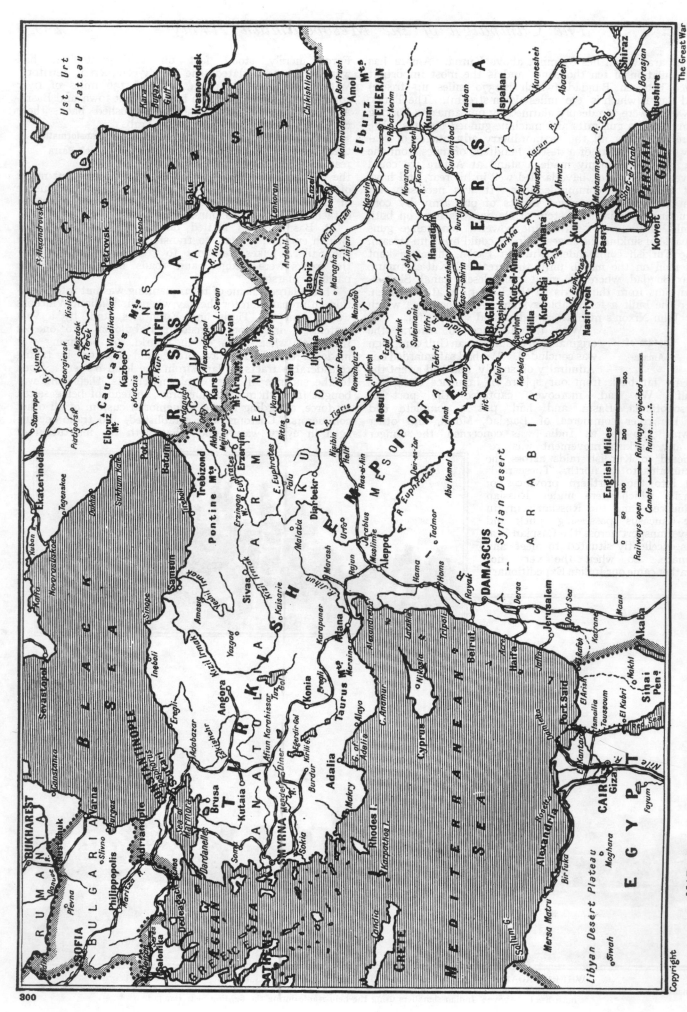

300

MAP OF THE TURKISH EMPIRE SPECIALLY DRAWN TO ILLUSTRATE THE CAMPAIGN IN MESOPOTAMIA.

Copyright

The Great War

settled and progressive government, the improvement of land and water communications and the public health system, the benefits of British occupation were brought home to the townspeople.

The result was that some of the Arab tribes began heartily to work for the new government, and did much to relieve our troops when the terrible heat was seriously telling on the white men. Not a shot was fired for months, and though it was believed by our soldiers that large quantities of firearms had been concealed by the Turks in the mosques, every Arab in the towns except the mullahs, was friendly. There was very little quarrelling or crime, and though our men still went about armed, they were never attacked. The hardest task that fell to our home regiments was that of guarding the date gardens and marshes in the Garden of Eden. Despite all scraps of archæological information doled out to them, the units of the garrison at Kurna refused to believe that the swampy land at the junction of the two great rivers was once so fertile, healthy and beautiful a spot that civilisation was born there, and the legend of its glory travelled down the ages to the Hebrews. The garrison only gave way to the general opinion of the army so far as to name some of the more important thoroughfares "Serpent's Corner," "Temptation Square" and "Adam and Eve Street." But with the steaming marshes around them, in which a few of the most wretched fishermen on earth won just enough food to beget children to share their misery, with a furnace-like air, buzzing all day with biting flies and humming all night with stinging mosquitoes, the unfortunate British soldiers guarding the paradise of the Sumerians reckoned that they could have given Dante and Milton some vivid information about the conditions of life in the infernal regions.

The Garden of Eden

This garrison work, though unexciting, was almost a relief after a skirmish in the desert. In the desert at times the temperature was up to 130 degrees in the small tents, and on very sultry days the sandstorms came. A dense khaki-coloured cloud rose on the horizon, and then rolled towards the encampment. The men rushed about strengthening their tent-pegs and ropes, and collecting all the loose kit; but often no preparation was adequate to meet the storm. The tents were blown down like packs of cards, and all had to hide their heads under tent-flaps, bedding, or boxes, as it was impossible to face the blasts of cutting sand. In violent tempests the sand made a black darkness which lasted for hours. When the storm passed, and the troops emerged, shaking themselves like dogs coming out of water, their eyes were bloodshot, their mouths and nostrils coated thick and black with sand and mud, and all their bodies were a mass of sand.

It was in these circumstances that the work of chasing down hostile Arab tribes and burning their camps had to be carried out. The actual conflicts with mounted bands of Bedouin guerillas were not much of a trial. As the Bedouins usually had no guns, they scattered among the dunes when our men offered battle, and our reconnoitring aeroplanes were hard put to it to trace the lines along which they were going to again concentrate. The Indian cavalry, with a section of horse artillery concealed behind them, managed at first by feigning a flight and leading the unsuspecting Bedouins towards our guns, to ambush some of the more daring Bedouin parties. But the Bedouin, being a born guerilla fighter, mounted on a fine desert horse, soon learned all the tricks of our cavalry, and had to be hunted down by converging columns of infantry. Infantry, however, had been hunting down the Bedouin for some ten thousand years; and when the Indo-British troops took up the work which Turk, Mongol, Persian, Assyrian, Babylonian and Sumerian had been unable to accomplish, the son of the desert resorted to his ancient tactics.

He retired deep into the sandy waste, where he could water by springs known only to himself. There he tried to outfight us by his last and most terrible weapon of defence—thirst. Our men had some narrow escapes from

THE "CITY OF THE CALIPHS."
Impression of a corner of Bagdad, showing, in the background, the pontoon bridge across the Tigris crowded with Arabs in their picturesque Oriental costumes.

the most awful of deaths. On one occasion a strong column of our troops was set the apparently easy task of rounding up some Bedouins whom our airmen had discovered camping only ten miles away. The men marched all night through the hot desert, charged the Arabs early in the morning, burned their tents, and hunted them over the sand-ridges for miles, and then returned to the captured camp for food and water. By this time the sun was terribly fierce, and the men, having emptied their water-bottles while marching in the hot night, were exhausted. And no water had been brought for them. It had apparently been thought that, as the river was only ten miles away, the column was in no danger of dying from thirst.

An awful march

At seven o'clock in the morning the troops began their march back to the river. But after covering only two miles the situation became desperate. The men began to stagger out and drop with exhaustion, and every hundred yards they went things looked blacker and blacker. At

WHERE "SULTAN AFTER SULTAN, WITH HIS POMP, ABODE."
On November 19th, 1915, General Townshend's Division attacked the Turks at Ctesiphon, eighteen miles from Bagdad. After sanguinary fighting, the position was captured, together with about eighteen hundred prisoners. This photograph shows the ruins of the great palace erected by Chosroes I. at Ctesiphon.

the end of four miles, when the sun was high and all the air was aflame, the column had to stop. The men—mostly Indians, and accustomed to tropical heat—could not get any farther. Some of the British officers, who had been very careful with their water-bottles, gave their last drop to Indian officers and other bad cases. Then the general ordered tents to be pitched, and sent his Staff and cavalry to bring water from the river. Meanwhile, the column was in an awful condition, the agony of many of the men being dreadful to witness. One British infantry officer, feeling he was about to die, thought he would make a struggle for it. He strung water-bottles round his neck and around the camp mules, mounted one of the chargers, and made for the river. He could not afterwards tell how he reached it. He was half unconscious. But the animals found the water, and the officer rolled in it on his charger, drank up something that was more mud than water, and filled the bottles. With his refreshed pack of mules he regained the camp before the cavalry arrived, and saved many lives.

This extraordinary story must always be borne in mind

when studying the operations in Babylonia during the season between May and September. Many of the Indian troops came from the desert regions in North-West India, yet even they could not march in the strong sun of the Mesopotamian summer through ten miles of waterless sand. In fact, as we have seen, they could not walk five miles when their water-bottles were empty. The heat from the sun above and from the scorching sand beneath dried up the blood in the body, and produced a condition of hallucination which quickly merged into coma, ending rapidly in death. Men did not sweat in the desert. Even with a good water supply they had not enough fluid blood to produce perspiration. They simply dried up. It was only in the steaming marshes and along the steaming rivers that a man could, by drinking much water, enjoy the luxury of perspiration. In daylight desert marching in the summer the human body just dried up; and a corpse, when left on the sand, baked. Practically all marching had to be done by night; and even then the heat in the sand so penetrated to the feet that an average progress of half a mile an hour was very good going. Eight miles in twenty-four hours was quite as much as any general could expect if he wished his men at the end of the eight miles to be in a condition to lift and fire a rifle. So we had to follow the immemorial custom of warfare in the land of the great rivers, and campaign in winter and rest in summer.

But the Bedouin, lean from the heat, and with a skin that resisted the flaming air, maintained his raids against our forces. There was a large and powerful Arab tribe, led by a picturesque fighter whom our soldiers called "Jamie." The tents of Jamie were pitched along the Euphrates between Basra and Nasiriyeh. Our pickets in the outpost line were attacked nearly every night, and the bullets sent by Jamie's men penetrated into the farthest corners of the camp. We had a good many casualties owing to these raids, but Jamie was a very sportsmanlike character. One night some of his men, evading all the pickets and guards, got into our slaughter-house, where the carcases of three hundred sheep were hanging, and cut the tails off all the sheep to show that they had been there. Unfortunately, Jamie was not fully aware of the resources of civilisation. The officer in charge of the slaughter-house rather hinted to his men that they need not be more careful than they had been; and the result was that eight more of Jamie's men got through the pickets and crawled to the building. But there were dynamite mines outside the door, and all eight raiders were killed. Soon afterwards two of Jamie's villages were stormed and burned, and Jamie himself began to think that he had better get on the winning side. The fact was that aeroplane reconnaissance had greatly altered the conditions of desert warfare, and as our force also employed armed motor-cars in places where the sand was fairly firm, even the Arabian horse was often outpaced and run down. The use of portable wireless instruments by airmen and troops increased the difficulties of the elusive Bedouin, and made him less elusive than ever he had been before.

The conversion of Jamie

A rest on the road almost within sight of the goal. After months of marching and fighting, our troops got within sixteen miles of Bagdad before lack of water compelled them to retire.

A transport on the flooded Shaiba-Basra road. While want of water caused the troops acute distress at some points of the march, excess of it elsewhere caused them infinite trouble. The Shaiba road is generally flooded, the water varying in depth from three inches to six feet.

Machine-guns manned by Indians in action in the desert. India's reply to the Kaiser's appeal to Mohammedanism was all the " more german to the matter," because she did " carry a cannon by her side," and used it most effectively—in defence of the British Empire.

By boats over the desert that lies before Bagdad. Another illustration of the discomforts and difficulties that attended the march to Bagdad. The desert was often flooded, and the troops had to wade through thick mud to the boats.

WITH HORSE AND FOOT ACROSS THE BLAZING SANDS AND FLOODED ROADS OF MESOPOTAMIA.

The upshot was that even in the heat of the summer the work of daunting and disarming the hostile tribes went on at a surprising speed. And as our armed vessels had a range of over a week's march down both the Tigris and the Euphrates, and the steamers were able to tow large flotillas of troop-filled bellums and barges to any point at which the hostile Arabs assembled, not only was the pacification of the occupied territory ensured, but far-distant raiding tribes could also be unexpectedly attacked. During this phase of the campaign the Turks had no flying machines, while our Indian Expeditionary Force had both aeroplanes and seaplanes. The eyes of Britain watched all the enemy's movements, and his remote entrenched camps were bombarded in a manner that shook the nerves of the Turkish, Kurdish, and Arabian troops. We lost a few machines, owing principally to engine trouble, arising from the flying sand, and perhaps from the extreme heat. On the other hand, there were some fine rescues of distressed airmen, such as that undertaken by Staff-Sergeant C. B. Heath, of the Australian Flying Corps. He helped to pole one of the long flat-bottomed boats—bellums—for twenty-eight miles, in order to bring back two aviators who had been forced to descend in enemy country. Sergeant Heath worked for twelve hours in the terrible heat of full summer, and effected a rescue.

About the beginning of July, 1915, the Mesopotamian campaign against the Turkish forces guarding Bagdad was undertaken. This was a profound change of policy, for which several reasons may be discerned. In the first place, our position in regard to Persia was becoming difficult. The German Ambassador at Teheran, Prince Reuss XXXI., was intriguing with various Persian politicians and Persian tribes, and was suborning the armed police and their Swedish officers. The police system had been established by Russia and Britain, with a view to keeping the highways free from brigands, and Swedish officers had been selected in order that neither Russian nor British interests should be especially favoured. It was not foreseen that some of these Swedes would so misuse their position as to transform their large force of 6,000

Intrigues of Prince Reuss XXXI.

armed men into an instrument of German ambition. But the intrigues that were going on in July among the gendarmerie, and among the mountain tribes on the Turco-Persian border, caused considerable suspicion. The Russian army in the Caucasus was apparently at a standstill, and part of the Turkish forces was extending towards the Persian highlands to co-operate with the mountain tribes and Swedish-led rebels.

The condition of the main Russian armies in Poland encouraged the Turks and the conspirators in Persia to plan a swift and complete Persian conquest, which would enable them to bring overwhelming forces against our Admiralty oil-fields and pipe-line, and then drive in on the flank of our Indian Expeditionary Force. Not only was this vast conspiracy to be countered, there was also our failure in the Dardanelles to be retrieved by some showy achievement which would restore our prestige throughout the Orient. It is, however, extremely improbable that Sir John Nixon planned the new campaign on his own initiative. His forces were utterly inadequate to the proposed task. A garrison was needed in the north to protect the oil-fields and pipe-line; troops were required for the occupation and defence of the string of towns running from Amara to Koweit; so that not much more than a division of Indian and British troops, with a brigade or so as a reserve, was disposable for an attack against the Turkish army in Mesopotamia.

Townshend's overwhelming task

General Townshend, who commanded the division, was set a task harder than that which Clive or Wellesley had carried out in India. With a tiny force, consisting two-thirds of native troops and one-third of British troops, he had continually to attack an enemy who possessed overwhelming numbers. The enemy was, moreover, well equipped, armed with guns of superior power, directed by German officers, and entrenched in difficult positions with all the skill of which German engineers were capable. The British politician was at his old game—trying to conquer a powerful empire by means of an utterly inadequate force. At the Dardanelles we had first thrown at the Ottoman Empire—which had six hundred thousand men under arms

LINED UP FOR INSPECTION ALONG THE PALM-SHADED BANK OF THE EUPHRATES.
British troops on church parade at Kurna, at the junction of the old channel of the Euphrates with the Tigris. The Turks put up a determined fight hereabouts during the summer of 1915, but surrendered when heavily attacked on the flank.

MODERN MAN-OF-WAR ON THE IMMEMORIAL TIGRIS.
The cruiser Odin arriving at Kurna, and going through the pontoon bridge which was temporarily " cut " to admit of its passage. An idea of the tropical vegetation which abounds in the neighbourhood of Britain's Meso-potamian war may be gathered from the dense mass of palm-trees on the farther bank.

—a single army corps, shipped in disorder, and unprovided with the heavy howitzers needed in the siege battles of modern times. When this operation had failed, and the Ottoman Government was reported to be waiting only for equipment in order to arm a million men, the British Cabinet sent General Townshend to operate on the other side of the Ottoman Empire and capture Bagdad, in a zone where the Turks were believed to have large forces.

From the nature of things the advance on Bagdad was doomed to failure. General Townshend's only chance of success was to defeat the Turks before their reinforcements arrived. These reinforcements began

A miracle of heroism

moving from the Caucasian front towards the middle of September, when the first heavy snow fell on the high mountain passes, and so strengthened the natural obstacles against the Russian advance that some of the troops could extend eastward in Persia, while others came down the Tigris. Before we could approach Bagdad we had to defeat a large Turkish force on the Euphrates at Nasiriyeh, which lay in a position to cut across the rear or take in the flank the advance we designed to make high up the Tigris. Then at Kut-el-Amara, at the junction between the canal connecting the Euphrates and the Tigris, General Townshend's small force had to meet the main Turkish army when it was strengthened by the force from Nasiriyeh. And all this had to be done in the season of intense heat, when neither the Indian nor the British troops could get along without water, and even then could get along only very slowly, and with much suffering. Having regard to the conditions under which the campaign was fought—the almost general outbreak of disease, the exhausting heat, sleepless, insect-haunted nights, and the bad diet of bully beef and Army biscuit

THE PONTOON BRIDGE AT KURNA.
This bridge was destroyed by the Turks with the aid of a floating mine. A British soldier is seen coming across with an Indian comrade.

supplied for this tropical campaign—it will be the considered judgment of the nation that General Townshend and his men performed a miracle of endurance and heroism. Indeed, we are inclined to maintain that the men who fought in the First Battle of Ypres and in the landing battles of Gallipoli scarcely showed such superhuman endurance as the columns that crawled to victory in Mesopotamia when they were dying of thirst.

The opening episodes in the Bagdad campaign showed how easily our men could have won the decisive battle if they had been properly reinforced from India for the closing effort.

305

GOING ABOARD A WARSHIP AFTER A FIGHT WITH THE FOE.
Campaigning was made comparatively comfortable for some of the troops who fought sufficiently near the Tigris to permit of their being re-embarked after an engagement on the warships that conveyed them up that river.

extending for about a mile on either bank

The Turks also had powerful detachments thrown out along the old channel of the Euphrates which runs through that vast sheet of water, Lake Hamar, to the junction with the Tigris at Kurna. There was a good deal of skirmishing round Lake Hamar between our armed motor-boats and steamers and the Thornycroft-built warships which the Turks employed. This river fighting had been proceeding since December 9th, 1914, when the capture of Kurna opened the old Euphrates channel to our ships and gun-tugs. The Arab snipers were gradually cleared from the great lake, and then, at the beginning of July, the Hampshire Territorials set out in a steamer to clear the Gurma Safha River, a stretch of the old Euphrates, running south - west to Lake Hamar, above the new channel.

In a fierce fight on July 5th along the Gurma Safha, Private H. W. Elkins distinguished himself by returning at a critical moment to the steamer for ammunition, and taking it, under heavy shell and rifle fire, to the firing-line. Private H. G. Wooldridge, another Hants "Terrier," also showed remarkable courage; on being knocked down by the blast of a shell and badly wounded in the shoulder, he went on fighting until ordered back to the steamer by the medical officer.

After fighting through the enemy's advanced position below Hamar Lake, our wonderfully-mixed flotilla arrived, at the end of the third week in July, at a distance of about seven miles from Nasiriyeh. The division was then split up. Two brigades were landed on the right or westerly bank, while to the other brigade was assigned the task of working through the groves of date-palms on the left bank. As a reserve, a fourth brigade was brought down from Amara, and held ready for action in river-boats. Each of these boats had four guns, and pushing slowly up the river it covered with its fire

The Battle of Nasiriyeh

our troops on either bank, and silenced some of the enemy's guns that tried to shell our flotilla. The reserve brigade did not come into action, so complete and rapid was the success of the division.

The battle began about half-past four on the morning of July 24th, 1915. For half an hour the brigades had been moving forward; but before the infantry charged, all our howitzers, field, and mountain guns bombarded the enemy's foremost trenches with high-explosive shells. For a full hour our batteries continued to smash up the enemy's entrenchments and gun positions; and then the 2nd West Kents advanced through the date groves, while eight of our machine-guns, with the supporting battalions, covered the advance by rapid fire on the opposing trenches

The Turkish force which had been beaten at Shaiba had retreated down the Euphrates to Nasiriyeh, and had there been joined by strong reinforcements, who brought more artillery, including three heavy siege-guns, transported from Adrianople. The Euphrates route, by which the Turks had made their previous attack on Basra, was the only practicable line for an advance during the flood season. The town of Nasiriyeh was also important as being the capital of the warlike Mustafik tribe of Arabs; and its junction with the cross-desert canal of Shat-el-Hai, running towards the Bagdad region, greatly increased its military importance. The capture of the town would prevent the enemy from advancing on Basra by the Euphrates route, with the result that in the season when the Tigris was in flood our position would be absolutely secure. The enemy, however, had taken great pains with his defences. His army was entrenched on both sides of the wide river, with long lines of very strong entrenchments,

On the rivers, flood-waters, and reed-grown marshes of Mesopotamia every form of craft was utilised. The river steamer shown above, and used for the passage of troops and supplies, was protected with armour-plates and sand-bags, and carried a gun on deck.

Indian mountain battery crossing the burning sands of the legendary site of Eden. So great was the heat that vigorous troops in the prime of life, marching at the top of their powers, seldom did more than eight miles a day.

How the heroes of the march to Bagdad entrenched themselves against Arabs and Turks. The belligerents, European and Asiatic, suffered less from each other's weapons than from the deadly little blood-sucking insects, which proved the real defenders of the land.

INCIDENTS IN THE AMAZING CAMPAIGN BETWEEN THE TIGRIS AND EUPHRATES.

Despite this covering fire, however, the West Kents were met by a terrible fusillade that swept their front lines. An officer in one of the regiments that was maintaining a covering musketry fire said the most magnificent sight he had ever seen was the West Kents going on under the enemy's terrific fusillade, and manœuvring as if they were on parade. As soon as they got up to the Turkish trenches, they wheeled round to the right, and, while their comrades stopped firing for fear of hitting them, they leapt into the trenches and were lost to view.

As they disappeared they got to work with the bayonet, and in a short time the spectators watching the game of life and death saw the Turks running as if the devil himself were after them. So the brigade opened fire again at the fugitives. Sergeant W. Wannell and Company-Sergeant-Major A. G. Elliott, both of the 2nd West Kents, were the first to reach the enemy's trenches. They each led several bayonet charges in the close fighting which followed the attack, clearing trench after trench with steel and bullet. Sergeant Wannell also showed himself a remarkable bomb-thrower, and Company-Sergeant-Major Elliott, after heading charge after charge, helped to rescue a wounded comrade under fire. When Lieutenant Hill was wounded, yet still fighting with his sword against a throng of enemies, Private Howe leaped to his help and, by shooting one Turk and bayoneting four others, saved his officer's life. Two others of the West Kents—Private E. T. Bye and Private W. Bridger—distinguished themselves in tending the wounded and searching for them under the enemy's fusillade. Company-Sergeant-Major E. J. Newbrook was a fine fighter. Badly wounded during the first attack,

Magnificent West Kents he remained directing his party till the close of the day's operations. Many soldiers have done this sort of thing in France and Flanders; but the climate in Mesopotamia in the fourth week of July was a trying one for a severely wounded man to keep fighting in until evening fell. In the Ypres battles the 1st West Kents—the regiment that never lost a trench—won the highest honours in the Army; and at Nasiriyeh, in Babylonia, the men of the 2nd Battalion showed themselves of the same grand cast of character.

After the West Kents wheeled and jumped into the Turkish trenches, the rest of the brigade advanced to support the attack, carrying all the ammunition they could collect. The brigade wheeled in the direction taken by its leading battalion, and picking their way through mounds of dead Turks, the men emerged into an open space where the Kentish heroes were taking cover by a low bank, and firing at the enemy in the date groves all around them. By this time the West Kents were using their last cartridges; but a battalion of Sikhs gave them some ammunition, and reinforced the firing-line by the low bank. Soon afterwards the order came to take two loopholed towers from which the enemy was maintaining a heavy fire. A double company of Sikhs and some twelve of the West Kents cleared the Turks out of the trenches on their right, and then shouting out "Hurrah!" like boys at a picnic, they stabbed their way along a communication sap, and took both towers in fifteen minutes.

Rout of the Turks

The Turks lost many men, for they fought with matting over their trenches to keep the sun out, and the Kents and the Sikhs stuck them with the bayonet through the matting while they were firing up rather wildly, without being able to see clearly what was happening over their covering. After capturing the towers and a considerable number of prisoners, the Sikhs and the handful of white men had ten minutes' rest, which they spent in binding up their wounded and putting them in the shade of the towers. Then the small force fought the Turks out of another long line of trench, running down to the edge of a creek which formed the extreme left of the Turkish position. Here there was a village with another couple of towers, and these were also stormed after long, terrible bayonet work above the last mat-covered trench. By this time the division had won the battle. The Turks could be seen running away on the left, and the Sikhs and the West Kents were signalled to hold the ground they had won, and not to advance any farther. So, posting guards, they slept by the last two captured towers that night.

Across the river our troops were equally successful. The Hants Territorials shared the honours of the day with the West Kents; for, despite the fact that the enemy's position was protected by barbed-wire entanglements, the Territorial battalion made a splendid storming charge. Two men—Private N. W. Player and Private J. Hill—raced in front of their line, and were the first to enter the Turkish trenches. There they fought with a skill and courage that made them a fine example to all ranks.

A FREQUENT INCIDENT DURING THE BRITISH MARCH TO BAGDAD.
Mule team in difficulties on the scorching desert sands that had to be traversed by the troops and supply columns during the memorable campaign in Mesopotamia.

BRITISH HEROES OF THE DESERTS AND MARSHES ALONG THE TIGRIS.
British troops, in sun-helmets and shorts, going on picket duty in Mesopotamia. On December 8th, 1915, the Turks began a fierce onslaught on the Indo-British position at Kut-el-Amara. They attacked persistently for three days, but without success, and their losses numbered thousands.

Another private of the Territorial battalion—E. G. Verrall—was wounded early in the battle after giving a fine exhibition of resourcefulness and daring bravery. Lance-Corporal R. Snow, who was in charge of a machine-gun, kept his weapon in action under a heavy shell and rifle fire. So terrible was the work he did among the enemy that the Turkish batteries singled him out as a target. They caught him at last with shrapnel, after he had been working his machine-gun for two hours; but in spite of his injuries the corporal continued to work his gun with steady and deadly skill for another hour, until it was put out of action by a Turkish shell. Another non-commissioned officer who won military distinction in the Battle of Nasiriyeh was Staff-Sergeant P. T. Wells, of the 2nd Cameron Highlanders. At a critical point and period in the attack, when the Turks were still unshaken, Sergeant Wells led his platoon with remarkable ability and coolness until he fell at last severely wounded.

Among the naval men who especially distinguished themselves was Lieutenant - Commander Seymour. He was in charge of the armed launch Shushan, and, working her gun himself in difficult circumstances, he sank an armed Turkish patrol-boat. Lieutenant Hugh Fortescue Curry, R.N., was in command of the stern - wheel steamer Muzaffri, and when our men on the right bank of the Euphrates were running short of cartridges, he landed under fire from the Turkish guns, and supplied the soldiers with ammunition. Lieutenant William Vesey Hamilton Harris,

R.N., while steaming along the river in the armed launch Sumana, observed that our troops had got into a very awkward position. There was a wide creek between them and the enemy, and both the mud and the water were so deep that they could not cross. The Turks were sweeping the creek with heavy gun and rifle fire, and it looked as though this part of our attack would be completely hung up. But Lieutenant Harris, with the ready ingenuity that marks the British sailor, jumped into a barge, and poled it into the creek. There, with shells bursting above him and bullets singing around his head, he turned the barge crosswise, and thus made a bridge for the troops. The Shushan, the Sumana, and other armed launches were uncommonly powerful vessels, because they had each in tow horse-barges containing a 4·7 in. gun. Most of our artillery was floating on the river, and if Turkish marksmanship had been good, the enemy's shells might have done a great deal of damage to our floating batteries. But our gunners had the whip-hand of the enemy all the time, and in our large but frail flotilla the guns were worked so quickly and so exactly that the Turkish batteries were silenced before they did much harm.

At the turning-point in the battle, the Shushan pushed up to the point where one of the main creeks entered the river, and so shelled the Turks that they broke and fled. At half-past five in the afternoon the Mejidieh steamer, from which the general and some of his Staff officers worked, reached this point, and soon afterwards the enemy's camp

GENERAL SIR JOHN ECCLES NIXON, K.C.B.
From April, 1915, to January, 1916, Commander-in-Chief in Mesopotamia.

GENERAL TOWNSHEND'S LINES OF ATTACK ON KUT-
EL-AMARA.

From the Dummy Camp on the north bank of the Tigris two Indo-British
brigades made a great surprise trek round the marshes on the northern
bank and almost encircled the fleeing enemy.

was occupied, all the remaining Turks bolting towards
the north. At the junction of the river and the
creek the Mejidieh found four 15-pounder Turkish field-
guns commanding the lower reaches of the river. If the
Indo-British force had not pushed through that evening,
it would have had a tough nut to crack next morning.
The river was two hundred yards wide, and another wide
creek served as a moat to the Turkish position. After the
battery had been discovered and silenced, Lieutenant
Seymour pushed ahead in the Shushan launch and reached
Nasiriyeh.

The riverside town of two-storied mud-brick houses was
fluttering with white flags, and it was just beyond the
town that Lieutenant Seymour spotted
two Turkish Thornycroft-built patrol-
boats, one of which he sank with a 4·7 in.
shell. As the Shushan returned past the
town she was fired on from the white-flagged houses. Had
our troops practised German methods, they might have been
tempted to sack and burn the capital of the Mustafik tribe.
As it was, the British and Indians camped in tents outside
the town for the night, and on July 25th some of them
went to the bazaar and peacefully bought what fresh fruit
there was for sale. Nasiriyeh was found to be a well-laid-
out town, but its sanitary conditions were so bad that our
troops camped in tents outside till our engineers had
cleaned up the worst filth. By the end of the month the
extraordinary heat and the arduous exertions of the
division had told so heavily on both officers and men that
ninety-five per cent. of the force was in quite an exhausted
condition.

The Turkish Commander-in-Chief, Nuredin Pasha, whose
base was at Kut-el-Amara, had despatched a large body

**Peace and War
at Nasiriyeh**

of reinforcements along the Shat-el-Hai Canal. If this
force had arrived during the battle, our sun-smitten, over-
worked division would have been compelled to retire.
Even if the Turks had collected the fugitives from Nasiriyeh,
and quickly attacked our exhausted men, the situation
would have been full of peril for us. Happily, things fell
out otherwise. The fresh Turkish troops met the routed
army of the Euphrates, and were so impressed by the tales
of the terrible valour of the British and the Indians, that
they, too, turned tail, and hastened back to Kut-el-Amara.
We captured some fourteen guns and a thousand prisoners,
at the cost of a casualty list of five hundred officers and
men. The work of our guns was dreadful; our shells
absolutely smashed the hostile trenches, and nine hundred
Turkish corpses were found in a small area.

But the work of fighting in a temperature of 130
degrees in the shade was not so distressing as the task of
cleaning up the mess and filth of the Arab town—which
engendered every tropical disease—and making it less of
a death-trap. The barracks were uninhabitable, and must
sadly have brought down the strength of the Turkish
troops who had lodged there. By the first week in August
our men were encamped in tents in the town, and were
living in comparative comfort, though in extreme heat,
and sorely troubled with flies. Towards the end of the
month, when Nasiriyeh had been cleaned and garrisoned,
the larger part of the force had another long voyage on
steamers and barges, with only grass mats shading them
from the sun. They went back to Amara in an attire
resembling that of the soldiers in Mr. Rudyard Kipling's
tale of the taking of Lung-Tung-Pen.

The men left behind at Nasiriyeh, to keep the warlike
Arabs in order, had a source of consolation similar to that
of the garrison of Kurna, though, like their comrades,
they did not appreciate it. According to the map illustrating Sir William Willcocks' last paper on Mesopotamian
irrigation, the country immediately north of Nasiriyeh,
and lying between the Euphrates and the Shat-el-Hai,
was the primitive Garden of Eden, where the Sumerians and
Akkadians built up the first great
civilisation of Babylonia. This happened   **The Garden of**
ten thousand years ago, and the British   **Eden**
garrison, suffering from heat, dysentery,
and fever, stared through the date groves at the barren
desert beyond the river, and wondered why intelligent
human beings ever chose such a place in which to live.

Meanwhile, General Townshend, based on Amara on the
Tigris, was working his ships up the great northern river
and getting on friendly terms with the powerful tribes of
the Beni Lam Arabs. These warlike Bedouins held most
of the land between the Tigris and the northern mountains.
They had also won considerable territory on the southern
side of the river, where the vast sandy steppes, with patches
of camel-thorn, extended for hundreds of miles. On the
southern side of the river, in the desert waste between
Amara and Kut-el-Amara, were other great confederations
of fighting Bedouins, such as the Abu Mohammed tribes,
who wandered in their black tents round our river base,
with the Abu Dir Diraye Arabs and the Makusis tribes, the
last being camped around Kut-el-Amara, and fighting as
light cavalry on the side of the Turks. All these nomads,
who had battled for ages among themselves for the spring
pastures along the rivers, were starkly independent
Ishmaelites, caring neither for Turk nor for Briton, but
possessed with a love for fighting and a very keen eye to
the main chance of winning booty.

Most of their mullahs were inclined, for religious reasons,
to urge their countrymen to fight against the infidels, and
help the Ottoman Caliph. On the other hand, our nation
enjoyed a high prestige in Mesopotamia, and especially
round Bagdad. There must have been thousands of
Arabs who proudly called themselves "Ingliz" and professed to be our fellow-subjects. This they did in the hope
of escaping the attentions of the Turkish tax-collector and

claiming the aid of the British Consul at Bagdad when they got into trouble. A British firm of shipowners, Messrs. Lynch, had maintained for many years an important traffic along the great river, and their steamers were, despite all fantastic German claims to the commerce of Bagdad and the Persian Gulf, the great trading vehicles of Mesopotamia.

Our victories on the lower rivers had made the sheikhs of the Beni Lam inclined to enter into a league with us; for, as some of their principal rivals had sided with the Turkish army, the Beni Lam had little to

Co-operation of the Beni Lam win if we were defeated, but they could look forward to acquiring new grazing grounds if they assisted us against the other Arabs and against the Turks. From our point of view the trouble was that the Bedouin looked on battle as a sport, and quickly rode away from the conflict if he met with a slight reverse. Fighting was more a pastime than a struggle to the death with the Bedouin. In many famous engagements between tribe and tribe, the dead could be numbered on one hand, and the wounded scarcely amounted to more than a score. The Bedouin did not like turning his winter sport into a deadly contest, and, trusting to the fine quality of his horse, he galloped away under the shelter of the sand-ridges when matters began to look serious.

The light Arabian cavalry was useful only after a battle was won. Then the Bedouin horsemen would readily ride down the beaten fugitive infantry. As a rule they did not mind who was beaten, so long as they could pursue; and at the Battle of Shaiba the defeated Turks had been attacked by their own Bedouin cavalry. All the Bedouin wanted was the rifle, ammunition, and other warlike spoil of the man he could kill without much risk to himself.

So long as the British force advanced victoriously,

General Townshend could count upon most of the Bedouin horsemen turning upon the Turk, in order to kill and rob him, and in order to make friends with the conqueror. Nevertheless, there were considerable bodies of sniping and raiding Arabs who continually pestered our expedition, and remained fairly faithful to the defeated and retreating troops of the Caliph. A fighting league with the great warlike confederation of Beni Lam enabled us to use a long stretch of the Tigris with little danger from musketry fire on both banks, and for a still longer stretch of the Tigris the northern bank was peopled with friendly Arabs. In these circumstances Sir John Nixon, as Commander-in-Chief, with the British Resident in the Persian Gulf, Sir Percy Cox, and Major-General Townshend, commanding the fighting division at Amara, entered into an alliance with the Beni Lam Arabs.

The advance towards Bagdad began as soon as the intense summer heat moderated in the middle of September. Our motor-boats explored the Tigris over the great distance between Amara and Kut-el-Amara. This work, indeed, had been going on for nearly ten months, and had been undertaken with increasing **The advance towards** vigour when the flood-water from the **Bagdad** melting snows in the Caucasus had subsided. The captains of the Lynch steamers, who had studied the Tigris for years, could not give full information about its navigation; for the great winding stream was restless in its bed, and in every flood season it changed its shoals and sandbeds, tore away its mud-banks, and altered its course in small or large ways. Only actual reconnaissance could reveal if certain marshes dried in the summer sufficiently to enable troops to ford certain difficult creeks. Steamers had to be prepared to find a newly-made mud-bank in the river blocking the line of advance, and the

LEADERS OF THE INDO-BRITISH EXPEDITION IN MESOPOTAMIA.

General Sir John Eccles Nixon, K.C.B., and officers of his Headquarters Staff. After capturing Kut-el-Amara at the end of September, 1915, a portion of Sir John Nixon's force, under General Townshend, reached Ctesiphon, eighteen miles from Bagdad. There, after its memorable march over the sands and swamps along the Tigris, the expedition suffered its first reverse.

GROUP OF TURKISH OFFICERS CAPTURED BY THE BRITISH.
Turkish officers captured at the Battle of Essinn, on September 29th, 1915. On that day and the day previous the Turks were defeated at Kurna and Amara by the British and Indian troops forcing the passage of the Tigris.

A CITY GATE ON THE ROAD TO BAGDAD.
One of the double-entried gateways of the city of Zobeir, a few miles south-west of Basra on the Tigris.

and the trying climatic conditions were to have an important bearing on the result of the battle. The two brigades demonstrated against the enemy on September 25th, but it was then discovered that the Turks had placed mines all over the south bank of the river. Thereupon General Townshend altered his plan of attack. On the night of September 27th the two brigades crossed the river by a flying bridge, leaving their tents standing, as a dummy camp to delude the enemy. A Turkish division remained facing our empty tents, and it was the absence from the real battlefield of this enemy force, during the critical period of the struggle, that enabled us to win the victory. Had all the Turkish forces been concentrated on the north bank of the river, our attack would almost certainly have failed. The **Deceiving the enemy** enemy's position was of great natural strength, and his entrenchments were almost impregnable.

Between the town of Kut-el-Amara and the hamlet of Nakhailat, the Tigris makes a sudden southward bend. A little north of the bend was a swamp known by its shape as the Horse-shoe Marsh. Then north of this marsh was a patch of firm ground; and beyond this ground, still going northward, was a larger swamp, known as the Suwada Marsh. North of the Suwada Marsh was another narrow strip of firm ground, with a third swamp north of it, which we may call the Circular Marsh. The Turkish entrenchments extended between the river and the Horse-shoe Marsh, and continued between this and the Suwada Marsh; and were further prolonged from the Suwada Marsh to the Circular Marsh. The heaviest Turkish artillery was sited near the river behind the Horse-shoe Marsh, close to a place known as the Hundred and Twenty-one Tents. South of the Tigris the enemy's entrenchments stretched for some miles opposite our abandoned tents. The river was blocked by a line of sunken dhows and a line of thick wire just above the water.

disposition of the riverside tribes, many of whom were in the habit of firing, even in peace time, at the Lynch steamers, could only be ascertained by steaming past their territory.

In the last week of September, 1915, our forces were safely transported to the neighbourhood of Kut-el-Amara. We had still only a single weak division, with a brigade in reserve. The Turks were three divisions strong, with a large medley of mounted Bedouins acting as light cavalry. In their position near Kut-el-Amara, about ten miles from our new camp, Nuredin Pasha's troops were deeply entrenched behind barbed-wire entanglements, and were supported by heavier artillery than we could bring up the river.

Plan of attack altered On September 23rd two of our brigades moved close to the enemy until they came within sight of the hostile tents. Our principal camp was then pitched on the south bank of the Tigris. Our steamers took up a position ahead of our tents, and laid their guns along the ground between the armies, ready to smash up any surprise attack. It is worthy of note that even in the short march of eight miles in the direction of the Canal of Shat-el-Hai, some of our men still dropped out through the heat. Though the summer was nearing its close, the sun was still very fierce,

The Turks, directed by German engineers, had spent months in fortifying their positions. Their trenches were ten feet deep, with bomb-proof communication trenches, overhead cover, and high wire entanglements, fronting which were wolf-pits, with pointed stakes at the bottom, and dynamite mines concealed beneath the sand. Moreover, all the Turkish guns were so dug in as to make useless anything but a direct hit with a howitzer shell. Our five days' operations were very trying, as it was distressingly hot in the day-time, though very cold at night; and the sand-flies prevented our troops from getting any sleep in the short time they could snatch for a rest.

During daylight and darkness on September 26th, 27th, and 28th, a column, under General Fry, gradually worked up to within four hundred yards of the Turkish wire entanglements round the Horse-shoe Marsh. The troops went forward slowly and carefully, digging themselves in under continual shell and rifle fire. Our guns in the open could not silence the Turkish artillery, which plastered our trenches and tried to curtain off our troops during their swift, short forward rushes.

Feint attack at Horse-shoe Marsh Luckily, the ground lent itself to our attacking operations, as every hundred yards or so there were deep dry ditches, which gave good cover. Still more luckily, the Turkish shells were of very poor quality. The segment shells, which we had sold to them after the Boer War, did as little damage to us as they had done to the Boers, while the shrapnel was so bad that our men went through bursts of it, and were only wounded if they were struck by the fuses and cases. The attacking brigade only had ninety casualties all told, during its task of holding the enemy round the Horse-shoe Marsh and by the river.

While General Fry thus pretended to attack the Turks in their strongest position where they wanted to be attacked, the second column under General Delamain, consisting of the brigades which had crossed from the south side of the Tigris, marched all night east of the Suwada Marsh, and after resting for two hours,

reached their new attacking position at a quarter to five in the morning of September 28th. The position at which they arrived was a neck of dry land between the Suwada Marsh and the Circular Marsh, where the Turks had constructed their most northerly entrenchments. General Delamain's column **Turks taken by** moving cautiously over ground which had **surprise** been only partly examined by one of our sapper officers, advanced for a mile between the marshes, and then came in full view of the enemy's trenches. But our airmen and one of our scouts had found that, right to the north of the last swamp, the Circular Marsh, there was no enemy position. So, before opening the decisive struggle, General Townshend detached part of the force under General Delamain, and, placing it under the command of General Houghton, directed it to march round the Circular Marsh northward, and make a flank attack on the Turkish entrenchments that barred the advance of General Delamain's troops.

The general's design was to outflank the enemy with General Houghton's column, and then to combine this column with General Delamain's column, and make another outflanking swoop on the enemy's main system of works around the Horse-shoe Marsh. It may seem extraordinary that Nuredin Pasha and his Staff of officers should have left their northern flank exposed to a turning

WHERE EAST JOINED ISSUE WITH WEST NEAR THE "CITY OF THE CALIPHS."
Wheelbarrows used by the Turks to convey ammunition, with metal shield attached to afford some protection under fire, and a muzzle-loading cannon. This primitive weapon, with the trolleys, was captured from the enemy at the Battle of Essinn. In oval: An old-world scene within the walls of Zobeir, near the Persian Gulf.

movement round the Circular Marsh. But the Turkish commander and his German advisers knew their business. The open road round the Circular Marsh seems to have been designed as a trap. There was a Turkish brigade hidden behind some ridges near the northernmost marsh ; and so well was it concealed that our reconnoitring airmen do not seem to have suspected its existence. But, on the other hand, General Houghton's column set out in the darkness and moved so quickly round the marsh that the Turks were taken by surprise when it appeared.

At 8.20 a.m. General Houghton was able to send a wireless message that he had reached the left rear of the Turkish lines. Thereupon, the skilfully-divided brigades of General Townshend's division gave battle. Along the river our flotilla of armed steamers, launches, tug-boats, and horse-barges had been bombarding the Turkish main position since daybreak on September 27th. Our river fleet, headed by H.M.S. Comet, first tried to dash in close to the bend in the stream, and work their guns at short range. But the Turks spotted the masthead and wireless aerials, and they dropped their shells so close that our vessels retired and struck their topmasts. Our

at some distance behind our fighting-line. But our holding troops were more seriously menaced in another direction, as early in the day the Turkish division south of the river discovered that our camp there was a dummy affair, and about nine o'clock in the morning it crossed the Tigris by a flying bridge and entered fiercely into action.

The larger part of this fresh division was directed beyond the Horse-shoe Marsh, in a counter-attack against General Delamain's column. This column, operating between Suwada Marsh and Circular Marsh, began its assault at 8.20 a.m. All our available artillery between the marshes was con- **Heroism of** centrated against a small portion of the **Mahrattas and Dorsets** enemy's front, and, covered by the fire of the guns and the Maxim and musketry fire of their supports, a double company of the 117th Mahrattas made a desperate rush on the Turkish trenches. Nearly half the gallant Indians were put out of action ; but the remnant went on, undaunted by the terrible losses, and, leaping into the enemy's deeply-dug line, bayoneted their way along it. A double company of the 2nd Dorsets was then hurled at the enemy's

GENERAL TOWNSHEND AND STAFF IN THE TIGRIS VALLEY. *[Copyright : " Illustrated London News."*
General C. V. F. Townshend, C.B., D.S.O., the indomitable commander of the force which advanced through the reputed Garden of Eden to Ctesiphon, eighteen miles from Bagdad, riding with his Staff. General Townshend is a descendant of the Marquis Townshend who fought with Wolfe at Quebec.

batteries on shore co-operated at high pressure with the guns of the river fleet, and the daring lieutenants command-ing our armed launches crept closer and closer to the enemy's field batteries and succeeded by noon in killing or scattering the Turkish gun-crews. Our ships were hit several times, but no vital damage was done to them. There was, however, one big Turkish gun that could not be silenced. One of our shore batteries managed to get within range by galloping closer. The **Dummy camp** Turks put one shell into the battery, **discovered** killing two gunners and wounding several others ; but that was the last shot the big gun fired, for our gunners got a shower of shells dead on it.

In the meantime, General Fry's brigade remained in front of the Horse-shoe position, under a violent fire all day long. A constant stream of shells burst, some one hundred yards behind the troops, coming from a group of hostile quick-firers, which seemed to be worked by German gunners. Whoever they were, they were certainly good artillerymen. They maintained a speed of fire like that of a huge Maxim. Having, however, no airmen to spot for them, these enemy gunners placed most of their shells

trenches, and when by furious fighting they also had secured a hold, the rest of the battalion followed. The sappers were consolidating the captured position when the leading troops of General Houghton came into action round the rear of the Circular Marsh. All the enemy's northern flank had been stormed in a frontal attack by a battalion and a half of Mahrattas and Dorsets ! But the Turks still held courageously to their southern flank, from which they sent a devastating fire against our men.

Hurrying into action from his position of advantage, General Houghton threw the Oxfords forward with the other battalions of his wearied brigade, and in an action that lasted from half-past ten to two o'clock, the encircled Turkish force was either destroyed or captured. Con-cealed in their ten-foot ditches, the Turkish soldiers fought with grim determination, and as our troops had to work above the mat-covered trenches in the scorching sunlight, they were much fatigued by their exertions. General Houghton's men, in particular, had been marching and fighting since the previous morning, and had had no water since the previous evening. They had just carried out a forced march of five hours round the Circular Marsh, and

INDIAN CAVALRY PATROLLING THE DESERT NEAR KUT-EL-AMARA.
The force which, under General Townshend, inflicted a severe defeat on the Turks at Ctesiphon, included a large proportion of Indian troops.
They were obliged to retire to Kut-el-Amara, owing to the arrival of strong enemy reinforcements.

while they were fighting down their trapped enemy, a scorching wind, laden with dense clouds of dust, swept the desert. General Delamain's men, who had also made a night march from the dummy camp on the other side of the Tigris, were likewise exhausted from want of water. By the time they had taken the enemy's position, with several guns and many prisoners, they were completely exhausted. The commander of the united victorious columns, General Delamain, hoped that by marching round the back of the enemy's position, between the river and Suwada Marsh, he could reach the Tigris at one of its bends, and there water his troops and horses before he again engaged the enemy.

Tropical heat and terrible thirst General Houghton's long - enduring troops were already making steady progress southward to the west of the Suwada Marsh. Early in the afternoon the Turkish division that had crossed the river at nine o'clock in the morning opened a furious counter-attack against the wearied brigade, while a force of Turkish cavalry tried to make an outflanking charge. But both infantry and horsemen were beaten back by our little flying column, though it was worn out by long marching in the tropical heat and consumed by a terrible thirst. After beating off first the Turkish infantry and then the Turkish cavalry, General Houghton's troops still struggled on southward towards the river, a mile or more in the rear of the main Turkish entrenched forces round Horse-shoe Marsh. But when the men had almost reached the water and completely

encircled the enemy, the heavy Turkish batteries near Kut swept the ground with a storm of shrapnel. General Houghton's column had to draw back, away from the water for which it was thirsting, and rejoin General Delamain's force on the western edge of Suwada Marsh. Both columns were then in the desperate position of Coleridge's Ancient Mariner, with "Water, water everywhere, nor any drop to drink."

The stagnant marsh water was so foul that, though our men felt that they could risk any disease for a long drink, they could not, happily, bring themselves to swallow it. Still, even the marsh water was, at dire need, good enough to pour into the jackets of our machine-guns and keep them from running out of action through over-heating. **Water only for the guns**

By this time the men had been marching and fighting for thirteen and a half hours, and after General Delamain's force had gone to the assistance of General Houghton's column, most of the troops had to be given a rest. They rested until five o'clock, and then the commander of the wonderful division, General Townshend, ordered by wireless a combined attack on the formidable Horse-shoe lines. General Fry's column, which had been making only very slow progress towards the Turkish centre, was ordered to wait until General Delamain's column got right on the enemy's rear.

Meanwhile, the two brigades under General Delamain and General Houghton wearily tramped along the south-

VICTORS ON A FIELD OF ANCIENT HISTORY.
Indian cavalry, with their British officers, riding in the desert near Kut-el-Amara. Fighting side by side with British troops, the Indians won
high praise from General Townshend.

315

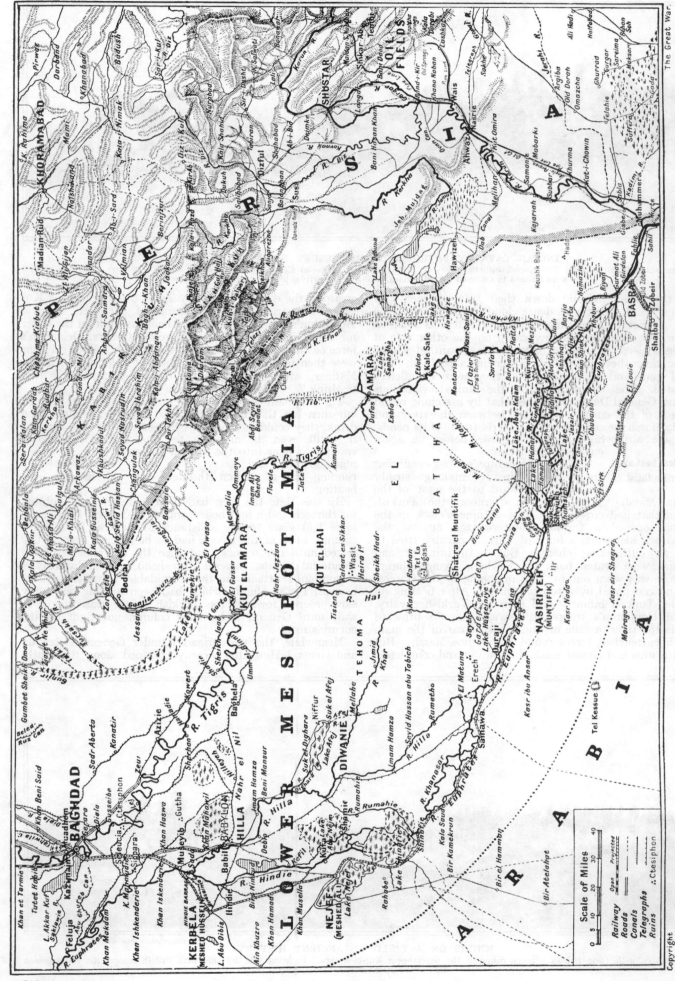

AREA OF OPERATIONS OF THE INDO-BRITISH EXPEDITIONARY FORCE ADVANCING UP THE EUPHRATES AND TIGRIS TOWARDS BAGDAD.

From the great desert triangle of Kut-el-Amara, Nasiryeh, and Basra, with its connecting river and canal lines, the heroic little Indo-British Division, commanded by General Townshend, tried to capture Bagdad and link with the Russian columns advancing into the Persian highlands on the north.

The Great War.

AN ORIENTAL VENICE: BASRA, A CITY OF "THE ARABIAN NIGHTS."

A picturesque scene at Basra, situated near the River Shat-el-Arab, about fifty miles from the Persian Gulf. Palm-trees grow here in great and beautiful profusion. The boats seen in the photograph are the principal conveyance in this Venice of Arabia. Basra's chief exports are dates and attar of roses. Basra fell into British hands on November 21st, 1914, General Barrett with two battalions taking possession of the city.

west edge of Suwada Marsh, and struck out once more towards the river, behind Nuredin Pasha's main position. Then occurred the most dramatic and extraordinary incident in this eventful day of tropical battle. A Turkish force of five battalions, with four guns, which had probably been detached to guard against General Houghton's out-flanking movement, abruptly appeared **Electrical bayonet** through the dust or mirage which had **charge** been hiding it. The Turkish column, when seen, was marching parallel with the British column, about a mile westward, slightly behind our troops. The effect of this surprising menace was electrical. With amazing rapidity, both brigades, which had seemed about to drop and die for want of water, wheeled to their right, and started to the attack as if it were morning, and they were fresh from sleep and breakfast. In one long, splendid charge, during which they hardly fired a shot, they broke in among the Turks with the bayonet, routed them in a single violent effort, captured all their guns, and shot them down as they fled in the gathering darkness towards the bridge of boats.

It was all over in an hour, and our exhausted troops, overtaken by the night, dropped down on the scene of their victory for a cheerless bivouac. Owing to the darkness and the absolute fatigue of the parched troops and horses, the encircling movement, which had begun at five o'clock in the afternoon, could not be completed. Nuredin Pasha was able in the night to evacuate his fortress, and move his troops across the bridge of boats to the southern bank of the Tigris. From there the Turkish force went by forced marches across the Shat-el-Hai, and on to Azizie, where another system of fortifications had been constructed

for the defence of Bagdad. According to Bedouin rumours, Nuredin was greatly perturbed at the thought of being overtaken by our troops with their river transport. The first day he marched his men thirty-five miles towards Bagdad, and the following day they had to do thirty miles in twenty-four hours. This was no bad marching feat, even for Turkish regular troops, at the heated end of a Mesopotamian summer.

Undoubtedly the impossibility of obtaining, on the spot, means for watering the two British brigades, which marched through or round the swamps almost to the enemy's rear, robbed General Townshend of a grand, decisive victory. His planning of the battle was as great a feat as stood to the credit of any British general in history; and his troops, in their qualities of endurance and fighting power, were as magnificent as any mingled force of Sepoys and Britons that Clive or Wellesley handled. A single Indo-British division had outflanked three Turkish divisions. The manœuvre against such heavy odds was a classic piece of strategy. Nothing but lack of water, in the critical afternoon of September 28th, **Townshend's classic** prevented our small force from surround- **strategy** ing and capturing an enemy of three times their strength, and conquering the whole of Mesopotamia as far as Bagdad by one swift blow. As General Townshend seems to have made his plan of battle on the spur of the moment, when he found the enemy was too strong on the south bank, and marched his main force across the river and around the marshes, the need for the large number of water-carts required to water two brigades could not have been foreseen. Moreover, such a number of water-carts was not to be had hundreds of miles down the river at

NEAR THE CITY OF "THE ARABIAN NIGHTS."
Turkish troops on the march over the desert sands near Bagdad.

IN AN INDIAN STRONGHOLD AT THE BATTLE OF SHAIBA.
Indians, wearing their newly-adopted shorts, firing on the Turks from behind a high breastwork built of earth and sand-bags.

our principal base. The officer who arranged the expedition had relied upon the troops operating always close to the water under the protection of the armed boats. But if General Townshend had fought in this manner at Kut-el-Amara he would have had to confine himself to frontal attacks against a strongly-entrenched enemy, and with his single division he would not have pierced the enemy's lines.

The Turks got away easily, and in good order. During the night the senior naval officer, Lieutenant-Commander Cookson, decided to clear the obstruction in the river and give chase to the fleeing Turks. When his ship, the destroyer Comet, with two smaller vessels, rounded the headland, the enemy opened fire with rifles, but the Comet steamed so close up to the obstacle that the Turks were near enough to throw hand-bombs. Our sailors soon found the big wire stretched across the river with dhows made fast to it. But as they were getting over their bows to cut the wire Lieutenant-Commander Cookson, who was leading them, was shot in seven places and killed. His last words were: "I am done. It is a failure. Return at full speed." When the ships steamed up again at daybreak, after burying their commander, they found the Turkish rearguard had vanished, and as our wreck-party had dynamited the obstruction during the night, the flotilla was able to proceed up-river to Kut-el-Amara, where the British cavalry were already in possession. It was the first place in the campaign at which the army had arrived before the navy.

Kut-el-Amara, which we occupied on September 30th, 1915, was 120 miles from Bagdad by road, and 220 miles by water. At about three-quarters of the distance was the riverside town of Azizie. Azizie was about 40 miles by road from Bagdad, and 116 miles by the winding river. The retreating Turkish army made a stand a little to the west of Azizie, to allow time for its engineers to prepare, near Bagdad, the last and most formidable system of defences in Mesopotamia. Meissner Pasha, the very able German railway engineer, who had given the best part

Turkish stand at Azizie

of his life to the service of the Turks, and had become the principal executive mind in the German attack upon our position in the Persian Gulf, had brought his line from Constantinople to within 380 miles of Bagdad. There were some important gaps in this line, where mountains required to be tunnelled, and much of the rolling-stock was in a deplorable condition. Not a few of its locomotives had gone to ruin, the boilers holed by rust, through Turkish neglect and incompetence.

After the outbreak of war, however, Meissner had been provided with the money and the skilled help he needed, and by the time our Expeditionary Force began seriously to threaten Bagdad, he, in all probability, had greatly extended his line across the desert, and had lessened the gap of 380 miles between Aleppo and the Tigris. This undoubtedly great engineer was also building a railway of invasion from the southern edge of Palestine to the Suez Canal, and laying a fresh-water pipe-line for the use of the army of Djemal Pasha. So he must have been at last abundantly provided with building material; and, as we have seen at Nasiriyeh, the Turks, with his help, had been able early in the year to bring heavy guns from Adrianople with considerable rapidity.

Meissner Pasha's railway work

While the snow was only light on the Caucasian Passes, most of the reinforcements for Nuredin Pasha's troops were, apparently, hurried up front Syria by the half-built Bagdad railway line. We found at Azizie, which we reached on October 13th, 1915, that the enemy had already received thousands of fresh troops. General Townshend's division stayed at Azizie until the beginning of November, with part of the Turkish force entrenched four miles up-river. Skirmishing went on daily and hourly, the cavalry and the Royal Horse Artillery getting, as they put it, most of the fun. Meanwhile, the infantry dug for all they were worth, in order to strengthen their position against a possible grand attack. Naturally, the British commander would have preferred the enemy to return and attempt to recover his lost prestige among the tribes by flinging his troops on our trenches, while our shore batteries and armed vessels swept the ground with shrapnel. But the pasha, after receiving reinforcements that made his force four times as large as ours, would not risk an assault. He threatened and worried, but he was too doubtful of his men to march out and attack. Our small columns of reinforcements that tramped along the river continued to have brushes with some raiding Bedouins between Kut and Azizie; and even in the second week of October marching was still a wearing ordeal with the temperature at over a hundred degrees. Twenty-four miles in twenty-four hours was very good going, and a mile or so away from the river the want of water was a source of great anxiety.

Our reinforcements did little more than restore the strength of the division, and though it was continually rumoured at Azizie that a large new force was coming from India in order to ensure the success of the advance on Bagdad, General Townshend only received enough men to fill up the gaps in his division and to provide a small reserve. As an officer in the little army at Azizie remarked, in a letter dated October 23rd, 1915, we then had in India men who had been training for ten months. " We shall shortly be heavily buoyed up by their arrival," said the officer. But for various reasons the Indian and British Governments decided to let the conquest of Bagdad be a wild gamble, like the Dardanelles affair, instead of either taking proper measures to ensure victory, or ordering Sir John Nixon and General Townshend to remain safely on the defensive in the Persian Gulf region, with Kut-el-Amara and Nasiriyeh garrisoned against attacks along the Tigris and Euphrates.

Turks' well-planned retreat

Meanwhile, General Townshend went on performing miracles with a force that never consisted of more than four brigades. Towards the end of October the Turks were so strongly established in their new fortifications near Bagdad that they left only a single brigade in their advanced position near Azizie. This rearguard had a large number of guns, by means of which it held the river against our gunboats, and pestered our camp with occasional shells. Our force preserved a grim silence, with the object of lulling the Turk, and making him forget his danger. On one very dark night two of our brigades made a long roundabout march in Kut-el-Amara fashion, with a view to getting on the enemy's rear and encircling him, while a third Indo-British brigade undertook a frontal attack at dawn. But the Turk showed himself capable of learning by experience. On this occasion his outposts were flung far into the desert, apparently with a portable wireless instrument well out on their flank. Long before our wide turning movement threatened their main position, the Turks were in full retreat, taking with them all their guns and most of their stores. Their movement looked like a headlong flight, but it was really a well-executed retirement in face of superior forces, which had carried out so well-planned a manœuvre that instant retreat was the only answer to it.

The Indo-British division at once embarked in pursuit upon its picturesque flotilla of bellums, launches, paddle-steamers, horse-barges, and gunboats. An unending series of unchartered mud-banks continually interrupted the progress of the extraordinary river armada,

boats sticking sometimes for a day on a shoal, and having to wait till the large steamers arrived and dragged them off. A couple of gun-launches scouted ahead for possible ambushes which our aviators might have missed, and our airmen in seaplanes and aeroplanes circled over Bagdad, and watched the enemy's lines of communication running across the desert towards Syria, and up the river towards the Caucasus heights. By November 9th General Townshend's officers knew that the great adventure was about to be undertaken. The small British force was set the task of breaking through to Bagdad with a view to linking on with the advanced columns of the Russian army in the Caucasus. One of these columns was rapidly working down the Persian border by Lake Urmia, and another was advancing much farther south towards the city of Hamadan. From Bagdad to Hamadan the distance was 250 miles, across difficult and mountainous country. But it seems to have been thought that, with the Turks beaten at Bagdad, and the German-Swedish-Persian force routed at Hamadan, the task of connecting the troops of Sir John Nixon and the army of the Grand Duke Nicholas would be fairly easy. On November 19th General Townshend's division, having captured the village of Zeur, marched against Nuredin Pasha's main system of defences. These works had been constructed eighteen miles from Bagdad, near the gaunt and imposing ruins of Ctesiphon, which loomed against the sky, at the edge of a reed-grown marsh, half a mile from the Tigris. Here, some thirteen hundred years before, Chosroes, the great Persian Emperor who contended for the dominion of the world with the emperors of Constantinople, had erected the noblest palace on earth. Just across the river a stretch of yellow mounds marked the site of a still more ancient imperial capital—Seleucia—which the Greek masters of Mesopotamia built after Alexander the Great made his march into India.

The attack on Ctesiphon

Nothing remained of Seleucia, and little or nothing of the mediæval glories of Bagdad under Haroun Al-Raschid. But even the all-destroying Mongol had not been able to overthrow the mighty work of the Persian architects. Yet Ctesiphon, with its great vaulted hall—the largest

KUT-EL-AMARA, THE CAPTURED TURKISH COALING STATION ON THE EAST BANK OF THE TIGRIS.
Arabs at Kut-el-Amara interested in the arrival of a river steamer. At this and surrounding portions of the Mesopotamian field of operations, the campaign was conducted on soil famous in history and in legend— the country of Haroun Al-Raschid and " The Arabian Nights." Above: Another view of Kut from the Tigris. The quaint circular boat, like an ancient British coracle, is called a " kufa."

existing vault in the world—and its magnificent Eastern curtain wall, rising from the reeds and desert sand in battered sublimity, was less a memorial of the imperial power of Persia than a memorial of the terrible striking force of Islam in the age of Mohammed. The conquest of Ctesiphon and the sack of the great palace of the Emperor of the Fire-worshippers was one of the first great warlike achievements of the army of the Prophet of Arabia. Turk and Kurd, Syrian and Arab, however unlettered, knew what the great ruin at Ctesiphon stood for, and Nuredin Pasha, while choosing the site chiefly for military reasons, was well aware of its strong appeal to the religious traditions which his medley of troops had received from the old Arabian conquerors. The battle for the ford of Ctesiphon was one of the most inspiriting stories of Islam. But now, by a strange vicissitude of history, the larger part of the descendants of the original warriors of the Prophet was inclining to the side of the British force. And in that force were many fighting Mohammedans from the North-West Provinces of India, brigaded with Mohammedans of the Deccan, Hindus of the warrior caste, Sikhs with a creed derived from both Mohammedan and Hindu elements, and Englishmen, with a sprinkling of Scottish, Irish, and Welsh officers.

Nuredin Pasha's army was greatly increased. He had four divisions strongly entrenched against our four brigades at Ctesiphon, with a large reserve of good troops encamped a little farther up the river near Bagdad, and composed probably of forces detached from the Caucasian front during midwinter. Yet, in spite of his overwhelming number of troops, his strong and well-planned lines, and his increased batteries of both heavy and light artillery, the Turkish pasha entered the battle a half-beaten man. He had

Nuredin Pasha outmanœuvred

been so continually outmanœuvred by British commanders with inferior forces that he could not trust his own judgment, and the truth is that we needed only one division of the new armies that had been training for ten months in India in order to conquer Mesopotamia and capture Bagdad and Mosul. On the military authority, or on the politician, who did not send General Townshend —a man of proved genius—the twelve thousand more bayonets he needed, rests the responsibility for all that afterwards happened.

On the morning of November 22nd the single Indo-British division attacked the four Turkish divisions, stormed their fortress lines, wiped out an entire enemy

THE VICEROY OF INDIA WITH THE SHEIKH OF ZOBEIR.
Viscount Hardinge, during his visit to the Indo-British Expeditionary Force in Mesopotamia, conferred with local chiefs. The Turks persistently circulated false reports among the Arab sheikhs regarding the treatment they would receive at our hands.

division, taking eight hundred prisoners and a large quantity of arms, and bivouacked victoriously in the captured works of defence. The Turkish report of the battle, spread through the world from the German wireless stations, estimated the number of our troops at 170,000. As a matter of fact, General Townshend, at an extreme estimate, could not have had more than 25,000 men all told, and his striking force could not have exceeded 16,000 Indian and British infantrymen. In spite of heavy counter-attacks by the reinforced Turkish army, our troops held on to the Turkish position at Ctesiphon till the night of November 24th, when want of water again robbed them of their full victory, and they had to retire four miles to the Tigris. Our position by the river, however, was too weak to be held, and as our small force had incurred heavy losses, many battalions being reduced to less than half their strength, a withdrawal was necessary. We removed our wounded to the boats, and embarked our prisoners, numbering 1,600, and then, after a rearguard action near Azizie, on the night of November 30th, our troops retired in perfect order on Kut-el-Amara. Two of our river-boats, which had been disabled by the enemy's shell fire, had to be abandoned after their guns and engines had been made useless, and the pursuing Turkish army arrived within two hours' march of Kut on December 3rd.

Retirement on Kut-el-Amara

Our losses around Ctesiphon were 643 killed, 3,330 wounded, and 594 men not accounted for, bringing the total to 4,567. Having regard to the fine achievement of our men, the list of their casualties was light, and if the British Government had given General Townshend and Sir John Nixon the comparatively small reinforcement of another division, Bagdad would certainly have been won at Ctesiphon. But, as at the opening of the Dardanelles campaign, our politicians in authority thought only of winning an empire on the cheap, and tried to overthrow a great military Power, first with a single army corps and then with four brigades. The attack on the Dardanelles, that began with a single army corps, cost us eventually, in dead, wounded, and sick, more than 200,000 men, and ended fruitlessly. How the attack on Bagdad, with a single division, was to end remained to be seen, for we lost the support of most of the Arab tribes, and the situation of our small, half-shattered force at Kut-el-Amara was one of extreme peril. General Townshend held out, however, with great skill and valour, and a relieving column was sent up the Tigris to his aid.

WHERE THE BAGDAD RAILWAY BRIDGES THE EUPHRATES.
A temporary bridge at Jeralbus, built during the operations in Mesopotamia, and seen from the eastern, or Mesopotamian, bank of the Euphrates. This bridge was about a mile long, and cost three million francs. Beyond it is seen the mound which marks the site of the ancient Hittite capital, Carchemish.

The cordial meeting of Lord Kitchener and the French Commander on Gallipoli.

Major-General Davies (extreme right), Lord Kitchener, Generals Birdwood and Maxwell looking towards Achi Baba.

Evacuation of Suvla and Anzac : Lord Kitchener's visit in November, 1915.

Lord Kitchener arriving on board a destroyer en route for Athens and the Greek Court.

The Secretary of State for War, the cynosure of admiring Anzac eyes, on Gallipoli.

Lord Kitchener inside a Turkish fort with Col. Sir Henry McMahon and a French General.

Col. Watson, Lord Kitchener, the French Commander, and Col. McMahon at Seddul Bahr.

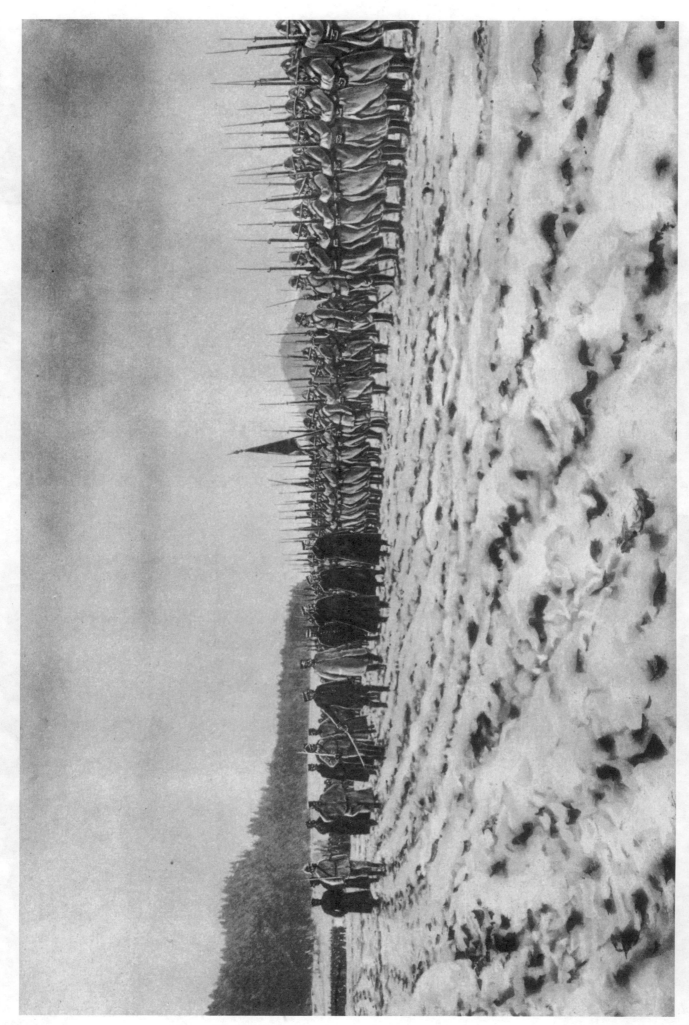

An echo of the panoply of former wars : General Joffre reviews his men on a snow-covered field of Lorraine.

CHAPTER XCV.

GREAT LEADERS OF THE ALLIES IN THE WEST.

Men Still the Raw Material of Armies—The Responsibility of Generals—Sir John French's Task—The British Expeditionary Force in 1915—Generals at G.H.Q.—Joffre's Tremendous Task—His Early Life—His Military Experiences—Named Generalissimo—Directs the Great Retreat—Takes the Offensive—French's Early Days—His Work in South Africa—His Duties at Home—His Work in France—Ferdinand Foch—His Valuable Services—General Pau's Career—General Dubail—His Campaign in Alsace and Lorraine—De Castelnau's Early Life—He Protects Nancy—Organisation of the French Army—France's New Armies—Maurice Sarrail—De Langle de Cary—Franchet d'Espérey—Maunoury—D'Urbal and Maud'huy—General Galliéni—General d'Amade—Gouraud and Sordet—France's Junior Generals—Sir Ian Hamilton—His Work in South Africa—His Leadership in Gallipoli—Sir Douglas Haig—His Services in Flanders—General Smith-Dorrien—His Services at Le Cateau—Sir Herbert Plumer and Sir Charles Monro—Sir John Nixon—Chiefs of the Staff—Commanders of Army Corps—Gough and Fergusson—Pulteney and Rawlinson—Cavalry Generals—Sir James Willcocks—Birdwood and Hunter-Weston—Our Dead Generals—Two V.C. Heroes among Them.

"They in all their deeds were so valiant that they ought to be reputed as sovereigns in chivalry."
—FROISSART.

THE remarkable development in recent years of weapons of all kinds—guns, machine-guns, howitzers, mortars, the reintroduction of bombs, the adoption of melinite, lyddite, turpinite, and other high explosives of every possible variety, to which must now be added poison gas and liquid fire—have altered the whole nature of war. But one thing they have not done. They have not made the human material—man—less important; rather the reverse. Without men to use and direct them, to follow up and complete their work of destruction, all the missiles of death are useless. Men —and masses of men— still form the backbone of all armies. In spite of all inventions men— men with munitions—are still necessary.

Men are indispensable, and equally so are generals. Modern warfare places a terrible responsibility upon generals. A slight mistake, a moment's hesitation, a little indecision when faced with a sudden difficulty, on the part of one of them, may cost a country thousands of trained and valuable lives; may even lose a battle and jeopardise the fate of a nation. The responsibility upon Charles Martel or William

the Conqueror, upon Hawkwood or Cordova, or any other great captain of the Middle Ages, even upon leaders of a later age such as Condé and Montrose, was trifling compared with that which to-day rests upon the shoulders of a general in command of an army corps, to say nothing of those in higher place. More than ever before it is necessary for generals to have brains, training, and experience, and to bring every ounce of every quality to bear upon the task before them. They must be men who think quickly and act promptly, who are neither unnerved by loss nor unbalanced by success; who know when to sacrifice life and when to conserve it, when to take advice and when to reject it. The difficult and responsible work done by some scores of British and French generals during the Great War has not been properly understood by the public, largely because it is unknown. Everyone has heard of French and Joffre, of Ian Hamilton, Douglas Haig and Smith-Dorrien, of Foch and Pau, but that is about all. Occasionally one saw a portrait of Sir Charles Monro, Sir Herbert Plumer, De Castelnau, or Franchet d'Espérey, but these men and many others were not known as they should have been. Yet it would be an insult to compare either their abilities or their actions with those of many second and third rate politicians whose names

FIELD-MARSHAL VISCOUNT FRENCH,
who was in command of the British armies in France from the outbreak of war till December 15th, 1915, when he relinquished his responsibility to General Sir Douglas Haig, to take over the appointment of Field-Marshal commanding the troops in the United Kingdom

BROTHER COMMANDERS OF THE SISTER SERVICES.
Admiral de Robeck and General Sir Ian Hamilton on board H.M.S. Triad at the
Dardanelles on the day of the latter's departure for England, October, 1915.

were in the papers every day, and whose features were familiar to all.

First of all, look at the work done by our own generals during the first year of the Great War.

Britain has never in the past given to anyone a task anything like so big as that laid upon many of her generals in 1914 and 1915. Confining the story to the first year, there were, in addition to Sir John French, at least four British generals who commanded twice the number of troops that Napoleon had at Austerlitz or Wellington at Waterloo, and far more than famous soldiers such as Gustavus Adolphus and Frederick the Great ever led to victory.

As for Sir John himself, British history has no parallel to his task. Neither Wellington nor Marlborough ever commanded 100,000 British troops at one time, while French had under him at least seven times that number. The armies which fought under Henry V. at Agincourt and Cromwell at Naseby would be swallowed up, almost unnoticed, in

his vast host, while the troops sent by Britain to the Crimea would be merely a useful little reinforcement.

But this is not all. Until to-day Great Britain has never been a great military Power, and Sir John's task should therefore be tested by foreign standards. Be it so. In the spring and summer of 1915 he could have supplied Napoleon with the equivalent of the Grand Army of 1812, and both the Russians and the Japanese with the numbers they put into the field at Mukden, and still have had a considerable army left. He had more than the total of the three armies with which the Germans invaded France in 1870, and more than Grant or Lee ever commanded in the American Civil War. Below Sir John and his three or four principal lieutenants there were many who commanded bodies of men which in former days would have been large armies, quite big enough to have turned the scale of the Civil War in favour of Charles I., or to have given William of Orange some sweeping victories over the French.

To illustrate this point, attention may be drawn to the organisation of a great army—say, the British Expeditionary Force in France as it was in the summer of 1915. At its head was the Commander-in-Chief, Sir John French, having under him—precision is impossible—perhaps 750,000 men. These were divided into armies—the First Army, the Second Army, and so on, each being commanded by a general and consisting of about 150,000 men. In their turn the armies were divided into army corps, each containing about 37,000 men, and each under its own general. Each army corps was divided into two divisions, each with a general of its own, and each division into three brigades, at the head of which was a brigadier-general. There the generals stop.*

This refers to the infantry only. But the cavalry were organised on somewhat similar lines. There was a cavalry corps, divided into divisions, and each of these divided again into brigades. At the head of each there was a general of one kind or another, while other generals directed the movements of the artillery.

Other generals must be mentioned, especially those who worked at that mysterious place called G.H.Q., or General Headquarters. One of these, the Chief of the Staff, was, after Sir John French, perhaps the most important person in the field. He was the Commander-in-Chief's principal adviser, and under his direction information about the enemy was collected, plans of campaign were worked out, and operations arranged. Then there was the Adjutant-General, who looked after the personnel of the Army, collected and arranged casualty lists, provided for reinforcements, etc., and the Quartermaster-General, whose business it was to supply the Army with food, clothing, and its other requirements. Other generals looked after auxiliary services, among which may be mentioned two of the utmost importance—the Flying Corps and the Medical Corps.

Task of the French generals

The task before the French generals was much bigger, and *a fortiori* the above remarks apply to them. At one time France must have had twenty men in the field for every British soldier, but gradually this proportion was reduced, until it stood, in the summer of 1915, at perhaps four to one. Accepting this as roughly correct, General Joffre's task was four times as great as was Sir John French's, and several of his generals had under them armies nearly as big as the one commanded by Sir John. Napoleon and

* A little later there were three divisions to each corps, but the above is true of the time to which the chapter refers.

THE NEW BRITISH GENERALISSIMO ON HIS WAY TO SEE GENERAL JOFFRE.
Sir Douglas Haig, on the right, inspecting French troops on the occasion of his visit to our ally's headquarters after being appointed to the supreme British command on the western front.

GENERAL JOFFRE'S CORDIAL HANDGRIP. HISTORIC MOMENT AT THE FRENCH HEADQUARTERS.
Sir Douglas Haig has just bidden farewell to the French commander and is looking towards General Joffre, who is shaking hands with a British Staff officer. Here in this quiet, prosaic environment some momentous manœuvre may have been decided. On the right an officer-orderly is waiting, ready with the General's fur coat, and a number of French officers and a guard of infantry stand at the salute.

"LE BON PÈRE JOFFRE,"

as our French friends christened him, returning from a review of his
stalwart "children." Portly of frame, and ever genial of expression,
General Joffre seemed to prove an exception among great strategists.
Certainly in no physical characteristic could he be compared with
Hindenburg, Mackensen, Napoleon, or Cæsar.

his marshals will always be prominent figures in the history
of war, but Joffre and his generals were set a bigger task.
The world's verdict upon their work has yet to come.

Joffre and French were undoubtedly the two dominating
personalities in the western theatre of war, and this is
still true if the Germans are included, for if they had
Hindenburg and Mackensen in the east, they had no one
on the other side of Europe to compare with the two allied
leaders. Kluck, a possible rival, disappeared as suddenly
as he had come, and even the high rank of Duke Albert of
Würtemberg and Prince Rupert of Bavaria failed to make
them other than shadowy figures.

Joffre and French   Joseph Jacques Césaire Joffre was
born at Rivesaltes, a little place near
Perpignan, in the Pyrenees, on January
12th, 1852, and was therefore eight months older than
Sir John French. When the Franco-Prussian War broke
out he was studying for the Army, and his first taste of
war was to assist in improving the defences of Paris. He
was with the artillery during the siege of the French capital,
and after its surrender he returned to the military school.
In 1872 he became a lieutenant in a regiment of engineers,
and, having spent some time in artillery practice at
Fontainebleau, he was raised to the rank of captain, and
set to work on the new fortifications of Paris.

Joffre's first experience of foreign service was in Indo-
China. Having just lost his first wife, he went to Hanoi, the
new French possession, in 1884, as chief of the engineering

corps, and he remained there for four years. On his
return to France he served as lecturer on fortifications at
Fontainebleau, and in 1892 he went to the Soudan, where
he planned and built a railway from the Senegal to the
Niger. While there he led a column to Timbuctoo, four
hundred and seventy miles from his base at Segou. Another
column, under Colonel Bonnier, had gone along the Niger,
but its leader was killed before Joffre, marching by land,
arrived. Joffre took over the command, fortified a series
of posts, and succeeded in pacifying the country. He
wrote an account of this little expedition which, under the
title of "My March to Timbuctoo," has been translated
into English.

As a colonel and a leading authority on fortifications, Joffre
went in 1895 to Madagascar to superintend the construction
of the fortifications of the new naval base
at Diego-Suarez, and coming home again   **Joffre's early**
he was made a brigadier-general.   **commands**
He then married a second time, and
rose rapidly in the service. First he commanded a brigade
of artillery, then was made Director of Engineering at the
Ministry of War, and then a general of division. In 1909
he was chosen to command the Second Army Corps at
Amiens, and in 1910 he became a member of the Superior
Council of War. In 1911, Joffre, then fifty-nine years old,
was selected by the Government to fill the position of Chief
of the General Staff and Vice-President of the Council. In

"THE MAN OF DUTY."

General de Castelnau, on the left, was General Joffre's right-hand man,
and was appointed Chief of Staff on the western front towards the end
of 1915. He was known to his brother-officers as "The Man of Duty."
When the news of his son's death in battle reached him, he did not allow
his personal feelings to interfere for one moment with the work he had
in hand.

THE WARRIOR-LEADER OF THE MEN OF THE BLACK MOUNTAINS.

King Nicholas passing through a Montenegrin village. King Nicholas, like King Albert and King Peter, personally directed the fortunes of his realm. Of Spartan temperament and simple tastes, this monarch was the most democratic of all aristocrats. From the outset of hostilities Montenegro took its stand by Serbia.

the Republic this office carries with it the position of Commander-in-Chief in the event of war, and he had been three years at his post, engaged in the work of re-organising the Army, when hostilities broke out. At once he was named Generalissimo of the Armies of France.

Then came the test of his life. How would this student of fortifications, this quiet elderly man who had seen less active service than many an English major, acquit himself in his tremendous task of driving back the ready armies of the first military Power in the world? Could he grasp the plan of a battlefield on which millions of men would manœuvre as well as he had grasped the plan of his forts at Hanoi or Diego-Suarez?

The answer to these, and many other such questions which Frenchmen—and not Frenchmen only—were asking in the anxious days of August, 1914, is recorded on the indelible pages of history. Certainly Joffre was surprised by the overwhelming strength which Germany had massed on the Belgian frontier, and certainly some of his generals failed him at crucial moments, the result being that a large part of France was overrun, and Paris itself was in serious danger less than a month after the outbreak of war.

Everyone knows Joffre's face and **Joffre's coolness** form, as shown in his portraits, and it does **and judgment** not need a thought-reader to tell the kind of man he is. The clumsy word imperturbable perhaps describes him as well as any other, and he faced the new and difficult situation with rare coolness and judgment. Ruthlessly he cleared the Army of incompetent generals, and he let his forces retreat steadily until they were only a few miles from Paris. It was a hazardous operation. and a costly one for France, and many thought

that Joffre should have turned and fought sooner—say, on the Heights of Champagne. But he did not. The main fact was that the long retreat did not demoralise his armies, and when the reserves, which had been concentrating in front of Paris, were added to them, the Generalissimo was able to strike hard.

On September 5th Joffre told Sir John French of his intention to take the offensive, and on the 6th he issued his famous order to his men. " We have," he said, " but one business on hand—to **The one** attack and repel the enemy." He had **Generalissimo** waited long, but at last the hour had come. The Germans were beaten on the Marne, driven back to the Aisne, and then began the long war of entrenchments. Throughout this Joffre continued to direct the operations, and from time to time his troops took the offensive. During the winter and the spring his methods did not regain much more ground, but none was lost, and he was steadily carrying out some plan. Perhaps there is truth in the story which represented him as saying that he was " nibbling away, nibbling away."

This is not the time or the place to sum up Joffre's merits as a soldier, or the extent of his services to France and the Allies; but one thing can be said—in spite of reverses and disappointments, he kept to a remarkable extent the confidence of the Army and of the people as a whole. More than once during the war one Prime Minister and one Cabinet gave way to another, but there was no question of another Generalissimo. Joffre had critics, but one and all realised that he was giving his very best to France, and that to change him for another would be sheer folly.

329

THE PERIL OF THE NON-COMBATANT : A THRILLING ADVENTURE WITH A RED CROSS WAGGON.

This exciting incident, which occurred somewhere on the western front, gives an idea of the perils of the non-combatant Red Cross worker. British soldiers in a support trench saw a horse ambulance rushing towards them uncontrolled, and swaying violently from side to side. Shells were bursting all round the vehicle, and a stray bullet had killed the driver, who was lying across the seat. In the nick of time some occupants of the trench dashed out and succeeded in bringing the waggon to a standstill before it careered wildly over the trench parapet.

Joffre's British colleague, John Denton Pinkstone French, was born in Kent on September 28th, 1852, being the son of a naval officer. For a few years he was a naval cadet and a midshipman, but evidently he grew tired of a quiet life at sea, for when he was twenty-two years old he left the Navy and joined the 8th Hussars. In 1884, having been transferred to the 19th Hussars, French went to Egypt on active service. During four years of peace he commanded the 19th Hussars, and then, having got a Staff appointment, he was able to gain experience of another kind.

In 1899, French, by then a major-general, went out to Natal to command Sir George White's cavalry, and he led them in much of the fighting around Ladysmith. He got out of that town by the last train that left before the enemy closed round it, and was given the task of holding back the Boers in the Colesberg district. He left this to lead 5,000 men to the relief of Kimberley, which he entered on February 15th, 1900 ; and then, without rest, he rode away to head off Cronje's army. Again he was successful, and some part of the credit for the surrender at Paardeberg belongs to him.

French in South Africa

French remained actively engaged in South Africa until the end of the war. He was one of the generals who helped to clear the Boers from the Orange Free State. Sweeping over the country to the west, he advanced with Roberts on Johannesburg and Pretoria, and he followed the retreating Boers, who were commanded by Louis Botha. During practically the whole of 1901 he was leading columns against the enemy, and his reputation was perhaps the foremost of those made in the war.

French returned to England as Sir John French, K.C.B., and in 1907 he was made a full general. He held several high commands — Inspector - General of the Forces, and finally, from 1911 to 1914, Chief of the Imperial General Staff. He was by then a Feld-Marshal, and it was generally understood that in the event of a great war he would take command of the British troops. So it came about. In August, 1914, Sir John went to Paris, where he had an enthusiastic welcome from our Allies, and then to the front. Sir John French's history during the following year is part of the history of the struggle in France and Belgium, and that does not need recounting to the readers of THE GREAT WAR. His balanced judgment and wide experience were great assets in dealing with the many difficult problems which confronted him from time to time. Like Joffre, he refused to be flurried. He conducted the retreat from Mons in masterly fashion ; he loyally co-operated with the French when it came to taking the offensive ; and, perhaps more difficult still, he arranged the transfer of his troops from the Aisne to Flanders. At Ypres his dispositions were highly tested, but events proved that in the circumstances they were thoroughly sound, and throughout the winter and the spring he carried out a plan of campaign which, though not spectacular, was in the best interests of the Allies. In December, 1915, Sir John resigned the onerous command which he had held for sixteen months, and was succeeded by Sir Douglas Haig. He was made a viscount, and was given the command of the troops in the United Kingdom.

Under General Joffre there were two or three other generals whose standing was not unlike that of Sir John French, or of Hindenburg and Mackensen in Germany, for they commanded not merely armies, but groups of armies. The enormous number of men in the field rendered something of this kind necessary.

Of these generals the most distinguished was Foch, and one careful critic, reviewing the first year of the war, declared that " he had some claims to be considered the first soldier in Europe." Ferdinand Foch was born in 1851, and fought in the war of 1870-71. When it was over, he studied for the Army at Fontainebleau, and soon became a lieutenant in an artillery regiment. He worked at the Ecole Supérieure de Guerre, and afterwards received a Staff appointment, which he vacated to take up an artillery command at Vincennes.

Foch was always a student of war. From 1896 to 1901

GENERAL ALEXEIEFF,
Chief of the General Staff of the Russian Army. One of the most remarkable men of the century, General Alexeieff rose to his exalted position from humble sergeant through sheer merit. The success of the great retreat from Warsaw was largely due to his skill and ingenuity, and he did much to keep up the spirit of the Russian Army all through this perilous period.

he was professor at the Ecole de Guerre, and some of his lectures there were published as " Les Principes de la Guerre " and " Conduite de la Guerre : la Manœuvre et la Bataille." In 1903 he became a colonel, and four years later a general, while from 1907 to 1911 he was commandant of the Ecole de Guerre, and a member of the General Staff. When his term of office came to an end he was made Governor of Nice, then head of the Eighth Army Corps at Bourges. When war broke out he was at Nancy, commanding the Twentieth Corps.

Foch as writer and fighter

After the first battles of the war Joffre formed several new armies, among them one called the Ninth, from the reserves which were assembling, and he gave the command of this to Foch, a man sixty-three years of age,

who had never seen a battlefield since 1871. However, he was soon to show that in the study and the class-room he had learned as much as some of his British colleagues had in South Africa and on the Indian Frontier.

The new army, consisting of three corps, came into line early in September, and fought at the Battle of the Marne. On the 6th it was in action with the Germans near Sézanne, and after two or three days of fierce fighting it fell to Foch **Foch at the** to make the decisive **Marne** movement of this battle. First of all he moved his left wing on to the flank of Von Bülow's army, and during the night of the 6th he pushed a division forward into a gap which he had discovered between Von Bülow and the German army on his left. His centre, after some hard fighting, drove the Prussian Guard with terrible slaughter into the Marshes of St. Gond, and when their flank was also attacked Bülow's troops fell back in something like disorder. The whole German line retreated to the Aisne, largely as a result of this success ; Foch and the French followed, and on the 11th he entered Chalons.

Foch's army fought around Rheims at the Battle of the Aisne, and then Joffre sent him to Flanders to exercise a general control over the French armies north of Noyon and Compiègne, and to act in conjunction with Sir John French. At first there were only two French armies, the Seventh and the Tenth, but they were soon joined by the Eighth. This work occupied Foch during the remaining months of the first year. The winter fighting, especially the Battle of Ypres, and, in January, the Battle of Soissons, taxed his resources most severely, but he came through the ordeal with an enhanced reputation as a strategist. He personally superintended the French offensive between Arras and Lens in May, and in June and July his men were also busy.

General Pau held for a time a command not unlike that of Foch in Flanders. Marie César Gérald Pau was born in 1848, and as an infantry subaltern served in the Franco-Prussian War. At Fröschwiller he was seriously wounded, and his arm was amputated, but he returned to the battle-line, and took part in the later stages of the struggle. He rose in the Army step by step, and became remarkably popular among the soldiers, who called him " le premier troupier du monde." In 1903 he was made a General of Division, and from 1909 to 1913 **General Pau's** he was commander of **popularity** the Twentieth Corps at Nancy and a member of the Superior Council of War. Pau's popularity was very useful to the Government when he helped to pass the Three Years' Bill through Parliament. He was one of the three generals—Joffre and De Castelnau being the others—who assisted M. Millerand to reorganise and strengthen the

RESPONSIBLE RUSSIANS IN SLAVDOM'S CRITICAL HOUR.
The Emperor of Russia, who assumed supreme command of his forces on September 5th, 1915, photographed with several near relatives, including the Grand Duke Nicholas, the Grand Dukes Peter Nicholaievitch and Michaelovitch, Prince Peter Alexandrovitch of Oldenbourg, officers of H.I.M.'s suite, and the Staff of the Grand Duke.

Army. In 1913, being then sixty-five years old, he retired owing to the age limit, but on the outbreak of hostilities he was recalled to active service, and was sent to command on the eastern frontier. This, however, turned out to be only a secondary theatre of war, and just before Joffre took the offensive in September he gave Pau a general supervision over the turning movement which resulted in the victory on the Marne. In 1915 the general

Pau's mission to Russia visited Russia and the East, presumably to arrange for more concerted action between the Allies.

About the time that Foch was sent to command the northern group of armies, the direction of the southern group, those operating between Noyon and Belfort, was entrusted to General Dubail. Born in 1851, Augustin Yvon Edmond Dubail fought as a lieutenant in the Franco-Prussian War, and was taken prisoner in October, 1870. After the struggle was over, he lectured in a military school, became a captain, and later a professor at the Ecole de

Guerre. He served as a Staff officer, both at home and in Algiers; he was colonel of a regiment of Zouaves and commandant of the Ecole Spéciale Militaire. In 1908 he became a general of division. Three years later Dubail was at the War Office assisting the Secretary, M. Berteaux, and he was Joffre's predecessor as Chief of the General Staff. He found time to write two books on military matters: "Le Livre de l'Officier" and "L'Education Militaire."

When war began Dubail was commander of the Ninth Army Corps at Tours and a member of the Superior Council of War. He took the field as leader of the Army of the Vosges, and directed its early and, as events proved, premature movements into Alsace. Having retired from there, he devoted his attention to defending the heights between the Valleys of the Meuse and the Meurthe, the unfortified gap between Toul and Epinal, where in August and September the four corps under his command successfully resisted the German attempts to break through.

THE COMMANDER-IN-CHIEF OF THE RUSSIAN ARMY AS AN ADMIRAL OF THE IMPERIAL FLEET.
The Tsar at Sebastopol, with Admiral Grigorovitch and Naval Staff. From Riga to Sebastopol is a far cry. The Tsar took a personal interest in the whole Russian front, one time directing the military situation on the eastern front, another inspecting the Imperial Navy in the Black Sea.

MAJOR-GENERAL SIR SAMUEL HUGHES,
Canadian Minister for Defence, at Toronto Camp with General Lessard,
who commanded the Toronto Division.

Before the Battle of the Marne Dubail's force was drawn upon for assistance elsewhere, and as it became clear that the main theatre of war would be away to the north, the Army of the Vosges became smaller and smaller until it was not an army—hardly an army corps. About the end of the year it was handed over to General Putz, while Dubail, who had received the Grand Cross of the Legion of Honour, took general command of the armies south of Noyon. Somewhat later he divided this responsibility with De Castelnau, who took the northern section, leaving the southern one to his senior colleague.

The chief events of Dubail's winter and spring campaign were the desperate struggle for the Hartmannsweilerkopf and the fighting around St. Mihiel and Les Eparges. Metz was neared, but for some reason or other Joffre decided to press the main offensive elsewhere. Progress was made **Dubail in the** by one or other of Dubail's armies along **Vosges** the Fecht Valley, and all through the summer he directed the continuous fighting in the Vosges and around Les Eparges.

Marie Joseph Edouard de Curiéres de Castelnau was, with the sole exception of Foch, Joffre's most trusted lieutenant. Descended from a very old family and born in 1851, he was intended for the Army, in which more than one of his ancestors had earned distinction, and he fought as a subaltern in the Franco-Prussian War. Afterwards he passed through the Ecole Supérieure de Guerre, and as a lieutenant-colonel he joined the General Staff in 1896. Four years later he was made chief of the Mobilisation Department, and then he commanded in turn a regiment, a brigade, and a division.

In 1912 De Castelnau went to the War Office as Joffre's principal assistant, and aided him in putting into execution the provisions of the Three Years' Law. This increased the standing Army by 200,000 men, and so made a new scheme of mobilisation necessary. It was drawn up under the supervision of De Castelnau, who, in 1913, was rewarded with a seat in the Superior Council of War. This general is a man of very attractive personality.

When war broke out De Castelnau took command of the Second Army, called also the Army of Lorraine, and, in conjunction with the Army of the Vosges, he led a prompt offensive. But this premature movement failed, and he drew back his forces to protect Nancy. At one time it seemed as if this old city would fall to the Germans, but the defences im- **Castelnau's defence** provised by De Castelnau on the Grand **of Nancy** Couronne proved impregnable, and assault after assault was beaten back. De Castelnau then moved forward, drove off the Germans, and on September 12th, when he entered Lunéville, the danger to Nancy was over.

In September a new army, the Seventh, was formed for service in Artois, and De Castelnau was chosen to lead this. He attacked Von Kluck, and retook Noyon, but after a three days' battle he was obliged to fall back. On a line from Albert to Ribecourt he repulsed fierce German onslaughts, and during the winter this army fought under the general direction of Foch. In the spring General Petain took over the command, and De Castelnau was sent to supervise the movements of the central group of armies. It should be said that this leader lost, during the early stages of the war, two of his five soldier sons.

In December, 1915, when the campaign in Greece had begun, a change was made in the French command. Joffre was given the supreme direction of all the French armies, and De Castelnau became his Chief of Staff. Apparently

BRIGADIER-GENERAL LUKIN, D.S.O., C.M.G.
He was appointed to the command of the 1st Brigade of the South
African Infantry for the European Campaign.

the idea was that Joffre from Paris should direct all the operations, while De Castelnau should control those in France and on the frontiers.

It may be well here to say something about the organisation of the French Army for war, and so to gain an idea of the places filled by its leading generals. In peace, military affairs are directed by the Superior Council of War. The president of this is the Minister for War, and the vice-president the Chief of the General Staff. The ten other members are all generals, the understanding being that in time of war the Chief of the Staff will take supreme command, and the other **French war organisation** generals, who have worked with him in peace, will serve under him. In time of war a perfectly free hand is allowed to the Generalissimo, as the Chief of the Staff becomes. He selects his army commanders both from within and without the Superior Council.

At the outbreak of war France put five armies into the field, numbered one to five, and counting from the south upwards. As already seen, Dubail and De Castelnau, both members of the Superior Council, were appointed to the First, or Army of the Vosges, and the Second Army. Ruffey, another member of the Council, took the Third, while the leadership of the Fourth and Fifth was entrusted to De Langle de Cary—an older man who was recalled to active service—and Lanrezac respectively. The latter was not

GENERAL THE RIGHT HON. LOUIS BOTHA.
Striking photograph of the South African Premier acknowledging the plaudits of the crowd on the occasion of the thanksgiving service after the capitulation of German South-West Africa.

a success, and after Charleroi his place was taken by Franchet d'Espérey, hitherto one of his subordinates.

Such was the start, but soon five other armies were formed from the reserves, and all were sent to the cockpit between the Marne and the sea. They were numbered six to ten, but they did not appear in the field quite in this regular order, and to command them Joffre took full advantage of his powers of free selection.

For the Ninth, as already stated, he selected Foch, and for the Seventh he called De Castelnau from Lorraine. For the Sixth he recalled another general, Maunoury, from the retired list, but to command the Eighth and Tenth he promoted two junior generals, D'Urbal and Maud'huy. The story must now concern itself with these leaders of armies, each consisting of 150,000 or 200,000 men. **General Maurice Sarrail**

About Ruffey there is little to be said, for his place was soon taken by another. His army stretched, in August, from Montmédy to Rocroi, whence it advanced towards Luxemburg, only, however, to fall quickly back before the German armies. Before the end of the month a big battle was fought, after which the obsolete fortresses on the Central Meuse, such as Mézières, surrendered, and Ruffey retreated to the Argonne region.

Maurice Sarrail, who succeeded Ruffey about this time as leader of the Third Army, was commander of the Sixth Army Corps at Chalons when hostilities began, and this corps

GENERAL THE HON. CHRISTIAAN SMUTS.
General Botha's right-hand man, this distinguished lawyer-soldier helped greatly to bring about the success of the Union forces in German South-West Africa.

formed part of Ruffey's force. When Joffre was planning the Battle of the Marne, he ordered Sarrail, whose army lay south of Verdun, to defend that fortress and the line of the Meuse. At first he fell back a little, but a series of savage attacks failed to break his army, and its firmness helped the others to win the Battle of the Marne.

The German attacks on Sarrail's force were repeated, if possible with more violence, during the Battle of the Aisne, but on the hills around Verdun the French engineers had prepared some very formidable obstacles, and aided by these he was able to beat back the onsets of an army much larger than his own. Once or 'twice the Germans came very near to success, but after a final repulse on October 3rd, 1914, they abandoned the attempt.

Throughout the winter Sarrail continued to protect Verdun, pushing forward his trenches little by little, until in March he got well across the Meuse, and took the offensive. He only got a little way, however, and then in June and July he was called upon to meet another attack delivered by the army of the Crown Prince, who was evidently anxious to retrieve his reputation as a soldier. Sarrail's defence of Verdun marked him out for still higher things. In the autumn of 1915 the position in the Balkans, owing to the entry of Bulgaria into the war and the defection of Greece, became most threatening. Britain and France decided to send help to Serbia, and Sarrail was chosen for the supreme command in this new theatre of war. Under his direction the Allies advanced to help the Serbians and then fell back to Salonika, which they fortified.

General de Langle de Cary Next comes the leader of the Fourth Army. Fernand Louis A. M. de Langle de Cary was born in 1849, the son of a naval officer. He passed into the Army in 1867, and was an artillery officer during the Siege of Paris. He was very severely wounded, but happily he recovered, and rose in the service. Having commanded a battalion, he was made professor at the Ecole Supérieur de Guerre; in 1895 he became a colonel, and in 1900 a brigadier-general. Then followed the command of a division (1906), of an army corps (1908), and a seat in the Superior Council of War (1912). Being sixty-five years old, he had just retired from active service when Germany declared war.

Joffre at once entrusted Langle de Cary with the command of the Fourth Army, which was to hold the Valley of the Meuse in the neighbourhood of Sedan. He made a slight advance in August, but was soon compelled to fall back and to join in the great retreat. The attempt to defend the Meuse was given up, and in a series of battles the Fourth Army suffered very severely indeed. However, it recovered to some extent when the Marne was reached, and during the battle on that river fought hard against the army of Duke Albert of Würtemberg near Vitry. **General Franchet d'Esperey**

For some days the issue swayed hither and thither, but when a fresh corps arrived to assist the Fourth Army, the Würtembergers had to give way.

Langle de Cary was one of the French leaders at the Battle of the Aisne. Again his task was to tackle the Würtembergers, but he was unable to drive them from their positions in Champagne, and a war of entrenchments began there. In February an advance was ordered in this district, and some ground was won.

Near the Fourth Army the Fifth fought a similar battle. Its commander, Louis Marie F. F. Franchet d'Espérey, was the son of a soldier, and was born in 1856. Unlike most of the French generals of 1914 and 1915, he was too young to serve in the Franco-Prussian War, but, in spite of this, he saw more fighting than most of them during the next forty years. He was in Tunisia and in Indo-China when a young man, in 1900 he served in the expedition to Peking, and in 1912 and 1913 he commanded troops in Western Morocco. In the meantime he had served on the General Staff, commanded a battalion and then a brigade.

On the outbreak of war, D'Espérey was in command of the First Army Corps at Lille, and he led this into the field, being present at the Battle of Charleroi. In this disastrous encounter he appears to have rendered good service to France, for he was appointed a Grand Officer of the Legion of Honour, and was selected to take the place of General Lanrezac as commander of the Fifth Army, of which his own corps formed part. This promotion took place just before the Battle of the Marne.

In this battle D'Espérey was pitted against Von Kluck, who was pushed across the Grand Morin near Esternay, and was followed over the Petit Morin to the Marne and then to the Ourcq. In their advance the Fifth French Army won a strong position at Montmirail, and joined up with the British near Chateau Thierry.

GENERAL DE LANGLE DE CARY.
On the left, with his Chief of Staff, Colonel Paquette. General de Langle de Cary was leader of the Fourth French Army, and one of the generals who directed at the Battle of the Aisne.

GENERAL MAUD'HUY.
In charge of a brigade at the beginning of the war, General Maud'huy (right) rose to command the Tenth Army within two months. Later he was transferred to the Army of the Vosges.

MASTERS OF STRATEGY WHO COMPRISED THE ALLIES' GRAND COUNCIL OF WAR.

Representatives of the Allied Powers outside the French General Head-quarters, where the Grand Council of War met on December 6th, 1915, under the Presidency of General Joffre. From left to right : General Count Porro (Italy), Sir John French, General Joffre, and General Jilinsky (Russia). General Wiellemans represented Belgium, and Colonel Stefanovitch, Serbia.

Like the British on their left, D'Espérey's troops crossed the Aisne under heavy fire, and advanced against the Germans entrenched on the Craonne plateau. There, however, their progress was stopped, and although they fought with the utmost gallantry, it was in vain. A little later D'Espérey settled down to a long spell of trench war-fare, his business being to hold the line while other armies made the grand assaults.

To command the new Sixth Army Joffre recalled another general from his retire-ment. Michel Joseph Maunoury, born in 1847, entered the Army as a youth, and fought in the Franco - Prussian War. He rose to the rank of colonel in 1897. Four years later he was made a general, and he held the ap-pointments of Com-mander of the Artillery in Paris and Director of the Ecole Supérieur de Guerre. At the time of his retirement (1912) he was a member of the Superior Council of War, and he was then made Military Governor of Paris.

Maunoury's army, one of not less than four corps, was fresh,

not having shared in the hardships of the retreat, so to it was given a big task at the Battle of the Marne. Early on September 6th Maunoury's men were advancing to the Ourcq, where, in conjunction with the British, they turned the flank of Von Kluck's army, and compelled it to fall back. Soon they were in possession of the line of the Ourcq, and the first victory for France and her freedom was won.

Maunoury had another responsible task at the Battle of the Aisne. His army, advancing on the left of the British, forced the passage of that river between Soissons and Compiègne, and made some progress up the heights on the other side ; but on the 15th it was attacked and driven back, almost to the bank of the Aisne. However, reinforce-ments arrived, and this loss was made good. Trench warfare then became the order of the day, and to Maunoury was entrusted the defence of this section of the French line. In January his right wing fought the Battle of Soissons, but for some time afterwards the

SIR JOHN FRENCH LEAVING THE MINISTRY OF FOREIGN AFFAIRS IN PARIS.

On December 7th, 1915, the members of the Allies' War Council went to Paris for a luncheon given in their honour at the Ministry of Foreign Affairs. On the 8th the Council was resumed to deliberate on the situation of the Allies in relation to the Balkans.

Sixth Army did nothing more than hold its ground. Passing over the Seventh Army, led by De Castelnau, and the Ninth, at first under Foch, two armies remain, the Eighth and Tenth, and the names of the generals in command of these are especially familiar to readers of Sir John French's despatches, mainly because they— D'Urbal and Maud'huy—under the supreme direction of Foch, were mostly in touch with the British troops.

Victor Louis Lucien d'Urbal was born of a military family in 1858, and after the usual training entered a cavalry regiment. He passed through the Ecole de Guerre, and held several Staff appointments before 1903, when he was made a lieutenant-colonel. When war broke out he was a brigadier-general. D'Urbal at once made his mark as a leader, and was promoted rapidly, first to

D'Urbal's rapid promotion

a division and then to an army corps. In October, when a new army was formed to hold the threatened line along the Yser and to support the Belgians, he was appointed to command it. It was called the Eighth Army, and in it were some Territorials. It came into position about the end of October, and from it D'Urbal sent assistance to the British during the Battle of Ypres. The savage German rush was driven back, and D'Urbal's was for some time one of the quieter parts of the front. His command ceased

THE FRENCH COMMANDER-IN-CHIEF AT THE DARDANELLES.
General Bailloud, who succeeded General Gouraud as Commander-in-Chief of the French Expeditionary Corps at the Dardanelles, when the latter was wounded in July, 1915, and until General Sarrail's appointment in August, 1915. Formerly General Bailloud commanded the famous Twentieth Army Corps at Nancy, and the Nineteenth at Algiers.

later to be of any great importance, and in March or April he succeeded Maud'huy as commander of the Tenth Army.

Louis Ernest de Maud'huy was born at Metz in 1857, two years before his soldier father was killed at Magenta. He studied at St. Cyr and the Ecole de Guerre, and entered the Army; served on the Staff and was a captain of Chasseurs before being made professor at the Ecole de Guerre in 1896. Two years later he obtained a high position in the War Office, but soon he was again occupying a professorial chair, lecturing on tactics and military history. In 1909 he became a colonel, and in 1912 a general. In August, 1914, he was in charge of a brigade, but in less than

General de Maud'huy

two months he was commanding an army, the Tenth, which took its place in the line about the end of September. It occupied the region between Arras and Lens, and at once fought the Germans at the Battle of Albert.

In the great campaign in Flanders in the winter of 1914-15 Maud'huy's army was on the British right. He advanced to Arras, but was soon forced to retire to the heights behind that city, where he just succeeded in repulsing a serious and strong German attack. From October 20th to 26th his position was well-nigh as desperate as was that of the British at Ypres a little later. Masses and masses of men were hurled at Arras, and at one moment they got near enough to bombard the city; but the French line remained unbroken, and as the Germans weakened and retired, Maud'huy gained ground from them by a vigorous and well-planned counter-attack. Like the British, his army kept to the trenches through the winter. In March

THE VICTOR OF THE VOSGES.
General A. Y. E. Dubail, one of General Joffre's right-hand men, and commander of the Southern French Armies operating between Noyon and Belfort. When the war began, General Dubail was leader of the Army of the Vosges.

or April Maud'huy was transferred to the Army of the Vosges, and D'Urbal succeeded him as leader of the Tenth Army.

To two of the most distinguished of the French generals, Galliéni and D'Amade—both members of the Superior Council of War—special tasks were given. Joseph Simon Galliéni, born in 1849, has been likened to Lord Kitchener. He fought with the Colonial infantry in the Franco-Prussian War, being made prisoner in Sedan, and soon after the conclusion of peace entered upon a long and fruitful career in France's Colonial Empire. In 1875 Galliéni was sent to Senegal, and some ten years later was made commander of the Upper Sudan Territory. There he not only put down rebellions, but he organised the country, and improved its defences, its education, and its roads. In 1892 Galliéni was transferred to Tongking,

Swaine.]

LIEUT.-GENERAL SIR RONALD CHARLES MAXWELL, K.C.B.

When Sir William Robertson was appointed Chief of the General Staff in France in January, 1915, Lieut.-General Sir Ronald C. Maxwell succeeded him as Quartermaster-General of the Forces.

where he was put in command of a military district, one especially exposed to the raids of Chinese pirates. An end was put to these, and defensive works were erected, after which the administrator was able to do something to introduce needed and beneficial reforms. Being then a general, Galliéni was appointed in 1897 French Resident in Madagascar. For four years he did the same kind of work there, the new colony being thoroughly organised by him, the enemy crushed, and measures taken to restore order and introduce prosperity.

Galliéni at Paris When Galliéni returned to France he was chosen inspector of the African troops, and in 1906 he took command of the Thirteenth Corps and then of the Fourteenth. From 1908 to the beginning of the Great War he was a member of the Superior Council, being retained, in spite of his sixty-five years, because he had commanded in chief before the enemy in Madagascar.

Towards the end of August, when the Germans were rapidly nearing Paris, Galliéni was made its Military Governor, and at once he took

steps to put the capital into a state of preparedness. But his dispositions were not tested; instead, he had the satisfaction of leading the troops under his command against the retreating foe. At the end of October the general was made Minister for War under M. Briand, another parallel between his career and that of Lord Kitchener.

Albert Gérard Leo d'Amade was born at Toulouse seven years later than Galliéni. He served when young in Algeria and Tunisia, and also in Tongking, after which he gained a good knowledge of China during a period spent as military attaché at Peking. As the representative of France he watched the operations of the British Army in South Africa during the Boer War, and was afterwards military attaché in London. In 1908 D'Amade was made a general, and was sent to command the French army in Western Morocco. After his return to France he commanded an army corps, and became a member of the Superior Council of War. **D'Amade at the Dardanelles**

At the beginning of the Great War D'Amade commanded a Territorial corps stationed at Arras, which moved forward to assist the British Army after its retirement from Mons, but more important work was soon found for him. In April he was chosen to command the French detachment which landed at Kum Kale on the Dardanelles. He superintended this, and also the crossing to the Gallipoli

[*A. Tear.*

GENERAL SIR EDMUND H. H. ALLENBY, K.C.B.

Commanding the Cavalry Expeditionary Force at the beginning of the war. In April, 1915, General Allenby succeeded Sir Herbert Plumer as Commander of the Fifth Corps.

MAINTAINING THE RULE OF THE ROAD IN FRANCE: ON "POINT DUTY" BETWEEN THE FIRING-LINE AND THE RESERVES.

A police-officer, khaki-clad, yet still in the familiar pose, administering the rule of the road—but in a shell-wrecked French village within range of the German guns. The imperturbable figure, wearing the red-and-black armlet of the Military Police, was to be seen standing in a sea of traffic, the large, uplifted hand, with its half-contemptuous flick, reviving memories of Central London during business hours. The busy crossing was in the same relation to a portion of the British front and the reserves behind as the Strand-Wellington Street corner is to the City and the West End. The crowded traffic consisted of guns, transport waggons, officers' cars, ambulances, and despatch-carrying motor-cyclists, riding on the business of war, but still ruled by the authoritative hand and thunderous voice of "Robert," from London.

Peninsula, and commanded the French in the attacks made early in May on the Turkish positions ; but just after this he returned home invalided, and his place was taken by General Gouraud.

Born in 1868, Henri Joseph Eugene Gouraud, almost the youngest of France's generals, earned the title of " the lion of the Argonne " when he commanded a division and then a corps in that region. On June 30th, soon after he arrived at the Dardanelles, he was wounded, and, without his right arm, was compelled to return to France. Sir Ian Hamilton described him as " a happy mixture of daring in danger and of calm in crisis, full of energy and resource."

Another general with a reputation was François André Sordêt, also a veteran of the war of

Gouraud and Sordet
1870-71. Having entered a cavalry regiment, he became in due time a general. In 1912 he was chosen to command the Tenth Army Corps at Rennes, and in 1913 he became a member of the Superior Council of War and Inspector of Cavalry.

In August, 1914, Sordêt took the field at the head of a cavalry corps, and he was stationed a few miles behind the British army at Mons. During the retreat Sir John French visited Sordêt and asked him for assistance, but the latter could do nothing owing to the tired condition of his horses after a prolonged and difficult march. The same thing happened on the following Wednesday, the 26th, " the most critical day of all." After this, however, Sordêt came up, and his help was very useful to the harassed British troops. Soon, his corps was incorporated in the new Sixth Army, but opportunities for cavalry action were few, and little was heard of him.

What of France's younger generals, the men who led the army corps and the divisions ? Some of them had undoubtedly a big future before them, for they had learned war in the great school of experience. Among them was Bailloud, who succeeded Gouraud in Gallipoli ; Putz, who, in turn, commanded little armies in the Vosges and on the Yser ; and Petain, who succeeded De Castelnau as leader of the Seventh Army. Paul Grossetti, the commander of the Sixteenth Army Corps, and Dubois, the commander of the Ninth, both made reputations in the early battles, and both assisted the British at Ypres. Conneau, Moussy, and Bidon are other names which will surely be heard again. Let the final glance at these men be at Grossetti, sitting in an armchair in the square at Pervyse, not far from the burning church, and giving his orders under the constant fire of the German guns.

Among our British generals the best known after Sir John French is, undoubtedly, Sir Ian Hamilton, and to him was entrusted a most difficult task. Sir Ian had a temperament very different from that of Sir John, for versatile or mercurial describe him better than do stolid or phlegmatic.

Ian Standish Monteith Hamilton, a grandson of Viscount Gort, was born in January, 1853, and twenty years later entered the Gordon Highlanders. The Gordons are generally

Sir Ian Hamilton
to the front when there is fighting, and so was Hamilton. He was in the Afghan War, and was one of the survivors of Majuba Hill, where he was wounded in the hand ; in 1884 he went down the Nile to the relief of Gordon, and later he was fighting in Burma. After a few years of peace he was a colonel in the force that marched to Chitral, and in the Tirah campaign he led a brigade. After commanding the Musketry School at Hythe he went to South Africa, and there, like French, he made his name.

Ian Hamilton was in Ladysmith with White at the outbreak of the war, and he remained there until General Buller's relieving force entered. He was chosen by Lord Roberts to command the mounted infantry, and he led the right wing of the army which advanced on Pretoria. He did

GENERAL SIR HORACE SMITH-DORRIEN, G.C.M.G.
Appointed to command of the Second Army of the original British Expeditionary Force, General Smith-Dorrien saw much service in the early critical days of the war. In December, 1915, he was given supreme command of the expedition against German East Africa.

good service in rounding up the Boers, and as Chief of the Staff to Lord Kitchener he had a great share in directing the final operations and in conducting the negotiations for peace.

After the war Hamilton was for a short time Quartermaster-General, but in 1904 the outbreak of the Russo-Japanese War gave him an opportunity to see warfare on a grand scale. As the principal British military attaché he was with the Japanese Army in Manchuria, and in " A Staff Officer's Scrap-Book " he wrote down his impressions. In 1909 he was made Adjutant-General, and in 1910 Inspector-General of Overseas Forces, in which capacity he visited Canada and Australia, and advised the authorities

"THE SOUL OF ANZAC."

Lieut.-General Sir William Riddell Birdwood, K.C.S.I., K.C.M.G., C.B., A.D.C., D.S.O., commanded the Australian and New Zealand Army Corps above Gaba Tepe, Gallipoli. He was slightly wounded on May 14th, 1915, but did not relinquish his command. Pending the arrival at Gallipoli of General Sir Charles Monro, who succeeded General Sir Ian Hamilton in the command of the Mediterranean Expeditionary Force, in October, 1915, Sir William Birdwood took temporary command of the force.

there on measures of defence. In 1907 he was made a full general, and later awarded the G.C.B.

During the earlier stages of the Great War Hamilton continued at his post, which also included the office of Commander-in-Chief in the Mediterranean, one then of great importance. Later, when the British troops were divided into armies, he was appointed to command the Fourth Army, and in March, 1915, he was sent to take charge of the attack on the Dardanelles.

Hamilton's despatch of May 20th tells something of his work there. He saw the "stupendous events" of the bombardment by the allied warships, and this having failed proceeded to make his plans. Readers of THE GREAT WAR are familiar with the story of heroism which enabled the British to get a footing on those narrow beaches. But then followed one disappointment after another, a few yards of ground won at great cost, and then perhaps, of dire necessity, abandoned, until there came the crowning failure of Suvla Bay. This was a great blow to the general, and in October he returned to England, his place being taken by Sir Charles Monro.

Early in 1915, when our new armies began to reach the front, a new organisation was necessary, and Sir John French's force was divided into armies. The leadership of the first two armies was entrusted to Sir Douglas Haig and Sir Horace Smith-Dorrien; later Sir Herbert Plumer

Sir Ian Hamilton at Gallipoli

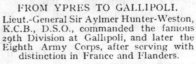

FROM YPRES TO GALLIPOLI.

Lieut.-General Sir Aylmer Hunter-Weston, K.C.B., D.S.O., commanded the famous 29th Division at Gallipoli, and later the Eighth Army Corps, after serving with distinction in France and Flanders.

took Smith-Dorrien's place, and when a third army was formed Sir Charles Monro was chosen to command it. On Sir John French's retirement in December Monro succeeded Haig at the head of the First Army, while General Allenby followed Monro in command of the Third.

Sir Douglas Haig was born in 1861, and after an Oxford education entered the 7th Hussars. In 1898 he served under Lord Kitchener in the advance to Khartoum, and in the next year he went to South Africa, where he did good work in command of flying columns. But Haig was only a lieutenant-colonel then, and it was not until 1903, when he had been in command of the 17th Lancers, that he began to come to the front. He was noted for the excellent work he did as Inspector-General of Cavalry in India, and in 1906 he became Director of Military Training and then Director of Staff Duties. Again, for three years, he was in India as Chief of the Staff, after which he returned home to take command at Aldershot. When the Great War broke out the First Army Corps went from Aldershot, and at its head went Haig, and he retained this command until he was promoted to that of the First Army.

Sir Douglas Haig

Sir Douglas came through the first year of the war splendidly, and made a reputation which no later event could destroy. He arranged the successful retirement of his corps from Mons to the Marne, and the men got away from their perils at Maroilles and Landrecies on August 25th "mainly owing to the skilful manner in which Sir Douglas Haig extricated his corps from an exceptionally difficult position in the darkness of the night." His services at the Battle of the Aisne were also praised by Sir John French. "I cannot," he said, "speak too highly of the valuable services rendered by Sir Douglas Haig." And further on he mentioned his "particularly marked and distinguished service in critical situations." On September 14th the action of the corps under his command was "of so skilful, bold, and decisive a character that he gained positions which have enabled me (Sir John

French) to maintain my position for more than three weeks of very severe fighting on the north bank of the river."

At the First Battle of Ypres Sir Douglas had a very anxious time. His corps was attacked again and again with savage ferocity and by overwhelming numbers, notably on October 31st, and by the Prussian Guard on November 11th, but its commander's nerve and judgment never failed. Reinforcements, the few available, were employed by him to the very best advantage, and his dispositions, coupled with the bravery **Haig at** of his troops, fewer every hour though **Neuve Chapelle** they were, enabled the line to be held to the end, as Sir John French said, "with marvellous tenacity and undaunted courage."

The Battle of Neuve Chapelle was largely directed by Sir Douglas Haig. Here again, Sir John French must be quoted. "I consider that the able and skilful dispositions which were made by the General Officer Commanding the First Army contributed largely to the defeat of the enemy and to the capture of the position. The energy and vigour with which General Sir Douglas Haig handled his command show him to be a leader of great ability and power." As at Neuve Chapelle, so at Festubert in May, the First Army did the bulk of the attacking, and again Sir Douglas Haig rendered valuable services, and so he did until the end of

GENERAL SARRAIL.

Appointed in January, 1915, to the supreme command of the Franco-British Forces at Salonika. In the west he had successfully withstood all the German attempts to break through in the region of Verdun.

LIEUT.-GENERAL SIR BRYAN T. MAHON, C.B., K.C.V.O.

He was appointed in October, 1915, to the command of the British Forces in Serbia. This photograph was taken outside his headquarters. General Mahon was formerly in charge of the 10th Irish Division on the western front.

the year. When, in December, 1915, Sir John French returned to England Sir Douglas Haig was chosen as his successor. Comparatively he was a young man, and this was not the least of the points in his favour, for on him the hopes of Britons were set.

Sir Horace Lockwood Smith-Dorrien was born in 1858, and entered the Sherwood Foresters when he was eighteen. Three years later he received his baptism of fire in the Zulu War, and he served under Sir Garnet Wolseley in Egypt. In 1884 he was in the Nile Expedition, and in 1885 and 1886 he fought in the Sudan. In the 'nineties he was in the force that marched to the relief of Chitral and in the one that fought the Tirah Campaign. In 1898 he was again in the Sudan.

Except for a year or two on the Staff in India, Smith-Dorrien had been all his life with the Sherwood Foresters, rising step by step until, when the Boer War broke out, he was colonel of one of its battalions. He took this to South Africa and soon **Sir Horace** attracted attention by his ability as a **Smith-Dorrien** leader. He commanded the brigade which took the leading part in the Battle of Paardeberg, and led a column during the later stages of the war.

His work in South Africa being finished, he passed six years in an Indian command. In 1907 he returned to England and was chosen Commander-in-Chief at Aldershot, where he made himself remarkably popular with the men, and in 1912 he was transferred to take over the Southern Command at Salisbury.

When the Great War began, Sir Horace was not chosen to go abroad. The Second Army Corps was sent out under Sir James M. Grierson. However, Grierson died in the train a day or two after reaching France, and Smith-Dorrien was sent out to take his place.

The Second Corps was under Smith-Dorrien when the fighting began, and during the retreat it had the harder task. Against heavy odds it fought the Battle of Le Cateau, and its general's services on that critical day won the very highest praise from Sir John French. The passage has often been quoted, but it will bear reproduction: " I say without hesitation that the saving of the left wing of the army under my command on the morning of August 26th could never have been accomplished unless a commander of rare and unusual coolness, intrepidity and determination had been present personally to conduct the operations."

Sir Horace led his troops through the fierce autumn

Sir Herbert
Plumer

fighting until after the Battle of Ypres it was exhausted by the enormous losses it had suffered. It was then given a rest, while reinforcements were sent out to bring it up to strength again; with these it was again ready for the front early in 1915. About this time the corps were grouped in armies, and Smith-Dorrien took command of the Second Army.

Sir Horace superintended the demonstrations made by the Second Army at the Battle of Neuve Chapelle, but the next that was heard of him was that he had returned home. In December, 1915, it was announced that he had been appointed to the supreme command in East Africa. He arrived at Cape Town on January 12th, 1916.

Sir Herbert Charles Onslow Plumer, who took Smith-Dorrien's place, was fifty-eight years old, and like most of our general officers, had made his reputation during the Boer War. He entered the York and Lancaster Regiment in 1876 and was in the Sudan in 1884. In 1896, when there was trouble in Bechuanaland, he raised a regiment of mounted rifles, and he was in Rhodesia when the Boer War broke out. With a force of about 1,000 men he pressed northwards to the relief of Mafeking, and this difficult operation first made his name known to the British public.

The war being over, Plumer, then a major-general, returned to England, and in a little while became Quartermaster-General. Later he held various commands at home, and in 1914 he was in charge of the northern district at York. Since 1906 he had been Sir Herbert Plumer, K.C.B.

During the earlier months of the Great War Plumer remained in England busily occupied in training men, until early in 1915 he was sent out as commander of a new Army Corps numbered the Fifth. This was put into Smith-Dorrien's Second Army, and on March 14th and 15th it took the leading part in the fighting at St. Eloi.

This was just a baptism of fire; but Sir Herbert's conduct must have commended itself to Sir John French, for in April he took over the command of the Second Army, which he led during the Second Battle of Ypres. He had then very much the same task as the one which had fallen to Sir Douglas Haig in the previous November, and his dispositions, together with the courage of his men, were successful in checking the German rush. His " fine defence of Ypres " was mentioned by Sir John French.

HISTORIC INCIDENT IN THE DARDANELLES.

General d'Amade about to disembark from H.M.S. Lord Nelson after visiting Admiral de Robeck. The band was playing the " Marseillaise," and the admiral, officers and men stood at the salute. The first photograph is of General Gouraud, successor to General d'Amade in command of the French Expedition against the Turks. General Gouraud was severely wounded on Gallipoli in July, 1915, and succeeded by General Bailloud.

The fourth of our Army leaders bears a name which, before the Great War, was quite unknown to the general public. Charles Carmichael Monro was born in 1860, and entered the Royal West Surrey Regiment in 1879. He saw service on the Indian Frontier in 1897 and 1898, and, of course, in South Africa, where he was on the Staff. In military circles he was chiefly known as a musketry expert, and he was made Chief Instructor and then Commandant of the School of Musketry at Hythe. From 1912 until he was sent to France he commanded one of the London Divisions.

As one of Sir Douglas Haig's chief lieutenants, General Monro made his reputation. He led his Division through the thickest of the fighting from August to November, and during the Battle of Ypres he was knocked unconscious by a shell. Early in 1915 he succeeded Haig as commander of the First Army Corps, and he directed its operations throughout the spring and summer. A **Sir Charles** little later, when the Third Army **Monro** was formed, Monro, by then a K.C.B., was chosen to command it. And then came a surprise.

In October it was announced that Sir Ian Hamilton was returning from Gallipoli, and that his successor would be Sir Charles Monro, who left at once for the Near East, and reached Salonika in November. He superintended the successful withdrawal of our troops from the Peninsula, and then returned to Flanders to succeed Sir Douglas Haig as Commander of the First Army. Evidently the new British Commander-in-Chief had a high opinion of Sir Charles's abilities, and his future was watched with interest. He belongs to the type of general associated with Wellington's campaigns in Spain, and these were among the best that Britain has ever produced.

In the war against Turkey the names of three other prominent generals claim notice. Sir John Eccles Nixon, K.C.B., was, like French and Hamilton, one of our commanders-in-chief during the Great War From April 9th, 1915, when he succeeded Lieut.-General Sir Arthur A. Barrett, K.C.B., till January, 1916, when he also retired from the command on account of ill-health, he directed the operations against the Turks in Mesopotamia. General Nixon was born in 1857 and, having entered the 18th Bengal Lancers, went through the Afghan War of 1879-80 and various expeditions on the Indian Frontier. In the Boer War he led a cavalry brigade, and after his return to India he commanded at Meerut and Peshawar, becoming finally head of the Southern Army. He was responsible for the British victory at Shaiba and for the advance on Bagdad. His successor was Lieut.-General Sir Percy Lake, Chief of the General Staff in India.

General Barrett, who was in command in Mesopotamia before General Nixon's arrival, was a man of like age. He had marched with Roberts to Kandahar, and had been in many expeditions on the Indian Frontier before he was made Adjutant-General in India in 1909. When the Great War broke out he was commanding at Poona. Chosen to lead the Indian Expeditionary Force, he arrived in Mesopotamia in November, and was responsible for the first Turkish defeats and the capture of Basra and Kurna. His principal assistants were Walter S. Delamain, William H. Dobbie, and Charles I. Fry.

During the Great War Sir John French had in turn two Chiefs of the Staff, and their responsibilities can hardly be exaggerated. The first was Sir Archibald J. Murray, who had served in the South African War with his regiment, the Royal Inniskilling Fusiliers, and was there severely wounded. Afterwards he filled high positions at home, including those of Director of Military Training and Inspector of Infantry, and he was Chief of the General Staff when war broke out. He went to the front with Sir John French, who spoke very highly of his services in his first despatch, and he remained there until early in 1915. In October, Murray succeeded another general of the

GENERAL GALLIÉNI.

Appointed French Minister of War in succession to M. Millerand in October, 1915. General Galliéni was invested with the responsibility of the Paris defences on the outbreak of war, and under his supervision many notable improvements were made to strengthen the city against a siege.

same name—Sir J. Wolfe Murray—as Chief of the Imperial General Staff, and in December he was sent to succeed Sir Charles Monro as British Commander in the Near East.

As Murray's successor French selected Sir William Robertson, who had entered the Army as a private, and had obtained a commission in the 3rd Dragoon Guards in 1888. He served as an intelligence officer in India and South Africa, and was severely wounded during the Chitral Campaign. After 1902 he was on the Staff at Aldershot, Commandant of the Staff College, and Director of Military Training, so he should know something about war.

In August, 1914, Robertson went to France as Quartermaster-General. During the retreat from Mons his duties were especially onerous, for it was not easy to provide for the wants of an army which was marching in the wrong direction. However, he **Sir William** met " the almost insuperable difficulties " **Robertson** with his characteristic energy, skill, and determination, so Sir John French said, and it was " largely owing to his exertions that the hardships and sufferings of the troops—inseparable from such operations—were not much greater."

Robertson entered upon his new duties just before the Battle of Neuve Chapelle in March, and in describing this Sir John spoke of his " able and devoted assistance " in arranging the operations. Some of the credit for the successful stand at Ypres and for the advance of Loos must also be given to him. In December General Robertson returned to London to succeed Sir A. J. Murray as Chief of the Imperial General Staff.

As Chief of his new Staff Sir Douglas Haig chose Major-General L. E. Kiggell, a name unknown to the general

GENERAL JAMES G. KING-KING, D.S.O.
Standing between two members of his Staff, before his headquarters in the Balkans. The house was constructed with mud and sticks.

public, although not to students of war. Kiggell served in South Africa, and was afterwards Director of Staff Duties, Commandant of the Staff College, and Director of Military Training, while he also filled the position of Professor of Military History and Strategy at the Staff College. With his wide knowledge of the science of war he seemed just the man to beat the Germans in the subject in which hitherto they had excelled all others.

A word may be said here about the Sub-Chief of the General Staff, Sir Henry Hughes Wilson, K.C.B., who entered the Rifle Brigade in 1884. He was wounded in Burma and served in South Africa, but much of his military life was passed in Staff work. For three years he was Commandant of the Staff College, and for four years before the war Director of Military Operations. During it, he served as chief assistant both to General Murray and General Robertson, and for his services was made a knight. No officer won more golden opinions in the war.

As Chief of the Staff in Gallipoli, Sir Ian Hamilton had Major-General Sir W. P. Braithwaite, an officer who had served for many years in India, becoming **Major-General** finally head of the Staff College at Quetta. **Braithwaite** Sir Ian's opinion of his services is unmistakable. He was " the best Chief of the General Staff it has ever been my fortune to encounter in war. I will not pile epithets upon him."

The Adjutant-General in France in 1914-15 was Sir Cecil F. N. Macready, K.C.B., a man then fifty-two years old. He was a Gordon Highlander, and served with his regiment in Egypt in 1882, and during the Boer War. He remained in South Africa after the war was over, and then joined the General Staff in London. More than once Sir John French spoke highly of his services at the front. Finally, Robertson's successor as Quartermaster-General was Sir Ronald Charles Maxwell, K.C.B.

To command his army corps Sir John French had a number of able generals. The First Corps, after being led by Haig and Monro, was given to Hubert de la Poer Gough,

a member of a distinguished military family, and the son and brother of generals who had won the V.C. Gough entered the 16th Lancers in 1889, served with that regiment in South Africa, and in 1901 became its colonel. He was in command of the 3rd Cavalry Brigade in August, 1914, and he took this to the front, where his rise was rapid. Soon he was in charge of a division, and just before the Battle of Loos he had taken command of the First Corps. According to Sir John French, he soon proved himself to be a cavalry leader " of a high order."

Smith-Dorrien's successor as commander of the Second Corps was Sir Charles Fergusson, a Scottish baronet, the seventh **Sir Charles Fergusson** of his line. He was one of the very few British generals who had not served in the South African War, for during that time he was with the Egyptian Army. He returned to England in 1904 to command a battalion of his old regiment, the Grenadier Guards, and from 1909 to 1913 was Inspector of Infantry. He took the 5th Division, which he was then commanding, from Ireland to France, and this had a very bad time in the retreat. However, Fergusson managed to get it away, and his " great skill and tenacity " in maintaining a difficult position at the Battle of the Aisne were praised by Sir John French. Throughout the spring and summer of 1915 he remained in charge of the Second Corps.

MAJ.-GEN. BRAITHWAITE.
Chief of Sir Ian Hamilton's General Staff on Gallipoli.

For the whole of the first year of war, the Third Corps had only one leader, Sir William Pulteney Pulteney, who started his career in the Scots Guards. He was at Tel-el-Kebir, and served through the South African War. In 1914 he was commanding the 6th Division, and when the Third Corps was made up of that division and the 4th, he was selected to lead it. During the Battle of the Marne Pulteney " showed himself to be a most capable commander in the field," and at Ypres the success of his men in repulsing constant attacks, made in great strength, was partly due to " the skilful manner in which the corps was disposed by its commander." For his services Pulteney was made a knight.

The Fourth Corps, too, only had one commanding officer during the same period, Sir Henry Seymour Rawlinson, Bart. Rawlinson had served in Burma, in the Sudan, and in South Africa, first in the 60th Rifles, and then in the Coldstream Guards, and had been in charge of the Staff College and afterwards of the 3rd Division. As everyone knows, he was sent out in command of the incomplete Fourth Corps when Antwerp was in danger, and in a few weeks constant fighting reduced it to a shadow. Early in 1915 it was re-formed as a complete corps, and was one of the two selected to storm Neuve Chapelle. There, one of the brigades of its 8th Division had a cruel experience in front of some unbroken barbed-wire, and two days later its 7th Division had one almost as saddening.

Rawlinson's reputation suffered as a consequence of Neuve Chapelle. Sir John French stated in his despatch that " the difficulties above enumerated might have been overcome at an earlier period of the day if the general officer commanding the Fourth Corps had been able to bring his reserve brigades more speedily into action." However, he retained his command, and his corps took a leading part in the attack on Festubert. Later, it distinguished itself at the capture of Loos.

The Fifth Corps passed from Sir Herbert Plumer to Sir Edward Henry Hynman Allenby, K.C.B. Born in 1861, Allenby began his military life in the famous Royal Inniskilling Dragoons, and served in Zululand and the Boer War. Then he became colonel of the 5th Lancers and general of a cavalry brigade. At the outbreak of war he was Inspector of Cavalry, and he was in charge of the British cavalry at Mons. He soon earned Sir John French's commendation, and when the cavalry were organised in a corps he took command of it. His men served like the infantry in the trenches, and about the end of April Allenby succeeded Plumer as commander of the Fifth Corps. In June he directed a successful attack on the Bellewaarde Ridge near Ypres, and in September his corps did good work at Loos. So meritorious were his services about this time that he was chosen to succeed Sir Charles Monro in command of the Third Army.

Allenby's successor as leader of the Cavalry Corps was Sir Julian Hedworth George Byng, a son of the Earl of Strafford. In 1883 he entered the 10th Hussars, and after serving in the Sudan and South Africa rose to be colonel of his regiment. He commanded a brigade and later a division, and from 1909 to 1912 he held a high command in Egypt. Early in October, 1914, Byng went to Belgium in command of the 3rd Cavalry Division, and his men saw some very hard fighting indeed around Ypres. Byng's " eminent services " were constantly brought to Sir John French's notice by Sir Douglas Haig, and his reward came when he was chosen to lead the Cavalry Corps.

The Indian Army Corps was under Sir James Willcocks, a veteran soldier with a long record of service in Afghanistan, the Sudan, Burma, the Indian Frontier, and especially West Africa. In 1900 he led the Ashanti Field Force to the relief of Coomassie, and for this deed received the freedom of the City of London. In 1914 he was the commander of India's Northern Army, and in **Sir James Willcocks** charge of the Indian Corps he reached France in October. In January he directed an attack on the German position at Givenchy, which was not very successful, but at Neuve Chapelle the Indians did excellent work, and something also was due to Sir James for keeping their martial ardour aflame in the trying conditions of a European winter with its endless wet and cold. When he retired later in the year his place was taken by Sir Charles A. Anderson, hitherto one of his lieutenants. Finally, the Sixth Corps, formed about July, was commanded by Sir John L. Keir, K.C.B., who had taken the 6th Division to the front in the previous September, and had led it successfully since then.

Among the most distinguished of all the corps commanders were the two who served under Sir Ian Hamilton in Gallipoli—Birdwood and Hunter-Weston. Sir William Riddell Birdwood, henceforth known to fame as the " Soul of Anzac," was born in 1865, and passed nearly the whole of his military life in India. In South Africa he was severely wounded, and after his return to India he acted as Military Secretary to Lord Kitchener, Quartermaster-General, and then Military Secretary to the Government. From the desk Birdwood went straight to the field. He took command of the Australian and New Zealand troops in Egypt, and under him they landed in Gallipoli. His powers of leadership and resource were fully proved during the anxious days that followed, and the dauntless courage and unfailing cheerfulness of his men were largely due to his example. A wound which he received did not keep him out of the field, and before Monro's arrival he acted as temporary Commander-in-Chief.

By this time many people have forgotten the name of the major of Engineers who assisted Lord Roberts' march to Pretoria in March, 1901, by blowing up an important railway culvert. It was **Birdwood and** Aylmer Hunter-Weston, who afterwards **Hunter-Weston** served Sir John French as Chief of his Staff. He had previously been in several of the campaigns on the Indian frontier, and after 1908 he held high positions at home—Assistant Director of Military Training and Commander of the 11th Infantry Brigade—and in August, 1914, he took his brigade to the front. After distinguishing himself at Ypres, Hunter-Weston was chosen to command

[*Elliott & Fry.*

LIEUT.-GENERAL SIR PERCY H. N. LAKE, K.C.M.G., K.C.B. Sir Percy Lake's succession to Sir John Nixon as Commander-in-Chief of the British Forces in Mesopotamia was announced on January 11th, 1916. From 1912 to January, 1916, he had been Chief of the General Staff in India.

the Immortal 29th Division proceeding to Gallipoli, and during the landings there and the subsequent attacks his abilities were severely tested. However, he came through the ordeal with credit, and showed that he had "very special qualifications as a commander of troops in the field." Later he was invalided home, but this was only a pause in his career.

A name which cannot be omitted is that of the Canadian leader, Edwin Alfred Hervey Alderson. He went through the Boer War of 1881, the Egyptian War of 1882, and the Nile Campaign of 1884-85. In 1896 he commanded some mounted infantry in Mashonaland, and he did the same during the Boer War, while from 1903 to 1912 he held various commands in England and India. In 1914 Alderson was selected to command the Canadian Division, and with it he reached the front early in 1915. He pulled it together after its terrible experiences at the Second Battle of Ypres, and showed himself a most capable leader throughout.

A long list of brave men remains, and about them, too, a great deal could be said. Among them were cavalry leaders such as Michael Francis Rimington, whose knowledge of South Africa enabled him to raise a body of scouts or guides at the beginning of the Boer War. When

THE CIVILIAN HEAD OF FRANCE WITH THE MILITARY LEADERS.
M. Raymond Poincaré, President of the French Republic, studying a map near the firing-line during a visit to the French front.

the Great War began he was Inspector of Cavalry in India, and as leader of the Indian Cavalry Corps he took part in the fighting in Flanders. Other cavalry generals were Sir Philip W. Chetwode, the first man to be mentioned in Sir John French's first despatch, and Charles T. McM. Kavanagh, whose "personal bravery and dash" were cited at the Battle of Ypres. Both won the D.S.O. in South Africa, and both went to France at the head of brigades of cavalry. So also did C. J. Briggs, H. de B. de Lisle, and the Hon. C. E. Bingham.

Among generals of division, Sir Thomas D'Oyly Snow earned a foremost place. He hurried up **Other leaders of** his Division, the 4th, to protect the re-**distinction** treat from Mons, and his work during the Second Battle of Ypres was singled out for special mention. Other generals who commanded divisions with distinction were Sir H. F. M. Wilson, J. A. L. Haldane, and R. C. B. Haking. Sir A. J. Godley, the leader of the New Zealanders, was Birdwood's assistant in Gallipoli, and Sir W. Douglas led there the heroic Division of Lancashire Territorials. The Divisions of the Indian Corps were commanded by Sir C. A. Anderson and H. B. B. Watkis, the former being an artillery officer who had

served on the Indian frontier and commanded troops in China. Another leader of proved resource was Sir Bryan Mahon, the reliever of Mafeking, who commanded the British contingent in Greece.

Of the younger generals, those still nearer to the firing-line, it is perhaps invidious to mention only one or two, but certainly the Earl of Cavan, Edward S. Bulfin, and F. C. Shaw made reputations as leaders. Lord Cavan, an Irish peer, led the Brigade of Guards in some of the hardest fighting of the war. On many occasions he was conspicuous "for the skill, coolness, and courage with which he led his troops, and for the successful manner in which he dealt **Generals who fell** with many critical situations." At the **on the field** head of the 2nd Brigade, General Bulfin went through the thick of the fighting until November 2nd, when he was rather severely wounded.

Sir David Henderson, the head of the Flying Corps, was another general who did excellent work, to which Sir John French repeatedly drew attention ; and so did Surgeon-General Sir A. T. Sloggett, the chief of the Medical Corps. Artillery leaders mentioned included Brigadier-Generals F. D. V. Wing, G. F. Milne, D.S.O., and J. E. W. Headlam. The Chief Engineer, Brigadier-General G. H. Fowke, has also performed services as valuable as any.

Finally, some mention should be made of the generals who fell on the field of battle, for the Great War took toll of them as it did of humbler men. General Hubert I. W. Hamilton, a brother of Sir Bruce Hamilton, and the commander of the 3rd Division, was killed by the explosion of a shell near La Bassée, on October 14th, 1914. The 1st Division and later the 7th also lost their leaders, as Samuel Holt Lomax, of the former, was wounded at Ypres on October 31st, 1914, and died in London in the following April ; and Sir Thompson Capper, of the latter, was killed at Loos on September 26th. All three had risen from one rank to another in infantry regiments, had served in various wars, and were able and useful generals in the field. Another loss to the Army was the death of Brigadier - General John E. Gough, V.C., a brother of Hubert Gough, and a son of the late General Sir Charles Gough, V.C., who died of wounds on February 22nd, 1915. He had won his V.C. in Somaliland, and had also fought in South Africa. John Gough was on the Staff, and had a good deal to do with planning the attack on Neuve Chapelle. Speaking of his services, Sir John French said he regarded him as "one of our most promising military leaders of the future." After his death he was made a K.C.B.

Another general who had earned the V.C. was killed during the war. This was Brigadier-General C. Fitzclarence, one of the defenders of Mafeking, and a descendant of William IV. He fell at the head of the 1st Brigade at Ypres on November 11th, 1914. Two Divisions, in addition to the 7th, lost their leaders during the Battle of Loos. G. H. Thesiger, C.M.G., commanding the 9th, was killed on September 27th, and F. D. V. Wing, C.B., of the 12th, on October 2nd. N. D. Findlay, of the Artillery, was the first general killed during the war. Two brigadiers, Julian Hasler and J. F. Riddell, fell during the Second Battle of Ypres, the latter while leading a brigade of Territorials, and a little later the Army lost two others, A. W. G. Lowry-Cole and G. C. Nugent.

The expedition to Gallipoli cost many valuable lives. One of these was that of William T. Bridges, the Australian leader. Brigadier-General H. E. Napier was killed during the fight for the landing, and Brigadier-General Noel Lee died of wounds a little later. To the dead honour, and to the living trust ; so did Britain and France feel towards the leaders of their armies in the field.

British airman dropping a wreath on a comrade's grave in the German lines.

All eyes on skycraft: British cavalry and French gunners contemplate the winged enemy.

Belgian observation balloon ascending to search the horizon for German artillery positions.

Observation post fitted with instruments for gauging the height and speed of enemy aircraft, a giant searchlight, a listening post, and a "75" gun installed round Paris.

TYPE OF BRITISH SEAPLANE

CHAPTER XCVI.

TAKING THE WATER.

THE AERIAL WAR ALONG THE WESTERN FRONT.

By G. Valentine Williams, Author of "With Our Army in Flanders."

How the Airmen Dispelled "the Fog of War"—Tactical and Strategical Scouting by Aircraft—Aerial Photography that Revolutionised Warfare by Revealing the Enemy's Dispositions and Intentions—Air Raids Generally Organised on Information Obtained by Aerial Reconnaissance—Aeroplanes more Effective against Zeppelins than Anti-Aircraft Guns—The Self-Sacrificing Heroism of the Pioneers of Aerial Combats—Martyrs in the Cause of Man's Ever-Growing Ascendancy in the Air—General Joffre's Thanks and Praise for the Efficiency of the Royal Flying Corps, which Flew an Average of Two Thousand Miles a Day during the First Months of the War—British and French the Best Airmen though they Learnt from the Germans—Enemy Aeroplanes Armed with Captured Canadian Guns—Thrilling Individual Exploits by British Aviators—Inciting the Indian Troops to Revolt by Pamphlets dropped from German Aeroplanes—A British Airman's Attempt to Bomb the Kaiser—How the Air Service Helped the British Victory at Neuve Chapelle—A British Aviator's Amazing Sang-froid—All Records for Daily Mileage Eclipsed Prior to the Great Advance on Loos—The Destructive Air Attack on the Railway Junction at Valenciennes—Braving Death in Many Forms in the Frailest of Craft—Some Heroes of the Royal Flying Corps who Lost their Lives but Won the Airman's Honourable Epitaph : "He Made his Report"—The British Aviator who Lived with the German Troops—Enemy's Respect for our Aerial Prowess—Discretion the Better Part of German Valour in the Air—Fighting in the Clouds at Five to One—Flying Corps Casualties Small in Proportion to their Immeasurably Valuable Services—German Chivalry towards' the Royal Flying Corps Born of the Freemasonry of the Air—British Airmen Prisoners not Treated Harshly—The Splendid Work of the Naval Wing of the Royal Flying Corps—Their Daring and Successful Raids.

THOSE who, less than half a dozen years ago, crowded to the flying meetings and watched with fascination those gallant pioneers of aviation—the Wrights, Blériot, Hubert Latham, Bertram Dickson, Colonel Cody, and the rest—disporting themselves in space, little guessed that they were assisting at the development of a science which was calculated to affect war more deeply than any invention since the magazine rifle. For the aeroplane has revolutionised warfare. Its effect has been more far-reaching than even the most sanguine supporter of the new arm ever dared to prophesy.

Curiously enough, however, its usefulness has not laid along the lines foretold by its disciples in the past. The aeroplane has not taken the place of troops as a weapon of attack. Its enormous importance lies in its functions as a scout. It has done away for ever with "the fog of war." It has become the eyes of the army. By means of it the commanders, working undisturbed with their maps and telephones and wireless at their headquarters far in the rear, are able to spy out the enemy's movements, to see deep back into the enemy's country. It is on account of the revolutionising influence that the development of aerial reconnaissance has had on warfare that, when the time comes for the lessons of this, the greatest of all wars, to be reckoned up, the arm which will emerge as the most important innovation in the history of war will undoubtedly be the aeroplane. Reconnaissance falls roughly into two branches—(a) tactical and (b) strategical. Tactical reconnaissance aims at the gathering of information upon which the tactics of the army may be based— that is to say, information of the enemy's dispositions and movements in a limited area of the front, close behind the firing - line. Strategical reconnaissance, on the other hand, is undertaken with an eye to the strategy of the army, therefore, rather for the purposes of the General Staff, and is on a more extensive scale, penetrating much farther into the enemy's country, for the purpose of getting more general information regarding the whole of the enemy activity in a particular part of the theatre of war.

AT THE AVIATION HEADQUARTERS IN FRANCE.
British aeroplane about to start on a reconnaissance over the enemy lines.

DESTRUCTION OF AN AERIAL CRUISER IN "PORT": THE BURNING ZEPPELIN SHED AT EVERE AFTER THE BRITISH RAID.

The exploit of Flight-Lieuts. J. P. Wilson, R.N., and J. S. Mills, R.N., who on June 7th, 1915—the same day that Lieut. Warneford destroyed a Zeppelin in the air near Ghent—successfully bombed and destroyed Zeppelin LZ 38 in its shed at Evere, north of Brussels, was a legitimate military raid and a just reprisal for the deliberate murder of women and children by Count Zeppelin's aerial cruisers. It also proved that the German dirigibles, when their "ports," could be located, were extremely vulnerable to bomb attack. Making a long flight in the dark, over territory occupied by the enemy, the two daring aviators dropped their bombs on the shed that lodged the Zeppelin, observed the flames that burst out from both sides, reach to a great height, and then flew safely back to the British lines, although exposed to heavy fire from German anti-aircraft guns. In this illustration is depicted the scene after the British raid. To the left are some Belgians watching the burning ruins; to the right are German anti-aircraft guns, one mounted on an armoured car, and stretcher-bearers about to collect the killed and wounded.

354

Tactical and strategical reconnaissances form the bulk of the work of the airman at the front. On tactical reconnaissance, undertaken with a specific objective, or consisting merely of trips to and fro over a stated strip of the front in order to observe anything of interest, his aim will be to look out for any change in the clear-cut line of the trenches, indicative of the laying out of fresh lines or communication trenches, to keep his eyes open for reliefs or any movement behind the lines, to divine the strength of the enemy at the part of the line in question by the number of transport columns seen ; to watch the railheads for signs of unusual activity, to locate hostile batteries and Staff headquarters. In this reconnaissance work photography plays a very great rôle. Aerial photographs, which were extensively taken by the airmen of the British, French, and German armies, reveal even more clearly than the human eye can focus the lines of trenches. It is by means of these photographs that many of the army maps are made.

Strategical reconnaissance takes the airman farther afield, right into the enemy's country, where above important military centres, railway junctions, airship sheds, camps, etc., much may be gathered of supreme importance to those who are engaged in patiently framing the jig-saw puzzle of the enemy's dispositions and intentions as a basis for the strategy of the supreme command.

Part and parcel of this daily reconnaissance work is the duty known as "spotting for the guns." Day by day, in all weathers, save in rain and fog, which are the only protection that modern armies enjoy from prying eyes in the air, the aeroplanes sally forth to hover over some point in the enemy lines which is to be the objective of the artillery, to watch the effect of the shells, and to signal back by wireless or smoke signals the result. An important part of this artillery work is the "spotting" of suitable objectives for the artillery (villages occupied by troops, an ammunition depôt, a supply park, etc.), and also the location of hostile batteries.

Aerial raids for destructive purposes do not form part of the daily programme of the military airman. Air raids are generally organised on information obtained by aerial reconnaissance showing the location of some suitable objective, such as an enemy flying-ground, or a Staff headquarters, or reporting activity at some railhead or military centre. Thereupon a bombing squadron is sent out, escorted by swift scouts to repel aerial attacks by the enemy on the slower bomb-carrying machines, to pour down a rain of destruction on the point to be attacked, and afterwards to return as swiftly as may be to its home aerodrome.

When military operations are in progress, the activity in the air increases. At such a time it is essential for the army command to be kept exactly and promptly informed of the precise strength of the enemy at given points, and of the location and disposition of his reserves. Every move is preceded by days of incessant flying on the part of the airmen reconnoitring or raiding strategic points in the enemy lines. Once the move has started, in addition to the aeroplanes which are out from dawn to dusk "spotting" for the guns, others are despatched on bombing expeditions against the enemy lines of communication, to destroy the railway, to blow up trains and bridges —in short, to do everything possible to delay the bringing up of reinforcements.

Before a great attack

Finally, the aeroplane has come to be regarded as the most efficient defence against hostile aircraft. Therefore, aeroplanes are employed day after day to chase off the enemy airmen who sally forth over the lines on reconnaissances or bombing raids. In 1915, London awakened to the fact that the aeroplane, properly utilised, is a more effective source of protection against Zeppelin raiders than any number of anti-aircraft guns, and on the rare occasions that hostile airships ventured forth over the towns and villages in the British zone of operations in France and Belgium, our aeroplanes drove the invader off before he had time to inflict any great damage.

In the vast and unprecedented military effort which this war demanded of the British people, nothing demonstrated more strikingly the adaptability of our race than the development of military airmanship. When the war broke out, next to nothing was known about the practical uses of the aeroplane in war. Its utility had been surmised and tested as far as might be under peace conditions, but it stands to reason that nothing could be known of such things as the effect of anti-aircraft projectiles on aeroplanes, or the tactics of aerial combats.

History and the aviator

All this the British airman had to find out for himself. Every pilot became a cog of the great organisation of the Flying Service. Every flight undertaken over the enemy lines added its quota to the store of experience of active service upon which the whole tactics of aerial warfare had to be based. Of no man who has laid down his life on the altar of the Motherland in the service of the Royal Flying Corps can it be said that he died in vain. Every man of

THE MOMENT BEFORE GILBERT'S LAST FLIGHT.
M. Gilbert, second from the right, discussing plans for his attack on the Zeppelin sheds at Friedrichshaven in June, 1915. Unfortunately he was compelled to descend, through engine trouble, on Swiss territory, and was interned in the " Island of Peace."

the gallant dead of the R.F.C. is as truly a martyr as any doctor who ever sacrificed his life in the cause of science. And history, when it eulogises the ever-growing ascendancy of man in the air, shall pay a tribute to the self-sacrificing heroism of the gallant airmen who lie buried beneath the broken propeller—the noble tombstone of the airman who falls on the field of honour—on the blood-soaked fields of France and Belgium and the Gallipoli Peninsula.

On the night of September 9th, 1914, at the height of the Battle of the Marne, General Joffre, the French Generalissimo, sent the following message to the French Mission with the British Expeditionary Force:

Please express most particularly to Marshal French my thanks for the services daily rendered by the British Flying Corps. The precision, exactitude, and regularity of the British airmen's reports are evidence of their perfect organisation, and also of the perfect training of pilots and observers.

It was a first tribute to the amazing efficiency of the British Air Service, which came as a complete surprise to all the belligerents. It was the British military airmen who discovered Von Kluck's famous swing-round from his

AN AIR DUEL IN PROGRESS.
British observer using an automatic gun against a German Albatross machine. What looks like a horizontal cog-wheel is the drum of cartridges feeding a Lewis gun, and on the right, falling rapidly into the car, are the expended cases. The gunner's right hand firmly grasps the trigger handle, while the left holds the spade grip controlling the weapon.

perhaps vain to debate whether or not the German air service showed itself the better versed in aerial strategy and tactics on the outbreak of war. It is probably true to say that the German fliers, on first taking the field, showed that they had made a profound study of the whole theory of the tactical employment of the aeroplane in war, and that the Allies had still something to learn from them as far as theory went. But the French and British were the better airmen, and they lost no time in learning the game, and establishing that mastery of the air which they very steadily increased as the war progressed. Moreover, in certain points, the British were far ahead of the enemy, notably in aerial photography and in the arming of aeroplanes. The Germans made great efforts to improve their aerial photographs, which were of incalculable value to the Intelligence, but they remained still far behind the British, while in default of a light and efficient automatic gun for aeroplane work the Germans after a while used Canadian Colt guns, captured in the gas attack at the Second Battle of Ypres.

Reconnaissance being the first rôle of usefulness of the aeroplane in war, the British airmen were primarily employed at Mons, during the retreat, and on the Marne and the Aisne, on strategical and tactical reconnaissance work, the scope and object of which have been already explained. But before the war settled down to the long period of siege warfare, operations in the open offered our airmen opportunities which they were not slow to grasp. Raids were frequently made on German camps and supply depôts. On one occasion, while the Army was advancing from the Marne, an incendiary bomb was successfully exploded right in the centre of a German bivouac, and on another day, a high-explosive bomb dropped on a column of German cavalry, hit an ammunition waggon, and killed fifteen men outright, besides wounding many others. By the end of the second week in September our airmen had shot five German fliers in the air, and brought their machines to earth. Before the British Expeditionary Force had reached the Aisne, it was already possible to speak of the mastery of the British military airmen over the Germans.

Mastery from the beginning

These were the early days of the war, but, though our airmen were almost in the learning stage, they showed themselves the possessors of all that infinite resource and glorious courage which still distinguish them now that they have perfected and mastered the whole theory of aviation in war. Thus in September, 1914, a pilot and observer of the Royal Flying Corps were forced by engine trouble to

march on Paris to the south-east, and by their timely intimation of this change of direction enabled the Allies to make in season those dispositions which inflicted on the Germans the great decisive defeat of the war.

Our air scouts had little rest during those days of ceaseless marching, of relentless fighting. During a period of twenty days up to September 10th, 1914, a daily average of more than nine reconnaissance flights of over one hundred miles each, was maintained by our airmen in France. How their efficiency increased with practice under actual conditions of war is shown by the fact that up to September 21st of the same year the total air mileage accomplished by our airmen since the beginning of the war amounted to 87,000 miles, an average of 2,000 miles per day, 1,400 hours representing the total time spent in the air.

In view of the indubitable ascendancy which our airmen established over the German military fliers, it is

MR. CHARLES BRIGHT.
Member of the Aeronautical Institute, who did much to expedite aircraft production.

PROFESSOR G. H. BRYAN, Sc.D., R.F.S.
The well-known authority on mathematics, thermodynamics, and flight.

[Portraits: Elliott & Fry.

MR. L. B. DESBLEDS.
Another prominent member of the Aeronautical Institute.

land in the enemy lines. They sprang out of their machine and bolted for cover to a small wood. The Germans lost no time in possessing themselves of the British aeroplane, but failed to find the prisoners, who eventually managed to creep away under cover of darkness to the steep banks of the Aisne. Here they cast away their Flying Corps field-boots, and descending to the water, swam across in the dark, and reached their aerodrome in safety, but barefoot.

A little later one of our most successful military airmen was out scouting in a single-seater monoplane when he came across a German machine. Being alone, he had no rifle, so promptly manœuvred his monoplane so as to get in a revolver shot at the enemy. As he was mounting above the German, the German observer winged him with a well-aimed rifle shot. The Briton never lost his presence of mind, but turned and flew for home, landing in our lines,

with the propeller behind the driving seat), which he recognised to be an Otto machine. At first sight, therefore, he was able to make two important observations—namely, that he had the advantage of speed, and that his adversary, owing to the position of his propeller, could not fire from behind. The Briton had two rifles clamped down one on either side of his engine, and at once started out after the enemy, taking good care to keep well in the latter's wake. At sixty yards' range he opened fire without any apparent result; then, as his speed was bearing him past his opponent, he turned and came back and gave the Boche the contents of the other rifle. The German wavered and began to descend. **A thrilling aerial combat** The British airman's rifles were empty. He was alone. He had no one to reload. Depressing the elevating plane, he planed down at a dizzy angle, and was thus able to take his hands off his steering wheel for a moment and recharge his weapons. The rifles jammed, but the airman managed to cram four cartridges home, and loosed them off at the stern of his adversary, who a minute later disappeared in a swelling cloud-bank. The Briton instantly dropped steeply down through the sky after him, but in the clear azure below could see no trace of his enemy, who must have come to earth in the French lines over which they had been manœuvring. The Germans made a number of spasmodic raids with isolated aeroplanes on towns in our zone of operations. They

A LESSON IN MOBILITY.
French "75" gun elevated against enemy aircraft on an improvised platform consisting of an old gun-carriage.

close to a motor-ambulance, which carried him off to the nearest dressing station.

The importance of the position of the propeller in an enemy machine is seen in the following account of a thrilling aerial combat which took place between a British and a German airman on the Aisne. One of our airmen, who was flying a speedy scout, caught up with a German biplane of the "pusher" type (i.e.,

"ARCHIE" AMONG THE SAND-DUNES.
German anti-aircraft machine-guns, or "Archies," as our R.F.C. called them, in action against British aviators flying over the enemy lines in Belgium.

357

GERMAN OBSERVATION BALLOON ABOUT TO ASCEND TO SEARCH THE HORIZON FOR ALLIED ARTILLERY.

If all the belligerents' aeroplanes differed considerably in point of construction and power, the enemy and Allies possessed at least one aircraft which was identical. Such was the captive balloon, seen in the above illustration, used universally as an artillery "spotter" The great quality of this gas-bag was its stability. This was guaranteed by the appendix seen on the right.

seldom if ever organised raids with "convoys" of aeroplanes such as the British and French organised with remarkable success, especially on the eve of and during an advance like that at Neuve Chapelle, or the general offensive of September 25th, 1915. These German air-raids were for the most part innocuous. The material damage they did was very small and their victims were generally unfortunate civilians. St. Omer, Bailleul, Béthune, Merville—these and other places in our lines in France at one time or another received the visit of hostile airmen. A house or two would be **Frightfulness pre-** wrecked, a few wretched women and **ferred by Germans** children and a couple of horses or mules would be killed, but these raids never possessed the slightest military importance.

At Bailleul on October 21st, 1914, a German airman dropped a bomb on the hospital. The projectile had a so-called "sensitive" fuse—that is to say, a fuse that would make it explode on impact. The shell burst accordingly as it went through the roof, and the greater part of the force was expanded in mid-air in one of the wards which forty patients had just left. A solitary patient remained, and he was wounded.

On the same day two German airmen who were brought down with their aeroplane in our lines were made to cut a very sorry figure. Their machine fell into a part of the line held by the Indian troops. On searching the machine the British officers found large numbers of circulars, written in very faulty Hindi, inciting the Indians to mutiny, and announcing that the Caliph had proclaimed the Jehad, or Holy War. The German airmen watched with amazement the British officers distributing these circulars to the Indian troops who, to the further stupefaction of the discomfited Boches, laughed with childish glee at the clumsy grammatical mistakes of the German Orientalist who had composed the proclamation. For a time the Germans were extremely uncomfortable, for they were apprehensive as to the penalty for their violation of The Hague Convention by inciting belligerent troops to mutiny. However, they suffered no harm, but they undoubtedly received an unforgettable lesson on Great Britain's methods of Imperial administration.

On November 1st the German Emperor was given an ocular demonstration of the prowess of the British airman, which he is not likely to forget to the end of his days. The Emperor had been visiting Thielt, in Belgium, where the German General Headquarters were then established. There is every reason to believe that his Majesty was in the General Staff building, when a British airman created something like a panic by suddenly appearing from the clouds and dropping bombs into the middle of a knot of motor-cars assembled outside. By way of retaliation the Germans bombarded Furnes from the air on the following day, in the belief that President Poincaré was in the place on a visit to the Belgian lines.

Despite high winds and drenching rain, in snowstorms and sleet-showers, all through the cold and wet season of the first winter of the war, our airmen carried out their reconnaissance work on an astonishing number of days. All the time they were improving their knowledge of this totally unfamiliar kind of warfare, fitting themselves for the great services they were destined to perform when the coming of spring heralded a forward movement after the dreary monotony of winter in the trenches.

The British success at Neuve Chapelle was largely due to the invaluable co-operation of the military air service with the Staff. It was our airmen who were in the main responsible for the selection of the slope running from the village of Neuve Chapelle to the Aubers-Fromelles ridge as the most suitable spot for a thrust at the enemy line. They ascertained the weakness of the Germans at that point and were able, moreover, to undertake that a series of carefully-prepared and daringly-executed air raids on important places on the German lines of communication would give the British thirty-six hours in which to make good any advantage they might gain before the enemy could bring up reinforcements.

Our aeroplanes furnished the General Staff with the information upon which its strategy for this operation was laid. While our troops were massing for the attack our airmen hovered out over the German lines, watching with hawk-like eyes for any sign that the enemy had

THE EVIL RESULT OF A LUCKY ENEMY SHOT.
Aeroplane brought down by the Germans in Flanders. The ill-fated craft fell headlong on to the roof of a picturesque villa. So terrific was the impact that the machine embedded itself in the tiles, and stood upright until removed by a squad of German soldiery.

divined our intentions. Despite the hazy weather prevailing on that fateful March 10th, our sky scouts went forth and, in the words of the British Commander-in-Chief, "continuous and close reconnaissance was maintained over the enemy's front." When the preliminary bombardment began, one of the most severe that the war, up to that date, had brought forth, our airmen were up, "spotting" for the guns while others went raiding into the enemy's country in order to hamper his movements along his lines of communication.

Bombs were dropped on the railways at Ménin, Courtrai, Don, and Douai; a wireless installation near Lille is believed to have been destroyed, while one of the branches of the German Great General **British airman's** Staff installed in a house in a suburb of **audacious ruse** Lille was set on fire. The airman who raided Courtrai Station displayed quite astonishing sang-froid. A troop train was in the station at the moment that the British aeroplane glittered into sight far aloft, and the German soldiers swarmed out of the carriages to shoot at the audacious invader. The Briton glided down to only a few hundred feet above the ground, whereupon

A JUST REPRISAL AS WELL AS AN ATTACK OF MILITARY VALUE.
On June 15th, 1915, twenty-three French aviators flew over Karlsrühe and dropped some hundred and thirty bombs on the city, thereby carrying out a just reprisal for Zeppelin raids on Paris. This photograph shows a street of houses near the barracks, which were set alight by the bomb explosions.

the soldiers and station officials rushed gleefully into a thick cluster in order to seize the prisoner, believing that his machine had been hit. Suddenly the airman dropped half a dozen bombs right into the heart of the crowd, and, with a jerk of his elevating plane, soared aloft again and made off. His bombs executed hideous slaughter among the soldiers and railwaymen. Another airman came down to within one hundred and fifty feet of the important railway bridge at Ménin, in order to make sure of his mark, and destroyed one of the piers of the bridge with a bomb.

During the fighting that took place in the spring and summer, the Second Battle of Ypres, the British offensive on May 9th against the Fromelles ridge, the operations in the Festubert region and about the ruined Château of Hooge, the aeroplanes continued to play their part quietly, modestly, usefully. But it was in the great Franco-British advance on September 25th that the airmen on the British front again had a great opportunity for showing what they had learnt in thirteen months' active service. They availed themselves of their opportunity to the full, and once more earned the admiration of their enemy and the warm eulogy of their commanders.

Three weeks of success Probably all records for air mileage per day were eclipsed by the Royal Flying Corps in the three weeks or so preceding our advance against Loos on September 25th, 1915. The weather was by no means invariably favourable, but, notwithstanding this, our airmen were out daily on reconnaissances of the enemy trenches, watching for any indication of the Boches being aware of the great events taking place, or of taking measures to meet the " big push." On more than one occasion our aeroplanes remained for two

360

hours at a stretch over the German lines, sometimes hovering at no greater altitude than seven thousand feet, the low-lying clouds preventing reconnaissance from anything like a safe distance above the enemy anti-aircraft batteries.

The great offensive was preceded by air attacks on the German railway communications south of Lille, the routes by which they would naturally bring reinforcements from Belgium. Events subsequently showed that these systematic air raids materially delayed the arrival of reinforcements to stem the collapse of the German front line under the sledge-hammer blows struck by our First and Fourth Corps. On September 23rd, two days before the day fixed for the attack, a German goods train was wrecked on the railway near Lille, and the line torn up in several places by bombs dropped from our aeroplanes. On the following day the railway was damaged in three places, while on the morning of the attack, despite hazy weather, our airmen sallied forth once more and bombed a train rushing up troops to the Loos region, damaging three coaches, and afterwards derailing a goods train and tearing up the railway line at three points.

Air attacks near Lille

On the day after the attack, when our troops were well through the German front line, and looked like getting on to Lens, one of our airmen appeared over the station of Loffre, east of Douai, on the railway between Valenciennes and Douai, two most important German military centres, and dropped a bomb on a troop train there. As the airman sped away he noticed that the German soldiers were swarming out of the train, and were gathering with a number of railway officials about the wrecked carriages. This airman must have remembered the feat of his comrade-in-arms at Courtrai during the Neuve Chapelle affair, for he turned back, and, gliding down to only about five hundred feet above the ground, unloosed a 110 lb. bomb he carried slung beneath his machine into the midst of the group. The explosion was so violent that it made his machine rock in the air as he clambered aloft and sped away unscathed.

On the same day the engine and six coaches of a troop train were derailed by aerial bombs dropped on the railway at Rosult, near St. Amand, on the line from Valenciennes to Orchies. Probably the most destructive raid of our flying men, however, was the air attack on the new railway station at Valenciennes, a railway junction of vital military importance to the enemy, as here the lines from Brussels and Maubeuge meet with the lines going out to Lille, Cambrai, Tournai, and Douai, the great military supply depôts in the northern part of the German western front. That the Britons were not permitted to accomplish these fine feats unopposed is shown by the circumstance that in the single week preceding our offensive there were no less than twenty-seven fights in the air between British and German machines, all of which save one terminated in our favour. One German machine was definitely known to have been wrecked.

Twenty-six British wins

Every time an aeroplane went out on duty over our lines on the western front its occupants braved death in half a dozen forms. The one thought inspiring every member of the Royal Flying Corps was to make his report—that is to say, to accomplish his mission successfully and return home to submit the results to headquarters. As the aeroplane hovered out over the German lines the German anti-aircraft batteries spat out their pear-shaped globes of pure white smoke with the characteristic "pom—pom—

MODERN MERCURIES AND THE MESSAGE OF MARS.
French motor despatch-rider handing a message to a comrade of the Air Service, somewhere near our ally's first line.

pom," a sound which will haunt for ever the memory of every man who has served in the trenches on the western front. The German firing-line machine-guns and rifles poured their stream of lead upwards against the invader in the sky, but the pilot kept his aeroplane steadily on its course with one thought uppermost—to make that report.

There are dangers in flying quite remote from war, those defects of the engine or in construction which no amount of care can guard against with absolute certainty. To these must be added the ever-present risk that a rifle bullet or the merest splinter of shell may, all unknown to the pilot, inflict irreparable injury on a vital part of the machine which will reveal itself at a critical moment in his flight, perhaps when he is assailed in the air by two or three hostile aeroplanes. Death from machine-gun, rifle, or shell fire in the air, death on the cruel earth many thousand feet below, wounds, capture—these are the risks which confront every member of the Royal Flying Corps as he fares forth on his frail bark of canvas, wood, and metal over the tortuous scars in the earth's surface marking the belligerent trench lines. But such was the spirit of the Royal Flying Corps—part and parcel, be it said, of the spirit of our Army in the field—that our airmen counted these risks as nought, so be it they might "make their report."

Modesty of the brave

Thus it is that the annals of the Royal Flying Corps in this war may be said to be the most amazing record of thrilling adventures which the world has ever known. The rules of the corps prevent the names of the heroes of some of the most fantastic of these experiences from being given, but this rule may be relaxed in the case of three gallant airmen who made the supreme sacrifice of their lives in the country's service. They are Rhodes-Moorhouse,

IN THE "IRON BIRDS'" CRADLE.
Belgian mechanic repairing an aeroplane motor at the Allies' aviation base in Northern France.

V.C.; Mapplebeck, D.S.O.; and J. Aidan Liddell, V.C.; all of whom were killed flying.

"Eye-Witness" made Britain ring with the heroism of Rhodes-Moorhouse. While on reconnaissance work he sustained a terrible wound from a shrapnel which burst close beside his machine and maimed him in an appalling way. Nevertheless, he fulfilled his mission, and then turned his machine for home, and landed at his point of departure with a grim jest on his lips at the expense of himself for the horrifying nature of his injuries. Before he would consent to be attended by the doctor, he insisted that he must "make his report." That was his honourable epitaph: "He made his report," for when the doctors came to him he was past human aid.

Captain Aidan Liddell, a comparative new-comer to

A NOVEL EMPLACEMENT.
French genius in adapting anything and everything to further the cause of war was demonstrated in innumerable ways. This photograph shows once again the clever way in which an anti-aircraft mitrailleuse was fixed to a revolving platform improvised from an old barrel and cartwheel.

flying, came from a famous Highland regiment. At the beginning of August, 1915, he was piloting his machine on a strategical reconnaissance in Belgium in the heart of the enemy's country when a high-explosive shrapnel from a German anti-aircraft gun burst right over his machine. His leg was simply riddled with bullets, and all but severed. The pilot lost consciousness on the spot and collapsed over his steering-wheel, while, to the horror of the observer, the machine dived nose foremost earthwards. The jerk jammed Liddell hard between the steering-wheel and the sides of the driving-seat, while it flung the observer between the machine-gun and the struts, fortunately enough, as it proved, for the aeroplane proceeded to turn a complete somersault. Luckily it was at a great height when the mishap occurred, and it thus had time to right itself.

Liddell regained consciousness as the machine regained

a horizontal position. Faint as he was with the loss of blood—he had some fifty separate wounds in his leg—he turned the machine round and made off straight across country for a Belgian aerodrome which he knew to be his nearest haven. He knew that he could not last very long, so would not waste time by climbing out of range of the enemy guns, but headed straight for the Belgian lines. He made a good landing at the flying ground, and said to those who ran forward to greet him: "You must lift me out. If I move I am afraid that my leg will drop off."

This brave man died in hospital a week or so afterwards, without living to receive the Victoria Cross which was laid on his bier in recompense for his deathless endurance.

Lieutenant Mapplebeck, who was killed while flying a new machine in England, was the hero of one of the most remarkable adventures of the war. He was shot down on a reconnaissance flight one day in the neighbourhood of a large town in the German lines. He was able to make a landing, but as his engine was badly *Mapplebeck's memorable exploit* damaged he could not hope to get away, so concealed himself, abandoning his aeroplane to the enemy. Presently German troops arrived, and started with loud hallo to search for the enemy airman, whom they knew must be somewhere in the vicinity.

They searched in vain. This remarkable young man, who spoke English, French, Flemish, German, and Dutch with equal fluency, managed to procure civilian clothing, and for about a week actually mixed with the German soldiers in the town, and even went so far as to attend their sports. The town was covered with placards announcing the flight of a British airman, and threatening dire penalties on whomsoever should venture to harbour him. Mapplebeck eventually succeeded in making his way through Belgium into Holland, doing thirty miles a day, a noteworthy performance, seeing that, as the result of an accident, one of his legs was shorter than the other. In a month he was flying at the front again.

It has been remarked already that pilot and observer had to work in closest harmony in their work at the front. Circumstances indeed frequently made it necessary for one to supplement the other. Thus, one day in October, 1915, while two Royal Flying Corps officers were reconnoitring over the German lines, they were attacked by a German machine. First the pilot was shot through the hand, and then the pilot, wounded in the arm and shoulder, lost consciousness and collapsed in his seat.

The observer, a man of exceptionally cool courage, promptly clambered through the back struts, wounded as he was, and took control of the machine. But the engine was damaged, so the officer cut off the petrol and started to glide earthwards. He actually managed to effect a landing in the French lines, where his unconscious companion and himself were tended by the French Red Cross.

The tenacity and fearlessness wherewith our airmen engaged and pursued any hostile machine they encountered gave the Germans a very healthy respect for our aerial prowess. For many *Effects of British ascendancy* months the ascendancy established by our fliers over the enemy was so complete that the German airman seldom waited to engage battle in the air, but made for home as soon as it appeared that the advantage was not immediately and obviously on his side. The British airman on the contrary, was not only always ready for a fight, but looking for a chance to close with the enemy, and destroy him in the air or drive him to a forced landing.

One day in October, 1915, a British aeroplane with pilot and observer sighted on patrol duty two German machines approaching from the eastward—that is to say, from the enemy's country. They let the first German machine come within fifteen yards, and then opened with their machine-gun. The German did not wait to reply. He hurriedly dived for the earth at a very steep angle. The

SQUAD.-COMM. BIGSWORTH,
who destroyed with bombs a German
submarine on August 26th, 1915.

FLIGHT-LIEUT. VINEY,
who was awarded the V.C. for sinking a German submarine on November 29th, 1915.

Briton did the same, the pilot firing at the enemy as long as he had a clear field of vision, and then passing the light automatic gun, with which our aeroplanes were fitted, to the observer, who gave the Boche the rest of the "drum" (or charger containing forty-seven cartridges).

The German machine, which was obviously quite out of hand, crashed heavily to earth in our lines. Our troops found the pilot stone dead in his seat, with a bullet through his heart, and the observer wounded. The British airman character-istically disdained to do any gloating over his prize, but, without even troubling to look at it, clambered aloft again, without landing, and went after the second German machine. Unfortunately the engine of the British aeroplane began to missfire, so the chase had to be abandoned, and the airmen had to content themselves with a single prize.

A few days after this one of our machines, while patrolling — *i.e.,* looking out for German machines on reconnaissance—saw a British aeroplane hotly pursued by a German. The British patroller, who was at a very great height, dipped downwards to attack the Boche. The latter seemed to lose his head for the moment, for he turned and flew directly beneath his two assailants, who "let him have it" from their machine-guns as he passed. The British machine which the German had been pursuing went away, leaving the field to the patroller and the foe, who circled round each other, firing rapidly, drawing ever nearer to the earth. Suddenly the German dived for his lines under a steady stream of fire from the British machine, turned, "banked" steeply, lost his equilibrium, and flopped upside down to earth. Pilot and observer were killed.

No odds were too great for our airmen. Thus a British battle-aeroplane, while on escort duty to a "covey" of slower aeroplanes out raiding, lost its way in the clouds

while heading off a German machine which looked like interfering with operations. The fighter could not pick up its bearings, so decided to run for home. Suddenly two powerful German biplanes dived straight out of a cloud-bank at the Briton, firing through their propellers. The British air-men instantly took up the challenge, and got their machine-gun at work so promptly and to such good purpose that the leading German "reared up" on its tail and dropped like a stone. The British observer, craning his head over the side of the driving-seat, saw his adversary vanish in a high pillar of dust among some trees far below.

M. RENÉ BESNARD.
Under-Secretary for Aeronautics at
the French Ministry of War.

Enough was as good as a feast for the other Boche. Discretion was always reckoned the better part of valour in the German Flying Corps, and he made off.

On another occasion a big German battleplane, of the very latest type with double fuselage and twin engines, declined to give battle to one of our machines. The British machine, which was flying at a height of some 5,000 feet, sighted the German about 2,000 feet above it. The big Boche seemingly did not spot his little adversary until the reverberating boom of his own "Archies" (as our airmen called the anti-aircraft guns) drew his attention to the latter. Then he wheeled slowly, powerfully, above his antagonist for a space, firing in a desultory fashion. But the Britons reserved their fire, waiting for the chance of a round at close range against a vital spot. It was the Boche himself who robbed them of their oppor-tunity. He seemed to think better of the encounter, for all of a sudden he turned and made off, his superior speed allowing him to get clean away before the British aeroplane could open fire. On the homeward journey the same British machine fell in with another German who also ran without showing fight.

Four or even five to one were no uncommon odds against

SEC.-LIEUT. D. A. C. SYMINGTON.
Awarded Military Cross for attacking an enemy
train on September 26th, 1915.

CAPT. JOHN A. LIDDELL, R.F.C.
Posthumously awarded the V.C. for bravery
in reconnaissance during August, 1915.

CAPT. ROBERT LORAINE.
Awarded the Military Cross for bringing down
an Albatross machine on October 26th, 1915.

our airmen in these aerial combats. Two Royal Flying Corps officers, on escort duty over the German lines on October 22nd, noticing a German machine some five hundred feet below them, dived at it, firing as they glided. The German did not wait, but made off. It was probably a trap to draw the Britons into action against vastly superior forces, as subsequent events seemed to prove. As the British aeroplane was pursuing the German it was suddenly attacked from behind by two German machines which opened with their machine-guns at a range of about one hundred and fifty yards. The moment the British airman returned the Germans' fire, the enemy machines dived to right and left, letting in a fourth aeroplane which came soaring down from on high, with engine stopped and

Victory against odds

VEDRINES AND HIS CAPTIVES.
The popular French airman standing between two German aviators whose "Aviatik" was brought down by Vedrines.

machine-gun rapping away merrily. The British airmen kept their heads, but the new-comer gave them no chance of a fight, for he never stopped his glide, but planed past them, firing all the time, to earth. In the meantime the other three Boche machines had disappeared. The British machine encountered and chased away yet another German machine before it reached home on that day.

On November 4th, 1915, a British machine fought and beat off three German machines in succession. The first machine passed at a distance of some two hundred yards, and immediately a second German opened fire from the rear, while a third passed to the right, firing from its machine-gun. The British observer, with the bullets snapping about his head from three sides, picked the last-named machine for his quarry and got in a round from the Lewis gun which effectively drove the Boche away. The other two machines kept manoeuvring about the Briton for about

twenty minutes, firing like mad, but they did no damage, and finally they also sheered off.

These fights in the air became part and parcel of the airman's life at the front. Never a flying day passed—in winter there was often too much haze to allow any flying whatsoever—but that at some point or other one of our airmen was at grips with the enemy in space. On the last Sunday of November, 1915, for example, there were no less than fifteen fights in the air between British and German machines. One of these encounters is well worth describing for the Britons "took on" and defeated four German aeroplanes which attacked a single British machine at the same time.

The British machine, with pilot and observer, was chasing away a big German Albatross that had been making a nuisance of itself prying over our lines, when the Boche was joined by two Fokker aeroplanes. Our men's endeavour was to head the first German machine away from its own lines and force it to descend behind our trenches. They therefore ignored the two Fokkers for the time being, and, rising level with the Albatross, got their machine-gun to work at very close range. The Albatross was apparently hit, for it suddenly dived steeply to earth and, as it landed, was seen to turn completely over. Meanwhile, two more German aeroplanes, with one of our fast scouting machines in swift pursuit, joined the two Fokkers which were coming up hand over fist, so to speak. Presently all four Boche machines were circling round the British, firing from their machine-guns. The Britons "stood their ground," for it was not the habit of the Royal Flying Corps to run away from the enemy. They returned a brisk fire to the stream of bullets poured in at them from four quarters, and by dint of very skilful manœuvring managed to let each adversary come under their fire in turn. The Germans finally cleared off and made for home.

Not all our machines came home, of course. On service so cheerfully undertaken in all weathers, among risks so bravely faced, there were inevitably casualties, though the number of airmen killed or wounded on active service was remarkably small and out of all proportion to the immeasurably great services they rendered to the Army. When a machine set out from the flying-ground at the front, with pilot and observer wrapped up to the eyes with fur hoods and leather overalls to protect them against the bitter cold up aloft, nobody could say whether it would return. One might sometimes see at one of the flying-grounds behind the lines—and it was an unforgettable sight—a little group of Flying Corps officers in their neat uniform, with the khaki forage cap and cross-buttoned tunic and mechanics in blue slops straining their eyes skyward in the hope of sighting a missing machine. Through long familiarity with the different types of machine, these airmen at the front could identify an aeroplane in the air and name pilot and observer long before the layman had made out anything beyond a shimmering grey and silver moth. They recognised the drone of the motor, the way the machine was handled in the air, with such infallibility that as soon as the missing machine appeared high above the green stretch of the aerodrome, a sigh of relief would go up from the waiting group. Great fires might often be seen burning on the flying-ground at night to guide the homeward path of wanderers who had not returned—fires kindled in the hope that the missing machines had been delayed by nothing more serious than a breakdown.

Chivalry from the Infinite

But often the airmen at the flying-ground searched the skies in vain. That night there were two empty seats at a Royal Flying Corps mess. Sometimes it was the enemy himself who relieved the subsequent uncertainty as to the fate of the missing airmen, for this war developed between the belligerent airmen a kind of freemasonry of the air which was the more remarkable in view of the complete absence of chivalry on the part of our foemen on land and sea.

SEAPLANES SET OFF ON TERRA FIRMA FOR THEIR NATURAL ELEMENT—THE SEA.
Powerful Royal Naval motor-lorries transporting seaplanes to "somewhere" on the South Coast, where they were to be refitted and tested.

It is hard to say whether it is due to the common bond of danger which unites all airmen or the respect which our fliers exacted from the enemy by their unmatched disdain of death, but certainly the Germans went out of their way to be chivalrous towards the members of the Royal Flying Corps, who, in their turn, repaid the enemy by the most scrupulous courtesy.

Thus it was more or less a custom between the airmen of the two nations to send back word by aeroplane of any airmen who had been shot down in the hostile lines. A message was dropped by streamer—that is to say, enclosed in a small metal case to which a long pennant was attached to attract attention—and flung out over the enemy lines with the news that Flight-Lieutenant X had been unfortunately killed and his observer, Captain Y, seriously wounded ; or that Squadron-Commander Z had been forced to land in hostile territory and had been captured. On one occasion, it is said, the Germans let the Royal Flying Corps know that a certain British airman had been killed on duty and that his funeral would take place on a certain date. Thereupon two of the friends of the deceased took a wreath up in their aeroplane and dropped it in the vicinity of the military cemetery where their comrade was laid to rest. The Germans respected their desire to pay this last honour to the memory of a brave man, and neither going nor coming was the British aeroplane shot at.

The brutality with which the Germans habitually treated their British prisoners was, apparently, not extended to the British airmen. Certainly, on the British side, the German airmen were treated with the most scrupulous courtesy ; but then all prisoners were well treated by their British captors.

There was a good deal of good-natured humour in the relations between the two air corps. Before the Battle of Neuve Chapelle, in his proclamation to the troops which were to take part in the attack, Sir John French, alluding to the ascendancy established by our airmen over the enemy, said that the Germans had been driven from the air. A few weeks later, on the eve of Easter Sunday, a German aeroplane raided a town in the British zone of operations and threw some bombs, which did practically no damage, and claimed no victims. With the bombs they dropped a message by streamer. The message ran something to this effect : "Hearty Easter greetings from two Bavarian airmen who have been 'driven from the air.'—Uncle Ignatius and Cousin Tony."

In the same way, our airmen occasionally sent by air to the Germans news which it was thought they should know, and which there was reason to believe was not allowed to appear in their newspapers. More than once, it is reported, British airmen dropped packets of British newspapers over Lille and other French and Belgian towns in German occupation for the consolation and encouragement of the unfortunate civilian inhabitants.

No modern battle picture would be complete without the aeroplane, glittering up very high aloft, ringed about with tiny white balls of shrapnel smoke gleaming dead white against the background of clouds or clear sky. The airmen were highly popular figures with the men in the firing-line. The man in the trenches knew that the aeroplane was, so to speak, the periscope of the Army. Every aeroplane he saw he knew to be out guarding against any form of "frightfulness" that the ingenious German might be preparing for him— the man in the fire-trench— the man who was first to get the knocks. If a well-concealed battery made itself a nuisance by shelling our trenches, smashing up the dug-outs, and knocking down the parapet, word was sent back post-haste by telephone for an aeroplane to locate the hidden nuisance and reveal its emplacement to our guns. If our patrols ascertained

A TALON OF THE BIRD-MAN.
How a quick-firing gun was carried aboard a British aeroplane. It could be elevated or depressed according to the position of the hostile machine.

of disappointment, when the German, as so often happened, broke away and headed out " home to mother "; but, if the British airman, with a well-placed burst of fire, sent his adversary hurtling, a limp rag of torn canvas, to earth, such a burst of cheering rang forth to heaven from the narrow trench-line as might have reached the ears of the airmen even above the roar of their propellers.

It was a rare and precious satisfaction to the men to be able to rush forward and secure the prize, to make prisoner the hostile airmen if they had escaped unscathed. If the men were wounded, how-
ever, all the innate humanity of the British soldier came out, and he set **Succouring the fallen foe**
about succouring his fallen foe with just as much enthusiasm as he had only a few seconds before displayed in applauding the attempts to encompass his utter destruction.

A highly humorous scene occurred one day when a German aeroplane was forced to descend in our lines. When our men reached the enemy machine they found pilot and observer engaged in a hot and angry discussion. The observer declared that there had been no need to land, and accused the pilot of cowardice, to which charges the

SEPARATE COMPARTMENTS FOR PILOT AND OBSERVER.
A late type of French warplane, the chief value of which was the arrangement whereby the crew could sit alongside instead of one behind the other. The circle photograph above shows a 37 mm. mobile cannon affixed to a French Voisin aeroplane. Captain Jaffrelot is seen in the car setting off on a reconnaissance.

that undue activity was going on in the trenches opposite them, if they heard the clink of entrenching tools night after night, and by day caught glimpses of fresh earth accumulating behind the enemy trenches, an aeroplane was despatched for a " look-see."

Some of the most thrilling of the aerial combats which have
been described in this chapter were
An enthusiastic audience fought out before the most enthusiastic audience to be found anywhere in the world—a couple of thousand or so of British soldiers on active service. As the two aeroplanes wheeled in great circles round one another, so close that even the " Archies " ceased " popping off " for fear of hitting their own man, and the faint " rap-rap " of the machine-guns drifted downwards from the sky, one could have heard a pin drop in the British trenches, so tense was the interest wherewith the men followed the vicissitudes of the fight. With one muddy hand screening their eyes, they strained their gaze upwards, hoping with all their hearts that their man would win. There was a gasp of relief, mingled perhaps with a touch

THE MOBILITY OF THE 37 MM. GUN.
Companion photograph of the first one on this page, showing how the cannon could be moved to fire at an opponent on a lower level.

pilot replied with equal vehemence. The two nearly came to blows over the matter, and sulked with each other all the time they were detained at the front pending their examination by the military authorities.

The flying-grounds at the front were admirably organised. They were all self-contained, with their own motor-lorries, which daily journeyed forth to the railheads to fetch rations, supplies, and stores. The motor-lorries in their turn had their own travelling workshops where ordinary running repairs could be carried out. On the ground in and among the aeroplane sheds, solid wood constructions or tents, were the repair shops, from which echoed all day long the clink of tools and the hum of the lathe To these sounds of activity the droning of the motors of the aeroplanes circling the ground on testing flights, and the loud roaring of engines being tried on machines on the ground or on the bench in the shops, formed a continual accompaniment.

In one part of the ground the petrol store was found, with stacks and stacks of petrol-cans, at another the magazine with ammunition for the machine-guns, and all sorts and varieties of bombs, from the round, dumpy, incendiary kind to the long and swollen 110 lb. monsters, which were slung beneath the aeroplane, and loosed by an ingenious mechanism to drop on their objective. At the Flying Corps headquarters there were large stores where **Work of the** every imagin- **Naval Wing** able kind of spare part was kept ready for use, and repair shops and work-rooms where aeroplanes could be put together or completely renewed with fresh planes, struts, and other accessories.

The object of this chapter has been to throw some light on the work of the aeroplane in the war on the western front, and has therefore dealt exclusively with the Military Wing of the Royal Flying Corps, an integral part of the British Army in the field. A word should be said, however, of the splendid work accomplished by the Naval Wing of the Royal Flying Corps, which for long had its headquarters at Dunkirk, and distinguished itself by a number of daring and successful raids into Belgium and Germany, principally against the sheds in which the Germans harboured their Zeppelins with a view to air raids on England. On September 22nd, 1914, Flight-Lieutenant Collet flew to Düsseldorf—a distance of some two hundred miles from his point of departure—and, descending to a height of only four hundred feet, dropped his bombs upon the Zeppelin shed there. Though the airman had his machine hit, he managed to return in safety. About the same time a similar raid was executed on Cologne, but the aeroplanes

THE PICTURESQUE SIDE OF AERIAL "FRIGHTFULNESS."
The above remarkable photograph of a Zeppelin over "the London district" was taken by an amateur, and has been only slightly retouched to give increased clearness to the details. The bursting of the shells from the anti-aircraft guns and the faint light of a street lamp in the foreground are noteworthy features of an unique photographic record.

returned without dropping their bombs, having been prevented by the haze from locating the airship sheds. In the following month—on October 8th—two parties of aeroplanes repeated these performances. At Düsseldorf, Lieutenant Marix literally flattened out the Zeppelin shed and the Zeppelin harboured there, and though the raiders' machines were damaged, they all managed to get back safely. At **Marix's exploit** Cologne the great military railway- **at Dusseldorf** station was badly damaged.

Next came the turn of Friedrichshafen, the baptismal font, as it were, of Zeppelinism and of baby-killing generally. On November 21st, Commander Briggs, Lieutenant J. T. Babington, and Lieutenant S. V. Sippe executed a daring and most successful raid on Count Zeppelin's aircraft factory from Belfort, a distance of some two hundred and fifty miles. Much damage was done, but unfortunately

WHEN THE RAIDERS HAD PASSED.
The effect of two Zeppelin bombs, one of which fell on the roof of a house in a London suburb; the other in the garden.

ENGLISHMEN'S HOMES AFTER A ZEPPELIN VISIT.
Ruined homesteads in the London district. The tragic result of bombs which fell in a working-class neighbourhood.

Commander Briggs' machine was shot down and the airman taken prisoner. His companions got away unscathed. In December the Naval Wing made several successful incursions into Belgium, always making the airship sheds their objective. It will be remembered that Lieutenant Warneford, who earned immortal fame by his splendid exploit of destroying in mid-air a Zeppelin which had returned from a raid on England, belonged to the Naval Wing of the Royal Flying Corps established at Dunkirk.

The service which the Royal Flying Corps rendered to our Army in the field cannot be over-estimated. In his despatches Sir John French repeatedly rendered homage to the splendid efficiency and the unflinching courage of our Army airmen. The Germans, for all their aptitude for war, their organising talents, and their thoroughness in everything they undertook, despite the fact that they had the start of Great Britain in military aviation—through

ANNIHILATION'S WASTE.
Old houses that suffered from the new terror. Impression of the debris caused by a Zeppelin bomb falling in the fourth area mentioned in the official report of the aerial raid on London in October, 1915.

no merit of theirs, but solely owing to the supineness of our military heads—were outclassed in the air. The human element is not everything in flying, but it plays a role which can never be eliminated. The typically British qualities of grit and coolness, combined with a touch in the hands which has made Englishmen the finest hunters and steeplechasers in the world, proved them admirably adapted to the craft of airmanship, which has revolutionised war.

The enormous progress in flying, both in airmanship and in the elaboration of safe and reliable types of machine which the present war brought forth, will ultimately accrue to the advantage of the world at peace. The heroes who have uncomplainingly and unflinchingly laid down their lives in the air service of the Empire will have deserved doubly well of the Motherland. Not only have they sacrificed themselves in defence of the Briton's birthright of liberty; they are martyrs also in the cause of the progress of the world.

Freakish effect of the raid on a suburban villa. The roof of the house was torn off intact, disclosing a small room, the walls of which were unaffected.

Where a bomb fell in the street of a London suburb, making a large hole, which was filled in, and destroying the doors and windows of ten houses.

Effect of a Zeppelin bomb on a well-known London thoroughfare. The wood paving was displaced as if a squad of navvies had been working.

Six houses wrecked by one bomb. Scene of devastation where a Zeppelin's infernal machine found a mark in the London district.

Wreckage caused by a bomb on the roof of a house. While the explosion shattered the roof, the house next door was comparatively undamaged.

Room in a London business man's office, which suffered indirectly, but none the less heavily, from the explosion of a bomb in the garden.

DAMAGE IN THE LONDON DISTRICT AFTER THE AIR RAID OF OCTOBER 13TH, 1915.

Russian soldiers erecting a strong barbed-wire entanglement at a strategic point on the Bessarabian front. An officer was giving an order to a soldier who is seen standing at the salute. The thick foliage is typical of the country at this extremity of the Russian line.

In the Dwina forest—a machine-gun section in action against the advancing enemy. In spite of the obstinate nature of the soil, formidable trenches will be seen to have been constructed, consolidated with tree-trunks, and covered with brushwood. An officer is surveying the German movement through his field-glasses.

THE MACHINE-MADE WAR IN SYLVAN SURROUNDINGS ON THE RUSSIAN FRONT.

CHAPTER XCVII.

THE STRUGGLE ON THE DWINA AND THE RESURGENCE OF RUSSIA.

Position of Russia after her Fortress Line had been Broken—Enormous Losses on Both Sides—The Unbroken Fighting Spirit of the Village Communities—Guerilla Bands Form along the German Rear—Hindenburg Fights for Comfortable Winter Quarters—Importance of the Riga-Rovno Railway Line—Dvinsk, the Fortress Gate into Real Russia—Terrific Attack by Massed Armies of Germany—Wonderful System of Russian Defences—Two Hundred Miles of Death-Trap Trenches—Unprecedented Losses Admitted by the Germans—Hindenburg Despairs of Taking Dvinsk and Tries to Storm Riga—How the British Submarines in the Baltic Helped to Defeat Hindenburg—Northern German Army Trapped between the Sea and the Swamp—The Rout at Kemmern, Anting, and Ragasem—Dimitrieff Advances across the Marshes and Captures the German Lines—Extraordinary Preparations Made in the Enemy's Entrenchment—Russky Plans to Wear the Germans Down by Winter Sickness—Guerilla Fighting in the Marshes and Kidnapping of German Generals—Woyrsch's Army Defeated and Thrown Back—Struggle Round the Styr and the Strypa—Appearance of First New Russian Army with Drum-fire Accompaniment.

HINDENBURG'S encircling movement against the Russian forces near Vilna in September, 1915, was the final manœuvre to obtain a grand decision against the armies of the Tsar. With the failure of this movement the plan of campaign, begun by Mackensen's Phalanx on April 30th, 1915, came to a conclusion. The only important advantage which the Germans and Austrians had won by their tremendous artillery power and their unparalleled sacrifice of life was that they had shortened their eastern front by nearly three hundred miles. The prisoners taken by the Russians numbered by the end of September more than 1,100,000; and the enemy troops, killed or disabled, reached a very much larger figure. Allowing for the multitude of cases of slight wounds which recovered sufficiently to enable the men to resume military service, the total permanent losses of the Teutonic Empires on their eastern front was incomparably

greater than any hitherto known in history. The pick of the Germanic populations was destroyed. Russia suffered even more heavily than her opponents in man power, and much more in equipment, while the loss of some of her busiest industrial regions further crippled her forces.

Yet she retained important elements of strength. In the first place, she had a far larger reserve of men capable of bearing arms than Germany and Austria, and when the Tsar in person took over the command of the armies, with the greatest of his fighting men, General Alexeieff, as his Chief of Staff, a vast new army was already in course of training. Then behind Russia, invisible, remote, and ignored by the Russian peasantry, was the sea-power of Britain, dominating all the ocean-ways of the earth. And behind the British Fleet was the money-power of London, which was also used in the service of Russia. With all the seas clear of German warships and the money markets still largely ruled from London, the munition

A COUNCIL OF WAR.
Russian Staff officers discussing the military situation at a farmhouse headquarters on the eastern front.

factories of Japan and America were linked with the Russian firing-line in such a way as to compensate Russia for the loss of her Polish factories. Moreover, the harvest in Russia in the autumn of 1915 was good, there were millions of fugitives from Galicia and Poland who helped to gather it, and all the captains of industry and mechanics in the Russian cities threw themselves with fierce earnestness into the vital labour of making high-explosive shells.

The struggle between the bureaucracy, based on the North Russian primitive system of village communism, and the young Parliamentary party, representing the plutocracy of the large towns and the important demo-cratic forces in South Russia, was checked by the necessity of saving the Empire before attempting to better its form of government. Although the Duma was suspended, and the old reactionarism established by the creation of a Chancellorship for M. Goremykin, yet some of the most violent revolutionaries returned from exile to serve in the Army. There was a feeling that the old machinery for controlling the village communities would **Patriotism versus revolution** prove more immediately serviceable for the purpose of war administration than any new political system hastily con-structed on the Western model. After all, the strength of Russia resided in her innumerable little systems of peasant communities, which, by hard work, hard living, and the continual production of swarms of children, had built up the Empire of the House of Moscow. Half the peasants could not read or write; their oral legends and traditions were still the chief source of inspiring national action in the country; so that the Tsar alone, acting directly as Imperator in the ancient Russian way, could evoke the full fighting spirit of the race.

From the point of view of the Allies of Russia, the action of the Tsar in placing himself at the head of his armies and creating a Chancellor to organise the Empire com-pletely for war had a great and striking effect upon the international situation. This abrupt, intense concentra-tion of actual power in Russia put an end to German intrigue for a separate peace. All the subterranean work which had been going on in Petrograd failed of effect when the Tsar removed from his capital, and lived in business-like seclusion with his Staff and some of his Council of Empire at general headquarters behind the firing-line.

The Russian communities were still full of fight. Even the peasant refugees of Polish, Lithuanian and Lettish race, who formed an immense **Hostility to** trail of utter misery far into Russia, were **premature peace** sternly hostile to anything like a prema-ture peace. An American observer, who spoke to thousands of them, said that the general sense of all their statements was : " We must win now, no matter the cost or the time it takes. The sufferings we have undergone are too great to stop at anything short of victory." The Letts of Courland, who had been one of the main forces of the revolutionary movement in 1909, came in tens of thousands to General Russky at Riga and Dvinsk and volunteered for any kind of service as guerilla troops or regular soldiers. Many of the Polish peasants between the German frontier and the Pinsk Marsh remained on their farms during the Russian retreat, confiding in the word of the German Emperor that they should be well treated. The Austrian troops seem to have acted in a civilised manner, but the German soldiers soon began to pillage the lonely farm-houses and small villages. The systematic marauding was conducted with great severity beyond the line of the Vistula and the Bug Rivers. The German Staff seems

A MASS OF BOG-LAND PATCHED WITH COPSES AND PINE-WOODS.
Some idea of what the Russian marshes were like when saturated by the autumnal rains may be gathered from this photograph of a horse which, lured by thirst, had wandered into the danger zone and got mired in a mudbank.

COLD COMFORT ON AN ICY MORNING, BUT ENOUGH FOR ARDENT PATRIOTS.
" Daddy Frost " is the modern Moujik's name for Russia's two most famous commanders—Generals January and February. He has no terror for them, and they fought more stoutly on a cup of cold water, which they had to break the ice to obtain, than the Germans fought on hot coffee.

to have regarded the land within the rivers as definitely acquired territory, which could at need be held by fortified lines, and which it would therefore pay to foster and keep well peopled in order to increase the national resources. In any case the Polish, Lithuanian, and Lettish peasants beyond the rivers were used with extreme rigour. Their goods were taken from them without payment ; they were subjected to insult and grievous injury ; and their women were not respected.

The upshot was the creation of guerilla bands, composed of men driven to extreme desperation, who knew that they would receive no mercy if they were caught, and who therefore gave no mercy to the German soldiery. For some months there were no continuous lines in the eastern theatre of war. Both contending forces manœuvred in the open field, with gaps between their main areas of concentration, and in the wide gaps there were only patrols and thin screens of observing troops. The guerilla bands were therefore able to work more freely than would have been the case if the opposing armies had firmly entrenched against each other all along the front. Most of the country was rough, with vast tracts of woodland and immense regions of lakes and swamps ; therefore, the fighting peasants, with their special knowledge of the ground, had numerous places of shelter. By the winter many of the guerilla bands seemed to have crossed into the Russian line and taken service as regular soldiers. This was especially the case in Courland, where the work of defending Riga and Dvinsk was conducted by the young Letts, supported by the ironsides of Siberia and the sharp-shooters of Livonia and Pskov. Although the Letts became regular troops, wearing the Russian uniform, the German commanders refused, against all international law, to treat them as soldiers, and shot them out of hand when captured.

This naturally did not make the young Lett any gentler in his treatment of the German. By this time the Lett was well aware of all that he owed the Germans for seven

Huns' inhumanity to Letts

centuries of serfdom, land robbery, and bloody repression, culminating first in the acts of the German barons of the Russian Baltic provinces in 1909, and then in the deeds of the German army of invasion in 1915. So when the Lett met the German in the autumn and winter of 1915, in the continuous battles around Riga and Dvinsk, there were not many prisoners taken on either side.

The struggle for the northern river-line of the Dwina, from Riga to Dvinsk, and then southward in the lake region above Vilna, was the principal feature of the eastern campaign throughout the autumn of 1915 ; for after Hindenburg had failed to capture the central Russian army round Vilna in September, 1915, there was nothing left for him to do but to prepare for a possible advance in the spring of 1916.

It will be seen from the map that there is a continuous line of railways running from the Gulf of Riga to Lemberg in Galicia. This railway line is made up of different sections—some double-tracked, a part of the grand European trunk railway, a stretch of single-line railway across the Pinsk Marsh, and bits of other systems. But it could be used to transport troops and guns north and south. Wherever the Russians were forced back from this Riga-Lemberg line, they destroyed the rails as thoroughly as possible. But they could not blow up the embankments running through the marsh, or annul the primary engineering work of levelling the country for railway-making. The country was flat and there were few tunnels ; most of the rivers were not broad, and there were only half a dozen bridges that could not be rapidly reconstructed. Therefore, in spite of all the damage that could be done to it by the retreating Russians, the possession of the Riga-Lemberg line was of great value to the Germans.

Riga and its railways

It spanned the entire Russian front, and if the Teutonic armies could align themselves some miles east of it, their position during the winter would be admirable. Not only would their troops be rapidly fed and munitioned, but they

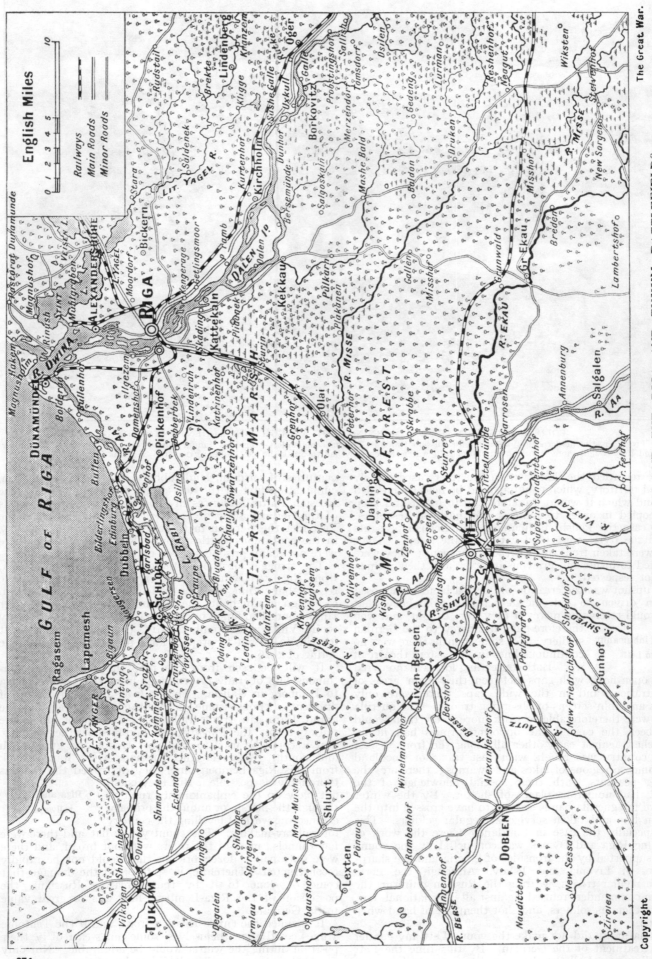

Copyright

LARGE SCALE MAP OF THE TIRUL MARSH AND THE RIGA AND TUKUM BATTLEFIELDS.

In this region of swamp and forest covering Riga, the hero of Bulgaria, General Dimitrieff, won a series of smashing victories over the Germans, which brought about the final failure of Hindenburg's grandiose plans.

The Great War.

could be moved up and down the six-hundred-mile track in such rapid concentrations that the three Russian armies, based on Petrograd, Smolensk, and Kieff, with no cross-country railway connecting them, would be unable to help each other. But until the Riga-Lemberg railway line was won, the Germans and Austrians had no better communications than their opponents. In many respects they were worse off, as their system of motor traffic had sadly broken down in the Polish mud, and the unsuspected appearance of a British submarine flotilla in the Baltic cut their important sea-line supplies.

Our submarines, indeed, did very much to save the Russian Army from losing its hold upon the Riga-Lemberg line. First of all, as has been already related, our brilliant and daring sailors broke up the naval attack on the Gulf of Riga in August, 1915, when our underwater craft torpedoed the battle-cruiser Moltke and put out of action some smaller warships, after attacking, in the previous month, the battleship Pommern and doing her much damage.

The submarines with British crews were so cleverly handled as to escape observation, while moving to the attack on the German Fleet, and thus our men got home a series of blows which crippled German sea-power in the Baltic. According to the plan arranged at **British submarines in the Baltic** Libau between Field-Marshal von Hindenburg, representing the German Army, and Prince Henry of Prussia, representing the German Navy, the conquest of the Riga-Dvinsk section of the railway was to have been accomplished by a seaborne supply of shells and other munitions; for even when the existing railways in Courland had been extended by the building of a new light railway, the German guns could not be served quickly enough to beat down the Russian defences. The German admiral transformed the Courland port of Windau into a provisional munitioning base for Hindenburg's northernmost army, in the expectation that this army would conquer Riga, which would then become a base of seaborne munition supplies for the drive against Petrograd.

But after the failure of the great German naval attack on the Gulf of Riga, in August, 1915, the channel by which the German ships had entered the Gulf was closed by a very difficult minefield and other obstructions. At the same time the German traffic through both Libau and Windau was disorganised by British and Russian submarines, with the result that Hindenburg continually ran short of shells in Courland, where his local commanders. Below

and Lauenstein, were relying upon their superior artillery to save their infantry. They had the two great siege trains which had shattered Kovno and Novo Georgievsk, and General Eichhorn, who had swung his right wing towards Riga early in the campaign, now moved the bulk of his forces from the Vilna sector towards the river-line of the Dwina. The condition of the roads prevented him from bringing up his heaviest howitzers, but he had hundreds of 6 in. pieces and a host of 8 in. howitzers. The point he selected for attack was the river-fortress town of Dvinsk, which guarded the junction of the Riga-Smolensk and Vilna-Petrograd railways. Dvinsk, sometimes known by its older name of Dunaberg, was one of the most vital positions in Russia, for it guarded the river-line of the Dwina and the vast lake district that covered Petrograd. For more than four hundred years the military importance of Dvinsk had been recognised by its being strongly fortified; and in 1812 Napoleon's army of invasion had met with a severe repulse at the bridge-head before carrying the town. Any advance on Moscow had to be protected by the capture of the great northern flanking position, to prevent the Petrograd army from driving down on the rear of any advancing forces.

The attack on Dvinsk

Hindenburg at the time was very close to all the line of the Dwina River from Riga to the lakes south of Dvinsk.

HOW THE RUSSIANS TOOK THE HEART OUT OF THE ADVANCING GERMANS.
Every conceivable difficulty was put by the Russians in the way of the pursuing Germans, who had to make temporary bridges for their transport over every stream and ditch they came to. Above: Prince Leopold of Bavaria studying a war map with some of his staff.

He had stormed the bridge-head at Friedrichstadt on the Dwina on September 3rd, 1915, while General Russky was working to save the army far to the south of Vilna. But after snatching this advantage from his hard-pressed opponent, the German Field-Marshal, who also threw every man he could spare into the Vilna fight, found that he had to rearrange his plan of operations on the Dwina front; for Russky had meanwhile received strong reinforcements from Petrograd, and had closed the gap at Friedrichstadt in the vital river-line. During the close of the grand struggle with the armies of Russky and Evert round Vilna, the German commander tried to distract Russky by hammering at Dvinsk, and there threatening to break through and entirely turn all the Russian forces based on Petrograd, Smolensk, and Moscow. But the Russian fortress-town was defended in a different way from Kovno or Brest Litovsk, and the other frontier strongholds. General Russky knew as much about fortification as any German, for he had stormed through the Austrian fortresses in Galicia in the first period of the war; and among his commanders was Radko Dimitrieff, whose long series of victories against Turk, Austrian, Hungarian, and German had only been broken by Mackensen's thousands of guns

A RUSSIAN GENERAL'S QUARTERS NEAR THE PRIPET MARSH.
So that it stood on Russian soil the rudest hovel satisfied any Russian, even of the highest rank. On the dreary plains of the Pripet Marsh, beyond which the Germans could not penetrate, this was the best temporary home that could be found for one general officer.

on the Dunajec river line. Since Dimitrieff in 1912 tried to carry the Chatalja lines near Constantinople by an infantry attack he had led the Russian infantry against the Przemysl forts, and had been at last blown out of his own lines by a million high-explosive shells. So he also well knew what modern artillery could do, and the defence of Riga and Dvinsk was therefore conducted by men who abounded in experience.

Their task was to hold out for two or three months between Riga and Dvinsk until their own artillery and their own shell supplies were raised to German level. Hundreds of heavy guns were coming from the Putiloff Works at Petrograd and from Japan and America; and the shell factories of three great countries were working at high pressure to save the Dwina line. As a matter of fact, General Russky had been given most of the best available artillery in Russia; and though his shell supply was still much inferior, in September, 1915, to Hindenburg's, it was greater than that of any other Russian general.

How Russky defended Dvinsk

The original fortress at Dvinsk was an insignificant affair, the works being thrown out scarcely more than a mile beyond the old citadel. Russky arranged his new defences in an immense circle more than twenty miles in diameter, which swept through a country so spotted with small and large lakes that it looked like an irregular piece of lace. Despite the watery nature of the ground, the fortified Russian trenches ploughed up the whole district. Each important position was arranged somewhat in the form of a crescent. Every frontal attack was caught on both flanks from the horns of the position. The horns in turn were strengthened by advanced trenches.

A 200-mile death-trap

The general result was that, when the hostile infantry charged, it was held up until its pressure became more than the men in the advanced trenches could sustain. These men, having done all their work, retired down the communication trenches, in as great a disorder as they could assume. The charging mass of enemies, seeing the opposing line give way, advanced through the central gap, where they met with the exact degree of resistance as would herd them together inside the crescent. Then from each horn and arm, and from the main trench behind, there came three crossing sheets of musketry and machine-gun fire, which mowed down the trapped battalions, while a storm of shrapnel from the Russian batteries burst over their heads, and also curtained off their reinforcements. All that the Russian infantryman afterwards had to do was to walk over the bodies of his fallen foes and resume his garrison work in the advanced trenches. Sometimes the Russian went forward, with the bayonet, when his fire had broken up the enemy. But, whether he worked with steel or bomb, he went forward. In other words, the Russian front line was made to break. Only the horns of each crescent, which could not be distinguished from other advanced trenches, resisted the pressure of an enemy attack. Russky's front was about two hundred miles long, and there were over a thousand places in it which the German infantry could occupy whenever it liked. The new system of constructing positions with a false front, flanked by strong arms, seems to have been a German or Austrian invention; but it was left to Russky and his engineers to develop the idea in so complete and gigantic a manner as to make a two-hundred-mile front into a death-trap. In order to defeat the hurricane fire tactics of the German gunners, all the Russian works were kept unusually narrow, and except by the edge of the water, they were dug very deep. There was seldom more than a target a yard wide for the heavy German artillery, firing miles away. The result was, according to M. Keri, the Hungarian war correspondent with Hindenburg's forces, that "the army could not make use of its heavy artillery, for it proved quite useless owing to the extreme narrowness of the hostile trenches." In the lake district south of Dvinsk, Keri said that the Russians made the utmost of the natural defences, and even the advanced trenches there were only occupied after very heavy losses, and then retained under most trying circumstances. The circumstances were, indeed, so trying that the Russian troops broke through the German lines in several places, and recaptured the positions around Sventen Lake and Ilsen Lake. Again, Keri said that "unprecedented losses on our part were incurred in taking Novo Alexandrovsk," a small town in the lake region on the Courland border. When an enemy is forced to make a confession of this kind a few days after the event, with several censors watching for any indiscretion, it is fair to

Lieut.-Gen. Sir Percy H. N. Lake, K.C.M.G., K.C.B., Commander-in-Chief in Mesopotamia.

Cossack cavalry on the alert in the snowbound Caucasus.

Austrian munition column crossing a stream in the Pripet Marshes.

Another wonderful photograph of Cossacks on the march in the frozen Caucasus.

Austrian supply column passing over a pontoon bridge in the Pripet Marshes.

German gas=attack on the eastern front photographed by a Russian airman.

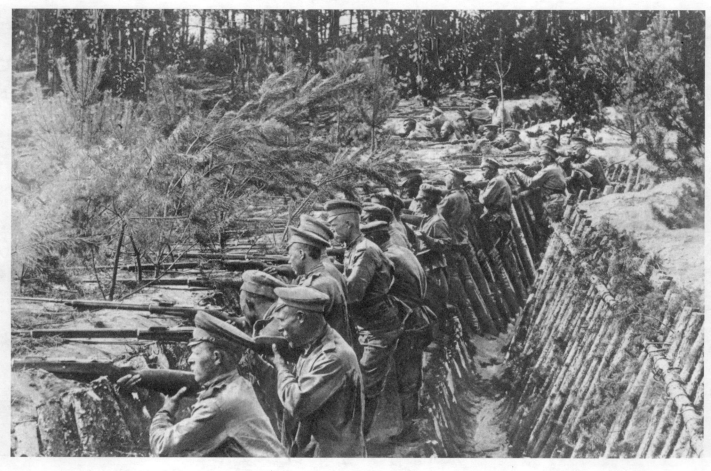

Russian trench on the edge of a forest on the Dwina front.

assume that the casualties of the attacking army must have been enormous.

And so they were. In the course of three months' fighting, General Russky—a weak, ailing invalid, whose brain worked with strange brilliance in his sick body—first fought Hindenburg to a complete standstill, and then advanced and drove him back from the Riga line. It is impossible to describe in detail the incessant furious fighting that went on for months between the Gulf of Riga and the wilderness of swamps and marshes north of Vilna. The great river fortress itself was never in serious danger, though the enemy approached from the west to the railway town of Illukst. The railway enabled him to bring up heavy guns and shatter village after village with gusts of his fire ; but the Russian troops, feeling at last that they also had good guns behind them, continually counter-attacked with extreme violence. By September 27th, it was reckoned that one-seventh of the northern German armies had fallen in front of Dvinsk. The last attack was pressed ten days and ten nights, and it increased in strength towards the end, eight army corps being massed around the fortress. The trenches often changed hands half a dozen times in the twenty-four hours, without weakening the ferocious determination of attackers and defenders.

Hindenburg's futile mass attacks

Finally, the Germans made a grand effort in the old-fashioned massed formation, but the masses were broken up by rapid fire from the Russian rifles, Maxims and guns. Three times in one day did Hindenburg launch a massed infantry assault, but without effect. On each occasion the Russians held back their fire to the last possible moment, and then annihilated the grey swarms at a range of two or three hundred yards. According to the official statements by the Russian Staff, all the fighting which had gone on for fourteen months in Poland and Galicia was mild when compared with that of Dvinsk. Hindenburg apparently thought that, as he had stormed Kovno at a cost of 100,000 men, he could take Dvinsk at the same price in man-power. A single Russian regiment on Monday, September 29th, had to withstand ten thousand rounds of high-explosive shell from the German siege-guns, and then beat back line after line of charging infantry. It was only the extreme narrowness and depth of the Russian trenches that saved the men from shell-blast, shell fragments and poisonous fumes. In the last fortnight of September the enemy did not advance more than a mile in two days against the new works of Dvinsk, and at the end of a month he was still ten miles from the town, with the last line of lake defences in front of him. He tried to turn the position from the north and from the south side ; but whatever move he made he had to continue his frontal attacks, as the circle of Russian defences was complete. At the beginning of October the Germans again struck at the Dwina, forty miles north of Dvinsk ; but having got off the main metalled road, their artillery was bogged in the mud and their convoys were disorganised by the guerilla bands.

By this time the effect of the Franco-British blows against the western German line in Champagne and Artois were felt on the Russian front. The enemy's offensive movement perceptibly slackened everywhere except at Dvinsk, and General Russky began to advance through the southern lakes and also in the north around Riga. The Germans meanwhile laboured at the construction of a field railway running along the Wilkomir road to Dvinsk, so that the largest howitzers and heaviest shells could be brought near the firing-line. Steam cranes were erected in large numbers at the new railhead to lift the monster cylinders into motor-waggons, and all the siege machinery from Kovno and Grodno was brought up to facilitate the working of the great arc of artillery at Dvinsk. The Lithuanian guerilla bands between Dvinsk and Vilna were checked in the first week of October, when Hindenburg at last closely linked his two armies and formed a continuous line from the Dwina to the Pinsk Marsh. Bands of peasant fighters, however, still wandered as far as seventy miles in the rear of the German firing-line, and wrought havoc among the enemy's communications.

By the middle of October the German pressure on the southern lake-line had been relieved, and Hindenburg, seeking the line of least resistance, brought his main forces to the north of the town, where there were more facilities for employing his heavy howitzers. After thirty-five days of continual storming attacks, Russky still faced the enemy with a strong semicircle of earthwork

STRATEGIC WRECKAGE IN THE RIVER NAREW.
Ruins of a railway bridge over the River Narew, that was blown up by Russian troops operating in Poland.

fortifications extending for thirty-five miles in front of Dvinsk. The town was bombed by Zeppelins and monster aeroplanes, but the Russian aviation service had greatly increased the output of aerial craft. The Russian Armies, possessing giant machines, bombarded the enemy's ammunition depots, and, what was still more important, maintained a regular and far-reaching system of reconnaissance over the enemy's lines. By this means it was found that Hindenburg, in the third week in October, was massing against Riga, having apparently come to the conclusion that Dvinsk was impregnable.

While still attacking the great fortress from the north-west, the German commander brought six army corps against Riga, and, heralded by bomb-dropping Zeppelins, an assault was made some miles south of the town, where the broadening Dwina is split by a large island. Dalen, as the river-island is called, lies just north of the farm of Bersemunde. Only a comparatively narrow stream separates it from the bank which the Germans were approaching. A crossing, therefore, could easily be effected, and there was high ground on the northern tongue of the island, from which the broad main eastern stream could be dominated. An immense swamp, ending in a large lake, Babit Lake, stretched to the Riga Gulf from the

Six army corps against Riga

RUSSIAN SCOUTS AMIDST THE BENDING REEDS OF THE PRIPET MARSH.
Scouts on the alert between a Russian outpost position and the enemy lines in Poland.

SCANNING THE ENEMY'S LINES.
Russian officer and Cossack, stationed in the fork of a tree and watching the German position.

A LONELY WATCHER IN THE RUSSIAN VAN.
Scout on outpost duty at an exposed position near the enemy's trenches.

north of the German line of advance. The great swamp known as Tirul Marsh served to protect the attacking army from any flanking movement; and immediately between the swamp and the sea there was only a tongue of sandy soil shaded with pine-woods, along which ran the railway from Schlock to Riga. In addition to the long stretch of water of the Babit Lake, a wide, winding river, the Aa, ran around the swamp and flowed along the seaward tongue of land into the estuary of the Dwina. Altogether, the position on the northern German flank seemed excellent, especially as the seaward peninsula was held by strong forces, entrenched with artillery against any sally from Riga.

But the Russian fleet in the Gulf of Riga began to assert its power in a disconcerting way, and while the enemy was trying to close on the town a Russian force landed far to the rear at Domesness, just by the entrance to the Gulf, and menaced the railways from Windau and Libau. The more immediate object of this surprise landing was to destroy a German force on the coast, which was trying to remove the obstructions in the channel between the mainland and the island of Oesel. With a **Surprise by the Russian fleet** loss of only four men wounded, the Russian landing-party scattered the Germans, destroyed all their works, strengthened the obstacles that kept all German ships out of the Gulf, and produced confusion along the enemy's rear. This neatly-handled little affair had a considerable effect upon the operations on the Dwina, for it enabled the Russian admiral to maintain complete mastery over the waters of the Gulf. He had four 12 in. guns in the old battleship Slava, and many 4 in. and 6 in. guns in vessels of lighter draught. With this considerable power of mobile artillery, he continually shelled the German batteries along the Courland shore of the Gulf, and, like our bombarding squadron off the Belgian coast, held up a considerable force of the enemy by the threat of a landing.

All this, it must be remembered, was achieved in the Baltic waters, where the Germans could employ a much stronger fleet than the Russians possessed. But the Russian Navy had some small but deadly helpers. In both a direct and indirect manner our submarine flotillas exercised much influence upon the land battles along the Dwina, by making the German Admiralty Staff fearful of risking their capitals. Remarkable was the tale of German warships sunk or damaged by our submarines in the Baltic during Hindenburg's operations against the Dwina line. The Pommern, the Moltke, the Prince Adalbert, Undine, Bremen and Gazelle were torpedoed, the Bunz, a mine-layer, was destroyed, and three destroyers and four torpedo-boats were sunk. In October, 1915, the seaborne commerce that German steamers had been carrying on with Sweden was stopped, after the enemy's mercantile marine had suffered great losses. German munition factories began to lack Swedish ore, which was needed for special purposes. Most of the lighter German warships were lost while attempting to clear the Baltic of our underwater craft by chasing them with **Loss of German warships** Zeppelins acting as scouts. Our seamen showed such splendid fighting power and trained ingenuity that all through the critical period of the campaign against Riga they remained practically masters of the Baltic Sea.

The German Admiralty, discovering itself unable to protect the last remnant of its merchant steamer traffic, was averse from resuming its operations in the Gulf of Riga. The British submarine was not the only and chief danger. New Russian battleships were either in commission or approaching completion. In order to engage the increasingly powerful Russian Navy, the Germans would have had to use a large number of their finest battleships and battle-cruisers, with an excellent chance of losing many of them even if a victory were won. The new head of the German Naval Staff, Admiral von Hötzendorff, who was a cautious man, with his weather eye always on our Grand Fleet, refused to indulge in any further Russian adventure, and left Field-Marshal von Hindenburg, the falling idol of Teutondom, to get along as best he could with an outworn army and inadequate railway communications.

TABLE REFINEMENTS UNDER DIFFICULTIES.
Russian officers at an alfresco luncheon behind the firing-line in Poland.

WITH TSARDOM'S FORCES ON THE POLISH FRONT.
Cavalcade of Russian field-guns and ammunition supply waggons passing a house used by Russian Staff officers, and on their way to a new position on the Polish front. In circle : Russian outpost sentry on the plains near the Pripet Marsh.

A RESPITE FROM THE TRENCHES: HARDY SONS OF SLAVDOM ENJOYING A "VACATION" AT A REST CAMP.

After a long spell in the trenches, fighting stubbornly against superior numbers of Germans, these sturdy Russian soldiers were enjoying a brief and well-deserved respite from actual fighting and from the roar of the guns, at a rest camp in a village behind the front lines. Hanging between some of the stacked rifles are their clothes, being dried; the men in the foreground are using a pail as a cooking utensil; behind are two travelling field kitchens, where steaming tea and the soldiers' favourite soup, "stchi," are being prepared.

In these circumstances the old Field-Marshal, with Generals Below, Lauenstein, Eichhorn, Scholtz, Litzmann, and Ludendorff under his control, resolved on a supreme effort against Riga towards the end of October. The troops, who were already suffering badly from the cold, damp climate, were told that the new operations would close the war. First of all, they would win warm, comfortable, healthy winter quarters in the ancient Hanse town of Riga, and add the historic German-founded city to the Empire; and then the great Slav enemy, having lost the last line of defence and the railway from the Baltic to Galicia, would be compelled by hopeless disaster—military, naval, and economic—to sue for peace. There was a smattering of truth in this official statement. The **The mirage of German success** German Chief of Staff, Erich von Falkenhayn, had fixed on Riga as the northern limit of the Teutonic advance. When the Dwina line was secured and strongly fortified, it was intended to swing a large part of the army through Poland into Galicia, with the object of reaching Odessa.

It was expected that Mackensen's forces, operating in Serbia, would quickly clear the road to Salonika with Bulgarian aid, and be released for the Odessa expedition about the same time as certain of Hindenburg's armies were set free for work in the south. The comparatively mild climate and great productiveness of the wheat region of South Russia made it a favourable ground for a winter campaign. Falkenhayn considered that Russia would need at least six months to arm her new formations, and from his point of view, therefore, it was a matter of vital importance to press her as hard as possible during the winter, and deliver a decisive blow early in the New Year before her new armies were ready.

But before all this could be done, and a great slice cut permanently out of Russia from Riga to Odessa to form the new kingdom of the Eastern Slav Confederation, Riga had to be captured. Hindenburg's forces had been terribly weakened by the continual storming mass attacks against Dvinsk. So a large body of fresh troops, most of whom were only half-trained, was railed into Courland, and collected round Tukum and Mitau. As will be seen on the map, both these towns are close to Riga, and are connected by a railway that skirts the large swamp of Tirul. From Mitau the railway runs along the eastern side of the swamp by the village of Olai to Riga. Hindenburg's design was to attack Riga from the south through Mitau and Olai and the island of Dalen, and at the same time to close in on the north from Tukum, **Riga blocks the way** along the peninsula and the shore of Lake Babit. At the beginning of October the three northernmost German army corps advanced from their strong entrenchments between Tukum and Schlock and spread along both sides of the Babit Lake. By the sea the land narrows in places to less than a mile; and the enemy had to go forward in a formation of great depth with an exceedingly narrow front. All the fighting had to be done by a small front rank which could be held up by a few well-entrenched machine-guns and quick-firing batteries. And

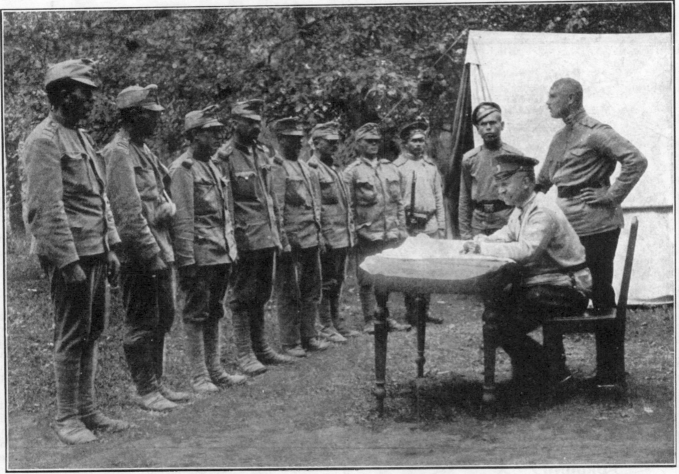

PRISONERS BEING INTERROGATED ON THE DWINA FRONT.
Russian Staff officers interrogating Austrian prisoners in an endeavour to elicit useful information as to the enemy's strength and possible movements.

when the front German lines were checked, the dense masses behind jammed together, and in many places interfered with the gun teams. This alone would have been sufficient to enable the Russian heavy artillery, working with aerial observers, to blast the masses away. But to add to the difficulties of Hindenburg's men, all the Russian warships in the Gulf of Riga steamed close to the shore and opened fire on their flank.

General Russky, with Radko Dimitrieff in immediate control of the Riga army, had his foes again in a death-trap. It was far worse than the bottle at Lodz into which he lured two of Mackensen's army corps. Between the anvil of the warships and the hammer of the heavy Russian batteries near Schlock, the German advance was completely broken up with little expense to the Lettish and Russian infantry. Then, on the south-west of Lake Babit, where the Germans managed to storm some Russian trenches, a strong defending column recovered the position and turned round the western edge of the lake, and there joined with the victorious force advancing along the peninsula. By the end of the first week in November all the German operations along the north of the marsh of Tirul came to an end, and before Hindenburg could reorganise his battered divisions Dimitrieff closed on Kemmern and took it by storm.

Kemmern taken by storm

Above Kemmern is Lake Kanger, with the village of Anting on the southern shore and Ragasem on the north. All the ground in the late autumn was a mass of bog-land, patched with copses and pine-woods, and the forces on both sides were frequently fighting waist-deep in the slimy morasses. The struggle lasted nearly a fortnight, the German commander throwing fresh troops into the fighting-line as his front continually weakened. But these new men were unfit for their work, being half-trained levies whose lack of discipline, shown by their marauding exploits, had already made them a byword among the veteran German troops. The German Staff had intended them only to be used with an overwhelming force of siege artillery to make a mass attack preparatory to the charge of the more experienced troops.

But the German commander on the Dwina front had lost so many of his best men that he had to use the raw levies in important holding positions. They were strengthened with an extraordinary number of machine-guns; in many places there was one gun to every ten infantrymen. This reliance on the machinery of war did not help the enemy. At Kemmern especially the new troops, many of them discontented Social Democrats, broke and fled in **German reliance on machinery** utter panic before the pressure of the Russians became really severe. The previous long and wearing fight in the bog-land had taken the heart out of the northern army, and it was only the heavy German guns of position, placed immediately around Tukum, and provided with a good store of shells, that prevented the German line in Courland from being turned. The victorious Russian column, by the third week in November, had pushed the enemy beyond Lake Kanger, and had arrived within seven miles of the railway at Tukum. Only the impossibility of bringing the heavy guns of the Riga defences across some twenty miles of swamps, soaked with autumnal rain, stopped General Dimitrieff from reversing the Russian and German positions, and laying siege to the Tukum defences.

As it was, the victorious Bulgarian commander at Riga devised a more subtle means of wearing down the remaining strength of the German forces. The chief German position had run from Kemmern along the River Aa; and after capturing this line the Russian soldiers were astonished at what they found there. It was well known that the German Emperor had stated that if any of his commanders had any men in winter suffering from frost-bite and chill he would be tried for negligence. This sounded at the time like a vain boast; but it was found

The Great War

MAP ILLUSTRATING THE RIGA LEMBERG RAILWAY SYSTEM.

that the organisation of the German lines in view of the winter campaign was a marvel of efficiency. The Germans had suffered terribly along the Rawka in Poland in the previous winter; but since then their ingenious engineers had devised a scheme for keeping the army warm during the hardest frost. Light metal buildings, manufactured in great quantities in standardised parts and fitted with steam-heating apparatus, were erected in dug-outs beneath the trenches. Each man had a sleeping-sack; a large daily supply of alcohol was provided, and orders were given that the soldiers should rub themselves all over with the spirit regularly every day. The officers had to act like doctors, and see that their men did not suffer from frost, Hindenburg's orders being that the officer who lost a single man from the frost deserved to be shot.

Even more astonishing than all these medical preparations was the great accumulation of cotton and linen goods found in the captured positions. Collections of domestic linen had been made through-out Germany; and all the houses in the Russian provinces occupied by the enemy **Trench-making by dynamite** had been systematically pillaged of calico, linen and holland, and any material of white colour. Then there were tripod devices for carrying a vast expanse of light white material, sometimes square for the troops to bivouac under it, sometimes narrow and long to cover an advancing line. The idea was to hide the troops when the snow fell, and enable them to creep across the frozen marshes for a grand surprise attack, with all uniforms and supply carts covered in white material, making them invisible on the snow. The Germans had also accumulated an amazing quantity of boring tools and blasting explosives. In the Courland winter the ground freezes to a depth of four feet and more, and trench-digging, under battle conditions, becomes impossible. So the ingenious and foreseeing Germans organised a large boring corps, whose duty it was to creep forward and plough up new trenches by means of dynamite as cover for the advancing forces.

But in the early part of the winter the boring corps around Riga and Dvinsk used all their energies in making land-mines by the hundred thousand, for it was found that the ordinary system of wire entanglements became quite useless in Courland. The ground froze, the rivers iced over, and the snow ceased to melt. It piled above the wire entanglements and buried them; and, as the snow thickened and hardened, there was at last enough hard material above the wires to enable the troops to climb safely over the entanglements. So a vast system of dynamite mines was constructed by the German engineers. Then a large number of infantry were trained in ski travelling. In the previous winter the Germans had won some small successes in East Prussia by means of ski work. After three days of snowstorms the Russian troops had sunk up to their chests in the snow, and while in this difficult posture they had been attacked and defeated by German troops on skis. So at Tukum the entire German army was trained in Arctic sports, and provided **Methods of arctic warfare** with sledges and skis in preparation for a great raid on the Russian lines after a heavy snowstorm. Naturally our allies, from whom we derive all this information, took steps to counter this Arctic method of warfare, in which cotton-dressed troops, white-washed sledges, and ski-ing divisions were expected, and the result we have to relate in our next Russian chapter.

Meanwhile, when the first light frosts of winter only were felt, General Dimitrieff's troops worried the enemy back to Tukum on the north and Mitau on the south. The German position at Olai was stormed in the first week of November, and the creeping movement continued on the line of lakes south of Dvinsk. Only a single company, or at the most a regiment, was usually employed in this kind of fighting, which the Russians called "little war." The object was to rob the enemy of small stretches of

Picturesque impression of a band of refugees taking cover in a wood. With the typical Russian waggon, they had come miles away from the danger zone, and were about to pitch their camp for the night. The womenfolk are preparing an evening meal.

Russian artillery descending into a dale in the neighbourhood of Grodno in order to take up a new position facing the enemy, whose advanced trenches may be faintly discerned on the horizon.

Russian engineers repairing a road in a pleasantly-wooded section of the eastern front. An engineer officer seated imperturbably on a grey charger superintends the pressing work. The sturdy proportions of most of the soldiers seen in this illustration will be remarked.

THREE PHASES OF THE STRUGGLE BETWEEN TSARDOM AND THE CENTRAL EMPIRES.

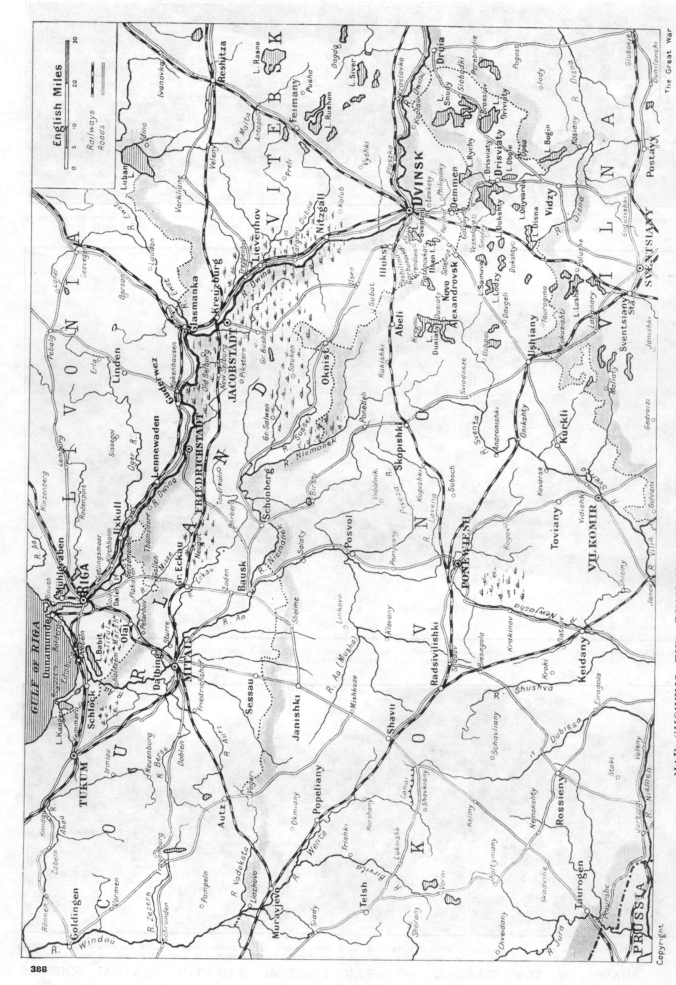

388

MAP SHOWING THE RUSSIAN NORTH FRONT LINE FROM RIGA TO DVINSK.

The great lake district between Riga and Dvinsk is of immense strategic importance, as it covers Petrograd. The country is so spotted with lakes, large and small, that it resembles an irregular piece of lace.

The Great War

his highly-organised trenches, and throw him back a few hundred yards where he would feel the stress of the weather. It was the patches of dry ground that the Russians coveted, and, having a manifest superiority over their foes, they pushed them into the bogs and low-lying watery ground by the river-courses. All this was done in accordance with a systematic plan; and when General Russky, the army group commander over Dimitrieff, had at last to retire from his command through illness, he left his successor in a happy position. The Germans held some healthy hill-country at Tukum, but their lines round the Tirul swamp and along the Dwina and the lake district, were calculated to sicken them of war. General Evert, who took control of all the Russian lines, from the Gulf of Riga to the Pinsk Marsh, became only the assistant to the two most famous of all Russian commanders —"General January" and "General February." These were their names, at least, in the days of Napoleon, but the modern moujik combined them into one personification—"Daddy Frost."

Most of the work of the little war was carried on by local volunteer forces and other new formations of fresh, spirited troops. Owing to the numerous bogs and lakes between Riga and Brest Litovsk, the enemy was unable to construct and hold an unbroken fortified front. There were hundreds of gaps in his trench system, and these had to be watched day and night by mobile forces which were generally scattered along the firm tracts marked on the Staff maps. But there were many other paths known to the local peasantry, and as the weather changed under recurring spells of frost and rain, the geography of the marshes altered in a way that only the inhabitants could foresee. A hard frost at night would open new lines of attack along ways unguarded by

Where Staff maps failed

THE WAR BY NIGHT.

Russian soldiers fixing a powerful searchlight in position on the outskirts of a wood. This apparatus was essentially mobile, and could be drawn rapidly from place to place by a horse attached to a small waggon. At the desired point, it was only necessary to elevate the light, the supports of which were horizontal with the shafts of the conveyance. It was then connected with the battery and a telephone-post, so that the light, artillery, and trenches were inter-communicable.

any German patrols, and the consequence was that there were hundreds of little raids through the German lines which were never mentioned in the official reports. But their cumulative effect throughout the winter campaign did more to wear down the strength of Germany than any of the ordinary methods of the war of position followed on the Franco-British front. In Courland, especially, the Germans were too far from their own country to make full use of their resources. In the previous winter they had had immediately behind them the splendid Prussian railway system, but along the Dwina their communications were so bad that they were beaten to a standstill for want of high-explosive shells, at a time when their munition factories were producing a quarter of a million shells a day. And,

seeing that they could not transport sufficient shells from their abundant home magazines, it may be taken that the lack of other less important but very useful supplies was more severely felt by the troops, particularly when they lost their well-organised positions and had to improvise new trench systems.

Their convoys were raided by the guerilla bands, and by adventurous parties of regular soldiers, who broke through the marshes. The most famous exploit took place in the Pinsk Marsh in November, near the little town of Nevel. Here the commander of the 82nd German Division had his Staff headquarters in a comfortable country-house, standing in a garden with no other houses near it. A young Russian officer in charge of a scouting party learnt from the peasants in the swamp that the place was not closely guarded. With a local guide the

ON THE TRACK OF ADVENTURE.
Spirited impression of Russian soldiers about to attack an enemy patrol.
An officer precedes the company.

UNDER SAFE COVER.
German troops engaging a Russian outpost from behind a sand-bag barricade.

PRISONER AND CAPTOR FRATERNISE.
The genial Slav apparently bore the Hun little or no malice if he could dine with him, as is seen in this illustration.

raiders set out one dark night with snow falling, and, after a fifteen-mile tramp across the bog-land, they came within sight of the lights of Nevel. The small band had a short rest, and then crossed the Stochod River, and got among the enemy's detachments. Working forward quietly, they entered the garden, and, crawling up through the snow to the house, found sentries guarding the back and front.

Swift, silent death overtook the unsuspecting sentries, and the Russians entered, and were at first mistaken for German soldiers. They slew the telephone-operator, and then, with bayonets and hand-grenades, worked through the house, capturing two German generals in their beds, with two other officers, a doctor, and some privates. Meanwhile, the shots roused the German division, and the nearest regiment hurried to the rescue. But a few Russian riflemen held them off till all the prisoners had been taken across the river, and were lost to pursuit amid the bogs. The little rearguard also got away with the loss of only two men, and after another tramp of fifteen miles, the raiders reached their own lines in the morning with their amazing capture. It is clear that when German generals could be captured in this manner at their headquarters, well behind the fighting-line, the risks run by company officers and their men, while trying to hold the marsh regions, were very great.

German generals captured

General von Woyrsch's army, which had advanced from Brest Litovsk to the wildest part of the Pinsk swamp, was utterly worn out by guerilla bands in its rear and skirmishing Russian parties along its front. In his first strong sweep Woyrsch drove far along the Pripet River and its northern tributaries, and reached, at the railway junction of Luninetz, the most easterly point gained by any invading force. Luninetz is 142 miles east of Brest Litovsk and about 36 miles east of the town of Pinsk. The railway line from Riga to Lemberg passes through it, also the railway from Brest Litovsk and Moscow. The position was therefore one of high strategic importance. But though General von Woyrsch fortified it, and brought up his main force as a garrison, he could not keep what he had won. For he was in the worst part of the 33,600 square miles of marshland, generally known as the Pinsk, or Pripet, Marsh, but referred to in both German and Russian communiqués as the Polyesye—which is Russian for waste forest-land. The drainage operations, begun in 1875, had only affected the swamp region near Brest Litovsk, and the region at which Von Woyrsch's army arrived was still primitive bog-land, which only the defending forces knew how to use.

They cut up the German convoys, starved the invading army of munitions, and then, in a series of terrible conflicts, threw the Germans out of Luninetz and pursued them along the swamp beyond the town of Pinsk. At the time when the German generals were captured by the marsh trappers, General von Woyrsch, instead of commanding the most advanced of the Teutonic forces, had his line bent farther back than any other German or Austrian Army leader. On his left hand Prince Leopold of Bavaria fought for months round the railway junction of Baranovitschi, 125 miles south-west of Vilna. On his right hand Linsingen, Ermolli, Bothmer, and Pflanzer tried in vain to advance from Kovel and Eastern Galicia and get command of the Rovno section of the Lemberg-Riga line. In this southern area of

Enemy held by Ivanoff

battle General Ivanoff continued to hold the enemy by a continual swaying movement along the Strypa and Styr Rivers, with the little town of Czartorysk, near the southern skirts of the Pinsk Marsh, as the chief pivot of conflict.

The process of attrition proceeded with a very high wastage on General Ivanoff's front. For the Austrian and German generals were as active on this right wing as was Hindenburg on the left wing. They had been set the task of clearing the Russians out of Galicia and making the great drive towards Kieff and Odessa. The forces of Austria-Hungary were mainly devoted to this scheme of operations. German reinforcements were also sent to Linsingen, and all the German centre was weakened to strengthen

PROFESSIONAL CURIOSITY.
Guns captured by our Russian allies from their western "neighbours." As the photograph shows, the Russian soldiers were much interested in the mechanism of the guns and in the marks indicating the place of their manufacture.

WITH THE TSAR'S VANGUARD ON THE DEFENSIVE.
Russian infantry advancing to the attack, having crossed a narrow stream by means of an improvised bridge. The centre illustration depicts a ruined railway reservoir near Kelze. The edifice was neatly sectioned by artillery fire.

the wings. Battles of large scope were fought along the Strypa and the Styr every week. Sometimes, indeed, there were three great battles a week, in which ten thousand prisoners were taken and a score of guns. All through the late autumn until Christmas, 1915, General Ivanoff and his brilliant army commanders stood on the defensive; for even their sudden victorious thrusts into the enemy's front were only designed to keep him quiet, and knock the attacking power out of him.

Everywhere the Russians were fighting for time. They had new levies, amounting to four million men, and they were arming and training them by the hundred thousand, as rifles and guns came from Japan. The terrific series of blows dealt by Falkenhayn had left Russia too weak to make any attack upon Bulgaria and save the Serbian armies from complete disaster. But feeble though Mother Russia was, with the flower of her young manhood destroyed or disabled, she yet managed to withstand the last blows by which her enemies sought to overthrow her. The cost of weakening her had been so great that Germany and Austria were also too much exhausted in man-power to carry out their plan of campaign. Thus there was produced in the eastern theatre of war a position of stalemate similar to that existing for a year in the western field of conflict.

Towards the beginning of December, Erich von Falkenhayn made one last effort to reach a more favourable line of fortified entrenchments. Linsingen and Ermolli, who had been trying for ten weeks **Provinces of** to conquer Sarny and Rovno, gave **barbed-wire** up all attempts to make a serious advance, and dug themselves in near the Rumanian frontier behind ten and more lines of wire entanglements. As a Russian officer put it, they created provinces of barbed-wire; and behind the wire were thousands of machine-guns and the remnants of the older manhood of the Dual Monarchy. What fresh troops were immediately available were sent far north to Mitau, where Hindenburg made one more essay to capture Riga.

He selected for attack the large river-island of Dalen,

lying in the Dwina within gunshot of Riga. He advanced against this island from the south along the little stream Berse which flows into the Dwina at the farmstead of Bersemunde, fourteen miles south of the coveted seaport. The farm was captured by the Germans on November 24th, and preparations were made to occupy the river peninsula and pass over to Dalen island, and thence force a passage across the Dwina at a spot where a series of islets half bridged the main western current. As a matter of fact, Hindenburg's forces had twice won a foot- ing on Dalen island since the summer of **The fight for** 1915. They had been driven out of it **Bersemunde** owing to their weak hold upon some dominating hills in the neighbourhood. These hills rose along the Berse stream near the farmstead, and on November 24th, 1915, the Germans, besides occupying the farm and all the area between the rivers, stormed the heights and occupied them with machine-guns and light artillery, and began to haul up their siege trains for the bombardment of the south- western sector of the Riga defences.

The positions they had won, quite close to the town, and with excellent means of crossing the river, seemed to promise victory at a time when all hope of further conquest had been abandoned. But most of the heavy guns had to be brought around the Tirul swamp, and across the marshy land and forests farther south, where both the Courland guerilla bands and the Russian scouting parties were working actively. And long before the guns and reinforcements arrived, Radko Dimitrieff, while repulsing an advance on Kemmern, designed to distract his forces from the points of importance, launched a division of fighting Letts against the lost farmstead and hills. For three days the struggle went on with increasing fury. The farmstead was recovered and lost and again recovered. Then after a hill had been carried and some machine-guns captured, the enemy was pressed back and thrown over the Berse in a shattered condition. As in most of the struggles round Riga, the Russians had but few prisoners to show the extent of their victory. This was merely a sign that the eighty-hours' fight had been conducted by the Lettish volunteers.

"GONE TO EARTH," A PHENOMENON OF SIEGE WARFARE IN RUSSIA.

Owing to the scarcity of accommodation behind the firing front our Eastern ally resorted to underground quarters, building spacious dug-outs and endowing them with some semblance of home comfort. This photo- graph shows such an encampment. Underneath the large mounds dozens of soldiers resided, and people from the adjacent village assisted in the preparation and embellishment of these subterranean dwellings.

THE VICEROY OF THE CAUCASUS IN THE FIELD. GRAND DUKE NICHOLAS IN CONSULTATION WITH SOME OF HIS STAFF.
After withdrawing the Russian forces from their perilous situation on the eastern front, only abandoning Warsaw at the last moment, the Grand Duke was appointed Viceroy of the Caucasus in October, 1915, so that the Tsar in person could take over command of the armies in Western Russia. In spite of a lack of munitions, the Grand Duke's strategic ability was recognised as having saved Russia from overwhelming defeat. The importance of the Caucasus front could not be over-estimated, and only a large army led by a cool and far-seeing commander could prevent the Turco-Teutons from swooping down on Persia and making this country a base for operations against India.

The Germans in Courland paid for their long tale of crimes against non-combatants within a few months of the time when they committed their misdeeds. So heavy was the continual wastage that a considerable part of the army of Prince Leopold of Bavaria had to be moved up to garrison the Dwina front during the winter.

Meanwhile the first new Russian army, which was armed too late to help Serbia, became ready to take the field in the last week of December, 1915. Had the bold Russian Commander-in-Chief, General Alexeieff, been able to choose his attacking point, he could have broken the German front as soon as the frost solidified the marsh-ground. The German centre especially was very weak, and as the Russian gunners had some millions of shells for immediate use, they could have equalled the hurricane fire effect of Mackensen's Phalanx. But the need of bringing pressure to bear on Bulgaria and helping Rumania to retain her freedom of action, and assisting the stricken Serbians in Albania, compelled the Russian commander to attack the enemy on his right wing. In other words, General Ivanoff received the new army as a re-inforcement, with orders to begin a strong offensive movement against the German and Austrian troops on the Styr and Strypa. The movement developed on December 30th, 1915, and its immediate effect was to bring Mackensen in haste from Serbia, check the Austro-German-Bulgarian attack upon the Franco-British camp at Salonika, and

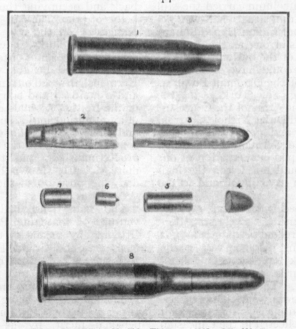

USED CONTRARY TO THE LAWS OF WAR.
Cartridge found on Austrian soldier.—1. Brass case. 2. Case for explosive bullet. 3. Lead lining. 4. Lead bullet at head of cartridge. 5. Cylinder containing explosives. 6. Pin which strikes cap attached to cylinder. 7. Cylinders in which the pin is placed. 8. Cartridge complete.

relieve the pressure upon the Serbian and Italian troops in Albania. So desperately hard pressed were the Teutons that they had not sufficient men to resist the Russians, and a Bulgarian force of 30,000 men had to be brought into Bukovina to strengthen the defence. Some of the Bulgarians, dressed in Austrian uniforms, were captured, and they readily revealed all the facts of the situation—with which they naturally were not pleased.

Such were some of the immediate results. But the mere appearance on the battlefield of the great new Russian army, that fired heavy shell continuously for twenty-four hours, was an event of mighty import. By an effort of recuperation unequalled in the history of her struggles against Mongols, Swedes, Prussians, and the Grand Army of Napoleon, Russia had, three months after the battles in the Vilna salient, shown herself capable of striking harder than she had ever done before. Reckoning from the date of the appearance of Mackensen's Phalanx at Gorlice, it had only taken Russia eight months to organise an artillery power as formidable as that of the enemy, and to create a new army as large as that which had been lost. And all this had been done while the Teutons were hammering their way through the frontier fortresses, capturing province after province, and straining the Russian power of resistance to breaking-point.

Moreover, while engaged on the double task of holding back the enemy from the Riga-Rovna railway line, and building up a

DEATH'S EYRIE AMONG THE PEAKS OF THE CAUCASUS.
"Eagle's Nest" is a peak 5,000 feet high in the Caucasus, where Russian sharpshooters were posted to pick off the enemy. Every man was a crack shot, and the place was a veritable eyrie whence Death swooped down upon the foes of Russia.

new army and a gigantic siege train, Russia—colossal Russia—had sufficient strength left over to extend her armed forces into Persia and prevent the Turks, Germans, and Swedish police-officers from conquering the country and making it a base for operations against India and our Persian Gulf possessions. The help we rendered Russia by our submarine flotillas in the Baltic was repaid by the aid which the Russian Army of the Caucasus rendered us in Persia. About the middle of December one Russian column, after breaking the Swedish-officered gendarmerie and the German mercenaries at Bulak, **Russian successes** captured Hamadan on the road between **in Asia Minor** Teheran and Bagdad. Soon afterwards another Russian column carried the still more important enemy centre of Kum, situate half-way between Hamadan and Ispahan. If our Indian Expeditionary Force in Mesopotamia had been as strong as the occasion required, the combined operations of the outlying forces of the Russian and British Empires could have struck such a blow against the eastern flank of the Ottoman Power as would have broken the prestige of Turkey in the Mohammedan world. As it was, the Army of the Caucasus, under its new commander the Grand Duke Nicholas, carried out its work in Northern Persia, and prevented another country from being flung into the German fighting-line. This greatly helped to relieve the perilous situation of our forces on the Tigris, though it could not lessen the high prestige which the Turks had won in Gallipoli and in the battle for Bagdad.

The Persian campaign developed with great rapidity until the victorious Russian force and the sorely struggling British columns on the Tigris were only separated by a fortnight's march. The intervening distance was nearly two hundred miles, but the track ran through difficult mountainous country, where Kurds and other hostile tribesmen could hold up an army. The Turks, however, were much alarmed by the narrowing gap between the British and Russian columns, and in the first week of January, 1916, strong forces were collected in the Caucasian region, and marched over the Persian frontier, with a view to beating back the Russian expeditionary force. At the same time a band of Persian freebooters, numbering a thousand men under Khan Kassandan, swept down to

the shore of the Caspian Sea and ravaged a couple of towns there, and tried to cut the line of communications with the Russian column. But the Russian commander flung out detachments on his menaced rear. In parties of about three hundred men, the men covering the line of supplies toiled over snow-covered mountains, and by a remarkable little piece of accurately-timed strategy surrounded the band on all sides, and destroyed it.

This defeat made the Turkish commander yet more anxious to deliver, at all costs, a staggering blow against the Russian expeditionary force in Persia. By still further strengthening the army he had sent over the frontier, he succeeded in pushing the Cossack vanguard back and occupying the town of Kermanshah. The main body of the Russian expeditionary force was then at Kangavar, on the way to Kermanshah, and it looked as though the Turks, having effected a junction with the rebellious Persian police and their Swedish and German officers, would be able to cause grave trouble in Persia. Kermanshah stood on a mountain fifty miles from Kangavar, and a hundred and sixty miles from Bagdad. It was one of the frontier arsenals of Persia, with a considerable store of ammunition and an important garrison of regular troops, and since the autumn of 1915 the Germans had been in control of it. With the Russians held up strongly in front of Kermanshah, and the British still more violently thrown back from Bag- **Why the Grand Duke** dad, the position of the Allies seemed **went south** very gloomy.

The man who had designed this seemingly wild venture of snatching Persia and Mesopotamia from the Ottoman by means of two small columns that could not meet was the Grand Duke Nicholas. After conducting with success the retreat of the Russian armies from Galicia, Poland, and Lithuania, the Grand Duke had apparently retired under a cloud from the command on the Eastern Front, his disgrace being, it seemed to some critics, merely mitigated in consideration of his Royal birth and undoubted personal merit, by his appointment to the command-in-chief in the Caucasus, where only routine defensive work was required.

This was the common superficial view taken of the affair. But the truth of the matter was far different. During the extraordinary battle in the Warsaw salient Russia had discovered that in the son of one of her non-commissioned officers of the last generation she had a leader of great capacity, who had won slowly forward by success after success during the Manchurian campaign and the European War. This officer of humble origin was General Alexeieff, and his successful stand against overwhelming odds along the Bzura, along the Narew, and at Vilna proved him to be a man of daring and coolness. The Grand Duke Nicholas, on the other hand, appeared rather a man of talent. He was a cautious calculator and an experienced organiser, but he was supposed to have given some of his army commanders rather too free a hand. Alexeieff was reckoned to be bolder in action, as when he let Russia apparently dance on the edge of death at Vilna, in order that his assistants, Russky and Everts, might trap the over-confident Teuton. Alexeieff was also a firmer disciplinarian than the Grand Duke. There was more of the drill-sergeant in him, and by working over the Russian Army battalion by battalion he removed all the weak links in a way that the Grand Duke, who trusted largely to his Staff, had not done.

Alexeieff to the fore

But the Grand Duke, with all the defects of his aristocratic temperament, was a master of war, and he was given the command of the Caucasian front because a fine intellect was urgently needed there. About the time that the Russian armies escaped from the enveloping movements of Mackensen and Hindenburg, the Franco-British expedition to the Dardanelles suffered a complete and decisive defeat. This led Ferdinand of Bulgaria to conclude that the day had come for him to assist the Germans, Austrians, and Turks, in order that he might share fully in the spoils of victory. It could be foreseen that, with railway communications restored between the Ottoman and Teutonic empires, guns, shells, and other munitions of war would rapidly be poured into Turkey. One result of this would be that newly-armed Turkish levies would largely strengthen the existing armies, and these armies would have an increased artillery power. The Caucasian front would become, in the spring of 1916, one of the principal theatres of war; for the German Staff would arrange for the main striking force of Turkey to be hurled against the Caucasian line, with a view to distracting large Russian forces from the European field of conflict.

Importance of the Caucasus

So important, therefore, was the Caucasian front that if the Grand Duke had not gone there Alexeieff would have been sent. The Grand Duke was at last on his mettle. When he had taken over the commandership of all the Russian armies there had been no general of any genius in his nation against whom he could measure himself, for all the generals then rested under the dark cloud of the Manchurian campaign, in which Kuropatkin, by aimless vacillation, had prevented his subordinate commanders from showing the best that was in them. But in the European War, thanks in large measure to the Grand Duke Nicholas' sound and steady leadership, Russia had produced a fair number of competent leaders.

The Grand Duke then received the impetus which comes of contact with other fine minds, and the result was that he came to the Caucasus in a mood of daring as great as that of Alexeieff. Many of his former successes were not of his design. The first smashing Galician campaign had been worked out by Russky, and it was Russky who chiefly engineered, with the assistance

RUSSIAN ADVANCE GUARD ENTERING A TURKISH VILLAGE IN THE CAUCASUS.
Though the Russian Army of the Caucasus was very silent for months it was by no means idle. At the end of August, 1915, it fought a series of small engagements, in which 2,000 Turks were killed, took 5,000 prisoners, and captured a number of guns.

of Ivanoff, the destruction of a large part of the Austro-Hungarian first-line armies. It was also Russky who had trapped Mackensen near Lodz, and had it not been for the recurring illness of this great Russian strategist he would probably have won the supreme position that Alexeieff gained.

However, in the Caucasus the Grand Duke at last had a clear field for displaying his personal powers of mind. And we think it will be generally admitted that he showed a combination of subtlety and strength such as Russky and Alexeieff only equalled. In order to take the Turk completely by surprise, he chose the apparently impossible season of midwinter for his swoop across the grim, frozen, snow-mantled heights. The physical strain he thus put upon his men was terrible, but he mitigated it by procuring strong reinforcements from Western Siberia and Manchuria—regions where men were hardened and toughened by a very rigorous winter climate.

Opposed to him was a Turkish army of about a quarter of a million men, based on Erzerum, the capital of Turkish Armenia. The Turkish entrenchments, dug under the

STRONG ENOUGH TO HOLD AN ARMY AT BAY.
If one machine-gun could hold up a battalion, one can imagine the destructive power of a whole section of these deadly weapons. This illustration shows a squad of Russian machine-gunners in action on the Bessarabian front.

supervision of German engineers, stretched northward along the Deve Boyun range to Lake Tortum and eastward past Koprikeui. The former commander of the Russian Caucasian Army had attacked the Turks in November, 1914, near Tortum Lake, and had routed two Turkish divisions. But in December, 1914, Enver Pasha arrived at the head of the main fighting force of the Ottoman Empire, and, by an outflanking movement with superior numbers, drove the Russians over the frontier towards Kars. In very violent mountain fighting on Russian territory, between large bodies of troops.

Turks vanquished on the heights the Turks were again defeated and thrown back to their own land, and before Enver Pasha could again bring all the Ottoman reserve forces to bear against Russia, our Dardanelles expedition relieved the pressure upon our ally.

The Turk then turned the Caucasian front into an affair of siege warfare, and each side deeply entrenched on the mountain slopes and drew off many troops to participate in the more important operations in Europe. The con-

ditions of the parallel battle in the Caucasian Mountains were similar to those afterwards obtaining in the High Alps between the Italians and Austrians. Long and laborious engineering operations were needed to capture merely one useful observation peak, so that the line scarcely altered for a year. The former Russian commander extended his operations to Lake Van and the Persian frontier, seeking merely for easier ground in which to engage the enemy. The Grand **Britain and Russia** Duke Nicholas' plan of sending a strong **draw near** expeditionary force into Persia seemed to be merely a continuation of this routine and almost mechanical extension of the fighting-line. But as it was combined with a British advance up the Tigris, the outlying Russian and British columns threatened a great turning movement against the Turkish forces entrenched in the Caucasian Mountains. The natural answer to this was to move a fairly considerable body of Turkish troops from the Caucasus front into Persia and this, we have seen, was done. Apparently Field-Marshal von der Goltz, supposed to be the grand modern master of strategy, directed all the Turkish movements. He merely did what seemed to be the sound, sensible, ordinary thing, in weakening his mountain front, which was safely buried in snow, in order to check the eastern extension of the Russian and British lines towards Bagdad.

He did, in fact, what the Grand Duke Nicholas calculated he would do, and on January 8th a little incident occurred on the Turkish Caucasian centre, near Tortum Lake, which seemed to be without significance. A party of Russian scouts dropped down from the snowy heights and threw the Turks out of the village, while a stronger force of Russians stormed the hamlet of Tev by the lakeside. The Russian commander sent up local reinforcements which met with unexpected resistance. Then, at other places along the fortified line, skirmishes of the same kind occurred. In all of them the Russians bombed and bayoneted their way into advanced posts from which they could not be expelled. The Grand Duke was testing the strength of the enemy's system of entrenchments, and the result was so satisfactory that on January 17th, 1916, a general attack was delivered against sixty miles of the Turkish mountain line between Lake Tortum and Chariansu River.

At several places the Russian troops had to climb over heights towering above the clouds, and dig trenches in the deep snow in blinding, freezing snowstorms. But the terrible severity of the weather amid the mountains was one of the contributing causes to the Russian victory. The Turks were completely overwhelmed in their fortified lines by the Russian attack and they retreated in disorderly haste on their second positions along the Deve Boyun mountain range north of Erzerum. Then it was that the great physical powers of endurance of the Russian troops, and the masterly strategy of their Royal commander, told with full effect. The Turkish centre was broken, and the three army corps, entrenched on the mountains, were routed with great slaughter, and scarcely more than half the Turkish troops won to the shelter of the Erzerum forts, for the Cossacks got among the fugitives

THE DERBY RECRUITING CAMPAIGN.

The Splendid Initial Response of Britain's Finest Men—Thirty Thousand Men a Week Required—The Apparent Exhaustion of the Voluntary System—The Vain Calls for Fresh Men—The Hesitant Two Million—The Desire to be "Fetched"—Feeling in the Highlands and the North Country—Our Traditional Opposition to Conscription—The Feeling Among the Working Classes—The Ridicule of Lord Roberts—Mr. Asquith and Lord Kitchener Confer with Labour Representatives—Lord Kitchener's Guarantee of Victory—The Organisation of a Fresh Recruiting Campaign—Lord Derby to the Fore—A Summary of his Services—Lord Derby as an Advocate of National Service—The Recruiting Director's New Scheme—The National Register as the Basis of a Recruiting Canvass—Volunteering under the "Group System"—The Forty-six Groups—Lord Derby's Optimism—The One Weak Point in the Scheme: The Case of the Married Men—Mr. Asquith's Declaration of Policy—His Pledge to Married Men—Lord Derby's Official Statement—The Appeal from the King—Sir George Pragnell's Armlet Suggestion Adopted—Growing Resentment Against the "Slackers"—The Foolish "White Feather" Campaign—Women's Attitude to Unenlisted Men—District Directors of Recruiting—The Sudden Lapse of the "Boom"—Mr. Bonar Law Voices the Threat of Compulsion for Single Men—Lord Derby Reaffirms the Promise to Married Men—His Letter to Mr. Asquith—Local Tribunals Appointed with a Central Appeal Tribunal—Net Results of the Scheme Disappointing—The Appeal of the Joint Labour Committee—The Final Revival in Recruiting—Extending the Time Limit—Lord Derby's Significant Statement—The Thirty Opponents of National Service—The Anti-Conscriptionists' Suggested Way Out—Serious Dissension in the Cabinet—Sir John Simon's Opposition and Resignation—Lord Derby's Report—The Figures—The Introduction of the Military Service Bill—Those to be Exempted—The Premier's Clear Statement: "We Must Keep our Promises"—Sir John Simon States the Case Against the Bill—General Seely's Passionate Speech—Mr. Herbert Samuel's Reply to Sir John Simon's Facts and Figures—The Dwindling Opposition—The Bill Passes its Third Reading by a Majority of Three Hundred and Forty-seven Votes.

BY the autumn of 1915 the question how to maintain a regular and sufficient supply of recruits was causing great anxiety to the authorities. There had been a magnificent response to the appeals for volunteers. At the outbreak of the war hundreds of thousands of young men, the very pick of the nation, had flocked to the Colours, many of them before any public call for recruits was made. Elaborate advertising schemes promoted by the War Office had forced the question upon every man in the country. Recruiting meetings, recruiting marches, military displays, public lectures, and private canvasses had all been used on a scale and with a persistence never dreamed of before. And the response to these had been larger than even the warmest advocates of voluntaryism would have deemed possible in the days preceding the war.

But if the response had been great, the requirements were still

THE CHIEF RECRUITER AND HIS ASSISTANT.
Lord Derby with General Sir Henry MacKinnon, who resigned the Western Military Command at Chester in order to assist Lord Derby in his recruiting campaign.

greater. The war was eating up men. At the Dardanelles alone close on 200,000 were, up to the autumn, killed, wounded, missing, or invalided. In Flanders, infantry battalions were losing an average of fifteen per cent. a month from one cause or another. At least 30,000 new men were required every week to make up "wastage." By September, 1915, the voluntary system had apparently almost exhausted itself. Meetings were redoubled. Posters and placards calling for volunteers were more abundant, more artistic, and more persuasive than ever. But the recruits now joined in mere driblets. Skeleton battalions, their ranks swept by war and disease, called vainly for fresh men. The fresh men did not come.

There were over two million single men of military age in the country who had not offered themselves for enlistment. There were many more married men, with family claims, who felt it unfair and unjust that they, with wives and children to support, should be called upon to

397

SIEGE OF THE RECRUITING OFFICES IN OUTER LONDON.
As the test period of Lord Derby's scheme drew near its end, volunteers besieged the recruiting offices. At Camberwell the waiting queue was dense, and at Southwark the men, who were in high spirits, as the upper photograph shows, cheered enthusiastically when they were admitted into the Town Hall.

serve, while others, unmarried and having no one dependent on them, were going free. It was obvious that some among those who had not volunteered were engaged in necessary war work at home. But many had no good excuse ; some said that they would not come until the Government fetched them. There were large districts, let it be said, where practically every man of military age had offered himself. This was particularly true in the Highlands of Scotland and in the North of England. The Government tried, by a more liberal scale of allowances to soldiers' wives and families, and by other means, to make it possible for men to come who had others dependent upon them. But it soon became clear that something more must be done.

In endeavouring to form a fair estimate of the attitude of the British people at this time, it must be remembered that the greater part of the nation was by tradition and instinct strongly opposed to conscription in any shape or form. It had been our boast for generations that ours was a voluntary Army. "One volunteer is worth three pressed men" was a favourite but ridiculous English adage. The Englishman was accustomed to compare the British volunteer soldier with the Continental conscript, very much in favour of the British volunteer. In the mind of the average Briton, voluntaryism was associated with freedom, and conscription with the system of State regulation of the lives of its citizens, such as

Germany maintained. Among the working classes, in particular, the feeling against conscription was deep rooted. There was a belief that conscription, if it came, would be the rich man's dodge to make the poor man's son serve, and that conscription for the Army would be followed by conscription for labour purposes, forced work, low wages, and industrial servitude.

This prejudice was so strong that for years it stood fast against every attempt to move it. Hatred of conscription caused many Britons, with great shortsightedness, as events afterwards proved, to shut their eyes to the German peril. Lord Roberts, the greatest soldier of modern times, realising the danger facing our country, gave up the last years of his life to organising, pleading, and writing on behalf of national service. He was sneered at, publicly rebuked by Cabinet Ministers, held up to scorn by a section of the Press, and ridiculed as an old man in his dotage. Papers like "The Times," the "Daily Mail," and the "Morning Post," supported him, and he won many followers, but not enough to carry the country. What the pleadings of Lord Roberts and the warnings of the Press had failed to effect in the past, was now, however, being slowly accomplished by the progress of

A SUNDAY MIDNIGHT SCENE AT A SOUTH LONDON RECRUITING DEPOT.
No "eight hours' day" was possible during the recruiting campaign. Many offices were open throughout the whole twenty-four. This photograph was taken at midnight on Sunday in one depot in South London.

events. Mr. Asquith and the majority of the members of the Cabinet had always been avowed advocates of the voluntary system, but Mr. Asquith himself admitted, as the war went on, that if sufficient recruits could not be induced to volunteer, they must be brought in by other means. The safety and honour of Great Britain came first.

At the end of September the Prime Minister and Lord Kitchener met a representative group of Labour leaders in conference. Lord Kitchener clearly put the facts before them. Men, many more men, must be secured for the Army, Navy, and munition work. Would the Labour organisations throw all their energy into the work of securing these men? There can be little doubt but that Lord Kitchener, backed by Mr. Asquith, solemnly warned the Labour leaders that if the recruits were not had by voluntary means, compulsion must follow. Mr. Will Thorne, M.P., told afterwards how Lord Kitchener said that if he could have seventy divisions—about 1,500,000 men—in the field, between then and the next spring, he would guarantee victory. He staked his honour upon it. A discussion followed, in which the Premier was told that voluntary recruiting would be more successful if the Government

ATTESTATION AND CONFIRMATION.
Above: Recruits at Southwark Town Hall taking the oath on attestation under the Derby Scheme. Below: A recruiting officer at Hammersmith Town Hall distributing the official khaki armlets to already accepted men in confirmation of their enlistment.

would frankly state the actual requirements and the number of men who had come forward. Some speakers declared that many more men would volunteer but for the attitude of the employers. In the end, the conference pledged itself to do its utmost, and it set about organising a big campaign. This campaign was to include meetings of the workers throughout the land, the preparation and distribution of special recruiting literature, and the sending of deputations to Trades Councils and other influential Labour organisations to explain the needs of the country and to secure their co-operation in meeting them.

A big recruiting rally was held throughout the country on the first Saturday in October, with marches of troops and special meetings everywhere. The rally was very successful, despite rain. But people were now coming to see that spasmodic efforts could scarcely ensure the regular inflow of men necessary.

A new and very important step forward was made on October 5th, when Lord Derby undertook, at the request of the Secretary of State for War, the direction of recruiting for the Army. Lord Derby had already done great public service. Head of the house of Stanley, and the leading territorial magnate in Lancashire, he was above all things a Lancashire man—blunt of speech, a hard worker, shrewd and genial, a good sportsman, and a born leader. As a young man he joined the Grenadier Guards, and served for some time

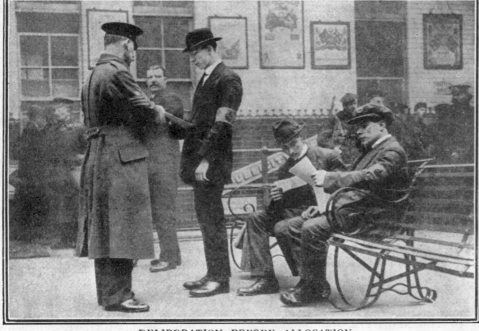

DELIBERATION BEFORE ALLOCATION.
When the Derby Groups were called up the men were allowed to choose the regiment to which they preferred to be allotted. Sergeants from many regiments attended to help them in their choice, and were eager to secure the finest men for their own battalions.

A GLAD SIGHT FOR MEN JUST HOME FROM THE FRONT.
Men home on leave reading the proclamation calling up the Derby Groups. Above: Sir Pieter Stewart-Bam appealing for fighting men from the Nelson Column, Trafalgar Square.

THE HELPING HAND TO THE NEOPHYTE SOLDIER.
An assiduous sergeant who was one of the most successful recruiters. Helping the men whom he secured on to the plinth, he swore them in, and had them into khaki at once, to show the improvement uniform made in the wearer. The effect was electrical.

as aide-de-camp to the Governor-General of Canada. In the South African War he was at first chief Press Censor, and then private secretary to Lord Roberts. Returning to England, he became Financial Secretary to the War Office and Postmaster-General. He threw himself into the life of Lancashire, and won the confidence and goodwill of Lancashire men—men who pride themselves on being the hardest headed and "canniest" in England. In a county noted for its great business he became a leading business organiser, director of a prominent newspaper, foremost in all public duties, trusted and followed by all who knew him. Lancashire thought of Lord Derby not so much as the earl of ancient lineage and owner of some 70,000 acres, but as a man among men, who talked in its own speech, who knew its ways, and who was equally good at a directors' board table, on the race-course or hunting field, or in some great department of philanthropic work.

When the news that Lord Derby had taken over the direction of recruiting was published, Lancashire chuckled. "Now," it said, "London will see what can be done." "You of the South of England do not know Lord Derby as we of the North," said one writer at the time. "It is true that he has been Financial Secretary of the War Office, Postmaster-General, and a **A John Bull** Member of the House of Commons. Such **Englishman** achievements, however, indicate but little. The seventeenth Earl of Derby has the same courage as had the first earl who took part in the Battle of Bosworth, in 1485. He is a strongly-built, red-faced, John Bull Englishman. He is hail-fellow-well-met with everyone, has a complete absence of ' side,' and has great knowledge of men and things. We who have stood by him in many arduous periods of his career know that he will not flinch from the task. We know that he will throw his unbounded enthusiasm and genius for organising into the work. We know that he will inspire the canvassers in their unpleasant rounds, and that just as he has sacrificed every moment of leisure and peace at his palace at Knowsley since the war began, so he will work, from morning till night, writing, speaking, travelling, and inspiring."

Political opponents joined with others in praising him. Thus Mr. T. P. O'Connor, the well-known journalist, himself M.P. for a Liverpool constituency and on the opposite side in politics, described him as good-humoured, rough-and-ready, brusque-spoken, genial. "For the work of recruiting this was the ideal man; for he knows his crowd without study, by sheer instinct, by the roots of his being. He is an Englishman with the Englishman's infallible instinct for taking the common-sense view; he is an

NAVAL RECRUITING MARCH IN THE METROPOLIS.
Men of the Royal Naval Division marching through London, under Commander the Hon. Rupert Guinness, to be reviewed by the Lord Mayor, who by virtue of his office was the Admiral of the Port of London.

aristocrat who thinks like the people and with the people. Like the people, his heart comes straight and authentically from the soil of his great and proud country. His was the voice of voices to reach the nation at the moment of the nation's direst need. He can best appeal to men in the language they understand for all the sacrifices of personal interest, of sweet affections, of ease of limb, of life for the good old country that gave them and him the heritage of her glory, her power, her history, her freedom."

Lord Derby was himself a believer in national service, but since the beginning of the war he had sunk his personal

Lord Derby on his task

preference and worked strenuously to make the voluntary system a success. He had led recruiting in Lancashire with much originality and marked success. He referred to his appointment at a meeting at Waterfoot, Rossendale, on October 5th. He told how, ten days before, he had asked two questions of the Government—whether it had decided on the number of men it had to put in the field ; and whether, having decided that, were it prepared, if it could not get enough men by voluntary means, to employ other means ? "I had the question answered in a rather peculiar way," he continued. "Lord Kitchener has asked me to become director of all recruiting throughout the United Kingdom. I have accepted out of personal loyalty and friendship to Lord Kitchener. It is not a position to be envied. I feel something in the position of a receiver who is put in to wind up a bankrupt concern ; but I hope I shall be able to do it with such satisfaction as will enable the creditors to receive their 20s. in the pound. I myself am an advocate of national service, but I do not think that even those who have been my most bitter

REFLECT—AND BE A MEMBER OF THE "KING'S NAVEE."
Among the many ingenious devices resorted to to convince the hesitant eligible of his country's needs was the one illustrated in the above photograph. The blackboard was placed outside the Royal Naval Division office in the Strand. A curious and likely recruit, reading the notice, would see himself reflected in the mirror, whereupon the businesslike-looking handy-man would help him to make up his mind.

adversaries will deny that I have done my level best to make the voluntary system a success. I have done all I possibly could to get men under the voluntary system."

The appointment of Lord Derby was quickly followed by radical changes in the recruiting organisation. Ten days after his appointment, Lord Derby issued details of his new scheme. These details were elaborated in a notable speech at the Mansion House on October 19th. Every recruiting organisation at work was to be employed, the Parliamentary Recruiting Committees taking prominent place for a grand canvass of unenlisted men of military age. Their work was to be systematised and thoroughly co-ordinated. The National Register, which had been taken some weeks before, was to be used as a basis for this canvass. Civilians were to be asked to volunteer under a group system.

THE HISTORIC SCENE IN THE HOUSE OF COMMONS WHEN THE MILITARY SERVICE BILL PASSED ITS THIRD READING.

On January 24th, 1916, one of the greatest changes in the British Constitution was sanctioned by Parliament in the interests of national salvation—the Military Service Bill passing its third reading in the Commons. By 383 votes against 36 the measure became law. At the first reading a total of 105, including Irish Nationalists, voted against the Bill, but during the second and third reading the number, principally owing to Mr. Redmond and his followers abstaining from the poll, dropped to 36, headed by Sir John Simon. The tellers were Mr. J. H. Thomas (Labour) and Mr. J. H. Whitehouse (Liberal). This detailed drawing illustrates the historic moment as the overwhelming "Ayes" proceeded to the lobby to vote, while the few "Noes" waited on the benches.

There would be forty-six groups —twenty-three for single men and twenty-three for married men— arranged according to age. The single men who volunteered would be called up for service in the order of their groups; the men in the twenties being used in their order before the men in the thirties were called upon. The married men would not be asked to serve until the lists of single men were exhausted. Those who wanted to join the Colours at once could do so. The others, after joining their groups, would go back to their ordinary vocations until wanted. "Starred" men—*i.e.*, men working at trades such as munition production, necessary for the war—and un-starred men found indispensable in their employments would be sent back at once to their employments after attestation, if necessary. But Lord Derby clearly intimated that even in "starred" trades there might be men who could be liberated from their employment. He evidently had in view the developments of women's labour in munition work, which were to be so marked a feature of the industrial development of Britain in 1916.

FIRST STARTERS IN THE DERBY VOLUNTEERS' FINAL.
Armleteers studying the proclamation pasted up outside the Mansion House calling the first four Derby Groups to the Colours.

"There are people who seem despondent about the spirit of the country," he said, at the close of his speech at the Mansion House. "I am not. I believe the heart of the country is right. Only the heart of the country has got to be touched. I believe we can do it. I believe that if men can only realise now, by their individual effort, they are going to secure for their children, and their children's children, a lasting and enduring peace, they will be prepared to make some sacrifice, or even any sacrifice. I believe implicitly that if we can get the country at the back of us now, we are going, even at this eleventh hour,

Attitude of the Press

to make the voluntary system an unqualified success." Lord Derby's proposals were received with a chorus of approval. The section of the Press which defended voluntaryism was naturally pleased, because it realised that here was a possibility of saving its position. But those newspapers which upheld national service were also perfectly loyal, and declared they would do everything possible to forward Lord Derby's plans. They kept their promise. During the weeks of the canvass they gave the scheme the utmost publicity and the warmest advocacy. "The new recruiting campaign starts under the most favourable auspices, and without the slightest sign of opposition," "The Times" declared. "Everybody wishes it well, and Lord Derby has a host of eager helpers."

The "Daily Mail," which had good reason to be pleased that the plan of "single men first," for which it had fought for many months, was now officially adopted, pledged itself to co-operate. "We wish Lord Derby every success in his scheme," it wrote, "and so far as the 'Daily Mail' is concerned, we will support it most strongly now it is a case of 'single men first.' We hope that our readers will give it every assistance in their power. It is not the first time that the 'Daily Mail,' though believing firmly in the justice and necessity of national service, has put forth all its efforts in the cause of the voluntary system."

While the substitution of a direct canvass for the old haphazard system was widely praised, one weak point was at once pointed out in the scheme. If large numbers of married men volunteered and comparatively few single men, the married men

INSPECTING THE PAPERS OF PROSPECTIVE SOLDIERS.
Derby men handing in their armlets at the White City Central Depot in exchange for a full uniform.

THE "SCRAP OF PAPER"

These are the signatures and seals of the representatives
of the Six Powers to the "Scrap of Paper"—the Treaty
signed in 1839 guaranteeing the independence and
neutrality of Belgium.
Palmerston signed for Britain. Bulow for Prussia.

The Germans have broken their pledged word
and devastated Belgium. Help to keep your
Country's honour bright by restoring Belgium
her liberty.

ENLIST TO-DAY

FACSIMILE OF BRITAIN'S "CASUS BELLI."

might be called upon before they ought to be, despite
the promise of "single men first." Thus we might
still see young "slackers" walking about the streets,
while married men with families were taking upon
themselves the responsibilities of the firing-line. This
point was brought before Lord
Derby by the Town Clerk of
Chiswick. Lord Derby's reply
was: "It is clear that if sufficient
young single men do not enlist
under the scheme, some other
steps must be taken to fetch
them. This would occur before
the married men are taken."

People, however, asked something more than a general statement from the Director of
Recruiting. It was felt that the
Prime Minister himself ought to
make a definite and unmistakable declaration of policy. Mr.
Asquith did so in a notable speech
in Parliament on November 2nd.
He admitted that there had been
differences of opinion in the
Cabinet over the recruiting question. The question of compulsion
was one of practical expediency.
He admitted that our system
of voluntary recruiting operated
in time of war in a hap-
hazard, capricious, and somewhat

unjust way both as regard individuals and classes.
His objection to the introduction of compulsion was
that under existing conditions it would forfeit the
maintenance of national unity. If it were applied without
something in the nature of general assent, the nation
would be disunited. He believed that the result of Lord
Derby's recruiting scheme would be wholly satisfactory.
" But," he said, " if there should still be found a substantial
number of men of military age not required for other
purposes, who without excuse hold back from the
service of their country, I believe that the very same
conditions which make compulsion impossible now—namely,
the absence of general consent—would force the country to
the view that it must consent to supplement, by some
form of legal obligation, the failure of the voluntary
system."

Then he went on to refer to the doubt among married
men whether they might not be called upon to serve,
if they joined their group while younger, unmarried men
were holding back and not doing their duty. " Let them
disabuse themselves of that idea," declared the Premier,
in a statement that affected the whole future history of
Britain. " So far as I am concerned,
I should certainly say the obligation of   **Mr. Asquith's**
the married man to enlist ought not   **famous pledge**
to be enforced, or binding upon him, un-
less and until—I hope by voluntary effort, and if not by
some other means—the unmarried men are dealt with
first."

Even this declaration did not suffice. Married men
when canvassed said that the Premier had merely given
an expression of personal opinion. They wanted more
than that. Nine days afterwards, on November 11th,
1915, an official statement was circulated to the Press
which placed the matter beyond doubt :

Lord Derby is authorised by the Prime Minister to express his
surprise that his statement in the House of Commons on November 2nd should be considered in any way ambiguous.

The Prime Minister on that occasion pledged not only himself
but his Government when he stated that if young men did not,
under the stress of national duty, come forward voluntarily, other
and compulsory means would be taken before the married men
were called upon to fulfil their engagement to serve.

Lord Derby is further authorised to state definitely that if young
men medically fit and not indispensable to any business of national
importance, or to any business conducted for the general good of
the community, do not come forward voluntarily before November
30th, the Government will after that date take the necessary steps
to redeem the pledge made on November 2nd.

PATRIOTIC APPEALS—VISIONARY AND EUPHONIOUS.
The monster poster erected in Aldwych, Strand, London, in front of which a recruiting band is giving
a patriotic selection.

"I rejoice in my Empire's effort."—*His Majesty King George.*

Pied Pipers of London Town: How the wild music of the Highlands helped to swell the ranks of Britain's fighting men.

The Queen with Princess Mary and Prince Albert watching the march=past of Irish cavalry at Aldershot.

The moment of farewell: A touching scene at Victoria Station during war time.

Home on leave: After the arrival of the trench "special" at a London terminus.

The new scheme was further supported by a direct appeal from the King to the people of Great Britain:

Buckingham Palace.

TO MY PEOPLE.

At this grave moment in the struggle between my people and a highly-organised enemy, who has transgressed the laws of nations and changed the ordinance that binds civilised Europe together, I appeal to you.

I rejoice in my Empire's effort, and I feel pride in the voluntary response from my subjects all over the world who have sacrificed home, fortune, and life itself, in order that another may not inherit the free Empire which their ancestors and mine have built.

I ask you to make good these sacrifices.

The end is not in sight. More men and yet more are wanted to keep my armies in the field, and through them to secure victory and enduring peace.

In ancient days the darkest moment has ever produced in men of our race the sternest resolve.

I ask you, men of all classes, to come forward voluntarily, and take your share in the fight.

In freely responding to my appeal you will be giving your support to our brothers who, for long months, have nobly upheld Britain's past traditions and the glory of her arms.

GEORGE R.I.

Lord Derby and his assistants felt that their campaign would be greatly helped by introducing some badge that would openly and publicly mark off the volunteer from the "slacker." This was provided by the adoption of an idea advanced some months before by Sir George Pragnell—the issue of armlets to all men who offered themselves for enlistment in the groups, and to other qualified persons. The khaki armlet was undoubtedly a dramatic stroke. The difficulty at first was that in some cities, particularly in London, young men did not care to wear their badges. They were driven to it more and more by public opinion, and by an appeal from the King.

An enormous mass of feeling in favour of military service had been gathering force in this country during the summer of 1915. Sometimes it found crude and foolish expression, as in "white feather" campaigns, when irresponsible young women presented young men in the streets with white feathers, the symbol of cowardice. But essentially the feeling was sound. The young man out of khaki or without his armlet soon found himself in a painful position. Young women formed leagues, pledging themselves not to marry any man who had shirked his duty of enlisting. Mothers who had lost their sons, wives who had lost their husbands, would stop young civilians in the streets, or turn to them in omnibuses, and demand why they were not doing their duty. "I've lost my son and my husband in this war," said one lady in an omnibus, where three young civilians were sitting. "I am proud of them, and would not have **Public opinion** kept them back; but I am ashamed **and the slacker** when I see young fellows like you, as fit as they were, lolling in London and enjoying yourselves in place of doing your duty, and I hope you are ashamed of yourselves." This was the kind of talk which met the "slacker" at every turn.

The new canvass was launched on October 25th, and was to last for six weeks. Leading men in different parts of the country accepted the posts of directors of recruiting for their districts. Thus, for instance, Lord Wimborne, the Lord-Lieutenant, undertook the duties of director-

general of recruiting for Ireland. The machinery of political organisations was enlisted. Liberal and Unionist canvassers joined together, and people volunteered by the thousand to do the necessary work of canvassing without pay. The campaign began with a unanimity rarely witnessed in Britain. Every newspaper gave it day by day the leading place in its pages and urged its importance in its editorial columns. "The Times" published a special recruiting supplement. Municipal authorities gave up their public buildings to the workers. **Extension of the time limit**

Every house in which a man of military age lived had to be visited and the man invited to join the Army. If he refused he had to be asked his reasons for refusing. The local Parliamentary Recruiting Committee responsible for the canvass in each district was at work often day and night, meeting difficulties, solving problems, and pushing on the campaign. The nation as a whole quickly came to learn that Lancashire's opinion of Lord Derby was right. He was an ideal man for the post, prompt in business, ready to face difficulties, frank and willing.

The campaign had its ups and downs. It was launched

EVOLUTION OF THE ANCIENT CATAPULT.
Machines for hurling bombs that worked on the principle of the catapult. This photograph was taken at a "school" for grenade-throwing at a training centre in England.

by what seemed to be a great boom, but that did not yield so many men as expected. All classes joined—civil servants, schoolmasters, many ministers of religion, and business men galore. In some cases the entire staff of a business house went and attested in a body. It seemed as though the great wave of enthusiasm would sweep every eligible man in. Then the boom suddenly exhausted itself. A statement made by Mr. Asquith in the House on November 15th—that no attempt would be made to apply compulsion in any shape or form without the consent of Parliament—was used in some quarters against the campaign. An attempt was quickly made to remedy this, and Mr. Asquith repeated and emphasised his earlier pledge to the married men. "What the Prime Minister meant," said Mr. Bonar Law, speaking for the Government, "and what we mean, was not if they do not come in, but if there is a general shirking of their duties then they will be made to come in before the men with wives and families."

The effect of the misunderstanding was, however, unfortunate, and for a week or two things looked very bad. The time limit for the canvass was extended to December

A MIMIC BAYONET CHARGE.

At a competition between men in training, where points were awarded for skill and speed in bayonet work by the Earl of Kerry, who acted as judge. The men were required to bayonet cards placed on sacks while leaping across trenches.

A WARLIKE SCENE IN RURAL ENGLAND.
Machine-gunners defending a bridge in a village where men of the New Army were in training.

TRAINING FOR TRENCH WARFARE.
Practising rudimentary bayonet work. Charging the trenches, the men endeavoured to transfix scraps of card placed on sacks.

11th, and Lord Derby, in speeches at Edinburgh and Glasgow, reaffirmed the promise to married men. "What more can I say to you on the subject," he asked, "except that as one who has been responsible for this scheme I should give you my own personal pledge? To the fullest extent in my power I will see that absolute faith is kept with those married men who have joined under the assurance given. I am not a member of the Government. I am only a recruiting sergeant. I have no personal power, but I have behind me in this matter an overwhelming power—the power of public feeling of the country. The country is long-suffering, and has stood a great many things, but it is not going to stand anything that would be like bad faith with those ready and willing to risk their lives for it."

On November 19th, in order to leave no room for misunderstanding whatever, Lord Derby wrote a letter to the Prime Minister, in which he clearly stated the position as he understood it:

Derby House, Stratford Place, W.
November 19th, 1915.

My dear Prime Minister,—As some uncertainty exists as to the effect of the various statements recently made in Parliament and the Press on the subject of recruiting, may I endeavour to put the position in a few words?

Married men are not to be called up until young unmarried men have been. If these young men do not come forward voluntarily, you will either release the married men from their pledge or introduce a Bill into Parliament to compel the young men to serve, which, if passed, would mean that the married men would be held to their enlistment. If, on the other hand, Parliament did not pass such a Bill, the married men would be automatically released from their engagement to serve.

Lord Derby makes sure

By the expression "young men coming forward to serve" I think it should be taken to mean that the vast majority of young men not engaged in munition work or work necessary for the country should offer themselves for service, and men indispensable for civil employment and men who have personal reasons which are considered satisfactory by the local tribunals for relegation to a later class, can have their claims examined for such relegation in the way that has already been laid down.

If, after all these claims have been investigated and all the exemptions made mentioned above, there remains a considerable number of young men not engaged in these pursuits who could perfectly be spared for military service, they should be compelled to serve. On the other hand, if the number should prove to be, as I hope it will, a really negligible minority, there would be no question of legislation.

Yours sincerely,
DERBY.

The Prime Minister replied:

10, Downing Street, S.W.
November 19th, 1915.

My dear Derby,—I have received your letter of to-day. It correctly represents the intentions of the Government.

Yours sincerely,
H. H. ASQUITH.

One of the urgent questions that arose during the canvass

CROUCHING PRELIMINARY TO AN ADVANCE.
Men of the 4th Batt. City of London Regiment (Royal Fusiliers) learning the rudiments of charging at a training camp. They are in the first position for advancing in extended order over open ground and under fire.

was how to decide which men were indispensable to the industries of the country, and which would serve the country better by enlisting in the Army. Lord Derby here laid down the cardinal principle that it was for the State, not for the employer, and not for the man himself, to say whether he was indispensable or not. It was the duty of the man to attest, and then to submit his case to the authorities. Local tribunals were appointed in which the various authorities interested were represented, and these authorities were empowered to decide.

Besides local tribunals, a central appeal tribunal of five members was appointed. At the head was Lord Sydenham, a famous artillery officer and Army organiser; Sir George Younger, the second member, was a Scottish Unionist whip, and chairman of a well-known firm of brewers; other members were Sir Francis Gore, who was formerly solicitor to the Inland Revenue; Mr. Cyril Jackson, a prominent educationalist; and Mr. G. J. Talbot, K.C., a distinguished ecclesiastical lawyer.

On December 3rd, despite all that had been done, it was felt by those behind the scenes that the net results of the scheme had been very disappointing. Lord Derby and the other leaders issued another appeal to all men of military age in the United Kingdom, pointing out to them once more that it was their duty to express their willingness to serve their country in the field. If they had difficulties which made it hard for them to do so, impartial tribunals would weigh their arguments, and, if necessary, exempt them from immediate service. " Let him "—the available man—" join the Army under the Group System, and show his country that he puts her interests before his own, and show the world, the Allies, neutrals, and enemies alike, that there are hundreds and thousands of our citizens who are ready to fight for her." At the same time the Joint Labour Committee, which had been working hard among the working classes, issued its final appeal " to the free men of Britain to respond to the call of their country, and to enrol themselves at once in the great volunteer army which stands between us and the loss of our rights and liberties."

Churches backed up the messages. The Free Churches of North Wales issued a stirring manifesto calling on Nonconformists to fight for Christianity, and all that Christianity stands for. " If any war in the whole history of the world can be called a righteous war, this is it."

Four days before the end an amazing final " boom " began. The recruiting officers suddenly found themselves overwhelmed by thousands of men pouring in. From all parts of the country, from Great Scotland Yard to East Ham, and from Manchester to the South Coast, the news was

Great eleventh hour response

PUBLIC SCHOOL MEN IN TRAINING.
Learning to hurl bombs from a small trench mortar—a necessary accomplishment in accordance with the exigencies of siege warfare.

WAR'S ALARMS IN ENGLISH FIELDS.
The explosion of a bomb fired from a small trench mortar by recruits of a Public Schools Battalion.

ANZAC INTERLUDE AT CAPE TOWN.
Men from " down under " giving a Maori war-dance display at Cape Town before his Excellency the Governor-General of South Africa.

looked for. After a few days rumours began to be circulated that the total results were not quite so good as had been hoped. Very many men had joined—that much was certain—but a large number of these were married, and quite a considerable proportion of single men had not attested. Soon it became clear that there had been enormous numbers of single men " slackers." Under the terms of Mr. Asquith's pledge, the Government must either compel these men to serve or not call upon the married men who had attested.

On Wednesday, December 15th, Lord Derby made a significant statement in the House of Lords. He said that the first part of his report, dealing with the figures the same. Long lines of men were waiting outside the doors of the recruiting offices to attest. In some cases the men had to wait for half a day before they could be seen to. In other cases the offices were kept open all night. It was not, however, really known how great this rush actually had been until Lord Derby published his report. Then it was shown that in these four days, from December 10th to December 13th, a total of 1,070,478 men had attested.

In the last two days it became evident that it was impossible to make the medical examinations. The only way of coping with the rush was to swear the men in, take their names, pay them their attestation money, 2s. 9d., and let them go away, and be examined more carefully later. In Manchester on Thursday evening the long corridor of the Town

Dramatic closing scenes Hall became so packed with men that the police decided to close the doors. In London bodies of young men marched to the recruiting depôts singing, and concerts were arranged for the crowds waiting their turn. Men in silk hats and men in fustian, employers and clerks side by side, lads not yet twenty and middle-aged men—fathers of families—hustled one another to get in.

Despite the fact that it had been repeatedly stated that no further extension of the time would be made, the time had to be extended in the end. It was found impossible to take the names of all offering themselves before midnight on Saturday, so attestations were continued during Sunday, December 12th, and those whose names were taken on that day, who even then could not be attested, were allowed until the following Wednesday to offer themselves.

These dramatic and surprising closing scenes gave every encouragement to the advocates of the voluntary system. They proclaimed that conscription had been killed once and for all. Lord Derby's report was eagerly

WARRIORS FROM THE WEST INDIES.
The Lord Mayor of London inspecting a fine body of men from Trinidad drawn up before the Mansion House. His Worship is wearing the uniform of the National Guard.

up to November 30th, had been submitted to Lord Kitchener and Mr. Asquith on the previous Sunday, but no judgment could be formed from it. Then Lord Derby added : " I ask your lordships to support me in saying that it will be absolutely impossible for any action to be taken which will necessitate the calling up of married men until the country is absolutely convinced that the single man has come forward to such an extent as to leave only a negligible quantity unaccounted for. We must, above all things, keep faith with the pledge the Prime Minister gave to the married men." The meaning of this was unmistakable. On the following day a group of some thirty resolute opponents of national service, led by Mr. J. H. Thomas, the railwaymen's Member of Parliament, requested the Prime Minister to receive them as a deputation on the subject of the compulsion of single men. The proceedings were private, but there can be little doubt about what the deputation asked. They were anxious to induce the Prime Minister to consent to a plan for yet another canvass of the single men who had refused to come in.

Eton boys drawn up on the platform of Didcot Junction about to assist in unloading war stores.

Members of the famous college hauling waggons off the railway trucks.

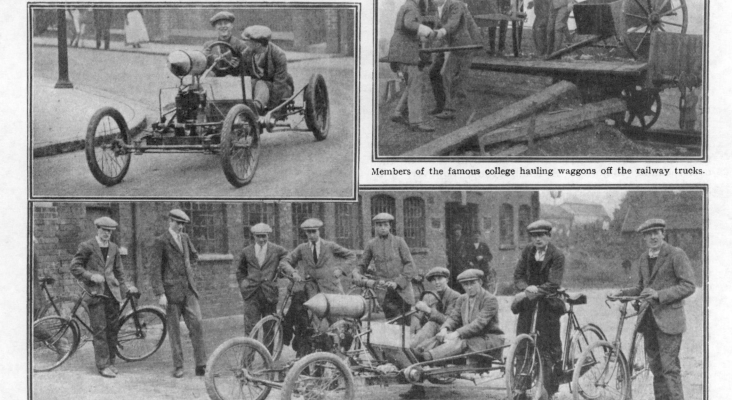

Some of the afternoon shift of Eton College munition workers who arrived considerably before the regulation time to sign on.   Centre (left) : To the munition works by car.   Two Eton boys who made shells in their leisure hours at the local munition works going " to business."

"FLOREAT ETONA PRO PATRIA": MEMBERS OF THE FAMOUS COLLEGE WHO WERE UNOFFICIALLY ENGAGED ON WAR WORK.

GETTING ACCUSTOMED TO THE
DEADLY BOMB.
Some of the Sherwood Foresters getting their
hands in at bomb-throwing, one of the most
difficult and hazardous branches of scientific
warfare.

were satisfied he would keep it to the full. Some newspapers, however, and a few politicians urged that the Government and Parliament were not bound by the Prime Minister's pledge, but that it was merely a personal promise which the Cabinet could break or not as it saw fit. Sir John Simon, the Home Secretary, led the opposition to compulsion in the Cabinet, and two other Ministers, Mr. Runciman and Mr. McKenna, were understood to be strongly against it. They feared the effect of a further considerable increase of our forces upon our economic position and our production of wealth, which must be maintained for success in the war.

The majority of the nation had by now made up their minds that if the Derby scheme did not succeed, compulsion for the slackers must come. Men of all classes, Labour leaders, Liberal Members of Parliament, religious teachers, who had for years consistently fought conscription, now declared that circumstances alter cases. They did not like conscription, and they did not want it, but better conscription than that Britain should lose the war. If the Government decided, with all the facts before it, that conscription was necessary, they would submit. This was the loyal view of the overwhelming majority. A small group, however, still stood out, including some members of the Cabinet. They asked, in the hope of delaying conscription, that a measure should be passed

Another Opposition plan directing all single men who had not attested to come before specially appointed tribunals and give the reasons why they did not join. If these reasons were satisfactory, the man should be marked off. If, however, in the opinion of the tribunal the reasons were not satisfactory, the man's name should be recorded. The total of the unsatisfactory men should be ascertained, and if this total was considerable, then, and only then, should a measure of compulsion be passed for them.

During the end of December it was an open secret that a serious struggle was going on with the Cabinet between the compulsionists and the non-compulsionists. Lord Derby's final report was to hand, but the Premier had delayed giving it publicity.

It was known that Mr. Lloyd George had taken a firm stand in favour of compulsion, declaring that to create further tribunals would merely be to postpone the struggle over the question. It was known, too, that Lord Derby had insisted rigorously on the maintenance of the pledge given by him. The compulsionists announced their faith in the Prime Minister's pledge, and said they

TRAINING IN THE HOME COUNTIES.
Members of the 3rd/19th Batt. London Regiment taking cover in a trench
preparatory to attacking the imaginary enemy with bombs.

A NERVE TEST FOR THE PHOTOGRAPHER.
Officers undergoing instruction in the use of the rifle. To pass through
a military college was only the beginning of an officer's training. Before
proceeding on active service a rigorous course of drill, trench-digging,
and other warlike duties, was imperative.

As 1916 opened it became clear that the voluntaryists were defeated. Sir John Simon resigned his position as Home Secretary, and Mr. McKenna and Mr. Runciman fell in with the views of the rest of the Cabinet. On January 1st a whip was issued to members of the House of Commons stating that on the following Wednesday the Prime Minister would introduce a Bill dealing with military service. Between the Saturday and the Wednesday those opposed to conscription used every possible effort to coerce and persuade the Cabinet even at the eleventh hour. Vague threats were made of a general strike of labour should compulsion be attempted, and particularly of strikes of railwaymen and miners. The Irish

DISLODGING THE IMAGINARY " BOCHE."
Men of the 3/5th Batt. London Regiment for home defence undergoing a course of instruction in bomb-throwing. An attacking party is proceeding along the trench. One of them has just hurled a harmless missile at the retreating figure in the foreground

BOMB-THROWING FROM TRENCH TO TRENCH.
Bombers of the 3/19th Batt. London Regiment having presumably taken part of the enemy's first-line position, are hurling grenades preparatory to a further advance.

Party, which had been from the first opposed to national service, was swayed by confident assurances from Sir John Simon's friends that at least 150 Radicals would oppose compulsion, and decided to aid them. "The first mutterings of a labour storm are coming from the country," wrote one political correspondent. Dismal pictures were drawn of the economic ruin that would follow a big increase of the Army. All these threats and forebodings failed, however, to affect the Cabinet.

On Tuesday, January 4th, Lord Derby's report was made public. In it he gave a careful and luminous statement as to the whole recruiting problem, the difficulties raised by starred men, and the problems that often prevent single men as well as married men from offering themselves. But public interest fastened on the figures, which showed that over 1,000,000 single men of military age had not attested under the scheme, and that after allowing for those who were starred (or marked with a star as required for some indispensible post at home) there still remained unaccounted for 651,160. Following is a table of the figures :

	SINGLE.	MARRIED.	TOTAL.
Total Men 18 to 40	2,179,231	2,832,210	5,011,441
Went to Attest	1,150,000	1,679,263	2,829,263
Did Not Attest	1,029,231	1,152,947	2,182,178
Of these are Starred	378,071	465,683	843,754
Unaccounted for	651,160	687,264	1,338,424
Total Attested	840,000	1,344,979	2,184,979
Of these are Starred	312,067	449,808	761,875
Unstarred	527,933	895,171	1,423,104
Deduct unfit, indispensable, and in reserved jobs ..	184,547	407,495	592,042
Actually Available	343,386	487,676	831,062

OFFICERS IN TRAINING FOR ACTIVE SERVICE LEARNING THE ART OF SIGNALLING.

Canadian officer delivering a lecture on the art of modern trench-digging.

Harmless bombs were exploded to accustom the men to the noise.

Work at the practice trenches. The exhilaration of the charge.

Bomb-throwing from a trench whence a charge was about to be made.
SONS OF THE EMPIRE TRAINING NEAR LAKE ONTARIO, CANADA, TO FIGHT FOR THE MOTHERLAND.

"This," said Lord Derby, referring to those who had not attested, "is far from being a negligible quantity, and in the circumstances I am very distinctly of opinion that in order to redeem the pledge mentioned above (the pledge to married men), it will not be possible to hold married men to their attestation unless and until the services of single men have been obtained by other means, the present system having failed to bring them to the Colours."

On the day after the publication of the report Mr. Asquith introduced the Military Service Bill into Parliament. This Bill applied only to England, Wales, and Scotland (not Ireland), and affected all single British men and widowers without children dependent on them who were between the ages of eighteen and forty-one on August 15th, 1915. The men were offered the choice of voluntarily joining the Derby Groups; if they did not do so a day would be appointed five weeks after the Bill passed, and on that day, unless they had been exempted, they would be deemed to have enlisted for the duration of the war. Certain exemptions were made. Persons to whom compulsion would not be applied were clergy and ministers of any denomination, persons with certificates of exemption, those medically rejected, men necessary in national employments, men who supported relatives and would leave dependents without support, necessary civil servants, and conscientious objectors to combatant services.

The dawn of compulsion

The scene in the House of Commons on the afternoon when the Bill was introduced was striking. The House was crowded, the benches and side galleries were full, and members sat even on the steps of the gangways. Many soldiers, Unionist and Liberal alike, had come straight from the front to record their votes. Some, like General Seely, himself formerly Minister of War, had only left the field of battle early that day. The atmosphere of the House was electric.

The Premier rose to the occasion and gave a clear statement of his position. He was opposed to general compulsion, and did not think that any case had been made out for it. This Bill was confined to a specific purpose, the redemption of the pledge publicly given by him to the House on November 2nd. This pledge was given because at the time overwhelming evidence was submitted to him that if the pledge was not given there was serious danger of the whole campaign breaking down. The Premier dismissed the idea that when he spoke he was not defining the general policy agreed upon by the Cabinet. After he

MODERN CANADIAN CAVALRY GARBED LIKE THE KU-KLUX-KLAN.
For protection of the men and horses while practising sword fighting with the real weapon, the Canadians were supplied with hoods and pads. The effect was grotesque when the troops were lined up for the attack. Above: The hoods thrown back during an interval.

MAGNIFICENT YOUNG MANHOOD OF OUR OLDEST COLONY.
Newfoundland, our oldest Colony, raised the first regiment she has ever had, to help the Empire at the great crisis of its history, and the men, who were of exceptionally fine stamina, came "home" to train. The photographs of them starting on a route march and at bayonet exercise well exhibit their superb physique.

from their obligations, and the second course would be to treat the single men of military age, without exemption or excuse, as though they had attested or enlisted. "This course," he said, "we propose to adopt in this Bill. I mean to keep my promise. We must keep our promises, and do not let it be said that we dallied and delayed in the performance of an obligation of honour."

Even now the voluntaryists did not give up hope. They thought that they had a considerable strength in the House, and they placed much reliance upon Sir John Simon. Sir John Simon was known as an able lawyer and a skilled Parliamentarian, but when he sat down after a long speech, which was evidently meant to be one of the great efforts of his life, everyone knew that the case against the Bill had broken down.

"It was full of cleverness, of course," said the "Daily Telegraph" in describing the speech, "for it revealed the involved windings of a legal conscience.

What to others was a plain pledge was to him something amazingly subtle, governed by one consideration here and **Sir John Simon's conscience** another there, and contingency A and contingency B, and some ingeniously concealed 'whereas.' His main complaint seemed to be that the Prime Minister was performing the letter of his bond before the conditions had been fulfilled, and yet it was clear from his whole speech that, however long the Prime Minister had waited and whatever the result the final investigation showed, Sir

gave the pledge in Parliament he had received neither then nor subsequently any sign of protest or remonstrance. He could not treat the estimated number of the unmarried men who had not attested—650,000—as anything but a substantial and even considerable amount, even when all possible deductions were made from it. "Our primary obligations, mine at any rate, must be to keep faith with those to whom I have given that promise." There were only two ways in which the promise could be fulfilled. One would be releasing the married men—over 400,000—

Men of the 3/1st London Divisional R.E. crossing a pontoon bridge of their own construction.

A sturdy specimen of "The Pioneers," the 25th Middlesex Regiment, at work among the barbed-wire entanglements.

Above : Sergeant Milner, motor despatch-rider, showing how to take cover while riding.   Left · Members of the Inns of Court O.T.C. returning to camp after trench-digging.   Right : Men of the Hackney (189th) Gun Brigade, enlisted at 2 p.m. and in uniform at 2.45 p.m. the same day !

LEARNING THE ARTS OF WAR : BRITONS IN TRAINING AFOOT AND AWHEEL.

John Simon's conscience—the late Home Secretary is pure conscience—would have led him just the same to make 'the grand refusal' at the end. And he claimed that there were others on the Treasury Bench who held identical views with himself, and were anti-compulsionists on strict principle, and did not regard the question, like the Prime Minister, as one of expediency only, or like Mr. Redmond as one to be judged by the degree of necessity.

" It was one of those speeches of resignation which widen the gulf between colleagues who have parted company. It was bitter—Sir John resembles Mr. Dillon in not being able to get certain newspapers out of his head—and seems also to agree with him that the Prime Minister was trapped into making the pledge and bullied into keeping it. So with a great show of civility he yet spoke to wound."

Two more speeches drove home the Premier's declaration. One was from Mr. Bonar Law, who had during the last weeks of 1915 steadily strengthened his position in Parliament as a businesslike statesman. The other was by General Seely, who spoke with a passion, enthusiasm, and emotion that stirred the House. The Liberal War Minister of other years, looking now the soldier he was, for he was serving at the time as a brigadier-general with the Canadian Division, told how he had long opposed conscription, but since the Prime Minister and Lord Kitchener said this Bill was necessary, he held it his clear duty to support them. Then he turned on **General Seely speaks out** those who denounced the Bill in the name of liberty. "Liberty to do what ? " he asked. " When the Lusitania had been sunk, when poisonous gases have been turned on, when thousands of innocent lives have been destroyed in defiance of every law of war and humanity, when overwhelming masses of your countrymen have risen in horror and said, 'We will not be ground down by Prussian despotism and tyranny.' Then you are going to appeal to liberty— liberty that you may send another man in your place."

The debate was concluded on the second day, when an amazingly eloquent speech from Colonel John Ward, the well-known leader of the Navvies Battalion, thrilled the House. Mr. Herbert Samuel pulverised Sir John Simon's figures and arguments. When the division came there was a majority in favour of the Bill of 298—403 against 105.

The result was a great disappointment to the anti-compulsionists, who had hoped that many members would abstain and many more vote against the Government. When the division came to be analysed the disappointment was still greater. The minority of 105 included no fewer than 60 Nationalists. The action of these in voting against a Bill which did not apply to Ireland created so much unfavourable comment **The majority for** that when the second reading of the Bill **compulsion** came on the Nationalists decided not to vote. The opposition thus dwindled to 39, and the second reading was carried by a Government majority of 392. On Monday, January 24th, 1916, the Bill passed the House on its third reading by a majority of 347, the opposition having now fallen to 36 votes. The members who voted against the Bill, either on the introduction or on the second reading, found in many cases that their action created great resentment. The Liberal organisation in Sir John Simon's own constituency asked him to resign. Another member pledged himself after the first reading not to vote against the Bill again. Great efforts were made to enlist the Labour party as a whole against the Bill, and a conference of Labour delegates carried a resolution against compulsion, which it was at first thought would compel the Labour members of the Government to retire. It was soon found, however, that all hopes of united and solid Labour opposition were vain. Many labour representatives were among the Bill's warmest advocates. The Government took pains to reassure those who believed that conscription for the Army might lead to industrial conscription. The few men who had whispered a threat of a general strike of labour against the Bill were silenced by their friends.

NEW ZEALANDERS ENCAMPED ON THE EGYPTIAN SANDS PREPARING FOR A THREATENED ATTACK ON THE SUEZ CANAL.
Their long and severe training finished, these New Zealanders were sent out absolutely ready and intensely keen to prove their superiority over the soldiers of militarist Germany. They occupied much of the brief period before entering the firing-line in keeping their marksmanship up to form on the rifle ranges.

CHAPTER XCIX.

SERBIA'S HARD FATE, THE ALLIES' RETIREMENT, AND MONTENEGRO'S OVERTHROW.

By Robert Machray.

Some Bright Gleams in Serbia's Dark Sky—Heroism of Vassitch and his Soldiers in the Babuna Pass—Sarrail's Attempt to Join Up with Vassitch Across the Hills—Battle of Mount Arkangel—Failure of the French—The Crushing of Serbia Proceeds—Advance of Kövess, Gallwitz, and Bojadieff—Serbians' Great Fight in the Katshanik Pass—A Five Days' Struggle—Numbers Prevail—Serbians Hemmed in on the Famous Kossovo Plain—Remorseless Enemy Drive—Fall of Mitrovitza and Pristina—Retreat of the Serbians—Last Stand at Prisrend—Terrible Retreat through High, Snow-clad Mountains—Struggle in Macedonia—Fall of Monastir—Position of the Allies on the Vardar—Object Gone—A Dangerous Salient—Equivocal Action of Greece—Naval Pressure Applied by the Allies—Retirement of the Allies—British 10th Division Gets Out of a Tight Place Triumphantly—Allies Across the Frontier—Brilliant Military Achievement—Bulgar Boasts—Allies Retire Unmolested on Salonika—A Great Place of Arms Constituted—Arrest of Enemy Consuls—Corfu Occupied—Action by Italy and Russia—Invasion of Montenegro—Capture of Lovtchen by the Austrians and Fall of Cetinje—"Capitulation" of Montenegro—The Facts of the Case—King Nicholas Retires to Italy and then to France—Austrians in Possession of Montenegro—Calm at Salonika.

HE disastrous week which saw the fall of Nish on November 5th, 1915, and the enemy in occupation of the greater part of Serbia, did not, however, close without witnessing a splendid vindication of the fighting qualities of the Serbians. If by this time the general situation of the little kingdom was becoming gloomy, the dark sky was not entirely destitute of gleams of light. As narrated in the concluding paragraph of Chapter XCIII., the soldiers of Bojovitch and of Vassitch respectively had repelled all assaults of the Bulgarians on the Katshanik Pass, north-west of Uskub, and the Babuna Pass, south-west of Veles, two places of extreme strategic importance, as subsequent events clearly showed. The heroic Vassitch did far better than merely hold the Babuna Pass against repeated attacks, for he was victorious in it in a battle which, had circumstances been more propitious, might have favourably influenced the whole course of the later phases of the struggle for his country's existence. During that first week of November, 1915, Vassitch, in and around the Babuna Pass, had only 5,000 men to pit against over 20,000 Bulgarians, who besides had much heavier artillery. Day after day, night after night, his small force of Serbians, often without

GENERAL MARTINOVITCH.
Owing to his influence Austria's infamous peace terms to Montenegro were rejected. General Martinovitch tried his best to defend Mount Lovtchen.

food, always under fire, but cheered by their commander, and singing their plaintive national airs, fought dauntlessly on, repulsing with serious loss to the invader all his most stubborn and persistent efforts to force the pass. They did more. From November 4th to November 6th an incessant and sanguinary hand-to-hand fight, in which the combatants made free use of their knives, raged in the deep and narrow gorges of the defile, ending in the complete rout of the Bulgarians, who were driven through Izvor pell-mell into Veles.

And on the other side of the hills the French, under General Sarrail, were only a few miles away—almost in touch. It looked as if the Allies might effect a junction, and telegrams were despatched from Greece which actually asserted that not only French but also British troops had united with the Serbians. The truth, unfortunately, was altogether otherwise.

A thoroughly capable soldier, who had already proved his merit in France, General Sarrail did wonders considering the shortness of the time at his disposal and the inferiority of the facilities at his command, but the numbers of his men were utterly insufficient for their task, and he could not achieve the impossible. He made a great, an even desperate, attempt to join up with

SCOTTISH NURSES RETREATING WITH THE SERBIAN ARMY OVER A DANGEROUS MOUNTAIN ROAD.

With the remnant of the Serbian Army retreating over the Albanian Alps, the first Serbian unit of the Scottish Women's Hospital trekked every inch of the way as philosophically and courageously as the sternest infantryman. The unit travelled through Montenegro to Scutari and San Giovanni di Medua, whence it proceeded by ship to Italy and London. Part of the way the nurses were compelled to walk, but at Ipek some pack-horses were requisitioned. This illustration gives an idea of the perilous passes which had to be negotiated, frequently narrow, snow-covered ledges round precipices. A lack of food and Arctic cold contributed to the hardships endured by these valiant Scots women.

Vassitch, and so nearly accomplished it that nothing but the absence of reinforcements at a critical moment robbed him of success. In this effort his troops were entirely French, the British, lying around Lake Doiran, being well to the south and east on his right flank.

As soon as possible after his arrival at Salonika, he railed all his available forces up the Valley of the Vardar, towards Veles. He had only a single-tracked and indifferent railway for the transportation of both men and supplies, yet he pressed on with surprising speed. The line followed the snaky twistings of the river, and parts of it, built on shelves cut out of the solid rock, passed through deep gorges, the longest of which, known as the Demir Kapu Ravine, extended for ten miles. As possession of this defile by the enemy would have been a fatal bar to his advance, his first business was to get it into his own hands, and after some fighting at Strumnitza station, a few miles to the south, he secured it without further opposition. Then he pushed on north of it to Krivolak, about 110 miles from Salonika. He reached Krivolak on October 19th, but at first he had only a handful of troops, and could do little till more had come up.

By a magnificent thrust Vassitch recaptured Veles from the Bulgarians on October 22nd, and managed to hold it for a week. This town lay along the railway some thirty-five miles north-west of Krivolak, but **Vassitch robbed** the French were not sufficiently strong to **of success** push their way up the line to it, and they had to fight hard, as it was, to maintain themselves. It was not till after they had gained possession of a steep and forbidding height, called Kara Hodjali, three miles north of Krivolak on the road to Ishtip, that they established their position, and, defeating furious assaults of the enemy on October 30th and November 4th and 5th, made an effective bridge-head on the east side of the Vardar. In the meantime Vassitch, far outnumbered and out-

gunned, had been compelled to evacuate Veles again and withdraw to the Babuna Pass.

Krivolak was twenty-five miles almost due east of the pass, and Sarrail's problem now was to bridge the distance which intervened between himself and Vassitch. The first part of the way was easy, fifteen miles across an undulating plain to the Tserna, a tributary of the Vardar, but the remaining ten miles, on **Sarrail assaults** the west side of the former river, were over **Mount Arkangel** very difficult country, consisting of rugged hills and mountains, interspersed with water-courses, the whole of this terrain, on which the Bulgarians had erected fortifications, lending itself readily to a powerful defence.

Having secured Kara Hodjali, which the French soldiers renamed Kara Rosalie, after the pet word for their bayonets, Sarrail, for whom reinforcements had all the while been arriving at Krivolak, marched south-west across the plain through Negotin and Kavadar to the Tserna, an unfordable stream of considerable width, with but one bridge over it, and that of wood, at a place called Vozartzi. On November 5th the French moved over the bridge, and occupied the adjacent crests of the precipitous slopes which, often rising above 1,000 feet in height, line for miles that side of the river. Here they were so near the Babuna Pass that they could hear the thunderous rumble of the artillery taking part in the fierce battle in which Vassitch was victorious. Advancing northwards along the west bank of the Tserna, Sarrail next day began an assault of Mount Arkangel, ten miles down-stream from Vozartzi, and the centre of the Bulgarian position, which had to be stormed if a junction was to be made with the Serbians.

Mount Arkangel, however, was an extremely hard nut to crack. The Bulgarians had strongly fortified it, were numerically much superior to the French, and, moreover, were constantly being reinforced by Teodoroff from his main army. In war, "L'audace!" typified the spirit of the French, and on this occasion, with their precarious communications and relatively small numbers, it needed all their boldness and courage to make the attempt. After skirmishes with outposts at the base of the mountain, they drove the Bulgarians out of the villages of Sirkovo and Krushevitza, and on November 10th they carried, by an encircling movement, with great dash the village of Sirkovo, situated some distance up the side of the eminence. But they did not get far above this point. By the close of the second week of November the Bulgarians concentrated upwards of 60,000 men, with a corresponding strength in guns, on Mount Arkangel and along the west bank of the Tserna, and on the 12th they took the offensive.

Their obviously best course was to cut the French off from the Vozartzi bridge, the latter's sole

Bulgarians take the offensive

line of supply and retreat, and then hem them in against the impassable river in the rear. For three days, in fighting of the most violent description, they made the most determined efforts to carry out this purpose, but the French, combining higher skill with equal determination, held their ground, and in a grim conflict, which took place on Mount Arkangel itself, inflicted a severe defeat on the enemy, who was forced to retire in great disorder, leaving 3,500 dead on the field. In this battle the Bulgarians charged to within twenty yards of the French trenches, but, faltering under a withering fire and then counter - charged by the French with the bayonet, broke, turned, and ran. Mr. G. Ward Price, the authorised representative of the London Press with the Allies in the Balkans, reported that if only there had been enough French troops to throw into the struggle at that moment, the retreat of the Bulgars would have been made a rout.

GENERAL SARRAIL IN THE NEAR EAST.
The famous French leader, who was in supreme command of the allied armies in the Balkans, going on a tour of inspection with some officers of the British Expedition.

Vassitch held out in the Babuna Pass, ten miles away all the next day, November 15th, but the French could not get across the hills, and as he was compelled to retire, in order to escape envelopment, on Prilep on November 16th, the opportunity passed. The French, still hoping to assist the Serbians in some way, retained their positions. It was November 20th, nearly a week after the Battle of Mount Arkangel, before the Bulgarians, freshly strengthened, renewed the attack, and they were again heavily checked, but Sarrail was unable to advance, the plain fact being that he neither had nor could get men in adequate force. And, meanwhile, in other parts of the country the progress of events, moving from disaster to disaster for the brave but unfortunate Serbians, had rendered

Sarrail's lack of men

it evident that the enemy's overrunning of the rest of Serbia was a question of but a very short time, on which the venture of the Allies would exercise little or no influence.

Up to the fall of Nish, the true crisis of the campaign, the policy of the Serbian Chief Command had been to retreat slowly before the enemy on all sides, delaying everywhere his advance as much as possible by stubborn rearguard actions, so as to give time for the expected effective co-operation of the Allies. Even after Nish had been occupied by the Bulgarians and the larger part of Serbia was gone, the great mass of the Serbian people still thought that the assistance of the Entente Powers would suffice to enable their armies to hurl back the invaders, and the Serbian leaders themselves seemed to have been for a short time under a similar illusion. M. Pasich, the Premier, declared that the Serbian " General Headquarters, as well as the members of the Government and the whole

SEEING THAT " ALL'S WELL."
Above and in circle : Two impressions of General Sarrail personally conducting members of the French Parliamentary Mission round the camp at Zeitlenlick, near Salonika

FUGITIVES: THE TRAGIC EXODUS OF THE SERBIAN PEASANTRY BEFORE THE ADVANCE OF THE GERMAN-BULGAR INVADERS.

Unlike the Belgians, the Serbian population had time to retreat, and most of them, fearing the brutality of the arrogant invader, elected to withdraw with their soldier-compatriots. One can but faintly imagine the interminable procession of old men, women, and children, some trudging over the rain-sodden highway, others riding in cumbersome bullock-waggons. Frequently, owing to the intense cold, a lack of food, and unwonted physical strain, an aged peasant or frail child would fall prostrate by the roadside

people," were convinced that as soon as the allied troops had arrived in sufficient numbers and entered into action, "success would be rapid and sure." This was on November 7th, and the same policy was continued a little longer, but it soon was clear that there was one thing—and one thing only—left to Serbia, and that was the salvation of her Army from capture or destruction.

On the north and north-east the crushing of Serbia went on unrelentingly, as the Serbian main armies were steadily pushed back towards the frontiers of Montenegro and Albania by Kövess, Gallwitz, and Bojadieff, in spite of the more difficult, because more mountainous, character of the country they had to take into account. The Serbians had no reserves from which to make good their losses, whereas the enemy kept bringing up reinforcements; his greater numerical strength and the efficiency of his long-range guns told heavily in his favour. Now becoming woefully short of supplies of both munitions and food, the Serbian armies, whose *moral* remained undiminished, fought bravely on in a struggle daily more hopeless. The fortnight after the fall of Nish saw the development of a great converging movement of the three enemy commanders on the historic Kossovo Plain, with the object of rolling up and encircling the Serbian principal forces.

At the end of the first week of November, Kövess with his Austro-Germans was marching towards Mitrovitza on the north side of the plain from Kralievo up the Valley of the Ibar, an affluent of the Western Morava. After a bitter fight he drove the Serbian rearguards out of the hills north of Ivanitza, and occupied that town on November 9th. Four days later, having driven the Serbians from their positions in the district of the Stolovi range, he forced his way to Rashka, a town on the Ibar, well on the road to Mitrovitza, and a few miles from Novi Bazar, which he took on November 20th, finding in its arsenal—the last the Serbians had left—fifty large mortars and eight guns that were, as the German official communiqué admitted, " of a somewhat ancient pattern." Farther east, Austrian troops were in possession of Sienitza and of Nova Varosh, close to the Montenegrin boundary, about the same date. Thrown back near Zhochanitza, the Serbians retired on Mitrovitza, from which Kövess on the 22nd was only five miles away.

East of Kövess, Gallwitz with his Germans had also been advancing southward, his objective being Pristina, on the east side of the Kossovo Plain and some twenty miles south-east of Mitrovitza. He had to negotiate the high mountain ridges of Central Serbia, and the Serbians, fighting desperately in the Jastrebatz and other ranges, made him pay a heavy price for his progress, but on this front they furthermore had to endeavour to stem a rising tide in the shape of Bojadieff and his Bulgarians, and against the two they had not the ghost of a chance. Starting out from Krushevatz about November 8th,

Serbians retire on Mitrovitza

WAR-BITTEN FRENCH VETERANS MARCHING OUT OF KAVADAR.
French troops retreating from Kavadar via Negotin to the Salonika lines. Owing to a superior concentration of Bulgarian forces, our allies were compelled to withdraw over the mountains, using pack-horses for transport in the absence of railways. This illustration shows the familiar steel-helmeted infantrymen leaving Kavadar.

Gallwitz, following the course of a small tributary of the Western Morava, struck south-west towards Brus with one part of his troops, and with another due south across the high hills of the Jastrebatz in the direction of Kurshumlia. He soon reached Ribari and Rabaska Bania (Baths), and subsequent to what the Germans themselves described as desperate local fighting, stormed the chief pass on the road over the mountains, and gained entrance to the Valley of the Toplitza, a river flowing westward into the Morava, the main stream of that name which in this section of the country was changed into the " Southern " or " Bulgar " Morava. After a week's hard struggle Gallwitz entered Kurshumlia, which the Serbians had evacuated, stripping it first of everything of military value, but being forced to leave several hundreds of their wounded, who fell into the hands of the Germans. Moving on from this town, which lay about midway between Krushevatz and Pristina, Gallwitz pushed across to Prepolatz, east of the Kopaonik Mountains, occupying it on November 20th, and then advanced southwards over the intervening ridges. The Serbians struggled on, but the same day which saw Kövess within striking distance of Mitrovitza beheld Gallwitz, from the north of the Lab Valley, threatening Pristina as closely.

Enemy occupies Old Serbia

Vienna announced with triumph, on November 20th, that on the preceding day the Serbians had been driven by force of arms from the last portion of Old Serbia by the three allied armies. Included in these were the operations of the Bulgarian divisions under Bojadieff, whose right wing had joined up with Gallwitz in the march on Pristina. The Bulgarians, however, had had anything but a walk-over.

RUDE SHELTER FROM WIND AND WEATHER.
A Serbian soldier's resting-place during the great retreat.

After withdrawing from Nish, the Serbians, under Marshal Stepanovitch, retreated to the west bank of the Morava, destroying the bridges as soon as they had got across, and, encouraged by the presence of King Peter in their midst, held up the Bulgarians there for some time. But farther north and farther south in the Morava Valley they were at first less successful in checking the enemy. On the north the Bulgarians captured Alexinatz on November 7th, the Serbian Army of the Timok, in retreat from Zaitchar, barely succeeding in crossing the bridge over the river in time. On the south, and on the same day, the Serbians had to abandon Leskovatz. With the capture of these towns and other points on the line, the enemy secured complete possession of the great trunk railway from Belgrade through Nish to Sofia and Constantinople and of the Nish-Salonika railway as far south as the French entrenchments at Krivolak.

Of these two gains, the former was infinitely the more important. The passing into Germanic occupation of the international highway, reaching from the North Sea to the Bosphorus and beyond, was up to that time one of the most striking features of the war, which, with free communication opened up between Germany and Asia, showed itself more manifestly than ever a world-war.

From Alexinatz the hard-pressed **Heavy defeat of** Army of the Timok had only a single **Bojadieff** line of retreat, the road to Prokuplie and Kurshumlia, and, in danger of being cut off by the Germans on the west, it marched swiftly, though fighting rearguard actions all the while, and was able to unite with the army retiring from Krushevatz. Prokuplie did not fall to the Bulgarians till November 16th. North-west of Leskovatz, where the pressure was not quite so extreme, Stepanovitch made a determined stand, on November 11th and 12th, and heavily defeated Bojadieff's centre, throwing the latter's troops into confusion, and taking prisoners and guns. But this success could not, unhappily, be followed up ; on the contrary, the Bulgarians, much reinforced, renewed the conflict two or three days later, and drove the Serbians down the road to Tulare and on to Pristina.

Meanwhile the Bulgarians were advancing on Pristina from a more southern direction—from Uskub. Here they were strongly opposed, and this sector of the campaign witnessed the Battle of the Katshanik Pass, in which the Serbians made their greatest effort subsequent to their magnificent resistance to the Austro-Germans on the Danube and the Save. By this time it had become apparent to the Serbian Chief Command that they could not receive from the Allies the expected assistance for their main armies. Indeed, it was strange that they had

SERBIANS' SPLENDID FIGHTING SPIRIT AFTER MANY DAYS OF BATTLE.
Our Serbian Allies entered the European War as veterans, having just previously fought in two stubborn wars with the Turks and Bulgars. That fact doubtless accounted for their wonderful stand against such overwhelming odds. One has only to contemplate this illustration, showing a rearguard which had kept the enemy at bay for days and preserved communication with the Montenegrins to realise the splendid physique and endurance of the race as a whole. The circle photograph depicts a typical Serbian outpost.

BROKEN IN THE WAR OF AGGRESSION.
It is idle to speculate on the mortality which the taking of Serbia cost the enemy. The true figure may never pass the German censor, but the losses were undoubtedly great, to judge only by the hosts of wounded shown in official photographs.

cherished the idea so long, as they must have known of the comparatively small numbers of the troops which had landed at Salonika and the difficulties of various kinds, such as the scarcely veiled hostility of the Greek authorities, with which the allied commanders had to contend. They now perceived that the only hope of saving their armies intact was by keeping open or forcing a way to the south through Uskub.

This meant first of all that the Katshanik Pass, which in the **Battle of Katshanik Pass** second week of November was still in the hands of the Serbians, but was beleaguered on the south by the Bulgarians, had to be cleared of the enemy, who thereupon was to be driven out of Uskub, whence the Serbian armies would retreat west to Kalkandelen (Tetovo), and then south by the road through Gostivar and Kichevo to Monastir. This was the plan, and a most heroic attempt was made to accomplish it. It failed, but not without shedding fresh lustre on the Serbian arms. Certainly it was the most hotly contested fight that took place between the Serbians and the Bulgarians; it was protracted for five days, and nothing except the overwhelming strength of the enemy prevented a decisive Serbian victory.

About November 10th Bojovitch's slender army of 5,000 men was reinforced by three regiments, including one from the Shumadia and one from the Morava Divisions, which were sent by the railway—the only bit remaining to Serbia—from Pristina to Ferizovitch, some ten miles from the Katshanik Pass. The weather was intensely cold, and the roads were indescribably bad. The Serbians, though exhausted by much marching, and weak from want of food, pressed on to the pass, and Bojovitch began the attack without a moment's delay. According to one account he had a hundred guns, mostly of the French 75

and 155 type (3 in. and 6 in.), which rained thousands of shrapnel and high-explosive shells on the trenches of the Bulgarians, who, under this terrible fire, retreated south for four miles. Then the Serbian infantry drove on, falling wave after wave on the reeling Bulgarian ranks, which, however, rallied as their supports came up. One Serbian regiment charged desperately seven times, each time capturing and then losing six Bulgarian guns. In several parts of the field there was a savage hand-to-hand mêlée, in which the combatants, throwing down their rifles, fought with daggers, knives, fists, and even teeth, the wildest, fiercest scenes in the envenomed fighting on the

NEAR WHERE THE KAISER DINED.
A strong position at Nish, fortified by barbed-wire, steel stakes, and sand-bags.

A HOUSE OF MARS ON THE BATTLE-PLAIN.
Typical Balkan blockhouse on the Serbo-Bulgarian frontier, in the neighbourhood of which much heavy fighting took place.

Timok being far outdone. For some time the Serbians on the whole made progress, the enemy's centre being pierced by a prodigious effort of the Shumadia and Morava troops, and it seemed as if Serbian valour would prevail. But here, once more, the Serbians had no reserves to ensure success. The Bulgarians were all the time being strengthened by large numbers of fresh men railed up from Uskub, and in the end this superiority was the deciding factor. On the 15th the battle was lost, and the Serbians were forced out of the pass, retiring by the passes of the Jatzovitza Hills on Prisrend.

Thus the plan of the retreat of the Serbian armies to the south completely collapsed, and its effect was immediately seen in the withdrawal from Mitrovitza of the Serbian Staff, such members of the Serbian Government as had remained there, and the personnel of the Legations of the Allies. The Bulgarians had not been unconscious of the scheme that lay behind the Battle of the Katshanik Pass, and had sought to forestall part of it by attacking Kalkandelen, a point which had been taken and retaken more than once. On November 15th they captured it for the last time, and driving the small Serbian force that had occupied it before them, they took Gostivar on the following day, the Serbians retreating to Kichevo, on the road to Monastir. About the same dates, or a little later, Boja-dieff, after a stiff fight, stormed the heights near Gilan, north-west of Katshanik, and occupying Gilan itself, advanced towards Pristina, being on November 22nd no more than two or three miles from the last-named town.

The enemy had now succeeded in his great object of rolling back on to the Kossovo Plain the Serbian main armies, which were united, but in considerable confusion and hampered by vast crowds of fugitives fleeing from all parts of the north, centre and east of the country. Near Mitrovitza, on the north of the plain, near Pristina on the east of it, and at Katshanik at its southern extremity, the Austro-Germans and the Bulgarians had, in the beginning of the fourth week of November, absolutely rounded up and hemmed in all the chief forces of the Serbians, for whom nothing really was left but surrender, destruction, or a terrible retreat into the mountains of Montenegro and Albania, now in the grip of winter, deep in snow, and swept by biting winds.

Serbia decided to make a last stand on the plain, and then, if that failed, to retreat, thus defeating the principal strategic purpose of Mackensen, which was the surrender or destruction of the Serbian **The "Field of the** Army. King Peter himself was present, **Blackbirds"** and the Serbians fought well, but by this time the Serbian Army, though in the military sense intact, had been greatly reduced in numbers by constant fighting and perhaps also by desertions, for the ordinary Serbians did not understand that a retreat was not a defeat, and in all probability no longer preserved that high *moral* which had distinguished them throughout the earlier stages of the campaign.

Known as the "Field of the Blackbirds," thus styled from the great quantities of those birds which frequent it, the Plain of Kossovo, a high plateau forty miles long and ten wide, had depressing memories for the Serbians, for there Lazar, the last of their ancient Tsars, in the days when Serbia was a powerful kingdom, was defeated and slain along with the flower of his nobles and chiefs in 1389. King Peter, old and bent with rheumatism, but shouldering a rifle, went up and down the ranks of his soldiers, heartening them to endure to the bitter end, and declaring that he was prepared to share Lazar's fate. But the enemy was far too strong for the Serbians. Kövess, having swept away the Serbian entrenchments north of Mitrovitza, entered that town on November 23rd, taking, by his own statement, 10,000 prisoners, 19 guns, and much railway material. On the same day Gallwitz, with his Germans, and the Bulgarians under Bojadieff captured Pristina, the former attacking it from the north and the latter from the south and east, capturing many thousand prisoners. That evening an official Sofia bulletin stated that Pristina was taken after bitter fighting, and said that when the Bulgarian army closed in on the Serbians the latter made the "most desperate efforts to hold" the town, "but were unable to withstand our pressure, and, driven out of their last position, were forced to retreat to the west."

BRITISH AND NEUTRAL WAR ACTIVITIES IN THE LEVANT.
Highlanders repairing a broken trench parapet at the extremity of a British line in the Balkans. In circle : A Greek five-wheeled transport lorry being driven through Salonika. From the moment of the allied occupation of this port the Greeks made preparations for the eventuality of war.

Some of the first contingent of British troops arriving on the Balkan front. A group of French soldiers who preceded them are contemplating their British comrades and transport waggons with interest.

After the arrangement with Greece regarding the temporary occupation of Salonika by the allied forces had been settled, Greek soldiers evacuated the ancient port. A large body of these men, whose uniforms were singularly like those of our own troops, are seen on the march to another base.

Preparing for a massed attack. Some idea of the enormous number of men involved in the Austro-German advance in the Balkans may be gained from this impressive picture. As far as eye can see along the river bank are troops and war equipment about to proceed across the river by the several improvised pontoon bridges.

ALLIED, ENEMY AND NEUTRAL MOVEMENTS IN THE BALKAN COCKPIT.

LAYING IN STORES FOR A LONG CAMPAIGN: FLOUR AND FODDER ON THE QUAY-SIDE AT SALONIKA.

Impression of the accumulation of stores at the French base, Salonika. Fully realising the extent of the campaign in the Balkans, France transported from her various Mediterranean ports an ample supply of munitions and provender. The whole quay-side was lined with trusses of hay and sacks of flour. Two officers, moving from the camera in this snapshot, are superintending operations, while a sentry is about to go on guard.

From Mitrovitza a part of the Serbian Army, accompanied by multitudes of civilian fugitives, retreated to Ipek in Montenegro, and some proportion of them eventually arrived at Scutari. by way of Podgoritza. after suffering the cruellest hardships and privations—the rest perished miserably from cold and starvation. Retiring from the same town, another part of the force which had opposed Kövess stood and fought him again at Vutshitrin, but was beaten and pursued across the Sitnitza, on the western bank of which stream it was still fighting on November 25th. But the main line of retreat of the Serbians was along the high road. from Pristina to Prisrend, and the Bulgarians pressed on quickly behind in this direction, took the heights west of Ferizovitch, and also advanced northerly towards Ipek, against which town Kövess had sent a detachment. The retreat to Prisrend was covered by the Shumadia Division. On November 27th upwards of 80,000 Serbians stood at bay in front of this town, but next day, after a most sanguinary conflict, and having fired their last shell, they spiked their guns, and fled across the frontier into Albania, making along the White Drin for Kula Liuma, sometimes called Lum Kulus, while several thousand prisoners fell into the hands of the enemy.

Serbian rout at Prisrend

As her forces still fighting in the south, in Macedonia, were inconsiderable, and were already being heavily pressed by the Bulgarians, the rout at Prisrend and the consequent flight signalised for the time being the end of Serbia. The Serbian Government, with the venerable Pasich at its head, had left Prisrend a few days before the débâcle, and arrived without misadventure at Scutari on November 30th. King Peter, attended by two or three devoted soldiers told off to see to his personal safety, made good his escape, and after wandering among the snow-covered mountain paths, reached the Adriatic, whence he was conveyed to Brindisi, and later to Salonika. The Crown Prince Alexander, with the Princess Heléne, succeeded in getting to Cetinje, having suffered much from hunger and cold in a wild ride through Montenegro.

Marked by horrors unspeakable, the retreat of the Serbian Army will remain one of the most terrible in history. Day by day thousands of men, ill-clad, ill-shod, or with bare and bleeding feet, and, crazed with famine, eating raw horse-flesh with avidity, stumbled painfully and wretchedly along the two available roads, and these no better than mule-tracks, from Kula Liuma, one going west to Scutari, and the other south through Dibra to Elbasan. Saddest of all, with these wearied and war-worn soldiers there travelled long, mournful processions of the aged of both sexes, of the women and children, of Serbia, exhausted and starving, but preferring to face anything than to fall into the hands of the Austro-German and Bulgarian conquerors. Each *via dolorosa* was strewn thickly with the bodies of these unfortunate people. It was estimated that out of half a million civilians, who sought refuge in flight into the Albanian mountains. more than 200,000 died. The ranks of the Serbian Army also were woefully thinned in the retreat, but not to anything like the same extent.

Horrors of the flight

On November 28th German Headquarters issued an extraordinary report, in which it announced that with the flight of the scanty remains of the Serbian Army into the Albanian mountains "our great operations against the same are brought to a close. Our object of effecting communication with Bulgaria and the Turkish Empire has been accomplished." After briefly describing these operations from a German standpoint, and admitting the "tough resistance" of the Serbians, who had "fought bravely," this communiqué asserted that **Germany's objective** more than 100,000 of them, "almost half **realised** the entire Serbian fighting forces," had been taken prisoners, while their losses in battle and from desertion could not be estimated. These statements, calculated to give the world the impression that the Serbian Army had been annihilated, were gross exaggerations, after the familiar German pattern, the truth being that on the date mentioned Serbia had 200,000 men left.

But it was true that Germany had effected communication through Bulgaria with Turkey. Her engineers and military railway staff had the trunk line from Belgrade through Nish to Sofia and Constantinople in running order by the middle of December. Having got the railway, she withdrew most of her own troops from Serbia, leaving the Bulgarians to finish Macedonia, and the Austrians Montenegro.

While the main Serbian armies were being driven out of their native land, the Bulgarians, after taking the Babuna Pass and Kichevo, as well as Krushevo on November 20th, did not forthwith advance to the capture of Monastir, and that city was subjected to many alarms for days, most of its population making haste to remove into Greece, whither the railway was still open. Vassitch had retired from the Babuna to Prilep, and there awaited the assault, which, however, did not materialise. When the Bulgarians at last moved, and took Brod with a view to cutting off his retreat, he quitted Prilep, and fell back on Monastir, which he evacuated on December 2nd, withdrawing his small band of heroes to Resna. The last fight of importance by the Serbians took place near that town, from which Vassitch retired on December 5th, and marching round the southern shore of Lake Ochrida, effected the escape of himself and his men into Epirus. There were some encounters between small groups of Serbians and Bulgarians at Ochrida and Struga, but the retreat of Vassitch marked the conclusion of Serbia's glorious resistance against overwhelming odds.

Just about ten weeks had passed since the Germans had begun shelling Semendria on September 21st. While the struggle was still going on Serbia might have come to terms with the enemy.

On November 14th Marshal Mackensen made an offer of an armistice to Prince Alexander, the regent, and the Serbian Government, with a view to a separate peace, the basis of which was the cession to Bulgaria of a tract of territory on Serbia's eastern frontier, including Pirot, Kniashevatz and Zaitchar, and the whole of Serbian Macedonia. By that date the most optimistic of the Serbian leaders **Separate peace** must have realised that, from the military **rejected** point of view, their country was doomed if the conflict was continued, but the proposal was rejected. In the Council of Ministers which considered it Pasich declared: "Our way is marked out. We will be true to the Entente, and die honourably." And in honour Serbia went down, fighting to the last.

With the disappearance from Serbia of her armies, the French and British forces which had come to endeavour to save them had no longer an object in remaining on

BRITISH MULE CONVOY TRAVERSING A PLAIN IN MACEDONIA.

HOW THE SERBIAN GENERALISSIMO WAS CONVEYED TO SAFETY.
The aged Marshal Putnik, whose able command of the Serbian Army was one of the remarkable features of this unique campaign, was too ill and frail to retreat on horseback. He was therefore carried in a crude Sedan chair by four faithful bearers.

attitude to the Entente Powers caused them much anxiety. The question was how she would comport herself in the event of the retirement—seen to be possible after the fall of Nish—of the forces of the Allies from the Tserna-Vardar and the Vardar-Doiran positions. Would she give them complete freedom of communication south of the frontier to Salonika, or seek to disarm and intern them and such Serbians as crossed the border ?

M. Skouloudis succeeded M. Zaimis as Prime Minister of Greece, but he was a mere mouthpiece of King Constantine, who had taken the reins of government into his own hands. Venizelos was not silent, but was no more than a voice crying in the wilderness. At the start Skouloudis expressed the opinion publicly that Greece's " benevolent neutrality " did not extend to protecting the allied troops — whether French, British, or Serbian—from the operation of international law, and that, therefore, these troops would be disarmed and interned on their passing over into Greek territory. Of course, Germany backed him up. His words created a painful impression throughout the allied countries, which was deepened when it became known that Greece had concentrated 200,000 men in menacing positions in and about Salonika. A report that she had signed a treaty with Bulgaria further increased the tension. The question now was whether Greece was to be permitted to carry out her declared intentions or not, and the Allies unanimously replied in the negative.

Ordinary arguments proved valueless, and time was lost in talk. Opinion and feeling grew heated in France and Britain over the delay, as well as over the question itself. France in particular called for immediate and energetic action, urging that it was necessary to show the iron hand under the velvet glove. The iron hand was a figure of speech for the fleets of the Allies, which could not only bombard and destroy the coasts of Greece, but deprive her of her supplies. It was a very powerful argument, and after a meeting of an urgent War Council in Paris it was brought to bear upon her in the form of a partial embargo of her shipping. Two visits paid to King Constantine while the crisis was acute had a favourable influence upon it. One was from M. Denys Cochin, a member of the French Government, and a man held in the highest estimation in Greece ; the other was from Lord Kitchener, who was on his way back from Gallipoli, whither he had been despatched by his colleagues in the British Cabinet to report on the advisability or the reverse of abandoning that peninsula. Yet the negotiations were spun out, and it was not till November 23rd that matters were brought to a head by the presentation of a combined Note to Greece.

This Note demanded formal assurances that the allied troops should in no circumstances be disarmed and interned, but should be granted full freedom of movement, together with such facilities as had been already promised. On the other hand, the Note categorically stated that the Allies would make restitution of all territory occupied, and pay suitable indemnities. Two days afterwards, the Greek Government replied in friendly but somewhat vague terms,

The Allies' Note to Greece

Serbian soil, particularly as they were not of themselves able to undertake an offensive, though during November large reinforcements arrived at Salonika. The rumours of military action by Russia on behalf of Serbia had proved unfounded, and a second bombardment of Varna had no effect on the general course of the campaign. Italy had done nothing in the Balkans to help her Allies, except to shell Dedeagach on November 11th. A month later she landed an army at Valona and elsewhere on the Adriatic coast, but this action had no influence on the immediate fortunes of her friends. That the allied forces in Macedonia would be unable to unite with the Serbians had been demonstrated in the Mount Arkangel fighting. For several days after November 20th, when the French on the west bank of the Tserna repulsed the Bulgarians on that portion of the front, nothing occurred. The first sign of what was about to happen appeared on November 27th in a Paris official communiqué, stating that, in consequence of the situation of the Serbian armies at that time, the French troops that had occupied the west bank of the Tserna had been brought to the east side of that river—a movement which was made without any difficulty. A general withdrawal into Greece, with Salonika as base, had been decided on by General Sarrail, in accordance with instructions from Paris and London.

But Greece was a doubtful quantity, and all through November and part of the following month her ambiguous

Gen. Sarrail, who assumed command of the Allied Forces at Salonika, January 16th, 1916

General Putnik, Serbia's invalid chief, conveyed in a Sedan chair across the River Drin.

Serbian engineers directing the transport of their pontoons over Mount Voshibatz.

French troops, withdrawing from Kavadar, transporting supplies by pack=horse.

A study in physical energy: Serbian heavy gun being dragged up a steep incline.

435

The fugitive King Peter and his escort crossing the River Drin at the foot of the Albanian Alps.

which were not considered satisfactory, and on the 26th the Entente sent a second Note, asking for a precise assurance regarding the liberty of movement of the troops. The Greek answer was liked so little that the iron hand had again to be displayed, with the result that a fortnight later Greece gave in, accepting practically all the Allies' demands, and withdrawing most of her men from Salonika, while the Gevgheli-Salonika and the Doiran-Salonika railways, with the adjacent roads and land, were handed over to the Allies. King Constantine complained that he was between the devil and the deep sea, or words to that effect, and protested that Greek neutrality was violated. But Greece, owing to her having invited the first Entente troops, was not genuinely a neutral. The King, anxious to be rid of his unwelcome guests, let it be understood that if the Allies would only retire from Greece altogether, he and his Army

CROSS AND CRESCENT.
British sentry outside the Turkish Consulate at Salonika after the arrest of the Consul and his Staff.

would ensure their safe embarkation against all comers. But the Entente Powers had come to the resolve that Salonika was to be held, and Constantine's suggestion fell very flat.

Although no arrangement had been concluded between Greece and the Entente by the beginning of December, the French, under the direction of Sarrail, with General Bailloud in local command, began their retirement on the 2nd of the month. There was good reason for anticipating the result of the Greek negotiations. The French position had become a most dangerous salient, with the Bulgarians surrounding it on the north-east, north-west, and south-west. Teodoroff had brought up large forces, with plenty of artillery, from the other Bulgarian fronts where they were no longer required, and greatly outnumbered the French.

Under cover of a feigned attack on Ishtip from Kara Hodjali, Sarrail drew in his men from the Tserna, and before the enemy had realised what was going on, had

retired from the Kavadar Camp with all his stores, of which there was a tremendous accumulation, and entrained at Krivolak, blowing up the bridges and tearing up the railway behind him. On December 5th he reached the north end of the Demir Kapu Ravine practically without opposition, but in the gorge he had to fight hard to get out of it. He had had the prevision, however, to form a strong bridge-head near its entrance, and this enabled him to repel the Bulgarian attacks, in spite of their being pressed home with the utmost determination. The retreat through the ravine was an extremely difficult operation, as there was no way of egress save by the single track of the railway lying on a narrow shelf cut out of the rocks beside the Vardar. Yet by December 8th the French emerged, still with all their stores, and, after having destroyed a tunnel and another bridge across the Vardar, continued their retirement to Gradetz, which had a fortified bridge-head. And here the Bulgarians attacked violently both on the 8th and 9th, but were driven off with heavy losses. On the 10th the French announced that they occupied a new front, defined by the course of the Bojimia, a tributary of the Vardar, and were in touch with the British.

Sarrail's fighting retreat

It will always seem a somewhat strange thing that, though British troops arrived in Salonika in the first week of October, two months should elapse before they took any prominent part in the fighting. General Mahon reached Greece on October 12th, and General Monro a month later, but the British made no move of importance. There were some trifling encounters with outposts, and these the Athens lie-factories magnified into battles. The French bore the brunt of the struggle on the Tserna—perhaps because they were more numerous than the British, who were not actively engaged in force until the first week of December.

GUARDS OF THE ALLIES AT THE AUSTRO-HUNGARIAN CONSULATE, SALONIKA.
Three enemy aeroplanes having thrown bombs on Salonika, General Sarrail, on December 30th, 1915, arrested the Consuls of Germany, Austria-Hungary, Turkey, and Bulgaria, with their Staffs and families, and sent them on board a French warship. The Austrian Consulate, when examined, was found to be " a regular arsenal."

Their trenches lay north and west of Lake Doiran, among bleak hills covered with snow, spreading out fanwise in the direction of Strumnitza, and they had taken them over from the French when the latter had gone up the Vardar to Krivolak. One of the difficulties of Sarrail's retreat was that while it was going on he was unable, owing to the nature of the country, to maintain close communication with the British prior to the 10th.

On the east side of the Vardar Teodoroff had massed four divisions—or roughly 100,000 men—and he made his first great assault on the British in the grey of early morning, and under cover of a fog, which permitted him to get close up to the British trenches, without being clearly perceived, on December 6th. The British force opposed to this Bulgarian army—for it was nothing less—consisted of the 10th Division, which had come from Suvla Bay, and could hardly have been in anything like full strength, and supports drawn from the Salonika base. The enemy first of all poured a rain of high-explosive shell on the British trenches, which were held mainly by the Inniskillings, the Connaughts, the Munsters, and the Dublin Fusiliers—the pick of Ireland—and the Hampshires. After very heavy fighting, often

hand-to-hand, with the advantage now on one side and now on the other, the overwhelming strength of the Bulgarians told, and the British were driven out of their first line. The battle had raged all day, with hardly a pause, and it was renewed next morning with equal or even fiercer intensity.

As on the 6th, the conflict commenced with a tremendous bombardment by the Bulgarians of the British lines, and then the enemy came on, hurrahing and cheering, and threw himself in successive waves on the 10th Division, which resisting stoutly, gave ground slowly, its rate of retirement being about two miles a day, which was wonderfully little considering the enormous pressure exerted by Teodoroff's four divisions. More than once the British looked like being annihilated, but a free use of the bayonet, added to Irish and English pluck, succeeded in extricating them from the most dangerous situations. According to all accounts, the losses of the enemy far exceeded those of the British, who, however, lost about 1,300 men and eight field-guns. The War Office announced at the end of the second week of December that the 10th Division had retired to a strong position from Lake Doiran westward towards the Valley of the Vardar in conjunction with the French, and it complimented the division on its gallantry, especially the Munster Fusiliers, the Dublin Fusiliers, and

10th Division's memorable stand

A CORNER OF THE BRITISH CAMP AT SALONIKA.
Stable dug-out at the foot of "Mount Arrowroot," as the soldiers called it—an official photograph, of which the Crown copyright is reserved.
Above: British patrol marching through the streets of the ancient Greek port.

the Connaught Rangers, by whose bravery the withdrawal had been successfully accomplished. It explained the loss of the guns as being due to the mountainous nature of the country, the guns being placed in a position from which it was impossible to withdraw them when the retirement took place. On December 11th the Bulgarians attacked the Allies at Furka, and were repulsed with a reported loss of 8,000 men.

Without much further fighting, the Franco - British troops on December 12th gained the other side of the frontier, having torn up the railway behind them, and fired Gevgheli and other points on the Macedonian side, so as to delay the Bulgarian advance.

ON THE SERBO-BULGARIAN FRONT.
British troops on their way to the first-line trenches. At the time the photograph was taken fighting was proceeding on the hill in the distance.

CONTRAST IN TRANSPORT.
British and Greek transport passing in the vicinity of Salonika. The small two-wheeled native carts aroused the active interest of the British soldiers.

By a fortunate coincidence Greece had on the previous day agreed to accept the proposals of the Allies by which their forces were to have free and unimpeded liberty of action. Considering the difficulty of the operations in face of the immense strength of the enemy, the whole retirement, which reflected the greatest credit on General Sarrail, had been carried out most successfully. Although his men had at their disposal only one line of railway and no roads, their retreat was executed in such an orderly manner that they were able to save and withdraw all their stores, while the total of their casualties did not exceed 3,500, a very moderate figure in the circumstances.

In reality a brilliant military achievement, the Franco-British retreat, in less skilful hands, or with less steady troops, might easily have been turned into a serious disaster for the Allies. That the expedition had to withdraw from Serbia without effecting the object for which it had entered the country was, of course, very unfortunate; but the best was certainly made of a bad job. It was satisfactory that everything which could be saved was saved, and it was something more than satisfactory that the Bulgarians were taught several severe **Brilliant military achievement**
lessons. According to their own version of the fighting they were everywhere victorious. One of the features of the Balkan Wars had been the extravagance and the bombast which had characterised the communiqués issued by the Bulgarians, but their statement, announcing the close of their operations in Serbia at this time, far outdid them all.

This document, published about December 14th, stated : " December 12th will remain for the Bulgarian Army and nation a day of great historical importance. The Army on that day occupied the last three Macedonian towns which were still in the hands of the enemy—namely, Doiran,

AMMUNITION FOR THE BALKAN FRONT.
Huge stacks of supplies at Salonika brought oversea, and being transferred by motor-waggons from the quays to the British lines.

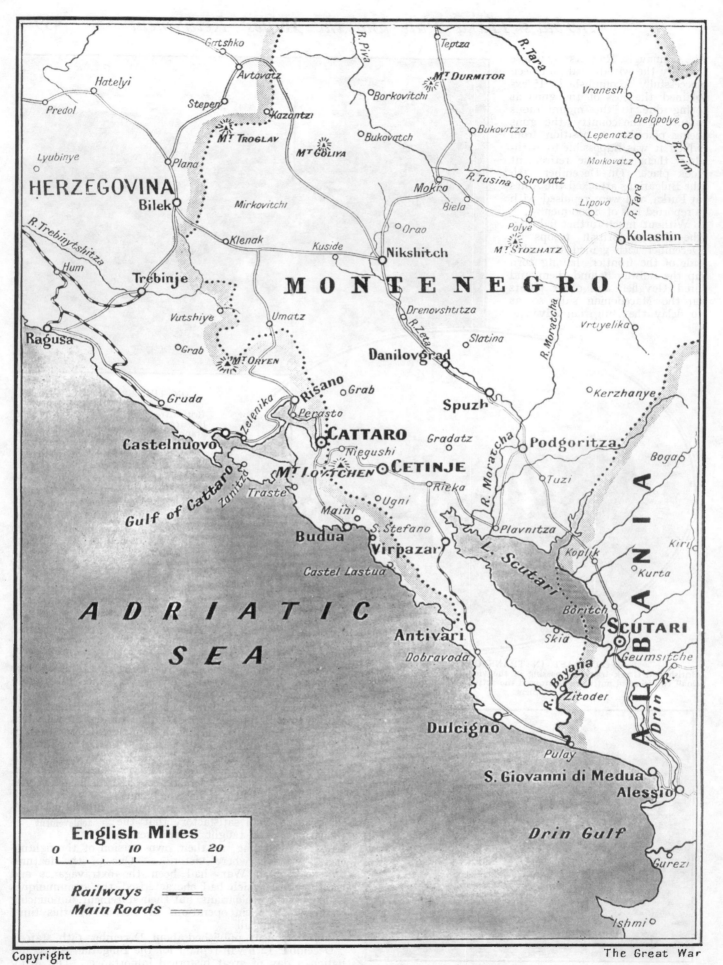

English Miles

0   10   20

Railways   ━ ━ ━

Main Roads ═══

The Great War

MAP OF THE ROADS AND RIVERS OF MONTENEGRO.

Specially drawn to illustrate the story of the Austrian invasion of the little Slav State and the line of retreat of the Montenegrin forces after the fall of Mount Lovtchen and Cetinje.

TERMINUS OF THE ONLY RAILWAY IN THE LAND OF THE BLACK MOUNTAIN.

The terms of surrender demanded of Montenegro by the Austrians included a clause that all communications, especially railways, should be given up to the Dual Monarchy. Owing to the mountainous condition of the country, there was only one small narrow-gauge line, which ran a distance of fourteen miles from Antivari to Virbazar on the shore of Lake Scutari. In spite of its diminutive character, this particular line was invaluable to British nurses and a detachment of naval men from Belgrade. Our striking photograph shows the terminus at Virbazar on the Lake of Scutari. The entrance to the station is the small gate seen at the foot of the bridge on the left.

Gevgheli, and Struga. The last fights against the British, French, and Serbians took place near Doiran and Ochrida Lakes. The enemy was everywhere beaten. Macedonia is free! Not a single hostile soldier is to be found on Macedonian soil . . . . In the course of ten days the expeditionary army of General Sarrail was beaten and thrown back on neutral territory. On December 12th the whole of Macedonia was freed. The pursuit of the enemy was immediately stopped when the neutral frontier of Greece was reached." This communiqué boasted that Bulgaria had beaten Serbia in forty, and the British and French in ten, days. A semi-official paper in Sofia declared that the victories won over the " Franco-British hordes " were even more glorious than those won over the Serbians, and declared that Bulgaria had given a lesson to the so-called Great Powers, Britain and France, showing them at the same time the manner in which small nations could fight for their independence.

Bulgarian braggadocio

These preposterous statements had a certain effect throughout the Balkans, especially in Rumania, which had had, not unnaturally, very little to say, but thought a great deal, while Serbia was being crushed out of existence. Yet so far as the withdrawal of the Allies was itself concerned, the simple truth was that it was a conspicuous success, the retirement being resolved on for sufficient reason on a given date, and on the motion of the Allies themselves.

Somewhat contrary to the expectation of the Entente Powers, the Bulgarians, in obedience probably to orders received from Germany, did not cross the boundary in pursuit of the retiring allied troops, for whom there was now free passage from Doiran to Salonika, as the Greek forces, in accordance with an agreement which had been at length arrived at, had evacuated that part of the country. Germany sarcastically inquired of the Greek Government whether Greece was still neutral, but the Greeks, in whom hostility to the Bulgarians was ingrained, waited anxiously to see what turn events would immediately take.

Sofia published the most reassuring things about Bulgaria's friendliness to Greece, but somehow Athens could not quite bring herself to put her trust in these protestations —perhaps recalling how Bulgaria had similarly proclaimed her good intentions before suddenly falling on Serbia. Greece stated in almost minatory language that she could not permit her hereditary enemies, the Bulgarians, to pass the boundary. She changed her tune afterwards, but at the moment it was this attitude of hers which was at the bottom of the orders from Germany to Bulgaria, and which gave the latter pause. At any rate, Bulgarian troops did not venture across the frontier into Greece after the Allies.

Meanwhile, the French and the British had fallen back, slowly and in a somewhat leisurely fashion, on an entrenched line two or three miles on the south side of the border. This line stretched from Karasuli on the Vardar to Kilindir on the Doiran-Salonika railway, the whole presenting a sort of bridge-head of about fifteen miles, the western moiety being in the hands of the French and the eastern in those of the British. The distance from the eastern end of this (British) front to Salonika was about thirty miles. The Allies now set strenuously to work on fortifying this line, and made it particularly strong, not so much with a view to holding up an immediate enemy advance—though that was looked and prepared for—as with the intention of

Allied line of resistance

441

SEARCHING THE HORIZON FOR SIGNS OF THE AUSTRO-GERMANS.
Montenegrin outpost looking for enemy artillery from a fortified position in the fork of a venerable tree.

was more or less prosperous as a shipping centre, owing to the business of the town being conducted by Jews, who formed the vast majority of its population.

When Greece got it, little change took place, and when the troops of the Allies began to disembark there in the beginning of October, 1915, they were at once confronted with a serious difficulty in the fact of the absence of large harbour or docking accommodation. There was, besides, the further serious difficulty of obtaining space ashore for the camps and marching ground for the troops, as well as suitable stretches of level surface for aeroplanes, Greek troops being in occupation of all desirable spots. Moreover, the railway facilities, as already mentioned, were distinctly inferior.

Very little progress was made by the Entente Powers in the direction of fortifying Salonika in great strength until after the Allies were actually in retreat and on Greek soil again, because Greek troops simply blocked the way, and even interposed obstacles. It was no good-will on the part of Greece that gave Salonika to the Allies and kept it theirs during October, November, and the first half of December, but it was the powerful allied fleets, standing out in the bay, ready at any time for action, that really determined its ownership. Naval guns had been landed and placed in position; from the ships, the country for ten or twelve miles inland was covered, and these supplied the convincing argument.

A very different state of things prevailed in and around Salonika on and after December 12th, the Entente having at last succeeded in bringing Greece to her senses. As the Greek troops withdrew, French and British troops took their place, some being fresh arrivals, for troopships were arriving every day, and others coming from the front. The guns, munitions, and stores of all kinds that had been evacuated from the other side of the frontier were sent on to Salonika with a minimum of delay. There were many reports that the enemy contemplated marching at once to the attack and capture of the place, and the Allies worked at fever heat to make it as formidable as possible. Steps were immediately taken to organise the semicircle of hills lying some distance to the north and north-east of the town, many Serbian refugees in addition to natives being employed on the works. In the course of a week or ten days a strongly-fortified front of hills and lakes was prepared, some fifty miles in extent, reaching on the west from the Vardar to the Gulf of Orphanos on the east, and enclosing a very considerable area, over which good roads were built, giving the Allies sufficient freedom of movement.

On December 20th Salonika saw the arrival of one of France's greatest soldiers, General Castelnau, the Chief of General Joffre's Staff—that is, of the whole French Army. He had come—rather unexpectedly, it was said—on a tour of inspection. No doubt a certain anxiety was felt in France and England with respect to the security of the Salonika position, and Castelnau had been despatched to

Salonika position consolidated

checking and delaying him for a length of time sufficient to allow of the easy retreat of the main body of the troops to Salonika, and of the fortification on a great scale of that important sea base.

Just at first when the Allies landed at Salonika there was some uncertainty whether the port should continue to be occupied if it was found the expedition failed to save the Serbians, but the great value of the place was speedily perceived by the Entente Powers. Even if it was the fortune of war that Serbia should temporarily be lost, they came to the conclusion that it would be a grave mistake to relinquish Salonika, the possession of which was of high advantage from the military, political, and commercial standpoints.

Further, naval men suggested that if it ever passed into the power of Germany it would be made special use of as a submarine base in the Eastern Mediterranean, which would be most damaging to the allied fleets in these waters, already the scene of considerable hostile submarine activities, as was demonstrated by the sinking of not a few liners, transports, and other vessels by the enemy. As the terminus on the sea of the great natural high-road across Serbia and Macedonia from Belgrade through Uskub to the Ægean, Salonika, an old town with a history of over twenty centuries behind it, ought to have been—and could have been—made one of the strong places of the world. Austria had long been aware of the high significance of the port; her policy in the Near East prior to the outbreak of the war turned on its acquisition sooner or later by her; and it was a profound disappointment to her when its possession fell to Greece as one of the results of the Balkan Wars, but she still kept her eye on it. In Turkish hands, Salonika

The Key of the Levant

BRITISH ENGINEERS LAYING TRACKS IN GREECE TO FACILITATE TRANSPORT OF MEN, MUNITIONS, AND GUNS.

HOLT "CATERPILLAR" TRACTOR HAULING HEAVY ORDNANCE ALONG A MAIN ROAD OF SALONIKA.

LIGHT-HEARTED WARRIORS OFF TO THE FRONT.
Hardy Montenegrin soldiers going to the trenches to hold a mountain
position against the invaders.

PICKABACK FOR THE SLIGHTLY INJURED.
Montenegrin Red Cross workers carrying their wounded comrades out of
the danger zone. They were about to embark on the Lake of Scutari.

AN URGENT CASE.
The difficulties of the ambulance men were augmented by the rough ground
over which their suffering burdens had to be carried on crude stretchers.
Above : A sorely wounded veteran is seen on his way to a field hospital.

report. With Sarrail he made a thorough investigation
of the French or western portion of the defences, and with
General Mahon he undertook an equally searching tour
of the British or eastern section. Having thoroughly
satisfied himself that all was well, he stated in an interview
that the situation of the Allies in the Salonika sector was
excellent. After spending nearly a week with Sarrail and
Mahon, he paid a short visit to King Constantine on the
26th. On the same day Paris issued an official communiqué
which announced that Castelnau, in concert with Sarrail
and Mahon, had settled upon the plan of action by the
Allies, and that he had assured the French Government
that the arrangements which had been already made
rendered the safety of the whole expedition absolutely
certain.

This statement came as a handsome and effective set-off
to a declaration which emanated about this time from
Berlin that the Germans would be in occupation of Salonika
on January 15th. Perhaps an even more remarkable and
satisfying answer to the German boast
was given by the appearance of Salonika   **Christmas Day**
on Christmas Day, which was celebrated   **in Salonika**
with great enthusiasm by the troops of
the Allies. The Commander-in-Chief, knowing that everything was well in hand, and that his men had been having
a hard and heavy task in trench-digging, gave them a
holiday. The day itself was warm and bright, which
helped the merry-making. Thousands took part in football,
races, and games of all kinds. In the evening the camps
were alive with entertainments and sing-songs. Never
had Salonika seen such a Christmas Day. But the best
reply of all to the German brag was the constant disembarkation of troops, many of them belonging as it happened
to Scottish regiments, in large numbers, and of quantities
of guns, including several batteries of heavy calibre.

The year did not close at Salonika without some sensational incidents. At ten o'clock on the morning of
December 30th the enemy directed his first attack on the
town by dropping bombs on it from three or four aeroplanes,
which did a certain amount of damage. Two hours later
other aeroplanes appeared over the town. But neither in
life nor in property was there much loss to the Allies.
One bomb, however, fell on a detachment of Greek troops
which was carrying out manœuvres in the presence of
Prince Andrew of Greece. This bombardment from the
air by the enemy was a flagrant act of war, and General

Sarrail, now in chief command of the allied forces, immediately retaliated. The warships lying in the gulf opened fire with their anti-aircraft guns, but the aeroplanes were at a height of over 10,000 feet, and were not hit. French aeroplanes went up in chase of them, but were equally unsuccessful. As some such contingency as that of this air raid had been expected, certain plans to deal with it had been prepared in advance, and they were swiftly put into operation.

At four o'clock in the afternoon of the same day troops of the Allies suddenly descended on the German, Austrian, Bulgarian, and Turkish Consular buildings, and arrested the enemy Consuls and Vice-Consuls, with their families and their entire staffs. Taken completely by surprise, the Consuls and their **Exeunt the enemy** personnel offered no resist-**Consuls** ance, and were shortly afterwards all marched down to the quay, where they were put into boats and transferred to a battleship of the Allies. The four Consulates were taken over at once as billets for French troops. On the following day the Consuls and their belongings were on their way across the Mediterranean to some unknown destination. Later the Norwegian Consul, a pro-German, also was arrested. One of the numerous disadvantages under which the Entente Powers lay at Salonika was that the place was a nest of spies; the Consuls who had been arrested and deported had long been suspected of espionage, and abundant evidence that this was the case was discovered when their houses were searched. The Greek Government protested at this breach of Greek

AT CETINJE, THE CAPITAL OF EUROPE'S SMALLEST KINGDOM.
The palace of King Nicholas, the venerable monarch of Montenegro.

KING NICHOLAS SEEKS REFUGE ON FRIENDLY FRENCH SOIL.
The arrival of the Royal fugitive at Lyons on January 24th, 1916, in company with members of his suite. The centre group photograph, taken in France, is the Royal family. Reading from left to right: Princesses Vera, Xenia, and Militza (wife of the Russian Grand Duke Peter Nikolaievitch), the President of the Council, M. Muskovitch, and Prince Danilo. Seated: The King and Queen of Montenegro.

"sovereignty," and the enemy Powers also protested, threatening reprisals. General Sarrail made reply that he had acted from military necessity, and he took the opportunity at this time of clearing out the swarms of spies with which Salonika was infested, and who had been unquestionably giving valuable information to the enemy. The Austrian Consulate turned out to be a miniature arsenal, hundreds of Mauser and Mannlicher rifles, besides numerous revolvers and dynamite cartridges, being found in it. Perhaps there had been a scheme to arm the mob in Salonika.

The strong measures taken by General Sarrail roused the wrath of Germany and her friends, but were welcomed in the Entente countries as evidence that the Allies were determined to carry on their campaign in the Balkans with the utmost energy and decision. A proof of this had been already exhibited a few days previously in the occupation by the Allies of Castellorizo, an island lying between Rhodes and the mainland of Asia Minor, and commanding the Gulf of Adalia. French troops to the

The iron hand in the velvet glove number of five hundred had been landed, with a view to using the place as a base in case of operations in that part of Asiatic Turkey. The Greek Government protested, as it also did when, during the first week of January, 1916, the Allies arrested the German, Austrian, and Turkish Consular officials at Mitylene for reasons similar to those which had led to the arrests in Salonika, and placed these men and their belongings on board a ship of the Allies. Greece made a still louder outcry when, on January 11th, a detachment of French soldiers took possession and military control of the island of Corfu, but she offered no opposition. She had been informed that the Allies intended to make the island into a vast sanatorium for the Serbians. The place, however, was of considerable strategic value.

While the French and the British were strengthening their hold on Salonika in every possible way, two movements were taking place on the part of the other Allies— one, by the Italians, having a very direct bearing on the whole situation in the Balkans; and the other, by the Russians, exerting an influence less direct but of great importance.

Early in December, Italy had enormously increased the force with which she had laid her grip on Valona (or Avlona) months before. This town, often described as the "Gibraltar of the Adriatic," was not much more than fifty or sixty miles from the Italian coast, and its possession by an enemy was highly undesirable in Italian interests. On December 1st, Baron Sonnino, the Prime Minister of Italy, made a speech in which he declared that Italy was determined to do everything possible to assist the Serbian Army, and that the presence of the Italian flag on the other side of the Adriatic would also constitute a reaffirmation of Italy's traditional policy, which included the maintenance of Albanian independence.

In the first week of that month Italy despatched troops in large numbers, but almost in secret, to Valona, and continued landing them there until an army, reported to muster over 50,000 effectives, had been accumulated. With part of this force she occupied Durazzo in strength on December 21st, joining up there with Essad Pasha, the famous Albanian chief, whose sympathies were entirely pro-Serbian and anti-Austrian. Within a few days it was officially announced that he had declared war on Austria. Meanwhile Austrian warships had been active in the Adriatic, sinking provision **Italian troops at** ships destined for the starving Serbians; **Valona** but they received a severe check on December 29th, when, in an attempt to bombard Durazzo, they were attacked by Italian and other allied vessels and defeated with a loss of two destroyers.

Though the Russian offensive between the marshes of the Pripet and the frontier of Rumania had nothing to do directly with the Balkans, so far as fighting in that region itself was concerned, it yet materially assisted the Allies at Salonika by drawing off from Serbia large German contingents which otherwise might have been employed in an assault on the Greek port. It was on December 27th that the Russians launched a determined and most violent attack on the Austrian positions near Czernovitz, between the Pruth and the Dniester, and simultaneously assaulted the Archduke Ferdinand's army on the Styr, and other enemy forces on the Strypa, with such embarrassing results to the Austrians that German troops had to be sent in all haste from the Balkans to their aid, and German plans, in consequence, entirely changed for the time being. In spite of these substantial German reinforcements, the Russians made considerable progress before they were

GERMAN TRANSPORT COLUMN IN DIFFICULTIES SOMEWHERE IN SERBIA.
Climatic conditions and incessant transport rendered the highways of Serbia as impassable as were the roads of Flanders during the first winter of the war. This track was little better than a ploughed field, and the difficulties of conveying ammunition and supplies from place to place can well be imagined from this illustration, which shows an officer's car being pushed out of a rut.

HOW THE MONTENEGRINS CARRIED AMMUNITION.
Owing to the absence of roads, wheeled traffic was an impossibility. Therefore, the Montenegrin gunners had their munitions transported on the backs of their sturdy mountain ponies.

held up. While this struggle was going on, Rumania remained silent and "neutral" as before ; but she must have been greatly struck by the recuperative power evinced by Russia after Germany had asserted that she and the Austrians had reduced the Tsar and his armies to impotence.

While this Russian movement was holding the stage of general attention, and nothing particular was happening at Salonika—albeit at Gallipoli there had been a startling development in the withdrawal of the Allies from that peninsula—events were taking an untoward course with respect to Montenegro. During the ten weeks in which the fourth invasion of Serbia was taking place, the world heard very little of Montenegro, though the warriors of the Black Mountain were engaged in supporting their kinsmen the Serbians all the time. Indeed, the Montenegrin Army, which for some length of time held a slice of Bosnia that it had conquered from the Austrians, formed the right flank of the whole Serbian position, and did good service during the earlier stages of the conflict, holding the enemy round Fotcha and on the Lim, a tributary of the Drina.

When Serbia was overrun, Mackensen redistributed his forces, various German and Austrian divisions being sent north to watch the Russians who, at that juncture, were rumoured to be about to make a diversion in the Balkans, either through Rumania or by a descent on the Bulgar shore of the Black Sea. German troops were transferred to Bulgaria, and even to Turkey, both of which countries were now openly "run" from Berlin. But troops were not withdrawn from the Montenegrin front ; on the contrary, they were greatly increased. Just as Austria hated Serbia with a deadly hatred, so she hated this still smaller Slav State which, with a population of less than half a million, had been long independent **Fate decides against** of her as of Turkey. Austria determined **Montenegro** to destroy it. The undertaking was difficult, because of the almost inaccessibly mountainous character of the country and the bravery of its inhabitants, who were inured to war and every kind of hardship, like the Serbians ; but it was not impossible, if men and guns were provided in adequate strength. What could be done in Serbia could be done in Montenegro.

As far back as the beginning of November it was announced from Rome that Austria was assembling a force of three army corps in Herzegovina to attack Montenegro from that side. There were also available the Austrian troops already in Serbia on the Montenegrin eastern frontier, to say nothing of the Bulgarians who so far assisted Austria as to take Djakova on December 3rd. The whole expedition was placed under the direction of Von Kövess shortly after the fall of Mitrovitza. King Nicholas was not ignorant of what was coming. At the **Lovtchen and** end of November, after Serbia had **Cetinje capitulate** been crushed, he issued a proclamation to his people, in which he said that Montenegro, faithful to her traditions, would resist to the death, preferring death to slavery. He went on to state that the Allies had charged themselves with the supply of the Army and population of Montenegro. Supply was always a great trouble in that poor little land, and, when the Serbian refugees came flocking in, it became an insoluble problem, unless with much help from outside, which was not always forthcoming.

Although the Austrians advanced during December some distance on the east side, or Sanjak front, capturing Plevlie, Ipek and Bielopolie, their great offensive did not start till January, 1916. In the interval the Montenegrins had at least one considerable victory, at Lepenatz, but in general they were driven steadily back. In the last days of the year Mount Lovtchen was heavily shelled, and then attacked in some force, but the Montenegrins were successful in repelling this assault on their stronghold. It was not till January 6th that Kövess began decisive operations by a series of concerted violent attacks on the Montenegrin east front, on the Tara, the Lim and the Ibar, while at the same time warships in the Gulf of Cattaro opened a terrible fire on Mount Lovtchen.

Desperate fighting continued for four days. Berane, on the Lim, was captured by the Austrians on the 10th ; and, far more important, Lovtchen succumbed on the same day to infantry assaults prepared by the fire from the warships. Some surprise was expressed among the other Allies that the fortress should have fallen in such a short time, but the feeling changed when it became known that the place was defended by less than 6,000 men—starving, with insufficient clothing, and lamentably short of guns and munitions. With Lovtchen gone, Cetinje could not be held by the Montenegrins, and it was occupied by the Austrians on the 13th. Four days later the announcement was made in the Hungarian Parliament that Montenegro had "surrendered unconditionally," but the subsequent telegrams that almost immediately arrived from Italy and Montenegro dealing with the subject cast a great deal of doubt and uncertainty on what had exactly occurred. And this obscurity cannot be said to have been wholly cleared up at the time this chapter of the Balkan story was written (February 5th, 1916).

When it was publicly announced that Lovtchen had been taken by the Austrians there was great rejoicing in Berlin, and the tremendous strategic importance of the stronghold, as against Italy, was dwelt on with enormous complacency by the Germanic Press. But when the news flashed over the wires that Montenegro had capitulated there was the wildest jubilation throughout Germany and Austria, and the other Allies were bid to see in her fate and in that of Serbia a sure prophecy of what the future had in store for themselves. Then were published in a well-known Vienna journal what purported to be the conditions imposed by the victor, and they proved to be harsh and brutal in the extreme. Next there was a curious, a strange silence. Things did not seem to be going just as anticipated by the enemy.

Meanwhile among the Allies, who had not expected that the Montenegrins would give in so quickly, there was much criticism of the little State's surrender, which it was suggested—and not without some show of reason—had been inspired for dynastic purposes by the pro-Austrian section of the Montenegrin Court. It was even asserted that King Nicholas had secretly come to terms with Austria weeks before the fall of Lovtchen, and that the resistance put up by the Montenegrins was unreal and of a purely theatrical character. It was recalled that the wife of the Montenegrin Crown Prince was a German princess. It was said that a compact was in existence, and had been in existence for a couple of months, by which Montenegro agreed to hand Lovtchen over to the Austrians in return for Scutari. While these things were being canvassed and discussed, it was rather forgotten that the Montenegrins had been short of food—and short, in fact, of everything—and that their small Army, plus such Serbians as were able to fight in its ranks, was outnumbered by the Austrians by more than twenty to one, a circumstance quite sufficient in itself to account for the capitulation.

THE MASTERY OF THE ADRIATIC.
After the capture of Mount Lovtchen, Cetinje, and San Giovanni di Medua the Austrians advanced south towards Durazzo, which had been captured by the Italians.

Then, in the midst of this strange silence from Germany and Austria, there appeared an official statement from Sir J. Roper Parkington, the Consul-General for Montenegro in London, who said that King Nicholas and his Government had peremptorily refused all the Austrian conditions, and that Montenegro would continue to fight to the last. This communiqué also said that the false insinuations of which Montenegro had been the victim, based on the mendacious reports of the enemy, had caused a most painful impression A somewhat similar statement was issued from the Montenegrin Consulate at Rome. People hardly knew what to think, till in the fourth week of January the Montenegrin Premier, M. Muskovitch, issued a Note admitting there had been negotiations with Austria, but asserting that the purpose behind these negotiations had been to gain time to ensure the retreat and evacuation of the Montenegrin Army towards Podgoritza and Scutari, as well as to give opportunity for the Serbian troops to leave Podgoritza and Scutari for Alessio and Durazzo. On January 23rd King Nicholas was in Rome, and shortly afterwards he journeyed to Lyons, where his queen had preceded him, and there, thanks to the courtesy of the French, the Montenegrin Government was temporarily established. The Austrians continued their advance, occupying Scutari on the 23rd, and San Giovanni di Medua on the 25th. By the end of January Austria was in full occupation of Montenegro, and was advancing south towards Durazzo, to meet Essad Pasha and the Italians.

Little happened for some weeks at Salonika after the arrest of the enemy Consuls and the clearing out of the spies. Everywhere the place was made stronger and stronger. East of it General Sarrail made its position still more secure by blowing up the railway bridge at Demir Hissar, on the line running towards Bulgarian territory. Additional reinforcements were constantly being landed at the Greek port. But up to the end of the first week of February no attack had been attempted by the enemy except by occasional aeroplanes. This was hardly what was meant when King Ferdinand of Bulgaria saluted the German Kaiser at Nish in the middle of January as " Imperator, Cæsar et Rex."

. A vivid personal narrative of the tragic retreat from Serbia across the snow-bound passes of Montenegro will be included in Volume VI. of THE GREAT WAR. This chapter will be from the pen of Mr. and Mrs. Claude Askew, the well-known novelists, who did much valuable hospital work for the Serbian Army, shared its adventures, and were among the last to leave.

END OF VOLUME 5.

THE GREAT WAR

VOLUME 6

Frontispiece Vol. VI "THE GREAT WAR".

From the Painting by C. M. PADDAY.

H.M.S. Spitfire torpedoing a German Cruiser on the Night of May 31st. 1916.

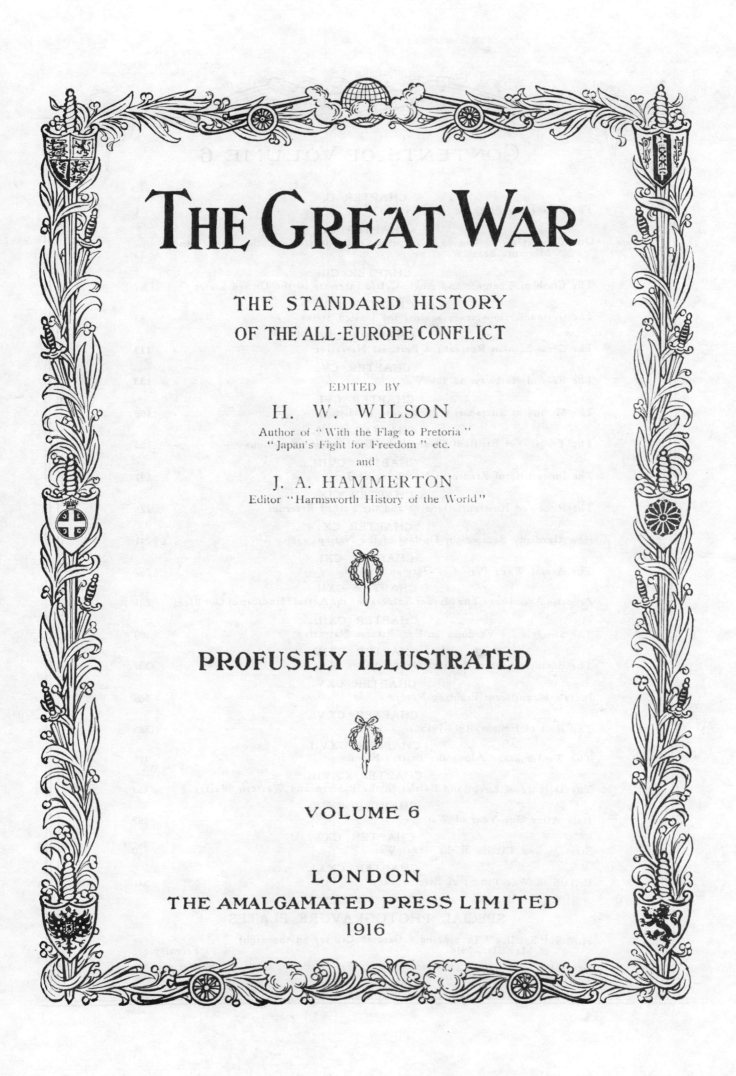

THE GREAT WAR

THE STANDARD HISTORY
OF THE ALL-EUROPE CONFLICT

EDITED BY

H. W. WILSON

Author of "With the Flag to Pretoria"
"Japan's Fight for Freedom" etc.

and

J. A. HAMMERTON

Editor "Harmsworth History of the World"

PROFUSELY ILLUSTRATED

VOLUME 6

LONDON
THE AMALGAMATED PRESS LIMITED
1916

CONTENTS OF VOLUME 6

SPECIAL PHOTOGRAVURE PLATES

THE GREAT WAR

THE STANDARD HISTORY OF THE ALL-EUROPE CONFLICT

VOLUME 6

CHAPTER C.

Resurgence of Blood-Madness in Germany when U Boats Attacked Liners—Military Reason why the Enemy Risked his Trained Submarine Crews—Enormous Rise of British Freights and Crippling of our Commerce—Enemy's Submarine Blockade Seriously Increases our Economic Losses—Sinking of Goliath, Triumph, and Majestic—Hersing Appears like a Wolf among a Flock of Sheep—Scattering of Allied Mediterranean Fleet—Army Deserted by its Big-Gunned Ships—Arrival of the "Chinese Pagoda"—Anti-Torpedo Monitor with 14 in. Guns—Dowagers of the British Fleet Turn Up in Waist-Belts—Foiled by our Novel Inventions, the Germans Organise Secret Bases in the Greek Islands—Beginning of Attacks on our Troopships—Southland Torpedoed but not Sunk—The Royal Edward Goes Down with a Thousand Soldiers—Troopships Ramazan and Marquette Sunk by German Submarines—Atrocious Cruelty of the Attack on the Ancona—Women, Children, and other Non-combatants Shelled by U Boat Flying Austrian Flag—Grounds for Thinking that the Submarine was Really a German U Boat—Destruction of French Passenger Steamer Ville de Ciotat—Again the Submarine Crew Jeer the People they are Murdering—Finest and Newest Japanese Liner Torpedoed—P. and O. Liner Persia Sunk in Five Minutes—Piratical Attack upon American Tank Steamer—Heavy French and Italian Naval Losses by Submarine Attack—Complete Defeat of U Boats during Transport of Troops to Salonika—Extraordinary Request from Austrian Government, asking for Austrians to be Protected from Attack by Austrian and German Submarines.

FTER the murderous destruction of the Lusitania on May 7th, 1915, with which our last chapter in naval history concluded, very little information was published concerning the work of our fleets. A highly-critical period of intense activity had opened, and upon its results depended in large measure the fate of our island kingdom and our Empire. Even our naval power was not secure; for though our main Fleet had improvised means of defence for its capital ships, the Franco - British armada, operating off Gallipoli, and the supply ships and transports of our unhappy Dardanelles Expedition were in much danger. Our entire operations, naval and military, round the Dardanelles seemed, so the enemy thought, likely to collapse in over-whelming disaster. In home waters our oversea food supplies and our ocean-borne commerce were seriously im-perilled, and our general position was one of great anxiety.

Germany rang with braggart clamour. With the Russian line breaking

in the east and the source of British power apparently weakening in the west, the people of Berlin became again intoxicated, in the spring of 1915, with the dream of world-dominion. By far the most popular piece of war art was a bronze showing an old, bearded Triton, with the face of Tirpitz, rising from a sea of wreckage. A well-known minister of the Lutheran Church, Pastor Laibel, in a sermon delivered in Leipzig, acclaimed the destruction of non-combatant men, women, and children on the Lusitania as a God-like act. In the course of his sermon he said : " Our deep sense of our mission allows us to congratulate ourselves, and abide content with a heart full of gratitude, when our marvellous submarines—instruments for executing the ven-geance of God—send to the depths of the sea thousands of the non-elect. With every means in our power we must fight the wicked ; their sufferings must cause us joy ; their cries of despair must not move German hearts. There should be no compromise with hell—no mercy for the servants of Satan. They have all been con-demned to death by

COMMANDER M. E. NASMITH, V.C.
The gallant commander of submarine E11 (in the foreground) is here seen "stretching his legs" on the more spacious deck of a battleship in the Dardanelles.

A "FEATHER" IN BRITANNIA'S CAP.
One of the torpedoes from the notorious German cruiser Emden, which was exhibited with other trophies on the Horse Guards Parade in London. The Emden was sunk on November 10th, 1914, off Keeling Cocos Island by H.M.A.S. Sydney.

Divine decree." Professor Rheinold Seeby, the chief theologian of Berlin University, and preacher in Berlin Cathedral, wrote in a strain of similar diabolical aversion and inhuman cant. Another Berlin preacher, Pastor Fritz Philippi, expounded the Hun doctrine thus: "The Divine mission of Germany, O brethren! is to crucify humanity. Satan himself has come into the world in the form of a Great Power — England — and must be crushed. On Germany is laid the Divine command to bring about the destruction of those who are the personification of Evil. When this work is carried out the redemption of humanity will be achieved. The kingdom of righteousness will be established upon this earth, and the German Empire, having created it, will remain its guardian."

When the leaders of the Protestant Churches of Germany spoke in this manner against another nation, also largely composed of Protestants, the state of mind of the people, whose anthem was the "Hymn of Hate," can scarcely be described. It resembled that of a mob of Haytian negroes in the blood-frenzy of the rites of human sacrifice brought from the jungles of Africa and mingled with faint, strange touches of Christian worship. But in the case of the Germans, who had been converted to Christianity by Irish and English missionaries some twelve hundred years ago, this outburst

of collective homicidal mania was infinitely more degrading than any lapse into hysterical savagery by negroes. It is a pleasure to observe that the Hungarians did not yield to the movement of the mob-mind of Germany, and that the Austrians also escaped for some time from this insanity of the soul; though, as will afterwards be seen, there were officers and men in the Austro-Hungarian Navy who could jeer at the men, women, and children they were drowning when they sent the Ancona the way the Lusitania had gone.

All these things must be recorded and kept in memory for the sake of ensuring the safety of the human race in future. The state of mind of the German people at the end of May and the beginning of June, 1915, was an even more striking revelation of the fundamental qualities of the race than had been their rejoicings in August, 1914, over the atrocious deeds of their armies in Belgium and Northern France. The first explosion of collective blood-madness had been excused by various neutral nations and persons in Britain, France, and Russia, who sympathised with the best qualities of Germanic culture. It was palliated as a transient product of a general system of Prussianisation carried out by schoolmasters, drill-instructors, reptile journals, and the intellectual serfs who were appointed to German professorships. But since the first period of national enthusiasm for methods of terrorisation, the German

WEAPONS OF VON TIRPITZ IN BRITISH SAFE KEEPING.
Big naval gun dismounted from the Emden and placed in position on the Horse Guards Parade. The centre illustration shows a powerful German mine containing a 220 lb. charge, which was picked up by a patrol off the East Coast of England.

people had been sobered by great defeats and checks in France, and by the long, wearing, terrible winter campaign on both fronts. The manhood of Germany had learned by personal experience the ghastly realities of modern warfare; and despite all official falsifications, the truth regarding the immediate causes of the outbreak of hostilities was known to the larger part of the German public, and quietly and discreetly discussed by them. Their most brilliant publicist, Maximilian Harden, had frankly written that Germany had willed the war because she thought it was worth winning and she could win it.

Such were the circumstances in which a few remarkable successes by German submarines aroused the German people from a mood of self-pity, floundering excuses, and appeals to humanitarian neutrals, and made them leap up, blood-maddened barbarians, screaming in their churches that the submarine had been given to them by their God so that they might wage "a war without pity," and "crucify humanity." It was in this very frame of mind that the Germans and Austrians had slain and tortured each other by the million in the Thirty Years' War of the seventeenth century. In the twentieth century they combined in a scheme for depopulating Europe, and though it was our task to save our women and children from "the chosen instruments of the Almighty," our descendants must not expect that a race with such potentialities as the German will, despite the genius of their musicians and the talent of their craftsmen, ever become truly civilised in soul. There is a demoniacal element in the "blond beasts," as their favourite philosopher called them, which transforms them always in moments of passion into the foulest and most cunning of human brutes. It is ineradicable.

In the last vain attempt to disguise from Americans, Scandinavians, and Dutchmen the pure, **Ineradicable Prussian** instinctive resurgence of their blood-lust **blood-lust** in the hour of their new victories, the Germans pretended that their campaign of submarine piracy, which formally opened in February, 1915, was merely intended as an answer to our plan for starving out the Central Empires by a naval blockade. As a matter of fact, our Foreign Office was as fearful of blockading Germany as was President Wilson of going to war with any country that chose to murder citizens of the United States. The British Government was afraid to interfere with the enormous trade carried on by Germany with America, Scandinavia, and Holland, lest the plutocracies, who had a ruling voice in the affairs of these neutral nations, should either declare war against us and our Allies or help to cripple us by refusing supplies, and especially

A PERILOUS "FISH" OUT OF WATER.

Section of a German sea-mine being placed in position on the Horse Guards Parade. One of the most devilish inventions of science, the mine was constructed in two parts, the upper portion containing a charge of fulminate of mercury, which fires the mass of gun-cotton occupying the lower half. Buoyancy of the machine was assured by air admitted to the upper portion. The mine case was studded with "pushers," and these, when pressed by collision with a vessel, would make the electrical contact which fired the fulminate.

munitions of war. When Germany opened her submarine campaign against non-combatants in cargo and passenger steamers, she was being fed by the Americans with fat and cotton for making smokeless powder, and large food supplies were reaching her from the Balkans and through neutral ports. The only real hardship the German people had to endure at times was that their cost of living was increased, largely owing to military necessities, that caused a great lack of labour, and to railway and canal transport difficulties also due to war conditions, and partly owing to the fact that the cost of their ordinary sea-borne supplies was increased by transhipment and railway charges from foreign ports. Fluctuations in the foreign exchanges, and the cornering of certain goods by neutral middlemen who wanted to make their fortunes quickly, were among the other causes that augmented the cost of living in Germany, and the German farming class was far from being averse to creating very profitable local monopolies in its produce.

We employed our naval power, not merely in as mild a manner as possible, but in a manner negligent of our purely warlike interests. The Liberal Government, which had tried to force the Declaration of London upon the Navy, did not, when hostilities opened, extend its list of contraband to the raw material of such things as dynamite, nitro-glycerine, and gun and rifle ammunition. Even when

Politicians and the Fleet

the Coalition Government was formed, no member of it had sufficient first-hand scientific knowledge to enable him to know what was properly contraband. For instance, Sir F. E. Smith, the Attorney-General, afterwards tried to excuse the new Cabinet's amazing ignorance in the use of our naval power by saying that lard, oil, and similar substances were overlooked in drawing up the contraband list because their use in the manufacture of nitro-glycerine was quite a new development. The development was about fifty years old ! We let both food and materials of war enter Germany through neutral ports, apparently with the idea that the extra cost of transhipment and

GERMAN U BOATS' WAR ON COMMERCE.
Russian steamer Anna foundering after being struck by a torpedo from a German submarine on July 10th, 1915, She was bound from Archangel to Hull with a cargo of timber.

railway carriage would gradually—very gradually—inconvenience the German people, and add to their financial difficulties, and thus tend, with the burdens placed upon their export trade through neutral ports, to impoverish and weaken them. And all this, our amiable Foreign Office thought, could be done without creating any irritation among the neutral States, which were growing rich by the stoppage of Germany's mercantile marine.

Admiral Tirpitz was well aware of the plan of our Foreign Office, for he had Herr Ballin at hand to keep him informed in the matter. And the German admiral and the German shipping magnate saw that the burden of the naval war, as our Foreign Office was conducting it, fell almost as heavily upon the British people as upon the German people. In the first place, the shortage of labour, caused by taking able-bodied men for the war, greatly delayed the unloading of shipping in our ports. A steamer which might only have been three or four days in port under ordinary peace conditions had at times to remain three weeks. The result was often that where a ship previously made three voyages in a given time, she now made only two—so that there was a reduction of thirty-three per cent. in actual carrying power. In the

second place, our Navy and Army had taken over something like two thousand steamers for warlike purposes, and this produced, in conjunction with the removal of the large German mercantile marine from the traffic of the world, a further large reduction of carrying power and a consequent rise in freights of enormous proportion. Our unenterprising and uncourageous Government, which lacked organising genius and knew it, was afraid to undertake the great task of commandeering our remaining merchant ships and using them to keep down the carrying cost of both our overseas supply of food and raw material and of our exports of coal, cotton goods, and other manufactured articles, with which we were partly paying our way in the war. The result was that our sea-borne commerce was almost as heavily taxed by continually rising freights as German exports and imports were by the extraordinary mild pressure of our naval power. The German Naval Staff wanted to increase the cost of our sea-borne traffic until it amounted to as much as the cost of German sea-borne commerce to neutral ports. This was the veritable military reason why many of the best German submarine flotillas, with their valuable trained crews, were launched against our mercantile marine.

The pretence of blockading our islands, and the pretence that the German people were starving, served to cover a sound, workable scheme for further increasing our freights. Our Government met this subtle move only in a partial manner, by instituting the national system of marine insurance against war risks ; for, low as were the Government rates, they helped to heighten the working expenses of our import and export traffic, and thus tended to equalise the conditions of the naval economic struggle between the weak but blood-mad German Fleet and the strong but feebly-handled British Fleet. The feeble handling, of course, was the work of our politicians ; our fighting sailors were eager to act according to our ancient sea law as developed by Abraham Lincoln.

Meanwhile, freights continued to rise. Between two hundred and three hundred British steamers were sold to neutrals, partly with a view to avoiding the submarine menace. At the same time our shipbuilding declined, and less than half as many new steamers were built as in normal times. All this lessened our control of freights. Then, though our merchant seamen showed all the fighting spirit of their race, and " carried on," usually without any defence against the U boats, they naturally asked for higher wages in consideration of the risks they ran and the increased cost of living borne by their families. So freights rose higher, till competition among shippers achieved to the full the submarine plan of campaign of the German Naval Staff.

In 1914 the cost of carrying rice **Rise of shipping** from Burma to the United Kingdom **freights** was about 21s. 9d. per ton. By the end of 1915 the freight was 150s. per ton. The freight on Calcutta jute rose from 18s. to 152s. 6d. The normal freight on Argentine wheat was 18s. a ton, which increased during the German submarine campaign to 150s. It was calculated that on some important lines of traffic the homeward and outward freight, after deducting the shipowners' extra expenses, amounted to thirty-nine times as much as the pre-war profit. Our special income tax of fifty per cent. on excess profits still allowed the shipowner

Hospital-ship Anglia, which struck a German floating mine in the English Channel on November 17th, 1915, and foundered with a loss of some eighty souls.

Broadside impression of the Anglia going to her doom. A destroyer is standing by to pick up some of the three hundred wounded and crew who were saved.

A third illustration showing the Anglia already down by the head. Most of the survivors having been got off, the destroyer is backing in order to clear the coming vortex. Several of the nurses sacrificed their lives in order to save their wounded charges.

HOSPITAL-SHIP ANGLIA SINKING AFTER STRIKING A MINE IN THE ENGLISH CHANNEL.

cost us more. Almost everything cost us more. Our farmers and stockbreeders naturally did not try to undersell foreign wheat and meat, but, as in all belligerent countries, profited by the continual rise of the markets to make money. In some working-class districts even the landlords attempted to put up their rents, in order to keep in line with the development of British and foreign shipping. Most of our working classes agitated for higher wages in order to maintain their standard of life. This increased the cost of our exports, and further tended to protect German markets abroad from conquest by us. In fact, with the general enormous rise of freights, the German manufacturers thought that their foreign markets were fairly well guarded against **Herr Ballin's** enterprising neutrals as well as against **economic strategy** a half-crippled enemy. They accumulated goods with a view to flooding the world after the war with cheap articles that would bring back all their customers.

Behind the whiskered face of Tirpitz-Triton, rising from the sea of wrecks in the Berlin bronze piece of war art, there should have been shown the features of the greatest shipping magnate in the world, Herr Ballin. To this German of remarkable genius is personally attributed the order for the sinking of the Lusitania, and he it was who worked out the economic strategy of the German submarine blockade. The man in our Government set to fight him was Mr. Runciman, son of a large British ship-owner, and manager of several lines. But Mr. Runciman for some time lacked the courage and the skill to organise both our import and export trade, and control our mercantile marine during war time, to keep the price of our food down, cheapen our imported raw material, and enable our exporting manufacturers to develop our industries as a whole in the way best calculated to

COMING ALONGSIDE.
Bird's-eye view of the hospital-ship Newralia, taking aboard some of the crew of the s.s. Marere after the latter had been sunk on January 20th, 1915.

to tax our import and export trade enormously, to the disadvantage of our existing and future commerce and of the financial power by which we were waging the war. This assisted the enemy by increasing the cost of all our raw imported material and producing, by high food prices, wide and deep suffering among our poorest classes. It was estimated that in the first nineteen months
           of the war the indirect cost to our
Assisting   people of the rise of freights was
the enemy   £400,000,000. The net profits in the
           shipping industry were reckoned at
£250,000,000 for 1915, as compared with £20,000,000 for 1913. Even when the tax of fifty per cent. on war profits was deducted, there was an estimated increase of five hundred and forty-three per cent.

The German submarine campaign did not create this condition of things; but it greatly aggravated it, and directly brought it to a very critical state. Therefore it might be maintained that the submarine policy of the Teutonic Empires was a very notable success. Our food

THE LIFEBOAT'S FULL LOAD.
Survivors from the s.s. Marere being rowed to the hospital-ship Newralia, which picked them up.

strengthen our financial power and prepare our commercial expansion after the war. Mr. Bonar Law later considered this scheme, but was fearful of commending it. Yet only by this gigantic effort of organisation, planned and executed with ability, could the subtle and far-reaching menace of the German submarine campaign have been annulled.

For many months our Government let things drift helplessly. The total British tonnage lost in 1915 was 997,992 tons, and our shipbuilding output in the same period was only 650,000 tons, as against an output of 1,360,000 tons in 1914. The British loss of ships of more than 500 tons each was increased by submarines, mines, and other enemy devices to 317 vessels. In addition to

DARDANELLES INCIDENT: TURKISH SHELL WASTES ITS POWER IN A WASTE OF SEA.
Shell fired from a Turkish land battery and intended for H.M.S. Louis exploding in the water considerably wide of its mark, falling at least a hundred yards from the destroyer, which is seen in the second illustration on this page.

the German submarine campaign in home waters and the Mediterranean, there were many fires and explosions in vessels bound from North and South America to Europe. During the year 321 British vessels and 212 foreign vessels were directly sunk by German agency, but there were other heavy losses through incendiary fires, which accounted for much of the grand total annual loss of 726 vessels of 500 tons gross register and upwards, of the value of nearly thirty million pounds. Putting the matter briefly, the losses of British and neutral shipping in 1915 exceeded 1,800,000 tons, while the heaviest loss in any year before the war was 500,000 tons. And as our shipbuilding industry was diverted by war conditions to the making of munitions and the construction of warships, the losses which would have been made good in normal times became very serious.

We shall relate in a future chapter the history of our naval blockade and its relation to the Declaration of London, the pro-German movement in Sweden, and the problems of domestic politics in the United States. All that we wish now to do is to bring out clearly the results of the economic strategy underlying the German submarine campaign against our merchant ships. The British public regarded the affair from a characteristically sportsmanlike point of view, and after first watching with keen anxiety the successes of the enemy, concluded that we had practically won on all points when the underwater raiding flotillas were destroyed, captured, or hunted away. The military side of the struggle is always more interesting than

its economic aspect. And our view of the results of the German blockade of the British Isles is falsified by the fact that, in rejoicing over our military success in the matter, we overlook our extremely heavy economic losses. Germany made a great sacrifice of her trained submarine crews and submarine vessels, but her losses in this respect were more than repaid by the heavily-increased economic pressure exerted upon our nation by the murderous campaign against our mercantile marine. When the freight on Argentine wheat rose from eighteen shillings to a hundred and fifty shillings per ton, and even the freight on American grain was increased more than fourfold, while the cost of exporting Welsh coal was in places increased eightfold, the German Naval Staff had no reason to think that its submarine activity had been vain.

Success of submarine piracy

We cannot at present estimate what effect the German submarine campaign, combined with the lack of Government control of our shipping, produced upon that class of our population which lived below the poverty line. The great, incessant call for labour of every kind no doubt benefited our poorest people, and gave many of them the chance of learning some skilled trade and getting better nourishment. We had also some splendid war charities, and in many towns private efforts of large scope were made to feed the infants and young children of poor mothers. Sir Henry Campbell-Bannerman once reckoned that about thirty out of every hundred men, women, and children in our islands had not sufficient food to maintain the proper

BRITISH DESTROYER IN ITS DEATH THROES.
Dramatic impression of H.M.S. Louis, which ran aground in the Dardanelles during a south-westerly gale. The photograph was taken before she parted amidships, and shows the tremendous sea running at the time.

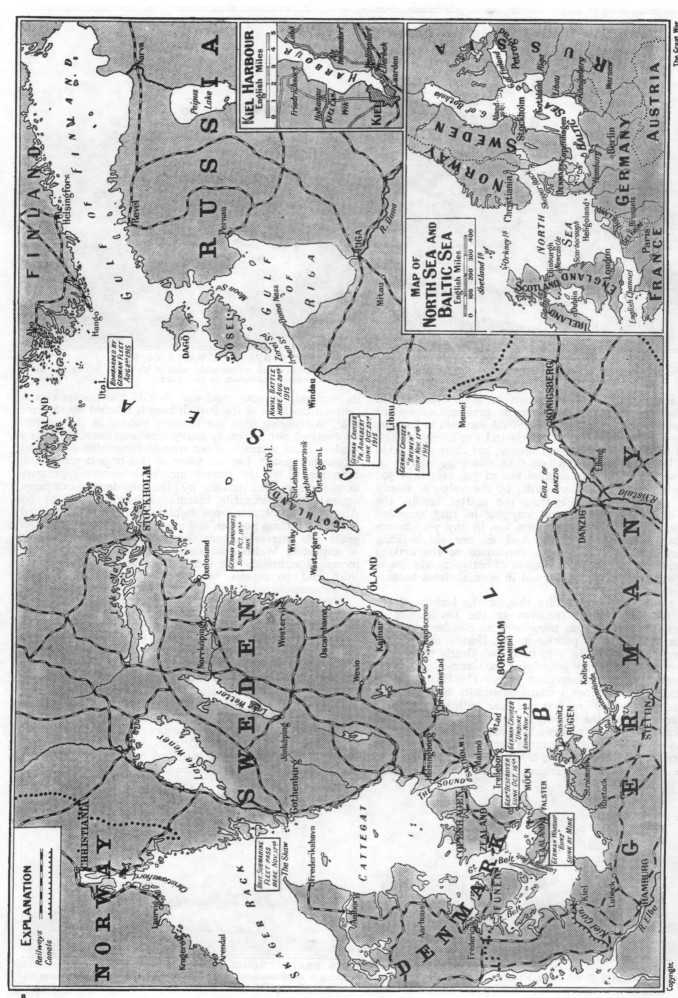

Explanation
Railways
Canals

KieL HARBOUR
English Miles
0 1 2 3 4 5

MAP OF NORTH SEA AND BALTIC SEA
English Miles
0 100 200 300 400

BOMBARDED BY GERMAN FLEET AUG 8th 1915

NAVAL BATTLE HERE AUG 20th 1915

GERMAN CRUISER "PR. ADALBERT" SUNK OCT 23rd 1915

GERMAN CRUISER "BREMEN" SUNK NOV. 17th 1915

GERMAN TRANSPORTS SUNK OCT. 18th 1915

BRIT. SUBMARINE FLEET HERE NOV.17th 1915

GERMAN CRUISER "UNDINE" SUNK NOV. 7th

GER.DESTROYER SUNK OCT. 16th

GERMAN WARSHIP "BUNZ" SUNK BY MINE

Copyright.

The Great War

MAP INDICATING THE LOCALITIES AND DATES OF THE GERMAN NAVAL LOSSES IN THE BALTIC.

If the German U boat found its way into the Mediterranean, at least two intrepid British commanders forged the Skager-Rack—Commanders Max Horton and Laurence—and made even the Baltic a dangerous sea for German naval activity. The British submarines scored many triumphs, the most important being the destruction of the German cruiser Adalbert on October 23rd, 1915. They also took part in the naval battle off the Gulf of Riga on August 20th, 1915, when the Russian Navy frustrated a German attempt to land troops.

8

strength of body. The enemy's submarine campaign might, by co-operating with other causes in the rise of food prices, have brought out a third of our population in hunger riots. We did not escape all the consequences of the defects in our national organisation, which had left us, at the close of a century of industrial development, with an enormous wasting slum class. The proportion of unfit men in our country, despite our athletic habits of body, was very large. But, on the other hand,

The Dardanelles factor the most menacing of all the enemy's operations against us does not seem to have hindered the unexpected, happy, uplifting movement which tended permanently to reduce the number of our people living below the proper standard of life.

With this fortunate and magnificent exception, the campaign of the German U boats had a grave economic effect upon our money power, industrial activities, and food supplies. The difference between the freights at the end of 1914 and those at the end of 1915 cannot, of course, be accepted as the measure of the enemy's success. The British Government took for war service about half the available tonnage, and by grave lack of initiative and foresight neglected to buy a large number of foreign vessels in the early weeks of the war, when neutral ship-owners were timid and ready to sell cheaply. Instead, it was we who lost some hundreds of vessels, after hostilities opened, by sale to neutrals. Our disastrous Dardanelles adventure—by reason of the huge fleets of merchant steamers, trawlers, and other trading vessels it distracted from commercial work—was a factor of high importance in checking our supply of wheat, iron ore, and other food and materials. Then the extension of our operations in the Persian Gulf to Bagdad diminished the number of steamers engaged in our Oriental trade. Our Government attempted in November, 1915, to concentrate our shipping resources on our own import and export needs, by forbidding British ships to trade between only neutral ports to the neglect of the carrying requirements of ourselves and our Allies.

But towards the winter of 1915, when the Dardanelles adventure was about to close and release a considerable part of our shipping, the new Salonika adventure, in which still larger armies needed transport and seaborne supplies, made a still larger deficiency in the commercial carrying power of our mercantile marine. But it might fairly be maintained that we could have borne the burden of the Dardanelles, Bagdad, and Salonika expeditions without being seriously inconvenienced by them if the murderous blow struck by the U boats had not turned our muddle into complete economic disorder.

From the purely military point of view, however, the enemy was not so successful. In the period under review he developed his submarine campaign by a series of very rapid and striking victories, which caused both us and the French much

perturbation. But the fighting British seaman, by reason of his extraordinary versatility and intelligence, rose quickly to the occasion, and in a long, bitter, wearing struggle, conducted in absolute silence, defeated the Germans. Never had our great silent Navy so well deserved its epithets. Its greatness was stupendous. Sir John Jellicoe had at last 3,000 vessels under his orders; and Admiral de Robeck could also number his large and small craft by the thousand. Its silence was still more amazing, for the Admiralty did not announce the victories of our seamen though these victories occurred every week. The German Marine Office seldom knew at any time what was its own strength in underwater craft. The boats went out, and stayed often with means of supply lasting for weeks, but very many of them did not come back. And it was not known where, when, or how they had been destroyed. The deadly silence of our victorious men told on the nerves of their foes far more than any triumphant announcement on our part would have done. It is credibly reported that the trained and well-disciplined sailors of Germany were at last **Our Navy's silent efficiency** wrought up into such a state of dread that they could not be got to volunteer for submarine work. The small crews needed were offered work on Zeppelins, which they regarded as much less risky, and after being removed for this supposed purpose from their comrades, they were dragooned into service in the U boats.

Yet the enemy had a remarkable run of successes soon after the sinking of the Lusitania. On May 13th, 1915, a Turkish destroyer threaded the Dardanelles in the darkness under the command of a German naval officer, and in a

ANOTHER VICTIM OF THE U PIRATES.
White Star liner Arabic, outward bound for New York, sinking off Kinsale on August 19th, 1915, with a loss of thirty-two lives. This photograph was secured by Professor Still, of Purdue University, U.S.A., as the lifeboat was leaving the vessel's side. The circle portrait is of Captain Finch, of the Arabic.

B

surprise attack torpedoed the British battleship Goliath, which was assisting the French Expeditionary Force. Owing to the unexpectedness of this very daring and brilliantly-conducted attack, our loss in men was extremely heavy, and out of a crew of seven hundred and fifty men and officers less than two hundred and fifty were saved. The Goliath, though fifteen years old, was a very useful bombarding ship, with her four 12 in. guns and her twelve 6 in. guns. A successful submarine attack, like that which had been made on the Formidable, would not, in the circumstances, have been extraordinary; but that a capital ship, belonging to the finest-trained Navy in the world, should have been sunk by a Turkish destroyer was a matter calculated to provoke some serious misgivings. Our Dardanelles fleet seemed to have grown somewhat careless in the use of its great striking force, so that proper precautions were not taken against action by the small, obsolete Turkish Navy.

About the time when the Goliath went down with five hundred of our men there came to the combined French and British fleets off Gallipoli a rumour which caused intense anxiety. The rumour ran from Gibraltar to Malta, and from Cape Matapan to Smyrna. German submarines of the most powerful type, it was said, were coming from the North Sea into the Mediterranean. As a matter of fact, Lord Fisher had been expecting for months the appearance of enemy underwater craft round the Dardanelles. One of the reasons why he may have disapproved of the expedition was that he foresaw serious difficulties, arising from the facts that Austrian submarines could escape the blockade of the Adriatic, and the latest type of German U boat could voyage from Emden to Constantinople. But when the Cabinet decided on the great adventure, Lord Fisher prepared to help in the days of trial. So at home great new naval machines of war were being made in haste to counter the submarine menace to our Mediterranean forces. But meanwhile a single German U boat—U 51, under Lieutenant Von Hersing—showed what serious injury could be done to our Fleet. Hersing seems to **Von Hersing** have worked around Scotland to the **outwitted** Bay of Biscay, where by arrangement he was met by a neutral ship, that supplied him with oil. With extreme boldness he tried to pass Gibraltar without submerging, but was spotted by a French destroyer, and forced by gun fire to dive.

He obtained another supply of oil, either from a secret base at Sollun, on the Egyptian coast, or at one of the numerous secret bases off the islands and mainland of Greece. His periscope was first clearly seen by the British fleet at 1.30 p.m. on May 22nd, 1915, near Rabbit Island. All our battleships, cruisers, and transports were at anchor, presenting a series of easy targets, but the Prince George fired two rounds that made the submarine dive, while our destroyers dashed out and screened the helpless fleet in dense columns of black smoke. Had Hersing been ready to venture the lives of himself and

NAVAL AND MILITARY WORK WITH THE GRAND FLEET.
Marines going through their drill on board a battleship. The smaller illustration shows British sailors storing munitions on a war vessel. The projectiles, after being put into the special cases seen in the background, were lowered into the magazine by means of a crane.

SEARCHING THE PERSIAN GULF FOR GUN-RUNNERS.
British naval officers aboard an Arab dhow, and examining the vessel's papers. An important feature of the work of the British Navy in the Persian Gulf and the Eastern Mediterranean was the war against the Arab gun-runners' efforts to smuggle rifles ashore.

his men, he might have got in a blow at some of our modern capital ships. But he was hunted away by the destroyers, and every warship, with the transports that were under steam, began to act as if her helmsman had gone crazy. All the ships started a series of evolutions at full speed, heading to all points of the compass, then rounding on their wake in the hope of being able to ram the enemy, and next spurting off in another direction. Each helm was shifted every minute to give the vessel a zigzag course. When the alarm subsided the ships returned to their anchorage, with the tireless destroyers forming a guard round them. But it was recognised that the protection of the destroyers was inadequate, and in the night all the valuable new battleships and battle-cruisers departed for home waters, and the work of making Mudros Bay a submarine-proof harbour was hurriedly **German menace in Ægean** carried on. The task of supplying the armies at the Dardanelles was seriously interrupted, as no unarmed steamer had a fighting chance against the German U boats. But the Swiftsure remained at her old anchorage, off Cape Helles, with some old battleships, while the Canopus, Vengeance, and Albion patrolled the coast round the Anzac position.

Had Hersing been watching near Gaba Tepe at dawn on May 23rd, he would have had a couple of easy victims; for the battleship Albion went ashore near the promontory in the early morning mist. The Turkish field batteries opened a furious fire upon her, while the Barbarossa, working in the Strait, dropped 11 in. shells over the hills, but through lack of good spotting could not hit the stranded British battleship. Happily, the Turkish land forces could not bring any heavy guns to bear upon the hapless ship, which remained firm on the bottom. A flotilla of destroyers clustered round, and answered the Turkish batteries, and the famous old Canopus, that had come from the Battle off the Falkland Islands, stood close in to the Albion, and under heavy fire got a wire hawser aboard and tried to tow her off the sandbank. The first cable snapped, but two other cables were made fast, and the towing started again. Most of the crew of the Albion jumped on the quarter-deck, **Stranding of the Albion** in rhythmic movement, to try to shift her bows, and at the same time all the fore guns opened a high-speed fire on the Turkish positions, with a view to shifting the ship by the concussion of the guns. For more than four hours the crew jumped, the guns roared, and the Canopus pulled—all without making any apparent impression. But at ten a.m.—six hours after the great, heavy ship had ploughed deep into the sandbank—she moved outward, and glided, under the tug of the Canopus, into deep water. More than two hundred Turkish shells—shrapnel and common shell—had struck her, but her armour gave such protection that no serious damage had been done, and few of her crew had been hit.

By this time the tension on the men of our Mediterranean Fleet was very wearing. They passed day after day, night after night, expecting to be blown up by an enemy they could not even see. Yet our active service ratings, most of whom had come through the ordeal of the Grand Fleet in the previous autumn, seemed to regard the new submarine menace as a form of sport, and got up sweepstakes, the stakes to go to the man who first actually sighted a periscope. The older reservists, fathers and even grandfathers well over fifty, felt the strain more than the

THE WASH OF THE NEXT AHEAD.
British warships in line patrolling the North Sea. A heavy swell was running, and the vessel in the distance has just been swamped by a huge wave, though its guns are discernible projecting from the cloud of spray.

younger men. In moments of danger young and old seamen changed in a remarkable manner, swelling out beneath their clothes as they blew up their safety waistcoats to enable them to float in the water.

At eight o'clock on the morning of May 25th Hersing spotted the Swiftsure off Cape Helles, and ran within three hundred yards of her, but being met by rapid fire disappeared without shooting. The Majestic and Agamemnon were quite close to the Swiftsure, and it is inexplicable why the German officer did not release a torpedo. Two and a half hours afterwards he tried a shot at the Vengeance, but missed, and then came up again, and caught the Triumph as she was steaming slowly near the Anzac position. The battleship had her

Loss of the Triumph nets down at the time, but they were utterly useless. Two terrible missiles either cut through them or went beneath them. The great ship listed, and in about eight minutes rolled over and turned upside down. Then after floating for half an hour bottom upwards she disappeared in a great cloud of steam.

Fortunately, not many lives were lost, as a trawler and destroyer were quite close to the stricken vessel, and at once went to the aid of the crew. But the ship herself, built in 1904, with four 10 in. and fourteen 7·5 in. guns, was a severe loss. At the beginning of the war she had taken part in the operations against Tsingtau, and had then steamed some thousands of miles to the Suez Canal, where she stood by in the hope of getting an opportunity to train her guns on the Turks. But the Turkish advance on Egypt was broken up so easily that the aid of her guns

and her seven hundred and ninety officers and men was not needed, so she joined the Dardanelles bombarding fleet, and by close fire smashed the entrance forts, the Albion working with her. She was struck badly in an attack on Fort Dardanus, her deck being pierced, and a fire started in the gun-room. But, happily, another Turkish shell burst the water pipes in the bath-room, and so put out the fire. She was sister ship to the Swiftsure, built for Chili, but taken over by our Government. Her crew's experience at Tsingtau in operations against modern and heavily-gunned fortifications had proved valuable to the Fleet. So her loss was badly felt.

But worse was to follow than the destruction of the Triumph. The submarine that sank her was perceived, and pursued until nightfall by our destroyers. But Hersing escaped in the darkness, and two days afterwards again approached the Anzac position. Here the old battleship Majestic, built in 1895 and armed with four 12 in. and twelve 6 in. guns, was acting as a huge heavy battery in support of the Australasian Expeditionary Force. Something like twelve destroyers were ranged about the Majestic, to protect her against hostile underwater craft. But the German submarine officer, whose skill cannot but be praised even by his foes, got under the powerful guard of the battleship and torpedoed her in so deadly a manner that she quickly sank. Had it not been for the presence of the destroyers, the loss of life among our brave fighting seamen would have been very heavy. Some of the destroyers emitted a black cloud of smoke to veil the scene from the Turkish **The Majestic torpedoed** gunners on Sari Bair, and others steamed in for rescue work, with the happy result that most of the crew—about seven hundred and sixty officers and men—were saved.

But the blow, by reason of the skill and daring with which it had been delivered, entirely upset Admiral de Robeck's plan of naval co-operation with our Mediterranean Expeditionary Force. It was quite clear that the British and French admirals had no defence against the German submarines operating around Gallipoli Peninsula. One U boat, with a good officer and thirty men, practically drove off the battleships, battle-cruisers and armoured cruisers collected by Britain and France against the Ottoman Empire. Thus was vindicated, in at least a partial manner, the opinion delivered before the war by our great gunnery expert, Admiral Sir Percy Scott, concerning the triumph of the submarine over the battleship.

When the army on Gallipoli Peninsula was deserted by its big-gun ships, the Turks imagined that a complete disaster for the Allies was imminent. The enemy went so far as to issue appeals to the allied soldiers, pointing out that they had been abandoned to destruction by the routed fleet and that no hope remained for them; but it was stated that if they would surrender they would be certain of receiving good treatment in the prison camps round Constantinople. Apparently, both the Turks and their German officers thought that, as the British and French battleships had been chased away, they would be secure from big-gun fire. Lord Fisher, however—who had disapproved of the Dardanelles campaign, but had been overruled by the Cabinet and by a certain politician whose audacity was equalled only by his ignorance—had foreseen the disasters which had occurred, and had taken precautions to meet them. Nearly all the shipbuilding yards of the United Kingdom were working at high speed under his orders, while the Turk and German exulted in their apparent triumph.

For the next two months things went well at the Dardanelles for the enemy. All he saw off his coast was an occasional battleship, some small cruisers, and the indefatigable destroyers. Most of the capital ships retired to sheltered harbours, where they could be protected by booms and nets; and though we had no further losses of importance, except in submarines, the mobility and

Commander Max Kennedy Horton, R.N., D.S.O., one of Britain's heroes of the Baltic.

Hide-and-seek in the Baltic: Zeppelin flies over British submarine in the stormy sea.

Blockade incident: British destroyer overhauls a neutral ship to search for contraband

A battle of four elements: British monitors shell German land batteries near Nieuport.

The Admiral's eyes and ears: Dramatic impression of British destroyers on the alert.

A Parthian broadside from H.M.S. Cornwallis, the last ship to leave Suvla Bay.

The last of flaming Anzac Town as seen from the deck of H.M.S. Cornwallis.

concentrating power of our naval striking force were sadly diminished. Hersing took his submarine through the Strait to Constantinople, and tried to fight our submarines. The Turk on the hills waited like a cat crouched to spring on a mouse. He reckoned that, as our fleet had been forced to retire, our army would soon have to embark, and that he would be able to leap down upon it during its withdrawal, with no big hostile guns out at sea ready to curtain him off with shrapnel.

But in the month of July the latest creation of the energy of Lord Fisher and his designers waddled into the Mediterranean. It was a raft floating almost flush with the waves. In the bows was a 9˙2 in. gun, in the stern a long 6 in. piece. What with the fire-control and the general get-up, it looked more like a Chinese pagoda than a warship. But when it spoke to the Turks they had good reason to recognise the latest addition to Britain's sea-power. The new-comer was followed by a smaller monster, armed with only two 6 in. guns. Then came **Huge torpedo-proof** Lord Fisher's supreme contribution **monitor** to the naval art of attacking land fortifications. It was a thing that neither sailed, steamed, nor floated, but came, in a sort of alternate lopsided motion, into Kephalos Harbour with the gait of a gigantic overfed goose which was growing too fat to live. The extraordinary object turned out to be a huge torpedo-proof monitor, carrying only two 14 in. guns, and some anti-aircraft armament. The sides bulged some ten feet, and then slanted under, forming a platform just washed by the waves. This ten feet of fatness made the vessel steer badly, and reduced her speed to a wobbling crawl. But despite her antediluvian slowness, the new monitor had little dread of any hostile submarine overtaking her; for on both sides she had a ten-foot wad of secret composition which would resist the rending force of a torpedo, and save the real inner hull. Despite her awkwardness and her defects, she was a portent and a prodigy. She was possibly the British battleship of the future in the state of a first rough draft. The American Navy had a novel gun-torpedo, likely to be developed into so formidable a weapon of penetration as to force all warships to submerge; but in the meantime our new wadded monitor outfought the submarine.

The 14 in. guns were not of British make, and they showed it. But despite their serious faults they were able to pitch in the enemy's trenches a shell weighing three-quarters of a ton at a range of fifteen miles. Four vessels of the 14 in. gun type came into action off Gallipoli, and, with a large number of other monitors of various shapes and sizes, they set to work to convince Turk and Teuton that the island race had not lost command of the seas. Then some ancient dowagers of the British Fleet turned up in strange disguise. They were twenty-five-year-old cruisers, decorated with a ten-foot waist-belt which hung from their sides by wire ropes and steel stanchions. But with the new anti-torpedo protection they did some good work, and the Dardanelles operations proceeded for some months with remarkable security so far as our surface vessels were concerned.

There seems to have been only one German U boat besides Hersing's operating off the Dardanelles at the close of May, 1915, but quite a large flotilla of hostile underwater craft at last collected in the Mediterranean. Many of the vessels appear to have been built or assembled in the Austrian ports along the Adriatic coast; others continued to make the long voyage from Germany. The U officers changed their flags according to circumstances, showing the Austrian ensign when torpedoing Italian vessels, and flying the Crescent when there was danger of provoking President Woodrow Wilson's talent for writing Notes. Even the Bulgarian flag seemed to have been used by the German submarine officers who controlled, by reason of their superior skill, nearly all the boats used against the

THE ILL-FATED SUBMARINE E13.

This vessel ran aground on the Danish island of Saltholm on August 19th, 1915. A German war vessel completed the frail craft's destruction with shells, in spite of the utter helplessness of the crew, many of whom were killed.

Allies. But, skilful though the Germans were, it cannot be said that they made the most of their opportunities. They found our battleships and transports floating motionless at anchor, and presenting such an opportunity for enormous achievement as submarine commanders dream about but very seldom find. Yet they did less damage than our submarine officers wrought in the Baltic Sea and the Sea of Marmora in circumstances of much greater difficulty.

The German was not a sportsman. He was just a little too cautious with regard to his own skin to bring off a great stroke like that which Lieutenant Noel Lawrence delivered against the **Treachery of Pro-** Moltke. The organisation of the German **German Greeks** submarine campaign in the Mediterranean was, however, magnificent. They seem to have bribed to treachery every Greek worth bribing, and the hunt for their secret bases in the Greek islands occupied our men for many months. Even some Greek cargo steamers trading to England appear to have met German submarines on their voyage and to have supplied them with oil. The fact that there was a very strong pro-German movement in Greece may have facilitated the work of the German organisers of the Mediterranean submarine campaign; but let us bear it ever in mind that it was the ordinary Greek, far removed from Court and political influences, who worked for the destruction of our ships and the murder of non-combatant crews and passengers. It was very disillusioning to find that Hellas, for which Shelley sang and Byron died—modern Hellas, born of Codrington's victory off Navarino—became

GREY DAWN ON THE EVER RESTLESS SEA.
Stern of a British war vessel patrolling the North Sea. The bleak and dreary atmosphere of the moment has been admirably caught by the lens, and the sinister naval gun lends to the illustration an essential effect of the great world-tragedy of our time.

PREPARING FOR BATTLE ON A BRITISH WARSHIP.
A.B.'s piling earth sacks round a gun emplacement while the crew is getting ready for action.

the base for the attacks made on the Ancona, Persia, and Ville de Ciotat. But disillusionment has at least the virtue of clearing the mind of false sentiment and perniciously false romance.

Apparently it was between May and August, 1915, that the power of German gold prevailed with certain Greeks of the labouring and merchant classes. The enemy's principal submarine campaign in the Mediterranean opened in the first week of September, 1915. By this time our warships were boomed or waist-belted against torpedo attack, and the German U boats sought and found easier victims in the allied troopships. By way of a beginning the Southland was torpedoed on September 2nd, but was not sunk. On September 14th, 1915, however, we suffered the first loss of a transport in the war, for the great troopship Royal Edward was torpedoed in the Ægean Sea with the loss of a thousand lives, most of the drowned soldiers being drafts for the famous 29th Division, which had won high honour round Seddul Bahr. Five days after the Royal Edward was destroyed, a German submarine, operating south of Greece, caught another of our transports, the Ramazan, and sank her by gun fire, causing the loss of three hundred men. Another transport, the Marquette, carrying Indian troops, was torpedoed in the Ægean on October 26th, when a hundred lives were lost. On November 5th two enemy submarines attacked one of our

armed boarding steamers, the Tara, and sank her after thirty-five of her men were killed. The troopship Mercian was shelled by an enemy U boat on November 10th, and one hundred and three men were killed or injured, but the vessel was not sunk.

A French steamer, the Indien, was also torpedoed and sunk by a U boat in the Ægean Sea on September 8th, 1915. In the same waters the Provincia was destroyed on October 3rd, and a French transport, the Calvados, was torpedoed and sunk off Algiers on November 4th, 1915. Altogether the toll taken by enemy underwater craft in the Mediterranean in six months in legitimate attack on warships and vessels employed for warlike purposes was considerable but not decisive. Our naval losses at the Dardanelles, in addition to those already mentioned, included a mine-sweeper, the Hythe, sunk in collision on October 28th, and the destroyer Louis, which was stranded and wrecked the following month. We also lost four submarines in circumstances that will be described later, and the same number of underwater craft were also lost by the French either in the Strait or the Sea of Marmora.

Naval losses at the Dardanelles

But the principal feature of the allied naval operations in the Mediterranean in the autumn of 1915 was that the British and French fleets did not succeed in defeating the activities of the German and Austrian submarines. Some of these enemy vessels were sunk, and some of their shore bases discovered. The U12, of Austria, was torpedoed on August 10th by an Italian submarine, and the U13 was sunk by a French destroyer, the Bison, on August 13th. But we, the French, and the Italians could not clear the sea and make it fairly safe for passenger liners and cargo steamers. For some time, indeed, a reign of terror prevailed over the great midland waters, by reason of the scientific savagery of German and Austrian submarine officers. Despite the continual assurances given by the Teutonic Empires to the President of the United States, French, Italian, Japanese, and British passenger liners were

MINED! THE LOSS OF A STEAMER DURING OPERATIONS OFF BELGIUM.
Incident during a British naval bombardment of the Belgian coast. Auxiliary steamer strikes a mine and founders. The crew are leaving the vessel in a naval cutter.

torpedoed without notice, and at times sunk with circumstances of diabolical cruelty.

The destruction of the Italian passenger liner Ancona on November 8th, 1915, was an act of atrocity carried out in a more devilish spirit than the sinking of the Lusitania. The unarmed liner, proceeding from Naples to New York, stopped at Messina for more passengers and cargo. The people were mainly Greeks and Italians with large families, going to the United States to settle there, the majority being women and children. At one o'clock in the afternoon of Monday, November 8th, as the liner was steaming between Sardinia and Tunis, a submarine appeared at a great distance and fired a shot across the bow.

Destruction of the Ancona

It was not a blank shot, but a live shell, and without observing any of the formalities accompanying the right of search, the submarine, while gaining rapidly on the steamer, continued to shell her when she had stopped. Not only was the wireless apparatus struck, but the sides and crowded decks of the ship were swept with shrapnel fire; even the lifeboats in which passengers sought for shelter were destroyed. Many of the non-combatants were killed outright by the exploding shells; others who leapt into the water and swam towards the submarine in hope of rescue were driven away with jeers. A wild panic broke out when the shelling began.

Screaming women, crying children, and frenzied men rushed for the boats, the first of which overturned before they were free from the davits. The panic might have been subdued, but the gunners of the submarine continued to fire shot after shot almost at point-blank range. The shells did not again hit the ship, but exploded all round the vessel, increasing the terror and confusion among the hapless people. One of the passengers, an American woman doctor, Dr. Cecile Greil, who jumped into one of

THE BIRD-MAN'S VIEW OF TRANSPORTS AT SEA.
British troopship somewhere in the Ægean, as seen by an aeroplane observer from a height of 1,000 feet. Even from such an altitude the vessel seemed to present an easy target for a bomb-dropper. The smaller photograph shows the deck of a captive balloon ship off Gallipoli.

THE CRADLE OF THE METAL FISH.
Interior of a German torpedo factory where hundreds of these weapons, for use against British merchantmen, were manufactured. A torpedo complete and ready for the U boat tube is seen on a trestle in the foreground.

the eight boats that escaped with the survivors, stated that the shrapnel continued to strike many of the small boats and kill or wound the passengers. The liner was quickly torpedoed and sank in seven minutes, more than two hundred men, women, and children being murdered. The submarine flew the Austrian flag, and was afterwards acknowledged by the Vienna authorities to be one of their vessels; but some Italian naval officers maintained that it was a German U boat with an expert German commander that wrought the atrocity, the Austrian flag and the Austrian uniform being merely used to avoid complicating the Lusitania case between Washington and Berlin. And it is remarkable that, on the same day and near the same spot, a French transport, La France, bringing invalided soldiers back from Mudros, was sunk by a submarine showing the German flag. For various reasons connected with the Italian blockade of the Adriatic and events in the Strait of Gibraltar, it seemed more probable that the submarine that riddled and sank the Ancona was German.

The enemy afterwards admitted that people were still visible on the ship when the torpedo was launched; but with a cunning as foul as the cruelty that

Foul cunning and cruelty   had been used, the Austro-Hungarian Government alleged that the Italian crew had saved themselves in the boats and left the passengers to drown. It was allowed that some loss of life had been caused by shells hitting the vessel, but all the deaths by drowning, witnessed by the jeering submarine crew, were falsely attributed wholly to the conduct of the Italian sailors. According to the formal statement of the Austro-Hungarian naval authorities, the commander of the submarine " had in view the rescue of all the passengers and crew, but apparently neglected to take into consideration the panic, which rendered disembarkation difficult." So to the most inhuman act of cruelty in the history of naval warfare there was added, in order to avoid war with the United States over the murder of American citizens, a sickening exhibition of hypocrisy.

Then, while both Germany and Austria-Hungary were protesting to the President of the United States " that the sacred laws of humanity should be taken into account in war " and insisting that they had given " numerous proofs of the most humane feeling," the French passenger steamer Ville de Ciotat was torpedoed. She was passing Crete

on Christmas Eve, bound from Japan for Marseilles, with one hundred and thirty-five passengers and one hundred and eighty-one officers and men. It was ten o'clock in the morning, and a minute after passing near a Greek steamer, a terrific explosion shook the ship, and a submarine flying the Austrian flag appeared on the surface a short distance away. The crew worked steadily and coolly, and lowered five lifeboats and two rafts before the vessel sank. Seventy-nine lives were lost, including the women and children in one boat which capsized. Again, it was reported, on the evidence of eye-witnesses, that the crew of the submarine circled in their vessel round the survivors and jeered at them. About the same time one of the newest liners of the Nippon-Yusen fleet, the Yasaka Maru, was torpedoed without warning on her way to the Suez Canal. Happily the ship did not sink for forty-nine minutes, and owing to the admirable skill and coolness of the Japanese officers and men, all the passengers and crew were saved. This was the second Japanese steamer torpedoed in the Mediterranean.

Apparently the commander of the submarine operating off Crete thought that he had given the Austro-Hungarian Government as much trouble with the United States as

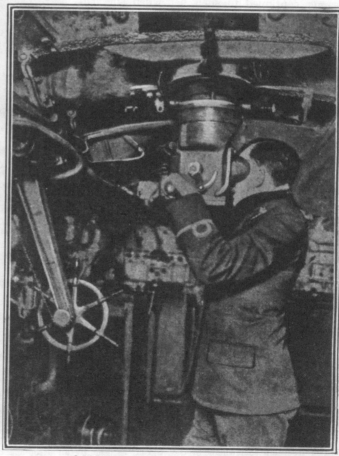

LOOKING FOR A LIKELY VICTIM.
German submarine officer at the periscope of his craft.

it could safely carry. On December 30th, 1915, he attacked the P. and O. liner Persia, and torpedoed and sank her in five minutes. But instead of coming to the surface to enjoy the death-struggles of drowning men, women, and children, he kept his vessel out of sight under water. It was well for his country—Germany or Austria—that he did so, for among the murdered passengers was Mr. Robert Ney McNeely, the American Consul for Aden, who went aboard the ship under a safe conduct from both Germany and Austria. As a matter of fact, the track of the torpedo was seen by the second officer of the Persia one second before it struck; but President Woodrow Wilson, being more anxious to avoid war with the Teutonic Empires than to hold them to accountability for the murder of American citizens, was glad to escape from the task of writing more Notes. He considered that, as no submarine had been seen, Consul McNeely might be supposed to have been killed in some vaguely accidental way.

Submarine pirates had merely to keep out of sight when committing their murders in order to fully satisfy official

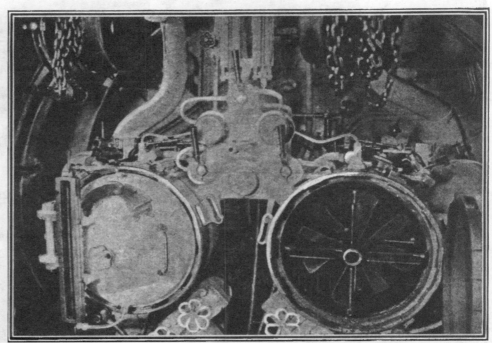

THE FAVOURITE WEAPON OF ADMIRAL VON TIRPITZ.
The two torpedo-tubes within a German submarine. One has been opened, displaying the propeller of this, the favourite weapon of Von Tirpitz.

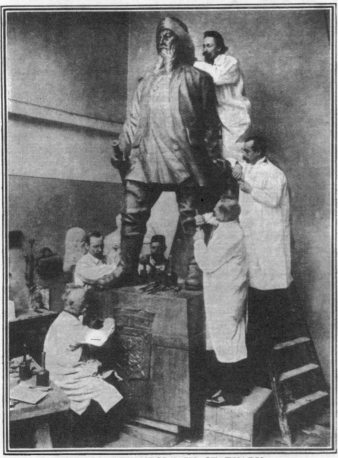

"FRIGHTFULNESS" IN STATUARY.
Patriotic German artists doing their bit for the Fatherland by making a grandiose statue of Von Tirpitz, who instituted the submarine war against Great Britain. "Old Turnips," as he was christened by our sailors, unfortunately does not appear to have made a very elegant subject for the art of Praxiteles.

America's ideas of humanity and justice. The loss of life in the Persia was very heavy. There were three hundred and fifty persons on board, and only one hundred and eighty were known to have been saved. Eleven of the survivors, including Lord Montagu of Beaulieu, were picked up after being thirty-two hours in the sea without water or food. The conduct of both passengers and crew was splendid. There was no struggling and no panic. But through the ship heeling over immediately she was struck, all the boats on one side were useless, and as the great liner went down in five minutes most of the other boats were smashed, only four of them getting off clear. Soon afterwards another Japanese steamer—the Kenkoku Maru—was torpedoed. There was also an attack on an American tank steamer—the Petrolite—on December 5th, 1915, which had an important sequel. The Petrolite was shelled in the Mediterranean by a submarine flying the Austrian flag, and the shelling continued, as in the Ancona case, after the steamer had stopped. The submarine then came alongside, and the commander offered to buy supplies. The captain of the Petrolite refused to sell, and the Austrian officer thereupon seized one American sailor and held him as hostage, while some of the submarine crew boarded the steamer and forcibly took supplies. **Sinking of the Persia**

Here we may conclude our survey of the first phase of the enemy's submarine campaign in the Mediterranean area. It was in this area that the hostile underwater craft achieved their most remarkable military successes, which included the sinking of two battleships and two troopships on the British side, as well as the destruction of several important French and Italian warships. The French cruiser Léon Gambetta was torpedoed in the Ionian Sea by a hostile submarine on April 26th, 1915; the French submarine Mariotte was sunk on July 26th, 1915, in the Sea of Marmora, apparently by a German submarine; one French armed merchantman—the Indien—was torpedoed in the Ægean Sea on September 8th, 1915; and the French troopship Calvados was sunk off Algiers in the first week of November, 1915. Italy lost a fine cruiser—the Amalfi—which was torpedoed in the Adriatic on July 7th, 1915; and eleven days afterwards a smaller cruiser—the Giuseppe Garibaldi—was also torpedoed in the Adriatic. Italy also lost a destroyer, a submarine,

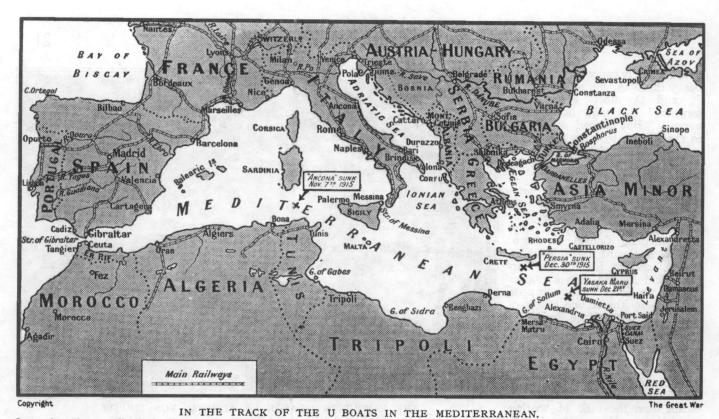

Copyright   The Great War

IN THE TRACK OF THE U BOATS IN THE MEDITERRANEAN.

Soon after the expedition to Gallipoli was launched enemy submarines found their way into the Mediterranean, and made themselves a menace to the allied movements. As was the case in the Atlantic Ocean and North Sea, merchant and passenger vessels were their principal victims, these including the Ancona, the Yasaka Maru, and the Persia. The positions and dates of these disasters are indicated in the map.

and a torpedo-boat; and the Austrian submarines sank one of her transports during the expedition to Albania.

But having regard to the long period of warfare covered by this survey, and the large area of operations in Mediterranean waters, crowded in places with allied warships, troopships, and supply steamers, the military damage wrought by the flotillas of Teutonic submarines in ten of the most critical months of warfare was much less than might have been expected; for in the Mediterranean circumstances favoured the attacking underwater boats. The water-gate of the Strait of Gibraltar was in one place only about nine miles wide, and from the great British fortress rock there were only eleven and a half nautical miles of sea stretching to the Moorish coast. But it was impracticable to employ nets to stop or capture the submerged raiders coming from German ports; for the water was remarkably deep—some nine hundred and fifty feet—with a powerful current running in from the Atlantic at a speed of three to six miles an hour, beneath which swept a strong counter-current flowing outward from the Mediterranean. Just beyond the Strait, the midland sea deepened to three thousand feet, and went down in a large tract to more than six thousand feet. Except in the shallowing waters of bays, the use of nets against enemy submarines was, therefore, not very efficacious. The German naval experts helping the Turks could not even net the very narrow Dardanelles

Ferreting out the water-rats against our underwater craft. Natural conditions generally favoured the attacking submarines.

The enemy had bases on the strip of Anglo-Italian coast-line in Africa, dominated by the warriors of the Senussi confraternity, and more bases along the Asiatic shores of Turkey, as well as numerous secret depôts on Greek islands. The task thrown upon our destroyers, light cruisers, and seaplanes was enormous, and though our sailors were helped in their work of ferreting out the water-rats by the French naval forces, the burden of incessant labour was such as often tested the men to the full stretch of their powers of endurance. We had some remarkable successes in capturing and destroying German submarines in the Mediterranean, but as these were not reported by our Admiralty they cannot yet be mentioned. Our curious policy of silence was founded on good tactics and on sound

psychology in regard to the Teutonic temperament. We may have discovered a base, and laid an ambush there, or captured a mother ship and used her as a stalking horse, or simply lighted by happy chance on an enemy ship and destroyed her. The Germans and Austrians seldom knew where and how their underwater boats had been snared. But it is worthy of remark that when the Salonika expedition was on the way, and the withdrawal from the Dardanelles was being undertaken, the military power of the U boats was reduced, **Austria's amazing** for the time at least, to a negligible **appeal** factor. Armies numbering a quarter of a million men, with their vast war machinery and material, were transported over the midland sea without disaster, despite the German and Austrian underwater craft. While the Teutons were killing non-combatants in unarmed liners, such as the Ancona, Ville de Ciotat, and Persia, they were shunning, more from fear than from ignorance, their proper work of impeding the Salonika, Albania, and Dardanelles operations. In fine, for practical warlike purposes, they were beaten; and, in the manner of baffled bullies, they turned upon undefended passenger liners, and vented their wrath of defeat in jeers at drowning non-combatants. The kingdom of hell is within us as well as the kingdom of heaven, and it seems as if the officers and men of the U boats were only able to save themselves from self-contempt by unloosening all that was hellish in their own souls. There was, however, one extraordinary note of humour in the ghastly history of Teutonic submarine work in the Mediterranean. On December 7th, 1915, the Austro-Hungarian Ministry of Foreign Affairs sent an appeal to Sir Edward Grey, through the American Embassy in London. Certain Austro-Hungarian subjects—chiefly women and children—were being repatriated from India in the British steamer Golconda, and an Austrian petition was forwarded to the British Government, pleading that the Golconda should be specially protected from the German and Austrian submarine attacks, and adding:

The Imperial and Royal Government will hold the British Government responsible for the lives and well-being of these passengers, *the majority of whom are better-class people.*

Sir Edward Grey's reply was a masterpiece:

With regard to that portion of the petition which asks that special precautions may be taken to prevent danger to the lives of

BRITISH MAKE-BELIEVE BATTLESHIP OFF MUDROS, LEMNOS ISLAND.

Dummy craft beached to serve as a breakwater and thereby assist naval and military operations. Lemnos acted as a base for the Gallipoli Expedition, affording excellent anchorage for shipping, transports, and hospital-ships. Turkey had intended to cede Lemnos to Greece after the Balkan War, but the treaty not having been concluded when the Great War broke out, the Allies occupied the island.

the Golconda passengers by submarine attack, I feel bound to express my astonishment that the Austro-Hungarian Government, itself one of the authors of the danger, should have thought it seemly to endorse this request.

Not content, however, with doing this, the Austro-Hungarian Government further states that it will hold his Majesty's Government responsible for the lives and well-being of those passengers, "the majority of whom are better-class people." I am at a loss to know why "better-class people" should be thought more entitled to protection from submarine attack than any other non-combatants; but, however that may be, the only danger of the character indicated which threatens any of the passengers in the Golconda is one for which the Austro-Hungarian and German Governments are alone responsible. It is they, and they only, who have instituted and carry on a novel and inhuman form of warfare which disregards all the hitherto accepted principles of international law, and necessarily endangers the lives of non-combatants. By asking for special precautions to protect one of their own subjects on board a British merchant vessel, the Austro-Hungarian Government recognises what is the inevitable consequence of their submarine policy, and admits that the outrages by which the Lusitania, the Persia, and numbers of other ships have been sunk without warning were not the result of the casual brutalities of the officers of enemy submarines, but part of the settled and premeditated policy of the Governments whom they serve.

It is needless to add that his Majesty's Government does not propose to take any precautions on behalf of Austro-Hungarian subjects which it does not take on behalf of its own, and that if they suffer any injury from submarine attack on the part of his Majesty's enemies the responsibility must rest solely with those who have made such attacks part of their ordinary methods of warfare. The proper and sufficient protection from this danger is that Austria-Hungary and Germany should observe ordinary rules of humanity in their methods of warfare.

Sir Edward Grey's reply

Much could be written on this affair. From it we could explain the sentimentality of the Teutons in regard to themselves and their barbarous treatment of other peoples. We could even illuminate fully the problem of reprisals for Zeppelin raids, and discover the method of breaking down the spirit of the decivilised Germanic herds. But we shall let the matter stand where Sir Edward Grey left it.

Before concluding this chapter, we must relate the extraordinary capture of Captain A. Stanley Wilson, M.P., and Colonel Napier. The two officers left Corfu for England in the Greek steamer Spetzai, carrying with

them some important despatches. On December 6th, 1915, when the steamer was a hundred and twenty miles off Patras, a submarine appeared about a mile away and fired a shell, causing the Spetzai to stop. The U boat then approached, and, hoisting the Austrian flag, ordered the skipper of the steamer to come on board with the ship's papers. Captain Wilson threw his despatch-bag overboard, but the bag floated, and was recovered by the Austrians. This, however, was not so serious a matter as it appeared; for the bag did not contain the most important despatches, which were hidden by Captain Wilson with, it is said, the help of an American passenger. Finding the names of British officers on the passenger-list, the Austrian commander sent a boat to the steamer for Captain Wilson, Colonel Napier, and Dr. Finlay. The latter, being a Red Cross medical man, was released, but the other two officers, after obtaining a portion of their baggage, were made prisoners. The submarine remained by the steamer for about an hour, and then set off on a cruise lasting two nights and a day and a half.

Capture of Captain Wilson, M.P

The prisoners were well treated, and had some exciting experiences in the enemy U boat. Among their companions were two French naval officers, who had been captured on December 5th from a French submarine that had run ashore. According to a letter received from Captain Stanley Wilson, the Austrians were of a different breed from those who jeered the drowning passengers of the Ancona. They treated their prisoners like guests, and made everything as pleasant as possible for them, until they were delivered into one of the naval fortresses on the Adriatic. There was at first a suspicion of collusion between the Greek skipper and the Austrian submarine commander; for the capture of British officers, bearing very important despatches, seemed unlikely to be the work of mere chance. But it would appear that this suspicion was baseless, and that the extraordinary stroke of ill-luck that fell on Captain Wilson and Colonel Napier was just one of the strange fortunes of war.

ENEMY SUBMARINE PASSING ONE OF THE TORPEDO-BOATS OF THE OTTOMAN NAVY IN THE DARDANELLES.

CHAPTER CI.

OUR SUBMARINE DEFENSIVE CAMPAIGN AND INVASION OF THE BALTIC AND MARMORA SEAS.

The Secret Arts of Submarine Hunting—How our Deep-Sea Fishermen Rose to the Occasion—Following the Submarine Wave and Netting the Great Steel Fish—Invention of a Detector for Locating Submarines Twenty Miles Away—German Accounts of our Nets Across the Narrow Seas—Wenninger's Adventures in U17 off the East Coast—Hersing is Netted on his Way to the Dardanelles—Fishing for a British Submarine in the Mouth of a German River—Magnificent Fight Between an E Boat, a Zeppelin, and Four German Destroyers—British Aviators' Successes against Enemy Submarines—Another Fight between a British Submarine and a Zeppelin—Why the German Marine Office Yielded to the President of the United States—End of the First Submarine Blockade of the British Isles—Germans Steal an American Idea and Build Mine-laying Submarines—Our Underwater Craft Invade the Baltic and Practically Complete the Blockade of Germany—Did we Use Captured German Submarines Against the German Baltic Fleet ?—Strange Adventures in the Sea of Marmora—British Lieutenant Swims from a Submarine and Blows Up Turkish Railway Line—Germans Renew their Submarine Campaign by Means of a Flotilla of Underwater Monitors—Our Occasional Naval Losses from Mines Sown by Enemy Submarines—Inexplicable Explosions in Ships in Harbour—The Strange Case of the Italian Battleship Benedetto Brin.

WHILE in the secondary field of naval operations, the Mediterranean, hostile underwater craft continued to cause much anxiety, and compelled several important steamship lines to avoid the Suez Canal and go round by the Cape, in home waters our anti-submarine campaign developed in intensity and scope. At present, no definite information can be given about the details of the long series of British victories which saved us from famine and defeat, and thus had a vital effect upon the general course of the war. It is doubtful whether our principal secret means of combating submarines will ever be revealed. What our men purchased by long, arduous, and terrible experience will not be discussed in despatches for the enlightenment of foes, but will remain rather a hidden fund of working knowledge to be handed down in training with other valuable traditions of our Senior Service.

The new art of submarine hunting was developed with deadly passion after the sinking of the Lusitania. With their wide experience in delivering submarine attacks in the Heligoland Bight, the Dardanelles, and the

"H.M.S. MIGHTY ATOM."
The tiny craft seen on the left—the smallest motor-boat in the Service—was christened " H.M.S. Mighty Atom." The men on the right are cleaning out a gig—a pleasant variation from the ordinary naval routine on a fine day.

Baltic, our officers knew so fully what the submarine could do, that they were able to devise ways of combating the class of vessel they used so well. Our Sea Lords also called men of science to their aid, with the result that strange devices of many kinds were constructed. Many hundreds of small, fast, handy vessels were added to the Grand Fleet in order to extend and accelerate the operations against U boats. It was during this great increase in the number of our warships that one grand and happy discovery was made. Our long-trained officers and men could be relied on to carry out their varied tasks with fine skill and flexibility of mind. But long-service naval men were not sufficient in number to man the immense number of small craft added to the Home Fleet. Even the Royal Naval Reserve was not large enough to supplement the ordinary ratings ; for our capital ships were increasing in number, with swarms of new light cruisers, destroyers, and little motor-vessels of terrific speed. Many fishermen, therefore, were called up for service.

The fishermen were the least experienced of all our fighting seamen. They began on the humble but dangerous job of trawling for mines and keeping

THE GERMAN SAILOR IN WAR-TIME—THANKS
TO JELLICOE.
As the Imperial German Fleet was for many months at a
time inactive, most of the men were diverted to shore
service. This photograph shows some German sailors
wearing respirators at rifle practice.

THE POISON CLOUD AT SEA.
Smoke from German gas shells seen from a British warship.

squadron of fishing boats, they watched
for German submarines as they used to watch
for a school of mackerel. There was a certain
wave for which the look-outs always searched.
No matter at what depth an 800-ton submarine travelled, it produced a curious wave
on the surface of the water, and the trained
eyes of the fishermen were able to discern
this wave with exceptional quickness. Naval
ratings knew how to handle guns, torpedoes,
and intricate machinery, but deep-sea fishermen, who had searched the waters since boyhood for schools of fish, had a quicker knack
of spotting a submarine wave. This disturbance was often very small, especially when
the water was broken or choppy; but the
fishermen on Beat 1 did not
let many underwater craft **Spotting the**
go unperceived and un- **submarine wave**
attacked. There was that in
their hearts which quickened their eyesight. One of them
said that almost every time when he was watching the
water he seemed to see the floating hands and drifting hair
of the women and children who were drowned in the
Lusitania. A cold, sustained Berserker rage against the
assassins of the sea nerved the fishermen to their unending,
weary, deadly task. Men of slow minds, patient and quiet
in trouble and hammered by a hard seafaring life into a
sort of mild endurance, it took much to rouse them into
lasting passion; but their ordinary quality of patience
became terrible when it was bent by the hands of dead
women and children to the work of retribution. Their
methods of attack cannot be explained. But it may be
said that any U boat they perceived far under the water
seldom rose again. It was trapped—the great, steel-
built, mechanical fish—before it could rise and use its
weapons; and as the trap closed round it, something came
down through the waves and cut the great steel fish in two.
There was no fight, though the German Marine Office
often complained that our fishing vessels caught their

clear the fairways to our ports. The noble courage
of these men was displayed in the Dardanelles and
on the Belgian coast, where they coolly fished up
enemy mines under heavy fire from hostile land-batteries.
This was only what one would expect from the best
deep-sea fishermen in the world. After years of
perilous endurance, by which they won food for the nation
at the risk of their lives, they were not the men to flinch
from the work of saving the Fleet. At first, however, their
labour was rather of a passive kind. Few of them could
take part in the active work of sinking enemy ships. Yet
by an extraordinary vicissitude of circumstances, these
quiet, steady drudges of the Grand Fleet became the most
deadly active fighters of the modern scientific school.
They it was who developed submarine killing into a science
that staggered and daunted the most adventurous spirits of
the German Navy.

The most important beat along our shores was held by
a band of fishermen, with a naval officer partly directing
them and partly learning from them. Manning a small

unsuspecting submarines on the surface and shattered them with quick-firing guns. This was not how the work was carried out, though there may have been some artillery duels in the opening phase of the campaign. The main work of destruction was done by "fishing," with fishermen in fishing boats matched against an unseen submarine that did not even show her periscope.

There is, however, no objection to referring to one method by which the U-boats were hunted down. An account has been published in an American periodical, the ' Popular Science Monthly," by the inventor, Mr. William Dudilier. He devised a mechanism for the Allies by means of which a submarine travelling fully submerged could be located within a radius of twenty miles. The mechanism consisted of a microphone which picked

Use of the microphone

up the hum of the electric motors used in a submerged submarine. There was a sound-sieve which kept out all other noises coming through the water—the vibration of engines, and beating of propellers in passing vessels—so that only the whine of electric motors used in submarines was picked up.

Two detectors were submerged at a considerable distance apart, and made so that they could be turned to get in direct line with the submarine. An increase in the volume of sound received told when the detector was being turned in the right direction ; and when both detectors were fully responding, a rapid and simple trigonometrical calculation gave the position of the submarine. The tract of water covered by the detector had been mapped out beforehand in numbered squares, known to all the guard-

ships. At the signal, they steamed to the square the submarine was approaching, and there began their trapping and killing operation, while the detectors and the detecting officers kept them informed of all further movements by the hidden German war-shark.

There is no special information concerning the methods by which the enormous transport of troops and war material across the Channel was protected against the German submarines. All that we know is that this protection became stronger as the war went on, the mining of the hospital-ship Anglia being a disaster of a rare kind. According to an enemy source, the " Vossische Zeitung," the French and British naval authorities closed the narrow seas by huge steel nets, sometimes forty miles long, in

THE DISASTER TO H.M.S. NATAL.
Survivors of H.M.S. Natal, which was blown up in harbour on December 30th, 1915. Each man has received a new kit, and is about to proceed on leave. Captain E. P. C. Back, R.N., of the ill-fated cruiser, is seen in the circle portrait. The Natal was a cruiser of the Warrior class, with a displacement of 13,550 tons, and was completed in 1904.

which hostile submarines were entangled until their crews were suffocated. The enemy's account, which we give for what it is worth, is as follows :

A net has been drawn from Dover to the French coast opposite, and another from Portland Bill, near Weymouth, to Cape La Hague. Between these two nets there is a space of over one hundred and fifty miles, sufficient for all transport service. Further, a net extends from the Mull of Kintyre in Scotland to Ireland, and another from Carnsore Point in Ireland to St. David's Head in South Wales, in order to protect the Irish Sea.

To allow the passage of trading vessels and the warships of the Allies, these nets have been fitted with gates which can be shut and opened, like pontoons. These passages are known only to the British Admiralty, and are often changed. Since submarines can descend to three hundred feet under water, these nets reach to sea-bottom, as the Channel is never deeper than two hundred and sixty-five feet.

The upper edge of the net is fastened to buoys, and both upper and lower edges are anchored so that storms and ebb and flood tides cannot change the position of the net or damage it in any way. The anchor-chains are also so shortened that the buoys are a few feet below the level of the water, consequently the submarines cannot see the nets either above or below the water. If one of them plunges into the net, it becomes entangled and so damaged that it is an easy prey to the enemy.

Small nets were largely employed by both British and German surface vessels engaged in hunting under-water craft. From Lieutenant Wenninger, commander of the German submarine U17, we have a lively account of his escape from our modern net-throwers off the East Coast. He left his base early one morning, and passed into the North Sea with hull submerged and periscope awash. On looking through the periscope he could see a red buoy behind his boat. He looked again ten minutes **Lieut. Wenninger's** later, and saw the buoy still at the **adventures** same distance behind him. He steered to the right, he steered to the left, but the buoy followed him. He descended deep into the water, and then rose until his periscope was again awash, but still saw the buoy floating on the surface above him. He had caught the chain of the buoy and was dragging it along with him, and a small British patrol-boat had observed the strange voyage of the buoy, and was intently following it, and calling with her wireless.

Wenninger then revealed the fact that the German submarines hunted down our ships by means of microphone detectors, which have a longer range than the periscopes ; for he said that his sounding apparatus indicated that two steamers were approaching, and soon afterwards he saw five British torpedo-boats coming from the north. The German officer first increased the speed of his vessel with the intention of attacking the foremost torpedo craft. But he noticed that they were ranging themselves around him in a menacing semicircle ; and, giving up the idea of an attack, he dived as deep as possible, and began to crawl away. Suddenly it seemed that an accident had happened to his boat. It rolled in a most alarming manner, and rose and sank uncontrollably, as though the steering-gear had got out of order.

But Wenninger discovered that it was not his steering-gear which was wrong, but his boat. One of the hunting torpedo-boats had steamed in front of him and had dropped a steel net. The U boat had **Caught in a** driven into it, and had got entangled in **steel net** an almost hopeless manner. For an hour and a half the netting carried the submarine with it, and though Wenninger made every effort to get clear, pumping up and down, and trying to work under the net, it was all in vain. His boat was always dragged back. He then resolved to increase the weight of the submarine as much as possible, and attempt to tear through the netting. He was fortunate in having pumped in about six tons of water when he started. He now filled all the tanks to their limit, and drove clear of the netting. He then descended as low as he could ; and with his menometer marking thirty metres, he stayed under for eighteen hours. But when at last he rose, his menometer still showed thirty metres, and his compass and rudder also refused to work. Moreover, the torpedo-boats were still watching close above him. Down he went again to the bottom of the sea for another six hours, by the end of which time he had repaired his steering-gear, and had got his compass to work. Once more he lifted his periscope, only to bring a vigilant torpedo-boat charging straight at him. So he went again to the bottom for two hours, and at night managed to crawl away unobserved.

Lieutenant von Hersing had a somewhat similar adventure in a British net on his way to the Mediterranean and his victories over the Triumph and the Majestic.

TARGETS WHERE NO MARKER WAS NEEDED TO RECORD THE HITS.
Floating mines off the Belgian coast provided our Marines with movable targets for rifle practice. As each hit involved the explosion of the mine, there was no uncertainty about the scoring.

THE "EARS" OF THE FLEET HAVE HEARD THE WIRELESS CALL FOR HELP.
Full speed ahead on a T.B.D. in answer to the S O S from a merchant steamer sinking as a result of a pirate's torpedo. Destroyers have been called " the eyes and ears of the Fleet." Certainly during the submarine blockade of Britain they did excellent work in hunting down the U boats, as well as in rescuing a large number of innocent victims of German piracy.

Our own submarine boats had some horrible escapes from German nets. The enemy used aircraft to spot our submerged boats. One of these was seen from above when she was lying in the mouth of a German river. There was only five feet of water over her conning-tower, so that even a torpedo-boat would strike her while steaming over. The British commander thought that all was lost, for he heard the rasp of a wire trawl sweeping over his hull. But to save the nerves of his men he turned on a gramophone, which made a noise covering the deadly outside sound. Happily the wire trawl did not catch on the boat, and after conducting the search in a most thorough but fruitless manner, the Germans went away, and in due course the submarine got home.

In another case, one of our submarines ran her nose into a German net, and rose to the surface so that the entanglement could be cut away. But as soon as she rose, down fell an aerial bomb. A Zeppelin was waiting above the net, while calling with her wireless for destroyers to come and finish the British vessel. Escaping the bombs, the entangled submarine descended very carefully and slowly, in order that the net should not get more closely wrapped

LIEUT. VON HERSING.
One of the most daring of Germany's submarine commanders. He sank both the Triumph and the Majestic, but had a thrilling experience on his way to the Mediterranean, being, like his compatriot, Lieut. Wenninger, caught for a time in a British net.

around her. The British commander wriggled and manœuvred his vessel, listening for the scrape of the steel links on his hull, and guessing blindly at the results of all his workings. At last he drew quite clear of the web of death, and sat his boat on the bottom of the sea and thought out the next move. His problem was to decide whether it would be better to push away under water and warn other British submarines of the snare, or wait until the German destroyers arrived in answer to the call of the Zeppelin, and attack them when they thought they had an easy victim still tangled up in the net. Our officer resolved to try for the double event. When his sound detectors told him that there were four destroyers searching above him, he rose, and going towards the sound of the nearest screw, got a torpedo home on one of his enemies and crumpled her up. He then dived and waited, following the sound of the next destroyer that came to take the damaged vessel in tow. Again the British submarine rose, and with her last torpedo she smashed up the second destroyer. Then she went on to the rendezvous, and reached it in time to warn other British underwater craft.

D   29

IN READINESS FOR THE LURKING ENEMY SUBMARINE.
Gun crew on a British destroyer ready for action against lurking enemy craft.

A good deal of the submarine hunting was done by seaplanes on our part, and by Zeppelins on the enemy side.

Our naval airmen who flew above the water seeking for U boats running awash or partly submerged, had two striking successes.

On August 26th, 1915, Squadron-Commander Bigsworth, who had previously distinguished himself by bombing a Zeppelin that raided Ramsgate, swooped down on a German submarine which he had spotted off Ostend.

The U boat turned her gun on him while he was manœuvring for position, and the German shore batteries tried to bring him down by a tempest of shrapnel. But with great coolness and skill, Squadron-Commander Bigsworth descended to 500 feet, and after several attempts to get a good line over the zigzagging enemy boat, he mastered her movements and dropped his bombs with shattering effects.

Then on November 28th, 1915, Flight-Lieutenant Viney, accompanied by a brilliant French lieutenant, the Comte de Sinçay, attacked another enemy submarine off the Belgian coast.

Lieutenant Viney, as pilot, manœuvred the machine and got it in line over the U boat, and the Comte de Sinçay, as bomb-dropper, launched the missiles which destroyed the hostile vessel.

On the other hand, one of our own submarines, submerged near the German coast, came up for air and found a Zeppelin waiting for her.

The monster airship was hovering so low down that her immense shining belly shut out the sky when the astonished British officer looked up. She launched her bombs at high speed, but by happy chance the E boat had come to the surface beneath the harmless end of the aerial leviathan. Moreover, the airship had to work against a strong wind, and could not therefore quickly get her stinging end over the British submarine, which was wildly dancing about on a rough sea. Meanwhile, the gun was manned by a sailor, who, though half-drowned in the breaking seas and washed about like a rag, clung on to his gun and got in a few shots between the walls of water that broke over him. He ripped a large patch out of the Zeppelin, and she made away with a list on her; but turned up a fortnight later with a new bright piece of covering on her port side. The shells supplied at that time to our submarines were apparently not powerful enough to smash a Zeppelin.

All this, however, was the rare, romantic element in naval submarine warfare. The labour

ANSWERING THE "S O S."
British torpedo-boat destroyer going to the assistance of a steamer torpedoed without warning by a German U boat. The S O S message having been flashed far and wide, a number of vessels soon arrived on the spot and removed the crew from the steamer as it was sinking by the head. The circle illustration shows how the patrol ships met the mine peril. One of these deadly machines is being exploded harmlessly by British sailors who have found the contact.

of maintaining a successful defence against the flotillas of U boats trying to blockade our islands was mainly a wearing, monotonous affair of incessant hard work and endurance. The glimpse of a periscope was a grand event.

Many of our small patrol boats had merely to watch neutral steamers, help them through new mine-fields laid by the enemy of civilisation, and endeavour to find if any of the neutral vessels was acting as supply ship to the U boats.

Thousands of our medley of naval recruits—yachtsmen, motorboat owners, retired admirals, pleasure sailing-boat runners and others—spent months at sea without bringing off any fine stroke against the enemy. Most of them had a beat, and in course of time many of them had a gun, and they patrolled their stretch of water hoping to catch a mother-ship of the U boats among the neutral vessels that passed, or to have a duel with a German submarine. Few of them were so fortunate, but the great, systematic, unending search they maintained had important general results in ensuring the safety of our Navy and mercantile marine.

Among the watchers of the seas there were some crews, like the crew of the Baralong, who crowned many months of alert but uneventful activity with a great

THE BLOCKADE AT WORK.
Lowering a boat and crew from a destroyer for the inspection of a doubtful-looking craft.

success. The case of the Baralong was not at all unique; there were other British ships as successful as she was, and many of the awards of the Distinguished Service Order given to officers on patrol cruisers, on August 7th and September 13th, 1915, were indicative of our victories over enemy submarines. There will be stories of many adventurous duels to relate when the war is over. The case of the Baralong has only become famous through its extraordinary sequel and through the advertisement given to it by the German Press Bureau. As a matter of fact, the Germans made a great blunder in regard to this British patrol cruiser; and, as will afterwards be seen, there was more than met the eye in Sir Edward Grey's seemingly simple proposal to submit the matter to the judgment of a Board of American naval officers.

There was a certain British naval officer who had, for reasons that need not at present be fully described, a very keen desire to fight a German submarine. He was given a merchant steamer, which he transformed into a patrol cruiser and renamed the Baralong, and disguised it in every possible way. For months he hung about one of the scenes of German submarine activity, hoping to be attacked, but the enemy did not like the look of his boat, and

THE OLD ORDER AND THE NEW IN WAR-TIME.
Gun crew at work on a British destroyer. The weapon is just being laid. The centre photograph shows a destroyer patrol racing after a sailing ship about to be overhauled for possible contraband.

NO DOUBT ABOUT HIS SEA LEGS.
Member of the crew of the E14 standing on the forepart of his vessel running awash somewhere in the Dardanelles.

kept away from it. So he built a contraption which concealed his armament, and made the vessel appear like a harmless tramp, and when the great British passenger liner the Arabic was torpedoed and sunk without warning off the Irish coast on August 19th, 1915, the commander of the Baralong steamed towards the scene of the murder. Meanwhile, another British steamer, the Nicosian, with a cargo of Army mules, and some twelve American cattlemen looking after the animals, approached within sixty miles of Queenstown. The German submarine which had sunk the White Star liner was lying almost awash across the course of the cattle-ship, and she fired a torpedo which struck the Nicosian. But the bulkheads of the steamer held out, and she only sank a foot deeper with a heavy list to port. The submarine then began to shell the ship, and after some seven shells had been fired the British captain and his British crew put off in a boat.

The American cattlemen, however, refused to take to a second boat which had been made ready for them, as they reckoned that the Nicosian was still safe. It was then that the Baralong appeared, steaming up at a great speed behind the Nicosian. She was a **Baralong avenges** clumsy-looking vessel, flying, it was **the Arabic** alleged, the American flag, and the submarine officer saw in her an easy prey. He seems to have had only one torpedo left, and in any case he did not wish to waste one of these valuable five-hundred-pound missiles on the vessel that he had winged and reduced to helplessness. So he sent a bombing-party in a boat to the cattle-ship to finish her off cheaply. But just as his boat's crew clambered up the side of the Nicosian the Baralong performed a transformation act. Her false upper structure of painted canvas and lathes fell away, revealing her fore and aft guns, and, with the gunners ready to fire and the white ensign flying, she drew clear of the cattle-ship that had screened her, and avenged the Arabic in two shots.

The men in the Baralong were angry because they had seen the submarine shelling the cattle-ship while the British crew was getting into the lifeboat. As our patrol steamer came round the bows of the Nicosian the submarine again fired, but the shot went wide over the Baralong. The Marines in the Baralong then opened musketry fire, and with one well-aimed volley swept the decks of the submarine, and demoralised her crew. The Germans at once left their guns, and rushed for the conning-tower, several going overboard, either from panic or because they were wounded. The Baralong then fired her port and stern guns. The first shot hit the U boat below the water-line, the second struck the conning-tower and split it in half. The battle was not an unequal one in regard to armament. The submarine was one of Germany's latest and largest, being about 300 feet long, with a displacement of about a thousand tons. She had two guns mounted fore and aft, which were of slightly larger calibre than the two guns of the Baralong. But the action scarcely lasted four and a half minutes, the submarine gunners only firing the one wild shot. If they had stuck to their guns they would at least have stood a fighting chance, but, as one of the gunners on the Baralong afterwards put it, "apparently German submarines, although always ready to attack defenceless merchant ships and kill or maim their passengers and crews, have no stomach for fighting armed ships of his Majesty's Navy, even when the odds are in their favour."

We had no casualties. As the shattered submarine sank, the German officer and the rest of his crew set out for the Nicosian in their second boat. Their intention was, of course, to secure **German Govern-** a footing on the cattle-ship, and there **ment's allegations** hoist the white flag in token of surrender.

Thus far, the facts as stated were admitted on both sides. But in regard to the final scene the German Government published a curious version of the affair, set out in alleged affidavits by some of the American cattlemen. The sum of the allegations was that the crew of the Baralong murdered the men of the German submarine as they were struggling in the water. In a series of Notes sent to the American Ambassadors in London and Berlin, the German Government demanded that the British Government should try the officers and crew of the Baralong for murder. Sir Edward Grey replied by offering to submit the case to the arbitration of a board of American naval officers if Germany would, at the same time, submit to the investigation of three atrocities committed within forty-eight hours of the Baralong incident. These atrocities were: (1) The torpedoing of the Arabic without notice, whereby forty-seven non-combatants were drowned; (2) the attack made by a German destroyer on the helpless crew of the British submarine E13, stranded in Danish waters; (3) the firing by a German submarine on the unresisting crew of the steamer Ruel, after our men had taken to their boats.

This offer the German Government rejected, stating in its answer that:

The German Government protests most sharply against the unprecedented and unprovoked accusations of the British Government in regard to the German Army and Navy, and the imputation that the German authorities have not dealt with any such crimes as have come to their attention. The German Army and Navy in this war observe the principles of international law

The hero of various daring submarine exploits in the Baltic—Commander Max K. Horton, R.N., D.S.O., in the centre, on the deck of the E9 with Lieut. Essen, of the Russian Navy (right).

Commander Horton's submarine, its decks coated with ice and snow, returning to harbour after sinking the German destroyer S116. On September 13th, 1914, the E9 sank the German cruiser Hela.

Submarine E9 cutting her way through the ice-packed Baltic, and risking the dangers of the ice-floes as well as braving German mines and destroyers.

Commander Max Horton's submarine entering harbour after undergoing a two-days' vigil among the ice-floes and enemy mines.

The submarine forging her way through the ice-floes. Among the enemy ships sunk by the E9 was the battleship Pommern.

WITH COMMANDER MAX HORTON, THE UNDERSEAS HERO OF THE BALTIC.

GERMAN INVENTION FOR SAVING LIFE.
Germany started the war so fully prepared with man-killing machines that it was almost a matter of surprise to learn that they were capable of creating something for preserving life. This photograph shows a special buoyant cage worked by a crane and fitted to the hospital-ship Sierra Ventana.

and humanity, and the higher authorities insist that in the event of offences being committed they shall be investigated most closely and punished sternly. . . . Inasmuch as the British Government has declined to make amends for this outrageous incident, the German Government feels itself compelled to take into its own hands punishment for this unatoned crime and to adopt measures of reprisal.

Sir Edward Grey, in a final statement, said with grim humour :

Some surprise is expressed that the nation whose armed forces are responsible for the sack of Louvain, the murder of hundreds of unoffending men, women, and children on the Lusitania and other ships, the execution of Edith Cavell, the introduction of poisonous gases, the poisoning of wells, attempted torpedoing of hospital-ships, and countless other atrocities should describe their methods of warfare as humane. . . . With regard to the German refusal to submit the Baralong case and the three cases put forward by the British Government for investigation by an impartial neutral tribunal, this action seems hard to explain if the Germans are really so convinced, as they say, of the guilt of the British commander and the innocence of the perpetrators of the three outrages cited by the British Government.

Meanwhile, a great cry for reprisals went up from the German Press. The Berlin "Lokal Anzeiger" said :

What form the reprisals will take we can safely leave to the responsible authorities. The main thing is that the blood of the foully murdered brave German seamen will not remain unavenged. The day is coming when British treachery, hypocrisy, and murderous lust will receive their just punishment. There is still justice in the world.

The "Frankfurter Zeitung" told the world that :

The indignation of Germany is enormous. The nation's demand for reprisals is enormous. The German Reichstag has experienced an hour of greatness. . . . . The Reichstag supports the Government when it sets itself appropriately to rebuke and brand before the world English perfidy and arrogance.

Under the whip of the German Press Bureau the tempest of indignation in Germany increased in violence, the purpose being to reduce the people to a state of mind in which a system of greater naval atrocities could be established by the Government, with popular approval, during the second phase of German submarine warfare. A number of submarine monitors, so rumour ran, were nearing completion in the German yards. These new underwater vessels were armed with very powerful guns, calculated to outfight easily all our armed merchantmen. The intention was to institute a pitiless campaign of murder against all our mercantile marine, and the Baralong case was worked up by the German reptile Press, under Government direction, with a view to stilling all objection to the ghastly work prepared for the submarine monitors.

Meanwhile, however, a strange and disconcerting rumour floated from Norway to Germany. A Christiania newspaper, the "Aftenposten," stated that the American muleteers on the Nicosian were responsible for the destruction of the German submarine crew. As a matter of fact, no British subject took any part in the final act of the Baralong case. The captain and crew of the Nicosian left the cattle-ship in a lifeboat, and the commander and men of the Baralong, after sinking the submarine, remained only puzzled spectators of one of the most thrilling tragedies that ever took place on the sea. When the cattlemen found that the Nicosian was quite buoyant, they began to pride themselves on their courage, and think scorn of the British crew that had **American cattlemen's** rowed away. They studied the German **revenge** submarine with calm interest until the small boat put off from the underwater craft, and it could be seen that the German seamen were carrying bombs. The quick-witted Americans realised at once what the Germans designed to do, and, while the boat was approaching, they saw the Baralong behind them clearing for action and resolved in turn to make a fight for their lives. The American cattleman is a notoriously ugly customer, and these men were as rough, strong, and fearless a gang as ever breathed.

Lacking firearms, they armed themselves with furnace-bars, consisting of pieces of steel, three feet in length and as thick as a man's wrist. The unsuspecting Germans, thinking they had only to deal with a few intimidated men who would be overawed by their revolvers and bombs, came alongside the ship and climbed on deck. As soon as they were aboard the cattlemen rushed them, and gave them little time to use their firearms. Caught in the act of laying bombs in a ship with men on board, the pirates who had sunk the Arabic could expect mercy from no man, and least of all from the group of infuriated American cattlemen, who were far from being "too proud to fight." The heads of some of the Germans were beaten in as soon as they reached the deck, and those that escaped the first rush were chased about the ship in all directions. Some took refuge in cabins and lavatories, only to have the doors smashed in upon them. Two sought for shelter in the tunnel of a propeller-shaft, only to be dragged out

The pirates' doom and brained. Their shrieks for mercy could be heard in the Baralong, but the puzzled British sailors could not divine what had happened. The German submarine officer and the rest of his crew also heard the cries and the scurry, but the first affair was over when they in turn came alongside and climbed up to the deck.

The cattlemen were waiting for the second batch, their steel bars wet with the blood of the first boat's crew. The terrible slaughter that followed was carried out more quickly than the first affair. Only the German commander seems to have escaped from the rush attack near the ship's side. He made for the bridge, apparently hoping that he might be seen and saved by the men on the Baralong. But it is doubtful if the presence of the Grand Fleet would have prevented him from falling into the hands of the blood-mad cattlemen. They tore his revolver from him, lifted him down bodily, tied two firebars to his feet, and threw him overboard on the side away from the Baralong. Then, very coolly and very mildly, the Americans received the visit of an officer from the Baralong. Not a man in the Nicosian had been injured, and the damage done to the ship was so slight that she was able to proceed slowly on her original course to Avonmouth.

At present we have not all the material necessary for forming a judgment upon the action of the cattlemen. Having regard to the falsely-sworn evidence concocted

DARING EXPLOIT FROM A SUBMARINE.
Lieutenant Hughes leaving his submarine to carry out a single-handed bomb attack on a Turkish position. The first photograph shows some Mohammedan prisoners huddled on the deck of the underseas craft.

by the German Embassy in Washington about the Lusitania, which was wrongly alleged to have been carrying guns, it would be rash to assume that any of the American cattlemen in the Nicosian tried afterwards to avoid being prosecuted by giving false testimony that the work of slaughter was done by the Baralong's crew. There does not seem any good reason why the Americans should not assume the responsibility for their deeds. They were non-combatant neutrals, fighting for their lives against heavy odds. The Germans

HOW A BRITISH SOLDIER ESCAPED FROM A MEDITERRANEAN WRECK.
Wearing a lifebelt he was lucky enough to reach a piece of planking, whence he was picked up by a passing ship, after being, for some hours, exposed to the buffetings of wind, weather, and sea.

were well armed, especially the crew of the first bomb-carrying boat, and if they had shot quick and straight they could have brought down all the cattlemen, who had to get within arm's length in order to use their steel bars. In any case, we can now see the irony of Sir Edward Grey's proposal that the case should be put before a tribunal of United States naval officers, and the reason why both the American and the German Governments refused to have the matter settled in this way.

Loss of the India In addition to Fleet auxiliaries like the Baralong, and patrol boats of peaceful build with a gun mounted on them, we employed large numbers of small warships for hunting down enemy submarines, especially a very fast new motor-boat, armed with steel rams and quick-firers. Our losses in action in small warcraft were very slight, being confined to a couple of slow coastal vessels. These were torpedo-boat No. 10 and torpedo-boat No. 12, which were sunk off the East Coast on June 10th, 1915, when trying to destroy a U boat. The German vessel turned on its pursuers and torpedoed both of them. On the other hand, one of our submarines sank a German destroyer of the G

THE TORPEDOED LINER PERSIA.

The P. & O. liner Persia was sunk by an enemy torpedo in the Mediterranean on December 30th, 1915. Some one hundred and sixty souls were lost, principally through the rapid sinking of the liner. The size of the vessel may be judged from this photograph. The portrait is of Captain W. H. S. Hall, who perished with his ship.

class in the North Sea on July 26th, 1915. The enemy soon afterwards avenged this loss by torpedoing our auxiliary cruiser India in Norwegian waters on August 8th. On the same day there was a sharp little naval outpost affair in the North Sea, in which the German auxiliary steamer Meteor played a telling part. She sank one of our small patrol boats, the Ramsey, by means of her heavier guns; but before sinking, the Ramsey gave a wireless call, and some of our cruisers overtook the Meteor and blew her up, after the German crew had abandoned her. But even when the Meteor rested on the mud at the bottom of the sea, her power of damage survived. Before sinking she scattered some mines; and, the day after she vanished, a fine British destroyer, the Lynx, was blown up and sunk by one of these floating masses of trinitrotoluene.

A week later, a quiet and remote part of the British coast was abruptly brought into the area of war. A German submarine sailed round Scotland and apparently passed the Mull of Kintyre. On August 16th, 1915, she opened fire on some Cumberland coast towns. The small manufacturing and mining town of Whitehaven was struck by shells which caused fires. The railway embankment at Parton, a northern suburb of Whitehaven, was damaged slightly, and some fires were produced at Harrington, three miles to the north of Parton. The bombardment took place between half-past four and twenty past five in the afternoon; the damage done was very small, and no persons were reported to have been killed or wounded. It is difficult to discover the reason for this freak performance by an enemy submarine. She only advertised her presence in the Irish Sea, and excited the hunting ardour of all our anti-submarine craft in the theatre of her operations, thus causing hindrance to her work against our shipping. Perhaps it was because she could not find any ships open to easy attack that the submarine turned her guns upon some of our small undefended coast towns; for it is an historic fact that at the time when German submarines began to emulate the feats of Zeppelins by trying to murder schoolchildren, the first grand Teutonic campaign against British and neutral shipping in the war area of the British Isles was failing by exhaustion on the part of the attackers. The enemy's sense of his failure was reflected in his negotiations with the United States over the problem raised by the sinking of the Lusitania. To the surprise of foes and neutrals, and to the angry disappointment of the German people, the German Government began to adopt almost a reasonable and civilised tone in its answers to the Notes of President Woodrow Wilson. The American Press was somewhat misled in the matter, and with considerable self-complacency loudly hailed the change in Germany's attitude as a glorious tribute to the diplomatic genius of their Note-writing President.

Mr. Balfour's famous letter

But our First Lord of the Admiralty, Mr. Balfour, revealed the springs of German conduct in regard to the submarine campaign by a famous letter of such importance that it deserves to be cited at length, for it is the epitaph upon the grave of all the hopes with which the German Marine Office entered upon its first scheme for the submarine blockade of our islands.

Much has been written about Germany's military methods and aims on land; not so much about her methods and aims at sea. Yet in truth the two are so intimately connected that neither can be understood apart from the other.

DEEP-SEA FISHING FOR MEN.

Having sunk an enemy vessel, the British sailors set to work to save the crew. One hauled in the lifeline, while a second helped the foe aboard.

PRESERVING THE BRITISH TRADITION AT SEA.

A German watching his comrades in the sea while his captors are busily engaged in rescue work forward. Above: Another Hun being hauled aboard the submarine. These photographs are an effective answer to the German libels on the British Navy.

"PERISCOPE ASTERN TO STARBOARD!"

A moment of suspense aboard a British destroyer patrolling the North Sea. Out of a choppy sea there suddenly appeared a periscope. With a hiss of foam astern, the destroyer swung round—and then a gleam of sunlight revealed the top of a floating spar, riding upright in the water!

with naval forces inferior to those of some third Power. This is the policy clearly, though cautiously, expressed in the famous preamble to the Navy Bill. It is unnecessary to add that the German Navy League entertained much more ambitious designs.

So far, however, neither the designs of the German Government nor those of the German Navy League have met with any measure of success. The British fighting Fleet has become relatively stronger than it was thirteen months ago, and there is no reason to suppose that during the future course of the war this process is likely to be arrested. It is, indeed, plain that after six months of hostilities Admiral Tirpitz and the Government which he serves arrived at the same conclusion. They saw that the old policy had broken down, and that a new policy must be devised. Submarines, they thought, might succeed where Dreadnoughts and cruisers had failed.

The change, no doubt, was adopted with extreme reluctance and many searchings of heart. The admission of failure is in itself unpleasant; and, though we cannot regard the Government responsible for the Belgian atrocities as either scrupulous or humane, even the most reckless of Governments does not desire to perpetrate unnecessary crimes.

As to what the German Navy must have felt about the new policy, we can only conjecture. But German sailors are gallant men, and gallant men do not like being put on a coward's job.

They know well enough that in the old days, which we are pleased to regard as less humane than our own, there was not a privateersman but would have thought himself disgraced had he sent to the bottom unresisting merchant ships with all hands on board; and it can have been no very agreeable reflection, even to the German Navy League, that the first notable performance of the German Fleet should resemble piracy rather than privateering.

We may, therefore, safely assume that nothing but the hopes of a decisive success would have induced the German Ministers to inflict this new stain upon the honour of their country. Yet a decisive success has not been attained, and does not seem to be in sight.

I claim no gifts of prophecy I make no boast about the future. But of the past I can speak with assurance; and it may interest you to know that, while the losses inflicted upon German submarines have been formidable, British mercantile tonnage is at this moment greater than when the war began.

It was in 1900 that Germany first proclaimed the policy of building a fleet against Britain; and from the point of view of her own ambitions the policy was a perfectly sound one. She aimed at world domination; and against world domination the British Fleet, from the time of Queen Elizabeth to the present day, has always been found the surest and most effectual protection.

The Germans have every reason to be aware of the fact; for without the British Fleet Frederick the Great must have succumbed to his enemies; and without the British Fleet Prussia would scarcely have shaken off the Napoleonic tyranny. Whatever may be thought about the "freedom of the seas" in any of its various meanings, the freedom of the land is due in no small measure to British ships and British sailors.

It takes, however, time as well as money to create a great fleet, and German statesmen were too wise to suppose that they could at once call into existence a Navy able to contend on equal terms with the Power which—as they saw clearly enough—was the most formidable obstacle to their aggressive projects. But they did not, on that account, doubt the immediate advantages which their maritime policy conferred upon them.

They calculated that a powerful fleet, even though it were numerically inferior to that of Britain, would, nevertheless, render the latter impotent, since no British Government would dare to risk a conflict which, however successful, might leave them in the end

It is true that by this method of warfare many inoffensive persons, women and children, as well as men, neutrals as well as belligerents, have been robbed and killed. But it is not only the innocent who have suffered. The criminals also have paid heavy toll. Some have been rescued and are prisoners of war. But from the very nature of submarines it must often happen that they drag their crews with them to destruction, and those who send them forth on their unhonoured mission wait for their return in vain.

Herein lies the explanation of the amazing change which has come over the diplomatic attitude of Germany towards the United States. Men ask themselves why the sinking of the Lusitania, with the loss of over 1,100 men, women, and children, was welcomed throughout Germany with a shout of triumph, while the sinking of the Arabic was accepted in melancholy silence.

Is it because in the intervening months the United States have become stronger or Germany weaker? Is it because the attitude of the President has varied? Is it because the arguments of the Secretary of State have become more persuasive? Is it because German opinion has at last revolted against lawless cruelty?

No. The reason is to be found elsewhere. It is to be found in the fact that the authors of the submarine policy have had time to measure its effects, and that deeds which were merely crimes in May, in September are seen to be blunders.—(Signed) ARTHUR JAMES BALFOUR.

At the beginning of September, 1915, we had behind us six months' experience of the most cruel and illegal form of piracy ever practised by a nation. But the ruthless destruction of merchant vessels entering our ports had not been accomplished. In the first place, we were far from having been starved, though we had **Captain Persius' admissions** suffered economic loss. In the second place, it did not look as though neutral ships had been terrified into avoiding our harbours, for the arrivals and sailings were increasing in numbers. And in the third place, our merchant seamen, instead of being intimidated by the new school of pirates, had their fighting instincts exalted to a remarkable height.

One of the chief German naval experts, Captain Persius, who wrote for the "Berliner Tageblatt," was uncommonly frank about the matter. In the course of his article he wrote:

It will be remembered that at the beginning of February high hopes were cherished in Germany in regard to submarine warfare. Many persons believed that, as the British Fleet had cut us off from overseas imports, it would not be difficult to do the same to the British people by means of our submarines. Some of our newspapers must, unfortunately, be held responsible for the extravagant expectations raised in our public with reference to the submarine war against commerce. Again and again we have counselled patience. It is now evident how necessary this was from a consideration of the simple fact—the concealment of which would seem dishonest—that the result of the activity of our submarines in their war on commerce is regarded in many circles as being very modest. Only a child would accuse the British of being bad seamen. They know how to defend themselves, and have devised many kinds of protective measures. It becomes more and more difficult for U boats to get near enough to hostile ships to launch a torpedo. Skill of almost a miraculous kind is required to avoid all snares, escape from destroyers, and yet make a successful attack.

How many U boats, with the finest-trained crews in Germany, were lost by Grand Admiral von Tirpitz and Herr Ballin remains a matter of speculation. As the work of destruction often took place far under the water, our men were not always able to say definitely that they had destroyed their enemy. Sometimes bubbles and oil appeared on the surface, and these were fairly good evidence of a killing; sometimes a submarine with its suffocated crew was found in the nets. But there were many doubtful cases, and it was not to our advantage to over-estimate the number of enemy boats and crews we had put out of action. It may indeed have been the aim of the Germans to deepen our new sense of security, and put us off our guard, by spreading the report that more than forty German submarines had been sunk by September, 1915. It was reported that by October, 1915, sixteen had been destroyed by ramming, gunfire, and other ordinary methods; and that twenty-seven had been

trapped in British nets. And the extraordinary statement was made that the German Marine Office protested against our defensive steel-net system as being inhuman!

As the Russians had also sunk two German submarines in the Baltic, and as at the opening of the war Germany had merely some fifty submarines built or approaching completion, she was, if the figures cited were correct, left with barely five U boats. This was a ridiculous calculation. Even allowing that a fairly important number of large underwater vessels had been constructed by German shipbuilders between August, 1914, and October, 1915—such as the 1,000-ton U boat sunk by the Baralong—it would be misleading to place Germany's submarine losses in fifteen months as high as forty-five boats. She sent at least two underwater craft into the Mediterranean in May, 1915, gave two to Bulgaria in September, 1915, for Black Sea work, and despatched a powerful flotilla into the Mediterranean on November 2nd. At the same time, the operations against our liners and cargo steamers in home waters were continued, though with less

A submarine's field of vision through the periscope, with marks denoting measurements by which the distance of the objective can be gauged. Here a German warship is seen, "hull down" in a rough sea. at a distance of a few hundred yards.

The man behind the periscope, on whose keenness of eye depends the safety of the submarine. In these illustrations, by a naval officer, the "look-out" man is taking the measure of an enemy vessel, prior to the launching of a torpedo.

THE "EYE" OF A SUBMARINE: SURFACE VIEW FROM BENEATH THE SEA.

intensity. For example, the Allan liner Hesperian was torpedoed off the Irish coast on September 6th, 1915, the U boat launching her torpedo at 8.20 p.m. in the darkness. The liner carried three hundred and fourteen passengers and two hundred and fifty crew, but she floated thirty-six hours after being struck, and the loss of life, including one American, was thirty-two persons.

Germany must have carefully retained a useful number of highly trained submarine crews and new model U boats, for she needed them for vital military purposes in both the North Sea and the Baltic. No doubt she went to the safe limit in her underwater campaign against the British Isles, with the result that her losses in northern waters precluded her from taking powerful action in the Mediterranean during both the Dardanelles and Salonika expeditions of the British and French forces. In other words the early anti-commerce operations of the German Marine Office were conducted at such heavy expense that sufficient far-ranging U boats were not left to undertake a deadly, comprehensive scheme of attack against British and

Our Mediterranean losses

WATCH AND WARD IN THE MIDDLE SEA.
On the bridge of a French warship in the Mediterranean. Officer and men of the watch, with gun trained, alert for hostile submarines and enemy mines.

French troopships, supply ships and warships in the Mediterranean.

After Hersing's surprise victories over the Triumph and Majestic in May, 1915, the only important naval success achieved by the Teutonic underwater craft in the midland sea against the Franco-British fleet was the destruction of the French cruiser Amiral Charner. This old ship, launched in 1893, and carrying a complement of three hundred and seventy-five officers and men, was torpedoed off the Syrian coast on February 8th, 1916, practically all the crew being lost. A raft was afterwards sighted off Syria, carrying fifteen French sailors, of whom one only, a Breton gunner, remained alive. He said his ship had been torpedoed early in the morning of February 8th, and had sunk so rapidly that there was no time to lower boats. So apparently the Amiral Charner, despite her age and slowness, had not worn an anti-torpedo waistbelt or been guarded by destroyers. But with the exception of this easy victim, the U boats in the Mediterranean made no progress in the attrition of the Franco-British fleet, while they were being hunted and trapped or caught in their secret bases.

In our home waters, in 1915, the enemy submarines became shyer but more wildly dangerous. This was the result of the appearance of a new type of U boat, designed as an underwater mine-layer. These vessels carried a certain number of mines outside their hulls, which could be detached as required. One of them is reported to have been sunk in shallow water in the summer of 1915. A vessel of this class was probably responsible for the destruction of the British cruiser Arethusa, in February, 1916.

These new mine-laying German submarines proved a terrible nuisance to both our Home Fleet and our mercantile marine. The stealthy, elusive, furtive assassins crept out of harbour without being seen, and working beneath the waves in some busy route of sea-traffic, floated off their mines and returned to their base. The new boats had an airtight chamber in which the mines were placed ready to be sown.

Each mine rested in the chamber on steel fingers, a hawser running from the end of the mine to the wrist of the metal hand. The fingered hand formed the sinker. On reaching the spot where it was proposed to make a small, new, unexpected mine-field, the door leading from the mine chamber to the hull of the submarine was shut, and the upper trapdoor of the chamber was opened, letting in the sea water.

The mines were then released. As each mine descended with its sinker, the explosive mass, which was lighter than water, was detached from the steel fingers by an ingenious mechanism, and allowed to float to the surface. Meanwhile, the heavy sinker sank to the bottom of the sea, and turning over as it sank, brought the steel fingers underneath and converted them into a kind of anchor that clutched the mud. Then, according to the length of the connecting hawser, the light, floating mine was dragged out of sight to the nicely calculated depth below the surface at which it would do most damage to the vessel that chanced to strike and explode it.

Working in this manner at night, the new German underwater craft could seldom be detected. It was a most despicable engine of slaughter. It worked blind havoc among belligerent and neutral ships alike, and gave non-combatant crews and passengers as little mercy as it allowed fighting sailors on warships.

Indeed, men in well-designed large warships, built with a system of watertight bulkheads to save them from instant destruction, were better off than Scandinavian, Dutch, Greek and American merchant sailors on ordinary cargo boats. Yet none of the neutral nations, despite the heavy losses which several incurred from mines laid by the new German submarines, dared strongly to uphold the general right to the safe use of the seas.

Fear amongst neutrals

In one or two cases, a downright fear of Germanic invasion prevented any forcible measures of reprisal being taken—such as the stoppage of exports to the Teutonic Empires. In other cases, Court intrigues, intrigues with powerful military leaders in neutral States, intrigues with politicians of the reactionary school, and wide control over new agencies and other organs of popular expression kept the suffering neutral people silent over the wrongs done

Lieut.-General H. S. Horne, C.B., commanding an Army Corps.

[*Lafayette.*

Keeping off a night attack on the Western Front.
Handful of British soldiers firing star pistols and rifles at once to make believe that the position is held in force.

British soldiers clearing debris after an advance into enemy territory.

Tragic relics of "No Man's Land"—pathetic documents, photographs, discarded rifles, buckets, boxes, etc.

From billets to trenches by motor = bus : British soldiers about to board the familiar London vehicle somewhere in Flanders.

to their seamen and their ships. In the Germanic point of view, they had to balance their losses in shipping against the enormous wealth won by their forwarding firms supplying the German market. International law, which was but a convention without the sanction of force behind it, vanished, even from the fringe of non-belligerent countries round the volcanic area of war. Only fear and self-interest ruled. At the Hague Conference the modern German Machiavelli, Baron Marschall von Bieberstein, who took a very humanitarian, high-minded view of the restrictions of civilised warfare, observed that if any country abused mine-laying tactics it would be effectively checked by the dread of reprisals by neutral nations. This was an example of the opiate methods by which the most subtle and clever of modern German diplomatists stilled all fears, while his own robber State was completing her preparations for the conquest of the world. When Germany used mines in an absolutely reckless manner against the merchant shipping of all neutral nations it was too late for many of these nations to think of regaining their sea rights by reprisals. Germany had won in various ways the whip-hand of them.

Those neutral nations of Europe which had no reason to love Germany, but were growing rich at the expense of all the combatants, left the matter unsettled, hoping it would be decided by the power of the British Fleet and the final victory of the Allies. Meanwhile, many of them shared the burden of mercantile losses with us, but we had, at the beginning of 1916, a serious naval disaster in the destruction of H.M.S. King Edward VII.—a fine pre-Dreadnought battleship, launched in 1903, with a main armament of four 12 in. guns, four 9·2 in. and ten 6 in. guns. She had a speed of nineteen knots, and carried about eight hundred and twenty officers and men. With her seven sister ships, she constituted a swift, powerful, and homogeneous battle squadron of the second class. Struck by a mine in a heavy sea on January 9th, 1916, she foundered quickly, but happily, the ship's company was taken off without any loss of life, and only two men were injured.

Our Fleet was always ready for a decisive general action. Sir John Jellicoe's plan was to have everywhere stronger forces more immediately available than the forces which the enemy could send. Hence a curious kind of chess play between the opposing commanders. The appearance of a flotilla of German submarines in the North Sea would be answered by the movement of a flotilla of British destroyers; if the enemy submarines called for help and brought up their destroyers, with probably a reconnoitring Zeppelin, our flotilla would wireless to the British light cruisers. And here, as a rule, the affair stopped and the enemy retreated. Had the drawing-out process gone on to the battle-cruiser and battleship stage, the German High Sea Fleet would have been brought into the fray, and then the British Grand Fleet would have concentrated and the great struggle taken place.

Loss of the Edward VII.

Our warships were always exposed to Zeppelin reconnaissance and submarine attack, and to the peril of the new enemy mine-fields and drifting mines. We lost a mine-sweeper, the Arabis, on the Dogger Bank on February 10th, 1916, when four British mine-sweepers were chased by a German destroyer flotilla.

On February 11th, 1916, we had another loss from mines laid furtively by the new type of German submarines. The most famous of our light cruisers, the Arethusa, struck a mine off the East Coast, losing ten of her men and becoming a total wreck. The splendid fast little ship was one of the most popular craft in the Navy; and as a signal act of honour, the Admiralty had had engraved on a prominent place on her deck, beside her battle honours, the first verse of the ancient ditty:

> Come all ye jolly sailors bold,
>> Whose hearts are cast in honour's mould,
>>> While English glory I unfold,
>>>> Huzza for the Arethusa!
>>> Her men are staunch
>>>> To their favourite launch,
>> And when the foe shall meet our fire,
>>> Sooner than strike we'll all expire
>>>> On board the Arethusa.

She was the first oil-fired cruiser in our Fleet, having a speed of thirty knots, and was commissioned a few days after war was declared as the mother-ship of our leading destroyer flotilla. Under Commodore Reginald Y. Tyrwhitt she nobly distinguished herself in the Battle of Heligoland Bight, fighting till all her guns but one were put out of action and her speed reduced to six knots. Again, in the Dogger Bank Battle, she played a fine part and torpedoed

FLOATING PALACES ON WAR SERVICE.
The s.s. Olympic and Aquitania, which were utilised for war purposes, arriving simultaneously somewhere in the Mediterranean.

the Blücher. Among our other important losses during the period under review was the stranding of the armoured cruiser Argyll on the Scottish coast on October 28th, 1915. The Argyll had been launched in 1904, and with her four 7·5 in. and six 6 in. guns, and nominal speed of over twenty-two knots, she was a useful ship of a rather antiquated class. Another armoured cruiser of greater tonnage and heavier armament, the Natal, was blown up in harbour on December 30th, 1915, with a loss of three hundred officers and men out of her ship's company of seven hundred and four. The Natal was one of our crack gunnery ships, and her commander, Captain Eric P. C. Back, was a very fine gunnery officer. The mysterious destruction of the Natal reduced the thirty-four armoured cruisers with which we began the war to twenty-seven. But great as were our losses in this class of ship, the proportion of wastage was much higher among the enemy. The Germans started with a total of nine armoured cruisers, and of these only three remained at the end of 1915. So the war of attrition did not seem to be working well from the Teutonic point of view. To complete our list of naval losses we must mention the blowing-up of the Fleet auxiliary steamer Princess Irene, at Sheerness, on May 27th, 1915. Altogether we lost by mysterious and suspicious explosions the battleship Bulwark, the armoured cruiser Natal, and the ammunition steamer Princess Irene. One could not help thinking that there was a daring German agent at Sheerness who found means of entering some of our ships and leaving an infernal machine. The Italians lost an oldish battleship, the Benedetto Brin, by explosion in Brindisi Harbour on October 4th, 1915. In this case it was rumoured that a fascinating lady was conducted round the ship by an admiring officer, and that, by appearing very ignorant of everything she saw, she was able to put her guide off his guard and manage to leave in a dangerous place a little, timed explosive memorial of her visit.

A later naval mystery was half concealed and half revealed on February 1st, 1916, when the Elder-Dempster liner Appam, bound from the West Africa coast to Plymouth, was brought into harbour at Norfolk, U.S.A., by a German lieutenant of the naval reserve and a German prize crew. There were four hundred and nine British subjects on board, including the Governor of Sierra Leone, Sir Edward Merewether, and his wife, and the British crew and passengers of the Appam. In addition there were the crews of seven similar British steamers—the Corbridge, Farringford, Dromonby, Author, Trader, Ariadne and Clan MacTavish. The Corbridge and Farringford had been sunk off Cardiff on January 10th, the Appam captured off Madeira on January 16th, and the Clan MacTavish was sunk in a sharp action the following day. The German lieutenant said the name of the new commerce-raider was Moewe, but the British prisoners stated that the ship which captured them was the Ponga, commanded by Captain Count Dohna and worked by a company of three hundred and fifty picked men.

She was fitted with a false forecastle head that fell in an instant, leaving clear for action a powerful armament of 6 in. guns. The captain and crew of the Clan MacTavish, that mounted a 3 in. gun, had refused to surrender to this array of artillery, and had fought with splendid courage until the small gun jammed and the big German guns wrecked the steamer, killing some eleven men and wounding others. It was reported that the Ponga had been armed at Kiel and sent through the North Sea under the Swedish flag, and that six more German commerce raiders of the same power were ready at Kiel waiting to set out. But this extraordinary tale of evasion of our Grand Fleet's blockade cordon, after seventeen months of war, stood, at the time of writing, in need of verification.

The mystery of the Moewe Undoubtedly the Teuton was not lacking in subtlety, but we answered his attacks generally by both downright fighting strokes and tricks that were not always vain. While the battle-cruiser squadron and battleship squadrons on either side delayed to come to a decision, our submarine officers showed themselves superior to the commanders of the German U boats. They had no opportunity of striking at the German High Sea Fleet in the North Sea, as Admiral von Pohl seldom ventured to send his battle squadrons beyond the Heligoland mine-fields. But they carried the war into enemy waters—the Baltic and the Sea of Marmora—with a skill and venturesomeness in which the highest

traditions of our Navy were well maintained. We have already related the opening incident of our submarine campaign against the Turks, in which Lieutenant N. D Holbrook dived under five rows of mines in the Dardanelles and torpedoed the Turkish battleship Messudiyeh, which was guarding the mine-field. The extraordinary difficulties which Lieutenant Holbrook overcame in contending with the strong current in the narrow strait, and in keeping his boat on a true course, were illustrated by the disasters which befell Lieutenant-Commander T. S. Brodie in submarine E15. His boat was swung out of her course by the Dardanelles current, and stranded at Kephez Point on September 17th, 1915. It was feared that the fine modern submarine would fall almost undamaged into the hands of the enemy. But Lieutenant C. G. MacArthur in a small, old-fashioned boat, B6, made two very enterprising reconnaissances off Kephez **Heroism under Turkish fire** Point on the same day, and though shelled by the Turkish batteries and very seriously endangered, saved his ship and brought back valuable information. Thereupon Commander Eric Robinson, with the picket-boats of the Triumph and Majestic, each officered by a gallant midshipman, made a night expedition to Kephez Point on April 18th, and torpedoed E15 to prevent her from falling in a serviceable condition into the hands of the Turks. The enemy forts swept the picket-boats with a heavy fire, and the Majestic's boat was holed and sunk.

We seem to have lost altogether four submarines in the Dardanelles. AE2, the submarine of the Royal Australian Navy, was sunk by Turkish warships in May, 1915, when trying to enter the Sea of Marmora, the commander and his men being made prisoners. The E7, missing since September 4th, 1915, was supposed to have been snared in proceeding to a rendezvous in the Sea of Marmora. E20

THE SHIP THAT DEFIED THE DISGUISED GERMAN RAIDER.
The Clan MacTavish, the vessel which pluckily defied and fought the disguised German raider Moewe or Ponga, continuing to fire her single 3 in. gun after she had been set afire by the German shells Ultimately she was torpedoed and sunk. Inset portrait: Captain W. N. Oliver, of the Clan MacTavish

was sunk in the same waters on November 5th, 1915, four officers being taken prisoners. One of these disasters seems to have been connected with the loss of the small French submarine Mariotte, which was rumoured to have been sunk by a more modern and more powerful German submarine in the Sea of Marmora on July 26th, 1915. It is thought that a note of the place fixed for the rendezvous of British and French underwater craft in the Marmora Sea was discovered by the Germans in the wrecked Mariotte. A still smaller French submarine, of only 386 tons, the Turquoise, was also sunk in the Sea of Marmora on October 30th, 1915, while early in May the Joule, a 550-ton boat, was mined in the Dardanelles, and in January the Saphir, of 390 tons, was lost while attempting to equal the feat of Lieutenant Holbrook.

But all these losses were outbalanced by the achievements of our submarines in the Sea of Marmora. Lieutenant-Commander E. C. Boyle, in command of submarine E14,

THE CAPTURED APPAM.
With a German flag at her stern, the Appam was taken to the port of Norfolk, Virginia, after being captured off Madeira, on January 16th, 1916, by the Moewe, the German cruiser that prowled the Atlantic disguised as a tramp.

won the V.C. by an eventful voyage through the Dardanelles on April 27th, 1915. After fighting his way through the enemy mine-field, he had great trouble to escape the currents that had wrecked the E15, and after overcoming the currents he was in danger from hostile patrol boats and shore batteries. But he remained in the narrow waters of the Strait, where he sank a Turkish gunboat before entering his easier field of activity, the Marmora Sea. In this wider and more tranquil stretch of waters he opened operations on April 29th by sinking a Turkish transport; four days afterwards he destroyed another Turkish gunboat and sank a large transport full of troops. On May 13th he forced a steamer to run aground, and on May 18th he returned safely through the Strait. It was Commander Boyle's work in extending Lieutenant Holbrook's warlike explorations of the Strait which completely opened the Sea of Marmora to the allied underwater craft. By the end of September, 1915, the E boats, ranging from Constantinople to our Mudros base, had so interrupted and disorganised the sea-borne supplies of the Turkish army on the Gallipoli Peninsula that if Germany, Austria, and Bulgaria had not opened the land route through Serbia to Constantinople our Mediterranean Expeditionary Force might have won the Dardanelles "gamble" though the exhaustion of the enemy.

Our submarine campaign in the Marmora Sea was conducted in as chivalrous a manner as possible, yet its military results, and its effect upon the civilian population in Constantinople, were very striking. Especially when our torpedoes exploded about the arsenal of the capital, the Turkish people were ready to give up

E14's brilliant work

the struggle, and a strong peace party was formed headed by the heir to the throne, whom Enver Pasha afterwards assassinated. The Germans tried to net the Strait against our underwater boats, and brought their best submarine officer, Hersing, to Constantinople to devise more defensive measures, and six or more German submarines operated round the Ottoman capital. But no defence was found against our astonishingly daring underwater attacks. In one extraordinary action, of which no official details have yet been given, a British submarine rose by the Turkish coast and fought against a squadron of Ottoman cavalry. The men on deck, handling the gun and sniping with rifles, were swept by the enemy's fire, but they stuck to their strange work, and routed the hostile horsemen.

Still more remarkable was the feat of Lieutenant G. D'Oyly Hughes, serving in submarine E11. On August 21st, 1915, he swam alone from the submarine to the shore near the Ismid railway line. He took with him on his long swim some explosive, and with this he blew up the brickwork support of the Turkish railway. There was an armed guard scarcely a hundred and fifty yards from the spot, in the enemy's line of communication, which he attacked. The gallant lieutenant fought a running fight with them for about a mile, and then dived back into the sea, and swam for another mile in his clothes, being at last picked up utterly exhausted by his comrades in E11. This submarine, of which Lieutenant-Commander Martin Nasmith was chief officer, spread terror through the Sea of Marmora to the capital of the Ottoman Empire. In June, 1915, Lieutenant-Commander Nasmith sank a large Turkish transport, a vessel containing a large quantity of ammunition, and then chased a supply ship filled with stores, and

COMMANDER OF THE GERMAN PRIZE CREW
Lieutenant Berg, chief of the prize crew from the Moewe that took the Appam to Norfolk, U.S.A. Left: Mr. Hamilton, collector of the port, who demanded the release of the British passengers.

THE MEN WHO CAPTURED THE APPAM.
The prize crew from the German raiding cruiser which, under Lieutenant Berg, captured the British liner. The German warship's exploit forms a romantic incident in the drama of the war at sea. In addition to being disguised cunningly as a tramp, the raider feigned distress, and thus deceived the Appam into steaming to her assistance.

torpedoed her alongside Rodosto Pier. A small store-ship was next met and forced to run ashore, and as a crowning exploit the British submarine officer penetrated into the harbour of Constantinople and torpedoed a transport lying alongside the arsenal. The Goeben, Breslau, and other warships were, however, protected by heavily laden boats being moored alongside them to form a rampart, and they could not be reached.

Lieutenant-Commander Cochrane, in E7, did some great work before his boat was sunk in September, 1915. He swept the Sea of Marmora of much enemy shipping, and then turned his gun on the Turkish railway line near Kava Burnu. After blocking the line by bombarding it from the sea, he shelled a troop-train and blew up three ammunition waggons attached to it.

Lieutenant-Commander K. M. Bruce, with Lieutenant W. B. Pirie, likewise made a prolonged cruise in the Sea of Marmora, during the course of which they did much damage to enemy shipping, and outfought by gun fire a Turkish destroyer and a gunboat, put both to flight, and returned to their base, after extricating their submarine from a very difficult position. Their work of destroying Turkish shipping was continued in November, 1915, by Lieutenant-Commander David de Beauvoir Stocks. Another British submarine officer, whose name has not been published, torpedoed on August 8th, 1915, the last Turkish battleship, the Hairredin Barbarossa, a 10,060-ton ship, carrying six 11 in. and eight 4·1 in. guns, built in 1891 for the German Navy, and sold in 1910 to the Ottoman Government.

Turkish shipping destroyed

Down to October, 1915, it was reckoned that there had been sunk in the Dardanelles and the Marmora Sea, mainly by British submarines, two battleships, five gunboats, one torpedo-boat, and one hundred and ninety-seven supply boats. And as E boats continued to operate in November and December, 1915, in the waters around Constantinople, the total damage done to Turkish shipping must have sadly impeded the transport of war material and troops from the European to the Asiatic shore during the winter campaigns in Mesopotamia, the Caucasus and Persia. Thus the strength of our new arm in underwater warfare told on the fortunes of land wars in places far distant from the scene of the operations of the E boats.

Effect on Baltic operations

And while telling heavily against the Turkish military and naval power in the southern waters of the Dardanelles and the Marmora Sea, the superb submarine force of Britain bore still harder upon the industrial military and naval power of Germany in the northern waters of the Baltic. In the spring and summer of 1915 the Germans were able to bring strong naval forces to the Courland coast to help the advance of the army under General von Below. On March 23rd, for example, seven German battleships and twenty-eight torpedo craft cruised off Courland, shelling towns, villages, and roads used by Russian troops, and Libau was captured on May 9th. Early in June enemy surface warships, with submarines and reconnoitring aircraft, began to appear off the Gulf of Riga, and the Russian transport Yenissei was torpedoed and sunk on

UNDER THE BROAD SKY AND ROCKED ON THE RESTLESS SEA.
In place of a bunk, the iron deck of a destroyer and a few tarpaulins. How British sailors on patrol duty in the North Sea managed to secure a brief respite from their trying vigil round our coasts.

THE LEVANTINE MECCA OF TWO WESTERN POWERS: MUDROS HARBOUR IN WAR TIME.
Just as all roads once led to Rome, so did all courses in the Mediterranean during the war lead to Mudros. This ancient port of Lemnos Island was a sort of half-way house to the allied positions in the Levant. A scene of unparalleled animation confronted the eye from the harbour. Ships of all sizes—ironclads, transports, windjammers, and cutters—found their way here on the business of war. Our allies also made Mudros a base.

June 6th. On the other hand, three German vessels were likewise sunk, and soon afterwards an attempt to storm Windau from the sea was defeated by our ally's torpedo-boats, which sank a German mine-sweeper. Then on July 2nd an enemy mine-layer, the Albatros, was driven ashore on Gothland during an action between Russian and German battle squadrons.

It was in this action that our Baltic submarine flotilla won its first striking success. Commander Max Horton, the "double-toothed" pirate who had sunk **The Pommern torpedoed** a German light cruiser and a German destroyer in the North Sea, had penetrated, in E9, far into the Baltic, and on July 2nd, 1915, he torpedoed the enemy battleship Pommern —the first German capital ship damaged by the British. She was a vessel of the Deutschland class, ten years old, with four 11 in. guns and fourteen 6·7 in. guns, six torpedo-tubes, and 9¾ in. armour amidships. Her fighting value was rather higher than our lost Formidable.

Then, on July 30th, when Below was pressing forward in Courland and in need of reinforcements, one of his large transports, full of troops, was torpedoed by another British submarine, under Commander Noel F. Laurence. The same gallant officer played a decisive part in the great naval action in the Gulf of Riga that lasted from August 18th to 21st, 1915. We have already described, from the Russian point of view, the principal events of this naval attack on Riga. A German fleet, consisting of nine battleships, twelve cruisers, and strong destroyer flotillas, tried to force the passage of Moon Sound and the northern entrance to the gulf. Fog interrupted the execution of the enemy's plan to capture Riga from the sea, and the old

Russian battleship Slava and the gunboat Sivoutch fought splendidly inside the gulf and destroyed several small craft. But the blow that staggered and daunted the German admiral was delivered by Commander Laurence outside the gulf. The enemy's battle-cruiser squadron, including the Seydlitz and Moltke, was acting as a supporting force to the ships engaged near Riga, and the British submarine succeeded in stealing quite close. Commander Laurence released a torpedo at the Seydlitz, and narrowly missed her; then he shot at the Moltke, and struck her in the bow, crushing in one of the torpedo chambers. Four hundred and thirty-five tons of water entered the hull, but as 1,500 tons was needed to overcome the buoyancy of the watertight bulkhead system, the battle-cruiser was able to get safely to a repairing port. Nevertheless, Commander Laurence's blow at one of the finest of the enemy's ships had an effect more decisive than Lieutenant-Commander von Hersing's attack on the Triumph and Majestic in the Dardanelles earlier in the year. The German admiral, **Disaster to the E13** reported to have been Admiral von Ingenohl, feared to risk any more of his capital ships against British submarines, and broke off the naval operations against Riga and the right wing of the Russian armies.

On the same day as the Moltke was torpedoed there occurred the first disaster to our Baltic submarine flotilla. E13, under Lieutenant-Commander Layton, was passing in darkness through the Sound, but he grounded in the early morning on the Danish island of Saltholm, near Copenhagen, in the southern mouth of the Sound. At 5 a.m. a Danish torpedo-boat appeared by the island and the officer gave

AFTER A BRUSH WITH THE TURKS NEAR THE TIGRIS.
British troops re-embarking on board one of our ships on the River Tigris after a fight with the Turks in Mesopotamia, along the desert way to Bagdad. Note the machine-guns at the side.

thirty men were interned, which was a loss of a finely-trained crew. Yet another boat was stranded and lost a few days later.

These strandings, however, were the only British submarine disasters in northern waters reported since D3 was mined off Yarmouth in November, 1914. As against them, we had in the Baltic operations a long, magnificent series of successes. After the murderous attack on Lieutenant-Commander Layton and the crew of E13, the Germans laid a new mine-field in the Sound between Denmark and Sweden, and later they so increased the extent of this field that only the narrow, shallow strip of Danish and Swedish territorial waters was left open. Moreover, the Swedish Government put out the lights on their coast in order to make the passage through the Sound on the Swedish side impossible during the night. But our E boats continued to penetrate, by mystic ways, into the Baltic.

On October 13tn, 1915, a remarkable naval action was witnessed off the Danish island of Moen, by the east coast of Zealand. Through the mist flashes were seen and the slam of guns came on the air. A German cruiser and three German torpedo-boats were fighting a single British submarine. The enemy vessels manœuvred in circles at high speed in order to avoid being torpedoed, but a loud explosion was heard and one of the torpedo-boats vanished. The cruiser and remaining torpedo craft then fled, and the grey form of E19 emerged and remained visible for some time. The next day there was another action between E19 and a German torpedo-boat off the island of Faroe, in which the enemy vessel was sunk. A greater British success was achieved off Libau on October 23rd, when the German armoured cruiser Prinz Adalbert, laid down in 1900, and armed with four 8·2 in., ten 5·9 in., and twelve 3·4 in. guns, was torpedoed by one of our submarines. Two torpedoes struck home, causing the ship to sink so quickly that most of her company was lost,

The German naval men in the Baltic were thoroughly "rattled" by this rapid series of British strokes. Among other wild things showing the condition of their nerves was an attack, on October **Undine and Bremen** 21st, 1915, on the Swedish submarine **sunk** Hvalen, which was swept by gun fire by a German U boat and damaged, an officer and a man being badly wounded. Lieutenant-Commander F. N. Cromie was among the British submarine commanders who won distinction in the Baltic as winter approached. He began his passage through the Sound during a severe bout of influenza, and directed operations from his bed. On November 7th he tried a spot in open waters where the train ferry between Germany and Sweden passed, but his plan was spoilt by two German destroyers and a cruiser, who stopped him in an exciting chase after the ferry. He dived when they left him,

the commander of E13 twenty-four hours in which to try and get the boat refloated. At the same time a German destroyer arrived on the scene, and stayed close to the E boat until two more Danish torpedo craft came up. The enemy vessel then withdrew, but at nine o'clock in the morning two German destroyers steamed in from the south, and at a distance of three hundred yards one of them fired a torpedo, which hit the bottom of the sea close to the stranded British boat and exploded. At the same time the enemy destroyer opened fire with all her guns and machine-guns. The helpless British crew was taken unawares by this illegal, murderous attack. The E boat was in Danish territory, with three Danish torpedo craft anchored close to her, and in her stranded condition she could not fight. Our men were cut down by shrapnel and machine-gun bullets while struggling in the water, and fifteen of them were killed before one of the Danish torpedo-boats steamed between the submarine and the German destroyer and made the murderers cease fire and withdraw.

We lost another submarine also by stranding, on January 6th, 1916, on the Haags Bank, off the Dutch island of Texel. The crew of thirty-three men and officers were happily rescued by a Dutch cruiser. The rescue occurred outside Dutch territorial waters, but the three British officers and

The s.s. Clacton under fire in the Dardanelles. Just prior to the taking of this photograph three men were killed by shrapnel. Another projectile is seen bursting in the same spot. The picture was secured as the Australians were landing at Gaba Tepe.

In view of the activity of Turkish artillery on the days when Gallipoli was being evacuated, it was nothing short of a miracle that so few casualties occurred. The above photograph shows a Turkish shell bursting near the pier at Lancashire Landing, Cape Helles.

HOW THE BRITISH ENTERED AND EVACUATED FATEFUL GALLIPOLI.

MAP OF THE ÆGEAN SEA, ONE OF THE PRINCIPAL AREAS OF ALLIED AND ENEMY SUBMARINE
ACTIVITY IN 1915-1916.

OUR "MOSQUITO FLEET" ON PATROL DUTY.
Destroyers setting out to look for "fun" in the shape of U boats, or even bigger game, in the North Sea.

reckoning they would soon return to renew their search after him. So it befell. The cruiser was the Undine, convoying the German steam ferry Prussia from Trelleborg to Sassintz. When she returned for battle, with her two assistant destroyers, Lieutenant Cromie torpedoed her and set her on fire. Then, as a glimpse through the periscope showed him she was not sinking, he dived his boat beneath her stern, and gave her another torpedo on the opposite side.

The Undine was a small cruiser of 2,715 tons, thirteen years old, armed with ten 4·1 in. guns, ten one-pounders, and two torpedo-tubes, with two-inch deck armour. A more improved vessel of a similar class was the Bremen, a 1903 ship of 3,250 tons, with the same armament and armour, but larger size. The Bremen, with other light cruisers of the town class, was sent out with destroyer flotillas, swarms of trawlers, and Zeppelin airships, in a determined effort to hunt down our E boats in the Baltic, as our Grand Fleet had hunted down the U boats round the British Isles. But the E boats fought with daring and skill. They sunk the Bremen on December 17th, 1915, and another German torpedo-boat. About the same time the German patrol boat Bunz was sunk, and to complete the list of German naval losses to the end of 1915, on the remote waters of Lake Tanganyika the armed enemy steamer Kingani was destroyed by British sailors on December 26th.

Meanwhile, our fighting underwater flotilla in the Baltic was ruining German trade with Sweden, **Panic in German** and completing the blockade cordon **Baltic ports** round the Central Empires. Had our Foreign Office allowed, a formal blockade of Germany could have been proclaimed by October, 1915, for the E boats, without resorting to furtive mine-laying, and with mighty German naval forces actively opposing them, broke down both enemy seaborne trade and enemy troop transport in the northern midland sea. The cargo steamers stopped and sunk were very numerous, and the import of fine Swedish iron ore, vitally needed for military purposes, was impeded until the Swedish port from which it came was icebound. German and Swedish insurance rates greatly increased, and some underwriters even refused to cover the German risks against British submarines. All German ships taking the Baltic north and south route had to keep within territorial waters. This augmented the difficulties of navigation, owing to the irregular coast-line of Sweden and the long fringe of islands. Moreover, an enormous number of mines got adrift in the Baltic, and added to the danger to shipping. The German mine-fields in the Sound were ineffective, the mines continually break-

ON ESCORT DUTY.
Scene aboard a British destroyer, on escort duty, while she was convoying an oil vessel to her destination.

ing loose; even in the Great Belt the Danish mines could not be made to keep their anchorage. The intense activity of our submarines, amid all the deadly confusion, produced a feeling of panic in German Baltic ports. So great were the losses to German shipping that information concerning most of the lost steamers was suppressed in the enemy's newspapers. As the Danish Government organ, the "Politiken," observed :

The tables are now turned on Germany in waters where the Germans have hitherto been unchallenged masters. This form of British warfare is no doubt exceedingly inconvenient to Germany, though the rigour of it is much mitigated, no neutral ships being molested ; but Britain nevertheless hits harder than her opponent, because the effective isolation of Germany is being brought about. The submarine war against British commerce was a mere pinprick, as British supplies were in no way impeded, but the loss of a similar amount of tonnage would lame Germany.

We conclude this chapter with the following rough statement of allied and enemy naval losses up to January, 1916, so far as these can be established from official and well-informed sources.

ALLIED AND ENEMY NAVAL LOSSES:
AUGUST, 1914, TO JANUARY, 1916.

BRITISH NAVAL LOSSES.
BATTLESHIPS.

Name.	How Lost or Damaged.	Date.	Tonnage.	Place.
Bulwark	Blown up (accident)	26–11–14	15,000	Sheerness
Formidable	Torpedoed	1–1–15	,,	Eng. Channel
Irresistible	Mined	18–3–15	,,	Dardanelles
Ocean	,,	,,	12,950	,,
Goliath (500 lives)	Torpedoed	13–5–15	,,	,,
Triumph	,,	25–5–15	11,800 (normal displacement)	,,
Majestic	,,	27–5–15	14,900	,,
K. Edwd. VII.	Mined	9–1–15	16,350 (normal displacement)	—

CRUISERS.

Name.	How Lost or Damaged.	Date.	Tonnage.	Place.
Good Hope	Gun fire	1–11–14	14,700	Off Chili
Aboukir	Torpedoed	22–9–14	12,000	North Sea
Cressy	,,	,,	,,	,,
Hogue	,,	,,	,,	,,
Monmouth	Gun fire	1–11–14	9,800	Pacific
Hawke	Torpedoed	15–10–14	7,350	North Sea
Hermes	,,	31–10–14	5,600	Dover
Amphion	Mined	6–8–14	3,440	North Sea
Pathfinder	Torpedoed	5–9–14	2,940	,,
Pegasus	Gun fire	20–9–15	2,135	Zanzibar
Argyll	Grounded	28–10–15	10,850	East Coast, Scotland
Natal	Blown up	30–12–15	13,550	In harbour
Arethusa	Mined	14–2–16	3,520	Off East Coast

GUNBOATS.

Name.	How Lost or Damaged.	Date.	Tonnage.	Place.
Speedy	Mined	3–9–14	810	North Sea
Niger	Torpedoed	11–11–14	,,	Eng. Channel
Arabis (mine-sweeper)	,,	10–2–16	—	Dogger Bank

DESTROYERS.

Name.	How Lost or Damaged.	Date.	Tonnage.	Place.
Lightning	Mined or torpedoed	30–6–14	290	Off East Coast
Recruit	Torpedoed	1–5–15	350	North Sea
Maori	Mined	7–5–15	1,035	Belgian Coast
Lynx	,,	9–8–15	935	North Sea
Louis	Stranded	Nov. '15	965	E. Mediter.

SUBMARINES.

Name.	How Lost or Damaged.	Date.	Tonnage.	Place.
AE1	Foundered	14–9–15	725	Australia
E3	Destroyed by enemy	18–10–15	,,	North Sea
D5	Mined	3–11–15	550	,,
E15	Stranded	17–4–15	800	Dardanelles
AE2	Sunk, gun fire	30–4–15	725	,,
E13	Wrecked	19–8–15	?	Saltholm Is.
E7	Sunk	20–9–15	?	Dardanelles
E20	Sunk	5–11–15	800	,,
?	Wrecked	6–1–16	?	Dutch Coast

TORPEDO-BOATS.

Name.	How Lost or Damaged.	Date.	Tonnage.	Place.
No. 10	Torpedoed	11–6–15	255	North Sea
No. 12	,,	,,	225	,,
No. 96	Sunk in collis.	1–11–15	130	Str. Gibraltar

ARMED MERCHANTMEN AND AUXILIARIES.

Name.	How Lost or Damaged.	Date.	Tonnage.	Place.
Oceanic	Wrecked	8–9–15	7,333	North Sea
Rohilla	Wrecked	30–10–15	4,240	Off Whitby
Viknor	Sunk	Jan. '15	—	North of Ireland
Bayano	Torpedoed	11–3–15	5,984	Firth Clyde
Clan Mac Naughton	Sunk	3–2–15	4,985	—
Pncss. Irene	Blown up	27–5–15	—	Sheerness
India	Torpedoed	8–9–15	—	North Sea
Ramsey (patrol)	Sunk, gun fire	,,	—	,,
Tara	Torpedoed	5–11–15	—	Eastern Med.
Hythe	Sunk in collision	28–10–15	—	Gallipoli

FRENCH NAVAL LOSSES.
BATTLESHIPS.

Name.	How Lost or Damaged.	Date.	Tonnage.	Place.
Bouvet	Mined	18–5–15	12,000	Dardanelles

CRUISERS.

Name.	How Lost or Damaged.	Date.	Tonnage.	Place.
Leon Gambetta	Torpedoed	26–4–15	12,350	Ionian Sea
Amiral Charner	,,	8–2–16	,,	Syrian Coast

GUNBOATS.

Name.	How Lost or Damaged.	Date.	Tonnage.	Place.
Zelee	Gun fire	28–10–14	680	Tahiti

DESTROYERS.

Name.	How Lost or Damaged.	Date.	Tonnage.	Place.
Mousquet	Gun fire	28–10–14	303	—

SUBMARINES.

Name.	How Lost or Damaged.	Date.	Tonnage.	Place.
Saphir	Sunk	Jan. 1915	390	Dardanelles
Curie	Destroyed	Dec. 1915	398	Pola
Mariette	Sunk	26–7–15	530	Sea Marmora
Turquoise	Sunk	30–10–15	386	,,
Joule	Mined	1–5–15	550	Dardanelles
Fresnel	Destroyed	5–12–15	400	Adriatic

TORPEDO-BOATS.

Name.	How Lost or Damaged.	Date.	Tonnage.	Place.
347	Collision	9–10–14	98	Iles de Porquerolles
338	,,	,,	97	
Dague	Mined	24–2–15	730	Antivari

French Naval Losses (continued)

ARMED MERCHANTMEN AND AUXILIARIES.

Name.	How Lost or Damaged.	Date.	Tonnage.	Place.
Casa Blanca (mine-layer)	Mined	3-6-15	—	Ægean Sea
Indien . .	Torpedoed	8-9-15	800	,,

RUSSIAN NAVAL LOSSES.
CRUISERS.

Name.	How Lost or Damaged.	Date.	Tonnage.	Place.
Pallada . .	Torpedoed	11-10-14	775	Baltic
Jemchug . .	,,	28-10-14	3,050	Penang

GUNBOATS.

Name.	How Lost or Damaged.	Date.	Tonnage.	Place.
Donetz . .	Gun fire	29-10-14	1,200	—
Sivoutch .	,,	20-8-15	875	Riga Gulf

ARMED MERCHANTMEN AND AUXILIARIES.

Name.	How Lost or Damaged.	Date.	Tonnage.	Place.
Prut . .	Scuttled to avoid capture	29-10-14	5,500	—

JAPANESE NAVAL LOSSES.
CRUISERS.

Name.	How Lost or Damaged.	Date.	Tonnage.	Place.
Takachiho .	Mined	17-10-14	3,700	Kiao-Chau
Asama . .	Aground	Feb. '15	9,750	Mexican cst.

TORPEDO-BOATS.

Name.	How Lost or Damaged.	Date.	Tonnage.	Place.
33 . . .	Mined	11-11-14	110	—

ITALIAN NAVAL LOSSES.
BATTLESHIPS.

Name.	How Lost or Damaged.	Date.	Tonnage.	Place.
Benedetto Brin . .	Fire and explosion	4-10-15	13,214	Brindisi Harbour

CRUISERS.

Name.	How Lost or Damaged.	Date.	Tonnage.	Place.
Amalfi . .	Torpedoed	7-7-15	10,000	Adriatic
Giuseppe Garibaldi	,,	18-7-15	7,240	,,

DESTROYERS.

Name.	How Lost or Damaged.	Date.	Tonnage.	Place.
Turbine	Torpedoed	24-5-15	—	Adriatic

SUBMARINES.

Name.	How Lost or Damaged.	Date.	Tonnage.	Place.
Medusa . .	Torpedoed	June '15	241	—
Nereide .	Sunk	Aug. '15		Adriatic

TORPEDO-BOATS.

Name.	How Lost or Damaged.	Date.	Tonnage.	Place.
Torpedo-boat	Torpedoed	26-6-15	—	Adriatic

GERMAN NAVAL LOSSES.
BATTLESHIPS.

Name.	How Lost or Damaged.	Date.	Tonnage.	Place.
Pommern .	Sunk	2-7-15	12,997	Baltic

CRUISERS.

Name.	How Lost or Damaged.	Date.	Tonnage.	Place.
Scharnhorst	Gun fire	8-12-14	11,600	Falklands
Gneisenau .	,,	,,	,,	,,
Yorck . .	Mined	3-11-14	9,050	North Sea
Magdeburg	Gun fire	27-8-14	4,550	Gulf Finland
Koln . .	,,	28-8-14	4,350	Heligoland
Mainz . .	,,	,,	,,	,,
Emden . .	,,	9-11-14	3,600	Pacific
Nurnberg .	,,	8-12-14	3,450	Falklands
Leipzig . .	,,	,,	3,250	,,
Ariadne . .	,,	28-8-14	2,660	Heligoland
Hela . .	Torpedoed	13-9-14	2,040	North Sea
Geier . .	Interned	9-11-14	1,604	Honolulu
Cormoran .	—	6-11-14		Tsingtau
Konigsberg	Ashore in (destroyed by monitors)	July '15 4th-11th July '15	3,400	East Africa
Bluecher .	Gun fire	24-1-15	15,600	North Sea
Friedrich Karl	—	Nov. '14	8,858	Baltic
Kolberg. . Reported by German pnr.	Gun fire	24-1-15	4,280	North Sea
Dresden .		14-3-15	3,544	Pacific
Karlsruhe .	Explosion	Nov. '14	4,822	West Indies
Prinz Adalbert	Torpedoed	24-10-15	9,000	Baltic (Brit. submarine)
Undine . .	,,	7-11-15	9,000	Baltic
Bremen . .	,,	17-12-15	3,200	,,
Hertha . .	Sunk	Oct. '14	—	,,

GUNBOATS.

Name.	How Lost or Damaged.	Date.	Tonnage.	Place.
Tiger . .	—	6-11-14	900	Tsingtau
Iltis . .	—	,,	,,	,,
Jaguar . .	—	,,	,,	,,
Luchs . .	—	,,	,,	,,
Mowe . .	Gun fire	9-9-14	650	S.W. Africa
Hedwig von Wissmann	Captured	20-8-14	199	—
Tsingtau .	Interned or sunk by Germans	17-8-14	168	Canton or Kiao-Chau
Vaterland .	Interned	Aug. '14	,,	Nanking
Eber . .	,,	Sept. '14	977	Brazil
Gunboat .	Ashore	3-8-15	—	Nr. Windau
Soden . .	Captured	30-9-14	—	—
Cormoran .	Sunk	8-10-14	—	Kiao-Chau

DESTROYERS.

Name.	How Lost or Damaged.	Date.	Tonnage.	Place.
V187 . .	Gun fire	28-8-14	650	Heligoland, by British
S126 . .	Torpedoed	6-10-14	487	—
S119 . .	Gun fire	17-10-14	,,	Sunk as S115
S118 . .	,,	,,	,,	,,
S117 . .	,,	,,	,,	,,
S115 . .	,,	,,	,,	North Sea
S90 . . .	Driven ashore by Japanese	20-10-14	400	Tsingtau
Taku . .	,,	6-11-14	280	,,
G196 Class .	Torped. & snk. by B. sub.	26-7-15	650	Nr. German coast
Three (?) .	Sunk by R.	20-8-15	—	Riga Gulf
? . .	,,	22-8-15	—	Off Ostend
? . .	Torpedoed	14-10-15	—	Baltic
Unknown .	Sunk by German mine	4-8-14	—	North Sea
Taku . .	Sunk	8-14	—	Heligoland
S116 . .	,,	7-9-15	—	Kiao-Chau
? . .	,,	6-10-14	—	North Sea
? . .	,,	29-1-15	—	Off Denmrk.
? . .	,,	17-8-15	—	G. Riga
? . .	Sunk in col.	24-8-15	—	Off Ostend
? . .		15-10-15	—	Baltic

German Naval Losses (continued)
SUBMARINES.

Name.	How Lost or Damaged.	Date.	Tonnage.	Place.
U18 . .	Rammed	23-11-14	650	Off Scotland
U15 . .	,,	9-8-14	250	,,
U? . . .	—	24-10-14	,,	,,
— . . .	—	4-3-15	,,	,,
U8 . . .	Sunk by Dest. flot.	5-3-15	,,	Forth ? Dover ?
U12 . .	Rammed by Ariel	10-3-15	—	Firth Forth
U29 . .	Sunk	Mar. '15	—	—
Two (?) . .	Destroyed	26-3-15	—	Hoboken Air Raid
U14 . .	Sunk	June '15	—	—
U30 . .	Foundered	25-6-15	—	Mouth of Ems
U? . . .	Rammed by Thordis	28-2-15	—	Beachy Head
U ? . .	,,	—	—	Dantzic Bay
U? . . .	Bombed by aero. by Bigsworth	26-8-15	—	Off Ostend
U27 . .	Missing (Germ. offic. report)	10-8-15 about	—	Off Hebrides
U8 . . .	Interned	7-11-15 about	—	Terschelling
U? . . .	Destroyed by patrol boat	July '15	—	Irish Sea— (after encounter with s.s. Cottingham
U? . .	Bombed by aero. and sunk	28-11-15	—	Off Middelkerke
— . . .	Sunk	24-9-15	—	Off Belgian Coast
— . . .	,,	,,	—	,,

TORPEDO-BOATS.

Name.	How Lost or Damaged.	Date.	Tonnage.	Place.
Torpedo-boat	Torpedoed	29-1-15	—	Baltic
Two . . .	Sunk	1-5-15	—	Off Dutch Coast
? . . .	Collision	15-10-15	—	Baltic
? . . .	Torpedoed	17-12-15	—	,,
? . . .	Sunk by mine	28-6-15	—	,,
? . . .	Sunk	24-9-15	—	Off Belgium

ARMED MERCHANTMEN AND AUXILIARIES.

Name.	How Lost or Damaged.	Date.	Tonnage.	Place.
Cap Trafalgar	Gun fire	14-9-14	9,854	Off Brazil
Berlin .	Interned	Nov. '14	9,834	Trondhjem
Kaiser Wilh. der Grosse	Gun fire (sunk)	27-8-14	5,521	West Africa
Bethania .	Captured	7-9-14	4,848	Jamaica
Karnak .	Interned	Nov. '14	4,437	Chile
Markomannia	Captured or sunk	12-10-14	2,840	Off Aimaur Island
Spreewald .	,,	12-9-14	2,414	North Atlantic
Grætia . .	,,	10-10-14	1,697	Gibraltar or N. Atlantic
Locksun .	Interned	8-11-14	1,020	Honolulu
Konigin Luise	Gun fire	5-8-14	945	North Sea
Ruchin . .	—	6-11-14	—	Tsingtau
Ophelia .	Captured	7-10-14	1,153	London
Itolo . .	Gun fire	Sept. '14	165	Off West Africa
Rhios . .	,,	,,	150	West Africa
Soden . .	Captured	,,	,,	,,
Macedonia .	,,	March '15	4,300	Las Palmas
Prince Eitel Friedrich	Interned	,,	—	Newport News
Kronprinz Wilhelm	,,	April 15	—	,,
Albatross (minelayer)	Ashore in Gothland	2-7-15	—	Baltic
Meteor . .	Blown up to avoid capture	8-8-15	3,613	North Sea
Prinz Adalbert	Captured	Aug. '14	—	Off Falmouth
Sudmark .	,,	15-8-14	—	,,
Max Brock .	,,	Sept. '14	—	Duala
Gneisnau .	Sunk	,,	—	Off Antwerp
Komet . .	Captured	14-10-14	—	Off New Guinea
Eleonore Woermann	Sunk	6-1-15	—	Pacific

TURKISH NAVAL LOSSES.
BATTLESHIPS.

Name.	How Lost or Damaged.	Date.	Tonnage.	Place.
Messudieh .	Torpedoed	13-12-14	10,000	Dardanelles
Haireddin Barbarossa	,,	9-8-15	,,	Marmora

CRUISERS.

Name.	How Lost or Damaged.	Date.	Tonnage.	Place.
Hamidieh .	Mined, seriously damaged	12-12-14	3,830	Bosphorus
Medjideah .	Mined	3-4-15	3,400	Near Odessa

GUNBOATS.

Name.	How Lost or Damaged.	Date.	Tonnage.	Place.
Burak Reis	Scuttled to avoid capture	31-10-14	500	—
Issa Reiss type	Sunk	Dec. 1914	420	Bosphorus
Issa Reiss type	,,	Jan. 1915	,,	,,
G. B. (?)	,,	15-2-15	—	,,
Two . .	Sunk (E14)	May, 1915	—	Marmora
Berk-I-Satvet .	Torpedoed	8-8-15	163	
Boura Kreis type	Sunk	—	—	Black Sea
Malatia type	,,	—	—	,,

DESTROYERS.

Name.	How Lost or Damaged.	Date.	Tonnage.	Place.
Yar Hissa .	Torpedoed	3-12-15	280	Marmora

TORPEDO-BOATS.

Name.	How Lost or Damaged.	Date.	Tonnage.	Place.
Demir Hissa	Ashore	17-4-15	97	Chios
Three . .	Lost	Feb. 1915	—	Bosphorus

ARMED MERCHANTMEN AND AUXILIARIES.

Name.	How Lost or Damaged.	Date.	Tonnage.	Place.
Transport .	Sunk	2-1-15	—	Bosphorus
Transport (empty)	Torpedoed	Aug. '15	—	Dardanelles
—	—	12-8-15	—	,,

AUSTRIAN NAVAL LOSSES.
CRUISERS.

Name.	How Lost or Damaged.	Date.	Tonnage.	Place.
Kaiserin Elizabeth	—	6-11-14	4,000	—
Zenta . . .	Gun fire	16-8-14	2,300	Adriatic

GUN-BOATS.

Name.	How Lost or Damaged.	Date.	Tonnage.	Place.
Temes . .	Mined	23-10-14	440	Save

DESTROYERS.

Name.	How Lost or Damaged.	Date.	Tonnage.	Place.
Lika . . .	Mined	29-12-15	780	Adriatic
Triglav . .	Gun fire	,,	,,	,,

SUBMARINES.

Name.	How Lost or Damaged.	Date.	Tonnage.	Place.
U12 . . .	Torpedoed	11-8-15	—	Adriatic
U3 . . .	Sunk	12-8-15	295	,,

TORPEDO-BOATS.

Name.	How Lost or Damaged.	Date.	Tonnage.	Place.
T.b. 19 . .	Mined	17-8-14	78	Pola

THE CAPITOL.

CHAPTER CII.

WASHINGTON.

THE CLASH OF TEUTONIC AND ANGLO-CELTIC INTERESTS IN THE UNITED STATES.

War Creates New Lines of Divergence in Persons of American Politics—Enormous Number of Teutonic Stock—German Attempts to Organise Teuton-Irish Vote—Historic Grudge against British People—President Wilson's Policy of Reconciling the A.B.C. League—Majority of Americans Hostile or Indifferent to Allies—Blood is not Thicker than Water—Cry for an Embargo on Munitions and on Wheat—Sharp Protest against British Interference with American Shipping—Extraordinary Prosperity of Farmers, Manufacturers, and Railway Companies—Why Roosevelt Wished to Side Actively with Allies—Remarkable Attitude of President Wilson—American Jealousy and Suspicion of Britain—Great Increase in United States Shipping—The Beef Trust of Chicago Outmanœuvred by British Government—President Wilson's Strange Outburst in Kansas—Germans being Born Blunderers, Save Britain from Grave Trouble—German Press Prematurely Celebrates the Triumph of German-Americanism—Beginning of Teutonic Submarine War on Commerce and Warning from President Wilson—German Dynamiters Open their Campaign against American Manufacturers and Workmen.

LIKE all modern communities which have felt the full stress of the industrial revolution while retaining the forms of popular government, the United States is a virtual plutocracy. The people, while nominally living in a democracy, are controlled, through indirect, subtle means, by a small, capable, and somewhat ruthless class, which holds most of the shares in railways, steamships, coal and iron mines, great manufacturing businesses, and plays a large part in fixing the prices of food. The American Trust magnates broke the power of American labour during the Homestead strike of 1892, and after this they kept American workmen in subjection, while Canadian, Australian, and British working men were comparatively free, by the large, simple method of flooding the American labour market with cheap, unorganised European labour. In recent years the subject races of Austria-Hungary provided a considerable portion of the new industrial army by means of which the American plutocracy kept the American working man in his place.

There remained, however, sufficient of the spirit of freedom in the enterprising Americans to prevent their Republic from becoming a polity of industrial feudalism in name as well as in fact. At times some members of the plutocratic class openly admitted that they needed the help of a warlike aristocracy in order to consolidate their powers, and after the fall of the old corrupt Republican system, and the resurgence

MR. ROBERT LANSING.
Appointed Secretary of State in President Wilson's Cabinet, June, 1915.

of Theodore Roosevelt, there was a very marked decline in the political power of the great plutocrats. President Thomas Woodrow Wilson owed his astonishing rise to the same deep movement of democratic feeling which Roosevelt had tried to interpret. Yet when the Great War broke out, the two anti-plutocratic movements under Roosevelt and Wilson were still powerfully checked by the small caste that ruled the labour market, controlled the railways, and fixed the prices of most of the necessities of life. Some of the most potent means of public expression were controlled by Trusts, newspapers, theatres, moving-picture factories and shows, and even churches and well-known preachers. The champions of freedom relied for public expression on certain weekly periodicals and monthly illustrated magazines, published at a cheap price and enjoying wide circulation. In some cases the managers of these periodicals and magazines found it hard to resist the pressure brought upon their advertising departments by the well-organised plutocracy. But on the whole the new organs of liberty managed to win a sufficient advertisement revenue to enable them to carry on their campaign.

Then came the new divergencies of feeling and thought created by the European War. There were, it was calculated, about eleven million persons of Teutonic descent in the United States, including two and a half millions who had been born in Germany, and nearly two millions born in Austria-Hungary. The Anglo-Celtic stock amounted to about seventy millions, derived from English, Irish and Scottish sources, with Scandinavian, Italian, and ancient French, Dutch, and Spanish elements. Part of the Irish element, however, was still fiercely anti-British, and though Mr. Redmond and all the Nationalist party at Westminster agreed to co-operate with the British party during the war, some of the Irish-Americans went over to the spoilers of Belgium and the ravagers of Northern France. Notwithstanding this, the proportion between the actively hostile Teutonic stock of the United States and the indifferent or friendly Anglo-Celtic stock was probably very much less than one to seven. For it must be remembered that the first large wave of Germanic immigration came about 1850, at the time when the Junkers of Prussia succeeded in defeating all the large, Liberal, semi-democratic, semi-plutocratic forces in Germany. The second large wave came after 1870, when many Southern Germans fled from the Prussian system. There were thus many men and women of German origin in the United States who had received from their fathers sound traditions of freedom, and these traditions had prevented them from joining the organisation for a Germanic uprising which had been prepared after the visit of Prince Henry of Prussia to the United States.

On the other hand, the German-Jewish financial houses in New York, Chicago, and other important centres were connected with the German-Jewish money-lords of Germany. The fighting alliance which Britain, Belgium, and France maintained with Russia had the effect of throwing most of the Jewish money-power in America at first against the Allies; for the Jews were embittered against the Russians, and even English Jews, such as Mr. Israel Zangwill, were sometimes tempted to lament the prospect that a Franco-British victory would involve their race in apparent defeat. The American Jew did not allow fully for the fact that both in Britain and in France his race had full liberty of development and exercised considerable political and social power, while in Germany, even the most influential and ablest Jews, who enjoyed the personal friendship of the Kaiser, rested under a shadow, and were deprived of certain rights enjoyed by German Christians. When the war broke out, the American Jew sided with the Germans, and as the entertaining author of "Potash and Perlmutter" pointed out, the Jewish

THE NOTORIOUS DR. DUMBA.
Dr. Konstantin T. Dumba, the Austrian Ambassador to Washington (marked with a X), was recalled in September, 1915, for fomenting strikes.

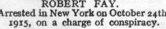

CONGRESSMAN BARTHOLDT.
Head of an organisation inaugurated at Washington in the German interest.

ROBERT FAY.
Arrested in New York on October 24th, 1915, on a charge of conspiracy.

CAPTAINS KARL BOY-ED AND VON PAPEN.
German Naval and Military Attachés. They were recalled in December, 1915, at the request of the State Department in Washington.

banking system was employed even against Russian Jews in New York who failed to show an active sympathy with the Hohenzollern cause. They could not get the large and easy credits to which they were accustomed in their business unless they made at least some show of following the leadership of Dr. Dernburg and the busy agents of Herr Ballin's steamship company.

In direct, vigorous work for the Germanic interest the German Jews surpassed the German Christians in the United States. The officials of the Hamburg-Amerika line provided the best secret service men employed by the German Embassy, and worked on the public opinion of the nation by a series of ingenious devices. Certain well-known writers, who were either in monetary difficulties or were willing at any cost to earn more money, were set up in luxurious apartments to write abuse against Britain. This was discovered by a brilliant English writer of the younger generation, Mr. Madox Brown, who by disguising himself in ragged clothes and sitting forlornly on a bench in Madison Square, New York, received from one of Herr Ballin's agents an invitation to earn a good living by attacking his countrymen. Clever German-Americans of the decadent school, such as Viereck, were suddenly lifted up into editorial chairs, while men of the stamp of that former light of British Nonconformity, Dr. Aked, were induced to illumine the people of the United States concerning the crimes of Englishmen.

But even reckoning all the American Jews, who numbered two and a half millions, with the Germanic party, there could not have been one American in seven ready to take an active part in helping the Germanic cause. Very likely the proportion was much less than this; for, in addition to the German families who had fled from Prussian oppression, there were large bodies of immigrants from Austria-Hungary, belonging to the subject races of the Dual Monarchy, and much less inclined than even the German of the Liberal school to take the part of the oppressors from whom they had fled. As the war proceeded, and the evidence of German atrocities in Belgium and France was confirmed by the sinking of the Lusitania, Ancona, and Persia, the large freedom-seeking element in German-American stock drew away from the criminal intriguers and murderous plotters housed in the German and

Austrian Embassies. Had anything like a Germanic rebellion been attempted in the United States, as was foolishly hinted by certain German writers, it would have been seen that the real force of the movement was dissipated at the very time when the agitators were making the most noise.

The German organisation in America had been founded as a social affair. Purely as a social affair it had attracted, by power of honest sentiment, many German-Americans who **Illusion of a** were glad of the opportunity of **German President** keeping in touch with the art, literature and science of the land of their origin. From the remote Berlin standpoint of the German Military Staff, the system of German social clubs in the United States loomed through the mists of the Atlantic in a very important and significant manner. It led to the illusion that, with the help of Sir Roger Casement and the Irish vote, a German President of the United States might be elected by playing the Democratic and Republican parties against each other. But men who are attracted to social clubs are not necessarily ready to sacrifice their lives for a cause in which most of them do not believe. Even the last small waves of German immigration had consisted mainly of Social Democrats, who despaired of their country, and of young men who wished to avoid the Prussian drill-sergeant. The Teutons of fierce, bellicose temper, who had come to America merely to make money and return with it to their native land, probably numbered less than half a million.

Some of them were very active and very clamorous, and a few were eager for the most desperate adventures. As we shall afterwards see, men of this class ended by doing considerable damage to American life and property, but it cannot

FAY'S SPEEDY ACCESSORY.
High speed motor-boat owned by the German Lieutenant Robert Fay, who confessed himself leader of a German plot in New York to blow up vessels carrying munitions to the Allies. In centre: Box containing a bomb found in Fay's apartments.

be said that they succeeded in swaying the American mind against the Allies.

What the Germanic element in American life did was to increase, by a heavy deadweight, the balance of policy against Great Britain. The native American had a traditional grudge against our country, and such was the condition of his feelings in the matter that for some generations every good American politician had had to practise the art of "twisting the lion's tail." The British Empire had also been disliked, and almost feared, because it held in Canada, the West Indies, Honduras, Guiana, and the Falkland Islands such important stretches of territory and such important strategical points in and around the American continent as interfered with the political plan of the plutocracy of the United States. That plan, as was explained by President Polk, Secretary Fish, Secretary Olney, and other developers of the Monroe Doctrine, aimed at the absorption of both Northern and Southern America by the United States. The design had been openly expressed by responsible American statesmen as late as 1895, when Richard Olney proclaimed: "The United States is practically sovereign on this continent." One result of this forthright frankness was that some of the most powerful and **South America and** progressive South American Re- **Monroe Doctrine** publics grew anxious about their economic independence, and sought for capital from Britain and France, so as to engage the interests of Britain and France in their existence as free States. Argentina, Brazil, and Chili went so far as to form a fighting league known as the A.B.C., which was largely directed against any possible aggression by the United States.

THE LAIR OF THE CONSPIRATORS.
Shack in the woods near Port Lee, New Jersey, where Robert Fay and his co-intriguers kept some of their explosives and carried out experiments.

Another impression of the fire at Trenton, which was attributed to German agency. The firm was one of several turning out munitions for the Allies.

Part of the industrial section of East Youngstown, after strikers had sacked and looted it on January 7th, 1916. Certain of these plants were employed in making munitions for the Allies.

MUNITION FACTORIES DESTROYED IN THE CAUSE OF KAISERISM.

Trying to cope with a fire of unproved origin which occurred on November 10th, 1915, at the premises of John A. Roeblings, Sons & Co., Trenton, New Jersey.

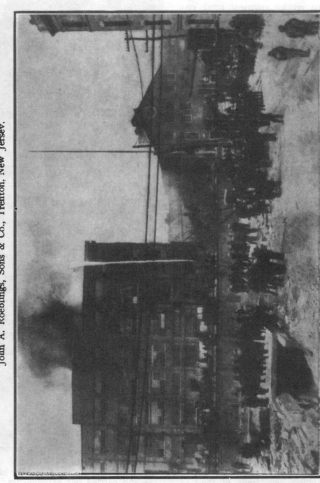

Works of the Bethlehem Steel Company destroyed by fire on November 10th, 1915, by alleged incendiaries. £250,000 worth of war material, including 800 guns, was destroyed.

THE REIGN OF TERROR IN NEUTRAL AMERICA:

France financed Brazil, while Britain lent to Argentina and Chili. Then Mexico, seeking for both capital and protection against her powerful neighbour, tried to develop her enormous oil resources by means of British capital. Lord Cowdray was ready to take the matter up, but the Rockefeller group of magnates became alarmed for the rich monopoly they enjoyed in all American petroleum products. The Standard Oil combination is alleged to have had some part in throwing Mexico into civil war, with a view to removing from power the Mexicans who had granted the oil concession to British contractors. Our Government stood aside completely, letting British interests and British lives be lost, while the Mexican revolutionary armies destroyed each other ; but the situation was saved by the unforeseen attitude of President Woodrow Wilson. This man, elected by his people to reform the economic machinery of the country and save it from plutocratic control, proved to be a true successor to Abraham Lincoln. The plutocratic party, which had done something to promote the Mexican troubles, got up a popular case for armed intervention, the natural sequel of which would have been the annexation of the country with its rich mines, great oil-fields, and other vast unexploited resources. Sufficient American men and women were murdered to provoke the indignation of the American people, until even Theodore Roosevelt proclaimed himself anxious to fight. But President Wilson refused to make war, and watched the struggle gradually subside under General Carranza, with Mexico still independent; and the A.B.C. League convinced at last that the Monroe Doctrine was not a gospel of aggression.

President Wilson and Mexico

It was a great victory for President Wilson, and its influence on the future development of the nations of the American continent seemed likely to be very important. It was practically a single-handed fight between one quiet, strong-minded thinker, called from a Presbyterian university to direct the intricate affairs of a great empire, and the mightiest oligarchy that had existed since Cæsar and his nephew broke the power of the Roman money trusts. It remained to be seen whether in the coming Presidential election Woodrow Wilson would receive sufficient support to enable him to ensure the independence of Mexico, and maintain his policy in regard to the European War. In any case, it must be admitted that his conduct of the Mexican situation did much to improve the relations between the United States and the British and French Governments. Sir Edward Grey, in particular— a man of the democratic school, very honest-minded, yet fierce against tyranny—recognised in President Woodrow Wilson a kindred spirit, and trusted him in a way in which he would not have trusted a figure-head of the American plutocratic party. On the other hand, it cannot be said that President Woodrow Wilson gave any help whatever to the Allies. He did not consider that it was in the interests of his people that he should do so, and, moreover, he seems personally to have had, during the first eighteen months of the most terrible struggle in Christendom, a Quaker-like aversion to drawing the sword. He resisted the strong current of warlike passion when the Lusitania was sunk,

and amazed friend and foe alike by saying that there were occasions when a nation felt " too proud to fight." In uttering this historic phrase, however, he appears to have been thinking rather of the reasons against intervention in Mexico than of the wrongs done by the German pirates against the honour and interests of the United States.

The President of the greatest commonwealth that ever existed in the world was certainly most anxious to avoid being drawn into the war. There were several reasons for his strangely patient and long-suffering attitude. In the first place, it may have been thought that the course of the movement of domestic reform in his country would be checked and perhaps perverted by war conditions. In the second place, the international position which the United States was winning quietly and peaceably, while most of the other great Powers were wasting themselves in conflict, would be compromised if America also entered the field of battle.

In the third place, the power of making war was not in the hands of the President, but was the supreme function of Congress, and a large majority of Congressmen desired peace with Germany. It was estimated that before the

"ANOTHER LINER SUNK!"

Judging by their expressions, these members of the Austro-Hungarian Embassy at Washington, who were entrusted with the delicate task of explaining the deaths of American citizens caused through piracy, did not take things too seriously. Reading from left to right they are : Baron Erich Zwiedenek, Councillor and Chargé d'Affaires ; Prince Alfred zu Hohenlohe-Schillingsfürst, Attaché ; Baron Stephen Henry de Hedri et de Genere Aba, Chamberlain to his Imperial Majesty Franz Josef, Second Secretary ; Consul-General von Grivicic ; Herren K. Schwenda, Josef Schoedel, F. J. Sobotka, Charles Pollak, all secretaries of the Chancellery.

sinking of the Lusitania the larger part of the American electorate was indifferent to the cause for which Belgium, France, Britain, Russia, Serbia, Montenegro, and Japan were fighting. Only in the Eastern States was there a distinct and strong movement of mind against Germany and Austria. The Middle States were partly friendly to the Germanic cause, but mainly indifferent to the results of the European War. It was in the Middle States that the German immigrants formed a large and well-organised voting power, and in some twenty-nine cities, including Cincinnati, Milwaukee, Louisville, and St. Louis, they were predominant over all other foreign stocks. Then in the Western States, with a coast-line far removed from Europe, and with a labour organisation concerned in preventing Japanese immigration, the presence of Japan by the side of Britain, France, and Belgium checked what natural sympathy there might have been with the champions of democratic civilisation. The Western States, which had been looking to the opening of the Panama

Pro-Germanism in the Middle States

Night scene, during the war, on the Avenue de la Gare at Nice, the news centre of the French Riviera. On receipt of the war telegrams the news was posted on bulletin boards which almost covered the façades of the offices of "Le Petit Niçois" and "L'Eclaireur." Reading these despatches there was always an interested cosmopolitan gathering of British officers, convalescent or on leave, Frenchmen, Italians, Belgian, sand Russians, with a few Americans. Amusing mistakes were sometimes made in the British news, but usually nothing more serious than "Sir Grey," "Lord Winston Churchill," or "Sir Lloyd George."

STUDYING WAR NEWS AT NICE : A COSMOPOLITAN CROWD ON THE FRENCH RIVIERA.

Canal to save them from the rather shadowy Japanese menace which continually troubled them, regarded the cause of the Allies with as great an indifference as did the Middle States. Even men of British stock were tinged with the prejudice against the European nations which had entered into a fighting alliance with the Far Eastern island race.

The prejudice against Japan seems to have become almost as strong in some circles of the American plutocracy as it was among the working classes on the Pacific slope. The governing circles in the United States—men acting behind the political bosses and the politicians whom the bosses helped to nominal power—were not wanting in patriotic ambition. For some years they had been quietly and thoroughly conquering a large part of Central America by the ancient Roman method of pacific penetration, and they intended to win the mastery of the Pacific Ocean by means of the Panama Canal and naval bases in Hawaii and the Philippine Islands. The sea-power of Japan, backed by a large and efficient Army, tended to disturb the American plan in regard to the Pacific, and by reason of our alliance with Japan we were at times looked upon with suspicion. The aspersions cast upon our general policy by some American journalists of the rampant school were quite ill-founded, but these attacks left a certain odium attaching to Britain.

The general upshot was that, for about the first ten months of the war, the majority of Americans were indifferent to Britain. At best, we were regarded as being so strong on sea that we stood to lose little and to gain much. The struggle between us and the Germans was regarded as a very dramatic gladiatorial contest, from which good Americans might learn to appreciate the blessings of peace. When a Chinese mandarin was asked what he thought of the war, he said : " We take no interest in the clan fights of Western barbarians." This was in large measure the view of the average American. He reckoned that we were a benighted remnant of the feudal ages, burdened with a king, princes, dukes, lords, and esquires, lacking the pure inspiration of Republican government, and engaged at the behest of our **View of the average** aristocracy in a struggle for dominion with **American** another remnant of the feudal ages that was better equipped for war than we were. The German legend of the encircling tactics engineered against Germany by King Edward was widely accepted in the United States as the ultimate origin of the conflict. Except in German-American and Swedish-American circles, there was no more sympathy with our chief opponent than with ourselves. It is true that thousands of Americans went to Canada and enlisted as Canadians in order to fight for our cause. The former President, Theodore Roosevelt, was at times half inclined to fight for the Allies. But this movement of feeling was at first confined to a very small section of the vast white population of the United States.

Blood was not thicker than water, and our public was not well served by its newspaper correspondents in America during the critical periods of strain. As a rule, our papers only reproduced passages from daily journals in the Eastern States which were very friendly towards the Allies. The Eastern States, which possessed great cities on the coast, well within the range of action of battle-cruisers, felt themselves to be a part of Europe. To them the struggle was no clan fight of the feudal barbarians of the effete Old World. They recognised that the oil-

burning battleship and the super-submarine had reduced the Atlantic Ocean to less than the size of the Mediterranean in Farragut's days. They knew also that modern troop transports were almost as speedy as oil-burning battleships. For this reason many of the leading minds in the Eastern States felt far more uncomfortable in regard to Germany than the men in the Western States did in regard to Japan. Americans could be found in considerable numbers in the great manu- **America's chief title** facturing coast-towns, who were ready to **to nobility** admit, with Admiral Mahan and Homer Lea, that the British Fleet defended the United States as well as France and Britain. The Eastern Americans were those who felt most keenly the wrong done to the Belgians, and who did most to build up that magnificent system of Belgian relief which history is likely to recognise as the chief title to nobility of the modern American people.

The population was much denser in the Eastern States than in the Middle and Western States ; but the country was so very large that no daily current of journalism bound together the minds of the different communities. The Eastern view of the war, therefore, spread with extraordinary slowness through the Middle States, and even in January, 1916, one of the representatives of Missouri, Mr. Mann, stated in Congress that if the United States went to war it would not be against Germany, but against Great Britain. To the British public, nourished only on extracts from the Eastern American Press, the statement made by Mr. Mann seemed an inexplicable freak of mind. But the fact was that the currents of opinion in Congress still remained confused and very conflicting, and the ancient plan of establishing an embargo against Britain and her Allies was still being debated. The device of an embargo had first been employed in the Napoleonic era, when the Orders-in-Council of Great Britain and the Milan Decrees of Napoleon caused serious interference with the sea-borne trade of the United States. The American President forbade his countrymen to trade with the belligerents ; but the main effect of this embargo was to help Canada to build up her commerce, to produce a national system of smuggling, and to lead the New England States to open negotiations with Great Britain with a view to seceding from the American Union. Many of the modern Americans who talked lightly about reviving the embargo seemed not to have fully studied the history of their country. The great manufacturing Eastern States were much too powerful to be coerced. Both their trade interests and their political feelings made them the champions of free commerce, and the gigantic suicidal device of an embargo was calculated to wreck the American Constitution.

MR. BRAND WHITLOCK.
The United States Minister to Belgium during the German occupation, whose earnest pleading on behalf of Nurse Cavell was ineffective.

COLONEL HOUSE.
President Wilson's special envoy to Europe. After visiting Paris, Geneva, Basle, and Berlin, he arrived at the U.S. Embassy in London on February 2nd, 1916.

MEN WHO ARRANGED THE U.S. LOAN FOR THE ALLIES.
Sir E. Holden, Bart., and Lord Reading leaving their hotel in New York
in September, 1915, after arranging, with leading American bankers, the
loan of £100,000,000 on behalf of the Franco-British Financial Mission.

Yet it is extraordinary how quickly the cry for an
embargo was raised by some important American newspapers. It began in January, 1915, when organs of the
calibre of the New York "World" and the Philadelphia
"Evening Ledger" advocated an embargo on wheat.
The United States had then had a bumper crop of
900,000,000 bushels, and owing to the hold-up of Russian
wheat by the closing of the Dardanelles, there was a huge
European demand for the American crop. The result was
a run of high prices in the American wheat pit, which
exceeded the highest normal record of fifty years, excluding
the prices reached when the market had been cornered.
The price of bread rose in the country, which was abound-
ing with wheat, and there was great prosperity in the
farming States. But the Detroit "Times," for example,
did not wish so much to cheapen bread
The cry for an   at home by an embargo as to starve out
embargo   Europe and "make it necessary for the
                  nations at war to quit their fighting and
go back to ploughing." Britain, being the least agricultural of the warlike states, was the one aimed at.

By February, 1915, the agitation had spread from wheat
to munitions. A Press poll, conducted among a thousand
representatives of American newspapers, indicated that
the leaders of opinion favouring an embargo on munitions
were outnumbered by two to one by those who favoured
the export of arms. In towns where the population was
more than fifty thousand, the majority against an embargo
was nearly four to one; but in the smaller towns the two
parties seemed almost equal. In other words, the large
manufacturing cities in the Eastern States sympathised
with the Allies in as active a manner as possible, and
heartily enjoyed the growing prosperity brought to them
by the trade in war material. But in the small agricultural
towns there was a very powerful class which was indifferent

or hostile to the allied cause. The farmers were averse
to an embargo on wheat, but many of them were not
unwilling to consider an embargo upon the articles by
means of which the manufacturing cities were tiding over
a period of great depression. The widespread agitation
for prohibiting the export of arms was conducted in an
irresponsible and mischievous manner. The numerous
newspapers that printed columns of inflammatory abuse
against the munition-makers were, in a real sense, part
instigators of the terrible series of outrages that followed.
Many of the writers may have done their work unwittingly,
but there were deadly German and Austrian plotters
directing the gigantic Press campaign, which was to lead
to a state of terrorisation in important branches of American
industry.

Even before the outrages began, the preliminary Press
agitation became so wild and violent that the American
champion of pacifism, Mr. Bryan, felt compelled to point
out to his countrymen that the export of arms and other
materials of war was quite legal. "There is no power in
the Executive," he said, "to prevent the sale of ammunition to the belligerents. The duty of a neutral to restrict
trade in munitions of war has never been imposed by
international law or by municipal statutes. . . . If
Germany and Austria-Hungary cannot export contraband
from this country, it is not, because of that fact, the duty
of the United States to close its markets to the Allies.
The markets of this country are open on equal terms to all
the world—to every nation, belligerent or neutral." The
Press of the Eastern States was pleased with this sound
statement on the matter made by Mr. Bryan in his capacity
as Secretary of State; but the German
and pro-German papers, such as those of   **Attitude of**
Mr. Hearst, cried down Mr. Bryan as a   **Mr. Bryan**
defender of Britain and England's ser-
vant. In view of the attitude Mr. Bryan afterwards
adopted as a man of peace at any price, the German
attacks upon him at the beginning of 1915 were very
mistaken.

As a matter of fact, both President Woodrow Wilson and
Mr. Bryan seemed at the beginning of 1915 to be drifting
rather into a war with the Allies than into any act of
hostility against Germany and Austria. Our interference
with the sea-borne commerce of the United States was
eliciting much passionate protest from the American
people; and in December, 1914, President Woodrow
Wilson addressed to our Government so sharp a Note that
a conflict seemed impending. We cannot go fully into all
the grave problems of the Franco-British naval measures
for stopping contraband of war and restricting the German
export trade. This matter will have to be discussed at
length in a separate chapter, not merely with reference to
the United States, but with regard to the even more
delicate position of Sweden, and with reference to Italy,
Norway, Denmark, and Holland. But we may point out
that during the American Civil War the Federals contended
that a coast-line of three thousand miles could be blockaded
successfully with an insignificant number of warships,
which were sometimes absent for five days from the principal
Confederate ports. Though it had only thirty-five modern
vessels available when the blockade began, the United States
maintained that goods sent to neutral ports could be
seized on the way as contraband if it appeared likely that
such goods were intended to be forwarded from neutral
territory to the Confederate States. In addition, President
Abraham Lincoln had proclaimed cotton, the staple of
his enemies, to be contraband of war, although it was not
then used for warlike purposes. Our cotton-workers
starved in multitudes for want of work, and our cotton
manufacturers were ruined. Lincoln seized cotton simply
with a view to cutting off the main source of wealth of his
enemies and reducing them by famine. There was no
ground in international law for the high-handed, terrible
form of blockade which the American President employed,

yet our suffering country, with its famished cotton-spinners rioting for bread, accepted both the doctrine of continuous voyage and the inclusion of cotton as contraband. It was largely due to our working and middle classes' sympathy with the abolition of slavery, and to Queen Victoria's passionate desire to avoid war with a country planted with British stock, that our Government acquiesced in the new American doctrines of the use of sea-power.

But when we in turn were compelled to apply the American doctrines under the new conditions caused by submarine warfare, the President, Congress, and people of the United States seemed to be inclined to stand to the letter of international law. The curious fact that it was a Virginian professor of jurisprudence who occupied the seat of power of Abraham Lincoln gave a certain piquancy to the situation. A representative of the descendants of the Confederates became the virtual judge of our use of sea-power. We cannot pretend to indicate the principle on which President Woodrow Wilson based his case against us. He never clearly stated that the alterations made by Abraham Lincoln in the early days of steamship traffic were the final developments of legal methods of interfering with an enemy's sea-borne commerce. He never clearly stated that the increasing range of action of submarines, which could operate from the German coast to the New England coast, together

PROCESSION OF "THE ALMIGHTY DOLLAR" IN NEW YORK.
Part of the convoy of twenty-three motor-waggons conveying fifty-two million dollars shipped by the Bank of England to uphold British financial prestige in the American markets. The waggons, guarded by forty men armed with rifles, and a detachment of mounted police, were photographed on their way to the Sub-Treasury in New York.

voyage. Sweden held that even Abraham Lincoln and his Secretary of State had been high-handed, lawless infringers of the law of nations, and refused to acquiesce in the French and British Fleets following the precedent established by the United States. Yet it was largely American wheat, American cotton, and American manufactured goods which were passing through the neutral ports of Sweden into Germany.

For the French and the British Governments did not, during the first eight months of the war, interfere with the roundabout import of food and many important materials of war by the enemy. The cry raised in Germany that the Franco-British squadrons were starving the German people was utterly false. For the first eight months of the war all the neutral countries bordering on the Teutonic

Empires did an enormous forwarding trade in both food supplies and war materials. The allied fleets even permitted Germany and Austria to import all the raw materials they needed for the manufacture of the propellent explosives used by their armies and navies. The Franco-British list of contraband of war was miserably inadequate from the point of view of the Allies. We did not even follow Abraham Lincoln's example in regard to cotton, though cotton in the American Civil War was a harmless staple, while in the European War it was veritable cannon-fodder. Yet, despite our unparalleled solicitude for the commercial interests of neutrals, the Government and people of the United States showed themselves in December, 1914, fiercely indignant over our treatment of their shipping.

ARMED ESCORT FOR BRITAIN'S TREASURE.
An armed guard watching part of the consignment of treasure being unloaded at the Sub-Treasury, New York. Two-thirds of the fifty-two million dollars were sent across the Atlantic in gold, and one-third in securities. The cargo journeyed from England on a battleship, guarded by a flotilla of destroyers.

with the much-extended and accelerated range of action of oil-burning warships, did not fairly allow a further development of the American doctrine. But some passages in his Notes seemed to imply that he did not even accept in their full consequences the principles laid down by Abraham Lincoln.

The general opinion in Britain and in France was that the American wanted it both ways, with a special law for himself when he was at war, and a very different law for belligerents when he was a trading neutral. The position of affairs was further complicated by the fact that certain other trading neutrals, such as the Swedes, would not even admit the validity of the American doctrine of continuous

We cannot explain the American attitude. If we understood it, we might be able to excuse it. But we cannot pretend to have arrived at an impartial view of the

Neutrals and contraband

situation as it developed in the very critical period that ended with the opening of the German submarine campaign in February, 1915. In the first place, we had no reason to suppose that the American exporters were suffering generally by our search after a very restricted list of contraband; for American oversea trade in the year 1915 was of incomparable volume. Often £20,000,000 worth of goods was sold abroad in one week. The Dutch and Scandinavian ports were clogged with American imports

Interior of the aeroplane-engine erecting shop, showing a number of mechanics working at lathes, vices, etc., and generally learning all about the integral parts of the "iron bird".

Members of the Royal Flying Corps dining alfresco at one of their camps. A military cook is helping each man to a second portion of his palatable fare.

At the headquarters of the Administrative Wing of the Royal Flying Corps. Scene in the rigging shop, showing (to the left) a single-seater biplane and (on the right) a parasol Blériot monoplane. Rigging and tuning up Service aeroplanes was considered one of the most responsible of the skilled duties of this corps, for on the thoroughness of such work depended the lives of pilots and observers.

IN THE NEST OF THE MECHANICAL BIRDS OF PREY: CAMERA VIEWS OF THE ROYAL FLYING CORPS IN TRAINING.

and the lack of shipping, due to the disappearance of the German mercantile marine and the conversion of a large part of the British mercantile marine to warlike purposes, was the only important hindrance to the gigantic expansion of American oversea trade. But even the great rise in freights did not oppress the American exporter. He placed the extra cost of transport on his goods, and his foreign customers made no complaint.

In the period preceding the outbreak of the European War the condition of American industry had been very bad. The great depression may not have been due altogether to natural causes. The American plutocracy had been seriously alarmed by the movements towards an economic reformation, led by Theodore Roosevelt and Woodrow Wilson. These two reformers, while using different

THE FINISHING TOUCHES.
Engine fitters at work on a six-cylinder 120 h.-p. Beardmore aero-engine.

FOR RAPID REPAIRS.
Lorry carrying equipment of lathe, drill, emery tool-grinder, forge, etc., all of which were electrically driven.

prevent the taxes on imported goods from enabling large American manufacturers to extort from their customers unconscionable profits. The reformers also attacked the system of political bosses and corrupt national and municipal politics, by means of which the plutocracy had governed the country in their own interests while maintaining a stucco facade of democratic institutions.

President Woodrow Wilson had made his name in New Jersey, where he had been put in as a figure-head by the political boss, and had much surprised that man by becoming a very live and sweeping reforming force. There was a quiet trenchancy about Woodrow Wilson which alarmed the plutocrats and excited the admiration of the

methods, agreed in their larger aim. They desired to restrict the overwhelming power of monopolists, by making railway rates as low for small business as for big business; they wanted to break certain monopolies, which seemed to be in restraint of trade, and to

Members of the Royal Flying Corps at work on plane-building and sailmaking, two of the special trades opened up for men during the war.

MACHINERY, PLANT AND ACCESSORIES OF THE ROYAL FLYING CORPS AT SOUTH FARNBOROUGH.

rather emotional American electorate; and when Roosevelt split the old Republican party, Woodrow Wilson was able to walk through the rift to the White House. Had the old Republicans been able afterwards to reduce Roosevelt to insignificance, they could have combined with the corrupt elements in the Democratic party, and have defeated all the reformers. But Roosevelt was too masterful a personality to be quelled and annulled. A volcano of emotion, he blazed continually on the horizon of American life, and even when he went on a long hunt in the tropics of Africa, the thoughts of his countrymen

Woodrow Wilson as idealogue went with him. Woodrow Wilson did not seem so dangerous, because he had none of the expansive power of emotion of the rival reformer; but the big business men reckoned him to be the more deadly of the two. He was what Napoleon used to call an idealogue. Robespierre, the incorruptible, was an idealogue; and allowing for differences of creed and sentiment, the Virginian lawyer, who had taught jurisprudence in Princetown University, was as stern a reformer of the philosophic school as the lawyer of Arras.

Certainly there was a reign of terror in big business

A LITTLE AFFAIR IN THE MIDDLE SEA
Engaging an enemy submarine in the Mediterranean. British 4·7 in. gun in action against a U boat, December, 1915.

circles when President Wilson extended his power into Congress. And when his men began to attempt to control railways and steamships in the national interests, break up the great Trusts, and lower the tariff, the plutocracy in turn resorted to severe measures. Apparently they agreed upon some self-denying ordinance, whereby their profits should be temporarily lessened, for the sake of giving the working classes a practical lesson in the danger of interfering with big business. Unemployment greatly increased, railway after railway went bankrupt, and trade slackened all round. Part of this depression was due to the disturbance created among the moneyed classes by fear of Woodrow Wilson and his reforming Senators. But it is fairly evident from the subsequent course of events that there was a large artificial factor in the forces making for American commercial depression.

It would not be too much to say that the war saved the President and the reform parties. What with the bumper crop of 1914, and the enormous demand for horses, harness, boots, and motor-vehicles, tinned meats, clothing, cotton, medicines, optical glass goods, machine tools, and crucibles, aeroplanes, and ordinary munitions of war, the American employers and the American working class had more work than they could perform. Even the railways, which had been in a desperate position, improved

in spite of themselves. Fewer miles of new track were built than in any year since 1864, and there were 41,000 miles in the hands of receivers in 1915—the greatest stretch of bankrupt line ever known. Yet the net revenue of the railways was more than a thousand million dollars —the greatest sum ever recorded. But, as against this remarkable profit, the four leading unions of American railwaymen were emboldened by prosperity to combine solidly together for the first time and agitate for an eight hours' working day, with time and a half for overtime. Thus, while the moneyed classes earned larger revenues almost in spite of themselves, the lightening of the economic pressure upon the working classes made these more independent, and increased the forces behind Roosevelt and Woodrow Wilson. By the beginning of February, 1916, the plutocracy was almost buried under its own unexpected new riches, and the general opinion was that if the big businesses could not come to terms with Theodore Roosevelt, President Woodrow Wilson would win the next election and carry on with greater thoroughness his campaign of reform.

All these abrupt and extraordinary changes in the domestic politics of the United States had an important bearing upon the American attitude in regard to the war. Both Roosevelt and Wilson regarded the prosperous condition of the country as a factor favourable to the reform parties; for the only real check to the economic reformation was widespread unemployment, causing such popular suffering that the people would accept any remedy which the bosses of the old school offered them. Roosevelt, however, thought that American democracy had nothing to lose by actively siding with the Allies. He reckoned that war conditions in the United States would be similar to war conditions in Britain, and would lead to so immense a call for labour of every kind, skilled and unskilled, that a considerable portion of the wealth of the plutocracy would be deeply spread through the lowest strata of American society. There would be splendid opportunities for following the fair-minded lead of the British oligarchy in the Napoleonic era, and establishing an income tax, and even imposing death duties in order to meet some of the war expenses. Roosevelt was also sincerely moved by the fate of Belgium and the tearing up of treaties. He was by nature a fighting man, as he had shown during the South African War and the recent Mexican imbroglio. There were times when he would rather have been a brigadier-general in France or Flanders at the head of five thousand American volunteers than a third-term President of the United States. He was one of the most powerful friends the Allies had in the New World, and one of his principal rivals in the Republican party, Mr. Elihu Root, was also an outspoken champion of the allied cause. Dr. Eliot, the President Emeritus of Harvard University, and many other leaders of American university life, also sided openly and strongly with Belgium, France, and Britain. And many of them agreed with Roosevelt's policy of armed intervention in Europe.

Roosevelt and the Allies

President Wilson, on the other hand, was neutral in thought as well as in word. He was as neutral as his Congress, without whose co-operation he could not, even had he so willed, have made war. When many Americans were at last aroused from their indifference or converted

Lieut.-General Sir E. H. H. Allenby, K.C.B., promoted for distinguished service in the field.

The U.S. destroyers Benham and Parker full speed ahead.

Torpedo being fired from the United States destroyer O'Brien.

White foam and black smoke: American destroyer Benham racing after a submarine during manœuvres.

Twentieth-century war kit: Trench equipment of a French officer.

A present for the Boches: Loading a French howitzer.

from partiality for the Germans, the President remained, with his First Secretary of State, an embodiment of pacifism. The same doctrinaire rigidity which made Woodrow Wilson so formidable a reforming force made him also one of the principal keepers of the peace. He was a man of solitary mood, who had worked out his ideas in his study, deriving his inspiration from the dead masters of knowledge rather than from large and various experience of life. He was not like Burke, whom he admired, a man who had first felt the stress of living forces

Doctrinaire keeper of the peace and had then worked out his conception of them. He was like Robespierre, who fed his mind on the works of Rousseau, and then tried to reduce Rousseau's ideas to practice. He had thought over other men's thoughts, criticised and shaped them to his own views, and it was the shock between his political idealism and the extraordinarily corrupt state of things in New Jersey which had made him more of a fanatic for reform than even Roosevelt was. Men of this sort, apparently quiet, unpractical scholars, have a tendency to grow as strong as chilled steel when they find that their long-meditated master-ideas are belied by the corruption of the State. They have little sentiment, and none of the give-and-take and geniality

creative mind. What creative spirit there was in the matter in America resided in Theodore Roosevelt, who, while lacking the great learning of his rival, adopted with tremendous energy the plain man's view that the tearing up of treaties of neutrality, and the breaking of The Hague Convention, to which the United States had been a party, had completely unsoldered the fabric of international agreements. Many men began to think that no international law existed, since there was no power to enforce the law when it had been broken. But President Wilson maintained an attitude resembling that of a lawyer in a country invaded by barbarians, and defended by a civilised army which was destroying certain buildings in order to get a clear field of fire. He noted with equal solicitude the injury done to property by both sides, with a view

CANADIAN AMBULANCES FOR RUSSIA.
Motor-ambulances presented by the Salvation Army in Canada to the Russian Red Cross. They were inspected by General Booth at the Guildhall before being despatched to Petrograd.

to bringing future actions against both of them. He did not seem to see that, if the barbarians won, there would be no redress for injuries, and that he would be in danger of his life.

To the Allies, therefore, during the very critical period of their struggle, the attitude of the President of the United States seemed to be based on a pathetic fallacy. France in particular, who had been the midwife of American independence, and was still the leading democratic force in the world, could not understand the attitude of the President, Congress and majority of the American people. French thinkers had supplied the ideas of the American Commonwealth, and French soldiers and sailors had done more than New England farmers and Virginia planters to ensure the triumph of the young Republic. From France had been obtained, more by friendship than by the money paid, immense territories west of the Mississippi which had enabled the United **France and the** States to expand. If the people of the **U.S.A.** United States had an historic grudge against Britain, they had in far larger measure an historic grateful friendship for France, especially for a France which had returned fully to Republican ideals. But except in the Eastern States, in which as we have seen there was sympathy also with Britons, his debt to France, in the supreme crisis of her national fate, did not move the average American to anything like active amity.

All the indifferent or hostile parties tried to damp down sympathy with France by falsifying the origin and conditions of the war, and making it appear to be only a duel for world-dominion between Germany and Great Britain. Our Government rather helped to impress this false image of the struggle upon the American people by not troubling to make it perfectly clear that the allied policy in regard to contraband was a French and Russian, as well as a

GENERAL BRAMWELL BOOTH.
The distinguished leader of the Salvation Army posing for his photograph between two members of his staff, after inspecting the Red Cross cars.

of men who have spent their lives in the practical study of human weaknesses. On the other hand, until they are violently brought up against the sombre side of mankind, they incline to interpret all things from their own high-minded standpoint.

And unfortunately for the Allies, the President of the United States looked with the eyes of a lawyer-professor on the problems of international conventions which he had been studying for many years. In other words, he was still a bookworm in regard to matters of international law, though he had become a very practical man in regard to the domestic policy of his country. There was no stress of forces in the United States making for the further development of the broken conventions between civilised States, there was no call for an American President again to become a lawgiver instead of a lawyer in regard to international rules. So there was nothing to transform Woodrow Wilson from a professor of jurisprudence into a

British policy. In particular, had more French warships been used for stopping and searching American ships and ships carrying American cargoes, the traditional irritation against our interference with the shipping would not have been so fully revived. Take, for example, the well-known case of the Dacia. This was a German-owned vessel, interned in a United States port, and wrongly purchased by a German-American, Mr. Breitung, and sent with a non-contraband cargo up the English Channel for the purpose of being seized by our Navy. The German plotters wished to provoke an outburst of warlike indignation among the American people when a vessel flying the Stars and Stripes was captured by a British warship. But the Dacia was seized and taken to Brest by a French warship and adjudged a prize without the least movement of popular anger appearing in the United States. French sailors were indeed allowed to go far in exercising the rights of search and capture against their enemies. In December, 1915, the French cruiser Descartes was reported to have stopped three American ships, plying between New York and Porto Rico, and to have seized four Germans and four Austrians who were on board. American newspapers contended that this was an affair parallel with the Trent case during the Civil War, when a Federal cruiser stopped a British ship and seized two Confederate commissioners, an act which almost brought Britain into the war. But though the American newspapers, especially

Case of the Dacia

those of Germanic colour, criticised the action of the captain of the Descartes, the American people were scarcely interested in the affair. The fact that the incident occurred long after the sinking of the Lusitania, and some time after the destruction of the Ancona, had no doubt some bearing upon the tranquillity of the American mind in regard to it. But even then there would have been loud and general protest if a British cruiser had appeared to infringe the settlement of the Trent case. From our point of view, there were several early incidents in contraband affairs between belligerents and neutrals which were not satisfactory. The Pass of Balmaha was a ship which had changed from British to American registry, and was sent with a cargo of cotton for Russia early in the war, when the Allies were freely allowing the shipment of American cotton to Germany. But the vessel was seized by a German warship, and was confiscated by a German Prize Court. Also, at a time when we were allowing wheat to pass to neutral ports without troubling whether it might be conditional contraband, a United States vessel, the William P. Frye, with a cargo of wheat for England, was torpedoed and sunk by a German submarine. Yet neither of these remarkable acts by Germany elicited from President Wilson and the American Press a hundredth part of the indignation which our mild measures in regard to contraband shipping did.

German use of sea-power

We are afraid that the American attitude in regard to

"DAUBING" IN THE FLEET: WASH-CLOTHES DAY ON BOARD A BRITISH PATROL.
Keeping up their reputation as clean fighters. Jack Tars washing clothes on a British monitor in the North Sea, an occupation known as "daubing."

"FRIGHTFULNESS" IN CANADA.
The Canadian Parliament House, Ottawa, on fire, the result of German incendiary bombs. The damage was estimated at £600,000.

FIRE, SNOW, AND WATER.
Another view of the Parliament House at Ottawa during the conflagration. The disaster occurred on February 3rd, 1916, and the death-roll, in all, amounted to seven, including two lady guests of the Speaker. The Minister for Agriculture, the Hon. Martin Burrell, was among the injured.

our use of sea-power had in it elements of jealousy, distrust, and suspicion. The plutocracy of the United States calculated that if they could keep their country out of the war they would emerge the virtual victors from the terrible, long struggle. With German industries diverted largely to war work, with the export of German manufactures blocked by the British Fleet, and at best weighted with transport rates to neutral ports, the fields left unoccupied by the Germans in the markets of the world were open to the Americans. In South America especially there was a grand opportunity for the United States exporters to make large conquests. Britain, France, and Belgium could not profit much by the stoppage of German foreign trade. With her splendid mines and highly-developed industries, Belgium lay under the foot of her outrager. France had also lost her chief industrial districts, and her energies were absorbed in war work. Great Britain, after trying vainly to carry on business as usual and capture German trade, had to follow the example of France, and employ most of her working people in the production of military material. We could not even export coal in sufficient quantity to an important ally like Italy, who needed the fuel for her armament works. Sweden had to threaten to stop the transit of our goods by land to Russia in order to get coal from us. Our country, therefore, was not in a position to compete with the United States in the capture of German trade. On the contrary, so immersed did we become in war work that some of our large, important markets at home, in the Colonies, and in foreign countries were left open to the Americans.

U.S.A. and British markets

One result was a great increase in the American mercantile marine. After eleven months of war in Europe, the tonnage of the merchant shipping under the American flag was equal to that under any other two flags combined, except the British. By June 30th, 1915, the increase in registered tonnage was three times as great as any which

had occurred in American history. About 523,600 tons of foreign-built vessels were transferred to the American flag, the total increase in shipping registered for foreign trade being 795,311 tons. There was enormous activity in the shipbuilding yards, owing to the impetus of the extraordinarily high freights. After first looking forward to possessing at the end of the war the third greatest merchant fleet in the world, the Americans began to think, as the struggle in Europe lengthened out, that they would finally develop, when peace was made, a mercantile

75

DIRECTORS OF ORDNANCE AND ARTILLERY.
Major-General Sir Stanley von Donop, K.C.B., Master-General of the Ordnance (right), leaving the War Office with Brigadier-General H. G. Smith, C.B., Director of Artillery.

marine greater than that of Germany, and able to compete with that of Britain. It must be remembered that before their Civil War the Americans had swept the seas of the world with their clippers, and had possessed the fastest ships in every trade. We afterwards clean outraced them, and took the carrying trade from them, by constructing first iron, and then steel, steamers, while their unenterprising shipbuilders were still constructing wooden vessels. It was not so much their Civil War as their lack of large inventiveness which prevented the Americans from keeping their mercantile marine at the height of its power. Long afterwards the high cost of skilled labour in the United States and the undeveloped condition of many of their shipyards hindered them from competing not only with Britain but with Germany. But the enormous rise in freights more than compensated for the cost of skilled American labour during the war. There

American suspicions of Britain were occasions when a ship could earn her cost in a couple of voyages. Shipbuilding therefore became once more a great American industry, though some observers wondered whether it would survive the strain of competition when all the British and German plant engrossed in war work was liberated for peaceful purposes, together with hundreds of thousands of skilled men, hungry for employment.

Meanwhile, however, the extraordinary increase in the American mercantile marine rapidly continued, thus providing the American industrialists, reaching to new markets, with the great cargo fleets they needed. And now we come to the ticklish point which lay at the root of our chief troubles with the United States. The great Trust magnates, who still exercised large powers in Congress, were suspicious of our methods of searching for contraband,

and conceived that these methods were subtly designed to hinder the development of American shipping. We were supposed to have adopted a dog-in-the-manger policy, with the aim of checking neutral shipping trade, until such time as our own manufacturers and shipowners could devote all their energies to peaceful commerce. There is no need to inform British readers that the American suspicions were utterly groundless. From the British point of view, Mr. Asquith and Sir Edward Grey were the very reverse of Machiavellian statesmen, and, indeed, rather endangered the existence and the interests of the Empire by a trustful innocency of soul, which, like the similar quality of Mr. Bryan, might have been angelic if it had not been childish. But all Americans had learned at school the legend of English perfidy, and, like Frenchmen of a bygone generation and Germans of our days, regarded the politicians of our unfortunate country as being capable of anything.

We must also remember that some of the measures employed by certain powerful American Trust magnates, when struggling with their own countrymen for power, were as base and as subtle as any used in Italy in the age of Machiavelli. The morals of industrial America were at times those of the wildest period of the Italian Renaissance ; but having no splendid bloom of art to spread an iridescence over the corruption of the Puritan conscience, the antagonists allowed their womenfolk to develop an artless, shoddy idealism that blossomed into the Higher Thought and Christian Science. But beneath all the idle, uncreative sentimentality of the superfatted American middle-class soul, a fierce, strong, and very practical plutocracy eliminated the smaller men **Methods of the** and organised itself in a permanent **Trust magnates** manner by means as pitiless as any known in history. Nothing, indeed, could compare with the great American plutocrats except the financial magnates of the Roman commonwealth just before the rise of Marius. And it is said that the wicked are always suspicious.

But Sir Edward Grey's countrymen, at least, were convinced that he was absolutely sincere in his desire to deal with all neutral shipping as fairly as the circumstances created by Germany allowed. Our Empire could not afford to misuse its sea-power. Did we do so, we should have raised up too many enemies against us. We held the seas for about a hundred years after Trafalgar, without any serious challenge from any Great Power, simply because we had the good sense to be fair to all other countries. Foreigners used our world rings of ports and coaling-stations with practically as much freedom and convenience as if they had been Britons. Our policy of Free Trade would have been worth little or nothing to other competing industrial nations if we had not maintained at the same time the policy of free ports and coaling-stations. And this we did without any pressure or agitation from our trade rivals. Rightly or wrongly, we almost gloried in rivalry in commerce, in the expressed faith that the more closely interwoven were all the international strands of trade and finance, the stronger was the permanent basis of peace between the leading Powers.

Yet, unjust and unfounded as were the suspicions of the American plutocracy in regard to our manner of stopping and searching American ships and American cargoes, these suspicions tended at times to endanger the relations between the Allies and the United States. Sometimes the magnates began by being merely greedy, and when their greed was checked became hostile. Such seems to have been the case with the Beef Trust of Chicago, which before the war was so powerful that it was said to be able to fix the price of meat in London markets. The Trust had considerable power of control over the export of cattle in the Argentine, and when our Government tried to get Argentine beef for the troops on fair terms, the Trust established practically a monopoly, and raised the price in an extraordinary manner. But one of our official representatives at Buenos Ayres had an original sweep of mind, unusual in

Viscount French reviewing troops in camp after his appointment as Field-Marshal Commanding-in-Chief in the United Kingdom. Although a comparative relief after the strain of his sixteen months at the front, these new duties were by no means light.

An inspection by the Field-Marshal of practice trenches at a training centre for recruits who enlisted under Lord Derby's Group System. Lord French took keen interest in watching troops engaged in learning to dig trenches on the latest model, to handle machine-guns, and to throw bombs.

Viscount French of Ypres watching " Derby " recruits at bayonet practice. Splendid appreciations of the Field-Marshal's brilliant work were published in the French Press, the following extract being typical: " He takes with him on his return to England our admiration and gratitude, and he can be assured that France will never forget the incomparable service which he has rendered her."

VISCOUNT FRENCH OF YPRES INSPECTING MEN OF HIS HOME COMMAND.

ALONG THE " L. OF C." IN THE HOME COUNTRY.
Guarding the lines of communication somewhere in England. All over
the Empire was this vigil kept day and night, for every road from Van-
couver, Fiji, Tasmania and Cape Town led to Flanders, and was therefore
kept inviolate.

Since the Germans were the first
to restrict the free sale of American
wheat by the violent, illegal method
of sinking an American-owned
wheat-ship sailing for England, it
might be fancied that President
Wilson was in this passage sternly
warning the Kaiser. But he was
not. He was preparing to show
France and Britain that Kansas
had the right to feed the armies
that ravaged Belgium, Northern
France, Poland, and Serbia, and
to provide bread for the submarine
crews who murdered non-combatants in passenger liners, and for
their mates in the Zeppelins.

a bureaucrat. He answered the American move by
getting control of all the vessels with refrigerating chambers
available for the Argentine trade. The Trust could not
can its meat in South America, and had to come to terms
with the British official who had all the refrigeration
steamers. But the Trust wanted to feed with bully-beef
the German and Austrian Armies, as well as the British
Army. Naturally its cargoes were seized on the way to
neutral ports as conditional contraband. In many of
these cases our Government was ready to buy the captured meat at a fair price. But this just solution of the
difficulty did not please the Trust. It wanted to obtain
full facilities for selling in both the British and the German
military markets at war prices, to break the blockade and
at the same time reap the profit caused by the blockade.
By this means it could set the German commissariat
department outbidding the British, and finally extort,
from which side it did not care, a much higher price for
its goods.

This seems to have been the general source of complaint
by Americans in regard to our contraband policy. We
were alleged, when we stopped goods that seemed destined
for the use of the Teutonic armies, to be creating a new kind
of monopoly—a monopoly of purchase.
The Americans had to sell to us and to
our Allies, because the allied market was
the only one within reach. This was
undoubtedly so in regard to the larger part of goods on the
contraband list, especially when this list was extended in
answer to the German proclamation of a submarine blockade
of the British Isles. The Allies' purchasing monopoly in the
market for contraband goods was a natural consequence
of our possession of sea-power. The chief American makers
of contraband goods, such as rifles, guns, and shells, did
not complain that they could not raise their prices against
the Allies by getting also the Teutonic markets. But the
wheat-growers of Kansas and the beef barons of Chicago
became, as the war went on, increasingly indignant that
they could not feed the German and Austrian Armies as
well as the soldiers and civilians of Britain, France, Italy,
and all the neutral States.

The condition of feeling caused in the Middle States by
the restriction of their markets augmented in violence
down to February, 1916, when President Woodrow Wilson,
in a speech in Kansas, said :

The Germans
born blunderers

America has the right to feed the nations of the world with your
wheat. When there is a blockade we recognise the right to blockade,
but the world needs wheat from Kansas, and America has the
right to see that the warring nations get it. To do this the country
must prepare itself to show other nations that it is determined
that its ideals shall be respected.

THE SILENT AND INTERMINABLE WATCH.
Keeping guard in a railway-yard barracks. Many of the men on home
service were requisitioned in this, certainly one of the most responsible
duties of the soldier.

Between Great Britain and the United States there was,
happily, a treaty for the arbitration of difficulties that
tended to postpone any possible war for at least a year,
and give the two peoples time for full consideration. Thus,
if treaties meant anything to English-speaking nations,
there was never any immediate danger of an outbreak of
hostilities, though the irresponsible threats of establishing
an embargo, first on wheat and then on munitions, might,
if carried out, have dealt a very serious blow to the Allies,
while evading in a nominal manner the dishonouring of the
treaty for arbitration. Had the Germans in both Berlin
and Washington been clever enough to be quiet in regard
to the United States, and refrain from intrigue in America
and the murder of American citizens on the high seas,
things might have gone badly with the Allies through
Great Britain getting into trouble over her contraband
policy and American shipping. But the German, with
all his thoroughness, talent for organisation, and steady
patience in preparatory labour, was a born blunderer.
Owing to the overweening conceit of his strength, he could
never adopt an attitude of masterly inactivity. He was
the champion of organised efficiency, and, disregarding
the proper feelings of neutral nations who seemed likely
to be of service to him, he proceeded energetically to organise
them. In some countries his work was remarkably successful. Nothing like it has been seen since the ages when

Philip of Spain and Louis of France succeeded in bribing the Stuart Kings of England to check English interests. In Italy, Sweden, and Spain powerful aristocratic, political, and religious forces were subtly transformed into Germanic streams of power, and men of genius and high reputation, such as Sven Hedin, came forth as fervent admirers of the spoilers of Belgium.

The sprawling, loosely-ordered mixture of races in the United States seemed to offer a more important field for the organisation of opinion by German methods. The Germans themselves reckoned that there were twenty million German-Americans standing helplessly on the farther side of the Atlantic Ocean, and watching their Fatherland surrounded by a ring of flame and steel. The impulse to do something was irresistible; and on January 30th, 1915, some fifty-eight representative German-Americans launched in Washington an organisation, the aim of which was declared merely to be the establishment of "genuine American neutrality." We have already given details in Volume III. of THE GREAT WAR of the principal leaders of this dangerous Neutrality League. Among them, we may now add, were Congressmen who tried to pass Bills establishing an embargo on munitions, and other men who aimed at bringing about a war with Britain.

SOMETHING LIKE HOME.
Officer's quarters on the lines of communication.

The German-American Neutrality League excited much attention in Germany and America. It was denounced by the Press of the Eastern States, some newspapers reprinting an illuminating passage from General von Bernhardi's work, entitled "Germany and the Next War." The passage, written in 1912, ran:

In our direct interests we cannot withdraw from the duty of supporting Germans in foreign countries in their struggle for existence, and keeping them loyal to their nationality. Isolated groups of Germans abroad greatly benefit our trade, since by preference they import their goods from their Fatherland. But as we are discovering in America, they may also be useful to us as a political force. The German-Americans have formed a political

alliance with the Irish, and in this combination constitute a power in the United States with which that Government must reckon

In February, 1915, the German Press began to celebrate the execution of the scheme confidently revealed beforehand by Bernhardi. The "Frankfurter Zeitung" said:

Suddenly, in the hour of need and peril to their old home, the Germans have rallied, and it is seen they are a political power of first rank in American life. For these German-Americans number more than three million voters. By reason of their numerous associations, they are splendidly organised, and able to defy the despotism of English opinion.

Then, as the Krupp organ, the "Rheinisch Westfalische Zeitung," prophesied, the German-American party, uniting with the Irish-Americans," will soon be so strong that not only will it be sure of being treated with the greatest consideration, but it will in time direct the course of affairs in the United States." The first exercise of power by the German League began with the cry raised in February, 1915, that Britain's only scheme for winning the war was to cut off the food of German babies. But it was the German Government which made wheat, grain, and flour conditional contraband on February 1st, 1915, by requisitioning all the supplies in the German Empire, and placing the consumption under official control.

And some time before this, as we have already seen, the captain of the Prinz Eitel Friedrich had sunk by a dynamite bomb the American wheat-ship, William P. Frye, bound from Seattle to Falmouth, declaring that wheat was contraband. It was not, therefore, the Allies who instituted the stoppage of food supplies; and, as the world afterwards learned, the first idle charge against the British of starving millions of German women and children was merely a dramatic effect, intended to palliate the inauguration of the Teutonic plan of submarine piracy. The desired effect was fully obtained in German-American circles, and the agitation against our alleged cruelty to German babies was used to nerve the conspirators against American life and property, and to maintain at white heat the passion against the Allies. In the course of a year a monster petition, supposed to have been signed by a million American woman interested in the fate of the babies of Germany, was brought into the American Senate.

In a more indirect manner, the creation of a strong German-American organisation led to the defeat of President Woodrow Wilson's Ship Purchase Bill in February, 1915. On entering upon office, the Democratic President

Ship Purchase Bill defeated

"WHO GOES THERE?"
Sentry on the lines of communication gives the familiar call and lowers his bayonet until he is assured by the friendly countersign.

In his despatch of October 15th, 1915, Viscount French described how a field-gun was brought up to close quarters to support a threatened infantry position during an attack on a German salient between Boesinghe and Ypres. "To reach its position," the despatch stated, "the gun had to be taken over a high canal embankment, rafted over the canal under fire, pulled up a bank with a slope of nearly forty-five degrees, and then dragged over three trenches and a sky-line to its position, seventy yards from the German lines." In campaigns previous to the Great War artillery was used extensively in advanced positions, when the gun fire had failed to reach certain points which, held by the enemy, might have wrecked an infantry attack that was unsupported by artillery brought forward with its advance.

ARTILLERY BEING BROUGHT UP TO SUPPORT A BRITISH INFANTRY ATTACK NEAR YPRES.

had resolved to lower freights by establishing a marine controlled by the Government. Seeing the waste of shipping caused by the internment of German vessels in American ports, the President proposed to spend some eight million pounds in purchasing some of the ships, and using them for the expansion of American commerce. The matter could probably have been arranged with the Allies, if the purchase money had been held in trust until the end of the war on conditions that would have left the enemy lines incapable of raising money on mortgage and heavily mulcted in internal expenses. But Congress was suspicious of sinister forces being behind the Ship Purchase Bill. The condition of Congress during the fight excited more apprehension than the fortunes of the Bill. One large banking firm was attacked unfairly as being the agent of Ballin and the Kaiser; and another banking house was assailed, equally without proof, for lobbying in British interests. The upshot was that the Hamburg-Amerika line was not relieved of its great internment charges. On the other hand, freights to Britain continued to rise enormously, to the disadvantage of both the American and the British people, and to the profit only of a small ship-owning class. In retrospection it seems as though President Woodrow Wilson had been remarkably foresightful in making his ship-purchase plan, and that if it had been carried out, as he proposed, in such way as would leave no disturbed conditions of neutrality, it might have relieved some of the economic pressure in our islands due to lack of shipping.

Meanwhile, the farmers of Kansas found something else to think about than a wheat embargo. The crop in their single State had sold for twenty million pounds, but little of the profit had come to them. Many of the farmers got two shillings and ninepence a bushel for their wheat; but in the Chicago pit the price rose to seven shillings a bushel. The wheat-growers wanted to know who had taken the other four shillings and threepence at which the wheat had sold. The famous bumper crop had made millionaires among the speculators in Chicago and New York. There was a widespread fear that they would let their own people starve in order to make more money out of the European market.

But, by a strange vicissitude of mind, some authorities in the Eastern States began to advocate a wheat embargo. The Mayor of New York, for example, addressed the President on the matter. Woodrow Wilson replied with the calming statement that the store of American wheat was so enormous that export could safely continue until the next harvest.

But the wheat problem was soon forgotten in the anxiety over the German submarine campaign against both neutral

Mr. Wilson's Note to Germany

NIGHT ON THE WESTERN FRONT NEAR YPRES.
With a British patrol on night-duty, leaving our lines to get into touch with troops cut off by a hurricane fire. The illumination from the burning houses and farm buildings added to the perils of the men. The above drawing is from a sketch by a member of the patrol.

and allied ships of commerce trading to the British Isles. There was at first very little sympathy with Britain in the matter. We were judged to be as lawless as our enemy. "Is it recklessness or desperation that moves England and Germany to imperil our neutrality in their frantic efforts to starve each other into submission?" asked the "Literary Digest," a fairly representative journal of New York. Our method of stopping and examining cargoes under neutral flags was placed on the same level as the Teutonic method of torpedoing or mining merchant ships and murdering their crews. President Woodrow Wilson tried to meet the difficulties by sending Notes to Britain and Germany. In the Note to Britain he expressed a hope that British vessels would not make a deceptive use of the United States flag in the area of submarine blockade defined by the German declaration. The Note to Germany was more important. In it President Woodrow Wilson stated on February 4th, 1915:

" If the commanders of German vessels of war should destroy on the high seas an American vessel or the lives of American citizens, it would be difficult for the Government of the United States to view the act in any other light than as an indefensible violation of neutral rights, which it would be very hard, indeed, to reconcile with the friendly relations now happily subsisting between the two Governments. If such a deplorable situation should arise, the Imperial German Government can readily appreciate that the Government of the United States would be constrained to hold the Imperial Government of Germany to a strict accountability for such acts of their naval authorities, and to take any steps it might be necessary to take to safeguard American lives and property, and to secure to American citizens the full enjoyment of their acknowledged rights on the high seas."

The sinking of the William P. Frye—not known until her destroyer, the Prince Eitel Friedrich, steamed in March, 1915, into a United States port—had created, the situation to which President Wilson referred. Submarine and aircraft attacks on other American vessels quickly followed, and on May 7th, 1915, came the crowning act of piracy, in the torpedoing of the Lusitania and the murder of more than a hundred citizens of the United States. At the same time, the murder of American citizens on land and the destruction of American property increased, as the Austro-German dynamiters became more daring. Germany was at last engaging with all her strength in the secret war against the people of the United States, the plans for which had been developing for quite a quarter of a century. The United States Government was to be attacked by a great political plot while the armament works were blown up.

A NATION AT VULCAN'S FORGE: SCENES IN THE FRENCH MUNITION FOUNDRIES.

Every other trade having practically come to a standstill, all France may be said to have been busy turning out gigantic quantities of munitions. The two photographs reproduced above show respectively a moulding foundry where gun parts were being removed from the moulds, and consignments of 370 mm. shells being placed on the rail side in one of the works preparatory to being sent to the front.

THE GERMANIC CONSPIRACY AGAINST THE UNITED STATES.

German Attempts to Found Colonies in America—Organisation of German-Americans in the Samoan Conflict and the American-Spanish War—Great Britain and the United States Form an Entente Against Germany—Plot to Drag America into a War with Huerta of Mexico—Papen Tries to Make a Corner in High-Explosives and Poison-Gas—Austro-Hungarian Intrigue to Control Congress —Rebuff to the Teutonic Plotters in Illinois and Chicago—Three Million American Slavs Organise Against the American Germans —Remarkable Story of the Midvale Company, and Victory of the American Business Men—Plotters Try to Terrorise the United States' Manufacturers and Workmen—Numerous Fires and Explosions on Munition Ships—Robert Fay and His Special Bombs —Koenig Tries to Blow-up Welland Canal—One of Tirpitz's " Big Six " Sets Out for the American Front—His National Peace Council and its Congress Leaders—Another Attempt at an American-Mexican War—Germany's Puppet is Arrested, and Rintelen Finds a Home of Rest in England—Bernstorff, Papen, and Boy-Ed Continue Rintelen's Work—The Austro-Hungarian Ambassador Retires Hurt—The Great Secret War Between the American Secret Service and the Teutonic Conspiracy—Papen and Boy-Ed are Defeated—The " Idiotic Yankees " and the Affair of the Papen Papers—Berlin Sues for Peace in the Matter of Bomb Warfare, and Renews the Political Intrigue—President Wilson Asks for a Great Navy and Army—Bernstorff and Tirpitz Try to Trap the American Government—Recoil of President Wilson and Critical Relations With Germany.

ALTHOUGH many Americans do not yet recognise the fact, Luxemburg, Belgium, Serbia, Montenegro, France, Russia, and Britain might have been saved from war if our country had let Germany work her will upon the United States. The Kaiser was wont to remark in confidence to his English friends that his new Navy, the second in power in the world, was not directed against British sea-power. It was primarily intended to overreach the Navy of the United States, and ensure the expansion of Germany in the Gulf of Mexico and in South America. It was an instrument for abolishing the Monroe Doctrine, which prevented Germany from obtaining that place in the sunshine of Brazil which her emigrants were trying to found in two of the most important Brazilian states. There were the German Brazilian Bank, the Bank of Chili and Germany, the Bank of Central America, and the German Overseas Bank engaged in the work of pacific penetration. More than two hundred million pounds of German capital was sunk in Brazil, Venezuela, Colombia, Argentina, Peru, and Chili.

This represented the greater part of Germany's oversea investments, and the figures were published in detail by the German Marine Office to convince the German people of the necessity of building a three-hundred-million-pound fleet of Dreadnoughts and

LORD ROBERT CECIL
[*Elliott & Fry.*]
Under-Secretary for Foreign Affairs. He entered the Cabinet, February, 1916, as Minister in charge of the new department for the control of blockade and contraband.

super-Dreadnoughts. The menace of that fleet to the Navy of the United States was much greater, and at one time much more imminent, than its threat to the Navy of Great Britain. Indeed, it might be said that the threat to British sea-power was partly in the nature of a disguise for what seemed to be the more practical operations against the vital interests of the United States. The Germans and the Americans had first clashed in 1889, in Samoa. Each wanted to dominate the islands and to construct a naval harbour and coaling-station. It was during the Samoan conflict that the German-American plotters first displayed their widespread, sinister power; for when the American flag had been fired upon in Samoa and the warlike feelings of the American people were stirred, nearly two hundred German organisations met in Chicago, and, with much cheering for the Fatherland, banded themselves together for common action. Similar meetings were held in Kansas City and in Toledo.

During the Spanish American War in 1898, the German-American organisation was greatly strengthened, and throughout the German Empire a campaign was carried on against the Americans with as much malignant violence as the later German movement of passion engineered against the British people during the South African War. The German Admiralty and the German Great Staff thought at the time that the Americans would be defeated by the Spaniards. They tried to profit through the strain on both belligerent nations, by acquiring a coaling-station in the Philippines. There is also considerable evidence that the German Main Fleet prepared for a rush to South America, portions of which were intended to be seized as a foundation for a new Colonial Empire. Our country prevented the attack upon Admiral Dewey's squadron in the Philippines, where our warships cleared for action in support of Admiral Dewey, after the German flag had been fired upon and a German launch had narrowly escaped being sunk. The German swoop on South America was also prevented by a large British naval concentration at Gibraltar.

Germany and the Monroe Doctrine

Meanwhile, Great Britain and the United States had come to an understanding with regard to measures of precaution against the enemy threatening both of them. Our Government knew that the Germans were plotting in South Africa to raise the Boers against us, in order so to weaken us that we should not be able to assist the United States in maintaining the Monroe Doctrine. So, by way of preparing for the coming conflict, Britain and the United States, in 1897, entered into an entente of a loose and defensive nature. Both Governments agreed that German colonies or protectorates in the Gulf of Mexico, South America, and the Philippines would be dangerous to American and British interests. There was a rearrangement of affairs in the Gulf of Mexico, by which Britain sacrificed certain advantages in order to strengthen the power of the United States. An understanding was also arrived at in regard to the action which each country would take should certain circumstances arise. There was, however, no reference, in the British-American entente, to the possibilities of a great European war; for neither Lord Salisbury nor President McKinley foresaw that the check to German expansion in America would lead to the thrust towards the Persian Gulf and the stroke at Serbia and Russia which brought about the most terrible war in history.

There are grounds for believing that the German war-party still hankered after a settlement with the United States, at the very time when the war against Russia and France was being urgently prepared. The first of the papers found in the possession of Captain von Papen, at Falmouth, on January 2nd, 1916, related to intrigues with Mexican revolutionaries, the design of which was to force President Woodrow Wilson to engage in a long, wearing, and costly war against the guerilla bands of Mexican peons. Captain Boy-Ed, the German naval attaché at Washington, wrote to Captain von Papen, the German military attaché, favouring the selection of General Huerta as the champion of German interests. From Boy-Ed's letter it appeared that Rear-Admiral von Hintze thought that Huerta was too weak a character to carry on a successful war with the United States. The admiral wanted the German Fleet to sail for Mexico in May, 1914, and make the position there uncomfortable for the American nation by forcing international intervention in Mexican affairs. A Hamburg-Amerika liner sailed to Vera Cruz with a cargo of ten thousand rifles, fifteen million cartridges, and some machine-guns, and though the United States had landed an army at Vera Cruz to prevent the import of arms for General Huerta, the German munitions were delivered to the man. When, in spite of this aid, Huerta was defeated, Captain Kohler, commanding the Dresden, offered him his ship "for any use he cared to make of it," and Huerta left Mexico on July 20th, 1914, on the German cruiser. The day after Huerta sailed in the Dresden the German Foreign Minister at Berlin told the British Ambassador that there would be no outside interference in the quarrel between Austria and Serbia, and two days later the Austrian ultimatum was delivered.

German intrigues in Mexico

IN THE RANKS OF THE MUNITION MAKERS: WOMEN OF BRITAIN BEHIND THE GUNS.
"Assembling" shell-fuses in a munition factory, an important part of the diversified war work almost entirely carried out by women of all social grades in machine shops. Few upheavals resulting from the world-war were more remarkable than the enthusiastic incursion of women into munition factories, where they accomplished all the work necessary for the completion of some types of shells.

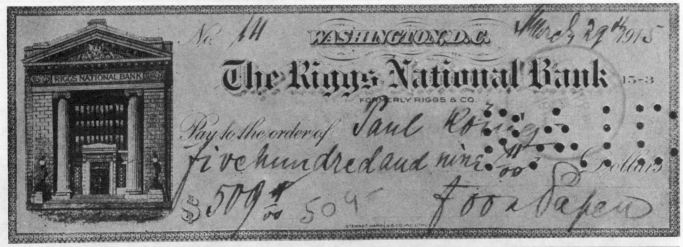

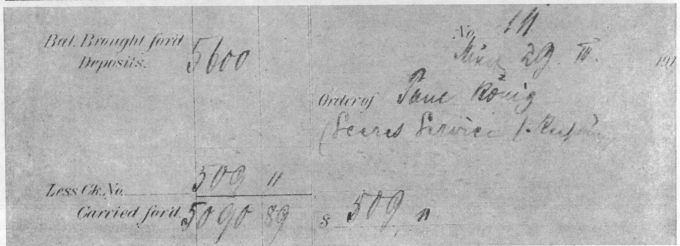

TO THE ORDER OF THE GERMAN SECRET SERVICE IN THE U.S.A.

Facsimile and counterfoil of one of the numerous cheques made payable to Paul Koenig, and specifically naming Secret Service. Paul Koenig was arrested in the United States on December 17th, 1915, and charged with having conspired to destroy the Welland Canal. The facsimiles, with many others, appeared in the Parliamentary Paper Miscellaneous No. 6 (1916): "Selection from papers found in the possession of Captain von Papen, late Military Attaché at Washington, Falmouth, January 2nd and 3rd, 1916."

There was a close connection between the German intrigues to draw the United States into a struggle with Mexico and the outbreak of the European War. The Germans knew something about the loose, verbal entente between Britain and the United States, but could not be certain of its scope. As a matter of fact, it was merely an unwritten friendly arrangement concerning common localised interests in Central and South America, and referred only to possible German aggression. But, by reason of its very looseness and vagueness, the common enemy of both English-speaking Powers could not be certain that there was not a wide scheme for mutual defensive action underlying the entente. Therefore a design was made to cripple the small military power of the United States by means of a Mexican war. Afterwards, when President Woodrow Wilson, by a policy of masterly inactivity, let the other Mexican generals fight out their quarrels of personal ambition, the German Embassy at Washington brought forth its puppet, Huerta, and made another move against the United States in February, 1915. German officers were sent to Mexico and Guatemala to drill the people, and according to letters published in "La Voz de la Revoluçion," a newspaper of Merida, Mexico, President Cabrera of Guatemala and General Huerta entered into an agreement with Germany to raise a new army in Mexico, overthrow General Carranza, and provoke war with the United States.

Soon after this plot was made, the Germans settled General Huerta on Long Island, New York, in the character of a peaceful American citizen. Huerta bought a small estate, and announced he was tired of war and desirous only of keeping his lawn trim and his garden flowery. But, for reasons we shall see later, his protestations did not delude the American Secret Service men. They allowed him to make, with the help of Germany, all preparations for the new stroke in Mexico. But when he tried to cross the Mexican border he was very neatly arrested, under a charge of conspiracy to violate the neutrality of the United States.

The German idea underlying this last plot for an American-Mexican war was more practical and better based than the early Vera Cruz intrigue. It aimed at stopping the supply of American munitions to France, Russia, and Britain by forcing the United States into a difficult struggle with her southern neighbour, in a barren, mountainous country held by large bodies of veteran fighters. So arduous and prolonged would the struggle have been that the German plotters calculated that the American armament firms would have been too busy supplying the needs of their own armies to spare any considerable munitions for the Allies.

The failure of this great scheme compelled the German conspirators to develop the other means they had been employing for interfering with the export of arms. They

REAR-ADMIRAL SIR DUDLEY DE CHAIR,
Adviser to the Foreign Office on questions connected with foreign trade and blockade.

RUN AGROUND AFTER ENCOUNTER WITH U BOAT.
French transport torpedoed in the Mediterranean, but run ashore in the neighbourhood of the allied operations to save valuable stores destined for Salonika. Two of the pack donkeys were let loose to graze in the adjacent fields.

used three principal methods of hindering the munitioning of the allied armies. The least objectionable method consisted in trying to monopolise certain war material and in making arrangements with American armament firms for buying up all their products. Mr. Thomas Edison was induced to sell his large output of phenol, used in the production of high explosives, to a German medical man, Dr. Schweitzer. The doctor **How Edison** made a public declaration that the phenol **was deceived** was only to be used for medicinal purposes, and Edison in an interview prided himself on his pacifist principles and the saving of German lives he was effecting by selling his phenol to the humanitarian Teuton. But from a military report to the Ministry of War at Berlin, signed by Captain von Papen, and dated August 20th, 1915, it appears that the public declaration concerning Edison's phenol was only made as a blind. And other written evidence discovered on Papen at Falmouth suggests that some of the high explosive was used in blowing up American factories. The Etna Explosives Company was also indirectly connected with the German intriguers through the Bridgeport Projectile Company, of Connecticut. Towards the end of April, 1915, the Projectile Company was apparently bought over by the Germans, Captain von Papen showing great skill in his management of the affair. A Russian and British Commission was negotiating with the Bridgeport Projectile Company for a large supply of shrapnel shell. The German design was for the company to undertake the contract and fail to fulfil it, making such large promises in the meantime as should keep other and more eager American firms from getting orders for shrapnel. According to Captain von Papen's statement, British Secret Service men, working in the United States, discovered this subtle intrigue, and enabled the Allies to break off negotiations with the Bridgeport Projectile Company in good time to find other firms ready to supply the shell.

Wider in scope was the attempt to make a corner in all the liquid chlorine in the United States—the chlorine being intended for the manufacture of poison gas. This failed through the Castner Chemical Company, one of the principal chlorine makers, being friendly to Britain. Another important scheme, which did not come to anything, was a series of negotiations to buy up the aeroplane patents of the Wright Brothers. It was at first thought by the German Embassy that the Wright Brothers held such a master-patent that the purchase of it would enable the agents of the German Government to stop the Curtiss Company from making machines for the Allies. It was, however, afterwards discovered that the Wright patents could not be used in this manner; and negotiations with the company were therefore broken off. The Austro-Hungarian Ambassador, Dr. Dumba, entered into relations with Mr. Meagher, a partner in the Chicago firm of Armour & Co., which, with the firm of Swift & Co., controlled the meat market. After yachting together, Dr. Dumba and Mr. Meagher discussed a scheme for bringing Britain and France to terms, by refusing to send any meat from the United States and the Argentine. But, as Dr. Dumba explained on August 20th, 1915, in a letter to Baron von Burian, Austro-Hungarian Minister for Foreign Affairs: "At the present moment Mr. Meagher and his companions are paralysed in the Argentine by the action of the British Admiralty, for the latter have commandeered most of the English freight-ships intended for the transport of Argentine meat." In the same letter Dr. Dumba remarked that he was in touch with the leaders of the American Cotton Trust, but feared that the threat of confiscation, under the British proclamation of a cotton **Dr. Dumba** contraband, would make the magnates **outwitted** agree to sell the greater part of the crop to Britain. Another audacious attempt at general control made by the Teutons was to try to purchase the entire business of the American Associated Press, which supplied news to about eleven thousand American newspapers. As in most of the other cases, the negotiations were conducted under cover of a middleman, apparently unconnected with the German and Austrian Embassies; but, happily for the Americans and the Allies, the American Press Association was not for sale to anybody at any money. Mr. Edward Lyell Fox, general manager of Wildman's Magazine and News Service, was won over by means that may have been quite fair, though his conduct was not always correct.

The sum spent by the German Government in the United States was enormous. In the ordinary way it would have quickly led to a very heavy fall in the value of the mark. But the Deutsche Bank, which supplied the huge funds, seems to have sent over American securities held by Germans and collected by the Government for war purposes. Out of this fund a powerful Press campaign was financed in order to bring pressure to bear upon American politicians. According to the report made by Dr. Dumba to the Foreign Minister of Austria-Hungary, the Austrian and German Embassies at Washington had won over the legislative bodies in certain States, and could have got them to vote for the prohibition of the export of munitions. Schwegel, the Austro-Hungarian Consul at St. Louis, Missouri, seems to have been **Pro-German Press campaign** one of the chief agents in conducting the political intrigue. Schwegel thought, on August 11th, 1915, that he could get a vote passed in the House of Representatives in favour of a measure of embargo. But he stated that he feared the measure would be wrecked in the Senate.

" And in any case," he continued in his Political Report No. 81, " there would not be forthcoming, in either House, the two-thirds majority necessary to put the resolution, when passed, into force against the President's veto. It follows that the delivery to the

Allies of arms and munitions and other materials of war will continue undisturbed. . . . But an agitation should be set on foot to introduce total separation of passenger traffic from transport of munitions. This is a point which can be carried through Congress. President Wilson would not be in a position to veto a Bill in that direction."

The last sentences enable us to measure the estimated power won by the alien conspirators up till August, 1915. Count Bernstorff and Dr. Dumba regarded themselves as being in a position to bring **Mr. Bryan and the intriguers** about the making of laws in Congress which American citizens would have to obey. They also apparently had control of the legislation in certain individual States, but thought there was no advantage in getting these local legislative boides to vote parallel resolutions for an embargo on munitions. The former Secretary of State, Mr. William J. Bryan, who had also for many years been the leader of the Democratic Party, went over to the Teutonic intriguers. One of Captain von Papen's paid agents, George von Skal, made the introductory speech at the Madison Square Garden meeting, at which Mr. Bryan addressed twenty-five thousand people in favour of a German peace. After Mr. Bryan had finished his oration, a member of the United States Congress—Mr. Volmer—spoke justifying the slaughter of Americans on the Lusitania. The Austrian Ambassador, the Turkish Minister, Captain von Papen, and Captain Boy-Ed were on the platform from which Mr. Bryan spoke. Mr. Bryan, who had thrice run for the Presidency as candidate for the Democratic Party which was in power, had resigned from President Wilson's

ON GUARD IN THE ALLIED CAUSE OFF SALONIKA.
French torpedo-boat ploughing through a choppy sea off the Gulf of Salonika, on patrol duty to watch for enemy submarines in the Ægean, and to guard French and British troopships and transport vessels steaming to the Gulf.

FUSILIERS AT BAYONET EXERCISE.
Learning to lunge at the enemy when he is entrenched. Recruits of the Royal
Fusiliers bayoneting sacks in place of Germans.

Cabinet in June, 1915, because he held that the second
Note sent by the United States to Germany in connection
with the torpedoing of the Lusitania was too strongly
worded. And four months before the second Note was sent,
Mr. Bryan, according to a statement published by him after
his resignation, had had a conversation with the Austrian
Ambassador, and had intimated that President Wilson's
first Note with regard to the Lusitania should not be taken
seriously.

Can it be wondered that the Teutonic plotters regarded
themselves as being at least part masters of the destiny
of the American nation ? They had the old leader of the
Democratic Party in the sphere of their influence, they
controlled the legislatures of certain States, and by playing
on the self-interest of the wheat States, cotton States, and
certain powerful Trust magnates, they calculated they

could pass Bills in the House of Representatives,
and, with a struggle, get the Bills through Congress. According to Dr. Dumba's report to
the Foreign Office at Vienna, only President
Woodrow Wilson towered above the web of
Teutonic intrigue.

"Last autumn," Dr. Dumba complained to his chief,
Baron von Burian, "the President, through his personal
influence, forced the House of Representatives to take
his view against their better judgment, and in the
Senate he overthrew a resolution already voted in favour
of prohibiting the export of guns and munitions."

Matters were not, of course, quite so favourable to the Teutons as Dumba supposed. Many
of the politicians in the House of Representatives
and in the Senate who appeared ready to vote
for an embargo on munitions were trying as
much to trick and capture the German-American
electorate as they were to make things uncomfortable for
their President. There were Republicans who would have
voted with the Democrats simply because they thought the
measure was sure to be unpopular and likely to destroy
the power of the Democratic Party for a generation. A
good deal of the political oratory in the United States
is extravagant and irresponsible, because
it is designed for a transient purpose and **Fishing in troubled**
is quickly forgotten alike by the speaker   **waters**
and by his audience. The conductors
of the intrigue were all foreigners, such as Bernhard
Dernburg, Count Bernstorff, Captain von Rintelen, Captain
von Papen, and Captain Boy-Ed. It was only their
subordinate agents who had any close acquaintance with
either the surface eddies or the strong undercurrents of
the strange, wild, frothy waters of American politics.

FROM CAVALRY TO INFANTRY.
Training Royal Horse Guards in infantry duties—digging and fortifying a trench on a golf-course near London.

NOVEL DUTIES FOR THE ROYAL HORSE GUARDS.
A machine-gun in position on a golf-course, where men of this famous cavalry regiment were taught to act as infantrymen.

Outside Congress, and outside the White House, there were strong, masterful, native Americans eagerly watching for President Woodrow Wilson to make a false step against the country's permanent vital interests, so that they might overthrow him and resume control over American policy. Some of the most prominent of these men, such as Colonel Roosevelt, Mr. Taft, and Senator Root, were not in the least afraid of the German vote, or of the two thousand German societies scattered about the United States.

The veritable strength of the foreign intriguers had already been tested by a couple of fighting elections. The first contest took place in October, 1914, when Mr. Roger Sullivan stood as Democratic nominee in the campaign for United States Senator from Illinois.

Roger Sullivan's striking defeat

He was supported by the German-American League, which issued a statement that:

All of us know he has been a friend of the Germans; his most intimate friends are Germans; his daughter is married to a sturdy young German; several times he has visited Germany, and he admires the German nation and its people. He is also an honorary member of several German organisations.

The pressure was too strong for the Democratic Party to resist. The chairman of the Democratic National Committee came to Chicago, and spoke from the platform with two leading German lawyers. The chairman revealed the fact that in the Baltimore Convention it was Roger Sullivan who had made Woodrow Wilson President of the United States. But simply because Sullivan was openly and strongly supported by the German organisations he was heavily defeated, and a Republican was made Senator from Illinois.

This striking defeat angered the German intriguers, for it had taken place in Chicago, which was the headquarters of the German propaganda and the stronghold of the German spy system. All the newspapers in Chicago, with one exception, seemed to be amenable to German influence. For the sake of Teutonic prestige, another attempt had to be made to dictate candidates and control the elections. It was in the municipal campaign in March, 1915, that the Germans in Chicago made a supreme effort to recover the ground they had lost. Their candidate, Mr. Robert M. Sweitzer, defeated the retiring mayor, Mr. Harrison, by a large majority in the Democratic primary. The Republican candidate for mayor, Mr. Thompson, was not well known, and he had the support of only one paper in Chicago. This paper received notice that it would not get a line of advertising unless it supported Sweitzer. A circular was widely distributed just before the election, in an English and a German version. It was one of the most extraordinary documents in the history of American politics. It ran as follows :

Chicago has a larger German population than any city in the world, excepting Berlin and Vienna, and the German, Austrian, and Hungarian Americans should at this coming election set every other consideration aside, and vote as a unit for Robert M. Sweitzer.

American v. German in Chicago Stand shoulder to shoulder in this election, as our countrymen in the trenches and on the high seas are fighting for the preservation of our dear Fatherland. The election of a German-American would be a fitting answer to the defamers of the Fatherland, and would cause a tremendous moral effect throughout the United States, and re-echo in Germany, Austria, and Hungary.

Leading Chicago politicians, such as Peter Reinberg, President of the County Board, put their names to this historic appeal. The result of it was that the German candidate, Sweitzer, was defeated in a smashing manner. Thompson, a man scarcely known before he came forward

THE EMPIRE WAR BY THE WATERS OF OLD NILE.
Indian troops transporting fodder and war material across the Nile by means of a floating bridge.

as an unhyphenated American candidate, received a vote larger than Roosevelt had done in 1904. But this victory of the American spirit over German intrigues was not so complete as the election returns indicated. Scarcely any man holding public office or seeking office in Chicago could escape from making the German confession of faith. He had to state that he was opposed to the shipment of war supplies from the United States. The same confession was required of nearly every public man in Illinois, and it was readily given, wrapped up in platitudes concerning the peace movement.

On November 2nd, 1915, the German vote defeated the Democrats in Maryland and Massachusetts, the Republican candidates being elected, from the Teutonic point of view, as a warning to President Wilson. In the Middle West both Democratic and Republican politicians, when bidding against each other for the German vote, often showed as little regard for the American spirit as the Teutonic intriguers. And, as we have seen in the previous chapter, President Wilson, when touring Kansas for the coming election, spoke with amazing sharpness against the Franco-British interference with the supply of American wheat to

the German Government. In some of these jerky flings against the Allies, however, there was a subtle movement against the alien directors of the Germanic conspiracy. Some American politicians tried to quieten and soothe the large peaceful elements of the German-American population, and win them by gradual means to an affirmed loyalty to the country in which they were settled.

The leaders of the German intrigue also met with opposition from a large body of recent emigrants from the Central Empires of Europe. On September 11th, 1915, representatives of more than three million Slavs—Bohemians, Poles, Croats, Ruthenians, and Bosnians—opened a two-days' conference in Chicago, the American capital of Germanism. They vigorously condemned the interference in American affairs by the Austrian Embassy at Washington, and they made specific charges that Dr. Dumba had subsidised Croatian newspapers for illegal purposes, and had fomented strikes and other lawless demonstrations.

At the time when this great Slav meeting was held, the Germanic conspirators recognised that they had been beaten in the political game. The torpedoing of the Lusitania had undone Dr. Dernburg's propaganda, by which he had temporarily convinced many Americans that the German invasion of Belgium and Northern France had been generally conducted according to the rules of civilised warfare. When Dernburg vanished, after losing, through lack of success in America, the reputation for great capability he had won as Colonial Secretary, Captain von Papen, Captain Boy-Ed, and Count Bernstorff showed more ability in trying to corner the munition supplies, while working with Captain von Rintelen and Dr. Dumba towards control of Congress. Had they been content to fight secretly or openly in the market for war supplies, and to manœuvre secretly or openly with the Germanic electorate, pacifist groups, and groups hostile to Britain and Japan, they would probably have won a certain measure of success. They would not have stopped the export of munitions, but they might have worked up trouble for the Allies with regard to the interference with American shipping.

But the plotters could not bring themselves to work entirely by comparatively peaceful means. They were men trained on the principles contained in the notorious German "War Book." They believed that great and highly-developed modern nations could quickly be subdued and reduced to impotent timidity by a swift and audacious system of terrorisation. They organised strikes in the factories where machine tools were being made ; and according to a statement contained in the Papen papers, they so checked the delivery of machinery and tools that even **Organisation of factory strikes** the delivery of shells being made to the order of the German Government was delayed for several months. Strikes were organised among the Hungarian and German working men at Bethlehem, Pittsburg, Bridgeport, Cleveland, and many other places. This was done by buying up newspapers read by the working classes, organising mass meetings and picnics, and sending—to quote a report despatched by Dr. Dumba to the Austro-Hungarian Foreign Office—"soap-box orators, who knew how to start a useful agitation." According to Dr.

Shabkadar Fort, north of the Khyber Pass and Peshawar, whence the British Division commanded by General Campbell moved out to attack the turbulent Mohmands. On September 5th, 1915, ten thousand of these rebel Pathan tribesmen were defeated near Hafiz Kor.

Armoured cars employed to cover the cavalry brigade in action and on reconnaissance duty during the operations against the Mohmands on the North-West Frontier of India. This minor campaign was due to Turco-German intrigue among the Mohammedan tribesmen.

An interesting contrast during the Indo-British activities near Hafiz Kor: Ancient and modern "Ships of the Desert"; an armoured car and a troop of transport camels with their native drivers on the North-West Frontier. The Mohmands are a powerful Pathan tribe living partly in Afghanistan, partly in independent tribal territory within the British frontier, and partly in districts around Peshawar.

Dumba's report, Captain von Papen was the mover of the attack upon the Bethlehem Steel Works and the munition factories of the Middle West, and he thought, in August, 1915, that he could disorganise and hold up for months some of the chief centres of the manufacture of munitions. The range and depth of this very ingenious scheme of munition strikes was remarkable. Even Slovak newspapers, representing the most downtrodden Slav race in Austria-Hungary, were transformed into machines for the great Germanic intrigue. The Slovaks, Croats, and Bosnian Serbs might sullenly rebel in their native country, where they were under martial law, but in the free, democratic land of the United States these Austrian Slavs were

GERMAN OFFICER PATROL ON THE BELGIAN SAND-DUNES.

FORMIDABLE TRENCH TRAP.
Cheval-de-frise suspended above an enemy trench about a hundred yards from the British line. During an assault such a trap would be let down, impeding the attackers and exposing them to a violent fire from behind the barricade in the middle of the trench.

sold into the hands of the Germanic plotters by their newspapers, their Union agitators, and other organs of intellectual representation.

But the American business men who ran the munition factories were not beaten by the strikes. Wages went up twenty-five to fifty per cent., and steel increased in price from one-half to double. All this was due more to the enormous demands of the Allies than to the strikes and secret purchases of the Germanic agents.

Steel magnates again in business But the most powerful American business men were only stimulated to great activity by the plots made to check the munition works. The tale of the Midvale Company brilliantly illustrates the final result of the intrigues of the German and Austrian Embassies. The Midvale Company had for thirty years been building big guns and armour-plate for the United States Government, but for twelve months it refused to accept orders from France, Britain, and Russia. About the time when the first clear revelation of Germanic intrigue was made, several retired steel magnates, who had worked with Mr. Carnegie and made immense fortunes, went into harness again. They secured an option on three hundred million tons of Cuban iron ore, bought up the Midvale Company, and formed a combination with the Remington Arms Company and the Worth Brothers Company, manufacturers of pig-iron.

By September, 1915, a rival to the Bethlehem Works had been created, and modern equipment on a vast scale was laid down for turning out big guns, large shells, armour-plate, machine-guns, and rifles for the Allies. The practised master-men, who thus returned to business, had made their money in creating the largest steel plant in the world ; and they at once recommenced at Midvale and its associated plants to aim at excelling Krupp in warlike productiveness. For practical purposes the Allies commanded the assistance of a new munition firm, that grew with enormous rapidity into a business capable of arming a great State. The size of the new corporation, of which Midvale was only the nucleus, was so vast that it was feared in some quarters that a new steel Trust had arisen. The magnates who returned to affairs had each millions of pounds to spare from their huge fortunes. They picked out many of the best of the younger minds in the sciences of steel-making and ordnance construction, and prepared not only to arm the Allies, but to make their own country secure from conquest. Captain von Papen, the directing intellect in the fire and explosion attack upon American munition plants, must have been a sadly **Mr. Wilson's defence programme** disappointed man when he learnt about the new Midvale Corporation. It was about this time that President Wilson astonished both friend and foe by putting forward a great national programme of defence. He proposed to spend about £80,000,000 in battleships and machinery and raise a new Continental army, estimated to number at the end of six years 1,200,000 men. This programme, regarded merely from the point of view of the Allies, served to encourage all American munition firms further to increase their plant and their output, in the prospect of large home orders after the foreign war orders had dwindled and ceased. Thus, in spite of all that the German intriguers could do, the industrial skill and energy of the United States continued to be devoted in increasing volume to the help of Russia, France, and Britain.

Then it was that the German policy of terrorisation was pursued with desperate audacity. Captain von Papen had begun to use violent methods in a desultory manner in September, 1914. His cheque-book shows that he then financed two spies, Von der Goltz and Caserta, both of whom tried to get work under the British Government, and opportunity for doing damage. On January 14th, 1915, Papen provided money for Kuepferle, the German spy who committed suicide in England the following

July. On January 18th, 1915, Papen gave seven hundred dollars to Werner von Horn, the man who made an attempt to blow up a railway bridge at Vanceboro, in Canada, on February 2nd of the same year. Then came the damning evidence in the cheques found on Papen at Falmouth. On May 11th, 1915, he drew a cheque for five hundred dollars to the order of the German Consulate at Seattle, a seaport in the State of Washington. The name of an agent—Schulenberg—is given on the cheque, and it is remarkable

Disclosures of Papen's cheque-book that a dynamite explosion occurred in Seattle Harbour on May 30th of the same year. On July 10th, 1915, Papen's cheque-book showed that he paid Tauscher, the American agent for Krupp, for a purchase of picric acid. Only about £14 worth of this high-explosive was purchased; it was not a large enough quantity to trouble about trying to smuggle into Germany, where there were large manufactories of the chemical. There were many cheques made out to Paul Koenig, with notes on the counterfoils that they were in payment for Secret Service. Koenig was the chief detective of the Hamburg-Amerika Line Bureau in New York, and we shall meet him at his work later. It was not unconnected with a curious note on the counterfoil of Papen's cheque-book on October 15th, 1915: "Bearer (G. Amsinck & Co.) for Berg. Fuse factory. Six hundred dollars." Fuse factories, picric acid supplies, and negotiations with manufacturers of dynamite are among the things that can be clearly traced in the cheque-book of Captain von Papen between September 1st, 1914, and December 10th, 1915.

By the end of November, 1915, there had occurred forty fires or mysterious explosions in American munition plants, causing more than a score of deaths and damage to property amounting to more than a million pounds. In one week the newspapers reported a great fire in the Baldwin Locomotive Works, where engines were being built for the Russian Government; the destruction of two buildings of the Midvale Works, which, according to American reports, was making Lee-Enfield rifles for the British Government; damage amounting to £300,000 to the ordnance plant of the Bethlehem Steel Company; a fire at Trenton, causing a loss of £200,000 to the Roebling Company, which was manufacturing wire cables for the Allies; and a fire in the ordnance plant of the Skelly Bolt Company, in Philadelphia. In the same period a great fire occurred in the chemical factory of the Synthetic Colour Company, of Stamford, Connecticut. The fires and explosions continued to the end of the year.

The works of the Du Pont Company, which manufactured explosives, were attacked first and frequently, and bomb explosions occurred in other American powder plants. On March 5th, 1915, the Du Pont Plant, at Haskell, New Jersey, was attacked; on April 1st, the Equitable Powder Plant, at Alton, Illinois, was damaged; on April 4th, a store of shell-fuses was exploded in a freight depôt at Pompton Lakes, New Jersey; on May 10th, the Du **Fires and bomb explosions** Pont Plant, at Carney's Point, New Jersey, was partly blown up; two bomb explosions occurred in the same plant on May 15th, and ten days later there was another explosion. On August 29th an attack was made on the Du Pont Plant, at Wilmington, Delaware. Among other outrages in the same period were a bomb explosion in the Westinghouse Electric Plant, Turtle Creek, Pennsylvania, and an attempt

THE ENEMY IN THE VOSGES: RESERVE TROOPS WAITING TO ADVANCE.

Reserve detachment of enemy infantry, sheltered behind rising ground, and awaiting orders to advance to the firing-line. It was in the Vosges that the German troops found themselves faced by the fierce valour of those renowned mountaineer-soldiers of France—the Chasseurs Alpins. After suffering badly at the hands of these picturesque warriors, the Germans nicknamed them the "Blue Devils."

FIRING RIFLE-GRENADES FROM A FIRST-LINE BRITISH TRENCH.
This striking photograph, obtained in a British firing trench, shows a grenade about to leave the barrel of the rifle the instant after the trigger had been pulled by the man on the left. Rifle-grenades were used as extensively as hand-grenades in trench fighting. Attached to a rod fitting into the barrel of the rifle, they were projected by a cartridge from which the bullet had been extracted.

in the spring of 1915 a German-American doctor named Kienzle, living in New York, wrote a letter to his father, Herbert Kienzle, who was the head of the Black Forest Clock Company in Würtemberg, said to be the largest clockmaking firm in the world. The firm was, of course, using its skilled clockmakers to make fuses for shells and bombs, and the manager had considerable influence with the Great German Staff. At the suggestion of his son in New York, he communicated with the German Secret Service, who in turn asked the military authorities for a man capable of undertaking desperate work.

Robert Fay, according to his story, was selected, and Herr Jansen, of the German Secret Service, gave him £800 and sent him to New York. But, before leaving Germany, Fay was ordered to study and commit to memory the documents sent by Dr. Kienzle to his father, the Black Forest clockmaker. The documents contained particulars of the sailings of various ships from American ports with munitions for the Allies, and detailed manifests of their cargoes. Railroads engaged in the transport of munitions were specified, particularly the New York Central and the New York, New Haven, and Hartford. Various firms were also mentioned as having turned over their plants to the manufacture of munitions, including the Allis-Chalmers Company, manufacturers of machinery, with factories at Chicago, Milwaukee, Stranton, and West Allis, and the Brown-Sharpe Company, of Providence. According to Fay's statement, he had to memorise the leading points in all this information, so as to identify himself when he reached the United States. On reaching New York, he immediately went to Dr. Kienzle, mentioned the names of the New York Central and New Haven Railways, the Allis-Chalmers Company, the Brown-Sharpe Company, and the contents of Kienzle's letter to his father.

Fay worked for six months in Weehauken and Grantwood, New Jersey. He was an expert mechanic, and he invented a special bomb that could be attached outside a ship and timed to explode when the vessel was well out at sea. Everything was ready, including a motorboat for transporting at night the bombs to the ships. But on October 7th, 1915, Fay was arrested with another murder plotter—his brother-in-law, Walter Scholz—as the two were making their final experiments with explosives in a wood near Grantwood. In their rooms at Weehauken the United States Police were reported to have found documents connecting Fay with the German Foreign Office, a map of New York Harbour, with all details of the docks and piers, four suit-cases containing disguises, mechanism for the new bombs, and a quantity of high explosive. In the last we can trace the destination of some

Plot against munition ships

to wreck the grain elevator of the Central Railroad at Weehauken.

There were also many attempts to sink steamers by means of infernal and incendiary machines. Among the ships attacked were the Cedric, on September 26th, 1914; the Touraine, on March 6th, 1915; Devon City, on April 27th; Lord Erne and Cressington Court, on April 29th; Sandland and Lord Downshire, on May 1st; Kirkoswold, on May 2nd; Strathtay and Bankdale, on May 8th; Minnehaha, on July 9th; Craigside, on July 24th; Athinai, on September 8th; Sant' Anna, on September 13th; and the Arabic, on August 4th. Twenty-three ship fires, damaging vessels carrying goods to the Allies, were known to have occurred up to December 31st, 1915. One of the most remarkable German agents in the attacks on ships carrying American munitions of war to the Allies was a man who called himself Robert Fay, and who averred he was a Prussian lieutenant sent by the German Secret Service to carry out the work of blowing up munition ships. According to Fay's confession, the German bomb plot against steamships began in the following manner: Early

of the picric acid shown, by Captain von Papen's cheques, to have been purchased through Krupp's agent in America. Nothing, however, was apparently discovered to incriminate Papen, Boy-Ed, Bernstorff, or Nuber, the Austrian Consul-General. But the younger Kienzle was found to be in the plot, and also Max Breitung, of Chicago, already notorious in connection with the Dacia case. Fay and his associates were found to have spent six thousand pounds in the previous six months, and to have command of very much larger sums of money. It could be clearly divined who were Fay's financial backers; but the former German Army officer fought with praiseworthy loyalty to protect his directing chiefs. By his signed confession he put all the blame on himself and Kienzle, and stated that his plans had been repudiated by Captain von Papen and Captain Boy-Ed, who advised him to make Canada the field of his operations. The plotter's story, however, carried evidence of its falseness. For how could he, an officer, sent to the United States by the German Government to blow up ships there, have disobeyed the commands of the German naval and military attachés at Washington if they had ordered him to confine his operations to Canada? While, however, both Fay and the German Embassy were maintaining that the outrages were merely the work of undesired and irresponsible adventurers, a German-American newspaper of New York, the "Deutsches Journal," rose to a supreme height of entertaining audacity in its explanation of the affair. To quote:

Fay's signed confession

More and more confirmation is being obtained of the view which judicious persons suspected from the beginning was the right one. This view is that the talkative Lieutenant Fay is neither a German officer nor a member of the German Secret Service, but an English *agent provocateur*. The suggestion was already put forward yesterday that Fay was no German at all, but an Irishman in the pay of the British Secret Service, and that it was his business to embroil as many prominent German-Americans as possible in his concocted plot, and then give them away at a convenient moment. On the English side this was expected to have a gigantic effect upon public opinion and upon the position of the administration. We cannot avoid the suspicion that Washington is anxious to forget the case as soon as possible.

But the American Secret Service men were not at all inclined to forgetfulness. Having caught Fay, Scholz, and Breitung, they found a connection between these plotters and Paul Koenig, the chief detective of the Hamburg-Amerika Line in New York, whose name occurs so frequently in the cheque-book of Captain von Papen. Koenig was trying to protect the German Embassy by substantiating Fay's suggestion that Canada had been designed as the proper field of operations. To this end an attack was planned upon the important waterway the Welland Canal, which connects Lake Erie with Lake Ontario and the

Atlantic. The canal was important because it prevented the Canadian railways from being choked with traffic in times of crises, by taking much of the wheat and other grain cargoes directly through the great lakes. The canal circumvented the navigation difficulties of the Niagara Falls; a fleet of small steamers plied through it, and in December, 1915, a larger canal was being made alongside the small cut, to enable ocean-going steamers to take grain direct from Duluth to Liverpool.

Koenig and his wife, with an art dealer of Fifth Avenue, R. E. Leyendecker, went to Buffalo and Niagara Falls to arrange the blowing up of the Welland Locks. Koenig's wife acted as his secretary, and jotted down shorthand notes of all the details of the plans. These shorthand notes, however, fell into the hands of the American police. This was due to Koenig's manner of treating his subordinates. One of his men was named George Fuchs, and to him Koenig had given the job of placing the explosives—dynamite and nitro-glycerine—and firing them. Fuchs was certainly the

SYMBOLICAL IMPRESSION OF THE SPIRIT OF FRANCE.
A sculptor, desiring to carve a French war monument, could scarcely devise a composition more vigorously effective than the compact group caught by the camera in this remarkable photograph. The soldiers were leaping from the trench for a charge. The regimental colours were being held aloft by the commanding officer, Colonel Desgrées du Loü, who, a moment after waving his men to the assault, fell mortally wounded. The men of the "garde du drapeau" were also killed or wounded, though the flag was saved.

man for the job. For several years before the war he had worked in the Union Carbide Company's factory in Welland. He knew every important feature along the twenty-five-mile stretch of waterway, and he was well acquainted with the various munition works and chemical companies on the Canadian side of the border. He worked under the name of Fox, and the guards on the Niagara Bridge and the soldiers along the canal let him pass as a loyal Englishman, knowing he was connected with the Carbide Company.

German spy's revenge   Fuchs therefore might have carried out the wrecking of the canal had he been given a free hand. But it was the policy of Koenig to trust nobody. He had a Germanic tendency to over-thoroughness. After sending a man on a mission, he sent another man to spy on him, and despatched a third man to watch that there was no collusion between the first two. Fuchs discovered that he was being followed by German Secret Service men as well as being shadowed by American detectives. Taking a train to New York, he burst into Koenig's office in the Hamburg-

GERMAN PLOTTERS AND THE WELLAND SHIP CANAL.
Among the many schemes of the German plotters on the American Continent was one to destroy the Welland Ship Canal, connecting Lakes Erie and Ontario, which would have disrupted the passage of wheat and munitions to England. Thanks, however, to the vigilance of the Canadian Secret Service in New York, the plot was frustrated.

Amerika building in Broadway, and apparently had a violent quarrel with his chief. For when he came into the corridor he shouted in anger : " That Westphalian, bull-headed swine ought to be arrested for what he is doing ! " Thereupon an American police-officer in the lobby of the building promptly arrested Fuchs himself, and Fuchs, in order to be avenged upon Koenig, willingly made a full statement of all he knew. Koenig was then caught when he least expected it, and his office and his two homes were thoroughly searched, with the result that several large boxes of incriminating papers were carried away by the American police, and examined by the new section of the American Secret Service popularly known as the " bomb squad."

Evidence was found that millions of pounds had been transmitted from the Deutsche Bank of Berlin to bankers in the United States in order to finance the numerous plots. For example, a single German agent in New York, Captain Franz von Rintelen, had been supplied with the remarkable

sum of £7,000,000, merely in order to start a great plot, designed to corrupt the labour leaders and produce a violent pro-German movement in all American trade unions. Franz von Rintelen was also the gold conduit in the plot to raise and arm the new army in Mexico for General Huerta. The sum of £300,000 was spent at the opening of the war by Dr. Karl Buenz, of New York, a director of the Hamburg-Amerika Line, in fitting out twelve vessels as supply ships for the German cruisers that were then raiding British and French shipping. Another large sum of money, received from the Deutsche Bank, was spent on an affair in San Francisco known as the Crowley plot, the purpose of which was to destroy munition plants in the Western States. Then a Wall Street financier, David Lamar, was found to have received from Rintelen large sums of money to organise a National Peace Council.

In outward form the National Peace Council was as innocent-looking as our Union of Democratic Control, Anti-Conscription Fellowship, and other pacifist organisations, supported by such papers as the "Labour Leader," the " Herald," and " Forward," and helped by politicians like Mr. Philip Snowden, Mr. George Lansbury, and Mr. Ramsay Macdonald. The National Peace Council in America had the support of Mr. Frank Buchanan, an Illinois Congressman, Mr. H. Robert Fowler, former Congressman from the same State, Mr. Frank S. Monett, the former Attorney-General of Ohio, Mr. J. C. Taylor, and Mr. Henry Martin. Yet at the close of 1915 all these men, with David Lamar, the " Wolf of Wall Street," stood indicted by the Grand Jury of the United States on a charge of conspiracy. For the National Peace Council, though ostensibly a strictly neutral organisation of peace-loving friends of labour, who wished in the interests of humanity to stop the war in Europe, was the master-weapon of intrigue forged by the master-mind in the German Embassy. It was not Papen, Boy-Ed, or Bernstorff who directed this grand affair, but an apparently humble person who called himself Mr. Hansen, or Mr. Gates, or Monsieur Gasque. Sometimes he was a Scandinavian, at other times a good American, and when he came to England he was a Swiss business man. He had, however, some inconvenient moments ; for instead of living in an obscure way, he frequented some of the best clubs of New York, where he was seen with an effect of considerable surprise by an officer of the United States Navy, who was well acquainted with the leading men of the German Marine Office.

We have already given the real name of this man of many aliases ; he was Franz von Rintelen.   **" Tirpitz's Big Six "**   Like Boy-Ed, he was a captain in the German Navy, but his rank was no measure of his power ; for besides being an intimate friend of Prince Henry of Prussia, he was a member of the small inner ring of German naval authorities known as " Tirpitz's Big Six." With five other naval officers and Tirpitz as director of the circle, Captain von Rintelen took part in selecting squadron leaders, fleet admirals, and the Naval Staff, watched all their work, and removed the men who seemed incapable. Such a man as Rintelen, therefore, could not have been spared by Tirpitz in the midst of a

Elliott & Fry.

Lieut.-General Sir Nevil Macready, K.C.B., K.C.M.G., Adjutant-General to the Forces.

Terraced path of the Achilleion and two Chasseurs guarding the sealed entrance to the Kaiser's private apartment

Modern France among the Immortals in the Achilleion grounds.

The Kaiser's White Palace, the Achilleion at Corfu, c

French soldier and the German Emperor's Achilles.

At the gates to the Imperial Palace.

Humility for the Hohenzollerns: The Tricolour over the Achilleion.

nto a Red Cross Hospital by our Allies in occupation.

After the fleeting furlough : British veterans awaiting the Flanders trench special at Victoria.

naval struggle on which the fate of the world depended unless there had been something for him to do in America of tremendous importance. As we have seen, this work was important enough for Rintelen to bring with him to New York, by way of preliminary expenses, the sum of £7,000,000. With this money he created the National Peace Council. He took offices in the buildings of a bank connected with the Central Powers. He engaged David Lamar to begin promoting strikes, paying him £100,000 on account, and he also employed some men who had an exceptional knowledge of Mexico. The National Peace Council was financed through Lamar with the design to produce a great labour agitation, ending in a strike for an embargo on the export of munitions.

But this great work of organisation and corruption did not exhaust Captain von Rintelen's energies. He adopted the idea of Papen and Boy-Ed in regard to Mexico, and had the final word in the decision to select Huerta as an instrument for diverting munitions from the Allies. He was ready to finance the war between Mexico and the United States with £1,400,000 as a first instalment, and a much larger sum as a reserve fund from which Huerta could draw when he had crossed the border and opened his campaign. Rintelen, like all skilful commanders, had two plans of attack, but he made the mistake of developing them both at the same time. His attack on the armament firms by means of the National Peace Council was apparently not fully discovered at the time, but his negotiations with Huerta, who landed in America the same month as he did, excited the interest of the American Secret Service men. There was a meeting in a Fifth Avenue hotel, at which Huerta and various Mexicans of his school discussed in detail the plan of the new revolution. But one of the Mexicans, instead of representing a dissatisfied section in his unfortunate country, was acting as a secret agent for the United States. Meanwhile, all the preparations were made, and in June, 1915, Huerta left New York for the Panama Canal Exhibition at San Francisco, changed trains during his journey, and struck through New Mexico for the border. But before he reached Mexico he was arrested at Newman, and put in gaol to await trial for conspiracy.

This was a disaster for Captain von Rintelen, and it was followed by a series of sad disappointments in regard to the National Peace Council. The American workmen were obstinately disinclined to strike except for small and very practical purposes of their own. The skilled trade unionists especially rejoiced in the prosperity caused by the enormous war orders, while many of their leaders would not sell for any money their conviction that Britain, France, and Russia were fighting for the root principles of all democracies ; and, as we have seen in the previous chapter, the Eastern States, the centre of the manufacturing energies of America, were largely favourable to the Allies. Even in New York, with a population of 359,000 naturalised Teutons and Hungarians, Rintelen could not arrange a strike of the longshoremen to hold up the ships carrying munitions. He spent £200,000 on the scheme, but the American Secret Service frightened the bribed agitators so that they fled,

Gompers' impassioned outburst

and Rintelen only provoked by his intrigue an impassioned declaration of faith in the cause of the Allies from Mr. Samuel Gompers, one of the great American labour leaders.

Mr. Gompers deserves recognition in any history of the Great War. Born in London in 1850, he worked for some years as a cigarmaker, and from boyhood agitated strongly for the rights of the working classes. Emigrating to the United States, he wrote a good deal on labour problems, and became, as one of the founders of the American Federation of Labour, an important public man. Owing to his position he was one of the first men to feel the sinister pressure that Rintelen was exerting on the working classes through the National Peace Council. Mr. Gompers does not seem to have been able to track the conspiracy directly to Tirpitz's chief agent ; but he knew sufficient about the great sums of money that were being spent in the bribery of even small labour leaders to divine that the affair was one of vast scope, with Imperial resources behind it. When American-born Congressmen of British stock

Eleven thousand conspirators

READY FOR ANY EMERGENCY.
Canadian soldiers on board a transport wearing lifebelts as the ship approaches the danger-zone. At any moment a torpedo from a German submarine might have struck the vessel.

were falling into the great golden net, it was only to be expected that some weak men would be found in some of the trade unions, and still more unprincipled persons among the unabsorbed or half-absorbed masses of recent immigrants, who had not been brought into vital relationship of co-operation with the alert and somewhat superior American working men. Most of the Swedes went over to the German side, and practically all their newspapers fought against the interests of the Allies and against the general attitude of the Eastern States. Still more unexpectedly, a large body of recent Dutch emigrants was led by devious ways into the Teutonic camp, where they met Slovaks, Croatian Serbs, and a certain class of Irishmen and Englishmen.

It was estimated that there were eleven thousand Englishmen—or men who seemed by their speech to be Englishmen—working for Rintelen, Koenig, and other leading German intriguers. Some of the notorious eleven thousand began their career in the Hamburg-Amerika building in Broadway as street orators. Afterwards they seem to

WELL-SCREENED FRENCH CANNON SOMEWHERE IN THE MARNE SECTOR.

agents. So, at the beginning of August, Rintelen set out on a neutral ship for a neutral State in Europe, in order to reach Berlin and discuss with Grand-Admiral Tirpitz the way in which stronger measures should be employed against the munition makers of the United States. The ship on which he travelled was brought by a British cruiser to a British port for examination, and Monsieur Gasque, the Swiss business man, who possessed a perfectly correct passport, was removed from the ship and placed in a British prison. Apparently there had been other men in the clubs of New York, besides the captain of a U.S.A. Dreadnought, who had recognised that Mr. Hansen, Mr. Gates, and Monsieur Gasque could be amalgamated into one of "Tirpitz's Big Six."

Even from the point of view of a German court-martial, Rintelen deserved the fate that overtook him in England. The love of parade and luxury that led him to frequent clubs where he was known to American naval officers and British visitors was a crime against his own Emperor. He should have worked in the background of American life in complete obscurity. He had more power than Dernburg, Bernstorff, or Dumba, but he went out of his way to attract the notice of the secret agents of the country he was directly working against and of the guardians of the interests of the allied nations he was indirectly attacking. His intelligence was eclipsed by his vanity and overweeningness. We could wish that, as Rintelen rose by apparent merit into the governing naval coterie around Tirpitz, he really was representative of the finest flower of intellect and character in the German Navy. But this is too large a hope. He belonged to a military autocracy which was decaying into Byzantine favouritism, but the process of decay had been checked by the emergence of an extremely efficient industrial oligarchy, whose managers and research directors were able to frame magnificent weapons for the fighting forces. An English engineering expert said, after he joined a technical section of our Army and found himself overruled in an important scheme by a "dug-out" colonel without practical knowledge: "In a war like this the men who know are at the bottom, and the men who don't know are on top." We had somebody on top who did not know much about the limitations of modern naval gunnery when we sent a fleet to blow up all the Dardanelles forts. Rintelen was on top, but his incapacity, unfortunately for us, was scarcely an indication of the general qualities of the officers of the German Navy.

Due to overweening vanity

After Captain von Rintelen retired to a place of rest in England, the work of bringing the American people into the German camp was vigorously pursued by Captain von Papen, Captain Boy-Ed, Count Bernstorff, and Dr. Dumba. Bernstorff was reckoned by his immediate subordinates to be a man of high talent, and much more capable than Dernburg and Rintelen. There was, indeed, some talk across the water with Maximilian Harden and the Prussian circle around this brilliant Jew of making

have been despatched in groups of a hundred or two hundred to important American munition works. There, by some mysterious means, they obtained employment; though, having regard to their general lack of mechanical skill, it is difficult to see how many of them escaped dismissal on the evening of the day in which they were engaged. Their real work was talking; it was for this that they were kept on the pay-sheet of Rintelen's agents. They had to talk the men into striking. But though they produced some sporadic interruptions to the manufacture of munitions, they could not induce the American mechanic to kill the goose that was laying golden eggs for him. And loud above the mutterings of the conspirators, who talked of peace and humanity while assassinating their fellow-workmen with bombs, rang the voices of the true apostles of democracy, such as Mr. Samuel Gompers.

Rintelen spent many millions of pounds on his hopeless task, providing a rich harvest for every alert blackguard in the United States. So far as can at present be seen, he confined himself to political action, helping Bernstorff and Dumba to win over politicians, newspaper proprietors, and labour leaders. He left to lesser men like Papen, Boy-Ed, Koenig, and Fay the work of blowing up factories and starting fires in buildings and ships. But on August 3rd, 1915, Rintelen came to the conclusion that he had failed in both his campaigns. Mexico was becoming more peaceful, and in the United States munition work was so increasing in volume that the export of manufactured goods was rising to ten million pounds' worth of goods a week. The most important thing that Rintelen had accomplished was to get Huerta and many other of his dupes into trouble. The American Secret Service men were even able to track down, in munition factories employing 15,000 men, each of the two hundred agitators financed through Rintelen's

Rintelen's double failure

Bernstorff the Bismarck of the new era, and entrusting to him all the peace negotiations and the general settlement of the war. Bernstorff was a man of the Falkenhayn type, an audacious fascinator and soother, who used words merely as counters, and was quick to say and promise anything in order to surmount an immediate difficulty in his path.

It was the opinion of practically all the Teutons that the personal fascination of Bernstorff and his skill in conversation had brought about the **Bernstorff and his** apparent defeat of President Woodrow **creatures** Wilson in regard to the Lusitania case and all the submarine disputes. The Germans did not truly estimate the patience and power of recoil of the very honest-minded and tenacious American President, neither did they appreciate the force of domestic political circumstances against which he was quietly but strongly struggling. He was in very great difficulties with his own party, as many of his leading men in the House and in the Senate had been seduced by personal ambition, pacifist principles, or German-American intrigue to a state of opposition against him. He could not carry out his vindication of international law against the more errant group of belligerents, because the Democratic Party seemed almost ready to sacrifice the sovereign rights of the United States in order to keep well out of European affairs. This was the mother cause of all the apparent vacillations of President Woodrow Wilson and his new Secretary of State, Mr. Lansing. But Count Bernstorff and his creatures self-conceitedly attributed the continual strategical retreats of the President in the field of diplomacy to the German Ambassador's talents in smiling and subtle mendacity.

Had Bernstorff been half as clever as he thought he was, he would have abandoned the policy of violence, while pursuing the far more effective policy of political, social, commercial, and financial intrigue. But we have sound evidence that the Count deeply committed himself to acts of secret war against the American people after Rintelen resigned the supreme command on the " American front "—as the conspirators called the United States in their private correspondence; for in the Papen papers there was a letter from Captain Boy-Ed to Captain von Papen, indicating that in August, 1915, the American Secret Service, while discovering some of Papen's crimes, had not been able to discover incriminating evidence against Bernstorff, though such evidence existed. But it may be doubted whether the American secret agents were at the time as much at fault as the German military attaché thought. It seems rather that President Wilson thought it unwise to use the evidence against Bernstorff and to insist upon his recall; for this step would probably have brought about war between the United States and the Central Powers at a period when there was still some danger of a Germanic rising in America if hostilities were opened with the German Empire.

With all the facts before him, President Wilson decided upon a slow but safe method of offensive defence. The American Secret Service men organised a large campaign of protection over the munition factories, railways, and shipping, which the plotters were attacking. For some months they failed to get the mastery of the bomb-makers and bomb-setters who worked in the harbours against ships. It was suspected that Koenig, of the Hamburg-Amerika Line, was one of the directors of the bomb and infernal machine attacks, but the man **Koenig's colleagues** could not be caught in action. It was **in crime** not known at the time that he worked with Frederick Schleindl, a clerk in the foreign department of the National City Bank of New York, who was able to trace the sums paid to manufacturers by the Allies and to note all large orders for munitions made by cable, and learn the contents of every cargo that left New York for Britain and France. Still less was it known that one of the warrant squad of the New York detective bureau was an agent of Koenig, and acquainted him with the moves being made against him.

FAIRYLAND! BEAUTIFUL ENVIRONMENT OF THE FEARFUL GERMAN ONSLAUGHT AGAINST VERDUN, FEBRUARY, 1916.
It is hard to reconcile this lovely scenic effect, obtained in the Vosges during the great German effort to capture Verdun. The verdant glades are white with purest snow, the trees silvered by the frost, and every-where a natural tranquillity reigns absolute. Only the two sombre Chasseurs remind us of the terrible red carnage on the other side of the forest in this vital sector of the French front.

Within a repairing shop on the eastern front. A Russian officer giving a mechanic instruction in the use of the lathe.

Russian motor-transports being overhauled and generally tuned up, prior to being put into commission. SECTION SOMEWHERE ON THE EASTERN FRONT.

Tea-time in a Russian Army training camp. New recruits to the automobile section resting after a course of study.

Happy Slav soldiers belonging to the automobile section at ease, playing with the regimental mascot. A DAY WITH THE RUSSIAN MOTOR-TRANSPORT

In the flourishing period of the grand conspiracy Koenig often had his secret agents shadowing the American Secret Service men, and things used to get complicated when the American secret police put on more men to shadow the Germans, who were shadowing Americans, who were shadowing Germans. For Koenig would lengthen out the trail by sending out more of his agents in turn to spy upon the second team of the American Secret Service; and so the game would go on. But though the Americans failed to protect many ships and had some im-

Efficiency of the bomb squads portant American factories burnt or blown up, they saved their country from the great systematic destruction of railways, waterways, and manufacturing plant which was attempted; for, according to statements afterwards made by American Secret Service men, the secret war assumed, in the autumn of 1915, a terrible character, a fresh impetus to the wholesale murder of workmen and general destruction of plant, depôts, and traffic routes for munitions arising from the failure of the Mexican plot and the arrest of Huerta.

The Eastern States especially might have suffered as much as Eastern Belgium and North-Western France had it not been for the patriotic efficiency of the "bomb squads." The wonder is not that one or two men in the detective departments were ready to betray the country of which they were Government officers, but that in a nation of recent origin, containing millions of late emigrants, many of them in positions of wealth and power, the fabric of American law and order proved so strong and effective. It was the party in power, the Democratic Party, with all the spoils of office for distribution, which contained the larger Germanic element. And no doubt the German intriguers confidently built upon the fact that tens of thousands of men likely to sympathise with them had been lifted by the Democratic victory into seats of widespread influence, from which they could promote the cause of the Kaiser. This undoubtedly was so in regard to many spheres of politics; but despite the well-known and ancient corruption of part of the American police system, in which police-officers had been found to be in league with "gunmen," or hired assassins, the American Secret Service system did not fail the country in the time of its greatest need. Mr. William J. Flynn, Mr. William M. Offley, and Mr. A. Bruce Bielaski were among the chiefs of the American Secret Service who saved their land from great disasters. The United States District Attorney, Mr. H. Snowden Marshall, of the southern district of New York, was also a fearless and tireless defender of civilisation, and he had the amazing experience of seeing one of the marked men in Congress trying to impeach him in a vain endeavour to escape arrest.

The conspiracy was gradually overcome in regard to its campaign of murderous destruction by striking at some of the principal alien directors. The Austro-Hungarian Ambassador, Dr. Dumba, was convicted of organising strikes and other illegal disturbances, and sent back to Europe. The Austro-Hungarian Government took the affair calmly, but instead of appointing another Ambassador, made Bernstorff its virtual representative, and Consul-General Nuber its nominal chief agent. Then, by way of

indicating to Count Bernstorff that he was not clear of suspicion of crime, his two attachés, Papen and Boy-Ed, were informed, towards the middle of December, 1915, that the evidence against them was overwhelming, and they must leave the country. The British Government was asked for a safe-conduct for the two murderers, and readily agreed not to take them prisoners on their voyage or hurt their persons. But when the ship containing Captain von Papen was brought into Falmouth, on January 2nd, 1916, our ingenious and polite naval officers explained that the safe-conduct related only to Papen's person, and that his papers must be given up.

Two days were spent in searching for secret despatches and other documents of interest, and some of the results of the search were indicated in newspapers soon afterwards and officially published by the British Government in February, 1916. In one of Papen's letters he had laughed at "the idiotic Yankees," but his conduct in trying to pass our blockade cordon with incriminating documents showed a want of intelligence, for he knew that our naval men were interested in German and Austrian secret despatches. He

TSAR OF ALL THE RUSSIAS EMERGING FROM A DUG-OUT.
His Imperial Majesty leaving a shell-proof shelter after making an inspection of the trenches somewhere on the eastern front. Members of the Russian Staff are saluting the Tsar in amused deference.

himself had endeavoured, in August, 1915, to report in cipher to the German War Staff and enable Dr. Dumba also to make secret reports to his Government, by entrusting a bundle of letters and despatches to an American journalist, Mr. James F. J. Archibald, who was travelling to Germany as a war correspondent. Archibald had been searched at Falmouth, and it was mainly from the papers found on him that the Austro-Hungarian Ambassador had been convicted of organising disorders in the United States. Yet, despite this warn-

Papers found on Archibald ing, Papen had taken with him to Falmouth evidence of the criminal activities of himself, Boy-Ed, Koenig, and many other subordinates, and, what was most dangerous, suspicious references to the part that Bernstorff had played as general director of the plots.

Meanwhile, the civilian element in the German Government, led by Bethmann-Hollweg, and including most of the industrial magnates and great financiers, had become alarmed over the probability of war with the United States. For many months there had been a struggle between Bethmann-Hollweg on the one part, and Falkenhayn and

Tirpitz on the other part, in regard to the questions of international law raised by President Woodrow Wilson in his Notes on the submarine piracy. The naval authorities, backed by the military authorities, regarded with contempt the actual fighting power of the American nation, and were eager to pursue the submarine campaign in the most outrageous manner possible. For their anger against the American people was enormous. The British were, in fact, regarded in the higher German military circles with professional respect, for we were giving millions of lives and all our treasure to help in winning a decision. But the German High Command was moved to blind fury by the thought that, whichever way the war went, the United States would stand victor at the end of it, not only wealthy beyond comparison, but possessed of a group of munition plants whose combined power of output surpassed that of Krupp and Skoda. In other words, Uncle Sam was not only supplying the Allies with munitions, but making himself thereby terribly strong in all the machinery of war. "Let us bring him into the fray," said the German military party in effect. "We can make him spend some blood and treasure, and perhaps break him up by a civil war that will prevent the export of arms and material to the Allies. In **German anger** any case, we lose nothing, for the **against America** American Navy can do no more than the British Navy is doing."

Some of the amazing Germans even had the ineptitude to suggest to the French, Russian, and British that the contending European Powers should make peace in order to prevent the United States from emerging the virtual winner of the war. Details of the idea underlying the proposed peace were not clearly stated, but they could easily be divined ; both belligerent groups were to unite in blackmailing America and making her largely contribute to the general war expenses. Brazil, with its large German settlements, was to be the ransom of Belgium, and other parts of South America were to be the ransom of the north-eastern departments of France.

This extraordinary hint of a settlement, however, was only vaguely shadowed forth by some of the organs of German industry and finance, which were trying to reconcile the views of their military and civil authorities. The scheme was not regarded as practicable by those men who suggested it. It was thrown out in the very faintest hope of attracting the attention of the selfish, ruthless, greedy Machiavellis of Britain ; we were still regarded as being the supreme masters of political craft, compared with whom Bethmann- **Amazing peace** Hollweg was an honest but babbling child. **suggestion** Apparently it was some subtle, restless minded, worried German-Jewish financier of Frankfort who threw out the suggestion to relieve his own anxieties.

The keen and brilliant Jews, who largely controlled the finance, shipping, and electric industry of the German Empire, were becoming more afraid of the United States than of Great Britain. They studied the future, and wished to keep on terms of friendship with the Americans, and Bethmann-Hollweg and the Emperor William, in his saner moments, agreed with their point of view. They were thinking of methods of recovery, following a war that seemed likely to them to end in a stalemate, and they wanted as many open and friendly markets as possible. Much of the German propaganda in neutral countries was designed chiefly to this end.

The commercial German party and the military German party were thus at loggerheads in regard to the attitude to be maintained towards the United States. When Tirpitz was confident of his power seriously to damage the merchant shipping of Britain, he prevailed, and even won Ballin over to his policy. But when his first submarine campaign failed, by reason of a great loss of U boats and trained crews, the commercial party began to regain its influence with the Emperor. It is quite likely that Bernstorff and his attachés began to receive, in the autumn of 1915, contradictory orders, each of which they carried out. But at the close of the year, when all the methods of violence were defeated by the American Secret Service men,

WOUNDED RUSSIANS AT WORSHIP IN A FIELD HOSPITAL.

The deep religious faith of the Tsar's soldiers is proverbial. "The religious ceremony is absolutely necessary to the opening of any hospital in Russia," said Mr. Ian Malcolm, M.P., a British Red Cross Commissioner in Russia. "The soldier feels, in some mystic way, that his chances of recovery are small indeed if his bed and the room in which he sleeps have not been blessed by the priest." Wounded Russians are here seen receiving the blessing of the Church at a portable altar in a field-hospital tent after a short "Te Deum" service.

BRITISH OFFICERS EXAMINING A CAPTURED GERMAN TRENCH.
The position did not appear to have been seriously affected by shell fire.

and discredited by the banishment or indictment of many of the principal conspirators, the German Chancellor made a final attempt to soothe the American nation. He tried to sacrifice Koenig, Fay, Fuchs, and hundreds of other plotters of murder and devastation to the cause of German trade in the future. So there vibrated from Germany to the American shore the following wireless message :

The German Government has never knowingly accepted the support of any person, group of persons, society, or organisation seeking to promote the cause of Germany in the United States by illegal means, by counsels of violence, by contravention of law, or by any means whatever that could offend the American people in the pride of their own authority.

Apparently, the enemies of Germany have succeeded in creating the impression that the German Government is in some way, morally or otherwise, responsible for what Mr. Wilson has characterised as anti-American activities, comprehending attacks upon property and violations of the rules which the American Government has seen fit to impose upon the course of neutral trade.

This the German Government absolutely denies. It cannot specifically repudiate acts committed by individuals over whom it has no control, and of whose movements and intentions it is neither officially nor unofficially informed. It can only say, and does most emphatically declare, to Germans abroad, to German-American citizens of the United States, to the American people, all alike, that whoever is guilty of conduct tending to associate the German cause with lawlessness of thought, suggestion, or deed against life, property, and order in the United States, is, in fact, an enemy of that cause, and a source of embarrassment to the German Government, notwithstanding anything he or they may believe to the contrary.

Captain von Papen somewhat spoilt the effect of this direct and downright Government statement by his indiscretion in

Von Papen's indiscretion travelling to Falmouth with a large bundle of documents of an incriminating nature. His cheque-book and his letters showed that Count Bernstorff, Boy-Ed and he had not only knowingly accepted " but provided funds for " groups of persons seeking to promote the cause of Germany in the United States by illegal means." Moreover, the President and Secretary of State had received through their Secret Service abundant and almost terrifying evidence of the criminal activities of the German and Austro-Hungarian Embassies, and the German Consul-General at San Francisco and his attachés were under arrest. What the German Government intended by its audaciously false declaration was really to acknowledge defeat in its secret campaign of violence against the United States and beg for a tacit peace. In other words, it did not

want Bernstorff to go the way Dumba, Papen, and Boy-Ed had gone.

The campaign of terrorisation in regard to American workmen and American manufacturers was seen to be a complete failure. Not only were some of the chief agents banished, indicted, or condemned, but hundreds of German-American business men knew they were in great danger of arrest and conviction, and, losing courage, broke away from the conspiracy of violence. And at this psychological crisis the President surprised everybody by a speech of great power. He pleaded fairly with the large and fundamentally loyal section of German-Americans, but denounced the traitorous element with a force of invective that shook

ALLIED OFFICERS AT SEDDUL BAHR.
Major Churchill, brother of Mr. Winston Churchill, and a French Staff officer standing alongside a shell fired during the Turco-Italian war for Tripoli, and later set up as a monument at Seddul Bahr.

the nation. He surpassed in effect the utmost fury of Roosevelt; for in his fierce outburst of long-pent passion there was that deadly quality peculiar to the final explosion of anger in a very patient man. Nothing had been felt like it since Lincoln lived.

The professor of jurisprudence, as he himself frankly admitted, had travelled in a year of tragic experience from the quiet universe of peaceful theories of international law on to the appalling, vertiginous world of actualities, where war was a department of politics. He was disillusioned, and reacted with all the abrupt violence of the visionary brought up against the wall of human sins, defects, and weaknesses. At first he apparently wanted to hammer

The packing-room of an Army clothing depot. Thousands of khaki greatcoats are seen packed in compact bundles, and about to be stitched up into bales for despatch overseas.

Numbers of crates and packages of clothing and provisions, ready for despatch to the front, being loaded into motor-lorries at a military depot.

A busy scene in a corner of an Army cloth factory. Every yard of the many miles of khaki cloth that had to be made was examined by hand, and then folded and pressed by machines.

Munitions to fight "General Winter." Some of the millions of thick Army blankets, folded and pressed into uniform bales by machinery, and ready for delivery.

THE BRITISH GOVERNMENT AS "UNIVERSAL PROVIDER": PHASES OF THE HUGE WORK OF THE ARMY ORDNANCE DEPARTMENT.

all mankind into brotherly kindness. Roosevelt had long been preaching the sound doctrine of national preparedness. But the Democratic President made the Republican programme of defence seem very modest. Dr. Wilson wanted a stronger navy than that of Great Britain, together with an army calculated to grow into Germanic size. Seemingly he was at first bellicose in a general way; all the belligerent nations were alike guilty of being engaged in a war that had broken upon his dreams of a life devoted to social reform. While on his first speech-making tour, in preparation for a Presidency election, turning upon the Democratic and Republican programmes of national armament, he suggested to the Western States that he wanted a more powerful fleet in order to be able to sell American wheat to German and Austrian soldiers, and he

A masterstroke of intrigue indicated to the Southern States that he needed a navy of overwhelming strength, so that he could feed German guns with ammunition made from American cotton. It was the extravagance of disillusion, and his extravagance of speech quickly recoiled upon him.

The Germanic forces in the American Press were quick to seize and expand this side of the President's movement of general reaction. Even newspapers in the Eastern States that had favoured the cause of the Allies began to publish articles on such subjects as "The Growing Irritation with England." The contraband situation was rigorously exploited, and poisonous calumnies against our country were launched from the Senate. It was there stated, for example, that the censorship at Liverpool was being used, with official consent, as an instrument for capturing American trade. The silence of our Foreign Office in regard to the Baralong case was widely taken as evidence of the inhumanity of our sailors, and our chivalrous reticence in regard to the part played in the affair by American cattlemen in the Nicosian was mistaken for the glumness of convicted criminals. Papers served by Mr. W. R. Hearst's International News Service published some thirteen pages of telegraphic matter on the Baralong case, composed from the German standpoint, and preparing the American mind to acquiesce in a system of reprisals, to take the form of a renewed campaign of submarine piracy against all merchantmen trading to our shores. According to the "Kölnische Zeitung," the support of Mr. Hearst was worth three army corps to Germany.

Amid this extraordinary rapid veering of American opinion, Count Bernstorff essayed a masterstroke of intrigue. He proposed that unarmed merchant ships and unarmed passenger liners of the allied nations should be sunk by German submarines, but with opportunity for crews and passengers to take to the boats. But all ships carrying a small gun were to be regarded as warships, and to be sunk without warning, like the unarmed Lusitania, with all persons on board. As British, French, and Italian seamen resembled the animal described by the French satirist—

"Cet animal est très méchant,
Quand on l'attaque, il se défend"—

and were so criminal as to incline to attempt to defend their ship when menaced by submarine pirates, the new proposal practically meant that all the conventions of sea warfare, for the maintenance of which President Wilson had been contending for many months, were to be abandoned in favour of a race of murderers.

It was reported at the time that some of the naval authorities of the United States had been converted to the Germanic view of submarine warfare. These authorities decided that as their country could live in war-time without imports, but had thousands of miles of coast to defend, the new system of piracy against all merchant shipping should be adopted and used by the United States. The American naval code and the supreme American court of law had both recognised the right of merchant ships to resist capture, this being in fact one of the fundamental

A COLOURED HERO AT THE INVALIDES, PARIS.
Dinah Yalifou, son of Behanzin, the last King of Dahomey, being decorated with the Legion of Honour by a French general.

principles of international law. But President Wilson and Mr. Lansing seemed inclined, under pressure from the German Embassy, some of their own naval authorities, and a large body of Democratic representatives in House and Senate, to abolish international law.

After secret negotiations between Count Bernstorff and Mr. Lansing, the proposal was submitted to the allied Powers. Some American newspapers hinted that merchantmen carrying a light gun against German submarines would be denied entrance to **Lusitania problem** American ports for the purposes of com- **all but settled** merce; they would be treated as warships and compelled to leave in twenty-four hours. While the astonished Governments of France, Italy, Russia, and Britain were considering the extraordinary American proposal, the Berlin Government, flushed with gratitude to President Wilson for the great victory he was winning for them, offered to settle the Lusitania controversy. After some trouble over the nice wording of the draft, the German Ambassador "recognised liability" for the loss of American lives and agreed to pay an indemnity. The matter would thus have been settled, but for the lucky accident of Bernstorff, Tirpitz, and the wilder spirits in the inner ring of German government being attacked by a frenzy of overweeningness. They showed their hand too quickly, when they had every reason for playing with extreme caution in the turning period on the "American front."

Instead of waiting until President Wilson and Mr. Lansing had received the answer of the Allies to the proposal regarding armed merchantmen, and had become entangled

SLEEPING QUARTERS OF FRENCH TROOPS IN THE ARGONNE.
These straw-constructed huts, presenting the appearance of part of a native African village, were admirably designed for the comfort of the inmates and security from the notice of passing enemy airmen.

CONFERENCE ABOUT THE CHAMPAGNE OFFENSIVE.
French general addressing a number of officers on the successes and failures of the great offensive in Champagne, September, 1915.

in this pro-German scheme, the Berlin Government assumed that America was too deeply implicated to withdraw and make a stand for neutrality and international law. Stooping to the vilest intrigue in order to ensure that the American Secretary of State would not change his mind, Count Bernstorff revealed to newspaper reporters, and exaggerated in revealing, the course of the confidential negotiations known only to himself and Mr. Lansing. President Wilson at the time was conducting his tour of oratory in the Middle West, and appears to have left the matter to his Secretary of State.

And as Bernstorff made his revelations, Tirpitz from Berlin rounded off the great intrigue by proclaiming a new submarine campaign upon the lines of piracy seemingly advocated by the United States. In the

new phase of the underwater war upon commerce, the operations were not to be restricted to the area around the British Isles, for Germany had built more powerful submarines that could range to New York and back. All armed merchantmen that might be thought to possess a light gun were to be sunk without warning, and unarmed merchantmen, if they could be recognised as unarmed through a distant periscope, were to be sunk after a warning shot. The negotiations with the United States with regard to the settlement for the Lusitania were thus abruptly and prematurely disclosed as the greatest diplomatic trap that had ever been engineered. All the munition activities of the American factories on behalf of the Allies were to be rendered ineffectual; for every ship, armed or unarmed, trading to the countries of the Entente Powers could be torpedoed and sunk   **President Wilson** with the apparent consent of the United   **angry** States Government. Even in regard to passenger liners Count Bernstorff could only give it as his "personal opinion" that, if they were unarmed, there might be no danger of non-combatants being murdered.

But Bernstorff and Tirpitz, acting as the Hindenburg and Mackensen of the encircling movement against the United States, had unveiled their heavy batteries before they had closed the gap. There was a quick and powerful movement of retreat by the American President and Secretary from the perilous submarine salient in the diplomatic battlefield. Dr. Wilson interrupted his election tour, and came back to Washington in a violent fit of anger. Mr. Lansing wished to send Bernstorff down the path that Dernburg, Dumba, Papen, and Boy-Ed had taken, and there was some talk of breaking off relations with the German Government.

THE "EARS" OF THE ARMY.
French engineers erecting one of the mobile "wireless" installations somewhere behind the lines. Complete, in two automobiles, the "wireless" rapidly arrived at any given place, and was installed in a few minutes, ready to transmit and receive messages.

The transport Norseman, which was sunk off Salonika. The circle photograph shows Commodore Keyes and Wing-Colonel Sykes in consultation at Cape Kephali, Imbros.

Signal station erected on the square rock off Port Ereo, in the Bay of Mitylene. It was the work of the men of H.M.S. Canopus, and looked quite substantial and formidable, with a naval gun ready for emergency.

MARITIME DESTRUCTION AND CONSTRUCTION IN LEVANTINE WATERS.

FUEL FOR THE FLAMES OF WAR.
Warship taking in coal by means of the Temperley Transporter apparatus.

But Bernstorff was not yet defeated. He possessed, to put it metaphorically, in addition to his heavy batteries, a great machine for the delivery of a poison-gas attack. In plain words, he had accomplished the extraordinary political intrigue mentioned by Dr. Dumba in the Archibald papers. He controlled a majority in the House of Representatives and in the Senate, and by means of his agents and dupes he was able to attempt to get a law passed that American citizens should lose their national rights to travel upon liners and merchant ships carrying any kind of armament. They were only to travel in ships which German submarines could sink without a fight. Both Democratic leaders in the House and Senate were strongly

OFF SALONIKA.
French torpedo-boats taking in oil from a supply ship.

in favour of this Germanic law for their people. There were also serious defections in the Republican Party, which still stood as a whole for international law and the maintenance of the sovereign rights of the American nation. For example, Senator La Follette, who had been the originating force in the Progressive movement which Roosevelt joined, now came forth as the champion of the German peace, and therefore as a virtual enemy of the French race from which he had sprung.

But President Wilson was at last roused, and he fought down the sinister and cowardly elements in Congress, in private discussions with the errant leaders, and in ringing appeals to the nation. Much had been said against his talent for letter-writing, as shown in the *Lusitania* case.

But when he began to write open letters to the Democratic leaders in Congress, he produced a series of bomb-shell effects. His strangely patient treatment of the German-American problem seemed to have been effective, transforming a vast medley of conflicting races into a nation that would hold together in any struggle. Still he delayed to strike at Bernstorff, and the baffled German, made doubtful at last whether he had any real power in American politics, asked his Government to postpone for a month the new submarine campaign.

While matters were thus in a state of suspense at Washington a remnant of the German-American assassins found a way of escaping capture and pursuing their work by crossing the Canadian border. At the beginning of February, 1916, they burned down part of some factories engaged in work for the British Government, and a great fire that burned out the Parliament House at Ottawa, on February 3rd, 1916—one of the finest buildings in the Dominion—was attributed to them.

Meanwhile Count Bernstorff waited to see what President Wilson would do, and President Wilson waited to see what Tirpitz would do.

ARCTIC CONDITIONS IN THE ÆGEAN.
Signalling on board a British warship near Salonika during exceedingly cold weather.

BRITISH TROOPSHIP

CHAPTER CIV.

NEARING SALONIKA.

THE GREAT SERBIAN RETREAT: A PERSONAL NARRATIVE.

By Alice and Claude Askew.

The Editors of THE GREAT WAR have thought it not inconsistent with the aim and scope of the work to introduce a chapter of a peculiarly personal character. The work, as a whole, is intended to be an impersonal narrative of events in all theatres of the war, arranged as nearly as possible in chronological order, but naturally modified even in this respect by the delays that must take place in the publication of official despatches. Although a full historical account has already been given of the retreat of the Serbian Army in Chapter XCIX., it has been thought worth while to supplement this with the following personal narrative, expressly written for THE GREAT WAR by two of our most popular novelists, who, early in the war, suspended their literary work in order to " do their bit," selecting Serbia as their field. By their writings in the Press, Mr. and Mrs. Askew had succeeded in raising a very considerable sum of money for the help of the Serbians, and themselves went out with the first British Field Hospital, Mr. Askew receiving the rank of Major in the Serbian Reserve. During the typhus epidemic, which ravaged the country in the earlier part of 1915, they rendered good service, and when the terrible retreat of the Serbian Army began they remained with the Army to the end, being among the last to leave San Giovanni di Medua before the Austrians arrived.

O N September 28th, 1915, we left Mladenovatz, where, attached to the Second Serbian Army, we had spent a couple of happy months under canvas, and it is from that date that we may reckon the beginning of the long and eventful journeying—nearly four months—that carried us across Serbia, Montenegro, and Albania, and only found its end when we came to harbour at Brindisi.

We were bound for Pirot, a little town on the Bulgarian frontier, where our Army was concentrating against an attack, which was regarded as imminent. We and our friends upon the Staff, in those days, viewed the Bulgarian menace with a certain equanimity. True, there was a tremendous frontier to be held, and the withdrawal of the Second Army meant a serious weakening of the Danube defences, but Serbia placed infinite confidence in her great Allies; with their assistance, Bulgaria would receive the punishment she merited if she were really foolish enough to attack.

The journey from Mladenovatz took us three days—under ordinary circumstances it could be accomplished in eighteen hours or less—but we did not mind being held up for indefinite periods at this little station or that, for, naturally, troop trains must take priority, and it was always a pleasure, not unmixed with excitement,

to watch the thronging crowds upon the platforms, and now and then to join in the cheering that went up for the brave lads as they swarmed into the cars that awaited them, filling them to overflowing, and quite regardless of the formal " forty men or six horses," with which words each truck was inscribed.

" Jiveo! Jiveo!" The cry was already very familiar to us as a toast at banquets, as an expression of approval in public halls, as a greeting to some popular personality, but it took on a wholly new significance now. For it had in it all a nation's care for its stalwart sons, the father's pride, the mother's tears, the sweetheart's desire, the child's faith; and one's voice grew husky, one's eyes a little dim in sympathy. And yet, of course, one smiled, for everyone was smiling; and as for the young soldiers themselves they were garlanded with flowers as if they were going to some fête, and not to risk their lives amid the horrors of the battlefield.

But if one could have lifted the veil that hung over the next few weeks, if one could have foreseen only a tithe of what was to come!

In this connection we had rather a curious experience. At one of the wayside stations we recognised a familiar face. It was that of a soldier who had been a patient at the Skoplje Hospital when we were there a month or so earlier; he had been wounded in the previous fighting with the Austrians, not

[*Elliott & Fry.*

MR. AND MRS. CLAUDE ASKEW.
The popular novelists, and authors of this chapter, went to Serbia with the first British Field Hospital. Mr. Askew was given the rank of Major in the Serbian Reserve.

AUSTRIA'S WINTER CAMPAIGN IN MONTENEGRO.

Austrian artillery in action on some picturesque, snow-covered slopes near the Montenegrin frontier. Reinforced by a Serbian corps, the Montenegrin Army resumed the offensive on December 22nd, 1915, and drove the Austrians from Montenegrin territory. In January the enemy launched a great offensive in Montenegro, up the valleys of the Tara and Lim in the north, and against Mount Lovtchen, overlooking Cattaro. On January 17th, 1916, Count Tisza, the Hungarian Premier, announced the unconditional surrender of Montenegro but three days later a Montenegrin official statement said that our ally had refused the onerous Austrian terms.

a serious wound in itself, but dangerous blood-poisoning had supervened. An intelligent, well-educated man, he had taken part in all of Serbia's recent wars, and his hatred of the Bulgars was unqualified. He was never tired of recalling their treacherous attack in July, 1913, which began the Second Balkan War—an attack that was made the very night that Serbian and Bulgarian officers had been dining together in apparent harmony, toasting the peace, which, so far as Serbia was concerned, had already been concluded.

"We did not pay them out sufficiently," he often used to remark. "Some day our chance will come again."

Well, now it had come, and that was the observation with which we greeted him. But he showed little of the old sanguine spirit; his demeanour was in strong contrast to that of the cheering crowds that surrounded him.

He stretched out an arm and showed us that it was thin and gaunt.

"It's too soon—too soon," he muttered. "There are so many of us like myself who have not been long enough out of hospital to put up a good fight. People don't get over typhus in a hurry, and there are hundreds and hundreds of men back in the ranks who were down **An ominous** with it in the spring, and who ought **experience** hardly to be out of their beds."

He shrugged his shoulders with a sort of passive resignation and smiled.

"But, of course, if one was at death's door one would want to get up to fight the Bulgars," he remarked.

At parting we said that we hoped we should meet again. He re-echoed the sentiment, and added:

"I wonder where it will be?"

He may have meant nothing by those words, but they sounded—and were—strangely ominous.

We met him twice afterwards in the course of the great retreat. The first time was at Prokuplie, when, marching with his company, he passed us in the road that leads out

of the town. We could not speak, but he recognised us, and greeted us with a look that showed very clearly that he had not forgotten the conversation of a few weeks ago.

And then, in January, we met him again at that tragic spot—Alessio. We were standing by the door of the hovel that called itself facetiously the "Grand Hotel." He came with other stragglers, trailing across the wooden bridge. He had lost his regiment, and had eaten little or nothing for days; bread was never forthcoming for the unfortunate men who had failed to keep pace with their comrades.

He was so dirt-begrimed as to be almost unrecognisable. His feet were bare; he had sold what remained of his boots for a fragment of **Bread practically** bread. His face was pinched and seared **unprocurable** and ashen-grey—it was a tint that we knew only too well by now, for it was common to the men of Serbia's phantom Army.

Once more he recognised us, and he came to a halt, leaning for support against the low stone wall of the filthy courtyard. His lips extended into a ghastly grin.

"So it is here that we have met again," he said.

We gave him food from our own small stock. Bread was what he especially craved. It was the want of bread that caused the greatest havoc among the Serbian soldiers, for at home, upon their farms, it is bread that forms their staple diet. The Serbian peasant eats but little meat.

At Scutari and Alessio, except from the Army authorities, who dealt it out as scrupulously as they could, bread was practically unprocurable. Not even the extortionate prices—ten to twelve dinars (francs) or more for a loaf—asked and paid at previous places on the line of march, would purchase it. For ourselves we were lucky enough, both at Scutari and Alessio, to receive a daily dole, though it used to vary considerably in quality and quantity.

Sometimes it was white bread, freshly baked and delicious —a veritable treat to people living under famine conditions —more often coarse and brown, occasionally of unpalatable maize, and now and then, not very often, there was nothing but apologies, and we had to consider ourselves lucky if we had any over from the previous day.

At Alessio we were in the habit of carrying thick slices of bread about with us, carefully concealed, in order to give them surreptitiously to hungry soldiers when the occasion presented itself. It would not have been wise to do so openly, as the demand would very soon have exceeded the supply, and serious trouble might have resulted.

Destiny's stern finger

We did all we could for our poor friend, but the stern finger of destiny pointed in one direction only—onwards, where his regiment had preceded him, along the marshy, repellent road that led to Durazzo.

"Shall we meet again at Corfu?" he asked grimly as he bade us farewell.

Poor fellow, did he ever reach Corfu? It is unlikely. That same afternoon we were talking to a British officer who was engaged upon road repair on behalf of the Adriatic Mission. He had just come from Durazzo.

"We are doing our best," he said, "but the men are dying like flies. The roadside is strewn with corpses. It is ghastly."

We had seen that for ourselves many a time already upon the other side of Alessio; and the grim irony of it was that in the earlier days of the retreat, when it became obvious that all Serbia must be overrun by the invaders, we, like everybody else, had fondly believed that once Scutari was safely reached all dangers and privations would be over and done with.

It was this assurance that had encouraged the already disheartened and weary men to face the terrible fatigue of the march across the Montenegrin and Albanian mountains. The decision to proceed was reached by the "Quartier General" (Army Headquarters) after much deliberation,

and, indeed, it was not arrived at without definite Montenegrin promises of food, support, and assistance within the confines of their country. There was no talk of Corfu or Tunis in those days; it was confidently anticipated that the retreating but undefeated Serbian Armies could be gathered together at Scutari, where they could enjoy the rest that was so essential to them and where the work of reorganisation could be undertaken.

"There will be food in plenty when you reach Andreavitza," so the already half-famished men were assured when at Ipek (Petch) they found themselves confronted by the great range of snow-clad mountains that barred their farther passage.

It was a long march, five or six days at least under the conditions that prevailed, but the men faced it with the dogged bravery and determination that characterised them. The horrors of the way have been told many a time and need not be repeated here, but to the most tragic event of all those tragic days little notice has been so far given.

It is the complete failure of the promised food supplies at Andreavitza. Think of it! Before they entered Montenegro the Serbian Army had already undergone terrible privations; they had marched hundreds of miles, fighting rearguard actions all the way; they were tired and footsore, hungry and dispirited; their clothes were falling from them; dysentery and sickness were running rampant. Nevertheless, in the fond hope of better things in store, trusting blindly in the

Mirage of Andreavitza

promises made to them—that in a few days' time they would find rest and nourishment—they cheerfully faced conditions worse by far than any which had gone before.

At Andreavitza food in plenty, the bread they pined for; thence, refreshed and strengthened, they could proceed to Scutari, where the ghastly ordeal of enforced flight—a flight the reason for which but few of them could understand —would have its end.

They reached Andreavitza after sufferings that will

A SCENE OF ANCIENT CONFLICT.
Serbian sentry, his horse knee-deep in mud, on the plain of Amselfeld, south of Pristina. It was here and on the Kossovo Plain that the Serbian Army was defeated by the Turks on June 15th, 1389.

ON THE TRAIL WITH A NATION OF FUGITIVES: "A LIVING SNAKE WITH HEADS FOR SCALES."

Part of the cavalcade of tragedy and pain on the trail during the retreat of the Serbian soldiers and civilians towards the Montenegrin frontier. "The whole road was a living snake with heads for scales;" it coiled across the plains, zigzagged up the mountains, and writhed down again into the valley."

Thus a member of Dr. Berry's medical unit described the unhappy throng of soldiers and villagers struggling westward. At frequent intervals during this terrible retreat of a whole nation furious blizzards of sleet and blinding snowstorms broke over the suffering fugitives.

HEROIC RED CROSS WORKERS IN STRICKEN SERBIA.

never be fully described—not all of them, for there were many that fell by the way—and it was to find no food awaiting them, no rest. Perhaps it was not the fault of the Montenegrin authorities; they had been anticipating the arrival of supplies via Italy, and these had not arrived; once again "too late" was to be the horrid burden of the song.

And so the cry was "On to Scutari!" There was, indeed, no choice in the matter. But the element of doubt had stepped in by now—one no longer felt quite sure of Scutari as a haven of refuge, a land flowing with milk and honey. Since supplies had failed at Andreavitza it must mean that they were deficient farther on, and then vague rumours were percolating through, rumours of enemy advance and of an eventual attack upon the Albanian coast towns. Scutari would not be spared. Where then would be the promised rest?

It is a wonderful thing that in face of all this the Serbian Army at Andreavitza behaved with such astonishing fortitude. It must stand to their eternal credit that they did not give way; many of their officers feared they might get out of hand and loot the town. Instead of that, they clenched their teeth, remembering the honour of their country, and with invincible bravery prepared to set out anew, weary and unrefreshed **Disaster's inexorable tide** as they were, upon the long march, double the distance that they had covered from Ipek and hardly less difficult, to Podgoritza and Scutari. We know the fate that befell them there.

It is terrible to have lived through days such as these. To us the privations that we endured, the discomforts, the frequent lack of food, were as nothing in comparison with the sense of participation in so hideous a tragedy, the knowledge of one's utter inability to stem, in the smallest degree, the inexorable tide of disaster.

We, too, at Ipek, regarded the future hopefully, once those grim mountains were crossed.

"We must hurry through to Velika," so an optimistic friend, who was sharing our flight, declared. "Once there we shall be in Old Montenegro and there will no longer be any danger from marauding Albanian bands. We may do it in two days, more

DECORATED BY KING PETER. Commander H. S. Cardale, R.N., of the British Naval Mission in Greece, who was decorated by the King of Serbia for distinguished service in the field.

likely three. At Velika the mountains are past and it is a clear road on to Andreavitza."

Our soldier servant—he was a Montenegrin named Chirovitch, naturally shortened into "Cheer-oh!" and a voluble rascal—agreed.

"They are good people beyond Velika," he said.

They were certainly not people to be trusted at Ipek or anywhere in the neighbourhood. Ipek is now in Montenegrin territory, though why they should have coveted it, heaven alone knows. It is essentially an Albanian town; the whole of the Sanjak territory, wrested from Turkey, is largely peopled by Arnauts, as they are called in Serbia. Some of the fiercest and most dangerous tribes have their home along the Drenitza River, which lies between Ipek and Pristina; the Second Army passed that way upon its retreat, and it was a sorry thing for the stragglers or for any who fell out of line in those days.

Certainly the dark, repellent mountains offered greater hope of security than an over-prolonged stay at Ipek. There had already been a massacre of unarmed transport carriers at Djakova, which is, being translated, the "Field of Blood," and this before the Bulgarians reached the town. We had heard other grim tales of Albanian aggression; there was an occasion, too, between Djakova and Ipek, when we ourselves **Grim tales of Albanian aggression** spent a night in the greatest danger, and one could not help feeling, when one walked in the thronging streets, that one was constantly being regarded furtively and menacingly, with something of the fierce light that one may see in the eyes of a wild beast caged.

Yet we made quite a long halt at Ipek, though it was not for love of the place. We were there from November 24th to December 3rd. There were various reasons for this prolonged stay. From Pristina we had travelled by a different route from that of the Army Staff, and arrived before them; we had to wait for them and also for the great decision as to the fate of the Army. There were many members of British and other missions at Ipek when we first arrived, but they had all gone on before we left. They could no longer work for Serbia; they had lost all their

PART OF A TRAGIC CAVALCADE.
Portion of the weary procession of soldiery and peasantry, with some British Red Cross men, along the road near Kralievo during the great Serbian retreat.

It was upon that occasion that we were in imminent danger of attack from the Arnauts, and, indeed, during the night there were marauding parties that stole out to investigate; but we were well armed, and M. Brabatz, the head chauffeur of the Second Army, who was conducting our little party, had also devised a plan that was successful in circumventing them. He had had fires lit in several places so as to give the impression that we were much more numerous than we actually were.

It was about half-past five when we reached Ipek, bitingly cold, and the moon still shining brightly. The empty market-place, where we drew up the cars, looked peaceful and wonderfully picturesque with the houses all white with frost and moonlight, and the great snow mountains towering in front. And we had leisure to enjoy the scene, for it was a full hour before we could obtain access to either of the so-called hotels. Luckily, for we were very cold and hungry, having had practically nothing to eat since breakfast the day before, we came across a Turk who was selling cups of " salep " to early risers, a hot, aromatic-tasting drink that has a powder called " iciote " sprinkled over it. What the actual ingredients may be we have never attempted to decide, but certainly that morning we owed a debt of gratitude to " salep."

Early morning at Ipek

When the hotels actually opened there was no food to be had, only coffee and " rakia," the coarse spirit universally drunk in the country, which is not unlike the German " schnapps." And, later, when a few of the shops opened—very warily, for they knew the Serbian Army was coming, and were afraid—there was little enough that could be purchased. Luckily one of our party was able to produce some bread, which went down very well with " karmak," the native cheese.

We secured a room at one of the hotels. We had journeyed far since the retreat began, and stayed in one or two strange places, but we had not yet been compelled to accept an apartment half so dirty or so miserable. We were told, however, that we might take it or leave it, and, later on, when we came to realise the condition of the town, we were glad that sheer fatigue had prompted us to stay.

Oh, the dirt of that squalid room! Not once during the ten days that we occupied it did we venture to sleep

medical stores long ago, and so they were in a hurry to leave the country. It was different with us. We wished to remain with the Army until the end.

Very fresh in our memory is the day we reached Ipek. We had come from Prisrend by way of Djakova—where we were hospitably lodged in a Turkish house, though it was a case of sleeping five in a bed—and the car in which we were travelling, a new one purchased by the Second Army at the cost of nearly a thousand pounds, had stuck irretrievably in the mud. We had to stay where we were till two o'clock in the morning, by which time the frost of a bitter cold night would have hardened the ground sufficiently to enable us to proceed.

beneath the bed-coverings, while we had always to wrap something about our heads before we dared make use of the pillows. Yet we could not have found better quarters in the town, overcrowded as it was, for love or money, and there were many who envied us the luxury of having a room to ourselves.

"Comme c'est chic chez vous," said M. Brabatz, when he first came to see us after we were installed. Absurd as it sounded, the remark was not exactly meant to be ironical, for he himself was sharing a tiny room with half a dozen others; while as for the Staff, when they arrived, most of them had to be contented with the floor.

We soon got accustomed to it, and, indeed, the room was luxurious in comparison with many which it was our fate to occupy later on. Yet we acquired quite a reputation for being lucky in finding accommodation superior to that obtainable by others.

On one occasion we spent a perfectly ghastly night, drenched to the skin with rain, in a filthy room, on the quay of Plavnitza, where we were waiting to take the boat to Scutari. The watchman, to whom the room belonged, was absent, and his son, a boy of fourteen or so, very kindly gave up his bed. How could we blame him because, at the same time, he gave shelter to five or six others —genial, good-natured fellows enough, but whose manners did not recommend them as companions for the night? We shall never forget the atmosphere of that room, what with the wet clothes, the incessant smoking, the spitting, and the malodorous fish that was produced by one of the men as a luxury; and it was blowing a gale outside, so that one could not open door or window.

Our little host was not uninteresting in his way. He had intelligence beyond his years, and his behaviour was that of a grown man. He was deformed and palpably consumptive, his face pinched, pallid, and wan. He smoked incessantly. His feet were bare in spite of the bitter cold, and his garments were ragged; we knew that they were verminous, and we trembled because of the bed upon which we lay in the wet clothes that we could not remove. Yet there were those who envied us our quarters; they mentioned the fact some days later to a mutual friend.

Storm-bound at Plavnitza

Perhaps it was not to be wondered at if they had failed to find shelter from the storm that prevailed that night.

If that storm had continued—which, luckily, it did not— we might have been held up for many days, and how we could have supported the conditions for so long, it would be hard to surmise.

At Ipek things were not really so bad when one got used to them, and we improved the look of our room as well

MARCH OF HEROIC SCOTTISH WOMEN FROM SERBIA.

During their terrible journey of two hundred miles through Montenegro, Dr. MacGregor and the other valiant Scottish nurses who braved the horrors of war to help Serbia suffered additional hardships through the frequent blizzards and snowstorms which swept the mountain paths and made travelling almost impossible.

as we could by purchasing a mat for the dirty floor, a couple of cheap rugs for the beds—it was really wiser, and they might come in useful afterwards—and a bright-coloured cloth for the bare table. Washstand, or anything of that sort, we did not possess. It is a luxury that you must not expect even in quite nicely-furnished houses. You are expected to wash outside, and you are lucky if there is more than one basin for the whole household. At one or two places we stopped at—they were little more than hovels, certainly—when we asked for water for washing purposes we were met by stares of blank amazement; finally the water was brought—in a tumbler. And we had to make it do.

In many Turkish houses, or where Turkish habits prevail, they will not let you wash your hands for yourself. Your hostess will consider it her duty to bring basin and ewer, and she will pour the water over your hands while

MAP OF THE BALKANS ILLUSTRATING MR. AND MRS. CLAUDE ASKEW'S PERSONAL NARRATIVE OF THE GREAT SERBIAN RETREAT.

The route followed in its withdrawal from Pirot to San Giovanni di Medua and Alessio by the Second Serbian Army, to which Mr. and Mrs. Askew were attached, is indicated by arrows. The writers'
long and tragically eventful journey across Serbia; Montenegro, and Albania, from Mladenovatz to Brindisi, described so vividly in these pages, took nearly four months to accomplish.

you rinse them, and for politeness' sake you have to pretend to be quite satisfied.

We did not only sleep in that room at Ipek, we had our meals, entertained our friends, and spent the greater part of the day there. At first we had dinner and supper in the one public room, but this very soon became impossible. The gradual deterioration of that hotel café might present a series of pictures fascinating in their very horror to the imaginative mind.

At first all was conducted with order and precision. The room was small; it contained only some **"Table d'hôte"** four or five tables at which one sat upon **under difficulties** long wooden forms. There was no attempt at napery, which perhaps was as well. But the "table d'hôte," such as it was, was evidently an old-established institution; the same clients came to it every day, and if there was no room for all, the late-comers had to wait. The service was of the simplest, but it sufficed. The landlord knew what he had to provide, and he went about his daily work in placid content of spirit.

Then the crowd of refugees poured into Ipek, and the town soon felt the strain. Food prices went up, and the "table d'hôte" could no longer be maintained at its former level. The café was filled all day to overflowing, people struggled for seats at the table when meal times came; the demand for food exceeded by far the possibilities of which the hotel was capable. Respectable clients stayed away. The landlord was in despair.

And then, with the influx of the Army, things became ever so much worse. It was no longer possible to serve a meal at all. The "table d'hôte" was given up, and nothing was sold but wine, coffee, and rakia. There was no drunkenness or disturbance, for that is not the way of the Serb; but the restaurant was a restaurant no longer, it was a rest-house for weary soldiers and refugees.

As for ourselves, we could no longer take our meals downstairs; there was no room for us. The refugees sat there wearily amid their belongings scattered haphazard about the room; some scarcely moved during the whole of the long, dragging day, and when night came they stretched themselves out on the floor and slept. They were all hungry, but there was no food, nothing but rakia, for which they had no appetite. There was no complaining and very little noise, only now and then a child would whimper pitifully.

We had difficulty in getting food in those days. The much-worried cook refused to do any further work, and it was a daily task for "Cheer-oh!" to persuade her to make an exception in our favour. One could only reach the kitchen through the restaurant, and at last the landlord, to prevent incursions by the soldiers and refugees, blocked the way altogether.

Then we had to cater for ourselves, and get our meat cooked at some other house in the neighbourhood. It was not easy at all, especially as prices were going up terribly, and the shops had practically nothing to sell. We can recall a day when our chief meal consisted of baked apples; we cooked them ourselves upon our little stove. But even apples, abundant at first, soon became hard to find; we paid eight francs a kilo for the last lot we bought. As for bread, it was eight to ten francs a loaf.

Our little stove was a source of trouble, too. It was necessary to keep it going, for the cold was at times intense;

but wood was very hard to get, and the price one paid for it exorbitant. When one did get it, it was usually so damp that one had to spend all one's time blowing it into reluctant flame. As for "Cheer-oh!" he belied his name, for day by day he would come to us with tales of impending disaster; if we did not take to flight immediately the least that could happen to us was that we should all be massacred in our beds.

And night after night the sky was red with ominous flame. All manner of property was being destroyed lest it should fall into the hands of the advancing Bulgars. Mitrovitza had fallen on the 26th, Pristina on the 27th, and on the 30th the Bulgars were already at Djakova; they were closing in upon us from every side. An Arnaut rising was reported from a mountain village along the route that we should have to take in our flight.

Towards the end, the unfortunate hotel took another step on its downward career. There was a great disturbance one day, the sound of much shouting in the courtyard and in the street. We soon learnt the reason.

An excited gentleman, armed however with power from the military authorities, had turned up and proposed to requisition the whole of the hotel for a hospital. He had come, with a number of wounded men, from Prisrend, and

TYPES OF SERBIA'S DAUNTLESS DEFENDERS.
A typical crowd of sturdy Serbian soldiers, recruited mainly from the hardy peasantry, and trained to bear arms almost from childhood.

he had searched Ipek in vain for any place to lodge them. And, indeed, it seemed almost futile to have undertaken the painful journey at all, for how was it to be continued? Sorely wounded men could not face the path across the mountains.

The landlord did not approve of this transformation of his hotel, and protested loudly in voluble Albanian. But of course he was powerless, as, too, were the unfortunate refugees who saw themselves deprived of their shelter. One by one they drifted out into the cold street, still silent and resigned, wandering forth to God knows what fate. Those were the days **Hotel requisitioned** of heavy snow and intense cold, when **for hospital** the mountain path was reported so dangerous that it was folly to risk one's life upon it; there were stories in circulation of accidents that had already happened, of women who had slipped over the precipice, of children frozen to death.

And then the patients arrived. The common room—the restaurant that a little while ago had been the daily resort of a genial, if unrefined, clientèle—was prepared for their reception. It was a simple task, consisting merely in the removal of tables and benches, and the laying down of straw. A Red Cross flag was suspended over the door. This was the new hospital.

And soon, as was only to be expected, it became an abode of horror. The wounded men lay huddled together, and there were no comforts for them, no means of alleviating their suffering, little, if anything, in the way of medicaments and bandages. Cleanliness was out of the question; the unfortunate patients still wore the clothes in which they had fallen—these were the only coverings they had. There was no lack of willing workers, but what can be done without material? It is on occasions such as these that one stands appalled, sickened, at one's utter helplessness. How we longed for our rich hospital stores, all swept away by the enemy at Krushevatz!

Sleep was next to impossible for us for the next night or two, the little while that we remained at Ipek. The night was filled with horrid sound; there were those who groaned the long hours away, those who muttered and talked in their delirium, one who sang.

We were glad, with a relief to which words can hardly do justice, when we received our instructions to prepare for

departure. We thought that at Ipek we had witnessed the limit of human endurance. Perhaps it was as well for us that we could not see into the future, that no nightmare vision arose to mock us with a glimpse of the hell that Alessio called its hospital.

We left Ipek at six one morning, after a frugal breakfast of tea, bread and margarine. We always made tea for ourselves, taking it after the manner of the country, very weak and very sweet, and drunk out of a tumbler. A little lemon was a useful addition, but rarely obtainable. Fresh milk we practically never saw from the time the retreat began; our substitute was Nestlé's, the sweetened for choice, taken by itself or with cocoa, and very delicious we found it. The only trouble was that we had not enough.

The margarine had been purchased at Ipek, and presented to us by a considerate friend. We had a big drum full, one of several left behind by some mission departing in a hurry, and it was a great find, for we had not tasted anything in the way   **Ipek tragic to** of butter for many weeks. Unfortu-   **the end** nately the drum was too big to carry with us; all we could do was to fill a moderate-sized biscuit tin. "Never mind," said our friend, M. Brabatz, who was going to accompany us on our journey, "you've got enough to last you till you get to Scutari. We shall find everything we want there in abundance."

It was the prevailing sentiment—Scutari, the haven of refuge!

We were advised to carry food enough to last us to Andreavitza, or preferably to Podgoritza, as it was hardly likely that we should find much on the way. It was advice easily given, but not so easily carried out, for the simple reason that Ipek could provide us with nothing suitable whatever; so we had to depend upon our own very narrow store, which we had hoarded for emergency ever since leaving Prokuplie many weeks earlier. How we wished now that we had been more lavish in our purchases.

Ipek was tragic to the end. On the outskirts of the town we came across the blazing remains of the Second Army motor-cars, the new ones in which M. Brabatz had taken such pride. He might have sold them, at some

WAR-WORN SERBIANS AT CORFU: IN HAVEN AFTER THE TERRIBLE RETREAT.
A gipsy-like encampment of the first Serbian soldiers to arrive on Vido Island, north of Corfu, from Albania, after suffering the horrors of the great retreat. Here they were fed, clothed, washed, and generally cared for. Above: Serbians enjoying the luxury of a toilet at Corfu.

SERBIAN SOLDIERS RE-EQUIPPED.
Serbians donning clean garments that had been distributed to them upon their arrival at Corfu, where they recuperated after the hardships of the great retreat.

ridiculous figure, to Albanian purchasers, but as this would have meant their resale to the enemy, he preferred to destroy them.

Others were less scrupulous, but it was little enough that they put in their pockets. A good stout donkey was worth more at Ipek in those days than any motor-car.

We had anticipated having two horses, one to ride and one to carry our baggage, such as it was, for by now we had practically nothing left. The greater part of our belongings was lost with the hospital stores at Krushevatz, some things were stolen at Pirot, others left behind in our hurried flight from Nish. We had learnt not to grumble. The less one had the easier it was to travel.

We were disappointed of our second horse, and so we had to pack our belongings upon the one that had been lent for riding purposes. This was a fine cavalry charger named Pigeon, and we were both extremely fond of him. He was the property of our friend, Captain Jean Gworsditch, aide-de-camp to the Staff of the Second Army.

An army in flight This arrangement meant that we must both walk, but we promised ourselves to look out for another horse en route. It was likely that we could get our baggage transferred to one of the Army transport horses.

Very soon after Ipek is left behind the path narrows and plunges into a ravine between the mountains. Here we soon came up with a marvellous turmoil of fugitives: an army in flight—orderly, but without definite order—a sort of "go as you please" procession. The loaded pack-horses rubbed shoulders with long-horned bullocks, flocks of goats, sheep, and pigs, whose destination was, no doubt, some mountain village, blocked the way embarrassingly; civilian refugees, too—men, women, and children. One wondered at first, seeing the long trailing line of humanity and beasts of burden clambering laboriously up the mountain path, how one was going to make any progress at all.

Pigeon could not get through, but for us on foot it was possible, though by no means easy, to thread a way through the congestion. But we were often squeezed against the rock or nearly pushed over the edge, so we had to walk warily.

Nevertheless, M. Brabatz wanted to push ahead. We had caught up part of the Army Staff, but there were others who had gone on in advance.

"Leave Pigeon with Chirovitch and the Staff," he said.

"We can wait for them wherever we decide to spend the night."

We agreed to this, and it was to our undoing, for Pigeon carried our wraps and coats, and all the food that we possessed, and, as events turned out, we saw nothing more of him till near noon the following day.

So it was our own fault, in a great measure, that we spent twenty-four hours of horrible discomfort. We were hungry by midday, when we caught up the rest of the Staff; but they had finished their meal, and we did not care to beg. Then we pinned our faith upon the possibilities of a "rest house"—the first on the route—a little farther on, but it proved to be a barn, and there was nothing to be had.

We should have been wise if we had waited at that barn, for it was there that the Staff, with Chirovitch and Pigeon, spent the night; instead, we allowed ourselves to be beguiled by stories of the supposed possibilities in the way of food and lodging of a village called Kuchista. It was still a long way to go, and we were tired; nevertheless, we determined to struggle on.

And so it happened that night threatened to overtake us when we were still at least an hour's walk from the

TRAGIC FIGURE OF THE RETREAT.
Little imagination is needed to visualise something of the tragedy of the Serbian retreat after a glance at this photograph of a Serbian soldier who was little more than a skeleton when he arrived at Corfu.

village. The path had descended sharply into a narrow, inhospitable valley, and before we had proceeded far along it we found that we were quite alone—M. Brabatz and ourselves—which is exactly what we had been most seriously warned against. Everyone else, all the crowding traffic of the day, had already gone into camp.

"We are in a most dangerous country," said M. Brabatz encouragingly. "It is more than likely that the Arnauts are watching us from the woods on the other side of the river. And we are within easy range if they elect to shoot."

It was a characteristic speech. He was disposed to be an alarmist. But in the circumstances it was very discomforting, especially for a lady who was so worn out with fatigue and want of food that, as she declared afterwards, she would not have minded much if the Arnauts had elected to shoot and so put an end to it all. Indeed, she was so done up that it seemed as if we should have to stay where we were, Arnauts or no Arnauts, without wraps or food, and await the morning. Luckily, however, just as it seemed inevitable that she must give in, two things

A ROADSIDE SCENE NEAR NISH.
Serbian soldier talking with a peasant family, driven destitute from their homestead by the tide of war and resting at a roadside.

happened; the first was that we came across three men sitting round a fire and making tea, which they allowed us to partake of with them; there was nothing to eat, but the tea acted as a much needed stimulant, so much so that we were about to set out again when the second event occurred. This was the appearance of several belated officers, with their orderlies, on horseback; they were quite unknown to us, but with characteristic Serbian thoughtfulness and generosity, recognising our plight, they dismounted and proffered horses.

Jack-a-Lanterns on a marsh   And so, in darkness, we approached Kuchista, and at first we were under the impression that we had come not merely to a large village, but even to a considerable town. The whole hill-side was aglow with lights. Here, certainly, we should find rest, warmth, and refreshment.

Rarely in our lives had we been so bitterly deceived. Kuchista was no town—hardly even a village—half a dozen poor cottages spread about over the hill, no more. Those lights that had seemed so full of promise came from camp-fires and not from houses; like Jack-a-Lanterns on a marsh

they had beguiled us to hopes doomed only to be shattered. There was nothing for it but to ask hospitality at one of these camp-fires, and, cold as we were, we wasted no time in selection. We plunged into a half-dismantled barn, open at both ends and with its roof and walls already partially pulled to pieces for firewood; it was occupied by some half-dozen groups of men, each with its own fire. There were three such barns in a cluster, all tenanted in the same way; there was a more solid structure, too, a stone-built house, though half in ruins; but this had apparently been appropriated to the use of sick men, and one look inside was enough to make us turn shuddering away.

Hospitality in a derelict barn

We were not readily accorded the hospitality we sought. At one end of the barn there was a large group of men, and they had food in abundance; bread was being cut up and passed round, while there was an entire sheep roasting upon a spit before the fire. But they would admit no one else to their circle, and as for food, money could not purchase it that night. Perhaps in the morning, if any fragments should remain—small solace was this to us!

Eventually we found friends. They were strangers to us, but the kindness they displayed merits the term. It was near midnight when they invited us to join them; till then we had been sitting, with practically no cover whatever from the cold wind, before a fire for which we must find fuel ourselves, for none had been laid in beforehand, and fuel was by no means easy to get; also we had to sit bolt upright upon a plank, any deviation from which landed one, perforce, into mud and filth. Without wraps or overcoats, without food since the early morning, well might M. Brabatz remark resignedly when we accepted our fate, "This will be a long night!"

Our new friends, however, were better placed. They were farther in the barn, had a good and well-fuelled fire, and they had erected a sort of screen against the wind. Also the ground was firmer, less foul. No doubt it was the feminine element in our party that aroused their pity, but they were equally kind to both sides. Here is a note from one of our diaries:

"The old man who lay alongside me had a big rug to cover him. As I had none, not even a coat, he insisted on putting me between himself and the fire, and in such a position that I could get a little support for my back against the wall. In the middle of the night, when he thought I was asleep, I felt him unroll a goodly portion of his rug and surreptitiously throw it over me. He had offered earlier to share it, but I had naturally refused to rob him of his covering. That's what I call a graceful act."

It was a weird sight in that barn with the full moon shining right through it, a sight not soon to be forgotten.

In the morning, as soon as it was dawn, our friends prepared tea. They were no better off than ourselves in the way of food, but they were lavish with their sugar. It is astonishing how much nourishment one can get, when one is really hungry, from sucking a piece of sugar; this was by no means the only time that we learnt to realise that fact.

Of course we were famishing by now, but we encouraged each other with the assurance that the Staff, with Pigeon

[Elliott & Fry.

Lieut.-General Sir John S. Cowans, K.C.B., Quartermaster-General to the Forces.

Rustic stairway communicating with a higher level trench on the French front.

The Eternal Vigil: French sentries keeping a steady eye on the German positions.

French soldiers, fully equipped, with respirators and steel helmets, advancing against the German lines.

PERILOUS WORK BY ENGINEERS.
In this striking photograph military engineers in the Balkans are seen placing their last charge at the side of the bridge they were destroying. The centre of the bridge had been demolished already by explosives.

and Chirovitch, were bound to turn up quickly—at seven perhaps, certainly not later than nine—and the Staff would have food in plenty.

The barn emptied by degrees. Our kind acquaintances of the night took leave of us. We replenished our fire from the remains of the others, and waited with all the patience we could muster. Very soon the day's traffic began; from where we sat we could watch the endless procession as it wound down the mountain-side to the rickety wooden bridge across the river by the side of which we had spent the night.

Nine o'clock—ten—eleven. Again and again we imagined we saw the white form of Pigeon, led by Chirovitch, descending the slope, but again and again we were at fault. By half-past eleven we were really desperate. All manner of people kept passing along the road, and many had food, but one could not beg of strangers, and we knew that it would be the same with others as with ourselves—they must hoard what they had against the long journey in front.

Thirty hours without food

And then relief came, in the shape of a French officer of our acquaintance. He was travelling with a division of the Army and had access to their stores. No sooner did he hear what had befallen us than he provided us with food in plenty. We had hot coffee, condensed milk, preserved meat, sardines, bread, and biscuits.

Hardly had we settled down to our meal—it was thirty hours since we had had anything to eat—than the Staff arrived. They were munching potatoes, the only food that they could muster just then. When they saw our lavish meal they fell upon it eagerly; so, in the end, it was we who fed them instead of they who fed us.

It may be imagined that we were glad to take our departure from that spot of such uncomfortable memories. But we were not to get away without another incident which, though we thought little of it at the time, gave us food for reflection later.

While we sat round the fire with our friends of the Staff enjoying our meal a Serbian soldier had approached and laid himself down at full length, outside our circle, but as near to the fire as he could get. We had so much to talk about that we hardly noticed him, nor did he attempt to address us till we were about to depart. Then, very

A MILITARY CONTRAST.
Transport waggons passing over a pontoon bridge built by military engineers across the Morava after the destruction of the permanent bridge to which the boats were moored.

faintly, he asked if he might draw nearer the fire, also if we could give him a small piece of bread. For a man of his station his voice was curiously refined.

We gave him all we had left over from our meal, which was not much, though far more than he had evidently expected. Then we went away, and new difficulties to be confronted soon engendered forgetfulness.

But afterwards—weeks afterwards—with knowledge garnered from experience, we often recalled to mind that sick soldier, his desire for rest and warmth, his hunger for bread.

For with our own eyes we had seen men die of starvation and fatigue. We had seen the dead lying by the roadside with none to bury them. And we could not forget how a young officer friend of ours had once attempted to rest by a camp-fire very similar to ours **Dead men by a camp-fire** at Kuchista. Out of twelve men huddled around it, pressing together for warmth, four were dead.

With these things in mind the memory often revives of a pale, pinched face, young and handsome, that of a man with his life before him, and of a weak, refined voice begging for warmth and bread; and then we ask ourselves if we could not have been more helpful than we were, and we wonder what that young soldier's fate may have been. We shall never know.

Starting so late, we could not make much progress that

day. The path was difficult, mainly owing to the mud, and our experiences of the night had hardly left us fit for great fatigue, and yet fatigue was inevitable when one could not take a step without having literally to drag one's feet from mud into which they had sunk up to the ankles. Feminine footgear, not made for this sort of thing, suffered severely, and progress was constantly impeded by the loss of a shoe which had to be dug out with some difficulty. It

seemed as if a shoe-horn would become as necessary to carry in hand as the stout stick which was so invaluable.

Luckily, before we had proceeded far, the kind offer of a pack-horse brought relief. Pigeon was once again turned to his true purpose, and all was well. But it was a terrible path, a path the horrors of which might well affect the nerves even of the strongest. Carcases of dead beasts, horses and oxen in all stages of decay, were to be met with every few yards. Pigeon did not like them, and now and then would shy dangerously. Sometimes the poor creatures were not quite dead ; **Pathway strewn** they would lift their heads and stare at **with horror** the passers with glazing eyes. More pitiful still, the horses that had stuck in the mud and could not be extricated, and those that had been abandoned as useless. Poor brutes, if only they could have been shot ! But no one had ammunition to spare. There were eagles that hovered low, and at night the wolves would come down.

A cruel, repulsive path through a narrow valley without sign of human cultivation or habitation. The mountain sides were bare and precipitous, and there were rocky masses which one's imagination could easily lend human

CAUSE AND EFFECT IN CENTRAL EUROPE.
Austrian artillery column, in proceeding to take up a new position, comes across the bodies of fallen Russian soldiers. In circle : Montenegrin women fugitives trudging out of the war-zone. A sturdy mountain pony is conveying their immediate belongings.

AUSTRIAN PRISONERS AND SERBIAN PATRIOTS.
Austrian prisoners captured by the Serbians. Below : Serbian troops at Salonika. Here, after having rested and recuperated from their terrible experiences during the retreat, Serbian soldiers were re-equipped prior to joining the allied forces.

shape to. Demons that mocked us as we dragged ourselves along, that is what they seemed to us. There was one weirdly fantastic figure that haunted us for quite a long way. It was like a giant ape, with lean arms extended and long fingers that clutched the missile which it was about to hurl ; so real did it appear, standing up alone on a ledge of rock across the river, that one had to look well before one realised that it was no more than the remains of a lightning-blasted tree.

After our recent experiences we were terribly afraid as to what our fate for the night might be ; and when we reached Byeluk, at the foot of the great **Night time on** mountain which the Serbs call Cachak, **Mount Cachak** beyond which it would not be wise to venture that day, our hearts sank within us. For it was a ghastly place.

Two or three wooden sheds stood in a field of mud, and you could not turn in any direction without your eyes resting on some dead thing. Camps were already being formed. Were we, too, destined to spend a night among these abominations ?

Luckily we found shelter, and such was our relief that we could hardly find words to express it. We had a tiny room to ourselves, like a cabin on board ship, with two berths one above the other. Straw was laid down in these, and if the straw had been clean it would have been quite comfortable ; but we were really too tired to mind. There was a stove, too, and Chirovitch, who slept on the floor, kept the fire going all night, which was a good thing, for it was bitterly cold.

Pigeon, well fed—it was not always that we could feed him well—was tethered just outside. There was no stable, and we dared not leave him far away for fear of thieves. Chirovitch was very emphatic on the subject.

"We are not yet among the good people," he said.

This meant across Cachak and into Old Montenegro, where we hoped to be the next day.

Our cabin did not boast a window, only a little sliding trap, and soon after we had climbed into our berths we were startled to see the trap opening slowly ; somebody was palpably manipulating it from the outside. It seemed most certainly a case for holding one's revolver in readiness.

Very slowly the trap was thrown back, and presently we saw that this was due to no human hand ; in the dim light we could distinguish a queer-shaped white thing, and it was a few moments before the mysterious apparition revealed itself for what it was.

It was no more nor less than Pigeon's nose. Pigeon was still hungry, and was asking for bread, of which he was particularly fond. Needless to say, he got it. Dear Pigeon, he was a fine horse, **A mysterious** and served us well ! We only parted from **apparition** him when we took ship at San Giovanni di Medua, and it was no doubt his fate to proceed to Durazzo, perhaps farther still. We would give much to know that he came safely through that terrible journey.

The following day, well rested, we crossed the dreaded Mount Cachak in safety, and reached Velika in good time. We were cheered and happy. We were "beyond the mountains." They stood up in grim semicircle, but they were behind us now, not before, as they had been at Ipek. We were nearing Andreavitza, the outskirt of the "Land of Promise."

Velika was distinctly an improvement upon Byeluk, though there were dead horses there as well. We obtained accommodation in a farm—a bed made up upon the floor in a little room where the family seemed to keep all their possessions, for it was with the greatest difficulty that we could induce them to leave us to ourselves. There was a stable for Pigeon, and Chirovitch decided that he would sleep there, too.

We pointed out that he himself had declared we should find "good people" when we got to Velika. He admitted this—nevertheless, he slept in the stable.

This meant nothing to us at the time, but we might have taken it as a presage for the future. Chirovitch and his "good people"! When we met with overcharging and incivility at Andreavitza, we were told we should find the "good people" on the road as we proceeded; when we were literally robbed upon the road, we must wait till we got to Podgoritza; when Podgoritza failed to come up to the mark, the "good people" of Montenegro were finally limited to Nikshitz, which was our orderly's native town. We never went to Nikshitz, so we were unable to dispute the claim.

Our spirits were high when we set out the following day for Andreavitza, and they were maintained until we reached that little town. The morning was sunny and warm—were we not on the sunny side of the mountains? When we reached Podgoritza we should eat pomegranates. We fully imagined that we were coming to a Riviera-like climate.

It was certainly very different from what we had gone through. The road lay along a broad, green valley, and there were plenty of houses scattered about, and peasants came out to sell fruit, wine, and rakia to the soldiers as they passed.

The soldiers were happy, too. The promised rest and refreshment were so near at hand. From every side one heard the sound of shooting—it is a way they have of marking their pleasure.

And so at night—full of expectation—we came to Andreavitza; and it was only with great difficulty, through the kindness of a friend, that we obtained a room at all—a bare room that contained nothing whatever except a couple of beds with scant coverings to them, for which

luxurious apartment we were expected to pay ten peppers (rather more than ten francs) a day. And there was no food to be had, none at all. We had to go hungry to bed.

But of the real tragedy, the failure of supplies to the Army, we only knew later. We regarded Andreavitza as a disappointment; but when, after a two-days' rest, we set out again, Scutari, our objective, was still to us the "Land of Promise." Of three things, at least, we felt confident—of sunshine, of immunity from enemy attack, and of kindly treatment from the people of Old Montenegro.

Delusions—like so much that had gone before, so much that was to come; for not far out from Andreavitza we were startled by an enemy aeroplane hovering over our heads; then that afternoon, descending after a most fatiguing climb into another valley, we found a cold mist prevailing, and this mist hardly lifted during all the weary travelling that ensued through a country so bleak, desolate, and grey that our very souls revolted from it; and finally, that night, and many other nights that followed, we slept under conditions that vied in horror with what we had endured at Kuchista.

Never after we reached Andreavitza—it was on December 6th—did we hear a Serbian gun fired in jubilation. The day of hope had departed, the night of despair had set in. In closing this chapter it may be of interest to jot down the route we took in our flight across Serbia and Montenegro to the Albanian coast. Starting from Pirot, on the Bulgarian frontier, our first retreat was to Nish. Thence we passed in succession through the following towns: Prokuplie, Kurshumliya, Pristina, Prisrend, Djakova, Ipek (Petch), Andreavitza, Podgoritza, Scutari, Alessio (Liesh), and San Giovanni di Medua.

The main part of the Second Army followed this route, save that it took the direct, but more dangerous, road from Pristina to Ipek by way of the Drenitza. The artillery and heavier transport were conveyed from Ipek to Andreavitza by a somewhat longer but easier route via Rozhai.

A large portion of the Army did not go through Montenegro at all, but marched direct from Prisrend to Scutari across Albania. It was a terrible journey, and fraught with the greatest danger. A smaller proportion escaped to the south through Monastir.

TROUBLE FOR THE ENEMY ON THE WAY TO NISH.
Inclement weather and incessant transports turned the Serbian roads into little better than ploughed fields, and such an incident as that pictured above was of regular occurrence. A German Staff officer's car having stuck fast in a rut, five hefty Teutons are grappling with the situation.

SUNSET, SALONIKA: BRITISH CONVOY MAKING FOR THE HILL POSITIONS.

ARRIVAL OF THE WATER TRAIN

CHAPTER CV.

SOMEWHERE IN S.W. AFRICA.

THE RÔLE OF RAILWAYS IN THE WAR.

By Edwin A. Pratt, Author of "The Rise of Rail-Power in War and Conquest."

Railways Become a New Arm in Warfare—Germany Prepares them in Time of Peace for Purposes of Conquest—Strategical Railways and Welt-Politik—Germany's Iron Road to the Persian Gulf—How she Yearned for the African Continent, and Hoped that Railways would Help her to Get It—German Troops Rushed across the Belgian Frontier by Rail—French Railways Fully Prepared—First Victory in the Great War Won by French Railwaymen—Strategical Services Rendered—British Railways also Ready—Basis of their Operation, under State Control, by Railway Executive Committee—What they Accomplished—Railways and the German Invasion of Russia—Overcoming Differences in Gauge—German Dependence on the "Railway Machine"—Italian Railways and the War—The Rail Factor in the Balkans—Rôle of the Railways in the Attack on Egypt—Various Purposes Served by Railways in War—Easily Destroyed but Readily Restored—Some Conclusions.

FROM the earliest days of their introduction railways have been regarded as offering the most efficient means for meeting the special needs of military transport in time of war ; and, in becoming a new arm in modern warfare, they have helped to alter its scope and character.

While, however, the use which may be made of railways in war is great, varied, and comprehensive, much practical and even disastrous experience established the fact that this use was only likely to be efficient when the employment of railways for military transport had been the subject of well-planned organisation in time of peace.

Hence it was that since, more especially, the War of Secession in the United States, schemes for the organisation of military rail-transport had been adopted more or less completely in all the leading countries of Europe, according to what were regarded as the special needs of the national situation ; and the outbreak of war in 1914 found the railway authorities in the countries concerned ready to respond at once to the demands that the military Powers were likely to make upon them. This, as will be shown later on, was certainly the case in Britain and France quite as much as it was in Germany and Austria.

The preparations

STUDY IN CRANE-POWER.
German locomotive being lifted bodily on to a lighter which conveyed it to a Danube harbour, whence it was used in the transport of troops to the Balkan field of war.

made by Germany went, however, far beyond those measures in the way of peace-time organisation which had been adopted in other countries, as a matter of prudence and precaution, in the interests of national defence.

Germany was the first of the great nations to recognise the importance of the rôle that railways were likely to play in warfare. As early as 1842 a scheme was put forward in that country for the construction of a network of strategical railways which would allow of operations being carried on simultaneously against France and Russia, should the occasion for so doing arise.

Nor was the said scheme to be regarded as merely a project on paper, since in this same year M. Marschall pointed out in the French Chamber that the German Confederation was already converging a formidable system of "aggressive lines" from Cologne, Mayence, and Mannheim on to the frontiers of France between Metz and Strassburg, leaving no room for doubt as to the nature of Germany's intentions. "Studies for an expedition against Paris by way of Lorraine and Champagne can," he added, "hardly be regarded as indicative of a sentiment of fraternity."

In the Schleswig-Holstein campaigns, the Austro - Prussian War, and the Franco-Prussian War, Germany made increasing use of her railways, revising and

RAPID REPAIR OF COMMUNICATIONS.
South African Engineer Corps repairing the De Viature Bridge, blown up by the Germans during their retreat inland.

improving her organisation with each fresh experience gained.

After the war of 1870-71, France showed so much activity in strengthening her defences in the north-east, alike by an extension of her railway system and by the construction of a series of formidable forts, that in 1896 Germany began to build along the Belgian frontier a railway which, subsequently to 1908—when her policy in this direction was suddenly developed with almost feverish activity—expanded into a complete network of strategical lines radiating from Aix-la-Chapelle, the Rhine, and the Moselle to the new Malmédy-Stavelot line (crossing the frontier of Germany and Belgium), the said network affording the means by which troops from all parts of the German Empire could be poured in an endless succession of trains on to Belgian territory, with a view either to the conquest of that country itself or to an attack on France at points more vulnerable than were then to be found in Champagne and Lorraine.

In the direction of Russia, Russian Poland, and Austria there was built by Germany another network of strategical railways which connected various military centres with lines running parallel to the frontier, and having branches to points within a few miles thereof, so that troops could be concentrated wherever they were wanted. Intersecting or transverse lines afforded a ready means of communication between one of these direct lines and another.

Germany had also reorganised her rail-
Frontier railways of Germany way system on the frontiers of Holland in such a way that she could assemble an army there and invade Dutch territory no less readily than Belgium ; while, simultaneously with these developments, she had so improved or adapted her railway system in the interior of Germany as to provide alike for the speedy mobilisation of her troops, for their despatch by well-defined routes to any one of her frontiers, and for their ready transfer from one front to another in the event of war having to be carried on in two or more directions at the same time. The programme recommended in 1842 was, in fact, accomplished in all its essential details.

Here it may be explained that strategical railways differ

from ordinary railways in so far as the former (1) are built expressly to serve strategical purposes, as distinct from ordinary traffic, and (2) have such provision of siding accommodation, long platforms, and other special facilities for the entrainment or detrainment of troops, horses, guns, munitions, and supplies that they are able to ensure the transport of large bodies of men and material, which many ordinary railways would not be able to do.

A railway is thus not necessarily of military significance simply because it has been made in the direction or in the neighbourhood of a frontier. For this reason ordinary railway maps may be misleading, unless the capacity of the lines for military traffic is understood. On the other hand, when one finds concerning German lines on the frontiers of Belgium, for instance, that many of them were not wanted at all for the ordinary needs of the district, and that the double lines, the extensive sidings, the long platforms, and the general station arrangements at places where the local traffic was quite insignificant in extent would permit of a complete army corps and all its necessaries being dealt with, no reason was left for doubt that such lines as these were purely strate- **Railways and** gical railways, deliberately designed **Welt-politik** for the furthering of a national policy either of defence or of invasion. Which of these purposes was the more likely to have been paramount in the case of Germany is a point that, as it happened, left little ground for speculation.

One has, in fact, only to look at Germany's policy in regard to railway expansion in order to understand how thoroughly, and over what a prolonged period, she had prepared for world-conquest, or, at least, for the acquiring of supremacy in the exercise of world-power.

Among the chief measures to which she resorted for ensuring the success of her Welt-politik were (1) railways, (2) commerce, and (3) a more powerful Navy. Railways were to afford her the means of either penetrating into and obtaining greater control over countries whose possession she coveted, or, alternatively, concentrating her armed forces within striking distance of such countries ; her commercial men were to be advance agents for the furthering of political no less than of economic interests ; and her expanded Navy was being prepared for that conflict with Britain to which, it was foreseen, her bid for world-supremacy would inevitably lead. But in these three essentials to the attainment of one great aim it was the railways that took the place of primary importance. Without them, Welt-politik must have remained a dream, since railways were indispensable to any practical attempt to effect its realisation.

The Bagdad Railway, regarded in Germany as a German line, was to be the means by which she would (1) strengthen her hold on the Turkish Government, through the consequent financial and political complications ; (2) convert Turkey in Asia into practically a German State ; (3) secure —with the help of railways in Europe which she either controlled already or hoped eventually to control—direct lines of communication from Hamburg and Berlin to the Persian Gulf ; (4) neutralise, as far as that Gulf, the sea-power of Great Britain; (5) acquire a strategical position from which she might add Persia, no less than Mesopotamia. to the German Empire; and (6) create at the head of the Persian Gulf a stronghold which, with a stream of troops and munitions conveyed thither. without fear of interruption, alike from Germany and from her vassal State, Turkey, would enable her to threaten the gates of India and the ocean highway to Australia, and start on fresh schemes of conquest in the Far East in general.

With western sections of the Bagdad Railway linking up with the Hedjaz Railway, and having extensions or branches which would afford greater facilities for reaching the eastern bank of the Suez Canal, Germany also looked forward (1) to the creation at Alexandretta of a great port from which she could exercise sea-power in the Mediterranean and control commerce expected to pass between that inland sea. Turkey in Asia (otherwise Germany in Asia), and the Far East, via the Bagdad Railway; (2) to bringing the whole of Syria under her influence; and (3) to the eventual conquest of Egypt, thereby not only acquiring a land of great value in itself, but making what was predicted in advance to be a deadly thrust into a vital part of the British Empire.

Railways, again, were to enable Germany to effect the

THE WAR ALONG THE NARROW GAUGE.
British scouting party setting out on a war train for a raid on the enemy's positions from Omarieru, South-West Africa.

The German East African Railway, connecting the Indian Ocean with the shores of Lake Tanganyika, was to enable German troops (1) to make raids into British East Africa; (2) to secure the eventual supremacy of Germany in the Belgian Congo, with its vast potentialities in the way of mineral and other resources; and (3) to join with German troops coming via the north-east corner of German South-West Africa in the seizure of Rhodesia.

Then, as originally designed, the northern railway of the German Cameroon was to be continued to Lake Chad, whence, it was hoped, Germany would get control alike over the Sudan and over the French possessions in North Africa, linking up Lake Chad with Algeria and the Mediterranean by what would then be a German railway across the Desert of Sahara. The line which was to lead to the realisation of this ambitious scheme was not carried, however, more than a comparatively short distance, and other proposals (1) for bringing the trade and traffic of the Belgian Congo under the direction of Germany, by securing it either for the German East Africa Railway or for new German lines connecting the Congo with the chief port of the Cameroon; (2) for a coastal railway connection between German South-West Africa and Portuguese Angola (helping to ensure the ultimate possession thereof for Germany); and (3) for the extension of the Lobito Bay railway to the southern districts of the Belgian Congo as part of a German line of rail

German projects in Africa

LINESMEN IN S.W. AFRICA.
Owing to the prevalence of sand-storms in South-West Africa, large squads of men were continually employed in keeping the tracks clear. In some districts a few minutes sufficed for the rails to be buried deep in sand.

conquest of the African continent; and here, once more, we have to deal, not with the visionary ideas of irresponsible dreamers who were merely planning schemes of world-conquest on paper, but with lines of railway actually constructed and in full working order—with still others definitely projected—for the express purpose of furthering the aims in question.

Aided by the strategical railways already built in South-West Africa, German troops were to join the Boers—whose rising when "Der Tag" arrived was confidently expected—in acquiring possession of British South Africa.

UNWIELDY MACHINE AND NIMBLE ENGINEERS.
South African Engineers pontooning a locomotive over the Orange River, which was in flood during the operations against German South-West Africa.

SIMPLE AND EFFECTIVE.
Ingenious arrangement for carrying wounded Austrians from place to place. It was in the form of a stretcher fixed between two bicycles, and proved highly satisfactory.

communication from the west coast across Central Africa to the east, had all failed of realisation at the time that war broke out ; though here we get still further evidence as to the nature of the aims that Germany was cherishing.

Had all these plans been realised, the world might eventually have seen, not only the transformation of Africa into a German Empire, but continuous lines of German-owned or German - controlled railways stretching from Hamburg, first to Constantinople, and thence in one direction to the Persian Gulf, and in the other to Cairo and the Cape.

With the failure of the Boer "rising" on the outbreak of war, and with the capture of German South-West Africa by General Botha's forces, the schemes of conquest so laboriously prepared and so long cherished came to grief at what was to have been the initial step towards their fulfilment. The railways in South-West Africa, on which Germany had spent over £8,000,000, were not only annexed by the victorious British forces, but were made use of for their own movements, and joined up with the railways of the South African Union, to serve thenceforward the purposes of peace in the development of South-West Africa under the administration of the Cape Province Government.

The railway policy thus adopted by Germany in Asia and Africa must, in the circumstances here narrated, be taken into account no less than what we have already seen she was doing in the same direction in Europe.

On the outbreak of the Great War the strategical railways which Germany had constructed towards, along, and, jointly with the Belgian Government (owing to the pressure she had brought to bear upon them), even across the Belgian frontier, enabled her at once to concentrate and to throw into that country great masses of troops for an invasion of France. But although these railways afforded her material aid in rushing troops on to Belgian territory, Germany had not anticipated so vigorous an opposition, at Liège, by the brave-hearted Belgians, who

thus thwarted her design, first to make a sudden descent on France by rail, and then to rush the main body of her troops, also by rail, back through Germany for the attack on Russia.

From the railway point of view the action taken by Belgium was of exceptional value to the Allies, since it meant that, although Germany crossed the frontiers of Belgium and Luxemburg on August 3rd, it was not until the 24th that she was in a position to attack the French Army, which by that time had not only completed both its mobilisation and its concentration, but had been joined by the first arrivals of the British Expeditionary Force.

When once the Belgian opposition had been effectively crushed, the close network of railways in that country became a powerful auxiliary to Germany's further operations against France. While, however, she had attached so much importance both to the perfection of her own railway system (from a strategical point of view) and to the control of the Belgian and Luxemburg systems, she had made the mistake of not allowing sufficiently for what the French and British railways could also do—especially with the practical advantage which, though at so terrible a cost to herself, Belgium had secured for them by her own heroic struggle with so powerful and merciless a foe. **How Belgium helped her Allies**

It certainly was the case that, in the Franco-Prussian War of 1870–71, military transport in France speedily assumed chaotic conditions, and that these were, in fact, among the direct causes of the disaster by which the country was so speedily overtaken. It cannot be said, however, that the disorder leading to those conditions was due to any lack of zeal or efficiency on the part of the French railway companies, who made the most strenuous efforts to deal with the traffic, and themselves accomplished marvels in this direction. The faults that arose were attributable, rather, to the absence in France of any organisation co-ordinating the military and the civil elements by the creation of authorities through

TRAMS AND AUTOMOBILES IN AMBULANCE WORK.
For conveying wounded rapidly from place to place at Prague a number of tramcars were utilised. This photograph shows the ordinary conveyance, with blinds drawn, and marked with the familiar emblem, en route for the hospital. The oval illustration shows a number of Red Cross autos which skidded and were put out of gear owing to the treacherous condition of the roads in France.

French supply column defiling along an open road behind the battle-line. This column was by no means exceptional as to length. Trailing away into the far distance, it took considerable time to pass a given point. In the oval illustration a similar convoy is seen halting at a Marne village.

About to proceed to the front. French supply section somewhere on the western line. Though motor transport was, to a great extent, employed by all the belligerents, a large number of powerful team-horses were found to be indispensable.

Empty war waggons, having delivered their contents at a junction for the first-line trenches proceeding to the base for a further supply of the necessities of life along the battle-front.

WITH OUR ALLIES' SUPPLY COLUMNS IN THE MARNE SECTOR.

WHEELS WITHIN WHEELS.
German locomotive going into
Russian territory on a rail truck.
The Russian gauge being too
broad for German engines, this
was the only means of conveying locomotives on to Russian
territory, to be used on lines
constructed by the Germans.

whom all orders and
instructions for rail transport would pass, the
military element further
adopting such methods of
control and regulation as
would avoid congestion
and delay at the stations,
while leaving the railway
element free to attend to
the working of the lines
without the risk of having
to deal with impracticable and
conflicting demands by individual
military officers acting on their
own responsibility without regard
for the physical limitations of the
railways or for the needs of the
situation as a whole.

In the interval which had elapsed
since 1870-71 an organisation for
the conduct of military rail-
transport in time of war, on the
lines here indicated, had been
planned and worked out in France
in a way so comprehensive and so
exhaustive that it provided in
advance—as far as the combined
wisdom of military and railway
authorities could foresee or suggest—for every contingency that
was likely to arise.

At the same time, also, France
had greatly improved her railway
system, from a strategical point
of view, and more especially in
regard to better connections with
the Franco-German frontier and
the linking up of cross-country
lines in such a way as to facilitate

speedy mobilisation and concentration in case of need

So it was that Germany's proclamation on July 31st, 1914, of
" the state of danger of war "
found the French railways prepared to take instant action.

The transport of "troupes de
couverture"—otherwise, the troops
despatched to the frontier to meet
the first attack of the enemy—
began at nine o'clock the same
evening, and was completed by
noon on August 3rd (before there
had been any suspension of the
ordinary railway traffic), although
this initial operation itself involved
the running, on the Eastern system
alone, of nearly six hundred trains.

The general mobilisation began
on August 2nd, and the despatch
of troops, etc., from the depôts to
the points of concentration at the
front, in accordance with the
time-tables prepared in time of
peace, was started at midday on
the 5th and completed on
the 19th. Between the
two last-mentioned dates
the number of military
trains run was nearly
4,500 (exclusive of 250
trains carrying siege supplies to the fortresses),
and of this total more
than 4,000 had destina-
tions on the Eastern
system.

At the end of this
period the French Gov-
ernment issued a notice
expressing to the railway
officers and railway
workers of all ranks the

TO THE FRONT BY LIGHT RAILWAY.
One of the many methods used by our French ally for conveying troops and provisions to the trenches.
In centre : French Chasseurs Alpins repairing a broken rail in the Vosges.

warmest acknowledgment of the patriotic zeal and the admirable devotion with which they had toiled day and night; while the "Journal des Transports," of January 30th, 1915 in announcing this fact, declared on its own behalf: "One can justly say that the first victory in this great conflict has been won by the railwaymen."

These earliest movements were, however, to be followed by a succession of others, which imposed a further abnormal strain on the railway organisation to an extent far greater than had been anticipated and already provided for.

No sooner was the concentration of France's seven armies—six along the front and one in Paris—accomplished than the railways had to ensure, between August 12th and August 20th, the conveyance to Mons of the officers and men of the British Expeditionary Force who had by that time arrived at Boulogne, Nantes, and St. Nazaire. This alone involved the running of 420 transport trains. Provision had likewise to be made for the transport across France, from Marseilles, of 60,000 French troops from Africa, and, also, of the troops arriving there from India.

The masterly retreat of the allied centre and right to the south of the Marne, which followed the fall of Charleroi, on August 26th,

BY SHINING STREAM AND SILVER BIRCH.
French soldiers repairing a light railway in the reconquered territory of beautiful Alsace.

called for an especially prodigious effort on the part of the French railways; and this effort—crowned with complete success—had to be made concurrently with the need for facilitating the flight of many thousands of refugees from the invaded or threatened districts of Belgium and Northern France.

Thanks to the results attained, there was secured for the defence of Paris so speedy and so strong a reconcentration of the allied forces that not only was the advance of the invaders checked, but the enemy was himself thrown back in some disorder successively to the Petit Morin, the Marne, and the Aisne. Thus the first great object of the German offensive failed, and Paris was saved.

Meanwhile, the railways had been further engaged in the removal of the French Government —as a precautionary measure— from Paris to Bordeaux, whither they conveyed the President, Ministers, secretaries, officials, and the more important of the State papers.

Many of the most precious of the art treasures in the museums of Paris were also taken to Bordeaux, while the continuous flight from Belgium and Northern France was now supplemented by a not inconsiderable exodus of the population of Paris.

QUEER MACHINES SEEN ON THE IRON WAY.
Freakish type of locomotive, used for transport purposes, taking in water. Attached to the engine is a waggon conveying small tree-trunks to assist in consolidating trenches. Above will be seen two similar engines constructed in England for use on the network of light railways laid down behind the French lines.

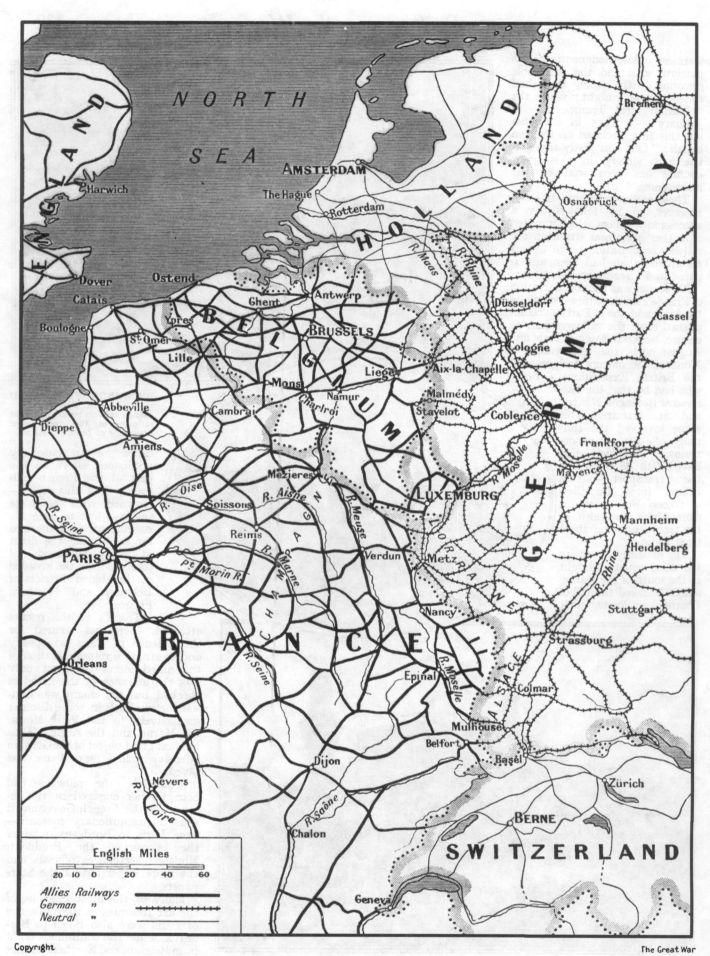

MAIN ARTERIES OF WAR: THE IRON WAYS OF THE ALLIES AND GERMANY.

As in the matter of men, equipments and armament, the Germans were equally prepared with rail service for their war of aggression. This map shows the railway systems of Germany and the Allies. The two distinct lines, one on each bank of the Rhine, greatly assisted in the enemy's rapid mobilisation.

BRITISH ABOUT TO REPEL AN ATTACK AT DAWN ALONG THE UGANDA RAILWAY.

On January 17th, 1916, enemy attacks on the Uganda Railway were repulsed by the British forces operating in East Africa. This picture gives a graphic impression of the manner in which these numerous surprise assaults were resisted. Along certain parts of the railway the lines run over an embankment slightly raised above the surrounding country, and the excavations at the sides of the lines provided excellent shelter.

Early in October came another great achievement of the French railways. The plan had been formed of transferring the entire British force, then located near Soissons, on the Aisne, to St. Omer and other points near to Western Belgium, with a view to carrying out a wide sweeping movement which would turn the right of the enemy, who, foiled in his dash on Paris, was now preparing to stretch out his line towards the coast in support of the threatened march on Calais. In the circumstances it became a matter of the greatest importance that the transfer of the British troops, with horses, guns, kit, and transport, should be effected with the utmost despatch.

The distance to be covered—allowing for a wide detour via Amiens, Abbeville, Boulogne, and Calais—was about 180 miles, and, although the operation involved the running of over 600 trains, with about 16,800 carriages and waggons, and had to be carried out "almost under the nose of the enemy," it was completed with conspicuous success in sixteen days. The cavalry, who started on October 3rd, were in contact with the enemy, to the south of St. Omer, on October 11th. The Second Army Corps arrived in the

evening of the same day, and took up position beside the cavalry. The Third Army Corps detrained at St. Omer also on the 11th, and the First Army Corps reached the same destination on the 19th. Thanks to the railways, the race for the sea was won by the Allies, and, although the contemplated turning of the enemy's flank was not accomplished, an effective check was put to the realisation of his designs on the Channel ports.

Under the conditions of trench warfare, demands made upon the French railways settled down mainly into the less exciting, though scarcely less exacting, continuous transport of French, British, and Belgian troops; of vast quantities of food supplies and of heavy guns, munitions, and other war material to the western front, together with the conveyance therefrom of sick and wounded, of men on leave, and of prisoners of war. Nor must one omit to mention, also, the very considerable masses of postal matter carried by the French railways to and from the trenches, or the obligation which devolved upon them to provide, as well as they could, for the needs of the civil population.

In Great Britain the

RAILWAYS AND MUNITION TRANSPORT.
Part of a siege-gun, in process of manufacture, being hoisted on to a truck for transference to the finishing shop of a French munition works.

ELEPHANT IN WAR-HARNESS.
A Sheffield munitions firm hired an elephant, finding that it could do the work of five horses.

United Kingdom, or any of them, or the plant belonging to any railway company apart from the railway itself; while the directors, officers, and servants of the railways concerned were to "obey the directions of the Secretary of State as to the uses of such railroad or plant for Her Majesty's service."

Down to 1912, however, there existed no executive body to which, in the event of their taking control of them under the provisions of this Act, the Government could entrust the operation of the railways; though the need for such a body, as an essential link in the chain of organisation, was obvious. Hence the appointment, in that year, of a Railway Executive Committee consisting of general managers of the leading railway

need for creating, in time of peace, some practical organisation which would ensure the efficiency of military rail-transport in the event of war was first brought under consideration in 1860, as the result of reports concerning French plans for the invasion of this country. Five years later there was formed an Engineer and Railway Volunteer Staff Corps which, composed of general managers and other officers of the principal railway companies, eminent civil engineers, and leading contractors, was to collect information concerning the facilities offered by the railways of the United Kingdom for dealing with the transport of troops and military necessaries, and to prepare such plans as the War Office might direct.

THE ANCIENT AND MODERN IN LOCOMOTION.
Primitive oxen-drawn carts with a motor-car at the railway-station at Mirovtze. During the Allies' campaign in the Balkans such contrasts were common.

In 1896 this corps was supplemented by a smaller body known first as the "Army," and afterwards as the "War," Railway Council, and constituted of railway managers, military officers, naval officers, and a Board of Trade inspector of railways. This new body was to take over some of the duties already discharged by the above mentioned corps, and others besides, though it was to act in a purely advisory capacity. Among the duties it discharged was that of drawing up rules for the working of a system of Railway Transport Officers—that is to say, military men who were to act as intermediaries between the troops and railway-station staffs in ensuring the efficient conduct of military rail-transport, without hampering or interfering with those staffs in the actual working of the traffic.

Our War Railway Council

The War Railway Council did good work in this and other directions; but it was, in turn, superseded by another body, known as the Railway Executive Committee.

Under the Regulation of the Forces Act, 1871, the Government was empowered, in the event of a national emergency arising, to take control over the railways of the

companies, presided over by Sir Herbert A. Walker, general manager of the London and South-Western Railway Company, such committee being charged, in the first instance, with the duty of preparing plans with a view to facilitating the working of the Act of 1871.

On the outbreak of war in 1914 the Government duly took control over the railways of Great Britain, by authority of an Order-in-Council, and it was then announced that such control would be exercised through the Railway Executive Committee. A notification issued by the committee explained that the action taken by the Government was designed to ensure that the railways, locomotives, rolling-stock, and staffs should be used as one complete unit in the best interests of the State for the movement of troops, stores, and food supplies; though the staff on each railway would remain under the same control, and receive their instructions through the same channels as before.

Under the arrangements made with the Government, the railway executive sat *en permanence* at its headquarters in London (some members being in attendance both day and night), and there acted as a sort of clearing house in regard to matters affecting the railways of Great

Britain as a whole, dealing more especially with what might be described as "main principles" in the exercise of the Government control.

In this way they (among other things) issued "general instructions" on a great variety of subjects affecting all the companies. These instructions were addressed in each instance to the general manager of the company, and by him, or by some responsible member of his staff, were communicated to and carried out by the respective departments.

The executive committee further discharged the important duty of co-ordinating the requirements of (1) the War Office and the Admiralty, (2) the travelling public,

"DERNIERES NOUVELLES DE LA GUERRE."
French soldiers, going up to the front in automobiles, buying newspapers from a villager in order to read the latest news of the Verdun Battle.

BATTLE-SCARRED MOTOR-CARS ON THE PERMANENT WAY.
Staff Officers' automobiles, which had been wrecked by hard going or shell splinters, on their way to a base for repairs.

concern which had all the necessary machinery ready for immediate use,* while this machinery had, in turn, been designed on a principle remarkable for its practical but efficacious simplicity as compared with the complications of the Continental systems, on which so vast an amount of effort had been spent.

When we come to inquire how, with the help of this organisation, the British Expeditionary Force was mobilised and safely transported to France, we gain evidence of what a military correspondent of the "Morning Post" justly described at the time as "a veritable triumph for all concerned," and "one of the best feats ever performed in the preliminary stages of war."

and (3) the traders; so that while the needs of the Army and Navy received first attention, those of the other interests dependent on rail-transport were studied and provided for so far as circumstances would permit.

As regards the actual traffic demands of the War Office and the Admiralty these, while being duly communicated to the executive committee, were, in order to save circumlocution and delay, sent direct by the military or the naval authorities respectively to the superintendents or traffic managers, who, keeping in close touch with one another, provided for all the necessary working details in respect to the route by which the traffic should pass and the arrangements to be made for its conveyance with all possible despatch and efficiency.

The system, which thus meant one control, one management, and the operation of the railways of Great Britain as one unit, was admirably conceived and, apart from inevitable delays, under war conditions, in the handling of ordinary merchandise, worked with complete efficiency. It was brought into operation (subject to certain financial conditions) by, as it were, the stroke of a pen, as a going

The order to mobilise was given on August 4th, at a moment when the railways were already crowded with holiday traffic. They speedily became still more crowded with reservists travelling from every part of the country to their respective headquarters. Meanwhile, the Government gave the railways a time-limit of sixty hours to get ready no fewer than three hundred and fifty trains, with an average of thirty vehicles each, for a special emergency movement. The necessary arrangements were all completed by the railway companies within forty-eight hours.

British railway triumph

For the conveyance of the Expeditionary Force to Southampton troop-trains were sent from every part of Great Britain, including remote places in Scotland and Wales; but in no single instance, it was afterwards declared, were the troops kept waiting for a train, while practically every train, without exception, reached

* At the ordinary general meeting of the shareholders of the London and South-Western Railway Company, on February 23rd, 1915, the chairman of the company, Mr. Hugh W. Drummond, said: "I think I may say that if the country was not prepared and equipped for war, the railways of the country were, at any rate."

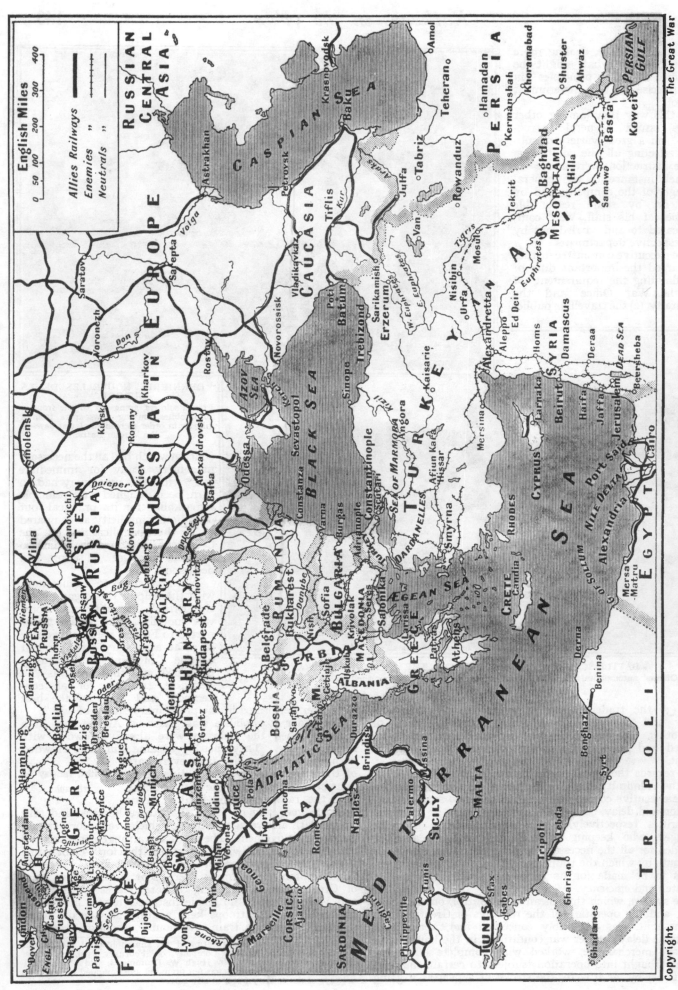

Copyright

Map illustrating the principal railways of Europe and Asia Minor, the most interesting of which was the Berlin Constantinople-Bagdad line. A glance at the diagram will give some idea of the enormous preponderance of the Central Empires' rail-power over that of Russia.

RAIL-POWER COMPARED: NETWORK OF COMMUNICATIONS IN EUROPE AT THE TIME OF THE GREAT WAR.

The Great War

Southampton in scheduled time. During the first three weeks of the war no fewer than seventy-three military trains, arriving at an average of twelve-minute intervals, were dealt with per day at Southampton, the work including the running of them to the boat-side, and the unloading alike of troops, guns, ammunition, horses, etc.

On August 17th a statement issued by the Press Bureau announced that " The Expeditionary Force, as detailed for foreign service, has been safely landed on French soil. The embarkation, transportation, and disembarkation of men and stores were alike carried through with the greatest possible precision, and without a single casualty." Sir John French wrote from France : " The transport of the troops from England, both by sea and by rail, was effected in the best order, and without a check. Each unit arrived at its destination in this country well within the scheduled time." On August 22nd—only eighteen days from the date when the mobilisation order had been issued in Britain—Sir John French was able to make dispositions to move his force to the positions he considered most favourable for commencing operations, and on that same day the advanced squadrons, he wrote, " did some excellent work."

In the House of Lords, Earl Kitchener said of the part played by the railways in the feat which had been accomplished :

" The railway companies, in the all-important matter of the transport facilities, have more than justified the confidence reposed in them by the War Office, all grades of railway services having laboured with untiring energy and patience."

Speaking in the House of Commons on November 16th, Mr. Walter Long said :

" The control over the railways has not only worked without a single hitch, but with the most wonderful regard for the convenience of the public at **Strategic results of** large. It has been, I think, one of the **railway transport** most successful enterprises ever undertaken in this country."

In the course of an article published in the " West Australian Railway Gazette," Mr. J. T. Shillington, who was in England at the time of the outbreak of war, wrote concerning the mobilisation and transport of the Expeditionary Force :

" The silent moving of thousands upon thousands of men, horses, guns, baggage, and all the equipment of an army was carried out in such a manner as to merit the highest approbation. I had the good fortune to see some of the inner working of this gigantic movement. In my humble opinion the mobilisation of troops was carried out with greater success in England than in any other part of the world. The system arranged for the conduct of the business was a masterpiece, and the staff carried it out faultlessly."

If we look at the strategic results of this great achievement in military transport, we find that they were of the utmost value and importance, since the arrival of the British force in support of the French was effected at a supremely critical moment, and became a potent factor in the checking and driving back of the German invaders at a time when Paris itself seemed to be at their mercy.

Had the organisation of the British railways been less perfect, or less ready to respond instantly to all demands ; had railway officers and railwaymen of all grades been less efficient, or less untiring in their zeal, devotion, and indomitable energy ; and had there, in consequence, been a breakdown in the transport arrangements in this country, involving delay in the arrival of the British units at their appointed destinations in France—then it is quite possible, if not in the highest degree probable, that the Germans would have forced their way to Paris, and that the further developments of the conflict would have been even graver than they actually were.

In these conditions the railway companies deserved

well alike of their country, of their country's Allies, and of supporters throughout the world of those principles which Britain was seeking to maintain in the greatest war on record.

The exertions thus made by the railway companies and their staffs were, however, only the beginning of a continuous series of untiring activities, the full resources of the railways in men and material being placed at the disposal of the Government so far as they could be utilised or made available in the prosecution of the war.

In addition to a considerable amount of military traffic carried by the ordinary trains, many thousands of " specials," in the aggregate, were run for the conveyance of troops, horses, baggage, guns, munitions, food supplies, fodder, timber for huts, coal for the Fleet, and other necessaries. The needs of both permanent and extemporised camps for the housing or the training of troops prior to their departure for the front made further

A FOOTHOLD ON GALLIPOLI.
Corner of a British military camp on the shores of the Gallipoli Peninsula ; a scene at " W Beach," with a glimpse of white tents in the distance.

considerable demands on the resources of the railways. Ambulance trains, meeting the sick and wounded, at the ports, distributed them over all parts of the country. Special trains were, at one time, no less wanted for the conveyance of Belgian refugees, of whom on one day alone no fewer than 6,000 were brought by South-Eastern and Chatham steamers from Ostend to Folkestone, while the total number of those who came to this country was considerably over 100,000.

In dealing with all this immense traffic, some of the companies had to lengthen their platforms, lay down new sidings, build special vehicles for heavy artillery, or provide further cranes and other necessary appliances for loading and unloading ; but these needs were invariably supplied with remarkable celerity, while the general arrangements were so complete that there was practically no delay whatever in the handling of military traffic. The companies, too, acquitted themselves of all these tasks notwithstanding

MAKING TRACKS.
Type of automobile used by French engineers in the construction of roadways to facilitate transport to and from the front.

the fact that about 120,000 railwaymen (out of a total of 622,000 employed at the commencement of the war) eventually joined the Colours, and that it was necessary to maintain the food supplies of the country and to provide, so far as circumstances might permit, for the continuance of ordinary trade and travel.

Then the railway companies of the United Kingdom placed at the disposal of the Government the full resources of their locomotive, carriage, and waggon works for the construction of ambulance trains (to be used either in this country or in France), road transport waggons, motor-lorries, gun-limbers, etc., together with the production of ordnance, munitions, military equipment, stretchers, and a wide range of other necessaries. This, in itself, must have been of great advantage to the Government, since the ordinary manufacturing establishments of the country would have been unable to provide all that was wanted, while the productive resources of the railway companies were on a very large scale indeed. **Valuable work on** A list compiled by the present writer a **land and sea** few years ago for his "History of Inland Transport" showed that the number of persons then being employed by leading companies at their various works was: London and North-Western, 14,800; Great Western, 11,700 (all at Swindon); Midland, 8,300; North-Eastern, 8,000; Great Northern, 6,000; Lancashire and Yorkshire, 5,800; Great Eastern, 5,200; Great Central, 4,300; London and South-Western, 3,600; Caledonian, 2,700; North British, 2,300; London, Brighton, and South Coast, 2,200; and the South-Eastern and Chatham, 2,000.

Excellent service was further rendered to the naval and military authorities by those of the railway companies' steamships which were also taken over by the Government, and were used as transports or as hospital ships. The fact that the railway companies had expended a large amount of capital on the construction or improvement of docks and harbours offering great advantages for overseas traffic, some of them being capable of accommodating the largest ships afloat, offered another great advantage to the Government, and one, indeed, of inestimable value in the greatest emergency through which the nation had yet been called upon to pass.

While the Germans on their side of the Russian frontier had an elaborate network of strategical lines, built for the

THE WAR-HORSE SLAKES ITS THIRST AT A POOL IN THE PRIPET MARSHES.
Austrian convoy crossing the treacherous Pripet Marshes. During the bad season this territory was impassable, and any offensive hereabouts would have proved disastrous. Above: Where tyres were dispensable. Motor-car with wheels made to fit the French railway gauge.

express purpose of facilitating an invasion of their neighbour's territory before she could mobilise and concentrate her own troops, Russia had only comparatively a few lines to the frontier, designed to serve the needs mainly of international traffic, and, unlike the aforesaid network of the Germans, having no transverse lines connecting them and facilitating tactical movements from one part of the frontier to another.

There had, however, been indications of late years that Russia, who had already been active in extending or improving railway communications in the interior of her vast Empire, would shortly turn her attention to those in the direction of her western frontier, and inasmuch as she already possessed what Herr von Jagow had called " an inexhaustive reservoir of fighting men," Germany may well have thought it desirable to bring off the apparently inevitable trial of strength with her eastern neighbour before, in addition to having this inexhaustive reservoir, Russia acquired any such power of mobility as that which Germany herself controlled.

Under these conditions the war opened with the advantages in the way of military rail-transport greatly in favour of Germany ; and when Russia, having

German v. Russian railways

completed her initial mobilisation in the unexpectedly short period of sixteen days, proceeded to invade East Prussia, a large body of German troops was withdrawn from the western front and sent across Germany in order to repel the Russians, and then, when they withdrew across the frontier, to follow them up by an invasion of Russian territory in turn.

The facilities thus offered by the German railways—whether avowedly strategical or otherwise—for the transfer of troops from one front to another were afterwards taken advantage of so frequently as to become one of the ordinary incidents of the war. In regard to Russia, however, Germany did not have, as an invader, the same advantage as in Belgium, Luxemburg, and France.

The railways of these three countries have a gauge similar to that of Germany and Austria, namely, 4 ft. 8½ in., so that the locomotives and rolling-stock of any one of the systems can run on the lines of any of the others. In order, however, to render invasion of her own territory more difficult, Russia had chosen a gauge of 5 ft., and the same principle was also mainly adopted in Russian Poland.

THE MAXIM MOTOR.
Armoured motor-car with a machine-gun mounted on the body, used for scouting and raiding on the East African front.

REPLENISHING STORES ON THE BRITISH FRONT IN MACEDONIA.
British mule transport passing through a typical Greek village near the Allies' base. The circle photograph illustrates an adaptation of the tri-car to war purposes. Each is armed with a Maxim. These are machines of the 25th Cyclist Battalion (The London Regiment).

RUNNING THE GAUNTLET OF GERMAN SHELLS: MOTOR-AMBULANCES UNDER FIRE ON THE WESTERN FRONT.

Most of the roads leading back from the trenches were subjected to heavy bombardment, and the work of conveying the wounded to the advanced field hospitals was attended by great danger. This picture (from a sketch by an eye-witness) shows a portion of the road behind one sector of the British front.

One motor-ambulance driver wrote: "We had gone about a hundred and fifty yards when a shell hit the ditch beside the car I was on; fortunately, it burst 'away,' and we only got its dirt, Almost immediately another struck the road behind the last car, which miraculously was not hit."

Germany was thus unable to take her ordinary railway rolling-stock across the Russian frontier and run it on the lines there, while the Russians, when retiring before the Germans, were careful to take their locomotives, carriages, and waggons with them, to prevent the seizure and utilisation thereof by the invader. The Germans are reported to have had a certain amount of rolling-stock fitted with readily adaptable axles, for use on lines of either gauge, and in Courland they relaid the Libau-Romny line with the 4 ft. 8½ in. gauge; but what they mainly relied upon was the hasty construction of light narrow-gauge railways by means of rails already fixed on sleepers so that they could be laid in complete sections (requiring only to be fixed together) along an ordinary road. Impromptu military railways of this type, and able to convey traffic at a speed of about nine miles an hour, are put down with such speed that, according to one authority, "a line seventy miles long can, by means of four railway battalions, be laid in two weeks; but in case of need, if the number of workmen be increased, it can be done in a week only."

Sections of line for light railways of this type are known to have been prepared in Germany in great quantities before the war, and to have been kept stored for any occasion when they might be wanted. They were taken to the Russian frontier on the ordinary railway trucks, other waggons conveying the diminutive locomotives by means of which the lines were to be worked for the conveyance of troops or supplies. Heavy artillery and ammunition were taken into Russia by similar narrow-gauge military railways, though in this case horses were generally employed as the motive power.

GERMAN TROOPS FOR THE EASTERN FRONT.
Scene on the Memel, the most northerly river in Germany. Schooners and barges were used to transport troops and munitions to Russian territory.

The organisation and the training in peace-time of railway battalions which—among other duties—were to carry out such construction work as this in time of war had long been followed up in Germany; and when, a few years ago, certain German critics suggested that the strength of these battalions was unduly large, it was replied that this was not the case because, in the event

Differences of railway gauge

of war, Germany might have to be prepared to deal with both France and Russia at the same time, and, in the case of the latter country, would also require to have a force large enough to overcome the difficulties likely to be presented by the difference in railway gauge.

Once more, therefore, we see from her action in regard to railways how well Germany had prepared for just such eventualities as those she was the means of bringing about in the autumn of 1914.

While the invasion of Russia was greatly facilitated by these pre-war preparations on the part of Germany, it became the policy of the Russians to draw the invaders such a distance alike from the frontier and from their network of strategical railways on the other side thereof that a maximum of possible difficulty in the matter of transport between the frontier and the positions they took up would be caused to them. It was then the Russians —still controlling railways which communicated direct with the country in their rear—who had the advantages of mobility and supplies. There were occasions—as, for instance, in the fighting north of the Lower Vistula in the early spring of 1915—when the Germans were reported to be "suffering disastrously" from shortage of supplies owing to the combination of unfavourable climatic conditions, bad roads, the distance from the nearest base, and the absence of available railways of any kind.

So much, in fact, and more especially in the earlier days of the war, did the Germans depend on "the railway machine" for their movements, and for their supplies, that as soon as they got out of touch of that machine, and were dependent more or less on themselves, they lost

After their long and uncomfortable sea voyage, mules of the Zouave contingent are being drawn, somewhat reluctantly it appears, down the gangway to be used for transport work.

An old German steamer, which was requisitioned in the transport of troops from place to place along the Mediterranean. Crowded with the men of France, it was on its way to Salonika.

On the French landing-quay at Salonika. Lined with great ships, crowded with men, horses, and stores, the quays at Salonika presented an unforgettable scene of animation.

Another view of the French quay at Salonika. A team of horses is dragging a waggon of stores away from the ship's side. The work of unloading the transport is practically completed.

TRANSPORT OF MEN, MULES, AND MUNITIONS TO THE MACEDONIAN FRONT. THE GREAT FRENCH EFFORT IN THE LEVANT.

much of their strength and their power of initiative, and were, as fighting men, in no way superior to the Russians, to whom railways were not so indispensable.

In view of all these various circumstances and conditions, the reader will more readily understand how it was that the story of the fighting, more especially in the Baltic Provinces, in Western Russia, in Russian Poland, in Galicia, and in the Carpathians, turned mainly on struggles, battles, or tactical movements directed to securing or to retaining control of certain lines of railway or of certain "railway knots," often of the greatest strategical importance whether for the movement of troops, the maintenance of supplies, the ensuring of the lines of communication, or the possibility of dividing the enemy's forces and even of cutting off and encircling a considerable portion thereof.

That her railways would constitute an important element in military strategy in any war in which she might be engaged with the Northern Powers had long been foreseen by Italy.

Genoa and Venice are the gateways through which an immense amount of Mediterranean traffic passed in the pre-war period to or from Germany and Austria, but the railway lines used for the purpose were also the lines by which, in case of war, the troops of those countries might, if unchecked, be expected to come in overwhelming strength both for the invasion of Italy and the securing of control over the ports in question, in the interests of the said important traffic.

One of these south-to-north lines to which particular importance was attached, from a military standpoint, was that from Venice and Verona to Franzenfeste (south of the Brenner Pass), whence it continues as the through route to Munich, Leipzig, and Berlin. There were other lines, besides—and notably those between Milan, on the north-west, and Udine, on the north-east—the security of which it would be imperatively necessary to ensure in the interests of national defence.

Hence the organisation of military rail-transport had been provided for in Italy on a basis no less efficient than that adopted in other countries. Italy had, in fact, her corps of railway troops who, composed mainly of recruits already having some experience of railways, underwent a thorough training—either at the Railway Technical School at Turin or on the ordinary railways—in all essential matters connected with construction, destruction, repairs, and operation, such instruction being facilitated by a series of technical books or studies prepared by a committee of officers appointed for that purpose. Practical experience was also gained through the working of two small standard-gauge lines belonging to the State.

When, therefore, Italy became involved in the world-war, she was able to take instant action for ensuring the protection of those of her railway lines on which so much depended, and this result she accomplished, notwithstanding that Austria possessed greatly superior forces, and that

Italian railway organisation

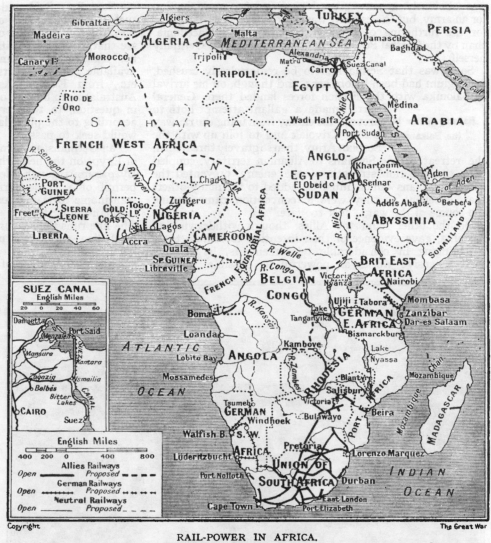

RAIL-POWER IN AFRICA.
Plan of the railway communications in being and under construction over the African Continent. The remarkable connection between Morocco and Lake Chad across the Great Sahara, if it is completed, will constitute an even greater triumph of engineering than that of the Cape to Cairo line.

the northern lines passed through such exceptionally difficult mountainous country.

Railways were the fundamental factor in the Balkan campaign as regards alike the purposes for which the campaign was undertaken, the means by which they were to be attained, and the strategical movements of the forces concerned.

Germany sought to "hack her way" through Serbia—with the help of Austria and Bulgaria—partly in order to provide the Turks with some much-needed ammunition and to stimulate their defence of Constantinople, so as to prevent its fall and the consequent opening of the Black Sea to the British and Russian Fleets, and partly with a view to increasing her hold on the Turkish capital, alike for its own sake and in the interests of her further designs against Egypt, Mesopotamia, Persia, the Persian Gulf, and India.

To the achieving of these purposes, control of the railway from Belgrade through Nish, Sofia, and Adrianople to Constantinople, with its branch from Nish to Salonika, was essential. This railway offered, in fact, the only means of transport through Serbia—a country of mountains and unnavigable torrents, and possessing practically no road at all until the single-line iron road in question was carried through tunnels and deep gorges or ravines, where it followed closely the numerous windings of the rivers, passing, at times, along what were mere shelves cut into the rocks above the tortuous streams.

Such a highway as this—to Constantinople and beyond—

was obviously a very precarious line of communication for an army, but the use of it was desired no less by Bulgaria, for the furthering of her own aspirations in Macedonia, than by the Central Powers, and more especially by Germany herself.

So it was that Serbia had to be remorselessly crushed, as Belgium had been before her ; and though, on his arrival at Salonika with the French forces landed there, General

Railway factor in the Balkans

Sarrail made a gallant attempt both to prevent the enemy from using the railway below Krivolak and to join up with the Serbian Army, then so gravely threatened, the retreat of the Serbians to Albanian territory, coupled with the superior strength of the enemy, prevented the success of plans which must be added to the many others that, excellent as they were in conception, came, during the course of the war, " just too late."

On the other hand the Allies, though withdrawing to Salonika, gave evidence of their intention to remain there by bringing in considerable reinforcements, by making their defensive works as powerful as possible, and by

WINE TO HEARTEN FRENCH TROOPS.
Wine carried on special railway trucks containing huge casks at a French base.   Here it was decanted into smaller casks and sent to the trenches.

destroying a number of railway bridges (including the iron viaduct, two hundred yards in length, over the Struma at Demir Hissar) in order to prevent the Bulgarians from approaching by their coast route.

Strategically speaking, the Egyptian railway system is admirably adapted to defence against any such attack from the Asiatic side of the Suez Canal as that which Germany had long been planning, while the practical difficulties in the way of carrying out the attack were such as to doom it to failure.

Along the entire length of the canal bank, on the Egyptian side, there runs a standard-gauge railway which, though having only a single line, permits of the ready transport of troops to any part of the canal where defensive measures are needed. The length of the line, from Port Said to the Suez docks, is one hundred and seven miles. Equidistant, approximately, between these termini is the junction of Ismailia, whence another single line runs, at right angles, to Zagazig. There it becomes a double line, and so continues to Cairo, with branches to other garrison towns, as well as to the port of Alexandria, on the southern shore of the Mediterranean. Alexandria is the military port of Egypt inasmuch as, under the Suez Canal Con-

vention, Port Said and Suez are to remain neutral, only such troops being sent or stationed there as may be necessary for the purposes of protection ; but the reader will see that, so long as Britain commands the Mediterranean, her transports can land at Alexandria any number of available reinforcements, and any quantity of munitions, etc., from Europe, Asia, South Africa, Canada, and Australasia, to be sent on from there, by the railway lines in question, to the very banks of the canal over which, according to the plans laid down by Germany, the invaders would seek to pass.

Pan-Germans, in turn, based their dreams of a conquest of Egypt on the help which could be secured from railways. By passing through Aleppo, the Bagdad Railway was to permit of a Turco-German force being sent from Constantinople to Damascus, where it would connect with the German-built, though Turkish-owned, Hedjaz Railway. The line runs thence for a distance of eight hundred miles, to Medina, which is situated two hundred and fifty miles north of Mecca.

The military value of this " pilgrim " line was, however, greatly reduced by its distance both from the Egyptian frontier and from the Red Sea. On the failure, therefore, in February, 1915, of the first Turkish attack on Egypt, the construction of an alternative route, as recommended by the German railway engineer, Meissner Pasha, builder of the Damascus-Medina line, was then pressed forward with all possible speed.

This alternative route, starting from the Damascus-Haifa section of the Hedjaz line, was to cross the Jaffa-Jerusalem railway at Lydda, and continue thence, in the first instance, to the Turkish base at Beersheba. In the eagerness that was shown to complete the work, the rails between Jaffa and Lydda were torn up for use on the new line, and press-gangs obtained labour from cinemas and other places of public resort. In the result, the laying of the lines to Beersheba was completed by August 9th, 1915, when the first locomotive arrived there. The extension of the line in the direction of the canal was proceeded with at once.

It was, however, extremely improbable that even this further railway would materially advance the Turco-German plot for the conquest of Egypt. Apart from the distance of Constantinople from Germany, whence most of the necessary munitions would have to come, there was the journey of more than 1,000 miles on the succession of single-track lines between Constantinople (Scutari) and Beersheba, while the latest addition thereto is, for part of its length, within **The railway factor** twelve miles of the Mediterranean coast, **in Egypt** whence it could readily be destroyed by British men-of-war. Then, even at the Turkish base of Beersheba, the troops would still have to cross— whether by a further complete extension of the military railway or otherwise—one hundred and fifty miles of practically waterless and foodless desert, with all their supplies, guns, munitions, and other necessaries, before they came within reach of the Suez Canal, to face British and Egyptian forces, having behind them such vastly superior transport facilities, alike by land and sea, with Egypt, France, Great Britain, and the whole British Empire in addition, as a readily available base for supplies.

Major-Gen. Sir A. J. Godley, honoured with the K.C.B. for services on Gallipoli.

General view of Gully Beach, Dardanelles, showing Anzac dug-outs, tr

Before the Great Withdrawal : French encampment at Seddul Bahr. Stores of

..orses, waggons, and men congregated amid typical scenery of Gallipoli.

..tion are in the foreground, while the transport River Clyde is seen on the left.

Seddul Bahr as seen, during the allied occupation of Gallipoli, from the bridge of the historic troopship River Clyde.

Thus the advantages of the strategical position in Egypt were from the first in favour of the defenders rather than of the would-be invaders. In addition to the heavy military traffic they provided for in connection with the defence of the Suez Canal (further facilitating that traffic by supplying the single-track lines with a number of new crossing-places), the Egyptian State Railways distributed throughout Egypt the wounded men and the Turkish prisoners received there from the Dardanelles. Then for a considerable period, as was pretty much the case in Great Britain, the staffs in the railway workshops were engaged day and night in the equipment of hospital trains, in the preparation of the armoured trains and the searchlight armoured trucks used with great success on the Suez Canal bank railway, and also in the making of iron bedsteads for the troops, mechanical devices to be employed in the trenches along the canal, and other military requirements.

Apart from the conveyance of troops, sick and wounded, prisoners, supplies, guns, and munitions in the different countries concerned, and apart, also, from their employment for the carrying out of tactical movements at the seat of war, railways were used for (among other additional purposes) the transport into Germany of the plunder taken on a wholesale scale from the occupied territory in Belgium and France; the deportation of Belgian and French citizens into Germany, and the removal of trainloads of dead Germans from the battlefields on the western front to furnaces in the Liege district, where they could be consumed by fire. In the transport of those exceptionally powerful guns and of those huge quantities of munitions which were among the leading features of the conflict, the railways allowed of war becoming a more terrible business than ever before. Russia introduced an innovation in the form of a bath train for soldiers, and in Britain those of the railway companies on whose lines there was an exceptional amount of military traffic gave facilities for the opening at stations in London and elsewhere of buffets at which free refreshments were supplied to troops arriving or departing by train.

The destruction of railways, in order to interrupt the enemy's lines of communication, prevent invasion, or, in case of a retreat, check pursuit, is an inevitable accompaniment of the use of railways in war, and one for which preparations are made by the organisation of special forces to undertake the work of destroying or of repairing the lines, as the case may be. One unprecedented feature in the Great War was the extensive use of aeroplanes for **Repairs and reconstruction** damaging railway lines, as well as for wrecking important railway stations, and especially railway junctions.

As a rule, the arrangements for repairs and reconstruction were so complete that the reopening of communications was speedily effected. The work on the French lines of restoring, temporarily or permanently, the large number of bridges blown up, either by the enemy or by French engineers seeking to prevent his advance on Paris, was, together with the relaying of lines and much other reconstruction during the course of the war, greatly facilitated by the sending to France of a large force of bridge-builders, permanent-way men, and other railway workers from England. The British railway companies

also placed at the disposal of the French railways large quantities of girders and iron which they had in stock, together with all the necessary implements, etc., so that the work could be commenced and carried on with the utmost speed.

A general review of the circumstances and conditions attendant upon the employment of railways in the Great War leads to the following conclusions :

1. That Germany had provided for an extensive use of strategical railways along and across her frontiers, in the interior of her Empire, in her Colonial possessions, and in foreign countries **Teutonic abuse of** as a section of her war-machine, and **rail-power** one indispensable to the efficient working thereof ; but had not taken sufficiently into account the use which other countries, in turn, could make of their railways in resisting the accomplishment of her designs.

2. That whatever the conditions of unpreparedness in which the outbreak of war found the Governments, the military services, the politicians, and the peoples of the allied countries, the railway systems of France and Britain

GERMAN WOMEN RAILWAY WORKERS.
Digging for an underground railway in Berlin. Women were doing the heavy work in place of the men at the front.

were—thanks to an organisation in each case no less complete in its way than that of Germany herself—able to respond instantly and effectively to all the demands made on them for military transport, while even Russia, faced by greater difficulties, had completed her initial mobilisation within sixteen days.

3. That such ready response on the part of the railways of France, Britain, Russia, and subsequently, also, of Italy, was a powerful factor in checking Germany and Austria in their abuse of that fundamental principle of rail-power, under which it is dependent for initial success on the rushing of a great force across a frontier by rail, and the overwhelming of an antagonist thereby, before the latter can complete the mobilisation and concentration of his own troops.

4. That the same conditions influenced no less powerfully the whole course of the subsequent campaign, neutralising to a very considerable extent the advantages which the enemy had counted upon gaining from his own highly-developed system of aggressive railways which had been developed in the special interests of Germany's eventual world-supremacy.

THE STEAM-ROLLER IN THE ARCHIPELAGO.
French engineers making roads at Port Ereo, Mitylene.
On the right : French Senegalese soldiers preparing an
aqueduct.

Preliminary operations to road-making. French Colonial troops in charge of white officers breaking stones to make tracks for transport at Ereo.

THE ISLAND OF MITYLENE UNDERGOES TRANSFORMATION AT THE HANDS OF OUR
FRENCH ALLY.

THE MUTINY AT SINGAPORE: A FOOTNOTE TO HISTORY.

The following vivid narrative, supplied by one of THE GREAT WAR correspondents, throws light for the first time on a plot which, promoted by Pan-German intrigue, might have had serious consequences for the Empire. The plot, conceived by Prussian agents in the United States, led to the mutiny at Singapore in February, 1915. Happily, prompt action on the part of the authorities, the loyal support of Europeans, Japanese, and Sikhs, the latter homeward-bound from the storming of Tsingtau, quashed the rebellion in the nick of time, though—unfortunately—not before a number of brave British civilians had been murdered and several combatants killed and wounded.

STARTLINGLY unexpected in the face of the great loyalty of the Indian peoples and troops, the mutiny of the 5th Light Infantry, a native regiment forming the principal part of the garrison at Singapore, on February 15th, 1915, placed in grave peril for three days the security of that important Eastern fortress and caused heavy loss of life among the British civil and military population.

Breaking out of barracks at half-past three in the afternoon, the mutineers first fired on their officers rushing down to inquire into the cause of the disturbance. They killed Captain Maclean and Lieutenant Elliott and mortally wounded Lieutenant Boyce. Major Cotton and Captains Ball and Hall escaped and ran for assistance to Normanton Camp, a quarter of a mile away, where a company of the Malay States Volunteer Rifles was under training. The volunteers, eighty-three strong, quickly got under arms, and drove back the mutineers as they were advancing on the house of Colonel Martin the commander of the regiment.

Heroism of R.A.M.C. corporal

Meanwhile a body of one hundred mutineers was making its way to Tanglin Barracks, where the German prisoners of war were interned. The guard at the prisoners' camp, seeing the native troops advancing in skirmishing order, took no notice, believing that they were engaged in field exercises. It was not until a well-aimed volley laid the majority of them low that they realised there was trouble. A corporal of the Royal Army Medical Corps heroically dashed across the space swept by the fire of the mutineers to the telephone, and fell dead at the instrument while giving to headquarters the first intelligence of the catastrophe.

After overcoming the guard, which only numbered twenty men, the mutineers opened the gates and offered arms and ammunition to the Germans inside. The prisoners in the camp numbered three hundred and nine, consisting of German residents of Singapore and the Malay State who had been interned when war broke out, crews of captured ships, and a few of the Emden's crew. To their great credit they refused to have anything to do ith the mutineers.

"War is war," they said, "but this is a mutiny."

The majority of them stayed peaceably in the camp, and even telephoned for a doctor to attend to the wounded men of the guard, in the meantime rendering first-aid themselves. Seventeen took advantage of the opportunity to escape, but declined the invitation of the mutineers to lead them in an attack on Singapore. Three of these were recaptured, but the rest got away in native boats to the neighbouring Dutch islands.

Simultaneously another party of mutineers was engaged in a ghastly orgy of murder at Keppel Harbour and Pasir Panjang, suburbs lying between Alexandra Barracks and Singapore. Officers of the garrison and peaceful citizens, riding on the Pasir Panjang Road in motor-cars and rickshaws, were shot dead. Across the Keppel Harbour golf-links there rang out a volley which laid many unsuspecting players low. Englishmen riding with their wives were shot, the murderers sparing the women. In one case a lady refused to obey the order of the mutineers to stand away while they killed her husband and, **Ghastly orgy of murder** clinging together, both were shot in another case having shot an Englishman driving in a car with two ladies, two of the murderers got into the car with the ladies, and compelled the Malay chauffeur to drive them into the city. Three young men sitting on the veranda of their house at Pasir Panjang saw some men of the 5th Light Infantry enter their compound. The answer to inquiry as to what they were doing there was a volley, instantly killing all three. Among those murdered were the district judge and two artillery officers.

Darkness was now falling, and the authorities were working frantically to grapple with the situation. The crew of the warship Cadmus had been hurried ashore, artillerymen brought over from the forts, the volunteers fully mobilised, and the city put under martial law. Wireless messages were also despatched to warships at sea, and a telegram sent to the Viceroy of India for military assistance.

The safety of the white women and children and the maintenance of order in the city, with its cosmopolitan population of a quarter of a million Asiatics, were the first considerations. Armed motor-patrols were despatched to the residential areas to bring the women and children into the city and to instruct all civilian white men to go to the police-stations to receive arms for their protection. The women and children, numbering two thousand, were put on refugee ships in the harbour, while the men were organised as special constables. Every white man in the city shouldered a rifle on that night of terror, and clergy men and missionaries, including the Bishop of Singapore, patrolled the streets or formed pickets at danger points.

For the women, herded on the ships, suffering every discomfort, it was a time of suspense and terrible strain. The constant sound of firing on shore

Sufferings of the women filled them with anxious fears, while their sufferings were increased by the lack of comforts and conveniences which, in the hurry and confusion, there had been no time to provide. Included among them were women who had seen their husbands shot before their eyes only a few hours earlier, one of them a young bride of only a fortnight, whose white dress was stained with her husband's blood.

The situation was full of menace. The mutinous regiment numbered eight hundred and fifteen, and with them were one hundred men of the Malay States Guides mule battery. It was not known how many had actually mutinied, and there were fears that if the men of the battery were disloyal they would turn the guns on the defenders of the city, though these fears were greatly relieved by the report of friendlies that the gunners had fled, leaving their guns, which the others could not work.

At nightfall the Malay States Volunteers, with the officers of the 5th Light Infantry and Mrs. Cotton, were besieged in Colonel Martin's bungalow, while the sailors, artillerymen, and pickets of volunteers and police barred the way into Singapore. The mutineers occupied their barracks and the surrounding country, but beyond desultory sniping, did not venture any further move during the night.

At daybreak the sailors and artillery, reinforced by Singapore volunteers and twenty-five armed civilians, who had pluckily volunteered to accompany them, advanced from Keppel Harbour to the relief of the party in the bungalow. Commanded by Colonel Brownlow, R.G.A., the little force numbered only one hundred and seventy-six, and of these only the eighty men of the Cadmus were trained to infantry fighting. It was soon seen that the enemy were in greatly superior numbers, but the white troops pluckily pushed on, over the intervening hills, to Alexandra. Colonel Brownlow, in his report, paid a tribute to the bravery of the civilians, who despite their lack of training, stood firm under heavy fire at a critical moment, when if they had given way the whole operation must have failed.

Since daybreak the defenders of the house had been subjected to a heavy fire from the mutineers. The reply of the volunteers had been so accurate and well sustained, however, that all attempts to get up the hill and rush the house were frustrated. When the relieving force swept down over the opposite hill and into the barracks, with fixed bayonets, the mutineers broke and fled, leaving thirty-seven of their number dead and wounded. The British casualties were one killed and five wounded, one mortally.

Not being in sufficient force to hold the captured barracks, the relieving force, with the rescued party, retired into Singapore, taking with them the guns of the mule battery which had given so much anxiety during the night. They were heavily sniped all **Warships called up** the way, and at one stage the column **by wireless** was held up while the sailors with their machine-gun and the Malay States Volunteers cleared the hills commanding a road junction.

Now concentrated on the city, the defence forces were formed into a chain of pickets, linked up by motor-patrols, to await the arrival of the warships hastening to the rescue in response to the wireless calls. Fortunately, the mutineers contented themselves with sniping and isolated attacks in small bodies, which were easily beaten off.

The redeeming feature of the situation was the loyalty of the other Indians in the city, and the tranquillity of the

TWILIGHT SOMEWHERE IN THE LEVANT: PHOTOGRAPHIC EFFECT FROM A BRITISH BATTLESHIP.

REVIEW OF JAPANESE SAILORS AFTER THE MUTINY AT SINGAPORE.
Our Far Eastern ally sent a warship to Singapore to assist in quelling the rebellion which broke out there on February 15th, 1915.

populace. There was a detachment of the 36th Sikhs in Singapore, on their way home from the storming of Tsingtau, and, true to the traditions of their race, they remained staunch, and lent valuable assistance. The Indian police also were perfectly loyal. The native population, consisting mainly of Chinese, carried on business as usual in the city, quite unperturbed. Their reply, when asked if they were not alarmed, was that the affair was not their "pidgin" and so long as they were not disturbed they did not concern themselves with it.

Nevertheless, a sigh of relief went up from the city on the morning of Wednesday the 17th, when the French cruiser Montcalm sailed into the harbour. Russian and Japanese warships followed, and bodies of Marines, with machine-guns, were landed. The governor of the French colony of Indo-China had also wired on hearing of the outbreak, offering to send troops if necessary. In this faraway corner of the world there was thus afforded a striking demonstration of the solidarity of the Alliance.

In addition to this representative gathering of allied troops, the arming and organisation of the white civilian population of the city had brought together what was probably the most heterogeneous assembly of nationalities that has ever taken up arms for a common purpose. There were British (including, besides natives of the United Kingdom, Australasians, Canadians, and South Africans), Americans, French, Russians, Spaniards, Greeks, Danes, Norwegians, Swedes, Italians, Swiss, Portuguese, and Dutch—thirteen different nationalities. There was also a body of two hundred Japanese special constables organised by the Japanese Consul.

A few brushes with the troops now advancing against them served to convince the mutineers that their doom was sealed. They broke up into small bodies and fled into the jungle. Large numbers threw away their arms and surrendered. On the afternoon of Thursday the 18th the Government was able to announce that the situation was completely in hand.

With some hundreds of well-armed men still ranging the island, it could not be said that all danger was over. There had been a good many surrenders, and on the night of the mutiny eighty men had come in and declared their loyalty. After the arrival of the allied warships, **Flight of the mutineers** large bodies of mutineers fled across the Strait of Johore to the mainland, but here they were rounded up by the Sultan of Johore's Malay army and handed over to the British authorities. On Saturday the 20th the Government announced that there remained some two hundred and thirty men of the regiment still unaccounted for.

Rounding up and capturing or killing these was a task of considerable difficulty for the troops, who were reinforced on Saturday night by six companies of the 5th Shropshire Territorials from Rangoon. Their arrival released the British sailors to go back to their ship, and the artillerymen to return to the forts, while with the disbanding of many of the special constables the city became more normal, and business was able to be resumed.

A remarkable circumstance was that although the houses had been so hurriedly abandoned on the night of the 15th, and in many cases left for two or three weeks, there was not a single case of looting or even of petty theft. The Chinese servants in every case remained at their posts and waited patiently for their masters and mistresses to return. The mutineers made no attempt to interfere with them.

Though the thick jungle, over a large part of the island in which they had taken refuge, offered the mutineers excellent opportunities for sniping, their one object now seemed to be to avoid capture by the troops. Many threw away their arms and accoutrements and attempted to pass themselves off as milkmen and bullock drivers, in which occupations numbers of **Man-hunting in** their fellow-countrymen are employed on **the jungle** the island. Rewards were offered for their apprehension, and many gave themselves up to stationmasters and headmen of the villages.

During the week the French, Russian, and Japanese Marines returned to their ships, but the Territorials and Malay States and local Volunteers were kept busy manhunting in the jungle for another three weeks. Recourse was finally had to Dyak headmen from Borneo to track down the fugitives On March 15th a Government communiqué stated that there were fewer than a dozen men of the regiment now at large, so far as could be estimated, allowance being made for some having died in the jungle. The troops were withdrawn from the jungle areas, the capture of this remnant being left to the police.

As soon as the mutiny had been quelled, a field courtmartial was constituted to try the captured men. Large numbers of them were sentenced to be shot, the first execution taking place exactly a week after the mutiny broke out. All the executions took place in public, in the presence of enormous crowds. On one occasion, twenty-two men were shot at once, the firing-party numbering one hundred and ten. Others were sentenced to transportation for life, or to long terms of imprisonment. The remnant of the regiment having expressed a wish to expiate their offence, they were sent to West Africa on active service.

The sequel to the mutiny was the trial and execution for treason of a leading Indian merchant of Singapore. He was proved to have written letters to the Turkish Consul at Rangoon asking for a Turkish warship to take away the Indian troops to fight for Turkey. Probably the seed of disloyalty was sown by Indian agitators, who returned from America at the beginning of the war and visited Singapore on the way. That German intrigues in America were responsible for the return of these dangerous conspirators to the East during the critical period of August, 1914, there can be little doubt.

Singapore now has compulsory military training for every British-born inhabitant of the colony between eighteen and fifty-five. The mutiny proved the necessity for it. From first to last the British casualties including fourteen murdered civilians, were forty-seven. The French had one man wounded, and the Russians three.

THE GRAVEYARD OF THE GREAT OF TWO NATIONS: IMPRESSION OF A BATTLEFIELD ON GALLIPOLI.

In the foreground are the French trenches, while in the middle distance to the right a "75" is bombarding the position of Krithia. The smoke of two Turkish shell explosions can be clearly seen. No photograph gives a better idea of the difficult, undulating country of the terrible Peninsula

CHAPTER CVII.

THE TRAGIC YET BRILLIANT CLOSE OF THE DARDANELLES OPERATIONS.

Sir Ian Hamilton's Last Despatch—Defect of Tactics in Regard to Crest Positions—Poor Digging by Untried Troops—Attacking Column at Anzac Misses the Path to Chunuk Bair—" General Inertia " and " General Muddle " Lead the Suvla Army to Disaster—Major-General De Lisle Arrives with the 29th Division—Battle again Lost through Two Brigades of 11th Division Missing their Path—Allied Armies on the Peninsula Become Too Weak to Undertake a Main Attack—Russell and his New Zealanders Win an Important Hill—Ian Hamilton Reports that Evacuation is Unthinkable, by Reason of Terrible Losses it would Entail—Sir Charles Monro and Lord Kitchener Come to Dardanelles and Decide on a Withdrawal—Floods and Frosts Try Our Men and Hinder the Germans from Bringing Up 10 in. Guns—British Sentries Frozen Dead at their Posts—Our Own Troops are Deceived about the Withdrawal—Subtle Manner in which Small Reinforcements were Landed by Daylight and Large Bodies of Troops Withdrawn at Night—The Critical Sunday, when only the " Last Ditchers " Remained in Suvla and Anzac—Absolute Blindness of Germans and Turks—None of the Beaches Shelled at Night when Crowded with Our Troops—Moonlit Night of Bonfires and Farewell Explosions—Automatic Bomb-Throwers, Trip-Mines, and other Welcomes Prepared for the Turks in Our Abandoned Lines—The Armies of Helles Attack Krithia Gully—Increasing Difficulties of Completing the Evacuation—Enemy Masses all his Troops Round Achi Baba to Force Us to Stand Battle—After Beating him Off, Our Troops Embark in a Perilous Storm—Marvellous Success of the Withdrawal.

INCE the appearance in Chapter LXXXIII. of our last account of the battles in the Gallipoli Peninsula, the story of our failure to carry Chunuk Bair and the Anafarta Ridge has been illuminated by the publication of Sir Ian Hamilton's final despatch. In regard to Chunuk Bair, we have also been able to gather the opinions of certain of the Anzac men who took part in the critical struggle for the commanding height. The general impression is that some of the officers of the British and the Australasian forces suffered from the use of tactics acquired in the South African War. We had learned marksmanship from the Boers, but we had also acquired from those very mobile sharpshooters rather too cautious and slow a mode of attack, and an inadequate appreciation of the force of the orthodox Continental mass formation assault.

It is possible that on Chunuk Bair, won by the New Zealanders and some of the New Army, the brigadier-general

may have been too much swayed by the local lessons of the Boer War. He placed his men a little below the ridge, as both Boer and Briton used to do, so that enemy sharpshooters, standing out against the sky-line, would be shot before they could shoot. But in Continental war with large masses, the crest was the conquering position. The side that held the crest, by means of well-covered observation-posts, with the infantry on the slope close at hand, could concentrate for a massed charge, so as to take unawares the opposing forces holding the opposite slope. Moreover, the introduction of bombs that could be rolled down on an enemy in mountain warfare further emphasised the importance of holding the crest position. The British race, however, had a tradition against crest positions. Our winning tactics, even in the Napoleonic wars, had been to nestle under the slope, as a protection against direct gun fire and musketry volleys, and shoot down the enemy almost at point-blank range when he charged over the crest.

LORD KITCHENER AT THE DARDANELLES.
The Secretary for War inspecting trenches and dug-outs.

VAST COLLECTION OF STORES AT MUDROS HARBOUR. THE FRENCH BASE IN THE MEDITERRANEAN.

This was Wellington's system, and it had been revived in the experience of the South African War, and methodically practised at all manœuvres afterwards. Sir John French had employed it admirably during the retreat from Mons; but when Sir Douglas Haig tried to break the German line on the northern plateau of the Aisne, we clung too long to our favourite slope position, and the German commander, General von Zwehl, by maintaining his hold on the crest at heavy sacrifice, stalemated our superb but old-fashioned attack.

In France and Flanders the value of the crest position was soon known by experience to the private soldier as well as to his superior officers. Gun fire made the ridges almost uninhabitable, but well-dug-in observers with periscopes became the eyes of their army. Along the greater part of the Italian front the struggle for observation ridges was the moving force of both the strategy and the tactics on either side. But in August, 1915, after a year of war, some of our officers did not seem to be generally alert to the vital need for holding crests as much for defence as for attack preparations.

Such is Sir Ian Hamilton's explanation of one of the causes of our check at Chunuk Bair. But the men of Anzac engaged in the affair, consisting of the Auckland and Wellington Mounted Rifles, the New Zealand Infantry Brigade, and two battalions of the 13th Division, with the 26th Indian Mounted Battery—all under Brigadier-General F. E. Johnston—attribute the failure to another cause. The brigade fought for three days and three nights without ceasing, and conquered the south-west half of the main knoll of Chunuk Bair. They won the crest dominating the Narrows, and the roads leading to Bulair and Constantinople; but they withdrew their main line twenty-five yards from the summit, and did not retain look-out posts to watch the enemy on the opposite slopes below. The fact was that the brigade was **Battle of** half dead from fatigue, and in dire need of **Chunuk Bair** water and food. So hot had the fighting been that they had not had opportunity to dig trenches, but had merely scraped a few inches of earth out of the ground, when groping for cover from the enemy's fire. All the Anzac men knew that the spade was mightier than the sword. They had discovered a new term of insult which bit deeper than anything used by the roughest tongue in civilian life. Call a man a coward, and he might laugh at you. Call a man a liar, and he might treat it as a joke. But call him a bad digger, and a fight was inevitable. Thus, if the New Zealanders had not dug proper trenches, it was not because they did not appreciate what they had failed to do—they were simply too sorely pressed during the terrible long action, and too utterly spent at the end of it, to do more than hold their ground.

On the third night of the battle, two battalions of the New Army—the 6th Loyal North Lancashires and the 5th Wiltshires—relieved Brigadier-General Johnston's Brigade on Chunuk Bair. It was then, according to the point of view of the New Zealanders and their British companions, that the great mistake was made. The North Lancashires arrived in good time, but the 5th Wiltshires, being delayed by the intricate country, did not come up until four o'clock in the morning. The Lancashire men began to strengthen their trenches, while the belated Wiltshires were ordered by their officers to lie down in the mere scrapings. But none of the superior officers of these two bodies of fresh, untried troops grasped fully the needs of the situation. Both battalions should have dug for their lives with every ounce of energy, got well under shelter, and, if possible, erected some defence against bombs rolled down the slope. Digging was all they were required to do, for the shattered Turks attempted no attack, and the relieving battalions were as fresh as possible in the circumstances, and would be in turn relieved by the rested veteran brigade. In fact, they had been sent for to dig rather than to fight. Apparently they were not instructed with sufficient emphasis by the retiring brigade, composed of veterans who thought that no soldier needed to be told to dig any more than he needed to be told to breathe.

An hour and a half after the Wiltshires arrived, the enemy batteries swept the slope with a storm of shrapnel, and a large Turkish column of fifteen battalions concentrated on the opposite slope and, storming over the crest in a huge mass, broke the North Lancashires and the Wiltshires, and then outflanked another British column. Had

Overwhelming disaster averted

it not been for a young New Zealand officer of the machine-gun section, who had reckoned upon the eventuality of the new battalions near the crest breaking, and had arranged ten Maxims in the rear to guard against that eventuality, there might have been an overwhelming disaster in Anzac. As it was, the Turks were driven back —but only after they had badly mauled our main column, killing the general and his Staff, and had thoroughly defeated the British attempt to carry the heights. The 13th Division of the New Army had lost more than half its men, ten commanders out of thirteen had been put out of action, and General Birdwood's total casualties were nearly half the striking force he had employed. The wonderful men were still game for more fighting, but they were too exhausted physically to attack again until they had rested and reorganised.

Putting aside the dispute about the bad siting of the trenches by the New Zealanders, owing to the unfortunate failure to appreciate fully the value of the crest position, and about the bad digging of the two new, untried British battalions, there was a far more serious cause of unsuccess. We hold that the New Zealanders and their comrades - in - arms accomplished more than could be expected of them, and showed such superhuman powers of endurance in actual battle, that their trench siting was no more their fault than were their hunger and thirst. And as for the Wiltshires, who were almost annihilated, and the North Lancashires, many of whom fell in the climax of the four days' fighting, they suffered only from the absolute inexperience of new levies, thrown into the fieriest furnace of battle where they could not at once grasp the needs of the situation. Like all untried troops fresh from the training-field, they thought more about fighting than about digging, and they needed hardening by a preparatory spell at Ypres to acquire the knowledge which had become to the New Zealanders a matter of instinct.

The main cause of the failure to hold Chunuk Bair lay elsewhere. Three columns were used in the attack. The first column, under Brigadier-General Johnston, was originally required only to gain Chunuk Bair and extend to the south-east. A second column of Australian, British, and Indian Brigades, under Major-General H. V. Cox, had the task of attacking Hill Q on the Chunuk Bair Ridge, and two of its battalions—the 6th Gurkhas and the 6th South Lancashires—reached the crest, broke the enemy, and went in pursuit down the opposite slope towards the waters of the Hellespont. With Column 1 holding the Chunuk Bair Ridge, and Column 2 over the neck of Hill Q, the Dardanelles seemed to be won on the critical day of battle—August 9th, 1915. For these two columns were only designed to be road-sweepers to Column 3, under Brigadier-

General A. H. Baldwin, which was to make the main attack. So much ground had been rapidly and gloriously won in the preliminary work of the first two columns that a swift and assured conquest of the key to the Dardanelles was prepared by nightfall for Baldwin's men. He was to mass behind the trenches held by the New Zealanders, and launch his battalions in successive lines over the high ground. But the main attacking column never arrived. It lost its way in the dark in the shrub-covered mountains, and when General Baldwin was a long way from Hill Q, and still groping for his path, the Turks re-formed, and with strong reinforcements drove back the Gurkhas and South Lancashires, and then massed against the New Zealand troops and the two New Army battalions. Baldwin's column never reached the neighbourhood of the crest, but was caught and outflanked at daybreak on August 10th, when the 6th North Lancashires and the 5th Wiltshires were broken on Chunuk Bair. In Sir Ian Hamilton's opinion, the straying of Baldwin's column, in a night operation along routes which could not be carefully studied in detail for lack of time and opportunity, was a mischance of war rather than a fault on Baldwin's part.

AT THE MOMENT OF THE RECOIL.
French "75" gun in full blast against an enemy position. It was hidden with a thoroughness which defied all efforts to locate the weapon

And after the British forces had been repulsed from the crest, they were taken on the left flank by the farm below Chunuk Bair by strong forces of the enemy, which should have been held back to meet the advance of our New Army corps advancing, under Lieut.-General Sir F. Stopford, from Suvla Bay. We have already given many details of the Suvla Bay battles, but at the time of writing our previous chapter we had only un- **The Suvla** official information concerning the root **Bay battles** cause of the failure, and, in justice to the commanding officers, we naturally refrained from going fully into the story of the disaster. But now that Sir Ian Hamilton has published the facts, we are able to complete our earlier story by a fuller relation of the critical details. The force under General Stopford consisted of the 11th Division, under Major-General Hammersley, the 10th Division, called the Irish Division, under Sir Bryan Mahon, and the 53rd Division, composed of Territorial troops, without artillery, under General Lindley. The 54th

PRIMITIVE SUCCOUR.
Wounded French soldiers arriving for treatment at an open-air ambulance station on Gallipoli.

Division, also consisting of Territorial troops without artillery, was brought into action as well. It is not made clear whether we had not sufficient guns and trained gunners, after a year of war, to arm these Territorial Divisions, or whether it was reckoned that the naval guns of the Fleet were so overpoweringly strong that no more field-guns and 6 in. howitzers were required by the Army.

On August 6th the 11th Division landed around Suvla Bay, taking the Turks completely by surprise, but the generalship was in certain respects bad. On Hill 10 there was confusion among our men, and near the Karakol Dagh, where the 11th Manchesters had advanced with great pluck, there was no leader who could take hold of the two advancing brigades, and launch them in an attack. During the period of hesitation the Turks tried to drive our men back, but again the 11th Manchesters took them on with the bayonet, and, with the 9th Lancashire Fusiliers, broke them and drove them in disorder over Hill 10. The Turks retreated towards the Anafarta Ridges, followed by the 34th and 32nd Brigades, who were joined by some of Sir Bryan Mahon's men— the 6th Inniskillings, the 6th Dublin Fusiliers, and the 6th Irish Fusiliers. With more troops of his 10th Division, Sir Bryan

delivered a spirited attack to support the plucky and dashing Manchester men of the 11th Division, and conquered nearly all the ground as far as the Anafarta Hills. The 6th Munster Fusiliers especially distinguished themselves.

A swift and decisive victory seemed within our grasp. The Turks had only four thousand men in the field, and they were not well-trained regular soldiers, but local levies and gendarmerie. We had an army corps, less a brigade, landed, and twelve thousand more riflemen coming up as a reserve, with another twelve thousand behind them. So the odds against the Turks in infantry alone at the beginning were nearly 24,000 against 4,000. We had, moreover, a squadron of warships with long-range guns to strengthen our army corps artillery. But there was an extraordinary amount of mismanagement and indecision among some of our generals. Major-General Hammersley, especially, seems to have acted as though he were manœuvring on Salisbury Plain, and would lose on points if he forgot the lessons of caution learned in the South African War and tried to rush his weak enemy. As Sir Ian Hamilton afterwards put it in his report, the real commanding officer in the opening phase of the Suvla Bay battles was

AMID THE BARREN HILLS OF GALLIPOLI.
French mountain 65 mm. gun screened by stones and brushwood. Oval: Celebration of Mass on the shore of the Dardanelles. In the background the s.s. River Clyde is discernible.

A DUMB CASUALTY: DARDANELLES INCIDENT.
Disposing of the carcase of a mule, killed during a Turkish bombardment of the French positions on Gallipoli.

"General Inertia." "General Muddle" was also conspicuous, especially in regard to the arrangements made for watering the troops. It had been clearly foreseen that in the heat of the tropical summer, and in a country where the water resources were not fully known, there was most urgent need to prevent the troops from being disabled and killed by the tortures of thirst. Sir Ian Hamilton had had his lesson in the matter in the cool spring of the year, when we almost lost the landing battles at the tip of the Peninsula through lack of foresight in regard to water supplies. At Suvla Bay the corps and divisional Staffs had been ordered to work out schemes for the distribution of water, and to select men of energy and experience for carrying out these schemes. But judging by results, the Staff work was extremely bad. In the Irish Division especially men died of thirst, and even in the 11th Division, which worked over country where fresh water existed in some abundance, the resources were not developed. The material preparations for a water supply were well made. But the hoses were pierced in some cases by soldiers whose thirst overcame their discipline, as there were no guardians of the water to hinder them. In other cases Staff officers showed a lack of *nous* in missing the fresh water that existed in

BIRDS OF ILL-OMEN.
Two vultures captured by French Marines in the Dardanelles, and appropriately christened by them "Guillaume II." and "Francois Joseph."

the country. Putting it briefly, both in leadership in the field and in attention to the vital feature of the commissariat, some of the commanding officers of our Ninth Army Corps were certainly not the best men that could have been found.

Examples of bad Staff work

Things were so bad at Suvla at dawn on August 8th that Sir Ian Hamilton sent one of his Staff officers to observe and report. The Staff officer telegraphed that no Turkish gun was in action, that Turkish rifle fire was small, and that the enemy was very weak, but that our troops were missing golden opportunities, owing to the inaction of their commanders. In these circumstances the Commander-in-Chief surrendered his control of the Anzac and Achi Baba battles, and sailed for Suvla Bay, arriving there at five o'clock in the afternoon of August 8th. All the day had been wasted, while the Anzac men and their comrades of the 13th Division had taken the height known as Table Top and the ground beyond, where they should have connected with the Suvla Bay army. Even the patrols of the 11th Division had not carried out orders—pushed forward in force and occupied, without serious fighting, positions that were waiting for them on the Anafarta Hills. A priceless twelve hours had been lost by "General Inertia" and "General Muddle," and our airmen reported that the Turkish army was on the march to Suvla.

Sir Ian Hamilton urged that the 11th Division at the eleventh hour should make an attack upon the hills. By this time the troops were well rested, watered, and fed. But the commander of the division did not like the idea of an advance by night, and General Stopford did not care to overrule his subordinate. Major-General Hammersley declared that the division was much too scattered for a night attack. Sir Ian Hamilton found, however, that one brigade—the 32nd—was fairly well concentrated and ready to move. Sir Ian Hamilton therefore overruled his generals, and ordered that the single brigade at least should try to make good the heights before the enemy occupied them. He gave his orders about 6 p.m. on August 8th, but the four battalions did not begin their advance until 4 a.m. on August 9th. One company of the East Yorks' Pioneer Battalion topped one of the Anafarta Hills, but the rest of the battalion and the 22nd Brigade were attacked on their flanks, and forced back. The hill that had been thus reached by a single brigade on the morning of August 9th commanded the whole battlefield.

It is quite probable that if the troops had been pushed up on August 8th, when even all difficulties about water had been overcome, the Turkish army marching on Suvla would have been thrown back, a connection with the Anzac army would have been established on the high hills, and all the enemy positions in the Dardanelles dominated. As it was, the 11th Division, under Major-General Hammersley, made its long-delayed attack on the Anafarta Ridges when the Turks had brought their guns back and had been strongly reinforced. The 32nd Brigade was pushed off the slopes of the hill, and though Sir Ian Hamilton brought up his general reserve, the Territorial Division and gave it to General Stopford, no advance could be made. Many of the Territorial battalions fought with great gallantry, the Herefordshire men being remarkable for the impetuosity of their attack. On August 10th the division was launched against the Anafarta Ridge, but failed to take it. Then, on August 12th, the infantry of the 54th Division, which was just landed, was sent against the northern Anafarta position. They took one Anafarta position in difficult and enclosed country, but it was here that the Norfolk Territorials, after breaking the enemy's line, lost their King's Sandringham Company, which charged into the forest against the yielding enemy, and never returned.

On August 15th General Stopford was retired from his command, being replaced by Major-General De Lisle. By this time the 10th Division, the 11th Division, the 53rd, and the 54th Division, originally consisting of 44,000 infantry, were reduced to less than 30,000 rifles. The Australasian and British forces at Anzac were reduced to 25,000, the British forces under Achi Baba numbered only 23,000 rifles, while the French corps consisted of 17,000 men. Sir Ian Hamilton estimated the Turkish forces in the Suvla Bay and Anzac region at 75,000. But the enemy had all the advantages of ground, sufficient ammunition,

Company which never returned

and drafts to refill all ranks depleted in action. On the other hand, the British divisions alone were 45,000 under their establishment, some of the finest fighting battalions being so shattered that they had to be withdrawn from the fighting-line. Sir-Ian Hamilton, however, felt confident that if all his battalions were made up to strength and his munition depots were re- filled, he could still take the Narrows in the autumn of 1915, and clear a passage for our Fleet to Constantinople. But at this time our main army in Flanders was preparing for the great effort by which we won Loos. Neither the men nor the ammunition Sir Ian needed could be spared for the Dardanelles operations.

Our feeble resources

To put the position plainly, our munition output, after a year's experience of war, was so small as to conduce to our defeat in the Dardanelles, and our arrangements for raising, training, and arming soldiers, after twelve months' experience of war, were tragically inadequate to all our needs. Sir Ian Hamilton could only be given one chance of making an attack in force; the attack failed, and the military resources of our Empire were so comparatively feeble in comparison with those of our enemies that the Dardanelles had to be abandoned.

The main fault rested with the British Government. It proved unequal to the task it assumed so confidently and with so much fine rhetoric. We believe it is a fact that our Cabinet was informed some six years before the war of the military significance of the enormous increase of the German production of machine-tools.

ANZACS IN THEIR CAMP ON CHESHIRE RIDGE, GALLIPOLI.
Innumerable dug-outs were made in the side of the hill to shelter the men from Turkish fire, and afford them places of refuge for the night. Gallipoli being almost devoid of human habitation, the opportunity of billets such as are obtainable on the western front was quite out of the question.

AN INCIDENT IN THE EVACUATION OF ANZAC AND SUVLA.
In broad daylight, yet undetected by the Turks, some of our guns and troops left the ill-starred shores of Suvla Bay in the manner shown in this photograph. A naval launch, tugging a raft containing a field-gun and its crew, is seen steaming out of the bay.

We started far behind Germany in regard to this fundamental factor of modern military strength—the machine-tool. But instead of making the best of a bad case, and organising all these tools and the men who worked them for the sole purpose of war production at the outbreak of hostilities, we erected the strange policy of "business as usual," and let both our Dardanelles army and our Flanders army struggle on with insufficient munitions. The reorganisation of our output had not been effected by August, 1915; it was not effected by October, 1915, when we had to cease battling for Lens because we had exhausted our store of heavy shell, and our factories could not maintain a large, constant supply.

Our strange policy

All this was a general defect of national organisation which told on our failure at the Dardanelles. But in the tropical summer weather on the Gallipoli Peninsula there was another special source of weakness that should have been remedied, had the men concerned been distinguished by inventive common-sense and the best and widest knowledge obtainable. We refer to the enormous sick-list, running up to a hundred thousand cases. The food was wrong, and the preventive measures against insect-borne diseases were inadequate. The men were overwhelmed with bully beef when they clamoured for light foods like sago, tapioca, and rice. Dates might possibly have saved a good deal of dysentery, and salol, the drug that disinfects the intestines, should have been given to every soldier frequently and regularly, if better but more expensive keratin-coated bowel disinfectants could not have been supplied by the ton. In the highest medical science our nation was ahead even of Germany. We were leading the way in the battle against insect-borne diseases and in the epoch-making campaign against bacterial toxic parasites. Had the foremost disciples of men like Sir Ronald Ross, Sir Almroth Wright, and the directors of the London and Liverpool Tropical Schools of Medicine, been placed in supreme command of our medical corps in the Dardanelles, Mesopotamia, and East and West Africa, we should have saved tens of thousands of our men from death, and hundreds of thousands of them from enfeebling maladies. A bold, inventive man might even have used gas to conquer the plagues of lice and flies, even if it were not desired to do to the Germanised Turks what the Germans had done to us. Gas of a deadly kind could have been had in abundance, without interrupting the home manufacture of the intoxicating fumes used at Loos. Our Empire has large and strange resources, and men already well practised in the use of certain things. There was plenty of material handy for an inventive mind, had such a mind only been in full control of our medical service.

Lack of medical prevision

When Sir Ian Hamilton found that he could not depend upon receiving drafts to fill out his wasted forces, he was afraid to attempt another attack on a large scale; for he was likely to lose so many men in attacking the Turks, now strongly entrenched around Suvla Bay, that his weakened lines might be broken by a counter-attack. He therefore restricted himself to action on a small front, and selected the Anafarta Valley as his line of advance. The famous 29th Division was transported from the southern Krithia area to Suvla Bay, and connected with the 11th Division. These two divisions were set the task of winning the Anafarta Ridge, while the gunless Territorial army corps, composed of the 53rd and 54th Divisions, held the enemy on the north. The attack was planned by General De Lisle, and launched on August 21st.

"THE SOUL OF ANZAC."
Lieut.-General Sir William Riddell Birdwood, K.C.S.I., K.C.M.G., C.B., C.I.E., D.S.O., who commanded the Australian and New Zealand Army Corps at Gallipoli. On May 14th, 1915, he was slightly wounded, but retained his command.

But two mischances in the work of part of the 11th Division led to another British defeat. The 34th Brigade rushed the Turkish trenches near Hill 100, practically without loss; but the 32nd Brigade, which should have connected with the victorious battalion and taken the south-west corner of the hill, was misdirected. The brigade lost its

COMMANDERS OF SISTER SERVICES ON GALLIPOLI.
Lieut.-Gen. Sir W. R. Birdwood, Commander of the Anzacs, with Rear-Admiral Sir C. F. Thursby, K.C.M.G., at the Dardanelles. Rear-Admiral Thursby's squadron assisted in the first landing, north of Gaba Tepe, on April 25th, 1915.

path in a light sea mist, and arrived at the north-east instead of the south-west corner of the spur. With magnificent courage and disregard of death, the men of the 32nd Brigade still tried to carry the Turkish position, but could not succeed in rectifying the mistake of the Staff officers. Then the 33rd Brigade, sent up in haste to capture the Turkish position at all costs, fell into precisely the same error, and instead of reaching the vital south-west corner, wasted its effort in a north-easterly and south-easterly direction. Meanwhile, the superb veteran 29th Division, which set out half an hour after the 11th Division, stormed Scimitar Hill, and despite the fact that one brigade was checked by a great forest fire across its front, the division pressed on up the Anafarta Valley until it was checked by the failure of the two brigades of the 11th Division to take the south-west spur of Hill 100.

Staff miscalculations One brigade of the 29th Division tried to carry out the work of the 11th Division, but as it moved eastward across the spur of Hill 100 it was swept by a cross-fire of shell and musketry from the unattainable height and from another ridge. The leading troops were brushed off the top of the spur by storms of shrapnel and bullets, and the brigade had to fall back to a ledge near Scimitar Hill. It was then that the English Yeomanry Division came into action in a magnificent manner. Under a steady and accurate fire from the Turkish batteries, it advanced in open formation across a plain for a mile and a half, moving like men marching on parade, while the Turkish shells made curtains of shrapnel bullets in its path. After traversing the plain the English yeomen formed up beside the 29th Division, and as darkness fell, the troopers of Bucks, Berks, and Dorset pushed up the valley between

Scimitar Hill and Hill 100. They took a knoll near the centre of this horse-shoe of heights, but the combined charge by the Yeomanry Brigade and the 29th Division could not carry the amphitheatre of Turkish trenches on the top of Hill 100. The 29th Division lost nearly 5,000 men, and the yeomen also suffered very heavily. The poor Staff work, which had allowed two brigades of the 11th Division to work forward in a wrong direction, had brought about a general disaster which no skill or courage could retrieve.

Towards the end of the month of August, however, Major-General Cox, with a fine Anzac force, captured a very important height known as Hill 60, which overlooked one of the Anafarta valleys. During the vain attack of the Suvla Bay army on Hill 100, General Cox with 2,000 New Zealanders, 2,000 Irishmen, and a battalion of the South Wales Borderers, reinforced by the 18th Australian Battalion, had carried one of the northern foothills of the Sari Bair clump, enabling trenches to be strongly made connecting **Success against odds** the Suvla Bay army with the Anzac army.

Then on August 27th, General Cox again thrust out towards the Turkish lines around Anafarta. He used only a small force, consisting of detachments from the 4th and 5th Australian Brigades, the New Zealand Mounted Rifles, and the 5th Connaught Rangers.

Owing to the depletion of our store of shell, our preliminary bombardment was ineffective. As soon as the Anzac troops swarmed out into the open they were smitten by a terribly hot fire of enemy field-guns, rifles, and machine-guns. But after this hurricane of death was loosened at short range against our men, some distant heavy Turkish guns flung out a shower of big shells, with such bad aim that some of the terrible missiles pitched into the Turkish trenches and helped our attack. The Australians on the

INSPECTING A TURCO-BRITISH BATTLEFIELD.
Flag-Lieut. H. S. Bowlby, R.N., explaining the use of barbed-wire by the Turks. Left to right : Lieut. the Marquess of Anglesey, Flag-Lieut. H. S. Bowlby, R.N., Lieut.-Com. Grattan, R.N., and Lieut. Paul.

right were held up by a battery of machine-guns, but in the centre the New Zealanders stubbornly fought upwards, and, after four and a half hours of fighting, took nearly nine-tenths of the summit. Then, on the left, a single company of the 5th Connaught Rangers made one of those grand charges in which the Gael shows at his best. In five minutes, by the swiftness and cohesion of their movement, they carried out their task and stormed the northern communication trenches of the Turks. All the battalion then entered upon a ferocious bomb fight along the other Turkish trenches. The men drew many of the enemy's supports, and were promised the help of fresh troops by midnight. But before our fresh force arrived, the hostile commander launched some of his general reserve against the Connaught men, and drove them from the trenches as the 9th Australian Light Horse were **New Zealanders** coming up. The Australians made a **hold firm** plucky attempt to retake the lost communication trench, but were repulsed.

This left the New Zealand Mounted Rifles isolated on the top of the hill. But the New Zealanders were made of rare heroic stuff. Their holding was reduced to a hundred and fifty yards of trench, and all the night and all the next day they were bombed, shrapnelled, blasted with heavy high-explosive shell, and attacked by dense masses of bayonets. But nothing that the Turk could do could shake them, and early in the afternoon of August 29th, while the top of the hill was still in our possession, the Turkish communication trenches on the left were carried and held by the 10th Light Horse. Thus was won an important height, from which our artillery officers gained an outlook over the Anafarta Sagir Valley, while our lateral communications between Anzac and Suvla Bay were thus made much safer. Brigadier-General Russell was mainly

NAVAL HERO OF THE V.C.
Captain E. Unwin, V.C., C.M.G. (left). Lighters forming a bridge to the shore having broken adrift, Captain Unwin left the River Clyde, under fire, to get them into position, and then saved three injured men.

responsible for the handling of the men who won this final victory on the rugged Peninsula of ancient romance where much of the finest blood in our Empire was vainly shed.

Despite the failure to reach the Narrows across the Anafarta Ridges and the vast rampart of Sari Bair, Sir Ian Hamilton reported that the troops remained confident that, with more help from their country, they would carry to victory the last and the greatest of the Crusades. But in September the flow of munitions and drafts fell away, and sickness began to work still more terribly among the survivors of many arduous conflicts. Then, on October 11th, the decision to withdraw was reached by the British Cabinet. Lord Kitchener cabled to Sir Ian Hamilton, asking for an estimate of the losses likely to be involved in an evacuation of the Peninsula. Sir Ian Hamilton, in a mood of extreme despond- **Thoughts** ency, replied in such terms as showed **of evacuation** that in his judgment an evacuation was unthinkable. No doubt he was unwittingly led to regard the cost of such an operation as very heavy, because of his strong desire to carry the operations on to a successful end.

He was, moreover, overweighed by his experience of the high cost of the landing battles ; and being despondent over a withdrawal that meant the end of all his hopes, he lacked the freshness and resiliency of mind needed in the new study of the extremely difficult problems of an evacuation. The Government therefore decided to obtain a fresh, unbiased opinion in regard to the probable withdrawal losses from another experienced commander. So, on October 16th, Sir Ian Hamilton was recalled to London, and Sir Charles Monro, a general who had greatly distinguished himself in the campaigns in France and Flanders, was appointed Commander-in-Chief of the armies on the Gallipoli Peninsula. And such was the anxiety of the

DARING SUBMARINE OFFICERS.
Commander M. E. Nasmith, V.C., and Lieut. G. D'Oyly-Hughes, D.S.O., heroes of the E11, which sank several Turkish ships in the Sea of Marmora in June, 1915.

Government in regard to the evacuation that, in the middle of November, Lord Kitchener sailed for Mudros, and proceeded to study our positions on the Peninsula, and to discuss matters with the commanding officers.

Among the reasons that greatly weighed with our Government was the lack of highly-experienced troops to meet the German, Bulgarian, and Austrian thrust at Salonika. The Salonika Expedition had been planned by General Joffre and the French Staff, and Sir W. Robertson and our Staff were at first as much averse to this new adventure as General Joffre and General Castelnau had been to our Dardanelles scheme. But even as General Joffre had given way out of loyalty to the common alliance, and had sent a French army corps on what he considered was a hopeless business, so our authorities and newly reconstructed General Staff were moved by loyalty to co-operate with General Joffre in the Salonika Expedition. The fact was that, through a naval and military muddle—

FRENCH COMMANDER ON GALLIPOLI.
General Brulard, who was Commander-in-Chief of the French Army in the Dardanelles during the allied evacuation of the Peninsula.

complicated by the sudden weakness of the Russian Army which prevented the despatch of a strong Russian expedition to the Turkish territory north of Constantinople—our idea of a thrust at the Dardanelles had failed of realisation. But in the French plan of the Salonika Expedition there was none of the amateurishness which Mr. Winston Churchill had stamped upon our Dardanelles scheme. No politician interfered with French Staff work. General Joffre came to London, and was able to prove that his idea was well thought out in all its technical detail, so that the execution of it was perfectly practicable.

The evacuation, therefore, was officially determined upon, and Sir Charles Monro was given the task of reducing our withdrawal losses to a minimum. These losses, however, were still expected to be very high, the estimates ranging from one-half of all the men on the Peninsula, and many guns and large stores, to, at lowest, only five per

cent. of the British, Australasian, Indian, French, and French Colonial armies.

The miraculous conclusion of the campaign must not blind us to the difficulties which pressed most sombrely upon the minds of all officers and men upon the Peninsula.

"Gallipoli is terrible," said one of the British officers there in November, 1915. "It is like a narrow ledge on which two men are fighting. There is no place to retreat to. The side that weakens first goes over the ledge into the sea. Neither side can withdraw troops, for that would mean that one side at last would have more men than the other, and the stronger would sweep the weaker to destruction in the ocean."

The hazards of our intended operation were not lessened by an indiscreet revelation in the House of Lords that the evacuation of Gallipoli had been decided upon, and that Sir Charles Monro was about to undertake it. The Germans were exploiting their great success in Serbia against us, and using their opened route to Constantinople for forwarding 12 in. and 8 in. howitzers and large supplies of shells and charges. One of the chief reasons why we had been so close to a great success in the Dardanelles was that the Turks had been very short of ammunition. The penury of our Army in munitions had almost become wealth by September, 1915, in comparison with the condition of the Turkish magazines. When the Teutons, with the help of Bulgaria, had won a clear road to Constantinople, the positions in the Gallipoli Peninsula began to be reversed. Happily the new 12 in. howitzers could only be moved up very slowly by bullock teams, and in many places the road had to be widened and reconstructed in a solid manner to allow the great siege pieces to be hauled along. Our battleships shelled the route, destroying the bridge of Kavala, over which the new guns had to pass. A large part of the Turkish army laboured at road-making, and their work was much aggravated by the sodden condition of the ground at the end of autumn.

Indeed, the clerk of the weather was so kind that he saved us from the full shock of the effect of the conquest of Serbia. **Inclement weather our ally**

He acted like one of the Homeric gods in the ancient struggle between the Greeks and Trojans on the windy plain of Troy, where the "Creeping Carolines" were firing with black-powder charges on our Helles position.

It had been expected that the autumn weather would do more to overpower the Allies than even the Turks could do with their new guns. The Gallipoli Peninsula and the neighbouring islands which we were using as bases were subjected to a series of terrible storms in the autumn and winter. British destroyers, which had been on duty off the coast since the opening of hostilities against the Ottoman Empire, showed by their logs that sudden and very heavy gales were to be expected; and it was widely thought in Britain that the storms would make it impossible for ships to ply to Anzac and Helles, so that the troops would be cut off from all supplies and unable to withdraw. But the handy naval men, surely the most ingenious set of fighting men in the world, prepared against the south-west gales by building breakwaters at Suvla, Helles, and Kephalos Bay. They filled with sand a considerable number of old ships, each of which they sank with nice calculation, so that the wrecks extended in solid lines from the landing-places, and formed large harbours of fairly calm water. The French engineers at Helles were equally inventive, and even sank a very old battleship to strengthen their system of sheltering piers. But a northern hurricane at the beginning of November undid some of this work, and damaged the lines of ballasted wrecks by rolling upon them with terrific fury from an unexpected direction. The breakwaters had been built against south-westerly gales, so that the northerly hurricane cleared the harbourages and made it necessary to reconstruct the extraordinary rows of sunken steamers.

The great and memorable Gallipoli storm was that which began on November 26th, 1915. In the night a violent thunderstorm broke over the Peninsula, bringing

British ambulance-waggon, with its wheels and the horses caked with mud, driving through the Great Gully on the way to Krithia after a heavy rainstorm. On the cliffside is a dug-out, roofed with sand-bags, on which soldiers are resting.

Busy scene in the horse-lines on the shores of Suvla Bay, near the British base, and formed there after the landing on August 6th, 1915. Here, during a series of fierce battles, we lost a large number of men because the " attack was not developed quickly enough."

THE BRITISH FOOTHOLD ON GALLIPOLI'S BEETLING SHORES.

GENERAL SIR IAN HAMILTON'S PERSONAL STAFF.
Left to right: Lieut. McGregor, Lt.-Col. Pollen (Military Secretary), Major Maitland, A.D.C. Standing outside their headquarters at the Dardanelles.

down a cloudburst torrent of rain. The flood streamed downward for about twelve hours, in a volume of water for which our sappers were quite unprepared. By the end of the first hour the trenches in some places were three feet deep in water, which cascaded down the saps, turned the dug-outs into drowning-pits, burst a dam of earthworks at Suvla, and then rushed down in all directions. Salt Lake was flooded in two hours, and some of the trenches were full to the parapets, and men had to swim to avoid being drowned. Indeed, we lost a number of men, overtaken in dug-outs and low ground by the bursting of the earthworks. Many dug-outs collapsed and buried their occupants; and in the trenches much of the equipment of the troops was washed away.

But though the Turks were on higher ground, they suffered more than did our men. In certain parts of their line they had to stand on their parapets, where they were shot down by our machine-guns. In other places, they had to crawl out into the open ground between the opposing lines, and there also they were shot down, our men standing up to their thighs in water potting at the Turks, who ran about like rabbits in front of them. But on one occasion, at least, the men on both sides were too much overcome when daylight arrived to hurt each other. Our troops held a position of advantage, but they were so weak they could not raise their rifles and fire. As one officer put it, "We could only stand and grin at the Turks."

It continued to rain on and off all the next day, and the Turkish artillery opened a heavy fire on our hill positions at Suvla, reckoning that we had been forced by the torrents to crowd on the high ground. The bombard-

PULLING WITH A WILL.
Lt.-Gen. Altham, Deputy Inspector-General of Communications, endeavouring with other officers to get his motor-boat off the beach.

ment lasted four hours, and was resumed the following night; but it was far from doing the injury the enemy designed, for all our men stuck to their trenches in order to kill the Turks as they left theirs. Then, in the night of November 27th, a still more terrible ordeal was imposed upon ourselves and our enemies. A northern wind of Arctic severity swept over the hills of the Peninsula. Many of the men of Anzac saw snow for the first time in their lives; and after the snow had fallen upon the soaking wet clothes of all the troops, a hard frost set in and froze the greatcoats of the men, so that these garments could be stood upright by themselves. There were men who had been up to their necks in water for a day, and had gone without food for thirty-six hours, as their ration parties had been lost; then their clothes had frozen upon them like boards. There were men crying with the cold; others were too far gone to cry, but moaned all night; while some were too bad to utter a sound. Soldiers were caught and frozen as they lay sleeping in utter exhaustion in the puddled mud of the trenches, in a climate which scarcely a month before had been warm with the waning glow of a tropical summer.

The plight of the enemy, however, was again worse than ours. When it thawed on December 1st, their bodies came floating down flooded gullies, where our men had died of thirst in August. The Turks had no blankets or waterproof sheets; some of them were killed while they ran about looking for fuel; and large numbers gave themselves up in the hope of getting near a fire. As a matter of fact, there were then no fires in our trenches; both officers and men were lucky who had cold bully beef and biscuit to eat. For the previous torrent had washed away the furniture of many dug-outs. It was far worse

A REMINDER OF GALLIPOLI.
Photograph taken immediately before the evacuation of Suvla, showing Captain A. Leigh, Captain Renton, Lord Howard de Walden, and Captain Cunningham before their dug-out.

VIEW OF A TURKISH TRENCH ON THE GALLIPOLI PENINSULA.

Teuton-led Turks in a trench on one of the Gallipoli heights facing the allied lines.   The difficulties experienced by our airmen in locating enemy trenches are apparent in this photograph.   It will be seen that the sandy soil is well-covered with bushes and hillocks, which could not fail to baffle an aerial observer.

than fighting. Frost-bite was common, men by the score losing toes and fingers ; and there were some tragic cases of sentries being found dead at their posts. In most cases the rifle was still clutched in a rigid grip, and the blackened face still leaned against the parapet under the sackcloth curtain that veiled the loophole.

Frozen and buffeted by wind and sleet, and barely able to move sufficiently to keep their blood circulating, all the troops endured agonies. But the Anato-

Sufferings of the   lians, lining all the northern heights of
      Turks   the Peninsula, were even more exposed to
the blast and the blizzard than our men on the Anzac cliffs and the hills near Suvla Bay. The Anatolian Turks were accustomed to severe winters, but the combined action of the great flood and the great frost took the heart out of them. Brave men they had proved themselves to be, with a gallantry that excited the admiration of Australasians, British, and French. But after the blizzard they became quite incapable of attacking. In many cases their clothes were a disgrace to the men who commanded the resources of the Ottoman Empire. Thousands of them were put out of action by the weather, and a still larger number were so enfeebled that they could not be made to charge. Liman von Sanders and his Turkish generals had therefore to rely upon the quick arrival of the new artillery and the immense new supply of shells.

The extraordinary weather entirely upset the enemy's new plan of operations. The roads for the heavy howitzers were washed away in many parts, and the great vehicles, with their bullock-teams, were first bogged in the mud and then frozen there. Road-building in heavy autumn rain was bad enough, but when the ground alternately froze and thawed at the end of November, while the men failed in thousands from both sickness and frost-bite, the German engineers directing the job must have been reduced to a mood of black despair. In fact, they did not get their heavy guns into position until there was nobody on the Peninsula remaining as a target for 12 in. shells. Even the shell supply was so delayed by bad communication and by our naval bombardments that the Turks could not,

even by the first week in January, 1916, maintain that intensity of gun fire which was required to level our trenches and inspire their infantry with sufficient confidence to attack. It is a sad fall from the rank of sky god on Olympus to the position of that modern mythical creature the clerk of the weather, but in spite of it all, Zeus remained a good European. Overseeing once more the new battle round Troy, renewed after a period of some three thousand years, Zeus acted on the precedents recorded by Homer, and favoured the cause of the Europeans against the Asiatics.

Meanwhile the Turks began to bombard small sections on our line, but did not launch any infantry assault. Notwithstanding the dangerous statement made in the House of Lords, the German and Turkish commanders did not apparently believe that the allied armies were preparing to evacuate the Peninsula. It was known that the French general on the Helles front, General Sarrail, had gone to Salonika, and that Sir Bryan Mahon, with the Irish Division, had followed General Sarrail. But the enemy was of opinion that the immense difficulties of a general withdrawal, as well as the problem of maintaining our prestige in the Mohammedan world, would compel us to remain on the Peninsula and await strong reinforcements for another attempt to storm our way to the Narrows. Now and then the Turks stole out in large numbers to
reconnoitre our positions, under cover of   **Beginning of the**
night, and see if there were any sign of   **" bluff "**
weakening in our forces. For the most part
these explorers were not molested, as our commanders wished to lure them out of their trenches in larger forces. But some of the Australian Light Horse would not encourage the enemy's curiosity, and cut up a large Turkish patrol.

All visible signs went to show that we were about to renew the battle for the heights before the new and very heavy pieces of German artillery could be got into position.

Our novel flotillas of motor-lighters, which had first been used in the landing battles of Suvla, again became busy. The directing Teutons and their Turkish subordinates, spying through glasses from the hill-tops, could see that we were landing fresh troops in large numbers. But what they did not see was that more troops left the Peninsula at night than had been landed by day. This was one of those simple tricks by which the British sailors, who were carrying out the re-embarkation, delight to deceive their enemy. In the landing battles the Navy had shared only part of the honours with the Army. Though the naval work had been admirably designed and excellently executed, a footing had been won only by the terrible cliff **Ottomans suspect** battles in which the soldiers prevailed by **nothing** a display of fighting quality of an incomparable kind. But the re-embarkation was more of a sailor's job than a soldier's, and it was the neatest thing in all the history of amphibious warfare.

The troops on land still had to do most of the work. They had to mine forward towards points of the Turkish line of tactical importance, so as to maintain the impression that they were preparing the way for the final, desperate assault. They had to intensify their bombing work and their employment of aerial torpedoes, until even in the official Turkish communiqués remarks were made upon our renewed activity. Both the British and French armies threatened an advance. They blew up parts of the enemy's line, and when he rushed forward, filled his trenches, and brought up his reserves, the allied heavy artillery went into action and caused him heavy losses.

All this meant much hard work for the troops, but it was only a cover for the intense and sustained labour they were employing in secret directions. Excavation work went on in the trenches as though all our sappers were making

tunnels against another and still heavier cloudburst. But the new diggings were filled with high explosives, and above the high explosives was placed a device of a deadly kind. Some of the things were trip-mines, which could be set so as to explode when anybody passed by. There were a good many miners in Anzac with much experience in explosives, and considerable powers of invention. According to rumour it was they who had suggested to the British War Office that donkeys would be very useful in transporting stores from the beach to the heights. The British official agreed that donkeys would save the lives of troops, but he wondered where they could be stabled, or something of that kind. The donkeys at Anzac were of course a simple mechanism used in the Australian gold mines, consisting of wires, up and down which suspended carriers could be hauled and lowered. The men who had first thought of these donkeys entered into confabulations with the regular military engineers, and Colonial ingenuity and British experience between them produced a series of infernal machines, which were placed in large quantities at all spots where inquiring Turks were likely to venture.

None of the troops was informed of the intentions of the British commander. At Anzac and Suvla the armies were settling down to spend Christmas on the Peninsula, when the news of the evacuation began to be known. The common opinion was that Sir Ian Hamilton had put down his probable casualties in a withdrawal at fifty per cent. of his men, and it was feared that the troops might be so disturbed at the possibility of such terrible losses as to fall into a panic towards the end. The **Guarding against** first part of the evacua- **panic** tion was, therefore, conducted in such a way as to deceive our own men. All the slightly wounded men, and the slightly sick, were first taken off at night, together with horses, stores, motors, and other machinery. But large quantities of empty boxes were piled up in conspicuous places to make the positions look as though they were going to be held for the winter. The operation began on December 4th, and by the 14th the only troops left were those completely fit. On this day all the regimental officers were informed that, if the sea remained calm for one week, the withdrawal would be carried out. The

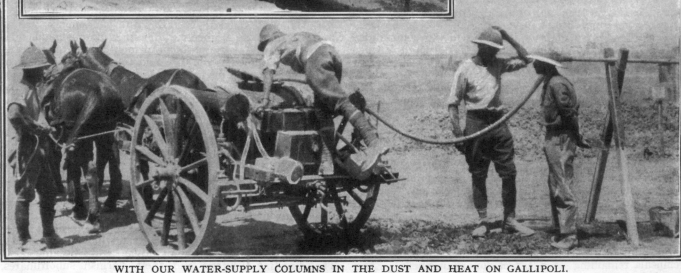

WITH OUR WATER-SUPPLY COLUMNS IN THE DUST AND HEAT ON GALLIPOLI.
Water being pumped from a well into a military water-cart on Gallipoli. Picture above: Distilling sea-water for drinking purposes. As mentioned in this chapter, "General Muddle" was conspicuous in regard to the arrangements made for watering our troops on the Peninsula. Many men died of thirst through lack of proper arrangements or deficiency of foresight in this respect.

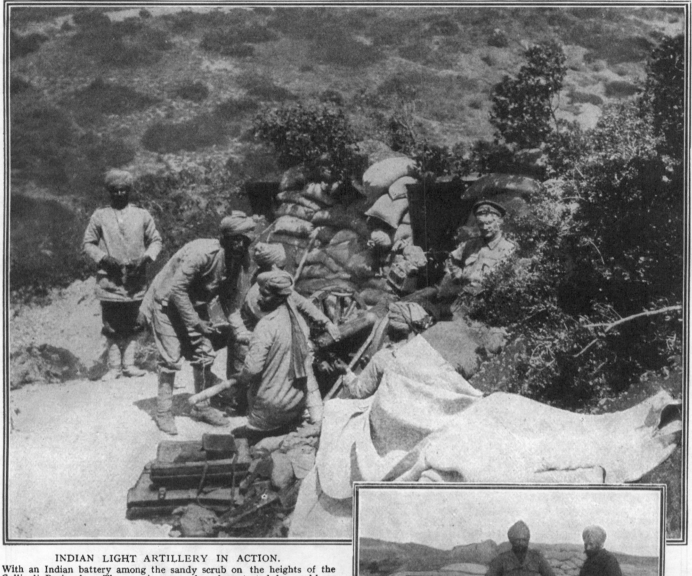

INDIAN LIGHT ARTILLERY IN ACTION.
With an Indian battery among the sandy scrub on the heights of the Gallipoli Peninsula. The gun is screened and protected by sand-bags and foliage.

INDIAN OFFICERS ON GALLIPOLI.
Colonel Kisham Singh Sardar Bahardur and Dr. Sampuran Singh, two officers who rendered valuable services in getting all the mules and carts off Gallipoli.

whole thing was largely a gamble on the weather, with the odds against us; for December was usually a month of heavy storms; and the moon was waxing, making the nights so much brighter that it seemed impossible for the Turks on the heights above to fail to see the ships which stole in empty after dark, and stole out full up at early dawn.

Meanwhile, our troops became suspicious. They kept asking awkward questions about the destruction of serviceable material, and to their questions the officers had to return answers as non-committal as possible, and maintain an assumption of indifference in the matter which they were far from feeling. For the period of suspense was naturally extremely trying. The horrible thought of fifty per cent. losses weighed on every officer, and day by day their anxieties increased and the suspicion of the troops deepened. At last the withholding of

Suspicions of the rank and file general confidence could not be delayed, and the men were told exactly what was expected of each of them. The idea of anything like a panic, especially among the new troops at Suvla, was then seen to be wildly absurd. The men behaved splendidly. Setting immediately to work with a will, they destroyed beyond repair almost everything of use that had to be left behind.

The guns were removed, then the baggage was sent on three days in advance, till by the middle of December most of the heavy stuff had been got away. The Turks became much more vigorous. They shelled the beaches and main positions continually all day, and in addition brought up some heavy howitzers behind the hills, that

caused our armies considerable trouble. Our balloon-ship came up to find the new batteries and help our gunners to knock them out. The gentle, moist south winds, which were making the weather perfect for embarkation, kept the clouds very low, and our aerial observers could not see anything. This lowness of the clouds saved us from far more serious trouble than the heavy howitzer fire. For the Turco-German observers in turn were unable to find anything extraordinary about the British positions, and the enemy's bombardment was interrupted at night, when our beaches were crowded with furiously busy men, with hundreds of lighters by the water-edge, and transport steamers close at hand.

Six o'clock on Saturday evening was the first critical hour at Anzac. Our warships cleared with all the men

Copyright   The Great War.

MAP OF GALLIPOLI INDICATING THE LANDING-PLACES FROM SEDDUL BAHR TO SUVLA.

All along the Ægean coast English words mingle with the ancient Arabic. Their names will go down to posterity, even though they were of temporary application, for there is not one that does not commemorate some immortal deed.

in their action stations, every gun trained in readiness to shatter any Turkish attack in force on our weakened lines. By seven o'clock in the evening the first big transport was in, and the embarkation began. It continued in absolute silence all night. The sky was clear, and the moon three-quarters full, yet the Turks never moved. Three-fifths of the total forces were embarked without mishap, and as the last transport slunk away at dawn Sir Charles Monro, Sir William Riddell Birdwood, Sir Michael de Robeck, and their chief officers began to think that all might go well.

Sunday, December 19th, was the day of culminating crisis. Nobody could be sure that the Turk had guessed nothing, and

NEAR THE FIRING-LINE.
Another impression of the difficulties of ambulance transport on the way to Krithia.

ON THE SUVLA HEIGHTS.
Brigadier-General F. F. Hill, C.B., D.S.O., speaking to a man wounded by a shrapnel splinter, but still puffing cheerily away at his briar pipe. At the time he was wounded he was standing near the General.

north of Suvla, to Lone Pine Plateau, south of Anzac Cove, was held by picked riflemen, one to seven or more yards. These "last ditchers," as they were called, were not so weak as they appeared to be. They had only six old guns behind them, but their guardian fleet had all the ranges nicely calculated to a yard, and could maintain an impenetrable curtain of shrapnel fire for a long period over all the first Turkish line and over the ground across which a charge must be made. There were also thousands of traps and mines with tripwires, and a very ingenious automatic bomb-thrower awaiting the enemy. But the Turks did not move. Even their patrols had

was not concentrating for an attempt to break through Anzac and roll up the Suvla Bay forces. The warships remained broadside on to the Turkish positions, with all men waiting for the signal for action. But the day wore on, and still the Turks made no sign. They shelled the beach as usual, but the sight that cheered every Briton, who laughed as he watched it, was the Turkish bombardment of a low hill from which every gun and every man had been removed. It seemed almost too much to hope that the Turks and Germans should be ignorant of what was going on beneath their eyes. But the only foragers in the half-deserted Anzac camp were a few men from Suvla Bay who had heard that among the medical comforts left behind for destruction were some cases of champagne. Suvla decided that medical comforts of this sort should not be wasted, and raided some of the abandoned stores.

On Sunday night the moon rose on a flat, oily sea, through a slight mist which hung low on the water and flowed on the wind into nullahs and valleys running up into the hills. Again the transports came in, miraculously unattacked in the clear moonlight, and the last men began to leave. The firing-line of trenches from Karakol Dagh,

been so severely handled that they had lost all their former spirit of adventure. One deserter who came in the last week of the operations surrendered in disgust at the apathy of his countrymen. He was asked if it were likely that his side would make an attack. "Attack?" he said. "It is as much as our officers can do to get the men into the trenches!"

The Australians, however, could not bear to see so historic a scene end without some sort of struggle. So their brigades began to quarrel for the honour of being the last men at Anzac. Many soldiers paraded before their commanding officers, and protested vigorously against the orders to go on board the transport while men who had arrived on the Peninsula later were staying with the rearguard. At Suvla two hundred men, who formed the ultimate rearguard, were selected from those who had made the first landing in the bay, and the final barrier they held was close to the spot where they had made their first rush in August and suffered heavy losses.

Quarrelling to the last

The most touching thing about the withdrawal was the time the troops spent, during the last week, in the little mountain cemeteries and the burial-places by Suvla Lake. At any time of the day small parties of men were to be seen carefully lettering in, on rough wooden crosses, the half-obliterated names of their comrades, or lovingly raking the mould, and bordering it with fuse-caps of enemy shells. The demand for wood for crosses was extraordinary, and some Australian chaplains were seen sowing wattle on the graves of their countrymen.

Courage of ambulance sections On Sunday night some of the ambulance sections were called upon to show great courage. They agreed to be left behind if necessary with the rearguard, and attend the wounded during the evacuation, and remain with them and take their chance with the Turks. But the enemy made no attack. At about 3.30 on Monday morning, December 20th, 1915, the embarkation was practically completed, and the rearguard at Anzac exploded a huge mine between themselves and the Turks on Russell's Top. This was a neck of land between the two ridges along

ARMY STORES AT SUVLA BAY.
Lieut. Cassidy collecting the lanterns that were used at night-time during the evacuation operations at Suvla Bay in December, 1915, after which the troops were "transferred, with insignificant casualties, to another sphere of operations," to quote Mr. Asquith's words, delivered in the House of Commons on December 20th, 1915.

which it was undesirable that the Turks should follow us. The terrific explosion had the desired effect ; the Turks thought the Australians were attacking, and kept up a furious rifle fire for forty minutes. On our side we maintained a desultory but effective reply by a series of automatic devices. Along our vacant trenches were candles and slow matches, so primed as to imitate rifle fire and make a show of activity sufficient to discourage Turkish snipers and patrols from reconnoitring our abandoned lines. About half an hour after the vast mine was fired, forty-five feet deep under the enemy trenches, a great fire blazed out at Suvla, and four other store-dumps burst into flame. There was soon one mighty bonfire two hundred yards long. The Anzacs also fired their abandoned heaps of bully beef, and a large motor-lighter, which had run ashore and could not be refloated, was blown up with a terrific report.

Still the Turks did not move, though the bonfires threw a red glow up to the sky, and dimming the moonlight, irradiated the whole scene with fiercer glow. The enemy

pitched a few shells on a hill and a beach at Suvla, the total result of which was that one of our men was wounded in the arm. But the Turkish and Teutonic gunners did not make a curtain of fire as they so easily could have done. With watchful gait the rearguards came down in Indian file through the saps, followed by the happy forlorn hopes of the ambulance sections. After many stops and starts, and keeping well within the shadow of the saps, all the "last ditchers" reached the transports by four o'clock in the morning. The army of Anzac embarked at four o'clock, and the army at Suvla left a little earlier. By five o'clock both positions were evacuated, but some midshipmen in picket-boats waited by the piers to see if they could find any stragglers.

When the sun rose, the Turks began a grand bombardment, but instead of trying to reach our warships and transports, they shrapnelled the vacated trenches, shelled the empty beaches, and in a state of utter mystification, even put large high-explosive shells into the flaming bonfires. Our warships also opened fire on everything that had been left behind—sunken lighters, the wrecked steamers forming breakwaters, and all structures likely to be of any use to the enemy. So the unique spectacle was enjoyed of Britons and Turks shelling the same targets simultaneously. When the sun had climbed out of the morning mist, the Turks and their baffled German directors discovered at last that something was wrong, and trained some of their guns on our bombarding squadron. But their shooting was wild, and they never got within a hundred yards of our nearest ship. Late on Monday night one of our battleships lay a dozen miles away from Suvla, and the glow of the bonfire was still visible.

The next morning a furious southern gale sprang up and drove huge seas before it into the little bay, further wrecking the breakwaters of sunken sand-filled steamers, and breaking off all connection between the coast and the sea. Our armies had just escaped the storm by twenty-four hours. In the meantime, the Turks had become as over-rash as they had been over-cautious. They tried to crowd into our abandoned trenches, with the result that the automatic bomb-throwers, the trip-mines, land mines, and all the other hidden machines of death caught them by the thousand. A report from Athens said that five thousand men were killed or disabled in the vast death-trap between Karakol Dagh and Lone Pine Plateau. But the Athenians, in the matter of veracity, had as low a reputation as the Cretans in the age of St. Paul.

There is no doubt that the Turks were badly punished during their first great rush for plunder into our abandoned lines. **Fatal rush for plunder**

Our total casualties were one officer and two men wounded at Suvla, and four men wounded at Anzac ; which was less than the ordinary daily casualties in the trenches under gun fire, sniping, and an occasional bomb. Two of the six guns left behind to support the rearguards in case of attack were venerable howitzers that had served in the South African War. All six guns were destroyed at the last minute, and though there seem to have been some stragglers who did not reach the Suvla beach till 8.30 a.m., not a man was lost.

General Sir Ian Hamilton (×) and Staff photographed before leaving Gallipoli

Admiral de Robeck (centre) and Staff, six of whom won mention in the Honours List.

Sister ship to the rescue: H.M.S. Canopus haul

M.S. Albion, which ran aground on Gallipoli.

Thrilling incident on Gallipoli: Horses rescued by Munster Fusiliers from a waggon shattered by Turkish gun fire.

The entire operations formed a wonderful piece of organisation. There had been at various times, both in the Dardanelles battles and the attempts to break the German line in Flanders and France, some severe criticism of our Staff work. It cannot be denied that, in the Suvla Bay landing, for example, some of the Staff work was very bad. But against all this we must put the extraordinary, perfect smoothness of the withdrawals from the Gallipoli Peninsula. There was little or nothing for the troops to do, as the enemy refrained from an attack. It was practically Staff work alone that achieved such a result. Sir Charles Monro oversaw all the arrangements, with Admirals de Robeck and Wemyss looking after the naval side of the affair, and General Birdwood looking after the military situation. In a special Order of the Day, Sir Charles Monro wrote an appreciation of the tactics of the withdrawal from the Anzac and Suvla positions, which deserves quotation for the plain truths that it sets out concerning the brilliant close of the most tragic episode in our annals of war :

The arrangements made for withdrawal, and for keeping the enemy in ignorance of the operation which was taking place, could not have been improved. The General Officer commanding the Dardanelles Army, and the General Officers commanding the Australian and New Zealand and Ninth Army Corps, may pride themselves on an achievement without parallel in the annals of war. The Army and Corps Staffs, Divisional and subordinate Commanders and their Staffs, and the Naval and Military Beach Staffs proved themselves more than equal to the most difficult task which could have been thrown upon them: Regimental officers, non-commissioned officers, and men carried out, without a hitch, the most trying operation which soldiers can be called upon to undertake—a withdrawal in the face of the enemy—in a manner reflecting the highest credit on the discipline and soldierly qualities of the troops.

It is no exaggeration to call this achievement one without parallel. To disengage and to withdraw from a bold and active enemy is the most difficult of all military operations ; and in this case the withdrawal was effected by surprise, with the opposing forces at close grips—in many cases within a few yards of each other. Such an operation, when succeeded by a re-embarkation from an open beach, is one for which military history contains no precedent.

During the past months the troops of Great Britain and Ireland, Australia and New Zealand, Newfoundland and India, fighting side by side, have invariably proved their superiority over the enemy, have contained the best fighting troops in the Ottoman Army in their front, and have prevented the Germans from employing their Turkish allies against us elsewhere.

No soldier relishes undertaking a withdrawal from before the enemy. It is hard to leave behind the graves of good comrades, and to relinquish positions so hardly won and so gallantly maintained as those we have left. But all ranks in the Dardanelles Army will realise that in this matter they were but carrying out the orders of his Majesty's Government, so that they might in due course be more usefully employed in fighting elsewhere for their King, their country, and the Empire.

There is only one consideration—what is best for the furtherance of the common cause. In that spirit the withdrawal was carried out, and in that spirit the Australian and New Zealand and the Ninth Army Corps have proved, and will continue to prove, themselves second to none as soldiers of the Empire.

British diversion from Cape Helles While the armies of Anzac and Suvla were withdrawing, the allied forces south of Achi Baba, at the tip of the Peninsula, undertook a diversion. The idea was to prevent the withdrawal of Turkish troops from the Cape Helles front for any closing attack upon the Anzac army and the Suvla Bay forces. We have seen that the enemy had no offensive movement whatever in contemplation ; but this could not be known to Sir Charles Monro, and, leaving nothing to chance, he ordered an attack upon the top of the Krithia Ravine. At two o'clock in the afternoon of December 19th all our artillery posts were manned beneath the rounded outline of Achi Baba—the familiar, unattainable, hateful object in the landscape, at which our soldiers had been staring since April. The country looked unutterably peaceful in the warm sunlight. The heights that bound the Trojan plain were reflected in the quiet surface of the Hellespont. Imbros raised her rugged **Beauties of the Classic Plain** peaks into the whitened sky, while Tenedos was stretched upon the waters like a sleeping lion. Nothing moved on land, though from innumerable points the smoke of cooking fires indicated something of the forces concealed in the mazes of trenches. But behind the eastern islands and in the northern mists our new monitors were hidden with their 14 in. and 15 in. guns ready for action. And up by the Krithia Nullah, in seven mine galleries driven beneath the

THE LAST OF A DERELICT IN THE DARDANELLES.
Destruction of an old vessel that proved a danger to navigation. One of the odd jobs of our handymen with the Fleet in the Dardanelles.

road, our infantry was waiting in darkness with bomb, revolver, bayonet, and sand-bag. There was only about a foot of earth between them and the Turkish trench which stretched end on to the mine galleries. The mines had been driven so quietly that the enemy suspected nothing. Instead of blowing them up and killing only a few Turks in their machine-gun posts, the British plan was to make seven infantry rushes through the mines, grab a few hundred yards of trench before the Turkish brigadier knew that anything had happened, barricade the captured position, and work down the saps until the Turkish reserves arrived. The Navy began the operation by dropping a 14 in. shell into Krithia. Then, in a seemingly desultory manner, more heavy shells were pitched into the enemy second and third line, as in an ordinary daily bombardment. Meanwhile, more monitors emerged from the northern mists and the attack opened in force. Three mines were sprung under the Turkish first line, and all the land batteries let go with lyddite and tritol shrapnel, while the monitors and destroyers intensified their gun fire.

In about five minutes the Turkish gunners replied, but being unable to perceive if a blow had fallen, or if a blow

A LEADER AT CAPE HELLES.
Lieut.-General Sir F. J. Davies, K.C.B., K.C.M.G., outside his dug-out on Gallipoli, where he commanded the Eighth Army Corps.

had been struck at all, they shot wildly about the Peninsula. No movement of our infantry could be perceived; yet, invisible in the dust and smoke, our soldiers had burst through their seven galleries. Some drove the Turks up the trench, while others built a barricade across the nullah, and with sand-bags made a parapet connecting our lines with the captured position. Eighty yards up, the Turks made a stand by their first barricade, and our bomb-throwers replaced the men with revolvers and bayonets. In another direction a brave Turk pulled his machine-gun into the trench and caught one of our companies, bringing down the captain and fifty men.

The rest went back to cover, but twenty yards behind them the new parapet was already four feet high. Five feet above the fighting infantry swept the shrieking shells from our land artillery and ships, and crossing them, a little higher in the air, was another line of roaring missiles by which the Turkish gunners were trying to keep back our supports.

What with the smoke and the noise, nobody could hear and nobody could see. Meanwhile, another trench had been taken with little difficulty, and the main group of Turkish soldiers remained ringed around by our infantry. The Turks fought on bravely behind their barricades where no help could reach them, and after combating all night, our men only made another ten yards' progress. The affair ended with two pieces of Turkish trench remaining in our hands—two hundred yards in all—with the Turks sandwiched between the ground we had gained.

Then the news came that Anzac and Suvla had been evacuated without the

enemy trying to move. There was then no reason for winning, at the cost of a man a yard, more of the ground we intended to abandon quickly. So the demonstration at Krithia abruptly ended, with the Turks still sandwiched between our two little pushes. No men could be spared for any general diversion, for with the evacuation at Anzac and Suvla the position of our forces at the southern point of the Peninsula became one of great peril.

In the first place, the enemy was able to concentrate overwhelming forces of men and guns, with increased munitions of all kinds, on the short front at the edge of Achi Baba. In the second place, another surprise re-embarkation by the allied armies seemed impossible of achievement. Not only had the Turks been put on their mettle by the extraordinary stratagem used against them, but the angry German General Staff, working with the still more furious Enver Pasha, despatched a large body of picked Teutonic officers to watch our last position by the Dardanelles, and see that we did not again steal away without standing battle. In the third place, the period of very heavy storms had set in, making the approach of ships to the shore almost impossible, despite the rough-and-ready breakwaters erected round the landing-beaches. Moreover, the moon was rounding into the full orb, so that when the night was by chance calm, the coast and a large stretch of sea were clearly visible to enemy observers. No transport could expect to approach the land without provoking furious gun fire, both from the Asiatic shore on the right flank and the Achi Baba lines in front.

Apparently our Government could not make up its mind to run the terrible risks of evacuating the southern end of the Peninsula. But it is very likely that this indecision

DUTY AND "SPADE WORK" AT THE DARDANELLES.
Major-General G. F. Ellison, C.B., C.M.G., who was mentioned in Sir Ian Hamilton's despatches, taking physical exercise on Gallipoli. Picture above: Major-General Sir William Douglas, K.C.M.G., C.B., D.S.O., in a tree from which he watched and directed operations on the Peninsula.

COM. HON. L. J. O. LAMBART, D.S.O.
Commended for services in action on
Gallipoli, and awarded D.S.O.

CAPT. H. C. LOCKYER.
H.M.S. Implacable. Mentioned
by Vice-Admiral de Robeck.

COMMODORE O. BACK-
HOUSE, C.B. On Staff, R.N.D.,
awarded C.B.

CAPTAIN J. W. L. McCLINTOCK,
D.S.O. In command of H.M.S. Lord
Nelson; inflicted severe damage on enemy.

REAR-ADMIRAL SIR C. F. THURSBY, K.C.M.G.
In H.M.S. Queen, was in charge of the landing of the
Australian and New Zealand Forces.

CAPTAIN A. V. VYVYAN, D.S.O.
Beachmaster at Anzac, and frequently
exposed to heavy shell fire.

REAR-ADMIRAL S. NICHOLSON, C.B., M.V.O.
Served from the landing of the Allied Forces on
Gallipoli to the evacuation.

COM. J. R. MIDDLETON, D.S.O.
Took part in operations in Dardanelles
and three times entered mine-fields.

CAPT. B. ST. G. COLLARD.
Assistant Beachmaster, "W"
Beach, in the landing.

COM. HON. P. C. G. C.
ACHESON, M.V.O. Awarded
the D.S.O. for his services.

COM. J. F. SOMERVILLE, D.S.O.
Fleet Wireless Officer, with duties of
exceptional difficulty.

LIEUT.-COM. E. L. C. GRATTAN,
D.S.O. In charge of wireless at Helles;
praised by Vice-Admiral de Robeck.

LIEUT.-COM. H. W. WYLD.
Awarded D.S.O. for services
during the operations.

LIEUT.-COM. R. H. L. BEVAN,
D.S.O. On the Staff of Rear-
Admiral Wemyss at evacuation.

LIEUT. F. H. SANDFORD, D.S.O.
Specially commended for good work
when attacking mine-fields.

HONOURED FOR SERVICE IN THE DARDANELLES: HEROES OF THE ROYAL NAVY.

Portraits by Russell & Sons, Elliott & Fry, Speaight.

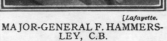

MAJOR-GENERAL F. HAMMERS-
LEY, C.B.

BRIGADIER-GENERAL P. A.
KENNA, V.C., D.S.O.

COLONEL E. G. SINCLAIR-MAC-
LAGAN, D.S.O.

LIEUT.-COLONEL W. J. MILLAR,
D.S.O.

Major-General F. Hammersley, C.B., commanded the 11th Division of Lieut.-General the Hon. Sir Frederick Stopford's force at Suvla Bay. Brigadier-General P. A. Kenna, V.C., D.S.O., A.D.C., who was on General Sir Ian Hamilton's Staff at the Dardanelles, died of wounds. He was mentioned by Sir Ian Hamilton for his services. Colonel E. G. Sinclair-Maclagan, D.S.O., Princess Alexandra of Wales' Own (Yorkshire Regiment), was mentioned in despatches and promoted to colonel for his services in the Dardanelles. Lieut.-Colonel W. J. Millar, D.S.O., King's Own Scottish Borderers (T.F.), was awarded the Distinguished Service Order, mentioned by General Sir Ian Hamilton and promoted for his services on Gallipoli.

was only another ruse to steady the nerves of the troops and mislead, if possible, the enemy. There were several good reasons for holding on. There was a considerable amount of elbow-room for the troops, enabling them to burrow away from the enemy's shell fire, while on the plateau which we occupied the flood-water from the hills inconvenienced our men less than it did the Turks on the higher slopes. The ground commanded the entrance to the Strait, giving us the power to share fully the control of the historic waterway with the Ottoman Empire. A brilliant American military correspondent, Captain Granville Fortescue, who had studied the position carefully from the Turkish side, and had talked to the German and Turkish officers there, published a pamphlet in London strongly advising the British people to hold on to the plateau at the end of the Peninsula, and so remain the outer guardian of the channel between the Black Sea and the Mediterranean. The enemy was quite aware of the power of leverage we could exert for generations on the traffic through the Dardanelles by maintaining our grip upon the southern plateau. He saw that the valid reasons for evacuating Suvla and Anzac, where we had been cramped, did not apply to our position on the tip of the Peninsula. Therefore, he was not at all sure that we intended to withdraw entirely. The Turks were not pleased with this state of things; they would have much preferred to see us attempt an evacuation, and then sweep down from the hills upon us. Even had we managed to leave without a battle, it would not have seriously distressed any Ottoman, except Enver Pasha, who badly wanted a victory for reasons of personal ambition.

LIEUT.-GENERAL THE HON. SIR FREDERICK W.
STOPFORD, K.C.M.G., K.C.V.O., C.B.
Who commanded the Army Corps operating from Suvla Bay.

Enver's malignant ambition

All the German commanders and advisers of the Ottoman Empire were determined to prevent another such withdrawal of the British and French troops as disastrous to their interests. They wanted to use the Turkish army to inflict a heavy blow on us, which would tell on both the material and moral elements of the allied strength. They reckoned that if they could only get their heavy howitzers in position

and accumulate a great store of shells, they could employ the hurricane fire artillery tactics used on the Russian and French fronts. Only one of our landing-beaches was protected from the enemy's guns; the newly munitioned Turkish gunners, with German, Austrian, and Hungarian artillerymen, working the new heavy howitzers, would therefore be able, it was calculated, to wear us down. By Christmas the Turks around Achi Baba had trebled their supply of ammunition; they had brought up guns from the Sari Bair area, and the heavy howitzers were being hauled along southward for the closing battle. New squadrons of German airmen were sent to Constantinople, and, reaching the Gallipoli front a few days before Christmas, they began to show unwonted energy and audacity in their scouting work. No doubt there had been sharp upbraidings and dismissals of commanding officers in connection with the Suvla and Anzac operations. The officers who were the Teutonic leaven in the Ottoman lump were, at any rate, resolved not to be surprised again. German aeroplanes boldly hovered over our bivouacs, though our gunners filled the sky with shrapnel all around them, and our machine-guns spouted bullets at them when they swooped down to get a clearer view of our activities. The German air-scouts would not go away until they had made a close study of our arrangements. They were certainly brave and skilful men, having been lashed by one desperate failure into a disregard of cautious tactics, which was rather unusual in the Teuton.

At the beginning of the strange struggle to prevent us from departing, the enemy used his new shell supplies in **Turks "make sure" of Helles**

an alarming manner. As soon as we got away from Suvla and Anzac, he tried to make life intolerable to the men at Helles. Every part of the ground was open to his fire. He shelled the communication trenches, along which the troops were to withdraw, and the beaches from which they had to embark. During the week after Christmas, our daily toll of casualties from shell fire became very heavy. So, by way of making the enemy anxious about his store

British mule transport at work in the Levant.   Right : A machine-gun is seen ready in the event of a Turkish charge.

Trying to convince a four-footed shirker that its services are indispensable.   Rough-rider's horse which strongly objected to being put into the shafts to draw transport waggons from place to place on Gallipoli.

WITH THE TRANSPORT AND MACHINE-GUN SECTION ON GALLIPOLI.

FRENCH OFFICERS HONOURED BY KING GEORGE.

General Sir Ian Hamilton addressing three French officers, Commandant Berthier de Sauvigny, D.S.O., Lieut. de la Bord, and Lieut. Pelliot, prior to decorating them with the Military Cross for their services on Gallipoli.

ALLIED GENERALS DECORATING FRENCH HEROES. .

Lieut.-General Sir Bryan Mahon, K.C.V.O., C.B., D.S.O., and General Bailloud, the French Commander-in-Chief at the Dardanelles, decorating officers and men of the French Army for bravery on Gallipoli.

of shells, Major-General Davies, commanding on the Helles front, launched another infantry attack against the Turkish lines. On December 29th a British division broke into the Turkish centre, and captured and held part of the fire trenches. This infantry movement was, of course, prepared by a terrific bombardment from our side, in which the great guns of the monitors joined with our heavy howitzers in watering all the enemy positions with shells that wrecked the deepest dug-out.

This show of activity on our part had the effect designed. Liman von Sanders calculated what his available shell resources were, and found that if he used them lavishly in desultory bombardments of our beaches and communica-

tion trenches, he might lack ammunition to repel a great and sustained attack in force. So he slackened his daily gun fire, especially at night, when his gunners were likely to waste shells by the hundred if our beaches were empty. He decided on a new and far more effective plan of action. He reserved his shells until his armies at Sari Bair and Anafarta were marched into position around Achi Baba. His idea was to put to a direct test the strength or weakness of our lines, by making a grand attack with all his Gallipoli forces.

By this time Sir Charles Monro had come to Helles with General Birdwood, and these two experts in the art of perfect evacuation studied the more difficult problem of Helles with General Davies; then, with Admiral de Robeck, Admiral Wemyss, and the military and naval Staffs, they worked out all the preparations. The French army corps started to embark towards the beginning of the New Year. Their departure could not be hidden from the enemy, who soon found out that he had British uniforms and British voices in front of him on the Kereves Dere front.

French leave for Salonika

By this river gully the opposing trenches came within a few yards of each other, so any concealment was impossible. Happily, the enemy was not disturbed; for knowing that the French had set their heart on the Salonika Expedition, and disapproved of the Dardanelles campaign, the Turco-German commanders naturally supposed that we had freed the French so that they might work under their own Commander-in-Chief, General Sarrail. But a British division and the English Yeomanry left about the same time as the French army corps, and the weakening of the lines went on in an apparently perilous manner to the first week in January, 1916.

At first the departing troops left their artillery behind them, so that the "last ditchers" could make a brave show of gun fire to the last possible moment. The method of embarkation was the same as that employed at Suvla and Anzac. The men came down to the beaches at night, and the transports came in under cover of darkness, loaded up, and stole out before dawn. Horses were used to drag down many of the big guns, and were then taken away by the French Navy, which gave skilful assistance to us in the work. Again it seemed extraordinary that the enemy could not discern, by means of star-shells, searchlights, and night-glasses, the difference between a nocturnal movement of reinforcement and one of general evacuation.

On January 7th, 1916, however, it looked as though the anxious Germans, watching from the hill behind Krithia and from the large, round hump of Achi **Terrible Turkish** Baba, had discovered all that was going **artillery fire** on. At eleven o'clock in the morning our position on both sides of the great ravine was swept with gun fire which continued for hours, while our guns replied fairly vigorously. Then came the surprise-packet for us. At three o'clock in the afternoon the enemy's fire suddenly assumed a speed and intensity exceeding anything known on the Peninsula. It was a true drum fire, or hurricane artillery attack, such as the French had invented in Champagne and Mackensen had perfected in Russia. It lasted only half an hour, so as to maintain the surprise effect, and prevent us from getting up all our reserves. At half-past three the enemy exploded two mines on Fusilier Bluff, which overlooked the sea at the extreme end of our line. The moment for the great infantry attack had come. All our left line was shrouded in black smoke, our trenches were blown in at many points, and several communication saps were blocked. Part of the New Army from Suvla Bay occupied some of the lines round Fusilier Bluff, and so desperately eager were they for a fight that they were on the firing-step before any Turk leapt over the opposing parapet. One of the battalions had lost its colonel, and the men were seeing red.

Johnny Turk did not want to fight. In some places the Turkish officers could clearly be seen driving their men out with whips. The men who came out were not many, and they were shot down. A real assault was only attempted opposite Fifth Avenue and Fusilier Bluff, where the Staffordshires clean broke up the feeble movement by bringing down most of the Turks who had been lashed out of the trenches. But all this was only the beginning of trouble for the Turkish infantry, for as they stood, packed and unwilling to move, in their front line near the sea, the experienced gunners of our destroyers, who could get their bearings to an inch with regard to the enemy position, opened a heavy sideways raking fire on the closely filled trenches. What then happened in those trenches between some of the officers with whips and some of their dismayed and angry men with bayonets need not be told. The German officers especially, accustomed to the fine, stolid discipline that continually carried their own troops through the horrors of a mass formation attack, must have brimmed over with despairing bitterness, at the way the Turk was turning out. The Turk was sick of the war. From the beginning he had not liked the idea of fighting against his old friends the French and British. His many hand-to-hand encounters with Australasians, Britons, French, and French Colonial troops had not lessened his personal respect for the fighting qualities of the Allies. He was a good fighter himself, and he knew that he had met at least his peers in battle; and what with frost-bite, enteric, dysentery, poor food, and bad clothing, he was only too willing to let his former friends go away quietly if they so desired. His only fear was that they would not go, and that he would be whipped forward to attack **Ottomans tired** us until he turned round and shot the **and discouraged** Germans.

It must be fairly admitted that though we lost, and lost badly, in the struggle for the Dardanelles, the soldiers of the British Empire were at the close of the operations very near to grinding down the Turkish infantry. Johnny Turk was a good man; but in continual conflict with him in soldiers' battles, our men, with little good leading except from their regimental officers, wore down practically every Turkish peasant. He was overawed and dismayed by our naval guns; they were, from the beginning, one of the chief reasons why he was averse to coming

LOOKERS ON: CONVALESCENT SOLDIERS WATCHING A MILITARY MOVEMENT.
Scene somewhere in the Levant. British Engineers hauling, with the aid of a traction-machine, a heavy gun up a steep gradient, while in the background a number of convalescents were looking on with interest.

out into the open to attack. Then our long superiority in air power, and rumours of our far-reaching submarine operatons, shook his moral, and made him think with bitter regret of the days when Britain and France were in fighting alliance with his country. At the time we were retiring from the Gallipoli Peninsula, the Russian Army of the Caucasus under the Grand Duke was beginning to break into the Ottoman Empire eastward. Had we

Why withdrawal was inevitable held on to the Dardanelles, and brought up two hundred more 6 in. howitzers, with large and constant shell supplies, and a hundred thousand more well-trained troops, under a general of strong character, we could have turned defeat into victory. The only great difficulty was the interruption of our sea communications by heavy storms.

But we still lacked the infantry reinforcements, if not the shells. Our commitments in Flanders, France, Egypt, Greece, Mesopotamia, German East Africa, and elsewhere made impossible any revisal of the decision of withdrawal from the Dardanelles. In particular, the repulse and encircling of General Townshend's column at Kut-el-Amara, after our feeble swoop towards Bagdad, necessitated a complete evacuation of the Gallipoli Peninsula. And things were made wonderfully easy for us by Liman

ON THE SICK LIST.
Invalided sailors coming aboard a vessel at the Dardanelles to be conveyed to a hospital base.

von Sanders and his subordinate officers. After the extraordinary check to the Turkish advance at Fusilier Bluff, the commander of the Ottoman forces decided that we were resolutely fixed at the entrance to the Dardanelles. The weakness of his infantry forbade him attempting another attack, and in his drum-fire bombardment he had spent so much shell that he had to be very careful in using what remained in store. Thus all circumstances compelled him to await the arrival of the new German and Austrian heavy artillery, with larger shell supplies, before trying to drive us into the sea.

In the meantime, nearly all our artillery was taken away. The Battle of the Bluffs ended in the evening of January 7th, 1916, and by dawn on January 8th most of the field-guns and howitzers we had used against the Turks had been taken to the beaches and shipped on gun lighters. January 8th was the day of culminating crisis at Helles. It broke clear and calm, with a perfect sea for the great event, but about four in the afternoon a gale blew up, increasing in violence at night till the wind tore along at a speed of thirty-five miles an hour. This was an extreme peril. Had the Germans in the Turkish army but known, our remaining forces on the Peninsula were at their mercy. In the overwhelming hurricane one of our principal embarking places, Gully Beach,

A FAREWELL SHOT FROM THE TURKS.
Exploding shell which narrowly missed a transport column about to evacuate Gallipoli from "W" Beach. Note the stores piled ready on the foreshore.

Twenty-four hours before the evacuation of Suvla. Scene on "W" Beach showing a number of lighters laden with stores, Red Cross waggons, trollies, etc. Preparations for the coming "bluff" were being made at the time this photograph was taken.

High-explosive shell bursting within fifteen yards of the official photographer, and shaking up a mule transport, but apparently having no terrors for the impassive Oriental, who has not even taken the trouble to fling himself down flat on the ground.

LAST DAYS ON GALLIPOLI PENINSULA: TWO OFFICIAL IMPRESSIONS.

WARM WORK AND HARD GOING.
R.N.D. despatch-rider on Gallipoli carrying a message to the Brigade Headquarters, along a communication trench.

was made impracticable, and a lighter was wrecked there. At the chief place of embarkation, W Beach, just above Cape Helles, the connecting piers were washed away. There were collisions with rafts and hospital barges, troop lighters, and gun lighters, the engines of other lighters broke down, and another steam lighter was wrecked. Moreover, a hostile submarine had been seen off Cape Helles at nine o'clock in the evening.

In the thick weather our bombarding squadrons would not have been able to help our last weak line of infantry. Happily, however, the effect of the great storm was of a double kind. It enormously increased **Day of crisis** the ordinary difficulties of the beach- **at Helles** masters, engineers, and lighter skippers, but it saved them from extraordinary dangers. The German landsmen directing the Turkish army were certain that no large military force, with numerous heavy guns and immense stores of war material, could be embarked in a thirty-five-miles-an-hour gale. The result was that the Turkish gunners went to sleep in their dug-outs. On our principal beach only six shells fell after darkness set in. It was pitch dark on land and sea, and the enemy was confident that the hurricane was working for him and preventing all traffic on the British beaches.

At midnight, January 8th, our firing-line was quite empty of troops; but not a single Turk or German re-connoitred our trenches. Zeus, in his sombre character as the lord of darkness and tempest, was still fighting against the Asiatics, and protecting the Europeans. For some years our seamen had hoped that when they met their enemy the weather would be rough. They desired a heavy sea in the great battle, so that the seamanship of their opponents should be put with utmost severity

to the test of battle. The German commander and Turkish generals on the Gallipoli Peninsula did not guess that our fighting seamen rather preferred storm to calm in the most critical phase of a struggle. Owing to this ignorance of German and Turkish soldiers in regard to the somewhat remarkable capabilities of the British sailor, the evacuation of the southern part of the Peninsula, in face of a much strengthened enemy, was conducted with even more success than the withdrawal from Anzac and Suvla. Our total casualties were—one man wounded. We left behind ten worn-out 15-pounders **"One man wounded"** which were not worth moving, with one good gun to help the "last ditchers" in case of need. The French army corps also left six old naval guns. All these seventeen pieces of artillery were destroyed before being abandoned.

The programmes of embarkation at W Beach and Y Beach were completed at 2.30 a.m. on January 9th, 1916. Meanwhile, the troops originally marked for evacuation at Gully Beach marched to W Beach, and got on the lighters by 4 a.m. As the naval beach party was just casting off, a military officer and three men, who had failed to clamber into a lighter at another pier, finished a two-mile walk, and barely arrived in time to catch the last boat. All the bonfires were already fused, and also the magazine piles and bomb stores. This small party just reached the last lighter and cleared the break-water when the fires broke out. It was a close shave, for the lighter was barely a hundred yards from the shore when the magazine exploded. Happily, the lighter was specially constructed with a splinter-proof roof. The men went below but the officers and some of the beach party sat astern.

WITH THE FRENCH COLONIALS.
French Colonial troops in a first-line trench on Gallipoli, reading, resting, and sniping in the heat of the day.

Turkish shell exploding in the sea and merely killing numbers of fish. The cheerful nonchalance of the soldiers, resting under the cliff and heedless of the fact that the next shell might be better aimed, forms striking proof of the Briton's care-free optimism and disregard of danger.

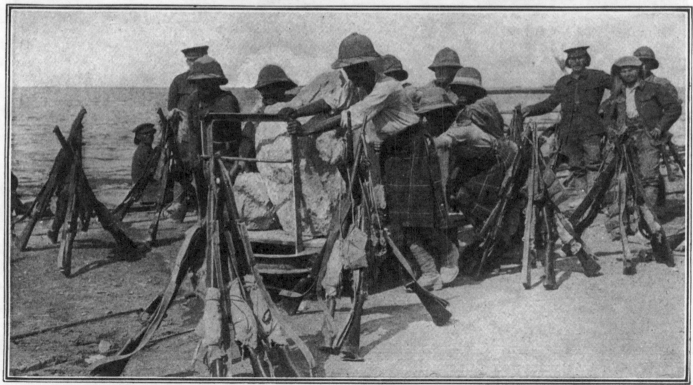

Highlanders pushing trollies loaded with rocks during the building of a breakwater by British Engineers at Cape Helles. Owing to submarine dangers, all reinforcements, ammunition, and supplies had to be taken from Mudros to Helles or Anzac by night in fleet-sweepers and trawlers.

AT WORK AND AT REST UNDER SHELL FIRE, GALLIPOLI.

The beach was in flames, cliff high from end to end, and from this line of lowering fire the explosion burst. The magazine contained the gun-cotton store of the Royal Engineers, and near it were clumps of small-arm ammunition, bombs, and other explosives. But the end of the gun-cotton pile was accounted by those who saw it the most spectacular thing in the war. A huge crimson mushroom rose in the reddened sky, with large lumps of black rock showing in the fearful flame.

Turk and Hun again outwitted It shook the sea and the ship, and the men who had cleared the breakwater thought their end had come. But the larger rocks fell short of them, only the fringe of the volcanic shower striking the boat. Six men were cut, but none severely.

It was then 4.30 a.m. The terrific explosion and the great line of flame aroused the Turk and the German, and their gunners began to shell the vacant lines and fiery beaches, and continued to waste ammunition until the slow, late winter dawn broke and showed them they had been again clean outwitted. On the Germans fell all the blame. Not only had they foreseen what would happen, but they had taken intense precautions to prevent Sir Charles Monro from getting his men entirely away without mishap. In addition to some of the best German aerial observers and some of the most practised German artillery observing officers, there were expert German naval officers studying wind and weather in connection with any possible evacuation movements by our three armies on the Helles front. But capable as the Teutonic seamen were in all the mechanical side of their profession, they did not allow for the fact that our sailors were of the old rough weather school, and delighted to

Ride in the whirlwind and direct the storm.

We at least graced the tragic theatre of the Dardanelles by our manner of leaving it. It was, however, an obscuring exaggeration on the part of the Prime Minister of the Coalition Government of the United Kingdom to say that the re-embarkation would take an imperishable place in our military history. What we hope will be imperishable in the memory of present and future generations of the Anglo-Celtic race are the causes, political, industrial, social, naval, and military, which led to the greatest defeat our nation had yet suffered—a defeat that occurred in circumstances in which victory could swiftly have been organised had we but possessed, in January, 1915, in the Cabinet, the War Office, and the Admiralty, men of merely fair capacity for co-operative warlike work.

LAST MOMENTS ON GALLIPOLI: TURKISH SHELL BURSTING NEAR THE RIVER CLYDE.

The Turks made desperate efforts to retrieve their failure in allowing our troops successfully to evacuate Anzac and Suvla, by furiously bombarding our positions at the heel of Gallipoli. This illustration shows a Turkish shell exploding near Cape Helles, and a French soldier, one of the last to leave, is protecting his head from flying splinters.

FRENCH REGIMENT

CHAPTER CVIII.

RETURNING TO CAMP.

THE INNER LIFE OF FRANCE IN HER TIME OF TRIAL.
By M. Henri D. Davray, the Eminent French Critic.

In the earlier volumes of THE GREAT WAR chapters have been included on the conditions of war-time life in Great Britain, Russia, and Germany, and also in America, as it has been thought desirable by the Editors that this historical survey should include every aspect of the war's effect on the belligerent nations, as well as its reflection on the life of the neutrals. It is now possible in the following chapter to add a highly important contribution to this series of studies in national life, and the Editors are fortunate in having been able to secure so distinguished a contributor as M. Henri D. Davray to write it. M. Davray has long held a foremost position in France as an interpreter to his compatriots of British life and character. As foreign editor of the "Mercure de France" he has introduced to the French public all the more notable English writers of our time, and for fully twenty years has been rendering the most brilliant service to the Entente countries by helping our French allies to a better understanding of ourselves. His knowledge of British life and character is profound and accurate, and the name of no living French critic commands greater respect among English scholars than his. It is, therefore, peculiarly appropriate that one who has done much to bring the two peoples together should enrich our pages with the following intimate account of the life of his own country during the earlier months of the Great War.

AN eminent English writer, who knows contemporary France as intimately as France of former days, has written : " We are all of one mind in admiring, and often with an admiration bordering on amazement, the magnificent temper in which the heroic French nation has faced its stupendous hour of trial." This "hour of trial" has assuredly been more "stupendous" than it is possible for an English islander to imagine.

Will war be imposed upon us ? Such was the question, repeated anxiously in all French circles, political and financial, commercial and industrial ; but the bulk of the population in the provinces, whether at manufacturing centres or in agricultural districts, was ready to believe still that the storm would pass. With more or less clearness, each imagined for himself the disastrous consequences which such a cataclysm would bring in its train for all those affected ; one pictured the losses and ruin which a modern war would accumulate with its

GENERAL GALLIÉNI'S SUCCESSOR.
When General Galliéni, owing to ill-health, resigned office as French War Minister, in March, 1916, General Roques (who is seen seated in the above photograph) was appointed to succeed him. For his services as commander of the First Eastern Army General Roques was awarded the Grand Cross of the Legion of Honour and the Croix de Guerre.

murderous arms and numberless masses of men, and the people refused to believe that there could be anywhere responsible heads of States mad enough to provoke such a frightful Armageddon.

When the definite rupture came between Austria and Serbia, public opinion realised that the conflict could not remain local, and that the efforts of the British and French diplomatists had been pure waste of time. A fortunate issue from the crisis was anticipated less and less, the fatal dénouement was perceived to be approaching, and one of the first effects of this pessimism was the almost total disappearance of gold and the scarcity of change. The difficulty arose of regulating purchases, and of changing notes of one hundred and fifty francs. Immediately, economists and bankers demanded that notes of twenty and five francs should be put in circulation. Very quickly public imagination foresaw the almost inevitable menace of war, and everywhere it was accepted without braggadocio or terror, even when hopes of intervention were reduced to a feeble

CAPTIVE HUNS IN COMFORTABLE BILLETS.
Scene in one of the depots in France where German prisoners of war were kept. Their quarters were comfortable and roomy, and they were allowed to follow any work they liked best.

glimmer. None the less, opinion awaited from Berlin the gesture which would arrest Austria on the slope, at the bottom of which lay fatal collision with Russia, and the letting loose of European war. But nothing could stay any longer the Austro-Germans in their mad coup. Suddenly, Germany proclaimed the Kriegszustand, which enabled her to complete in secret by mobilisation in its strict sense the preparation of the last eight days. At the same time she despatched an ultimatum to Petrograd, and put to the French Government a question which was in itself but an ultimatum in disguise.

The whole of France lived through those last days of waiting with calmness and gravity. No one concealed from himself the danger; everyone perceived distinctly the threat and its consequences for the country and for himself—in fact, it was this clear perception of danger which supported the efforts made to avert it, and which sustained the hope that the wise Governments of the Triple Entente would succeed in turning it aside. On the afternoon of July 31st the Senators and the most influential Deputies of all groups of opinion assembled at the Palais Bourbon, under the leadership of Jaurès, to examine what final sacrifice could be made to maintain peace and to spare civilisation the horrors of war. These men of good intentions were forced simply to record their own impotence.

Jaurès: An irreparable loss

The same evening Jaurès was killed by a madman. General consternation ensued. Jaurès was a great force; he wielded in France a powerful influence over the masses and enjoyed considerable prestige abroad. By every party it was recognised that his disappearance at such a moment was for France an irreparable loss. Already on the previous evening, in his journal "L'Humanité," his patriotic spirit had found noble expression in advocating national unity, on the ground that from that moment there was no question of politics, but of the country's very existence. This stupid crime—the act of an isolated individual—brought to a premature end the career of a man whose honour was unassailable; at a moment, no doubt, when Jaurès was about to become "le clairon du patriotisme"—to borrow a phrase from Gambetta—at a moment when his eloquence might have become an instrument of national defence.

FRANCE'S HUMANE TREATMENT OF GERMAN PRISONERS.
These striking pictures show how humanely France treated her German prisoners of war, in eloquent contrast to the harsh lot of allied prisoners in Germany. Above is seen the large and comfortable common room of a prison camp, where the inmates had plenty of games with which to amuse themselves. Their faces are an index to their contented lot. In circle: A corner of the prison hospital.

GERMAN PRISONERS WORK FOR FRANCE.
Scene at a noted French seaport, where a number of captured Teutons were employed in the construction of railroads, to facilitate military transport.

PLEASANT TOIL FOR THE CAPTURED HUN.
German soldiers at a French railway-station, where they were employed in useful and apparently not uncongenial labour. Nearly all Frenchmen having been called up, the manual service of German prisoners was distinctly useful.

For a moment reprisals were feared on the part of indignant Socialists, desirous of avenging their respected chief. But who could be made responsible for the act of a maniac? In a letter to Madame Jaurès, the President of the Republic expressed his regrets at the "abominable attack," at a time when "national unity was more than ever necessary." The Government placarded all Paris, and caused to be reproduced in every newspaper a manifesto, in which the Prime Minister, M. Viviani, rendered homage to the great orator so "basely assassinated," to the "Republican Socialist who fought for such noble causes, and who in these difficult days supported by his authority in the interests of peace the patriotic action of the Government."

The whole of France, with no distinction of party or of opinion, rendered to the great citizen a tribute of homage, inspired by a just and sincere feeling of the necessity of solidarity between all Frenchmen at such a tragic moment.

Covenant of "sacred unity" Gustave Hervé, in "La Guerre Sociale," found a formula, which concentrated in compact phrase the universal opinion: "National defence first. Jaurès has been murdered. We shall not murder France!" Over the dead body of Jaurès the covenant of "sacred unity" was sealed.

As was to be expected, numerous and contradictory rumours spread, which the public, for the most part, accepted without belief. On many occasions it was bruited that the war was becoming general in the Balkans, and that the Turks were attacking their enemies of the year before. But wiser heads were troubled especially by what might happen in Belgium. There was a general belief that the road of the invader was sufficiently barred on the Franco-Belgian frontier by the fortresses of Maubeuge, Lille, and Dunkirk; but the public did not know that, some years before, the military administration, in conjunction with Parliament and the Government, had reduced in importance one of these fortresses and dismantled the others.

Uneasiness, too, was to a large extent assuaged when the Belgian Government declared that the territory of Belgium would not be violated; but that, with a view to meeting all eventualities, it was preparing for resistance. Reassured in this direction, public opinion found elsewhere new reasons for confidence. Persistent information was forthcoming to the effect that Italy had already decided to remain neutral in the struggle. A conviction that war was henceforth inevitable had taken root in men's minds; there was a sort of rivalry among the more imaginative and the more ingenious to foresee what turn events would take in the near future. But the most general, serious, and constant preoccupation concerned Britain. Would she

MEMBERS OF THE ALLIES' PERMANENT WAR COUNCIL OUTSIDE THE FRENCH GENERAL STAFF'S HEADQUARTERS.

Reading from left to right: General de Castelnau, in charge of all French Armies on the west front; Sir Douglas Haig, the British Commander-in-Chief; General Wielemans, the Belgian Army representative; General Gilinski, the Russian Army representative; General Joffre, Generalissimo of all the French Armies engaged in the war; General Porro, the Italian Army representative; and Colonel Pechitch, the Serbian Army representative. The important Conference of leading representatives of the Allied Governments held at Paris, March 27-28, 1916, confirmed all the military measures agreed upon by the Permanent War Council.

remain neutral ? Would she suffer German naval squadrons to come and ravage the coasts of Normandy, to disembark troops in the French ports, before the French Fleet—for the most part in the Mediterranean—could arrive to bar the way ? We admired the Germanic cunning which, after the check in Morocco, had invented the pretext of a war with Serbia, which was bound fatally to involve the intervention of Russia, and finally the entry of France into the struggle, but which yet permitted a hope that Britain might discover no treaty violation, and no motive to join the ranks of the belligerents.

All this time, under the veil of Kriegszustand, mobilisation continued in Germany, where the General Staff was chiefly concerned with securing the success of its sudden attack, from which were expected immediately decisive results and crushing victories, which would render the enemy incapable of raising his head. The situation was of such gravity in the last days of July that public opinion began to reflect that even if it suited the wishes of France to insist on maintaining peace at any price, it was becoming particularly dangerous, in face of the German threats, not to make preparations to repulse possible aggression. It would be a crime against the country, it was said, "to postpone French mobilisation any longer," especially when the enemy by anticipatory measures was putting himself in a position to enjoy a striking advantage over France.

THE BRITISH COMMANDER-IN-CHIEF

General Sir Douglas Haig, photographed at the Second Great War Council of the Allies held on March 13th and 14th, 1916, at the General Staff Headquarters of the French Army. Along with other officers of high rank in the armies of the Allies he was appointed a member of the permanent War Council for the conduct of the operations as a whole.

On August 1st, at four o'clock on a Sunday afternoon, mobilisation orders were at last posted all over France. The country had been expecting for several days this measure, which was hailed with sensible relief. It was the first indispensable measure for the safeguarding of our territory, while it was at the same time a supreme means of aiding a pacific solution of the crisis. It was necessary to have an army to lean upon as a basis, and to discourage the aggressor, who would then be less inclined to attack a country in a posture of defence.

In an appeal addressed to the nation, **No parties—only one France** the Government explained and justified the reasons which had led it to decide upon that measure, and ended with the following declaration :

Strong in its ardent desire to reach a pacific solution of the crisis, the Government, protected by necessary precautions, will continue its diplomatic efforts, and it still hopes to succeed. It counts on the self-control of this noble nation to refuse to be led away into unjustified emotion. It counts on the patriotism of all Frenchmen, and knows that there is not one of them who is not ready to do his duty. At this hour there are no parties, there is only France—eternal, peaceful, resolute France ; there is only the Mother Country of right and justice, absolutely united in its calmness, vigilance, and dignity.

The nation rose to the level of the occasion. By its self-control, its unanimity, its calm, it fully justified the confidence reposed in it by the Government. No troubles broke out during the feverish and anguished days which

the country had just lived through since the threat of invasion had united all the citizens ; and since she has been engaged in defending her invaded soil France has not ceased to offer to the world the spectacle of unbroken unity and of inflexible resolution to ensure the triumph of justice and right, to obtain legitimate reparation, and guarantees against the return of such barbaric aggression.

Despite the reassuring explanations of the Government, no one doubted that there would be war, for it would have needed a miracle to calm Germany, seized with bellicose fury, and scenting already the pillage and booty to be reaped in the rich provinces of the East of France up to Paris itself. War, since German madness had imposed it, was accepted as a deliverance—a deliverance not only from the nightmare of torture of the last few days, but also from the continual alarms with which Germany had harassed France for years past—a deliverance from the threats and reiterated insolence of the brutal policy and arrogant diplomacy of a nation afflicted with megalomania —a deliverance, too, from the humiliation of defeat undeserved and unceasingly demanded for forty-four years past by a conqueror swollen with pride and satisfied with his own blackguardism. Moreover, it meant the abolition henceforth of the tyrannical clauses of the Treaty of Frankfort, which hindered and opposed the development of the whole economic activity of France. "We have had enough of it !" was heard on all sides.

Nowhere was there any manifestation of misplaced

GETTING READY FOR THE GERMAN ONSLAUGHT: FORTIFYING PONT-À-MOUSSON WITH SAND-BAGS.

The mitrailleuse and "75" proved so destructive during the terrific fighting for Verdun in March, 1916, that the Germans were seldom able to reach our ally's barbed-wire in large numbers. Sanguinary hand-to- hand fighting, however, occurred in Douaumont, Vaux, and other positions. This photograph shows how the French took precautions to reinforce the arcade of Pont-à-Mousson with sand-bags.

enthusiasm; there was no turbulent agitation, no dis- cordant voice. The spontaneous sacrifice of all provoked a patriotic impulse, which found vent in cheering and acclaiming the regiments on their way to the eastern frontier, in innumerable flags hung out at the windows as on the national fête day, July 14th.

It is difficult for an Englishman to realise what is meant by mobilisation in a country subject to compulsory military service. It means profound disorganisation of civil life, complete disintegration of national activity. Every French citizen at the age of twenty is forced to discharge military duties for a period of three years. After that he remains at the disposition of the military authorities until the age of forty-eight. Each man is furnished with a military booklet, which indicates his position in the Army; the same booklet contains a special notice on blue or red parchment, on which are printed particular directions which it will be his duty to carry out in case of mobilisation. The calling up of men extends over a period of several days, according to whether they belong to the Regular Army or the Regular Army Reserve, to the Territorial Army or the Territorial Army Reserve. The instructions given in the booklet are perfectly simple and impossible to misunder- stand. The name of the soldier, non-commissioned officer, or officer is followed by the name of the town where the depôt of his regiment is situated; next follows an injunction that the man must have rejoined his depôt by the first, second, third . . . tenth, or twelfth day after the mobilisation order has been posted. On the date given, the man sets out on his journey, being assured by his booklet of a free pass on the railway as far as the town where his depôt may be, and where he will be armed and equipped.

The call to arms

Thus, then, during the first days of August, 1914, several millions of Frenchmen responded to the call to arms. Whatever their social position or profession might be— rich or poor, townsmen or peasants—all went off gaily to the depôt to resume their rank, put on their uniforms, and shoulder their rifles. Several millions of men thus brusquely left their occupations or employments, abandoning desk or workshop. Banker and merchant, engineer and manu- facturer, writer and artist, lawyer and doctor, workman and agricultural labourer—all equalised by the same duty of defending the threatened country, leaving behind them home, wife, and children—set out for the great adventure. How many of them will never return!

This formidable movement of men was carried out with complete order, calmness, and regularity. In a few days the depôts and arsenals had equipped and armed these masses of men; the railways transported those who had been mobilised to their depôts, whence they set out again for the frontier, after being assigned to battalions and regiments.

Everything gave place to military necessity. The groups of railways had been militarised ever since the notice of mobilisation was posted, and were exclusively devoted to transporting troops, material, munitions, provisions, according to plans and time-tables drawn up long before and continually brought up to date. For the conveni- ence of civilians there remained on each line no more than four trains a day, one train every six hours. These were "omnibus trains," stopping at every station, of which the times were liable to be changed at any moment, if military necessities demanded, and they might, in case of necessity, be suppressed altogether. As for the transport of goods, only perishable goods were forwarded—by which I mean

Effects of mobilisation

in particular those articles of food which were indispensable for the sustenance of the population.

Under such conditions it is obvious that there could be no question of pursuing one's daily occupation "as usual." The sudden departure of so many men paralysed in a moment the whole activity of the country, and rendered impossible—for the moment, at least—all trade, every industry. Heads of administrative staffs, managers of banks and houses of business, of workshops and factories, etc.—all left their occupations if they had not reached the age-limit of forty-eight. In the large banks, offices, great business houses, and industrial enterprises, this brusque departure of an expert personnel and of specialised workmen caused dislocation. More than one firm was compelled to close its doors.

Response of the women of France In Paris and the great provincial towns the majority of small shopkeepers had shut their shops when they went off to rejoin the Colours at the same time as their assistants. On the shutters they had glued notices, mostly humorous, which revealed in what excellent spirits these modest breadwinners answered the call of duty and sacrificed their personal interests to the defence of the country. In many cases, however, wives bravely took up the task of carrying on the business in the husbands' absence, and a Tricolour placard pasted on the window would be inscribed with the words "Maison Française," followed often by the information that "the proprietor is with the ——th Infantry," artillery, or cavalry.

In the country-side, also, the sudden departure of so many men—farmers and labourers—could not fail to produce deep perturbation at a time when agricultural activity demands most effort, when reaping, harvesting, and vintaging are either begun or on the eve of being undertaken. In these circumstances the women of France showed of what they are capable. After bidding farewell, not without tears, to husbands, sons, and brothers, who exchanged scythe and plough for bayonet and Lebel, they

SHIPPING HORSES TO SALONIKA.
Horses for the French Army being taken on board ship at Marseilles en route for Salonika. Despite the trench warfare and the innovation of the motor-car, horses still had an important part to play.

UNLOADING SUPPLIES OF FLOUR FROM CANADA AT A FRENCH PORT.
Supplies of flour from Canada being unloaded from a ship at a French port. Thanks to the vigilance and efficiency of the allied fleets, the food supplies of Britain and France were maintained very much as in peace times. In circle: Hoisting an ox on to a ship at Marseilles.

AFTER A WAR COUNCIL.
General Joffre shaking hands with M. Briand, the French Premier, after attending a meeting of the War Council in Paris. Standing behind the Commander-in-Chief is General Roques, the French War Minister.

harnessed the few horses left behind by military requisition as being too old for utilisation by the Army, and went off harvesting, storing, and ploughing from the rising of the sun until the hour of its setting empurpled the sky with sanguinary hue. Grandmothers found new vigour in their old limbs; young girls renounced their games, and, with new seriousness in their looks, accepted before the time the heavy fatigue of labour on the farm and in the garden. At night, seated round the hearth at their frugal meal, their thoughts travelled towards the absent, from whom news was awaited with anxious patience; sometimes—too often, alas!—the news came, gloomy and glorious, a brief notification that the father, husband, brother had "fallen on the field of honour."

On the wrinkled faces of grandmothers, on the sunny cheeks of young women and young girls, tears would flow, bitter and burning, and the melancholy silence of the night would be broken by sobs and lamentations. But on the following day, with eyes reddened by a night of tears and features drawn with pain, the heroic women would return to their daily task with sorrow in their souls at the thought of their dear ones whom they would never see again, and who are sleeping their last sleep in the sacred soil which they defended at the price of their lives.

Women of France, all who have seen you at work during the long months of this accursed war **Tribute of respect** render you the homage of affectionate **and admiration** respect and deep admiration which are your due! You are, indeed, worthy companions of those who undertake your defence in the trenches against the fury and atrocities of the Huns.

While the whole country was preparing with so much calm, and in a unanimous spirit of sacrifice for the great trial, the President of the Republic, on August 2nd at noon, signed a decree, proclaiming a state of siege throughout France for as long as the war should last. At the same time the Council of Ministers decided to convoke the Chambers for the following day.

According to the report of the Minister of War, the

state of siege was justified by "the necessity of concentrating all power in the hands of the military authority." The declaration of a state of siege was authorised by various constitutional laws "in cases of imminent peril resulting from foreign war or from an armed insurrection."

The constitutional laws of free England do not permit under any circumstances the establishment of a state of siege. At all times, and in all places, the civil authority reserves to itself supreme power; the people has obtained for itself this prerogative after long struggles, in the course of which the Commons have maintained their independence and the liberty of the subject against all the encroachments of Royal power. In France it is different. The country is nominally a Republic, but its institutions are monarchical. Administration, formidably centralised, is there concentrated in the hands of the Government, which discharges its functions under the more or less efficacious control of Parliament. By virtue of the state of siege, the powers with which the civil authority was invested for the maintenance of order and of the police, passed wholly and immediately to the military authorities. These immediately assumed the right of making perquisitions by day or by night in private houses; of sending to a distance those claimed by the law, and those whose homes were not in the districts subject to a state of siege; of ordering the surrender of arms and munitions, and even of proceeding to search for and to remove the same; of forbidding publications and meetings considered likely to provoke or prolong disturbance.

In short, the administration of justice passed into the hands of military tribunals, whose duty was to take cognisance of crimes and **Suspension of** offences against the security of the State, **individual liberty** against the Constitution, against public order and peace, regardless of the position of the chief offenders and of their accomplices. In a word, as will be plain to anyone reading between the lines of legal jargon, this transference was nothing more or less than the virtual suspension of every individual liberty, of all rights guaranteed by the Constitution. In ordinary times the authority of the municipality, of the prefect, of the Government was constrained to respect certain legal formalities and arrangements, in default of which their decisions might come before the Council of State and were liable to be quashed in case of any legal irregularities. But from the time named—that is, the introduction of a state of siege—military governors might arrive at any decisions they pleased, these having then and there the force of law, without appeal.

It must be admitted that the military power never abused these prerogatives; quite the contrary. In practice it could not replace the civil authority, with which it was content to collaborate and to approve such decisions as the new circumstances required. Those few cases, in which the military power allowed itself to take the initiative, were undoubtedly fortunate instances and received the approval of all well-affected persons—one might say, of the vast majority of the population. And yet it attacked the privileges of two elements, which exercised an almost all-powerful influence on modern democratic society—the Press and the drink interest—to which civil government had always shown themselves full of discretion and of harmful indulgence.

For instance, when the crisis began, the newspapers vied with one another in sensational information, and it was far worse when hostilities had begun. Every hour, from ten in the morning till the late hours of the night, clamorous sheets were issued, special editions containing on each occasion news of which the authenticity was not always certain. The noisy vendors spread themselves over the most animated portions of the boulevards, and through almost the most hidden and peaceful suburbs, bellowing the name of the paper and the number of the edition. The passers-by would purchase the sheet, the inhabitants would come from their houses and purchase it, too, **Deadly blow to the Press** to be rewarded almost invariably by the same deception, since the news announced was almost always a rumour without foundation, or some trivial anecdote.

It must be admitted that the newspapers had some excuse. They were obliged to maintain a fierce struggle for existence. The formidable upheaval caused by mobilisation, and the state of siege which immediately followed, had dealt a deadly blow to quite a number of newspapers, whose existence had always been precarious. Since they subsisted penuriously on subsidies from certain political committees, or on financial enterprises of a more or less risky character, these sheets, suddenly deprived of resources, ceased to appear.

The great dailies were themselves sensibly affected; the majority of advertisement contracts, from which their chief receipts were drawn, were suspended or suppressed. On the other hand, the requisition of means of transport rendered extremely difficult the delivery of enormous quantities of paper, which they required every day, not to mention the fact that the manufactories, losing all their younger personnel, had to relax their production. The less rich appeared in the form of a single sheet of two pages, sometimes of reduced size, **Official control of news** while the more opulent retained a double sheet of four pages.

The problem before them was to maintain their circulation; hence the consecutive editions. Soon, the result of these noisy criers and sensational placards was evident. Public opinion grew visibly nervous and agitated by all this news, of which it was impossible to distinguish between true and false, and ended by believing in the most absurd rumours and the most far-fetched legends. To cut short a state of affairs which led to abuse and might involve dangerous consequences, the military authority did not hesitate to avail itself of the state of siege and to take energetic measures. It decided to publish three official communications a day (soon reduced to two) relating to war news, and that this official news only should be inserted to the exclusion of any other. It forbade the newspapers to appear with big headlines, to be cried in the streets, to be advertised by posters. No newspaper was authorised to issue more than one edition a day, which was bound to appear always at the same hour—an hour which the

SAFEGUARDS AGAINST ASPHYXIATING GAS.
Group of French officers donning their masks before passing through an asphyxiating gas manufactory situated within the battle area on the western front.

AA

GENERAL LYAUTEY VISITING HIS HOME AT CRÉVIC, WANTONLY DESTROYED BY THE GERMANS DURING THE FIRST DAYS OF THE WAR.

Before returning to his post in Morocco, General Lyautey paid a visit to the scene of his once beautiful home at Crévic (Meurthe-et-Moselle). This sector suffered terribly from the first blows of the German onslaught in 1914, and General Lyautey was not surprised to find his house in ruins—savagely destroyed by the Huns because it happened to be the property of one of the most respected chiefs of the French Army.

206

journal was invited by the military authority to fix for itself ; no exception was tolerated.

Finally, every publication, whether daily, weekly, or monthly (including books and pamphlets), must be submitted to the censorship of the military authority. Every newspaper must in convenient time communicate to the Press Bureau its complete "impression"—that is, the entire "proofs" of the paper, exactly as the letterpress would appear—nor must any modification be made except such as were demanded by the censorship.

Extension of the Censorship Protests being useless, the Press submitted to this new régime, with the happiest results for public opinion. Subsequently the censorship was extended to cover political comments, and the Government abused this easy means at its disposal for suppressing criticism, which "hit on the raw," but it is worth noting that this abuse proceeded from the Civil Government and not from the military authority. Disobedience to the orders of the censorship was severely and continuously punished.

The political veteran, M. Georges Clemenceau, an ex-Premier, dared to defy the censorship, which retaliated by simply suppressing "L'Homme Libre," in which newspaper M. Clemenceau exposed without mercy the faults of the Government. It is true that the paper reappeared on the following day under the new title of "L'Homme Enchaîné." But more than once there was left of the indefatigable fighter's article nothing but the title and the signature !

Few newspapers—not one, it may be said—escaped the vigilance of the censorship, which showed itself as inflexible towards the strong as towards the weak. Certainly it was guilty of slips, and even of glaring mistakes ; its severity frequently gave rise to violent protests and was the object of rather spirited debate in Parliament, but the Government had never much trouble in obtaining a large majority to approve of its measures.

The military authority also attacked the sacrosanct "bistro" —that is, the wine seller, café proprietor, the vendor of "apéritifs," of adulterated liqueurs, and other alcoholic poisons. The hours of opening were rigorously fixed. The sale of fermented liquor and of spirits was forbidden for soldiers, except at certain times—to wit, meal-times—while for women it was forbidden altogether.

For the last forty years Parliament had shown culpable weakness in its relations with the drink trade ; it could not have been otherwise, since the drink sellers, or "bistros," both in the towns and in the country, are the most influential electoral agents, to whom the majority of Parliamentarians owe their election. It may be granted that the manufacture and sale of alcohol were scandalously protected by public powers. The most violent and convincing campaigns against the dangers of invading alcoholism never succeeded in obtaining from Parliament the least restriction of the advantages attached to poisoning the public.

On the contrary, the liquor sellers obtained all they wished in the way of shameful concessions from those elected by universal suffrage. But the military authority was under no obligation to what was derisively called "the bistrocracy," and unceremoniously wrenched away its privileges. Soon it even attacked one of the most violent of alcoholic poisons—absinthe. By a simple decree of the Military Governor of Paris—then General Galliéni—the sale of absinthe was strictly forbidden in Paris and throughout the whole territory over which military government extended. Identical measures were enforced in the provinces. A popular movement arose among the better classes, which so strengthened the Government, that the latter ratified the decisions of the military power by forbidding the manufacture, sale, and consumption of absinthe throughout the whole territory of the French Republic, of its Dependencies and Colonies. To anyone who knows what ravages were wrought by the "green enchantress" on the working classes in huge industrial centres, how she filled the asylums with maniacs and weakened the race, this vote of Parliament must seem equal to winning a war.

Frenchmen knew that they had the necessary courage to sustain the shock of a formidable enemy, which attacked them treacherously by violating the frontiers of a neutral country, and they also knew that the success of their resistance depended on their will, their firmness of soul,

CHIEF OF THE FRENCH AERONAUTICAL DEPARTMENT.
Colonel Regnier, head of the French Aeronautical Department, entering his office in Paris.

their coolness. It must be confessed that they nourished strange illusions, shared by other opponents of Germany. Germans have committed a series of capital mistakes in assuming beforehand the complacency of Belgium, the indifference of Britain, the impossibility on the part of France of opposing invasion of her soil and capture of her capital. The military chiefs, advisers of the Kaiser, repeated during the first days of the war that our mobilisation would be hindered by sabotage, thwarted and disorganised by the workmen's syndi- **Teuton calculations at fault** cates ; that a revolution breaking out in Paris would upset the Government and create grave disorders, by which the German armies might profit to reach Paris without striking a blow. With all their foresight, the Germans had not foreseen the "sacred union" and Joffre. On the other hand, the French did not suspect the formidable power of their enemies, the crushing superiority of their arms and numbers. They clung to those antiquated ideas about the value of the individual combatant, about his superiority to mere material. They paid dearly for this mistake. Of what use was the dash of our troops against machine-guns, which mowed them

MAKING AND DESPATCHING SUPPLIES OF "TRENCH TORPEDOES."
Scene in a French munition factory where aerial torpedoes were made. These explosives, on reaching their objective, burst with terrific force and wrought great damage to the German trenches.

upon the eastern line of defence of France, failed ; and notwithstanding repeated efforts, were never able to break the barricade of the four great entrenched camps of Belfort, Epinal, Toul, and Verdun, defended by the élite of French troops. And in what triumphant tones would t h e speaker announce that the enemy had not even succeeded in taking Nancy, an open town, while the French secured the summits of the Vosges and penetrated Alsace, where they soon occupied nearly a hundred localities.

The French people grew daily more conscious of the seriousness of the conflict in which they were engaged. The enthusiasm of the opening days gave place gradually to uneasy calmness, and in spite of all the fears which might naturally be engendered by the deceptive development o f hostilities, the legitimate anguish experienced by all before the menace of invasion never assumed the proportions of panic.

down and prevented all close contact ? What could heroic bravery avail against the hurricane of shells rained on them by the enemy ?

One had dreamed of formidable encounters, in which the "furia francese" should have irresistibly flung back the hostile hordes and driven them as far as the farther side of the Rhine. The opposite to this happened, and public sentiment, taken aback at first, was not slow to accept this defensive war, preceded by a retreat, which might cause the worst disasters to be apprehended. But even while repeating to themselves that they would know how to resist the invaders, that they would " nibble " at them (according to the phrase attributed to General Joffre), Frenchmen refused to admit as an irrefutable dogma the material superiority of the German Army, the preponderance of scientific over heroic warfare. In conversation, an advocate was always found to maintain that it was to the personal value of the French soldier as a combatant that Germany was indebted for the two great checks to her western offensive ; to prove that, in spite of the great number of their machine-guns and their heavy artillery, the German armies of Strassburg and Metz, which rushed

The laconic nature of official communiqués left room for optimism. They confined themselves to speaking of the operations in Lorraine and Alsace, so that nothing was known by the people at large of the formidable Battles of Mons and Charleroi. It must not be forgotten that the newspapers were forbidden to publish the German communiqués. Still, rumours ran, putting things at their worst, in which the very exaggeration prevented sensible people from giving any credence, though they furnished Gallic imagination with a plentiful pabulum, since even the sturdiest optimists found in them a reason for contemplating disasters, in the possibility of which they refused to believe, but the consequences of which everyone accustomed himself beforehand to foresee. Thus the surprise was less violent when bad news arrived.

Government and public opinion

The manner in which news was distilled, a drop at a time, deserves to be related. The Government seems to have dreaded particularly the nervousness of public opinion. Was it justified ? Some praised its prudence, others found occasion for reproach. But when one reflects that in tragic circumstances the whole of a great nation was satisfied with the four or five lines of official news vouchsafed to it twice a day, it is hard to believe that it would not have supported at once the knowledge of the whole truth, however painful it might be. It even seems to those who at the time were in a position to feel the pulse of opinion, that the people of France felt humiliated by this lack of confidence. This was the impression of those who took part in the daily life of the population both in Paris and in the provinces.

In the luxurious cafés, frequented by merchants and others of the middle class, as well as at the bars of the "marchands de vin," where the spokesmen of the humbler classes love to perorate, conversation revealed the same

WOMEN'S WAR WORK IN FRANCE.
Women munition workers in a French factory welding together the parts of aerial torpedoes. It required great courage to undertake this critical task, and the women wore special shields to protect their eyes.

French munition makers working on nose=pieces of aerial torpedoes.

Jovial incident at a French railway-station: A "Poilu," laden with souvenirs, greets British soldiers with a cordial handshake.

1870—1916. A French soldier of to-day, visiting a military club, relates his experiences to veterans who fought the Huns in '70.

Modern men=at=arms: French infantry on furlough passing Notre Dame, Paris.

results ; nowhere was importance attached to the acts and attitude of the Government and of the Parliament. A few politicians who attempted to push themselves into notice drew upon themselves remarks that were the reverse of indulgent. Every heart was tortured by the same anxiety, and the hopes of all were centred on the Army, which was known to be at grips with a formidable enemy, and for which decisive and rapid triumph was desired with trembling fervour. All France seemed listening for the echo of cannon ; by a kind of collective intuition, in the poverty of news allowed to her, she guessed that the day of battle was near at hand—and with it the enemy.

When an official telegram made the laconic announcement that "German cavalry have occupied Brussels," public opinion was not extravagantly alarmed. For the invaded Belgians there was unanimous sympathy. In conversation, stress was laid on the solid support afforded to French resistance by the existence of such strongholds as Maubeuge and Lille. Also, when at a later stage one learned that "the great battle between the bulk of the Franco-British forces and the bulk of the German forces" was in progress, the most fantastic conjectures were rife. Ingenuity was taxed to imagine the details of a gigantic encounter on the historic field of Waterloo, where the Kaiser's dream of hegemony should be shattered like that of Napoleon. An impatient public awaited the issue of the great battle, concerning which one was told nothing in vague and embarrassed phraseology. Soon uneasiness drew closer, and suddenly a communiqué announced that "the parties of cavalry, which had shown themselves two days before in the regions of Lille, Roubaix, and Tourcoing, had appeared on the preceding day in the region of Douai." This was incomprehensible. Why did the communiqués speak no more of the great battle announced a week previously ? How had the enemy managed to cross the frontier and advance so far ?

It says a great deal for the French people that they were not yet alarmed, in spite of these reticences and obscurities. Men shrugged their shoulders at all this mystery, which was interpreted without anger as a sign of distrust on the part of a timid Government which doubted the patriotism of the nation.

But soon the gravity of the situation was such that it became impossible to leave the country and the capital any longer in ignorance of the danger which nothing now seemed able to avert. Those only had information who found in English, Italian, or Swiss journals the German communiqués, which the French Press was forbidden to publish. But this knowledge was confined to a very small number of persons in the more cultivated classes, and the bulk of the public had no idea of what was happening. All at once, falling brusquely in the midst of this uncertainty compounded of hope and anguish, like a stone dropped in a pool, appeared a short communiqué saying : "The situation from the Somme to the Vosges remains the same as yesterday."

Impossible to describe the consternation caused by this piece of news from end to end of France

The Germans had reached the Somme ! That meant Amiens, eighty miles from Paris—at the very moment when it had been hoped that they had been crushed by the Franco-British forces on the field of Waterloo.

The deception was bitterly cruel. One painful question tortured every heart : Are we already **M. Viviani's** defeated ? But no one would admit it, **Coalition Ministry** no one despaired, there was no loss of control, or panic.

The Government had been reconstituted two days before into a Coalition Ministry, presided over by M. Viviani, and including MM. Delcassé, Briand, Millerand, Ribot, and two Socialists, MM. Marcel Sembat and Jules Guesde. These statesmen inspired the whole country with confidence, and their presence in power undoubtedly contributed in a large measure to reassure the population.

Those who lived in Paris during the fortnight which preceded the Battle of the Marne will never forget their experience. Everyone now knew that the Germanic hordes were pouring like a waterspout on Paris. It was known, also, that the entrenched camp of Paris had been in an utterly neglected state at the beginning of the war, and that it could **Paris contemplates** not have been put in a state of adequate **Teutonic pollution** defence in the course of the three preceding weeks. The fate of Belgian towns proved that the double girdle of forts surrounding Paris was unable, even had the forts been furnished with the most powerful artillery, to prevent the Germans from entering the town. Was Paris to undergo Teutonic pollution ?

SOLDIER AND SAILOR TOO !
Rear-Admiral Lacaze, appointed Acting Minister of War in place of General Galliéni during the latter's indisposition. As Minister of Marine, he was one of the French representatives at the first meeting of the Allied Council of War in Paris, November 17th, 1915.

The population remained quite calm, in spite of certain wicked rumours circulated by one or two anti-Republican sheets, which falsely accused of treason such leaders as Generals Sarrail and Percin, whose sole crime was that before the war they had openly professed Republican ideas. These culpable attempts to break at such a moment the compact of "sacred union" had not the least success, and earned for those who ventured them the rebuke and the contempt of decent men. However, it is a common, historical phenomenon—when a nation suffers a reverse, obscure mischief-makers are always to be found to suggest to the credulous a suspicion that they are betrayed, and to hand over at once to vengeance the very men in some cases who have best served their country, as was most certainly true of the generals disloyally accused. But such was the moral of the French nation that these criminal insinuations took no hold.

PRECAUTIONS IN RHEIMS.
The vigilance of our ally was so strict that a spy seldom got through the lines. Even the inhabitants of Rheims had to carry their papers with them, and submit them for inspection.

BRAVE WOMEN OF SHELL-SHATTERED RHEIMS.
No men were left in the city of Rheims, all having gone on service with the Colours. This photograph shows a group of elderly French women round a milk-cart. In centre: A scene at Noyon, in German occupation. A queue of poor women are waiting for the distribution of bread.

The invasion spread. The enemy advanced by forced marches towards Paris, into which were already flowing streams of refugees from the north and the east, who disseminated tales of the atrocities committed upon the unarmed population. The worst was expected and prepared for. In the town itself and the populous outlying districts every facility was afforded to the population of departing before the arrival of the enemy. All those who were able to take refuge in the provinces on their estates, or with relations or friends, were invited to go, to diminish the total of useless mouths in case Paris should be invested or occupied. The trains which returned to the west or the south in quest of troops took away thousands of people. The central administration and the municipalities collaborated actively to ensure the feeding of the population, which remained large in spite of all the departures. The same bodies were also occupied in arranging ration lists and food tickets. All this was done in most orderly fashion, and carried out with diligent activity.

It seemed as if the capital could hardly escape from the lot which threatened it. If, in spite of all, Parisians—and with them all France—still clung to hope, there was some merit in doing so, for every day the news became less and less reassuring. However, the worst pessimists were obliged to recognise that three great facts dominated the situation. First, the unanimous impulse which had inspired the whole nation and its unalterable resolve never to yield, never to be influenced by the hardest reverses, and to resist to the bitter end.

Sources of encouragement

On the other hand, the news of the Russian advance encouraged the most despondent. The term "steam-roller" had captured popular imagination, which already pictured the Russian masses pouring out like a devastating torrent as far as Berlin. If the so-called "steam-roller" accomplished none of the miracles expected of it, it is undeniable that the certainly fabulous hopes founded on it contributed in a fashion which can scarcely be exaggerated to the preservation of the moral of the sorely-tried French population.

But what sustained in a manner infinitely less conjectural the courage of France was the collaboration of Britain—of the whole British Empire. Future historians will not find in official archives any documents to tell them with what eager suspense France, at the beginning of August, awaited the decision of Britain. Still, the fact should be known. The numerous friends whom the British possessed amongst the French followed attentively all that was said and done across the Channel.

The declarations in Parliament of Ministers indicated clearly for one who knows how to interpret reticences and reservations an inevitable decision. But certain opinions publicly expressed, and certain articles in newspapers, which the French Press commented upon very naturally, gave rise to some apprehension. "Is England going to help us?" Such was the question, universally debated and answered in the affirmative by those who had studied British politics closely during the last fifteen years.

In the public mind a conviction had acquired strength that if Britain made the irreparable mistake of abstaining from the conflict, Germany's chances of crushing France were enormously increased. But if the all-powerful British squadrons barred the North Sea to the Germans, and kept the French coasts intact, then our armies might hope to get the better of their formidable adversary. Accordingly, when on the morning of Wednesday, August 5th, the newspapers announced that Britain had grasped the sword of justice to defend the honour of treaties impudently violated by the modern Huns, there was all over France an outburst of joy. Men greeted one another with the words "England is with us!" And these four words were charged with a significance scarcely to be expressed by those who uttered them. They implied a certainty that French ports would not be bombarded and burned before the French squadrons could return from the Mediterranean; that the German army corps would not be flung on our coasts to take our defences in the rear. We gained confidence with the feeling that we were no longer alone, but had with us and near us both a friend and a support enlisted in the same cause, for our Russian ally was far away and we had never seen him as you might say, while the Englishman was a neighbour who visited us and whom we visited, and Britain was for France the Mother of Parliaments, the country of individual liberty, the great democracy. For ten years the popularity of the Entente Cordiale had increased a friendship which answered to the intimate feelings of two nations, once they had set aside all the old disputes which might have provoked estrangement.

In spite of all the quarrels which led them to fight one another so long and so often, ever since William of Normandy became King of England, French and English have never ceased to respect one another, having always observed in their struggles the code of honour and the rules of humanity.

Popularity of the Entente Cordiale

PROVIDING FOR THE POOR OF PARIS.
French soldiers' wives who waited daily at the Paris "Covent Garden" market for traders who sold, at low prices, vegetables left over from the previous day, thereby helping to solve the problem of housekeeping in a practical and sympathetic manner.

REPRESSING THE "PROFITEERS."
The French Government was determined not to allow traders to exploit the war situation and overcharge those who could least afford to pay. This photograph shows a group of French women collecting tickets for coal from a Government depot. In centre: Children attending a temporary school in Northern France.

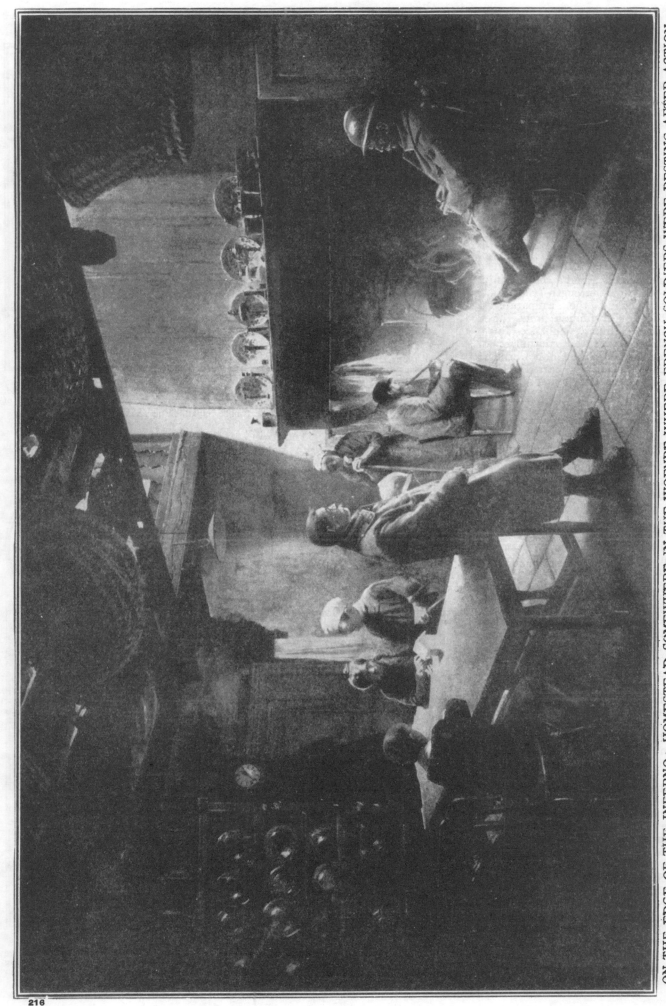

ON THE EDGE OF THE INFERNO: HOMESTEAD SOMEWHERE IN THE WOEVRE, WHERE FRENCH SOLDIERS WERE RESTING AFTER ACTION.

It is currently admitted in France that the word of an Englishman is his bond, and when such a conviction has been implanted in the popular mind nothing can eradicate it. It was this reputation and this flattering esteem which formed the basis of that feeling of sympathy that made possible the Anglo-French rapprochement and increased the popularity of the Entente Cordiale. Once more French confidence in Britain's word was justified,

French confidence justified and that under circumstances when the existence of two nations was at stake as well as the future of humanity in opposition to a people which was destroying the very foundations of that social contract without which civilisation is impossible. "England is with us!" It seemed as if henceforward all was safe. Britain and France united, with their allies present and to come, were defenders of right and justice, champions of a cause which could not fail.

Perhaps French public opinion did not thoroughly grasp the part which Britain was to take in the conflict. Everybody in France knew that the British Fleet was far superior to all the fleets in the world, and that it would very soon annihilate the German squadrons if the latter should risk an encounter. But the German ships prudently returned to the Kiel Canal as soon as the British appeared in the neighbourhood of Heligoland. So complete was their retirement that the British Fleet, having cleared the seas of a few "raiders," which professed to annoy it, was compelled to limit its rôle to a silent surveillance of the North Sea and to remain on guard at the mouth of the lair where the German men-of-war were hidden.

The naval actions off the coast of Chili and at the Falkland Islands were the only ones capable of striking popular imagination, which, meanwhile, was kept in breathless suspense by the alternate offensive movements on the western front. Soon certain difficulties and internal controversies in England found an echo across the Channel, and French opinion asked if the efforts made by Britain were proportionate to the risk she ran and to the sacrifices to which France had heroically consented from the beginning—frightful losses, the complete paralysis of her entire commercial activity, and the concentration of every effort and every energy on one sole end—the repulsion and the defeat of the aggressor.

This uneasiness was purely temporary. It was not difficult to convince French opinion that the British nation had realised the gravity of the danger and the importance of the interests at stake. Many contingents came to reinforce the British troops at the front; the importance of the naval battles and of the control of the seas was explained, the immense industrial efforts of Great Britain were described, and the formidable task which she had imposed upon herself of creating an army equal to those of the Continent; so the French confidence returned with its enthusiasm and cordiality.

In speeches, in the Press, in books there were constant allusions to "true, faithful Britain," and the Englishman replied to this recognition of an essential quality in his character by paying homage to "French heroism." On both sides a sincere effort was made towards a better

mutual understanding and a closer mutual appreciation, which effort was facilitated by reciprocal esteem that sprang from brotherhood in arms. If the French showed recognition of the prodigious task accomplished by the British Empire, the British rendered full justice to France, their testimony of admiration being greeted as a precious sign of approval. The series of articles on "The Achievement of France," which appeared in the "Times," was translated into French and circulated by the thousand. "The French are generous," said the author of these articles, "always ready to praise the good qualities of others, but we ought to say in our turn that it is they who have made the greatest efforts."

It is impossible to evaluate and difficult to compare anguish and moral suffering. The population has had a large share in these, without speaking of those endured by the inhabitants of the invaded regions. Right up to the Battle of the Marne, after a few days of hope, we beheld the black spectre of defeat, the almost realised menace of annihilation. Paris, in particular, had some dark hours to live through. Life there seemed to have stopped, all

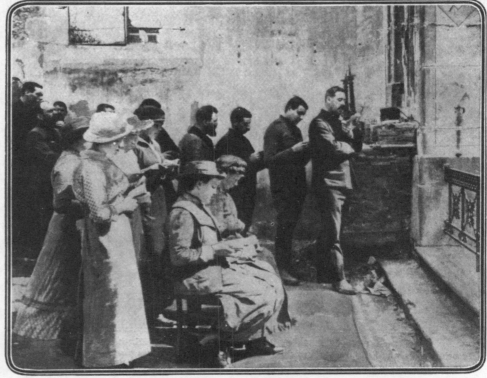

SUNDAY MORNING IN A SHELL-WRECKED CHURCH.
Service was still held in this ancient little edifice on the French front, though shells had intruded upon its sanctity. The congregation shown in our photograph was composed of girls from the adjacent village and men from the trenches.

activity to have dried up. Since the mobilisation order, the motor-'buses had been requisitioned; not a single one was running in the streets. The tramways, the Métropolitain, the Nord-Sud line, impeded by shortage of personnel, had considerably reduced their services, which ceased by nine o'clock in the evening. Theatres, cinemas, places of amusement were **German aeroplanes** closed. Cafés shut at eight, and restaurants at nine. National museums were **over Paris** closed, their most precious contents having been removed as far as Toulouse to save them at once from the dangers of bombardment, fire, and Teutonic pillage.

When German aeroplanes came to fly over Paris and dropped a few bombs, no one was afraid. Certainly it was a depressing sensation to feel that the Germans were descending the Valley of the Oise, where no line of defence could stop them. In those days of tropical heat it became a distraction for the populace to visit convenient spots

THE CAMP-FIRE IN THE SNOWY VOSGES.
French soldiers who had been through the inferno of Verdun resting in a pine-covered corner of the Vosges Forest.

talk to." "We, fresh troops," said the grinning Turcos and the black sharpshooters, bathed in sweat under the weight of arms and equipment. And some days later, under the command of General Maunoury, the impetuous attack of these valiant troops rolled the German regiments headlong back on the Ourcq, and began the great offensive, prepared and commanded by Joffre.

Being anxious not to let itself be imprisoned in Paris, if Joffre's plan should fail, the Government had prepared for departure, and sent to Bordeaux the archives and the employees of the Ministers. On the day following this departure, General Galliéni, the new Military Governor of Paris, issued to the Army and the inhabitants the following proclamation :

The members of the Government of the Republic have left Paris to give new impetus to national defence. I have received the order to defend Paris against the invader. This order I shall carry out to the end.

Although foreseen and expected, this transfer of the Government confirmed the fears of an investment or of an attack on Paris. But if even the most optimistic felt hope tottering, the Parisians greeted with superb coolness the decision taken by the Government from weighty motives and after mature reflection. It was necessary, above all, to ensure "national continuity," as was explained in a proclamation signed by the President of the Republic and by the fourteen Ministers who formed the Cabinet :

. . . Without peace or truce, without cessation or slackening, will continue the sacred struggle for the nation's honour, and for reparation of violated right. . . "Endure and fight on " must be the motto of the allied armies. Endure and fight on, while on the seas the British aid us in cutting the enemy's communications with the world. . . . Let us all be worthy of these tragic moments. We shall gain the final victory. We shall gain it by indefatigable will, by endurance, and by tenacity. A nation which does not wish to perish, and which, in order to live, does not recoil from suffering or sacrifice, is sure of victory.

Paris seemed emptier than ever, but the moral of the population was intact. Besides, one was reminded that the perimeter of the fortifications erected since the last war covered a circumference of nearly a hundred miles, and that investment would require a million men. Every sort of pretext for hope was found, even at that time, when the enemy had almost reached the gates of the capital. This was not due to levity **Civic courage in** or ignorance. Everyone knew the **the capital** gravity of the situation, and in the suburbs the industrial population was ready for every sacrifice to defend the town, as General Galliéni had promised.

The same civic courage inspired all and dictated one tragic duty—to confront the worst dangers with a firm heart. What would have happened if the Germans had been able to attempt to take Paris by a sudden stroke ? The answer is better left in the region of conjecture.

But the African troops had come in the nick of time

and watch for the arrival of Taubes in the sky, which continued unalterably blue. The crowd thronged about the Heights of Montmartre, the Arc de Triomphe, along the Champs Elysées ; on the terrace of the Tuileries and the stone balustrades which surround the Place de la Concorde people sat and remained for whole days at a time in order that they might lose no incident in the aerial spectacle, when murderous Taubes were chased away by French aviators. Between two bombs the airmen of the Boches would drop insolent messages, announcing their impending arrival.

On several evenings in succession, however, the promenaders, who profited by the comparative coolness of the evening to stroll about, were surprised by an extraordinary sight. Just at nightfall, along the wide roads which run from the south of Paris to the north, there passed an interminable procession of one regiment after another. All the African troops, those from Morocco and Algeria, passed thus through Paris in the night, seen only by those whom the chance of a capricious walk took that way. But the rumour very soon spread, and the Parisians knew that the army of Von Kluck was likely to " find someone to

A cannon, dating from 1881, of 155 mm. (6 in.) calibre, that did excellent duty in the defence of Verdun. In spite of its old pattern, this was a favourite type of weapon in the French heavy artillery. During one portion of the fighting at Verdun this particular cannon fired three thousand shells in forty-eight hours.

OLD BUT NOT OBSOLETE: CANNON THAT HELPED TO HOLD VERDUN.

to reinforce the army of Paris, and it was soon known that a battle was raging between our forces and those German troops which were trying to turn the entrenched camp.

One heard the cannons. The great guns of the forts, it was said, were firing on the enemy's advance-guard, but it was no more than the echo carried by the east wind. The anxiety of the whole population reached its maximum. It was as though people no longer dared to speak, but greeted one another in silence, as though they were awaiting sentence of life or death from a throw of the dice. Those were tragic hours which those who lived through them will never forget.

Victory of the Marne   Suddenly the communiqués, while retaining their brevity, lost their tone of vague embarrassment. They became more definite, and gave an impression that something decisive was happening. It was the communiqué of September 8th which announced that the battle was general, and during three days Paris and the whole of France anxiously awaited the result. Those three days were long. The defeat of our troops would mean the enemy in Paris almost immediately.

At last the communiqué of the 11th said that "the Franco-British troops had crossed the Marne," and on the 12th General Joffre, in his General Order No. 15, told the troops: "The battle which has been in progress for the last five days is ending in incontestable victory." On the 13th official despatches announced that "the general movement of retreat of the Germans was continuing before the Franco-British troops, who have reached the lower course of the Aisne," and from Amiens to Nancy, passing by Soissons, Rheims, and Verdun, the enemy was recoiling. It was the victory of the Marne, called by the Germans "a strategical movement," which the Wolff Agency was careful not to announce to the population of the Fatherland or to the world in general.

If all France felt relieved, Paris experienced veritable joy. This joy found no noisy expression in cries, acclamations, or in flying flags. The same coolness, the same calm and restrained temper which had faced danger, greeted victory. "Paris is saved," we said, "but the enemy is still formidable, and **Vandalism of the invader** a whole rich region of France still remains to be freed." This first benefit of the national effort was accepted by men who at once proceeded to think of new efforts to be dared.

The Germans had not succeeded in enclosing the Franco-British armies in their pincers, but they were still riveted to the soil of France and attempting a new envelopment in the north. There followed in turn the Battles of Artois, of the Yser, and of Ypres, which broke the great German offensive and annihilated the German hopes of victory on the western front.

In the course of those months of struggle the Huns, against whom it had been possible to establish proved acts of brigandage, murder, violation, pillage, and incendiarism, added to their record such feats of vandalism as

SYMBOLS OF "LA BELLE ALLIANCE."

On March 9th, 1916, following closely upon the decoration of a number of brave Canadian soldiers by the French military authorities, General Sir E. H. Allenby presented British honours to French units who had distinguished themselves at the front. This photograph shows a number of steel-helmeted veterans marching past General Allenby after the ceremony.

FRENCH CIVILIANS UNDER THE HEEL OF THE INVADER.

French villagers, chiefly old men and women, being marshalled by the German soldiery during the process of turning a captured village into a military position. The plight of the peasantry was pitiful. With their scanty treasures, snatched hastily from the homes they were forced to abandon, they were driven from place to place, often being left without food or shelter.

the bombardment and burning of Rheims, Arras, Soissons, Ypres, the destruction without strategic necessity of historic monuments and open towns. They came by night through the air to assassinate peaceful civilians by hurling bombs on habitations thronged with women and children. They waged war by the most cruel and treacherous methods, and the sole result of their crimes has been to heap up against the Huns a contempt and a hatred which will remain vividly intense in the hearts of many generations.

During the long months of defensive war which followed, France maintained this state of mind, inspired by calm confidence in her strength and in the justice of her cause, by her immovable resolve to repulse the enemy from her country and to shatter the militarism responsible for the war and for its horrors.

To reach this end her sacrifices were enormous. All the national resources were devoted to the war, to the detriment of economic activity, paralysed by the sudden and immediate call to arms of so many millions of men.

Stern resolve in sorrow No list of casualties was published, but from the number of people in mourning whom one met in towns and villages, in Paris, and in the provinces, a conviction was soon reached that perhaps not a single French hearth was to be found which had not been stricken by the death of some dear one. The seriousness of the first months of the war was sustained by the series of all these bereavements, and even, one might say, accentuated by a universal note of pathos and melancholy, which far from producing a feeling of lassitude, as no doubt the Germans expected, provoked a terribly grim earnestness about the prosecution of the war.

Certainly, the external aspect of life was radically changed. Fashion shed its extravagances, but the French-woman, even at the worst moments, remained a woman of taste, and with her instinct of elegance applied to her costume that simplicity which was at once becoming and attractive. All social festivities were by tacit consent abolished. How could amusement exist at a time when all the young and middle-aged men were with the Army, and when so many fathers and mothers, brothers and sisters, wives and fiancées had lost the sole object of their affections and their hopes ?

Spirit of Old France

There were no more receptions—luncheons, teas, dinners, or ceremonious parties. People continued, of course, to see one another, to meet, and exchange visits, but discreetly, almost silently, and to testify more clearly to this reserve they renounced all the outward signs of previous social etiquette. Women, as well as men, abandoned evening dress, and it would have seemed a violation of this tacit convention for a man to wear his " smoking " jacket or for a woman to be " décolletée."

All these changes, which were reflected in the most ordinary habits of daily routine, helped to deceive a super-ficial observer. Abroad, as in France itself, it was said and repeated in a hundred keys that a miracle had happened, and that a new France had suddenly been born. Do not believe it ! France who offered such obstinate resistance to German aggression is the same France that has always existed ; the army which fought at the Marne, at Nancy, at Ypres, at Arras, at Soissons, at Verdun is not composed of soldiers created by a miracle to suit the needs of the hour, but of men born between 1866 and 1896. And the rest of the French nation—men and women, old men and children—who endure the counter-strokes of war, its predations and sacrifices, its pains and griefs ; who give their manhood, their money, their labour, all they have in the world—the whole people of France has been during the war what it always was before. Only it was not fully known, it had been calumniated, and the nature of man is such that rather than admit himself to be in error, he prefers to assert that things have changed.

On the other hand, it should not be imagined that France had become a peevish and doleful country, where **Paris herself again** everyone wears a sour face. Gradually, as the certainty grew that the Allies held the enemy at bay and would finish by beating him, public life, while remaining serious, became more animated.

The trench war, which was drawn out to such interminable length, made it possible to grant frequent leave to the troops. In Paris, one by one, a few theatres reopened, reviving on their bills pieces that had been successes before the war, while others produced revues, in which actualities were caricatured, and, in spite of the tragic circumstances of the moment, satire and the comic spirit found free vent, so far as the strict military censorship allowed.

CELEBRATION OF MASS IN THE FIELD.
Artillery caisson as a Communion table. French soldier priest celebrating Mass in the presence of his company, not far from the zone of operations. The war gave a new solemnity to religious services.

Officers and soldiers on leave soon became assiduous patrons of all pleasure resorts ; the restaurants, thanks to them, resumed animation, and in concert-halls, music-halls, cinemas, steel-helmeted heads were undoubtedly the most numerous. During the entr'acte it was by no means a rare thing to see in the foyer of a theatre uniforms which bore traces of the campaign, and which the wearers had not troubled to change, so eager were they to profit without losing a moment by the three or four evenings which their leave put at their disposal. One of my friends, an interpreter in the British Army, having obtained a week's leave after nineteen months' campaigning, spent six evenings in the theatre and reserved only one to be spent with his family.

Another friend, an aviator officer, who had to come with his machine to a camp near Paris, and was obliged to fly off on the following morning, profited by the opportunity to pass an evening in town. Regardless of the fact that he had with him only his professional outfit—enhanced, by the way, by the Legion d'Honneur and the Croix de Guerre—he appeared in that garb at the rendezvous hastily arranged by telephone, and no one was surprised to see thus attired,

in a restaurant blazing with light and in a gorgeously decorated theatre, that tall young fellow, full of dash, gaiety, and youth, who had so often risked his life, and was prepared to risk it again as often as he should receive the order, and obtain honour by doing so.

Officially, or through the intervention of various societies, special performances were periodically organised for the benefit and entertainment of wounded convalescents of the Home Army and of Colonial troops. The great provincial towns followed this example, and the companies of the endowed theatres organised, under official patronage, tours in the war zone to supply men in the field with the distraction of the best pieces in their répertoire.

At the beginning of the war, during the long retreat to the Marne, grave anxiety had been felt concerning medical arrangements. The particularly murderous character of the battles, in which men were mown down by heavy artillery and machine-guns, overtaxed the organisation of ambulances both in the front and at the rear, and the removal of such an unforeseen number of wounded exacted efforts for which one was hardly prepared. In Parliament and in the Press serious agitation was manifested, and in fact it was owing to his vigorous reproaches in this connection that M. Clemenceau was indebted for the suppression of his journal, "L'Homme Libre," transformed on the following day into "L'Homme Enchaîné."

When the Germans had been defeated, and operations on the front brought to a standstill, the reorganisation of the medical service was most rapid, and it worked afterwards in such a way as to give general satisfaction. From the first it had been remarkably seconded by the admirable organisation of the Red Cross, composed of three societies—the Société de Secours aux Blessés Militaires (the Society for Aiding Wounded Soldiers), the Society of French Ladies, and the Union of the Women of France ; all three attached, by official decree, to the Service de Santé Militaire.

With branches reaching into the smallest towns of France, these societies had at disposal a body of volunteers, of ladies more or less instructed in the art of aid to the wounded. Since the outbreak of hostilities they were in a position to make use of more than 1,600 buildings—high schools, colleges, schools, large and small hotels, and private residences, where they installed in a few days more than 100,000 beds. From the Channel to the Pyrenees and the Riviera the women of France entered upon close rivalry of eager devotion to receive and attend to the countless maimed victims of that terrible carnage. A large number stayed in the war zone, in towns unceasingly bombarded by Teu- **Woman's mission of mercy** tonic barbarism, and paid with their lives the price of motherly devotion to wounded soldiers. Many were named in military Orders of the Day for acts of heroism and bravery which reflect honour on their sex.

From sheer sense of duty and love of country, women of every class multiplied their efforts to help in assuaging misery and mourning. The works founded and maintained by them form a list which, as compiled by M. Vallery-Radot, the son-in-law of the great Pasteur, fills for Paris and its outskirts alone a complete volume. It was a woman who had the idea of the "Army Orphanage,"

Men wearing respirators ramming home the powder charge into slender, tapered shells with mallets and mandrels, after the requisite quantity had been poured in. A scene in one of the great munition workshops of France.

Pouring "T.N.T." (trinitrotoluol), which was in the form of a thick brown liquid, into shells. Despite its thickness this deadly explosive could be poured quite freely through the funnels. The French called it "tolite."

SCENES IN FRENCH MUNITION FACTORIES: LOADING SHELLS WITH EXPLOSIVES.

founded for the purpose of taking under its protection the war orphans whose families lack means to support them.

The idea was barely broached before it was welcomed with boundless enthusiasm. The President of the Republic, the Presidents of the Senate and the Chamber, all the members of the Government, the most notable personages in Paris and the provinces, in business, in finance, in trade, in politics and art, accorded to this scheme at its birth the most eager patronage, and Parliament voted State aid to a project which in the first instance was to have been private.

The young father, stricken down by German shell or bullet while defending the liberty of his country and the independence of his fellow-countrymen, gained the assurance that his little boy or girl, left in a mother's charge with no other resources than the meagre sum **The Army Orphanage** officially assigned, would henceforth be cared for, brought up, and educated under the auspices of a great and noble institution, possessed of every means to make these orphans into men and women capable, when peace should come, of working for the greatness and prosperity of the country.

To women, too, must be attributed that charming idea of the "Godmothers" (Marraines)—an idea which quickly spread to England. Among the combatants at the front there was a fair number of "lonely soldiers"; there were also all those who came from the invaded provinces, and were deprived of all news of their families, so that they never received a letter or a parcel to sweeten the rough reality of life in the trenches.

Generous women undertook the rôle of "understudies," and with all sorts of attentions and much tact took the place of their families for these isolated sons of France. When the need of "Marraines" was satisfied, another woman invented the plan of "adopting a soldier at the front," and appealed to the young in schools, high schools, and colleges, both of boys and girls. A great many people had not the means of carrying out an "adoption" separately; but by co-operation, a group of children in a class would easily collect a sum sufficient to send the "poor, grown-up comrade" who was fighting for them a parcel of little comforts and a short letter of inspiriting sympathy. This plan, while rendering service to the soldiers, conveys a lesson of mutual aid, of patriotism and humanity, which might well exert a lifelong influence on the child engaged in it.

Side by side with these voluntary works, created and developed by feminine energy, was the collaboration of women in social activity to make up for the absence of men, and to carry on those activities and employments which lay within their power. The Frenchwoman, as a rule, has no desire for man's work, and there is no rush on her part for those more or less athletic posts which attract young Englishwomen of all classes. She hates the idea of becoming masculine; even in doing man's work she refuses to look unattractive, and she found a way of remaining pretty in spite of the caps and unsightly overalls which in certain cases she was compelled to wear. Externally, by this carefulness to remain "feminine," she signified her pride in being a woman; at the same time, by her energy, intelligence, and courage she signified her power of equality with man—with the husband, father, or brother who had gone off to fight.

Wherever possible, the working men's wives and daughters replaced their male relatives, punching tickets in the "Métro" and on the trams, becoming clerks and cashiers in banks, post-offices, large and small shops, and all places of business allowed by the war to continue. They were even in some cases entirely substituted for men, and assumed the management in milliners' and costumiers' establishments, and all the essentially feminine trades, even in provision trades, with the exception of those appertaining to butchers and bakers.

Yet in the country and in the small towns, women took upon themselves the arduous labour of making bread. The newspapers gave wide publicity to a letter which M. Poincaré, President of the Republic, wrote to a young girl of seventeen, who took the place of her father and brother at the furnace when they were called up, and supplied bread to an **President and** entire locality. Many similar letters were **girl baker** published, among them one addressed to a young country girl of sixteen, left alone on a farm with her invalid mother. She succeeded in ploughing, with a primitive implement and an old horse, fifty acres of ground, in sowing and harvesting the same. Innumerable were the examples of this masculine courage on the part of Frenchwomen.

German aggression, and the gigantic struggle which ensued, have revealed a France unknown—misknown—too often decried and slandered—a France which, while capable of every sort of heroism, showed itself also capable of tenacious endurance, of irrefragable firmness in resolution and sacrifice—a France which was the worthy ally of the unconquered and unconquerable British Empire.

TESTING GUN-CARRIAGES OF THE FRENCH "75's."
Method employed at the Creusot Works in France as a test for the carriage axles of the famous French gun. The carriage was driven round at such a speed that any defect became manifest at once.

MAGNIFICENT TYPES OF

CHAPTER CIX.

CAUCASIAN SOLDIERS.

THE RENEWED RUSSIAN OFFENSIVE AND THE FALL OF ERZERUM.

By F. A. McKenzie, author of "From Tokyo to Tiflis."

Opening of Russia's 1916 Campaign—Operations in Armenia and Persia Brilliantly Planned and Splendidly Executed—Russia's Use of Her Admirable Roads and Railways—Erzerum, the Metz of East Turkey, Described—Over-confidence Proves the Undoing of the Turks—Rapidity and Force of the Grand Duke's Blows—How the Tsar's Troops Endured Bitter Cold and Heavy Snows on High Mountain Roads—Storming the Turks' Carefully-Prepared Positions—The Big Fight at Keupri Keui on January 16th —Russians by a Clever Move Separate Tenth Turkish Corps from Erzerum—Unexpected Russian Advance Takes Place to the South—The "Miracle" of the Ascent of Karga Bazar on the Night of January 26th—Russians Twelve Miles from Erzerum on February 11th—Fight for the Surrounding Forts, February 11th to 15th—The Assault on the Main Fortress, February 16th— Official Statement of Russia's Captures at Fallen Erzerum—The Enormous Strategical and Political Importance of the Capture of Erzerum—Russian Troops Advancing through Stricken Armenia Find Evidence of Turkish Atrocities—Terrible Retreat of the Turks in Storm and Frost—Russian Advance from Many Points—Capture of Mush and Bitlis—By the End of March, 1916, the Position of the Russians in Asiatic Turkey and in Persia is Extremely Favourable—Effect of Russian Triumphs throughout Turkey—Situation along the European Front—Our Ambassador to Russia Sounds the Note of Closer Alliance between Britain and Russia—Russia Equipped with Men and Munitions—Significance of Reassembly of the Duma, February 22nd, 1916 —General Alexeieff's Plans on Western Front—Tsar's Visits to his Troops and Commencement of the Russian Offensive.

THE Russian campaign in Armenia and Persia at the beginning of 1916 was brilliantly planned and splendidly executed, and must rank among the boldest operations of the war. When the Grand Duke Nicholas was transferred by the Tsar from the supreme command of the western armies to the Caucasus, many regarded this step as virtually relegating the great Russian Prince to obscurity. The Grand Duke himself evidently did not see it in this light. In co-operation with his Chief of Staff, General Yanushkevitch, he planned what must have seemed, before it was attempted, a desperate and almost hopeless venture. He sent for troops from Siberia, picked men who had learned their soldiering under some of the most severe climatic conditions known. These Siberian troops are inured to hardship. They live largely in the open, and they work for many months in each year in a climate so cold that most soldiers would be unable to face it. Their very horses are trained never to enter a stable even in the bitterest weather.

The Grand Duke was able to

THE FIRST TO ENTER ERZERUM.
Captain Konieff, who was decorated by the Tsar with the Cross of the Order of St. George for being the first man to enter the captured Turkish stronghold.

back these soldiers with an ample supply of mobile artillery, including powerful siege-mortars, with abundance of shells. His original plan of campaign, prepared with the utmost secrecy, was to advance along the whole front, from the Black Sea to Lake Van, and to send out simultaneously numerous columns over a wide area, all converging on Erzerum, the great Turkish fortress in Armenia, or guarding the flanks of other columns centring on it.

It is difficult for those unacquainted with the country to realise what such an advance implied. The admirable roads and splendid railways constructed by the Russians in days of peace made it comparatively easy to bring forces to Kars, to Batum, and to the Caucasian border. But here the real difficulties began. The shortest road from Erzerum to Kars was about one hundred and thirty miles long, with inadequate paths buried in deep snows, maintaining a general level of from 4,000 to 5,000 feet above the sea, The whole district was subject to fierce blizzards. Time after time the troops would be compelled to haul their guns and munition trains many thousands of feet up ice-covered mountain sides. In January the normal

TYPES OF THE VANQUISHED FOE.
Sturdy Turks, captured during the fighting around Erzerum, going into captivity under Russian guard. To their fighting qualities our allies paid generous tribute.

A SLIGHT DELAY IN THE GREAT PURSUIT.
Officer's car being hauled through a difficult fording near Erzerum. The victorious forces of the Grand Duke Nicholas experienced some severe transport difficulties while pursuing the Ottoman Third Army north, south, and west of Erzerum.

temperature was twenty to twenty-five degrees below zero, and at times the cold increased to forty degrees below. Even the most hardened troops, accustomed to Siberian weather, might well shrink before this.

Nor was the road undefended. The Turks had along this route an army originally estimated at 250,000 men. There is reason to believe, however, that this force had been considerably weakened in order to meet the attempted British advance towards Bagdad. The Russians from the north and the British from the south were each very materially helping one another by causing a division of the enemy forces.

Erzerum, at which the Russians were aiming, has been well termed the Metz of East Turkey. Standing some 6,000 feet above the sea level, it is guarded by the slopes of

mountains from 10,000 to 12,000 feet in height. A town of some 50,000 inhabitants, it has for centuries been the great trade centre of Armenia, owing to its commanding position and to its situation as the junction of various important routes. The Turks had long recognised that, in the fight between them and Russia, Erzerum would be a vital point. In 1900, German military engineers began modernising the old forts, and in 1916 there were at least eighteen strong fortresses built on the granite hills, three of them new works, fortresses which should have made Erzerum impregnable. The Deve Boyun Mountains, which guarded the north-east route from the Caucasus, were supposed to be specially strongly fortified, and it was claimed that this mountain position was defended by nearly three hundred Krupp guns of heavy calibre and one hundred mortars, besides four hundred pieces of older type. Here again, however, most of the armament existed only on paper. Immediately fronting Erzerum, along the main route where the attack must be made, was another group of forts, also supposed to be splendidly armed. A German commander, Posselt Pasha, was responsible for the defence of the city.

Over-confidence of the Turks

Over-confidence helped to the undoing of the Turks. Many of the guns which were supposed to defend the position had been removed, probably to the south against the British forces. Others were evidently none too modern and in none too good condition. The Turks were doubtless suffering, in common with the rest of the Turkish

Army at that time, from inadequate food. They did not believe that the Russian armies could cross the mountains in any strength, and so did not prepare against such a move. But the factors which really overthrew them were the rapidity and force of the Russian blows. The Russian Commander-in-Chief first succeeded in producing a feeling among the Turks that there was no special reason to fear him. Then by a series of brilliant moves he caused such confusion among the Turkish Staff that it was unable to fathom his plans. The Russian armies advanced in such

Grand Duke's brilliant moves

a way that they might be going to make their main blow at any one of a dozen points. When they struck at the Turkish centre and broke it, they followed up their first success with a rapidity rarely equalled in the history of war. The Turks had never time to recover, never time to reorganise their schemes of defence, never time to strike a counter-blow. Kiamil Pasha, at the last moment, ordered the Tenth Corps on the Turkish left and the Ninth on the right to close in and help in the defence of Erzerum. The Russians had anticipated such moves, and fresh Russian forces were ready to meet them and check them, while the main body pressed on to Erzerum. The Russians deceived, outplayed, and overwhelmed their opponents at every turn.

In the middle of January the Russians, who had been greatly hampered by the heavy snow —snow which often came up to a man's waist —attacked a strong Turkish position, the village of Azankai, seventeen miles off Kara Urgan, and stormed an important mountain ridge, some 9,000 feet high. This fortified position of Azankai was typical of others. Here on the heights overhanging the roads was a labyrinth formed of several tiers of trenches

for infantry and artillery positions. They were dominated by a trench linked to them. All these works were carefully masked, and joined up by sheltered galleries. The Turks held the Russians up for three days there, but at the end of the third day the position was in the Russian hands. From here they aimed straight at the Turkish centre. The Russian artillery overwhelmed the Turkish fire. The Russian infantry went forward with amazing dash, and all opposition broke down before it. Russian cavalry completed the work of the infantry, and cut down the retiring Turks by the hundred.

Now followed an advance which future generations may rank beside Napoleon's passage of the Alps. Blizzards, bitter cold, heavy snows, failed to stop the Russians. The high mountain roads were in such a condition that it was impossible for horses or oxen to drag the great guns, so the Russian soldiers themselves pulled them along. Time after time they were confronted by strong, carefully prepared Turkish positions. These they swept through, one after another.

On January 16th there came a big fight at Keupri Keui, where three Turkish divisions tried finally to hold back the triumphant Russians. Two days later they had

DECORATED FOR VALOUR AT ERZERUM.
General Ewart, a Russian commander of Scottish descent, decorating heroes of the Grand Duke's hard-fought offensive at Erzerum and Bitlis. Picture above: The Grand Duke Nicholas, Viceroy of the Caucasus and commander of the Russian forces operating against the Turks, about to mount his charger in Teheran.

COSSACK AMBULANCE CONVOY IN THE MOUNTAINS OF CAUCASIA.

Cossack divisions have a method of carrying their wounded over difficult country that is both speedy and humane. A pair of long bamboo poles are made fast between two horses, one ahead, the other in the rear. The stretcher is slung midway between these poles, and thus the "give" of the supple bamboos serves the purpose of springs remarkably well, specially when the wounded are being conveyed over steep or rough ground, such as during the campaign in the Caucasus. In the above picture a troop of Circassian Cossacks is seen carrying wounded from the field over a difficult mountain road. A somewhat similar method of transporting the wounded, but in mule-litters, was employed by Wellington's army in the Peninsular War, and also by the medical department of the Napoleonic army in Spain.

reached Hassankale, a little over twenty miles from Erzerum. The Cossacks swept the Turks out of the place by one impetuous rush, and pursued them into the fire zone of the Erzerum forts, slaying large numbers before they could get away. Observers there at the time described the place as covered with the enemy's dead, and with the bodies of the horses and mules used in their transport service by the Turks. Three days later the Russian howitzers had come up and opened a deadly fire on the supposedly impregnable defences of the Deve Boyun Mountains. It must have seemed to the Turks that magic aided the Russians in getting their heavy pieces in such amazing fashion over the great mountain line.

While one Russian army under Generals Lastouchkin and Vorobeioff was then directed against Deve Boyun, a second army, under General Shevalsky, swept down on Erzerum from the north. It found itself opposed by the Turks, who held a number of fortified heights situated in lofty mountain positions. The Russians themselves paid warm tribute to the courage of the defence at this point. It needed some days' fighting before the Turks were driven out, mainly by a series of night bayonet attacks. The Tenth Turkish Corps which, as previously stated, had been brought up from the Turkish left, confronted the Russians here. The Russians, by a clever move, cut the Tenth Turkish Corps in two, and forced themselves between part of this corps and Erzerum, thus preventing it from sharing in the defence.

While these movements were going on to the north and northeast, a still more unexpected Russian advance was taking place to the south. The Turkish Staff was convinced that danger was least of all to be feared from this quarter, for the whole district to the south is covered with mountains rising to a height of 10,000 feet, and is without any roads. So confident were the Turks that they had left the defence of this region to Kurds. The Russians determined to attempt the "impossible," and accomplished it. Despite almost incredible hardships, a considerable Russian force struck through, and by **On Karga Bazar** February 12th was outflanking the main **in a snowstorm** southern defence of Erzerum, Fort Palandeuken.

To the north-east, Russian troops began to ascend the great mountain, Karga Bazar, on the night of January 26th. There was a blinding snowstorm, and it was bitterly cold. "By a kind of miracle," wrote one Russian correspondent (the whole storming of Erzerum was a miracle), "they even dragged up, not machine-guns, but field-guns. Camels transported shells for the guns, together with cartridges and food. On these 'inaccessible' heights also arrived the flying Red Cross detachments and the tea-vans of the Municipal Unions."

COSSACKS ON A NIGHT RIDE WITH HAND "SEARCHLIGHTS."

When tracking their way across the snow by night the Cossacks found many uses for the electric torches with which they were provided when on outpost or patrol duties. Many wounded Russians, fallen helpless at night in outpost fighting and overlooked in a rapidly-moving engagement, owed their lives to the Cossacks' hand "searchlights."

By the night of February 11th the Russians were holding a number of important positions, forming a kind of arc, about twelve miles from the city of Erzerum itself. But the Turks still held the town and the great fortress immediately protecting it. For the Russians to subdue the fortress by the ordinary method of siege attack would have been, in a climate like that of Erzerum, almost impossible. Storms and snows must in the end have wiped out the Russian armies as they waited in their unprotected positions around the Turkish front. The Russian commanders had resolved on another course. They were to take the city by storm. On the night of February 11th an advance was made from Karga Bazar. The Russians, advancing in three columns and dragging their guns and machine-guns with them, reached the edge of the mountainous plateau, slid down the snowy slopes, and attacked a series of stone and snow trenches. Thence the Russians pushed on with the utmost resolution. The Russian batteries planted on the heights of Karga Bazar covered the Russian assaults with sustained artillery fire. At various points the Russians, by successfully manœuvring, so isolated important Turkish positions that it was impossible to hold them. Fort after fort was assaulted and taken. Fort Tafta was stormed in the darkness. The Russian force moved through the deep snow in silence. Its approach was unseen, and the men fell upon a Turkish garrison and bayoneted it without firing a shot.

The main fight for the surrounding forts lasted for five days, February 11th to 15th. Day after day, assault after assault was made. The resistance was desperate and sustained. Several Turkish regiments were annihilated. Other regiments were made prisoners en bloc. Some Turkish army corps of three divisions (40,000 men) were reduced to between 3,000 and 5,000 men. All the remainder had been slain in the fighting, fallen into Russian hands, or perished from exposure. The Russians were the first to admit the resolution and the courage of the enemy. "During the five days' assault the fortress was defended by the Turks with a stubbornness to which the enormous quantity of killed and frozen corpses gives testimony. . . . The fortifications were full of Turkish dead," the Russian official account declared.

The assault on the main fortress was made on February 16th. Here the fighting was of a fierceness even beyond that already known. Whole regiments were wiped out. The works were blocked with the dead. The wounded were quickly frozen to death if not promptly attended to. The Turks had prepared their positions carefully. The Russians had to fight at many points through barbed-wire entanglements and over tremendous obstacles. The Headquarters Staff of Erzerum was mainly German, and while the assault on the fortress was in progress the Germans were the first to abandon the position, causing panic and disorder among the already demoralised Turkish troops.

The road to the west was open to the Turks, and those who could escape fled along it, quickly pursued by the Russian cavalry. The first report that reached Europe was that 100,000 men **German Staff** and 1,000 guns had been captured. This **leads the exodus** was an exaggeration. According to the official statement, the Russians captured 235 officers and 12,753 uninjured men, besides sick and wounded; 323 guns, nine standards, a vast supply of stores, and a very considerable quantity of ammunition. The Russians noted among the stores many evidences of German organisation, particularly an admirable Röntgen ray apparatus in perfect order.

The capture of Erzerum came as a surprise, not only to the world at large, but even to most Russians. It had seemed impossible that such a thing could be done, and those most familiar with the tremendous difficulties of the undertaking had been most doubtful of its possible success. The "impossible" had been accomplished. The Russian General Staff was careful that the Germans should be fully informed of what had taken place. Circulars printed in German, giving a full account of the capture and its significance, were scattered by aeroplanes over the German lines. In many cases the Russians stuck up big notice-boards opposite the trenches, "Erzerum kaput" (Erzerum finished). The usual response

TROPHIES OF VICTORY: TURKISH FLAGS CAPTURED AT ERZERUM.
Russian heroes with the nine Turkish flags captured by them in the battles for Erzerum, in that portion of Asia where the Turk was crushed between the Russian hammer and the British anvil. Above: Decorated banners captured by Russians at Erzerum.

THE TORTUOUS WAY THROUGH THE ICE-BOUND CAUCASUS.

A striking photograph of part of the left wing of the Russian forces operating in Armenia, as they were advancing on Bitlis. After storming and capturing Bitlis—an important centre one hundred and twenty miles south-east of Erzerum—on March 2nd, 1916, they gained notable successes over the Kurds south of Lake Van.

of the Germans was to open a tremendous burst of fire on the notice-boards.

The Turkish Headquarters attempted to minimise the victory. It stated in an official communiqué that the retreat of the Turkish army from Erzerum towards positions in the west had been attained without loss, and that the Turks abandoned in the fortress only fifty old guns, which they could not remove. But the Turkish communiqués had recently been too much even for some Germans, and the distinguished German war critic, Major Moraht, in a significant article in the "Berliner Tageblatt," advised Turkey not to be afraid to tell the truth when she had defeats, but openly to admit them. "Our people are united by so many interests with Turkey that they should have the right to be told the truth. No one can say otherwise than that the Grand Duke conducted his operations ably," added Major Moraht. "The Russian conquest of Erzerum is, of course, of import-

Major Moraht's consolations ance both strategically and politically." He consoled his readers by recalling that the geographical difficulties of advance in the territories of the Armenian Taurus were almost unconquerable, and that defeat might bring about a flaming-up of fanatical Mohammedan war forces. "History has often shown that only after bitter experiences does the Moslem become conscious of his strength."

The capture of Erzerum was of enormous strategical significance, largely because it opened up a very considerable area of country to the Russians. This one point protected Western Armenia and Anatolia from invasion. It commanded all the best roads of Transcaucasia and of the interior of Asia Minor. With Erzerum

in their possession, the Russians were now in a position to move forward quickly, and they did so.

The Russian armies found plenty to inflame their zeal in the country through which they were now advancing. The Christian population of Armenia had for centuries suffered cruelly from Turkish oppression. Earlier in the present war the Turks had carried out a massacre of the Armenians on the most tremendous scale, murdering, outraging, and torturing innocent and unarmed people to an extent rarely equalled in the history of the

Vengeance on the weak

modern world. As the Russian troops now arrived in district after district, they met with hideous evidences of how the Turks had wreaked their vengeance—villages forsaken, homesteads burnt, and bodies of country folk lying stark and mutilated by the roadside. The survivors related narratives of young girls and women outraged, of children slain, of old people murdered, and of the women folk of the nation carried off to be sold as slaves. One Armenian priest, who escaped from the Turkish lines, told how the Turks had sought to wreak their vengeance after their defeats in the field by wholesale massacre of the Armenians in the Mush vilayet. He declared that 13,000 Armenians had been slaughtered before his eyes at Mush alone; and two hundred Armenians, including two of the priest's own children, had been driven into a caravanserai, and there burnt to death. The priest declared that quite 100,000 people in that province had been slaughtered by the Turks. After making all allowances for exaggeration in the priest's statement, it was obvious that the Christians all around had been murdered wholesale, often in forms horrible beyond words.

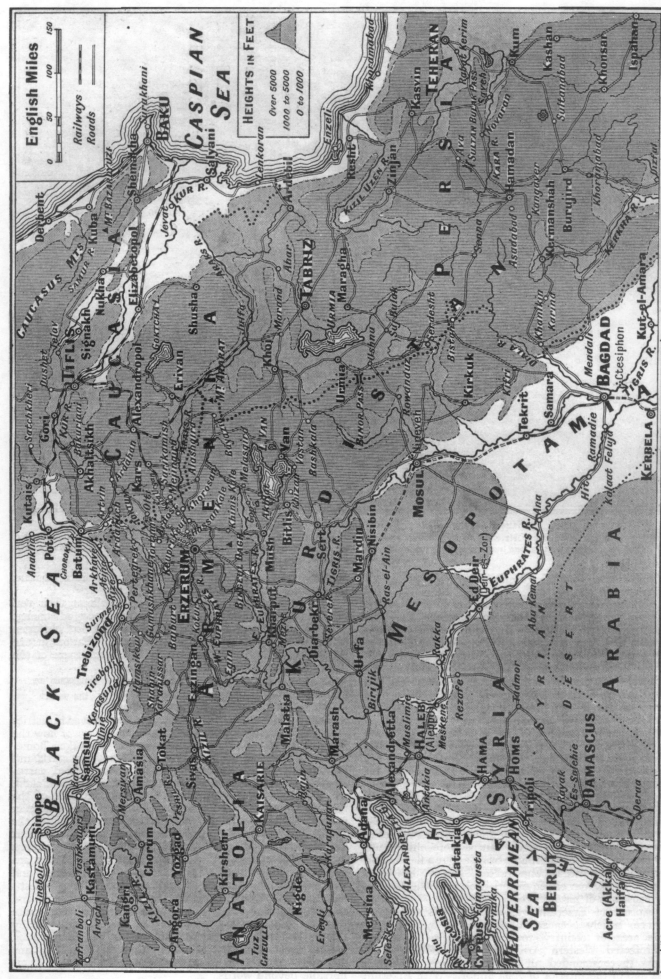

The Great War.

MAP OF THE CAUCASIAN FRONT SHOWING THE AREA OF OPERATIONS OF THE GRAND DUKE'S ARMY, ERZERUM, AND THE LINE OF THE RUSSIAN ADVANCE ON MESOPOTAMIA.

Enver Pasha was attempting the relief of the Erzerum garrison with a hastily collected force, including, as was stated, a certain number of Germans. But while it was yet a hundred miles away, the fate of Erzerum was sealed, and his new force was confronted by the quickly retreating fugitives. The Turks hastening away from Erzerum suffered heavily. The pursuit of them by the Russians was to some extent checked by very severe weather,

Trebizond and Bagdad threatened deep snow, which made roads almost impassable, and heavy frosts. But if this rendered it difficult for the Russians to advance, it made it equally difficult for the Turks to carry on their retreat. Large numbers of Turkish troops, caught in the storms and heavy frosts, were frozen to death. The Turks abandoned guns, ammunition, and anything that kept them from escaping more quickly. Nine out of ten in many a battalion were lost, and the remnants that finally escaped the frosts and the Cossacks were little more than a ragged, broken band.

The Russian plans soon became apparent. A big advance was being conducted, not from one point, but from many. On the Black Sea, Russian troops, aided by Russian gunboats, were making constant demonstrations in the direction of Trebizond. From Erzerum one Russian army corps was striking directly to Sivas. Another Russian army corps, advancing in Persia, captured Kermanshah, and from there moved to take Bagdad in the rear. Another great force pushed down from Erzerum southwards in the direction of Mosul and the Euphrates Valley. On February 18th this force captured Mush, seventy miles from Erzerum. By the beginning of March it reached and captured the very important position of Bitlis, one hundred and twenty miles away. Bitlis was a well planned and strongly defended mountain position, armed with heavy modern guns, and occupied by a considerable garrison. The Russian army moved forward at night-time during a fierce storm. Following the plan it had previously adopted, it came on in silence, without firing a shot, stormed the place, and took it with the bayonet. Scenes of terrible slaughter followed. The Russian troops knew well the story of Bitlis. They knew that here, in June, 1915, 15,000 Armenians, unarmed and helpless, had been tortured and done to death by the Turks. The Armenians were now amply avenged. Bitlis gave the Russians an entry into the main road down the river valley to the plains of Mesopotamia, and it gave them the whole Van region, cutting in two the Turkish forces operating in the Mush region and in the region of Lake Urmia.

The Russians in Armenia and Persia, in pushing forward as they were doing, were showing in the best way possible their co-operation with their ally, Great Britain, for every mile they advanced brought them nearer to Kut-el-Amara, where General Townshend's first Indo-British force, that had sought to reach Bagdad from the south, was surrounded, and unable to advance or retreat.

By the latter part of March, 1916, the position of the Russians in Asiatic Turkey and in Persia was extremely favourable. The enemy had brought up strong forces, but despite repeated endeavours had been unable to stay the Russian advance. In Persia, Russian forces occupied Ispahan, the southern capital, thus finally defeating efforts that had been made by Germany to make the Shah their

tool, and to use Persia in their campaign to win over the Mohammedan world. On the coast of Asia Minor their armies were steadily advancing until they were actually threatening Trebizond, which was now within two days' march of them. The army that had moved westwards from Erzerum towards Sivas was progressing in a way that would eventually threaten Constantinople, and the Turks were busy building strong defensive works from Sivas to Shabin-Karahissar to check it. The army moving southwards that had seized Bitlis had now reached Khizan, thirty miles farther south. Thence it was aiming at Sert, when the rich Euphrates Valley would be open to it.

The effect of these Russian triumphs was markedly felt throughout Turkey. The mass of the Turkish people had never been more than half-hearted in the war against the Allies. The Turkish troops against the British in the Dardanelles, for example, had displayed great courage but little venom, and had sought in many ways during armistices, and when our wounded fell into their hands, to show that, though fighting us, they fought as a matter of State policy, without individual ill-will. The steady progress of the Russians in Asiatic Turkey was only one of many indications to the Turkish people that the war

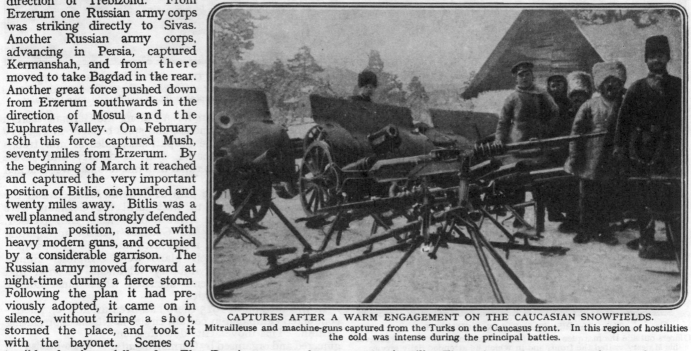

CAPTURES AFTER A WARM ENGAGEMENT ON THE CAUCASIAN SNOWFIELDS.
Mitrailleuse and machine-guns captured from the Turks on the Caucasus front. In this region of hostilities the cold was intense during the principal battles.

was going ill. Throughout the country the people were starving. Constantinople itself was almost in a state of famine. The Young Turk Party under Enver Pasha, who had brought the nation to this pass, found their influence daily weakening, while the Old Turks, traditionally friendly to Britain, grew in strength.

The Turkish Army in general, and Turkish officers in particular, disliked the dominance of the German officers over them, even while they were half-unwillingly forced to recognise their military efficiency. The Turkish people saw German officials daily acquiring more and more power throughout the land. **Turkey fighting without enthusiasm** Enver Pasha and his supporters were, however, in control of the Army, and it would take much to turn the Army against them. But day by day it grew more evident that Turkey was fighting, so far as the mass of her people was concerned, not only without enthusiasm, but with a stubborn conviction that the nation had made a great mistake in coming in on the German side. However much the original policy of despatching an allied army to Salonika may be open to question, it is undoubtedly true that the menace of the large allied force there, holding as it did an almost

THE VICEROY OF THE CAUCASUS AT A REVIEW.
Russian troops marching past their Commander-in-Chief, the Grand Duke Nicholas, who made an imposing figure standing to take the salute.

THE TSAR'S TRAVELLING CHURCH.
Officers outside the marquee church that accompanied the Tsar whenever his Majesty visited the front, and in which he attended daily service.

impregnable position, increased the Turkish uneasiness. It seemed more and more certain that Rumania would throw in her lot with the Allies, that Greece might follow suit, and even possible that Bulgaria might, late in the day, completely reverse her position. To the Turkish nation as a whole the spring days of 1916 were gloomy indeed.

While these important movements were proceeding in Persia and Asiatic Turkey, the situation was rapidly developing along the European front. **Anticipating the enemy** The Russians had no delusions about the plans of the enemy. They believed that Germany intended, as soon as weather conditions permitted in the spring, to launch an immense offensive against Russia, with the aim of crushing the new armies, occupying either Petrograd, Moscow, or Odessa, and bringing about a decision in the east before turning her full forces on the west. Even the sustained and costly German attack upon Verdun did not shake the belief of Russia that the real spring campaign would be in the east. "Verdun is an interlude. The main German armies are being concentrated along our lines, and they will attempt to repeat Von Hindenburg's old drive,"

234

Russian publicists declared. All along the German eastern front there were movements, and spies brought in at every point, from Riga to the Carpathians, tales of new troops being drilled and prepared, with a rigidity and severe discipline which even German drill masters had not reached before.

It was no part of the plan of General Alexeieff and the Russian General Staff to wait until the Germans were ready, and to let them strike a blow when they pleased. The Russians, adopting the German plan of anticipating the enemy's movement, resolved to hurl their troops upon the enemy before their plans were complete. Simultaneously with these military advances, internal and international developments occurred which must not be passed over without notice.

In the autumn of 1915 there had been an active, quietly-conducted campaign in certain circles in Russia depreciating Britain. This movement, doubtless engineered and organised by German agents, **Anglo-Russian relations** took the form of vague whispered charges that Britain was not doing all she ought in the war. She was leaving, so it was said, the main fighting and the main suffering to Russia and to France, while she remained comparatively quiet. When, at the beginning of the war, the British and French armies were endangered, Russia, by a bold and costly offensive in Eastern Prussia, had created a diversion. When, in the summer of 1915, Russia was in desperate straits, Britain had remained quiet.

Suspicions and rumours such as these, carefully fostered, were not without their effect in some small circles. Correspondents, returning to London from Petrograd, warned our people that where, fifteen months before, there had been nothing but burning enthusiasm for Britain, a certain coldness had now arisen. The British official methods of secrecy in war had done great harm. The Russian people did not know what we were actually doing, because they had no means of knowing. The work of the British Navy had been veiled in darkness. The real labours of our armies had only been partly revealed, and then in a way which officials who did not understand the art of publicity thought proper, rather than in a way which would make people really understand. The British Government saw that the situation was one that might develop unfavourably for us, and steps were taken to remedy it.

Sir George Buchanan, the British Ambassador to Russia, took occasion at the annual dinner of the new English Club at Petrograd, in January, 1916, to sound the note of closer alliance and still greater co-operation between Britain and Russia. The Russo-British Alliance was, he indicated, to be no mere temporary arrangement for the duration of the war, but was to continue indefinitely. Germany was to be rendered harmless. That was not all. The German commercial exploitation of Russia was not to be renewed, and Britain would have to learn so to adapt her commercial methods that she would oust Germany from the extremely valuable and growing Russian markets. In short, a permanent alliance, commercial as well as political, was the ideal to which the Ambassador pointed.

Sir George Buchanan's strong position in Russia ensured instant attention to such a speech. Our Minister was an Ambassador of the old type, the representative of his country, not merely a mouthpiece of the Government, but one who by his strong personality created an atmosphere favourable to his nation. There was much

Note of closer alliance favourable comment on his words. The British Government invited a number of representative Russian journalists to see for themselves what this country was actually doing. This did much good. The presence of British submarines and submarine officers, of a British Naval Air Service Contingent in Russia, and of numerous British Red Cross parties, also helped to dissipate misunderstanding. The early months of 1916 were marked by a notable increase in Russo-British cordiality and mutual understanding.

The Russian Minister of War was able to declare to a representative of the Paris "Journal," in February, 1916, that the shortage of munitions, which had brought about the retreat of the Russian armies in the summer of 1915, was now absolutely a thing of the past. Immense efforts and rigorous and inflexible measures had been required; there had been an absolute revolution, an absolute transformation of industrial activity and almost of national customs. "Now," he declared, "we can look to the future with confidence." Great masses of men had been mobilised, the number of military depôts had been doubled, and a permanent reserve of 1,500,000 recruits was being maintained in order to fill up gaps in the front line by despatching fully trained men.

During these trying months the Russian **Russia's confident** nation was passing through a period **outlook** of profound growth. The temporary movements in internal politics, the triumph or disgrace of particular Ministers, were of minor import. The Russian people were more and more understanding that the Government of a nation was the business not of bureaucrats but of the nation itself. "Things can never be the same again," men said to one another. The position of the Tsar, so far from being weakened, was strengthened. Never had he so surely held the hearts of his people as then. A great change was coming over the Army. The older type of Russian professional officer had been largely killed or disabled in the fierce earlier fighting. His place had been taken by professional and business men. This helped to break down the rigidity of much of the old military system. The great burst of enthusiastic self-sacrifice that was witnessed at the beginning of the war was making itself felt not only in the Army but in the civil life of the nation. Russia had suffered much, Russia had paid heavily, but it now became more and more evident that Russia was gaining much in this war, and was realising more and more through it the oneness of her peoples and the greatness of her national life.

The reassembly of the Duma, on February 22nd, 1916,

WITH THE GRAND DUKE'S FORCES NEAR THE BLACK SEA.
Russians bringing up a searchlight projector and its electric generator by means of a six-horsed team. The apparatus was covered with a tarpaulin. Searchlights were used to a very great extent by all belligerents, and were found of incalculable value for night artillery work.

was a significant evidence of the new developments of Russian national aspirations. The spirit in which the Duma of 1916 went to work was very different from the spirit with which the first Duma attempted to bring about revolutionary changes in Russia. The Tsar visited the Assembly on the opening day, and after addressing the members in the most friendly fashion, remained some time in the rooms of the President. All the Progressive and Central parties united in a declaration criticising the Government for not having more efficiently employed all the resources of the nation in the war, and urging it to use to better advantage the public enthusiasm and the public strength to bring the war to a successful end. The declaration of the Progressive groups, representing as they did the majority of the Duma, was of undeniable significance. It was proof that the nation was speaking, apart from officialism, and its voice declared for waging the war to the end. The influence of the Progressive groups was soon to be felt in yet more powerful fashion.

GATEWAY TO THE TURKISH CAPITAL OF ASIA MINOR.
Impressive gateway to the city of Erzerum, for long Turkey's most advanced bulwark towards Russia. A curious mixture of Roman and Byzantine architecture is traceable in the structure. The columns, apart for being chipped here and there by flying shrapnel, remained intact.

A few days after the opening of the Duma, M. Sazonoff, the Foreign Minister, in a great speech, voiced Russia's reply to Sir George Buchanan's message :

"I am happy once more to note that the fatal misunderstandings which so long obscured our relations with Britain have now been finally dispersed."

The plan of General Alexeieff on the Russian western front was the same as that of the Grand Duke Nicholas in the Caucasus—to keep the enemy guessing, to harass him in every possible way, and to keep him **Keeping the foe in** under constant apprehension of advances **suspense** all along his line, in order that when the right moment came a more effective attack could be launched against him. The policy of guerilla warfare, which had marked the closing weeks of 1915, was bound in the end to grow into something more. The one question was when and how the Russians would move.

The German armies occupying the long line from the Gulf of Riga southwards had endeavoured to protect themselves by a very thorough system of entrenchments, less elaborate naturally than that on the French front, for there had been less time to build it, but surprisingly

complete when the length of the front and the time available were considered. Concrete trenches, warm, movable houses for the troops, elaborate machine-gun positions, and splendidly placed artillery faced the Russians. The Central Powers had largely concentrated their forces on two areas. A great Austro-German army occupied the country below Pinsk, with a view to advance in springtime, as soon as the weather made it possible, to Kieff and Odessa. An immense German army under Marshal von Hindenburg was being accumulated around Dvinsk to attack Petrograd. **German threat** Between these two groups were the **against Petrograd** almost impassable Pinsk Marshes.

In February there were growing signs that either side might attempt to strike a blow before the spring thaw came on. The Russian Emperor visited his northern and western fronts, inspected the troops, and warmly congratulated them on their appearance and on their work. Violent artillery duels broke out on either side along the Vilna-Dvinsk-Riga fronts. It is probable that the Russians were at this time largely influenced by a desire to help the French, who were just then being heavily attacked at Verdun. The artillery duels were followed by infantry advances, and at point after point great bodies of Russians were constantly flung upon the German lines. The extent of this offensive may be judged by one significant sentence in the German official report that the Russians " employed against the German lines north-west of Jacobstadt such masses of men and ammunition as have not hitherto been known in the eastern theatre of war."

The idea that the Russians were attempting an immense diversion, knowing that such a diversion must of necessity be very costly for them, is strengthened when the weather conditions are remembered. The great spring thaw was nearly due. Once the thaw set in, the movement of troops on either side would be virtually impossible. The Russians could not hope at this time to launch their really big advance, and they knew it. What they could hope to do was to keep the Germans fully employed, to prevent any movement of German troops from the east to the west, and possibly to make some gains in position. A month at the most was available for them.

That month was used to the full. In the Dvinsk region attack and counter-attack followed each other in rapid succession. The movement of the Russian troops seemed to indicate that they were attempting to recapture Vilna, and the Germans hastily set about fortifying this place. The fighting was specially notable in revealing the great excellence of the Russian artillery and the abundant supply of munitions for the Russian guns. In the south the Russian armies moved in the direction of Czernovitz, manoeuvring there for position. Before, however, a real decision could be had by either side, the spring thaw set in. The ice-bound rivers broke up, the countryside became a quagmire, and the movements of armies were necessarily suspended for a few weeks. Throughout the nation there was confident hope that immediately the effects of the spring thaws were over, and it was possible to move troops again, the war would take on a fresh aspect.

Vice-Admiral Sir Reginald H. S. Bacon, K.C.B., in command of the Dover Patrol.

Missed !' U boat's torpedo passes just beyor

...a of a *British war vessel on the high seas.*

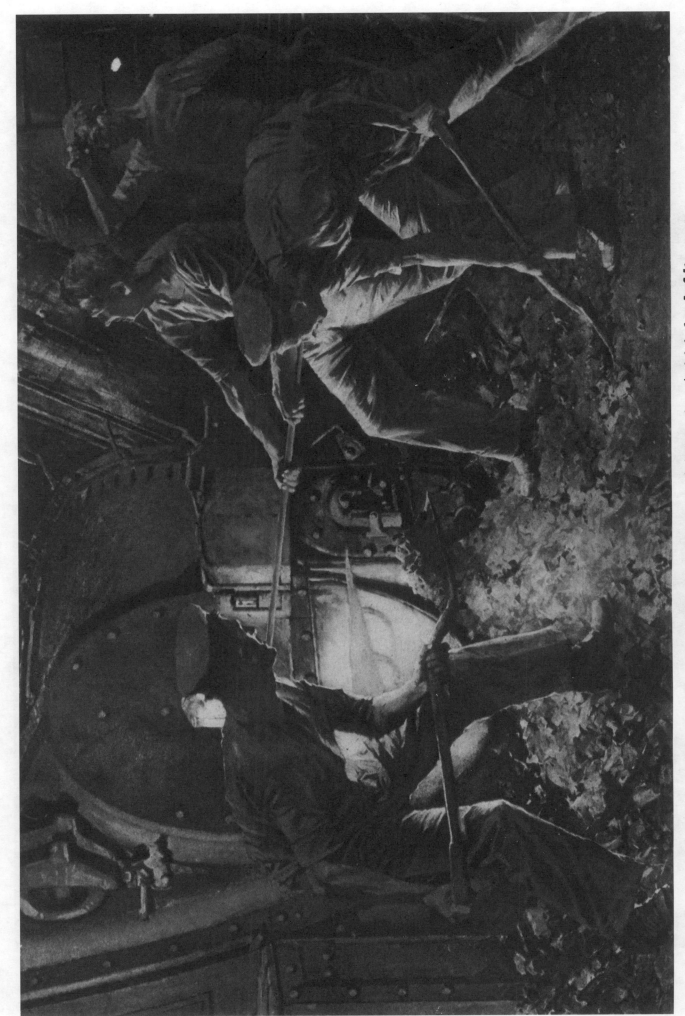

The "black squad" at work in the stokehold of a British battleship.

SUSPECTED SERBIAN SPIES

CHAPTER CX.

IN GERMAN HANDS.

HOW GERMANY BECAME THE OUTLAW OF THE NATIONS.
By Arthur D. Innes, M.A., author of "England and the British Empire," "The Hohenzollerns," etc.

The First Crime—Germany's Self-Outlawry—Character of the Evidence—" God is Just "—International Law—The Hague Conferences of 1899 and 1907—The Fifth Convention and its Violation—Articles in the Regulations Appended to the Fourth Convention—Summary of Violations—Von Bülow's Warning to Liège—Von der Goltz's Brussels Proclamation—Von Bülow's Namur Proclamation—The Warning to Wavre—Dieckmann at Grivegnée—The Crime of Louvain—Rheims Cathedral—Zeppelin Bombardment of Open Towns—Naval Bombardment of Open Towns (Ninth Convention)—Pillaging—Forbidden Weapons—Civilians Used as Screens—German Evidence—British and Belgian Evidence—Murder of Wounded (from German Note-books)—Massacres of Civilians (from German Note-books)—The Wenger Letter—Prisoners Set to Trench-digging—The Submarine Piracy—A Contrast—The German Apologia—German Charges against the Belgians—Belgian, French, and British Charges against the Germans—Conclusion.

GREAT BRITAIN flung her soul into the Great War in the summer of 1914, not merely because German aggression had thrown down a challenge to Europe, nor because she knew that if she stood by she would presently have to fight Germany single-handed. These things touched her material interests and appealed to her intelligence, but they did not move her soul. The thing which set the flame of righteous wrath ablaze was Germany's cynical denunciation by word and act of the fundamental principle of civilised society—that nations as well as individuals are bound by their pledged word.

Twice, in 1839 and in 1870, Prussia had solemnly bound herself not only to observe but to protect the neutrality of Belgium. The invasion of Belgium, and the Chancellor's fatal phrase about " a scrap of paper," revealed the atavism of the most powerful military State in Europe—the truth, which few people hitherto had succeeded in believing, that Germany was not a civilised but a barbaric Power.

Yet even then the completeness of German barbarism had not revealed itself. Germany had only shown that what seemed to be a short cut to victory offered a temptation to crime too strong to be resisted. She was still to

show that she held no pledge binding, no law of humanity sacred; that her triumph would mean the establishment of such an organised tyranny of blood and tears as the world had never known. She was still to prove, not only that her rulers were ready to override all laws, human and Divine, but that her people were ready to override all laws, save those ordained by her rulers.

It is well to take stock of the proofs, to remind ourselves of the reasons for the iron resolve of the Allies, after twenty-one months of the war, that it should be carried to such an issue as would make a revival of Prussianism for ever impossible.

The crimes systematically committed by the German army in the invasion of Belgium, in the invasion of France, on the seas, in the air, and in the fighting-line, under the direction of Prussianism, imposed upon the Allies a duty terrible but imperative ; so terrible and so imperative that we require to be satisfied beyond question that the indictment against Germany was proved up to the hilt.

The sum of the indictment is this—that to the rulers and to the bulk of the people in Germany the pledged word of a people was nought ; the established principles of humanity were nought; Christianity itself was less than nought. Deliberately, as the means to victory, Germany made herself the outlaw

Gott strafe England!

"GOTT STRAFE ENGLAND!"
Pictorial expression of the German lust for the blood of perfidious Albion.

IN MEMORIAM: EDITH CAVELL, OCTOBER 29TH, 1915. THE LORD MAYOR OF LONDON LEAVING ST. PAUL'S CATHEDRAL AFTER THE MEMORIAL SERVICE.

of the nations, sinning against the light with open eyes.

Our immediate aim in these pages is to summarise the evidence for these charges.

We have nothing, then, to say here to random accusations—we have to deal with proofs. In the heat of conflict the wildest charges are made, circumstantial evidence seems to be spontaneously generated, and a single misdeed is multiplied into a hundred specified crimes. No charges can be admitted as proved till they have been investigated and the witnesses examined by persons trained in the sifting of evidence and actuated by the single desire to ascertain truth. We have to be guided by the most rigid standards of a British court of law.

It is in accordance with those standards, therefore, that we frame an indictment **A damning indictment** blacker than any that has been formulated against a civilised people since the great German Civil War—the Thirty Years' War—nearly three centuries ago.

Of all the evidence, that which is most damning is established, not by the word of the enemies or the victims of Germany, but by the Germans themselves—by German official statements, or by German documents, the authenticity of which is beyond dispute. This evidence confirms and is supplemented by a great body of additional evidence tested and sifted by tribunals of experts, appointed by the French, British, and Belgian Governments, the names of whose members provide a conclusive guarantee of the strictest judicial impartiality, as well as of trained competence.

From the note-book of a German non-commissioned officer we extract as our text some sentences which admirably express the nature of the condemnation that Germany has called down upon herself:

October 15th, 1914.—The civil population had already been driven out of Billy, and everything movable had either been carried off or made useless. This fashion of making war is sheer barbarism. I am astounded that we can reproach the Russians for their behaviour—our behaviour in France is far worse. Time after time, on any sort of pretext, it is burning and pillage. But God is just and sees all. "The mills of God grind slowly, but they grind exceeding small."

Passing by the initial outrage, the violation by Germany of Belgian neutrality, in despite of the most solemn pledges, we turn directly to the great group of pledges which she had taken, in common with all the civilised sovereign States of the world **Meaning of "international law"** —actual w r i t t e n pledges, signed and sealed, not mere understandings established by general or even by universal custom—the pledges set forth in The Hague Conventions. But here a prefatory digression may be permitted, since it is not everyone who knows exactly what The Hague Conventions were.

The term "international law" is familiar, but the meaning of it is hazy. There is no code of international law to which we can point. Customs have grown up, occasionally formulated in specific treaties, to which everyone conforms as a matter of course, such as the inviolability of a flag of truce. Particular nations, again, have pledged themselves to the observance of certain rules in dealing with each other; but these agreements and customs have never been

PRINCE ALBERT JOACHIM OF PRUSSIA ON THE EASTERN FRONT.

codified into a system adopted by all sovereign States, which all are pledged to enforce.

So-called international law lacks the sanction of an international authority which can enforce obedience to the law, and the agreements cover only a very limited field.

The Hague Conferences were instituted with a view to the gradual establishment of a body of regulations which all civilised States should be pledged to observe in their relations to each other, with two specific objects in view— one being the settlement of international disputes without resort to arms, and the other the conduct of war, if war should break out, in such a manner as to reduce to a minimum the evils which necessarily attend it, whether affecting neutrals or belligerents.

The conventions or agreements arrived at by these conferences between official representatives of the sovereign States were regarded as morally binding **Precedents and pledges** upon all the signatories, but carried with them no positive obligation, except that each State should itself observe them, no obligation to take action against a State which disregarded its pledges.

Precedents for the common acceptance of definite regulations had been set by the Declaration of Paris (1856), dealing with certain questions affecting maritime war, and by the Geneva Convention of 1864, revised in 1906, which was concerned with the treatment of the sick and wounded. Neither of these, however, had attained to the position of acceptance by all even of the leading States of the world, when the First Hague Conference was assembled on the initiative of the Tsar of Russia in 1899.

That conference was a tentative effort to find bases of agreement for reducing the menace of war by the reduction of armaments, and by the practice of referring disputes to

arbitration, and for the observance of humane methods in the actual conduct of war. At that conference the Governments of twenty-six sovereign States were represented. The conventions then adopted, though having no compulsory sanction, were loyally observed by the belligerents in the Russo-Japanese War and in the South African War.

At the Second Hague Conference, in 1907, the earlier conventions were elaborated and expanded in the form of fourteen conventions, forty-four sovereign States being represented. They were signed on behalf of all the States except Nicaragua, with specified reservations on the part of particular States ; and in most cases, though not in all, the acceptances were **Second Hague Conference** ratified by the respective Governments — a condition necessary to make them technically binding upon the individual States.

Germany, Russia, France, Italy, Great Britain, Belgium, and Japan all ratified the conventions. Turkey and Bulgaria did not.

There were clauses stating generally that the conventions were obligatory only when all belligerents had adopted them. On that plea, for what it was worth, Germany was subsequently to claim that the belligerency of Turkey cancelled the obligation to observe the conventions. But, in plain terms, no technical excuse can evade the moral obligation upon every signatory Power to observe the conventions, except when in conflict with a Power which itself repudiates the obligation ; while, in any case, until the war had been in progress several months, all the hostile Powers were actually parties to the conventions.

The Fifth Convention of the 1907 Conference deals with the Rights and Duties of Neutral Powers in the case of War on Land. Article 2 declares that belligerents are forbidden to move troops or convoys, whether of munitions

THE GERMAN CROWN PRINCE AT WORK IN THE FIELD.

A PERMANENT MEMORIAL OF GERMAN VANDALISM.
West front of the Cathedral of Rheims after repeated German bombardments. One of the finest extant specimens of Gothic architecture, Rheims Cathedral became a more or less permanent mark for the German gunners. It was built between 1212 and 1430.

breaches of Germany's definite solemn pledges, were only the precursors of an appalling series.

The Fourth of The Hague Conventions of 1907 is concerned with the Laws and Customs of War on Land. To it is appended a series of Regulations. In Article 23 of the Regulations it is expressly forbidden to compel the subjects of the hostile party to take part in operations of war directed against their own country; to kill or wound an enemy who, having laid down his arms, and no longer having means of defence, has surrendered at discretion ; to destroy or seize enemy property unless such destruction or seizure be imperatively demanded by the necessities of war.

Article 25 forbids the attack or bombardment by any means whatever of undefended towns, villages, dwellings, or buildings. Article 46 insists that family honour and rights, individual life, and private property must be respected. Article 49 provides, in the case of the occupation of enemy country, that if the occupant levies money contributions they shall only be applied to the needs of the army or of the administration of the territory. Article 50 lays down that no collective penalty, pecuniary or otherwise, shall be inflicted upon the population on account of the acts of individuals for which it cannot be regarded as collectively responsible.

By Article 52, requisitions in kind and in services shall not be demanded from local authorities or inhabitants except for the needs of the army of occupation. They shall be in proportion to the resources of the country. Contributions in kind shall as far as possible be paid for in ready money. By Article 56, any

or of supplies, across the territory of a neutral Power. Article 5 declares that a neutral Power must not allow any of the acts referred to in Article 2 to occur on its territory. Article 10 declares that the fact of a neutral Power resisting, even by force, attempts to violate its neutrality, cannot be regarded as a hostile act.

Belgium, therefore, in offering armed resistance to the passage of German troops through Belgian territory, was not merely acting within her rights, but was actually carrying out what was stated to be her positive duty in a convention formally ratified by Germany. Nevertheless, Germany, in defiance of Article 10 of the convention, deliberately treated this fulfilment of her positive duty on the part of Belgium as a hostile act, and proceeded against Belgium as a hostile country.

From the moment when the first shot was fired, Belgium was treated no longer as a neutral, but as a declared enemy. The sole excuse put forward was the absolutely untenable plea of " military necessity."

The treatment of Belgium, then, as an enemy country was in itself a second crime, following upon the first crime of violating neutral territory. But those two crimes,

seizure or destruction of, or wilful damage to, institutions dedicated to public worship, charity, education, and to science and art, of historic monuments, and of works of science and art, is forbidden. Buildings of this class are also (Article 27) to be spared as far as possible in sieges and bombardments.

Every one of the foregoing clauses was violated in Belgium by the Germans ; sometimes by express order of the higher authorities, but, if not, with their tacit approval or sanction. Defenceless persons were killed, enemy property was wantonly seized or destroyed, Belgians were compelled to take part in operations of war, undefended **German official culpability** towns were bombarded, the sanctity of the family, individual life, and private property were not respected, money contributions were levied without even the pretext that they were needed for the army, collective penalties were imposed where there was no sort of collective responsibility, requisitions were not proportioned to the resources of the country, and the buildings and institutions expressly protected were deliberately despoiled or shattered by bombardment. One plea was regarded as adequate in every case—the bare statement or suspicion that one or more civilians had fired upon German troops.

We are not, be it observed, dealing with the wild misconduct of a soldiery which had got out of hand and paid no heed to the officers whom it usually obeyed. We are dealing in the first place with the positive orders given by the responsible authorities. Read this extract from a proclamation delivered to the communal authorities in Liège on August 22nd, 1914, by Von Bülow, the "general commanding in chief."

The inhabitants of Andenne, after having protested their peaceful intentions, made a treacherous surprise attack on our troops. It was with my consent that the general had the whole place burnt down and about one hundred people shot. I bring this fact to the knowledge of the town of Liege, so that its inhabitants may know the fate with which they are threatened if they take up a similar attitude.

The slaughter of defenceless persons, the destruction of property, and the infliction of the collective penalty—three of the ten points we have enumerated—are all expressly sanctioned, and the responsibility for them assumed, by the highest military authority, and justified on the plea that a treacherous attack was made upon the soldiery by the civilians of Andenne.

It is quite possible that the soldiers on the spot—who were, in fact, fired upon from the other side of the river outside of Andenne—rushed to the conclusion that the shots were fired by Andenne civilians, though there was nothing in the nature of proof, or even of a presumption, that this was so. What was the punishment inflicted for this hypothetical crime, the punishment on which the Commander-in-Chief bestowed his sanction and approval? If we accept only Von Bülow's own statement, the whole place was burnt down and a hundred persons, of whom it was not even suggested that they were personally implicated in the imaginary firing of civilians upon the Germans, were shot. Of the attendant atrocities reported by many independent Belgian witnesses, Von Bülow has nothing to say.

Massacre at Andenne

On October 5th, 1914, Field-Marshal Baron von der Goltz, the German Governor-General of Belgium, posted the following proclamation in Brussels :

During the evening of September 25th the railway line and the telegraph wires were destroyed on the line Lovengoul-Vertryck. In consequence of this these two localities have had to render an account of this and had to give hostages on the morning of September 30th. In future, the localities nearest to the place where similar acts take place will be punished without pity ; *it matters little if they are accomplices or not.* For this purpose hostages have been taken from all localities near the railway line thus menaced, and at the first attempt to destroy the railway line or the telephone or telegraph wires they will be immediately shot.

The shooting of hostages who could not conceivably have any hand at all in the committal of the hypothetical

THE GUARDIAN ANGELS OF ARRAS CATHEDRAL.
These beautiful pieces of statuary, one of the features of Arras Cathedral, were removed from a position high up in the nave and placed on the floor for safety, Arras having suffered so terribly from bombardment.

offence was not, we must suppose, in the eyes of Field-Marshal Baron von der Goltz the infliction of a collective penalty, and therefore, not being specifically prohibited, was permissible ! Or is Article 50 suspended on the all-inclusive ground of " military necessity " ?—which appears to be distinguishable from charity, in that it covers not merely a multitude of sins, but every sin that ingenuity can conceive if committed by (but not against) German military authority.

Let us call Von Bülow into court again, with his Namur proclamation of August 25th, in which the following clauses appear :

The Belgian and French soldiers must be delivered as prisoners of war before four o'clock in front of the prison. Citizens who do not obey will be condemned to hard labour for life in Germany. Every street will be occupied by a German guard, who will take ten hostages from each street, whom they will keep under surveillance. If there is any rising in the street, the ten hostages will be shot.

Observe that the penalty of hard labour for life was to be inflicted not for concealing French or Belgian soldiers, but for omitting to betray them. To repeat the previous comment on the hostage business is superfluous.

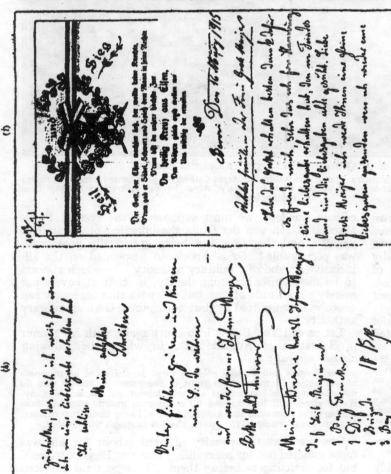

GERMAN CONFESSION OF FRIGHTFULNESS: FACSIMILE OF A LETTER WRITTEN BY A SOLDIER.

Through the courtesy of Professor J. H. Morgan, whose book "German Atrocities: An Official Investigation" was published in March, 1916, we reproduce above in facsimile a letter quoted among Professor Morgan's documents, but not received by him in time to be wholly included in his book. This typical document was written by a German soldier to a German girl in Hamburg, informing her, in the passage underlined in the reproduction, of his having bayoneted several French women and girls.

Following is a translation of the letter, which was found on a prisoner of the 86th Regiment:

"Berai, the 16th March, 1915.

"Honoured Miss or Mrs. Grete Mäyer.—Have received the parcel and best thanks for it. I was very glad to have received a present of comforts from Hamburg, for in the enemy's country presents are hard to find. Dear Greti Mäyer I will send you a small present when I find one again, a ring from one of those shells which threatens us with destruction. (?) Dear Grete Mäyer, I will arrange the ring so finely that you will be able to wear it on your arm at once and you have a nice souvenir from a German warrior who has been through everything from the start and has shot and bayonetted so many Frenchmen and I have also bayonetted many Frenchwomen. Dear Greti Mäyer, I have bayonetted seven women and four girls in five minutes. In an engagement near Batovile. We had a house to house fight, and these women fired at us with revolvers, and they shot at the Captain too, then he said that I should shoot them all. I bayonetted them and did not shoot them this herd of sows, they are worse than the men. We have dead and wounded every day. Dear Greti Mäyer, I am a bomb thrower, and have often crept up to within 10 metres of the enemy and have thrown him one into his trench; then they have fired flares to see me and fired at me, but have never hit me, and that is always the good thing. Dear Greti Mäyer if I live and get through it I will seek out Greti Mäyer; if this Greti Mäyer is still single and not engaged I take the liberty [? to ask] that she send me her photograph so that I too may know from whom I have received my present.

"I close my scrawl with many greetings and kisses if you were there, from far away, WENGER. Please answer soon. My address is:—Johann Wenger, Inf. Body Regiment 1 Bav. Army Corps, 1 Div. 1 Brigade, 3 Bav., 10 Kp.

The letter was obviously written by an illiterate person. Though the handwriting itself is passably good, several grammatical errors appear here and there, and the writer's punctuation and mode of address are erratic. A touch of sentimentality contrasts strangely with the acts of brutality confessed to by the writer. His allegation that the women were armed with revolvers has been repeatedly proved to be untrue.

246

So far Von der Goltz and Von Bülow, the Governor-General and the Commander-in-Chief, wiped out five of the ten points. This is the way in which Lieutenant-General von Nieber dealt with a sixth, speaking in the name of Von Bülow, in a letter to the Burgomaster of Wavre, August 27th:

War levy on Wavre

On August 22nd, 1914, the general commanding the Second Army, General von Bülow, imposed on the town of Wavre a war levy of £120,000, payable up to September 1st, to expiate the infamous conduct, contrary to the laws of the rights of nations and the customs of war, which they showed in making a surprise attack on the German troops. [Observe the general's tender solicitude for the laws, etc.] The town of Wavre will be set on fire and destroyed if the payment is not made when due ; without distinction of persons, the innocent will suffer with the guilty.

It is illuminating to note that no evidence was adduced to prove that any inhabitant of Wavre had fired upon the Germans. A German soldier had, indeed, been wounded by a bullet, but it was a German regulation bullet. Penalty imposed on Wavre because one German shot another—£120,000. Penalty if Wavre failed to pay within ten days —destruction of the town of Wavre.

After the generals, Commandant-Major Dieckmann acquitted himself as might be expected in a notice to the commune of Grivegnée on September 8th, 1914. He requires a list of persons who were to be held as hostages :

The life of these hostages depends on the population of the commune remaining quiet in any circumstances. From the list which is submitted to me I will designate persons who shall be hostages from midday to the following midday. If the substitute is not there at the correct time, the hostage must remain another twenty-four hours at the fort. After these twenty-four hours the hostage will incur the penalty of death if the substitute has not presented himself.

Morally, at least, the clause which forbids the occupying forces to compel the inhabitants to take part in operations of war covers the case of Von Bülow's Namur proclamation penalising citizens who did not betray French and Belgian soldiers.

There remain only to be dealt with in this connection breaches of the obligation to abstain from the bombardment of undefended towns, and from the destruction of churches, hospitals, and other institutions of analogous character.

It is true that neither Von der Goltz nor Von Bülow issued proclamations specifically ordering the destruction of such buildings ; but Louvain, one example out of many, is sufficient to prove that such destruction had the sanction and approval of the supreme command.

On August 26th, 1914, a German garrison was in occupation of Louvain. German forces advancing against Antwerp had met with a reverse, and were falling back upon Louvain. In the evening there was a report that Belgian forces were attacking the town. In the confusion German troops fired upon each other, and became possessed with the idea that the civilian inhabitants were firing upon them. As the inhabitants had already deposited their firearms, the thing was actually impossible, though it is conceivable that here and there civilians might have concealed arms.

The result was that Louvain was first bombarded for some hours, and that the town was then deliberately set on fire. The Cathedral of St. Peter, the University buildings, and the University library were destroyed. It is absolutely clear that no attempt whatever was made to preserve them, even if they were not deliberately chosen for destruction.

No bombardment could have taken place except by the orders of responsible authority. Louvain, therefore, completes the tale of proofs that in respect of the ten points enumerated the responsible German authorities, Von der Goltz and Von Bülow, or subordinate but immediately responsible commanders, swept aside the pledges given by Germany at The Hague Conference under signed conventions, upon no other plea than unsubstantiated reports that a civilian or civilians had shot at German soldiers.

The truth of those reports was not tested. It was simply taken for granted, although on the other side abundant evidence of improbability at least was forthcoming. Even if the reports had turned out to be true up to the limits within which their truth was at all possible, they would have proved nothing in the nature of a collective responsibility on the part of the inhabitants. Even if they had

A VENERABLE PATRIOT OF FRANCE.
Dr. Langlet, Mayor of Rheims, who kept in office during the war, performing numerous brave acts and helping in every possible way to mitigate the hardships of the unfortunate citizens.

proved such collective responsibility, the penalties exacted would have been monstrous and barbarous, and in no conceivable manner demanded by military necessity.

Palpably the exaction of those penalties had one single object in view—the terrorisation of the civil population of the invaded country. Only one other motive can be suggested—the desire to avenge on the civil population reverses sustained by the Germans at the hands of military forces.

The bombardment of open coast towns falls under another category than that which we have at present under consideration. But the Zeppelin bombardments in England and the destruction of Rheims Cathedral quite definitely belong to the immediate inquiry, though the evidence regarding them does not come directly from German documents.

Open coast towns bombarded

In the case of Rheims Cathedral, there are two alternative explanations of what took place on September 19th, 1914. One is that incompetent German gunners, legitimately bombarding the city of Rheims, tried to spare the cathedral, but failed ignominiously. The other is that competent German gunners deliberately made a target of the cathedral, with their usual success.

It would seem superfluous to ask which of those two alternatives is the more probable.

It is true that the Germans sought to evade the dilemma by propounding a theory that they did shell the cathedral, but with a justifiable object, because it was being used by the French for an observation-post, and for covering troops and war materials; but, as a matter of fact, the cathedral was not being used for any of those purposes.

At best the Germans could only have been acting upon unverified suspicions—a principle w h i c h would make a clean sweep of the rule against such bombardments, since such suspicions could be urged as justifying the bombardment of any buildings whatsoever.

JEWS BEFORE THE CAMERA.
Typical Polish Jews about to be officially photographed by the German authorities in occupation.

LOOKING PLEASANT FOR THE HUN.
Group of mothers with young children facing the camera for identification purposes. A photograph taken by an official operator in territory occupied by the Germans in France.

the claim that if a town on the coast possessed a couple of obsolete ornamental guns it was not an undefended town but a fortress, and that if it possessed a harbour it was a naval base. The conclusion was like that applied to the Zeppelin raids— that there were not on the English coast any towns or villages entitled to claim protection from bombardments under the Ninth Hague Convention.

It would be interesting to learn whether the same rule applied to the towns and villages on the French coast, but that question has not been put to the test, for lack of opportunity. The plain fact is that the German Government simply wrote off its obligations noted under the Ninth as under the Fourth of The Hague Conventions. It is curious, by the way, that in Germany Metz appears to be the only town which was not entitled to claim immunity from bombardment.

There remains yet another clause in the Fourth of The Hague Conventions—Article 28 of the Regulations — which was repeatedly **Teuton obligations** and indisputably overridden by the **written off** responsible officers of the German Army: "The giving over to pillage of a town or place, even when taken by assault, is forbidden."

It always has been a matter of great difficulty to prevent the soldiery from sacking a town taken by storm. In the Peninsular War the British troops broke from all discipline and obedience when they stormed Badajoz and Ciudad Rodrigo. But looting has been repressed, even if only on disciplinary grounds, by most strong commanders; those who have deliberately permitted it have for centuries been regarded as failing in their duty.

As to Zeppelin raids in England, the German practice involved the assumption that there existed in England no such thing as an undefended town or village, and therefore any town or village might legitimately have bombs dropped upon it. Or it might have been argued that every town or village was a potential munitions factory or camp, or depository of military stores, and might therefore properly be bombarded on that assumption —invalidating all prohibitions whatever.

Convention IX. deals with bombardments by naval forces. Article I forbids the bombardment of undefended ports, towns, villages, etc; but Article 2 excepts military works, military or naval establishments, depôts of arms or war material, and the like.

In the naval raids, and in the air raids against coast towns, undefended watering-places were subjected to bombardment, and the officers who took part therein were applauded and decorated.

The Germans were reduced to justifying themselves by

The Hague Conference has definitely embodied this principle among the recognised rules of civilised warfare. The German command in Belgium and elsewhere did not in set terms authorise pillage, except in the sense that the official sanction for destruction was equivalent to an official permission to pillage. Not only at Louvain, but wherever destruction was authorised, it was accompanied by pillage, for which no punishment was inflicted.

One circumstance, repeated over and over again, was in itself a tacit authorisation; on houses which were known to contain valuables officers affixed notices ordering that they should be left alone—and they were left alone. The pillaging was not the work of an infuriated soldiery who had broken from control, but of troops acting under discipline and obedient to their officers' orders.

Manifestly, in all these cases, the pillaging could have been prevented by a word from the right quarters. The word was not spoken. It was deliberately left unsaid, with full knowledge of the consequences.

The evidence is not indeed to be found in official German documents, but it is overwhelming, consisting not only in the statements of hostile witnesses or in the inferences to be drawn from the ruins at Termonde, Dinant, and a score of other places, but in the notes on events in which they had participated found upon killed or captured Germans.

The argument is the same throughout. It was admitted that "military necessity" may in particular cases compel a disregard for a principle generally accepted as binding. To terrorise the civilian population was a military necessity, therefore no rule which checks the terrorising of the civil population needed to be observed. The fallacy of the syllogism is too palpable to need emphasising.

Besides the prohibitions above discussed, Article 23 in the Regulations appended to the Fourth Convention forbids the employment of poison or poisoned weapons, and of arms, projectiles, or materials calculated to cause unnecessary suffering. At the conference of 1899 declarations were approved and ultimately signed by the Powers represented which explicitly condemned expanding bullets and asphyxiating gases, though with reservations on the part of Great Britain and the United States.

Those declarations retained their binding force after 1907. Nevertheless the Germans in German West Africa avowedly poisoned water supplies, and the Germans in Europe not only introduced asphyxiating gases, but employed gases which inflicted the most agonising sufferings upon their victims.

The pretence that this was forced upon them by the example of the French themselves was absolutely without foundation. Later they introduced also the discharge of liquid fire. The capture of projectors revealed the fact that these crimes had been planned and prepared long before the outbreak of the war, while their adoption was hailed with enthusiastic applause by practically the whole of the German Press.

We have confined ourselves hitherto to cases in which the German Government or the German command was palpably and directly responsible for gross breaches of specific pledges officially ratified; breaches of faith for which the only pretexts put forward were demonstrable falsehoods, obvious afterthoughts, or transparent fallacies.

We turn now to a different class of charges; in plain English, charges of blackguardism, charges which, however vociferously repudiated, are irrefutably proved either specifically or by cumulative evidence.

We may define blackguardism as conduct so universally condemned that its formal prohibition in set terms under agreement is superfluous.

Of all forms of blackguardism, none has been more universally condemned than the use of prisoners, civil or military, as screens for troops. The most damning evidence of the use of civilians **Prisoners as screens** for this purpose by the Germans comes **for troops** itself from a German source. The "Neueste Nachrichten" of Munich published, on October 7th, 1914, a letter from a Bavarian officer, Lieutenant Eberlein. Thus graphically writes the lieutenant:

But we have taken three other civilians. A happy thought strikes me. They are given chairs, and they are ordered to go and seat themselves in the middle of the street. On the one side entreaties, on the other blows with the butt of a rifle. We are slowly becoming shockingly hard-hearted! Well, there they are seated in the street. I am sorry for them, but the means are immediately efficacious. The fire from the houses on our flank diminishes at once, and we can now occupy the house facing, and so are masters of the principal street. Everything that shows itself in the street is shot. By seven in the evening I can report that Saint-Dié is cleared of enemies. I learnt afterwards that another regiment had a precisely similar experience. The four civilians whom they, like ourselves, had set in the middle of the street, were killed by French bullets. I myself saw them stretched out there near the hospital.

GERMAN PRECAUTIONS AGAINST ESPIONAGE IN LUBLIN.
Registration of Jewish inhabitants of Lublin by the provisional German commandant of the town. Each individual was given a brass disc with a number on it, and photographed in groups of twenty, all records being kept by the commandant for reference.

A TRUE DAUGHTER OF FRANCE.

Charming citoyenne of Rheims who displayed a laughing contempt for German shells.   She posed for her photograph in front of a factory which had all but collapsed from bombardment.

had been not to fire, but when we saw women and children shot, my sergeant said "It's too heartrending," and gave orders to fire, which we did.

Another British soldier stated :

I saw some men, women, and children actually brought in the front of the German position from the village. They were being pushed along by Germans. One old man was very old and bent. I noticed two women in particular who had two or possibly three children, and they were holding them close in, as if to shield them.   One of the women had a blue apron on.   Altogether, I suppose there were sixteen to twenty women there, about a dozen children, and half a dozen men.

Seven other similar cases were witnessed by British soldiers, whose evidence is recorded in the report of Lord Bryce's Commission, besides numerous depositions by Belgians. Perhaps the most flagrant example is in the deposition of a Belgian refugee, who was taken prisoner, but succeeded in making his escape after nine days' captivity.

I was taken, he says, to Tournai, where there were about four hundred civilian Belgian prisoners—men, women, and children.   A fight took place there between French and Germans. All the prisoners above referred to, including myself, were marched in front of the German forces to act as a screen. Two of these who did not move quick enough were shot by the Germans

Of unrestrained brutality, the evidence from German note-books is hideously convincing. The originals are in the hands of the French, British, and Belgian Governments. Photographs of them are in many instances published in their reports. They may be headed by an extract from the note-book of a soldier in General Stenger's Brigade, under date, August 27th, 1914. "A brigade order has been received to shoot a'l the French, wounded or not, who shall fall into our hands. We are to make no prisoners." From another note-book of the

The whole tone of this Eberlein letter, and the fact that it was published by a leading Munich newspaper, are extremely significant, and remove all hesitation in accepting the other evidence of similar iniquities given by hostile witnesses, of which four instances, among many, may be cited by way of illustration.

During the retreat from Mons one British officer deposed that the Germans, in order to cover a movement under fire, drove civilians across the firing-line ; and another, that while holding a barricade he and his men saw German troops advancing, pushing in front of them a crowd of civilians—men, women, and children. "The Germans," the deponent went on to say, "could not have advanced apart from the protection afforded them by the civilians, as the street was quite straight and commanded by our rifle fire at a range of about seven hundred to eight hundred yards."

On the same day, August 23rd, a British soldier affirms that the advancing Germans placed women and children in front of them :

They seemed to be pushing them on, and I saw them shoot down women and children who refused to march. Up to this, my orders

same date : "The French prisoners and wounded were all shot, because they mutilate and ill-treat our wounded" [a baseless statement]. "Brigade order."

"We are to make no prisoners"

Evidence of the murdering of the prisoners by order of officers is also voluntarily given in depositions of German prisoners of war, and in half a dozen note-books.

A prisoner of war signed the following statement :

We had been fired at from a house. We broke into the house and had orders to search it, but we could find only two women and a child. My companions declared that the two women had fired, and we did find some arms, revolvers. But I did not see that the women had fired. We told the women that they would not be hurt, because they cried a great deal. We took the women out of the house, and brought them to the commandant and were then given orders to shoot them. When the mother was dead, the commandant ordered the child to be shot, because it could not be left alone in the world. The child's eyes were bandaged. What I have written is true. I took part in it myself because we had the orders from Commandant Kastendick and Captain Dültigen. It grieved me to see it. I had tears in my eyes.

Here is a sinister note. "As we were going to look for water, a young girl with a revolver came in front of us. We killed her, and confiscated the revolver."

From the note-book of a Bavarian soldier:

On the night of August 18th or 19th, the village of Saint Maurice, as a punishment because German troops were fired on, was completely burnt by the German troops, the 12th and 17th Landwehr. The village was surrounded by our men at one pace interval so that no one could come out. Then the Uhlans set it on fire, house by house. No man, woman, nor child could come out. Anyone who tried to do so was shot. All the inhabitants of the village were burnt with it.

At Dinant : " At the entrance of the village lay about fifty civilians, shot for having ambushed and fired upon our troops. In the course of the night many **" Captain Hamann** others were similarly shot ; we could count **was drunk "** more than two hundred. Women and children carrying lights were compelled to help in the horrible scene. Captain Hamann was drunk." The last words were judiciously added in shorthand.

From three other note-books :

At Leffe, nineteen civilians shot—ten more men shot. Since the King of the Belgians has given the order to defend the country by any means, the order has been passed to us to shoot all the male inhabitants. At Dinant, a hundred men or more were collected together and shot. A frightful Sunday.—Creil, September 1st. Bridge has been blown up, so the streets have been burnt and civilians shot.—Orchies, August 25th. Houses were ransacked and all civilians arrested. A woman was shot because, instead of stopping when ordered to halt, she tried to run away. Then the whole place was burnt.

A Bavarian cavalryman, who disliked the business, said that by way of punishment " harsh and sometimes unjust orders have to be given, in consequence of which the worst elements think themselves authorised to commit any kind of atrocity, the Army Service being the worst offenders." An infantry lieutenant observed, " Our company behaves well—a contrast to some others. The pioneers are not worth much, and the artillery are downright brigands." But a grenadier

SHORT SHRIFT FOR SPIES.
Austrian soldiers escorting a suspected Russian peasant to be tried on a charge of espionage.

officer says the infantry are the worst of all!

A non-commissioned officer wrote, on August 12th. 1914 :

You get an idea of the fury of our soldiers when you see the wrecked villages. Not a house spared. You see heaps of men and women, shot by order. I am sorry for the people. After all, if they fight improperly, still they are only defending their country. Mutilation of the wounded is in the Order of the Day.

At Sommepy, September 3rd.

A frightful blood-bath. Village burnt. French thrown into the burning houses, civilians all burnt with the rest.

At Blamont.

We buried all the dead, about sixty. Among them a number of old women, old men, and one woman who was giving birth to a child—a horrible sight. Three children, all together, and all dead.

At Courey, October 22nd.

The village and the workmen's houses plundered and ransacked through and through. Horrible. There is truth in it when they talk of the German barbarians.

THE ENEMY IN POSSESSION.
German soldiers taking it easy at a Serbian house in company with the owner and his family.

We need not, perhaps, attach very great importance to the evidence of Private Wenger. The above extracts have been taken from the **Private Wenger's** note-books of German soldiers who could **letter** have no conceivable object in misrepresenting what they saw ; the Wenger document is a letter photographed and reproduced on another page. In the character of a " lonely soldier " the man would seem to have received a parcel from a well-meaning person in Hamburg who had never seen him, but had probably been given his name by some society ; so he wrote to his unknown friend a nauseous letter—which we may hope she would have been horrified to receive—with the evident intention of impressing her with his own exploits. Even so might Bardolph or Ancient Pistol have written. He mentions casually that some women had shot at his captain, who

THE TERROR IN BELGIUM.
Belgian workman, arrested on a charge of espionage, chained to a German cavalryman and dragged up to " justice."

then told him to shoot them ; whereupon " I bayoneted seven women and four girls in five minutes." But though we may doubt whether the heroic deed was actually done, it is a fact of repulsive significance that a man, writing to a woman, should expect to gain applause by professing to have done it, whether truly or falsely. Of the authenticity of this singularly disgusting document, as of the rest cited, there can be no manner of doubt.

German evidence of German misconduct on the Russian front is at present lacking, save for the statement of one German prisoner, whose name suggests that he was in fact a Prussian Pole. In a signed deposition he says :

> I have frequently seen Russian prisoners of war in Russian uniform employed upon the construction of the third-line trenches of my regiment. There were one hundred and fifty to two hundred Russians altogether so employed. During the course of the work they occasionally came under fire. Two were killed and four wounded. Seven Russians tried to escape—two succeeded, one was shot dead, and four were retaken.

Prussian Pole's deposition The employment of either civilians or prisoners of war upon work in connection with the operations of the war is expressly forbidden in Articles 6 and 23 of the Regulations of the Fourth Hague Convention. Trench-digging is manifestly an operation of war. Prisoners of war by scores or by hundreds could not have been set to trench-digging without the authority of someone in high command. The inference is obvious.

There is one particular form of German frightfulness which has especially affected ourselves and also neutrals— the application of the doctrine that the activities of submarines were not to be limited by the rules of the game as hitherto recognised and practised by all surface craft. There were no precedents for submarine actions as such; therefore a submarine, it seemed, might do as it pleased. **German submarine frightfulness**

It was a universally accepted doctrine that merchant ships might only be sunk in very exceptional circumstances, and then only if adequate provision was made for preserving the lives of passengers and crews. But according to the German doctrine, a submarine was at liberty to sink any merchant vessel at sight, even a neutral, because the submarine could not be certain that the victim was a neutral, and was therefore entitled to assume that she was not. The submarine could not capture her and take her to a German port ; therefore, she might sink her. The submarine might be sent to the bottom if shot at, so she was entitled to secure herself by making shooting impossible. The submarine could not herself take the crew and passengers on board ; therefore, she was under no obligation to consider their security.

THE MAYOR AND CORPORATION OF RHEIMS IN ANTI-POISON GAS MASKS.

Dr. Langlet, the Mayor of Rheims (centre) with the Mayoress, members of the City Council, and personnel of the Town Hall, wearing their respirators. Owing to the frequency with which the Germans hurled asphyxiating gas shells into Rheims, these masks were always held in readiness.

CHILD VICTIM OF THE GERMAN MILITARY JURISTS.
Charged with having retained in his possession an old flint-lock, after an order had been issued that all arms should be rendered up to the German authorities, this unfortunate ten-year-old French boy was sentenced to be shot.

It is superfluous here to discuss the argument, or to cite the series of crimes by which it was illustrated, from the sinking of the Lusitania to that of the Tubantia and the Sussex. The German Navy and the use of it displayed precisely the same characteristics as the German Army and the use of it, though some few German sailors knew how to behave like gentlemen, such as the commander of the Emden, the late Captain Weddigen, and

"Frightfulness" the commander of the Moewe, Count
at sea Dohna. It is safe to say, however, that, outside the German Navy, no sailors would have disgraced their service by such a performance as the bombardment of the stranded and helpless submarine E13.

We give this branch of the subject only scant notice, because the facts are too well known to require demonstration or illustration. We pass from it with one brief but significant note. After twenty months of war, British warships had not been responsible for the death of a single civilian; and they had saved from the sea something like 2,000 men of the German Navy. German ships of war had sent to the bottom of the sea some hundreds of women and children, and a vastly larger number of male non-combatants. The British had not sent one neutral to death nor attacked one hospital-ship; but the Germans——

We need not again tell the story of Edith Cavell's death, a crime committed under colour of law, but hateful in its impersonal inhumanity, stamping its perpetrators with infamy indelible.

Our case has been rested entirely upon (1) facts which are notorious and indisputable, such as the sinking of liners and the destruction of Louvain; or (2) upon the official proclamations of German commanders; or (3) upon the private memoranda of German soldiers, supplemented by the depositions of German prisoners of war. These extracts from note-books could be multiplied almost indefinitely, repeating the ghastly story of miscellaneous and unchecked lootings, **German White** of wholesale burnings, of the casual **Book analysed** murder of individuals, of the deliberate slaughter of civilians, women and children as well as men.

French, British, or Belgian witnesses have not in these pages been called in support, except of the single charge that French and Belgian men, women, and children were deliberately used as screens by the German troops.

There is absolutely no possibility of traversing the evidence. Still, it may be said we have only the evidence of one side; we cannot pass judgment without hearing the German answer.

Very well. We have the official German answer. And the answer is as damning as the evidence. It is contained in the German White Book, issued on May 10th, 1915. This official publication is not easily accessible, but it has been analysed, and its introductory memorandum has been printed in English by Professor J. H. Morgan, in his volume upon "German Atrocities." The defence rests upon the proposition (as concerns Belgium) that the resistance offered by the Belgian civil population

RUSSIAN PEASANT'S VAIN APPEAL.
Sentenced to death for espionage, this ill-fated Russian is seen protesting, but only appears to have elicited cynical smiles from his captors.

FIVE PEASANTS BEING TRIED BY COURT-MARTIAL IN GALICIA.

Dramatic incident on the Balkan front. A number of civilians near the zone of operations, being suspected of conveying information to the enemy, were tried by Austrian Staff officers and peremptorily sentenced. The masked figure on the extreme right is that of the female informant of the Austrian authorities. Below: The reign of terror in Belgium. Group of refugees between Malines and Brussels.

justified and necessitated all the severities exercised. It was open to the German authorities to argue either (1) that the resistance was unorganised, and an unorganised resistance where there has been time to organise is illegitimate under The Hague Convention; or (2) that organised resistance was legitimate *per se*, but was rendered illegitimate because the Belgians disregarded the rules of conduct applying in that case.

The German White Book tries to have it both ways, probably because the authorities had an uneasy sense of the palpable absurdity of pretending that the Belgians had had time to give the civilian resistance an organised shape. So half the time the resistance was punished " because it was not organised," and the other half of the time it was punished for the precisely opposite reason! But there is not even a pretence of proving that the defence was organised, or that there had been time for organising it.

In the second place, the White Book avers that the severity was justified by the " fury " of the Belgian resistance, as at Louvain and at Andenne, or by the atrocities committed upon wounded Germans by the Belgian population. The fury of the resistance at Louvain is demonstrated by the terrible casualty list of the Germans, amounting to no fewer than—five. Andenne is a place which once had 8,000 inhabitants; 7,000 German troops were marching through it. The fury with which they were

254

assaulted justified them in burning the whole place to the ground, slaughtering men, women, and children promiscuously, and then, by their own admission, shooting a hundred of the inhabitants.

As for the evidence of atrocities committed by the Belgians, its value may be gauged by a sample or two. While a German column was marching through a village, and clearing the inhabitants out of the houses, a private saw some little girls " armed with sharp instruments, busying themselves about the German wounded," unperturbed, of course, by the immediate presence of a column of German soldiers. A German patrol, separated from his comrades, walked into a farm where a dozen German wounded were lying, half of them horribly mutilated. There were half a dozen Belgians present, who may or may not have been the perpetrators of the outrage. We are invited to believe that they allowed that one man to walk out again and inform against them at his leisure!

Those two stories are not exceptional; they are typical of the kind of " information " which the German authorities put forward as conclusive proof of Belgian savagery, sufficient to justify wholesale massacres and burnings. The very men who give **An appalling** unqualified credence to these pre- **catalogue** posterous and palpable fabrications denounce as mere malicious inventions, too gross to need refutation, the whole mass of the carefully sifted and for the most part unimpeachable evidence of German atrocities published or expected to be published by the Belgian, French, and British Commissions of Inquiry.

We have scarcely spoken of the evidence given by Belgians, French, or British, because it is the evidence of witnesses with a hostile bias. It would be difficult to imagine a task more sickening than has been that of investigating the appalling catalogue of specific charges soberly made by a vast crowd of eye-witnesses and personal victims of crimes perpetrated by the Germans.

After making every allowance for wilful or involuntary

exaggeration, for inaccuracy of statement, for the possibility even of deliberate invention, in cases carefully sifted by tribunals whose one desire was to ascertain the truth, the evidence is overwhelming and unspeakably terrible.

It is impossible to doubt the truth of frequent and deliberate firing upon ambulances and hospitals, of sham surrenders made to trap the enemy, of abuse of the Red Cross. "Repulsive" is a word wholly inadequate to describe the hideous tale of outrages upon women and young girls; and this tale we know would be far larger but for the reluctance of the victims themselves to speak of what they suffered.

Women stripped and abused, mothers violated before their children, daughters violated before their mothers, husbands and fathers murdered for daring to attempt interposition, ghastly mutilations, slaughter of the victims for struggling against their captors or after they had been outraged—these things were not **German officers'** exceptional abominations, but a part of **guilt** the programme. Murders of helpless old men and boys, women and children, were commonplaces of the days when the invasions of Belgium and of France were in progress.

No other conclusion can be reached from a perusal of the depositions. No other conclusion has been possible for the commissioners; and perhaps the worst horror of the thing lies in this—that the German soldier, drunk or not drunk, gleefully sated his brute passions, his lust for blood and destruction, his taste for sheer filthy beastliness, and his instincts of brigandage, unrestrained by superior officers who not infrequently themselves set the example; although the discipline of the German machine was such that, whenever the higher authorities chose to give the word, such crimes were held completely in check.

THE GENTLE HUN IN SERBIA.
Serbian refugees in German hands. A photograph taken by the enemy.

CIVILIANS UNDER PRUSSIA'S IRON HEEL IN POLAND AND BELGIUM.
A scene that was typical of the hopeless misery suffered by the people of territory overrun by Germany's ruthless soldiery. A family of despairing Polish refugees stranded by the wayside, owing to the Germans having commandeered the horse from the cart that contained all their worldly goods. Picture above: Belgian village girl being interrogated by German sentries.

MOVING A CAPTIVE AERIAL SCOUT TO A NEW POSITION.

A French captive observation balloon, or "spotter," being shifted to a "healthier" position on the French front. The Frenchman who obtained this photograph wrote: "On reçoit trop de marmites; la saucisse céde la place" ("We are getting too many saucepans; the sausage yields ground"). "Saucepan" was the nickname given by the French to one of the larger types of German shells, while "sausage" was the term they applied to their balloon.

CHAPTER CXI.

THE AERIAL WAR: PERIOD OF GERMAN ASCENDANCY.

Amazing Small Number of Our Machines—Average Life of Engines only Six Hours—The Royal Aircraft Factory and the Road to Disaster—Air Commanders Who Could Not Fly—Our Large Resources Wasted for Want of Organisation—Germany's Magnificent Progress in Engines and Machines—The Enemy Gains the Command of the Air against Great Odds—He Encourages His Private Manufacturers while We are Strangled by Officialism—How Fokker Aped his Way to Fame and Power—Great Superiority of German Air Engines—Strange Tale of the R.A.F. and the German Engine—All the Burden of Aerial Warfare Falls on France—She Has to Help Russia, Italy, Serbia, and Laggard Britain—Crisis in French Aviation and Movement of Reform by Blériot and Clemenceau—Mr. Pemberton-Billing and Mr. Spenser Wilkinson Agitate for a Reorganisation of Our Air Services—The Derby Committee, Lord Montagu, and Pemberton-Billing—Extraordinary Allegation of Murder of British Pilots—Crisis in Russian Aviation—The Great Retreat and the Blinding of the Russian Army—Brilliant Exploits by Our Naval Wing at Dunkirk—Warneford Brings Down a Zeppelin at Ghent—The French Take Over Our Work of Raiding German Military Centres—Attacks on Karlsruhe and Stuttgart—We Lose More Men and Machines through Defects than through Hostile Attack—" You Cannot Start an Aeroplane Merely by Touching a Button."

FROM the end of March, 1915, to the end of March, 1916, the condition of things in our air services was so bad that we did not care to attempt to write the history of our aerial forces. It was not until certain Midland centres were roused by the Zeppelin raid of January, 1916, and until a remarkable degree of plain speaking was attained by members of the Houses of Lords and Commons, acquainted with the condition of our aerial resources, that we could discuss the matter with any profit.

After the extraordinary scandal in regard to guns and shells had been courageously ventilated in May, 1915, our warlike strength was sufficiently increased towards the end of the year for the new Minister of Munitions to safely make the statement that we had been producing only five thousand high-explosive shells daily against the German output of two hundred and fifty thousand shells of the same kind. It is not yet possible to indicate what was the proportion of aeroplane engines of high power produced in Great Britain and in Germany in May, 1915; but it will probably be found, when all the facts are known, that our Royal Aircraft Factory and the Advisory Committee for

BRITISH AIRMAN WHO BOMBED A ZEPPELIN.
Lieutenant Brandon, R.F.C., who attacked the raiding Zeppelin L15 on March 31st, 1916, from a height of 9,000 feet.

Aeronautics and the National Physical Laboratory working with it, did much less to assure victory for our naval and military airmen than the old Munition Committee had done to help our gunners in Flanders.

Our defects in regard to aerial resources were profound, widespread, and rooted in an apparently invincible system of officialism. A man of fine practical knowledge, large grasp of mind, and smashing force of character was needed to help our scanty pilots and still scantier designers of machines and engines of first-rate quality. Such a man did not emerge. By an unhappy chance, the only person in the British Government possessing the knowledge and the driving power likely to make us supreme in the air was Mr. Winston Churchill, who was thought largely responsible for the disaster in the Dardanelles. According to one school of naval opinion, the retirement of Mr. Churchill and Lord Fisher produced a more balanced and better connected scheme of general work in our Navy. We are not inclined to dispute this statement, which was made by Mr. Arthur Balfour, Admiral Meux, and newspaper writers alleged to be partial to Lord Beresford. But we can confidently maintain that with the disappearance of Mr. Winston Churchill from the Admiralty

THE GUNNERS WHO HELPED TO HIT THE ZEPPELIN L15—MEN CONGRATULATED BY VISCOUNT FRENCH.

there vanished from power the only man of standing who might have saved one, at least, of our aerial services from a condition of disastrous weakness.

Both our Navy and our Army owed to Mr. Churchill personally the small amount of good material they possessed at the outbreak of hostilities. By recognising the merits of certain proprietary machines, Mr. Churchill prevented many of our more important private manufacturers of aeroplanes from throwing up their business, and enabled them to supply our pilots in

Average life of engines August, 1914, with some better aerial scouts and fighting aeroplanes than the enemy possessed. According to a German report, it was merely two Vickers' gun-carrying machines that enabled us to win, during the vitally critical period that ended with the Battle of the Marne, the temporary command of the air. Our total service aircraft then appears to have been the ridiculously small number of thirty military aeroplanes, twelve naval aeroplanes, and twenty seaplanes—in all, sixty-two machines. The average life of many of the engines of these machines was *only six hours!*

For some years before the war our leading airmen had been asking for gun-carrying machines, the value of which could clearly be foreseen. But our Government works, the Royal Aircraft Factory, with its Advisory Committee, the National Physical Laboratory, its mathematicians, theorists, multitudinous officials, and routine-ridden workmen, could not, or would not, supply our fighting airmen with the machines they needed. Neither could these men, though backed by large subsidies and by incomparable means for making experiments, supply our Army and Navy with the aero-engine required to compete with the German motors. We did have a British engine, the Green engine, that could easily have been developed into a good prime mover for aerial work; but, being a private British invention, it suffered a fate like that of all private British flying machines, and was not taken up by the officials of the R.A.F. For some time these officials acted as Government inspectors of all private-made machines submitted for sale to the War Office. But they neglected so many machines which were afterwards found to be serviceable, that even the War Office had at last to appoint its own inspectors of machines and engines in order to get the material it wanted.

At the time of writing, nobody connected with the Royal Aircraft Factory seems to have had any feeling that he helped to lead us down the road to disaster. On the contrary, neutral journalists were proudly shown over the establishment at Farnborough, with its 3,000 workmen, and

were informed that the works were to be regarded as a glorious example of British science and organisation. The truth of the matter is that, since our coal-tar dyes industry was conquered by Germany, owing almost entirely to the lordly unpracticalness of British men of science and to their utterly unbusinesslike character, there has been no such monument of theoretic futility and of the narrow-minded jealousy that stamps so many of our scientific intellects as the Royal Aircraft Factory, which we owe to Lord Haldane, Brigadier-General Seely, and other politicians at the War Office. We can excuse a soldier, like Sir David Henderson—he was trained to obedience; and when he, as a mere officer who had learned to fly out of keenness for new developments in his profession, was opposed by politicians, official experts, and other men of authority, he was overborne by the show of superior intellect against him. His resignation would not have called the attention of the nation to the defects in the work of the men of science. There was no Board of Aerial Service, formed of practised fighting aviators, whose resignation would have told the public there was something vitally wrong with the service. Neither in the Army nor in the Navy were even practised flyers always put in command. As late as February 16th, 1916, Mr. Ellis Griffith stated in the House of Commons:

Of the six brigadier-generals in the air service, only one man has flown at the front from the beginning of the war. Men are promoted to the position of squadron-commanders with practically no experience in flying. A man who learned flying in December, 1915, is now an acting wing-commander of the Royal Flying Corps.

Such were some of the conditions in which the Royal Aircraft Factory, with its scientific experts and 3,000 workmen, was able to escape thorough investigation with regard to all the things it had done **Government aircraft production** and left undone from 1912 to 1916. A Parliamentary committee of inquiry—composed of men with practical personal knowledge of aviation, and helped by naval and military pilots of long experience, and by some good shop-managers of the speeding-up school—should have been appointed to examine into the great scandal of Government aircraft production, even to the point of discovering the reasons why good machines and engines made by private firms had been formerly passed over by R.A.F. men.

But long before such an inquiry had been even vaguely dreamed of, the cancer of academic futility had spread from the War Office to the Admiralty. This pernicious outgrowth seems to have been directly due to the resignation of Mr. Winston Churchill and to the appointment of Mr. Balfour to the position of First Lord. Mr. Balfour had followed the progress of flying machines from the days when Wright first flew in France, but he showed no practical mastership whatever of the problem his predecessor had left him. Mr. Churchill had promised the nation that a swarm of hornets should be ready to attack an invading squadron of Zeppelins; and it was reported that just before he resigned office he was busy creating the machines of defence. He had organised an amateurish corps of Naval Anti-Aircraft gunners, with pea-shooting pom-poms and a few little guns, some of which were sited around London; but it does not appear to have been expected that these queer weapons would be able to bring down a Zeppelin from a height of ten thousand feet. They were provided only with shrapnel, instead of incendiary shell, and the crews had practically no real training in firing at aerial targets. It does not seem to have been seriously desired to bring down a loaded Zeppelin on London or any other important English city, for fear that **Mr. Churchill's scheme** the burning airship and its cargo of bombs would do more damage than its destruction was worth. A mere gunnery demonstration, with a real fighting aeroplane defence around the coast and continual raids on Zeppelin sheds, seems to have been Mr. Churchill's scheme.

When he left the Admiralty this policy was not maintained; the new Lords of the Admiralty saw fit to adopt an air policy of inactivity. Naval pilots were no longer despatched on raiding expeditions across the Rhine to attack German airship sheds, and no further attack was made upon German bases for aerial reconnaissance in the North Sea. Part of the work of supplying material was allowed to fall into the official hands of the Royal Aircraft Factory, thus undoing some of Mr. Winston Churchill's historic achievement of finding new and larger sources of practical invention outside official circles. Our Naval Wing at Dunkirk was so impoverished in regard to machines that the pilots under Wing-Commander Longmore had to use foreign aeroplanes.

The fact that the R.N.A.S. airmen in Flanders did some remarkably good work with poor British material is no doubt a tribute to their airmanship. But what can we say of a country, rich in all industrial resources and distinguished by designing engineers of original genius, that leaves its fighting men, after twenty months of war, less well equipped against their foes than they comparatively were at the opening **Good work with** of hostilities? Our Army airmen in the **poor material** first month of 1916 were also mounted in some cases upon machines inferior in strength, speed, and climbing power to aeroplanes made by private British firms. There had been a much-desired reform, in October, 1915, in regard to the connection between the War Office and the Royal Aircraft Factory. An Army officer who was a good engineer was put in charge of all military aeromotors, with the result that engines were selected without any official bias against private makers, and with the sole aim of improving our aerial fighting power. But good engines could not be found, tested, made in large quantities, and built into admirable machines quickly under the conditions obtaining in our unorganised nation.

The general public still believed that we retained command of the air, and most of our aircraft workmen, especially the three thousand in the Royal Aircraft Factory, were averse to being speeded up when everything in official communiqués told of our aerial predominance; so, from the autumn of 1915 to the spring of 1916, the flower of our Royal Flying Corps was killed or captured, often because

THE LAST OF ZEPPELIN L15, LYING LIKE A GIANT WHALE HALF SUBMERGED IN THE SEA.
Zeppelin L15 raided the Eastern Counties during the night of March 31st-April 1st, 1916, and was brought down off the Thames estuary after being crippled either by gun fire or by bombs dropped by an airman. These two photographs show the wrecked aerial cruiser just before she disappeared beneath the waves.

their machines were of inferior make, as a British officer complained in a letter written from his German prison.

It is not extravagant to say that if the Royal Aircraft Factory, with its cumber of committee and officials, had not existed, we should have maintained the command of the air. This we won in the first weeks of the war by means of machines made by Mr. A. V. Roe, of Manchester, Messrs. Vickers & Maxim, of Sheffield and Barrow, Sir George White, of Bristol, and other private firms mentioned in our previous chapter on the **Germany's remarkable progress** development of aerial warfare. As it was, the Germans left us to the mercy of our Royal Aircraft Factory, and copied the fine features of the fast scouts and battle-planes which had been invented by private British manufacturers. The Germans also copied the Morane-Saulnier and other good French machines, and extended their own private aircraft works in an enormous manner. Dr. Hansen, who was in London just before the outbreak of war, took back with him drawings of the new Bristol scout biplane, which, with the latest Morane-Saulnier monoplane, was manufactured in a new aircraft factory founded in Cologne. Baron von Skoda, the maker of the

PREPARING FOR HOSTILE AIRCRAFT AT SALONIKA.
French airmen setting fuses in readiness for an enemy aeroplane.

famous 12 in. Austrian howitzer, established a large aircraft factory near Vienna, and a Dutch crack pilot, Fokker, after trying a machine of his own design that was of no use, undertook to manufacture Morane machines in Germany. The Bristol Company's works at Halberstadt were commandeered, rechristened, and much extended; and many other German factories were greatly developed, and in many cases set to work on standardised designs in order to supply German needs.

These needs were great. The German pilots had to meet the Russians in the east, the French in the west, and the British near and around the coast of Belgium and north-west coast of Germany. In other words, the German designer had to fight against the inventive brains of Britain, France, Belgium, and Russia, with the American inventor and the Japanese inventor intervening. The entrance of Italy into the war left Austria matched against the inventive Italians of the new engineering school, so that all the main burden of the first great aerial war fell upon Germany. We had only to compete with the German pilots on a front of some thirty miles during the first phase of trench warfare, while the Germans had a thousand miles of front to reconnoitre and defend against the airmen of France,

Russia, Britain, and Belgium. The Belgians counted because they were a nation of inventive engineers and skilled mechanics; though they had lost their mines and factories, their intellectual power and craftsmanship still told against the common enemy. It might fairly have been reckoned, at the outbreak of war, that Germany and Britain were well matched in regard to potential output of flying machines. Our private manufacturers had led the world in the quality of their products, and with the Royal Aircraft Factory and our vast resources in motor engineering and American supplies at our call, our race, which had invented the steam-engine, the railway, the principle of the dynamo, and other magnificent instruments of power, should have been fully able to keep pace with German engineers.

We ought to have been in a position in May, 1915, to help France and Russia in holding the dominion of the air on the combined lines of fifteen hundred miles, instead of having to cry for aid from French aeroplane makers to enable our airmen to hold their own on a thirty-mile front.

The odds against Germany in aerial warfare would have been overwhelming had we performed our duties to our Allies in regard to the design and manufacture of machines and the training of a large host of pilots and observers. Our position was shameful. The position of the Germans was glorious. Not since the English of the Elizabethan age outfought at sea Philip of Spain, with the resources of a continent behind him, had there been so superb a victory against great odds as the Germans won in the air. Their Zeppelins did not help them much in military matters. It was their swift reorganisation of the production of heavier-than-air machines which enabled them to hold their immense double front on land, and save their artillery from being blinded. The energy and organising ability with which they met the situation command our admiration.

In spite of the fact that their success was founded upon our delay, the efforts they made were magnificent. They had men of science to assist and stimulate their private manufacturers, but there was no Royal German Aircraft Factory standing between their enterprising private designers and their pilots in the field. Field requirements seem directly and quickly to have governed all the work of the designing engineers. The famous Taube, despite the advertisement it received throughout the world, was rapidly scrapped at the demand of pilots who **Albatross displaces** had proved its inefficiency. Other **the Taube** well-known machines of more power were also thrown aside, and the standardisation of new models with unusual qualities was undertaken. The new Albatross was tried in the spring of 1915, and then made by the hundred. Soon afterwards there followed a large gun-carrying machine with two engines, and then the deadly Fokker scout.

Scarcely any remarkable originality in design was seen in the new German engines. For example, both British and French aviators had for months employed a machine-gun firing through the propeller before Fokker adopted this idea. It is reported to have been the invention of the brilliant French airman Garros; and it was when Garros was brought down with his machine in German territory

Improvised anti-aircraft lorry in No Man's Land. The better to follow movements of a hostile aeroplane, R.N.A.S. gunners mounted their weapon on the chassis of a motor-'bus, thus being able to re-attack the enemy under more advantageous conditions.

Exciting incident with an armoured car in the first line. The vehicle sunk axle deep in the soft road, and was in process of being dug out when a German battery of 5·9 guns discovered it. Shells fell all round the car, which was preserved only by a miracle of luck.

ANTI-AIRCRAFT GUNNERS, AND A THRILLING AFFAIR ON THE WEST FRONT.

RETURNING FROM A NORTH SEA
FLIGHT.
German seaplane returning from a flight
over the North Sea.

and made a prisoner, on April 19th, 1915, that Fokker got to work imitating the new firing arrangement. Garros had made his propeller with deflecting blades, so that the small percentage of his machine-gun bullets which hit it were turned away without damaging the driving structure. The machine-gun was fixed in relation to the propeller through which it fired, and the entire machine had to be manœuvred in order to take aim at an opponent. Fokker merely copied this design and the French machine to which it was attached; but he installed a more powerful air-engine than the French were using. The use of armour was also copied by the Germans, especially from British machines, and, as we have already pointed out, the fast, small, German scouts and the German gun-carrying "'buses" were closely imitated from British designs. The Germans also copied a fine and very powerful Italian machine, the Caproni. In short, they showed scarcely any inventive gift in regard to machine design.

Their native source of strength resided in their aero-engines. These engines were much better than ours, and it took us nearly a year to produce motors as efficient as the best German ones. Again, however, there was no surprising inventive power in the German engineers. They won forward by careful workmanship and continual experiment with many failures. Even their best engine, the Maybach, seems to have worked badly in some of the new Zeppelins, having to be improved in 1916 by the slow process of trial and error. The success of the German makers of aero-engines was due almost entirely to the Government encouragement given to them before and throughout the war, and to the discouragement which the theoretic faddists of the Royal Aircraft Factory inflicted upon all British engineers who tried to produce something better than the 70 h.-p. air-cooled engine used on our slow Government craft. Our private aeroplane makers had first to rely upon the Gnome and other French engines, by reason of the repressive attitude adopted by Royal Aircraft

Source of Teuton ascendancy

officials, who apparently wished to wait until the great, wonderful, scientific, Government-designed engine arrived to triumph over all the world.

But as this engine never arrived, our condition in regard to readily-available British motors was disastrous. The history of the Royal Aircraft Factory and its Advisory Committee and Laboratory men of science, affords a fair measure of the effect which a system of State Socialism would have upon the inventive powers of the British race. Practically all our great inventions were due to private individuals. Bodies of ordinary men of science of the official type have done exceedingly little to help forward any great progress in mechanics, medicine, chemical

WITH THE AIRMEN OF THE GERMAN FLEET.
German sailors hauling a hydroplane out of the water at Wilhelmshafen.

industries, and other important forms of national activity. The official type of scientist can explain the theory of accomplished facts—never can he himself invent. The most he can do is to make some small improvement in the achieved work of more creative men. It is because we had an amateur of science, Lord Haldane, at the head of our War Office, who thought that invention was merely a matter of official organisation, that the Royal Aircraft Factory blundered into existence. The nation that Lord Haldane took as his model did not imitate him and Brigadier-General Seely, and make their progress in aviation depend upon a new, conceited, and petty-minded Government department. A Chair of Aeronautic Research was established in Berlin; but it was on private inventors and experimenters, such as Count Zeppelin and the leading engineers in the German motor-engine industry, that the practical, organising Prussian depended for quick results and warlike profits. The Germans had the Benz engine of 150 h.-p. to 180 h.-p., and in the winter of 1915 the Mercédès Motor-Car Company brought out a splendid aero-engine, which was used on the Albatross machines. We had quite half a dozen motor-car firms with just as good engine designers and fine mechanics as the Benz and Daimler Companies.

Our men needed only a little sunshine of Government orders to produce motors better even than the best German ones. Our motor-car trade was flourishing; we led the world with the Rolls-Royce, and in commercial motor-traction design we were also outrivalling the Teutons. Therefore, Britain's productive resources, progressive designers, and skilled workmen were very remarkable. Instead of failing, after twenty months' war, to hold German airmen on our small length of front, we ought to have been able to help crippled France, and export machines of incomparable quality to Russia and Italy. But for some time the Royal Aircraft Factory's adopted foreign engine remained our official type, with the result that many of our best pilots were outclimbed, outraced, outmanœuvred, shot, burned to death, or captured by German pilots who possessed better-engined machines.

R.A.F. and German engine As a matter of fact, the Royal Aircraft Factory tried at last to redeem its reputation by copying a captured Mercédès engine. Apparently, some special steel had been used by the German motor-car company. Our Sheffield steelmakers, who excelled both Germans and Americans, could quickly have manufactured something at least equal to the Mercédès material. But our Government aeronautic experts would not rely upon the private steelmakers of Sheffield any more than they would rely upon our private aeroplane makers. Disdaining all rule-of-thumb methods, they laboriously analysed the special material of the Mercédès engine, and then built up a synthesis of it, and after their grand scientific labours the thing was not a success.

Owing to our delay all the burden of aerial warfare fell on France. The French were quite as admirable as the Germans in aircraft production, for the French had to struggle on, with their chief industrial districts in the hands of the enemy and all their young men in the fighting-line. It was only when General Joffre was able to release some of the French Territorials—oldish married men of the Landsturm type—that the French war factories could speed up their production. The French seem to have obtained some help from the watch-making districts of French-speaking Switzerland, peopled by tens of thousands of men accustomed to very fine, exact metal-work. Many of the watchmakers, however, were required for making shell-fuses, and there had to be large dilutions of skilled labour in some of the aircraft factories. The result was that some French machines deteriorated in quality, and it was in these machines that some of our best pilots lost their lives.

The French were working at over-pressure. They had some of their best men—such as Paulhan—in Serbia with a park of machines, fighting the Austrians and training the Serbians. Then, in the summer of 1915, a still larger band of French pilots of the first class, with a considerable number of the best machines of the new type, went to Italy, and nobly helped in the aerial battles of the Alps, until the Italians expanded their production of machines and corps of flyers. Moreover, about this time our Admiralty authorities of the new régime abandoned the air

policy of Mr. Winston Churchill, and gave over arranging long raids against the enemy's Zeppelin bases in the Rhineland and on the shore of Lake Constance. The French not only took over this work, but greatly extended it in a long series of distant bombing expeditions in German territory. The French factories supplied Russia with practically all her machines, beginning with a thousand aeroplanes before the war, together with some fine French pilots, and continuing with new and powerful models as the conflict on the eastern front increased in violence. The Russians lost their old machines at a fearful rate, and really needed the entire output of France to keep the air. But much-enduring France, with all her best manhood in the trenches, and her chief coal-mines held by the enemy, could not supply all Russia's needs. Still, she continued to do all she could. And on the top of this demand from Russia, Italy, and Serbia, came Great Britain, with her adult male working population still unhampered by conscription, and asked for large supplies of French air-engines and French machines.

Germany had only to help the Turks, and later the Bulgarians; for Austria was able, with Skoda's great plant at Neustadt, Vienna, and smaller private factories

GERMAN AIR-RAIDERS BOMBING SALONIKA.
An anti-aircraft gun on a British warship firing at the three enemy aeroplanes which raided Salonika and dropped about thirty bombs, on the morning of December 30th, 1915. This flagrant act of war on Greek soil was followed by the arrest of the Consuls of Germany, Austria, Turkey, and Bulgaria, who the same evening were conveyed on board a French warship.

ABOVE THE CLOUDS.
Pilot's view of an opponent aeroplane.   Remarkable impression of two
machines at an altitude of many thousand feet.

elsewhere, to make all the machines required on the
Galician and Italian fronts. Germany had also many
first-rate mechanics in the industrial region of Russian
Poland and in Belgium who could be set to work on
apparently peaceful jobs, if they did not like making things
that could be clearly seen to be war-machines. There were
many parts of engine structures, magnetos, and metal
framework which the mechanics of the conquered non-
combatant population could be induced to make for a
living, without knowing that they were helping to slaughter
the Allies. Therefore, in the duel of aircraft production
between Germany and France, with Britain " slacking " all
the time, the material advantages of Germany were
enormous. She had the fine iron ores of Sweden fully at
her disposal ; and even when our submarines began to
operate in the Baltic the German accumulations of fine
iron ore carried them on through the
winter. France had the ores of Spain
within her reach, while British steelmakers worked for her, and Americans
also helped. But highly-skilled French workmen were
inadequate in number, especially in the aircraft factories,
and French officialism hindered the manufacturers.

The crisis in French aviation was similar to that in our
country. On September 14th, 1915, a Radical-Socialist
deputy, M. René Besnard, was appointed as a sort of Minister
of aircraft production, in the hope that he would prove the
Lloyd George of French aviation, and give his country
the material for winning the dominion of the air. But
though M. Besnard was an eloquent orator, he had little
practical knowledge, and none of the gifts of an organiser.
The French aeroplane makers struggled on like our own
in bitter silence ; while the French public, also like our
own, were kept, by official statements, proud and confident

**Crisis in French
aviation**

of their aerial services. The one thing upon which the
French especially prided themselves was the immunity of
their capital from German air-raiders. Paris was only
fifty miles from the German front at Noyon ; and for
many months no Zeppelin disturbed the Parisians, though
distant England was being raided frequently.

We were informed in great detail of the wonderful aerial
defences of Paris, and the extraordinary suggestion was
made that the Paris aeroplane squadron should cross the
Channel and organise the defences of London. It is only
fair to say that this suggestion was made by some admiring
Englishmen with no knowledge of the squadron of Paris,
for the squadron in question was not an entire success.
It was really the light French gun served by the superb
French gunner that defended Paris ; and when, early in
1916, a Zeppelin raided the capital under
cover of a fog, the French public at last   **How Paris was**
began to inquire into the merits of the   **defended**
Paris squadron. The inquiry soon
extended to the Aviation Department of the French
War Office and to the French Government. M. René
Besnard fell, and M. Clemenceau, the President of
the French Aerial League, began to agitate for the reform
of the general direction of French aviation. The situation
was explained by the famous French engineer and Channel
flyer, M. Blériot, in a letter published on February 5th,
1916, in M. Clemenceau's newspaper :

"The development of French aviation," said M. Blériot, " is
being retarded. The reason is very plain. The men who created
the science of airmanship have been removed from all technical committees, from the study of programmes of construction, and from
the general control of affairs. For the most part these men are
engineers, constructors, and airmen.   Let them be given the real
technical control, in collaboration with two or three pilots selected
from among the best of our fighting men. Then in four months
we shall almost recover the leadership we have lost. But there is
only just time to do it. Only a few men are necessary. They are
Voisin, Caudron, Bréguet, Saulnier, Bechereau, Délage, and Farman.
Let us form out of them an aerial committee for the defence of
France. Their past record would be a guarantee for the future."

In its origin, however, the French crisis was different from
ours. The controlling power in France had fallen into the
hands of men without up-to-date experience, who knew
nothing about what the Germans were doing, and so failed
to provide the men at the front with proper equipment. The
manufacturers knew what was wanted, but could not get
the officials to order the new models in time to cope with
the progress of German machines. In Great Britain, on
the other hand, it was not men who had once flown at
thirty miles an hour who retarded the development of
our material.

Our soldiers and sailors, even at the War Office
and the Admiralty, earnestly wanted the best machines
and the best engines they could get. But they had been
deluded by official assurances that a slow official machine
had more factors of safety than the swift machine built by
our private manufacturers. The real factors of safety in
aerial warfare were speed in passing the enemy's anti-
aircraft guns, escaping from better armed pursuing
craft, and climbing power that enabled the pilot to get
above his enemy. Until the Fokker arrived, neither the
French nor the British technical committees and departments, that drew up programmes of construction, understood the needs of the situation. In both cases there were
only two classes of men who could put things right—first,
the active service pilots ; and second, the experienced
designers in private firms, who had led the way in almost
every development of a warlike nature. In neither country
were these two classes of men consulted by the authorities. The result was that the Germans, who connected
field experience closely with design and experiment in new
engines and machines, were able to win a series of remarkable aerial victories.

By another curious coincidence, both in France and
Britain, the attention of the peoples was not drawn to the
defects of their military and naval machines by what was

The Belgian Royal Family at their villa in devastated Flanders.

In shell-wrecked Rheims: Two floors of a shattered house near the Cathedral.

Result of a single German shell that plunged through an office at Rheims.

Woman's tribute to heroic Womanhood - The Edith Cavell Memorial Service in St. Paul's Cathedral, October 29th, 1915.

going on at the front. It was Count Zeppelin, by a series of raids with his famous airships, who forced the French and British publics to take a general interest in aeroplane engines and aeroplane design.

The French people, however, showed themselves more alert to the needs of the situation. We produced no Blériot, ready to sacrifice if necessary all his future chances of Government contracts in order to obtain satisfactory conditions of manufacture. The root-causes of our lack of progress in design, lack of development in aero-engines, and general retardation in the production of large numbers of first-rate machines remained. What we required was a Board of Control on the lines sketched by M. Blériot for France, together with his implied plan of amalgamation of all private aircraft factories, with a view to a large standardised production of machines of a superior type. All the scientific

work of the Royal Aircraft Factory **M. Blériot's** should have been carried out for the **Board of Control** common benefit of all firms working on Government orders, and the three thousand workmen at Farnborough should have been placed under the control of foremen such as Messrs. Vickers employ in their speeding-up system of management. But no sign was to be seen in our country of a plan of a complete and enlightened reorganisation of our aircraft industry by a board of practical manufacturers and leading pilots, with some man like Lord Montagu of Beaulieu as Air Minister and Government representative.

From our service airmen, however, there came at last a violent agitation for the reform of our aerial policy. Mr. Pemberton-Billing, a well-known aeroplane constructor, who had joined the Royal Naval Air Service, resigned his commission as flight-commander, and after contesting the constituency of Mile End, was elected Member of Parliament for East Herts on March 10th, 1916. In the circumstances it was a very remarkable thing for an eager and capable flying man to leave the adventurous front of battle and do nothing but talk. But such was the condition of affairs in both our aerial forces that one talker who could attract the attention of the electorate was worth more than a score of silent, hard-working airmen. There was in the country a large and increasing body of opinion dissatisfied with the state of the air services, and Mr. Pemberton-Billing, from his practical knowledge and well-informed criticisms of our defects, seemed likely to prove a goad of sufficient poignancy to compel the Coalition Cabinet to develop all available resources for winning the command of the air.

Mr. Spenser Wilkinson, Chichele Professor of Military History at Oxford, unexpectedly came forward to support the attack which Mr. Pemberton-Billing made upon the British air authorities. Mr. Spenser Wilkinson had lost a son, an officer in the Royal Flying Corps, and he stated in regard to the Royal Aircraft Factory's part in the war :

Mr. Pemberton-Billing used strong language about the machines given to our men at the front. He spoke of machines " with regard to which every one of our pilots knew when he stepped into them that if he got back it would be more by luck and by his skill than by any mechanical assistance he got from the people who provided him with machines." *That is the truth, as all those know who have had any intimate conversation with airmen who have been at the front.*

Lord Montagu of Beaulieu, happily saved from the torpedoed P. and O. liner Persia, also came forward as a critic of our air policy, but after one telling speech in the House of Lords he was reduced to silence by being appointed assistant to Lord Derby on the new Air Committee. Mr. Pemberton-Billing, however, challenged violently, on March 21st, 1916, in a speech in the House of Commons, the merits of the principal members of the Committee.

I would like to ask what qualification Lord Derby has for deciding the destinies of the air service, and what that noble lord can do, when sitting at the head of a table with a multitude of counsellors

HIDDEN ON A MOUNTAIN PEAK.
Italian anti-aircraft gun ingeniously screened from enemy aeroplane observers.

counselling him upon a subject of which he knows, I regret to say, nothing. . . . His assistant, Lord Montagu, criticised the Government, and what is the result ? Within twenty-four hours he is roped in and told to sit on the Committee. Then he has to confess in another twenty-four hours that he would like to say a number of things in the interests of the country, but unfortunately his lips are sealed.

Then we have a gallant officer of the General Staff on this Committee. His peculiar knowledge of aeronautics is quite unknown to me. It may be very great, but I have been associated with aviation since 1904, and I have never heard his name in that connection.

Then we have Admiral Vaughan Lee, an able and gallant officer who has devoted the whole of his life to the noble profession of the sea, where, I believe, he has gained a very high reputation. But so surely as he is well advised and capable as a naval officer, so surely he is ignorant as a babe in matters of aeronautics. He is the naval officer to whom this country is looking to solve the problem of how we shall beat our enemies in the air. I fear that his name will be coupled with the names of other officers who have been sacrificed on the altar of the Government's ineptitude.

Then there is General Henderson, who is also on the Committee. I have never had the pleasure of meeting General Henderson. I know he is a very able officer, but so far as the air services are concerned I have heard him referred to as the De Rougemont of the air services. We then **Mr. Pemberton-** have Commodore Sueter. Commodore Sueter **Billing's challenge** is the father of the Naval Air Service, and he, together with Squadron-Commander Briggs, represents the expert opinion on that Committee. . . . I would suggest that whatever this Committee makes it is likely to be reactionary. When does it meet ? I understand that, in the last six weeks, it met on six occasions. That means to say that for over five weeks a policy of pondering or waiting to see has been adopted. Anybody appointed to deal with this very pressing question of the air should sit, not once in six days, but every day, and, if necessary, all day, until some solution is found to our third-class position as an air Power." ·

In a still more striking speech Mr. Pemberton-Billing thoroughly aroused the country by stating that our naval and military airmen had been " murdered " by being

BRITISH AIRMAN "STANDING BY" READY TO BE OFF AFTER ENEMY AIRCRAFT SOMEWHERE IN THE LEVANT.
Graphic illustration of the method by which the aeroplane was held in position until the engine speed was up and the signal was given to "Go!"

ordered to carry out their work on "rotten material," though we then possessed the finest machines in the world. He was apparently referring to our heavy losses in highly trained officers upon the slow, inferior Royal Aircraft Factory machines, which were being produced in standardised form in great numbers by Government contractors throughout the country, at a time when these machines were clean outclassed by the Albatross and Fokker productions, which, however, could have been met by superior machines already being manufactured by the leading men at the game—the private British manufacturers of aeroplanes. There was considerable outcry made in the House of Commons over the charge made by Mr. Pemberton-Billing, but the Parliamentary airman repeated his charge of murder at a great City of London meeting on March 27th, 1916, and the Government was at last sufficiently impressed to offer to appoint a committee of inquiry into the matter.

Thus affairs stood at the time of writing, with Great Britain reduced to the third position in regard to air-power, while Germany and France fought over Verdun for the command of the skies. According to Mr. Pemberton-Billing, we had lost 415 pilots and observers—150 dead, 160 wounded, and 150 missing. They had been shot down in many cases upon machines which, when fitted by local squadron smiths, had a speed of only sixty-eight miles an hour, as against a speed of one hundred and ten miles an hour made by Fokker and other German aeroplanes. Even the vast Zeppelins were faster than some of our official aeroplanes. The defectiveness of our aerial material was of long standing, as may be seen **Flying officer's evidence** from the following letter received from an officer of the Royal Flying Corps, who took part in the Battle of Neuve Chapelle:

I was flying a rotten old machine, with an engine that runs very badly and was missing from the time I left the ground. In ordinary circumstances I should have landed again immediately, but it was an important reconnaissance, so I had to do it. The highest I could get the machine to was 4,700 feet, and then as I flew towards the lines I could see our other machines up getting a hot time from "Archie." They were flying between 7,000 feet and 8,000 feet, and as soon as I was in range the Germans opened on my machine, and then, during the whole of the reconnaissance, which consisted of circling about a small area, they didn't give me a moment's peace, and I had shells bursting round my machine the whole time, simultaneously flashes of flame and loud bangs, some-

times on one side and then on the other, below the machine, above it, behind, and in front, and some of them bumped the machine about unpleasantly.

It was thoroughly uncomfortable. I twisted the machine about this way and that, made it side-slip outwards, and did everything I could to spoil their aim, but they kept me guessing the whole time. One shell exploded just in front, and I saw some bits of things flying off the engine, and thought the propeller was gone. I was very glad when the reconnaissance was over. On landing I found that the machine had been hit by rifle fire as well as by shrapnel.

Yet it was with material largely composed of machines of this kind that our airmen, as the Italian Aero League stated in May, 1915, "had carried out a continuous sequence of triumphant attacks, which placed British airmen far beyond any other air service **Our pilots' personal** in the belligerent forces." Both our mili- **ascendancy** tary and naval airmen were magnificent, and despite their inferiority of equipment they continued to show a personal ascendancy over the German pilots. There was, indeed, a crisis in German airmanship as well as in French and British flying. But in Germany it was the quality of the personnel that was the source of weakness. Flying officers of the stamp of Immelmann and Bölke were apparently rare. The small band of natural airmen among the enemy seems to have been largely recruited in the Scandinavian fringe of the Teutonic Empire. The ordinary German, in spite of the excellence of his machine, was not sufficiently given to taking fighting risks to make him a commander of the air. So the entire body of enemy airmen was formed into a flying army corps and thoroughly reorganised, with a view to producing pilots of a better type. But the fact that the officers, men, and mechanics of the German Flying Corps were numerous enough to form the material for a separate army corps organisation in the spring of 1916 indicated the unusual strength in both personnel and equipment of the enemy's military air service.

Mr. G. Valentine Williams has already related, in Chapter XCVI., from the point of view of a war correspondent at the front, many remarkable incidents of the work of our Royal Flying Corps. We must, therefore, forgo now to dwell upon the pleasant and inspiring side of our topic, and confine the present chapter chiefly to the technical aspects of our military and naval air services. Generally speaking the work of our principal air force in Flanders and France during the spring and summer of 1915 was strongly influenced by the course of events upon the Russian front. In April, 1915, the German Staff thinned its western lines of fast, scouting aeroplanes, in order to exercise an overwhelming superiority in the air against the Russians. A purely defensive attitude was maintained against British and French airmen, and the enemy battle-planes were seldom seen over our trenches. Thereupon both the British and the French began to assume they had recovered the command of the air, when, as a matter of fact, the enemy was as superior to all the Allies in aerial material as he was in artillery, the apparent decline in his power on the western front being merely the result of his most formidable concentration of forces on the eastern front.

The Russian Army was very badly off at the time in the matter of air resources. At the opening of the war, Russia was reported to have had a hundred pilots and a thousand machines. But her material, though apparently gigantic in comparison with our tiny total of thirty military aeroplanes, was of little value; for the machines were of a slow old French type, and even the much advertised Russian giant model, the Sikorski, was so slow and **Russia's air** feeble in defence that it needed swift **resources** battle-planes to protect it. The Russian pilots, on the other hand, were good. They had the dash, daring, and ingenuity that win battles. One of them was reported to have saved an army corps in East Prussia in March, 1915, when Hindenburg made his second great encircling movement, by discovering a gap in the Masurian forests and leading the almost enveloped corps through it. And again, in May, 1915, when Dimitrieff's army was broken on the Dunajec, one of his divisions,

which had been weakened by being extended to the Carpathians, was finely helped out of terrible difficulties by an air pilot.

The Russian airmen, however, could not by mere courage make up for the increasing defects of their old machines. They had suffered badly in the Carpathian battles through the extraordinary winds encountered on the mountains. In the winter all flights had to be made at a low altitude by reason of the intense **Her Dunajec** cold; 6,000 feet was a good height, and as **army blinded** the enemy anti-aircraft gunners improved in marksmanship, the Russian machines became fairly easy targets. Then it was that the Russian air crisis occurred through an unforeseen circumstance. The policy of buying aeroplanes in great quantities from France resulted in Russia being left, in the period of dire need, with no considerable body of mechanics trained in aircraft work. There were not even men enough to do field repairs to the much reduced number of old machines still available.

It was in this deplorable condition of affairs that the air service of our Allies was strained to breaking point by the sudden appearance, towards the end of April, 1915, of swarms of the fast new German Albatrosses, followed by the improved Aviatiks and twin-engined battle-planes carrying guns. On the Dunajec front, especially, the Russian Army was blinded, and Mackensen was able to prepare and deliver his terrific blow with such effect that it was a complete surprise.

Great as was his heavy gun power, its destructiveness was enormously increased by his still more telling superiority in aerial power. Throughout the great retreat

AFTER A NOCTURNAL RECONNAISSANCE: BRITISH AEROPLANE LANDING BY THE AID OF FLARES.
To other daily perils members of the Royal Flying Corps added that of reconnaissance work by night. The greatest difficulty in this connection was, of course, the one of landing. This obstacle was partly overcome in the manner illustrated above. To guide the nocturnal airman, aerodromes in France were provided with powerful searchlights which, illuminating the clouds, gave the pilot an idea of his whereabouts. Carefully planing down, the aviator searched for the landing-place. Hearing the approach of the machine, waiting mechanics at a given signal set fire to tins of petrol enclosing a square, into which the aeroplane alighted effectively or not according to the skill of the pilot.

the Russians were almost in the position of blind men fighting against men with telescopic powers of vision. General Alexeieff at last had to manœuvre his forces under cover of night and conceal them in forests, in order to prevent all his dispositions from being closely studied by German observers seated in swift and far-ranging aeroplanes. Even in January, 1916, the Russians had not been able to make good their lack of repairing

General Alexeieff's dilemma mechanics and their deficiency in fast and powerful machines. They had trained in the meantime another large body of keen and venturesome young pilots, but they remained very far behind their enemies in machine construction.

On the Franco-British front the energetic Germans succeeded in developing a strong aerial position while they were overwhelming the Russian airmen in the east. In May, 1915, our Assistant Director of Military Aeronautics made a remarkable speech in London, which did not receive the general attention it deserved. German airmen, he said, had been supplied with faster machines, and had become so much bolder that our scouts were no longer able to do their ordinary work; for we had found it necessary

AIRCRAFT AT THE RELIEF OF KUT.
British aeroplane being repaired on the desert in Mesopotamia during the march to the relief of Kut-el-Amara.

to send our machines out in couples—one to reconnoitre and one to beat off attacks. This was a fairly clear warning, by an expert in a high official position, that we needed to organise urgently a great national effort to maintain the command of the air. But, unlike the appeal for high-explosive shells made by the army in the field in the same month, the call for more powerful and faster climbing aeroplanes did not excite the public mind. Yet we had then suffered in the disastrous attack on Rouges Bancs as severely in our air service as in our infantry. In some of our squadrons every machine was disabled, and in addition to our immediate losses in highly-trained men and scanty material, we soon afterwards lost more first-rate men because good British machines were not available. In some cases we apparently had to use the leavings of the French air service in both our Royal Flying Corps and our Royal Naval Air Service, because our private manufacturers of machines and aero-engines had not been encouraged by our Government to expand their works.

It must therefore be borne in mind, while reading this section of the history of the war, that our military and naval airmen had continually to struggle against terrible disadvantages. They did not have sufficient machines; the machines they had were often of very poor quality; and when, at last, the Royal Aircraft Factory model was produced in large numbers, it was so obsolete as to become, with the fine men it held, only " Fokker fodder." Instead of grieving that our airmen did not continue the splendid series of long-distance raids on Zeppelin bases in Germany, we should rather be astonished that they, with their poor equipment, managed to do their duty brilliantly in the more restricted fields of operation in Flanders and the North Sea.

The most brilliant group of British pilots in the period under review was probably the Naval Air Wing No. 1 at Dunkirk, under Wing-Commander Longmore. This band of flying sailors succeeded the wing under Commander Samson that went to the Dardanelles to spot for the gunners of our Mediterranean fleet. Commander Samson and his officers had made a fine reputation for our Navy by their flights over the Rhine and Lake Constance; and though the fall of Antwerp and the German advance to the Belgian coast had since restricted the range of our old machines, and made it more difficult to fly to Cologne and Düsseldorf, the new wing under Wing-Commander Longmore found new opportunities for doing fine work.

The wing was both the advanced aerial guard of our south-eastern coast and the eyes of our bombarding fleet that shelled the Belgian shore and reinforced the artillery of the Belgian Army along the flooded Yser stream. Our naval airmen, however, had much less work to do for their gunners than our army airmen had, and their land reconnoitring flights were apparently less arduous, as the lines were held by the Belgian Army with its own artillery and aerial observers. Wing-Commander Longmore's wing, therefore, had more time for general fighting than any army air force. The sailors were open to attack anything—Zeppelins, submarines, harbour works, warships, war factories, hostile seaplanes, and aeroplanes—in short, anything warlike and German.

Among its achievements in 1915 were the destruction of two Zeppelins, one in the air and the other sunk at sea, and the sinking of two German submarines. A third Zeppelin would have been destroyed if our official designers of bombs for attacking airships had been competent to their work. For on May 17th, 1915, a Zeppelin which **Our naval airmen's** had attacked Ramsgate was pursued and **services** overtaken off Nieuport by Squadron-Commander Bigsworth. He swooped down within two hundred feet of the monster of the air, and dropped four bombs upon it, being thus the first pilot in a heavier-than-air flying machine to get the advantage of an enemy airship and bomb it. The gallant flight-commander risked his life of course; for if the enormous volume of gas had exploded two hundred feet beneath him, as he intended, he would have been unlikely to escape. But though one bomb, at least, exploded in the stern of the Zeppelin and damaged it, there was no vast flame; for our airship-attacking bombs at that time do not seem to have been composed of the ingredients necessary to introduce an explosive element into the volumes of hydrogen contained in the ballonets of a Zeppelin. Thus, through the defect of some of our

Type of man-lifting kite used by the French Army for observation purposes.

Kite ascending from a warship. The circle photograph shows the basket-like receptacle suspended from the kite which contained the observer.

Members of the flight section of the French Army preparing kites behind the lines for aerial reconnaissance work.

USE OF THE KITE FOR OBSERVATION PURPOSES BY THE FRENCH ARMY AND NAVY.

THE GUNNER AND THE GUN THAT DESTROYED A ZEPPELIN.

The French artilleryman, Adjutant G——, and the " 75," mounted on a motor-car, from which he fired
the incendiary shell that decided the fate of Zeppelin L77 near Révigny on February 21st, 1916.

ordnance experts, Squadron-Commander Bigsworth was
robbed of an historic achievement, after he had done
everything needed to bring off the affair.

But No. 1 Wing obtained proper bombs, and keenly waited
for another opportunity of cutting across the return course
of raiding Zeppelins with Belgian or Rhineland bases.
The position of the wing in the north-western corner of
France and the last remaining nook of free Flemish land
at Nieuport was awkward for all enemy airships returning
to Belgium in daylight. The British pilots could not do
anything when the raiders stole out across the sea to
Southern England under cover of night; but when the
news of a raid came quickly by wireless or by cable, the
aerial advanced guard of our shores flew up towards daybreak and patrolled the Belgian coast in the hope of
punishing the murderous German airships.

On the morning of June 7th, 1915, Wing 1 arranged
an attack upon the Zeppelin shed near Brussels. Flight-
Lieutenant J. P. Wilson and Flight-Lieutenant J. S. Mills
flew to Brussels and bombed the airship shed. The German
officers in charge were absent without leave, and their men
were merrymaking inside with wine and women. A great
flame spurted from the shed, showing that the gas ballonets
of the airship had been set on fire; most of the drinking

men and some of the women
seem to have been killed. Then
two motor-guns were brought out
against the victorious airmen.
The first gun ran into a railway
barrier and was smashed; the
second gun fell into a ditch and
broke from its carriage.

But all this was only the
beginning of trouble for the
Teutons. Flight-Sub-Lieutenant
Reginald H. J. Warneford had
started in the same raid and
lost his way. He was flying
between Brussels and Ghent, and
by happy chance the other
Zeppelin housed in Belgium was
up in the air, at a height of
only 6,000 feet, travelling towards
Ghent. Mr. Warneford was remarkably daring, even for a
British pilot. Like Flight-Commander Bigsworth, he swooped
barely two hundred feet above
the airship and dropped six
bombs. On this occasion there
were the proper chemicals in the
bombs, and the Zeppelin exploded
over a convent at Ghent, the
burning wreckage unfortunately
killing two nuns when it crashed
to earth.

The force of the explosion also
overturned Mr. Warneford's
machine and stopped its engine;
but while falling upside down the
young airman so controlled his
aeroplane as to right it. He was,
however, compelled to make a
landing in the enemy's country.
There he managed, after fifteen
minutes, to restart the engine,
and before any German soldiers
could draw near to him, he arose
and flew back safely to the
British aerodrome at Dunkirk.
Born in India in 1892, Mr.
Warneford had taken his certificate
as pilot at Hendon scarcely four
months before he destroyed the
Zeppelin. Owing both to youth and temperament, he
was one of the most reckless of flyers. Before his famous
stroke he had attempted to blow up a Zeppelin in her shed,
and finding the shed empty he had bombed all the men's
quarters at the aerodrome, flying very low down and doing
unusually terrible damage. But only ten days after his
exploit over Ghent he was killed at Paris while trying a
new French machine.

The destruction of two Zeppelins in one day by British
airmen on aeroplanes seems to have caused much anxiety
in Germany. For a considerable time no German newspaper was permitted to give news of the disasters; but
there was much Teutonic clamour over
the claim of an Austrian seaplane to have   **Anxiety caused**
destroyed the Italian airship Citta di   **in Germany**
Ferrara on June 8th. But our Italian
friends stated that their airship had been obliged to descend
owing to engine trouble, and had caught fire, and the fact
that the crew escaped showed that their version of the
affair was correct. Warneford's feat for long remained
unrivalled.

We described in our previous chapter on naval affairs
the other two remarkable achievements of No. 1 Wing
—the destruction of a German submarine by Flight-

All that remained of Zeppelin L77, brought down by a " 75's " incendiary shell near Révigny. All the upper structure was destroyed by fire. Only the aluminium tubing, flanked by the mangled metal trellis-work, was left amid the ashes on the snow.

The prow of one of the Zeppelin's wrecked cars, with a shattered propeller attached, shrouded in snow. The bodies of the officers and men of the L77 were found in the cabin boat.

French officers examining the wreckage as it lay at Brabant-le-Roi, near Révigny. After being hit, the Zeppelin burst into flames and crashed to earth. The murderous exploits of Germany's aerial cruisers obliterated any feeling of sympathy that might have been felt for the crew.

WRECKAGE OF ZEPPELIN L77, DESTROYED BY THE SHELL OF A " 75."

Commander Bigsworth and a similar fine piece of bombing and manœuvring work by Flight-Sub-Lieutenant Viney and Lieutenant Count de Sincay. Throughout the year the Naval Wing at Dunkirk constantly performed good work, in spite of the fact that in June, 1915, the Germans brought out another new model, an Aviatik with a six-cylinder Mercédès engine of 150 h.-p., that made rings round our fast scouts. The Belgian coast was frequently raided by No. 1 Wing, and according to German reports some

Raids on the Belgian coast of our other naval airmen in the autumn of 1915 made extended flights in seaplanes over the North Sea and bombarded the German shore.

Our Admiralty, however, preferred to publish nothing about our system of aerial reconnaissance over the critical battle area of the North Sea. Here the enemy's long-distance airships, with wireless receiving as well as transmitting instruments, had a very telling advantage over our machines. And though our air scouts, by skill, pluck, and endurance, managed to keep our main Fleet informed of the movements of enemy warships, their work was performed in a long silence likely to endure to the close

WEAPONS OF "FRIGHTFULNESS" DROPPED IN AN ENGLISH VILLAGE.
As many as twenty incendiary bombs were picked up in fields near a village in the track of the Zeppelin raiders. This photograph shows the exploded machines gathered together in a coal-cellar.

of the struggle. Their difficulties were such that it was not desirable to give the enemy any chance light upon the incidents of their task, save what he could gather from his own observation. On the other hand, the new chiefs of our Admiralty did not, for many months, display any initiative in designing aerial bomb attacks upon the bases of the Zeppelins that exercised a virtual command of the air in the North Sea. It was not until Mr. Pemberton-Billing invaded the House of Commons that a somewhat feeble attempt was made to revive the attacking strategy of Lord Fisher and Mr. Winston Churchill.

Throughout the summer, autumn, and winter of 1915 and the early spring of 1916, all the important long, daring raids by the Allies into Germany were conducted entirely by French airmen. In the old days our No. 1 Wing had been able to send a squadron to Belfort, under Flight-Commander Briggs, for a splendid and effective attack upon the principal Zeppelin factory at Friedrichshafen, on Lake Constance, near the Swiss frontier. But such was the deplorable condition of our aeroplane-making industry, under the fostering care of the Royal Aircraft Factory and its supporters at the War Office and the reformed Admiralty,

that after Commander Briggs had been captured by the enemy, we could afford no more machines and officers for great flights on true anti-Zeppelin principles.

But a single French machine resumed the work of Flight-Commander Briggs on April 28th, 1915, and dropped six bombs on a Zeppelin shed at Friedrichshafen, damaging the airship housed therein. At this period our ingenious allies had organised their air service, dividing it into large and rather slow bombarding machines and swift, fighting aeroplanes to protect both the light scouts and the heavily-loaded bombers. Their new bombs weighed 100 lb. and 25 lb. In April they blew up some German ammunition depôts by nocturnal aeroplane raids, wrecked a Zeppelin at Dunkirk by gun fire, and damaged by aerial attack the railway-station, bridge, and factories of Leopoldshöhe. It was on the 18th of the month that Garros, with his fine machine that Fokker afterwards copied, came to grief. He was fighting a troop-train at Hufte, in Germany, and after he had swooped close to earth and smashed the locomotive and broken the rails, his engine was struck and he was forced to land.

Then, on May 27th, a French force of seventeen aeroplanes carried out one of the most important raids in the air. Flying to the Rhine, the French airmen circled over the city of Lüdwigshafen and the neighbouring town of Oppau. In these two places were the old and new factories of the Baden Aniline Dye Company, which, with a largely increased staff, was busy making high explosives for the German Army and Navy. In the manufacture of coal-tar explosives the Baden Dye Company Works led the world, but they were less important when the French airmen had done with them. Several factories were struck and set on fire, only one French machine, an armoured aeroplane, being brought down by the enemy.

This was a classic example of a really effective aerial bombardment. There was excellent secret service work as the foundation of the French attack, and the result taught the Teutons not to put most of their trinitrotoluene eggs in one basket, especially when that basket was on the Rhine, and well within the range of French machines. On June 25th, 1915, as a reprisal for Zeppelin raids over England and France, three French aeroplanes raided Karlsruhe, the capital of the Black Forest country, and dropped bombs on the Grand Duke of Baden's castle, on the munitions factory, and the railway. The Germans then had for almost the first time a full taste of the new kind of war against non-combatants which they had been practising for nearly a year. According to Karlsruhe reports many people were slightly wounded, as the Government measures of **French raid on** protection worked very badly. The anti- **Karlsruhe** aircraft batteries were sadly inefficient— just like those of London about the same time—and the people crowded into the streets. Here, just as in England, the telephone service was not adequate, and the military and civil authorities did not work together. All of which afforded a certain unchristianlike consolation to Frenchmen, Belgians, and Britons living in places visited by Zeppelins.

Again, on June 28th, a solitary French aviator reached Friedrichshafen and bombarded the Zeppelin factory, dropping eight bombs upon it. The airman's engine

Complete devastation of a Paris tenement by a Zeppelin bomb. No fewer than five floors were sectioned by the explosion.

Freakish effect of a Zeppelin bomb on another Parisian residence. The bed, though comparatively undamaged, was left hanging over the floor.

Where a Zeppelin bomb fell in the centre of a Paris boulevard, making a clean hole in the roadway and penetrating to the "Métro," or Paris Underground Railway. A large crowd of Parisians turned out to see the damage on the morning after the raid, which accounted for twenty-five civilian lives and twenty-five wounded.

AFTER THE ZEPPELIN RAID ON PARIS DURING THE NIGHT OF JANUARY 29TH, 1916.

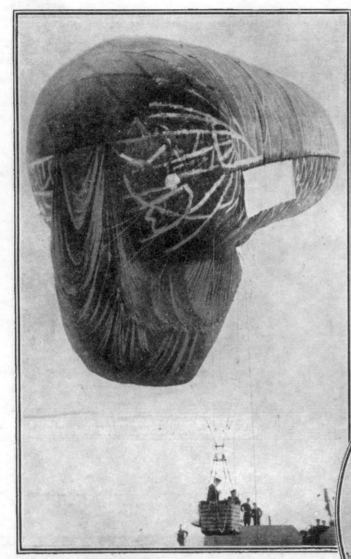

A "SPOTTING-POST" OF THE SKIES.
Captive naval balloon ascending from a ship at sea. This type of gasbag proved very serviceable as a "spotting-post."

spy worked in front of the airman and found very important objectives for aerial attacks—petrol factories in an Empire suffering from a petrol famine, explosives works, arms factories, aeroplane factories, and other productive military centres.

On August 26th the French Staff arranged an allied aerial offensive against German troops. A fleet of sixty machines, both aeroplanes and seaplanes, manned by French, British, and Belgian soldiers and sailors, attacked the German positions in **Foreshadowings of** the Forest of Houthulst, north of Ypres. **the future** There were German batteries, underground shelter chambers, and a maze of trenches in the Flemish wood, but by using incendiary and explosive bombs amounting to twenty tons the forest was burnt out. It was a very significant experiment—possibly indicative of a grand change in warfare. It was made in the section in which the enemy had first employed poison-gas clouds, and it seemed clearly to foreshadow how the great aerial fleets of the future, consisting of a thousand bombarding machines, would drive infantry out of their trenches and dug-outs and destroy dug-in artillery forces. On the other hand, the fact that France, Britain, and Belgium, when combining all their naval and military aerial forces which could be spared from routine work on the front, could

was struck, but he managed to land in Swiss territory. The next month—July—a despatch from Sir John French revealed the reason why—after twelve months of war—we had to leave all these raids against distant Zeppelin bases to our allies. The British Field-Marshal thanked the French Government for their supply of aeroplanes, "without which the efficacy of the Royal Flying Corps would have been seriously impaired." Yet in the same month our Under-Secretary for War, Mr. Tennant, was confidently replying to all criticisms made in Parliament in connection with our air services, and making out that everything was going so well that no marked improvement could be expected.

Meanwhile, the French alone continued to raid Germany. On July 30th a fleet of forty-five of their aeroplanes bombarded the enemy petrol factories **Brilliant work of** near Wissembourg and made a strong **French airmen** attack upon the air sheds at Phalsbourg. The next day, the excellent and dangerous Aviatik works, which had been moved from Mulhouse to Freiburg, were fiercely bombed, with the result that the Aviatik manufacturers fled with their staff farther towards the peaceful centre of their country So the raid was quite effective. The shifting of the Aviatik plant delayed the production of the new 150 h.-p. Aviatiks and thus generally benefited the Allies. The directive hand of the French General Staff, with its far-reaching espionage system, can be traced in most of these raids into Germany. The

TWO GLIMPSES OF THE CAPTIVE GASBAG.
Kite-balloon about to ascend from H.M.S. Canning. The centre illustration shows the balloon floating above the parent ship.

only collect in August, 1915, sixty machines for the great bombardment of Houthulst Forest, proved that the power of the aeroplane was not fully recognised.

But in our Royal Flying Corps there were still many expert airmen who were sceptical of the results of aerial bombardment. They reckoned that, at an altitude high enough to escape from anti-aircraft gunnery, a flyer could not expect to hit a mark much smaller than an acre. It seemed, therefore, to them that a great gun—such as our 15 in. naval gun mounted for military use on land—could interrupt the enemy's lines of transport behind his front more effectively and more continuously than squadrons of bombarding aeroplanes could do. This opinion, however, was formed at a time when our official designs in machines were so far behind the German aircraft that our flyers were in a generally despondent frame of mind. They still held their own, on the whole, by means of a desperate fighting spirit, but they felt they were outclassed badly

RISING AFTER INFLATION.
How the captive balloon ascends through the deck of the parent ship to make an aerial reconnaissance.

in material, and saw no way of getting an equality of weapons against their foes.

Meanwhile their comrades, the French airmen, who had begun to use at midsummer a new fast-climbing, twin-engined biplane, were discovering new forms of aerial warfare. On September 13th a French airman attacked some towns and villages in the southern part of the Black Forest, near the source of the Danube. He dropped some bombs on Donaueschingen and then pursued a troop-train, flying five yards from the ground and pouring a stream of bullets from his machine-gun into the crowded carriages. A German airman at last attacked him, but was brought down. Altogether it was one of the most extraordinary aerial fights recorded.

The new French twin-engined biplane, the Caudron, was employed, nine days afterwards, in a longer distance raid into Würtemberg. The capital city,

French attack in Wurtemberg Stuttgart, a busy centre of war industries, was bombed, and the airmen of the French Republic, regarding the Teutonic royalties as the principal authors of the war, attacked the palace of the King of Würtemberg as they had attacked the castle of the Grand Duke of Baden. Representatives of the leading Republican democracy on earth, they perhaps desired that enemy potentates should have the horrors of Germanic warfare brought home to them as it had been brought home to Belgian mechanics and French peasants. A Hendon pilot, M. Henri Salmet, was the leader of the Stuttgart raid, and with him was Sapeur-Aviateur Prévost, cousin of another famous French airman.

The previous day the Hendon pilot had attempted a single-handed raid on Stuttgart. When heavily loaded with bombs he was assailed by four German biplanes, but, despite his load, he had escaped his enemies by out-climbing them on his twin-engined Caudron. This shows the difference between our Royal Aircraft Factory machines of the period and the best type of French design.

But it must not be concluded, therefore, that there were not in England any fine climbing aeroplanes. In June, 1915, Mr. Harry Hawker had broken all British records in altitude by climbing more than 18,000 feet in a new Sopwith biplane, **Government and** which was at once offered to the British **Sopwith biplane** Government, but blandly neglected. All the time we had the material of aerial victory as well as the men, but we would not give our pilots the best, practical British machines, and enable the manufacturers of these machines to produce their superior designs in large, standardised quantities.

Even as late as March, 1916, a leading London newspaper, the "Daily Chronicle," accused Mr. Pemberton-Billing of wishing to promote the monetary interests of our private aeroplane-makers when he condemned the Royal Aircraft Factory machines as dangerous to the officers who were compelled to use them. The Elswick battleship-building works might as well have been accused of profiteering in the old days, when by reason of the superior gifts of its designers it produced better warships than our Admiralty. Our Admiralty, however, then had the sense to ask the leading Elswick man to come to Whitehall and direct its battleship design. Had our Government but ordered our leading aeroplane builders to combine together and take over the practical direction

RISING CLEAR OF THE SHIP.
Captive balloon about to ascend with two aerial observers in the basket.

of the Royal Aircraft Factory and its three thousand workmen, we should never have lost the command of the air that Messrs. Vickers, Mr. A. V. Roe, Mr. Sopwith, and Sir George White, with the Shorts, Martinsydes and others, won for us between Mons and the Marne.

In the first week of October, 1915, the French lost their airship Alsace, which had been bombarding the German military base at Vouziers, behind the Champagne front; but about the same time, in the eastern theatre of war, the first twin-engined German biplane was brought down. It was reported to be fitted with two 170 h.-p. Mercédès motors, which showed how the German engineers had improved upon their winter model of an aero-engine of the first class. In the same month the French air service resumed its expressed policy of bombing German towns in direct reprisals for the Zeppelin raids upon English villages and cities, but well as this was meant towards us, it scarcely reconciled our people to the extraordinary attitude of Tolstoyan non-resistance of our Government. Nearly all our air service men were eager to cross the Rhine and use the German people as they were using us. But they were apparently told that we had no machines for bomb-carrying work on long voyages. At the beginning of December, 1915, a British-built Caudron biplane, with two Anzani engines, appeared at Hendon, being the first successful twin-engined land machine constructed in our country.

The problem of reprisals

Yet Messrs. Short Brothers had made a promising twin-engine machine in 1912, but received no encouragement from our Royal-Aircraft-Factory-ridden Government to develop their design. In November, 1915, Mr. Louis Coatelen, of the Sunbeam Motor Company, who had already made one of the best aero-engines used in our machines, let it be publicly known that he was prepared to put on the market a 300 h.-p. aerial motor. There was another British firm, with remarkable inventive power, busy on a new aeroplane of uncommon qualities. In fact, the general engineering genius of our nation was deeply stirred to activity by private reports of the desperate anxieties of our pilots in regard to the poorness of their material. Strong forces were working, beyond the range of vision of our air authorities, and making for the reconstruction of our aviation equipment, but some months had still to elapse before the work started of reforming all the errors of the Royal Aircraft Factory and of the War Office and Admiralty officers who looked to Farnborough alone for sound, scientific ideas in aeroplane development.

Meanwhile, engines remained our principal source of weakness. By the end of 1915 we had lost more men and machines through motor defects than through the enemy's fire, our officially-designed engines being quite as bad as private motors, though the development of the latter had been checked for years to enable the Government works and their men of science to produce the perfect aero-engine. The Germans had relied upon private motor engineers, with the result that there was scarcely a case in which a German machine had been captured through its engine going wrong. The Germans had for several months applied the electric device of self-starting motor-cars to their aeroplane engines when our Under-Secretary for War, in January, 1916, said, in an inane attempt at sarcasm, in a Zeppelin debate: "You cannot start an aeroplane merely by touching a button." This was practically what the enemy had been doing for a very considerable time. One of our pilots, for instance, passed over Lille in the autumn of 1915 at a great height. But a German climbed up to him in seven minutes, attacked, and forced him to turn back. Notwithstanding the magnificent pluck and terribly daring skill evolved in our pilots by their heroic attempt to hold their front against all odds, we must candidly admit that the enemy, through his superiority of material, won the command of the air against us in the second year of the war.

Official attempt at sarcasm

ZONE OF OPERATIONS SEEN FROM A CAPTIVE BALLOON.
Scene from the basket of an observation balloon, taken on a dull day over the British western front. (Official photograph issued by the Press Bureau.

BRITISH "ARCHIES" IN FRANCE

CHAPTER CXII.

SHELLING GERMAN AEROPLANES.

ZEPPELIN ACTIVITIES: THE MURDER RAIDERS AND THE AERIAL HANDICAP OF OUR FLEET.

The Price We Paid for Old Age Pensions—Germany Spends in Aerial Experiments Seventy-five Times More Money than We Do—Commander Boothby and His Forecast of the Naval Value of Zeppelins—How a German Airship Destroyed Three British Armoured Cruisers—Enemy Battle-Cruisers Evade Our Trap through Our Lack of Large Airships—Fire-Control Possibilities in Naval Airships—The Queen Elizabeth's Experiment with Aerial Fire-Control—The Destruction of the Königsberg by British Airmen Directing the Severn's Guns—Strategical Importance of Zeppelins Throughout the Naval Operations—How Our Airmen Damaged the Von der Tann and Forced Three German Destroyers out of Harbour—Military Purpose of the Zeppelin Raids over England —Though Petrograd is Within their Range, they Prefer to Attack London—The Strange Conception of British Character on which the Enemy Based His Campaign of Terrorisation—Dr. Joseph Sticker and His Balloon Flights over London in Peace Time—Sticker Leads the Raids on Our Capital and Eastern Seaports—" Mine was the First and Only Ship over the City of London "—Attacks on Southend and Ramsgate—Sticker Reaches an Outlying District of London, and Many People are Killed on the North-East Coast—The Effect of the Zeppelin Raids upon the British People—Sir Percy Scott and His Troubles—The Attack on the Midland Towns and the Movement of Reform—L19 and the Grimsby Trawler—The Great Zeppelin Spring Campaign—Successive Nocturnal Attacks and the Aerial Invasion of Scotland—Aeroplane Raids and Adventures—Sir Alfred Gelder and the Dummy Gun—Lord Derby and Lord Montague Resign from Air Committee—Strong Reform Movement Begins at Birmingham under Lord Montagu—Our Defects and Departmental Friction and the Ministry of the Air.

IN 1908 the amount spent upon experiments in aerial navigation for military purposes by the British Government was £5,270. In the same year the German Government spent for the same purpose £133,731 from public funds, in addition to £265,000 collected by the National Zeppelin Airship Fund. This was at the time when Zeppelin IV. had been wrecked by explosion, and £100,000 raised for further construction within twenty-four hours of the disaster. The German Government continued to increase its outlay on aeronautic work to the astonishing sum of £4,000,000 a year. Our Navy, which was most keenly interested in airships, could not find any money. The naval estimate for guns, projectiles, ammunition, torpedoes, and gun-cotton had been reduced in two years from £5,270,000 to £3,351,000. With the sum available for war stores decreased by thirty-six per cent., a cheese-paring economy prevailed at the Admiralty, which made experiments in the con-

struction of large airships of the rigid type impossible. We had naval officers who understood what Zeppelin building meant for us. When the Germans were making ingenious toys representing London under the bombardment of a Zeppelin fleet, there were officers in our Navy lecturing upon the more immediate peril to our Battle Fleet in the North Sea. It was the extraordinary power of aerial reconnaissance which the Germans were winning with the Zeppelin that disturbed our naval experts. The airship could travel in favourable weather faster than any destroyer, and avoid all risk of fighting, while keeping her Fleet informed of hostile movements at sea. No mines or submarines could endanger her, and owing to the breadth of the North Sea practically no small enemy aircraft could attack her. She was the perfect scouting cruiser in favourable weather.

By 1912 this view of the Zeppelin was widely adopted in our Navy, Commander F. L. M. Boothby having discussed the matter with uncommon and prophetic thoroughness at the Royal

FLIGHT-COMMANDER R. J. BONE, D.S.O., R.N.
After bold and skilful manœuvring he brought down a German seaplane which had been engaged in a raid on the coast of Kent on March 19th, 1916.

BRITISH ANTI-AIRCRAFT GUNNERY IN THE EAST.

Commander C. R. Samson, D.S.O. (second figure from the right), watching the effect of a shot from an anti-aircraft gun in action somewhere on the eastern fields of operation.

United Service Institution. But no money could be obtained from the Government for the construction of large rigid airships, with sheds or mooring-posts, on the East Coast of England and Scotland. When Mr. Reginald McKenna was First Lord of the Admiralty he strongly pushed forward a Zeppelin programme, but his successor, Mr. Winston Churchill, was reported to have obtained from the Treasury so small a sum for aircraft that our Navy could not hope to win the command of the air over the North Sea. The money was barely sufficient for the experimental construction of one large airship of the rigid type. So Mr. Churchill, instead of risking all his money on one big gasbag, spent it upon a score of seaplanes, in the construction of which our private makers excelled the Germans. This was certainly a wise policy in the circumstances, but the circumstances were deplorable. We had to pay dearly for the Old Age Pension scheme, the financing of which was the cause of our severe economy in destroyers, battle-cruisers, and large naval airships. Besides suffering from Zeppelin raids, the loss of certain war vessels is known to have been due to fine reconnoitring work on the part of Zeppelin crews, and our operations in the North Sea were seriously checked by the command of the air being held completely by the enemy.

Mr. Churchill's seaplane policy

On the other hand, after the first German battle-cruiser raid on our coast, Sir John Jellicoe, in spite of his inferiority in weapons of aerial reconnaissance, trapped the enemy squadron off Scarborough. One of our battleship squadrons was closing round the enemy, and one of our battle-cruiser squadrons was completing the encircling movement. But when the enemy ships were at a range of only eight miles, a fog-bank intervened, and they escaped. Had we then possessed a couple of large naval airships with a speed of fifty or sixty miles an hour, with transmitting and receiving wireless instruments, and crews that included expert fire-control officers, the German raiders would have been sunk. It is worthy of remark that Commander Boothby had foreseen the case of low-lying fog-banks interfering with gun fire, and had shown in technical detail the use of a fire-controlling rigid airship in the circumstances. When war broke out the range of our 15 in. naval guns was limited by the vision of our " spotters " in the fire-control stations in our battleships. It is sometimes said that, if the Germans possessed a 17 in. naval gun, they would not be able to use it over a longer range than our 15 in., because the men in the fire-control had reached the limit of their vision. But though the curvature of the earth may definitely restrict all spotting operations from the mast of a battleship, it does not interfere with the fire of great guns directed from an airship by means of a long-range wireless telephone. If the fire-control in the airship worked

out their calculations correctly, they should be able to train a 17 in. gun on a target fifteen miles distant. In this case the battleship could only be blinded, in regard to its extraordinary range of striking power, by the bringing down of its fire-control airship.

Our Navy made two interesting experiments with aerial fire-control. During the Dardanelles campaign one of our balloon observers off the coast of Anzac saw a large transport packed with Turkish troops going at a good speed across the Sea of Marmora. The observer in the balloon signalled to the Queen Elizabeth, which was the ship with large guns nearest to him. She was moving a good distance from the Gallipoli coast, out of range of the Turkish batteries, and across the mountainous Peninsula the enemy transport was still on her way through the placid inland sea. But the observer in the balloon rapidly calculated the future positions of both ships, wirelessed the result to the Queen Elizabeth, and then gave the final signal. A vicious flame came out of her side, and a small cloud of rank yellow smoke ascended. The balloon observer saw the 15 in. shell strike home, sinking the enemy transport and nearly all the troops in it. The shot was certainly a marvel of accurate gauging, and the man who sent it home would have been much more useful in an airship in a North Sea battle than in a tethered balloon over the Gulf of Saros. We had the men capable of putting the command of the air to magnificent uses had we been able to build the airships and sheds they required.

Another fine example of aerial spotting in a naval operation was the destruction of the German cruiser Königsberg on July 11th, 1915. The German warship had retreated into the Rufiji, in German East Africa, and our first attack against it had failed through our loss of the aeroplane sent up to spot for our gunners. Then, on July 6th, the two river monitors Severn and Mersey anchored in a branch of the river, and two British aeroplanes circled above the tropical forest and marked the shooting. Both aeroplanes however, broke down owing to extreme hard work in a difficult tropical atmosphere. They worked watch and watch for thirteen hours, making total flights of 915 miles. When the machines were again ready for service on July 11th, the flying officers quickly got the guns of the Severn on the Königsberg. Hit after hit was rapidly signalled, and the Königsberg was set on fire by a small ship with much less powerful guns than hers, and completely destroyed in a few hours. If the Königsberg had had fire observers in a good aeroplane, she could easily have smashed both the Severn and the Mersey, instead of being burned and wrecked by one of the river monitors.

Aerial spotting in East Africa

It will thus be seen that the lack of fast and long-ranging

British airships in the decisive area of naval operations, the North Sea, was in various ways a serious disadvantage to our main Fleet. We endeavoured to make up for the death before birth of the McKenna squadron of Zeppelins by means of patrolling airships of small size and narrow radius of action, and by squadrons of seaplanes rising from mother carrying-ships. But we never exercised with these simple makeshifts the large reconnaissance powers of the Zeppelins and other large German airships with powerful engines and heavy supplies of petrol and lubricating oil. Our destroyers and armed patrols had to carry out most of the work which should have been done by large airships. Our Navy had to work harder and take more risks, and our submarine hunters could seldom or never work near the enemy's waters as hunters in airships might have done.

The German naval airships never fought. One or two of them suffered from the fire of our submarines, less through the desire to give battle than through a misunderstanding of the fighting spirit of our seamen. The German naval airships were designed to fly away from attack. Their function was to reconnoitre and study the movements of our warships. Even when they found one of our submarines trapped in a net, they usually **Function of German naval airships** wirelessed to their destroyers instead of trying bombing tactics. On some occasions, however, they stopped merchant ships in the North Sea, attacked some and examined others. But to examine a ship the Zeppelin had to descend and settle on the waves, and send out a small boat, or have one sent to her. This procedure, however, became risky as the war progressed, and powerfully-armed vessels were used in the patrol of the seas. Blockades could not be carried on directly by means of monster air cruisers, unless it was a blockade on the German system of sinking anything afloat in the war area— friends, neutrals, or foes.

But throughout the naval war the Zeppelins, assisted sometimes by Parsevals and Schütte-Lanzes, were a factor of strategical importance. The German Navy had especially large Zeppelins, each with a gross weight of thirty-five tons. Their engines gave them a speed of fifty miles an hour, afterwards developed to sixty miles an hour, and their fuel storage enabled them to reach, if need were, Land's End or John o' Groats. All the North Sea was easily within their power of wing, and even a moderately rough **A factor of** wind, which troubled them when getting **strategic value** in or out of shed, did not, as a rule, endanger them when in flight. No aeroplane or seaplane built in the first twenty-one months of the war had anything of their range of action, and no heavier-than-air machine could possibly have their staying power. For they were able to hang at a great height over the sea, drifting in the wind without using their engines, while they watched through telescopes the waters beneath them. They were, indeed, incomparable observation balloons as well as flying dragons. By reason of the stability of their metal framework and ballonets, they had such steadiness that they could receive long-range wireless messages and transmit messages for a distance of about one hundred and fifty miles, while on small heavier-than-air machines the vibration interfered with the working of the delicate wireless receivers. A Zeppelin could listen as well as talk, and this much increased her usefulness in long-range reconnaissance.

The only serious disadvantage of the Zeppelin was that her enormous shed was not only costly to erect but an unmistakable landmark for hostile aircraft at twenty miles distance. Had we possessed even long-range aeroplanes capable of a return journey across the North Sea we should have been able to dim some of the eyes of the German Fleet. Had we possessed, also, airships with the travelling power of the German, we should probably

METAMORPHOSIS OF THE MOTOR-OMNIBUS.
Two converted motor-omnibuses that plied for hire in the streets of London in pre-war days. The chassis of the 'buses were used for mounting anti-aircraft guns.

have blinded the German Fleet and made the sky over the North Sea an almost exclusively British possession. This would have meant that the enemy's submarine campaigns against our shipping would have been conducted in circumstances of much greater difficulty, for the hunting would have begun just out of gun-shot of the German coast batteries. Then, as at Zeebrugge in Belgium, which was within range of our machines, the enemy's warships, including his submarines, would have been frequently bombed.

In this connection it is illuminating to learn from a late report of our air raid on the **Effects of the** German coast at Cuxhaven that more **Cuxhaven raid** damage was done than was known at the time we described the affair. Our little squadron of naval pilots, mounted on machines of an early type and indulging from their point of view in a great practical joke rather than a serious operation, severely damaged the German Battle Fleet. When they appeared the German admiral, fearing that the bombers might make a lucky stroke at a funnel, moved his ships out in order to scatter them, with the disastrous result that one of his fine cruisers,

BRITISH ANTI-AIRCRAFT OBSERVERS FINDING THE RANGE.
The aeroplane was seen to be hostile, and the alarm was given. (Spirited official war photograph issued by the Press Bureau.)

the Von der Tann, was badly injured in a collision and put out of action for months. Before this incident was known it had been rumoured that the Von der Tann was crippled in collision in escaping through the fog-bank from our battleships and battle-cruisers after the Scarborough raid, but there is now reason to suppose that the damage to her occurred in the confusion round Cuxhaven when the British airmen appeared.

Many months afterwards there was a somewhat similar incident on a much smaller scale at Zeebrugge. There, on March 20th, 1916, a fleet of fifty French, British, and Belgian machines began to bomb the harbour, where three German destroyers were lying. The German warships were so hard pressed, or so alarmed, that they put out to sea, where a superior British naval force of four destroyers attacked and damaged two of them. This was an uncommonly fine bit of design between the wing-commander at Dunkirk and the commander of the British destroyer flotilla patrolling the Belgian coast. The two officers had forecasted what would happen at Zeebrugge, and had concerted their action accordingly.

All this indicates what could have been done by combining the command of the sea with the command of the air. As it was, the enemy used his fleet of airships against us in a military way as well as in a naval way. Not only did he scout over the coasts of Russia on both sides of the

Baltic, hunt our submarines that passed the Sound, patrol the coasts from Denmark to Holland, and watch the movement of ships in the North Sea, but he employed his airships against our armies in Flanders and France, Turkey and the Balkans. The Zeppelins did not bomb our far-scattered land forces, or if they did occasionally, it did not matter. Zeppelin power in the command of the air was employed against our troops in a more indirect and telling manner. Raids were made on England for the purpose of detaining in the Motherland large forces of anti-aircraft guns and crews and an increasing number of machines and pilots that could have been used at the front. Also, it is not extravagant to say that tenfold the money that our Treasury had saved from 1908 to July, 1914, on aeronautical research and large airship construction was lost by the country, chiefly through street accidents in darkened cities, interruption of railway traffic, the stoppage of factories in bombarded areas, and the damage done by the enemy to life and property. He never did as much damage as he claimed to have effected, but, when we reduce his destructiveness merely to a hundredth part of what he boasted it was, it remained on occasions something more than the sum our Chancellor of the Exchequer used annually to allow for a year's researches and experiments in aircraft.

Yet the British Government, under both the Liberal and Coalition Cabinets, continued during the war to take no active interest in Zeppelin construction. In January, 1915, Mr. Winston Churchill had one Zeppelin in the early stages of building, but work on it was interrupted, and it was not until the spring of 1916, under pressure from private members of Parliament, that Mr. Arthur Balfour resumed the work. We did make one large airship in this country, but it died of a broken back soon after it was born. The German engineers had the advantage over us in the matter of experience, which they had purchased by a series of terrible disasters with their earlier designs. A considerable time had to pass before we were able to produce great rigid airships capable of serving all the needs of our Navy.

In the meantime, the Germans had speeded up their Zeppelin construction, and after supplying all the requirements of their Fleet in the Baltic and the North Sea, were able to attempt to terrify the hostile populations of Russia, Britain, and France. The towns behind the Russian front were bombed with great violence, continual attempts being made, especially round Riga, Dvinsk, and more southerly cities, to reach the Russian ammunition depôts and dislocate the railway traffic. Much of this work was of a fairly legitimate military character, there being a large German element in the Riga district which it was scarcely good policy to terrorise in savage **Air raids on the** fashion. Moreover, several airships were **Russian front** lost on the Russian front, and this tended to make the Germans rely more upon bombarding aeroplanes with a short range of travel. Though Petrograd and its great munition suburb of Ochta were within the range of travel of the Zeppelin, no raids appear to have been undertaken in this direction.

In France also, where the German lines at Noyon were within fifty miles of Paris, the raiding Zeppelins, housed in Belgium and along the Rhine, did not attempt a campaign of nocturnal raids over Paris. Visits from both

Great activity in the anti-aircraft ranks. Men rushing in a body to take up their position, thence to fire at the marauder, so as to drive him off or bring him down—one of the most exhilarating branches of modern warfare.

The big gun in action from the essential mobile lorry. An officer was observing with critical judgment the effect of the shells.

"ARCHIE" ON THE OFFENSIVE: INCIDENTS WITH OUR ANTI-AIRCRAFT CORPS.

enemy airships and enemy machines became rare, owing probably to the fact that the French Army, with its search-lights, anti-aircraft guns, and night-flying pilots, was entrenched between the raiders and the capital. Paris also was ringed about by a considerable number of anti-aircraft batteries with special listening instruments for magnifying the distant drone of large aerial propellers.

England, therefore, became the chief target for most of the large German airships that could be spared from reconnaissance work. The length of our coast-line from Kent to Scotland lay open to attack. We should have required guns and searchlights every two miles or so, along a winding line of three hundred or more miles, in order to protect our coasts. We could not spare this enormous number of guns with their multitude of trained crews—it would have crippled our Army. But it was one of the objects of the director of the Zeppelin raids to excite our civil population to demand some complete protection of this sort and maim our striking power on the Continent, in order to meet the menace of half a dozen or a dozen Zeppelins at the most. During the Napoleonic Wars Napoleon had succeeded in distracting, by a threat of

ANCHORED WHILE THE WIND WAS HIGH.
Belgian aeroplane, temporarily out of action owing to a very high wind, being moored to the ground.

invasion, a considerable part of our energy to the construction of useless Martello towers round our southern and eastern coasts. In vain did Nelson point out that our battleships were our forts, and that one gun in a ship, that could be massed with other ships for battle, was worth more than a score of land guns fixed at points which the enemy could avoid attacking. Our forefathers of a hundred years ago were not generally as strong-nerved and confident as we sometimes suppose, and the useless Martello towers had to be erected in order to restore public confidence.

Moral of the Martello towers

The War Lord of Germany certainly thought that he could play upon our nerves, by means of frequent Zeppelin raids, in the way that Napoleon had done by invasion threats. He also thought that he could do very considerable military damage at important East Coast centres and in the Thames estuary. He even fancied there was a fair chance of terrorising our non-combatant element, and making them exert pressure on the Government to end the war. Certainly the Press and people of Germany thought that the last object could be attained, and the destruction of a large part of London by means of aerial bombardments was regarded by the enemy populace as a feasible operation.

It was, indeed, for this event that they had subscribed annually hundreds of thousands of pounds to the National Zeppelin Airship Fund. Count Zeppelin himself had prepared for it by sending one of the best German aeronautists, Dr. Joseph Sticker, to practise balloon flights over London, and thereby attain a complete personal knowledge of the air conditions and aerial topography of the British capital.

Sticker also practised ballooning at Paris in the days before the war, with results that were afterwards seen. He had first tried to become an aeroplane pilot, but after getting in a bad smash and failing to distinguish himself in any way, he worked for the brevet of a Zeppelin pilot, and conducted the first raid on the London district. Happily for us, he was killed during the raid of September 8th, 1915, when he again sailed over the neighbourhood of London.

Dr. Sticker's practice flights

One of his last letters ran (we quote it without regard to its truth or falsehood) :

We have a week full of events behind us which has brought me many interesting experiences. On the night of August 9th I crossed the Thames. Three days afterwards I was above Harwich, and—this is the principal thing—on August 17th mine was the first and only ship above the City of London. I will give all details in person later. But we had no hits that night, as conditions were so bad between London Bridge and Black-friars Bridge.

Afterwards, a certain Captain Mathy pretended to have been the leading raider over England, but we can confidently reckon that Dr. Joseph Sticker, who used to be so keen on taking part in balloon competitions in our country, was the chief murderer of our women and children until he disappeared mysteriously on the night of September 8th, 1915.

But the record of this balloonist shows that he had carefully and treacherously prepared, some years before the war broke out, to bomb the English city where he had received a friendly welcome as a keen aeronautist, apparently interested only in the scientific side of balloon competitions. He afterwards led a large body of German airmen into Denmark, arranging an important exhibition, so that that country could be well studied by German pilots with a view to future eventualities. After the war, all the peoples of the Quintuple Entente and other States in friendly lead with them will, it is hoped, see that no German air pilot, however genial and purely scientific in his aims, is allowed to make aerial reconnaissances over their territories.

Sticker and his chiefs, however, could not have worked so easily against us if there had not been a deadly leakage of weather information from our western observing stations. With the single exception of a weather station in Iceland under Danish control, our meteorological authorities held all the available sources of knowledge concerning the air disturbances that would affect German airships in the North Sea and in the Rhineland and Belgium area. Settled weather could be marked on the Continent, from which the great anti-cyclone systems usually spread to our islands. But our islands were the passing place for Atlantic cyclones. We were aware of trouble in the air a day or more before the Germans had warning of it. Their great raiding airships had to wait for moonless yet clear nights, in order to escape our anti-aircraft guns, and they had also to wait for settled weather, with no rain or snow

Commander of the L15, Captain Breithaupt, one of the enemy's leading raiders, wearing order obtained for bombing London district on October 13th, 1915.

Warrant officer of the L15. The man served on steamer trading between Hamburg and the East Coast before the war.

Ober-Lieutenant Kuhne, second in command of the L15. He had lived in England before the war, and was well acquainted with London and its environs.

at high altitudes and no strong gales, in order to carry their full cargo of bombs and avoid very strong head-winds on their return journey, when their store of petrol was becoming exhausted.

Had we possessed great airships, together with our practical monopoly of forecasting bad weather, we should have dominated the North Sea. As it was, the Germans, by means that are not yet known, succeeded in obtaining good weather forecasts. Our Government did all it could to block every means of communication. First of all, advertisements in the "agony" columns of our newspapers were rigorously checked, nothing being published to which the name and address of the sender was not attached so that it could be examined. Then the mailing of all newspapers to the Continent was regularly delayed, cabling

became more slow in operation, and letters took a longer time to reach Holland and the Scandinavian countries. But the enemy's meteorological department continued to forecast the state of weather in Britain with considerable exactitude, and it was a long time before we managed to let a storm loose on the raiders, similar to the tempest of snow that overwhelmed a Zeppelin and a Schütte-Lanz in the North Sea on February 17th, 1915.

This disaster seems to have staggered the German airship director. It was not until April 14th that he again launched his ships against our coast towns. The damage done was slight, and though some private houses were damaged, only two persons were injured. On April 15th another Zeppelin passed over the East Coast, but did no important damage to life or property. An official

Warrant officer, whose duties consisted in navigating the gasbag. He had lived in America, and spoke English tolerably well.

A leading mechanic of the L15 between two British guards. This man was responsible for the smooth working of the Zeppelin's engines. (All the photographs on this page are official, and were issued by the Press Bureau.)

AERIAL HUNS OF THE DESTROYED ZEPPELIN L15 PHOTOGRAPHED IN CAPTIVITY, APRIL, 1916.

German report stated that "defended towns" on the British East Coast had been successfully bombarded by naval airships, which were heavily attacked by gun fire, but returned undamaged. This was written, of course, to feed the lust for blood of a people anticipating the hideous programme of wholesale murder to be inflicted upon us from the air.

Soon after the war began, the picture of our urban populations, mad with terror under Zeppelin attack, was the most popular subject in all German humorous papers. We were regarded as being a nation of cowards, possessing sufficient brave men to conduct operations far away from our shores, but much too weak of heart as a whole to withstand any attack on our own land. Continental nations, in the German point of view, had been hardened by ages of invasive conflict, while the British people, since the union of England and Scotland, had grown soft through not being exposed, generation after generation, to the experience of invasion. It was thought that our stubbornness in carrying on all our Continental wars since the Elizabethan era was due to the fact that our population was so well protected by our sea-power that they fought longer than Continental nations not from any superior strength of character, but by reason of their exemption from the ghastly miseries that fell on civilians—men, women, and children—in countries with land frontiers.

Feeding the Teuton blood-lust

The German people it was that impelled the Zeppelins to make raids. The German military caste was not so anxious to raid us as the German populace was. The directors of the war had to maintain their airships at full strength for scouting purposes, and the need for them increased when the great thrust against the Russians was planned, and the Baltic coast as far as Riga became the highly important theatre of operations. Also, the entrance of our submarines into the Baltic made more work for the German airships, and thus checked the air campaign against England. But the raids were renewed with energy in May and June, 1915, when the British army in Flanders was trying to remove the pressure against the Russians by attacking the German front. Ipswich and Bury St. Edmunds were attacked by a German airship on April 29th, explosive and incendiary bombs being dropped. This was probably one of Dr. Sticker's preliminary excursions, in which he avoided Harwich because he knew there were guns there. Nobody, however, was killed, and the damage to private property was slight. The only casualty was one pet dog in a shop at Bury St. Edmunds, and here it was that a cottager showed the enemy of what stuff the civilians of East Anglia were composed. A bomb fell in an alley way between two cottages, and a man in one of them rushed out with a bucket of water, and, chancing whether it was an explosive bomb, came quite close up to it

A SCOUT OF THE SKIES.
Inflating a French observation balloon preparatory to sending it up to reconnoitre for the Intelligence Department.

and tried to put it out. There seems to have been another airship approaching the Suffolk coast in the evening, but a British machine went up to engage it, and it turned and disappeared in the seaward haze.

On May 10th the Zeppelins began a serious succession of raids. About three o'clock in the morning bombs were dropped on Southend and the neighbourhood in great profusion. The Zeppelin apparently carried a load of 5,000 lb., and nearly one hundred bombs of 50 lb. each were used. One lady was burned to death in her bed; her husband, a man of sixty-three, suffered from burns and shock; and damage to private property amounting to £7,000 was done. A six-months-old baby of a corporal of the Borderers had a narrow escape, and the soldier father sleeping with it was buried with it in the ruins of the house; but neither lost their lives. Thus the 5,000 lb. of bombs achieved only the death of one aged woman working in the Salvation Army. The people were not at all panic-stricken. It might have been better for them afterwards if they had been. They were all anxious to see a Zeppelin in action, and crowded out into the streets

BALLOONING IN A BLIZZARD.
One of the " eyes " of the French Army in Alsace being sent up, in spite of the blizzard that raged during March, 1916. The falling sleet is plainly visible.

to watch it, so that if our anti-aircraft batteries had poured shrapnel shell around the invader, the falling missiles would have killed more town-folk than did the bombs. This general spirit of curiosity remained in play throughout the year, despite the warnings given by our Government of the great danger from our own shells.

On May 16th a Zeppelin attacked Ramsgate, dropping bombs in one of the most crowded parts of the seaside resort, murdering two persons and injuring eight more. The Bull and George Hotel was wrecked by two bombs, which fell from such a height that they passed through the building and, bursting on the ground-floor, filled the cellar with the wreckage. This seemed to show that, contrary to general opinion, the cellar was one of the most dangerous parts of the house. Two guests in an upper room were recovered from the wreckage, badly injured, but they would probably have both been dead if they had sheltered in the cellar. On May 27th there was another raid on Southend, in which three persons were killed. One of them was a young lady visitor, who was alighting from an electric tram when a falling missile from one of our guns struck her on the head. Aeroplanes and seaplanes went up to chase the Zeppelin, but she escaped in arrogant security, flying over Sheppey and returning over Kent. She was faster than the machines sent against her, and none of our anti-aircraft shells went anywhere near to her. In the previous raid on Ramsgate, as has been related in a former chapter, Flight-Commander Bigsworth overtook the raider in Flanders and dropped bombs on it, which, however, failed to set it on fire.

On May 31st the Zeppelin raiders at last approached their principal goal. The outlying district on one side of London was reached, and bombs were dropped at places in Essex and Kent. The German pilot claimed to have reached Finchley. Three large fires and many small fires broke out, but our authorities reported that all the fires could not be absolutely connected with the airship attacks. Only eight persons, however, were killed, among them being a child of eight, who was coming home from a picture-palace with a girl of sixteen. The boy and girl apparently got lost in the crowd of spectators, and a falling bomb killed the child outright, and so injured was the girl that, after horrible suffering, she expired. A man and his wife kneeling in prayer by their bed were burnt **First attack on** to death by a bomb coming through the **London area** roof of their house. No public building was injured, but the damage to private property was considerable. Four children were killed, and two women were among the slain. Another raid on our East and South-East Coasts took place on June 4th, but no casualties were reported. Yet the German Press and the German military authorities made extravagant claims in regard to the destruction done by their airships. From Leipzig we learnt that England had at last found her master in Count Zeppelin. Along our coasts and in our inland cities flames and smoking ruins marked the path of the Zeppelins. Unrest was being created over Britain on a large scale, which would soon have a great influence on the course of the war.

BRITISH OBSERVATION BALLOON ASCENDING.
A " sausage," as the men called the balloon used for reconnoitring over the lines, going up to observe the effects of artillery fire on the British western front. (Official photograph issued by the Press Bureau.)

But the influence was not that foreseen by Count Reventlow, the loudest of the braggart murderers. The Germans were certainly bringing the war home to us, and on June 6th another Zeppelin raided one of our towns on the East Coast, started fires in a drapery stores, a timber-yard, and a terrace of small houses, killing twenty-four people and injuring forty. Nine days afterwards the North-East Coast was visited by a Zeppelin, dropping bombs that killed fifteen **Public feeling and** persons and injured fifteen more. There **the raids** was unrest among our population, but it was of a kind that did not in any way make for a premature peace. It helped the recruiting of our first-rate voluntary Army, and it hardened our women till they became as tempered as were their sisters in Belgium and Northern France. The Germans, in the early part of the war, complained about our sportsmanlike character, which in plain English meant our mixture of daring, good-humour, and chivalry. All good-humour in regard to the enemy had been knocked out of our soldiers, but at home there remained a large fund of easy-going sentiment in regard to the Germans. Our women, especially, could scarcely believe the evidences of general atrocity, such as had been collected by the Bryce Commission. Our working classes did not read reports by Government Commissions, and allowed too much for the excited state of mind of soldiers marching through hardly-contested hostile country.

It was the supreme function of Count Zeppelin and his pilots to engrave for generations, on all classes of our people, the entire truth about the nature of the Teuton, with such results as would become apparent at the end of the war. The remnant of our Free Traders continued to talk about the economic necessity for renewing relations with Germany when peace was made, but while they were trying to prepare us to deal with the German as an erring but repentant brother, the Zeppelins went on bombing the British electorate into a sterner frame of mind. Fires were started by the Zeppelin bombs which were not to be put out with water. They were fires in the soul of our race, and far away in Australia a Labour Government of an uncommonly progressive kind was

KK

RELIC OF THE SERBIAN
RETREAT.
Wrecked Serbian aeroplane found
lying in a mountain valley on the
Serbo-Albanian frontier.

taking the first steps towards
a longer struggle than Germany ever contemplated.
For the explosion of the
bombs that killed the women
and children of the Motherland echoed to the ends of
the earth.

On August 9th Sticker
attacked the East Coast,
claiming to have bombed
Harwich. He led a squadron
of airships over our shores
between the hours of 8.30
p.m. and 12.30 a.m. The
night was very dark, and a
thick fog over some of our
coast towns rendered night
flying by the British airmen
very difficult. At this time,
when the war had been going
on for a year, we did not seem
to have had adequately lighted landing-places for our pilots
returning from a nocturnal flight. One of our officers who
attempted to bomb a Zeppelin, Flight-
Fatality to Sub-Lieutenant Reginald Lord, a very
Sub-Lieut. Lord gallant Newcastle sportsman and aeroplane builder, was killed by landing in the
darkness. One Zeppelin, however, was seriously damaged by
gun fire from our land defences, and in the morning of August
10th some enemy patrol ships found it and towed it towards
Ostend. But a squadron of French seaplanes from their base
at Dunkirk attacked the crippled monster. It was first hit
by one of our naval pilots, but the French airmen dropped
upon it twelve 4·8 in. incendiary
bombs and six 3·6 in. bombs.
They quite destroyed the structure
by an explosion of its gas, and
then turned on the port of Ostend
and dropped forty-nine explosive
bombs among the enemy's patrol
vessels. Thus this Zeppelin raid,
in which we had lost twenty-five
persons killed or wounded and only
suffered immaterial damage to
property, was not a success for the
enemy. He had then lost more
than twelve Zeppelins, without
counting any hit by the Russians or
any loss of Parsevals. This was his
minimum verifiable loss of rigid airships on the western front, and his
full losses of Zeppelins on land and
sea was probably much greater.

A CAPTIVE ALBATROSS.
German aeroplane that was brought down by French airmen at Salonika.

The Zeppelins were often seen
off the northern coast of Holland
in the evening, going westward
with a guard of German destroyers.
The destroyer flotilla convoyed the
air squadron until night fell, so as
to beat back by gun fire any
British vessel that tried to bring
down the raiders. The Zeppelins
flew low because of their heavy
cargo of bombs and fuel, so that
while daylight held they were
unusually easy targets for any
hostile ship with anti - aircraft
guns. On the other hand, the
Zeppelins were scouting for the
destroyers that protected them,
and only our submarines,
by suddenly emerging off
the Dutch coast, could
have made a surprise
attack. The German
destroyer flotilla was employed against just this
eventuality, as one of our
submarines had badly ripped
a Zeppelin some months
before.

On their return journey
the Zeppelins usually kept
away from the sea for fear
of attack from our sub-
marines and patrols, and
often infringed the neutrality
of Holland by using the
Dutch islands and even the
Dutch mainland to escape
all danger from the sea.
We could have had fair
warning from the northern
coast of Holland that
Zeppelins were flying west-
ward, but, according to the Dutch Press, all telegrams
sent from correspondents from places where Zeppelins were
sighted were delayed by Dutch censors. German aircraft
were thus enabled to proceed to England and kill our
women, children, and other non-combatants without any
Hollander being able to warn us of the expected arrival of
the raiders. The well-known Dutch newspaper the
" Telegraaf " pointed all this out in the summer of 1915,
and contrasted it with their Government's tacit submission
to the violation of Dutch neutrality by Zeppelins.

From the " Telegraaf " we also learned about this time
that the Zeppelin sheds near Brussels were being removed

NUMBERED AMONG FRANCE'S MANY AIR TROPHIES.
A German biplane that was forced by French airmen to descend at Salonika. The machine was
practically undamaged.

AUSTRIAN WIND-TESTING BALLOON.
Austrians in Albania filling from a gas-cylinder one of the small balloons that were sent up to test the direction and speed of the wind.

for security to Antwerp. The airship that first attacked Ramsgate had been destroyed in its shed at Brussels, as already related. New sheds were also being erected, so that airships could be brought by daylight from the Düsseldorf and Hamburg bases, and then replenished with fuel or loaded up with bombs at Antwerp for nocturnal raids on England. Count Zeppelin, besides, was constructing a new model with increased protection against gun fire and aeroplane attack.

Antwerp as a Zeppelin base The anti-aircraft guns were to be defeated by giving the airship a larger volume of gas, enabling her to travel with her bombs at a height of two miles. Aeroplane and seaplane attack were to be met by adding another propeller, by increasing lifting power, and by placing two Maxims on the top of the huge vessel in addition to the machine-guns carried in the gondolas. The speed of the ship was also increased so that it could outrace our Royal Aircraft Factory machines. Whenever possible, all German aircraft went out against a steady fair wind, so as to have it helping them on their return.

But while the new model was being built in standardised quantities, which were said to have brought the total output of Zeppelins to the remarkable number of one hundred by the spring of 1916, the raids against England were continued by the excellent naval model of airship which was larger and more powerful than the military model. Admiral von Tirpitz seems to have been the director of the air campaign against England as well as of the submarine campaign against all merchant shipping found in or near British waters. On August 12th there was another raid on our East Coast by two Zeppelins that came over at 9.30 p.m. and 11.45 p.m. They killed and injured twenty-nine persons and destroyed fourteen houses. Our aircraft patrols went up, but could not overtake and outclimb the enemy airships, though one Zeppelin was thought to have been hit. Again, on August 17th, the Eastern Counties were raided by three Zeppelins, one of which was struck by a British motor-gun. Again our air patrols went up, but could not find and overtake the enemy. All the deaths and injuries occurred amongst civilians, one pathetic incident

being that of a little girl killed in her sleep, and still clasping in her arms her cherished doll. A surgeon, performing the operation of tracheotomy at a nursing home on the East Coast had the town electric current cut off, just when he was opening the windpipe of a child. Fortunately, the operator was prepared for Zeppelin effects. He had lamps ready, and with but trifling delay the operation was completed and the life of the child saved.

German newspapers were full of the tremendous exploits of their air fleet. By a stroke of the pen they had already destroyed most of the London docks, and they now went on and blew up Landguard Fort, at Harwich, by means of a Zeppelin bomb which penetrated into the magazine. The Dutch mail was destroyed at Harwich and postal communications interrupted for a week. But after reading all this, the Dutch were surprised to receive still the post from England in a regular manner, with no letters delayed except perhaps a few in which the British Censor was interested. Our Admiralty had settled on a policy of silence in regard to the places attacked by the raiders. Perhaps Mr. Arthur Balfour thought that a strategical silence and the repression of long and detailed newspaper reports would tend to keep the nation calm. **Mr. Balfour's policy of silence** The Germans answered this move by getting their agents in England to start rumours of enormous loss of life after every important raid.

On September 7th Sticker saw London, and died. According to the German statement, the western part of the London district was attacked, and large factories and harbour works and ironworks in the Eastern Counties. Between September 7th and September 8th the loss of life in the London district and the Eastern Counties was heavier than in any previous raid. The dead numbered thirty-seven, and the injured one hundred and twenty-five. Fires broke out, but happily were got under control, though the damage to small dwelling-houses was considerable. Yet the harm done by this aerial bombardment, maintained for two nights with all the power that Germany could spare, was insignificant in comparison with the dreams of

MYNHEER FOKKER.

The Dutch inventor of the German monoplane bearing his name. When the brilliant French airman M. Garros was brought down in German territory in April, 1915, Fokker adapted the Frenchman's device of a machine-gun firing through the propeller, and introduced a more powerful air-engine than the French were using.

destructiveness which the German populace had been cherishing for ten years. The German airship was first perceived moving at a fairly low level in the clear radiance of some of the London searchlights. The searchlight men caught her and held her, distinct and strangely picturesque, against the dim background of the starred autumnal sky. Had we then possessed, on certain high places round the capital, well-trained anti-aircraft guns, using incendiary shells, we should probably have made Sticker or Mathy pay for the damage he did.

We had practically abandoned the system of attacking airships with aeroplanes. There seems to have been a lack of nocturnal landing-places, with proper signal lights, and if any airman rose at his own risk over London and tried to equal the feat of Mr. Warneford, he **The defence of London** was only able to land in very hazardous circumstances. The defence of the capital appeared to consist of anti-aircraft guns of short range, firing almost useless shrapnel, because there were no high-explosive or incendiary shells available. Most of the men who manned the guns worked all day in bank and business offices, and were given no practice against kites or balloons. They were apparently intended only to serve as scarecrows, and induce the German airships to lessen their load of bombs in order to keep at a high altitude. The airship first seen over London, when the searchlights played upon her and the shrapnel bullets came near, put up her nose and rapidly ascended into a cloud, which she seemed to have manufactured for the purpose.

Most of the Londoners took the matter in a sportsman-like mood, standing in groups to watch the shooting, and

confidently expecting the raider to be winged. Great was the general disappointment when she easily escaped eastward, without showing signs of any damage. The fault was not in the gunners, but in the responsible authorities, who had not provided effective anti-aircraft guns or trained the gunners by sending them in batches to the front for actual work against enemy machines. The new German aeroplanes were beginning to operate at a height of 10,000 feet, which was the altitude at which Zeppelins travelled at night over dangerous localities. Any gunner that could hit a small biplane at a good height could have brought down a Zeppelin, caught by searchlights, if he had a gun that carried far enough, and an incendiary shell to explode hydrogen gas. But we have already seen that, during the Zeppelin attack on Ramsgate, Flight-Commander Bigsworth and his fellow pilots had no incendiary bombs for exploding Zeppelins. It would have been possible, also, to equip stationary anti-aircraft **Long-range guns** batteries with fire-control instruments, **needed** making a hit almost a certainty for a highly-trained gunner. But it was reckoned the instrument makers could not fully supply the Navy and our growing armies with fire-control installations if the capital and coast defences were fully equipped. Still London and a few more important places might have had good guns and a fire-control system. But our aerial defences, at the end of twelve months' warfare, were in a deplorable condition. Neither our Fleet nor our Army could spare the long-range guns needed against high-flying Zeppelins, and our supply of high-explosive shell was still, in August, 1915, much less than was required by our forces in Flanders, the Dardanelles, and Mesopotamia. And while in this condition of weakness, we had not strenuously developed the means of making attacks upon the sheds from which enemy airships operated.

The only attempt at reorganisation was the appointment of Rear-Admiral C. L. Vaughan-Lee as Director of Air Services in the Admiralty, in the place of Commodore F. M. Sueter, who became Superintendent of Aircraft Construction. The rear-admiral was a fine seaman, quite capable of introducing stricter discipline into the naval wings, but he does not seem to have had any practical experience whatever in flying. For gunnery experts our Navy went to first-rate gunnery officers, for torpedo experts it went to good torpedo officers, and for navigation experts it went to navigation officers. For a supreme air director, however, it turned to a flag officer who could not in person have carried out a successful attack against an Albatross. We had one flag-officer, Rear-Admiral Kerr, who was an experienced flyer ; but, for some reason at present unknown, Mr. Arthur Balfour and his Sea Lords thought that a director with practical knowledge was not needed in the Naval Air Service, one of whose functions at the time was to guard our coasts against hostile aircraft. Some weeks afterwards, Mr. Balfour said that he did not know why the air defence of London had been entrusted to the Navy. Apparently, the civil head of our Admiralty did not know that London was one of the principal seaports of the Empire, which was being attacked from the sea, the Naval Wing partly defending it from Dunkirk and patrol ships in the North Sea warning it of raids.

On Sunday, September 12th, the Zeppelins, according to the official German statement, tried again to reach the docks of London. The next night a Zeppelin crossed the East Coast. In both cases no persons were injured, and very little damage was done. Our anti-aircraft guns, fixed and mobile, were in action. They beat the raiders off. In the meantime, Admiral Sir Percy Scott was appointed to take charge of the gunnery defences of London against attacks by enemy aircraft. This was a better step than the appointment of a torpedo officer, who was also a Director of Naval Intelligence, to reorganise our air service. Sir Percy Scott had raised the shooting in the Navy to a very high level, and it was fairly certain that if

Lieut. Brandon attacking one of the Zeppelin raiders on March 31st, 1916.

294

Sikorsky biplane about to ascend for reconnaissance.

Quick-firers on British armoured cars shelling enemy aircraft over a French village behind our lines.

he was given the men, the guns, the fire-control instruments, and the special shell he needed, the Zeppelin flights over London would become very dangerous to the flyers. But the work did not go on in a rapid manner, and at intervals there were reports that Sir Percy thought of resigning from his position. Both soldier and sailor gunners took part in the anti-aircraft artillery work along our coasts, and for some months the Admiralty and the War Office worked together without any close organisation. Neither, seemingly, wanted the entire responsibility for failures to stop the nocturnal raiders. As they both relied mainly on the Royal Aircraft Factory for machines, they could not mount their pilots with the efficiency needed for aerial bomb attacks upon the raiders. The War Office, moreover, could not spare flying officers for defensive raids on airship sheds between Emden and Hamburg, Antwerp and Düsseldorf. Yet in the end it was the **The War Office** War Office that took over the defensive **takes control** work against hostile aircraft, though our sea patrols and Naval Wing exercised more or less control over the waters which the Zeppelins had to cross in reaching our shores.

There seems to have been an under-estimation on the part of our Government regarding the damage that could be done by the air raiders. It appears to have been considered that only a few hundred deaths and injuries to civilians and a comparatively small amount of damage to property could be effected by Zeppelin attacks. The fact that we had had a run of good luck with regard to the possible destruction of important war factories, naval bases, and centres of Government work seems to have lulled our leaders into a feeling of security. We had destroyed several German airships between June and September, 1915, in spite of our inferior means of defence. Our Government was content with this. Even Count Zeppelin, by twenty raids, could not arouse our Cabinet, our generals, and our admirals to a really acute sense of the warlike value of first-rate aircraft.

The last Zeppelin raid of the year took place on October 13th, when Zeppelins again visited the London area and the Eastern Counties. Fifty-five persons were killed, and a hundred and fourteen injured ; but, except for one chance shot, the damage was reported to have fallen wholly on property unconnected with the conduct of the war. The darkening of the metropolitan area helped to prevent the enemy from discovering the exact position of places of importance, but his bad marksmanship was still more attributable to the height at which he flew—some two miles—and to the speed with which he passed over the vast tract of dim streets. We have seen that Sticker, in a private letter to a friend, claimed to have distinguished the bridges over the Thames and discerned the misses he made. But an airship going at fifty miles at a height of two miles could not have any hope of hitting a target the size of an acre. Unknown currents of air in the lower altitudes would deflect the bombs, even if it had been possible to loosen them at the exact fraction of a second necessary to hit a mark in advance of the airship's route, which was being studied by an observer in the forward gondola. Our officers of the Royal Flying Corps in Flanders, after hundreds of bombing expeditions in which they swooped down to 1,000 feet or less, confessed that they seldom got home on their targets. They thought a long-range heavy gun was far more effective than any bombing machine. On this reasoning, a Zeppelin, at a height of two miles and going at high speed to escape a shell being fired at it, could not be expected to hit any building in London. It could only sow death and suffering indiscriminately amid the largest urban population on earth.

London, however, was not the most important object from a German point of view that could be attacked from the air. The bombing of our capital and our seaside resorts was a blunder as well as a crime. It was a blind expression of the " Gott-strafe-England " spirit, in which

IN READINESS FOR AIR RAIDERS.
French " 75 " mounted on a motor-waggon. These famous French guns were as useful against raiding aircraft as on the fighting fronts. It was a " 75 " that shot down Zeppelin L77 near Révigny in February, 1916.

ferocious exasperation over our entry into a well-planned war that we had upset misled the director of the Zeppelin squadrons. He aimed at London, in order to placate the German populace and carry out the tradition of the London bombardments of German toymakers and the pictures of the panic-stricken British capital given in German comic papers. Important military damage might have been done if all the twenty raids of 1915 had been directed towards our Midlands. On the other hand, the people of the Midlands had more energy of character than the vast, unorganised population of London. **Public spirit in** London was so large that it possessed no **the Midlands** corporate spirit. There " east was east and west was west, and never the twain could meet "—even on Zeppelin nights. But the leading Midland cities had each a soul and a vigorous creative temper. They were governed for the most part by practical men of business, used to handling large concerns, and capable of making great efforts to remedy our deficiences when these deficiences were brought vividly home to them. It was almost worth while, from the German point of view, to let the sleeping dogs of the Midlands lie, and from the middle of October, 1915, to the middle of January, 1916, no Zeppelin raid occurred.

But on January 31st, 1916, the Midland Counties were at last furiously attacked, sixty-seven persons being killed and one hundred and seventeen injured. Among the killed and injured were seventy-four women and fourteen children. Six or seven airships came over England and dropped bombs in Norfolk, Suffolk, Lincolnshire, Leicestershire,

Staffordshire, and Derbyshire. It was a foggy night that turned to rain, and the mist and moisture helped to defeat the enemy. Only in Staffordshire was any considerable damage done. A church and a chapel were badly damaged and a parish room was wrecked. Three railway sheds were struck, three breweries were somewhat shattered, and an engine-shed and a lamp factory seriously damaged. Minor damage was done to a munition factory, two iron-works, a grain shed, colliery and pumping station, and fifteen small dwelling houses were destroyed. Many of the bombs fell in country places, and merely disturbed the ground. The Germans made extravagant claims to have bombarded the docks, harbour, and factories in and around Liverpool, to have wrecked smelting furnaces at Nottingham and Sheffield, and large industrial works on the Humber. It is doubtful whether these claims originated from captains of Zeppelins who desired to win the Iron Cross, or whether some new Baron Munchausen was employed by the German Naval Staff for the delectation of the German populace, This populace was beginning to make trouble over the mild effects of our incomplete blockade. Britain, they were told, was starving them, in spite of the fact that in the early days of the war, when the German Zeppelin and submarine campaigns opened against us, we were still letting large supplies of both war material and food through the North Sea into Germany. But the legend of our starvation policy had been stamped into the German mind by the German Government, and, as the Zeppelin raids were popularly supposed to be a punishment inflicted on us because of our blockade, the results of every raid had to be exaggerated to satisfy German expectations.

The starvation legend

Had there been more guns in the Midlands, or even along the coast, the raiders would have suffered badly ; for some of them appear to have flown very low. One was seen hovering over a passenger train, but the train was not attacked. Another circled for ten minutes over a town, trying to bomb a goods yard, with the engine-driver sitting calmly looking on from his engine. A mission meeting at which a lady speaker, Bible in hand, was addressing a body mainly composed of women and girls, was struck by a bomb that killed or injured most of the audience, the lady speaker being cut in two by the missile. In one house the grandfather, grandmother, mother, and two grandchildren were all killed outright by a bomb. One Midland town, warned of the approach of the raiders, closed all its works down, stopped its tram-cars, and dimmed all lights. The Zeppelin passed over it without attacking, and unloaded its bombs on a neighbouring city which had not put out all its lights. Another town, after escaping one raider, was subjected to a long attack by a returning Zeppelin. But though thirty incendiary bombs were discharged on this town, not a single person was injured and little damage was done Nearly all the cargo of fiery death was emptied upon the open spaces of the town. There were two raids, one early in the evening and another about midnight.

On this occasion the raiders did not escape with impunity. Though the official German communiqué stated that all the airships safely returned, one of them was struck and another, L19, was winged, and fell in the North Sea. The Grimsby trawler King Stephen sighted the wreck on February 2nd. The cars and the gasbag were partly submerged, but the upper portion of the envelope rose fifty feet out of the water. Some sixteen men, with lifebelts round their waists, were at first

HOW THE ZEPPELIN FOUND ITS WAY BACK TO THE FATHERLAND.
These unpleasant visitants, seeking the cover of night for their sinister work, frequently arrived back in Germany during the dark early hours of the morning. To guide them safely to their sheds, a series of lighthouses were specially built all over Germany. Their method of illumination was various to a degree. Some projected a permanent beam of light straight up into the air. Others shone with a disappearing light, signalling a number which indicated a certain flying stadium ; others again were fitted with a revolving light. Our drawing is of one of these lighthouses in communication with a Zeppelin crew.

visible on the platform. The Zeppelin commander asked the Grimsby skipper to launch a boat and take the air crew off. He offered gold for a rescue. But on coming closer to the wreck the skipper of the trawler saw that there were at least twenty men on it, some of them being armed. It would have been easy for them to have overpowered the small crew of the King Stephen, and the skipper decided—and all his men agreed with him—that it was too dangerous to attempt a rescue. So the murderers were left on their sinking gasbag, and a gale blew that morning and sank the airship and her crew.

Prior to this L19 had been stationed at Hamburg and at Tondern, patrolling the west coast of Denmark and part of the North Sea. She was the first airship to stop and board a merchant steamer. Three months before she was wrecked she stopped a Swedish steamer in the middle of the North Sea, came down herself within a few yards of the water, and then launched a boat carrying the inspecting officers. She was also supposed to have been the Zeppelin which bombed and sank a collier belonging to Hartlepool on her way to England; her identity in this case, however, was far from being established. The German Press was furious over the fate of L19. The action of the crew of the King Stephen was stated to be a revelation of the brutality of the British character, and a greater act of cruelty than that of the American cattlemen in the Nicosian. But the deepest wound dealt to the Germans in the matter was the report from Holland, cited in a French official communiqué, which stated that L19 had finally been brought down by Dutch guns at the moment when, with the usual Teutonic contempt of neutrality, the commander of the Zeppelin was trying to pass over Dutch territory.

One result of the attack on the Midlands was a conference of Midland public authorities, held in Birmingham under the Lord Mayor of the city, Mr. Neville Chamberlain. They devised a scheme for organised and uniform action in connection with military authorities. They wanted public warning when hostile aircraft reached our shores, so that all districts could be placed in darkness and night-working munition factories dimmed some time before the aircraft arrived. Satisfactory arrangements, however, could not be made with the Home Office, the Post Office, and the Commander-in-Chief of the home forces. But Birmingham did not settle down quietly under official discouragement. Like Paris, which had been raided in a fog a few weeks before, Birmingham, with Coventry, Sheffield, and other important industrial centres, began to extend the inquiry into the general condition of our air services, the quality of our machines, our lack of large airships, and the loss of command of the air.

In the middle of February, Lord Kitchener made a short

Lord Kitchener and air defence

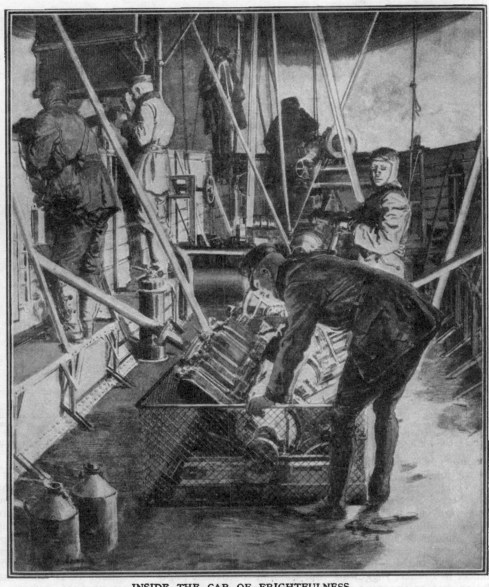

INSIDE THE CAR OF FRIGHTFULNESS.

Interior view of a Zeppelin cab, showing the powerful Maybach motors in the centre receiving attention from engineers. On the left the look-out man and machine-gun operators are seen ready to repel hostile aircraft. One of the large radiators for the water-cooled engines is situated just above their heads, while at their feet is a fire-extinguisher. At the rear of the gondola is a reserve steering apparatus.

statement on the problem of air defence during a debate in the House of Lords. He pointed out that up to the period of which he spoke, hostile invasions of England had effected no military purpose, and that some risks must be accepted in order to be strong at the most important point. He continued:

I may say at once, as regards Zeppelin attacks, that it is beyond our power to guarantee these shores from a repetition of incursions. But although we have only one example of a Zeppelin being destroyed by aeroplane attack—I allude to Lieutenant Warneford's gallant action—there have been several cases in which we have so disabled the enemy's aircraft as to bring them eventually to the ground, or to render them useless for further service. During the last raid, while we are sure that one airship was lost at sea, we have very good reason to believe that a second was placed out of action.

But these remarks did not cover the problem. The country was not only becoming thoroughly dissatisfied with the condition of the air services, but it was beginning to move strongly for a radical change in both the military corps and the naval wings. The position was widely esteemed intolerable. After more than eighteen months of war our aerial forces and anti-aircraft organisation were not set in order. Each new enemy air raid disclosed fresh defects and a larger lack of system. The Midland raid, for

ARMAMENT OF AN ENEMY AEROPLANE.

Drawing made from a German aeroplane brought down in the British lines, showing the two guns with which the machine was armed. The observer, seated in a gun-rest, turned his weapon the extent of a semi-circle. He could depress and elevate the gun according to the position of his adversary, firing through the metal tube in the framework if the enemy approached from below. To the muzzle of the weapon was fixed a telescopic sight. A lighter gun was mounted on the plane, which the observer, rising and turning in his seat, used for forward fire.

example, showed there was no uniformity of lighting restrictions and no uniformity in the sending of warnings. In London there were frequent rumours about Admiral Sir Percy Scott and the difficulties against which he was fighting to force effective measures of defence upon officialdom. And this after he had been engaged for four months on his special work !

About this time the chief organ of the Coalition Cabinet, the "Westminster Gazette" published an article by an officer in France, suggesting that the non-combatant population was as timorous as the Germans supposed, because they could not suffer in silence from occasional Zeppelin bombs, though the soldiers in the firing-line were constantly exposed to high-explosive shells. This was a vain and calumnious suggestion. Some British mothers with little children were perturbed when Zeppelins hovered above them ; so were some aged people and persons of nervous temperament who found themselves hopelessly without defence from the monsters of the air.

"In the firing-line" Many a man, too, had a feeling of utter helplessness when close to the bomb-line of a German airship, and uncertain of what the course would be. But in one of the great London raids the writer heard a woman say, after coming out in the street and leaving her two children asleep at home : "Now we know what our men at the front feel. We are in the firing-line !" Soldiers at home on leave confessed they were unnerved when under a Zeppelin, because they could not strike back. On the whole, the general spirit of the public was strong and high. But their wits were sharpened by their experience, and they at last began to examine the reasons for our loss of the command of the air.

Far from being terrorised into a desire for peace at any price, as the enemy designed, our civil population was stirred to agitate for more powerful weapons for carrying the war to a decisive victory. Even some conscientious objectors—which was often only a long name for the common coward—were "zepped" into the ancient courage

of their race and the recruiting office. The movement created by the Zeppelin raids was longer in taking definite shape. The people wanted, from instinct, the command of the air, but in the slow, roundabout English way, they made such gradual approaches to the object of their desire that an observant foreigner might have been inclined to charge them with stupidity. But the fact was that England was the slow, old **England the** "steam-roller," and not Russia. Had **"steam-roller"** Scotland been continually raided, the movement of reform might have started earlier and proceeded with more rapidity.

The Press Bureau issued a statement on February 4th, pointing out that, in all the raids that had taken place in Britain since the war began, 133 men, 90 women, and 43 children had been killed by bombs, whereas in the Lusitania alone 1,198 innocent civilians had been murdered. This contrast in figures was apparently intended to appease the people ; but it was reckoned extraordinary by certain critics that the supposed result of inadequate vigilance off the Head of Kinsale, in the matter of destroyers, should be put forward in mitigation of the later failure to build machines capable of raiding the Zeppelin bases. As was pointed out at the time, if the Germans were allowed to build a really great airship fleet capable of raiding us until tens of thousands of our population were killed, the Press Bureau could still point out that the deaths of women, children, and non-combatants only amounted to a fraction of our losses at the Dardanelles. But this manner of reasoning could not still the general agitation for the energetic construction of a great British air fleet capable of winning the command of the air, bombarding Zeppelin bases, and making reprisals on Cologne and Düsseldorf, as was urged by a Labour member, Mr. Hodge, in the House of Commons.

The German power of the air was shown towards the end of February, 1916, in direct military operations at Verdun, where all French machines had been prevented from reconnoitring and discerning the scope of the enemy's preparations, so that the blow against the French lines, the outermost of which was taken, was delivered with a maximum surprise effect. This showed that Germany had a large reserve of fast and powerful machines, and men to pilot them and fight from them, as well as a fleet of Zeppelins of considerable size.

The situation was full of danger to all the Allies, and the extraordinary slowness of Britain, the principal manufacturing power of the Alliance, in building an air fleet approaching in comparative strength her sea Fleet, was not a matter on which we could pride ourselves. It was, perhaps, well for us that Count Zeppelin continued to drive home the lesson that we had to learn, at any cost, ere it was too late for us to attempt to recover the leeway we had lost. The Germans clearly mistook the agitation of British public opinion for symptoms of weakening, and tried to stampede us into something like panic. On March 5th there was another air raid by three or more Zeppelins over eight English counties—Yorkshire, Lincolnshire, Rutland, Huntingdon, Cambridgeshire, Norfolk, Essex, and Kent. According to our War Office report, three men, four women, and five children were killed, while thirty-three were injured, of whom one afterwards died. No military damage of any kind was done, but two terraces of dwelling-houses were destroyed, a block of almshouses was badly shattered, and several other buildings—shops, a public-house, and café—were wholly or partly wrecked. Probably another great raid over the munition towns of the Midlands was intended, but the enemy's plans were upset by a snowstorm.

Upset by a snowstorm

The commanders of the airships were afraid that the great weight of snow on their envelopes would bring them down, and, in order to lighten their vessels and rise above the storm, they unloaded their bombs anywhere. Some fell in the sea near the shore, and most of the others were pitched out on agricultural land. Two of the Zeppelins seem to have sailed over our coast in daylight about five p.m. Apparently we had no patrols out at sea to give warning of their coming, so that no attack could be concerted against them when they reached the coast. One of the Zeppelins, however, that passed over Essex turned south and returned over Kent.

Under the pressure of public opinion the Admiralty,

on March 25th, arranged an attack by British seaplanes on the Zeppelin sheds in Schleswig It was delivered fifteen months to the day after our little experimental raid on Cuxhaven. It might reasonably have been expected that, after fifteen months' further practice and progress in construction and training of pilots, the Schleswig raid would have been conducted in an airmanlike manner. But it proved to be only a futile air operation, backed by a fine piece of naval work. A force of light cruisers and destroyers, under Commodore Tyrwhitt, convoyed two seaplane-carriers across the North Sea to the German coast of Schleswig-Holstein, near the Island of Sylt. The German anti-aircraft gunners are said to have been warned of the coming attack, after two armed German patrol vessels had been sunk by our destroyers. But this news came from the enemy, and was suspect. A German torpedo-boat was sunk, and, though we lost

OVER THE DUNES.
British seaplane flying low along the Belgian coast.

the destroyer Medusa in collision with the destroyer Laverock, the daring naval excursion was a success. The aerial force, however, was quite inadequate. A week earlier sixty-five allied pilots had been launched, with considerable success, against Zeebrugge. But against the more important Zeppelin base on the Schleswig coast, it seems only five seaplanes were sent. Three of the seaplanes were brought down either by engine trouble or by enemy gunners, and three of our pilots, with a midshipman and mechanic, were captured.

Our Admiralty stated that the object of the operation

ABOVE THE GREEK BASE OF THE ALLIES.
Twin-engined Caudron biplane in flight over Salonika.

was achieved, which may have been the case if no Zeppelin sheds were aimed at. There were from eight to ten sheds on the Schleswig-Holstein coast, each protected by very powerful anti-aircraft artillery, including the 4·1 in. gun, discharging every minute ten 39 lb. high-explosive shells to a height of 26,000 feet. If we had employed fifty seaplanes on an intensive operation against one or two sheds, the German gunners would have had so **The Schleswig** many targets that they could not have **raid** concentrated against them, and some of our pilots would probably have got home with their bombs on one shed or even on two. Our machines would appear to have concentrated against the Zeppelin station at Tondern, but there were not sufficient of them to distract and scatter the enemy's fire. The affair seems to have been designed, with incomplete knowledge of the developments of air tactics, for the political purpose of making a show of activity to silence critics in Parliament and reformers in the country.

We had arrived at a period when a raid of one hundred machines, in groups of thirty, could be regarded as a serious attack. But we were lacking in the first-rate and abundant equipment needed for businesslike raids. We lacked also any long-flight machine, capable of acting from a single fast seaplane-carrier, and undertaking a single-handed surprise raid at little cost even in case of failure. There were, it is true, seaplanes that could have been converted into long-range aeroplanes, powerful enough to travel to Germany and back, but they were not so used. All we did was to employ a considerable naval force, with an insufficient aerial force, and lose a destroyer equal at least to a couple of Zeppelins. Had a feeble raid of this kind been conducted at the outbreak of the war it would have passed, like the little Cuxhaven affair, as an interesting practical experiment. But being carried out after eighteen months of warfare, it confirmed everything that had been

said in the House of Commons concerning the condition of our air services.

After our little futile expedition to Schleswig, the director of the German Naval Air Service thought fit to give us an example of sound air raid tactics. On the night of March 31st two Zeppelin squadrons and one detached ship raided the Eastern Counties and the North-East Coast. On the night of April 1st two Zeppelins approached the North-East Coast. One turned back, and the other conducted a raid, killing and injuring about one hundred and sixteen persons. On the night of April 2nd six Zeppelins raided the coast of Britain and the inland districts. For the first time in the war Scotland was bombed. Three raiders travelled to the South-Eastern Counties of Scotland, cruising over them for some hours and dropping bombs. One Zeppelin attacked the North-East Coast of England, and the two remaining ships cruised over the Eastern Counties for nearly two hours. On the night of April 5th there was another Zeppelin raid on the North-East Coast, three Zeppelins apparently coming in from the sea at intervals.

This sustained and widespread operation did not affect all that the man who planned it designed. It included an attack on the munition factories in the London district, but the raiders were beaten off by the improvements in our artillery defences that Sir Percy Scott had effected. According to the   **A sustained** Under-Secretary for War, more than one   **operation** attack had been beaten back from London and the munition factories round the capital without the inhabitants becoming aware that Zeppelin raiders were menacing them. Yet in comparison with our Schleswig operation, the prolonged attack on both England and Scotland was a serious piece of work, pregnant with a larger menace. It showed what the Germans intended to do if they could further increase their rate of Zeppelin production. It had taken them a remarkably long time

THE " GERRARD " OF THE ZEPPELIN DEFENCES OF PARIS: ANTI-AIRCRAFT TELEPHONE EXCHANGE.
Interior of the telephone headquarters. The office was connected by telephone wires to every point within the Paris zone of defence. On the receipt of the alarm from an observation post, possibly on the fortifications, information as to the raider's whereabouts was telephoned all over the capital.

PRELIMINARY WORK BEFORE MAKING AN AIR RAID.

Scene at a headquarters of the French aviation section. Flying officers busily engaged studying the best cross-country routes by the map, making up meteorological charts, and compiling the latest information about enemy gun positions, railway junctions, munition factories, etc.

to extend their attacks to Scotland, but it looked as though they were at last forming designs against our northern naval bases, where some of the ships of our Grand Fleet might be found. In the Schleswig raid five German battle-planes and a Zeppelin had assailed our light cruisers and destroyers on their return journey, and though our well-handled ships had outmanœuvred both the gasbags and the machines, the Germans had certain experiences at Cuxhaven and Zeebrugge which encouraged them to think that an aerial attack over a harbour in which a battle fleet was anchored might bring some results.

According to the German Press, the Zeppelin campaign of the first week of April, 1916, was the last of the exploratory raids. As a mere work of exploration it was somewhat costly. We had seventy men, women, and children killed, and one hundred and eighty-five injured in the four attacks. In all, sixteen Zeppelins crossed the coast of our country between March 31st and April 5th. But one of the raiders was brought down in the estuary of the Thames, and another Zeppelin was hit somewhere on the coast. L15, which was beaten down in the mouth of the Thames, was hit by gun fire while over the Eastern Counties. The shell struck the upper part of the ship near the tail, and after being injured she dropped to a lower altitude, well down by the tail, and at last fell into the sea off the coast of Kent on Saturday morning, April 1st. The commander and crew surrendered to the steam-trawler Olivine, commanded by Lieutenant W. R. Mackintosh, R.N.R. An attempt was made to tow the Zeppelin to harbour, but she sank.

Sinking of the L15 On the same night on which L15 was brought down several officers of the Royal Flying Corps went up to attack the raiders. A New Zealander, who only gained his wings three weeks before his brilliant flight, Lieutenant A. de Bathe Brandon, rose 6,000 feet at a quarter to ten on the night of March 31st, and saw a Zeppelin about 3,000 feet above him. He climbed up this distance, got over the airship and attacked it, while the Zeppelin crew worked their top machine-guns against him. But he dropped

several bombs, three of which he believed took effect. Then, to make sure, he got over the Zeppelin again at ten o'clock and dropped two more bombs on her nose. It was a fine feat like that of Mr. Warneford, or rather like that of Flight-Commander Bigsworth, for, as the Zeppelin did not catch fire and explode, the bombs given to the officer may not have been proper incendiary bombs. At the time of writing it was not known what became of the stricken vessel. She may **Lieut. Brandon's** have been the airship that is known to **fine feat** have dropped a machine-gun, petrol tank, ammunition, and some machinery, so as to lighten herself, and possibly she may have been L15, which our gunners afterwards struck. Either way, we were not able definitely to claim the destruction of more than one Zeppelin out of sixteen. It was a casualty rate little calculated to disturb the enemy. It was very much less than our proportion of losses in the brief Schleswig raid.

In addition to all the Zeppelin attacks we have noted, there was a series of aeroplane raids mostly over the southern coast of England in daylight. On February 21st, 1915, a machine flew over Colchester at 9 p.m., but did not kill anyone. Then on April 16th there was a midday attack on Faversham and Sittingbourne, without injury to life. The raider was fired on and chased by British airmen, after he had killed a blackbird and a field-mouse, but his superior speed enabled him to escape; for it was an Aviatik biplane, and the British airmen who pursued it were on Royal Aircraft Factory machines. The following day the raider seems to have returned to the Kentish coast, dropping some bombs, smashing one house, killing one person, and wounding six others, nearly all of them women. After this there was a lull of some months in aeroplane attack, but on January 23rd, 1916, a hostile aeroplane travelled on a moonlight night over the Kent coast, and dropping nine bombs in rapid succession, caused some fires, killed one man and wounded a man, two women, and three children. In the afternoon of the next day two German seaplanes made another attack upon Dover, but were beaten back by heavy fire, and pursued. Four of our

FLIGHT-SUB-LIEUTENANT
I. H. W. BARNATO.
Took part in British raid on Constantinople. Son of the late Mr.
Barney Barnato.

SQUAD.-COMMANDER SMYTH-
PIGOTT, D.S.O.
Leader of the great naval aeroplane
attack on Constantinople, April
14th, 1916.

FLIGHT SUB-LIEUTENANT
DICKINSON.
Took part in attack on Constantinople. Son of Mr. W. H. Dickinson,
M.P.

FLIGHT-LIEUTENANT K. S.
SAVORY.
Also took part in Constantinople
operations. Nephew of Admiral
H. W. Savory.

military aeroplanes and two of our seaplanes went up in pursuit, but the raiders had faster machines and could not be overtaken. If any attempt was made to cut them off on their return by our Naval Wing at Dunkirk, the result was regarded as not worth publishing.

Again on February 9th, at half-past three in the afternoon, two German seaplanes bombed Ramsgate and Broadstairs. For some strange reason a girls' school at Broadstairs was selected for attack, and four bombs launched at it, which just missed the target. Two women and one child were, however, injured, and though our military and naval pilots ascended, they could not overtake the raiders. On February 20th the enemy extended his aeroplane raids, and two biplanes circled over Lowestoft, dropped bombs, and vanished. A quarter of an hour afterwards they returned and dropped more bombs. Five minutes before their return, two of our naval aeroplanes went up, but once more, and in more favouring circumstances, our officers failed to overtake the raiders. The British machines were clean outclassed in speed. Meanwhile two other German seaplanes were making for the Kentish coast, and after bombing the lightship by the Kentish Knock, one of the raiders made straight for Walmer, and reached that town at 11.27 a.m. It flew

FLIGHT-SUB-LIEUTENANT
KNIGHT.
Took part in raid on Zeppelin
sheds in Schleswig-Holstein, March
25th, 1916.

FLIGHT-LIEUTENANT G. H.
REID.
Another hero of Schleswig-Holstein air raid. He was reported
missing.

at the low altitude of 3,500 feet and bombed a church, missed it, and then bombed a roadway, killing two men and one boy, and wounding one Marine. But the remarkable thing about the Walmer raid was that two of our aeroplanes went up from Dover and came over Walmer at 11.15 a.m. This was twelve minutes

**Attacks on
Kentish coast** before the raider arrived at a low altitude. Again our inferior machines could not overtake the enemy, who was using one of the powerful-engined new models.

What was noteworthy in the Lowestoft raid was not the time it took us to get two seaplanes into the air, but the fact that the distance from the Belgian coast to Yarmouth and back was about the distance from Dunkirk to Düsseldorf and back. In other words, if our airmen had possessed as good machines as the Germans, they could have retaliated. Moreover, such a machine was in exist-

ence. It was built by Messrs. Sopwith, of Kingston-on-Thames, who for nearly a year had been making aeroplanes that broke all British records in climbing power. But the Sopwith machine had been offered to the Government about June, 1915, and neglected in favour of the Royal Aircraft Factory.

We are happy to be able to conclude our account of these tragic aeroplane raids with a comedy. On March 12th a German seaplane was sighted off the North Foreland at midday, but our Dover station was uncommonly alert, and sent up men who beat the German away from the land, and vainly pursued him as usual. The quickness with which the Dover station had previously sent men over to Walmer seemed to show that somebody was bent upon making the wing efficient. But on March 19th four seaplanes came over Kent. The first pair bombed Ramsgate, Margate, and Westgate, and the second pair flew over Dover at a height of about five hundred feet, bombed the harbour and the town, and dropped bombs on Deal. Three men, one woman, and five children were killed; sixteen men, five women and nine children were injured. One bomb fell on a hospital at Ramsgate, doing material damage but causing no injury to life.

But against all this our official report was able to add that Flight-Commander Bone, in a single-seater aeroplane, pursued one of the German seaplanes out to sea for many miles, killed the observer, damaged the machine, and forced it to descend. Then it was afterwards reported that a second enemy aeroplane had been shot down after the Dover raid. Even so, the state of affairs was not very satisfactory. One **Commander Bone's** machine was brought down by a naval **brave exploit** officer who was not on duty at the time. The other machine was shot down by a military pilot flying with a passenger from Farnborough to France, and meeting the retreating enemy by pure luck.

In connection with these raids on Kent, serious allegations were made by Mr. Joynson-Hicks in the House of Commons on March 21st. He alleged that in one town: the officers who should have been in control were not in control at the time. They were away, perhaps lunching, or something of that kind; but things are now so serious that while I believe a naval officer is entitled to have his lunch, there should be a subordinate in charge while he is away, in order that at the moment and at every moment throughout the day and night the amplest protection should be afforded to all our people against these German air raids.

A week afterwards, Mr. Joynson-Hicks further alleged that the captain whose duty it was to issue raid warnings at Ramsgate did not leave his house until after the bombs had fallen, and then drove about the town in a motor-car with two ladies showing them the damage. But this and other such allegations were refuted on behalf of the airmen. But still more striking and memorable was the speech of Sir Alfred Gelder, who was a resident of Hull. He said:

I remember a year ago that there was a certain raid on an East Coast town, which did very much greater damage than the Press Censor ever allowed to be published. I was near enough to hear the cries and shrieks of the people, and I never want to be in such proximity again. I thought it my duty to do everything I could to meet this difficulty, and the naval authorities replied: "In respect to the future, we intend to make the air service on the East Coast efficient. We intend to provide your large towns and cities with aircraft guns." I went so far as to discuss with them some suitable places for aerodromes in the vicinity of one large centre of industry. We found that, a week or two afterwards, one or two motor anti-aircraft guns were paraded through the streets of the city. We naturally imagined that they were for our defence, and the people were very delighted.

The matter was in the hands of the Admiralty for nine months, and at the end of that time, in the same East Coast city, there was another raid of a very terrible character. It is all very well when you have the power to reply. It is all very well if a man feels that he can hit back. Then his courage rises, but **Sir Alfred Gelder's** when you feel that you are up against a power **speech** and have no reply to it, the bravest hearts are liable to quail. I am free to confess that when I stood on my doorstep and saw bombs dropping two hundred yards away, and thought that perhaps the next one would drop on my head, and I had my wife and family near me, I felt that I could have fled anywhere and hid in any corner to be safe. This is not an isolated experience. It has been the experience of every man under similar conditions. There was a man who was on the flat roof of one of

the hotels, and a bomb dropped within thirty yards. That man was a soldier, and he said: "I have been in the trenches in France. I have been under the thickest shell fire, but I never felt so hopelessly helpless and so weak as I felt when this shell dropped near to me and I had no power of reply."

Therefore, when hon. members rise to speak, I would just ask them not to think that we are cowards. Let me tell you that the men on the East Coast, from Newcastle to Essex, and down to the South, are as brave as you on the **The dummy** West Coast, and we will stand our corner. **gun** Within a few days of the promise that I received from the Admiralty, on one of the large engineering works in our city a gun—a solitary gun—was fixed, and a military guard was mounted by day and night over that gun. We all thought that that was part of the equipment to protect our city, but we found afterwards that it was only a dummy gun. It was not done for a joke. Was it done in order to convey to the Germans the idea that we were fortified? It might be, although I think that is a very far-fetched idea. I think it was done to allay the fear, the suspicions, and the anxieties of the people. If it was done for that purpose, such deception was unworthy of our military authorities, and unworthy of any General Staff which allowed it to be done.

Sir Alfred Gelder's remarkable speech brought one change. A Joint Committee, of which Lord Derby was chairman, was set up as a sub-committee of the War Office, to advise the authorities in connection with materials and co-ordinate the duties of service between the Admiralty and the War Office. Lord Derby had spurred the Government by a strong speech in favour of a controlling Air Board, with power to accomplish reforms. Lord Montagu of Beaulieu was added to the committee, and appointed assistant to Lord Derby.

Lord Derby had considerable strength of character. His last recruiting scheme, with its promises to married men that all single men fit for service should first be taken, had not worked too well. Yet the Earl was not the man to allow the Government to screen our weakness in aircraft policy. Both he and Lord Montagu resigned, in the second week of April, 1916, from the Air Committee. Then, at a meeting in Birmingham on April 12th, with the Lord Mayor of Birmingham in the chair, Lord Montagu stated

THE AIRSHIP'S "MECHANICAL FOSTER-MOTHER."

Among the many wonderful mechanical contrivances used in the war, one of the most remarkable was the automobile hydrogen-generator for inflating airships and observation balloons of the French Army. Described as the airship's "mechanical foster-mother," it was specially fitted up with tanks and pipes, and could travel from place to place along the front, replenishing the gas required by the French airships and balloons.

AIR SCOUTING WITH "OUR SURE SHIELD."

Seaplane scudding swiftly over the waves, prior to starting on aerial reconnaissance duty. It formed a striking contrast to the sombre battleship riding at anchor.

fully and frankly what had led him and Lord Derby to resign. In the first place, he said, they had joined the committee because they thought it would become a Board of Aviation upon which an Air Ministry could be built. But after a few meetings they discovered the committee had no real power at all, and that no decisions could be arrived at unless all the members on it were unanimous. Lord Montagu could see at once it was unlikely that there would ever be a unanimous decision if any criticism or comment was put forward on the work of the military and naval services. The committee had no executive power, and Lord Derby and Lord Montagu thought it was lulling the public into a sense of false security. Lord Montagu went on to remark, in a speech that promised to make history :

North Sea, but we have only a few seaplanes and our magnificent service of destroyers and submarines. A navy that has a chance of seeing your stragetical arrangements from a distance of from seventy to eighty miles has an enormous advantage over a navy that does not possess eyes of that kind. I do not think our rulers can be acquitted of negligence in not having foreseen that point. [He might have referred to Commander Boothby's lecture in 1912.] In the case of our Army, our fighting planes, after twenty months of war, are not so fast as those of the Germans or of the French, and I believe the Russians, too, are in some ways ahead of us. The Government on the whole are responsible for the defects.

Then I come to our own shore. In the first months of the war, no Zeppelins came, and the whole thing was neglected. Now we have had twenty-eight raids, some of them very serious, and these raids will not only be repeated, but they will become more serious as time goes on. Yet in the twentieth month of the war we have only just begun to have a system of anti-aircraft defences in this country. **Lord Montagu's warning** I am not going to reveal secrets or talk about dummy guns, but I will say that there is hardly a town, with the possible exception of London, that cannot be properly defended against attacks from Zeppelins. But what can we do with guns that are too small and preparations that are inadequate ? It is almost incredible to me that things should have been left so long in this direction and in others. It must have been well known to the Government that we were running this risk

Is it possible to go on running the air defence of this country, or an air defence by two departments—sometimes three—without any link between them, and with traditional jealousies

A VENICE RAIDER.

An Austrian hydroplane captured while raiding Venice.

Let me tell you that you live here barely three hundred miles from the nearest Zeppelin shed, and are just as likely to be attacked as though you lived at Dover or Yarmouth. There is no part of industrial England to which a Zeppelin cannot fly and rain destruction. The more important a district, the more likely it is to be attacked. In this war the power of defence has grown so largely that it has largely stopped offence. This can only have one result. On sea it will drive warfare into the sphere of submarines, and on land it will drive it into the air. Warfare will be driven into new channels, and we are now only at the beginning of that struggle.

To-day we have no airships to act as eyes for our Fleet. The German Fleet has Zeppelins spread over the

GERMAN MACHINE THAT BRITAIN REFUSED.

The Fokker aeroplane, of which Germany expected much early in 1916. The type was invented, or largely adapted from a French model, by a young Dutchman. The British Government refused the machine when it was offered, as the first two patterns were valueless.

In a sea of cloud. Remarkable photographic study of the French Sub-Lieut. Navarre's machine mounting higher and still higher towards the infinite.

The machine, having passed through a great cloud-bank, was seeking its way back to the French lines after Lieut. Navarre had brought down his fifth German aeroplane.

A "MOSQUITO" OF THE UPPER AIR: STRIKING STUDIES OF A FRENCH FLYER ABOVE THE CLOUDS.

SOUVENIR-HUNTING IN FRANCE.
A British Red Cross nurse cutting away a piece of the plane of an enemy aeroplane that had been shot down.

Mr. Pemberton - Billing was able to state in the House of Commons that he could quickly find a hundred machines capable of outmanœuvring the best German machines, and also of making long raids into Germany. The mystery of our Air Departments is to find any shadow of reason why those responsible for material nearly always adopted inferior R.A.F. machines, and even standardised them and so had their defects produced in enormous quantities, when private British aircraft firms—as patriotic and able as the ordnance makers of Newcastle, Sheffield, and Coventry — were vainly producing models superior not only to the R.A.F., but to the latest German designs.

One suggested explanation is that the experts of the Royal Flying Corps and the Royal Naval Air Service simply played for safety instead of aiming at progress. If their officers failed in R.A F. machines they could at least escape responsibility in selection, by pleading that they had taken the best machines provided by the Government factory. If, on the other hand, a Sopwith, an Avro, or a Vickers, Bristol, Short, or Martinsyde failed, the expert who selected it would have to bear full responsibility for his choice. Before the war a great French writer, Emile Faguet, had **Promise of better** charged his country with suffering from **things** the general vice of being afraid of bearing responsibilities. The ordeal of battle showed that we suffered badly from the same kind of moral cowardice. Yet our experienced pilots were magnificently courageous, and wanted to test and find the best machines and put them to far-reaching uses. Therefore it was high time that two men of commanding personality, Lord Derby and Lord Montagu, the latter of whom was a flyer, should put themselves at the head of all the forces of public opinion making for an Air Ministry formed of men with ideas and, if possible, tact. Mr Pemberton-Billing, the organiser of the first raid on the Zeppelin shed at Friedrichshafen, was also becoming a recognised power making for reform. It looked as though Britain, at great cost and by a slow, arduous struggle, might end the war as mistress of the air.

existing between them ? The curse of all Government departments is that of thinking departmentally instead of nationally. A few days ago I turned round to certain representatives on the War Air Committee and asked if it was not time that they dropped phrases about competition between services, and had more co-operation. If circumstances demand the recasting of some of our administrative departments, I for one say that no departmental difficulties shall stand in the way of national necessities.

If we put into the Ministry of Aviation men of ideas and also men of tact, there will be great difficulties, but these cannot be compared with the danger of leaving things as they are. When the Ministry of Munitions was first established, there was a very tough fight with certain departments of the War Office, but the great point was that Mr. Lloyd George got the stuff, millions and millions of rounds and thousands of guns. It is something of the same kind I want to see established with regard to aviation. The question of the air is so important that in the wars of the future it will be a case of : Go up, or go under ! When we are trying to amalgamate two great commercial companies where does the opposition always come from ? From the administrative staffs, and not from the shareholders. The people are the shareholders in the British Empire, and opposition in regard to the matter of our air services does not come from them. We must have a strong air policy, or else this country will suffer far more in the coming months of the war than it otherwise would do. At the present time lives are being sacrificed, money is being spent, and time is being wasted. Action is needed. But I have faith in my cause, and because I have that faith I have no fear for the future.

A campaign for reform   Thus opened in Birmingham, one of the most energetic cities of our Empire, the campaign for the immediate reform of both our air services. One of the principal departments requiring reform was the Royal Aircraft Factory which, with more than 3,000 workmen, was stated by the Under-Secretary for War to be on March 28th, 1916, " not a producing factory in the sense of producing large numbers of engines or their parts, but a factory to assist us in the manufacture of designs. We do not produce quantities there, and it is not a manufacturing plant." Mr. Tennant did not go on to explain why huge buildings and thousands of workmen were needed in a place that was not a manufacturing plant.

ANTI-AIRCRAFT SERVICE ON THE FRENCH FRONT.
French gunners about to fire a special 90 mm. anti-aircraft gun at an enemy aviator who had ventured to cross the lines of our ally.

CHAPTER CXIII.

THE STRUGGLE FOR VERDUN: AN EYE-WITNESS NARRATIVE.

By Lord Northcliffe.

The Editors of THE GREAT WAR are happy in being able to print the following important chapter as a link in the long chain of narrative wherewith the multitudinous incidents and episodes of this prodigious conflict of the nations are being bound together in one great historic record. Lord Northcliffe had the honour of being invited by the French Government, in the initial stages of the German Struggle for Verdun, to proceed to the scene of that extraordinary battle as an eye-witness of events which will surely remain among the most memorable of the war. His lordship, a civilian with no exceptional claims to military knowledge, but with the true journalistic eye and the selective sense of the trained observer, was able, in his famous despatches to the "Times," the "Daily Mail," and other British, Colonial, and American journals, to give to the world a series of the most remarkable descriptions of the earlier phases of the titanic attack on Verdun that did more than the writings of any other war correspondent to establish in the public mind a really vivid, truthful, and lasting impression of one of the greatest episodes of the war. These despatches were quoted in the Press of every continent, translated into a perfect babel of tongues, and will probably be remembered as one of the most signal achievements of the art of the war correspondent in our time. This chapter, which is a connected narrative of events witnessed and opinions formed on the battlefield, was written in the second week of April, 1916, and in its reading the date of writing should be borne in mind. The subsequent evolution of the struggle for Verdun will be chronicled in due course.

VERDUN is, in many ways, the most extraordinary of battles. The mass of metal used on both sides is far beyond all parallel; the transformation on the Douaumont Ridge was more suddenly dramatic than even the Battle of the Marne; and, above all, the duration of the conflict already looks as if it would surpass anything in history. More than a month has elapsed since, by the kindness of General Joffre and General Pétain, I was able to watch the struggle from various vital view-points. The battle had then been raging with great intensity for a fortnight, and, as I write, four to five thousand guns are still thundering round Verdun. Impossible, therefore, for any man to describe the entire battle. The most one can do is to set down one's impressions of the first phases of a terrific conflict, the end of which cannot be foreseen. My chief impression is one of admiration for the subtle powers of mind of the French High Command. General Joffre and General Castelnau are men with especially fine intellects tempered to terrible keenness. Always they have had to contend against superior numbers. In 1870, when they were subalterns, their country lost the advantage of its numerous

SUN-SIGNALLING.
Working the optic heliograph on the French front.

population by abandoning general military service at a time when Prussia was completely realising the idea of a nation in arms. In 1914, when they were commanders, France was inferior to a still greater degree in point of numbers to Prussianised Germany. In armament, also, France was inferior at first to her enemy. The French High Command has thus been trained by adversity to do all that human intellect can against almost overwhelming hostile material forces. General Joffre, General Castelnau—and, later, General Pétain, who at a moment's notice displaced General Herr—had to display genius where the Germans were exhibiting talent, and the result is to be seen at Verdun. They there caught the enemy in a series of traps of a kind hitherto unknown in modern warfare — something elemental, and yet subtle, neo-primitive, and befitting the atavistic character of the Teuton. They caught him in a web of his own unfulfilled boasts.

The enemy began by massing a surprising force on the western front. Tremendous energy and organising power were the marks of his supreme efforts to obtain a decision. It was usually reckoned that the Germans maintain on all fronts a field army of about seventy-four and a half army

THE DEFENDER OF VERDUN.
General Henri Philippe Pétain, commander of the French armies defending the Meuse sector. As a colonel, he gained pre-eminent distinction during the retreat from Charleroi.

available total of one hundred and eighteen divisions, he massed his principal striking force of thirty-two divisions against the British army. Verdun was apparently only a secondary objective, against which first fourteen and, later, thirty divisions were concentrated. At the time of writing, the principal enemy mass is still placed, according to the last information I have, against Sir Douglas Haig's army.

So we come to the first problem in the German campaign. Did Falkenhayn first intend to follow General Joffre's plan in the Champagne and Lille operations, and strike fiercely at two widely separate sections of the hostile lines? Did he arrange to press the French hard at Verdun, and possibly attract British reinforcements there, and then renew the old attempt to break through between Arras and Ypres? Or was his **Falkenhayn's first** chief concentration against the British **intentions** army only a very prolonged feint? The last suggestion seems quite impossible in the circumstances; for, in order to mislead the British commander, a strong body of German troops had been withdrawn from the neighbourhood of Ypres and sent into action round Verdun with the clear design of making our Staff think that the forces opposing our men had been weakened. But for the rest, the affair remains at present a matter of speculation.

One effect of this massing of German troops against the new and longer British line was that the then French commander at Verdun, General Herr, scarcely expected the overwhelming attack made upon him on February 21st, 1916. General Herr's Staff knew—though he himself

corps, which at full strength number three million men. Yet, while holding the Russians from Riga to the south of the Pripet Marshes, and maintaining a show of force in the Balkans, Germany seems to have succeeded in bringing up nearly two millions and a half of men for her grand spring offensive in the west. At one time her forces in France and Flanders were only ninety divisions. But troops and guns were withdrawn in increasing numbers from Russia and Serbia in December, 1915, until there were, it is estimated, a hundred and eighteen divisions on the Franco-British-Belgian front. A large number of 6 in. **Germany's gigantic** and 12 in. Austrian howitzers **preparation** were added to the enormous Krupp batteries. Then a large proportion of new recruits of the 1916 class were moved into Rhineland depôts to serve as drafts for the fifty-nine army corps, and it is thought that nearly all the huge shell output that had accumulated during the winter was transported westward.

All this gigantic work of preparation could not be hidden. Even I learnt a good deal about it from my agents in Germany, who still send me definite and detailed information nearly every week. I looked forward to a terrific explosion of German force on both land and sea. The allied Staffs, with their various and wide sources of information, knew more fully what was about to happen on the western front, but I do not think they penetrated deeply into the German plan; for the hostile Chief of Staff, General Falkenhayn, made his dispositions in a very skilful manner. Out of his

IN CONFERENCE WITH GENERAL JOFFRE.
General Pétain talking with General Joffre. Before his great achievements at Verdun, General Pétain played a vital part during the allied offensive in Artois and the operations in Champagne.

A BATTLEFIELD BURROW ON THE WOODED MEUSE.
Entrance to a shell-proof " dug-out," behind the first-line trenches of the Verdun sector, in which ammunition was stored. The Chasseur Alpin
on the left is unscrewing with pincers the nose of a shell. The roof of the " dug-out " was well screened from the eyes of enemy airmen.

obstinately declined to believe it—that the enemy was
preparing a formidable assault in the woods north of the
old French frontier fort. But though the German airmen
were very active throughout January and February, a
good deal could be seen by the French aerial observers of
the vast secret work going on amid the misty tracts of
woodland. Lieutenant Immelmann and other crack
Fokker pilots joined the Crown Prince's army, and for
some weeks our allies at Verdun almost lost the command
of the air above their lines. Indeed, I have heard that on
one or two occasions German airmen were at last able to
swoop within four hundred feet of the ground, and bomb
French positions without being brought down. They
even attacked infantry with remarkable impunity.

It is true that one Zeppelin was brought down by gun
fire while trying to bombard the French railway line of
communication, and two German aeroplanes were destroyed
out of a squadron of fifteen that bombed Révigny. But
the triumph over the Zeppelin by the skilful French gunner,
working a " 75 " gun on a motor-car, did not in any way
alter the effective situation. Our heroic allies, as they themselves admit in their special account of the Verdun
operations, were at a very serious disadvantage in regard to
aircraft during the critical periods of
French handicap the German preparations and the enemy's
in aircraft main attacks. It was not until the
middle of March—nearly four weeks
after the opening drum-fire bombardment by at least two
thousand five hundred hostile guns—that the French
recovered fully at Verdun the power of reconnoitring the
enemy's positions and bombing his distant lines of
communication.

The French Staff reckoned that Verdun would be
attacked when the ground had dried somewhat in the
March winds. It was thought that the first enemy movement would take place against the British front in some
of the sectors of which there were chalk undulations,
through which the rains of winter quickly drained. The
Germans skilfully encouraged this idea by making an
apparent preliminary attack at Lihons, on a five-mile front,
with rolling gas-clouds and successive waves of infantry.
During this feint the veritable offensive movement softly
began on Saturday, February 19th, 1916, when the enormous
masses of hostile artillery west, east, and north of the
Verdun salient started registering on the French positions.
Only in small numbers did the German guns fire, in order
not to alarm their opponents. But even
this trial bombardment by shifts was a **Opening of the**
terrible display of power, calling forth all **offensive**
the energies of the outnumbered French
gunners to maintain the artillery duels that continued
day and night until Monday morning, February 21st.

Looking at the country from the observation point east
of Verdun, one can see why it was chosen by the German
Staff for a grand surprise attack. The scene has been
compared to that on the border of Surrey and Sussex, where
the line of the northern downs rises from the wooded clay
of the weald. But as I stood, with the flooded Meuse and
its high western banks behind me, and before me the
famous plateau crowned by the ruins of Douaumont Fort,
I was reminded of Scotland. Perth on the Tay, amid its
fir-wooded heights, is rather like Verdun in the basin of
the Meuse. It was the evergreen fir-woods that had
attracted the German Staff, as splendid cover for their
vast artillery preparations. As their aircraft at last
almost dominated the French aeroplanes, they completed
their concentration of guns by an arrogantly daring return
to old-fashioned methods Instead of digging any more
gun-pits, they placed hundreds of pieces of artillery side
by side above ground, confident that the French artillery
would be overwhelmed before it could do any damage.
Even in daylight some of the woods in the German lines,
when the decisive bombardment was going on, looked like
firework exhibitions. A French airman, sent to count the-

THE VALLEY OF THE SHADOW: REMARKABLE CAMERA VIEW FROM A FRENCH FIRST-LINE TRENCH NEAR VERDUN.

Churned up by continual shelling, with never a blade of grass and but a few shell-stricken trees, the land between the opposing trenches in the Meuse sector presented a sinister, terrible appearance. The sturdy stakes supporting the inevitable wire cut the sky-line with monotonous regularity. The ridge-like planes which stretch the whole breadth of the picture are numberless. German Infantry, thrown mercilessly against the French guns, and shattered piecemeal before. they could even reach the barbed-wire entanglements, so accurate and ruthless was the fire of our allies' artillery.

batteries in the small wood of Granilly, gave up his task in despair, saying there were more guns than trees.

The method of handling these great parks of artillery was as terrible as the force employed. It was a development of the phalanx tactics used by Von Mackensen in breaking the Russian lines at Gorlice; and according to a rumour, Von Mackensen was at Verdun, with his chief, General von Falkenhayn, superintending the disposition of guns and men. The commander nominally in charge, Field-Marshal von Haeseler, was a tall, thin man of eighty, of the type of Von der Goltz—excellent at drawing up schemes on paper, and accounted, before the test of war, the best military leader in Germany. He had, therefore, been given a position similar to that which Blumenthal occupied in the Franco-Prussian conflict, and placed in command of the Crown Prince's army, so that by his genius he might win personal glory for the Hohenzollern dynasty. But all he won in conflicts with General Sarrail and General de Langle de Cary, in battle after battle between Réthel, Verdun, and the Argonne Forest, was the dishonour of defeat that fell upon the figurehead of his army—the Crown Prince. Thus General von Haeseler, once the idol of both the German and Austrian Staffs, was under a cloud. He had, indeed, been replaced by General von Mudra during the later fighting at Fille Morte, in the Argonne Forest; but for some reason, that is not yet apparent, he was restored to his position.

In any case, it is clear that Von Haeseler either adopted and developed Von Mackensen's new system of attack, or that Von Mackensen in person directed the movement, with Von Haeseler in nominal command, in order to mislead the French Staff as to the way in which the movement was likely to develop. Certainly, General Herr, who had succeeded General Sarrail as army commander on the Verdun sector, did not anticipate the character or the tremendous violence of the assault that opened at dawn on February 21st, 1916.

Two army corps against seven For two days the German heavy howitzers had been battering at the twenty-five miles of defensive earthworks round Verdun. This was the orthodox manner of preparing for a storming infantry advance on a wide front, in order to make so large a gap that the hostile long-range guns of defence behind the third line could not close the rent by means of curtain fire. A break ten miles in length was thought to be necessary. General Herr and his Staff were prepared to meet such an attack; they had only two army corps to hold back the seven army corps that the Germans first brought forward, but the high, broken, difficult ground about Verdun favoured the defending forces. Moreover, the French engineers had worked in an astonishing fashion to perfect the natural difficulties of the terrain. In the

OBLITERATED IN A CLOUD OF BLACK SMOKE AND SULPHURIC DUST.
A vivid instantaneous photograph obtained at the moment a German shell burst on an isolated outpost station near Ornes, a little village north-east of Verdun. This was heavily shelled by the enemy just before the skilful tactical retirement of the French troops from the Bois de la Vauche.

low ground, such as that round the two Ornes heights held by the Germans, the French had tunnels running to a depth at which no shell could penetrate. In the three important woodlands between Ornes and the Meuse—Haumont Wood, Caures Wood, and Herbebois Wood—there were tunnels for protection against flame-projector attacks, deep, winding communication saps hidden in the trees, with shrapnel-cover, for escaping from intense gun fire, and land mines, entanglements, and spiked barriers with high-explosive attachments and trip-mines; in short, all the intensive system of protection that had been developed in the Argonne fighting. General Sarrail had only extended his lines to the woodlands in the plain between the Meuse and Ornes in the spring of 1915, snatching the ground from the enemy bit by bit when the German forces at Verdun were weakened through sending reinforcements to the Champagne and Lille fields of violent conflict. General Sarrail, however, seems to have extended his lines into the low-lying northern woodlands with considerable reluctance. He liked hill positions himself, and there was a dispute between him and the High Command regarding his manner of fortifying the newly-won ground. As a result he was sent

RUINS NEAR VERDUN.
So terrific were the artillery bombardments that almost every building was reduced to ruins during the epoch-making battles. Above: Water-logged shell-holes on a battlefield of the Meuse—a waste of mud, water and shattered trees.

DESOLATION IN THE VERDUN BATTLE-AREA.
Ruins of Hennemont after a snowfall. Half buried under the battered wall is a mangled gun-carriage. The great snowstorm of February to some extent upset the enemy's plans.

to Salonika, and the defence of Verdun in the new style was given to a new man, little known to the public—General Herr.

But the phalanx tactics of the Von Mackensen school were calculated to overwhelm any system of defensive works, new or old, in forests or on hillsides. It is tempting, but idle, to speculate what General Sarrail, the fortifier of Salonika, might have done in Verdun against his old opponent Von Haeseler, whom he had twice helped to defeat in 1914. Maybe, with only four divisions facing Von Haeseler, and the rest of the Verdun garrison holding the southern lines against Strantz's army of Metz, Sarrail would have fared worse than Herr; for the German attack was irresistible, and it was only the large space of country available for retreat between the Meuse and Ornes line and the Douaumont Plateau that saved Verdun from rapid capture.

The enemy seems to have maintained a bombardment all round General Herr's lines on February 21st, 1916, but this general battering was done with a thousand pieces of field-artillery. The grand masses of heavy howitzers were used in a different way. At a quarter past seven in the morning they concentrated on the small sector of advanced entrenchments near Brabant and the Meuse; 12 in. shells fell with terrible precision every few yards, according to the statements made by the French troops. I afterwards saw a big German shell, from at least six miles

Precision of German gun fire

distant from my place of observation, hit quite a small target. So I can well believe that, in the first bombardment of French positions, which had been photographed from the air and minutely measured and registered by the enemy gunners in the trial firing, the great, destructive shots went home with extraordinary effect. The trenches were not bombarded—they were obliterated. In each small sector of the six-mile northward bulge of the Verdun salient the work of destruction was done with surprising quickness. After the line from Brabant to Haumont was smashed, the main fire power was directed against the other end of the bow at Herbebois, Ornes, and Maucourt. Then when both ends of the bow were severely hammered, the central point of the Verdun salient, Caures Wood, was smothered in shells of all sizes, poured in from east, north, and west. In this manner almost the whole enormous force of heavy artillery was centred upon mile after mile of the French front. When the great guns lifted over the lines of craters, the lighter field-artillery, placed row after row in front of the wreckage, maintained an unending fire curtain over the communicating saps and support entrenchments.

Then came the second surprising feature in the new German system of attack. No waves of storming infantry swept into the shattered works. Only strong patrols at first came cautiously forward, to discover if it were safe for the main body of troops to advance and reorganise the French line so as to allow the artillery to move onward. There was thus a large element of truth in the marvellous tales afterwards told by German prisoners. Their commanders thought it would be possible to do all the fighting with long-range artillery, leaving the infantry to act as squatters to the great guns, and occupy and rebuild line after line of the French defences without any serious hand-to-hand struggles. All they had to do was to protect the gunners from surprise attack, while the guns made an easy path for them and also beat back any counter-attack in force.

But, ingenious as was this scheme for saving the man-power of Germany by an unparalleled expenditure of shell, it required for full success the co-operation of the French troops. But the French did not co-operate. Their High Command had continually improved their system of trench defence in accordance with the experiences of their own hurricane bombardments in Champagne and the Carency sector. General Castelnau, the acting Commander-in-Chief on the French front, was indeed the inventor of hurricane fire tactics, which he

General Castelnau's perplexing tactics had used for the first time in February, 1915, in Champagne. When General Joffre took over the conduct of all French operations, leaving to General Castelnau the immediate control of the front in France, the victor of the Battle of Nancy weakened his advance lines and then his support lines, until his troops actually engaged in fighting were very little more than a thin covering body, such as is thrown out towards the frontier while the main forces connect well behind.

We shall see the strategical effect of this extraordinary measure in the second phase of the Verdun Battle, but its tactical effect was to leave remarkably few French troops exposed to the appalling tempest of German and Austrian shells. The fire-trench was almost empty, and in many cases the real defenders of the French line were men with machine-guns, hidden in dug-outs at some distance from the photographed positions at which the German gunners aimed. The batteries of light guns, which the French handled with the flexibility and continuity of fire of Maxims, were also concealed in widely-scattered positions. The main damage caused by the first intense bombardment was the destruction of all the telephone wires along the French front. In one hour the German guns ploughed up every yard of ground behind the observing posts and behind the fire-trench. Communications could only be slowly re-established by messengers, so that many parties of men had to fight on

THE MOST POPULAR OF "POILUS."
French field-kitchen before Verdun. The cook contemplates a delicacy with the affectionate interest of a professional chef. The first illustration shows a number of cans filled with soup awaiting conveyance to the men in the trenches.

TRAVELLING KITCHENS BEHIND RUINED HOUSES ON THE HEIGHTS OF THE MEUSE.
Not the least remarkable feature of the war was the ready way in which the French epicurean temperament adapted itself to dining cheerily amid the discomforts of campaigning.

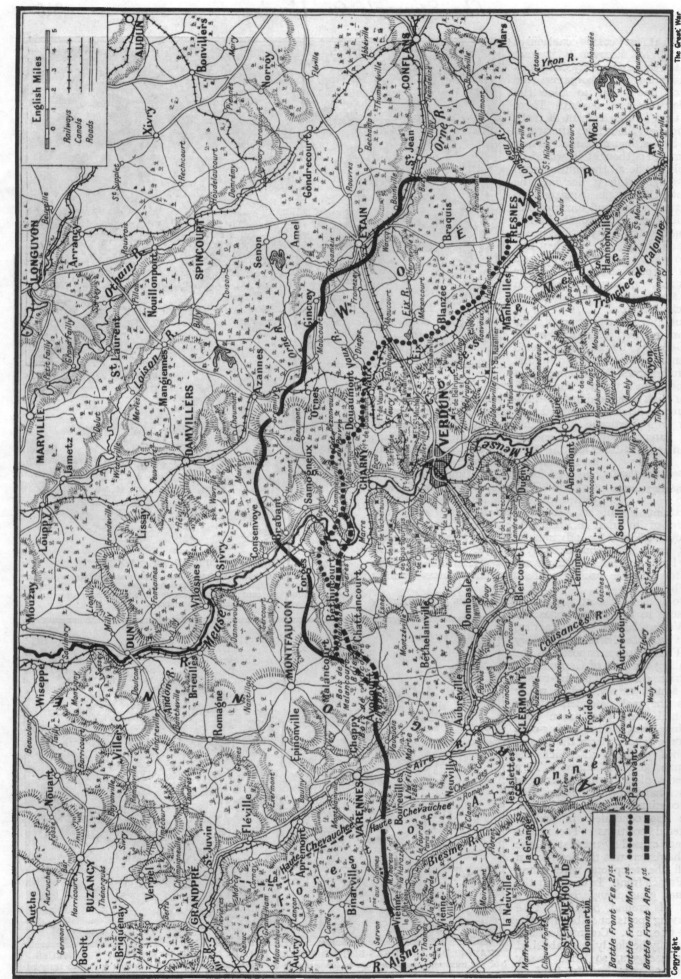

The Great' War

MAP SHOWING THE VARIOUS BATTLE-FRONTS IN THE OPENING STAGES OF THE FIGHT FOR VERDUN.

The thick black line indicates the French positions when the Germans launched their attack on February 21st, 1916. The Avocourt-Fresnes sector, to which our ally for strategic reasons had retired by April 1st, 1916, is shown in broken and dotted lines.

their own initiative, with little or no combination of effort with their comrades.

Yet, desperate as were their circumstances, they broke down the German plan for capturing trenches without an infantry attack. They caught the patrols and annihilated them, and then swept back the disillusioned and reluctant main bodies of German troops. First, the bombing parties were felled, then the sappers as they came forward to repair the line for their infantry, and at last the infantry itself in wave after wave of field-grey. The small French garrison of every centre of resistance fought with cool, deadly courage, and often to the death.

Artillery fire was practically useless against them, for though their tunnel shelters were sometimes blown in by the 12 in. shells, which they regarded as their special terror by reason of their penetrative power and wide blast, even the Germans had not sufficient shells to search out all their underground chambers, every one of which have two or three exits.

The new organisation of the French Machine-gun Corps was a fine factor in the eventual success. One gun fired ten thousand rounds daily for a week, most of the positions selected being spots from which each German infantry advance would be enfiladed and shattered. Then the French "75's," which had been masked during the overwhelming fire of the enemy's howitzers, came unexpectedly into action when the German infantry attacks increased in strength. Near Haumont, for example, eight successive furious assaults were repulsed by three batteries of "75's." One battery was then spotted by the Austrian 12 in. guns, but it remained in action until all its ammunition was exhausted. The gunners then blew up their guns and retired with the loss of only one man.

UNDER CROSS-EXAMINATION.
French Staff officers interrogating two German prisoners captured in the Verdun fighting.

Some of the Haumont guns got through the German fire curtain, and helped in the defence of the Caures Wood. Here there occurred some memorable exploits. First of all the wood was lost, despite its magnificent system of defences, by the smashing effect of the German heavy shell fire. The position was almost as strong as the famous German Labyrinth near Arras, and, knowing this, the enemy used his 16·8 in. Berthas in addition to the 12 in. Skoda guns. The deep roofs were driven down upon the men sheltering beneath, and the wood had to be abandoned. But the survivors of the garrison held the enemy back, while a lieutenant of engineers with his men laid a large number of mines with electrical firing wires. The German general, after his skirmishers and bombing-parties had been beaten off, went back to the old Prussian method of a mass attack, and launched a division against the wood. By arrangement, the French covering troops fled in apparent panic, and were hotly chased down the trenches and communication saps to the southern outskirts. As the last man left the wood, the lieutenant of engineers, who was near Beaumont waiting the signal, pressed a button. Many of the trees rose in the air, and though I can scarcely believe that the division was annihilated, as the survivors of the Caures garrison firmly maintain, I have no doubt that the Germans suffered very badly.

Defence of Caures Wood

Soon afterwards, Lieutenant-Colonel Driant, with two fine battalions of Chasseurs, recovered by a counter-attack the southern part of Caures Wood. Driant was the son-in-law of Boulanger, and Deputy of Nancy, and a magnificent soldier. His heroic end saddened the French people, and yet inspired them with fresh courage. The day after his fine

STAFF WORK UNDERGROUND.
Headquarters of the état-major of a French division established in a cellar fortified with stones and stout beams.

NN

WIRE SCREEN TO PROTECT SOLDIERS FROM FLYING BOMB SPLINTERS.
Economy in lives was undoubtedly the watchword of the French Command throughout the tremendous conflict for Verdun. Our ally, in addition to adapting the steel casque to practical usage. resorted to other life-protecting devices, such as the wire screen against flying bomb and shell splinters depicted in this photograph.

victory the forces on either side of him were compelled to withdraw, and the Germans closed round him on both sides. Arranging his two battalions in five columns, he made a splendid fighting retreat between the two German divisions which almost enveloped his force. With only a hundted men he rearguarded the retirement, and was found dead by the Germans on the battlefield. He was buried beside one of his captains close to the wood.

In spite of the vast forces employed by the enemy, the Germans achieved but little on the first day of battle, February 21st. They won a footing in the first-line trenches and in some of the supporting trenches—a thing any army could have done with a large expenditure of shell. The French still held Brabant and Haumont, with Colonel Driant in Caures Wood and the garrisons of Herbebois Wood and Ornes holding their own by a superb defence. But on the morning of Tuesday, February 22nd, the Germans worked up a ravine between Brabant and Haumont by means of burning liquids spurted from flame-projectors. At the same time the German artillery renewed its smashing, intensive fire, wrecking and

Haumont village flattened out

flattening out Haumont village and breaking up the French works for a depth of three or four miles. Fortified farms were bombarded south of Haumont Wood and transformed into volcanoes by the huge German shells, and when night fell trench warfare had come to an end so far as the northern part of the Verdun garrison was concerned.

All their earthworks had been swept out of existence, and the troops fought and worked in the open in a tragic darkness lighted by the enemy's wonderful star-shells. They had been hammered out of Brabant, on the edge of

the Meuse, and their centre had been driven in. On the right, however, the garrison of Herbebois Wood still clung on to part of their original position, under an intermittent hurricane of heavy shell, the intervals of which were filled by infantry attacks. Under the enemy's fire the French troops linked their Herbebois line with Hill 351, digging all night in a rain of death to connect the two positions for a fresh defence against an enfilading attack on Beaumont. When morning broke, the Germans began the attack on this new French line. After a desperate struggle lasting twelve hours, in which the enemy commander

French retire from Herbebois

continually brought up fresh regiments, the French retired from Herbebois and another wood below it, but still held on to the hill.

All along this side of the salient hand-to-hand fighting went on, from Ornes to Bezonvaux and the advanced position of the Hill of Vaux. Small French garrisons held advanced positions in the plain stretching towards the enemy's base of Etain. There was terrible fighting at Maucourt, where the French had some quick-firing guns, posted only five yards apart, and unmasked against German columns charging twenty men abreast in close ranks. The French soldiers themselves sickened at the slaughter they wrought. They were so near to the enemy at Maucourt that odds and ends of human remains almost fell on the top of them as their melinite shells exploded in the German masses. From Ornes to Vaux the ground was covered with dead or maimed men. According to one lucky French Territorial, in a detachment of four hundred and fifty men that fought for five days and nights near Ornes without losing one man, the enemy formed, in places, grey barriers. The

Territorial attributed the escape of his double company from all casualties to their deep defensive works, and to the fact that their captain withdrew them quickly when their own artillery support weakened. The French gunners suffered more in proportion than their infantry, especially in the centre and the left wing, where the guns had to fight a continual rearguard action in the open. Though they often caught German columns at short range, they were in turn smitten by the heavy German guns, enemy airmen circling over them and directing the fire.

Loss of Ornes and Fosses Wood Ornes held out until the afternoon of February 24th, when the garrison, attacked from three sides, retreated to Bezonvaux, from which a ravine ran up to Douaumont. Covering the country north of Douaumont was a superb set of fighters composed of Zouaves and African sharpshooters. They recaptured part of the wood between Herbebois and Hill 351, and then withstood a prolonged bombardment of terrific intensity. The din and concussion of the heavy shells were appalling ; the blood at times poured from the men's ears under the shock of the pressure of air, and yet they stuck to their job. They were pushed out of Beaumont and out of the wood they had recaptured, and they lost Fosses Wood, a little way below the Douaumont Plateau, towards which they retired.

Meanwhile, the centre and left of the French salient were hammered back with increasing rapidity. The division close to the Meuse, which had withdrawn from Brabant and Haumont, tried in vain to counter-attack from their second line at Samogneux, Hill 344, and a fortified farm near by. The enemy massed his guns against them across the Meuse, northward, and north-westward. They could not move out to attack, and by the evening of February 23rd their position was untenable. In the night they withdrew from Samogneux towards Pepper Hill (Côte du Poivre), which was practically their last dominating position. Pepper Hill was, indeed, the critical position of the entire defence of Verdun. Had the enemy won it he would have been able to advance along the Meuse and cut off a large part of the French forces in the salient.

General Herr and his Staff, however, devised a deadly system of defence for Pepper Hill. The enemy was pushing ahead in continual rush attacks, following the line of least resistance rather than making sure of his footing. Anyway —into Verdun at any cost. But Pepper Hill was not the way. Across the river at this point the French held several lines of dominating heights, from which they poured a flanking fire into every hostile force advancing from Brabant and Haumont. The nearer the Germans came to Verdun, on the Pepper Hill sector, the more terribly they suffered from the fire across the **Sanguinary struggle** Meuse. They came within range of rifles, **for Pepper Hill** machine-guns, and light field-pieces, as well as heavy howitzers and while their flanks were thus shattered, their front was hammered from the Pepper Hill position. At Vacherauville, a village just below Pepper Hill, the enemy's advance was definitely checked on February 25th. In one ravine near the village, as day was breaking, some French gunners on Pepper Hill espied a grey mass of hostile forces, and shelled it furiously. The Germans did not move. When the light was clear, it was seen that the figures were dead, though many still stood upright. They had been

FRENCH SOLDIERS DIGGING THEMSELVES IN ON THE SLOPE OF A VERDUN WOOD.
The Verdun sector of the French line abounded in woods and ridges, and these natural obstacles undoubtedly helped greatly in our ally's resistance to the German onslaughts. In this illustration a number of French soldiers are seen in the act of organising a new position during an enemy bombardment. Tactical withdrawals ordered by the French Command were frequent in the early days of the Verdun battles, but every inch of ground thus occupied by the enemy cost a price in German blood tragically disproportionate to the military value of such positions.

IN THE WAKE OF A SHELL-STORM.
The desolate aspect of a once wooded slope near Verdun. The ground had been torn into ruts, the trees sheared and riven, and tracks formed with logs twined over the deep mud.

caught the evening before by the heavy guns across the river and slain wholesale, more by shell-blast, apparently, than by shell fragments. Von Haeseler had made a costly mistake in driving up the Meuse towards Pepper Hill before he cleared the French from Goose Crest (Côte l'Oie), Dead Man Hill (Mort Homme), and Charny Ridge across the river. He afterwards tried to remedy his error by bringing his main artillery forces against Goose Crest and Dead Man Hill. But before thus widening the scope of his attack, he tried to preserve the intensive, narrow method of assault in the Von Mackensen style by thrusting into the centre of the flattened Verdun salient. That is to say, he shifted the point of the phalanx from Pepper Hill to the middle of the Douaumont Plateau. This was the right and plain course, for it removed the attacking masses and their immediate artillery supports from the French flanking fire across the Meuse, and brought them nearly within reach of victory.

The great thrust into the French centre also cleared the French out of the eastern edges of the Heights of the Meuse overlooking the Woevre Plain, for the Zouaves and Moroccans and the former garrisons of Herbebois and Ornes were farthest from Verdun, and

most in danger of being cut off. The Zouaves and Moroccans fell back on Douaumont, while the troops from Bezonvaux entrenched by the Douaumont Ravine and the Vaux Ravine.

Then the great snowstorm of February swept over the hilly battlefield and the lowland marshes of the Woevre. The storm was a disaster to the Germans. It robbed them in the crisis of the struggle of their tremendous power of artillery. Gunners and aerial observers were blinded, and from their point of view matters were not much improved by the mist that followed the snow. Snowdrifts in the valley paths delayed the forward movement of the guns and the bringing up of ammunition and supplies to the firing-line. This was when the original German plan for economy in men went all to pieces. The High Command could not wait for its guns to resume full action. The infantry, which had been promised so easy a task, had to undertake, with diminished artillery support, the terrible work of breaking the French front by hand-to-hand fighting. Verdun, after all, was to be purchased with German blood and not with German shells.

The great arc of artillery was, of course, still able to work by the map and by observers in the firing-line. It could pound villages, farms, and old forts, in which French troops might be sheltering, but it could not aim at the manœuvring columns and discern all the paths of communication. On the Plateau of Douaumont, some four hundred feet above the Meuse, the garrison of Verdun had the old entrenchments prepared at the outbreak of the war and improved by long labour. Then there were many improvised new defences—masked batteries of quick-firers, to be unmasked only against mass infantry attacks, hundreds of machine-guns detached from battalion service and acting as a sort of secondary artillery corps. And far behind the flaming, smoking plateau there was a superhuman outburst of activity in France, veiled from enemy air scouts by the falling snow.

General Joffre, General Castelnau, and their Staff were now convinced that Verdun was the enemy's first objective. The British army took over all the line where the second grand German offensive was expected, thus liberating important French reinforcements for the battle on the Heights of the Meuse. All lines and roads leading, roundabout or direct, towards Verdun, were crowded with men and material, and so remained when I made my way towards the scene of the great struggle. The main French force—the mass of manœuvre—was driving towards the enemy. The only matter of doubt was whether it would arrive in time to hold Verdun, or whether the supreme contest between French and German would take place on the western side of the Meuse.

Snowstorm aids the French

MUNITIONS TO FEED THE GUNS OF VERDUN.
Convoy of horses with panniers loaded up with munitions for the French machine-guns along the Meuse.

General Henri Philippe Pétain, the brilliant and resourceful defender of Verdun.

French reserves marching through a shell-shattered village of the Meuse.

Ashes to ashes: French military funeral procession on the Verdun front.

French scouts on the "qui vive" near Fort Vaux, some two miles east of Douaumont.

Our allies counter-attacking at Louvemont, near the famous Pepper Ridge.

Honour for Pétain's braves : Decorating French soldiers in the environs of Verdun.

After the ordeal in the trenches round Verdun : A pannikin of steaming broth.

This depended upon the staying power of the small, original garrison of Verdun. At heroic sacrifice they had to cover the massing of the great new forces. The situation had become very critical on the afternoon of February 24th, when large enemy forces debouched between Louvemont village and the hill in front of the Douaumont Plateau. General Herr flung all his remaining reserves into the fight, with the order that the line between Douaumont and Haudromont was to be held at any cost. Von Haeseler, in turn, using the raging snowstorm as cover, brought up all his available infantry and employed them in mass attacks of great ferocity and persistence. His aim was to wear down the physical power of endurance of the thin line of the French. On February 25th the Germans, after a long hand-to-hand wrestle, took all the village of Louvemont at the slope of the plateau, and climbed up the ridge, but were thrown down.

General Balfourier's timely arrival It was apparently about this time that General Castelnau came to Verdun to see how things were going on. He was not contented with what he saw. The Germans had won a magnificent artillery position on the high land at Beaumont, towards which they were dragging the main group of their heavy guns. The command of the air had been almost lost, and there were not enough pontoon bridges across the flooded Meuse to bring up quickly the needed reinforcements. General Herr was very properly relieved of his command (in contrast to the dangerous British policy of not punishing unsuccessful blundering generals), and a very fine engineer, who was also a specialist in handling heavy artillery—General Pétain—was entrusted with the reorganisation of the Verdun defences. Meanwhile, before General Pétain could get to work, there was the immediate task of checking the massed infantry attacks which the enemy was employing until the air cleared and his guns were sited on the new Beaumont position. General Castelnau could not bring up a large force—time and means were lacking. A picked body of fighters was needed, and, with pardonable favouritism, the general wired for the Bretons who had won the Battle of Nancy for him—the Bretons of the Twentieth Army Corps, under General Balfourier.

They arrived just in time on the plateau on February 26th. As was the case at Nancy, the Kaiser was present, watching the development of a " grand German victory." He stood, I was informed, on one of the hills near Ornes, with the Crown Prince by his side, and Von Falkenhayn and Von Haeseler. For reasons of domestic politics a purely Prussian force—the Brandenburgers—had been chosen to deal the decisive stroke. No doubt if the Prussian Guard had been available it would have been used. All the previous day and the previous night ordinary German

THE VERDUN SCAPEGOAT.
Field-Marshal von Haeseler, who, although over eighty years of age, was entrusted to throw the dice for Germany in the gamble for Verdun. He retired after the first phase of the great offensive.

divisions carried out the real work of smashing against the Zouaves and Moroccans, and bringing them to the limit of human endurance. One battalion of Moors was caught and broken by a shower of heavy shell, but rallied under a captain who spoke to them in Arabic of the honour of their race. Storming up in Islamic fanaticism, the Moors made a bayonet charge with a sustained fury almost superhuman when regard is had to the long, sleepless ordeal they had undergone since their first victory near Herbebois.

The Zouaves, who for generations have been the supreme pattern of picturesque heroism to every French schoolboy, were perfect. They were in front of Douaumont village, with the Moroccan Division and two infantry regiments. " I have given my word of honour that you will hold out," said their commander. " Your honour and my honour are the same." He shook hands with his men. They did not speak, and they fought quietly for two days and two nights without eating or sleeping. The houses of the village were blown up by 12 in. shells sent in a deluge, as the thick weather prevented aerial spotting. On February 26th, when Douaumont Fort was lost, the Zouaves and their comrades still held the village, and on

"RESTAURANT DES TRANCHÉES."
French cooks behind the first Verdun line engaged on the midday menu.

THE ROAD-MENDERS' CONTRIBUTION TO VICTORY AT VERDUN.

The successes of our ally at Verdun were due no less to the wonderful system and regularity of transport to and from the fighting-front than to the glorious courage and confidence of the French soldiery. Every precaution was taken to keep the highways to and from the zone of operations as perfect as possible. With such incessant and heavy vehicular traffic the danger of road wear was ever present, but scarcely was a stone dislodged by the revolving wheel than the military road-menders stepped forward to repair the damage.

February 27th, without help, they broke the long prepared attack by part of the German Fifteenth Army Corps. They let their foes come within two hundred yards, and then put a shrapnel curtain behind them to prevent retreat or reinforcement, and smote them down with "75's," machine-guns, and rifles. The struggle for the village went on to the end of the month, by which time the Germans had made eighteen attacks in force, all of which were broken. When the approaches to Douaumont were covered with dead and wounded the French made a counter-attack, and won a footing in a redoubt north-west of the village, from which the enemy had been pouring an uncomfortable machine-gun fire.

Stubborn, however, as was the stand made by the Zouaves, they would have perished on the critical day of the Douaumont fight—February 26th—but for the arrival of Balfourier's Bretons. On the afternoon of that day they were in extreme peril of being enveloped on their right. The dismantled fort had been taken by three thousand Brandenburgers during the heavy fog. Still working by the map, the gunners of the long-range German and Austrian artillery massed with remarkable precision against the fortress works, and then poured great shells about it, in a blind profusion which was expensive but effective. Every two or three yards there was a crater. After this bombardment had made the trenches of the troops untenable, the Brandenburgers, who had come in the night up the ravine from Bezonvaux and gathered in a wood, charged under cover of the fog, and won a footing on the plateau. Reaching next the dismantled fort, that crowns a swell of ground some 1,200 feet above sea-level, the men of the Brandenburg Mark tried to break through the French rearguard. But after withdrawing for a mile and a quarter, the French line remained unbroken, bent

The crisis at Douaumont

away from the fort, but still curving round the village. Friday night (the 25th) and Saturday morning were a period of extreme crisis. Open field fighting of the most desperate nature went on continuously. The Germans fought with great bravery, according to the best tradition of Prussian discipline. But the French, French Colonial, and African troops still bore up against the superior numbers of fresh enemy forces. Charging German battalions were counter-charged and stayed by French companies, or broken up by machine-gun fire and point-blank shrapnel fire. Fighting and working, our allies strove to establish themselves solidly on their new line of defence, while the Germans, with victory apparently well within their reach, tried to break through by overwhelming weight and unfaltering driving power. They took, without breaking, heavier punishment than their own theorists before the war expected modern national armies to stand. But firm as they were, the outnumbered French soldiers were firmer, and as twilight was falling, Balfourier, with the famous Twentieth Army Corps, came into action.

Balfourier surprises the enemy

The vehemence of attack of the fresh French force was terrific. The men went forward with such speed that the enemy was surprised. But after falling back some hundred yards, the Prussians proved worthy of their reputation as a crack corps, and resisted with great vigour. Many were Berliners of poor physique, judging from the prisoners I afterwards saw, but so strongly were they handled by their sergeants and officers that they in turn bent without breaking, under sudden and very severe pressure. The Bretons smashed onwards for more than a mile, joining on to the Zouaves at Douaumont village, and enclosing part of a Brandenburg regiment in the fort. The Germans on the slope of the ravine, however, managed to hold on to a sap running through a coppice and connecting with the fort. The enemy thus retained a valuable observation station on the plateau, from which he could direct his main batteries at Beaumont. But for the rest he was trapped.

The Kaiser in person had sustained a more disastrous defeat than he had received at Nancy. There he was at least able to retire from the crescent of embattled hills, when his cuirassiers and the Bavarian troops were thrown back. But at Verdun he could not retire. He had telegraphed to Berlin news of his great victory over the "hereditary enemy"; his officials had filled the German and neutral Press with glorious anticipations of the capture of Verdun, of which the principal fort

Kaiser trapped in his own boasts was alleged to have fallen. A special party of German-American, American, Scandinavian, and Dutch journalists had been brought to Etain, in order to proceed through Ornes and Douaumont to the plateau, and describe to a startled and apprehensive world the scene of the terrible and decisive display of Germany's inexhaustible power. Rumania, according to Teutonic opinion, was only being restrained from following the example of Italy by the tremendous energy with which the Germans were renewing their drive in France. The Kaiser's telegram concerning the conquest of Douaumont had been sent to Berlin as a transmitting station; its true destination, as the joyful Berliners themselves had recognised, was Bukarest.

I cannot think of any parallel in history to this new phase of the situation at Verdun. The War Lord of Germany was entangled in the web of his own prestige. At the time it may not have seemed dangerous to him or his military advisers. Certainly, on the night of February 27th, Von Falkenhayn and Von Haeseler could not have foreseen any disastrous difficulty. Far from desiring to withdraw from the attack on Verdun after the check delivered by the new French corps, they were merely made the more

eager to press on with increasing reinforcements and larger expenditure of shell before the French High Command could oppose them with equal forces. But to General Castelnau and General Joffre the operations at Verdun assumed a new complexion. If they could bring up and organise their forces in time, they had the enemy so fixed that they could bleed white one of his largest armies. They might also sap the strength of movements he was preparing in other directions, by compelling him continually to reinforce at all costs his Verdun army. Only so long as they kept the Crown Prince out of Verdun could they hold the Kaiser trapped in his own boasts, with all his people waiting for the fulfilment of their high hopes, in an intensity of spirit that might be an important moral factor if cheated of success. Verdun, in short, had become more than a military objective. For Germany its political and moral value had become even greater than its strategical importance. It was worth capturing Verdun at a cost of life that made the capture equivalent, in terms of ultimate resources, to a defeat. Two hundred thousand German casualties are alleged to have been the Kaiser's estimate of the worth of Verdun.

All this, however, greatly aggravated the burden on the mind of the new defender of the French frontier town, General Pétain, who, when **General Pétain** I saw him in the critical first week of his **in command** task, carried his burden easily. Tall, fair, blue-eyed, of the northern stock of France that has absorbed much Flemish blood, Pétain was radiant with energy of both character and mind. He was only a colonel of the engineers in August, 1914, but while developing his own special branch of knowledge and showing a fine gift of leadership in the handling of infantry, he became also a master-gunner—the new French heavy howitzers being his favourite weapon. In the last attack in Champagne,

"ALLONS, ENFANTS DE LA PATRIE!"
Impression of a nocturnal march of French troops along one of the roads leading to the Verdun fighting-front. In imagination one can hear the rhythmic, muffled thudding of the tramping feet as the men, bending slightly forward under the weight of their equipment, strode eagerly forward to take their places in the battle-line.

THE STRUGGLE FOR A MINE-CRATER: FROM A PICTURE BY A GREAT FRENCH ILLUSTRATOR.

In spite of the fact that the battles for Verdun were in the main gigantic artillery duels, some terrific hand-to-hand encounters took place. Such a struggle is here depicted with graphic forcefulness and tragic exactitude by the celebrated French artist M. Simont. Our allies, whose casques lend them the appearance of mediæval warriors, are surging forward with traditional élan to secure possession of a mine-crater. In the centre of the picture a bombing-party assaults a German barricade. Deep down in the calcined earth German soldiers, torn, wounded and bewildered, await captivity or death.

under General Castelnau, Pétain on the right wing achieved most success, taking the Hand of Massiges with less loss than occurred elsewhere, owing to his new system of using heavy artillery. It was as the master-gunner of France that he was brought by General Castelnau to Verdun to fight against the two thousand guns of the German phalanx, the largest pieces of which carried farther than the French heavy howitzers immediately available.

General Pétain, however, had a method of getting more out of his howitzers than the manufacturers expected. Even with his medium

SHRAPNEL BURSTING OVER THE MEUSE VALLEY.
Dreary waste near the enemy's trenches, where the ground was pitted with shell holes, and every tree left bore battle scars.

FRENCH ARTILLERY BEFORE VERDUN.
French battery moving into position along a Verdun road which had been heavily shelled by German guns.

General Pétain did not, however, pack his infantry into the restricted Verdun area. Under fire his men were scattered but fresh, the main force being well out of range of the German artillery, and used in short shifts at the front, a division at a time. On the other hand, no German within five miles of the French guns was safe. As the new French commander's shell supply quickened, by his constant improvement of his lines of communication, and as newly-rifled guns arrived regularly to replace those worn by firing, he gradually dominated the German artillery. It is quite likely that the guns in use on both sides throughout the operations amounted to six thousand, for the rifling of the heavy ordnance wore out rapidly under constant use, and had to be repaired.

pieces he could often overpower heavy enemy guns. He had, besides, worked out a method by which he could use these medium pieces with the flexibility of light field-artillery. But until he had constructed his telephone service, recovered the command of the air, and got his guns into the special positions required by his system, he had a desperately hard struggle to maintain his line and win time for completing his preparations.

After breaking against the Douaumont Ridge on February 26th, the German attack seemed to weaken. Fierce infantry fighting continued at Douaumont village till the end of the month. Then came an ominous period of calm, lasting three days. The enemy was moving his enormous parks of guns closer to Verdun. But the time thus spent by the Germans in the thick slush of valleys and ravines, into which the thawing snow drained, was like a gift from heaven to General Pétain. He threw bridges over the Meuse ; he augmented his gun power on the western heights at Dead Man Hill and Charny Ridge, making his flanking fire from this direction more deadly and far-reaching : he strengthened the Douaumont Plateau defences, and poured in guns, ammunition, and fresh troops by means of a special service of four thousand motor-lorries, each running a hundred miles a day.

In continual drum-fire bombardments, in which massed artillery acted like one gigantic machine-gun, it was not only shell stores, carefully accumulated for months, that were spent, but the life of the heavy ordnance.

The wasting of shell accumulation and the wearing out of the guns crippled the immediate offensive power of a nation in **Continual drum-fire bombardments**

a manner that no reserve of man-power could supply. General Pétain therefore had to provoke the hostile artillery into constant action, as well as induce the German infantry to fling itself against his quick-firers and machine-guns. Thus, even if he could have done so at once, it might not have been sound policy to overwhelm the enemy with a large part of the French accumulation of shell. Considerable subtlety in playing upon the mind of the German commander was needed, in order to induce him to exhaust all his resources thoroughly while not doing any grievous damage to France.

General Pétain was always willing to sell at a good price the pieces of ground he did not want. At the beginning of his operations it may be thought that he was perhaps just a little too easy in retiring from unnecessary positions. On the first day of his command he withdrew all French

CARE OF THE WOUNDED.
As each wounded man was brought out of the danger zone, a printed form was filled in with particulars of his injuries.

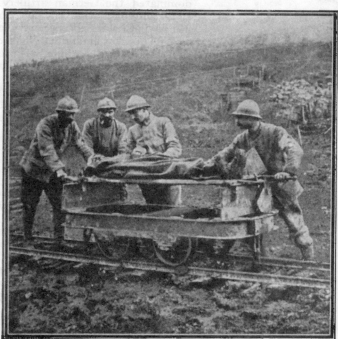

AMBULANCE WORK IN THE FIELD.
Members of the French Red Cross conveying wounded comrades to the ambulance.

TO HOSPITAL BY RAIL.
How light railways were used in the transport of French wounded soldiers from the trenches to the field-ambulance.

posts in the Woevre Plain and placed them upon the high ground. But afterwards he was not so sternly scientific in his concentrations of force. Instead of evacuating his weak points, he concealed machine-guns around them with observers at the end of a telephone wire, which ran not to a battery but to a central exchange, from which heavy guns by the hundred could be aimed. This gave the Germans something strenuous to achieve, and, going on the principle that the struggle was greater than the prize, they had, after accomplishing their object, something to celebrate in their communiqués.

In the first days of March they resumed their bombardment and infantry attacks upon the Douaumont Plateau, losing heavily, but not shifting General Balfourier's corps. This was the period when I became a spectator of the battle; but Douaumont, despite the enemy's activity round it, had then become a place of secondary importance. General Pétain had not waited for bridging material to transport his big guns across the Meuse. Instead **Abrupt change in the situation** of concentrating round the spot at which the enemy was striking, he ran his new heavy ordnance more quickly up the Argonne Forest to the hills above Verdun, on the opposite side of the stream. There, with a range of five miles, he could sweep all the reserve, support, and firing lines of the enemy's forces engaged on the front of three and a half miles between Pepper Hill and Douaumont.

This abruptly changed the situation, as the Germans viewed it. They had to take the hills across the Meuse—Dead Man Hill and Charny Ridge especially—in order to recover fully the power of making mass attacks on the Douaumont Plateau. So the tide of battle shifted—but at the masterly direction of General Pétain. The great batteries at Beaumont swung round to westward to make a flanking bombardment on the French positions across the Meuse, and east of these positions another mass of heavy German artillery near Montfaucon opened a hurricane fire. Then on March 6th infantry assaults began. Forges, a weak salient in the French line, was taken at great cost, but the enemy could not debouch from the hamlet on to the northern slopes of the Goose Crest. The force that attempted to do so was shattered. But the next day a fresh German division reached part of the crest, and worked down the railway to Regnéville, lying over against Samogneux, with the river between. The conquerors had, however, advanced against terrible machine-gun and artillery fire and were badly weakened, though the total French garrisons of Forges and Regnéville had been merely six hundred men! Again new forces were deployed on March 7th, and by another day of hard and good fighting the German commander made a brilliant stroke. He captured Crows' Wood (Bois des Corbeaux) and Cumières Wood, from which a decisive advance could be made on Dead Man Hill. If Dead Man Hill fell, General Pétain's power over the enemy's ground across the Meuse would be seriously reduced, and his more southerly position on Charny Wood would be menaced.

He at once threw reinforcements towards Dead Man Hill, and by an attack quite as fine as that of Balfourier's corps at Douaumont, the division recovered the greater part of the two woods. All the next day it withstood frontal and flank attacks, with the enemy's guns pounding it from the north, east, and south, the reverse fire coming from German batteries across the river near Pepper Hill. On March 10th another fresh, large enemy force of some 20,000 infantry worked again through part of Crows' Wood and Cumières Wood, suffering frightful losses and achieving no great result; for all that General Pétain had fought for was time. He had gained more than forty-eight hours in which to organise the works on and round Dead Man Hill in the way he wanted. This important advanced position had now become safe—for the crucial time at least.

The enemy commander also needed time to bring up his guns to cover the ground he had won in the woodlands and by the river. So there was a lull round Dead Man. But on the distant eastern side of the Verdun salient the German offensive was resumed with extreme violence. The new objective was the Fort of Vaux, south-east of Douaumont Fort and connecting with it in the old system of defence before the structures of armoured concrete were

Attack on Fort of Vaux

"CANNON FODDER" IN CAPTIVITY.
Types of German prisoners captured by the French in the early days of the Verdun onslaught.

OUT OF HARM'S WAY: MORE GERMAN PRISONERS FROM THE VERDUN SECTOR.
German prisoners on the march through a French village to the rear of Verdun, under a French mounted-guard with drawn sabres. The circle photograph shows General Joffre, with some Staff officers, personally inspecting a group of German prisoners.

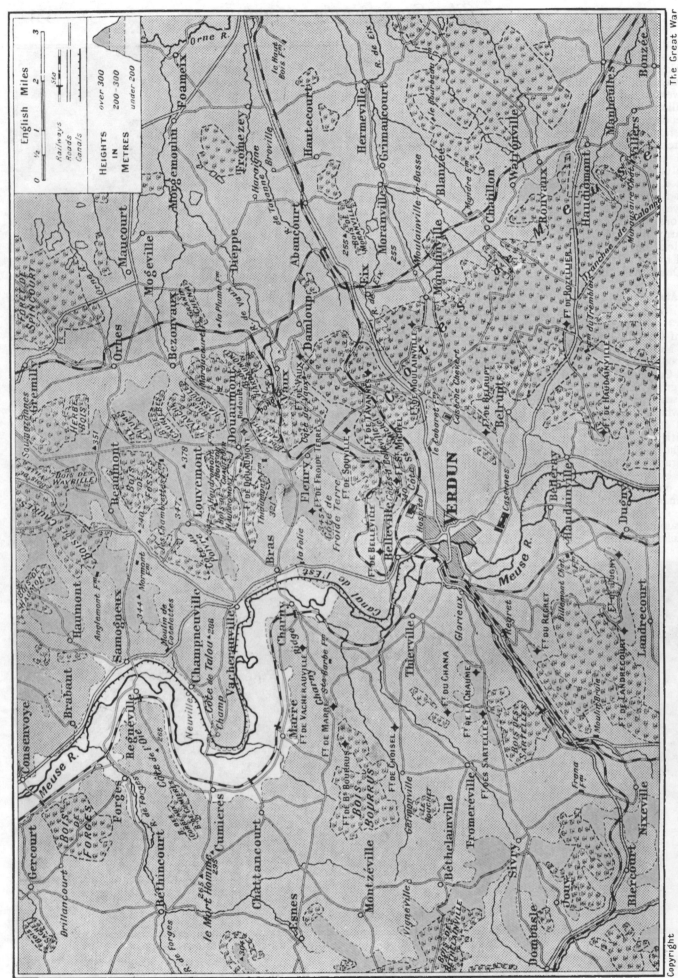

LARGE-SCALE MAP TO ILLUSTRATE THE FIRST PHASE OF THE GREAT BATTLE OF VERDUN.

The comparative heights of all the hills memorable in the titanic contest are shown, also the various woods lea the possession of which nerce fighting took place, and the course of the River Meuse.

The Great War

emptied of guns. The fort on the plateau was approached by a ravine in which lay the village of Vaux. Supported by their heavy artillery in the Woevre Plain, the Germans attacked round the mouth of the ravine on March 9th, and at night some 6,000 Poles, under General von Guretsky-Cornitz, got into the village, but were scattered by a bayonet charge

But, to the amazement of General Pétain and his Staff, the Berlin wireless spread the news that the Posen Brigade had stormed not only the hamlet in the hollow but the fort on the plateau. Paris was perturbed, and, at command of Headquarters, General Pétain had to send one of his Staff officers to Vaux. He found the garrison in merry mood with the soldiers off duty playing at manné, the Poilu's favourite game of cards. They had neither won nor lost any battle; the enemy had not come near them.

FRENCH TRENCHES ON THE MEUSE HEIGHTS.
A once beautiful valley shattered beyond recognition by the tempest from rival guns.

Meanwhile, the German Staff discovered it had made a ridiculous misstatement, and tried to palliate its blunder by ordering the fort to be taken. In ordinary circumstances the first attack on the village might have been a strong demonstration made with the object of misleading the French commander. But General Pétain now knew that the Vaux sector had become important, and that if he massed an unusual number of guns and men there, and improved his means of bringing up shells, his labour would not be wasted. Thus opened another general butchery of Germans, slaughtered for the sake of Prussian prestige. Vaux Fort had become Verdun in little. It had to be captured to save the reputation of a race of braggarts.

The price of Prussian prestige

But it was not captured, though the struggle for it went on for weeks with increasing fury. Even by the middle of March the ground below the fort was heaped with greyish forms, where the dead and dying had rolled down the slopes. The barrier of bodies grew so high that the living Germans refused at last to climb over it, stopping in horror, and thus becoming in turn easier targets for the defending gunners. In the ravine below, the Germans by the end of March won the eastern houses of the village, but could not for long advance farther. It cost them the larger part of a division to get this small footing, and when, at increasing heavy sacrifices, they occupied all the houses and began to climb the ravine, a terrific French bombardment, followed by a bayonet charge and bomb attack, cleared them out again. They had no time to dig cover enough to protect them from Pétain's heavy guns. Vaux Fort remained untaken, and the neighbouring Caillette Wood was recovered early in April, thus strengthening

NATURE WAR-SCARRED IN THE VALLEY OF THE MEUSE.
A panorama of mud, shattered and bare tree-stumps, abandoned trenches and dug-outs near the crest of the hill, and many shell-holes, mostly filled with rain-water. Above: A communication trench in the Verdun sector.

VERDUN REFUGEES.
Civilians about to leave the battle-zone. A common and pathetic sight at Verdun in February, 1916.

both the Douaumont and Vaux positions. It is difficult to decide, in some of these cases, if General Pétain suffered a temporary loss of any importance because his available forces had weakened, or because he deliberately refrained from strengthening his line. I incline to think that sometimes he preferred to seem weak where he was exceptionally strong, in order to get a mass of the enemy under the hammer of his guns. He had a deadly ingenuity. About this time it was revealed to the people of Paris that General Pétain was using 16·8 in. shells, filled with a more powerful explosive than German chemists had discovered.

The Germans began to show definite signs of "grogginess." The chief among these signs was their tendency to lies of a gross and childish nature. Their claim to the capture of Vaux Fort was possibly a bad mistake, due to some eager Staff subordinate's misunderstanding; it was a blunder that warned the French and pinned the Germans down to an operation they could not make **"Capture" of** a success. But in the middle of March, **Dead Man Hill** when the Vaux attacks were failing badly, the German Staff claimed the capture of Dead Man Hill. They were trying to win by the pen what they had so far failed to achieve by the sword. They stormed the Dead Man by conveying the name to a lower ridge of no decisive importance which they had occupied. Challenged on the matter by the French Staff, they tried to evade the charge of falsehood by stating that the words " Mort Homme," as lettered on the French map they used, extended to the lower ground. As though the best-informed War Staff in the world did not know every acre of ground near its own frontiers ! Dead Man Hill was a highly-important strategical height close to the Metz area, yet Field-Marshal von Haeseler could not, after nineteen

months' operations round Verdun, find the height that bore the name ! Perhaps it was a symptom of senile decay ; more likely it was an attempt to soothe the German people, whose anxiety in regard to Verdun was turning into angry despondency.

Von Falkenhayn had increased the Crown Prince's army from the fourteen divisions—that battled to Douaumont Fort—to twenty-five divisions. In April he added five more divisions to the forces around Verdun by weakening the effectives in other sectors and drawing more troops from the Russian front. **Crown Prince's** It was rumoured that Von Hindenburg **army increased** was growing restive, and complaining that the wastage at Verdun would tell against the success of the campaign on the Riga-Dvinsk front, which was to open when the Baltic ice melted.

Great as was the wastage of life, it was in no way immediately decisive. But when the expenditure of shells almost outran the highest speed of production of the German munition factories, and the wear on the guns was more than Krupp and Skoda could make good, there was danger to the enemy in beginning another great offensive likely to overtax his shell-makers and gun-makers. Von Falkenhayn's great concentration against our army, for example, remained perhaps only a silent demonstration because of the shell and gun difficulty. There was, of course, ample munition for a most violent and sustained attack, but if after another operation like that at Verdun our line was unbroken and our artillery power undiminished, it would be difficult for the enemy to turn against re-armed Russia.

At the time of writing it

PETAIN'S HEROES AND HARASSED CIVILIANS.
Refugees from villages in the Verdun sector on the steps of the mayor's house, and watching Algerian troops pass by. Above : Scene along a road behind the Verdun battle-front. Soldiers marching to and from the trenches, and civilians leaving the danger-zone.

DOUAUMONT'S TORTURED FIELD

A corner of the field of battle just outside the village of Douaumont, photographed in the interval between two series of German assaults. It was hereabouts that the grand counter-attack was made by Bretons and Colonial troops under General Balfourier on the critical evening of February 26th, when the Prussians were swept back, leaving part of the crack Brandenburgers all but surrounded in the fort. In the background is the glacis of the fort that was rushed by the Brandenburgers.

RUSHING A BOMB-MORTAR TO THE VERDUN FRONT.
The men were working like horses, inspired by the prospect of an advantage over the foe.

is still doubtful if the enemy's waste of shell and loss of men from February to April, 1916, have seriously interfered with his original plan for spring campaigns on both the Russian and British fronts.

The attacks continued on the Heights of the Meuse, and especially round Dead Man Hill, to the middle of April. Victorious Verdun was still being blown up in flaming ruin like Rheims and Ypres. Whenever an infantry assault failed, the Germans hurled incendiary shells into the unattainable town. Yet it was still to be attained by their forces, only the price at which the Crown Prince was to be allowed to ride by Vauban's citadel was much higher in April than it was in February.

General Pétain was a hard bargainer. **Pétain's menacing** And he could not be left alone. He had **position** forcibly to be kept in the position he occupied, for if the force against him weakened he might in turn employ his enormous artillery power to blast a path right through the German lines. This he had nearly done in the previous autumn, north of Massiges, with a mere fraction of the gun power he was now using. His position, at the eastern corner of the long German line stretching to the sea, was very menacing. Far from the Battle of Verdun being ended, there were possibilities in it of a decisive development

Immortal and indomitable France had won over her foe more power than she had possessed even after the Battle of the Marne. If her Allies, with the help of Japan and the United States, could soon overtake the production of the German and Austrian munition factories, it was possible that Verdun, so close to Sedan, might become one of the turning-points in the war.

STACKS OF SHELLS BEHIND THE VERDUN FRONT.
The Germans squandered more shells before Verdun than in any earlier battle of the war. With characteristic economy our ally only used shells where they were likely to be most effective—not, however, on account of any shortage, but rather with the idea of preserving their huge stock, part of which is seen in these two photographs, for a greater day—the day of the advance.

CHAPTER CXIV.

THE BUSINESS SIDE OF ARMAGEDDON:

How Men and Guns were Supplied and Unity of Control Effected on the Rival Fronts.

The Land of Work Behind the Fighting Fringe—Gigantic Labours of Organisation and Preparation—Our Million Men in Artois and Picardy—Standing Shoulder to Shoulder they Would Form Two Lines from London to Edinburgh—How this Great Number Shrank for Actual Fighting Purposes—Half a Million Infantrymen and their Servants and Assistants—The Transformations of the British Soldier—How the Petrol Engine Increased the Power of the Bayonet—Four Thousand Motor Lorries Save Verdun—Light Railways versus Motor Transport—In Order to Feed Our Men we Lose the Command of the Air—The Menace of the Motor Lorry—Petrol Power Signifies Attack, Steam Power Signifies Defence—Revolution in Strategy Effected by the Motor Omnibus—The Victory of London over Berlin in the Vital Element of Motor Traction—The British Invasion of the French Channel Ports—New Cities Spring Up in France to House Our Troops—French Shopkeepers and Farmers are Enriched by Our Soldiers—Mr. Thomas Atkins as a Millionaire on 1s. 2d. a Day—The Daily Rations of a Million Men—France Recognises the Patriotic Virtues of Refrigerated Meat—"Combing" the World for Horses and Mules—Prussian Foresight and the Telephone Factor—General Pétain's Genius—Marvels of the Underground City at Verdun—Scientific Progress Making Material Greatness Greater—War as a Huge Business Concern—Our Debt to Caledonia—French Liaison Officers and Unity of Control—The Allied Board of Strategists—French, German, and British Leadership Compared—The Duke of Plaza-Toro's Method Justified by Events—Prop Timber and the Paper Famine—The Great Central Railway and the Channel Tunnel.

 N practically all our descriptions of the operations of war we have left out the larger part of the picture. We have given only the fighting fringe of an immense area of intense and unending human activities. Battles are rare events in the modern war of entrenched positions, and their result depends almost entirely upon unexciting but gigantic labours of organisation and preparation, that often go on for months before the great guns herald an infantry attack in force. For the larger part of a year the opposing lines were strangely and uncannily empty in appearance, and at intervals almost silent. Along a stretch of hundreds of miles there was an apparent wilderness of desolation in which no human living figure could be seen Except for the tangles of barbed-wire and the parapet of the firing trenches, it seemed as though humanity and civilisation had ebbed from the earth. Pools of rain-water gathered in the shell-craters that pitted the vacant scene, whose silence was but the balance of the mightiest forces known on this planet. Here and there the shot of a sniper broke the stillness, and still more occasionally the explosion of a bomb from a trench-mortar party

FUEL FOR THE MACHINE.
British despatch-rider refilling his petrol tank.

revealed what enormous powers of slaughter were hidden underground in the apparently empty scene. When night fell there was more activity in the deep ditches and the intervening strip of ground between them. Sappers crept out to repair or strengthen their entanglements; adventurous patrols stole forward towards the enemy's bank of sand-bags to listen for information, find new sniping positions in some cases, and perhaps to harry a hostile machine-gun position with a few hand-grenades. But star-shells and light-rockets from the enemy's lines abruptly illuminated the zone of death; the explorers and patrols sought for cover in the shell-holes or threw themselves on the ground and looked as much like corpses as they could in order to induce their foes not to waste ammunition upon them, and all activity between the lines died down.

The great guns, however, often went almost to sleep in the day-light and awoke at nightfall. In the darkness they boomed over the firing trenches and the support trenches, leaving, for the most part, the hostile entrenched troops in peace, and pouring their shells a mile or two beyond the firing-line. Their aim was to interfere with some of the work going on behind the army, to knock over a motor-lorry, break up a railway track, or merely damage a road. The Germans at first used their long-range heavy guns in this way every night against all the Allies. It made things difficult for our transport columns behind Ypres and Armentières. But as we increased the range and weight of our artillery, added 9·2 in. guns to our 6 in. howitzers, and then produced in still increasing numbers siege-guns larger than the 9·2 in., the Germans found it was becoming very costly to shell at night our lines of communication when these were most busy with traffic.

Balance in heavy gun fire A gun that fires in darkness needs a heavy ground mist to hide its tongue of flame from hostile observers in a balloon. When British, French, and Belgians got heavy siege-guns into the position behind their lines the night became more silent ; for it did not pay the German gunners to make a chance shot at a supply waggon, when their shot was sure to be answered by a great blow at themselves, delivered with almost mathematical precision over a range of five or more miles.

On establishing something like a balance in heavy gun fire on both sides, the nights became more peaceful, and the German attacks on our lines of communication were made in daylight, when the position of the firing gun could not be so easily traced by its spurt of flame and little puff of fume. Had it not been for the invention of smokeless powder, daylight firing would have given the gun positions away in sunlight as well as in darkness by reason of the enormous cloud of smoke coming from a heavy piece of ordnance. But with smokeless powder a little desultory long-range firing was difficult to trace exactly to its source. On the other hand, the lines of communication immediately behind the front were almost empty in daylight, as hostile observers in kite balloons and aeroplanes could espy every movement. Most of the work was therefore done at night, and the volume of it can scarcely be visualised by any effort of imagination.

For instance, at the beginning of April, 1916, our army, lined out from the north of Ypres through Artois towards Albert, was reported to consist of a million men or more. Opposed to our soldiers was the greatest concentration of force that the Germans had ever gathered on a line so short as eighty-three miles—namely, three-quarters of a million men. It is easy to write about a million men, but hard to conceive their numbers in a concrete way. If the men under Sir Douglas Haig had been placed shoulder to shoulder in our country, the line would have reached from London to Edinburgh and then back again. If one man were to tick off their names on a pay-sheet and could do it at the rate of one hundred a minute, then, with twelve hours a day off for food and sleep, the task would take him over a fortnight, supposing he could keep up the pace of his work all that time. They were a mass of adults larger than the total male population of Ireland between the ages of fifteen and forty-five. If every man, young and old, were taken from Birmingham, Liverpool, and Manchester, they would not amount to a million ; neither could another group of our important industrial centres—Newcastle, Hull, Bradford, Sheffield, Leeds, Nottingham, and Bristol—acting together and calling out old and young, put a million men into the field.

As a matter of fact, Sir Douglas Haig could not do so either. His million men greatly shrank in number when he regarded them as **Sir Douglas Haig's** effectives in battle. To hold his line he had **million men** probably only about 500,000 infantrymen. The other 500,000 men were the servants of the troops of the line. During the summer of 1915, Germany, the greatest military Power, with the largest numbers of armed men in the field, only employed 1,000,000 infantrymen to hold the line from the North Sea to Switzerland. And they did not actually and constantly hold the line, for the larger part of them were kept well away from the firing trench, in billets out of range of hostile guns, and hundreds

CAVALRY PATROL HALTS FOR WATER.
Belgian cavalrymen pumping water for their horses. This illustration was secured during the great snowstorm of February, 1916, at a picturesque corner of the allied front.

A FRINGE OF THE BRITISH FRONT IN FRANCE.

This illustration is eloquent of the atmosphere of desolation in a foremost position. Weather and bombardment had turned the neighbourhood into a mud heap. Here and there a shell-crater reflected the ashen skies. To left and right and all around stout stakes supporting the barbed wire are visible, while a solitary shell-ruined farmhouse is a conspicuous landmark. Running up the centre of the photograph is seen a wooden track, quite a creditable piece of carpentry, laid down to facilitate transport and marching over the quagmire.

of thousands of them were held as reserves round distant railway junctions, ready to be transported to any threatened point. In the same way the first army of a million men that we placed on one great field of battle was used only in fractions and widely scattered behind the front. The work in connection with the soldiers would have been much easier if they had formed one great war city, in which they were crowded together regularly in underground rooms along the front, with a background of cottages and tent billets in the area beyond the reach of the enemy's siege-artillery. As it was, they were a colony of idle men, looking at them from an economic point of view, who did not work for their living, but had to be fed and clothed, doctored and bathed, lodged, supplied with ammunition, and kept cheerful. Like the well-trained athletes they were, they gave their bodies and minds to the task of winning victory, and, themselves tense in the prolonged effort of the struggle, they had to be seconded by a multitude of assistants. And the work done for them was, in its way, almost as remarkable as their own achievement. Certainly no other army was ever so well served as ours. This was the reason why they were maintained at the top of their fighting form.

There were some failures in fitting them out; they started with an insufficient proportion of machine-guns and an obsolete method of using this secondary armament; they were weak in the heavy guns needed in trench warfare, and still weaker in high-explosive shell; and after the French had found in steel helmets a valuable protection against shrapnel fire, our men had to wait long before being properly supplied with the new headgear. On the whole, however, the effectives of the principal British army were well looked after.

How our effectives were served

In the most modern of armies there was an extraordinary number of heavy guns. The artillery was rather an enormous siege train than a manœuvring force, such as all sides employed at the opening of the war. The corps' artillery was almost submerged in the heavy ordnance which often played a most decisive part in a battle. We may take it that in an army of a million there would be more than a quarter of a million artillerymen, with perhaps less than 100,000 cavalry. The men engaged in looking after the combatants would thus number 150,000. These figures, however, were liable to enormous changes. The Germans, for instance, would sometimes take all the artillery used with an army of a million men and employ with it only about a quarter of a million infantry and no cavalry at all. Over considerable periods we transformed our troopers into foot-soldiers and grenadiers, and let them practise the art of a gunner with trench-mortars. At the same time, we often temporarily reduced the number of our infantry by giving many of them sappers' work to do. In fact, our army was sometimes formed of nothing but sappers and artillery at night and infantry and artillery by day.

Figures liable to enormous changes

It was the extraordinary power of the German siege-artillery that brought about these transformations. For an entire year our cavalry almost ceased to exist, and new recruits were seldom accepted for cavalry regiments. Then, as our strength augmented, the mounted arm, which had done such splendid work in the retreat from Mons to the Marne, was restored to a position of distinct power in view of the intended general offensive movement by the Allies. In the meantime, however, the trooper had become more versatile, and while waiting for the guns and infantry, to clear a path for his charge against the hostile batteries, he had become practically everything that the infantry-man was—bomber, sniper, sapper, gas-dodger, dirk-fighter, and front-line burrower. He was really a mounted infantryman, so that we may add him to the effectives, and place the actual infantry forces of our army of a million at 600,000 men

On the other hand, this fighting mass was reduced in number and power by the loss of its machine-gun sections. These sections had usually been removed

Petrol power and infantry efficiency

from each battalion and formed into a semi-independent arm that constituted a secondary armament distinct from the guns and the rifles. The idea of detached machine-gun forces was a brilliant Prussian invention which—like the Prussian use of heavy howitzers in the field—showed that the inheritors of the traditions of Frederick the Great had not lost the remarkable power of making large and successful changes in military organisation and tactics. Nevertheless, the great and sometimes enormous increase in secondary, light, and heavy artillery did not diminish the supreme power of the infantry. Tremendous as grew the power of the guns, they were still the servants of the men with

WARM WORK IN THE SPRING SUNSHINE.
Indians engaged on earthworks and entrenchments some distance behind the first line in Flanders.

the bayonet, who alone could achieve victory by breaking through the enemy's lines.

What added to the infantryman's striking power was his use of the petrol-engine. In his arduous period of training he was still taught that his feet were more important than even his hands, and by long and frequent route marches he was prepared to wear the enemy down by outwalking him. It was more, however, to increase his general strength of body and to provide for accidents in a future stage of open field warfare that the training of a soldier's legs began before his musketry course and continued through it. For in actual battle practice the petrol-engine saved the legs of the soldier and enabled him to come fresh into battle. There were some breakdowns, of course, and in the struggle at Loos two of the new divisions seem to have been almost marched off their feet in order to get them in the firing-line, where their condition of fatigue prevented them from doing all that had been expected. This, however, seems to have been the result of an exceptionally bad piece of Staff work. As a rule, there were motor-omnibuses and lorries ready to take the infantry almost within gun-shot of the fighting-front.

In the allied armies in the western theatre of war the motor-lorry, with a range of a hundred miles a day, was the most important instrument of victory. On it in many cases depended the issue of a great battle. The railways of France and Germany were excellent. Many of the lines had been designed with a view of use in warfare, and after the outbreak of hostilities an extraordinary amount of material and labour was spent in developing mazes of light railways, starting from the old railheads behind the entrenched armies. But neither steam nor electric locomotives running on flanged wheels could supply the special needs of a manœuvring force. The railways became almost monopolised in periods of crisis by the service of the heavy guns. For example, in the first stage of the German attack on Verdun in February, 1916, the enemy used three million shells. A fifth of these were for heavy guns from 6 in. to 16·8 in., and with the lighter shells of the quick-firers the total weight of the projectiles was 47,000 tons. For the transport of this vast stack of metal and high explosive there were needed two hundred and forty long trains, each carrying two hundred tons, and afterwards an incalculable line of lesser carriages to carry these shells to the batteries. Then there were needed, besides, trucks for the fifteen hundred additional pieces of ordnance brought up to the woods around Verdun, and for the material used in building emplacements. Also, the very heavy guns wore out rapidly when employed in intense bombardments over a period first of weeks and then of months. The railway traffic was thus gigantic; the German railwaymen, who had several times made official complaints of being underfed, were subjected to prolonged and debilitating strains of work, and the rolling-stock, forming the shuttle between the enemy's eastern and western fronts, was far from being as good as it was in August, 1914.

Yet while using her railways in this manner, Germany was rearranging her infantry forces, and massing them in new groups of half a million and three-quarters of a million against Verdun and the British lines. Her railway system could not serve her great guns round Verdun, and also bring up the shells being accumulated from Roulers to St. Quentin, and at the same time remain free to transport the infantry. Potatoes had to be taken from the suffering German people and transformed into alcohol, which the Germans used for much of their motor traffic. They appear also to have employed steam traction.

The Allies, on the other hand, had an abundant supply of petrol, and their armies manœuvred largely by means of petrol or paraffin motor-omnibuses and motor-lorries. Behind the great working army of railwaymen in France there grew up a system of motor transport which

4,000 motor-lorries save Verdun

continually increased in size. Verdun was saved in March, 1916, by a force of 4,000 motor-lorries, which one of the French War Committees had been organising for months. The German guns at the time commanded the railway line from Verdun to Paris, but the French engineers threw a series of new pontoon bridges across the flooded Meuse. Over these bridges, day and night, the 4,000 motor-lorries fed the garrisons of Verdun and Dead Man Hill with reinforcements of men, guns, and shells. Each lorry could

Two members of General Sir Douglas Haig's escort in France resting awhile in a wooded district somewhere near Headquarters.

Indian cavalryman on sentry duty. Two typically French figures were looking down the road in the direction of the battle-front.

British officer making an inspection of Indian cavalrymen and their equipment at a picturesque camp behind the lines in France. Trench warfare, of course, deprived these expert horsemen of an opportunity to distinguish themselves in charges.

BRITISH AND INDIAN CAVALRY BEHIND THE LINES IN NORTHERN FRANCE.

341

OUT AND ABOUT AGAIN: WOUNDED HORSES IN CONVALESCENCE.
Having recovered from their injuries, these horses were being watered in a stream near the headquarters of the British veterinary service in France.

make a journey of a hundred miles a day with a great load. At first, the end of their journey was slow and perilous, for the Germans had 15 in. naval guns, with a range of twenty miles, and ploughed up all the roads behind the French front, making them not only impassable by any vehicle, but very dangerous to approach. If a 15 in. shell struck a train of motor-lorries loaded with ammunition the damage would not have been slight. Yet, despite this disadvantage, the new French motor service triumphed over the new railway of supply which the Germans had constructed north of Verdun. General Pétain got his new guns and new shell supply quicker than the enemy was able to accumulate another three million shells. When the enemy was at last ready to renew his hurricane fire tactics, the French commander was also fully prepared. On discovering this, the Germans postponed their second great infantry mass attack to the second week in April, and then failed completely to get anything like a decision. Verdun was a triumph of motor transport over railway transport. Of course, the French railways greatly helped in the victory, but it must be admitted that without the vast new fleet of motor-lorries Verdun would have been lost.

Probably our army was, on the allied side, the pioneer of motor transport. We had most experience in the matter; for it was against our small Expeditionary Force that the Germans launched their motor wing under General von Kluck. It was the speed with which the westernmost German army corps travelled in motor-omnibuses and motor-lorries that made our retreat so physically exhausting and continually perilous. We had not been prepared for so immense a use of motor transport concentrated on a small sector of the front. But after escaping from the full force of this surprising and yet finely logical piece of motor tactics, we became the leaders in military motor **Lesson learnt from** work. Some years before the war our **the enemy** Government had subsidised the motor-lorry squadrons of large business houses, when the vehicles were of a type acceptable to the War Office. But these subventioned lorries were soon found to be insufficient for the needs of the Army, and thousands of other motor-vehicles were hastily requisitioned. Omnibuses were taken off the streets and converted into ambulances or lorries; the entire output of leading manufacturers was taken over, and large regular orders were placed with practically every firm that could build a motor-vehicle.

There was certainly some "push and go" in the rapid organisation of our motor transport. Even in the early stages of the war the weekly supply of new lorries to our Government ran into three figures, and at last all our private motor-car makers were working for the Army or Navy. Motor-bicycles, sometimes fitted with machine-guns, were needed by scouts and despatch-riders, while armoured motor-cars, with machine-guns or quick-firers, were wanted by the Naval Wing for raiding the Uhlan and supporting airmen. **Motor transport** The gunners wanted ammunition lorries **rather overdone** to bring shell from the sea-bases to the firing-line quicker than the congested French railways could bring them, while the Army needed motor transport for nearly everything except a cavalry charge.

France had lost a very considerable quantity of rolling-stock during the enemy's drive towards the Seine. She was, of course, ready to share with us her diminished power of steam carriage, but as a loyal ally we had to do our very best to relieve the heavy burden upon the partly crippled French railway system. This we did by constructing what was probably the finest motor-transport system existing. Nearly all our motor firms enlarged their plant and speeded up their output, but their labours were not sufficient for the needs of our growing Army. A golden cloud of prosperity rose above the great centres of motor-lorry making in the United States, from which Britain, with France and Russia, obtained enormous supplies. Meanwhile, the Royal Automobile Club, the Automobile Association, and Motor Union sifted their members and their machines, and placed a remarkably large organised force of cars, drivers, and motor-cyclists at the disposal of the Government and certain municipal authorities.

We soon had motor fleets concentrated against possible invasion, with motorists guarding our telephone and telegraph lines at home until their work was taken over by military men. Then, in a considerable number of cases, the British motorist converted his car into an ambulance, and worked with it behind the firing-line. As a matter of fact, we at last rather overdid the motor-transport system, and did not pay enough attention to the light-railway system, which the Germans were developing with remarkable energy and the French with fine forethought.

In important places along the front the Germans ran their rails into the redoubts behind the fire-trench. They were the best military engineers in the world. They must have kept their troops labouring continually in a much harder way than we did ours. They brought their light railways through narrow cuttings, and even through tunnels, in order to shield them from gun fire, and the toy-like trains used in and just behind the lines were constructed in great quantities in the Westphalian industrial centres. The Germans were occupying practically all the Continental coalfields of Europe, together with the iron-field above Verdun, and all the mineral fields of Belgium. Steam power, therefore, was their main instrument of battle, and in the long pauses of trench warfare they set all their troops in shifts to help the engineering corps, until the network of light railways and the new lines of full-size track behind the narrow-gauge systems became a remarkable monument to the energy of the Teutons.

The British Army, on the other hand, was so absorbed in its motor-transport system that our mechanics, skilled in the making of internal combustion engines, had no time left for attending to the needs of our air services. We could not get a hundredth part of the number of first-rate aero-engines we urgently required, because the men that could have made them were engrossed in **Petrol power v. steam power** engine-making for the motor-transport department. It must, however, be borne in mind that the light-railway system went best with a stationary form of defence, and that a force which aimed at breaking the opponent's lines and making progress far behind them, would find in motor transport the very best possible means of manœuvring, especially in the months when the ground would be fairly dry. In the western theatre, at least, petrol power signified attack and steam power mainly defence. The first German rush towards Paris had largely been upborne by petrol, the most flexible and rapid source of power. The Germans had developed steam traction only when their great blow had failed, and, in spite of their rubber famine that told on the tyres, they still continued to use motor-omnibuses in shifting troops from one sector to the other.

The large development of motor transport by the western Allies produced a revolution in one of the fundamental elements of strategy. In the age of Moltke only one army corps could be moved along one road on the same day. If two or three corps were crowded into one road, the rear corps could not be used in a battle at the front. Moreover, if several corps were stationed close together, they could not be fed for more than a day or two. In our opening

BRITISH TRANSPORT WAGGON IN DIFFICULTIES.

FRESH FOOD AND FORAGE FOR MEN AND MOUNTS IN FRANCE.

Forage being distributed in the horse-lines at a British camp in France that was situated on fields of mud behind the front. Picture above: British soldier bargaining for cattle in a French market town. Whenever possible our men were provided by the Army kitchens with roast beef.

CAUGHT IN THE GLARE OF A GERMAN LIGHT-PRODUCING PROJECTILE: A BRITISH PATROL IN PERIL BETWEEN THE TRENCHES.

A British night listening-patrol trapped in the dazzling glare of a German light-shell rocket, and in momentary danger of being fired at by the enemy. The men, caught in the sudden brilliance while scouting in No Man's Land, between the trench-lines, are lying with faces to the ground, their revolvers clutched, ready for instant use in the event of discovery. Away to the left are visible the British wire entanglements and trenches, from which the listening-patrol had crept to within a few yards of the German trenches just behind the staked barbed-wire to the right. The brilliant, irradiating glare produced by one of the enemy's light-producing projectiles lasted for about fifteen seconds, making the space between the trenches as light as by day, and enabling artillerymen and scouts to locate their objectives.

battle round Mons each marching division extended for five and a half miles along the road, and took two and three-quarter hours to pass through a hamlet on the way. We had then speeded up the rate of movement since the age of Moltke, as many of our supplies were drawn by motor. Both time and space were saved. Yet the marching pace of infantry columns in their full kit still ruled all the allied strategy. But when, at the close of twenty-one months of war, our motor-transport system had been developed, the German Staff had to take into consideration the number of motor-vehicles at our disposal, and the speed with which they could transport both infantry and guns over many

SUPPLIES FOR THE FRONT.
Scene at an important railway station for the French front. A number of military transport waggons were loading up from rail-trucks, thence to proceed to the zone of operations.

MILK FOR THE FRENCH ARMY IN THE FIELD.
Interior of the large central military farm which supplied the French armies in the field with milk. The depot was organised with great thoroughness, and staffed by men unfitted for active service and by women.

wheels. Paris had been saved by its fleet of taxi-cabs, which transported the Paris garrison into the conflict along the Ourcq, and it seemed as though the motor-vehicle would end by becoming, with its assistant railways, the universal instrument of mobility.

Parks of motor-lorries were already spoken of as fleets, and it looked as if some of the future battles of manœuvres in the open field would more resemble naval and aerial actions than the old, crawling land battles of August, 1914. Railways were the factor that had concentrated for the conflict four and a half million men in Flanders and France, Alsace-Lorraine and the Ardennes. But with the exception of General von Kluck's motor wing, all these millions of soldiers, on leaving their railheads, had to work forwards and backwards on their feet. Their cavalry, which moved more quickly, was often the sooner worn out. The marching power of the men and the rate of progress of their supply columns decided the victory—the victory of the Marne.

Changes in war conditions

It was not be expected, however, that the next great open field battle would be decided by the same factor; for the western Allies were mastering at last the problem of moving men by the million—which had perplexed despots with great dominions since the age of Xerxes, and probably earlier. The internal combustion engine, linked with the steam locomotive, gave to the great modern army a mobility that terribly increased its striking power. The new type of motor-tractor that could rear up like a horse, break through a hedge, and cross ploughed fields, was significant of great changes in the conditions of war. Before the outbreak of hostilities, the enterprising Germans—and Krupp in particular—had begun to construct chassis for

miles of country. Two fairly parallel roads might serve the progress of considerably more than two army corps, if they were filled with motor-lorries going at ten or twelve miles an hour. Then, in regard to concentration of force, as the Germans themselves showed us at Verdun, sixteen army corps could be massed on a front of thirty miles or less without the slightest danger of starving. The entrenchments, with their machine-gun redoubts and the backing of light and heavy artillery, still tended to veil the extraordinary quickening of movement behind the lines. It was only in a renewal of open field warfare that the full result of the evolution in transport could be seen.

Meanwhile, concentrations of unusual power could be carried out with increasing rapidity, and with the curious consequence that less strength was needed in holding the trenches. Only so many men with machine-guns and bombs were placed in the firing-line as would be able to hold out until a fleet of motor-omnibuses reinforced the support trenches and enabled the supporting troops to enter the contest in front of them. Thus the complexion of the battlefield changed, for the army ran almost wholly on

ON THE ALERT FOR ENEMY AIRCRAFT.
Men of the "watch" on the look-out for hostile aeroplanes in front of a reserve trench in France.

"LINES OF COMMUNICATION."
"Signals"—the nickname given to men of the Signal Service, R.E.— telephoning to the trenches from a shell-swept village.

MESSENGERS OF MARS.
Motor-cycle despatch-carriers making their way across difficult country. These messengers of war won high praise from commanders for their daring and devotion to duty.

the rapid transport of light artillery. The motor-engine was used to haul the gun and its carriage up strong ramps into the motor-lorry, where there were depressions for the wheels to sink into. Very heavy artillery, on the other hand, was drawn by big traction-engines working with steam. The steam-tractor, however, was more dependent on constant renewal of fuel and water supplies than the petrol-engine, and even before the war the French military authorities were experimenting with three hundred tractors using petrol fuel. Without penetrating any secrets we can take it that, in the fleet of 4,000 motor-lorries that saved Verdun, there may have been some interesting examples of siege-gun transport at a speed of ten miles or more an hour.

In regard to the reserve of motor power behind the new British front of eighty-three miles, little or nothing can discreetly be said. We began with some advantages, and we certainly did not lose them. By one of those happy strokes of fortune which the British race strangely enjoys, we were in a position of supremacy in the industrial motor industry. We had in London and the country around a first-rate road system and a very scattered urban population of incomparable magnitude. Owing to the great distances in the London area and to our fortunate backwardness in developing a complete system of electric tramcar lines, London offered a field for motor transport without parallel in the world. Omnibus companies, large stores, and even our Post Office authorities, turned with fostering orders to the industrial motor trade, with the result that in both the number of vehicles and the manufacturing plant available we were superior to Germany. Berlin had so complete a system of electric tramcars that the motor-omnibus could not flourish there. In our country there were vastly more industrial motor-vehicles than our Army required, and, as a most important by-product, we had a large army of well-trained drivers, many of whom were drafted into the forces and set to dodge occasional German shells without any further training. Our manufacturers were also able to supply thousands of highly-skilled repairing mechanics for working in the field and keeping the engines and lorries in good order. Had our Army Council fully thought out the possibilities of a petrol war, our original Expeditionary Force might have been at the beginning a very mobile motor wing of the French Army. We had more motor-omnibuses than the Germans, more motor-vans, and more motor-drivers.

Our advantage over Germany

Of course, we had not got behind the front sufficient motor-vehicles to carry all our men, but we probably had enough for a swift manœuvring wing of considerable size; and this means something, as we can see if we reduce the transport problem to railway terms. An army corps of 40,000 men, with all its ammunition and guns, including the long-range heavy guns, needs at least one hundred and fifty trains to carry it. Supposing the trains followed each other at intervals of ten minutes, the last would arrive at its destination twenty hours after the first. This destination would only be a rail-**New cities spring** head, and it is unlikely that the corps **up in France** would come into action quite close by.

There would thus follow the task of marching the men and dragging the guns and supplies down lanes and roads to the firing-line. But a motor wing, consisting of an army corps with squadrons of flying men scouting before it, would not be confined to a single track. It could break into divisions and brigades, some of which would take roundabout roads in order to diminish the volume of traffic. In a manœuvring area of fifty miles the motor wing, if excellently equipped, would be able to come into action before the railway-carried corps. And the infantry, having had no marching from a railhead to do, would be fresher.

By the spring of 1916 our increasing motor transport enabled our army to cover with an intricate net of communications the 2,000 square miles of French territory over which we operated. The stretch of land was about the size of Norfolk, and included the Depart-ment of Pas de Calais and the free part of Nord. Then the Somme Department was added, and part of Normandy was also included in our area of communications, for, in addition to the northern ports of

Calais and Boulogne, we also had material at Dieppe and Havre. New towns were created by our troops in certain parts of France which excited the admira-tion of some of our French friends. Dunkirk was temporarily Belgian, and Calais was also largely needed as a port of supplies for the Belgian troops. So the British force extended southward. As our army increased and the volume of its oversea traffic grew vaster, the ports of Normandy became brisker with British war business. By extending our line towards Amiens and relieving our French comrades of the defence of the north-west front, we simplified the transport arrangements, leaving the French with Paris as their northern base, from which they fed all their line from Roye to Verdun. Paris had St. Nazaire, on the Bay of Biscay, as the great port for American supplies, and on the Mediterranean there was Marseilles, while from the great inland centre of Lyons the French eastern front from Belfort to Nancy could be fed. Much of the traffic from England and Scotland to Paris still came through the Normandy ports, but on the whole the northerly reach of the Channel, together with Artois, Picardy, and the upper part of Normandy, were the scene

BRITISH MOUNTS ON THE MUDDY FIELDS OF FRANCE.
British horse depot behind the western front. Some slight idea of the depth of mud encountered by our troops during winter operations is given in this photograph. It will be seen that the soldier's right leg is knee-deep in the wet mass. Picture above: Slightly wounded horses being taken to a veterinary hospital behind the lines, where injured mounts received as much skilled care as that bestowed on wounded men.

of a great British invasion about which the Germans never tired of warning the French.

Sometimes it did quite look like a real invasion, for we employed a great number of troops to guard our lines of communication and garrison the ports we were using. Probably well over a tenth of our army of a million men was on lines of communication work, engaged in watching the roads and in policing our sea-bases and towns in which troops were densely billeted. German spies were not entirely absent, and we had many stores of explosive material which the enemy was not averse to blowing up if he had the chance. There was a great deal of other war material of an interesting kind, which had to be kept from the eyes of the friendly French population, because of the danger that someone who was not in the service of France might get a glimpse of what was going on. Along the roads practically everybody was stopped for identification, any sightseer being regarded with especial suspicion. But our occupation of this large corner of France was not disagreeable to the French trading classes, for our soldiers,

Millionaires on 1s. 2d. a day

LOW TEMPERATURE BUT HIGH SPIRITS.
Some of the Spartan sons of Britain who composed the khaki line along the west front enjoying their morning ablutions at an icy stream behind their firing trenches.

with their pay of 1s. 2d. a day, were millionaires in comparison with any Continental troops.

Possibly both the French and the Germans were better off with their pence than our soldiers were with their shillings. The Frenchman had a Government allowance of wine and tobacco, and the German had a similar allowance of tobacco and beer. Neither had to pay for button polish, soap, and other little necessary luxuries as our soldiers did. On the other hand, the one thing about our Army provisions that struck the French soldier as the summit of wild luxury—jam—was really a very scientific element of diet which provided heat energy for our men.

The feeding arrangements for our million of men were properly generous. It was assumed that every man had the same appetite, and that this was a large one, as the troops were living in the open air. Every man had each day one and a quarter pounds of fresh meat, or one pound of preserved meat; he also had one and a quarter pounds of bread, or a pound of biscuit, four ounces of bacon, three ounces of cheese, four ounces of jam, three ounces of sugar, and a few spoonfuls of tea—five-eighths of an ounce. Eight ounces of vegetables were daily provided, but butter was rare. Only two ounces were given once a week; our

soldiers had to get their heat energy out of their liberal ration of jam and sugar.

With a million men consuming daily rations of this sort, the labour thrown on the Army Service Corps and its transport department was enormous. Six hundred tons of meat, six hundred tons of bread, more than a hundred tons of bacon and jam, and nearly a hundred tons of cheese and sugar had to be delivered every day. Then in addition there was an extraordinary private supply of provisions and little luxuries through the parcel post.

A day's fresh mutton for the Army would be represented by a flock of sheep spreading three miles down an ordinary country road, giving the Army butchers such an amount of work as would overcome them. In fact, they could not have carried it out, their numbers were not sufficient. Refrigerated beef and mutton were largely used to save space, cattlemen, and labour. The French authorities made a gallant struggle to provide their vaster Army with freshly-killed, home-bred meat, but they could not continue this estimable policy. As the war lengthened out, and the appetite of the French soldier increased with a year of open-air life, he threatened to eat up all the sheep and oxen of France. Farmers grew anxious about the probable condition of their stocks at the end of the struggle, and the upshot was that both the French troops and the French urban populations had to be gracefully educated by their Government into recognition of the patriotic virtues of refrigerated meat.

But the cattle-ships, in which animals used to be brought to Liverpool and London so that their flesh could be sold as home-killed meat, were transformed into more innocent uses; most of them became mule transports, like the famous Nicosian that avenged the torpedoed liner the Arabic. Where motor transport ended, the work of the mule cart began. The French and the British seem almost to have emptied certain American States of mules, and these hardy, rough, and far from gentle animals required a large force of men to handle them. Then there were the chargers of the cavalry and the enormous herds of horses used with the artillery. Even when motor traction developed, the horse could not be safely separated from the guns. Engines went wrong at critical moments, but a well-kept team of good horses, though slower in pace than a steam or motor tractor, was more reliable. We held to both methods of moving artillery; so did all the other armies. They had some form of mechanical transport—steam or petrol—but knowing that a shell might smash the track or an internal combustion engine break down from its own defect or a shrapnel bullet, they "combed" the whole world for horses. Germany drew upon Holland and Scandinavia, and got within sight of an eventual shortage. Russia had a practically inexhaustible **"Combing" the world for horses** horse supply in her own immense territories. France ran short, and drew on Spain and Ireland. Our Government having in Ireland the principal centre of fine horse-breeding, with, moreover, a lot of superb blood in England and Scotland, came to the help of Belgium and France, but found that the British reserve of horse-flesh was also running very low.

There was an astonishing rise in the price of British horses, and in everything connected with horses—oats, hay, bran, and corn. Poultry and eggs grew dearer, and

[Gale & Polden.

Major-General F. W. B. Landon, C.B., Chief Inspector of the Q.-M.-G.'s Services.

349

Rat catching : A spare-time diversion with the Canadians on the west front.

Sylvan surroundings of part of the Canadian line in France.

Canadian infantry in the trenches ready to repel an attack.

Lunch in the Canadian trenches within fifty yards of the German lines.

A Canadian officer, Lieutenant Kent, receives the Military Cross.

pork and bacon, because the food on which hens and pigs flourished was requisitioned for the vast herds of horses needed by the armies of the western Allies. Could we but have run the war by motor transport—that is on petrol—the cost of living throughout Western Europe, excluding the Central Empires, might not have risen so high. Britain and France, in particular, might have developed their poultry farms in a remarkable way if oats, bran, and grow- ing grass had not been so urgently needed by millions of horses and mules conscripted by France, Britain, Belgium, and Italy. The Italians also used, to a quite considerable extent, the antique oxen-drawn carts, while Belgium developed her dog trains for machine-gun traction. In Russia pony carts were used by the hundred thousand, and excellent they were, too, these little shaggy creatures and their primitive vehicles. They brought supplies through the Polish mud at a pace greater than that of the German motor-lorries, which often stuck deeply under their heavy loads. The able engineers of the Germans' transport department made the westerner's inveterate mistake in planning the great campaign against Russia. Like Napoleon, they were influenced by conditions of travel in Western Europe, and did not allow sufficiently for eastern mud. Another remarkable means of travel—used in winter by friend and foe in the French Vosges, the Italian Alps, and along the Russian front—was the ski. Sledges were also largely used in Russia— motor-sledges as well as horse and pony sleighs.

We have seen that, of all things behind our fighting-line, the motor transport was the most important. It fed the men and the guns, manœuvred the troops and the shell supplies, carried the wounded to the railhead, and enabled the generals and Staff officers to control all operations more quickly than they could have done by horse power. But there was another thing—quite a small thing in appearance—which was almost of equal importance with petrol power, and this was the telephone. As in most military matters, the Prussian Staff had been the first to foresee clearly the possibilities of telephone con- trol in warfare. In the great opening battles their overwhelming force of artillery had been remarkably well scattered in small groups of guns to prevent much damage being done to it, yet each battery was linked by a telephone wire to a central control, so that massed fire effect could swiftly be obtained from the dispersed and concealed guns. All through the war telephone control increased in importance, especially during the long and almost stationary parallel battle between the sea and the Jura
Pétain's telephone Mountains. Happily for us, it was our
fire-control alert and brilliant-minded allies the French who produced the man of genius capable of developing to perfection the telephone system of fire-control. General Pétain, the organiser of the successful wing in the Champagne Battle, and afterwards the defender of Verdun, was the master-gunner of the new era. From him we learned much, even as he learned something of no small value from us ; for our artillery tactics at Neuve Chapelle had been excellent of their kind, and it was only lack of high-explosive shell that prevented us from breaking through. General Pétain had the advantage of being a soldier of genius, who took up the study of heavy artillery

in the vivid experience of actual warfare. He began by knowing beforehand the utmost that could be done with the latest form of telephones, and by attaching his guns to a central telephone exchange in which he sat, with wireless instruments connecting him also with his aerial scouts, he became a virtuoso in artillery tactics.

At Verdun, for example, he sat in an underground city a hundred feet below the earth, and there directed his storms of the new French high explosive that was more powerful than melinite. **Underground city** His principal guns had a range of five **at Verdun** miles, but they were often more effective than the longer-ranged 12 in., 15 in., and 16·8 in. ordnance of the Teutons. His telephone wires, sunk out of reach of the heaviest shell, spread in a great network from three sides of his underground city, and enabled him to act like the gunnery lieutenant of an enormous battleship. His men and officers, tens of thousands in number, were almost his blind servants. They loaded the guns, but they did not aim and fire them. The new telephone system had produced an extraordinary simplification in the handling of the vast and scattered masses of artillery. General Pétain in person

A HELPING HAND TO THE SISTERS.
British soldiers helping Red Cross nurses at a camp-kitchen installed on the platform of a railway-station some distance behind the western front.

aimed and fired his two thousand or more guns. The result was that he often produced a volume of fire which made any German movement impossible. It was useless to attempt a diversion against his left flank in the morning, and attack his right flank in the afternoon. His guns could swing round quickly in response to a telephone message ; each new elevation or traverse was rapidly and clearly given, and practically the whole tempest of shell under the general's control was directed precisely on the new ground where the enemy's movement had been discerned.

Round the French lines were French artillery officers at the end of telephone wires, running, not to their battery but through to the central control, where a large staff of men rapidly organised all information and placed it before the general. All wireless messages from aeroplane observers were also organised and related to the general body of information. The range of every piece of ground in front of the French was registered to an inch and arranged for instant use, and of course, all the French positions were similarly registered. A good deal depended upon General Pétain's Staff, but they were all men of exact and ready mind, tested in the heat and rush of previous

BRITISH HEAVY HOWITZERS IN ACTION IN FRANCE WITH AIRCRAFT IN CO-OPERATION.

Battery of howitzers preparing to shell an enemy position. The gun on the left is laid ready to fire. That in the middle is being loaded, two men "ramming home" the shell while others stand by with hand-spikes with which to help to lay the gun. A small crane, used for lifting the charge into the "load" position, is attached to the gun-carriage. Behind and under the heavy wheels of the gun, which stands on a wooden platform, are ramps to check the recoil. Over each gun saplings are so arranged that they conceal the battery from enemy aircraft. In the foreground on the right are dug-outs for ammunition, telephone, and shelters, and a field-telephone is seen in use. A scouting biplane is setting out to "spot" where the shells fall and, report on the effects of the firing.

actions. Everything was carefully built up so as to put the French commander in single-handed control of practically all his guns. What we had done in battleship gunnery he had done in army artillery. If one could imagine Sir John Jellicoe being in such a position that he could personally fire every gun in his fleet, naval tactics would resemble the new military tactics as developed by General Pétain.

Of course, the stationary circumstances of trench warfare greatly assisted this strange development in the use of the telephone. In the mobility of a battle of manœuvres in the open field, with the new motor wings and central reserve of motor - omnibuses changing the dispositions in perhaps half an hour or an hour, the telephone control of all the guns would not be easy. The wires in most cases would have to be strung from trees or laid along the ground, and shells and changing batteries would damage them. Yet when the wireless telephone, with a range of some thousand miles, came into practical use, it was possible that the Pétain system of controlling the gun fire of entire armies might, before the end of the war, be brilliantly employed upon changing masses in the open field. The wireless telephone would indeed both answer and complete the new strategical element of motor traction, and combine with it to make the conflict of millions of men a rapid and most terrible clash of mighty nations, in which a decision would be obtained, in a final and definite manner, in a few days.

Military operations would more closely resemble naval operations. It was expected that a general fleet action between Britain and Germany would be over in a few hours. It would be, as the Germans say, a battle without a morrow. In the same way, a general military offensive in the open field, under the new conditions of warfare, was likely to terminate in a quick and overwhelming victory for one side or the other. It is well for us and our Allies that this process of development was late in occurring. If Germany had possessed at the outbreak of hostilities a mighty system of motor traction and a well-organised system of long-range wireless telephone control, her troops would not have failed from fatigue when they crossed the Marne. All these new developments increase the power of the country that can put quickly into the field most men and most guns.

Small States are growing smaller than ever. Only by a complete and loyal system of military federation are they likely to be able to make any effective resistance against great predatory empires. If, as **Tendency of scientific invention** a result of the war, the Central Empires were allowed to combine into a single effective military organisation, they would surely end by becoming the veritable masters of the world. It is a sad and deplorable thing, but the general tendency of scientific invention is to make, in both business and war, mere material greatness greater. A large London store, with its tentacles of motor-traction delivery, spreads rapidly into the country and impoverishes the shopkeepers in towns and

HUBS OF THE WAR-WORLD.
Units of the Motor-cycle Machine-gun Corps and some motor-cycle despatch-riders halting in the cobbled "place" of a French town.

villages. Then, a carburetter is discovered by which cheap paraffin can be used instead of costly petrol, with the result that large business houses are again able to extend their radius of action and save money on the expense of their delivery system. So, to their original advantage of being able to buy in larger quantities than small local shopkeepers and offer better bargains, motor traction and the progress of the telephone, both of which bring them into immediate touch with remote customers, add new advantages. **Conduct of war and business**

The conduct of war strangely resembles the conduct of an enormous business concern. In regard to our Army, for instance, there was a Board of Directors, of which the King was the chairman, and Mr. Asquith the vice-chairman, the other members being the Cabinet Ministers and their expert advisers. This Board of Directors met in London, and appointed as its general manager abroad the Commander-in-Chief, Sir Douglas Haig, chosen for his wide and practical knowledge of his business. But Sir Douglas Haig could not personally control his million of men. He divided his office work into departments, at the head of each of which was a departmental chief. There was a quartermaster-general to look after the stores, an adjutant-general to see to the discipline of the men and their reinforcements, and so on. Each departmental chief needed a hierarchy of officers, inspectors, and book-keeping and clerical workers. The controllers of food supplies, munitions, medical stores, railways, horse and motor transport, clothing and other things, conducted a business far larger than all the combined stores in British cities. Parts of a considerable town had to be taken over to house their men, and a great network of new telegraph and telephone wires constructed to carry on their business. They needed also a

A SOLDIERS' "SHOP" IN FRANCE.
Interior of a general store that was managed by some British soldiers at the front. Here additional commodities were purchasable by way of a pleasing extra to official fare.

post-office service of their own, large enough almost for the population of Australia, if that population were concentrated into one urban community, and this postal service, with its telegraphic and telephonic service, had to function alongside the ordinary French national organisation.

The life of the inhabitants went on almost normally in the town from which the great business of

Activity at General Headquarters

the fighting colony was controlled. And, except for the remarkable number of khaki uniforms visible in the main streets, and the remarkable number of motor-car and motor-cycles coming in and going out, there was little of the show of war to mark the General Headquarters of the Army, as the warehouses of the immense business were built elsewhere at points most convenient for supplying our lengthening front. Quiet but steady office work, combined with an intensive study of geography, formed the principal labours of the new community. Military clerks in long rows sat at desks, writing, calculating, or typing, just as one might see men in a large London bank, with the telephone in constant use, and in a calm atmosphere of businesslike efficiency. The results of their labours came in a condensed form to the sub-departmental chiefs, and were combined by them into a tabloid statement for the departmental head. He then handed his information to the General Staff, or, in cases of importance, discussed the matter with the commander.

But, as a rule, the energies of the Commander-in-Chief were concentrated upon the actual military use of all the forces and materials which were docketed for him by his principal assistants. In the rooms in which he worked with his Staff officers were large tables covered with maps, and on the maps were recorded every movement by his own troops and those of the enemy. He had also

under his eyes the disposition of his guns, the amount of shell accumulated by the batteries and available for instant use, and the store of shells in the field depôts and at the bases. He could tell almost to a minute the time it would take to make concentrations, and he had also clearly set out before him all that was known about the enemy's troops, their regiments, brigades, divisions, and army corps, the position of all their artillery and their probable amount of shell supply.

The modern system of aerial reconnaissance had much increased the recording work in the commander's working rooms. He had tabulated statements of the arrival and departure of all German trains opposite his lines, and all the transport columns that had been seen on the move, together with the results of the Secret Service work of the Allies that affected his forces. One of the chief branches of this business of war was strangely prosaic. The information about our troops and the enemy's troops was, of course, enormous, yet all the vital factors in it had to be instantly available. So filing systems and methods of displaying concretely exact, summarised information were very useful. Even the daily state of the roads and its effects upon the speed of our motor-vehicles was worth constant study by some member of the Staff when he came to work out the transport side of an offensive movement. Sir William Robertson, the new director of all the military operations of our Empire, had first distinguished himself by his study of the road problem in connection with the feeding of our troops during their retreat from Mons. It was this precise and very detailed grasp of the purely business operations of the Army in the field which made for great generalship. In the brain centre of our million of armed men there was no more heroic romance than was to be found in

COOKS' QUARTERS AWHEEL.
The kitchen of a French armoured train—a curious evolution of the luxurious Continental restaurant car of peace time—arranged as a ship's galley and manned by sailors.

AT A CANADIAN RED CROSS KITCHEN IN FRANCE.
Ambulance men line up for hot soup and meat at midday. On the right a member was piling up an abundant supply of French bread.

the office of Messrs. Vickers & Co., of Sheffield. The power of creative imagination and strength of character were, of course, needed in a commander-in-chief. But even he could do without a creative power of mind if he was a first-rate business man with strength of character and quick and sound methods of using his forces; but he had to be a good judge of men, so as to provide himself with a first-rate Staff, and in his Staff officers he required mainly the qualities that made for success in any business—a good memory, accuracy, grasp of detail, and quickness in coming to sound decisions.

In the early phase of the war, when our force was small and the situation often desperate, and the movements rapid and continually changing, the Irishman and the Englishman finely distinguished themselves. They were men of races with a romantic temperament, the born adventurers of the world. Sir John French was akin to Wellington, Gough, and Roberts, and other brilliant types of the swift-minded Irish gentry. But when the war settled down into a slow, parallel battle, the other British race, which had produced some of the greatest business men in the world, emerged as commanders. A Scottish private, William Robertson, who had won to high rank by extraordinary industry and width and grasp of mind, succeeded Lord Kitchener as general director of all military operations, and became, as our Imperial Chief of Staff, the practical peer of General Joffre, Count von Falkenhayn, and General Alexeieff. And to augment this triumph of hard-headed Scotland, Sir Douglas Haig succeeded Lord French as commander of a million men in France and Flanders, while another Scotsman, Sir Charles Monro, became leader of the Mediterranean Force, and yet another Scotsman, Sir Archibald Murray, took over the command in Egypt.

Our debt to Caledonia

SPARTAN JUVENILE IN THE RANKS.
Little waif discovered by the roadside in France and promptly adopted as a mascot by the cooks of a British camp.

It was an incomparable situation, and perhaps it would have been impossible to find in any part of the world, except Scotland and districts colonised mainly by Scots, any race capable of excelling the real Prussians in those virtues of mind which have made them successful. There is a good deal of Scottish blood in East and West Prussia, and it was only after the great Scottish emigration in the Jacobite period that Prussia showed signs of intellectual and military greatness. The greatest Prussian thinker Kant—or Cant, as his family sometimes wrote the name—was of Scottish origin, and, from the days of Field-Marshal Keith to the days of Field-Marshal Mackensen, the Scottish leaven in Prussia has been a great factor in the

THE COMMANDER-IN-CHIEF: A STUDY AT EVENTIDE ON A FIELD OF BATTLE.

His attitude suggesting the burden of care that rested on his shoulders—revealing, almost, the thoughts passing through his mind—the Commander-in-Chief, a lonely figure standing apart from his Staff, is silhouetted against an evening sky reddened by the flames of burning villages. What manner of thoughts and emotions are those of a General surveying the scene of destruction after a battle planned by him- self? The realisation of his terrible responsibilities—first, to the nation whose cause has been entrusted to him; secondly, to the soldiers whose lives are in his hands—must be vivid as his eyes rest on the battlefield. The tragic significance of such a scene has been emphasised by the artist in this fine illustration, which recalls many popular works among the paintings of military interest.

national success. Even in Gallipoli we were defeated by the descendant of a man named Sanders, who claimed to be English, but was probably of Scottish origin.

The success of the Prussian must be distinguished from the success of the German Empire that he made, and contemned in the making; for the success of modern Germany was largely the work of the German Jew, and his ostentation, his stucco-fronted luxury, and his worship of all signs of material success did not please the real Prussian. Many Prussian gentlemen still worked for their Government at a salary of three pounds a week, and in spite of some scandals in regard to corruption, they generally did their work earnestly and thoroughly, living simply and very frugally. It is very doubtful if the English or Irish gentry would work like them in our comfort-loving, week-ending, motoring age; so let us all be thankful that Caledonia, with her fine system of popular education and her great tradition of hard work and porridge, produced in our hour of need a band of men with

Sir W. Robertson's great services

the grand virtue of businesslike efficiency. Yorkshire used to reckon herself as hard-headed and businesslike as Scotland, but up to the time of writing, her most famous son, Mr. Asquith, does not seem to have shown in the conduct of the war anything more than a Ciceronian eloquence in explaining the failures of the two Governments of which he has been Prime Minister. Grasp of detail, foresight, and the power of organising in advance, are the supreme qualities in war. The English and Irish races have, however, shown these qualities in the organisation of our Fleet. We have yet to learn who were the men upon the original Munitions Committee that worked from September, 1914, to June 1915, with the result that we did not gain the Battles of Neuve Chapelle, Rouges Bancs, and Festubert because we were only producing 5,000 high-explosive shells a day against the German production of 250,000. Lord French was worn out by his anxieties, but he found, before he left France, most of the Scotsmen who so splendidly continued his work.

It was under Sir William Robertson that our army in

BRITISH AMBULANCE ON THE WEST FRONT.
Officer examining the engine of a British motor-ambulance on the completion of a journey from the field-hospitals.

France and Flanders was organised for trench warfare. He erected the headquarters system which we have been describing, and built up the Staff system, and it is to be presumed that the failure in the Staff work at Loos was not in any way his fault, as he was soon afterwards promoted practically to the supreme command in the Empire. The main lines of the system of military organisation which he adopted were commonplace. General Headquarters was placed centrally behind the three headquarters of each army. Then each army centre had, a few miles in front of it, the headquarters of each army corps, and closer to the enemy every army corps was divided into divisional, brigade, and battalion headquarters. A multitude of Staff officers connected these directing centres, but there were also in the British and Belgian armies new factors in the organisation- the international liaison officers. These officers maintained daily touch between the general and army headquarters of the British, French, and Belgian forces, travelling to and fro in motor-cars.

Much of this linking work was, of course, done by telephone, telegraph, and written reports, sometimes in plain language, sometimes in cipher. But the liaison officers still had much to do in amplifying communications, discussing points of difficulty, and bearing verbal messages of such importance that prevention of all possible leakage was a prime necessity.

New factors in organisation

After the French forces withdrew below the Somme, leaving the British and Belgian armies in control of nearly all the field of battle directly covering the French coast-line, General Foch, the brilliant lieutenant of General Joffre, still exercised a general power of command over Sir Douglas Haig and King Albert. Had there been any shadow of personal ambition or national pride among the British and Belgian leaders, the position of General Foch might have been difficult. In the earlier period he had direct control over a larger and more powerful French army than the Belgian and British forces with whom he co-operated. But the French concentration towards the centre and the

CORNER OF BRITAIN'S GREAT CAMP IN FRANCE.
Good food for good fighters. Roast beef being prepared at a field-kitchen behind the front as a welcome change from "bully."

east had left him with only a small force in front of Roye and north of Ypres, while he still exercised, by means of French liaison officers and personal intercourse, large powers of control over a million Britons and some quarter of a million Belgians. But there was a fine spirit of loyalty, comradeship, and personal friendliness among the allied commanders and Staffs on the north-western front, and the genius of General Foch was so well proved, and his powers of charm and tact so winning, that he held the three armies together with a light touch which yet secured thorough combination.

In this way an absolute unity of control was maintained throughout France and Flanders, which balanced the German unity of control along the other side of the western front. The British and Belgian forces in all their large operations were directed by the French Staff through General Foch, so that the western Allies in the field acted together like one military machine. If, for example, we did not attack the Germans by way of diversion when they were attacking Verdun, it was because General Joffre, General Castelnau, and the French Staff decided that the Germans on our front should be left for a while in peace.

Moreover, there had then come into **Allied Board of Strategists** existence a higher power of command than that which General Joffre wielded. There was an Allied Board of Strategists, on which Russia, Italy, Serbia, Belgium, France, and Britain were represented. It was this Board of General Control which arranged all movements of importance on all the fronts of battle. It had taken long for the Board to organise itself and obtain the general control of all the principal operations of the Allies. Great national ambitions, and even valid elements of national independence, had seemed to be threatened by this large, overruling organisation. Italy, for example, was only at war with Austria-Hungary, and

although she had been attacked by Bavarian infantry and German submarines, reasons yet remained why she should refrain from declaring war upon all the Teutons. The Allied Board of Strategy could not, therefore, arrange all matters in a purely logical way. It could not, for example, make use of Italy's superabundance of infantry in France, while strengthening the Italian offensive in the Alps by means of heavy French and British artillery and shell supplies. In spite, however, of the various political and economical difficulties, the **Political and** general plan of campaign was elaborated **economical difficulties** by the Board, and this reduced the power of all the allied commanders. Each had to wait until all were ready, and it was during this period of waiting that the enemy vainly tried to upset the allied plan for a general campaign by driving in upon Verdun.

Our study of the functions of the liaison officers at our General Headquarters has led us far afield. Now we must return from the Allied Board of Strategists and from the French General Headquarters and General Foch's Headquarters to the comparatively small areas in which our armies were collected. Our Second Army under Sir Herbert Plumer, and our First Army under the successor to Sir Charles Monro, held the line from Boesinghe, north of Ypres, to Grenay, south of Armentières. Our Third Army, under Sir E. H. H. Allenby, held the line between Arras and the Somme. Each of the three generals had his own Headquarters and Staff, his Headquarters often being some twelve or fifteen miles from the firing-line, and situated in a quiet little town close to some junction of highways from which the trenches could rapidly be reinforced. These places were smaller copies of General Headquarters, lapped in the same atmosphere of calm but energetic business. Some miles eastward of each Army Headquarters were the Army Corps Headquarters,

ARMY SERVICE CORPS IN A DRIFT.
British transport waggons partially snowed up near a camp in Flanders just after a severe snowstorm. Still, the almost Arctic weather prevalent during part of the winter of 1915-16 was "enjoyed" in a fine sporting spirit by our fighting men.

THE STRAIGHT ROAD TO THE BATTLE-FRONT.

Men of the British Cyclist Corps halting along a snowy roadway behind the lines in France. The severe blizzard of April, 1916, naturally added greatly to the difficult winter conditions under which our troops fought and worked at the front.

each of which was also a replica in miniature of Sir Douglas Haig's place of business. In our military organisation we seem to have come round to the Continental point of view, and made the army corps of two divisions the unit of military power. It did not consist merely of two divisions under a major-general, but of a complete small army of some 40,000 men. It had a special artillery corps for reinforcing any point of its line, a special Staff for linking all the operations together, its special **Enemy's two** transport, and so on. In some cases it **lucky shots** could be supported by the siege-artillery of the army of which it formed part, but usually it conducted all its business with its own armament.

Some miles beyond the Army Corps Headquarters were its two divisional headquarters, which were often within range of the enemy's siege-ordnance. Then, well among the ruined houses and scattered villages, were the six brigade headquarters, where the brigadier-generals and their small Staffs conducted the actual fighting. In many cases the brigadiers and their officers lived in an underground chamber in the firing-line, working their 4,000 men by means of telephone cables, running beneath the earth from their dug-outs and winding along the walls of the communication trenches to the firing-line and to the artillery observation posts, hidden in the neutral zone between the opposing fronts. Except for their daily rounds of inspection along the deep ditches, the brigadiers did not see much open-air life when in the firing-line. They were office men living in caves, or at best in some very quiet and modest house near the third line. Houses, however, were dangerous lodgings for the brain of a fighting force that was under fire, as enemy gunners naturally were keener to get a hit on the headquarters of a brigade than on a dug-out in a fire-trench. It will be remembered that in the most critical hour of the First Battle of Ypres, on October 31st, 1914, German spies discovered the

Headquarters of our 1st Division and 2nd Division, and enabled the German gunners to put the leader of the 1st Division, General Lomax, temporarily out of action, and also to stun Sir Charles Monro, besides killing six important Staff officers. It was these two lucky shots that produced confusion in our line, and almost led to a great defeat. Had not Lord French and Sir Douglas Haig been able to get quickly to the spot, and take up the duties of General Lomax and Sir Charles Monro, the day might have been lost, and Calais have become a German submarine base.

Most of us have laughed at W. S. Gilbert's creation, the Duke of Plaza-Toro, who always led his army from behind because he found it less exciting. But this rearward position became, for excellent reasons, the best method of leadership. The French seem to have retained, in divisional tactics, the old heroic style of leadership. For instance, in the Second Battle of Champagne, General Marchand went forward at the head of his men, with the result that he was quickly shot down, and his fine talent in handling troops temporarily lost. The Prussian method of keeping all officers behind their men is based on common-sense; for, if the men have a fine spirit, they will go forward when their guns have prepared the way for them, and with their officers guiding them from behind and keeping in touch with each other, manœuvres will be **Duke of Plaza-Toro** executed with more precision, rapidity, **justified** and general cohesion than if subalterns, captains, and even majors break up the machinery of the battalion in order to charge in front of the men. As a matter of fact, both the French and British have been rather given to sacrificing their officers by letting them head the charge. All officers should really be drivers—that is to say, their place should be behind the platoon, the company, or the battalion—where they can see what their men are doing and direct them quickly, and be in turn soon found by any Staff officer charged with a message that needs new

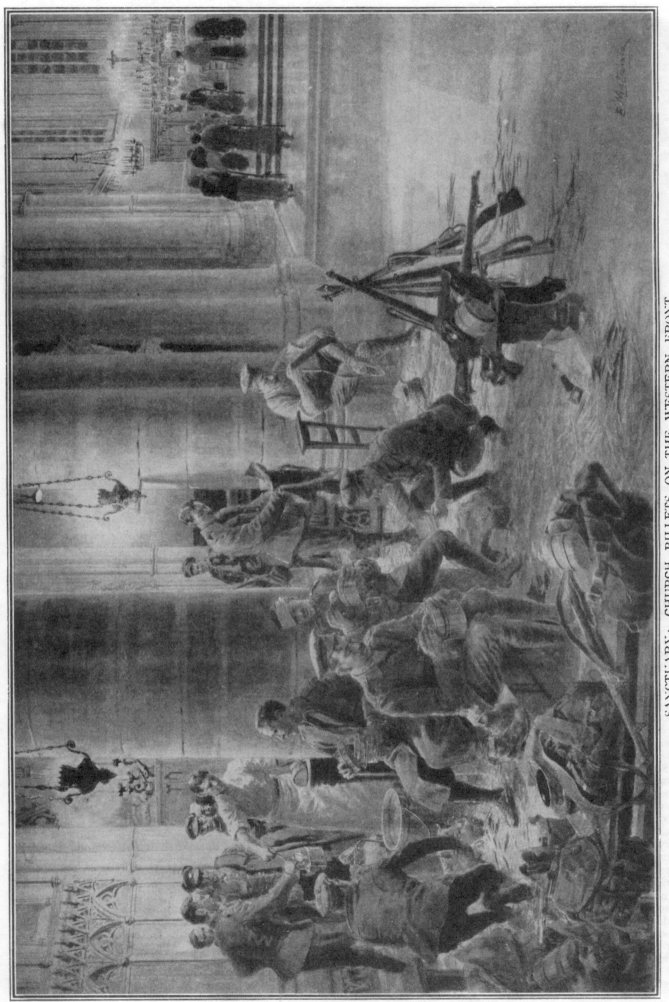

SANCTUARY: CHURCH BILLETS ON THE WESTERN FRONT

British soldiers making themselves comfortable in unusual quarters after a spell of duty in the first-line trenches on the western front. Describing this scene, an officer wrote: "It was an odd sight to see B Company 'at home' in a corner while service was going on before the lighted altar. The men first paid their respects to the cook. After that arms were piled on the floor of the church and wet boots and puttees removed, while the women congregated at the far end and went on unheeding, absorbed in their own cares, and the soldiers settled down to rest.

orders being given at once to the men. There have, however, been occasions when our directing officers and their Staff have been too far behind. One fine Scottish brigade at the Battle of Loos rushed on Lens at such a terrific speed that its brigadier could not catch it up. He did not want the brigade to swerve towards Lens, for just in front of it were one hundred and fifty German guns. We never got those guns. By the time the too rapid Scotsmen paused and pulled themselves together, the opportunity for a rush attack on the enemy's batteries had been lost

In the ordinary circumstances of trench warfare, in which grand charges were almost as rare as holidays, the actual fighting-line was about half a mile **Model German** beyond brigade headquarters. The fight- **trench-making** ing-line usually consisted of a fire-trench, a support-trench, and a reserve trench, connected by zigzagging, narrow communications, and diversified by excavations of every kind and engineering devices of great ingenuity. There were battalion headquarters by the hundred, linked by telephone to the brigadiers and to their own firing trenches and observation posts. The medical officer and the quartermaster lived near the underground orderly-room, where the colonel, the major, the adjutant, and their orderlies watched over the affairs of the battalion. Usually there were two of these battalion

knew precisely the limits of shell penetration in different soils, and constructed their own earthworks accordingly. German-like, they boasted of the impregnability of their line before the great tests came, but the tests proved that their boasts were justified. It was from them that the French and the British armies learned at last at heavy cost the complete science of trench-making, until, as we have seen at Verdun, General Pétain drilled a hundred feet below ground, and there made a city with electric-lighted corridors and air chimneys, with underground kitchens, dining-rooms, and dormitories, in order to beat the Germans in the science of defensive mole warfare.

What we did on our front between the Yser and the Somme cannot be described. But we had a large stretch of chalk which could be cut like cheese with power drills, and as it was notorious that the Germans had concentrated their largest existing force against us, and three thousand guns, beginning with 16·8 in. howitzers, 15 in. cannon, and 12 in. and 8 in. howitzers, coming down to 6 in. howitzers and guns, and ending in 4·1 in. and 3 in. quick-firers, trench-mortars, and aerial-torpedo throwers, it may be supposed that we, too, went rather deep into the ground behind our firing and support lines. The amount of timber sunk on both sides in France was enormous. In fact, the labour spent by Germans, Frenchmen, Belgians, Britons, and Canadians in digging, carpentry, and general and special

[*Photos by Elliott & Fry.*]

MAJOR-GENERAL SIR J. STEEVENS, K.C.B.   MAJOR-GENERAL T. P. BATTERSBY.   MAJOR-GENERAL SIR W. H. BIRKBECK,
Director of Equipment and Ordnance Stores.   Inspector of Army Ordnance Services.   K.C.B., C.M.G.   Director of Remounts.

organisations, one for the men in the fire-trench, and the other for the men in the support-trench. After working for four days as supports, each battalion usually went into the fire-trench for four days, and on being relieved had eight days in billets, which was sometimes a kind of a holiday and at other times was rather the reverse. In fact, some officers and men thought that true peace was to be found in the support-line, while others looked upon a dug-out in the fire-trench as the best place of repose, notwithstanding the bombs that occasionally came from the German trench-mortars.

Trench life had been an utter misery in the old days in Flanders, when the enemy held nearly every comfortable piece of high ground, while we occupied mainly ditches of water in the soaking lowlands. The German engineers then were the best in the world; they put more energy into their work than we and the French did, and introduced modern novelties in an alerter manner. For example, they used electrical power for lighting, pumping, and drilling. In answer to our bombardments they deepened their trenches to nine feet, constructed special winding, bomb-proof stairways to their dug-outs, built mazes of underground forts, and at last connected their fire-trenches with their support-trenches by means of tunnels. Their industry was ant-like and amazingly effective. Having at the time the most powerful armament in existence, the Germans

engineering work would have opened the vast coal-mines of China to the world, and brought down the price of coal by quite fifty per cent. if it had been employed for that purpose. Prop timber became scarce in our country and also in Germany because of the vast demands of the trench-makers. Probably one reason why we had to restrict the import of wood-pulp was that we and our western Allies wanted all available timber for the battle-line. Where it was marshy we had to board the bottom of the trenches; and then, as the trenches universally deepened in answer to the growing power of the artillery, more wood was needed to make the **Prop timber and** firing-step from which rifles could be **paper famine** fired through loopholes in the parapet.

An extraordinary amount of timber was also used for posts on which the barbed-wire was wound in line after line. The enemy destroyed the French and Belgian forests in his occupation in order to build his trenches; and though he had great plantations of fine timber in his own country, he also reduced both his wood-pulp imports and his wood-pulp industry in order to get more timber for military work. Perhaps also the Germans carefully conserved their own timber resources as a valuable asset after the war, having calculated the effect of the drain on all available forest trees during the long parallel battles on the west, south, and east. There were many other things going on behind the

A CAMP BAKERY.

The staff of life in the fields of war. Army bakers preparing bread at a British camp near Salonika.

German fighting-front to which no parallel could be found in the area behind the allied lines. The enemy was a methodical and foreseeing spoiler. Having captured a great amount of Belgian, Russian, and French machinery, he resolved that when peace came it should not work in the markets of the world against him. A good deal of it he removed to his own country, and the larger part of it he destroyed. The first part of his rolling-stock to wear out by constant use was that which he had captured in Belgium and France. Belgium, especially, was likely to need the help of most of the locomotive and carriage builders in Britain and the United States before she could get her railway service into good working order.

The Germans were able to save their own rolling-stock to a very great extent by reason of their admirable network of inland waterways. Happily, France also had a good canal system, and in our part of the front we were able to do a good deal of transport by means of barges. At home, where our canals were in a grievous condition of neglect and complete undevelopment, the situation was saved by the Great Central Railway. If this new line had not been constructed, the other **Had the Channel** northern lines would have been in- **Tunnel existed** adequate to supply London and the southern counties, and at the same time to serve all the needs of our Army and Navy. Our coastwise shipping traffic was seriously checked by the German submarine campaigns, by the commandeering of ships for military purposes, and by the extraordinary rise in freights. Our railways had to do much of the work hitherto done by our coasting vessels; but the fortunate construction of a new, great competitor with the Great Northern and Midland Railways enabled our system to meet the ordeal of a long Continental war. Had the Channel Tunnel also existed, the working connection with our first Expeditionary Force would have been greatly facilitated, and the shipping released would have been sufficient to bring down the cost of living towards something like normal rates. At the same time the freight expenses of our export trade would have been diminished, thus enabling us to seize more of the markets which the Germans had temporarily abandoned. Had we been governed by a master mind, he would have started driving the tunnel as soon as our grip on Ypres was assured. But we had leaders who had to be pushed forward at every step by the slowly gathering force of public opinion.

PROVISIONS AND PRISONERS AT AN ARMY BASE IN FRANCE.

German prisoners assisting in the unloading of supplies of meat for the French troops. Picture above: One of the tanks from which the British Army was supplied with drinking water. They were erected at camps in Britain, France, and Belgium, and held about one hundred thousand gallons of water.

BRITISH ARTILLERY PASSING

CHAPTER CXV.

INDIAN CAVALRY DIVISION

INDIA'S MAGNIFICENT FIGHTING RECORD.

By F. A. McKenzie, Author of "From Tokyo to Tiflis," "The Unveiled East," etc.

Divided Opinion on Employment of Indian Troops—Neither Great Fears nor Extravagant Anticipations Realised—New Conditions for Indian Army—British Officers in Indian Regiments—Indians' Part in Second Battle of Ypres—Tributes to their Gallantry on Other Occasions—Indian Troops' Splendid Dash at Battle of Loos—Indian Army Corps Withdrawn from France in December, 1915 —Prince of Wales Delivers King-Emperor's Farewell Message—Did it Answer to Send the Indian Corps to Flanders?—Indian Troops' Participation in Gallipoli Expedition—Admirable Service of the Indian Mule-Cart Corps—Sharing the Honours with the British North of Anzac—Playing a Prominent Part in Persian Gulf Operations—Fighting in Mesopotamia—Sir John Nixon's Tribute—Share of the Indians in Advance on Bagdad—The Fight at Ctesiphon and the Retreat to Kut-el-Amara—Gallantry of Indian Troops Revealed in Official Honours Lists—Heroes of Nasiriyeh—Further List of Decorations in the "Government of India Gazette"—Participating in the Military Movements in Egypt, at Aden, and in East Africa—How Subahdar Ghulam Haidar, of the 130th Baluchis, Won the 2nd Class of the Indian Order of Merit—Engaged Among the Tribes of Northern India —How Captain Eustace Jotham, of the 51st Sikhs, Won the Victoria Cross—German Attempts to Stir up Disaffection in India —Mutiny of the 5th Indian Light Infantry at Singapore—Plans of the Mutineers Carefully Laid—The Suppression of the Disturbances—The Lahore Conspiracy Case the Outcome of a Plot by Indian Seditionists—Story of Hardial, Leader of the Indian Revolutionists—The Loyalty of the Great Mass of the Indian People—Sir John Hewett's Tribute—The Aga Khan's Work for the Empire—Indian Princes Use their Wealth in the Imperial Cause—Lord Hardinge's Return—Mr. Chamberlain's Statement.

WHEN an Indian army was first despatched to France in 1914—as described in Chapter LXI—many were doubtful about the wisdom of this step, while others entertained extravagant anticipations of what the Indian soldiery would accomplish. The doubters declared it unwise to allow coloured troops to fight Europeans. Our rule in India had been built up on the prestige of the white man. We had refused to permit Indian native troops to participate in the South African War on the plea that this was a white man's war. Why should we alter our policy? To bring the Indian regiments to Europe, to engage them with white foes, to let them mix for a long period in the intimate daily life of European towns and villages, would inevitably shatter the prestige and authority of the white man in the East—so these critics declared.

Others, who supported the despatch of the troops to the West, boasted that Europe would now witness something amazing in war... Here we had, said they, the picked fighting men of the world. Races such as the Gurkha,

FINDING THE RANGE.
Indian artilleryman finding the range for an Indian battery during the campaign in East Africa.

the Rajput, the Dogra, the Pathan, the Garhwali, and the Afridi supplied us with stern warriors who had for untold centuries made battle their chief business. These were soldiers of untamable spirit, fierce, almost fanatically eager, welcoming death as a short cut to greater glory—very different from the town-bred, tender-souled Europeans. White troops had in the past subdued them because of better mechanical equipment. Now, armed with the weapons of the West, and trained in the use of them, they would burst on Europe as a revelation of what a fighting man could be. The tradition of the fierce Indian hillman went before him.

By the spring of 1915 it was possible to judge these forecasts by accomplished facts. Briefly, it may be said that neither the great fears nor the extravagant anticipations had been realised. The white man had not lost prestige. The discipline of the Indian regiments continued strict, and the conduct of the men singularly good. The elaboration of European war, the terrific nature of the instruments employed, the great guns, and the aerial war had probably given many an Indian soldier a fuller realisation of European strength than ever before. The Indian soldier had shown himself brave in action. He had proved his ability to fight by the side of European troops. So long as he had his European officers leading him, he had never failed to respond to any demands made on him. He had, time after time, taken part in advances with the greatest gallantry.

On the other hand, it was undoubtedly true that the Indian temperament severely felt the strain of modern mechanical war. The men of the hills were warriors from childhood and warriors by descent. The Indians of the plains were among the best-drilled and best-trained soldiers in the world. But to them war was a **Indians and** matter of personal combat. Let them **trench warfare** charge against a foe, and none could excel them in daring. Give them a forlorn hope, and they would prove their strength. Send your hillman out as scout or sniper, and he would show the utmost skill, subtlety, and courage in pitting his wits against the wits of his foe.

But in this war the requirements were of another kind. The soldier had to stand day after day, week after week, in the highways of invisible death. A large proportion of the men, even those in the front trenches, never came in touch with a single German from first to last. They waited in muddy trenches, facing a yellow, sodden country-side opposite them. They could see one or two slight ridges a few score yards ahead. The crack of shots fired from the opposite side, which could be almost continu-ously heard, was the main evidence that the enemy was alert.

Every now and then there would come a heavy cloud of greyish-black smoke on the ground among them, as a high-explosive shell burst ahead, or a sudden break of

ON GUARD.
Indian sentry on duty at a camp in France pitched in a scene of rural calm.

firelit white cloud in the sky as shrapnel exploded over-head. The Indian soldier had not been trained for this kind of warfare. The Indian Army was essentially one of cavalry and infantry, not of artillery. It had now to accustom itself to novel and terrible forms of death. Still more surprising and awesome to the men of the East were the aeroplanes which came scattering bombs among them and the submarines which threatened them with death when on the sea.

"We shall fight, even as tigers, for Jarj Panjam!" (King George) said the men. They were thrilled to the heart with pride that they were fighting as brothers side by side with white troops. They proved their valour by their casualties. In the first year of the war the Indians lost 22,935 men. Of these no less than 17,385 were killed or wounded on the western front. But it took all their courage and discipline to stand the strain. Added to the novel nature of the war, they were exposed to the most severe climatic con-ditions. Week after week they crouched in the muddy trenches and countryside of **Severity of** Flanders. They knew little of trench life, **climatic conditions** and understood even less than our white troops did at that time of the right way to modify its severity. These men of the East, accustomed to the sun and the bracing mountains, must have thought the terrible dampness and penetrating cold of the Low Countries a foretaste of their hell. They had few chances of showing their best fighting qualities. Of what they had they availed themselves to the full. They were at war under conditions least suited to their experience or temperament. They stood the strain, not only without demoralisation, but in a way that earned them the utmost credit.

As is well known, the British officer plays a large part in the life of the Indian regiment. He is the father of his

INDIAN CAVALRYMAN ON PATROL DUTY.
These men displayed marked pluck and resourcefulness.

troops, their leader and their chief in a sense that the white officer of a white regiment can hardly claim to be. The British officers showed in these days of great strain of what magnificent material they were. Time after time almost every British officer in a battalion was killed leading his men forward. Take, for example, the case of the 40th Pathans, popularly known as the " Forty Thieves." Shortly after their arrival at the front from Hong Kong they were faced by a desperate task—a night attack over open ground. One officer, Captain **Men worthy of** Dalmahoy, kept on until he was wounded **their officers** six times. Every other officer, save one captain and three subalterns, was wounded or killed, and two subahdars were killed. The men were worthy of their officers. They did splendidly in the charge, and despite all their losses, were ready for another after the fight was over. " They were in fine spirits after their ordeal," said a writer at the time. " They are proud of the worthy part of the ' Izzat ' they have earned, and ready for another slap at the enemy when reinforced."

The large death-rate among the officers had, in some cases, one very serious result. The men relied on their officers. With officers they knew and trusted, they would do anything. Without them, they were at times almost like sheep without a shepherd. It was impossible to find, at short notice, sufficient European officers who knew their language and were trained in their ways to fill the vacancies caused by the casualties.

In the Second Battle of Ypres the Indians played a creditable and costly part. The Lahore Division had one terrible experience. On Saturday, April 24th, 1915, it was marched off at ten minutes' notice to help to repel the great German attack. It was hurried north of Ypres, a march of thirty-three miles, and after a few hours' rest was thrown into battle early on Monday morning. It had to charge 1,200 yards of open country up a hill.

It was absolute murder (wrote one officer afterwards). The Germans had countless machine-guns and any amount of heavy artillery, and the whole country was being shelled for five miles back from our line. The result was that the brigade lost sixty per cent. of its strength, and the division, which went in twelve thousand strong, came out five thousand. We could not get up close to the Germans, but we got on a bit, and made them evacuate one ridge and accounted for many of them, and dug ourselves in, and that line has been held ever since. We thought the whole thing was a big success, as we thought when we went up to the attack that we were to push right through, but we found out afterwards that our division was only meant to do a counter-attack to hold up the German front—and this we certainly did

The division, by its bold advance, saved three other British divisions from being surrounded. Out of thirty-one officers in this officer's battalion, only four were left. The others had been killed, wounded, or invalided. At Ypres the Indians learned a fresh horror of war—poison gas.

Here is a typical narrative related by a correspondent of the " Daily Express " of the doings of the Indians.

A Saxon regiment had captured about fifty yards of one of our trenches held by Territorials, who were driven out by explosive shells blowing in a section of the trench and burying quite half of the defenders. The **Indian heroism** Saxons took possession, but were enfiladed **at Ypres** by rifle and machine-gun fire. Nevertheless, we could not drive them out. Regiment after regiment poured men into this small salient, which rapidly became an inferno, and the tide of German infantry looked like sweeping through our lines. At the critical moment the Territorials were reinforced by an Indian regiment, who got right into the broken trench and bayoneted all the Germans as they came in. The pile of dead became higher and higher, and the enemy retired, and at once the artillery bombardment began again.

The Indians suffered badly, and at the first lull made an attempt to pick up the wounded lying in front of the trench. The Germans at once opened fire with rifles. The Indians tried to charge, but came

TYPES OF INDIAN LANCERS PHOTOGRAPHED IN A SYLVAN ENVIRONMENT NEAR THE BRITISH LINES IN FRANCE.

STIRRING SCENE ON A SNOW-DRIVEN FIELD OF FRANCE.

Sir John French reviewing a body of Indian cavalry some time early in 1915. In spite of severe hardship due to climatic conditions and a total inexperience of the peculiar rigours of trench warfare, the Indians generally behaved with extraordinary gallantry, eliciting high tribute from the Empire's first generalissimo. In writing in his despatch of this particular body of cavalry, Sir John said : "They are magnificent, and will, I feel sure, give the best possible account of themselves when called upon." All ranks of our Indian Army showed the utmost bravery in fighting for their King-Emperor.

under a fire that cut them down as if with scythes. Their second charge met the same result. Three-quarters of the regiment were now out of action. Another Indian regiment came to their support, and two hours later the Germans reopened the bombardment, and followed it by an infantry charge, which was repulsed without much difficulty.

While the Germans were retiring both Indian regiments made a counter-attack, taking the enemy completely by surprise. The Indians' first rush took them right through the Germans, and they actually reached the enemy's trench, although a strong body of Germans were standing their ground between the trenches. An extraordinary position then developed, the Indians fighting with their backs to the German trenches and the Germans with their backs to ours. The Indians charged again, but were driven off. The second time they got through, and then charged back again. The scene as described to me was horrible. Men, slipping in their own and their comrades' blood, hacked and hewed their way through. An eye-witness describes it as "Hell with the lid off."

Too much for the Germans

The Germans fought well, but could not withstand the fury of the Indians, some of whom when wounded tried to struggle to their feet and have another thrust. The fight ended when the Germans surrendered.

Captain O. F. Smith, of the Governor of Bengal's Bodyguard, when describing the gallant behaviour of the Indian troops, told in particular of a company of Sikh infantry which he relieved upon one occasion. These men had lost all their officers but one; they were in a trench up to the waist in icy water. It was December, and they had been there for three days and three nights almost without food. As he waded up the trench he spoke to some of the men, every one of whom was grey with cold and practically frozen from the waist downwards. They all said the same thing: "Sahib, we cannot move but we can still shoot. Take your men away; we will stay here till we die." They had to be carried out bodily, and in thirty-six hours they were back again.

The Maharaja of Baria, on his return from active service with the Meerut Cavalry, said:

The Indian troops are quite cheerful and in excellent spirits, and proud of the fact that they were given an opportunity of fighting the Empire's battle. They have already adapted themselves to trench life, and I can say from my experience that they are fighting heroically. I have had occasion to talk to the Indian troops, who are simply in magnificent spirits and are extremely pleased with the hospital and other arrangements made for them. His Majesty, the King-Emperor, and Queen Mary are very solicitous for the comfort of the Indian troops, and so are Lord Kitchener and Sir John French. The Indian troops are not at all afraid of meeting the enemy, but in the trench fighting they cannot show their mettle. The Gurkhas, the Sikhs, the Rajputs, the Mahrattas, and the Mohammedans are all animated with one spirit—namely, that of upholding the Empire in this gigantic struggle and of adding to the glory of the King-Emperor. They have formed a good opinion of their comrades-in-arms the British and the French, and have been treated with great kindness and consideration by the latter.

The next summer passed for the Indian troops in routine work in and behind the trenches. For some weeks there was a comparative quiet and then, after elaborate preparation, there came, on September 25th, 1915, the great attack by the British forces at Loos. The Battle of Loos is fully described elsewhere in this history, and it is only necessary here to call attention to the particular work of the Indians in it. They fought side by side with the British. The Indian Corps formed part of the forces occupying the line north of Bethune and La Bassée Canal. The Meerut Division of the Indian corps attacked the Moulin du Piètre, advancing splendidly, capturing the position in one great rush. The Germans quickly brought up reserves against it, and after a long and sustained fight

the Indians, in common with the British troops fighting at this point, were obliged to retire to their own trenches. They had fully performed what was expected of them in holding large numbers of the enemy away from the main attack.

The experience of the winter of 1914–15 had proved that the cold and damp of Flanders very severely taxed the Indians. Their services were wanted in other quarters, such as Salonika and Egypt, more suitable to men of Oriental birth. So, in December, 1915, the Indian Army Corps was withdrawn from France. There was a memorable farewell parade when the Prince of Wales, as personal representative of the King-Emperor, delivered the following message from his father:

Officers, non-commissioned officers, and men of the Indian Army Corps:

More than a year ago I summoned you from India to fight for the safety of my Empire and the honour of my pledged word on the battlefields of Belgium and France. The confidence which I then expressed in your sense of duty, your courage, and your chivalry you have since then nobly justified.

I now require your services in another field of action; but before you leave France I send my dear and gallant son, the Prince of Wales, who has shared with my Armies the dangers and hardships of the campaign, to thank you in my name for your services, and to express to you my satisfaction.

British and Indian comrades-in-arms, yours has been a fellowship in toils and hardships, in courage and endurance, often against great

THROUGH THE JUNGLE IN INDIAN FILE.
Indian troops wending their way to the front in East Africa, and about to go into action against the German forces.

odds, in deeds nobly done in days of ever-memorable conflict. In a warfare waged under new conditions, and in peculiarly trying circumstances, you have worthily upheld the honour of the Empire and the great traditions of my Army in India.

I have followed your fortunes with the deepest interest, and watched your gallant actions with pride and satisfaction. I mourn with you the loss of many gallant officers and men. Let it be your consolation, as it was their pride, that they freely gave their lives in a just cause for the honour of their Sovereign and the safety of my Empire. They died as gallant soldiers, and I shall ever hold their sacrifice in grateful remembrance.

You leave France with a just pride in honourable deeds already achieved and with my assured confidence that your proved valour and experience will contribute to further victories in the new fields of action to which you go.

I pray God to bless and guard you and to bring you back safely, when the final victory is won, each to his own home—there to be welcomed with honour among his own people.

The sending of the Indian Corps to Flanders had been a great experiment. Had it answered? One writer, who had an opportunity of studying the Indians in Flanders for many months, Mr. G. Valentine Williams, supplies the answer:

King-Emperor's message of thanks

The Indian Corps has rendered a great, an inestimable service to the British cause. The first contingent came into the field at a moment when every man was wanted, and as its numbers were completed, it took over its share of our line and held it efficiently. Everything in trench warfare was new to the Indians, and for

INDIANS ON OUTPOST DUTY IN EAST AFRICA.

Infantrymen holding an advanced position, barricaded with boulders, in East Africa. In that campaign, where the forces under General Smuts' command were representative of the whole Empire, the Indian troops played a gallant part.

months they had no opportunity of displaying those qualities of dash that won fame in many a hard fight in their own land. But they showed themselves to be excellent marksmen, and on patrol work revealed a cool pluck and resourcefulness which brought in much valuable information. . . . Both for the Indians themselves and for the Empire the sending of the Indian Corps to Europe was a great adventure, in many respects the most remarkable event of the world-war. The future lies on the knees of the gods, but to those, like the writer, who have seen the British and Indian troops side by side in the field, one thing at least is clear, and that is, that this campaign has knit even closer than before the ties of affection and respect existing between the Indian

Gurkha gallantry on Gallipoli soldier and his British leaders.*

Indian troops participated to the full in the British expedition to Gallipoli. Indian infantry and artillery took part in the first landing. On May 11th the 29th Indian Infantry Brigade replaced the 29th Division, which had been for eighteen days and nights in the actual firing-line. This brigade just about the same time had a leading hand in a brilliant little affair. The Turkish right rested upon a steep cliff jutting out into the sea, which the enemy had converted into a powerful bastion, strongly defended by machine-guns which held up the left of our attacks. Two attempts had already been made to drive the Turks from this point, and both had failed. Then the Gurkhas struck. Their scouts descended to the sea, moved for some distance through the broken ground along the shore, and then crawled up the steep face of the cliff. As they reached the top they found the Turks were waiting, and ready to pour a heavy fire on them. It was impossible to capture the position then, but valuable information had been obtained, and next day Major-General H. B. Cox, commanding the 29th Indian Infantry Brigade, drew up a plan for a concerted attack on the bluff, which the army had named, in honour of the Gurkhas' advance, "Gurkha Bluff." The plan was approved. Heavy firing was opened upon the Turkish position by our warships, our divisional artillery, and some British troops. Under cover of this fire a double company of the 1/6th Gurkhas again crept along the shore. While the attention of the Turks was distracted by the heavy bombardment, the Gurkhas swiftly mounted the cliffs and stormed the position

with a rush. Then the machine-gun section of the Gurkhas was hurried forward, and a second double company was pushed up to join the first. These two companies extended and entrenched. They were joined by a third double company which rushed across the open under a heavy rifle and machine-gun fire, and formed another line. A fourth double company moved up as support. In the end not only was the position taken, but the British line was advanced by nearly five hundred yards.

The Indian Mule-cart Corps did admirable service in the very dangerous and difficult work of bringing up supplies. The mules employed by this corps were singularly fine animals. Happily they were all saved at Anzac, and nearly all at Suvla. The Indians managed the mules as though they were well-trained dogs, and behaved with the greatest patience under the severe trial of tempest and frost.

In the attack on the Turkish positions on June 4th and 5th, the 14th (Ferozepore) Sikh Infantry played a leading part. Sir Ian Hamilton, in a message to General Sir Beauchamp Duff, Commander-in-Chief in India, gave him a glowing description of what this regiment had done. When the main attack on the enemy's trenches failed, two companies would not retire, but held on to the edge of a ravine, losing all their British officers and forty-five per cent. of the men. The battalion went into action with a strength of fifteen British officers, fourteen Indian officers, and five hundred and fourteen rank and file. Next morning the unwounded numbered only three British and three Indian officers and one hundred and thirty-four rank and file. Even these heavy losses did not cause the Sikhs to waver. "In the highest sense of the word," wrote Sir Ian, **Sikh infantry's leading part** "extreme gallantry has been shown by this fine battalion; not an inch of ground was given up, and not a straggler came back. . . . The defence of the point gained in the ravine with an enemy entrenched on both sides above it speaks for itself, and is a very fine example of the way the Sikh bears himself as a stubborn fighting man." The general told how the Lancashire Fusiliers and the Worcesters were full of admiration for the gallantry of their Indian comrades. In conclusion, he

* "With Our Army in Flanders." By G. Valentine Williams.

wrote : " The history of the Sikhs affords many instances of their value as soldiers, but it may safely be asserted that nothing finer than the grim valour and steady discipline displayed by them on June 4th has ever been done by soldiers of the Khalsa."

In the tremendous fighting north of Anzac, early in August, Indian troops shared the honours with the British. The Indians co-operated with the New Zealanders in the approach on Sari Bair, and one New Zealand officer, Major Overton, was killed while guiding the Indian column through the night. In the fighting at Suvla Bay later in August the Indians carried out an attack on the northern flank of the Anzac position, and established themselves on a line from the hills to the plain where they were in touch. On Gallipoli India shared the common sacrifice and common glory with the British, the Australians, and the New Zealanders.

Meanwhile, events were developing in the region of the Persian Gulf in which the Indians were to play a prominent part. The Indian Government attempted to strike a blow at the very heart of Turkish Asiatic prestige by the capture of Bagdad. It aimed further so to establish the British position in Persia that an anti-British agitation, which had been carefully fostered there by German agents, should be completely broken up.

Indian troops in Mesopotamia

In November, 1914, a few days after the entry of Turkey into the war, troops from India reached the mouth of the Shat-el-Arab, in the Persian Gulf, and landed there. The Indian Government, knowing that the position of Turkey was very doubtful, had despatched a complete brigade, under General Delamain, with some mountain batteries to Bahrein Islands in October, ready to strike at the first moment. This brigade seized Fao on November 6th, and the important town of Basra immediately after-

wards. Severe fighting followed, the enemy being time after time repulsed. General Sir A. A. Barrett arrived with further troops on November 12th, and then the real advance began. Town after town was attacked and captured.

It is not the purpose of this chapter to tell in full the story of the Mesopotamian campaign—which is fully dealt with in other chapters in this history—except in so far as it directly affected the Indian troops. In the fighting under General Gorringe's command the Indians played a very large part. This general's force established itself, early in July, about two and a half miles from the junction of the Hokeike with the Euphrates. On July 5th the 30th Infantry Brigade, commanded by Major-General Mellis, advanced to attack the enemy. Among the regiments engaged were the 76th Punjabis, the 24th Punjabis, the 30th Mountain Battery, and the 2/7th Gurkhas. The troops advanced in part in bellums—local boats—through the flooded country. The 24th Punjabis had to carry their bellums across some sixty yards of dry land before they could cross the Euphrates to take possession of the enemy's position and batteries. An enemy detachment composed of 1,000 regular Turkish troops, 2,000 Arabs, four guns, and two Thornycroft launches armed with pom-poms opposed our men. Our troops captured one hundred and thirty prisoners, took four guns, and occupied the enemy position at a cost to us of twenty-six killed and eighty-five wounded. On July 13th and 14th the 24th Punjabis distinguished themselves by a gallant attempt to capture some sand-hills behind certain entrenchments held by the Turks. They met, however, with unexpectedly strong opposition. They were attacked in the rear by Arab tribesmen, and had to withdraw. In General Gorringe's operations for the capture of Nasiriyeh, which was occupied on July 25th, the Indians,

Notable services at Nasiriyeh

INDIAN PREPARATIONS TO CONQUER GERMAN EAST AFRICA.
Shiploads of camels, sent from India for transport work, were unloaded by means of these native boats. The " ships of the desert " naturally proved of immense value to the Indo-British troops during the East African campaign.

RAJPUT, DOGRA, AND SIKH: SOLDIER TYPES IN THE INDIAN ARMY CORPS.

Representatives of warrior races and castes of India—types sketched by a French artist at a camp in France. Left: A Rajput of the bluest blood of the Hindus, the Kshatriya, or warrior caste, descended from the ancient Scythian conquerors of India. Centre: One of the Dogras, a Rajput offshoot from the Himalayan foothill region of Kumaon. From these districts, too, came the celebrated Garhwalis, one of whom was the first Indian to win the Victoria Cross—Naik Darwan Sing Negi. Right: A Sikh, one of the famed warriors of Northern India.

like the British, responded to every call. One instance of special gallantry must be mentioned. Subahdar Major Ajab Khan and twenty men of the 76th Punjabis swam the River Kerkha under heavy fire—a river two hundred and fifty yards wide, with a rapid and deep current. They brought back a boat in which troops were ferried across until sufficient were collected to assault a stout mud fort strongly held by the enemy. Several other instances of gallantry at this time are described further on in this chapter. The first stage of the operations

Sir John Nixon's fine tribute was so successful that Persian Arabistan was cleared of the enemy, and the Arab tribes forced to submit.

Seldom, if ever (wrote Sir John Nixon in his official report), have our troops been called upon to campaign in more trying heat, but the spirit of the troops never flagged, and in the assault on entrenchments which the Turks thought impregnable, British and Indian soldiers displayed the gallantry and devotion to duty worthy of the highest traditions of the Service.

The expedition—one to possess a melancholy and glorious interest for Britain in the months ahead—that set out from Kurna early on the morning of May 31st, 1915, under the command of General Townshend, included, besides a number of British regiments, a strong Indian contingent.

Men who witnessed the work of both British and Indians in this advance had no praise too great for either. Thus Sir Mark Sykes wrote:

These British soldiers, so clean and so cheerful, have carried a wonderful load through this campaign; they have borne heat, vermin, mosquitoes, fever, double duty, heavy casualties in the field; sunstroke, heat stroke, malaria, and typhoid have exacted a dismal toll, and anyone who counts the casualties in the various actions, and compares them with the numbers engaged, will perceive that the fighting has in Mesopotamia been as severe, if not as persistent, as anywhere in the war. If the British soldier leads, the Sepoy has not been slow to follow.

The real significance of General Townshend's move began in time to reveal itself to the outside world. Here was an army that had slowly and laboriously made its way up from the Persian Gulf, braving the most appalling, the most critical conditions, working through fever-haunted zones, meeting strong enemies time after time, and shattering them one after another in steady succession. Its objective was Bagdad, the most famous city of

Arabia, the old-time capital of the Mohammedan world, and still the centre of Mohammedan tradition. Here our troops could stay and await the arrival of the armies of the Grand Duke Nicholas, already preparing to launch their amazingly triumphant march from the Caucasus southwards. Every Indian soldier marching in the toilsome advances northwards felt something of the touch of the greatness of his task. Even the British soldier, in the East for the first time, could not fail to understand—as he passed through cities whose very names proclaimed them to be the garden of the world, the site of Eden, cities that had been the home of humanity's most ancient civilisation—that here by his terrific work and tremendous sacrifice he was attempting something amazingly daring with very feeble resources.

It is difficult to describe the share of the Indians in this advance, apart from that of the British, for they were intermingled. Take, for example, the first fighting northeast of Kut. Here three or four months of preparation had converted a point of great natural advantages for defence into a really formidable obstacle. The Turkish commander, Nuredin Pasha, had an army of some 10,000 regulars, in addition to a large force of Arab irregulars. His position extended for six miles on either side of the Tigris. On the right bank the Turkish right wing had as its front a canal embankment, twenty feet high, topped by high watch-towers. On the left bank trenches extended for two miles to a marsh two miles wide, and on the other side of the marsh further trenches ran to still another marsh guarding the Turkish flank. The stream itself was dammed. Wire entanglements, carefully concealed gun positions, and several other obstacles barred the way of the attacking force. **First fighting near Kut**

Major-General Townshend laid down a plan of battle. A vigorous attack, in reality nothing more than a feint, was made on the Turkish right by Brigadier-General Delamain. A brigade, under Major-General Fry, came up in boats and held the Turkish centre on the left bank. While these operations were proceeding, a bridge of boats was quickly built. As soon as darkness fell on the first evening the main body of General Delamain's troops was transferred to the extreme Turkish left between the two

372

SIKH, GURKHA, AND INDIAN MOHAMMEDAN: WARRIORS WHO FOUGHT FOR THE KING-EMPEROR.

Left: Another Sikh. Men of this community of fighters neither smoke nor eat beef. Centre: A Gurkha, another race of Rajput ancestry, but now of mixed blood. The Gurkha gained prominence in France for his unflinching bravery in hand-to-hand fighting with his fearsome knife, the kukri. Right: An Indian Mohammedan, from which race our Punjab regiments are recruited. The Pathan (or Afghan) tribesmen of the Indian Army are in the same religious category. On duty their common tongue is Urdu, but ordinarily each uses its own language.

marshes. This was reinforced by a number of men sent by General Fry from the centre. On the morning of September 28th the 16th and 17th Infantry Brigades, under Brigadier-General Delamain, advanced in two columns against the extreme Turkish left. British and Indian troops fought for the honour of being first in the trenches. The first actually to arrive was the 1st Battalion of the Dorsetshires, the 117th Mahrattas, and the 22nd Company of Sappers and Miners. By two o'clock in the afternoon the whole of the enemy's northern position was in our hands.

The battle was fought under such physical conditions that it is difficult for people living in a temperate climate to realise them. The men had been marching and fighting since the previous morning, and had had no water since the previous evening. The day was very hot, and men and horses endured agony from thirst. There was marsh water, it is true, but it was so abominable that even the thirstiest could not drink it. Dense clouds of dust swept the desert the whole of the day, and added to the torment of the troops. General Delamain realised that his soldiers had almost reached the end of possible endurance and commenced to wheel his left round the marsh towards the river in the hope of finding water. Just then strong hostile reserves appeared from the south-west. Thirst and fatigue were forgotten. The enemy was routed with one magnificent rush. That night the troops bivouacked on the scene of their victory, about two miles from the river.

Tested almost beyond endurance They suffered tortures untold for want of water. Next morning, when the column reached the river, the horses got their first drink for forty hours. The Turks evacuated their main trenches during the night, and escaped along the bank of the Tigris. Our cavalry were not in sufficient strength to pursue them immediately, especially as they were covered by a strong rearguard of infantry and guns. The Turks lost 4,000 men in casualties, including 1,153 taken prisoners by us. Our own casualties were less than one-third of that amount, a large proportion of the men being only slightly wounded.

It is unnecessary to dwell here on the fight at Ctesiphon —almost within view of Bagdad—and the subsequent retreat. On December 5th the retreating troops reached Kut-el-Amara on the Tigris, a hundred miles south of Bagdad as the crow flies. Here they found their road farther south cut off. There was nothing for the general but to halt at this spot, to occupy the commanding positions around, and to repulse time after time the fierce assaults of the gathering Turkish armies, which already saw their prey within their grasp.

As soon as news came through of General Townshend's desperate plight a relieving force was sent out to his aid. A number of Indian and British troops were despatched, first under command of General Aylmer, and then under Sir George Gorringe, who was promoted to Lieutenant-General. Some of the Indian regiments included in this enterprise had previously taken part in the European campaign. They now found themselves face to face with still more desperate conditions, as they tried time after time—alas! in vain—to break through strong Turkish positions which lay between them and General Townshend's sorely-stricken force.

Examples in the Honours Lists

The official Honours Lists gave many illustrations of the gallantry of Indian soldiers. Here are some typical cases.

One lance-naik and two sepoys of the 76th Punjabis were gazetted to the Indian Order of Merit for conspicuous gallantry at Gurma Safha, where they attempted to move machine-guns out of an impossible position under a heavy fire. Several others had the Indian Order of Merit bestowed upon them for conspicuous gallantry near Nasiriyeh in July. Lance-Naik Gosain was decorated for carrying Captain Leslie Smith's body out of action under heavy fire and not abandoning it until isolated and surrounded by Arabs, when he tried to hide the body. Sepoy Parmodh, of the 24th Punjabis, was decorated for bringing back under heavy fire a wounded havildar and a sepoy. The party became isolated, and was attacked by Arabs. The wounded men helped each other back, while Parmodh Singh kept the Arabs at bay. He eventually brought the two wounded men to safety. Sepoys Gheba Khan and Feroz Khan were decorated for carrying Major Morton, who was mortally wounded, out of action. Both of these

IN SHORTS AND SUN HATS.
The Mohmand campaign on the North-West Indian Frontier. British patrol about to engage the enemy.

BRITAIN'S LITTLE WAR IN REMOTE ASIA.
The Empire's outpost attacking the Mohmands on the North-West Frontier of India.

Havildar Sarayun Singh who had fallen in an exposed position a hundred yards from the enemy. Kunda Singh hoisted the havildar on his back and attempted to carry him off, when he himself was shot down. Havildar Harbraj Rail, of the 2/7th Gurkhas, backed by only seven men, initiated an attack against an entrenched picket of thirteen men, and accounted for all of them. Rifleman Narman Rai, 2/7th Gurkhas, attacked a party of Turks who had fired after hoisting the white flag, and cut down seven with his kukri.

Another issue of the "Government of India Gazette" gave a further list of decorations. Resaldar Pren Singh and Jemadar Copal Singh, of the 16th Cavalry, were both gazetted to a

men were killed in endeavouring to save their officer. Subahdar Sohan Singh, 24th Punjabis, was distinguished for bringing up reinforcements under a heavy fire to the companies attacking the sand-hills. In the words of the official communication, "He displayed great courage and coolness."

Another sepoy, Mangal Singh, also of the 24th Punjabis, remained with Captain Simkinson, who was wounded, until sent back by him for ammunition. On his return he remained in the firing-line until rescued by a party sent up in a bellum at the end of the attack. Sepoy Lachman Singh, 24th Punjabis, made several efforts to go back under a heavy fire, after the withdrawal had begun and search for wounded officers.

A number of Indians distinguished themselves at Nasiriyeh on July 24th, and received decorations. Sepoy Partab Singh, of the 90th Punjabis, was wounded twice in the upper part of his right arm during an attack. He refused to go back or even to have his wounds dressed, but kept on advancing and fighting. Again he was struck by a bullet, and had two fingers cut off. He was now unable to use his rifle, but he still refused **Young sepoy's** to fall back, and busied himself **gallantry under fire** in helping to bind up the other wounded and generally assist them. He was a young soldier with only one and a half year's service to his credit. Lance-Naik Hari Tingri, 22nd Sappers, exposed himself to heavy fire in order to complete the upper structure of a bridge. He was severely wounded in the leg, but continued to work on, and completed his task before he gave in. When a pioneer bridging-party was attempting to bridge the Mejeninch Creek both Indian officers were wounded. Thereupon, Havildar Bhag Singh, of the 48th Pioneers, assumed command of the men and carried through the task with great coolness and courage. Lance-Naik Kunda Singh, of the 90th Punjabis, was killed while seeking to rescue

posthumous honour in the Indian Order of Merit; the one for courageously leading and the other for supporting a gallant charge into the middle of four hundred of the enemy at Bushire, who were thereby thoroughly disorganised. Sepoy Ramkishor Singh, 11th Rajputs, was decorated for conspicuous gallantry and coolness at the same place. Wounded, and the only man left, he nobly assisted Lieut. Staples in working one of the machine-guns under heavy fire. Another sepoy received the coveted order for continuing to fight after being twice wounded. Havildar Shah Nawaz Khan, 109th Infantry, received the Order of Merit on account of his great exertions at Lahej, near Aden, in bringing up guns during an ugly action. He handled his men well throughout, and showed much discretion in checking **Awards of the** two rushes of the enemy. These are a **Order of Merit** few instances selected out of very many.

In addition to the fighting in Mesopotamia, the Indian troops actively participated in the military movements in Egypt, on the Suez Canal, at Aden, in East Africa, and elsewhere during the autumn and winter of 1915-16.

One example of the work in East Africa was given in the "Gazette" in a notification of the posthumous bestowal of the 2nd Class of the Indian Order of Merit upon Subahdar Ghulam Haidar, of the 130th Baluchis, for conspicuous gallantry on May 5th, 1915, at Mouyuni, East Africa. While in charge of a patrol of fifteen men he boldly led them to attack a party of the enemy one hundred strong, with three machine-guns. "The conduct of this officer was most prompt and gallant," says the official notification. He was wounded and died from his wounds the next day. In connection with the same affair the Indian Distinguished Service Medal was awarded to Havildar Muhammad Ali, Jemadar Mehar Singh, and Sepoy Purna Singh, of the 130th Baluchis.

While large Indian forces were helping to maintain the honour of the Empire in these various parts, other forces were engaged among the tribes of Northern India. A notable instance of their work was made public by the conferring of the Victoria Cross upon the late Captain Eustace Jotham, of the 51st Sikhs. On **Notable work in Northern India** January 7th, 1915, during operations against the Khostwal tribesmen, Captain Jotham, who was commanding a party of about a dozen of the North Waziristan Militia, was attacked in a nullah and almost surrounded by an overwhelming tribal force of fifteen hundred well-armed Zadrans, Tannis, Gurbaz, and other Khostwal tribesmen, subjects of Afghanistan, who had crossed the frontier to British territory. Seeing that it was hopeless for thirteen or fourteen men to attempt to resist fifteen hundred, Captain Jotham gave the order to retire. He could have escaped himself, but he most gallantly sacrificed his own life in endeavouring to carry into safety a militia sowar who had lost his horse. The enemy were ultimately driven off by militia reinforcements which came up, and were later on attacked and heavily defeated by General Fane with a movable column, which inflicted salutary punishment on them.

The position in India itself was one of great interest. The German Government had made, in the days before the war, elaborate plans for stirring up Indian disaffection when war came. It was particularly hoped to appeal to the Mohammedans and to provoke a Holy War against the British. This

SIGNALLERS AT WORK.
Loyal native soldiers helping to guard their country from the Mohmands.

INFORMATION BY FLAG.
Another view of heliographers and signallers in communication with artillery.

attempt, which was described in Chapter LXI. of THE GREAT WAR, was resisted by the leaders of Indian Mohammedanism and by the great Indian Mohammedan chiefs. It failed in its main purpose. But the anti-British propaganda was not without some result. In a few districts, notably in Singapore, Lahore, Calcutta, and Rangoon, more or less serious trouble broke out. On the Indian frontier various Mohammedan tribes, notably the Bunerwals, attempted to stir up revolts against the British Raj.

The most dramatic disturbance came at Singapore, where the 5th Indian Light Infantry broke into open mutiny. On February 15th, 1915, when part of the European community at Singapore was in the park near the golf-course, enjoying the cool of the evening, rifle firing started, apparently from various points simultaneously, and several of the Europeans fell mortally wounded. An alarm was raised, and the local volunteers were quickly mobilised. Some men were landed from a British war sloop then in the harbour, and every available white man who could bear arms was enrolled. European civilians not belonging to the volunteer force were made special constables. Wireless messages flashed **The revolt at Singapore** across the waters, and word went out that an Indian regiment had mutinied and was shooting down Europeans wherever it could find them.

A number of Europeans, often with wives and children, were living in outlying bungalows. Others had been out driving or motoring that afternoon and were at the mercy of the mutineers. The greatest anxiety was aroused about their fate, an anxiety that in some cases proved only too well founded. Some were murdered in cold blood by the revolting soldiers as they drove unsuspectingly along; officers and civilians were shot down

MOHMANDS SIGHTED!
Getting ready to stop a sudden rush of Mohmands—one man is about to fix his bayonet.

GURKHAS WITH THE TIGRIS FORCE.
Turkish prisoners captured during the fighting along the Tigris being escorted by a guard of Gurkhas. Indians fought splendidly throughout the campaign for Bagdad, the ancient capital of the Mohammedan world.

mutinied was eight hundred and eighteen. There was no particular reason for their uprising save the general unrest. There was said to have been some discontent in the regiment over promotions, and the rank and file did not like the prospect of shortly having to remove to Hong Kong. The fighting began on the afternoon of February 15th. By the morning of the 18th the situation was well in hand. By March 1st not more than sixty-two of the rebels were still at large. Most of the others had surrendered, and fifty-six had been killed, wounded, or drowned. Fortunately their supply of ammunition was limited and was quickly exhausted. Before another week almost every one of the mutineers was accounted for, either as a casualty or as a prisoner.

without warning. The volunteers and other armed men were sent out to rescue and bring in all Europeans they could. All that night guerilla fighting was maintained.

Sailors and Marines were landed from several foreign warships within call. The Sultan of Johore volunteered the use of his land troops. A number of the Japanese residents enrolled themselves as volunteers, under the Japanese Consul-General. Admiral Huguet hurried to Singapore without waiting for instruc-

Dramatic arrival of the French tions, and landed a considerable French force on the morning of February 17th, at what was perhaps the most critical moment of all. Many of the people of Singapore openly declared that the French had saved the situation. It is at least certain that the dramatic appearance of the French shattered the hopes of the mutineers and prevented an extension of their revolt. The Russians co-operated splendidly, and a column was landed from a Russian warship on February 20th. The French Governor-General at Saigon telegraphed offering assistance and desiring to send additional troops. It was now no longer necessary.

The plans of the mutineers had been carefully laid. There is little doubt that they had been urged in their course by some of the Germans interned at Singapore. The mutineers took possession of the camp of the German prisoners shortly after the outbreak and released them. Most of these German prisoners were quickly recaptured, while others who succeeded in reaching a Dutch island not far from Singapore were interned there. The original scheme of the mutineers was to begin the outbreak after midnight on February 15th, to make their way into the town, and to murder as many Europeans as possible in their sleep. Happily some of the men were too impatient to wait for the appointed hour, and their premature outbreak gave the European community the chance to rally its forces.

The number of troops who

The Lahore conspiracy case was the outcome of a plot by Indian seditionists, originating in America some time before the war began. One of the leaders of the Indian revolutionists, Hardial by name, was the centre of the plot. Hardial was an Indian scholar who lived for some time in England and studied at Oxford, having been awarded a scholarship by the Punjab Government. While in England he became most intensely anti-British. As stated in the judicial findings, " He appears to have become imbued with an extraordinarily unreasoning race-hatred and to have developed into a monomaniac—dangerous because he appears to have possessed **Leader of the Lahore conspiracy** certain powers of speech, and because he thereafter devoted himself to inoculating others with the same race-hatred."

From England he went to America, where he matured his schemes. In the summer of 1914 he gathered a large number of Hindus together there, and sent them back to India for the deliberate purpose of warring against the Government. On the way back they were joined by other Hindus at various places in the Far East. When they reached the Punjab they scattered themselves

STUDYING THE WEAPONS OF THE WEST.
In an Indian cavalry camp near the British front. A French officer explaining the mechanism of the French carbine to Indian officers.

General Sir Pertab Singh leading the Jodhpur Lancers through a French village.

Saving a wounded comrade: Sikh sergeant keeps German patrol at bay.

The herb of Peace in the trenches of War: Indian troops around an improvised pipe.

379

For the glory of the Raj: Indian troops charging the German trenches at Neuve Chapelle, March, 1915.

round the countryside and then set about creating disturbances of every possible kind. Some of them worked at attempting to seduce troops from their allegiance to the British Raj. Arms were collected, dacoity was begun, and a number of isolated attacks on railways, bridges, and general communications was reported. The people were told that the British Government had retired from India to fight the Germans, and that the British no longer could rule them. The whole thing was to culminate in a general rising on February 21st, 1915.

The police could see by the unusual disorder that extraordinary trouble was in the air. The plans of the conspirators were carefully guarded, but the authorities obtained a clue to what was threatened, and raided the headquarters of the conspiracy on the day before the uprising was to begin. A series of sensational trials followed at Lahore. In all several hundred persons were convicted, and received sentences varying from death to six months' imprisonment.

At Rangoon a plot to murder all Europeans was discovered, but no details were ever made public. A native regiment was arrested in a body, five of the leaders were shot and the rest sent to an outlying island. For the time being the British volunteers took possession, and their place was afterwards taken by a Territorial regiment from home. There was also some trouble at Calcutta.

These isolated examples of revolt only served to throw into bolder relief the loyalty of the great mass of the Indian peoples. "The attitude of the Indian peoples in this respect, to my mind, is marvellous," said Sir John Hewett, one of the most eminent of retired Anglo-Indian administrators, after a prolonged visit to India at the close of 1915.

WADING THROUGH THE MARSHES OF MESOPOTAMIA.
Indian troops advancing to the support of a British attack in the Persian Gulf region. To the left is a machine-gun detachment, the dismantled weapon being carried in its separate parts.

The Ruling Chiefs, in particular, lose no opportunity of giving the clearest proofs of their loyalty to the King-Emperor and devotion to the British Empire. One must not forget that we are at war with a Mohammedan Power, and must make every allowance for the very uncomfortable position in which the Moslems of India are placed. Their behaviour generally—in the circumstances—has been all that we could expect, and there is no doubt whatever that the overwhelming majority of the people of India are heart and soul in our favour. Of course, there is no

Sir John Hewett's tribute

blinking the fact that there have been, even quite recently, seditious manifestations—as a matter of fact, when I landed there three tribunals were sitting in different parts of the country to deal with offenders, although before I left two of these, those at Calcutta and Benares, had concluded their labours—but such manifestations have been confined to particular areas, and have not indicated any sign of the general public being affected by them in the least degree. It would be unwise to shut one's eyes to the possibility of trouble on the frontier, but two comparatively new factors in war—high explosives and aeroplanes—will tend to deter the frontier tribesmen from rushing into hostilities with the Government of India. One thing that struck me forcibly was the fact that the term "the never-changing East" cannot in any sense be applied to India.

The only ground I discovered for uneasiness was the presence in some of the Native States of naturalised Germans, who are still, for some reason I am quite unable to fathom, allowed to remain at large.*

The Aga Khan, the head of the Ismaili Moslems, particularly distinguished himself from the first by his strenuous work for the British cause. In April, 1916, the King-Emperor bestowed the distinguished honour upon the Aga Khan of having for life a salute of eleven guns and the rank and status of a First-Class Chief in the Bombay Presidency. The Aga Khan's authority was spiritual, not territorial, which made the honour all the more exceptional. The King-Emperor's action gave the greatest satisfaction to the Mohammedan peoples. As one Indian writer said at the time, "It is chiefly due to the widespread influence which he exercises that the Moslems throughout the Empire have remained staunch in their allegiance at a time when their religious sympathies

* Interview in the "Morning Post."

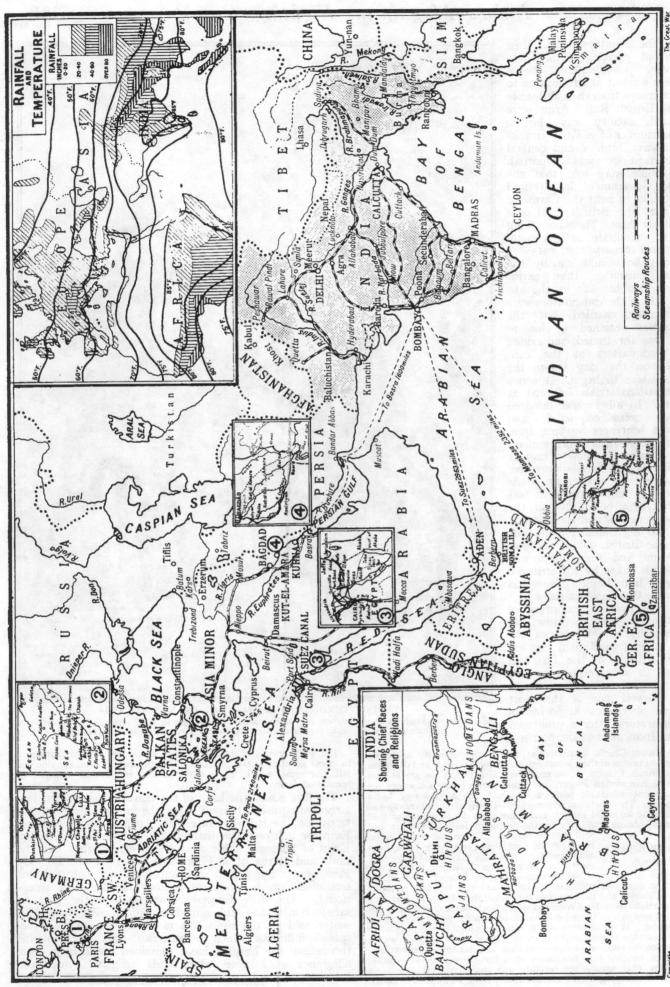

MAP TO ILLUSTRATE THE IMPORTANT PART PLAYED BY INDIAN TROOPS IN THE WAR.

All battle areas in which Indian troops were engaged are shown in larger scale (in squares). Top right-hand corner: Diagram illustrating climatic changes Indian troops had to contend with. Bottom left-hand corner: Map of India showing localities whence the various regiments came. The distances in miles they had to travel are also indicated.

The Great War

cannot fail to be with the unhappy Ottoman victims of German duplicity and intrigue. He has earned the bitter hatred of the enemies of Britain."

Indian princes continued to use their wealth in the Imperial cause. One typical list of their gifts published in September, 1915, included: From the Maharaja Scindhia of Gwalior, one lac of rupees to the Minister of Munitions and for the equipment of X-ray apparatus;

Typical gifts of Indian princes

from the Maharaja of Bhaunagar, a workshop and a State hospital for wounded Indians from the front; from the Rani of Dhar, £700 to the Queen's Fund for the relief of the wounded; from the Chief of the Sangli, 30,000 rupees for the purchase of motor-ambulances; from the Prime Minister of Nepal, 340 Nepalese mechanics to manufacture munitions; from the Maharaja of Kolhapur, 39,000 rupees subscribed by officers for motor-ambulances; from the Raja of Manipur, four motor-ambulances; from the Junagarh Durbar, three armed aeroplanes; from the Raja of Bariya, a State hospital for wounded Indians; from the Thakur Sahib of Morvi, workshops to manufacture munitions; from the Maharaja of Rewa, a second aeroplane; from the Maharaja and Maharani of Bikanir, £1,000 for relief funds.

Lord Hardinge, returning to England in April, 1916, at the close of a Viceroyalty which will be famous in generations to come as among the most brilliant and successful of modern times, was able to declare to questioners who met him as he reached London, "India is perfectly quiet."

Mr. A. Chamberlain, Secretary for India, in an interview published in the following month, was able to state that India, instead of being a cause of anxiety, had been a substantial help to the Empire in time of need.

INDIAN CARPENTERS
constructing a temporary bridge on the British front.

"She was able to send troops to aid in the great Battle of Ypres in those critical days when the Germans were striving to reach Calais. She has also sent troops to Egypt, Gallipoli, East Africa, Mesopotamia, Persia, and China. No less than twenty-one regiments of Indian cavalry and eighty-six battalions of Indian infantry, in addition to troops placed at the disposal of the Government by the rulers of Indian Native States, have been fighting the battles of the Empire far beyond Indian borders. These have been despatched completely equipped, and, in addition, drafts more than filling up the vacancies caused by casualties have been regularly forwarded, and the people of India, sepoys and maharajas, villagers and highly-educated public men, have given their support because they are deeply convinced that in this war the British Empire is fighting in a just and righteous cause. The rally of India to the Empire has, in fact, been one of the most remarkable events in its history. Directly the war broke out the rulers of the Indian Native States took the lead in asserting their enthusiastic loyalty to the King-Emperor. And from beyond the borders of India came additional proofs of support. The chiefs of Koweit and Bahrein, on the Persian Gulf, contributed to the charitable funds of India. The Dalai Lama of Tibet, on hearing of General Botha's victories in **Mr. Chamberlain's** South-West Africa, ordered flags to be **statement** hoisted on the hills round Lhasa, while the Amir of Afghanistan gave striking proofs of his friendship and of his determined loyalty to the British alliance. The leading Indians in the provinces directly administered by British government were equally decisive in their expression of loyalty."

IN FRANCE.
Gurkha with a French officer near our allies' front.

READY FOR THE TURK.
Gurkhas, with their British officers, waiting in Reserve Gully, Gallipoli Peninsula, and ready for action at a moment's notice.

BRIG.-GEN. J. F. RIDDELL.
Also served in Hazara and South African campaigns.

MAJ.-GEN. SIR T. CAPPER.
Saw much service in India, Egypt, and South Africa.

GENERAL S. H. LOMAX,
Officer commanding the 1st Division in Flanders.

BRIG.-GEN. GEORGE NUGENT.
He will be remembered as commandant of the Irish Guards. Killed in action.

BRIG.-GEN. J. E. GOUGH,
V.C., C.B., C.M.G. On the Staff. Killed while inspecting trenches.

BRIG.-GEN. G. B. HODSON,
C.B., D.S.O. Brigade Staff in the Mediterranean.

BRIG.-GEN. W. T. BRIDGES, C.M.G.
Australian commander.

BRIG.-GEN. N. R. MacMAHON,
D.S.O. Killed in an attack on the Prussian Guard.

BRIG.-GEN. F. D. V. WING,
C.B. Commander of the 12th Division at Loos.

BRIG.-GEN. J. HASLER.
The Buffs. He fell in his sixth campaign.

BRIG.-GEN. H. G. FITTON,
C.B., D.S.O. He had a long record of war service.

BRIG.-GEN. P. A. KENNA,
V.C., D.S.O. Commanded Notts and Derbyshire Yeomanry.

MAJOR-GEN. G. H. THESIGER.
In command of the 9th Division. Killed at Battle of Loos.

LT.-COL. LORD CRICHTON.
Heir to the earldom of Erne.

LT.-COL. H. C. BECHER.
1st Canadian Infantry.

LT.-COL. A. S. KOE.
King's Own Scottish Borderers. Fell in Gallipoli.

THE ROLL OF HONOUR, 1914-1915.

Photos by H. Walter Barnett, Elliott & Fry, Gale & Polden, Hills & Saunders, Lafayette, Russell & Sons, Swaine.

CHAPTER CXVI.

THE ROLL OF HONOUR, 1914-1915.*

Tributes to Dead Heroes—Speeches by Pericles and Lincoln—The Right Spirit Defined—Classes of Casualties—The Reporting of Casualties—British Casualties to the End of 1915—Contributions of the Different Parts of the Empire—Losses in Earlier Wars—Proportions Killed and Wounded—Losses of Officers—How the Casualty Lists Grew—Two Months of Awful Slaughter—Losses among Subalterns—Generals Killed—Colonels Killed in Action—Territorial Colonels Killed—Cavalry and Indian Colonels Killed—Prince Maurice of Battenberg—Losses of the Aristocracy—The House of Lords—Heirs to Peerages—Julian and Gerald Grenfell—Losses of Ducal Families—Losses of Earls and Barons—Baronets Killed—Two Gallant Baronets—M.P.'s and their Sons Killed—Only Sons: A Sad Record—Professional and Business Men in the Army—Losses to Literature, Music, Art, etc.—Clergymen Killed—Heavy Losses Among the Young—Oxford and Cambridge Men Killed—The Public Schools—Athletes Killed—Rugby Footballers—Losses of Marksmen—Sacrifices of Rich Men—Losses of the Rank and File—Losses in Humble Life—Regimental Losses.

" It is not well to think of death unless we temper the thought with that of heroes who despised it."—R. L. Stevenson.

L ONG before Horace wrote his immortal line, *Dulce et decorum est pro patriã mori*, special reverence and honour were paid to those who died in defence of their country, and this sentiment has endured in all parts of the world until our own day. Evidently it appeals to something which is universal and eternal in man, to something which takes no heed whatsoever of divisions of race and language, of time and space. It links together not merely civilised people, such as the ancient Athenians and the modern Britons, but the barbaric black of Africa with the red man in America and the yellow one in Asia.

The literature of the world contains two great orations on this theme, spoken by two of its outstanding orators. Four hundred and thirty years before the birth of Christ, Pericles addressed the citizens of Athens and spoke of the men who had fallen in the city's cause during the Peloponnesian War. His speech was reported by the great historian Thucydides, and one passage therein is specially memorable. Pericles said : " The sacrifice which they collectively made was individually paid to them ; for they received again each one for himself a praise which grows not old, and the noblest of all sepulchres—I speak not of that in which their remains are laid—but of that in

THE MARQUIS DE RUVIGNY.
The Marquis is seen engaged in the work of compiling a Roll of Honour of British officers and men who distinguished themselves in the war.

which their glory survives and is proclaimed always and on every fitting occasion both in word and deed. For the whole world is the sepulchre of famous men ; not only are they commemorated by columns and inscriptions in their own country, but in foreign lands there dwells also an unwritten memorial of them, graven not in stone, but in the hearts of men."†

It is a far cry from Ancient Greece to Modern America, but Abraham Lincoln, the greatest of American Presidents, had on this subject very much the same ideas as Pericles.

In 1863 he dedicated a cemetery on the battlefield of Gettysburg, and in his speech there he said : " We have come to dedicate a portion of that field as a final resting-place for those who here gave their lives that that nation might live. It is altogether fitting and proper that we should do this. But in a larger sense we cannot dedicate, we cannot consecrate, this ground. The brave men, living and dead, who struggled here, have consecrated it far above our poor power to add or detract. The world will little note nor long remember what we say here, but it can never forget what they did here. It is for us, the living, rather to be dedicated here to the unfinished work which they who fought here have thus far so nobly advanced."

In Britain to-day there are no orators of the high type of Pericles and Lincoln, but there are the

* This and other chapters of a kindred character will be completed in due course, so as to make the history complete. We feel sure our readers will be glad to have here and now this preliminary instalment of the stirring story of the heroic Britons who have died that Britain may live.
† The translation adopted here is Dr. Jowett's.

heroic dead ; and they deserve, as much as either Athenian or American, the glowing tributes quoted here. They gave their lives for their country ; they died while fighting to protect the hearths and homes of Britain ; and to their gallantry and devotion also no words are adequate. They, too, have the noblest of all sepulchres and the praise that grows not old. It is intended in this chapter to say something about those who fell in battle for Britain during the first eighteen months or so of the Great War.

Their sepulchre the whole world The subject, pile upon pile of dead, may easily become a morbid and unwholesome one, but there is no necessity that this should be so. With exquisite taste Robert Louis Stevenson has described the spirit which should animate reflections of this kind. We are to add to the thought of death that of the heroes who despised it. We are to think of the two together, and so to rob death of its chief horror. Looked at in this light the subject becomes an inspiration— one to fill all who reflect upon it with thankfulness and pride, rather than with melancholy and gloom. That Britain has lost thousands of young and valuable lives is a sad and depressing thought ; but that these and many other thousands have cheerfully faced death for their country is a great and heartening one.

THE CHURCH'S BLESSING IN A GREAT CAUSE.
The Bishop of London blessing motor-ambulances subscribed for by the inhabitants of Stoke Newington, and destined for service with the British ambulance section attached to the French Army.

Britons have every reason to follow the wise counsel of Stevenson. Every class, almost every household, has suffered grievously in the struggle; but about each one who fell, from general to private, those who mourned could proudly say that he despised the death which took him. And this was the habitual attitude. Those who did not feel so were that small class who, physically unwholesome, thought pain to be the worst of all evils, and that other class who, " having no creed or faith, and staking everything upon the present world, regarded loss of life as the ultimate calamity." Whatever happens, the Great War has driven away utterly all talk about the degeneracy of the British race.

For a good reason the loss of life in war should be brought before the nation. Direct taxation is advocated by economists on the sound principle that it brings home to each one the fact that he has a personal interest in the financial affairs of his country, and makes him realise his citizenship. In the same way the cost of the Great War in human life should be brought home to each one, and no worse service could be performed than that of leading people to believe that their country was defended cheaply. It was not. It was protected at a tremendous cost, at a price in flesh and blood, compared with which the millions

of money spent were as dust in the balance. " Liberty is never cheap," said Emerson, and the liberties of Britain have been bought with a great price.

The familiar word casualties is a military one, and expresses the ideas of the soldier rather than those of the civilian. It includes three classes which are, in reality, very dissimilar, although not so—for the time being at all events—to the military man. These classes are killed, wounded, missing and prisoners.

To the general in the field, intent only on active operations, the main fact is that a certain number of men have fallen out of the ranks. For the moment it does not matter whether they are killed, wounded, or missing. They are not available for fighting purposes, and so they are returned as losses or casualties. They are lost to the Army in whichever category they fall.

The civilian looks at the matter in a very different way. There is an immense difference, especially to relatives and friends, between being killed and being wounded or made prisoner. This is the point of view taken here. This chapter is mainly concerned with the " killed in action " and the " died of wounds," although casualties in general are discussed by way of introduction. Owing largely to the excellence of the medical service, the great majority of the wounded recover, and a high percentage, something like sixty, are able to return to active service ; and in time the prisoners may be restored to their friends. Neither lot is an enviable one, but they are divided from the other casualties—the dead—by the fact that they are still alive.

The reporting of casualties in the British Army is controlled by the Adjutant-General. His subordinates receive lists from the different regiments and other units at the front, and these are carefully checked by them before being sent to London. Each man reported as a casualty is identified by looking up his name and regimental number, and then his fate is appended thereto. Thirty copies of these checked lists are sent to the War Office every day, and from there information is sent out to the nearest relative of each before the names are sent round to the Press. As everyone knows each soldier wears an identification disc round his neck, and these are taken from all bodies buried, and sent to headquarters. The enemy also usually do this with the bodies which they inter. Even when every care is taken a certain proportion of men disappear, and nothing is known about them except that they are missing. In the Great War, however, the proportion untraced was not large.

On January 28th, 1916, it was stated **Total casualties to** in Parliament that the total of British **Jan. 9th, 1916** casualties down to January 9th, 1916, was 549,467. Details of this total are important enough to be set out in tabular form.

	Officers.	Men.	Total.
Killed	7,801	120,337	128,138
Wounded	14,176	339,107	353,283
Missing and prisoners ..	2,145	65,901	68,046
	24,122	525,345	549,467

Of the missing the great majority, but not quite all, were prisoners of war either in Germany or in Turkey. On December 1st Mr. H. J. Tennant stated that there were 32,000 British military prisoners in Germany, and there were certainly a good number—perhaps 12,000—in Turkey.

COL. F. H. FAIRTLOUGH,
Royal West Surrey Regt. A Deputy
Lieutenant for Surrey.

LT.-COL. H. C. SMITH,
Hampshire Regt. Served in
the Nile Expedition.

LT.-COL. A. L. ANDERSON,
Bhopal Infantry. He was
killed in action.

COLONEL A. P. BIRCHALL,
Canadian Infantry. He was killed
at Ypres.

COLONEL E. H. MONTRESSOR,
Royal Sussex Regiment. Killed at the
Battle of the Aisne.

COL. SIR E. R.
BRADFORD,
Bart., Seaforth Highlanders.

COL. C. S. CHAPLIN,
King's Royal Rifles.
Killed August, 1915.

COLONEL R. J. MARKER,
D.S.O., Coldstream Guards. Died of
wounds at Boulogne.

LT.-COL. E. R. A. SHEARMAN,
10th Hussars. Fatally wounded near
Ypres.

LT.-COL. R. ALEXANDER,
Rifle Brigade. Had distinguished South African record.

LT.-COL. E. W. R.
STEPHENSON,
3rd Middlesex Regiment.

LT.-COL. HON. P. C. EVANS-FREKE,
Leicester Yeomanry. Secretary of the
Cottesmore Hunt.

LT.-COL. A. FRASER,
Cameron Highlanders. He rejoined from
the Territorial Reserve.

MAJOR HON. SIR
S. McDONNELL.
Cameron Highlanders.

LT.-COL. W. T.
GAISFORD.
Fell while leading a charge.

LT.-COL. W. M. BLISS,
Cameronians. Fell in action at Neuve
Chapelle.

THE ROLL OF HONOUR, 1914-1915.

J. Walter Barnett Elliott & Fry, Hills & Saunders, Lafayette, Speaight.

SOMEBODY'S HOME ON THE NEUTRAL PLAIN.

Dwelling-house set on fire by shells. Caught in the barren neutral ground between the opposing trenches, this residence was shaken to its very foundations by the continual vibration of passing shells until an incendiary projectile found its mark and set the villa alight.

This total does not include naval casualties, which, to November 5th, 1915, amounted to 12,160, although it does include the losses suffered by the Royal Naval Division in Belgium and Gallipoli. It includes the losses of the Canadian, Australian, New Zealand, and Indian Contingents, and embraces those in every theatre of war except German South-West Africa where, however, they only amounted to a few hundreds.

At the end of the first year of the war—or, to be exact, on August 21st, 1915, just a year from Mons—the total casualties (including naval) were 391,088, and this can be apportioned with approximate accuracy among the different parts of the Empire. Down to July 25th, only a little short of the full year, the Indian losses were estimated by the "Pioneer" at 22,935, 17,385 being incurred on the western front, 3,852 in Mesopotamia and East Africa, and 1,698 in Gallipoli. Of these 166 officers and 4,732 men were **Home and Overseas losses** killed, and 18,037 wounded. The Australians suffered almost as heavily. In September their losses were officially returned at 19,183. Of these 4,604 were dead, 13,210 wounded, and the remainder missing or prisoners. By February 4th following, the number had grown to 24,539—6,595 being dead and 16,078 wounded. For New Zealand the total, to about the same date, was 6,138—78 officers and 1,231 men killed, 4,284 officers and men wounded, and 545 missing.

In spite of the gas, the Canadians came off more lightly. To September 30th their total casualties were 11,834. The dead numbered 129 officers and 2,435 men; the wounded, 275 officers and 6,675 men; and the missing and prisoners, 60 officers and 2,260 men. By the end of February, 1916, their total had increased to 13,868.

Of the above figures those relating to the Indians cover rather less than a year, while those of the other contingents cover rather more, but the discrepancies are not serious. In round figures the Indians lost 23,000 men, the Australians and New Zealanders, 25 000, and the Canadians, 11,000. Deduct this total of 59,000 from the 391,000, and 332,000 remains as the year's contribution of the Motherland to the Imperial roll of

sacrifice. Five months later, or at the end of 1915, the figures were approximately as follows: Australia and New Zealand, 30,000; India, 26,000; and Canada, 13,000; leaving for Great Britain a balance of 481,000.

The naval total of 12,160 was made up of 802 officers and 11,358 men. The great majority of these were killed—589 officers and 9,928 men. The wounded numbered 161 officers and 1,120 men, and the missing 52 officers and 310 men.

One minor point may be mentioned here. The grand total of 550,000 does not mean quite that number of individuals, for a small proportion figure twice and some thrice in the casualty lists. This is the case with those who are wounded and, having returned to the front, are wounded again, or perhaps killed, and of those who are wounded and are returned as such, and who afterwards die of their wounds. In the later months **Britain's most** of the fighting it was quite common, when **costly war** reading an officer's obituary notice, to find that he had been wounded earlier in the campaign, and this was also the case with many of the men. It would be mere guesswork to put down any particular figure for this, but the total is not inconsiderable, and it is some slight satisfaction to know that the big figure of 550,000 refers perhaps to only 500,000 individuals, or thereabouts.

It is hardly necessary to say that this total far exceeds that of any previous war in which Britain has been engaged. In the Boer War our killed amounted to 701 officers and 7,091 men, and the wounded amounted to 1,668 officers and 19,143 men, and in addition 9,553 were missing, making a total casualty list of 38,156, or almost exactly one-tenth of that for the first year of the Great War. In the Crimea we had about 45,000 casualties, but most of these were due to privation and disease, only 4,729 being killed and about 12,000 wounded. At Waterloo we lost just over 8,000 in killed and wounded, and at Malplaquet we and our Dutch allies

PART OF THE STEADFAST GATE TO CALAIS.

Corner of the British first-line trenches, showing a soldier shaving himself, quite oblivious to the proximity of the official photographer. The height and strength of the sand-bag barricade are more than usually apparent in this photograph.

LT.-COL. G. DU MAURIER,
D.S.O., Royal Fusiliers. Author of " An
Englishman's Home."

LT.-COL. P. C.
ELIOTT-LOCKHART,
D.S.O., 59th Scinde Rifles.

LT.-COL. F. D. FARQUHAR,
D.S.O. Fell at the head of
Princess Patricia's L.I.

LT.-COL. R. E. BENSON,
East Yorkshire Regiment. Fatally
wounded at the Aisne.

LT.-COL. F. G. JONES,
Royal Inniskilling Fusiliers. Saw much
service in Burma and South Africa.

LT.-COL. HITCHINS,
Manchester Regiment. Killed
at Neuve Chapelle.

LT.-COL. H. M. HANNAN,
Cameronians. Saw service in
South Africa.

LT.-COL. H. O. S. CADOGAN,
Royal Welsh Fusiliers. Believed killed,
October, 1914, near Ypres.

LT.-COL. GORDON WILSON,
Royal Horse Guards. Fell in First
Battle of Ypres.

LT.-COL. J. W. JESSOP
Lincolnshire Regiment.
Killed in action at Loos.

LT.-COL. McANDREW,
Lincolnshire Regt. Killed at
Neuve Chapelle.

LT.-COL. E. B. COOK,
Life Guards. He was killed in action at
Ypres.

LT.-COL. L. I. WOOD,
C.M.G., Border Regiment. Served in
India and South Africa.

LT.-COL. M. C. A. GREEN,
South Lancashire Regiment.
Killed at Ypres.

LT.-COL. G. B. LAURIE,
Royal Irish Rifles. Killed
at Neuve Chapelle.

LT.-COL. J. H. KNIGHT,
North Stafford Regiment. Missing,
afterwards reported killed.

THE ROLL OF HONOUR, 1914-1915.

Photos by Bassano, Chancellor, Elliott & Fry, Lafayette, Russell & Sons, Swaine, Vandyk.

lost about 20,000. It is impossible to give the totals for the campaigns of which these battles formed part, but neither during the War of the Spanish Succession nor the struggle against Napoleon did Britain lose anything approaching 500,000 men. In this matter, as in many others, the Great War has entirely altered our perspective; and it makes a Briton rub his eyes when he reads that at the famous Battle of Blenheim his nation had 670 men killed and about 1,500 wounded, while at Inkerman 648 were killed and 1,729 wounded.

Proportion of killed to wounded Other nations, however, have had losses in warfare more comparable with those of Britain in 1914-15. The enormous number of French soldiers killed and wounded under Napoleon, a case where it is probably not an exaggeration to speak of millions, leaps at once to the mind, and during the American Civil War no fewer than 700,000 lives were lost. During the Franco-Prussian War the Germans had 17,570 men killed and 96,000 wounded; the losses of the French were much heavier, their dead alone numbering

THE TRIPLE ENTENTE IN "TRENCH TOWN.
French, Russian, and British officers inspecting trenches constructed by men under General Haig's command. It will be noted that four of the company were in civilian clothes.

150,000. Russia, too, has lost heavily in her various wars. In the Russo-Turkish War of 1877-78 she had 32,780 killed and 71,268 wounded, but this total was far exceeded in the struggle against Japan, for Mukden alone cost her some 150,000 casualties.

But there is one fact in this sorrowful story which is wholly satisfactory. In previous wars the losses from sword and bullet had been as nothing compared with those from disease and sickness. The Crimean War, where for every Briton killed by the Russians four were carried off by disease, is the classic instance of this, but it was hardly exceptional. Even in the Boer War the losses from disease formed a very considerable proportion of the whole, as 339 officers and 12,911 men died from this cause. This, however, proved no longer the case. The German and the Turk, not dysentery and fever, were the chief enemies in Flanders and Gallipoli, and when the full tale of the Great War is told it will assuredly be found that the losses from the latter were small compared with those from the former.

The proportion of killed to wounded is a question of some interest. As already stated, the killed numbered 128,138,

and the wounded 353,283. This is 1 man killed for every 2·75 wounded, and 1 killed for every 3·3 wounded and missing. In the Crimea the ratio of killed to the number wounded and missing was as 1 to 4·4, or 22·7 per cent.; in the Franco-Prussian War of 1870 it was as 1 to 5·7, or 17·53 per cent.; in the Russo-Turkish War it was as 1 to 2·17, or 45·98 per cent; in South Africa it was as 1 to 5. or 20 per cent.

The proportion of killed to wounded and missing, therefore, during the earlier period of the Great War was somewhat greater than it was in the Crimea and in South Africa. The obvious conclusion is that the greater destructive power of modern weapons is almost, but not quite, neutralised by the improvement in the medical and nursing services.

These facts, of course, refer only to soldiers. With regard to sailors the reverse is the case. There the wounded form only a slight proportion of the whole, the great majority being killed outright. Of the 12,160 naval casualties, no less than 10,517, or over 85 per cent., were dead. There is nothing to compare with this huge proportion of killed in the old days of naval warfare.

Another question which may be answered is what proportion of the casualties fell upon the officers. They suffer, it is well known, far more heavily than do the men, but by how much? An army of twelve divisions contains roughly 5,700 officers and 168,000 men, or one officer to about every 29½ men. Put in another way, the officers number about 3·3 per cent. of the whole. The establishment of an infantry battalion is 30 officers and 992 non-commissioned officers and men, or just about 3 per cent. of commissioned officers; making an allowance for officers engaged on Staff and other special duties, the proportion of 3·3 per cent., or one to every 29½ cannot, therefore, be far wrong.

In the 549,467 military casualties under consideration, there were 24,122 officers and 525,345 men. This means that 4·5 per cent., or one to every 22, were officers, but this is only half the story. Among the killed the proportion of officers was much higher, while conversely among the missing it was much lower. The killed included 7,801 officers and 120,337 men, or 1 to every 15½, and the missing 2,145 officers and 65,901 men, or 1 to every 30½. Among the wounded there was one officer to every 24 men.

From these facts one or two broad conclusions can be drawn. The chances that an officer will be killed are just about double those of a private, but as regards wounds there is not much to choose between them. Officers, accustomed to lead not to be led, do not surrender anything like so easily as do the rank and **Losses among officers** file. These conclusions are obvious and **and men** do not need figures to prove them, but one is at first sight rather inexplicable. The proportion of officers hit was not very much greater than that of men, but the proportion killed was about double. Whereas for every officer hit there were 21 men, for one officer killed there were only 15½ men. Put in another way, of the officers hit, 1 in 3 was killed, but of the men hit only 1 in 4 was killed. It must be that the officers by exposing themselves more render themselves more liable to really serious wounds, presumably in the head, and also that when not completely

LT.-COL. DOUGLAS-HAMILTON,
of the Camerons. Awarded V.C.
posthumously.

LT.-COL. A. G. BURT,
of the 1st York and Lancaster
Regiment.

LT.-COL. R. F. UNIACKE,
Royal Inniskilling Fusiliers.
9th Divisional Staff.

LT.-COL. H. P. UNIACKE,
C.B., Gordon Highlanders, cousin of
Lt.-Col. R. F. Uniacke.

LT.-COL. G. K. ANSELL.
Dragoon Guards. One of the first cavalry
leaders to fall.

LT.-COL. R. L. BOYLE.
Commanded the 10th Alberta
Battalion.

LT.-COL. J. A. C. QUILTER,
R.M., Hood Battalion. Killed
at the Dardanelles.

LT.-COL. F. E. DANIELL, D.S.O.,
Seaforths. Fell in action during winter
of 1915-16.

MAJOR LORD C. M. NAIRNE,
Royal Dragoon Guards. Son of Lord
Lansdowne.

MAJOR T. P. LEES,
Queen Victoria's Rifles. Killed
in action near Ypres.

MAJOR LORD J. S.
CAVENDISH.
Duke of Devonshire's brother.

MAJOR R. T. ROPER,
Dorset Regiment. Killed in action at
Pont Fixe.

MAJOR HERBERT M. FINCH,
D.S.O., Royal Berks Regt. Served in S.A.
as Railway Staff Officer.

MAJOR HON. E. S.
ST. AUBYN.
Heir to Lord St. Levan.

MAJ. ANDREW B. KING,
A. & S. Highlanders (T.F.).
Major, Stirling unit since 1911.

MAJOR J. MACKENZIE,
V.C., Bedfordshire Regt. Took part in
Ashanti War and Chitral Expedition.

THE ROLL OF HONOUR, 1914-1915.

Photos by H. Walter Barnett, Elliott & Fry, Lafayette, Speaight, Van Iyk.

incapacitated by wounds they continue to fight and refuse to leave the field.

The majority of the casualties were, as one would expect, incurred on the western front, although the campaign in Gallipoli was probably more costly in proportion to the numbers employed. The figures supplied by the Prime Minister in January, 1916, give the losses in the different theatres of war. In France and Flanders the total casualties to January 9th, 1916, were 400,510; in Gallipoli they were 117,549, and in other parts of the world 31,408. The naval casualties may be put down on the same date at 13,000, or thereabouts.

This total of 550,000 represents, during the period under review, an average loss of 32,500 a month, or just over 1,000 a day; but it was not by any means uniform.

In an early report Sir John French estimated our losses at the Battle of Mons at 2,000, and on September 1st, 1914, a return gave them as 188 officers and 4,939 men, the greater number of whom, no fewer than 4,278, were missing. A few days later an official estimate put the total casualties at 15,142, and Sir John French stated that the Battle of the Aisne had cost him 561 officers and 12,980 men. In the first month of active operations the total losses were about 30,000, but of these something like one half were prisoners of war.

The First Battle of Ypres In October the First Battle of Ypres began, and this has supplanted Malplaquet as "one of the bloodiest ever fought by mortal man." By the end of that month the British casualties had grown to 57,000, but the ordeal of November, when the Germans tried to hack their way through to Calais, added quickly to this. By February 4th the total had increased to 104,000, or nearly double what it was on October 31st. Ypres was responsible for about 40,000 of these. By this time there had been five and a half months of active operations, so that the monthly average was just under 20,000.

In March, 1915, came the Battle of Neuve Chapelle with its 13,000 casualties, including 572 officers; and by April 11th the total had grown to 139,347, 35,000 having been added in just about nine weeks. This reduced the monthly average a little, but the respite was only of brief duration.

The two months which followed April 11th were a time of fearful slaughter, happily without previous parallel in the history of Britain. The time included the beginning of the campaign in Gallipoli, the Second Battle of Ypres, and the Battle of Festubert, and by May 31st these and other less costly operations had raised the total to 258,069. In less than two **Costly attack** months, fifty days to be precise, there **on Loos** had been 120,000 casualties, more than 60,000 a month, and not 1,000, but well over 2,000, a day. The landing in Gallipoli cost the lives of 600 officers and over 13,000 men.

Fortunately this rate was not quite maintained. Between May 31st and July 10th another 63,000 were added, making a total of 321,889; and a further 60,000 between July 10th and August 21st produced, exclusive of the naval casualties, the year's total of 381,982. During the comparative quietude of July and August, Britain was losing just about 1,500 men a day.

The lull continued until the Battle of Loos, at the end of September, and this was a most costly proceeding. In October the Prime Minister announced that the total casualties to the 9th of that month amounted to 493,294, an increase of 111,312 since August 21st. Further figures took the story down to November 9th, or a month later, when the total was given as 510,230. On the western front our losses during the months of August, September, and October had amounted to 95,000, and consequently an estimate of 60,000 for the attack on Loos is probably fairly exact. If this is so, and there is every reason to believe it is a moderate estimate, it stamps Loos as the most terrible battle ever fought by British troops.

AFTER A FIGHT: SEARCHING DEAD GERMANS FOR IDENTIFICATION DISCS.

After an engagement on certain parts of the front it was customary for contending forces to venture out to succour the wounded, bury the dead, and search for identification discs or any papers constituting proof of a man's identity. This chivalry could only exist, however, in sections where the tension between Briton and German was not too great. Our illustration shows such humane work proceeding under charge of a British officer.

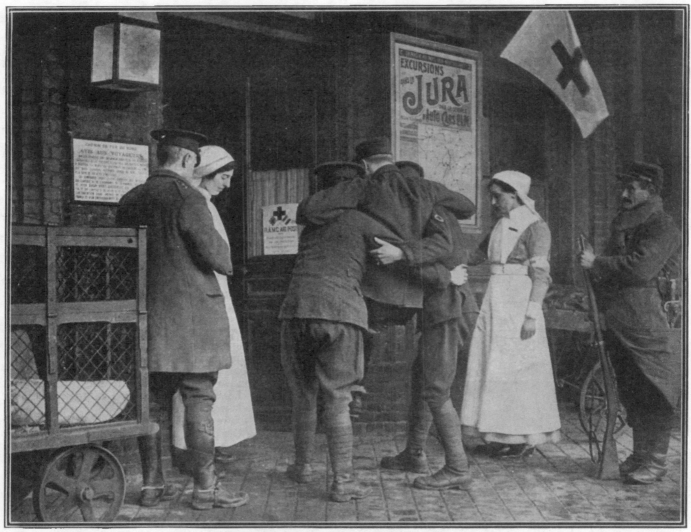

BRITISH AID FOR FRENCH WOUNDED.

R.A.M.C. orderlies carrying a wounded Frenchman into an "Aid Post" in France—the first of the St. John Ambulance depots at the western front, where both British and French wounded were treated.

The final operations in Gallipoli were also very expensive in human life. Before the last attack in August, 1915, the total casualties there, to July 10th. were only 46,622; but by August 21st they had grown to 87,630, or 40,000 in a little over a month. Still they mounted up through the autumn, and finally, when all was over, they totalled no less than 171,549. To the casualty totals issued in January 1916, will have to be added, in addition to the steady growth on the western front, a considerable total from Mesopotamia, the price of the attempt to relieve General Townshend at Kut.

Losses in proportion to population

The main theme, however, is not the casualties as a whole, but the dead; in a very literal sense the dead loss to the nation. Naval and military together amounted during the year and a half to approximately 140,000 men, an infinitesimal proportion out of the Empire's population of 400,000,000. But this is not the whole truth. The bulk of this loss, 135,000 white men, fell upon the 46,000,000 people in the United Kingdom and the 13,000,000 in Canada, Australia, and New Zealand, or—to be more correct—upon the younger men among this population. It is not, therefore, 1 in 2,860, or even 1 in 420, but one in a much lower number. What, then, is this number?

The census of 1911 stated that in England and Wales there were 5,989,202 males between 15 and 35 years of age. Assuming that the number of boys between 15 and 18 is about equal to the number of men between 35 and 40, we can say that there are 6,000,000 men between 18 and 40. This total is for England and Wales only, and for every 36 persons in England and Wales there are 22 in Scotland, Ireland. Canada, Australia, and New Zealand, and so the number of men between 18 and 40 in those parts of the Empire can be estimated at 3,600,000, giving a total of 9,600,000. The loss of 135,000 men has fallen upon these, and it works out at 1 in 71.

Looked at in this way the total is not large. The British proportion of loss is certainly far smaller than that suffered by Germany and Austria, or by France and Russia. The man-power of the Empire can stand a drain of this kind for a very long time indeed.

Look at the question in another light. In England and Wales during 1912 the number of boys born was 445,000, and to this a proportion may be added for the other parts of the Empire inhabited by whites. The result will be an addition of 271,000, or a total of 716,000 boys born. The number of births during the year of war would not be very different from this total, so it can be stated that the deaths in battle in a year—75,957—were just about one-tenth of the number of boys born. There again the loss, although serious, is by no means disabling.

In England and Wales during that same year 250,232 males died, and presumably 153,000 in the other countries under consideration. A death list of 403,000 and a birth list of 716,000 leaves, on balance, an increase in the male population of 313,000. This is sufficient to make good the losses in battle, not once, but more than four times. In these facts and figures there is no hope or consolation for our enemies.

Mortality amongst the young

But these figures, however satisfactory to the statistician and the statesman, are no consolation for the individual mourner. All talk about percentages or averages of loss is mere mockery to the bereaved wife or mother. Moreover,

[*Official photograph circulated on behalf of the Press Bureau.*]

SISTERS OF MERCY.
British nurses about to leave Boulogne to pick up wounded soldiers on their way back from the trenches.

it cannot and should not disguise the prime fact that 140,000 young lives had been destroyed, that many times that number of people had been plunged into mourning, and that, worst of all, these lives were the pick of the nation's manhood—the strongest, the healthiest, and the bravest. They were the daring and adventurous, the keen of eye and the quick of hand ; the kind of men who build empires and make fruitful the waste places of the earth. They were of the lineage of Drake, Clive, Rhodes, Livingstone, and Scott. Above all, they were the lost fathers of a lost race, the men who should have married women such as Kirstie Elliott was—she who " by the lines of a rich and vigorous maternity " seemed destined to be "the bride of heroes and the mother of their children." Without this re-

Lost fathers of a lost race

flection the nation's loss cannot be fully appreciated.

In modern warfare the bulk of the losses falls upon the infantry, and the Great War was no exception to that rule. Probably ninety per cent. of the British losses during the year fell on the Guards and the infantry of the line. The cavalry had one or two chances early in the war, before it became an affair of trenches, but they had very few afterwards, and it was only in exceptional cases, such as the retreat from Mons, that the artillerymen were hit in any numbers. The fact hardly needs elaborating, but one proof may be given. On May 17th, 1915, the heaviest casualty list so far published appeared in the daily papers. It contained the names of over four hundred officers killed, wounded and missing, and an analysis of it revealed the fact that just one hundred of these were dead, and that of these eighty-nine belonged to the infantry, eight to the Artillery, one to the Engineers, and one to the Medical Corps, the hundredth being General Lowry-Cole.

Still confining the story to the officers, the loss fell most heavily upon the juniors, and the chances of death became less as the higher ranks were reached. Generals, who are not supposed to expose themselves, suffered least of all ; colonels, being nearer the firing-line, were not quite so safe,

while captains faced still greater risks, and lieutenants and second-lieutenants the greatest risks of all. As a rule, it may be said that generals are free from all danger, except that which comes from chance shells ; colonels are safe as long as everything is going all right, but whenever their men are checked and shaken, they run very grave risks, for they must expose themselves. The rest of the officers take practically all the risks going.

These conclusions about the risks to officers are again fairly obvious ones, but some proofs may be given. For this purpose two lists may be taken as typical of the rest. One is that of May 17th, just referred to, and the other the one for the two days, November 5th and 6th, 1914, when the casualties in the great fight of October 31st were being made known. The one hundred killed on the former list were divided thus : Generals, one ; colonels, two ; majors, four ; captains, nineteen ; and subalterns— lieutenants and second-lieutenants—seventy-four.

In the November list there were forty-two names. One was that of a colonel, three were majors, eleven captains, and the remaining twenty-seven subalterns. The last-named class, therefore, suffered nearly three-quarters of the total casualties in **Six divisions lose their generals** officers, for the figures for the wounded show very similar proportions. Subalterns form just over half of the total number of officers in an infantry battalion, so there seems no reason to doubt that they lose more heavily, in proportion to their numbers, than any other class in our Army.

The generals, however, did not escape scathless by any means. During the period, at least six divisions lost their generals, and quite a number of brigades did the same. In the west, Hubert Hamilton, of the 3rd Division, was killed on October 14th, and S. H. Lomax, of the 1st, was seriously wounded a few days later ; in the following April he died in London. General W. T. Bridges, the leader of the Australian Division, was killed in Gallipoli on May 15th At the Battle of Loos Sir Thompson Capper, commanding the immortal 7th Division ; G. H. Thesiger, commanding the 9th ; and F. D. V. Wing, commanding the 12th, were all killed.

Generals in charge of brigades are nearer to the fighting-line, and so more of them lost their lives. General Charles Fitzclarence, V.C., was killed on November 11th, 1914, at the head of the 1st Brigade, and during the Second Battle of Ypres, Julian Hasler and J. F. Riddell, the leader of the Northumberland Territorials, fell. About the same time H. E. Napier was killed while trying to get his brigade ashore in Gallipoli, and in the same campaign Noel Lee, general of the Manchester Territorials, died of his wounds. Other generals killed during the spring and summer of 1915 were G. C. Nugent, A. W. G. Lowry-Cole, W. Scott-Moncrieff, and P. A. Kenna, V.C., the last named, who won the cross when with the 21st Lancers at Omdurman, being killed in Gallipoli.

Of the generals on the Staff, John E. Gough, V.C., was killed in February while inspecting some trenches. Brigadier-General N. D. Findlay, of the Artillery, was the first British general killed in the Great War, while another early death was that of Brigadier-General N. R. MacMahon, killed at the same time as General Fitzclarence, the day of the great attack by the Prussian Guard. Generals killed during the latter part of the period included G. B. Hodson, C.B., Hon. J. F. H. Stuart-Forbes-Trefusis, D.S.O., W. J. St. J. Harvey in Mesopotamia, H. D. Fitton, D.S.O., and F. Wormald.

The list of colonels killed while leading their battalions is far too long to cite, but some idea of its size may be given. On one day, May 4th, 1915, the names of seven colonels were reported as having been killed in action. Three of these— E. W. R. Stephenson, of the Middlesex, A. D. Geddes, of the Buffs, and A. G. Burt, of the York and Lancaster— were killed in the west while defending Ypres, and three others—R. A. Rooth, of the Dublin Fusiliers, A. S. Koe, of

MAJOR HON. HUGH DAWNAY,
D.S.O., 2nd Life Guards. Fell in action
while leading his men.

LORD ARTHUR HAY.
Capt. Irish Guards. Brother
of the Marquis of Tweeddale.

CAPT. SIR J. E. FOWLER.
Seaforth Highlanders. Among
the first baronets to fall.

CAPT. HON. T. C. R. AGAR-
ROBARTES, M.P.
Coldstream Guards. Heir of Visct. Clifden.

CAPT. LORD JOHN HAMILTON.
Irish Guards. Son of the Duke of
Abercorn. Killed, 1914.

CAPT. LORD PETRE.
Coldstream Guards. Died of
wounds received in action.

CAPT. VISCT. STUART.
Royal Scots Fus. Heir of the
Earl of Castlestewart.

CAPT. LORD GUERNSEY.
Irish Guards. Eldest son of the Earl of
Aylesford. Killed, 1914.

CAPT. LORD D. FITZGERALD.
Irish Guards. Brother and heir to the
Duke of Leinster.

LORD H. GROSVENOR.
Capt. Life Guards. Son of
the first Duke of Westminster.

HON. R. S. A. PALMER.
Capt. Hants Regt. Younger
son of Lord Selborne.

CAPT. HON. A. O'NEILL, M.P.
Life Guards. Son-in-law of Lord Crewe.
M.P. for Mid-Antrim.

CAPT. FRANCIS GRENFELL,
V.C., 9th Lancers. One of the first V.C.'s
of the war. Killed in May, 1915.

CAPT. W. HALSWELLE.
H.L.I. Served in South Africa
with Mounted Infantry.

LT. A. F. WILDING.
Royal Marines. Well-known
lawn-tennis player.

CAPT. REV. J. G. BUSSELL.
R. Sussex Regt. Priest-vicar of Truro
Cathedral. Master at Marlborough Coll.

THE ROLL OF HONOUR, 1914-1915.

Photos by Bassano, Elliott & Fry, Lafayette, Speaight, Vandyk.

the King's Own Scottish Borderers, and H. Carrington Smith, of the Hampshires—were killed in the first attack on Gallipoli. The seventh was C. H. M. Doughty-Wylie, a member of Sir Ian Hamilton's Staff, who received the V.C. for his gallantry in leading on some men whose officers had nearly all been shot down.

The various battalions of the Royal Welsh Fusiliers had four colonels killed during the first year of the war, and the Gordon Highlanders had three. The Gordons were H. P. Uniacke, of the 2nd Battalion, Colin Maclean, of the 6th, and S. MacDougall, of the 10th. The Welshmen were H. O. S. Cadogan and R. E. P. Gabbett, of the Regular battalions, F. C. France-Hayhurst, of the Reserve, and B. E. Philips, of the Territorials. Later the Gordons, lost J. E. McQueen and J. R. E. Stansfield, D.S.O., and the Welsh Fusiliers H. J. Madocks, and S. S. Binny, D.S.O.

Quite a number of regiments lost two colonels. The Grenadier Guards lost first L. R. Fisher-Rowe, and later, W. R. Abel Smith, C.M.G.; the Loyal North Lancashires lost G. C. Knight and W. R. Lloyd in quick succession, and the Royal Sussex, E. H. Montressor and H. T. Crispin; the Border Regiment lost R. O. C. Hume and Lewis I. Wood, C.M.G.; and the Royal Inniskilling Fusiliers, R. F. Uniacke and F. G. Jones. In addition to Stephenson, the Middlesex lost B. E. Ward; in addition to H. C. Smith, the Hampshires lost F. R. Hicks; and in addition to Rooth, the Dublin Fusiliers lost A. Loveband, C.M.G.

The first of the infantry colonels to be killed were A. M. Dykes, of the Royal Lancasters, and C. A. H. Brett, D.S.O., of the Suffolks, while the Battle of the Aisne cost the lives of Adrian Grant-Duff, of the Black Watch, Dawson Warren, of the Royal West Surrey, R. E. Benson, of the East Yorkshires, Sir E. R. Bradford, Bart., of the Seaforths, L. St. G. Le Marchant, of the East Lancashires, and W. S. Bannatyne, of the Liverpools.

Colonels killed during the First Battle of Ypres were W. L. Loring, of the Warwicks, C. A. C. King, of the Yorkshires, C. B. Morland, of the Welsh, M. C. A. Green, of the South Lancashires, and R. Alexander, of the Rifle Brigade. B. T. Pell, of the West Surreys, wounded and prisoner in this engagement, died later in Germany.

Among those killed at Neuve Chapelle, the next big fight, were G. F. R. Forbes, of the Royal Irish, G. B. Laurie, of the Royal Irish Rifles, G. B. McAndrew, of the Lincolns, W. M. Bliss, of the Cameronians, H. W. E. Hitchens, of the Manchesters, and G. L. B. du Maurier, D.S.O., of the Royal Fusiliers.

LT. A. G. MURRAY SMITH.
Life Guards; grandson of Lord Belper

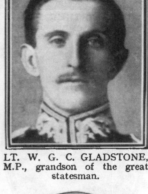

LT. W. G. C. GLADSTONE, M.P., grandson of the great statesman.

SEC.-LT. R. A. LLOYD.
King's (Liverpool Regt.), a well-known Rugby International.

SEC.-LT. SIR G. BAILLIE.
Royal Scots Greys. He fell in action early in the war.

SEC.-LT. HON. W. L. WALROND, M.P., of the Intelligence Department.

Photos by Chancellor, Elliott & Fry, Lafayette, Speaight.

SEC.-LT. G. W. V. HOPLEY.
Grenadier Guards. Died of wounds received in Flanders.

At the end of April, returns from the Mediterranean Force began to swell the total, and among the killed there was O. G. Godfrey-Faussett, of the Essex. Several of the colonels killed in the Second Battle of Ypres have already been mentioned, but there were others—A. de C. Scott, of the Cheshires, A. R. S. Martin, of the Royal Lancasters, G. S. Tulloh, of the Gloucesters, P. C. L. Routledge, of the South Staffordshires, and O. Clinton-Baker, of the Royal Irish Rifles. Later in the summer G. J. Hill, C.M.G., was killed at the head of the Berkshires. At Loos the Coldstreams lost A. G. E. Egerton, and the Buffs C. A. Worthington, but most of the colonels killed there belonged not to the Regulars, but to the Territorial and Service battalions.

Of the colonels on the Staff, F. W. Kerr, A. J.-B. Percival, a son of the Bishop of Hereford, and R. J. Marker were killed; the Medical Corps lost Lieutenant-Colonel C. Dalton, the Artillery Colonels C. N. B Ballard and H. T. Butcher, and the Engineers Lieut - Colonel G. B. Hingston.

By this time the Territorials had been in the field for some months, and several of their colonels, too, were among the dead. Colin Maclean, of the 6th Gordons, already mentioned, was probably the first to be killed. The Second Battle of Ypres was heavy on the Territorials. There were killed G. H. Shaw, of the East Yorkshires, J. Clark, C.B., of the Argyll and Sutherland Highlanders, A. Fraser, of the Camerons, C. L. Robinson, of the Monmouths, and J. W. Jessop, of the Lincolns. Others, W. J. Keys, of the Manchesters, J. A. Fallows, of the Lancashire Fusiliers, and A. Brook, of the Royal Scots, fell in Gallipoli. Later, the muchtried Royal Scots lost S. R. Dunn; the Cameronians lost H. M. Hannan, and the King's Own Scottish Borderers, John McNeile. At Loos the Black Watch lost H. Walker, C.M.G., and the 19th London Regiment H. D. Collison-Morley.

Before the end of August Kitchener's Army was in the field, and soon the colonels at the head of its battalions began to fall. Among the first were C. H. Palmer, of the 9th Warwicks, C. S. Chaplin, of the King's Royal Rifles, A. H. Allenby, of the Scots Fusiliers, and E. H. Chapman, of the Yorkshires. Others were Colonel A. R. Cole-Hamilton, of the East Lancashires, and M. H. Nunn, of the 9th Worcesters, and then came Loos, which took a heavy toll of these Service battalions. Among the many colonels killed there at the head of their men were W. T. Gaisford, of the Seaforths, A. G. W. Grant, of the Devons, E. T. Logan, D.S.O., of the Durham Light Infantry, A. de S. Hadow, of the Yorkshires, F. H. Fairtlough, C.M.G., of the West Surreys, B. H. Leatham, D.S.O., of the Wiltshires, A. Parkin, of the Northamptons, and A. F. Douglas-Hamilton,

CAPT. HON. A. T. SHAUGHNESSY.
Canadian Infantry. Son of Lord
Shaughnessy, President of C.P.R.

CAPT. LORD DE FREYNE.
S. Wales Borderers. Killed in
Second Battle of Ypres.

CAPT. BASIL MACLEAR.
R. Dublin Fusiliers. Famous
International footballer.

CAPT. J. NORWOOD,
V.C., Dragoon Guards. Won his distinction near Ladysmith, October 30th, 1899.

LT. H. OMMUNDSEN.
Honourable Artillery Company. Well-
known Bisley marksman.

LT. LORD WORSLEY.
Royal Horse Guards. Heir
of Earl of Yarborough.

**LT. PRINCE MAURICE
OF BATTENBERG.**
King's Royal Rifle Corps.

LT. LORD NORTHLAND.
Coldstream Guards. Earl of Ranfurly's
only son. Served in South Africa.

LT. C. T. MACLEAN.
Royal Fusiliers. Formerly a London
curate.

LT. PERCY WYNDHAM.
Coldstream Guards. Son of
late Mr. G. Wyndham, M.P.

LT. SIR R. W. LEVINGE.
Life Guards. Killed in action,
October, 1914.

LT. LORD CONGLETON.
Grenadier Guards. Killed in First Battle
of Ypres.

LT. H. T. CAWLEY.
Manchester Regt. M.P. Heywood Div.,
Lancs. Killed in action at Dardanelles.

LT. VISCT. HAWARDEN.
Coldstream Guards. Killed in
action at Mons.

LT. LORD BRABOURNE.
Grenadier Guards. Killed in
action, March, 1915.

LT. HON. C. T. MILLS, M.P.
Scots Guards. Heir of Lord Hillingden.
M.P. for Uxbridge.

THE ROLL OF HONOUR, 1914-1915.

Photos by Bassano, Chancellor, Elliott & Fry, Lafayette, Maull & Fox, Russell & Sons, Vandyk.

the heroic leader of the Camerons, who, after his death, was awarded the V.C.

The losses during the winter included G. H. Fowler, of the Sherwood Foresters, M. V. Hilton, of the East Lancashires, G. B. Stoney, D.S.O., of the K.O.S.B., A. S. Hamilton, of the Durhams, H. Stoney Smith, D.S.O., of the Leicesters, L. C. Howard, of the Somerset L.I., J. H. Knight and F. H. Walker, of the North Staffords, J. F. Radcliffe, D.S.O., of the Essex, F. E. L. Daniell, D.S.O., of the Seaforths, R. W. Fox, of the Devons, and F. J. Bowker, of the Hampshires.

Casualties among the cavalry Specially should be mentioned G. H. C. Madden, of the Irish Guards, and two gallant Camerons, L. O. Græme and C. H. Campbell, D.S.O.

Several cavalry regiments lost their colonels. Quite early in the war, G. K. Ansell, of the 5th Dragoon Guards, and I. G. Hogg, of the 4th Hussars, were killed. During the First Battle of Ypres the composite regiment of Household Cavalry, just out from England, lost E. B. Cook, colonel of the 1st Life Guards, and Gordon C. Wilson, colonel of the Royal Horse Guards. H. A. Lemprière, D.S.O., of

the 7th Dragoon Guards, was killed in December, and E. R. A. Shearman, of the 10th Hussars, and G. F. Steele, C.M.G., of the 1st Dragoons, in the Second Battle of Ypres. A later death was that of H. D. McNeile, also of the 1st Dragoons. To help the cavalry various regiments of Yeomanry were sent out, and soon P. C. Evans-Freke was killed at the head of the Leicestershire men, and S. G. Sheppard, a London stockbroker, at the head of those from Hertfordshire.

Several Indian battalions lost their white colonels. These included H. L. Anderson, of the 9th (Bhopal) Infantry, W. E. Venour, of the 58th (Vaughan's) Rifles, P. C. Eliot-Lockhart and C. C. Fenner, both of the 59th (Scinde) Rifles, C. O. Swanston, of the 34th (Poona) Horse, and G. H. Fitzmaurice Kelly, of the 34th Sikh Pioneers. These were all early deaths; later ones were those of F. A. Jacques, of the 14th Sikhs, in Gallipoli, C. A. Vivian, of the 15th, F. W. Thomas, of the 9th Bhopal Infantry, H. W. Beadon, of the 51st Sikhs, and F. Rennick, of the 40th Pathans.

H. A. Vallings, of the 29th Punjabis, was killed in East Africa, while the campaign in Mesopotamia was responsible for the deaths of H. L. Rosher, of the Dorsets, and T. X. Britten, of the 110th Mahratta **Death-roll of** Light Infantry. Lieut.-Colonel P. Maclear, **oversea forces** of the Dublin Fusiliers, and Lieut.-Colonel G. P. Newstead were killed in the Cameroon.

At Neuve Chapelle the Canadians lost Colonel F. D. Farquhar, D.S.O., and in the German gas attacks at Ypres they lost H. C. Becher, A. P. Birchall, R. L. Boyle, and W. F. R. Hart McHarg, the famous rifle shot from British Columbia. In Gallipoli the Australians lost G. F. Braund, H. N. Maclaurin, R. Gartside, E. R. Clarke, and A. J. Onslow Thompson. Finally, the naval contingents lost Lieut.-Colonel A. E. Maxwell at Antwerp, F. W. Luard, and E. G. Evelegh, of the R.M.L.I., in Gallipoli, and there also J. A. Cuthbert Quilter and W. L. Maxwell, of the Royal Naval Reserve.

But long as is this list, and it is not quite complete, it does not include all the battalion commanders killed. Not infrequently a battalion was in charge of a major,

[French official photographs.]

SCENES AT HAVRE, THE FRANCO-BRITISH BASE.
Bureau of the British camp at Havre. The circle photograph shows some soldiers transporting supplies in the neighbourhood of the base. The French port of Le Havre formed one of the principal bases of the two allied Powers on the Continent.

LUNCH-TIME AT HAVRE.
British soldiers entering the canteen at Havre for their midday meal.

members of the House of Lords, and two Irish peers. The three were Lord Brabourne and Lord Congleton, of the Grenadier Guards, and Lord De Freyne, of the South Wales Borderers; the two were Earl Annesley, of the Flying Corps, and Viscount Hawarden, of the Coldstream Guards. Lord De Freyne lost a brother, the Hon. G. P. French, also in the ranks of the South Wales Borderers. At a later stage four other peers, Lord Petre, of the Coldstreams, Lord Kesteven and Lord Vernon, of the Yeomanry, and the Earl of Seafield, of the Camerons, were killed.

Of heirs to peerages no fewer than forty-eight were killed. Such well-known public men as the Marquis of Lincolnshire, Lord Balfour of Burleigh, Lord Kinnaird, Lord St. Davids, Lord Ribblesdale, the Viceroy of India, Viscount Hardinge of Penshurst,

and quite a number of these commanding officers were killed. The Munster Fusiliers lost two, G. J. Ryan, D.S.O., and V. Pickard; Major Roper, of the Dorsets, was killed at Pont Fixe, and Major Bottomley, of the West Surreys, at Ypres. In November, 1914, Major the Hon. Hugh Dawnay, D.S.O., was killed while leading the 2nd Life Guards, and two other instances are those of Major H. M. Finch, of the Berkshires, and Major T. Roche, of the Wiltshires.

Socialists and Labour leaders have borne unsought and willing testimony to the gallantry shown by members of the British aristocracy during the Great War, and the Roll of Honour bears silent witness to this. It may be somewhat difficult in the modern democratic State to find any useful place for an aristocracy, but this only applies to times of peace. In times of war the "gilded popinjays" of other days gladly leave their luxuries and pleasures for the hardships of the field, and show there a cool disregard of danger which is the admiration of all.

Before dwelling on this subject in detail, the contribution of the Royal Family to the casualty lists should be mentioned. On October 27th, 1914, Prince Maurice, the youngest of the three sons of Princess Henry of Battenberg, and King George's cousin—incidentally the Kaiser's also—died of wounds received in action. The prince, who was a lieutenant in the King's Royal Rifle Corps, was then just twenty-three years of age.

During the first year five peers were killed in action, three being

and his kinsman, Baron Hardinge, lost their eldest sons—in several cases, their only sons. Lord Lincolnshire's case was as sad as any; not only did he lose his only son, Viscount Wendover, of the Royal Horse Guards, but also

Tribute of the titled families

his son-in-law, Nigel Legge-Bourke, of the Coldstreams. Others to mourn their son and heir killed in battle were the Earl of Castlestewart, Lord Stamfordham, the King's private secretary, Lord Redesdale, King Edward VII.'s old friend, Lord Willingdon of Ratton, the Governor of Bombay, Viscount Bridport, Viscount Clifden, and Viscount Goschen. The Duke of Leinster and the Marquises of Northampton and Tweeddale lost their heirs; in

AT THE GREAT FRANCO-BRITISH SUPPLY BASE.
Horse team at work in Havre. Oval photograph: Waiting for the tram. An everyday incident with the British troops domiciled at the famous French port. *(French official photos.)*

THE CROSS-ROADS OF GERMAN EFFORT AND BELGIAN RESISTANCE: A DRAMATIC WAR PICTURE.

The coast road to Calais, which was held by the Belgians throughout the critical days of October, 1914. On the left, the momentous Yser runs towards the sea. The river enters Flanders by several canals, some of whose locks and bridges are shown in this picture, the canals of Furnes, Yser, and Ostend. Immediately to the right of the column of smoke, the white spot marks the position from which the long-range German gun fired into Dunkirk. The weapon was well screened in the centre of a barn, but enterprising aviators discovered it and wrecked the gun with bombs. In the foreground is seen a Belgian battery, standing right across the road, suggesting a "gate of iron and fire," which the Germans, in spite of every effort, were unable to breach and thus control the highway to Calais.

these cases they were brothers, not sons—Lord Desmond Fitzgerald, of the Irish Guards, Lord Spencer Compton, of the Royal Horse Guards, and Lord Arthur Hay, of the Irish Guards. The Marquis of Bath lost Viscount Weymouth, the Earl of Yarborough lost Viscount Worsley, the Earl of Ranfurly Viscount Northland, and the Earl of Aylesford Lord Guernsey, all being eldest sons. Two Irish viscounts, Monck and Templedown, had their eldest sons killed, and so had three Irish barons, Lords De Blaquiere, Dunleath, and O'Neill. Lord St. Levan lost two sons, one, the Hon. E. S. St. Aubyn, being his heir.

Irish peers seem to have been particularly unfortunate, or their heirs particularly daring, for in addition to those already mentioned, Viscount Valentia lost **Deaths of the** his eldest son, the Hon. Arthur Annesley, **Brothers Grenfell** of the 10th Hussars, and the Earl of Westmeath and Lord Killanin lost brothers, who were also heirs to their titles. Turning again to England, Lords Aberdare, Manners, Knaresborough, Rosmead and Playfair mourned the untimely deaths of eldest or only sons ; and two peeresses in their own right, Lady Amherst of Hackney and Lady Kinloss, did the same. Lord Hamilton of Dalzell lost his brother and heir, Hon. L. d'H. Hamilton of the Coldstreams, and so did Lord Leconfield ; Lord Cottesloe and Lord Bolton lost grandsons, second heirs to their titles. The Earl of Loudoun lost his nephew and heir, and the Marquis of Lothian lost his second heir, Mr. D. A. Kerr.

The name of the Hon. Julian H. F. Grenfell, Lord Desborough's heir, is reserved to the last, and he was perhaps the most remarkable man killed during the war. He was in the 1st (Royal) Dragoons, and died in hospital on May 26th, 1915, from wounds received at Ypres. Grenfell, who had won the D.S.O. for skilful reconnaissance work in the previous November, possessed a combination of physical and intellectual gifts to which it is difficult to find a parallel. He was equally successful as a scholar and a boxer, and in the same week that he wrote those fine verses " Into Battle," which first appeared in the " Times " just before his death, he knocked out two professional boxers.

A little later, on July 31st, Lord Desborough lost his second son, his heir since his brother's death, as the Hon. G. W. Grenfell, of the 8th Battalion the Rifle Brigade, was killed in the attack on Hooge. He, too, was a remarkable man, not perhaps quite his brother's equal as a boxer, but good enough to represent his university in this sport. He also played tennis for Oxford, and both at Eton and Oxford he won high distinction as a classical scholar. In these two brilliant young men, and in their cousins mentioned later, the Grenfell family laid costly victims on the altar of patriotism.

But the losses of our titled families were not by any means confined to the forty-eight heirs to peerages. Almost every family had a member on the roll of honour. The Unionist leader in the House of Lords, Lord Lansdowne, lost his younger son, Lord Charles Mercer-Nairne, of the Royal Dragoons, the Liberal leader, Lord Crewe, lost a son-in-law, the Hon. Arthur O'Neill, M.P., and Lord Selborne lost a younger son, the Hon. R. S. A. Palmer.

Run down the list of dukes as given in any popular book of reference. There are twenty-six of them. The Duke of Abercorn lost a son, Lord John Hamilton, and so did the Dukes of Richmond and Wellington. The Duke of Devonshire lost a brother, Lord John Cavendish, and so did the Duke of Leinster. The Duke of Northumberland lost a son-in-law, Lieut.-Colonel A. E. Maxwell, the Duke of Beaufort a step-son, and the Duke of Bedford a brother-in-law, Lieut.-Colonel C. W. Tribe. Lord Hugh Grosvenor, an uncle of the Duke of Westminster, was another casualty ; and hardly one of the other ducal families escaped without the loss of some relative or other.

Further down the peerage lists come the earls. The Earls of Plymouth, Leicester, Dartmouth, Galloway, Bessborough,

GERMAN TUNNELLED TRENCH.
Bomb-proof enemy trench in France. The sides were built up with metal plates and it was roofed with sheets of corrugated iron.

Wemyss, Strathmore, and Glasgow each lost a son ; the Earl of Durham, a brother and a nephew, and Earl Cadogan a brother. Among viscounts, Falmouth, Downe, and Lifford received news of the death of a son ; and among barons, Cowdray, Sudeley, Rodney, Forester, Joicey, Tennyson, Macdonald, Saltoun, Dunalley, and Glanusk.

Lord Penrhyn lost two brothers, and Lord Lovat and Lord Stalbridge one each. The Marquis of Salisbury and Viscount Haldane lost at least two nephews each, and Lord Sempill and Lady Strathcona a son each. The new Canadian peer, Lord Shaughnessy, also lost a younger son. Others to suffer were Lord Camoys and Lord Sinclair ; and the casualty lists contained also such ancient names as Tollemache, Somerset, Wyndham, Crichton, and Cholmondeley.

Baronets, too, have lost very heavily indeed. Before the end of 1914, Sir G. S. Baillie, of the Scots Greys, Sir E. R. Bradford, of the Seaforths, Sir A. C. Gibson-Craig, of the Highland Light **Baronets on the** Infantry, Sir R. G. V. Duff, of the Life **Roll of Honour** Guards, Sir Roland J. Corbet, of the Coldstreams, Sir R. W. Levinge, Sir G. N. Ogilvy, Sir Frank S. Rose, Sir E. A. Stewart-Richardson, and Sir F. E. Waller had been killed. The roll quickly grew longer, Sir Mark Cholmeley, of the Grenadiers, Sir E. H. W. Hulse, of the Scots Guards, Sir J. E. Fowler, Sir W. L. Napier, Sir Robert Filmer, and Sir G. H. Houstoun-Boswall being added thereto. Two baronets on the Roll of Honour deserve special mention. One, Sir John P. Milbanke, a wearer of the Victoria Cross, colonel of the Sherwood Rangers, lost his life in that immortal charge of English yeomen on August 21st, 1915, which was described so vividly by Sir Ian Hamilton in his last despatch. A few days

REMNANTS OF A WOOD BEHIND THE BRITISH TRENCHES.

British soldiers creeping through undergrowth and broken tree-stumps that once formed a wood behind the British lines in France. The position was being shelled heavily by the enemy at the time this official photograph was taken.

before, in the same blood-stained region, Sir Horace Beauchamp, of the Norfolks, had led 16 officers and 250 men, "ardent souls" who charged into the forest and were lost to sight or sound. Nothing more was ever seen or heard of any of them; not one of them ever came back.

Many baronets lost their eldest sons. Sir Frederick Banbury, M.P., and Sir Edward Beauchamp, M.P., did so, and so did the late Sir Edward Antrobus, the owner of Stonehenge, Sir George Brooke, Sir **Norfolks who never** George Jenkinson, Sir E. St. L. Clarke, **came back** Sir Charles Dunbar, Sir C. Graves-Sawle, Sir E. Nugent, Sir C. H. Campbell, Sir Marteine Lloyd, Sir George Armstrong, Sir A. Osmond-Williams, Sir Ralph Forster, and Sir William Miller. Sir Humphrey Mackworth lost his brother and heir, and so did Sir Thomas Neave.

The late Sir Robert Lucas-Tooth lost two sons, one a captain in the 9th Lancers and the other a captain in the Lancashire Fusiliers, and Sir Walter Gilbey lost a son. A Naylor-Leyland and a Williams-Wynn may be added to this list. An American, Lawrence Breese, of the Royal Horse Guards, killed in action, was a brother-in-law of Lord Ancaster and Lord A. Innes-Ker.

The House of Commons did not suffer so much as did the House of Lords, but it did not go unscathed. The Hon. Arthur O'Neill, Unionist M.P. for Mid-Antrim, fell quite early in the war, and in the spring Mr. W. C. G. Gladstone was killed while serving with the Royal Welsh Fusiliers. The next was Captain H. T. Cawley, killed in Gallipoli, and then three others fell in quick succession. All were the sons of peers—the Hon. T. C. Agar-Robartes, a son of Viscount Clifden, Lord Ninian Crichton-Stuart, a brother of the Marquis of Bute, and the Hon. C. T. Mills, a son of Lord Hillingdon. Three were Liberals and three

Unionists; one represented Lancashire, one Middlesex, and one Cornwall; one was a Scottish, one an Irish, and one a Welsh member. In addition the Hon. W. L. C. Walrond, M.P., son and heir of Lord Waleran, died while on active service.

In addition to Sir Frederick Banbury and Sir Edward Beauchamp, several M.P.'s lost sons in the war. Mr. J. S. Ainsworth lost both a son and a son-in-law, A. G. Murray-Smith, of the Life Guards; Sir Frederick Cawley, Bart., lost two sons, Captain Cawley, M.P., and Major J. S. Cawley, of the 20th Hussars, and Sir Courtenay Warner lost one; Mr. W. Pearce and Mr. Donald Macmaster lost only sons; and sons of the Hon. E. A. Fitzroy, the Hon. W. G. A. Orde-Powlett. Col. D. F. Boles, Col. C. R. Burn, Mr. A. W. Soames. Mr. E. T. John, and Mr. John Hinds were killed in action.

The Prime Minister did not escape loss. Both Mr. and Mrs. Asquith had at least one nephew each killed in action, and two of his four soldier sons were wounded. Here may be mentioned another politician, the late George Wyndham, whose son, Captain **Capt. Percy Wyndham** Percy Wyndham, was killed during 1914. **killed** This death was another loss to his step-brother, the Duke of Westminster, his father-in-law, Lord Ribblesdale, and a wide circle of other kinsfolk.

A few scattered facts will show how severely the families of well-known men have suffered in the war. Among those who have lost only sons are Sir Wilmot Herringham, the Vice-Chancellor of London University, Sir Desmond O'Callaghan, General Sir Hallam Parr, Mr. Rudyard Kipling, Mr. H. A. Vachell, the novelist, Rear-Admiral Sir Charles Ottley, Kaid Sir Harry Maclean, Professor I. B. Balfour, of Edinburgh, Sir John Dickinson, the police magistrate, Sir Edwin Egerton, and Mr. Godfrey Walter.

Sons have been taken from such prominent men as the Bishops of Winchester and St. Asaph, Sir Beauchamp Duff, the Commander-in-Chief in India, Admiral Sir Michael Culme-Seymour, Sir Robert Chalmers, of the Treasury, Mr. Frederic Harrison, Sir W. M. Ramsay, Dr. Norman Moore, Sir Charles G. E. Welby, Bart., Dr. Wood, sometime headmaster of Harrow, Mr. C. J. Longman, the publisher, Mr. C. J. Stewart, the Public Trustee, the Rev. Marcus Dill, D.D., Sir George McCrae, Sir Isidore Spielmann, Sir Lauder Brunton, Sir Robert Hermon-Hodge, Professor Spenser Wilkinson, and many others. Sons of the late F. Marion Crawford, the late Bennet Burleigh, and the late "Ian Maclaren," an adopted son of Sir J. M. Barrie, and a nephew of Sir Rider Haggard, Captain Mark Haggard, of the Welsh Regiment, were also among the slain.

Sir E. Chandos Leigh, counsel to the Speaker, lost both his sons, two majors, just before his own death, and Mr. F. W. Grantham, a son of the late Justice Grantham, and his son were both killed. The late W. O. Danckwerts, K.C., was one of the famous lawyers who lost sons.

So far the story has been confined to the losses among a small section of the population, but both the middle classes and the masses contributed nobly to swell the total. In all Britain's former wars the soldiers were almost entirely composed of two sharply-divided classes, **Middle classes and** both comparatively small. The officers **the masses** were drawn from the wealthy, and a certain number of families with military traditions, and the rank and file from the poorer and more adventurous among the workers. The middle classes were hardly represented at all, and the more prosperous artisans by very few.

Upon these two classes the early losses of the Great War fell. In the obituary notices of the officers at that time we read nearly always that they had passed through Sandhurst or Woolwich, very often that their fathers were colonel this or captain that. Of the rank and file we read nothing, nothing whatever save that a certain number of Scots Guards, Durham Light Infantry, or Gordon Highlanders had been killed.

From about November, 1914, there was a change. It came slowly at first, but in a short time it was established. The dead officers were no longer all professional soldiers; we read of a barrister, a business man, an accountant who, having taken a commission in the Army, had fallen at the head of his men. As **Changes in the** regards the privates, the change was **rank and file** apparent when we began to read their obituary notices in the "Times." The private soldier of old, fine fellow though he was, had no friends able to do this last service for him, but many of the new ones had, and soon it was by no means uncommon to find a number of these notices in the same issue.

If this change must be dated it began with the arrival of battalions of Territorials at the front. In October, 1914, several of these—the London Scottish, the H.A.C., and the London Rifle Brigade among them—were in action for the first time, and in the fighting in April and May many Territorial battalions suffered heavily. From that time war became a terrible and near reality to many households where hitherto it had only been thought of as something far off in every way from their own sheltered and comfortable homes.

The following notice, taken at random from hundreds, must serve as an example of the class from which most of the new officers were drawn:

Lieutenant Brian Fargus, whose death was officially announced on January 7th, was killed on December 20th. He was a son of Mr. Henry Robert Fargus, and partner with his father in the firm of Clayton Sons & Fargus, solicitors, of 10, Lancaster Place, Strand. He was educated at Rugby, and joined the Queen Victoria's Rifles, T.F.

WHERE THE ALLIED LINE IN FLANDERS MET NEAR THE SEA.

Panorama of the extreme left of the allied line in Flanders. The region depicted is Nieuportville, showing the winding Yser. This position was held by the French Fusiliers Marins in the face of tremendous odds. During the course of their continued resistance these French "handy men" lost terribly from German gun fire, at one time the casualties numbering eighty-five per cent. of their effectives. German artillery wrought great havoc hereabouts, as indicated by debris in the foreground, but the Fusiliers Marins held firm, and their line never changed for a whole year.

The gallantry of these new officers, many of whom were without any desire for a life of danger, cannot be over-praised. In July, 1915, the President of the Law Society stated that sixty-seven solicitors and thirty-five articled clerks had lost their lives, and the lists of barristers serving given in the "Times" from time to time contained many names marked with an asterisk. By January the number of solicitors killed had increased to one hundred and thirty-one, and of articled clerks to seventy-six;

Gallantry of the new officers the Inner and the Middle Temple had lost fifty-five barristers and thirty-nine students. In November it was reported that forty-nine teachers under the London County Council had been killed, and a large number of masters in the public schools also lost their lives, including Mr. W. G. Fletcher and Mr. R. S. Durnford, of Eton, Mr. C. H. Eyre and Mr. R. O. Lagden, of Harrow, and Mr. J. R. Pound, of Shrewsbury.

Accountants, engineers, Civil Servants, and business men of every kind left their work to fight for Britain, and the casualty lists tell how daringly they fought. As showing the wide circle from which the new officers came, it may be mentioned that the Roll of Honour contained the names of Mr. Lionel Mackinder, the actor; Mr. Edward Mason,

FRENCH "75" GUN IN POSITION IN A VILLAGE STREET.
So furious were some of the Verdun battles that frequently house-to-house fighting took place in the villages of the Meuse sector.

the musician; Major T. P. Lees, Secretary of the Civil Service Commission; Mr. F. E. F. Crisp, the portrait painter; Mr. J. L. C. Booth, the "Punch" artist; and Captain M. A. F. Cotton, the editor of the "Weekly Dispatch." Lloyd's Bank reported in October, 1915, that twenty-nine members of their staff had been killed, and this is, no doubt, a fair sample of the losses suffered by the big business houses.

Even the Church did not escape. Several clergymen were among the officers killed. One of these was Captain L. F. Studd, an officer of the Rangers, 12th County of London, who was ordained in 1914; another was the Rev. J. G. Bussell, a master at Marlborough and a Rugby "Blue" at Oxford; and a third was the Rev. Hugh Speke, of the Lancashire Fusiliers. But perhaps the most remarkable of all was F. E. B. Hulton Sams, really a fighting parson. For three years he boxed for Cambridge against Oxford, and for six years he worked in Australia. He enlisted in the Army as a private, but had received a commission before he was killed on July 31st, 1915. Many of the fallen officers, and a few privates, were, previous to the war, students at the theological colleges.

But in reading the frequent obituary notices one fact soon became painfully prominent. So many of the killed were young men, with everything before them; fresh, gay, and irresponsible they had been robbed of their fullest and best years. To show this, we have taken from the "Times" six typical columns of the war's obituary notices. They are those of September 23rd, 1914, an early one; of November 4th and 17th, when the results of the First Battle of Ypres were being made known; of March 20th, 1915, just after Neuve Chapelle; of May 15th, the longest of all; and of August 5th. Most of the names therein are those of officers, but a fair sprinkling are privates.

Altogether the six lists contain 189 names. To 41 of them no age is given, so 148 remain. Of these 47, or just a quarter, were 21 or under, another 36 were between 21 and 24, and the remaining 65 were over that age. If these figures are representative, then 1,950 of the 7,800 dead officers were 21 or under, and another quarter were between that age and 25 or 26. But the exact percentage does not matter; the plain fact is known to all.

These six lists reveal another sad feature to which frequent attention has been drawn. So many only sons were among the dead. Of the 189 names no less than 39 are described as such, and, moreover, six of these were also the only child of their parents. The list of "killed in action," which appeared in the "Times" of May 15th is especially sad. It contains just fifty names, and as many as seventeen of these are described as only sons. In one place there are five of them in succession.

This means, of course, the end of many families, some of them families of distinction. Other cases are even worse, for in many two, three, and even four brothers have been killed. One or two of these have already been mentioned. Mr. R. E. Pollock, K.C., Lieut.-Col. R. Phayre, Sir J. Hayes Sadler, and Mr. J. G. Snead-Cox had each two sons killed early in the war; Sir Duncan Baillie, the late Mr. W. F. K. Lyon, and Captain Loder-Symonds lost three each; and the late Mr. R. H. Woodhouse, the well-known dental surgeon, and Mr. W. L. Field, of Streatham Common, four each. These were by no means the only cases of the kind.

Most of these young officers, probably the large majority, were fresh from the universities and the public schools. Many had not settled down to any particular career when the Great War broke out, and with one accord they flocked into the Army. It is quite safe to say that under ordinary conditions hardly one in twenty would have chosen this profession, and this makes their enthusiasm and gallantry more marked.

To take the universities. In June, 1915, Oxford published a roll of service containing 7,800 names, and among these were 300 dead. By the end of August the total was probably 400, and it has grown considerably since then. Without hyperbole, the deaths of one or two of these may be described as distinct **The Universities'** losses to the nation. Gerard Anderson's **contribution** name should be linked with those of Julian and Gerald Grenfell. At Eton he was a great athlete and a fine scholar; at Oxford he won the hurdle race in the University Sports; twice he won the English championship and once the Scottish for hurdling, and he ran in the Olympic games at Stockholm and against Yale and Harvard. By his scholarship he won a fellowship of All Souls' College, and on the outbreak of war he got a commission in the Cheshires.

[Maull & Fox.

Major-General C. St. Leger Barter, awarded K.C.B. for distinguished services.

Irish troops bombing enemy sap on the west front.

Connaught Rangers preparing to attack the German trenches.

Another view of bomb explosion on the enemy sap.

Officer of an Irish Division about to occupy a mine crater.

Rushing the German lines at St. Eloi: Glorious charge of the Northumberland and Royal Fusiliers.

All Souls' lost two other of its Fellows in the war, J. H. D. Radcliffe, of the King's Royal Rifles, and A. E. G. Hulton, of the Army Service Corps. Exeter College also lost two, J. W. Jenkinson, D.Sc., who was University Lecturer in Embryology, and C. F. Balleine. The former was killed in Gallipoli while serving with the Dublin Fusiliers, and the latter was in the Rifle Brigade. Brasenose **Notable Oxford and** College lost a Fellow, D. R. Brandt, who **Cambridge men** had played cricket for the university, and Magdalen lost R. P. Dunn-Pattison, of the Devons, at one time Lecturer in History there.

Three more Oxford men may be mentioned. Gilbert Talbot, a son of the Bishop of Winchester, had been President of the Union, and soon after the outbreak of war entered the Rifle Brigade. Frederick A. Rose, of the Gordon Highlanders, was one of the most learned of the younger scholars in the English language and its literature. George Calderon, poet, linguist, and novelist, though far above military age, laid down, in the Gallipoli Peninsula, a life that from Oxford days had been dedicated to ideals.

When on All Souls' Day, 1915, Cambridge held a service for those members of the university who had been killed in the war, no less than 490 were remembered. The best known, from the intellectual point of view, was Rupert Brooke, a poet of the rarest promise, who was a Fellow of Trinity, and who died on active service at Lemnos. J. W. Reynolds, Fellow of Sidney-Sussex, was a scholar of distinction, and so was the young historian A. A. Seaton, Fellow of Pembroke.

The other universities were not behind the two older ones. Before November 1st, 1915, London had lost 250 members, while about the same time Leeds reported 28 dead. The public schools have each a long roll of honour. The figures are of no use for comparative purposes, because the numbers at each cannot be given, and the totals are not all made up to the same date, but the losses at a few of the leading schools may be set down. In the autumn of 1915 Eton had had 462 killed, Harrow 181, Rugby 209, Clifton 156, St. Paul's 111, Bedford 102, Haileybury 100, Shrewsbury 66, Repton 63, and Aldenham 35. These schools were in no sense exceptional; they were just typical, and not only of the older public schools, but of schools of all kinds.

To find among the killed a large number of sportsmen is not at all surprising, but upon one form of sport the war has fallen very heavily indeed. This is Rugby football. R. W. Poulton-Palmer, the English captain in 1913-14, and one of the great three-quarter backs of the game, was killed in action, and so were his contemporaries, F. H. Turner, the Scottish captain, and R. A. Lloyd, the Irish one. R. M. Bain and A. J. Dingle, two of Poulton-Palmer's comrades at Oxford, and F. N. Tarr, another Oxford player, were also among the killed, and so were A. H. Wilson, C. A. Vintcent, and P. C. B. Blair, of Cambridge. To an older generation belonged Basil Maclear, the great Irish international, and P. Kendall, the English one. R. F. Simson, of Scotland, was another famous player killed, and others were Douglas Lambert, the Harlequin, W. P. Geen, the Welsh international, R. O. Lagden, L. A. McAfee, and Percival Powell.

In athletics, one of the greatest losses was that of Captain Wyndham Halswelle, of the Highland Light Infantry, who broke the record for the quarter-mile at the Olympic Games of 1908. Kenneth Powell, of the H.A.C., represented Cambridge at both hurdling and tennis, and his country at the Olympic Games at Stockholm in 1912. Boxers are represented on the Roll of Honour by George Mitchell, of the Black Watch, the amateur challenger of Carpentier, and G. W. V. Hopley, of Cambridge; golfers by John Graham, of Liverpool, and J. E. Balfour-Melville, also an amateur champion; and cricketers by Alan Marshall, of Surrey, and a number of university players and other amateurs, including W. S. Bird, of Surrey. Many oarsmen fell in battle, S. P. Cockerell, G. S. Maclagan, the Oxford cox, G. F. Fairbairn, and H. M. Goldsmith being some of them. A. F. Wilding, the lawn tennis champion, was killed in Gallipoli; and polo players who fell included Noel Edwards and the brothers Riversdale and F. O. Grenfell, of the 9th Lancers. F. O. Grenfell, a cousin of Lord Desborough's sons, earned the V.C. for gallantry in saving some guns during the retreat from Mons, and having

DOGS OF WAR ON THE BELGIAN FRONT.
Belgian war dogs under improvised shelters. From the first days of the war the Belgians made use of dogs for the purpose of transport of light cars, machine-guns, ammunition, surgical equipment, etc.

recovered from his wounds returned to the front. His death in the trenches at the end of May deprived the Army of one of whom it may be said, as was said of Gordon, that "no man ever combined in more harmonious proportions the qualities of the hero and the saint." In April, 1915, "Baily's Magazine" stated that five masters of hounds, or ex-masters, and a hundred hunting men had been killed, and this list was much longer six months later.

Marksmen, a class the Army can ill afford to lose, also suffered heavily. The most famous of these were Lieutenant Ommundsen, of the H.A.C., and formerly of the Queen's Edinburgh Rifles, and **Prominent sportsmen** Sergeant John Tippins, of Braintree, these **who were killed** two being considered as among the three best rifle shots in the country; both of them had represented Great Britain in international contests. Other fine shots killed were Private R. Roche, of the Queen's Westminsters, Captain Shattock, of the same regiment, Captain Newton, of the H.A.C., and Lieutenant Ker Gulland, of the London Scottish.

Where the German naval men were fighting. Marines on the Belgian dunes.

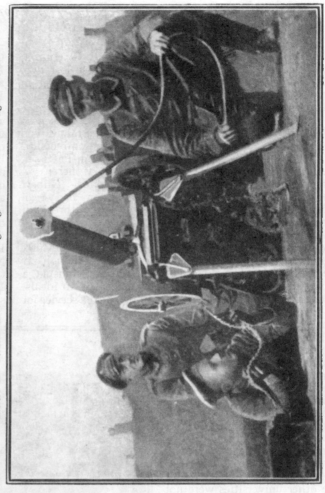

German machine-gun in action against hostile aircraft on the west front.

German Marines reposing on the sand-dunes of Belgium.

Bands of cartridges for enemy machine-guns.

GERMAN MARINES AND INFANTRYMEN AT WORK AND AT REST IN THE FRONT LINE.

410

Of the men who earned the V.C. during the Great War a goodly proportion are dead. Some, like F. O. Grenfell, W. H. Johnston, and Douglas Reynolds, were killed later in the campaign, but more died while winning it, and for them it was only a posthumous honour. Among other heroes killed were Captain J. Mackenzie, who won the cross in Ashanti in 1900, Captain J. Norwood, who won it during the Boer War, and Major H. A. Carter, who gained it in Somaliland.

Finally, the wealthy did not spare themselves. Many of those who fell in battle had great possessions, but these they left at the call of duty. One colonel's property was valued at over £400,000, and that of a Yeomanry captain at over £300,000. A subaltern in the Dorsets left £100,000, and a Liverpool accountant, who had joined the forces, about the same amount. Many other instances could

A typical human document

be given; for example, a colonel of the Guards left £118,000, a subaltern in the Leicestershire Yeomanry £112,000, and a captain in the Somerset Yeomanry £78,000.

So far the narrative has, with one or two exceptions, confined itself to the 8,000 dead officers, and has mentioned a mere selection of these. But 120,000 privates and non-commissioned officers were also killed, and although these had not the position and wealth of those named already, they were their equals in the things which really matter—in manhood, courage, and possibilities of life—and their loss, too, meant stricken homes, bereaved women, and fatherless children. Indeed, in some respects there is more need for compassion in these cases than in those of the officers.

As a rule, the dead among the rank and file left behind them larger families than did the officers, and quite certainly they were unable to make any provision for those dependent on them.

It is unfortunate, but true, that it is only by mentioning numbers that any idea of this loss can be given. Forget, however, for a moment, 120,000 or any other figure, and

consider this little document, taken from the "Times" of Saturday, March 13th, 1915:

REPORTED FEBRUARY 24th—KILLED.

KING'S ROYAL RIFLE CORPS.—Atkin, 3546 G.; Banks, 2503 S.; Chapman, 8400 J.; Cooke, 9293 J.; Farley, 9547 L.-Cpl. J.; Harrison, 9037 R.; Hill, 10099 T.; Jones, 860 Col.-Sgt. L.; Mixer, 10208 F.; Ovens, 9852 L.-Cpl. A.; Partridge, 8299 F.; Sanders, 9374 A.; Southcoat, 9499 C. E.; Thorne, 1243 C.; Trueman, 8864 L.-Cpl. G.

LEINSTER REGT.—Brennan, 3862 J.; Day, 8095 Sgt. C.; Downey, 3686 W.; Hurley, 7292 C.; Kent, 9323 J.; McGrath, 3081 J.; O'Brien, 8695 Cpl. P.; Parsons, 10145 P.; Patterson, 7734 Sgt. A.; Vanderhook, 8430 Sgt. H.

MIDDLESEX REGT.—Ailvey, 2228 W.; Dean, 14031 Actg. Cpl. R.; Gadd, 13750 H.; Wallace, 7097 J.

LONDON REGT. (T.F.).—Carpenter, 2767 C. G.; Cook, 2361 B.H.; Humphreys, 1344 D.W.; Rush, 1422 S.W.; Wing, 1591 W.

LONDON RIFLE BRIGADE.—Gardener, 9312 J. P.

RIFLE BRIGADE.—Chismon, 119 A.; Mansey, 5036 G.; Rycroft, 4575 L.

ROYAL IRISH FUSILIERS.—Dunne, 11119 M.; Graham, 6809 D.; Smith, 7571 J.; Woodhouse, 8355 T.

ROYAL DUBLIN FUS.--Leonard, 11734 T.; McCormack, 7644 J.

E. SURREY REGT.—Cronin, 10294 J.; Sadler, 10271 C.

A SHELL IN FLIGHT.
Remarkable photograph of a French 90 mm. gun at the moment of firing. The shell is clearly recorded in flight by the camera.

It contains forty-six names belonging to nine regiments, and it is a sample of the lists which appeared in the papers every day following September, 1914. Unhappily, it is one of the shortest. Every day lists like this were published, printed in the smallest possible type, yet the space available was severely taxed to make room for them. Multiply the one here by a thousand, double it, and then add five hundred more to that; reflect that each name meant a tragic message to some home, a wail of anguish, and then

GERMANS ON THE BELGIAN-DUTCH FRONTIER.
General Bissing, German Governor of Belgium (marked with a cross), examining barbed-wire on the Belgian-Dutch frontier. The notice forbids persons without passports to wander in this region.

a settled despair, and you will have some faint idea of the national sacrifice and loss.

From time to time some losses of an exceptional kind drew public attention to the price which humble folk were paying for their country's freedom. On September 27th, 1915, to take a concrete case, the following, under the heading "Six Brothers Killed," appeared in the "Manchester Guardian":

Private William Clarke, of the East Lancashire Regiment, now in the military hospital at Ormskirk, is a member of a Lancashire family of which the war has exacted a terribly heavy toll. He is one of nine brothers who were mobilised on the outbreak of the war, all in the same regiment, and of whom six are killed, another is without his right arm as the result of wounds, and the youngest is still in the trenches. The husbands of three of his sisters have also been killed, making a total of nine male members of the family killed out of twelve. Seven were killed in France and Flanders and two in the Dardanelles, where Clarke himself was wounded. The family lived at Rawtenstall, and the mother is a widow.

Another instance is that of ten brothers, eight of whom were in the Connaught Rangers. By the end of August five of them had been killed. Everyone has seen in the papers cases of the deaths at the front of four, three, and two brothers, and these serve to give a better idea of the

awful loss of human life than does the mere citation of figures.

Some day the losses in the various regiments will be made known; at present they can only be guessed at. The present writer, who has followed the subject with some care, hazards the opinion that it will be found that—so far as the first year is concerned, anyhow—the heaviest losses fell upon the Guards. The three battalions of the Coldstreams lost as many as any, and at one time the 1st Battalion was reduced to about eighty men. On one day, January 31st, 1915, not a time of heavy fighting, sixty Scots Guards were returned as dead, and in December it was stated that the Irish Guards had had 123 men killed to date. Probably by the end of the first year each battalion had some 400 or 500 dead.

Before the end of the First Battle of Ypres the 1st Royal Welsh Fusiliers had "practically ceased to exist," and about the same time the 1st Royal Scots Fusiliers were reduced to 70 men. At Neuve Chapelle the Cameronians, coming up against some **Losses in the various** unbroken barbed-wire, had 15 officers **regiments** killed and 9 wounded in a few minutes, and presumably an almost proportionate loss—over three-quarters—in men. In that battle the Middlesex Regiment had also a long list of dead.

But our worst losses were in April and May, the result of the fighting around Ypres, and the landing in Gallipoli. It may be said that if a battalion of nine hundred or one thousand men loses a hundred or more killed in a single engagement, it has suffered heavily, for its gross casualties will be four or five times that number, or something like half its total strength.

On June 7th it was reported that the King's Royal Rifle Corps had lost 102 in dead alone, the Lancashire Fusiliers 111, and the Dublin Fusiliers 157, the two last-named having suffered in Gallipoli, where the Munster Fusiliers and the King's Own Scottish Borderers had also heavy lists of dead. These were the casualties in dead alone for a single day, and to them must be added a constant stream of smaller totals, as well as a further number for those who died of their wounds. Only in this way can one get a proper idea of the total.

On the next day, June 8th, it was reported that the Black Watch had 119 dead, and the Seaforth Highlanders 164; about a fortnight earlier another list of dead had

BOARDING A HOSPITAL SHIP: BRITISH WOUNDED HOMEWARD BOUND.
Sick and wounded British soldiers boarding a hospital ship at a French port to embark for England.　Above: Cheerful invalids resting on the deck of a hospital ship during their homeward journey.

CONVALESCING IN SUNNY BOMBAY.
Wounded Indian soldiers in a ward of the Lady Hardinge Hospital, Bombay. Native attendants are seen at their duties.

service that 119 Post Office Rifles had been killed. The Monmouth and the Hertford Territorials had their share in these losses.

The early casualties in one of these divisions, the 7th (the late General Capper's), may be seen from the fact that by the end of November, 1914, its original strength of 12,000 had been reduced to 44 officers and 2,336 men, and this was before its very heavy losses at Neuve Chapelle and Ypres. By November 7th one of its three brigades, the 22nd, consisted only of 5 officers and 700 men. About the same time the 1st Brigade had been reduced to 8 officers and 500 men, and after the fighting at Ypres one Canadian brigade had not 1,000 men left.

About the brave dead much more could be said, and at the end the words would be inadequate. The deepest gratitude of all went out perhaps from the mothers of our land, from those who read of the little tortured children of Belgium and of Serbia, and then thought of their own little ones happily all unconscious of the horror of war. Let the epilogue be a few lines of thankfulness written by one of these :

> Mothers of dear brave dead,
> Whose fight is fought and won,
> I thank you in the name
> Of this, my tiny son—
> Dimpled and sweet and fair
> He lies upon my knee,
> His rosy limbs outstretched
> In baby ecstasy—
> For him, for us they died,
> Kept England undefiled,
> Saving from worse than death
> Maiden and wife and child.
> Oh, mother hearts that ache,
> My tears with yours are shed :
> Take from my inmost soul
> Thanks for your dear brave dead.

contained the names of 94 Seaforths. Other big lists of dead were 188 Royal Fusiliers from Gallipoli, reported on June 10th, and 104 Royal West Surreys on the 17th. Under date May 16th, 70 Dorsets were reported killed by poison gas, and in the previous October the same battalion had had 130 men killed in holding on to a position at Pont Fixe. Other regiments to lose heavily in dead at one time or another were the Rifle Brigade, the Gordon Highlanders, the Northamptons, and the Suffolks. But indeed it would be truer to say that every regiment in the British Army lost very heavily indeed.

Among the Territorials the chief losses fell upon battalions from Scotland, Northumberland, Durham, and London. Territorials belonging to the Cameron and the

Territorials' awful losses

Argyll and Sutherland Highlanders suffered heavily in the Second Battle of Ypres, the Royal Scots had the most terrible losses in Gallipoli, and the Black Watch and Cameron Highlanders at Loos. In the fighting for the Hohenzollern Redoubt some of the Territorial battalions—Lincolns, Leicesters, and North and South Staffords—had the most awful losses. On April 26th, 1915, the Northumberland Brigade—four battalions of Territorials—lost its general, 42 officers, and about 1,900 men, perhaps half its strength.

Of the London men the 13th (Kensington) Battalion of the London Regiment bore the palm. On Sunday, May 9th, 1915, it advanced against the Aubers Ridge, took three rows of German trenches, and was then compelled to fall back. At the end of the day the battalion was reduced to 4 officers and about 40 men, although a few others doubtless rejoined later. Ten days before, the London Rifle Brigade had had 170 casualties in a fight, and later in the year it was announced at a memorial

A STUDY IN SHADOW AND WHITE.
British Orientals who fought for the Empire basking in the sun before the entrance to the Bombay hospital.

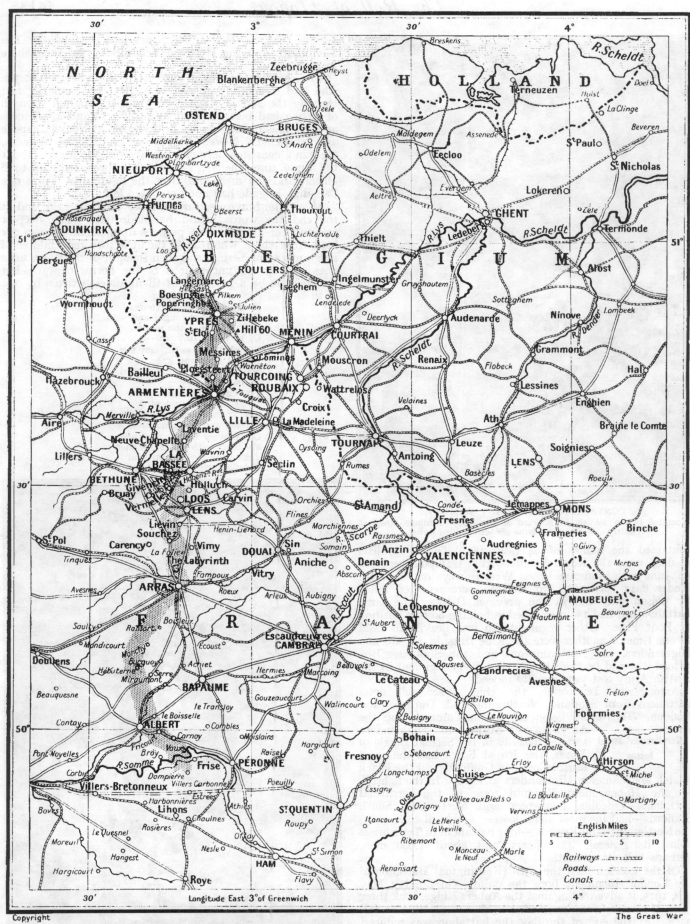

THE BRITISH FRONT IN FLANDERS AND NORTHERN FRANCE, MAY, 1916.

The miraculous growth of the British Army in the field may be judged by the fact that within two years it developed from 160,000 men to over a million. Thus Great Britain was able to hold nearly a hundred miles of fiercely contested positions, the line being extended in August, 1915, and again in March, 1916. The extreme left and right of General Haig's armies are Langemarck and Frise respectively.

The Great War

CHAPTER CXVII.

THE WINTER STAND ALONG THE BRITISH FRONT.

Revival of Seasonal Warfare—Industrial Reason for the Winter Pause—Remarkable Increase of British Strength and its Effect on German Strategy—General Changes in Our High Commands—Stick-in-the-Mud Warfare in Flanders—Suggestion of Swimming Races in the Trenches—Enemy Saves His Shells, Enabling us to Use Five to One—Important Result of Our Temporary Superiority in Artillery Power—The Canadians in their Boredom Invent Winter Sports—British Soldiers Rapidly Develop the "Little War"—Startling Effect upon the Moral of the German Forces—Nocturnal Raiding as an Offshoot from Sniping Operations—Story of the Old Farmer with Fine White Teeth—Our School for Snipers and its Victorious Pupils—Enemy Tries to Recover Ground by Mining—How Britons Developed the Art of Mole Warfare—Tales of Heroic Tunnellers at Fricourt—The Mine-shaft Kicker and His Extraordinary Work—How the Troopers of the Scots Greys Escaped from a Mine Tomb—Magnificent Charge by the Midland Division—Lieutenant Vickers Walls Himself in to Die—The Londoners Hold the "Tongs"—The Deadly "Bowling" of the Old Cricketer Nash—The German Poison Gas Attack of December 19th, 1915, at Ypres—How it Woefully Miscarried—The Poison Cloud Destroys the Plague of Rats—The Little Affair by the Quarries of Hulluch—Sailors Win D.C.M. in the Trenches—German Attacks on the Franco-British Lines at Frise, Carnoy, and Dompierre—These Attacks the Prelude to the Great German Drive against Verdun—British and French Modes of Defence Contrasted—Fighting for the "International" Trench—Fierce Local Activity all Along British Front during March, 1916—Germany's Spring Plans—The Gallant Dash of the Fusiliers at St. Eloi—The Rev. Edward Noel Mellish, the Clergyman V.C.—Our Men Wear the New Steel Helmets—Loss of Craters at St. Eloi and a Trench at Langemarck—Great Exploit of the Irish in the Loos Salient—Military Lessons Learnt by the British—Problems of Our Army.

IN ancient days tribes went to war when the harvest was gathered, and ended the fight in time for the spring sowing. Agricultural communities, such as the Balkan States, have still tended in our time to maintain this seasonal form of warfare. But thousands of years ago large and well-organised States were able to maintain the struggle throughout the year, as part of their peasantry was left to sow and reap and sustain the standing army. But even in the modern era climatic conditions in Northern Europe often compelled armies to go into winter quarters, and in the war of entrenched positions in Marlborough's days there was a winter standstill. Napoleon revived the rapid and decisive battle of manœuvres in the open field, and fought with extreme violence in blinding snowstorms and regions of mud in East Prussia. Moltke quickened the Napoleonic method by employing railways for his manœuvres and supplies, and at the beginning of the present struggle the nephew of Moltke designed, by a combined use of railways and motor traction, to reduce the war for the dominion of the earth to the limit of a seasonal campaign between

BRITISH AND GERMAN STEEL HELMETS.
Interesting comparison in head protectors. Neither design approached to the artistic appearance of the French helmet, but doubtless they were all equally useful for their purpose.

the harvest of 1914 and the spring sowing of 1915. When, however, his plan utterly failed and his successor had to fall back upon the old-fashioned and dreaded system of a parallel battle of entrenched fronts, there was an unexpected revival of the conditions of seasonal warfare. In winter a practical standstill obtained in both Russia and France. Soaked by the autumnal rains, the ground was so slippery and muddy that the attacking force lost more than the ground it gained was worth. It was not until the spring of 1915 that the Franco-British armies in the west and the Teutonic-Magyar armies in the east attempted an offensive movement in a large way.

There was, however, another cause for this apparent seasonal interruption in the attacking movements of the opposing forces. The state of the ground along all the fronts did not make attacking impossible. There were large stretches of porous soil in France, over which armies could advance even in February, generally accounted the most soaking month in the year. The compelling reason of the extraordinary winter pause on all fronts was rather to be sought in industrial conditions. It was impossible even for Germany, with her enormous number of machine

WINTER WEATHER IN THE WAR ZONE: BRITISH TRANSPORT CAUGHT IN A BLIZZARD.

tools and iron foundries, to manufacture the shells and guns needed for a continuous offensive movement. In 1915 she had persistently attacked for four months on the eastern front. But in order to do so she had been compelled to remain fairly quiet generally during the previous winter, and to adopt, for more than a year, a purely defensive attitude on the western front. In other words, she had to exercise a strict economy in **Industrial reason for** shells and guns along the larger part **winter pause** of her double front in order to employ a hurricane fire, first on a section of thirty miles in Galicia and then on another small section north of Warsaw.

The general result of these industrial conditions was, however, somewhat similar to the general result of the economic conditions of tribal warfare. Tribesmen could only fight while their supply of wheat held out. Modern empires in arms could only maintain a strong attacking movement while their accumulated store of shells and newly-rifled guns lasted. They had to break off their offensive while they still had in hand a safe margin of accumulated munitions to repel a grand hostile counter-attack. Germany, for instance, lessened her attempts to break the Russian line in the early autumn of 1915 because she needed to keep in hand sufficient shells and unworn guns to safeguard her against the threatened Franco-British offensive. Her calculations were exact, and when the storm broke over her lines in Champagne and Artois, she had quite a sufficient reserve strength to check both the French and British assaults. She recovered some of her lost ground from the French, notably the Hill of Tahure, and against our First Army at Loos she regained the hill near Lens and the fortified lines around the Hohenzollern Redoubt.

But by this time all the chief opposing forces were nearing the depletion of their stocks of munitions. Russia,

who had been the first to run out of war material, greatly benefited by the general pause. But while she was reorganising her armies she exercised so little pressure upon her enemies that they were able to spend the remainder of their heavy shell stores in crippling Serbia and threatening a new line of activities along the Constantinople route. This, however, was only a diversion from the main and decisive theatre of conflict. As soon as the Serbian Army was driven out of its country the heavy German and Austrian artillery, instead of being railed to Asia Minor, or even to Salonika, was moved towards France. There then followed that silent accumulation of tens of millions of shells which had become one of the principal activities in winter warfare of the new kind.

On the British front it looked as though we were winning at last the mastery of material over the enemy; for, as Mr. John Redmond remarked, in November, 1915, when he paid a visit to our lines, our gunners were using fully five shells to every one the Germans spent. But appearances were deceitful. The enemy was only exercising severe economy in order to concentrate all the main output of his war factories into a great blow he intended to deliver as soon as the ground **British strength and** on part of the front was dry enough for **German strategy** infantry charges and artillery advances.

His intention, of course, was known to the French and British Staffs. The preparations for a grand offensive last several months, and, provided the aerial reconnaissance forces on either side are active, the preliminary labour of organisation cannot be hidden. The British front seemed to be threatened most. Our growing numbers naturally attracted the main German force. Towards the end of the summer and autumn of 1915, Lord Kitchener had placed in the field a Third Army under General Allenby, which had taken over the French line from a point below Arras to a point just above Frise on the Somme River.

After the Battle of Loos ended in the middle of October, 1915, it was reported that there were a million British soldiers in France, who were expected to be increased to one million and a half by March, 1916. Behind this great force was our new Ministry of Munitions, together with certain armament firms of the United States. But for our excursions to Gallipoli, Salonika, Egypt, and Mesopotamia—occasioned by the entrance of Turkey into the struggle—we should then have approached in the decisive field of war the standard of a great military Power. Indeed, had we been able to concentrate all our growing forces against the German line in Flanders and France, we should, in conjunction with our western Allies, have begun to dominate the principal enemy on the ground where his main forces were arrayed.

Even as it was, the British army facing the Germans was of such power as to strain the human resources of the German Empire. In combination with our splendid allies the French we outnumbered the common foe. France was only in an inferiority of seven to ten against Germany originally. But Germany, owing to the weakness of Austria-Hungary, had had to undertake to garrison some five hundred miles of entrenched lines in Russia. Even in winter she needed eighteen army corps on the Russian front, which left her little more than fifty-seven army corps for use on the western front. Some of these had to be employed in keeping down the Belgian people and in garrisoning Antwerp and other important centres. Considerable forces in men and guns were also needed along the Belgian coast to prevent a British landing, and the Belgian Army along the flooded Yser also required watching. On the mountain line of the Vosges there was an important saving in German troops, owing to large tracts of wooded upland where difficulties of ground made any grand French advance impossible. Only in Lower Alsace, around Mulhouse, and in Lorraine, north-east of Nancy, were large defensive forces required. But from Nancy to the sea there were many openings for a great thrust, and the German army corps had to be placed closely to concentrate for attack and defence.

Germany's human resources strained

On the other hand, the continually extending line of the British army that covered Calais and Amiens could not be allowed to become irresistible. German humorists, conscious or unconscious, might continue to gibe at the quality of our fighting men, and ponderous German military experts might continue to prove to the satisfaction of their leaders that a great modern national army could not be improvised in a twelvemonth amid the confusion of a great world-war. But the German Staff, unfortunately, was not misled by the nonsense with which it fed the German Press. It paid Kitchener's men the remarkable but inconvenient compliment of massing against them the greatest German force in the field. Twenty German army corps, out of a total of seventy-five on all fronts, were at last concentrated against our armies. Yet our Commander-in-Chief was able to release the Indian Army Corps from the new winter campaign, and allow it to be despatched for operations in a warmer climate, without in any way diminishing the strength of our forces between Ypres and the Somme.

Changes in our High Commands

When the brave, skilful, and enduring Indian troops departed—after a last battle near Arras, where they won the admiration of their French comrades—important changes took place in the High Commands of France and Britain. On December 11th, 1915, General Joffre retired from the position of Chief of Staff, and his friend and fellow-

MEN OF THE ARMY SERVICE CORPS MOVING UP TO THE FRONT WITH PROVISIONS ALONG A SNOW-WHITE HIGHWAY

worker, General Castelnau, became the actual generalissimo on the western front, while General Joffre took over the conduct of all the French operations in Europe and acted for France on the new Board of Strategy, on which all the Allies were represented. Immediately afterwards, on December 15th, Sir John French, at his own desire, was moved from France to England, and given the work of organising and controlling all our home defences, the title of Viscount being bestowed upon him in recognition of the great services he had rendered to the Empire and the Allies. Sir William Robertson, his former Chief of Staff, was made Imperial Chief of Staff at the War Office, with Major-General R. Whigham as his assistant. The work of Sir William Robertson was somewhat similar to that of General Joffre. With his Staff he initiated and directed all new operations, and linked our movements with the general conduct of the war as worked out by the Allied Board of Strategy.

Lord Kitchener became responsible only for the administrative work of the Army, the new Imperial Chief of Staff being the principal directing mind of the forces. Sir Douglas Haig was promoted from the position of leader of the First Army to that of Commander-in-Chief of all the British armies in Flanders and France, and as his new Chief of Staff he was given a first-rate man in Major-General L. Kiggell, who had formerly occupied the positions of Director of Staff Duties, Director of Military Training, and Director of Home Defence. The general opinion in regard to all these great and fundamental changes in our Army commands was favourable. In the New Year's honours Major-General Sir H. S. Rawlinson and Major-General Sir J. L. Keir were promoted lieutenant-generals, and the honour of knighthood was given to Lieut.-General Edwin A. H. Alderson, to Temp. Lieut.-General Richard C. B. Haking, to Temp. Lieut.-General Hubert

Honours and promotions

De la Poer Gough, and to Major-Generals C. St. Leger Barter and Alexander Wilson, while twelve colonels were promoted major-generals.

Meanwhile, the army had rather wearily settled down amid the discomforts of a winter campaign. It was not so bad in some sections of the line as it had been the year before. Many of the trenches had brick floors and drains to carry the water away, and forests had been cut into logs to bridge over the boggy ways and build up dug-outs. The pioneer battalions had done splendid work in this way, and the Third Army in the wooded region of the Somme was well provided with timber. But there were parts of our front that could not be kept dry, and many battalion commanders had not watertight dug-outs in which to work. Even in August there were communication trenches through which men had to wade with water up to their thighs. A good many of our men were provided with waterproof waders reaching above the knee, but even these were not high enough in some stretches of low-lying ground. Cases of trench-feet began to pass down to the casualty clearing stations towards the end of November, for once more our long-enduring men were often inclined to withstand the danger to their legs for too long a period, instead of going at once on the sick-list. Trench-feet were easy to cure when taken in time, but it was a bad business if the men waited until their limbs were quite numb. Then the November storms in several parts of our line caused the parapets to silt down, and sections of the trench collapsed in a chaos of ooze and slime. The Germans suffered as much as we did, and pleaded in places for a temporary truce. Some of them crawled on to their slushy parapets to dry their legs, and begged our men not to shoot. But with much experience behind him, the British soldier did not encourage any more truces. White, clammy fogs crept out of the Flemish lowlands, making everything sticky to the touch, and veiling the quagmire battleground of the

Stick-in-the-mud warfare

BRITISH CAVALRY OFFICERS AND MEN ENGAGED ON A SCOUTING EXPEDITION THROUGH A WOOD ON THE WEST FRONT.

SEARCHING THE GROUND.
British sniper at work from behind a natural breastwork.

with frosts and lashing winds, that made all warfare in the winter lowlands a wearing, bitter misery. The elaborate comfort of the German dug-outs, with electric light, cottage pianos, and panelled walls, was found solely on the high ground, and reserved for officers only. A trench was a trench wherever it was, especially when there was three feet of water in it. At Hooge, for example, we had at last captured the higher ground, and there were rivers in the enemy's lines. The Germans, with enormous labour, drained the Belle-waarde Lake, which was oozing into their trenches. But though the draining of the lake saved them from swimming up to their para-pets, the ground in the neighbourhood remained a morass, in which men sank at times up to the neck. We had some bad positions in the marshlands, but the enemy had to share them with us in order to keep us off his main lines on the ridges.

Where artillery power told

It was against the weak spots on either front that the power of artillery told. In the winter of 1914 the Germans, with the siege-guns they had brought up from Antwerp, had our men at their mercy. When our parapets were soaking away in the rain and frost and the sides of the trenches washing in, a few German shells would complete the ruin and make the position hopeless. In the water-logged ground it was almost impossible to dig for fresh cover, for dig-ging would only produce a water-filled dike. But in the winter of 1915, when our factories were providing us with ample munitions, so that our gunners could use more shells than their rivals, we were able to retaliate on the enemy and give him, in the second winter campaign, a full taste of the sufferings we had endured the previous year. The increasing number

enemy's trenches. In the northern part of our line a bayonet charge would have been clogged in the mud after the first leap over the parapet, and to get even the lightest artillery forward would have been quite im-possible.

It was a stick-in-the-mud war, with the chance of swimming thrown in. The mud was intolerable. If a man leant his rifle against the traverse, it seemed nine chances to one that a drop of mud would fall down the barrel and foul it. When stumbling up a communi-cation trench a man had to put his hand out to save a fall, with the result that handling his ammunition

MARKING THE HITS.
Following through field-glasses the result of the shots.

afterwards would make it gritty, and perhaps cause a jam in the rifle when next a German head was spied. The soldier ate mud with his cocoa in the dug-out and consumed it with his "iron ration" in his last fight. Some of the men of

Indomitable sense of humour

the 20th Canadian Regiment put the state of things in a humorous way in a series of new brigade orders :

Commanders of submarines plying in the communication trench are requested to see that their vessels are not used by pleasure parties passing between the lines.

Non-commissioned officers and men are not allowed to bathe at No. 50 trench. This is reserved for officers only.

Owing to scarcity of material for filling sand-bags, any man who consumes more than ten pounds of mud a day will be severely dealt with.

Ration and fatigue parties must not engage in swimming races to the firing-line. This sport is dangerous owing to the presence of hostile submarines.

It was this indomitable sense of humour that saved our men. The discomforts were equal on both sides, but the German soldiers appear to have been more inclined to low, despairing spirits amid the horrible dampness, mingled

SWEEPING THE SKY.
Firing at an aeroplane. The machine-gun used is partly covered from observation by a sack.

of men who crawled over to our lines and surrendered was sound evidence of the demoralising effect of our increasing artillery power and of rain and frost on the physique of the German soldier.

But though the German was economical in the use of gun fire, he was not at all spent, and when he thought fit he could still pour a devastating hurricane of shell upon our positions.

The laborious German continued every day to strengthen his line and make up for his inferiority in man-power by labour-saving machinery and defences. Armoured and concrete forts continued to rise behind his trenches, enabling him to sweep the ground in front, and hold it with fewer men to a yard than were required in the old days. But every day there was a British bombardment on the German lines similar to the daily German bombardments of our lines in the previous year. We made the life of the German soldiers in the trenches and behind the trenches an infernal kind of existence, and in December, 1915, our "caterpillar" traction-engines were still bringing up "Aunt Marias," "Grandmothers," and other oddly-named heavy howitzers to bombard the German positions. Deep as was the mud, it did not stop the great caterpillar wheels, whose broad bands made moving platforms over rain-pools and rutted slush.

In the first week of December our heavy artillery destroyed an important German fortress in the neighbourhood of Messines known as the High Command Redoubt. Masses of masonry were blown up by our heavy shells, and concrete machine-gun emplacements were smashed up, leaving a **Important German** hole some thirty yards long and a line of **fortress destroyed** German parapets, through which the enemy's dug-outs were spotted and smashed, while two farms behind the earthworks were exposed to our machine-gun fire. No estimate could be made of the actual casualties produced in the German lines by our greatly superior expenditure of shell. But the weekly toll must have been a heavy one, for there was a deadly method in our work of destruction.

In the daylight, when the winter mist allowed, our artillery observing officers, working by telephone, would mass their batteries against a section of the enemy's wire entanglements and parapets. Then, before darkness fell, the machine-gun officers in our fire-trenches would train all their guns on the battered bit of line and the shattered stretch of wire. At night some of our men would be out listening for the Germans to come and repair the damage done to their defences, and when sounds of activity were clearly heard, our machine-guns would sweep the positions with mechanical precision, and with a scythe of bullets reap another little ghastly harvest on the field mown by the great shells in the daytime. By the time the enemy was ready to reply, our machine-guns had finished their work.

GENERAL CADORNA ON THE WESTERN FRONT.
[Official photograph issued by the Press Bureau.
The Italian Generalissimo, with some members of his Staff, inspecting the ruins of Rheims Cathedral on the occasion of his visit to the French Headquarters. The lower illustration shows General Cadorna inspecting the guard of honour (Artists Rifles).

CHEERY CHAMPIONS OF CIVILISATION.
Battalion of the Durham Light Infantry brandishing steel helmets on their rifles and showing a smiling front to the official photographer.

To the remnant of the "Old Contemptibles," who had survived the terrific bombardments around Ypres and Armentières in the previous year, the enormous increase in the power of our artillery must have been a matter of grim satisfaction. And ranking with the veterans were the first drafts of Kitchener's men who had enlisted at the outbreak of hostilities, and, after only three months' training, taken their place in the battle-front and become soldiers of the finest quality in a marvellously brief time. They had been joined by reservists, Territorials, and Indians—all of whom had felt for months the weakness of our small artillery power when brought up against the great German siege train. But in the second winter of the war we had built up a more powerful armament than was temporarily possessed by the twenty German army corps that were massing against us. The Germans were in larger force than the original armies of Generals Kluck, Bülow, Hausen, and the Duke of Würtemberg, which had invaded Belgium and Northern France and smashed through almost to Paris. But instead of the original British Expeditionary Force of about two and a half army corps, Britain had more than twenty-five army corps in the Franco-Belgian theatre of war, and her industrial population had been mobilised for the production of munitions. France was estimated to have two and a half million men at the front, with large reserves, and though her human resources had been diminished in the long struggle, she was still able to keep back her youngest classes longer than the youngest German classes. Her artillery also temporarily dominated throughout the winter the more economical German batteries, which had been placed on a strict shell ration in preparation for the Verdun operations.

The frugal tactics of the German Staff were in the meantime balanced by an increase in casualties from our gun fire. If the Germans were determined only to use one shell to our five, they had to pay in flesh and blood for the saving in material they effected. They prepared, however, to reduce their human sacrifices to the uttermost minimum by holding their fire-trenches with a few sentries and widely-spaced machine-gun sections, backed by sunken redoubts and tunnels. In this way they presented very few targets for our guns. It was then that the British soldier took steps to invent new tactics in trench warfare. No general had a hand in the new development. It was worked out

FROM THE LOWLANDS TO THE HIGHLANDS.
Six "Jocks" on leave from the battle plains of Flanders photographed in Edinburgh prior to going home farther north.

WINTER EQUIPMENT OF THE BRITISH SOLDIER.
The fur coat and woollen cap as seen in the horse lines in France.

IN FULL COLD-WEATHER KIT.
Warmly clad British soldiers looking out for the enemy in a wood not far from the German lines in France.

moonlight night, and the German position was heavily manned, but with something of the craft of the Redskins of their country, the Canadians not only cut through to the German position, but placed a bridge over the Douve River at a distance of only sixteen yards from the hostile parapet. When all these preparations were completed, the scouts guided a large bombing party into the German lines, and in the conflict which ensued thirty enemy soldiers were killed, and, what was still more remarkable, twelve were brought captive into our lines. The affair excited great attention, and General Joffre in person circulated a detailed account of all the work of preparation among the French armies, as a classic example of the new development in trench warfare.

Captain Andrew Henry Jukes, an officer in the Gurkha Rifles, attached to the Staff of the 6th Canadian Brigade, seems to have been one of the first men in a position of authority to discern the large importance of the soldiers' winter sports. The bored men, who started raiding in order to get some excitement out of life, were really following the old example of the Gurkhas, who in manœuvres in India in the days of **Canadians adopt** peace had captured an English battalion **Gurkha tactics** by a nocturnal raid. So the experienced Gurkha officer was able to give some sound tips even to the enterprising Canadians. He organised the training of the midnight fighters, and twice led them into the enemy's trenches with great success. The 10th Canadian Battalion produced in Lieutenant Younger, Lieutenant Trimmer, and Lieutenant Kent three leaders of fine skill and coolness. They quietly began by making reconnaissance crawls into the German line and discovering machine-guns for their batteries to destroy the next day. Then they took to felling German sentries, and finally they developed raiding operations in a more deadly way. After the wire was cut, bombing parties were led into the enemy's lines and a little noisy battle was openly conducted. In every case there was a sudden retreat on the part of the raiders, whose sole object was to make a quick kill before the German supports arrived, and get safely back into their own lines before any hostile machine-gun could direct an enfilading fire upon them. By the first week of December, 1915, the subalterns of our new armies occupying the fire-trenches were taking up the new form of warfare with great skill. The Cheshires soon distinguished themselves. Sec.-Lieutenant Harding, of the 1st Battalion, went out on the

apparently by some of the Canadians, and certain Yorkshire and other British regiments took up the new game with great zest until it became a general and regular feature. Both sides used to send out nocturnal patrols to scout in the zone between the two lines of wire entanglements. In many places there were little, concealed breaks in the wire through which snipers went out in the darkness with ammunition and food to work in the daylight hours. Our men began to be bored by the inactivity of trench duty at night, and with some of their subalterns indulged in what they called "winter sports." They crept out stealthily and cut the enemy's wire, climbed over his parapet, and knocked the sentry on the head by means of a spiked club. Sometimes instead of killing the Germans, they took them prisoners and carried them, gagged and bound, by stealth into our lines. Nothing was done to alarm the enemy, and never a bomb was thrown nor a shot fired unless the little nocturnal raiding party was surprised. Silence and stealthiness were the **The new** original marks of the new winter sports. **"winter sports"** The Germans, however, held their line so weakly that they invited more daring attacks, and in November, 1915, the Canadian force near Messines began to extend their raiding operations. On the night of November 16th two sergeants and four corporals of the 7th Canadian Battalion undertook a brilliant raiding operation. Sergeant Meyerstein and Sergeant Ashby, with Corporals Badcock, Odlum, and Weir, and Lance-Corporal Berry, worked for four hours cutting wire by a German trench. It was a bright night of December 6th with a fighting patrol that struggled through deep mud which was almost impassable. But the subaltern and his men reached the German line, smote down a considerable number of the enemy with bombs, and waded back through the mud carrying a prisoner. A week afterwards Captain Ellis Dean, of the 13th Cheshires, led a fighting patrol against the German salient at Le Touquet. The men obtained a footing for some forty yards along the enemy's parapet, bombed all the troops holding it, and returned to their own lines with only one of their men killed. They had some wounded, such as Corporal Jackson-Payne, who, though struck in three places, went on throwing bombs with extreme coolness until ordered to retire.

"Plug Street" raiders

On the night the Cheshires started their operations, the 1st Battalion of the Wiltshires, holding the famous lines in "Plug Street," also made a fine raid. It was led by Sec.-Lieutenant Macklin, who crawled through six yards of water, and then, with a German listening-post within twelve feet of him, cut a lane through the wire, and led the raiding party into the German position. Again, on December 16th, Sec.-Lieutenant Gordon, another subaltern of the 1st Wiltshires at Ploegsteert Wood, went out with a sergeant and cut his way into the German trenches. Two nights afterwards he returned with nine men, jumped into the German trench, killed ten of the enemy, and withdrew his party without casualty. This escape was largely due to Sergeant Loveday, who bombed all the Germans who attempted to counter-attack, and held them back until the Wiltshire party had withdrawn. Our men in the trenches then covered the gallant sergeant with rifle and machine-gun fire, and enabled him also to get safely away.

By the second week in December practically every battalion in the fire-trenches was sending out raiding parties at night. Among the regiments that distinguished themselves were the Gloucester Territorials, the 13th Durham Light Infantry, the 2nd, 3rd and 4th Grenadier Guards, the 2nd Highland Light Infantry, the 11th King's Royal Rifles, the 11th Lancashire Fusiliers, the 12th Middlesex, the 7th Norfolks, the Notts and Derby Territorials, the 10th Rifle Brigade, the West Belfast Rifles, the 9th West Riding Regiment, and the 8th Somerset Light Infantry.

The Yorkshiremen began early on the night of November 22nd, near Hooge. Their fighting patrol bombed the German lines, but lost a lance-corporal by the hostile trench. At this moment the German patrol came out to fight. Lance-Corporal Russell bombed the Germans back, and then with his sergeant picked up the wounded lance-corporal and brought him into our lines. Still earlier in date was the exploit of Private Mayes, of the 7th Norfolks. On the night of November 6th he left our position by the Hohenzollern Redoubt and, getting through the German wire, opened rapid fire down a German sap by which enemy bombers used to approach our line. On his way back Private Mayes marked down a hostile machine-gun; it was very foggy the next morning, and he went back with a comrade to the spot he had marked, dug out the machine-gun, and brought it back complete with its tripod. This put a complete end to the enemy's bombing operations from the sap in question.

Among the early raiders we must also mention the 19th, 28th, and 29th Canadian Battalions, and the 9th Yorkshires, who were conspicuous both for gallantry and for ability; then there were the West Yorkshires, who took to laying torpedoes under the enemy's positions, the West Yorkshire Territorials, the 12th Northumberland Fusiliers, the 2nd Suffolks, the 2nd Irish Rifles, the 8th Norfolks, the 20th Hussars, the City of London Regiment—9th and 10th Royal Fusiliers—the 2nd Welsh Regiment, the 2nd and 9th Welsh Royal Fusiliers, the 8th North Staffordshires, and many others.

Private Mayes' daring exploit

BRITONS IN THE GUISE OF THE ENEMY.   [*Official photograph issued by the Press Bureau.*

All the men in this group took part in a great charge across two lines of the enemy trenches, and each one secured a souvenir of the exploit. To make this amusing illustration they donned their trophies, consisting of helmets, badges, and the incongruous gas-masks used by German soldiers.

WITH THE "FIGHTING FIFTH": SCENE OF JUBILATION AFTER THE VICTORY AT ST. ELOI.

[Official photograph issued by the Press Bureau.

This striking illustration was obtained by the official photographer immediately after the Northumberland Fusiliers made their successful attack on the German trenches near St. Eloi. The photograph gives an idea of the high spirits of the British troops at this period of hostilities, the spring of 1916.

The Royal Engineers also produced some gallant and very skilful raiders. For example, Temp.-Lieutenant Duncan Shepherd, of the 171st Tunnelling Company, working near Armentières, led a fighting party into the German trenches in order to get at the enemy's mine-shafts from the rear. He could not find the shafts, so he smashed up a machine-gun fort with its steel dome, and withdrew without a single casualty. In single-handed exploits a tunnelling officer of the Royal Engineers, Temp.-Sec.-Lieutenant Eaton, was very remark-

Sec.-Lieut. Eaton's adventure able. He set out in the first week of January from our position by Moulin de Fragny, in the region of the marshes. He had an opinion that the enemy was mining from the shelter of a small wood, and, after dodging German patrols by hiding in the reeds, he swam behind the enemy's lines and lost his way. But a German battery opened fire from a wood, where no guns were known to be concealed, and the engineer carefully marked its position for the information of our gunners. Then, continuing his work of exploration, he stumbled in the darkness across a road and fell over a bank into a ditch close to some empty waggons. The noise attracted the German sentry, but the man thought it was some natural noise of the countryside, and Lieutenant Eaton remained quiet until the sentry was reassured. Then he sprang from behind at the German and clubbed him.

The clatter of his accoutrements made such a din that the British officer leapt into a waggon and hid under the covering, and soon afterwards the transport men came up with horses, yoked up, and moved the officer away. He dropped off behind, rolling again into a ditch, and taking the pennant number of the waggon with him as a souvenir. He made his way to the wood where he thought that mining operations were taking place, found out what he wanted, and, turning back towards the marshes, he reached the firing-trench and crawled along behind the shelter of the back parapet. By good luck, the Germans then began to bomb our line and our men replied, so that the noise and activity helped to cover Lieutenant Eaton's advance.

He came at length to a dug-out containing two German officers, and having in his wallet a hand-grenade of the waterproof kind, he profited by the tumult to bomb the dug-out. Then, while the Germans were attempting a small attack, he reached one of our communication saps after seven hours of the wildest adventure, bringing back information of a most important kind, which led to our heavy guns inflicting great damage throughout the German position.

The new raiding warfare had by this time developed along our line into a very serious kind of operation. All our generals recognised its high value; for though the results were small in appearance, the moral effect upon the German army, as we began to learn from startled prisoners, was of large and increasing significance. The German High Command was affected. Their men laboured under a sense of insecurity, and grew nervy and uncomfortable when left in darkness in the usual small numbers to guard the fire-trenches. Flares and other illuminating devices were employed in larger quantities, but it was not possible to keep the No Man's Land between the lines

radiant all night long. The German Staff had, therefore, to abandon its tactics of holding the front line very weakly against our dominating artillery fire. Also, in order to restore the courage of the troops, they were launched against our lines at night in imitation of our successes. The Germans, however, did not seem to have sufficient men of the right sort for the small, frequent raids that depended upon initiative and personality. Instead of undertaking the dashing "little war," they based their operations upon our latest form of combined nocturnal attack.

Some of our forward observing officers, who watched day and night the enemy's positions upon perilous sap-heads between the opposing lines, had become interested in the raids that went on around them. For example, Temp.-Sec.-Lieutenant Charles Stanley King, of "A" Battery, 96th Brigade, took part in the raid of December 15th, 1915. He directed the fire of his battery on to the enemy's wire, and cut it so as to help the raiders. When the sharp, brief bombing attacks increased in fury, owing to the Germans placing more men close in support of their fire-trenches, our forward observing officers began

[Official photograph issued by the Press Bureau.
BACK FROM ST. ELOI WITH TROPHIES.
Men of the Northumberland Fusiliers returning from the trenches after their successful attack on the German position. One is wearing a German greatcoat, and another has an enemy helmet badge affixed to his own steel casque.

to take a larger part in the tussles, and bring their guns down on the alarmed and disconcerted enemy. At the same time we answered the movement of the German supports by protecting our small bodies of picked bombers with large covering parties, and the artillery behind the larger supporting force was increased, until all the guns of a division, backed by shells from the corps' artillery, were at certain times employed.

But though the forces in the new war- **Object of the** fare grew stronger, the object did not **"little war"** change. In all our raids we never tried to conquer and occupy a hostile position, but merely to deal a sudden, unexpected blow and retire quickly before our own casualties were as heavy as the enemy's. Naturally, we were not always successful. There were times when the enemy opened fire with his machine-guns and illumined the land with flares before our bombing party got through their own wire. But, owing to the very small parties we sent out, we seldom lost more than half a dozen men in our failures, and they were more often wounded than killed. On the other hand, we were

[*Official photograph issued by the Press Bureau.*

TYPES OF THE MEN WHO FOUGHT AT ST. ELOI.
Some of the Northumberland Fusiliers trying on captured German gas-masks and helmets.

continually bringing off complete surprises, especially when the wind was blowing from the enemy's trenches, with a patter of rain to confuse the ear. In the raids practised by the Germans there was usually an artillery preparation, which went against all secret surprise. In this case, however, there was introduced another disconcerting element, of which both sides made use. Earlier in the war the Canadians had trapped their foes by preparing a bombardment in great style and getting the enemy to pack his front lines to resist an infantry attack, and then pouring high-explosive shell into the crowded trenches, without any movement of infantry from the British lines.

Developments of artillery raids This was how the artillery raid was conducted by both the British and the Germans in the winter of 1915 and the spring of 1916. The bombardments were often feints, made for the purpose of collecting targets for the heavy howitzers. Then, by way of reply to this, the common method was for the attacked side to retaliate by shelling the enemy's trenches; for if he had collected men for a nocturnal raid, they could be struck down before they attacked, and prevented from getting over their parapets. Then all the artillery of an army corps would be massed against a mile or two of front, while only a couple of hundred men would collect near one small section of trench, with all wires cut in front of them, to make a bombing raid. The enemy, in his answering bombardment, would waste his shell on a wide front, and yet would not know where the infantry attack against him would come.

At the appointed time the guns would lift from the front trenches and settle in a wide, deep rain of shell upon all points from which the enemy might reinforce the threatened position. Then the bombers would go out and quickly return, and the Germans the next day would proudly report that an attack had been made on their lines and repulsed. The Germans had hundreds of victories of this sort, large and small, because it was of the essence of

a raid that the raiders should return to their own lines in apparent defeat. Had they tried to occupy the enemy's positions, the German guns would have put a barrage round the trench, and we should not have been able to get ammunition and reinforcements to the bit of sand-bag line. As a matter of fact, we never tried to do such a thing. The entire object of the "little war" was to force the Germans to hold their front trenches more strongly, and thus expose more men to our dominating artillery fire.

Connected with the raiding operations was the art of the sniper. Our raiding was an off-shoot from our sniping. At the beginning of the campaign the Germans, much to our surprise, were generally superior to us in this deadly form of sharpshooting. The Jaegers, who first terrorised our trenches, could have been met by our long-trained regular soldiers if we had then had an army of a large size. But our first-rate men were small in number, and after withstanding superior forces from Mons to Ypres, they were terribly reduced, and the ranks were filled out with fresh recruits and reservists, against whom the German commanders could bring an army of Jaegers. In the winter of 1914 the German sniper was a pest to our forces. He was often a man of undoubted bravery and imperturbable ingenuity. Sometimes he lived in our lines, spying as well as sniping. At first these men stayed behind in disguise or in hiding-places when we were advancing, and with remarkable courage watched our movements and shot our officers and men.

Even as late as September, 1915, a sniper of this sort was discovered. It was at a spot where we were about eight hundred yards from the nearest German trench, and therefore in little danger from hostile rifle fire. About half a mile in our rear was a small stream, still farther removed from sniping enemies, but our men were constantly shot at when they went out at night for water. The colonel became

[*Official photograph issued by the Press Bureau.*

HAPPY IN CAPTIVITY.
German soldiers taken prisoners by the Northumberland and Royal Fusiliers at St. Eloi.

BRITISH TROOPS MOVING ALONG A COMMUNICATION
TRENCH.

TO THE FRONT LINE VIA A COMMUNICATION TRENCH.

savage and sarcastic with his officers, and just before dawn
one morning they threw out the battalion in a great loop
and gradually beat inward, but found nothing but a bent
old French farmer driving a ridging plough for potatoes.
The British subaltern asked him if he had seen any suspicious figure, but the old man told the soldiers to get off
the field, and not to injure his potato crops. " The old chap
got in a fearful rage," said the young officer to his chief,
" and absolutely showed his teeth at us. Jolly fine teeth,
and clean, too," said the subaltern reflectively.

" A man so old he cannot stand upright, and yet with fine
white teeth ?" said the colonel. " Take a couple of men
and have another talk with him, and pin him from behind.
Be careful you don't lose any lives, and bring in to me this
old man with nice, clean teeth."

The enlightened subaltern feeling rather ashamed of
himself, arranged his plan of attack very carefully, and it
was well he did so. The young German

Drawing a
" gorilla's " teeth
officer fought like a gorilla, and rolled the
three men over and over before they could
tie him up. He carried two automatic
pistols and a belt of rifle cartridges, and later in the day
his rifle was found in a dug-out in a ditch, under a heap
of brushwood.

But by the end of December, 1915, we had produced a
large force of master-snipers. We had set up a new
organisation run by big-game shots, backwoodsmen, and
musketry experts, and they called for volunteers, got them
by tens of thousands, and then condensed them to hundreds
by difficult tests. Gamekeepers came out in good numbers,
together with men from the outlands of the Empire,
accustomed to rough shooting. Many marksmen in the
new armies, however, had been taken into the new machine-
gun organisation, so that all naturally excellent shooters
did not become snipers. But nearly every battalion that

fought at the front had men with quick eyes, who were
very anxious to pay off old scores. So the rifle experts
collected ample material for the new training schools that
were established, and by the beginning of 1916 the British
sniper was the master of the Jaeger.

Our men were at least as good shots as the picked German
sharpshooters, and outdid them in daring ingenuity and
perseverance. It was our snipers who in nocturnal explorations first found ways about the neutral zone, where
some of them had to lie for hours in seemingly impossible
hiding-places, often in rain or frost, wet to the skin or chilled
to the bone. They had to scheme and scheme for days to
catch some German who was playing the same game. But
though a sniper might fire only one shot a day, his admiring
comrades could be certain that one spent cartridge meant

427

one dead German. The snipers became the petted darlings of the army. The colonels gave them any rifle. sight, or steel shield they wanted, and saw they got it quickly. They usually had the most comfortable quarters in rest billets, and little privileges were allowed them which the other men did not enjoy—for they were liberating our troops from the greatest of all dangers, and giving the enemy in turn a violent lesson in the art of sniping. The German infantry that used to stroll about carelessly behind their lines and show themselves in working parties in safe spots where they thought British riflemen could not harm them, began to cling to their ditches and never show a cap top.

Even their boldest Jaegers exhibited marked reluctance for hazardous expeditions beyond the fire-trench. No doubt, we had killed off, in eighteen months of warfare, most of the daring and highly-trained young marksmen of the German forces opposed to us. German officers, with the cool dare-devilry of the young man with the fine teeth who worked behind our lines, had perished by the unfair process of natural selection that goes on in war. Germany had put her best and bravest young men into the field at the opening of hostilities, while the full flower of the adventurous spirits of our Empire had only been gathered for training in the latter part of 1914, and had been brought into the field slowly, as arms were made for them. Many Germans had been extraordinarily brave during the first six months of the struggle, but it was of their bravest, finest spirits that we and our Allies had taken full toll during the long German offensive movement. And, although we lost in turn some of the flower of our race in our attempts to break the German line and capture the Dardanelles, yet incomparably far more of the fine, virile element of our race survived than did the similar element in the German race.

Toll taken of the bravest

In raiding and sniping we dominated the enemy, but he attempted to restore the balance of his losses by mining our front trenches. This was a matter of organisation, in which the Germans might fairly have been expected still to excel, for their engineering corps was vast, with immense supplies and superb machinery. The German engineers had displayed veritable genius in their gigantic system of fortifications and network of light railways, and, as we have remarked, their activities were ant-like—a sort of insect-like industriousness and persistence that seemed more than human. But our new armies, with hundreds of fresh young tunnelling officers, proved equal to the Germans in the art of mining. There were several important operations in which our miners and the Germans faced each other in order to blow a breach for an infantry attack. In these mole contests we usually won, as was seen several times round Ypres.

But there was another kind of mining activity, which prolonged the little war of the nocturnal raiders. It was intended only to annoy the enemy and make his troops in the fire-trench uncomfortable. Great holes were blown in the enemy's line, but nothing followed—not even a bomb struggle for the lip of the crater. The mining operation was merely a slow and laborious form of inflicting slight casualties on the opposing force. We had a perpetual mine-field at Fricourt, near Albert, on the southern section of our line. We took it over from the French after they had been fighting there for many months, round the Bois Français and the Tambour. It was the French who began mining in the woodland, and after we had continued their work through the winter no wood remained. Not even a fallen tree-trunk was to

BRAVE WOMEN OF FRANCE AND THEIR SHELL-SHATTERED HOME.
An interesting proof of the confidence of the French populace in their soldiery, as well as of their love of home, was the way in which they clung to their habitations near the fighting-line.

be seen. The place was a chaos of brown earth, in which so many craters had been made that they had merged shapelessly into each other. Our dug-outs were thirty feet below the surface, and well below this depth the tunnelling went on, until by January, 1916, our miners won the mastery.

Sapper J. Williams, of the 178th Tunnelling Company, showed conspicuous gallantry in the Tambour du Clos. He was always selected to work in difficult places near the enemy's galleries when speed was essential, and his wonderful skill and tremendous energy made him continually victorious. Contempt of death was only one of his smaller merits. What so distinguished him was the way his mind brightened and his power of work increased when he knew he was in great peril. He came to the front first on November 28th, 1915, when he found the Germans had almost completed a mine under our trenches. He then burrowed down so quickly that he was able to blow up the Teutons just before they retired to fire their mass of high explosive.

Before this exploit the Tambour had been marked by some brave deeds by Sergeant A. Watts, of the same tunnelling company, who had worked there with conspicuous gallantry from August, 1915. On November 5th nine men of his section were buried by the explosion of a German mine, and while the blown-in gallery was full of foul gas the sergeant began working in it, and led the rescue party.

His comrade, Sergeant A. McQuade, was also eminent by his daring skill in rescuing the buried miners, and Sergeant McQuade also laid, tamped, and exploded the charge in the gallery that Sapper Williams drove within ten feet of a German mine gallery on November 29th. At this time Lieutenant R. S. Mackilligan, of the 3rd Wiltshire Regiment, who had been attached by reason of his engineering ability to the tunnelling company in the Tambour, directed the sappers in their high-speed operations against the German miners. A good many young officers of the new school who went into the Army for infantry work were taken from their regiments and turned into human moles because of the ability they showed in the

Tunnellers' daring skill

most dangerous form of trench warfare. Temp. Sec.-Lieutenant Durrant, of the 8th North Lancashires, for instance, first won distinction as a tunnelling engineer at Frélinghien on Christmas Eve. Our sappers found a German gallery and placed a charge in it, but the charge only partially exploded, and so warned the enemy. There was instant danger that the Germans would explode their mine beneath our position. But one officer of the tunnelling company, Sec.-Lieutenant Eagar, guarded the entrance to the enemy's gallery, and shot a German down there, while Sec.-Lieutenant Durrant placed

KING ALBERT IN THE TRENCHES AT STEENSTRAETE.
His Majesty, wearing a steel helmet, was photographed while conversing with two of his soldier subjects.

a second charge in the enemy's underground works, and, firing it, blew in the gallery. In the same tunnelling company was Sapper G. E. Willis, who was a miner of genius like Sapper Williams. On December 3rd the Germans were found to be working towards our trenches, and we drove out a gallery in order to anticipate them. But they found out one of our shafts in which Sapper Willis and another man were working, placed a charge against it, and blew it in. Sec.-Lieutenant Eagar worked down the wrecked tunnel and dug out Sapper Willis and the other man after two hours' hard work. Willis was badly shaken and bruised, but after having his injuries dressed he insisted upon returning at once to work at the face of the gallery in which he had just been buried. He pointed out that the position was critical, and that if the wrecked gallery was not at once pushed forward the enemy would explode another mine. So Sapper Willis had his way, and though suffering from the poisonous fumes of the previous explosion and from the shock and bruises of the German mine, he went back to the wrecked gallery and worked it forward with such speed that the position was saved and the Germans lifted into the air.

The kind of courage needed by the human moles that fought each other with high explosives, pickaxes, and revolvers was the highest kind of which a man is capable. Airmen and submariners, nocturnal raiders and lonely snipers, were often hard set and strained ; but the nerves of the tunnellers, digging underneath the earth and racing against the miners of the enemy, were put

Mining and counter-mining

to terrible strains. In the chalk part of our front mining operations were simple, and almost comfortable. A pleasant, clean, roomy gallery could be cut in the chalk, and there was only need to be very careful in approaching the enemy's lines not to let the sound of a pick be heard ; for if there was a German mine-shaft in the neighbourhood—as there commonly was—listening ears would detect the noise of the burrowing, and a charge would blow it in. In course of time the surface of the chalk became so pulverised 'that the tunnellers had to sink shafts at a great depth ; but through the winter and the spring the work went on in this manner,

ROYAL LEADER OF A RESOLUTE NATION.
King Albert conversing with an officer of his Staff in a village near the Belgian Headquarters.

with the surface getting more churned up and the tunnels starting farther back and making a deeper curve towards the hostile lines.

But in the northern section of our line, that rested on the mud of Flanders, mining was often a more dangerous business. There were places in which a man had to burrow towards the enemy with little help from tools. After a hole was made, the sapper inserted himself feet foremost into it and kicked his way forward, passing over his shoulders the mud he dislodged with his toes. He would go forward in this manner, through earth which was just consistent enough to remain firm above his head when he had hollowed it out with his toes. Behind him crawled a string of men to collect the mud, pass it on and out, and shore up the narrow, underground drain with timber. But if the man who was kicking his way in front struck through the muddy earth into a vein of sand, death fell upon him and the men behind him ; for if sand was tapped in the sodden ground, the result was a stream of water that flooded the small burrow and drowned the men, who were so tightly wedged in the drain that they could not even make a struggle for life. By common consent of the men

in the Army, the greatest pluck of all was required by the mine-shaft kickers, toiling in suffocating darkness through the earth, and knowing their lives lay at the mercy of an accident which no skill or caution could avoid.

What with their duties of tunnelling, mine-laying, repairing broken wire out in the open at night in the zone of death, mending telephones under fire, rebuilding battered trenches, and reorganising newly-won positions, the Royal Engineers were the hardest worked and the most heroic corps in the long and wearing period of trench warfare. All the main burden of it fell on them, and it was well for their country that they were able to be reinforced by practical miners and skilled engineers, whom they were soon able to train into the most useful of all kinds of modern soldiers. Especially heroic were the continual rescues made of men buried by German mines exploded under our trenches. Helmets were provided to enable the rescuers to escape being choked by the foul fumes of the explosion, but it often happened that the helmets were not immediately at hand when the disaster occurred, and the rescuers went to work without protection, and often had to dig their comrades out while the enemy's batteries played upon them. Examples of heroism of this kind are so numerous in our official records that it is scarcely possible to attempt a selection.

But in order to illustrate the closing scene of the mining operations we have been describing, we will take the story of a bombing party of the Scots Greys. Seven of the troopers—Vessin, Ramsay, Jameson, McLeish, Carter, Dewar, and a man called Johnnie—were holding a barricade at a sap-head and throwing bombs at the Germans. In the night the first bombing section retired into a dug-out close by the post, so as to be at hand to help the second section which was on duty. But soon after they went for a rest into their shelter there was a great explosion behind them ; the chalk rose up and smashed in the dug-out, which collapsed on the top of the troopers. They did not at first know what had happened, but they could soon hear hundreds of bombs and grenades bursting above them in the pitch darkness. Trooper Carter was killed by the shock of the first explosion, and soon after he died another mine roared up and completely swallowed him, and also buried Johnnie up to the waist. The men still alive were all pinned down by the heavy timber of the roof and in total darkness. Ramsay, being nearest to where the door had been, began to scrape the avalanche of chalk away and make a hole. But when he had scratched an opening and lifted his head and shoulders out, a German bombed him full in the face, killing him instantly. The bomb also brought another part of the roof down on

Bombers' appalling experience

the dead man, pinning his body on the back so that he blocked up the door.

None of the other troopers still alive could move, but Dewar had his hands free. All night he wrestled with the body of Ramsay, trying to get it out of the doorway, but he could not move it. At the same time the other men were trying to disentangle themselves, and just before dawn Vessin, who was pressed on the top of Dewar's legs, managed to shift a little. Thereby, Dewar, getting more reach, was able to scrape an air hole over Ramsay's body.

Belgian cavalry exercising in the neighbourhood of the front. The Belgians adapted the French steel casque to general use.

A redoubt in the Belgian lines, christened the Elizabeth Redoubt in honour of the Queen of the Belgians.

The arrival of letters at a depot in the Belgian lines. Our ally adopted khaki when the supply of national uniforms gave out.

KING ALBERT'S ARMY ON THE FLANDERS FRONT: BELGIAN CAVALRY AND INFANTRY NEAR THE FIRST LINE.

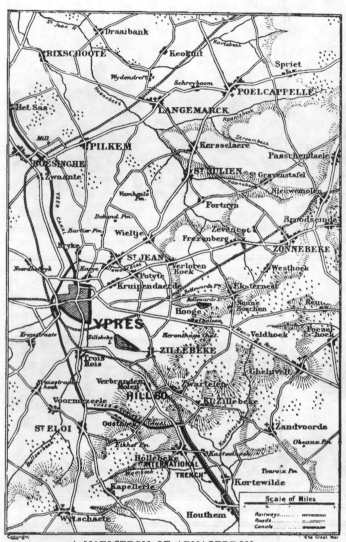

A MAELSTROM OF ARMAGEDDON.
Map of the war-scarred Ypres district and the fiercely contested "International Trench," which derived its name from the fact that it was taken and retaken several times by British and Germans.

Then he saw that the only thing to do was to dig down under Ramsay, so that his body would fall and leave a space above it. So Dewar started digging with his hands under the face and shoulders of the dead man. It was a terrible job, for the trooper could only work from his elbows, and he was already tired out and seized with cramp. But at last he made a hole big enough to squeeze through. When he got out he couldn't recognise the place.

It was nothing but a chaos of broken chalk, with the German trenches about thirty yards away. He expected to hear the whiz of a bullet, but none came. Dewar did not lose any time, but, dashing off in the direction of the British lines, came to one of the craters made by the mine explosions and there surprised one **Crippled trooper's** of his own snipers, who was looking over **splendid grit** his steel shield. From the sniper's nest Dewar reached a new British sap. Meanwhile, he had left more room in the sunken dug-out, and this enabled McLeish to dig out Johnnie's legs. Johnnie had been buried from the beginning, but never once did he complain, and when Dewar found it was impossible to bring a stretcher to him by daylight, the crippled trooper managed to drag himself out of the hole over Ramsay's body, and stagger into the sniper's nest. By this time the Germans were shooting heavily, but all the three sound troopers got away without injury, and were invited to the officers' mess for dinner. Johnnie was sent to the Ipswich Hospital, suffering from a wound in the neck as well as from half-smashed legs; but he got well, and was able to walk by April, 1916.

In regard to the main operations along the British front in the winter period, these were not of any great importance. Our offensive round Loos was concluded by a magnificent charge of the Midland Division on October 13th, 1915, that swung round the Hohenzollern Redoubt towards the "Big Willie" and "Little Willie" trenches. A brigade of Staffordshire men surged in four waves towards Big Willie trench, and, though swept down by machine-guns, cleared thirty yards of the German position by quick bombing. At night, however, they had to fall back towards our lines, after a most gallant struggle, in which Lieutenant Hawker showed great endurance. Another Midland Brigade, of Sherwood, Leicester, and Lincoln men, smashed through the barbed-wire of the Hohenzollern Redoubt and reached the Fosse trench that formed the northern base of the German salient. The men were severely tried, their first two lines being caught   **Midland Division** by machine-guns and the last two lines   **at Loos** by a hail of shrapnel. But some of the Lincolns pushed up with a machine-gun to a spot within sixty yards of the Fosse trench, while the Leicesters made a leap of three hundred yards up Little Willie trench, and the Sherwood lads forced their way along the nose of the salient.

Our men, however, were overpowered by their more numerous enemies, who came upon them from two or three sides. Then it was that Lieutenant Vickers, of the Sherwoods, made one of the most remarkable stands in trench warfare. For some time, with a party of his men, he kept a space of twenty yards clear in front of him. Any German who advanced was blown to pieces by a bomb. But the Germans came by another sap round the flank of the party, and some of the lieutenant's best men were shattered. When two men only remained, the lieutenant ordered the soldiers well behind him to build another sand-bag barricade, and thereby curtain him off so that he could not retreat. He wanted to die as hard as he could between the two barricades, so that when he fell the enemy would be still held up by the new obstacle. His two men carried bombs for him between the new barricade and the place at which he was making his stand, but energetically though they worked they could not keep him supplied. He was badly wounded, but he continued to throw bombs with quick and deadly precision, and reinforcements arrived just when he was growing faint and giddy. As eager hands reached to lift him over the barricade with which he had walled himself in to die, the officer only said "More! More!" He wanted more bombs to throw, though reeling with physical exhaustion and the effects of his wound.

All through October 14th the men of the Midlands held on to their ground in the Hohenzollern Redoubt, and some of the Sherwoods made an extraordinary advance in the eastern portion of the redoubt at the moment when the enemy was launching a counter-attack. Happily, the counter-attack was made at a different point, and the Sherwoods not only made a fresh conquest, but brought the main enemy's force round against them, and relieved the pressure on one of our weaker spots. On the night of October 15th a brigade of Guards came up to relieve the Midland Division, but the enemy was unfortunate enough to start another attack along the whole line of the redoubt when we had double forces at hand. It was a fierce, terrible, horrible bombing battle, in which men flung high explosives at each other with ghastly results. The Guards were fresh, like the Germans, but they were fewer in number. The Midlanders, however, instead of being tired out by their long exertions, also fought like fresh troops, and when day broke the enemy had been bombed back to their holes in the ground. The position we had gained was not a favourable one. We were sandwiched between Big Willie and Little Willie, with the enemy so close on the other side of our barricades that his guttural whispers could be heard.

In the southern part of our new salient at Loos there was a brilliant action after our offensive had ended. The

[Photo by Frederic Robinson.

Lieut.-General Lancelot E. Kiggell, C.B., Chief of the General Staff.

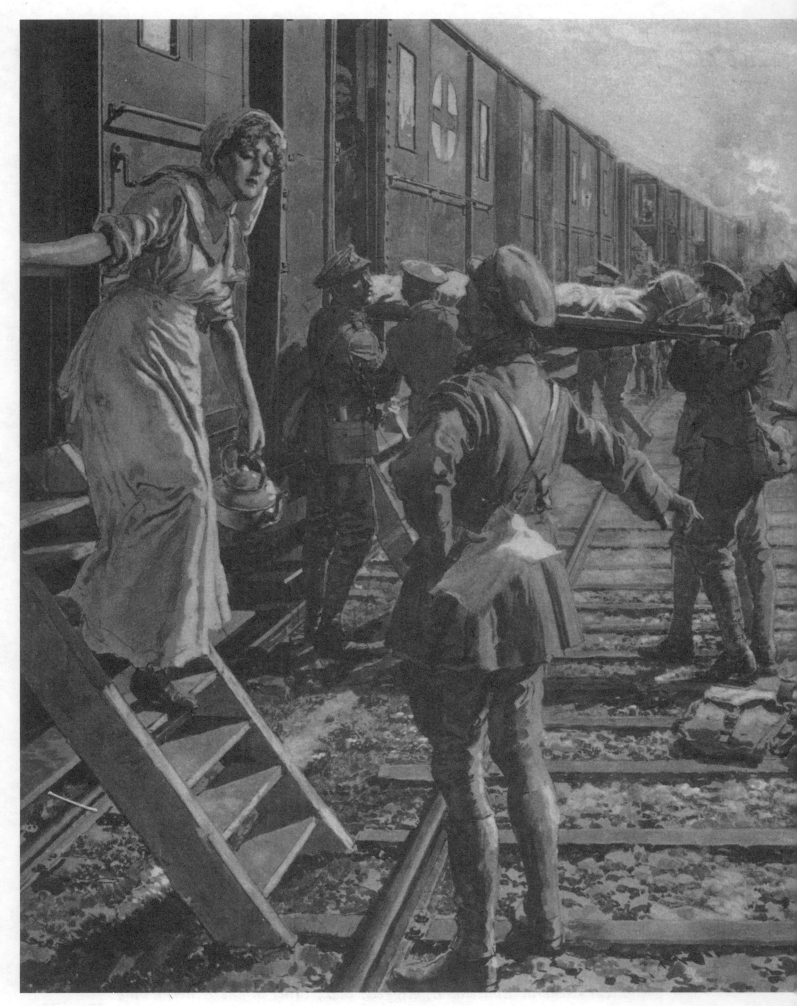

Wayside Calvary in France: Poignant scene as the woun

...rived at a junction to be put aboard the ambulance train.

In the heart of Arras: "Jack Johnson" exploding in the Grande Place.

LondonTerritorial Division, which had done so well in the battle, was filled out with fresh drafts, and sent up to the scene of its victory, when this was still dominated by the ungainly iron structure of the "Tower Bridge." In the front line there was a fantastic twist, such as is often found in the confused intricacy of entrenched warfare. Two of our trenches had been thrust forward until they connected with a bit of captured German trench, while an abandoned trench ran diagonally from one tip. The position was known as the "Tongs." One day the Germans bombed themselves back to the top of the Tongs, and thus restraightened their line, and a bombing party of Londoners was sent forward to recover the position. Many of them were fresh troops forming the new drafts, but they went about their business like veterans. The bombers stormed up the communication trenches into the German line, and then sowed death and destruction along the rows of dug-outs. It was a wild, rough-and-tumble affair, for the tangle of trenches running at every conceivable angle was as difficult a thing to race through as the maze at Hampton Court. Men who took wrong turnings sometimes lost themselves in the smoke and confusion, and Germans fell into our power when they thought they were working safely in their own second line.

One old cricketer named Nash jumped on the parapet of a German trench, and with deadly accuracy bowled his bombs into the enemy beneath until they killed him with a grenade. But there were some accidents in the mazy confusion. One British bomb fell short of the enemy, and landed among a group of Londoners. The margin of life left to them was two seconds, but Private Drewitt thrust his comrades aside and threw himself flat on the bomb. It blew him to pieces, but no one else was hurt. It was an extraordinarily fine deed, making the affair in the Tongs for ever memorable to the fighting men of London.

In the last two months of 1915 little of importance occurred along the front except our night raids and the incessant mining activity on both sides. But on December 19th the enemy, whose spirits had been shaken by our nocturnal attacks and increasing artillery fire, endeavoured to deliver a severe blow against us on the north-eastern curve of the Ypres salient. After waiting for some days for a good wind, the Germans unloosened

Private Drewitt's supreme sacrifice a vast, green, terrifying cloud of poison gas not far from the spot where they had first employed this method of frightfulness. But between April and December our defence against poison had been perfected. We had men watching day and night, and when the wind set anywhere along the front in favour of the enemy every soldier in the front line looked to his gas-helmet. And this was only the beginning of our preparations. The forward observing officers warned all their batteries in the rear, and the gunners prepared

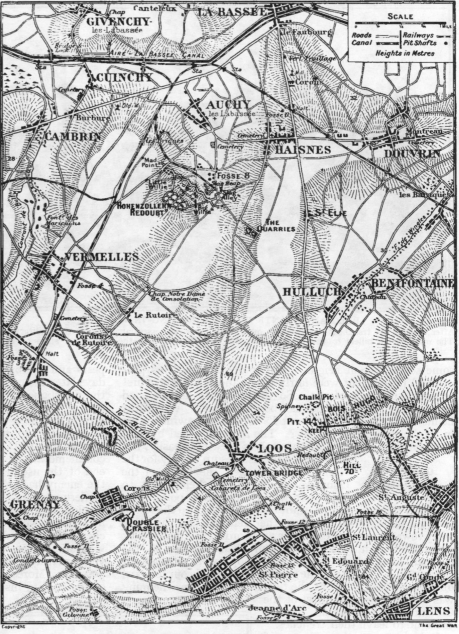

THE COCKPIT FROM GIVENCHY TO LENS.

Map of the Loos-Hulluch sector of the British line. Situated between Vermelles and Auchy is the famous Hohenzollern Redoubt. To the south of Loos the memorable "Tower Bridge" is indicated, that gaunt steel structure which figured in the British advance of September, 1915.

for a bombardment. Soon after daybreak a delicious scent was wafted into our lines by a light north-west breeze. It smelt as though a garden of lilac-trees had blossomed in midwinter. Some of the soldiers were delighted with the delicate odour, but their commanding officer burst among them, raging and shouting about goggles. The next moment all the regiment began to grow tearful, and every man fumbled frenziedly for his eye-protectors. The lovely scent arose from lachrymal shells, which the enemy had begun to use. The gas produced a violent inflammation of the eyes, calculated to blind the soldiers. But the goggles were adjusted all along the line with remarkable quickness, and five hundred black-avised monsters peered at each other through their mica eye-pieces. The artillery duel increased in fury and deafening power, and then the order came to put on gas-helmets.

The forward observing officers had seen a white mist creeping along the ground. It seemed at first only a foot high, but it gathered volume as it came onward, and when it arrived at our trenches it was a wall of grey-green vapour

BELGIAN INFANTRYMEN EXERCISING IN FLANDERS.
After days in the trenches, exercise was more than ever an essential part of the military routine.
The march from billets to the trenches was not sufficient to keep the men in a state of muscular
fitness

some seven feet in height. The troops holding this part of the Ypres salient were fairly fresh, and it was their first serious experience of gas. So their anxiety as the flood of poison rolled over them can be understood. Would the helmets absolutely keep it out? Would the awful feeling in the burning lungs be felt? The moments sped by, and the men were glad to feel themselves breathing easily, but they braced themselves up tensely for the terrible minute when the thick of the cloud would overwhelm them. But, to their happy surprise, the poison fog suddenly thinned, and the slant of wind picked up the tail of the foul fume, rolled it along the trenches, and carried it away towards the left rear. The great ordeal was over. But, meanwhile, hundreds of our guns had massed on the German lines, where the enemy troops were packed for the assault. The rise of the gas cloud had made our forward observing officers busy at the telephones. So overwhelming was our gun fire that most of the German forces could not be brought to leave their trenches.

Ordeal of the poison-gas

Only in one or two places did the Germans come forward to see if their poison cloud had cleared the way for them. In one place a hundred advanced, but the foremost of them died twenty yards from the German lines. Then all at once our infantry were startled by a dark mass of men surging along from a trench on our right. Our guns were still smashing up the parapets in the centre, and the new enemy seemed to have escaped the notice of our observers. The Germans came along in loose order, wearing gas-masks and looking like giant toads. On both flanks and in advance were companies of bombers, who began throwing their grenades when eighty yards away from their trench, so that the missiles burst harmlessly quite a hundred feet from our parapet. The

British infantrymen blazed away with their rifles, but could not kill the Germans fast enough. Nearer they came to our line. Then abruptly the affair was over. Our machine-guns had been waiting for the enemy to reach a marked range, and on a line about sixty yards from our front our rattling Maxims wiped away the entire mass of toad-like figures. Another feebler attempt made later was more rapidly checked by the machine-guns. All that was left of the assaulting troops seemed to be some hundreds of bundles of rags littering the yellowed plain. Now and then one of the bundles would drag itself along, but most were motionless.

The victorious troops had an unexpected pleasure and an unexpected disappointment. Their trenches had swarmed with rats, and they had been badly troubled by the vermin, but the poisoned c l o u d had destroyed all the pests and thoroughly disinfected the position. But some days later the regiment, which had been anxiously awaiting the newspapers in order to read of the great fight, found only a line in the British official report saying that a gas attack had been attempted, but that the enemy had been stopped by our fire

The action at Ypres on December 19th, 1915, deserves commemoration, for it probably marked the effective end of the use of heavy, visible poison-gas clouds, which the enemy had, with extreme inhumanity, introduced into modern warfare. The chlorine fumes which the Germans employed caused the most horrible, prolonged torture on men who were not prepared against the flesh-eating chemical. But by the winter of 1915 our fresh drafts were almost as well practised in gas drill as were our veteran troops, and no chlorine surprise was any longer possible. Moreover, as our artillery was as strong as that of the enemy, his use of gas only advertised the fact that

BEHIND THE INTERMINABLE RAMPARTS.
Impression of a Belgian trench consolidated with sand-bags. To the right of the figures is the entrance
to a dug-out in which a table is discernible. On the extreme left a soldier is attending to a machine-gun

he was preparing to make an infantry movement. Thus our observing officers knew when the German trenches were packed for an assault, and they were able to bring all their batteries down on the enemy's front line and kill the troops there before they could come out. Instead of being a surprise, gas had become a warning. By persisting in the use of this method of scientific barbarism, the enemy enabled the Allies to inflict upon him by artillery fire heavier losses than they had incurred from the early gas attacks. Except that we and the French lost some guns north of Ypres in April, 1915, the enemy did not in the end win any military advantage by the use of his poison cylinders, as in the total of his gas operations his failures were more numerous than his successes.

On December 30th, 1915, there was a little affair by the quarries of Hulluch, in which the Grand Fleet took part. Sir John Jellicoe had the happy idea of showing his seamen what the new armies were doing in France and Flanders. Men were accordingly picked from thirty ships of the Grand Fleet, representing all ratings, and sent on an excursion to the trenches. One party was making a sort of New Year's call in the new salient, when the Germans were preparing a great bomb attack. Five mines were exploded about the quarries with a deafening roar that was heard for miles. The Vickers gun team was buried, but the sailors rushed into the fighting-line, manned the machine-gun, and with rifles and bombs held the shattered position. They swept the ground over which the German infantry had planned to advance, and caught them in their trenches with rifle-grenades, so that no attack was possible. And, while holding the line, they dug out the soldiers buried in the mine, and happily found that the casualties were few. Petty-Officer William Bright and Ship's-Carpenter W. C.

PHYSICAL ENERGY AND MECHANICAL POWER.
Getting a Belgian 4 9 in. gun into position. The "caterpillar" wheels, first used by the Germans in moving their colossal siege-guns, are seen in working.

Hatherley had the peculiar distinction of winning the Distinguished Conduct Medal in trench warfare.

A few days afterwards the Germans exploded another mine, but again did not attempt to occupy the crater. This showed a lack of combativeness, for the side that exploded a mine could time a bombardment round about, launch a party of bombers into the crater, and make things very uncomfortable for the troops who had been surprised by the explosion. The process of attrition was carried out with more energy by the British, who, in the New Year, still continued to develop their raiding tactics all along the front.

Germans answer mosquito attacks

The Germans, however, at last answered our mosquito attacks by striking at the new junction point of the British and French armies at Frise, on the Somme. On January 27th an attack was made on the north-east of our salient at Loos, and when, after a tremendous bombardment, the German troops left their trenches, they were smashed up by our fire. But on the following day a still larger force of guns began to batter the Franco-British lines from Carnoy, about four miles north of the Somme stream, to Dompierre, south of the river marshes. We lost a few sap-heads and the Germans claimed to have taken 1,500 British and French soldiers. All the men we lost, however, consisted of a single patrol of five soldiers, two of whom escaped from their captors and returned to our line. The attack was made, after a hurricane bombardment, by the Silesian army corps. Twice the grey waves were driven back by the French gunners, who held Dompierre against all assaults. North of Dompierre the little village of Frise was lost. Nearly all the ground south of the village was recovered, but Frise was

PARADE DISCIPLINE UNDER DIFFICULTIES.
Belgian soldiers saluting their commander. Scene in a Flanders trench through which a platform of wood had been laid to facilitate manœuvres. In stepping from the platform one became ankle deep in mud.

AMERICAN WOMANHOOD AT THE SEAT OF WAR.
Member of the American Women's Mission to the western front being personally conducted through the French lines by an officer of the allied forces.

FROM "GOD'S OWN COUNTRY" TO NO MAN'S LAND.
Members of the American mission taking a discreet look at the German trenches in company with two French officers.

surrendered to the enemy because it was not worth holding. It lies on the fringe of a belt of marsh caused by the meandering and divided River Somme.

It was impossible to dig trenches in the wet ground or construct works of importance. We held strong positions on the high, dry ground north and south of the marsh, and left the enemy bogged and half drowned in the watery belt. The German commander only wasted men in the three sweeping movements he made from Carnoy to Dompierre. His losses in this local, unimportant attack were uncommonly great, for the men were sent forward in close order against the allied guns, which were at least as powerful as the German artillery employed. In our part of the line the British general withdrew most of his men when the bombardment became heavy, and after saving them and letting our guns do most of the work, he launched a counter-attack the next morning and recovered the saps at Carnoy, which were valuable. But the wedge of marshland at Frise he left to the enemy, and the Silesian troops must have had a terrible time of it when in February, a great snowstorm fell and, melting in March, turned the river swamp into a lake. It was almost

440

kindness on the part of the enemy to capture Frise and take over the impossible position there.

All these attacks were the opening of the great drive against Verdun. The aim of the German Staff was to distract the French forces by making strong demonstrations at every important point, and to keep our Staff anxious in regard to a threatened great offensive against our front. As we were still capturing prisoners almost every night, our Headquarters had continual means of verifying its calculations of the enemy's disposition. It was clear he had massed his main forces against us, and although we were very strong and eager to withstand the attack, our armies were not altogether in the best position to resist the new German offensive movement, as they were divided into two parts by the heroic French army that held Arras. The French, of course, fought as well as we did, but there was still some difference between French and British tactics. The French used their **Allied tactics** magnificent quick - firer almost like a **compared** machine-gun. Their infantry retired when it was scarcely in danger, let the terrible "75's" blast away the attacking force, and then returned to the trenches.

We, on the other hand, stuck to our positions, curtained the enemy off with shrapnel, and shot down with rifles and machine-guns the foes that got through our artillery fire. When the French came to our rescue at Ypres in the autumn of 1914, the difference between the methods of the Allies somewhat disconcerted our soldiers. Indeed, they thought it disastrous for infantry to abandon a trench as lightly as the French sometimes did, and it was some time before our fine regular battalions, whose boast was that they never budged, understood the deadly science underlying the tactics of the French. In spite of the enormous growth of our armies, we could not equal the artillery power of our French comrades. The French gunners had years of practice, and their skill was incomparable. They still formed a much more numerous class than the gunners of our new formations, and they knew their principal weapon as well as the most expert rifleman knew his rifle. Therefore, they could do things, especially with their quick-firers, which neither German nor British gunners could accomplish. Hence the difference in the tactics of the two allies.

The difference in the methods of the forces holding the line in front of Calais and Amiens did not make for homogeneity. Therefore, it was an advantage to both the French and the British when the Ninth French Army was released by our men soon after the first attack on Verdun, and all the line for some ninety miles between Boesinghe, north of Ypres, and Vaux, above the marshes of the Somme, became a solid British front. The French were sorry to leave the scene of their great battles between Souchez, the Labyrinth, and the shattered ruins of the lovely old city of Arras. But by giving up this section of the front they were able greatly to strengthen their hold on Verdun, and inflict on the Germans the severest defeat they had ever suffered. A small French force seems to have remained between Ypres and Dixmude, near the scene where the Moroccan troops and Zouaves had been overcome by the first German gas attack. But this remaining small French force did not disturb the homogeneity of the new allied dispositions. It was linked on to the Belgian Army, which was using French guns and ammunition, so that the same supplies did for both.

British front extended

Our extended army enjoyed freer communications when the French departed from the centre, and by a rapid reorganisation we prepared to resist any pressure the Germans could bring against us. All the country behind us was at last free for our needs and connected with our sea-bases, with the result that the enormous volume of munitions which would be required if 800,000 Germans moved against us was arranged to flow with the utmost speed through North-Western France. Neither side could bring up and store all the shell needed for a grand prolonged battle. The speed with which the guns worked depended upon the speed of the railways, light railways, and motor transport behind the front, and, in our case, upon the speed of our steamers and our home railways. Being much farther removed from our war factories than were the French and the Germans, we needed a good deal of elbow room behind us, and this we obtained when the growth of our armies and armament enabled us to join the Arras sector to the sectors already held by our First, Second, and Third Armies.

NEUTRAL VISITORS TO THE FIRST FRENCH LINE.
A mission of distinguished Spaniards paid a visit to the allied lines, and particularly inspected the damage wrought by German shells on French cathedrals and churches. The circle photograph shows two members of the mission learning the principles of siege warfare at first hand.

BRITISH HEAVY HOWITZER BOMBARDING THE GERMAN POSITIONS IN FRANCE.

Meanwhile, the enemy continued to demonstrate against our front. It was his way of explaining that it would be highly dangerous for us to detach any considerable force in order to help our allies when Verdun was attacked. The German bombardments of our lines increased in fury, resembling at times the rolling drum fire that heralds a great assault, when the heavy howitzers act together like a titanic machine-gun. The losses thereby inflicted upon our troops were not great, however, for as one of our gunners calculated, when he was punishing the enemy in turn, it took on the average about two tons of shell to slay one soldier in the new, deeply-dug entrenchments. But we answered the enemy's bombardments with at least equal power, shelling his gun sites with unusual vigour. At the same time our nocturnal raids developed, especially in the triangle formed by the railway from Ypres to Comines and the canal between the same places. We held a bluff by the canal, from which our men continually raided the German lines.

Shell price of a man

One night a British officer and a few men went across the canal bank, and found only one German sentry. They shot him down, and the noise brought up a rush of German troops. Our patrol waited for them to gather, and either wiped them all out with bombs or scattered in terror those who survived, for not a shot was fired back when the patrol returned to their own trenches. This kind of work went on regularly, subjecting the enemy troops to a continual nervous strain. The local German commander was compelled to do something. He drove one heavily charged mine towards the bluff, but it exploded without doing any damage. Then he made four tunnels, unfortunately under our position. Some of our miners heard what was going on, and began to drive a shaft to blow up the German moles. But it was too late, and on February 14th the German mines exploded at nightfall, creating such chaos that there was no longer a definable line for our men to hold.

Some two hundred German guns poured a smashing fire into our shattered position, and our troops fell back down the communication trenches to our support line when the mass of German infantry advanced. Thus only a few of our men were taken prisoners, and though we lost some six hundred and fifty yards of trench, the blow did not tell against us so heavily as it might have done. Two of our miners had an extraordinary escape. The gallery in which they were working was not injured, and when they ascended into the air to see what had happened the Germans were streaming into the bluff, and our two soldiers followed them unobserved in the darkness, and reached our support trench. Here we had prepared a great store of bombs; for the trench by the canal had continually changed hands during the war, and had thereby acquired the name of the "International Trench." So our bomb depôt near by was specially organised in view of a possible change in the ownership of the "International."

When our men hurriedly retired from the bluff it was with the aim of returning with the bombs, and they used these terrible missiles so well that all the Germans were smashed out of the high ground. A British group of three bomb-throwers, consisting of an officer, sergeant-major, and a private, threw 2,300 bombs in the night. They were uncommonly skilled men with a long training as grenadiers. But the fact that three men could command bombs by the thousand showed what our immediate resources were. The bluff became a No Man's Land, and after our bombing counter-attack our artillery, having exact ranges of the lost pieces of trench below the hillock, maintained day and night a heavy fire upon the position. For a fortnight our great howitzers shelled our lost line and the enemy trenches in the rear, and thus prevented the Germans consolidating themselves upon the high bank along the canal.

What three grenadiers did

The intensity of our fire increased on February 29th, and attained an extraordinary violence on March 1st from twelve to four in the afternoon. This clearly indicated that our infantry was about to storm out against the bluff. So the arc of German guns massed on our trenches, and made a curtain of fire far over our rear, as well as smashing at our front line. But we had no troops packed there for an assault. Our gunners were only trying to induce the enemy infantry to come forward with hand-bombs in the fire-trench, and there be killed. Our answering fire after the great feint was so tremendous that our men could hardly be restrained from rushing out and making an assault. Some of them got on the parapet and cheered. It must certainly have been exhilarating for them to see that, when the Germans by a supreme effort had brought at least two hundred guns of all calibres round the bluff, our resources enabled us to dominate completely the best that the enemy could do. All through the night our heavy howitzers gave the enemy " bouquets " of fire. The bouquet is a pretty name for a terrible piece of artillery tactics, which consists in swamping a position with high-explosive shell in sudden, short spurts. Between two of these spurts an attack could be made, but the enemy had no means of guessing at what interval the assault would come. Our guns also shot at any flame from the German **Giving the foe** artillery positions, as the Germans used to **" bouquets " of fire** do when they possessed an overwhelming superiority in siege ordnance.

After one bouquet the British infantry came out in the darkness without firing a shot, and running at top speed, found all the wire entanglements broken by our guns, and with little loss climbed over the German parapet. The enemy's front lines were apparently almost empty, not more than a hundred men being found alive. But the dead were thick in the maze of trenches, and our men stumbled across them. Most of the German troops had gone to cover in deep dug-outs, and they were in a pitiable condition after surviving our bomb attack—dazed by the

continuous shell fire and cold with terror. Our troops stormed on beyond their objective into a salient in the original German line, and there found more men alive in dug-outs, but could not induce them to come out. We had to threaten to blow them up before they would surrender. They were not desperate men who preferred to die fighting rather than to yield, but human beings crazed by a fortnight's bombardment with heavy howitzers.

Our attack had been organised with extreme attention to the most minute details, and all the work of taking up sand-bags and ammunition was carried out successfully, so that when the enemy **Veiled in the** began a counter bombardment with every **driving snow** available gun, and then launched wave after wave of German infantry against the bluff, not a yard of ground was lost by us. Through the thick snowstorm of the first week in March the enemy vainly tried to beat us back again from the canal. Our artillery could not then mark the German batteries and shell them down, but the position of all the German trenches around the bluff was precisely known, so our gunners retaliated on the hostile infantry. It was an extraordinary scene, veiled in the driving snow, and yet rocking with a double bombardment of British and German guns. Nearly all the troops on both sides were in deep dug-outs, but some heroic men had to stand amid the tornado of shell, deafened by the racket and blinded by the snow, yet still watching for a possible rush attack.

Fierce local activity prevailed all along the British front during March, for the enemy was anxious about our intentions during the critical period of the Verdun operations. He seems rather to have expected that Sir Douglas Haig would make a grand attack on his lines with a view to relieving the pressure upon Verdun. According to a French report, the British Commander-in-Chief informed

[*Official photograph issued by the Press Bureau.*
STRIKING ILLUSTRATION OF A 60-POUNDER GUN AT WORK ON THE BRITISH FRONT.

THE KAISER'S SON-IN-LAW IN FRANCE.
Duke of Brunswick greeting a member of the Staff in a village behind the German lines in the West.

THE BATTERY ON THE PLAGE.
German Marines who manned the coast positions of Belgium alongside their gun hidden between two villas.

Black Sea and to Petrograd. They wished to attack the new Russian navy in the Baltic by seizing its base by a land attack and assailing it with submarines and battleships from the sea. We had to remain as strongly menacing as possible, so as to keep not only guns and men against us but shell supplies, until Russia was ready and the snow had melted on the Alpine front of Italy. The Germans were using many 12 in. Austrian guns at Verdun, and by wearing them out and depleting their store of 12 in. shells, General Pétain was fighting for Italy and Russia as well as for France. In the French view, the Germans had made a great mistake in assuming the offensive at Verdun, and it would have helped them to recover from their mistake if we had begun in turn to use up our shell supply at a time when Germany could have concentrated against us the larger part of her resources.

So our commander waited for the time to arrive when the Central Empires would be fully extended in a desperate defence on the Russian front, the Italian front, and the Franco-British-Belgian front. In the meantime, we went on with our "little war," by means of nocturnal raids and even daylight raids, smashing bursts of artillery, and mining operations. In the last week of March we drove a series of mines under one of the strongest enemy positions round Ypres, south of the ruined town, and at the shoulder of our salient by the village of St. Eloi. The Germans occupied a mound between two forking roads; they had wired the position very thickly, and behind the deep lines of barbed cables they had a strong parapet nearly nine feet high, with machine-gun emplacements sweeping all the ground below the mound. The stronghold seemed absolutely safe against any sudden assault, but the German miners did not listen intently enough, and our sappers were able to drive their galleries well into the mound and place there an uncommonly large amount of high explosives. At

German stronghold at St. Eloi

General Castelnau that he was ready to make an attack, but the French Staff thought that it was in the best interests of the Allies to allow the enemy to waste his men by the hundred thousand against Verdun, without replying in another part of the line to the force he was exerting. As has been stated, we helped the French Army by taking over the Arras section, and then remained upon the defensive with some 800,000 Germans opposed to us. Both sides had enormous stores of shell ready for the most terrific battles of the war. If Verdun had fallen, our Army, which had increased to more than a million men, and outnumbered the greatest German army in existence, might have smashed forward, even at a heavy sacrifice and with an enormous expenditure of shell.

As General Pétain at Verdun was gaining the mastery over the enemy, it would have gone against the general interests of the Allies had we used up a large portion of the output of our Ministry of Munitions. The Germans wanted to exhaust the French and British winter accumulation of shell, so as to be able to turn most of the produce of their war factories against Russia and blast a road to the

half-past four in the morning of March 27th, 1916, the ground for miles around shook as with an earthquake, and on the mound tons of soil rose up like a black cloud beneath a flaming volcano and then fell through the darkness.

Before the explosion of earth came down, the two battalions entrusted with the attack—the Northumberland Fusiliers and the Royal Fusiliers—were over their parapets and rushing like footballers to the goal. So quickly indeed did they get away that when the enemy's machine-guns opened fire on our parapet our trenches were empty. The fences of barbed-wire had not been injured by the explosions, and the Fusiliers had no time to stop and cut through the obstacle. They went over it by climbing on each other's shoulders or working through with torn hands and clothes. The nine-foot parapet was also strangely intact, and the men again helped each other over into the hostile salient. At the apex of the salient there was a machine-gun with a crew of five men and an officer, which had escaped destruction. The Germans turned their gun on the two thousand Englishmen struggling amid the wires, so that, with the bullets streaming out at a rate of four hundred a minute, terrible havoc would have been wrought among the assailants.

Brilliant attack by Fusiliers

But a British subaltern, with three men, rushed straight for the machine-gun position, and the officer flung a bomb with such precision that he saved the situation. His missile knocked out the gun, killed the officer and two men, and before the others could recover they were bayoneted. Inside the stronghold there was no great and determined resistance. Trenches had been reduced to chaos, the dug-outs destroyed, while the communication saps were so blocked up by masses of earth that no reinforcements could come up and no survivors could escape. It was a young Jaeger regiment from Schleswig-Holstein, with a considerable number of Danish lads among them, that held the salient. A company of them perished in the explosion, and most of the dazed survivors were taken without any trouble. Only on the extreme right was there any attempt at a counter-attack. But by the time the German bombers arrived, the "Fighting Fifth" had discovered a store of enemy grenades, and they so smote the enemy with their own missiles that thirty-five of the German grenadiers who were sent up to make the counter-attack came over and surrendered.

Strengthened by the German hand-grenade depôt, the Fusiliers extended their attack into the enemy's second

CANADIAN INGENUITY.

Neat stove improvised from a petrol can. Several of these stoves were used in a certain section of the Canadian trenches.

BREAKDOWN WITH THE ARTILLERY CROSSING A RIVER IN FLANDERS.

Owing to the sudden overflow of a river the bridge collapsed and a heavy gun slipped into the stream, but was eventually hauled out. Circle: Cook at work. British soldier preparing food in a dixey for his comrades.

AN ENTENTE IN TRENCHLAND.
Canadians working at the front with their
Belgian allies.

the other attacking battalion of the Royal Fusiliers also fought with noble courage and skill, and behind the two battalions of the Fusiliers was a fine Canadian force, which took over the position. The Germans could not suffer patiently the defeat inflicted upon them. Their position across the marsh was so weak that it had to be strengthened at any cost. More heavy howitzers were brought round, and on March 30th the enemy's guns pounded to pieces the trench that carried our front across the salient. His infantry could not advance to make a frontal attack over the marsh, and our artillery put a curtain of fire round the eastern side. Yet the German troops were pushed through our tempest

line of trenches, beyond which there was a stretch of marshy ground nearly a hundred yards wide. The enemy had to fall back over the swamp, with the result that his front became most weak at the place in which it had been most strong. Among the men who distinguished themselves in the opening scene of the fierce little battle of St. Eloi was the Rev. Edward Noel Mellish, who won the Victoria Cross by rescuing many wounded men from certain death during the prolonged and intense bombardment with which the German artillery endeavoured to prevent us from consolidating the position. Not since 1879 had any Army chaplain won the V.C., and the men who stormed St. Eloi were proud to think that their padre, who looked after their

[*Official photograph issued by the Press Bureau.*]

BUSY CANADIAN SNIPER.
Canadian crack shot at work amid an environment of débris and desolation caused by eternal gun fire.
The sniper's work was perhaps the most exciting relief from the trench ordeal.

Army chaplain wins the V.C.

bodies as well as their souls, had won the highest distinction for heroism. It was also during the opening bombardment by the German batteries that there occurred one of the most comical incidents in the war. An officer, suddenly entering an apparently deserted traverse, came upon two men of the "Fighting Fifth," with a bareheaded Jaeger between them. They were two Tynesiders. They had put their rifles down, and one of them was unbuttoning his tunic and swearing most violently. The shrapnel screamed above them, and the German soldier did not seem to like the situation. But the two men went on preparing for their boxing match. They both claimed the prisoner, and could not come to an agreement about him, so they were going to fight it out, although the bombardment was growing more appalling every moment. The arrival of the officer, however, put an end to the extraordinary comedy.

In this attack our men wore the new steel helmets, and although there was some hard fighting, in which the "Fighting Fifth" especially distinguished themselves, the casualties were very small. The Londoners who composed

of shrapnel, and after much loss of life they bombed their way into one of the craters. Fighting went on day and night between the Canadians and the Germans. We in turn brought more guns up, and hammered at the bit of shattered mound which the enemy had reoccupied.

Then on April 2nd the Canadians recaptured the lost crater, and extended the British line well beyond it, fighting with magnificent endurance and taking a good toll of prisoners. But terrible as were the hand-to-hand combats with high-explosive grenades, they were not so wearing as the shell fire which the Germans poured on the position they had thrice lost. St. Eloi was worse than Ypres in the autumn of 1914, for the German artillery had much increased in power, and though ours was equal to it our guns could not win the local mastery. In this local battle there was only a given space in which either side could mass its guns. We were in a corner, just at the southern shoulder of the Ypres bulge; our arc of fire there was narrow, while the German arc of fire some miles in front of us was broad. All their large guns, from Messines to the Menin Road, could concentrate upon the heap of earth at

St. Eloi. The Canadians had to endure a battering such as that from which General Herr's men withdrew near Douaumont Fort. When the enemy thought the Canadians were annihilated, the German infantry again stormed up on April 5th, and maintained the attack for a day and a night. But at the end of the struggle only one crater out of five was in their possession. Then our guns played on the crater, and on April 9th the Canadians not only recaptured it but smashed their way along the German trenches lying to the south-west of the position. Two days afterwards, with a bombardment going on day and night, a fresh German force took two of the five craters; but though the Canadians were outnumbered, they held on to the main part of the mound and repulsed another great German attack.

By this time the German commander round Ypres had resolved upon a supreme effort. He had lost the bluff near Hill 60, and the small piece of chaos to which his men clung at St. Eloi had cost him thousands of lives, but left him with his line across the marshes. Our raiding parties were still continuing their work and fretting the nerves of all his men; so in Prussian fashion he tried to deal us a

NOTRE DAME DES CAVES.
Unique service at Rheims, held in a wine-cellar, with full champagne cases for pews and schoolchildren and steel-helmeted soldiers for the congregation.

stunning blow which would more than make good his losses. On the night of April 19th he opened a hurricane bombardment all round Ypres, from Pilkem in the north to St. Eloi in the south, and then launched four great attacks —at Pilkem, at Wieltje, at the Bluff, and at St. Eloi. The German infantry were successful in reaching some of our trenches, but they suffered so terribly from our machine-guns and from our artillery fire that our troops smashed up most of the remnants with hand-bombs and bayonets. We lost, however, the craters at St. Eloi, and also a trench on the Langemarck Road.

The Langemarck position had been lost by us owing to the condition of the ground. The mud between our support line and our lost front line was never less than kneedeep,. Not a few lives were lost by actual drowning in the quagmire. But our Staff did not care to leave the mud between us and the enemy as a sufficient defence. On the night of April 21st the King's Shropshire Light Infantry dragged themselves slowly over the ground in three columns, with the rain beating down on them and the enemy's shells burying them beneath geysers of the liquid earth. In places it took the column some hours to cross the two hundred yards to the German line. The men were up to their armpits in the mud, **Shropshires' gallantry at Langemarck** and as the uncertain bottom with its quicksands of ancient shell-holes would not support them and their rifles, they had to progress by holding their weapons at arm's length over their heads, leaning against the mire until they sank forward into it, and then drawing their legs after them to regain an upright position.

All the timing of the attack went to pieces, and the fighting with the Germans was a series of disconnected struggles between small groups of men, with bogged Staff officers groping for the groups in the rain and shrapnel tempest in order to join them together. One man, unwounded and quite sound, remained stuck in the mud, utterly helpless and undiscovered from April 21st till April 25th. But in spite of the extraordinary difficulties, the attacking line zigzagged at last into the German trenches, where few of the defenders escaped. One wounded private would not be removed, because he reckoned the Shropshires were not strong enough to resist the inevitable counter-attack. The wounded man remained for thirty-six hours, during which time he helped to beat off two counter-attacks, and

SCHOOL LESSONS UNDERGROUND.
Children of Rheims at lessons in a wine cellar. These little pupils of France went to and from their underground school wearing respirators, a necessary precaution against poison gas.

then had to be carried away on a stretcher. One important sap down which the enemy tried to advance was victoriously held by a single Shropshire private. In another part of the trench an officer directed his men though the enemy's fire had left him with one arm hanging to the shoulder only by a sinew.

But the main difficulty came when the order was given to consolidate the conquered position. "How can you consolidate porridge?" someone asked. What remained of the trench could be taken up and poured through the hand, and the following day the German official communiqué stated that the position had been abandoned because of the wetness of the ground. But our men found that during the two days the Germans had been in occupation of the position they had worked like beavers in the water-filled dyke, posting machine-guns, fitting steel loopholes, and cutting new communication trenches. It was not the flood of water that disturbed the Germans but the flood of Shropshire men, whose exploit ranks amongst the most remarkable in the war. One lance-sergeant took a wounded man to shelter over a distance of six hundred yards. He carried him first through the mud, until he was himself wounded in the shoulder. Then, with his unwounded arm, he let the man float on the mud,

Irish heroism at Loos

moving forward himself as best he could. It took him six and a half hours to cover the six hundred yards. It may be doubted if any other successful attack has been delivered through such a depth of mud against a heavily-gunned army like the German force round Ypres.

Another exploit of great brilliance and much farther-reaching importance was performed in the Loos salient on April 27th, 1916. The rising of the Sinn Fein conspirators was then causing suffering and misery in Dublin, and a violent band of Irish-German plotters in the United States was endeavouring to exaggerate the nature of the outbreak which they had organised and financed, and make it out to be a movement of revolt with a national force behind it. But at this crisis, when the German Emperor was trying to use Ireland both against President Woodrow Wilson in the dispute over submarine warfare and against the Allies generally, the German commander at Lille made a grave mistake. He enabled the real fighting men of Ireland to show beyond doubt and with instant energy for what cause they were ready to lay down their lives by ordering an attack upon **German commander's** that part of the British line which **costly error** was being held by an Irish division.

The Irishmen were feeling uncommonly sore and moody. A few days before Sir Roger Casement had landed in their country—Casement who, as was alleged, had tried to seduce Irish prisoners of war in Germany from their allegiance, and had left them to be starved and otherwise ill-treated when they refused to fight for the spoilers of Belgium. Then, to crown the sorrow of the Irish troops, the Sinn Fein rising had occurred. The Germans probably knew well what division it was that held the chalk-pit salient at Loos. The attack was one of those wildly fatuous essays in psychology in which the laboriously blundering Teutonic mind delights. The Germans calculated that the Irish troops would be so upset and distracted by what was happening in Ireland that they would not be able to hold their ground.

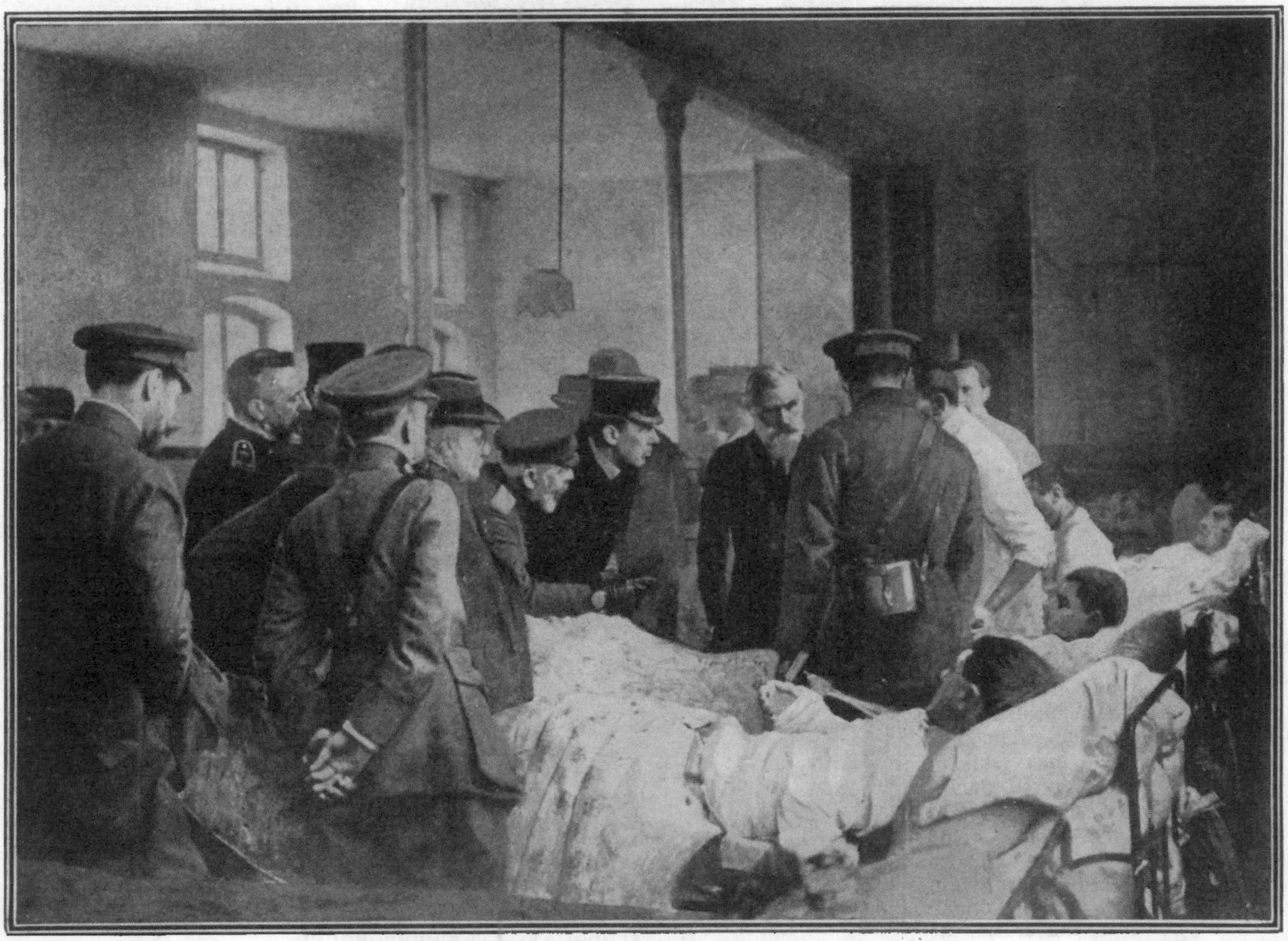

SOLVING THE PROBLEM OF TRANSPORT OF WOUNDED. [*French official photograph.*]
Expeditious transport of wounded soldiers from hospitals at the front to the base was one of the most difficult problems of the war. At one time the Allies appointed a joint commission to devise the quickest and best possible means of carrying out this work. This illustration shows the mission prosecuting inquiries among the doctors, attendants, and wounded soldiers themselves at a hospital in France.

CHAOS! THE RESULT OF ENEMY MARKSMANSHIP.
All that was left of a French chateau close to the Canadian lines after it had been wrecked by German shell fire.

[Official photograph issued by the Press Bureau.

Day broke clear and bright over the angle of lines in the chalk-pit between Loos and Hulluch, but there was a gentle easterly breeze blowing. An easterly breeze was suspect, and, though the enemy had attempted no serious gas attack for some months, there was no relaxation of defensive precautions in our lines. And this was well, for some forty minutes after day broke a thick, sluggish, greenish cloud rolled from the enemy's trenches on a front of more than a mile. "Poison gas! Put on your helmets!" cried the Irish officers. "I wish we could give Roger Casement a taste of it in his throat!" said one of the men. Quickly they put on their masks, and the cloud of agonising death rolled over the Dublin Fusiliers and Inniskillings who held the fire-trenches, and thinned out among their comrades in the rear. The sergeants walked among the men where the poison fume was thickest, patting them on the shoulder and making pantomimic fun of the Hunnish method of warfare.

As the gas was passing over, the enemy's artillery, which had been pounding all night at the salient, poured in a final smashing fire, and then lifted against the Irish support trenches and deluged them with blinding gas shells and shrapnel to prevent any reinforcement of the fire-trenches. Two columns of German infantry stormed across the neutral zone. The Dublin battalion was composed mainly of young troops who had not withstood an infantry attack, but, despite the gas cloud, the lachrymal shells, and hurricane fire of high-explosive shell, the men had that within that kept them as steady as veterans. Not a German got through what remained of the barbed-wire defence. The Dublins shot down both columns.

Then, on the northern side of the chalk-pit salient, held by the Inniskillings, the hostile commander launched another

TURNING HIS HANDIWORK TO HIS OWN HURT.
After the Huns had destroyed this church in Flanders by shell fire, the Belgians entrenched it and fortified it with its own masonry, in case the desecrators should try to pass that way.

attack in the same fashion. First came a great gas cloud, followed by a terrific artillery bombardment and a curtain fire on the Irish support line. In this case the German gunners were more expert, for they broke down the parapet at the angle of the trenches, blowing away the sand-bags and completely smashing up the wire fence in front of the position. The second German infantry attack, meeting with no obstacle whatever, reached the first Irish line, and the Inniskillings, with some of the Dublins, fell back down the communication trenches towards the support line. But when the Germans entered the destroyed fire-trench they had good cause to wish they were back in their own lines. The traverses as well as the parapets had been destroyed, and the result was that an Irish machine-gunner, surviving in a good position along the line, was able to enfilade the attackers and turn the trench they had won into a death-trap. In a very few minutes the Inniskillings returned with fixed bayonets. Their blood was up, and they did their work with fierce speed and terrible neatness. It was a complete clean up, for most of the Germans who tried to escape from the Irish bayonets were caught by the machine-gun near the end of the salient. Such was the answer of the true fighting men of Erin to the German and Germanised conspirators in Dublin and the United States.

The enemy then tried a third gas attack, but when the cloud was floated out the wind changed and swept it over the poison users. So the action ended with the balance of losses in effectives lying heavily against the Germans, while the victorious Irish battalions still held the chalk-pit salient, which they rebuilt in the night and made stronger.

It must be borne in mind, in the study of these small local affairs, that either side could at any time take a

A POPULAR FIGURE AT HEADQUARTERS.

The French Generalissimo receiving the salute of British Staff officers on the occasion of a visit to General Sir Douglas Haig's headquarters. Père Joffre was as popular with British officers and men as he was with his own "enfants."

the sea, would have allowed the Germans to acquire another strip of territory at the cost of bad tactical positions. There was, indeed, a rumour that our Staff was considering this move early in the spring of 1915, but for some reason not yet clearly known, and possibly rather of a political than a military nature, it was resolved that our army should hold fast to the lowlands about Ypres and the marshes around the plateau of Lille. We afterwards made a series of attempts to get on to the Lille plateau, but as we did not succeed in reaching the ridge or any of the hills held by the enemy, we had to abide in the fenland under the plunging fire of the German guns.

Our army, therefore, had more occasion than the German to undertake snatching attacks, especially along our northern sector. But after the Battle of Loos we seldom massed our guns in order to steal bits of the enemy's front line. Even at St. Eloi we only employed ordinary mining tactics, followed by the ordinary dash for the craters. We managed to keep the enemy at full tension by raids and mines that cost us little more than the average casualties of trench warfare. But the German commanders, though occupying the positions of vantage, were obliged, in order to return our continual worrying small blows, to employ all the mechanism of a grand attack. Yet thereby they achieved nothing.

Nearly all the valuable gains were made by us, and though the patches of ground we won were small, they not only afforded us points for developing further attacks, but the lessons that we learnt in these little successes contained the germs of methods likely to be of high value in the near future.

fragment of the opposing front by massing artillery against it and sacrificing a few battalions. A great concentration of guns, with a large expenditure of shell, could break into the fire-trenches of either British or German troops. It was a question whether the small gain was worth the lives and the munitions it cost. We really had throughout the parallel battle more reason to make snatches of this sort, because our original line was badly sited. In October and November, 1914, the Germans had seized upon practically all positions of military value, leaving us with the alternative of falling back to the next strong line or of clinging to low-lying ground of no tactical importance. Underestimating the possible length of the standstill on entrenched positions, our Staff chose to keep as close as possible to the German line, and occupy inferior positions which were dominated by the machine-guns, mortars, and light artillery in or near the enemy's front trenches. The mistake was inevitable at the time it was made, as no one thought the pause would last for long, and our chiefs desired to remain at grips with the enemy in view of a possible offensive. But the result was that in the first period of trench warfare our weekly average of casualties was larger than that of the enemy. He possessed also the power of launching attacks upon us from the higher ground which he occupied almost all along the line, and his artillery observing officers had wider fields of view than our forward observing officers usually had.

Probably a French commander would have given up the bad ground in order to save the constant toll upon his men, and, by retiring across the lowland marshes to higher ground nearer

Enemy's advantage of ground

WHAT A HIGH EXPLOSIVE DID IN A FLEMISH FIELD.

German 21 cm. shell-crater, whose size may be gauged from the figure of the Belgian officer standing in the centre. A Belgian girl, who was apparently contemptuous of the work of these monster projectiles, is seen posing on the crater edge.

French official photographs.]

IN THE LAND OF THEIR HEART'S DESIRE.

It was the Germans with whom the Australians chiefly desired to cross swords, and they were not content until they actually arrived in France, bound for the western front. The photographs show one of the regiments of Australian Cavalry, athletic and elated men, en route to their camp quarters.

We had a total British field army of some seventy divisions. Nearly all our privates were raw troops, mainly officered by inexperienced men, and directed by a Staff which had no practice whatever in handling such enormous numbers of men, guns, and supplies. Everybody in the army was a learner, from the Commander-in-Chief downwards. Knowledge had to be gained under the fire of the German siege-guns and amid the hurry and confusion of battle. The long period of trench warfare was therefore for us a blessing in disguise. We could never

Knowlege gained under fire have put into the field in the time a national army capable of manœuvring in mobile warfare against the well-led German forces. Our new recruits could not have done what our small force of regular soldiers had accomplished. Flung into the furnace of battle in the open field, the new divisions would have fared like the divisions of Prussian Landwehr in the struggle with Napoleon's veterans. Only after much battering, and probably some severe disasters, like that which overtook part of the New Army in Suvla Bay, would they have acquired the cohesion of the conscript forces of the Continent.

Going by the experiences of part of the Anglo-Celtic race in the Civil War of the United States, we could estimate what our fine-spirited, but inefficient, volunteer army might do in ordinary mobile warfare. The most hopeful men reckoned that we should pull through by tenacity of character, and, after great suffering, emerge with a diminished but veteran national force, officered by sifted men who had proved in the heat of battle their natural gifts of leadership. Happily however for us, we were able to train our New Army in a long period of trench warfare, in which the lines shifted much less than they had done in the great parallel battles between the Federal and Confederate forces of the United States. The great standstill on the western front was an extraordinary and utterly unexpected stroke of good luck for us. Our Staff, who had never handled more than a hundred thousand men, learnt to handle more than a million. We brought up our artillery fully to the Continental standard, discovered by experience every secret in the armoury of the enemy, and applied our own talents for invention and organisation in making surprise weapons against him.

It had taken Prussia more than a hundred years to develop her national Army from a broken professional fighting force, swelled by a horde of half-trained militia, into the mightiest military force in the world. Checked by France and wasted by Russia, the force that Prussianised Germany wielded still remained extremely formidable ; but we were able, by the happy accident of trench warfare, to train our new cadres, our new troops, and our amateur artillerymen into soldiers of the first quality in a manner so rapid as to constitute the greatest miracle in history.

In ancient days men could be made into warriors in a few months. Weapons were simple and short in range, and races that lived in the open air and often shot for their food—as men used to do in our islands before the industrial revolution—had an **A miracle in** abundance of natural marksmen for **history** battles that took place at a range of a few hundred yards. But when the technique and the machinery of human slaughter were intricately developed by the progress of modern science, the need for long training in all ranks made conscription inevitable. France, with a larger population than Prussia and the German States closely allied to Prussia, was overthrown in 1870 because she had abandoned conscription while Prussia had retained it. The French new army of volunteers, operating on the Loire, had one temporary success due to its fine spirit, but enthusiasm could not compensate for lack of training, and it eventually was severely defeated. Another hastily formed force in the north was also overthrown, and in the east and south-west more defeats followed. Narrowly did we escape at Ypres the risk of having to expose our New Army in similar mobile warfare against trained conscript forces.

Yet if the Germans had got to Calais, they might have been able to starve us by their submarine campaign. A national army would then have been almost useless to us. But by a supreme effort, which practically cost us all our finely trained but small regular force, and drained France for the time almost of her last available soldier, the enemy was kept away from the coast, and our strangely fortunate race was given a miraculous opportunity for accomplishing in two years what it had taken Prussia one hundred and ten years to carry out. According to a statement made by Mr. Asquith, on May 2nd, 1916, "the total naval and military effort of the Empire from the beginning of the war up to this moment exceeds five million men." The precise meaning of this was much discussed, but from another statement on May 3rd it appeared that our field army of white troops numbered eighty-three divisions of twenty-five thousand men each.. It could be fairly reckoned that the larger part of this great force was operating in France and Flanders, and there winning, with all its Staff machinery and its artillery and transport organisation, as alertly practical an experience of the latest developments of warfare as was possessed by the German army opposed to it.

In the trenches our rank and file felt themselves to be more spirited fighting men than the privates and corporals opposed to them, and our officers, though wisely appreciative of the powers of discipline and direction shown by the German regimental officers, began to think that we were catching up with the finest trained force **Germany's mag-** in the world. General Joffre had frankly **nificent organisation** admitted, towards the end of 1915, that the enemy opened the war with " a superiority in his subaltern cadres "—that is to say in his regimental officers ; and in the same passage in the French official review of the first phases of the war, it was also admitted that the divisional and brigade Staff work in the German infantry and artillery was in many cases at first superior to that of the French. It was also in even larger measure superior to that of the Russian. In short, Germany started with possessing the finest body of officers in the world. Our small band of finely trained professional leaders did not enter into the field of comparison any more than did the similar but not so small body of Serbian officers. Britain and Serbia did not count, though we both did good work. It was the clash of the grand Continental masses that first decided the course of the war, and, when Austria was badly crippled, Germany had to fight both France and Russia, and though she was able to use the Austrians as cannon fodder and take part of the Austrian

guns, her organisation was so magnificent that she was still able to make an effort far greater than Napoleon ever made.

Such was the standard of achievement which we had to equal when we took over the greater part of the north-western front. Germany was still able to organise against us an effort as tremendous as that by which she had broken the Russian line between the Vistula and the Carpathian Mountains. And our position was naturally weaker than that which Radko Dimitrieff had lost along the Dunajec and Biala Rivers ; for the Germans, as we have seen, held nearly all the dominating hills and ridges, while we clung to the lower slopes or wallowed in marshlands. But our difficulties helped to save us. They trained us in the hard and terrible school of adversity, until our new officers were transformed into veteran leaders and our grimly humorous, indomitable troops had learnt practically every trick of war, and were **Difficulties that** enabled to carry on the imperishable **helped us** traditions of the little regular British army that had fallen between Mons and Ypres. Owing to the inferior positions we held, the wastage of our army reached a proportion very unusual in parallel battles along entrenched fronts. The call for drafts for our units amounted to more than a hundred per cent. annually, according to a statement made by Lord Wimborne. Conscription, therefore, was forced upon us. We had either to retire from the field and submit to a German peace against ourselves and our Allies, or take steps to fill out our wastage by compulsory service.

The incidence of losses in parallel battles had been terribly aggravated since the Federal and Confederate States of America entrenched against each other from 1861 to 1865. In that long period the Union Army of some 2,800,000 men had only a total of 67,058 men killed in action, and 43,012 mortally wounded. Our small regular army in Flanders had more men killed in one year along a front of thirty miles than the two million and a half Union troops, stretched from Texas to Virginia, lost in four years. Machine-guns, long-range artillery, and high-explosive shell had made the war of entrenched positions far deadlier than it was in the days of Grant and Lee. There was a veritable process of attrition in the modern parallel battle, which was calculated to wear down in a remarkably rapid way the resources of the mightiest empires. Whether the Germans suffered as heavily as we did is, at the time of writing, a matter of speculation. Our increasing artillery power certainly helped towards a balance of losses, and the larger output of shell when Mr. Lloyd George got all his new factories going strengthened our gunners in a striking manner. But what the balance of all the results was by May, 1916, is a thing at which we can only guess. Probably we still had a good deal to make up.

FRENCH SOLDIERS IN THE TRENCHES WATCHING "SOME ARTILLERY ACTIVITY."
High explosives and shrapnel were bursting on the enemy positions, indicated by white lines in the background.

BRITISH CAMEL CORPS

CHAPTER CXVIII.

IN THE DESERT.

THE DEFENCE OF EGYPT AND BATTLES IN THE EASTERN AND WESTERN WASTES.

The Action at El Kubri—Turks Killed by Drinking Salt Water—Meissner Pasha Tries to Run Water-pipes Through the Desert—British Engineers also Water-pipe the Waste and Make Motor Roads—Indian Troops Occupy the Well of Moses—The Red Gibraltar of the Sin Desert—Tremendous Defence System Along the Suez Canal—German Water Supply Destroyed by Airmen—Anzac Swoop Into the Wilderness—Kressenstein Tries to Stay Our March Along the Serbonian Road—Heroic Stand by Ayrshire Men at Duweidar—Worcester Yeomanry Surprised at Katia—Turco-German Advance Broken by Our Air Attack and Katia Recovered —New Trouble in the Western Deserts—The Warrior-Prophet of the Sahara and the Mystery of the Senussi—The New Mahdi Descends Upon the Italians, but Befriends Shipwrecked Britons—Arrival of German Submarines at Sollum with Guns for the Senussi—Enver Pasha's Brother Incites the Senussiyeh Against Us—Intrigues of Turk and Teuton in Egypt and Attempts to Assassinate the Sultan—Extraordinary Letter from the Kaiser—The Tara is Torpedoed and Sollum Captured—Egyptian Garrisons Retire to Matruh, and the Senussi Raises the Tribesmen Against Us—Colonel Gordon's Stand Against Gaafar Pasha—Critical Battle on Christmas Day—Splendid Charge by New Zealand Recruits and Sikhs—Battle of Hazalin and Picturesque Victory of the South Africans—General Lukin Forms a Mobile Column and Springs on the Enemy—The South African Brigade Storms Agagia Ridge—Magnificent Charge of the Dorset Yeomanry—Enemy is Outflanked and Ridden Down, and Turkish Commanders Killed or Captured—Panic Flight of the Senussi into the Libyan Desert—South Africans Storm the Mountain Passes and Win the Key to Sollum—Duke of Westminster, with Nine Armoured Motor-Cars, Charges the Senussi Army—Thirty-two British Soldiers Capture All the Enemy's Artillery and Rout Six Thousand Troops—Wonderful Motor Race Into the Heart of the Desert and Rescue of Tara Men—British Forces Hem the Broken Foe in the Libyan and Sahara Deserts—The Bait of the Date and Return of the Tribesmen—Italians Recover their Tripoli Ports and Cut Off the Senussi from Sea Supplies.

AFTER the failure of the Turkish attack on the Suez Canal, in February, 1915, the operations of the enemy army in Palestine came to an end. Baron von Kressenstein, who was in actual command of the Turkish force which was nominally led by Djemal Pasha, pretended afterwards that the expedition was merely a reconnoitring affair, and that it fulfilled its end by discovering that the canal was safeguarded by so many British warships that a Turkish advance into Egypt was out of the question. The German commander calculated that he would have to extend the Syrian Railway down to Beersheba and undertake great engineering works across the desert before he could bring close to the Suez Canal a sufficiently large army to make the conquest of Egypt possible.

The famous German railway engineer, Meissner Pasha, could not obtain the material he needed to prolong the railway partly through the desert. All the Turkish lines were in a dilapidated state, and in the Asiatic region of the Empire especially the tracks were becoming very bad, and the boilers of many

MAJOR THE DUKE OF WESTMINSTER, D.S.O. (Cheshire Yeomanry).
Photographed on the terrace at Shepheard's Hotel, Cairo, after his exciting armoured-car exploit against the Senussiyeh at Sollum.

locomotives were rusting into holes. Our advance from the Persian Gulf and the Russian thrust into Armenia compelled Meissner to devote most of his energy and material to the Asia Minor and Bagdad lines. He seems to have been able to extend part of the Bagdad track, but his lack of rails, rolling-stock, and good engines prevented him from building a line of victory towards Egypt. When the war is over we shall probably find that Meissner worked magnificently within the limits imposed upon him by Ottoman ineptitude, negligence, and corruption. He seems to have provided the roadless waste of Palestine with good log tracks, over which guns could be moved with comparative quickness; but after destroying forests in this way, and laying water-pipes and constructing reservoirs in the desert between Palestine and Egypt, the German master-engineer, who had spent the greater part of his life struggling against the ignorance and short-sightedness of the Turk, had to leave Egypt practically unmenaced.

Our attack on the Dardanelles, combined with our threat against Mesopotamia, relieved the pressure against the Suez Canal. According to the Turkish official statement,

THE END OF THE FIGHT.
Wounded and dejected, these Bedouin prisoners were waiting to be sent to the base under an Indian guard.

KHAKI AND BURNOUS IN CLOSE PROXIMITY.
Arabs who were rather shy of the camera and a British armoured car commander photographed somewhere in the desert near the region of Bedouin hostility.

even the Yemen Division from Southern Arabia had to be diverted from the Egyptian frontier and sent to Gallipoli to oppose our Anzac army. Some skirmishing went on near Suez during the last week in March, 1915. The enemy then had about a thousand troops at El Kubri, a post opposite Suez.

On the morning of March 23rd an Indo-British force, under General Sir G. Younghusband, attacked and routed the Turks, who were reported to have been commanded by General von Traumer. The retreat of the 12,000 Syrians, Ottomans, and Arabs across the desert to Beersheba appears to have been a pitiful affair. In spite of the German organisers, the Ottoman commissariat department was an utter failure; the desert vultures hovered above the demoralised troops;

Turks killed by drinking salt water and large numbers of the men fell out and died before water was reached. The affair in March showed that the German engineers could not get water for a column of more than a thousand men, even in the season when the rainfall on the Sinai heights streamed into the desert sands below. According to a Berlin war correspondent who accompanied the Turkish expeditionary corps, the wells were frequently salty, and on more than one occasion there was a suspicion of petroleum about the taste. Yet in the blazing heat the soldiers rushed in an anguish of thirst to any kind of well, and filled themselves out with salt water rather than wait for a purer drink. The sufferings of an army that drank salt water do not need to be described, and it was reported that the force which vainly attempted to capture the canal

ceased to exist as a fighting unit when it was thrown back into the desert.

The British commander, General Maxwell, did not make any attack on the enemy. He did not care to expose his men to desert thirst when Nature in her most terrible mood was working against the enemy. Our cavalry patrols seldom went more than a few miles from the fresh-water canal that supplied us. But a French cruiser, in April, 1915, bombarded the enemy's coast camps at El Arish and Gaza, the fire being directed from a seaplane. At the same time our aeroplanes worked over the desert almost as far as El Arish, dropping bombs upon the tented encampments of the enemy, and tracing all the movements of the small Turkish forces that remained based upon the **Enemy's coast camps bombarded** oasis of the wilderness. The Bikanir Camel Corps, working with our reconnoitring aeroplanes, harassed the Turkish patrols from time to time, but nothing of importance occurred in the summer and autumn of 1915. The winter streams in the great wilderness dried up, leaving only scorching, stony beds; the water in the oases shrank, and the brief herbage around withered, giving scarcely sufficient sustenance for the hostile guards who had replaced the scanty Bedouin communities.

Meissner was working hard at Beersheba, trying to collect the waters of Idumea in large reservoirs of cement and convey them by pipe lines into the southern desert. Two thousand Germans were reported to be directing the works, which were gradually extended across the waste to the Hassana oasis, an important station a hundred miles east of the town of Suez. Here some of the winter streams from the Sinai Peninsula were collected in a large reservoir, which was protected by strong entrenchments. The Well of Hassana was within the bombing range of our aeroplane squadrons, but our pilots did not attempt any attack. Our commander thought that there was no immediate reason to discourage the energetic German engineers and make them see that their work was wasted. Had they given up their job owing to air attacks, they would have found better employment in the Dardanelles, the Caucasus, or the Bagdad regions. Their labours in the Desert of Sin were amusing to them and harmless to us, and our chafing pilots were restrained, for strategical reasons, from showing the Germans how hopeless was their task.

Nothing could be done on either side until the winter. We ran water-pipes into the desert, and laid light railways and motor tracks to our advanced posts in the wilderness. In the first attack on the canal, when the enemy could only bring small forces across the desert, the vital waterway between the Mediterranean and the Indian Ocean was defended by our warships, many of which afterwards took part in the Dardanelles operations. This employment of our naval force in a land battle was, however, only a temporary expedient, and after the Turks were thrown back from the canal, the British commander erected a system of military defences at a considerable distance east of the waterway. The Well of Moses, with its twelve springs of water and grove of palm-trees, was occupied by a battalion of Indians who came from Flanders, expert in trench work, and tunnelled through the rock and sandbagged the sands. Then Jebel Murr, a mass of redstone rising ten miles north of the Well of Moses, was transformed into a Gibraltar by means of blasting and quarrying. The red hill commanded the pass down which the enemy would have to come in his westward march, and before the winter rain fell, rooms, corridors, gun-pits, and

Gibraltar of the Sin Desert

machine-gun redoubts had been blown out of the great rock to enable the garrison to survive the fiercest hurricane of high-explosive shell that the enemy could fire from the Raha ridge rising farther in the desert.

There was at first great trouble in constructing trenches in the desert sand. Sandstorms made the work heart-breaking. The fogs of dust quickly filled the holes made for the guns, and the walls of the trenches were liable to subside under the pressure of the tempest-blown masses of sand, thus making vain all the labour spent on the earthworks. But the genius of our race proved equal to the occasion, and our engineers designed a new kind of trench which, though taking much longer to construct, withstood all the ravages of the desert storms. Road-making and railway construction were accomplished by Egyptian labourers, but all the defence works were carried out by our troops. They endowed Egypt with a great system of defence such as no Pharaoh had ever undertaken, and the glittering waste of sand, a picture of utter desolation in peace time, became in the days of battle a scene of the most intense human activity.

New Egyptian defence works

When winter came, it was open to the German Staff to make a second stronger assault against the canal. Perhaps if General Joffre had not initiated the great Franco-British

THE POWER OF SCIENCE IN THE TRACKLESS DESERT.

Bedouin prisoners being escorted into Mersa Matruh under a British guard. In the fighting with the Senussiyeh armoured cars played an important part, the Duke of Westminster's exploit being particularly noteworthy. The smaller illustration above shows one of the armoured cars in attendance on a squad of auto-ambulances waiting for the wounded to arrive after an engagement.

CHRISTMAS DAY ACTION AT MERSA MATRUH: BRITISH WESTERN FRONTIER FORCE ENGAGING BEDOUINS.

On Christmas Day, 1915, a heated engagement between a number of Bedouins and the British Western Frontier Force in Egypt took place at Mersa Matruh, a small seaport in Western Egypt. Early in the morning the Western Frontier Force moved out to the attack in two columns, frontally and on the enemy's flank. Aeroplanes and light-draught vessels off the coast also took part. The enemy's field-guns were soon put out of action, and the Bedouins retired on to successive ridges, but were eventually driven from these by bayonet charges. In the far background the foremost ridge held by the enemy is seen under shell fire, which formed cover to the advance of one of the sections of dismounted troops seen to the left of the drawing. Immediately in the foreground, artillery horses are being led out of action.

stand round Salonika, a couple of German and Austrian army corps would have been railed to Palestine to stiffen Kressenstein's army for a great movement of invasion over the Wilderness of Sin. Field-Marshal von der Goltz had collected a considerable force near Aleppo, from which he could move either towards Bagdad or towards Egypt. But General Townshend's advance up the Tigris determined the direction of Von der Goltz's reserve, and the strength of the Franco-British forces round Salonika made it impossible for the German and Austrian forces there to move into Egypt. Djemal Pasha, on the other hand, insisted on 25,000 German troops being sent to Syria to enable him to make another attack on the canal. He **Air attack on** refused to move if this reinforcement **German reservoir** were not sent. Owing to the course of events at Verdun and the great Russian sweep on Erzerum and Trebizond, neither Teutonic nor Turkish troops were sent to Djemal; so he did not move, and Kressenstein, his assistant, had but small forces to maintain a demonstration.

Peace, with her white wings extended, brooded over Egypt. Everybody was happy, except the troops who returned from Gallipoli and had nothing to do, after a period of rest, but to burrow in the desert and tunnel in the outlying rocks of the Sinai Peninsula. Probably the Australasians were the most depressed. Useless to attempt to console them by remarking that the winter climate of Egypt excelled that of the Riviera. The only health resort they were interested in was the tangle of freezing ditches between the Yser and the Somme. They put it that they had fairly earned in Gallipoli the privilege of getting into the thick of the Great War with the Canadians and the British. Had their old friend, Johnny Turk, been willing to follow them to Egypt and give Anzac an opportunity of showing what it could do in the way of defence, the Australasians still would not have been happy. They would have angrily wiped out the Ottoman as a nuisance, and turned again to meditate upon the remote delights of Flemish mud. Great, therefore, was their excitement when, with their ranks filled out with fresh drafts from the army of 300,000 men gathering in Australia and New Zealand, they learned they were going to France. But before they departed from the land of sand, sunshine, and pyramid they had some interesting excursions.

As the Turks refused to march again to the conquest of Egypt, our forces began to worry their advanced guards. Small parties of mobile troops, keeping in wireless touch with aeroplanes, broke into the enemy's screen of outposts. On February 20th, 1916, the long-delayed air attack on the new German reservoir at Hassana Well, a hundred miles from the canal, was delivered. The works had been so far advanced, after a year's designing and construction, that they were worth destroying. One of our patrols, surprised by a thunderstorm in a gully some fifty miles from the canal, had been almost overwhelmed by a torrent that deepened twelve feet in an hour. Thus there was water in the rainy season if only it could be stored. The reservoir, therefore, was able to water a very considerable body of Ottoman troops in an important region midway between the canal and the Turkish frontier. Two pairs of machines set out from different points according to a time-table arranged so that the second set of pilots should arrive over the wells when the first set had begun the work of destruction. The plan worked out like clockwork. Each pilot dropped ten heavy bombs on the reservoir and power station, destroying in an operation of half an hour work that the enemy had spent months in carrying out. According to one of the pilots, the place looked like a volcano in eruption when the bombs were striking home. Towards the end of the attack one airman saw some Turkish infantry firing at his fellow flyers. Swooping down upon them from behind, he got within seventy yards of the ground and then opened fire with his machine-gun,

BEDOUIN DRAGOMAN WHO WORKED FOR BRITAIN.
Loyal Bedouin guide who served with the British troops in Egypt, an old dragoman who claimed to know every desert track from Cairo to Turkey.

scattering them—officers and men—helter-skelter into the sand for cover. All the flyers returned safely after a round voyage of two hundred miles.

The damage done to the reservoir, when all the winter rain had come from the heights on either side of the Hassana Well and the rocky and stony wastes were heating in the springtide sun, was an irreparable disaster for the Teutonic engineers and the Turkish troops depending upon them. The forces near the canal had once more to be reduced in number by reason of the scanty water supply. But at a point nearer to the Suez waterway there was an oasis lying under a range of hills, where a large supply of water might, it was reckoned, be found by deep boring. Jifjaffa was the name of the well village, and an Austrian engineer made three borings there to a depth of three hundred feet, but without striking water. His labours had been perceived by our aerial scouts, and a detachment of the famous Australian Light Horse, the peers of the old Light Brigade, with some of the Camel Corps, came out in order to see what was happening.

Surprise, of course, was the essence **Australians' terrific** of the operation, and it was no easy **night march** work to catch off their guard the desert Bedouin who did the outpost work for the Turco-Germans. The Light Horse had to march one hundred and sixty miles in three and a half days, going over either soft, sinking sand or heavy, stony soil. Yet some thirty of the Australians, rather than be left out of the possible shindy, acted as camel drivers. No man had more than six hours sleep, and on the last day the troopers did forty miles and then fought. The Bedouin with his burnt skin stretched tight over his fine-drawn, wiry muscles, feeds on dates, sour milk, and coffee, and can afford so little flesh to eat that he practically incarnates all the virtues of a vegetarian diet. He comes of a race hardened by thousands of years of vigorous, hardy living, yet in qualities of endurance the heavy meat-eater of European stock usually beats him. When the Bedouin had half the known world under his

FFF

horse's feet, and all the pregnant forces of civilisation at his command, he could not carry on. Vehement as was his energy in the flowering time of the Arab genius, it was expended in a single, short burst of creative power. The Crusaders threw him back, and only failed to over- throw him completely because they were at last enfeebled by the tropical, insect-borne diseases of the lands they tried to hold. There is even more staying power in the meat-eating modern Briton, who has behind him the medical resources of modern bacteriology. He can surprise even the Bedouin in the desert, despite the fact that the Arab nomad has the fine physical qualities of the Arab horse.

The Australians, by their last terrific night march, came unperceived within three miles of the enemy's position, and as dawn was breaking they surrounded Jifjaffa north, south, and east, leaving only a westward outlet towards the distant Suez Canal. As the attack was developing in daylight, some of the enemy retired from their advanced posts toward the trenches by the well works, but a troop of horse cut them off, shepherded them together, and compelled their surrender. Every Turk, Arab, and Teuton was killed or taken prisoner, the plant and material were destroyed, a gun position was wrecked, and all the works completely demolished. The engineer in charge was an Austrian—the officer who had thrice bored deep for water without reaching it. He was much astonished when he was brought to the Anzac camp, where the men were all working in shorts. He thought from their magnificent physique and their scanty dress that an athletic tournament was taking place, but it was only the Austra- lasian soldiers in their Gallipoli mode of attire going about their ordinary work.

Actions at Hassana and Jifjaffa

The actions at Hassana and at Jifjaffa were small, but their results were large. They diminished the enemy's water supply, and thereby weakened the forces around his works of preparation in the desert, and compelled him to draw farther back from the canal. On the day on which the Australian Light Horse captured the Turkish camp at Jifjaffa, a small body of English Yeomanry took the Katia oasis, which lies forty-eight miles north of Jifjaffa, from which it is separated by a range of sand- blown heights, the Jebel Magara. This hilly country, however, was still held by the enemy, making our position at Katia insecure. The Katia oasis was of great importance. It lay some forty miles east of Port Said, on the old camel route by the coast, the famous Serbonian Road, along which armies have thirstily moved between Asia and Africa since the dawn of history. At Katia our mounted troops, consisting of the Worcestershire Yeomanry, the Warwickshire Yeomanry, and the Gloucestershire Hussars, were able to range towards the enemy's positions near the centre of the desert and raid the hostile Bedouin camps. Supporting the Yeomanry and Hussars was a small body of infantry nearer the canal at Duweidar, consisting of a company of the Royal Scots Fusiliers with two other companies on a hill some miles away. The Australian Horse were also within call, with some squadrons of the Royal Flying Corps.

Von Kressenstein's return stroke

All these forces, however, were small in number. Our army along the canal, with its reserves in Egypt, was exceedingly strong. In an ordinary way we should have held our newly-won advanced posts in the heart of the desert in considerable strength, but we were not allowed time to extend our fresh-water supply and our motor roads from El Kantara. Baron von Kressenstein made his return stroke before we could water any larger body of troops than we had collected round the oases. The weather at Easter favoured the Turco-German commander. A thick mist, the first for six weeks, obscured everything more than forty yards distant from the Duweidar post, which was held by a company of Ayrshire men. The enemy, some 2,000 strong, made a night march from the hill country, and at dawn on Easter Sunday charged through the mist on the Duweidar oasis. Had the Turkish force captured Duweidar they would have cut off all the Yeomanry and Hussars, who also were fighting against overwhelming forces sixteen miles farther in the desert along the Serbonian Road.

We may, therefore, regard the encircling swoop on our rear at Duweidar as the more critical of the two actions.

BEDOUIN PRISONERS IN CUSTODY OF DORSETSHIRE YEOMEN.
Dorsetshire Yeomanry particularly distinguished themselves in Western Egypt, where they obtained a decisive success against the tribesmen under the command of Gaafar Pasha and Enver Pasha's brother, Nuri Bey, taking many prisoners.

SORRY AFTER THE EVENT: WHOLESALE SURRENDER OF DEJECTED BEDOUINS.
Gaafar Pasha, a Turkish soldier, was in chief command of the Bedouins who rose against us in Western Egypt. After he surrendered the Bedouins gave themselves up to the British troops in large numbers and begged for forgiveness.

The little company of Ayrshire men had the odds of six to one against them, together with the disadvantages of a surprise attack in a heavy mist. The line they held was about two hundred yards from the fringe of the oasis, with a machine-gun redoubt on a height south-east of the well. The German officer commanding the Turks laid his plans admirably. He brought up machine-guns, which swept all the approaches to our Vickers' team on the crest, and when the alarm was given by the sound of heavy firing and a great burst of Arab cheering near the British machine-gun position, none of our men in reserve could go to the help of the south-eastern post. Every officer and man who attempted to reach this hot corner was hit by the enemy's machine-guns. And against this little isolated redoubt the main attack was made.

Ayrshire men's heroic stand

The British machine-gun was hit in five places, three of the gun-team were killed and one was wounded; but the rest of the men fought the gun to the end, and no Turk or Arab got within twenty-two yards of the position. Then to the left of the south-eastern post a small party held another British position on rising ground above the oasis. Close in front of them the Turks had a machine-gun in action, and they changed its position so frequently that it could not be located. Captain Bruce, of the Territorial Army Service Corps, was sent up with a few men to lengthen the line at this place, and there for three hours he fought the enemy off with cool, inspiriting audacity. At nine o'clock the first of the reinforcements were sent to the mound that Captain Bruce and his little band were defending, but the leading officer of the new troops, Lieutenant Crawford, was wounded while crossing the open space, and fell exposed to the murderous fire of the hostile machine-gun and rifles. For three hours Captain Bruce had been able to judge the effect of this fire; nevertheless, when the lieutenant fell he left the sand-bag which had served as his cover and ran out to try and carry in his comrade, but dropped mortally wounded. Yet his noble example was followed by Corporal Clifford, who, by amazing luck, got through the sweeping fire, brought in the wounded lieutenant,

and then went out again and recovered the body of the heroic captain, still without being hit himself. The Turks maintained the attack in a resolute and daring manner, and it was only by high skill as well as by desperate courage that the little band of Scotsmen held the position until reinforcements arrived from a hill seven miles away. A bayonet charge by two more companies of Fusiliers routed the Turks, who fled into the south-eastern hills, leaving a large amount of their ammunition behind, four machine-gun boxes full, five hundred rounds of small-arms munition, and a heap of shrapnel shell.

Meanwhile, a small force of Yeomanry at the Katia oasis had been almost surrounded by a strong column, consisting of 2,000 picked Turkish infantry who had fought at Gallipoli, and 1,000 German and Austrian troops. This Teutonic-Ottoman force was mounted on camels and provided with four mountain guns and many machine-guns. The main attack was delivered against the village of Katia, which was held by two squadrons of Worcester Yeomanry. The rest of the British cavalry brigade was three miles southward, completing a successful raid on the oasis of Magheibra, where the enemy's camp had just been burnt and prisoners taken. The brigadier heard firing in the direction of Katia, and though his small force had done a long march through heavy sand under a very hot sun, he **Yeomanry surprised** sent forward the remaining squadron **at Katia** of the Worcester Yeomanry to join the troopers holding the village, and then flung the Warwickshire Yeomanry in a curving movement to the south, while the Gloucestershire Hussars rode round the village to the north. In the meantime the two squadrons in the oasis were suffering heavily from shell fire. Their horses were destroyed by the enemy's mountain guns, so that the men had to make a fighting retreat on foot, while the mounted Germans and Turks continually overlapped them on either flank, and shot them down or took them prisoners. Nearly a squadron, if the Turkish report may be trusted, was enveloped. But the Warwickshire men succeeded in shooting the German commander through the head, and then the other Yeomanry and Hussars, by a vehement attack against their more numerous and better-armed enemy, smashed the Turks and Teutons back for a distance of two miles, and thus released the remnant of the trapped but still fighting farmer troopers of Worcester.

Our sweep of two miles, however, had brought us very close to the hostile mountain battery and to the enemy's reserve, and the British brigadier, knowing that both his horses and his men were worn out by two actions and the severe march, abandoned Katia. But this was not the end of the

Enemy advance broken by air attack operations in the mid-desert oasis and round Duweidar. At the latter point, when the Scots Fusiliers finished their charge, a regiment of the Australian Horse rode down the routed Bedouin and Turk forces ; and when the steeds of the Australians began to tire a squadron of aeroplanes took up the pursuit, and after bombing the fugitives, swooped down and raked them with machine-gun fire. Then, in the darkness of Easter Sunday night, more aeroplanes gathered by the canal, and set out in the darkness so as to arrive over Katia at dawn. The Germans had left a strong rearguard of five hundred men in the oasis, and the two British flying squadrons blew them up amid the palm-trees, taking the force by surprise, and planing with

ANCIENT AND MODERN MEANS OF TRANSPORT IN JUXTAPOSITION.
After the victorious campaign against the Senussi near Mersa Matruh the Yeomanry unloaded their horses and camels at a rail-head up the line and sent them down to the base in charge of native drivers.

stopped engines in long curves that came close to the ground before they rose again above the desert. Some seventy-one bombs were thrown on the encampment, with such good aim that when we reconquered the place half the Turkish force was reported to have been killed or wounded. Our mounted columns advanced again to Katia, but the Teutons and Turks did not care to stand battle, and retired for sixteen miles to the oasis of Abd. Half a dozen miles south of this spring of brackish water there was a smaller oasis with a tuft of palm-trees which sheltered a hostile camp. On February 25th our aircraft bombed the enemy out of this southern oasis and harried him as he fled towards Abd. Then Abd was assailed from the air by our Flying Corps, while our mounted patrol searched all the Katia district and cleared it of hostile troops. All our positions were recovered, and the heavy losses of the Worcestershire Yeomanry were more than balanced by the casualties of the enemy. At the beginning of May we were half across the desert on the road to El Arish. This, of course, did not signify any intention on our part to advance in force across the Wilderness of Sin in the flaming heat of the tropical summer. In the spring of 1916 we were still standing on the defensive on

the eastern frontier, and occupying the mid-desert oases in order to keep the enemy's camel corps far away from the canal.

Egypt at the time was threatened more seriously and somewhat unexpectedly from an entirely different direction. It was on the western frontier, where the Libyan and Sahara deserts stretch in vacant, blinding splendour under the African sun, that a new enemy had arisen. Small were his material resources, but he had mysterious, spiritual influences that made him for a time a formidable factor in the war. For he was Senussi the Mahdi—a strange, mysterious figure that had long excited the apprehensions of all the European Powers with interests on the North African coast.

For quite a generation the warrior-prophet of Islam had loomed from the Sahara in a haze of mystery and romance above the African coast washed by the Mediterranean Sea. He first fascinated and disturbed the imagination of the French, who expected him to descend suddenly upon Algeria and Tunis at the head of a new Saracenic host and menace Europe. It was against France that the new Moslem confraternity was originally directed. After the French conquest of Algeria in 1830, a sheikh of Oran, Seyyid Mohammed Es-Senussi, fled into the Sahara, and died in an odour of sanctity near the oasis of Jupiter Ammon, in the Libyan desert.

The aim of the Senussi had been to restore Mohammedan doctrine to its pristine severity, in order to make Islam again divinely powerful against its foes. The reformer seems to have been genuinely descended from the favourite wife of Mohammed ; but this was no great distinction in itself, as in every Moslem city there may still be found a seyyid, or lord, descended from the Prophet and acting as a leader of the local community. It was the reforming passion of the old man that made him eminent. His standing along the North African coast was insignificant ; but when he set up as a holy hermit in the unmapped wastes of the Sahara his fame travelled with the camel-men of the caravans, and his influence spread deep into the Sudan. The Seyyid died before he could build up his confraternity, but his work was continued by his son, Senussi the Mahdi, who was brought up in the desert oasis from 1853 to 1889. This Mahdi was the first great warrior-prophet of the Sahara. He was reported to have strange physical signs, this new leader of Islam—blue eyes, one arm longer than another, and a mysterious mark between his shoulders. His holiness of life and his rigour in doctrine made him revered and renowned, and his reputation spread from Jupiter Ammon to the oasis of Kufra, and thence to Lake Chad and Nigeria. A religious college was set up in the desert, where students were instructed in the reformed creed, and sent as preachers to the Moslem races, while negro slaves were freed, educated, and despatched as missionaries to their pagan countrymen in the Sudan.

The Mahdi of the Sahara

The work of the Senussi in converting the pagan tribes of Central Africa was very important. He was more successful than Christian missionaries, and performed a labour of high merit in raising pagan natives from a condition of hopeless superstition, and disciplining their minds and characters. Several European administrators in Africa reckoned that the severe deism of the Senussi sect,

[Photo: Vandyk.

Brig.-General H. T. Lukin, C.M.G., D.S.O., commanding South African Forces in Egypt.

462

Storm cloud on the battle front : British soldiers charging the enemy tr

through a screen of vapour produced by specially thrown smoke bombs.

The familiar emblem of mercy on the Nile: Cook's pleasure craft on war service as hospital ships.

British armoured cars confound the Senussiyeh: Juggernauts from the West dash into the enemy camp on Egypt's shore.

with the rigid and temperate rule of life that went with it, was more suited to the negro than were some of the loose, modern, emotional forms of Christianity. But the French Government, composed largely of anti-clericals, began to think that the missionary work of the Mahdi might be dangerous. They feared a great Mohammedan rising of Berbers, Arabs, and Touaregs from Egypt to Morocco, backed by negro converts from Equatorial Africa. It is not, however, yet decided whether the Senussi confraternity was then intended to be a fighting force, somewhat resembling our ancient Order of Knights-Templar, or whether it was a peaceful missionary society. Certainly there was great unrest on the thirteen-hundredth anniversary of Hegira, in 1882. But the prophet of the Sahara gave no sign. As he would not move, the son of a Nubian carpenter proclaimed himself the Mahdi, and after a long conflict the rising was quelled at Omdurman.

During this struggle the Senussi displayed towards us considerable friendship. He scornfully rejected the offers of alliance made by the false Mahdi, and in 1888 he opposed the westward march of the revolted troops that held Khartum. The Pretender of the Sudan had angered the great missionary by his arrogance and cruelty, and it may have been that the partial successes of the false prophet interfered with the execution of the more deeply laid and more slowly maturing plans of the Senussi. In any case, the Senussi by this time had missed his only opportunity of gathering together the Mohammedan races of Africa for a war, compared with which the revolt in the Sudan that took us so many years to overcome would have been merely a provincial concern. His policy of inaction during the critical period of unrest greatly abated his influence, and after General Joffre and other French commanders drove down through the Sahara to the Niger and to Lake Chad, Senussi the Mahdi fell, vainly fighting, in 1902, in a final futile attempt to win back some of his old prestige.

The Turkish Pasha of Tripoli had also swept down in force on the Senussi oasis of Jupiter Ammon, and this had led to the Senussiyeh retreating across the desert to Borku. After the death of the prophet, his nephew, Seyyid Ahmed, returned to the oasis of the desert and lived nominally under British rule at the Kufru oasis, from which centre he maintained a connection, along the caravan routes, with Tripoli and Egypt. But we had no power whatever over him, though one of his towns, Jupiter Ammon, or Siwa, paid an annual tribute in dates to the Egyptian Government. The inhabitants were a warlike race of Berbers and Arabs, who were in turn surrounded by hostile tribes, making all connection difficult. The ubiquitous German, however, managed to penetrate into the last retreat of the Senussi confraternity. In secret alliance with the Turks, the Germans in 1911 armed the desert tribes against the Italian army that invaded Tripoli, and Enver Pasha first distinguished himself in organising the Berbers and Arabs into a force that resisted the advance of the Italians. There was no evidence that the Senussi in Kufra waged war upon the Italians in 1911, and our Government could not find any ground for sending an expedition some four hundred miles into the Sahara, by way of Jupiter Ammon, in order to attempt to conquer the missionary society. Italy at the time was the ally of

Germany and the desert tribes

Germany and Austria, and, though there was a suspicion that the Germans and Austrians were supplying with munitions the Mohammedan forces in Tripoli, the remote and doubtful influence of the Senussi could not be traced in a clear manner on the conduct of the Italian-Turkish War.

The confraternity maintained a show of friendliness towards our Government during the most critical period of the Great War. The Italians in Tripoli were pressed back towards the coast, and the French outposts in the Sahara had to be withdrawn in places and concentrated under the menace of the Berber and Arab tribesmen. The brother of Enver Pasha, Nuri Bey, and Gaafar Pasha were organising all the warriors of the desert and forming them into an army to fight in the Turco-German interests, but no important attack was made against the western frontier of Egypt, though some of the tribe of Ulad Ali, occupying the coast of Egypt between Alexandria and Sollum, went over to the enemy. Even when the army of Syria advanced from Beersheba and tried to capture the Suez Canal in February, 1915, the Senussiyeh did not attempt to co-operate with the Turks by making an assault upon the western frontier of Egypt. Some races under the Senussi influence remained still actively friendly towards

Arab leader befriends Britons

WOUNDED AUSTRALIANS STARTING FOR A TRIP ON THE NILE.
Trips up the Nile in a pleasure-boat have long been a favourite prescription of fashionable physicians. They were a much-appreciated part of the treatment of wounded Australians recuperating in Egypt.

us. For example, a British steamer, the Niggem, carrying a cargo of cotton from Alexandria to Barcelona, sprang a leak and on Christmas Day, 1914, headed for the Gulf of Sidra. Captain MacIntyre and his sixteen men were fired upon by the Senussi tribesmen, and the captain was taken to one of the chiefs and tried as an Italian spy. All the seamen were stripped of their clothes and robbed of their money. But when the Arab leader, Sidi Ahmed, found that his captives were Britons, he tried to make amends by presenting the skipper with a tarboosh, and sending him with his crew over the frontier to the British station at Sollum. There the shipwrecked mariners were received by Major White, after a camel journey of thirty-eight days through the Senussi territory. All this happened at the time when the Turks were launching their attack against the Suez Canal. So it looked as though the attitude of active benevolence which Senussi the Mahdi had shown towards us when Gordon died at Khartum would be maintained by the new chief of the confraternity during our struggle against the Young Turkish party.

There seems to have been a rift in the matter of religion between the missionary sect of the Sahara and the free-thinking band of Ottomans and Jews which had won control over the Caliphate. The Senussiyeh had a respect

THE LURE OF EGYPT: A LAND OF PROMISE TO THE YOUNG TURK PARTY.
Turkish munition and Red Cross column on the way to the Suez Canal. Undoubtedly one of the strongest incentives to the Young Turk Party to go into alliance with the Central Empires was the latter's promise of Egypt as the eventual reward for Ottoman intervention on behalf of Germanism.

for the British power. It would be extravagant to say that they liked any Christians, but at least they preferred our very tolerant and very shadowy form of suzerainty. What was still more important, in the crisis of the Turkish attack against the canal, they remembered the tenacity with which we had fought down the false prophet of the Sudan, and they did not care to engage us. Naturally, they spied upon our forces in Egypt, where Australasia, India, Britain, and Egypt itself were represented in great strength. Nuri Bey and Gaafar Pasha were eloquent, but the leader of the Senussi would not move against us. Our operations in the Dardanelles and in Mesopotamia made him doubt the power of attack of the Ottomans.

Meanwhile, the Teutons and Turks plotted for a great African rising. Some Moslem tribesmen rose in Morocco, where the Germans had prepared a Holy War before hostilities broke out in Europe. A grandson of the famous Emir, Abdul Kader, was appointed leader of the insurgents, but he could at first only collect a force of 2,000 men. The French had, however, a very difficult time, as one of their columns was trapped and annihilated. The Government was inclined to withdraw to the coast, as the Italians did in Tripoli. But, happily, there was a man of genius and daring in Morocco—General Lyautey. He fed the armies in France with most of his regular troops, and mainly with Territorial French soldiers and native recruits put down all resistance, countered the intrigues of the Germans from the Spanish zone, and saved Morocco. By January, 1916, the remnant of the rebels was driven into the Riff Mountains. Many of the Moorish fighting men entered the service of France, and fought **General Lyautey's** with splendid gallantry from Charleroi to **success in Morocco** the Yser and from Champagne to Verdun. All that the revolt accomplished was to extend the French power into territories of tribes that had hitherto been unsubdued, and to prove that French rule, by its justice and humanity, had won the lasting respect of the general body of the Moorish people.

The Italians in Tripoli were most severely pressed. Their conquest was so recent that the Arabs and Berbers had not had time to see what advantage they would win under a settled and progressive government. The Senussiyeh were antagonistic to the Italian occupation, and the main strength of the tribes of the desert was massed against the Italian forces, and these forces were compelled to retreat towards the coast towns. As we have seen in the incident of the wrecked Niggem, a considerable stretch

466

of the Tripolitan coast was occupied by tribes under the Senussi influence, and there were German and Austrian officers directing the operations, in addition to the Turkish commanders.

When the German submarines arrived in the Mediterranean, supply bases for them were organised on that part of the African coast dominated by the Senussi. Vessels flying the Greek flag evaded our blockade and brought ammunition for the tribesmen and oil for the German submarines. Greek vessels also transported Turkish and Teutonic officers, but they were not always successful in evading the Franco-British-Italian blockade of the strip of coast which the Senussiyeh had occupied. The German submarines, however, made a profound impression upon the sheikhs of the coastlands. One of the Arab leaders was taken from Africa to Austria **Fairy-tales about** by an enemy submarine that crossed the **the Kaiser** Mediterranean, threaded the Adriatic, and brought the wonder-stricken sheikh safely to Pola. After consulting with the Austrian and German military authorities the Arab returned by submarine to his own people, deeply excited by his experiences of the strange powers of "Hadji Wilhelm Mohammed," the new Mahdi.

It was then that extraordinary fairy-tales concerning the weapons and intentions of the German Emperor began to spread through Mohammedan Africa. Camel drivers from the desert brought the stories into the bazaars of Egypt and the Sudan, and an army of spies worked to capture the imagination of the Bedouins by the desert fringe and of the peasantry along the Nile. It was related that some ancient Hohenzollern had married one of the descendants of Mohammed and that Hadji Wilhelm was, like one of the ancient German Emperors of the Hohenstaufen line, a Mohammedan at heart, who was only waiting for his crowning victory over Christendom in order to proclaim himself the new Mahdi. Meanwhile, he was using a fleet of magic airships fitted with magnetic instruments, and these airships had sailed over London, Paris, Petrograd, and Rome, and had magnetised King George, some mysterious French Emperor, Tsar Nicholas, and King Victor Emmanuel, had extracted them out of their palaces by magnetic power, and made them prisoners. German submarines, of course, held the absolute command of the sea, and, after sinking the Franco-British navy at the Dardanelles, were conducting regular underwater voyages to all parts of the world. The Senussiyeh were being supplied with artillery and ammunition by the submarine traffic, and they would soon be in a position to reconquer Morocco, Algeria, Tunis, Tripoli, and Egypt.

These fairy-tales of science and history made a considerable impression upon some of the Mohammedan people. The Bedouins, who had seen Austrian and German submarines on the Libyan coast, were ready to believe that everything was possible with such wonder-workers as the Teutons. In Egypt two attempts were made upon the life of Sultan Hussein Kamel. He was shot at on April 8th, 1915, by a young Egyptian merchant, but a bystander knocked up the assassin's arm and made the bullet go wide. On July 9th, 1915, a bomb was thrown at the Sultan as he was going to prayers, but happily the missile did not explode. Some of the Ministers of the Sultan were also attacked by assassins. In many of the villages of Egypt

German Emperor as the new Mahdi the German Emperor was supposed to have made the pilgrimage to Mecca and to be the new Mahdi, and as the fellaheen were nearly all members of some dervish order and passionately religious, there was some danger of their being influenced by the Turco-German intrigues. Happily, the fellah was a fairly sensible man. His mind was coloured by old traditions of the condition of Egypt under Turkish pashas, and he knew what Syria was like under Turkish rule. Our just, progressive, and prosperous government swayed his mind, especially the work that had been done under Lord Kitchener before the outbreak of the war. Though he listened to the wonder tales about Hadji Wilhelm, he did not see his way to rise against the British in order to let in upon himself the Turk and the Bedouin. The collapse of the Turkish attack on the Suez Canal confirmed the Egyptian peasant in his belief that the race which had recovered the Sudan from the false Mahdi could hold its own against all its new enemies.

On the other hand, a striking success by any force invading Egypt might have had serious consequences. The Senussiyeh were even more dangerous than the Turks, because of the religious influence of the reforming prophet of the Sahara. The military power of the Senussi was small. He had only a bodyguard estimated at some 4,000 men, and though his stock of munitions had been almost exhausted in the war in Tripoli, it had since been greatly increased from Austrian sources. The Italians themselves had landed considerable quantities of arms for the warlike tribes, and even when the Austro-Italian war was raging, Teutonic agents in Italy had continued

BRANCH OF THE "DEVIL'S WORKSHOP" IN THE CITY OF CONSTANTINE.

Turkey being almost entirely dependent on Germany for munitions and guns, Krupp's established a large factory in Constantinople, and despatched some four thousand skilled workmen to turn out shells for the Ottoman armies. Some German officers and their Turkish allies are seen outside the entrance to the factory. In circle: Djemal Pasha and officers of his Staff before leaving for the front.

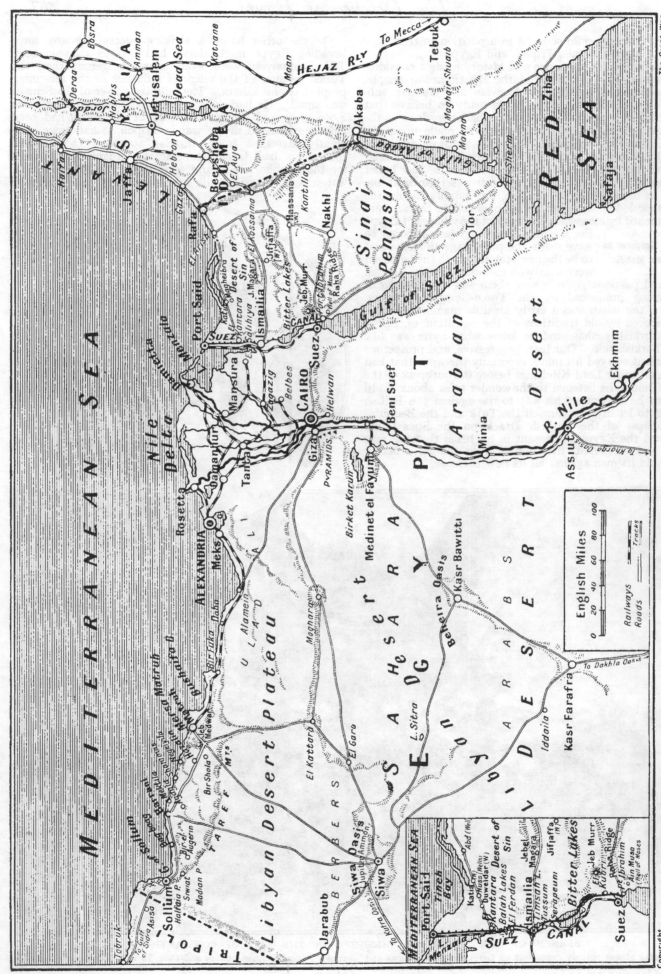

The Great War

DETAILED MAP SHOWING THE OPERATIONS IN EGYPT FROM THE DESERT OF SIN TO THE WESTERN, TRIPOLI, FRONTIER.

The eastern and western frontiers of Egypt are indicated in stipple. The area of fighting with the Senussiyeh was between Mersa Matruh and Sollum, almost on the border of Tripoli, and it was between here and Asisa that the Duke of Westminster rescued the men of the Tara.

Copyright

to send barrels of rifles to Tripoli in Italian and Greek ships. The munitions were ingeniously concealed in apparent cargoes of foodstuffs and other harmless articles of commerce, and it was long before the Italian port authorities discovered the daring traffic in arms between their enemies. Then, in August, 1915, a French torpedo-boat, patrolling the Tripoli coast, found a sailing vessel flying the Greek flag and carrying some Turkish officers, with £4,000 in German gold, and among other gifts an engraved casket containing a letter in Arabic from the German Emperor. The letter ran as follows:

Praises to the Most High God! Emperor William, heir of Charlemagne, Envoy of Allah and Protector of Islam, to the illustrious Chief the Senussi. We pray Allah to lead our armies to victory. Our will is that thy valorous warriors shall expel all infidels from the lands that belong to the true believers and to their commander. To this end we send thee arms, money, and experienced leaders in war. Our common foes shall fly before thee. So be it!

WILLIAM.

It was an extraordinary epistle for an Emperor reigning over Protestant and Catholic Christians to address to a Mohammedan missionary chief. For the "infidels" to whom the Hohenzollern referred, and wished to see exterminated by the Senussi, were the Protestant, Catholic, and Orthodox Christians in Egypt and Tripoli, Tunis, Algeria, and Morocco. Of all instances in history of hypocrisy, the vilest surely is the attitude of the Protestant German Emperor, praying to his "old God" before his own people, while exciting the wild and ignorant Bedouins to massacre Christians in the name of Allah, and the Hohenzollern, true believer and protector of Islam.

But Senussi the Mahdi was not inclined at the time to attack Egypt. The tribes he had gathered had enough to do in fighting the Italians in Tripoli, and they needed guns, machine-guns, and more ammunition before trying the strength of our outposts in the Libyan desert. At our frontier fort in Sollum Gulf, at the point where Egyptian territory joins that of Tripoli, we had two small, old coastguard boats, the Abbas and the Abdul Moneim, and, though their guns were small and antiquated, the Senussi confraternity could not easily drag through the desert any artillery to match them. The range of our sea-power gave us the means of rapid action all along the coast. At need, we could evade hostile submarines and bring troopships in the darkness, or even send waist-belted monitors by daylight, to dominate or reinforce our posts along the seashore. We had built a good motor road westward of Alexandria towards Matruh, Barrani, and Sollum. At some distance inland from the last three small seaports rose the waterless, unexplored ridge of the Taref Mountains, that form a great semicircle, with its horns near Matruh and Sollum. Beyond the mountain line was the waterless sand of the Libyan desert, that stretches south to the remote oasis of Siva, known in ancient times as the mysterious shrine of Jupiter Ammon, which Alexander the Great had visited. Our position, therefore, was one of considerable strength, and the Senussiyeh, who were camped near Sollum, had the sense to perceive that, so long as our sea-power was not crippled, our coastwise posts were practically impregnable.

But on November 5th, 1915, an Austrian submarine torpedoed off the coast one of our armed merchantmen, the Tara, which, before being rechristened and armed, had been a Holyhead steamer on the Dublin route. She was commanded by Captain Gwatkin Williams, and carried a crew mainly of Welshmen. Out of ten boats only three succeeded in getting away, and these the submarine took in tow, landing the men as prisoners with the Senussi. They were marched for nearly one hundred and eighty miles into the Libyan desert, and treated very differently from the former party of shipwrecked seamen whom the Senussi had rescued and brought to the British post at Sollum. They were compelled to work like slaves on a starving ration, lashed with rhinoceros-hide whips, and when ill left to die like dogs in a ditch.

Torpedoing of the Tara

THE PRINCE OF WALES IN EGYPT.

In the spring of 1916 the Prince of Wales visited several of the fronts. In Egypt he spent a considerable time among the troops, and on one occasion assisted at a general inspection.

No hope of rescue seemed possible, for the submarine that sunk the Tara also sunk by shell fire the Abbas, one of the coastguard boats, and so damaged the other that it had to run ashore. The submarine then fired fifty shells into Sollum, and afterwards convoyed a large vessel which had escaped the Franco-British blockade in some mysterious manner. There were two or three hundred Turkish soldiers in the steamer, with a band of German and Turkish officers, together with a few guns, a considerable supply of Maxims, and a large quantity of ammunition. The men and munitions were landed by the camp of the Senussi, and then in the second week of November an attack was made upon Major White's little force at the extreme frontier post.

The Senussi put to the test

The attack seems to have been made by the newly landed troops, led by Nuri Bey, the brother of Enver Pasha, and reinforced by some Bedouin tribes. The assault was severely repulsed, and the Senussi stated in a message published by a native Egyptian paper that the attack had been made against his order, and that he would not break his friendship with the British nation, and would punish the tribe that invaded Egyptian territory. The situation, therefore, remained ambiguous, and after consultation with the civil authorities, General Maxwell, commanding

A WELCOME REST AFTER CHASING THE ARABS.
British soldiers under Major-General Peyton photographed in the shade of palm-trees after a successful action with Arabs at Sollum. In both Mesopotamia and Egypt the Arab, that treacherous if picturesque figure, gave our men considerable trouble.

contingency, a strong column of reinforcements was collected near the railway ready to reinforce the small frontier guard at Matruh. The desert was patrolled by officers of the Royal Flying Corps, who watched the white-robed Arabs collect from Tripoli and the southern desert and march slowly eastward.

The situation was soon seen to be serious, for the Bedouins were coming forward in thousands. On December 11th our reconnoitring patrols, under Colonel Gordon, met a body of three hundred Arabs, defeated them, and drove them westward with a loss of eighty killed, thirty wounded, and seven captured. Two days afterwards a stronger Arab column of 1,200 rifles with cannon and machine-guns, led by Gaafar Pasha, vigorously attacked Colonel Gordon's troops at a spot some twenty-four miles westward of Matruh. Our outnumbered force held its own and inflicted heavy punishment on the enemy, but though only eight men were killed among our troops, we retired on our base in the night lest another strong enemy column should get ahead of us. The Senussi army gradually collected in a rocky donga some seven miles south of the little port, threatening to overwhelm it. But by this time British sea-power had come into play in a way that the new Mahdi had not foreseen. Part of a new brigade of New Zealand troops, which was completing its training in Egypt and thinking of spending Christmas quietly in Cairo, was railed to Alexandria and thence transported in trawlers and sweepers to Matruh. With the New Zealanders came the 15th Sikhs, some fresh troopers of the Australian Light Horse, and some of the English Yeomanry that had done so well in disastrous conditions in Suvla Bay. The water by the shore was brackish, and the fresh-water wells inland were either within range of enemy snipers or insufficient for the needs of the new little army. Drinking water had to be brought from Alexandria to the camp close to the beach. Here the force was safe from any attack, for, in addition to its own artillery, it was covered by guns mounted on the steam fishing vessels which had been used as trans- **Sea-power comes into play** ports. These vessels did not draw much water, so it was extremely difficult for any hostile submarine to torpedo them, and as the seamen were fresh from Gallipoli, they were well experienced in dodging torpedoes and helping in land battles.

After spending some days in trenching the hill above the port, erecting wire entanglements, and preparing generally a strong resistance, the British commander decided to attack on Christmas Day. A small party of the Senussiyeh and the Bedouin tribesmen were trying to carry in a night attack one of the sangars guarding our

the British-Egyptian forces, decided to put the Senussi to the test. Our troops at Sollum were a great distance from the nearest rail-head, in a rough country, with a line of communications that could easily be cut by enemies, gathering under cover of the mountain ridge. Therefore, for strategical reasons and political motives, the outpost at Sollum was withdrawn to Matruh, which was only about forty-two miles from the rail-head, and connected with it by means of a good motor track. Matruh then became a bait for the Senussi if he was hostile, as was strongly suspected. The country around Matruh was very valuable. The light, sandy soil produced, on the edge of the vast desert, a bountiful crop of barley that formed the mainstay of the Bedouin population. The Matruh barley was traded by a large caravan commerce to the oasis of Jupiter Ammon, from which dates were in turn exported. We could stop the barley trade if the Senussi confraternity were hostile. It was therefore certain that, if they intended any operations against Egypt, they would begin by attempting to get possession of the barley fields. To provide against this

PRACTICE THAT MADE PERFECT: REHEARSING A CHARGE OUTSIDE CAIRO.
Berkshire Yeomanry practising the charge on the outskirts of Cairo. Subsequently they fought with great gallantry in the desert, and at Matruh, on the Egyptian frontier, they completely routed the Arabs, who found their real onslaught irresistible.

SAPLINGS FROM BERKSHIRE STRAINING AT THE LEASH ON THE CAIRO COURSE.
Another photograph of the Berkshire Yeomanry, lined up awaiting the order to charge with the bayonet. Even in training, as here, and in the sham fighting of manœuvres this is an exciting moment which tautens every nerve and muscle; in actual battle it raised these men to the pinnacle of heroism.

base, but disregarding this local attack, our main force of some 5,000 troops made an early breakfast and, falling into line before dawn, marched out through the stray bullets with a view to making a rapid enveloping movement. Our base camp was left with scantily-manned sangars, but with some 6 in. guns protecting it from the sea. The dune tops were garrisoned by Army Service Corps men, who maintained a show of ferocious activity, while our fighting columns set out on a round of thirty miles' marching and fighting, that lasted twenty-six hours and included a Christmas dinner of two army biscuits and a drink of water. One column, composed of Sikhs and New Zealanders, broke camp at four o'clock and marched seven miles along a rough road towards some hills where the enemy was massed among the rocks and caves. Then the cavalry, consisting of the Australian Light Horse and some English Yeomanry, rode out in a sweeping movement round the enemy's right flank.

New Zealanders and Sikhs in action

The New Zealand and Sikh column, which was divided into two parties, first encountered a small advanced party of Bedouins, who retired after a skirmish, and then our mountain battery opened fire on the height occupied by the enemy, while our column broke up into artillery formation in anticipation of the work of the dusky gunners who had joined the Senussi. There were only two pieces of hostile artillery on the height, and after they had landed a few shells near the New Zealanders, our screw guns struck the top of the hill, then lobbed a shell over it among the white-draped Bedouins in the hollow, pitched a high-explosive shell into a stack of enemy shells that flamed aloft with a roar, and finally sent a direct shot on the larger of the two hostile guns, completely destroying it. The work of the British battery was wonderfully smart; the gunners got the range dead and quick. And soon after they had put out of action the large gun, a British warship lying off the coast, and firing with an aeroplane spotting for her, put a 6 in. shell on the smaller Turkish cannon.

By this time the Sikhs, who were leading with the New Zealanders' A Company reinforcing them, had come under fire from a strong body of natives on the first of a series of ridges. The Sikhs fought with great dash and courage, and their reckless daring won the admiration of every New Zealander. But the new troops of British stock proved themselves quickly to be worthy of charging with the veterans from the Indian frontier. They swept across the donga, often letting themselves go sliding down fifty feet of slope, at the foot of which they had some two hundred yards to rush at the concealed enemy. In all, three lines of infantry stormed up the ridge, and behind them came a squadron of armoured motor-cars, driven with wild courage along the rocky way close up to the top of the ridge.

The machine-guns in the cars swept the Bedouins, while the mountain battery threw up its shrapnel with deadly aim. The Arabs were tenacious, but the shock of our infantry charge and the extraordinary climbing power of our modern war chariots shook their nerve, and their white burnouses fluttered away to the second ridge.

The conflict then became mainly an infantry affair, and the newly-blooded battalion of New Zealanders, with the imperturbable Sikhs, warmed to their work. According to a British officer in the Egyptian service, who was keenly watching the fresh troops in their first battle, there could not be detected a single flincher along the whole line. Here and there was a face with a strained expression, but the spirit inside kept the anxious body moving forward over the rocks. Some men are like the great Frenchman, Turenne, who trembled when he came under fire and swore at his carcass. It was a battle in the old-fashioned style—a mix-up in which our men could see their foes, kill them, and pass their bodies with eyes fixed on the next ridge. Our khaki uniforms were finely fitted for blending with the desert ground, while the white,

An old-fashioned battle

streaming robes of the Bedouins, though excellent as a protection against the sun-heat in the hot season, made clear targets.

By two o'clock in the afternoon the enemy, commanded by Gaafar Pasha, had been driven from the ridges west of Jebel Medwar into a long, rocky valley, known as Wadi Majid. The Turco-Bedouin-Senussiyeh army then numbered some 3,000 rifles, and our infantry force deployed against them was about 2,000 strong. The long nullah in which Gaafar made his stand by his main camp was pitted with caves, that offered excellent cover for defensive purposes. In some places the sharpshooters had literally to be dug out from their hiding-places by our sappers, and the work of clearing the valley, bend by bend, went on somewhat slowly. The midwinter night was falling

Hurried flight of Gaafar Pasha when the camp was reached, and the darkness prevented a complete carrying out of our plan. The Australian Light Horse and the English Yeomanry had worked round on the enemy's rear, and the troopers were waiting there for our artillery and infantry to drive the Turks and Arabs against our expectant horsemen. But in the short daylight hours of Christmas Day the nullah could not be quickly forced, in order to shepherd all the fugitives towards the spot where our cavalry was waiting for them. They were able to escape in the darkness, and though the Australian and English troopers rode some of them down in the twilight, the enveloping movement did not "click."

We captured, however, all the stores in the enemy's main camp, including flocks of sheep and cattle, a herd of camels, and a large quantity of ammunition. Four hundred dead Arabs were left on the ridges and in the nullah and some fourscore prisoners were taken, while

Gaafar Pasha fled in such a hurry that all his private papers, containing information of great value in determining our future operations, fell into our hands. Our serious losses were light, consisting only of fourteen men killed.

But easily though we won the victory in the first trial of strength with the Senussiyeh, and small as were the forces employed on both sides, the affair was of importance. It is not extravagant to say that it was of more importance than any fighting that was taking place at that moment in Europe, for our hold on Egypt and the Sudan and our control of the Suez Canal depended upon rapid success against the Senussiyeh. The Egyptian and Sudanese peasantry and the tribes along the edge of the arable lands of the Nile

TURKISH LEADER OF THE SENUSSIYEH TAKEN PRISONER AFTER THE DECISIVE CHARGE OF THE DORSETSHIRE YEOMANRY.
Gaafar Pasha, Turkish Commander-in-Chief of the Senussiyeh, surrendered after the British had routed the tribesmen. Wounded by a sword thrust, he had to be assisted into the picket-boat which took him out to the warship for conveyance to Alexandria. Above: The pasha, still blood-stained, immediately after his surrender.

were watching and listening. It was not the wine-drinking Young Turkish Party that was now trying to rouse them to revolt, but the heir of a religious leader, whose pureness of doctrine, rigorous mode of life, and fine missionary work in the south deserved the admiration of his fellow-believers. Had the campaign opened with a series of small disasters, such as befell the Egyptian forces of 1882, when Mohammed Ahmed proclaimed himself the Mahdi, the flame of fanaticism might have spread like fire through dry straw.

Momentous issues in the balance From many points of view Egypt had become, for the time, the most important region of strategy of all the theatres of war. Momentous issues were being decided by comparatively small forces, fighting on difficult, waterless stretches of sand and rock. The rising of the Senussiyeh had been long prepared to time with the great Turco-German attack against the Suez Canal. The thrust through Serbia had been preliminary to this operation, and, but for the Franco-British stand at Salonika, which led the German Staff to alter their plan and strike at what seemed the weakened French front at Verdun, the battle for Egypt might have been an affair of very large scope. As it was, the more forceful part of the Turco-German

and thus opened the way for the Russian conquest of Armenia—the turn of events in Egypt remained uncertain.

And it was during this period of uncertainty that Nuri Bey and Gaafar Pasha induced the Senussi to act in open enmity against us. Our retirement from Sollum, instead of being correctly regarded as a sign that we were concentrating, struck the Bedouins as a symptom of our weakness. The little local successes of the tribes of Tripoli had fired the imagination of the Berber and Arab nomads, so that when we left part of the Egyptian coast open, they swooped upon it, and were joined by many tribes under the suzerainty of the Egyptian Sultan. It was a task for the British forces quickly to convince the revolted tribes that the Senussi was not a victorious Mahdi. The battle of Christmas Day was an important step in this direction, and, after dispersing a small advanced force of hostile Bedouins and capturing their camp on December 28th, 1915, we prepared for a strong sweep back to Sollum.

General Wallace, who was in command of the new Western Frontier Force at Matruh, waited some weeks for the arrival of reinforcements. These consisted of a Natal battalion, forming part of General Lukin's South African Brigade, which, after the desert warfare in German South-West Africa, had volunteered for service in Europe. General Lukin's men were many of them troopers, and though they had come to Egypt to train as infantry, in the hope of getting somewhere between Ypres and the Somme, they needed horses again to become a perfect instrument for the Libyan desert operations. In their long rides and battle manœuvres under Botha they had learned all there was to learn about desert warfare, and the ribbons on their deep chests told of victories they had won against more expert enemies than the Bedouins.

The camp by the shore of the Mediterranean, with its flotilla of sweepers, became bathed in a Colonial atmosphere, in which knots of old Anzacs and South Africans who had ridden with Botha swopped Boer and Virginian tobaccos, and talked about the Dardanelles and the road to Wind-

WHERE THE PTOLEMIES HELD IMPERIAL SWAY.
Red Cross supplies for the Anzac hospital at Alexandria. In the background are seen houses typical of this pleasant city halfway between the Occident and Orient.

operations was abandoned, and the army of Syria did not come into action against the eastern frontier of Egypt. The large forces originally designed to reinforce it were dispersed towards Bagdad and Armenia, while Mackensen's gunners, instead of crossing the Bosphorus, returned to the Russian front or travelled towards Verdun.

From the standpoint of the Ottoman and Teutonic commands, the unsupported rising of the Senussi confraternity and the massing of the tribesmen of the Libyan and Sahara wastes formed merely a promising diversion, which had a chance of developing into a great movement. It is difficult to say whether Kressenstein and Djemal were in a position to strike again at the canal somewhere about January or February, 1916, if the strength of our defence had then been weakened by the despatch of large bodies of troops and guns to the western marches of Egypt. But the energetic manner in which all our forces along the canal laboured in the winter on new and larger systems of entrenchments, shows that the menace of a Turco-German attack in force had to be countered by strenuous preparations. Until the plans of the enemy Staff were completely upset by the mistake made by Von der Goltz—who took an army corps from the Caucasus front to stop the progress of General Townshend's column at Ctesiphon,

hoek. The dismounted South Africans, finding themselves back in a desert, longed for their horses, and it was indeed a drawback that they were not again a flying column. But a horse wants a great deal of water, especially in a tropical desert, and the host we were collecting drank more than the wells of the country could supply. Water had to be brought in increasing quantities from Alexandria. Because of the water problem, the South Africans had to fight on foot, and the commander had to rely on the Australian and Yeomanry troopers for his enveloping movement, with some Sudanese camel drivers, and the motor-car battery under the Duke of Westminster.

The Battle of Hazalin

Our total forces were still considerably inferior in number to those of the enemy, and the disadvantage of this was seen in the Battle of Hazalin on January 23rd, 1916. The enemy had won over the large Ulad Ali tribes, spread about the Egyptian coast, and the warriors of Sheikh Harun, whose territory was east of Matruh. There were also the more regular army of the Senussi chief, together with large forces of Tripolitan Bedouins, a few hundred Turkish troops, some scores of Turkish officers, and Teutonic naval gunners and military engineers. Seyyid Ahmed the Senussi was only the religious leader; the actual

Truckload of jovial Australians photographed while taking camels from Cairo to the western frontier of Egypt.

Draft of camels "anchored" in a compound and waiting to be sent by rail for service against the Senussiyeh.

Camels en route for the western frontier.   Packed closely in rail trucks, the heads of the animals are fastened by means of ropes to the side of the truck.

WITH THE IMPERIAL CAMEL CORPS IN EGYPT: CONVEYING CAMELS TO THE WESTERN FRONTIER

commander-in-chief was Enver's brother, Nuri Bey, with Gaafar Pasha as his second in command. They occupied a position twenty-five miles to the west of Matruh. There 2,000 Senussi regulars in uniform, with some 4,000 Bedouins, occupied a well-designed series of entrenchments planned by the Germans and Turks, with numerous machine-guns under German and Turkish officers, backed by two pieces of artillery.

We set out on the evening of January 21st, with a strength of 4,000 infantry, 500 horse, one battery, and two guns. General Wallace's plan was to make a long, quick march under cover of night, and deliver a surprise attack at daybreak. The five hundred Australian and Yeomanry troopers led the way through a gap in the wire entanglement, and made towards the wells at Bir Shola, eighteen miles out. Then the Maoris headed the infantry, which was a fine-looking force, with its sinewy Indians, muscular New Zealanders, dogged Britons, war-seasoned South Africans, and dusky camel drivers from the Sudan. But it was the rainy season, and the rain came down upon the sand and clay and made the going extremely heavy. The troopers and the infantry slipped and ploughed along with great labour, but the high-powered armoured cars and many of the light motor-ambulances could not travel to the scene of action. Even the magnificent horses of the Australian divisional train could not pull their loaded waggons through the slough. The waggons sank axle deep in places where the sand and clay melted into a soft yet tenacious mixture; and, after prolonged **The Senussiyeh** and intense labour, the train was em- **full of fight** bedded nearly midway between the base and the battlefield. Meanwhile, the troops bivouacked for the night by the wells, and then set out at early morning and arrived at half-past nine near the enemy's camp

Our cavalry advanced and screened the movements of the main force, while our artillery opened fire at four thousand yards, and the Sikhs extended in a firing-line, with the South Africans in support. We tried to shake the enemy with shrapnel fire, but he was very well led, and dug himself in deeper while holding his ground. Full of fight, the Senussiyeh swept with fire the Sikhs in front, and by bad but effective marksmanship hit the South Africans who were in support. The hostile commander then seized the initiative and tried to envelop our right. His movement, however, was answered by the South Africans extending beside the Sikhs, while the New Zealanders came up in support. Then, for four hours, there was a ding-dong battle, with the artillery in full blast, and the machine-guns and rifles rattling away in a manner that reminded the Anzacs of the old Gallipoli days. German and Turkish officers worked the hostile machine-guns with great valour and precision, and the hostile artillery ranged with more accuracy than in the **A four-hours** Battle of the Ridges Our cavalry was **ding-dong struggle** compelled to withdraw by the enemy's heavy fire, and though the British commander pressed forward on both flanks in an attempt to make an encircling movement, he was not only matched at this game, but the Ottoman commander deployed his more numerous forces on both wings, and succeeded at last in overlapping us on the right by a force of six hundred Arabs with three machine-guns. In reply to this we strengthened our centre, while holding back the flanking movement with only three platoons of New Zealanders.

Few as these were in number, they firmly held their own, and then our cavalry, with three of our guns, made the first break in the hostile wall of fire. The guns were shifted to a new position so as to command all the ground on the left, and our cavalry there waited until it was again pressed, and then galloped away in apparent confusion. Excited by the victory, the Arabs charged forward in masses, and were blown to pieces by a tempest of shrapnel from our quick-firers. The enemy losses at this critical point were said by a prisoner to have exceeded the total casualties in the Christmas Day battle, and the shock of the blow we had delivered soon began to tell on the enemy's long line. We could not reach his artillery, as a mirage hung over the western sand, and made all spotting there a matter of great difficulty. But our guns, after breaking off the enemy's left flank, smashed away at the centre, and early in the afternoon the foe was completely dominated, and detached bodies of his shaken Bedouin forces began to move away to the north-west.

OVER A WATERLESS WASTE AND UNDER A PITILESS SUN.
Australian transport crossing the desert to meet the hostile tribesmen on the Egyptian western frontier. The expedition was harassed by the eternal difficulty, inherent in desert warfare, of watering so many men and horses, and the endurance of all was tried severely before they achieved victory.

NOTABILITIES OF THE SUDAN WHO WERE PRESENTED TO THE PRINCE OF WALES IN KHARTOUM.

Left to right, standing: Sheikh El-Agab Abu Gin, Chief of the Hamada tribe, Sennar Province; Sheikh Ahmed El-Sunni, Omda of Wad Medani town, Blue Nile Province; Sheikh Idris Habbani, Chief of the Hassania tribe. White Nile Province; Sheikh Bedawi Asaker Abu Kalam, Chief of the Gimma tribe, White Nile Province; Sheikh Ali Tom, Chief of the Kababish tribe of Northern Kordofan; Sheikh Mohammed Fagir, Chief of the Meseria tribe in South-Western Kordofan. Seated: Sheikh Ibrahim Mohammed Farah, Nazir of the Jaalin tribe of Berber Province (rendered valuable services to Lord Kitchener on his way to Omdurman, in 1898); Sheikh Mustafa Hassan, Omda of Shawal District, White Nile Province; Sheikh Hamid Suleiman, Omda of the Habbania tribe, dwelling west of the White Nile.

For one hour the Senussiyeh regulars doggedly rearguarded the retreat, but at four o'clock our firing-line was steadily advancing over the hostile camp, where half a mile of tents and stores went up in flames as the closing shots were fired in the twilight

Our victorious troops had brought neither greatcoats nor blankets. They were soaked through by the pouring rain and chilled to the bone by the bitter wind that swept in from the sea. No sleep was possible. The men first built a rectangular rampart, placed their machine-guns and artillery ready to beat off a night attack, and then bivouacked in the biting cold gloom until day broke. Then, happily, they were soon released from their anxieties by our airmen, who found that the enemy had been so desperately afraid of pursuit that he had marched some twenty miles eastward. Our troops were able to march back to their waggons and get greatcoats, blankets, bully beef, and water. The plight of the artillery and cavalry horses was pitiable. They sniffed at the sand and the mud, for they had had no water for thirty-six hours. The rain that fell had been at once soaked up and turned into slippery desert mud. But for the drenching rain, neither horses nor men would have suffered from thirst, and the waggons would have been able to advance and, with the machine-guns of the armoured car wing, the battle would have probably been decisive.

[Photo by Vandyk.

COL. SIR MOHAMMED ALI BEG, AFSUR-UL-MULK, K.C.I.E.

Commander of the troops of the Nizam of Hyderabad, that took part in the operations against the Turks in Egypt.

The South Africans and the Sikhs bore the burden of the fight, and about a hundred of the former distinguished themselves in a very picturesque way. The South African troopers felt the strain of the long, heavy march through the slippery mud; for, being originally cavalrymen, who had not done route marching for many weeks, their feet were not so hard as those of the long-trained Sikh infantry. They struggled on towards the enemy's position, and then a hundred of the troopers were sent back, as it was reckoned they were unfit to march any farther. But as the cripples set out to drag themselves back to the wells, our guns boomed, and the strange battle-cry of their own battalion came to them down the wind. Turning about, they sent the cry back again in a roar, took off their boots, and with rifle in one hand and boots in the other, went into the battle and fought it to the end.

The continual increase in the number of the Senussi's forces caused our general in command in Egypt serious thought. Notwithstanding successive defeats and the loss of the barley fields and large quantities of food and warlike stores, the tribes were still gathering for battle. They had quite doubled in number since the action on Christmas Day. We had to increase our forces also. So, in spite of our extreme difficulty in watering a large body of troops, reinforcements were sent to Matruh, where Major-General Peyton took command of all the operations. He turned to the experienced lieutenant of General Botha, Brigadier-General H. T. Lukin. and gave him a free hand to make a strong mobile column. General Lukin took under his orders all the South African Infantry Brigade, with a mountain battery, a squadron of the Dorset Yeomanry, the 1st Field Company Kentish Territorial Engineers, the 1st South Midland Field Ambulance, and a camel supply train. The column was also further strengthened by a company of the Australian Camel Corps and the armoured-car squadron under Major the Duke of Westminster.

Towards the end of January news began to come in through deserters that some of the Egyptian tribesmen were growing discouraged and inclined to return and make peace with the Government. It was then time to strike quickly ; but as the enemy had put nearly fifty miles of difficult desert country between his new camp and our base, our column had to be light in movement and yet strong enough to resist and break a large and well-armed force. It was possible that the Senussi would collect more men from Tripoli and the southern oases, so that the South African Brigade might have to fight a division. We were, however, able to move supplies by sea along the coast, and keep all the forces and the flotilla of sweepers in touch by wireless telegraphy and aeroplane pilots. The Senussiyeh army continued its retreat to a point nearly eighty miles from Matruh. Nuri Bey and Gaafar Pasha knew that the port of Barrani, between Matruh and Sollum, would be our first objective. Barrani had been one of the posts held by the Egyptian garrison **The Battle of Agagia Ridge** before the retirement in November, 1915, and the enemy army entrenched on a ridge at Agagia, some fifteen miles south-east of the little seaport. There our aeroplane scouts found the Senussiyeh and the Bedouins in larger numbers, which showed that more reinforcements had been obtained from the tribes. So, on the morning of February 20th, General Lukin's column marched out from Matruh.

For four days the column marched west, with airmen flying in front and a fan of cavalry guarding it against any small body of snipers. But no foes were seen, and in the evening of February 25th, 1916, we camped near the enemy's position, with the intention of making a night attack. But Nuri Bey and his Turco-German Staff believed in the sound Teutonic method of an attacking defensive, and just as we were about to make a general advance in the darkness, the German gunners began to shell our camp. The shrapnel was of bad quality, and though the bombardment lasted two hours no material damage was done. All night our men stood to arms, and at daybreak the yeomen of Dorset moved away from the infantry towards the flank of the Senussiyeh force. Being met by sharp machine-gun and rifle fire, the troopers dismounted, and brought into action their two machine-guns, opening battle at a range of about a mile. They pressed on towards the ridge on which the enemy's sharpshooters had retired, and about this time our infantry, who had been moving forward for two hours and meeting with little resistance, also came sharply into action. Our front was about five miles long after the South Africans had opened out and led the way. The advance took place over long, undulating swells, affording no cover of any kind, and the men soon began dropping as they advanced in short rushes over the barren ground. But splendidly were they led, and every man stuck valiantly to his work, and, with the Territorial artillery shrapnelling the ground in front, the infantry topped the ridge and threw the enemy down into the valley below.

Then came the unexpected factor in General Lukin's plan of

LOOKING FOR THE TRUTH IN THE BOTTOM OF THE WELL.
Greco-Roman reservoirs, long since dry, are among the antiquities of the desert frequently found near water. The Australian Camel Corps in Egypt bivouacked wherever they struck water, and they carefully searched these reservoirs, which the Senussiyeh used as hiding-places for ammunition.

action, which took the enemy completely by surprise. When his front began to waver, the Dorset Yeomanry, near the flank, received the order to mount and charge. They were commanded by Lieut.-Colonel H. M. W. Souter, of the Jat Lancers of India, and he led the yeomen of Dorset in one of the finest and most decisive of modern movements of cavalry. They swung out in line of squadron columns, and then, with drawn swords, swept in line across the wide, open valley, a mile and a half broad, against the ridge held by the enemy infantry with four machine-guns. On this occasion the German and Turkish officers directing the gun teams could not fire with their usual precision.

General Lukin, with his experience of desert warfare, had seen that a charge of cavalry against unbroken infantry was likely to succeed, for the sun was hot, and there was a very disturbing amount of heat shimmer over the scorching sand. None of the hostile machine-gunners could get the range quickly enough to wipe out the swiftly charging line of horsemen. First the Maxims on the ridge ploughed up the sand in front of the yeomen, and then the gunners, in trying again to get on their mark, raised the sights too much, and sent the streams of lead whistling over the heads of the oncoming horsemen. Colonel Souter splendidly led his men in front, and the yelling line swept on over the crest, sticking and slashing like furies. They were first met by Senussiyeh regulars, who inflicted upon them most of their casualties. Five officers were shot down, and Colonel Souter was brought to the ground right in front of Gaafar Pasha in a wide valley full of the enemy, who were all running like mad. Gaafar at once surrendered to Colonel Souter and another officer, Sec.-Lieutenant Blaksley, who had had two horses shot under him.

Meanwhile, the charging regiment was riding down the thronging fugitives in the valley, which extended below the long main ridge over which our infantry was working. The panic of the Bedouins when they were caught on the flank by the cavalry charge was complete and decisive. The English horsemen suffered heavily ; they went right through the valley and then rallied to the left in the hope of making another charge. But the long drive through the desert under a hot sun, with an uphill movement for a mile and a half at the beginning, had tired out the horses. The victorious regiment could not do much more; but it had decided the battle. Among the prisoners were Gaafar Pasha, Nehad Bey, Sami Bey, Yusbashi Senussi, Abdulla Mulazim-Ahmed Mukhtar, and other commanding officers and chiefs. Nuri Bey was reported to be killed, and most of the Turkish Staff were slain or captured.

Some notable prisoners

The victorious column, with the enemy fleeing in scattered parties before them, pushed on to the seaport of Barrani, and there prepared for the final stroke along the coast. Supplies were pushed forward by sea transport

ENEMY CONVOY WRECKED BY BRITISH AIRMEN.
During the fighting between Alexandria and Matruh, in February, 1916, two British aeroplanes dropped bombs on a Senussiyeh camp in the region of Baharia Wells. A camel convoy was at the spot, some of the animals being laden with high explosives. Great damage was done.

and land convoy until Barrani was made into a base for a final forward movement. The port was put into a state of defence and filled with a reserve force from Matruh, and on March 9th the mobile column under General Lukin moved out to retake Sollum, lying fifty miles west by the Tripoli frontier. The bay was encircled by the Taref Mountains, that came down to the coast, leaving only a narrow way of approach by the seashore. The mountain passes had to be occupied in order to ensure the capture of Sollum and prevent the enemy from using the escarpment as a screen for an infantry attack on the rear of our column. The troops at first marched along the rough track by the coast to the wells of Bag-boag. At this small Bedouin settlement the everlasting trouble in desert warfare became acute.

Small as was our mobile column there was not enough water for horses and men. General Lukin was, in fact, trying to accomplish with foot soldiers and horsemen a task requiring a camel mounted force. The enemy, who was amply provided with camels, was retreating with the utmost speed. The Senussiyeh and the Bedouins had had on the ridge of Agagia all the fighting they wanted, and they aimed to get into the heart of the desert, far across the Egyptian frontier, and there recuperate. It was a race in dead calm weather under a burning sun, first across a rough and stony plain and then up the mountain passes.

A FERRY ON THE NILE.
Some men of the Pioneer Corps crossing the Nile on a raft.

the motor-car battery held the Madian Pass. Then, on the morning of March 13th, General Lukin rearranged his forces.

The larger body of troops, with all the animals, moved along the plain and the coast to another pass midway between Sollum and the height where the empty Roman cistern had been found. General Lukin, in person, with the two South African infantry battalions, the armoured cars, and a mountain battery, moved eastward along the top of the Taref Mountains. With him also went the Australian Camel Corps and camels carrying the water supply. There was only enough water for eight pints a man until the water supply at Sollum could be captured. It might have been forty-eight hours before water was reached, and it might have been longer. So there was not much drink for the two thousand infantrymen and their comrades. The detached column on the ridge marched until nine o'clock at night, and then bivouacked four miles distant from the Halfaia Pass, where it was to meet the column in the plain. Every man who was not on sentry duty snatched a few hours' rest after a feed of biscuit and a mouthful of water. Then, early next morning, the armoured cars went out to reconnoitre and found the pass abandoned by the enemy, and also learnt that the Senussiyeh had evacuated Sollum the evening before and retreated to the south-west.

Along the Taref Mountains

The troops rested only for a few hours at night, and reached Bir-el-Augerin at noon on March 12th, after a trying march across the plain and mountain slopes. Then, after only a few minutes' rest, two battalions of African infantry were sent forward to carry the first pass, the Madian, and advance eastward along the heights. The South African Scottish Battalion, with the 1st South African Battalion in support, went upward to win the heights. The armoured-car battery, which came up from the south-east along the ridge, assisted in the operation. Meanwhile, the South Africans, worn down by the heavy marching and suffering fearfully from lack of water and the tropical heat, struggled up the Taref Mountains, and by a feat of magnificent endurance reached the summit in the afternoon, fortunately without meeting any resistance.

The sufferings of the men when they had won the key to Sollum after a gruelling task were not at an end. There was an ancient Roman cistern at the top of the Madian Pass, and it was expected that this reservoir would provide water for the whole column. But the enemy had emptied the cistern, and also pumped dry the wells at Siwiat farther eastward, intending thus to prevent any advance along the mountains. This he did to some extent. General Lukin had intended to water his troops at the cistern and the wells, and then move his whole force along the mountain ridge towards Sollum Bay. But in the absence of water his plan had to be modified. The main force bivouacked on the plain on the night of March 12th, while

Our aerial scouts reported that the Senussiyeh camp at Bir Waer, on the heights west of Sollum, was empty, and the Duke of Westminster was ordered to pursue the retreating foe with "reasonable boldness." Heading his armoured-car battery, which consisted of nine armoured cars and one open car on which a machine-gun was mounted, with some thirty-two men, the duke went forward with a degree of boldness that can hardly be described

PIGEON-HOUSE NEAR THE PYRAMIDS.
Egyptian pigeon-house in the Australian camp near the Pyramids.

AN AGREEABLE CHANGE FROM THE SAND.
Method of swimming horses across the Nile. The Great Barrage can be seen in the distance.

ON THE EDGE OF THE DESERT.
Australians in a practice trench near Cairo, on the very fringe of the desert.

as reasonable. It was incomparably daring. The squadron quickly passed through the enemy's camp at Bir Waer and then turned down the old road which starts in the desert and runs to the Tripoli coast town of Tobruk, ninety miles west of the Egyptian frontier. The road surface had worn rocky in the course of ages, but the armoured motor-car men regarded it, after their experiences in trying to get through the rain-soaked desert sands, as a magnificent track. On it they speeded up their motors to thirty-five miles an hour, which was lightning travel in the Libyan wilderness. It took them only half an hour to overtake the Senussiyeh army, which

IN THE PINK OF CONDITION.
Western Australians passing through Cairo on a route march.

was watering at the Asisa Wells, some twenty miles from Bir Waer. Detachments acting as rearguards sniped the modern war chariots but missed, owing to the speed at which the strange charioteers were going. Then, as the leading car whipped round a bend in the road, an extraordinary battle between thirty-two Britons and some six thousand Senussiyeh regulars, Bedouins, Turks, and Germans abruptly opened.

Charge of the motor-car squadron

The enemy was caught just as he was preparing to break camp. His camel supply train was standing loaded, and masses of his infantry were already on the move. Two guns had been removed from their position, but a third gun and two machine-guns still protected the rear of the retreating army. Some Turks manned the 10-pounder and the two Maxims, and opened fire with these as the leading car swung into sight. As the shells from the hostile mountain gun whizzed over his head, the Duke of Westminster shouted to his battery to form in line and charge. The ten cars formed up along the road, with the enemy facing them over some three hundred yards of rough ground formed of boulders, stiff scrub, and sandy patches. As the cars wheeled, our machine-gunners in them swept the hostile positions, and then, while two of the cars remained on the road and kept up a covering fire, the other eight cars attacked in infantry fashion. That is to say, each car made a short rush forward, supported by the covering fire of the cars that were standing still at the moment. Rapid and exact judgment with regard to range was needed from the machine-gun officers, while from the drivers there was required a nice appreciation of the intentions of the Turkish officer who was directing the mountain gun. But this officer could not get the range

of any of the charging cars. His 10 lb. shells, after whizzing at times just over the armoured tops of the war chariots, burst some two miles behind the scene of action. Not a single direct hit did the Turkish gunners register. Meanwhile, the British machine-guns were doing deadly work. They shot down, almost to a man, the Turkish officers and gun-crews, and then swept forward against the absolutely demoralised Senussiyeh army, which was scattering in every direction. To many of the Arabs our armoured motor-cars, with their terrible rain of death, were not human weapons of warfare, but horrible magical instruments that nothing could stop. Had they not come through the fire of the Turkish mountain guns and the Turkish battery of machine-guns? The cars dashed about the battlefield, breaking up every knot of men that still showed fight, and searching chiefly for Turkish officers, whose capture was of most importance.

Most of the Bedouins threw away their rifles and fled, utterly regardless of the direction in which they were going. There was one hostile officer who did not lose his head, and worked furiously to get away some fifty loaded camels of the Senussi's supply train. But as the

Enemy supply train blown up

animals were leaving the camp our machine-guns fired at them, and the result was a terrific surprise. The unfortunate beasts had been laden with petrol and bombs, and they were blown sky-high in a grand explosion. The charge was continued for seven miles, but the pursuit of the enemy had then to be abandoned for fear of a shortage of petrol. Three cars were left on the field to guard the booty and the prisoners, while the rest of the battery went back to Sollum for more petrol. Three mountain guns, nine machine-guns, a large quantity of shell, 300,000 cartridges, twenty-four

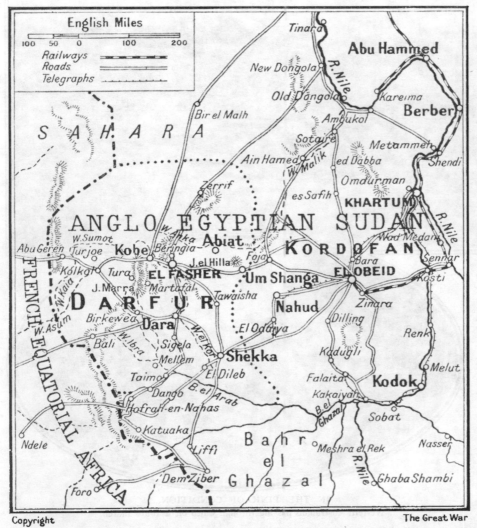

AREA OF THE OPERATIONS AGAINST THE SULTAN OF DARFUR.
Ali Dinar, Sultan of Darfur, who had long been truculent, gathered a force at Jebel-el-Hilla. in February, 1916. Colonel Kelly advanced from Nahud to Abiat and, after a sharp engagement at Beringia, completely routed the Sultan and occupied his capital, El Fasher, on May 23rd.

flock at Doctor's Well in boyhood, thirty years before. Thereupon, the Duke of Westminster resolved to make a great raid into the desert. Every man in the battery was up all night and all the next day tuning up the engines and getting the cars in order. The armoured war chariots were reinforced by squadrons of light cars carrying machine-guns, and all the motor-ambulances within travelling range of Sollum were added to the expedition, in order to provide space for the men of the Tara and the crew of the Egyptian patrol boat Abbas when they were found and rescued.

By midnight on March 16th, 1916, there gathered at the old Turkish fort on the ridge above Sollum the nine armoured Rolls-Royce cars, five open touring motor-cars with machine-guns, light cars, and motor-ambulances, forming together a fleet of forty-two vehicles. And no tourist trophy cars were ever more carefully prepared than these were. At three o'clock on the morning of St. Patrick's Day the Duke of Westminster led his strange squadrons across the desert for a few miles, and, picking up the Tobruk road, reached Asisa, the scene of the motor-car battle on March 15th, and there halted in the darkness until day broke and lighted the ancient Tobruk road. Thence the cars hummed along the old Roman way through illimitable stretches of bare desert, with an occasional halt to repair some burst tyre. When sixty-five miles had been covered a small party of Bedouins was overtaken and disarmed, but, as there was no room to spare for prisoners, the men were set free. The Duke of Westminster, at the time, was feeling somewhat like Robinson Crusoe at the sight of man Friday's footprint in the sand. In the dust on the old road the mark of motor-car wheels could be seen. Speeding along another sixteen miles, the column overtook a strange car and captured it. It was **The Duke** one that had belonged to our Royal **and the Arab** Naval Armoured Car Division, and it was fitted with sheet-rubber rolled up in camel hide and bound to the wheels with wire.

About this time the cars, under the direction of the two Bedouin guides, turned south into the desert, and after travelling for fifteen miles over desperately rough ground, the expedition came to a standstill. The man who had fed his flock at Bir Hakim thirty years before maintained with much eloquence that the column was going on a wrong track. The Bedouin who had guarded the prisoners was not inclined to argue the point, for he was doubtful himself, and yet held that his direction had been the right one. He was sincerely concerned about the matter, and desirous of making the expedition a success. The duke resolved to trust this man, though the desert was now becoming very stony. The hundred mile point was passed, and then the one hundred and five mile point, which had been thought to be the extreme limit of the expedition. The cars went on for another sixteen miles, and nobody in them spoke. The sense of failure weighed upon all. Then one of the Arabs espied in a mirage a

spare machine-gun barrels, military stores, food supplies, camels, and mules were among the material captured. We had only one casualty, an officer being slightly wounded in the head. Important among the enemy losses were thirty Turkish officers killed or wounded. What with the smashing up of the Turkish High Command at Agagia, the destruction of guns round Matruh, and the final capture of the rest of the artillery possessed by the Senussi and most of his ammunition and supplies, the campaign on the north-west frontier of Egypt seemed practically concluded. The Duke of Westminster's charge was a unique and decisive piece of work.

But one more strange and picturesque exploit fell to the gallant nobleman. A letter was picked up near the ruins of Bir Waer, written by Captain Williams, of the auxiliary boarding ship Tara, to Nuri Bey. The **Captain Williams's** British captain complained that the Tara **letter** prisoners were starving and ill, and begged that medicine should be procured for them at Sollum. The letter mentioned Bir Hakim as the place where the prisoners were being kept. All our Bedouin captives and refugees were questioned about the position of Bir Hakim, yet none of them had heard of Doctor's Well, as Bir Hakim reads in English. But in the first dash through Bir Waer the Duke of Westminster had captured a Bedouin straggler, and the man afterwards admitted that he had acted as guard to the Tara prisoners, and showed himself eager to guide the armoured squadron to the well. Then another Arab said that he had fed a

small height. But, happily, there was more than a mirage on the hill. There was a line of men running about with rifles in their hands. The armed men quickly disappeared, and the Duke of Westminster formed his armoured cars into line at two o'clock in the afternoon and then launched them on an attack. Meanwhile, other figures had appeared against the sky-line—strange creatures covered in sacking and dumb as statues. At last one of the figures faintly raised a British cheer.

Rescue of the Tara survivors The cars raced up to within two hundred yards of the mound, and as they opened fire the Senussi's soldiers bolted as fast as they could, which was not, however, very fast, as they had their women and children with them. Some of the armoured cars advanced in pursuit, while the tourist cars and the ambulances approached the prisoners, many of whom were now dancing and shouting with joy. Some of them, indeed, could not be persuaded to leave the fighting cars, and in their happiness at meeting their countrymen again they slightly hindered the battle with the guards. But while these were being hunted down, the remainder of the motor fleet was making a tremendous race to the rescued men, running abreast, careless of boulders and punctures, the crews cheering, and pulling out milk, jam, bread, and bully beef as they came.

The condition of the prisoners was dreadful. They had been living on snails and edible roots, but even these sources of nourishment had failed them, for their strength had so diminished that they could not travel far to find the roots. They were dying from famine. Despite their sufferings, they had, however, managed to get food for the dog of the ship-wrecked Tara, who was accepted as a mascot by the armoured-car battery. One of the Tara men said that he went almost mad when he saw the soldiers unloading packing-cases from the car, as he knew they contained food. Many of the prisoners ate three days' rations with such speed that their starved stomachs could not digest the unusual quantity of food. The result was a severe attack of indigestion. The wonderful and romantic episode in the tropical desert closed with a touch of sublimity. Most of the men on the old Holyhead steamer were Welshmen, and, going on their knees, they thanked their Maker for their happy deliverance from terrible captivity, and then sang together the old Welsh hymn, "O fyrniau Caer—salem."

After bringing the rescued men, numbering nearly a hundred, back to Sollum through a sand blizzard, the armoured-car battery returned to the workaday labour of patrolling. For some months the patrols continued to hunt out and destroy hidden stores of ammunition, of which another quarter of a million rounds were discovered after the occupation of Sollum. Then south of the port two German wireless sets were found in the desert and brought in. A cordon of troops was flung out in a semi-circle toward the Libyan and Sahara wastes. In the south the British and Egyptian troops at Kharga made reconnaissances in all directions, while our airmen flew over the oasis of Dakhla, and there broke up the Bedouins by machine-gun swoops and aerial bombardments. More to the north, round the Beharia oasis, a small body of the Senussi's followers continued until May, 1916, to terrorise the native population and rob them of their food. An epidemic broke out, with a famine, and the refugees came in a pitiable state down the old caravan tracks to our desert outposts. Along the northern coast our victorious frontier force came down to the edge of the plateau at Moghara, and, after closing all routes of supply to the western deserts, we opened markets along the line we were holding. This brought the Bedouins in from the western wastes. And they came in tribe after tribe. Along the coast the Ulad Ali tribe sent in their headmen to make submission, and the sheikh who had first assailed us near Matruh returned with the remnant of his people to make peace.

A NUT THAT OUR ARMY CRACKED ON CHRISTMAS DAY.
This cave stood on the side of a steep hill commanding the road from Matruh to Rakhum. It is cut out of solid rock, and had been strongly fortified by the Senussiyeh. They defended it stoutly, but it was carried by the British troops in the Mersa Matruh fight on Christmas Day, 1915.

INTERESTING OPERATIONS IN THE FIELD.
Field-kitchen in operation at the camp of the Australian contingent in Egypt.

The condition of the country was terrible. Not a grain of the barley of rare quality, grown by the coast, had been raised during the brief war. The hostile Arabs, once so well fed from their own land, had been living, like the Tara prisoners, on roots and snails. Many cairns in the desert told the price the natives had paid for listening to the false tales of Gaafar Pasha and Nuri Bey. Our soldiers were at first hot against the enemy tribesmen. In the long nullah near Matruh, on Christmas Day, the New Zealanders had found the bodies of some of our wounded left behind in one of our charges. The wounded men were not only dead, but their corpses showed that they had been slain by a race of torturers. Terrible were the things some of our troops were going to do when they got the Bedouins in their hands. But when the tribesmen came in—parties of starving men, women, and children—the usual thing happened. The British soldier went hungry and the Arab children shared his ration. In April the pets of the Matruh garrison were two small Arab children who, having been abandoned by their tribe on the Sunday, were found by a patrol and brought into camp. They were in the last stage of starvation, and it seemed impossible that they could live. At the beginning of May, 1916, the larger part of the Bedouin army was living on the biscuits and dried dates brought by our transports and motor-trucks to the coast towns. When the Bedouin had fed well and recovered his strength he needed only one thing to complete his happiness—a military pass enabling him to travel eastward with his family to safety and peace.

Starving Bedouins fed by British

Very unlikely it seemed that these men could ever again be induced to rise against British rule, and there was no need for us to punish them. In a few months they had been reduced to the condition under which the Sudanese races lay when Lord Kitchener broke the power of the successor of the former Mahdi at Omdurman. They now knew from experience the curse of barbarism and the blessing of a settled and progressive civilisation. By the middle of May, 1916, the complete submission of the western Arabs had still to be secured. An Italian force had landed at Moresca, after clearing the mines sown by enemy submarines round this Tripolitan port. The allied force then

PUTTING FRIENDLY SHOULDERS WHEN WANTED TO THE WHEEL.
Friendly Arabs took much interest in the doings of our troops in Egypt, and gave useful help in unloading a train with the baggage waggons of the New Zealand force at Alexandria. In circle: British soldiers at a hospital in Egypt.

"THE IMPERIAL SCHOOL OF INSTRUCTION OF EGYPT."

Third Officers Course, July, 1915.—Top row: P. T. Roberts, H. C. A. Sandford, C. R. Longden, D. P. Macdonald, R. Andrew, J. E. Lloyd, G. W. Akeroyd, J. H. Slater, H. Craig, G. Beith, W. T. Bichan, W. G. Galbraith, E. A. Davis, A. Skene-Smith.   Second row: F. D. Adamson, G. F. Langley, A. S. Robertson, V. C. Alderson, J. A. Lorimer, H. Smithram, J. F. Keelan, T. C. E. Godfrey, G. C. Maxfield, L. C. Roth, L. Elmiger, C. J. Thomson, B. Atkinson, G. M. Nicholas.   Third row: A. H. Ross, E. M. Bland, F. J. C. Sale, J. P. Stewart, E. J. Gaynor, P. G. R. Parkes, M. Kelly, K. V. Clinton, J. C. McCaul, N. Hill, W. H. Bunning, R. G. Raws, A. G. Brown, M. W. Sayce.   Fourth row: E. Catani, K. C. D. Dawson, A. C. Fogarty, Lieut, H. H. Sloane-Stanley (Staff), Capt. J. A. S. Cooke (Adjutant), Lieut.-Col. E. M. Colstan, M.V.O. (Commandant), Lieut. P. Clarke (Assist.-Adjutant). Capt. S. H. Chadwick (Quartermaster), J. M. Maine, J. C. A. Ellerton, W. R. Hunter.   Fifth row: W. F. Kinsett (Sergt.-Instructor), W. K. Miller (Sergt.-Major), J. R. Shed (Sergt.-Instructor). W. Gerahty (Sergt.-Instructor), C. C. Chick, H. E. Smith.

advanced by land to the port of Bardia, and thus secured the two centres in Tripoli through which munitions had been supplied to the Senussi and from which German and Austrian underwater craft had obtained supplies. The brother of the Senussi chief joined the Italian expedition, which encountered no opposition whatever from the broken army of Seyyid Ahmed.   The Senussi still retained his original base at Jupiter Ammon and his great central camp in the Kufra oasis.   But he was **Sultan of Darfur's** cut off from all supplies from the sea **threat** and encircled in the desert by French, Italian, and British forces.

At first one promising path of retreat had been open. In February, 1916, just before General Lukin broke the Senussi's power on the ridge of Agagia, the Sultan of Darfur, a thousand miles away from the scene of action, began openly to side with the Senussi and the Teutonised Turks. Darfur is the westernmost State of the Anglo-Egyptian territories of the Sudan.   It extends along the northern edge of the Sahara, some four hundred miles south of the Kufra oasis—the Senussi's headquarters—with which it connects by means of caravan routes running through Borku, in French territory. Darfur had been incorporated in the dominions of the false Mahdi in 1883, but the negroes and Arabs composing the population chafed under the rule of the dervishes and fought desperately for freedom until our victory at Omdurman in 1898 liberated the country.   The hereditary Arab leader of the then friendly Darfur people, Ali Dinar, was set free from the Mahdist prison and recognised as Sultan, under the suzerainty of the Anglo-Egyptian Government of Sudan, to which he paid an annual tribute of £500.

It was largely through the influence of the older Senussi that the Darfur chiefs had fought for fifteen years against the Mahdi and Khalifa and their dervishes of the Sudan. Owing to the strong influence of this missionary sect the younger Senussi had been able to induce the Sultan, in January, 1916, to attempt a movement of invasion towards Khartoum. El Fasher, the capital of Darfur, lies some five hundred miles west of Khartoum, in a mountainous country watered in the rainy season by tributaries of the Nile and streams flowing towards Lake Chad.   A farming nation of some four million brown-faced negroes and Bedouin settlers, who live in huts of clay and reeds in a burning climate, scantily people a country larger than the United Kingdom.   As, however, the high plateau is seamed by dry river-courses and broken by innumerable mountains, between 6,000 and 7,000 feet high, Darfur is a land of great natural strength, as the natives, indeed, had shown in their long struggles against the Khalifa.

Ali Dinar was not content to remain upon the defensive. Early in February, 1916, he gathered a force at Hilla, a great mountain a hundred miles east of his capital and close to the frontier of Kordofan.   His clear intention was to invade Kordofan, one of the centres of the former Mahdist revolt and peopled by half a million Arabs and Nubians. But in answer to this dangerous threat, the British Sirdar made a concen-   **The rebel Sultan** tration of a mixed Egyptian force of all   **outmanœuvred** arms under Colonel Kelly. The concentration took place at Nahud, a point three hundred miles south-west of Khartoum, and well to the south of Ali Dinar's centre of operations.   Colonel Kelly marched in a north-easterly direction towards the enemy's capital, thus menacing the line of communications of the rebel Sultan and compelling him to postpone his invasion of Kordofan and look to his own safety.   While the outmanœuvred Arab potentate was rearranging the disposition of his force, Colonel Kelly's column marched from Nahud in Kordofan to the Darfur town of Um Shanga, which was reached, after arduous skirmishing and marching, towards the end of March. At the same time another part of the column closed round the great mountain of Hilla, where Ali Dinar had made his first concentration. From Hilla the column moved along the lower edge of the Sahara, by the bed of the Nuere water-course, to the town of Abiat, the seat of Ali Dinar's power.

Our lines of communication were strengthened and broadened, enabling supplies and reinforcements to come from Khartoum and Kordofan. Six weeks were spent in strengthening the little column and preparing for the decisive advance.

Then, on May 15th, 1916, Colonel Kelly moved out from Abiat on a long fighting march towards El Fasher. The Sultan's outposts were driven in, and his larger advanced forces were shaken out of their positions by a series of sharp movements, which brought our column on the evening of May 21st close to the village of Beringia, twelve miles north of the Darfur capital.

A miniature Omdurman The enemy, some three thousand strong, was entrenched on the heights by the village, and Colonel Kelly was not inclined in the circumstances to make a frontal attack. On the morning of May 22nd, 1916, he sent out his camel corps on an outflanking movement, and this compelled Ali Dinar to abandon his entrenched position. But the Arab leader was as vehement in temperament as his old enemies the dervishes of Omdurman. Instead of retiring when he had been outflanked, he ordered a general attack against our lines. The battle that quickly ensued was an

Omdurman in miniature. The drive, tenacity, and absolute disregard of death of the mountain negroes and Arabs of Darfur were superbly heroic. Like Fuzzy Wuzzy, they would have broken the Egyptian lines had the troops been armed only with Martini rifles. But the new magazine rifle, machine-guns, and modern quick-firers stayed the terrific charge within ten yards of our front. Despite the rapidity of movement and desperate courage of the new fanatics, half their forces were brought down in the wild, vain rush that cost us only five lives to stem and then break in a victorious counter-charge.

Flying Corps officer's daring feat

When the enemy, reeling from the losses of his ineffectual onset, was trying to make a stand against our counter-attack, a strange, unexpected event struck fear into the hearts of Ali Dinar's reserve forces. He then had left a large body of mounted men and some two thousand foot soldiers. But over them swooped an officer of the Royal Flying Corps. He bombed the Arab horsemen and scattered them, threw his remaining bombs at the Darfur infantry, and then planed down—a wonder and terror to the ignorant, barbaric soldiery—and raked them with his machine-gun. They broke in disorder under his fire, as much through superstitious dread as through loss of physical courage. And while the gallant British officer was flying back, wounded in the thigh, to Abiat, Colonel Kelly and his column marched on to El Fasher. The capital was occupied early in the morning of May 23rd, 1916, and Sultan Ali Dinar, with only a small following, fled westward. He had fared worse in his intended attack on the Sudan than his master, the Senussi, had done in the intended attack on Egypt.

FROM THE RUGGED HILLS OF GALLIPOLI TO THE SANDS OF EGYPT.
Australian troops on their arrival at Cairo, where they recuperated after the glorious and strenuous days and nights of fighting against the Turks on the fateful Peninsula between the Ægean and the Dardanelles.

CHAPTER CXIX.

ITALY AFTER ONE YEAR OF WAR.

By Dr. James Murphy.

Interesting Questions Suggested by a Consideration of Italy's First Year Military Balance-Sheet—General Cadorna's Swift Thrust in Early Days of the War—How Austria Failed to Take the Italian Advance Seriously—Alpini Capture the Main Passes of the Trentino Salient and of the Dolomite and Carnic Alps—Their Skill and Ingenuity in Mountain Warfare—Austria's Dream of Invading Plains of Lombardy Abandoned—Italy's Defensive Warfare for Control of Strategic Positions—Difficulties and Hardships of the Alpini's Winter Campaign—Dangers of the Spring Campaign owing to Avalanches—Admirable Organisation of Mountain Transport—Objects of General Cadorna's Advance on the Isonzo—How Italy Lost Two Weeks through sheer Ill Luck—Siege Warfare—The Carso Battle-Front Described—General Position Along the Isonzo Described—Why Italy Did Not Participate in Other Theatres of the European War—Cadorna's Hope of Indirect Help to Allies in the Balkan Theatre—Italy's Vigorous Action in the Adriatic—Her Occupation of Valona and Durazzo—Intricacies of the Political and Economic Position in Italy—The Strength and Weakness of the Whole Italian Position—Wonderful Spirit of the Soldiers and Civilians—Democratic Origin of Italy's War a Source of Strength and Weakness—Italy's Aims and Claims not Understood by Her Allies—Explanation of Her Reluctance to Make Open War against Germany—The Great German Campaign for the Capture of Italy's Industry and Commerce—Compact between Baron Sonnino and Prince von Bülow—The People of Italy Annoyed with Britain over Exorbitant Prices for Coal—The "Trojan Horse"—Italy Becomes an Intimate Partner in the Alliance—Exchange of Visits between Allied Statesmen and Generals—Campaign for the Italianisation of the Banca Commerciale—Mr. Asquith's Visit Hailed as a Symbol of Alliance for which the Italian Soul had Long Yearned—"La Vittoria e Secura!"

IN casting up the net results of Italy's military effort against Austria during the first year of her campaign, a number of general questions suggest themselves. Can the sum total of the year's work be looked upon as a fulfilment of the high hopes inspired by the victorious onslaught of the first two months? How far was the Italian Army successful in its effort to redeem the lost provinces? What were the difficulties that lay in its path, and how far were they overcome? What were the indirect influences of the Italian campaign in the other theatres of the European War? How far was the political orientation of Italy deflected from Germany and directed towards the allied Powers? What was the effect of the war on the economic and social life of the nation?

Looking over the broad outlines of the military situation, one feature which stands out more boldly than all others is the admirable wisdom of General Cadorna's swift thrust during the very first days of the war. Italy was weak. Her Army was only in the process of formation, and her resources in munitions were meagre. To the last shell

GENERAL PAOLO MORRONE
When General Zupelli resigned the Italian War Ministry in April, 1916, to serve at the front, he was succeeded by General Morrone, a Neapolitan member of General Cadorna's Staff.

and the last rifle the Austrians had known what the striking power of their new enemy would be. Hence the neglect on the part of Austria to take the Italian advance in its full seriousness. The Austrian Staff allowed one month for the Italian mobilisation, in the belief that by the end of that time the Alpine defences would be fully manned against the approaching enemy. But Cadorna did not wait to mobilise. With the small army which for some months had been stationed on the frontier he immediately opened the attack along a front of nearly four hundred miles. Probably he had little more than a quarter of a million men at his disposal, and it was even said in Italian circles that his Staff was not unanimous as to the plan of campaign.

But Cadorna had his way. Within ten days after the declaration of war the main passes of the Trentino salient and the Dolomite and Carnic Alps were in the hands of the Alpini. Fortified positions had been taken with surprising rapidity, together with quantities of guns, munitions, and food supplies; for though Austria had her defences well prepared they were not yet manned by their full quota of soldiers.

487

"ALL'S WELL WITH THE ENTENTE."
Mr. Asquith and Signor Salandra, the Italian Premier, leaving the Chamber in Rome on the occasion of the British Premier's visit to Italy at the end of March, 1916, when Mr. Asquith made eloquent reference to the community of ideals and policy animating the two peoples.

Yet it must not be supposed that the work of the Alpini was a walk-over. It is true that the Austrians were not fully prepared, but it is also true that the Italians had not completed even the first stages of their preparation. The thin screen of advancing troops was practically unsupported. It moved against the most formidable defences in the world, seizing mountain positions which ten men might have defended against a thousand, scaling jagged rocks and icy peaks, and encircling important bodies of defensive forces through sheer skill and ingenuity in mountain warfare. Surprised by the swiftness and daring of the assault, Austria had to abandon her cherished dream of invading the Plains of Lombardy and Venice. She was driven back to the defence of the main arteries which opened into the very heart of her territory. Hastily, large **Swift daring** bodies of troops were withdrawn from **of the Alpini** Galicia. But it was too late to think of a counter-attack. The Alpini were in full control of every outlet into Italian territory.

A few weeks' delay in mobilisation would have given Austria a chance fully to man her positions and bring up the reserves which she would need in case an invasion of Italy were decided upon. At some points of the frontier, such as the Toscolano Valley, between Lake Idro and Lake Garda, she was within a long day's march of some of the most vital arteries of communication in Italy. A quick dash southwards from Garda might have brought her to the great railroad which runs between Milan and Verona. At the same time a series of bold onslaughts through the valleys of the Adige, the Brenta, the Piave, the Tagliamento, the Fella, and the Judrio might have overwhelmed the half-prepared Italian Army and given Austria command of the Lombardian and Venetian plains. Hence the plan of the Italian commander. His work had to be carried out with lightning dash and energy, not allowing a moment

of time for the Austrians to reinforce themselves. During those days of June and July, 1915, we all stood in wonderment at the marvellous advance which was being made in the Alps ; but not all of us realised that it was a matter of sheer necessity, a question of life or death. At the end of July the Italian positions on the vantage points were perfectly consolidated and the danger of invasion was over for the moment.

Such was the work of the Alpine soldiers along what I might call the high mountain sector of the battle-front. It was essentially a defensive warfare, a battle for the control of the strategic positions which Austria had secured for herself in the Treaty of 1866. Once the dominating rim of the mountain ridge had been gained, nothing remained but to consolidate defences, organise systems of supply, and settle down to a siege warfare. To press farther onwards would have brought the Alpini into the great valleys, where numerous masses of supporting troops and weight of metal would have been necessary. So the active onslaught on a   **The heroes** large scale was brought practically to a   **of the hour** standstill while the main forces of the Italian Army, concentrated on the Isonzo front, were hammering at Gorizia in an effort to break through the great Austrian defensive and invade the enemy's country.

Before speaking of the operations on the Isonzo it will be well to dwell for a moment on the difficulties and hardships of that strange form of warfare which the Alpini were called upon to wage throughout the long winter months. In August, 1915, during my first visit to the Italian front, I noticed that the Alpini were the heroes of the hour. At every café in the little town where Headquarters were established one heard of their heroic skill and prowess. Jauntily and gaily they passed to and fro, shod in spiked boots, an eagle's feather bravely borne in the hat as a symbol of their profession. Fine fellows they were, lithe of limb and hard of muscle, with sharply-cut features, keen eyes, and a clearness of complexion that told of long days spent in the glorious air of the mountains. None of the grimness of the warrior was about them ; sportsmen rather than soldiers you would have considered them—romantic, daring, battling against forces of Nature, and judging of their victories by the difficulties of the terrain which they had overcome rather than by the number of enemies they had slain.

Along the Isonzo and in the trenches of France and Flanders war meant slaughter ; but away on the hill-tops it was romantic and heroic, robbed of its gruesomeness, characterised by the sublime elements of ancient tragedy. Speaking with the Alpini in the wine-shops and sipping afternoon coffee with them in the piazzas of the little towns along the front, they told me of the glories of their mountain warfare. To be a mere unit in the military machine which crushes masses of human material and is crushed in turn is not a man's work, they would say. It is cruel, cold, mechanical slaughter, dull and terrible. You advance against a hail of shell, a murderous mass of machinery rather than human enemies. You fall without having looked into the face of an opponent, without having seen the hand that sped the shell or bullet. The men charge in masses and you are borne on by the fury of the crowd. But in the mountain it is man against man. " Ah, signor, you must come with us," exclaimed a mountaineer to me one August evening, as we sat in the piazza of a little hillside town when the sun was sinking in the west and the far-away hills looked like a mass of glowing coral. " With us you will be surrounded by the glory and mystery of Nature in her most heroic mood, the great shadows of the night lying in the valleys and the moon like dazzling limelight thrown on the glittering diamonds of the peaks, the artillery booming like the organ in a vast cathedral, and the echoes resounding from hill-top to hill-top like the strophe and the antistrophe of a great choir. Sometimes the wind sings

Elliott & Fry.

Major-General Sir G. J. Younghusband, K.C.I.E., in command of troops in Egypt.

Italian Alpine outpost ready to signal the approach of Austrian aircraft.

Peasant women of Italy welcome a cavalry patrol with words of cheer and spring water.

Italian gunners finding the range for mountain artillery amid the Dolomites.

Italian artillery column goes into action along a mountain road skirting a precipice.

Swept down the mountain side by tons of snow : Fate of an Austrian patrol caught in an Alpine avalanche.

gently through the pinnacles like the soft music of an æolian harp, and sometimes it is like the crashing of a great orchestra."

That was in the summer-time, when Nature invites the adventurer to taste the heroic beauty of the great hills. The Alpine soldier was then the happiest figure in the vast theatre of the European War. He was the hero of the drama, not only enjoying the plaudits of the world audience but also taking a keen zest in the work which he was performing. But when I again visited the front in the spring of 1916, I found the spirit of my Alpine friends had changed. Buoyant as ever they were, and confident of their power; but they did **Ordeal of the** not speak of the glories of their task. **winter siege** The grim siege of the winter months had told on them. They were weather-beaten and war-worn, telling you in serious and tragic tones of the terrible ordeal through which they were passing.

In the depth of the winter the task of the mountain warrior was grim and terrible. Not only had he to withstand the piercing cold, oftentimes ten thousand feet above sea-level, but day after day his trenches were being filled by the snowdrifts, so that he had to build new habitations and at the same time keep guard against his enemy. From the highest peaks to the saddles of the mountains the roads and pathways were being constantly blocked. It needed a whole army of workmen to keep the ways open so that food and ammunition might be supplied to the outposts. Rarely before had human beings ventured into these haunts of the eagle, which now became peopled by large bodies of soldiers.

But with the advance of spring the task took on an aspect of deeper tragedy. For the period of avalanches set in—Nature in violent outburst against the men who had occupied the outposts which she had reserved to herself. No longer was it the Austrian enemy which the Alpine soldier dreaded, but all day long and through the watches of the night he heard the muffled roar of the mountain, which told him that great masses of snow were being loosened from their foundations. His task became a very war of Titans. Down from the eternal heights the mountains of snow came tumbling, destroying the lines of communication and sometimes burying beneath their mighty bulk the trains of men who were bringing food and ammunition to the advanced positions. Day after day there were reports of new disasters. Sometimes as many as twenty positions would be cut off during the one day. How was help to be taken to the victims? In many cases it took ten days to build a new tunnel through the fallen mountain, and all the time the little company on the heights were without fresh supplies of food and ammunition. It was terrible and anxious work for the engineers. And oftentimes their labour was in vain. The mountain was taking its toll of lives, a toll in excess of what the Austrian took during the first four months of 1916.

I do not think that this sphere of operations, with its vastness, its difficulties, and its terrors, has ever been fully understood by outsiders. It must be remembered that the Alpine advance considerably lengthened the Italian line so that it now stretched over a distance of almost exactly eight hundred and fifty kilometres, or five hundred miles. About five-sixths of that line, from the Stelvio Pass to Plezzo, ran along one of the highest mountain ridges in the world. When one thinks of the immense organisation necessary to keep it supported and supplied one begins to grasp the magnitude of the Italian task.

The whole organisation which kept the plains and mountain saddles in touch with the heights was admirable in the extreme. The motor transports brought their cargoes along the roads which had been built in the main body of the hills; then the cargoes were shifted to the backs of mules, and sometimes to sledges whenever that was possible.

THE PRINCE OF WALES IN ITALY.
The King of Italy and the Prince of Wales visiting the Basilica of Aquileia, on the Isonzo, May, 1916. The Italian priest, Cavaliere Don Celso Costantini, is describing the antiquities of the building. Admiral Cito is seen in the porch.

The spectacle reminded one of the northern Icelandic regions, and it struck one as curiously incongruous to see men whose lives had been spent in the balmy plains of Tuscany and Latium clad in the dress of Eskimos, travelling over vast spaces of snow and glittering ice. From where the mule paths end, on the saddles of the mountain ranges, two further systems of communication led to the heights. Overhead railroads served to bring the ammunition, firewood, and boxes of preserved food to the men. At the last mule station the kitchens were situated. There the food was cooked, and it was brought to the outposts by trains of men who had become adepts at mountaineering. This was a most interesting and curious sight, these long rows of men laden with cans of meat and soup, vegetables and wine, bound to one another by a long rope and led up the hill-side by an expert Alpine guide. Generally the journey took about six hours, but the provisions arrived with **Marvels of Italian** remarkable punctuality. Remember that **organisation** these trains set out twice daily over a front of four hundred miles, and then you will have an idea of the vast organisation which was at the back of it all.

It has often been said that organisation is not a strong point with Italians. Nothing could be further from the truth. For the Italian is heir to the old Roman genius, and he has not squandered his heritage. He has a far stronger sense of organisation than the German; but his organisation is not mechanical. German organisation creates a machine which is blindly responsive to the man at the wheel, whereas Italian organisation is the resultant of that strong sense of personal responsibility which each individual possesses, coupled with that sense of solidarity

484

ROMAN CITIZENS ACCLAIM THE PROCLAMATION OF WAR.

Popular feeling in Italy was solid in favour of secession from the Triple Alliance and intervention in the Great War against Austria. When the decision of the Government was announced on May 23rd, 1915, an enormous crowd assembled before the Quirinal and gave enthusiastic demonstration of its patriotic enthusiasm.

which is inherited from the Roman genius. That is why you will find among Italian soldiers and engineers far more individual initiative and resourcefulness than among Germans. The directive power does not come from the Staff or the inferior commands; it is the result of the conscious co-operation of each unit in the mass. The German has not a genius for organisation, but he has a weakness for being organised, whereas the reverse is true of the Italian.

In grouping the different incidents of the Italian campaign and judging of their value in relation to the general aim, one must always make a clear distinction between the work of the Alpini on the high mountains and that of the main body of the army operating along the Isonzo line. The work of the former was defensive, that of the latter offensive. Therefore, once the passes amid the high mountains were secured, the main interest of the struggle centred round one or two points on the Isonzo line. In the present chapter it is not necessary to treat in detail of these operations, because the subject has been fully dealt with in Chapter XCI. of THE GREAT WAR. But I may be permitted to add some few details which came under my own personal observation.

It is generally taken for granted that the main object of General Cadorna's advance on the Isonzo was the capture of Trieste, but that is not entirely correct. The capture of Trieste formed only a part of the main object, for the Isonzo struggle was essentially a military one. Here Austria had drawn up her line of defence, and here the Italians decided to break through. It is true that the fall of the Carso would have opened the way to Trieste, but the Italians would never have been tempted to follow up their success by undertaking a march towards the great Adriatic seaport while the Austrian armies remained intact on the Middle and Upper Isonzo. Therefore, the essential purpose of General Cadorna's plan was to destroy the Austrian defence and open a way into the interior of Austrian territory.

To carry out that purpose Cadorna ordered a quick advance on both wings of the Isonzo army, at Monte Nero in the north and on the Carso in the south, **Advance on Monte Nero and Carso** while the centre would hold the ground opposite Gorizia and Tolmino, thus preventing an Austrian inrush. If an advance on the wings were successful an encirclement would have been the result, and the Austrians would have been compelled to retire from Tolmino and Gorizia. Here again everything depended upon time. It was only a question of hours—not of days. A series of unfortunate circumstances conspired to oppose the Italian plan and succeeded in converting what might have been a swift and smashing victory into a long and exhausting siege war.

On the eve of the outbreak of war the Italian cavalry was

A DREAM OF MEDIÆVAL BEAUTY.

Our Italian friends were not long in learning the lesson of Louvain and Rheims, and soon after war broke out the authorities removed to a place of safety all the stained glass for which Milan Cathedral is specially noted. The superb edifice, whose delicate spires look like shining crystal against the sky, is seen to advantage in this photograph.

stationed at Palmanova, one of the frontier towns nearest the Isonzo line. Its orders were that at the moment war was declared it should gallop to the river and prevent the Austrians from mining the bridges. But some hitch occurred, the exact details of which were not made public. The result was that when the army arrived at the Isonzo the bridges had already been destroyed. Furthermore, the Austrians had cut the banks of the canal which runs to Monfalcone and turned its waters into the Isonzo bed. This manœuvre, together with the heavy rains and the melting of the snows, overflooded the river and reduced the surrounding plain to a vast swamp. The infantry advanced knee-deep in water and mud under a terrific fire from the Carso, those that fell wounded being drowned in the shallow water. Circumstances of the same nature hindered operations around Monte Nero, for though the mountain was taken in the first onslaught, the terrific flood destroyed the bridge and rendered the sending of reinforcements extremely difficult. Thus two weeks were lost to the Italians, and the Austrians gained sufficient time to strengthen their defences along the Carso and Julian hills.

FOOD FOR THE FIGHTING MEN.
Military canteen under the direction of Italian ladies, who served refreshments to soldiers passing to and from the front via the Central Station at Milan.

Then commenced what turned out to be one of the most gruelling experiences in the whole European War. When the conflict comes to be seen in its proper perspective, the epic of the Isonzo will stand out as one of the most marvellous in military history. At Gradisca the great crossing took place. Nine times the bridge was built and nine times it was destroyed, but the Italian engineers stuck to their work. When the first battalion had crossed the river the bridge was once again destroyed, but though it had only one battery at its disposal, the little company blasted itself into the stony side of the Carso and clung there by sheer dint of grit and daring. The story is so rich in deeds of surpassing heroism that it would need a volume to itself, and I shall not attempt to dwell upon it here. Let me simply say that all the published estimates which I have seen of the numbers who fell and the sacrifices that had to be made do not exaggerate the facts as they were known to the authorities.

When I visited the Carso I had an opportunity of seeing close at hand the conditions under which the battle had been waged. As one stands on the bridge at Gradisca and looks at the frowning Carso—a great natural fortress throwing the shadow of its mighty **The epic of the** bulk across the waters of the wide Isonzo **Isonzo** —and remembers that during those first weeks in June every crevice in the side of the mountain was a veritable inferno, shooting forth tongues of living flame, it immediately becomes clear how impossible it would be to overestimate the courage of the men who built the bridge at Gradisca and charged the mountain side in the teeth of the enemy's fire.

Standing on the bridge and looking at the Carso, I could see the thin line of trenches stretched along the side of the hill. To one familiar with the almost mathematical symmetry of the battle-front in France and

Flanders, this Carso line presented a curious appearance. It was full of salients, wriggling in a sort of serpentine fashion for a distance of about eighteen miles. One could hardly call it a battle-front, because it was made up of many fronts. From Gorizia to Monfalcone several generals were in control, and though a strong sense of organisation was in evidence, each general seemed to act more or less independently. It seemed to be a question of jockeying for position. During the night the Italians would move forward their barricades of stones and sandbags, striving to gain the summit of a hillock which would give them control of the Austrian

DEVOTION TO THE WOUNDED.
Ladies well known in Milanese society who worked as nurses with the Red Cross. This illustration was secured at the station of Porta Vittoria on the arrival of an ambulance train.

trenches in the immediate neighbourhood. Then the Austrian would be forced to retire or allow himself to be taken prisoner. This detailed work, which went on incessantly throughout the winter months, accounts for the number of small victories which were daily recorded in the official bulletins. At the beginning of May, 1916, the Italians had gained many of the commanding heights, especially at San Martino and Sei Busi. On San Michele, which may be looked upon as the southern pillar of the gate which opens into the Vipacco Valley at Gorizia, the Austrians had been driven to the last ridge of the hill. In other words, after twelve months of incessant effort the Italians held that position on the Carso which they might have gained during the first two weeks of the war, were it not that sheer ill-luck had hindered their plans.

Moving northwards along the Isonzo line, we came to Lucinico and San Floriano, directly opposite Gorizia. Nestling cosily amid its cincture of hills, Gorizia did not seem to retain a very bitter recollection of the terrible duel which was fought here during October and November, 1915. From where we stood we could make out the names on the shopkeepers' signs. The Italian battery beside us was thundering away at the hills across the river. No soldiers were in sight and no advance was being prepared, but the officer said that the artillery attack was being kept up so that the Austrians might not send their heavy pieces to Verdun. It was a beautiful evening, with the richness and calm of early summer all around. Gorizia looked peaceful and idyllic, as if it had never known a day's unrest. An Austrian band was playing in the piazza, right under the muzzles of the Italian guns. "Why do you not throw a shell at them?" I said to the officer. "Ah, no," he replied. "That is not war." I was struck by the contrast between Gorizia and Monfalcone. The Italians might have destroyed the former as the Austrians destroyed the latter, but they had bombarded only a few isolated sections of the town, which were used for the mounting of guns and billeting of soldiers. The churches stood proudly intact—a far different story from that which the churches of Gradisca and Monfalcone have to tell.

Something of this humane spirit seemed to have crossed the river and found a home even in the Austrian breast. Italian soldiers walked along their trenches without paying much attention to the necessity of cover. Of course, a certain amount of sniping went on, but it was nothing like what one witnessed in France and Flanders. The Italians

A LEADER OF MODERN ITALY.
Gabriele D'Annunzio, the Italian poet, delivering one of his many patriotic orations from the pedestal of the Memorial to Garibaldi and the Thousand at Genoa.

said that nothing was to be gained by the shooting of individual soldiers, and the Austrians returned the compliment. There was no attempt at camaraderie, nor yet was there any trace of that senseless slaughter which the Germans practised on the western front.

In summing up the general position along the Isonzo, one can say that, though no spectacular victories had been won, steady and plodding progress had been made. At the beginning of May, 1916, the Italians were well established on the Carso, and in front of Gorizia they had moved forward almost to the bridge-head which formed the immediate defence of the town. On Monte Sabotino,

which is one of the sentinel mountains guarding the gate of the Vipacco Valley, they had secured positions which gave them a firm hold on the hill, though the Austrians still held the majority of the vantage points. At Monte Nero the Italian troops had gained many important positions, while in the neighbourhood of the Predil Pass they had secured a footing which seriously threatened the Austrian defensive. From the point of view of results gained, the Italian Army had one main achievement to which it could proudly point. It had closed the gates of Italy against the enemy and brought within the Italian fold about 1,500 square miles of the *terra irredenta*, with upwards of a hundred important communes. Furthermore, it had established its fame both at home and abroad as one of the bravest and most scientific fighting forces in Europe. But it had not broken the Austrian defensive.

Italy's main achievement

In other theatres of the war Italy did not seem to take as vigorous a part as was generally expected of her. In the foreign Press it was often stated that she had a large Army at her disposal, and could well afford to send a strong expeditionary force to the help of the Allies in the eastern war theatre. Great expectations were raised when she declared war against Turkey on August 20th, 1915, but little came of it, except the despatch of some forces to Tripoli to keep the Turks quiet in that section. When the Balkan disaster came, it was asked why no Italian troops were being sent to Salonika, and the answer did not help the outside public to understand the Italian position any more clearly.

Now that the whole question has become a matter of history, it is possible to speak openly and throw a little light on that dark chapter. During the month of July, 1915, it became abundantly clear to the minds of Italian statesmen that the defection of Bulgaria was already an accomplished fact.

BERSAGLIERI AT PHYSICAL EXERCISE.
Detachment of Bersaglieri practising their characteristic "trot" round the beautiful Garibaldi Memorial in the Italian capital. The Bersaglieri are among the most spirited and intrepid infantry in the world.

CANNONS THUNDER ACROSS ETERNAL VALLEYS.
Battery of Italian 6 in. guns in action among the mountains. These powerful weapons, the length of whose barrels is remarkable, were all but hidden in embrasures of shrubbery and earthwork. This graphic camera- glimpse affords some help to a realisation of the stupendous difficulties with which the Italian artillerymen had to contend in placing their guns in position amidst the mountain fastnesses of the Trentino.

This they made known to their friends in the Alliance. The Italian counsel was understood to be that a strong force should be immediately thrown into the Balkans, so that Greece might be won over to the side of the Entente and the hand of Serbia strengthened. Once Russia had been crippled in the Carpathians, the small Balkan nations were bound to be attracted to the orbit of the strongest Power in the neighbourhood. In July, 1915, it was already too late to depend any further on the power of diplomacy. Force was the only consideration which could then have weight. Had the Italian advice been followed, Italy would most probably have co-operated. Had an expeditionary force been sent to the Balkans early in August, it might have been strengthened by the addition of one or two Italian army corps, but not more.

Italy and the Balkans

For it must be always borne in mind that at no period during the whole course of the year's conflict were the actual fighting forces under General Cadorna's command so large as was supposed by outsiders. Naturally, there was no attempt to correct that impression, because everybody knew that Italy had large numbers of men at her disposal, and it would not have been wise to explain abroad how far the country had got on with the work of producing equipment and munitions. As a matter of fact, just as in the case of Britain, the Government was not at first fully alive to the needs of the moment. General Cadorna was getting the most out of the forces and equipment at his disposal, but he was not sufficiently supplied either with men or munitions to warrant the sending of a large expeditionary force to outside theatres of the war.

Moreover, Italy had to be very chary of the steps which she would take. Co-operation with the Allies in the Balkans must necessarily have brought her into open hostility with Germany. For that emergency she might have made preparations during July and August had there been a more frequent and open exchange of views between herself and the Allies. But as matters then stood within the Alliance, her position was not yet clearly defined.

When the Balkan crash came, it was found that the Italian statesmen and military authorities had decided on the only course which lay open to them. They struck hard and fast at Austria along the Isonzo front. There all their forces were gathered. Throughout the greater part of October and the whole of November, 1915, the Battle of Gorizia raged, a battle which surpassed in violence anything that had been witnessed in the European conflict up to the great onslaught at Verdun. It must not be supposed that General Cadorna believed he could break through the Austrian defence in the Vipacco Valley. The great battle was undertaken, not in the hope of any local success, but rather that it might be a source of help to the sorely-pressed Allies in the Balkan theatre. From that point of view it was eminently successful.

When it became clear that Serbia was lost for the time being, and that Austro-German forces were advancing into Albania, Italy took vigorous action in the Adriatic. She had already occupied Valona, and she now began to extend and strengthen her defences there. Valona is the Gibraltar of the Adriatic. Possessing a magnificent harbour, which might easily be rendered impregnable, it stands on a commanding position about forty miles from the Italian shore. The great Italian naval station at Taranto being outside the Adriatic, Italian ships would have to pass Valona in order to enter Adriatic waters. Therefore the possession of it is absolutely necessary to Italy for the defence of her eastern seaboard. This truth becomes abundantly clear when it is remembered that the eastern coast of Italy affords no facilities for naval defence, whereas on the Austrian side of the Adriatic there is a series of the best landlocked harbours in the world.

Durazzo occupied and evacuated

About sixty miles north of Valona Durazzo lies. It is in Albanian territory and is excellently sheltered. In order to save the Serbian Army and transfer it to Corfu, the Italians occupied Durazzo. There they were close to Cattaro, the southern naval base on the Austrian shore. The covering of the Serbian retreat was a matter of the utmost difficulty, yet they succeeded in bringing 150,000 Serbian soldiers, with horses and artillery equipment, together with 20,000 Austrian prisoners, safely to Corfu. On February 25th, 1916, the Italians decided to evacuate Durazzo. It was a rather dramatic proceeding. On the morning of the 24th it was discovered that the Austrians had succeeded in bringing their heavy artillery into position on the Albanian mountains overlooking the town and harbour. Suddenly great shells began to fall in the town and along the quays. There was no chance of opening an answering fire, so the Italians hastily took to their ships, having destroyed whatever war materials they could not bring away. The evacuation occupied three days, and though it had to be carried out during a violent storm and under a constant plunging fire from the mountains, not more than three hundred casualties occurred. The open and generous manner in which the Serbian Government acknowledged the great part which Italy had played in saving the Serbian Army, the remaining hope of the nation, did much to silence the sinister rumours which enemy propagandists had set on foot under the pretence of explaining why Italian aid had not been sent to the Balkans.

Serbian Army's debt to Italy   So interesting are they, and so vital to an accurate understanding of the course of the war, that we shall do well to examine with some care the intricacies of the political and economic position in Italy during the first year of conflict. At the outset it must be borne in mind that Italy's decision to enter the field on behalf of the cause for which the Triple Entente had unsheathed the sword was not the work of the Government or the Cabinet. It was the work of the people. Wrought to a white heat of indignation and horror at the spectacle of the atrocities committed by the Central Empires, the Italian people cried out for armed intervention on the side of right and justice. The country which had been the apostle of civilisation, religion, art, and science in Western Europe could not stand by with folded arms while Teuton barbarism triumphed over Latin culture. It has often been said that had the decision been left in the hands of the Government, Italy would never have ranged herself on the side of the Entente. **Voice of the Italian people** But the statement is, to say the least of it, gratuitous. The main point to remember is that the very intensity of the popular movement may have brought about a declaration of war sooner than it otherwise would have happened.

That fact explains both the strength and weakness of the whole Italian position. Being a thoroughly democratic movement, the war had a wonderful driving force at the back of it, especially during the early months of the campaign. The call of *Italia Irredenta* found an enthusiastic answer at every fireside throughout the country. That call was all the more effective because it was simply the torch which set light to the fire of wrath that had already been prepared. Every atrocity which Germany had committed, her brutal disregard of all humane laws and pleadings, her submarine murders, her destruction of ancient monuments of art and treasures of learning, brought horror and indignation to the Italian heart. The old Latin soul became incarnate once more, and cried out for vengeance. So that although *Italia Irredenta* became the war-cry, it was simply a formula which drew all its life-giving power from a source that was far deeper and wider. The war

MONSTER MACHINE OF DESTRUCTION: ITALIAN 305 MM. (12 IN.) GUN IN ACTION.

The terrific power of Italian ordnance was one of the surprises of the war. This, the largest weapon used on the Alpine front, weighed upwards of twenty tons, and fired a 12 in. shell weighing something between seven and eight hundredweights a distance of twenty miles. These guns are comparable with the modern naval weapons used in the Italian Fleet and the coast defences of the peninsula kingdom.

THE SPIRIT OF ITALY IN FACE OF HER ETERNAL FOE.

At the end of a year of war Italy was more than ever defiant of Austria, her immemorial enemy. Her high courage and proud independence of soul are beautifully symbolised in this bold and dramatic picture by the Italian artist Signor Buffa.

reminded one of the outpourings of religious ecstatics. "This is the noblest and most precious moment of my life," wrote a peasant soldier to his parents. "My manhood is glorified. I give it to my country, and I make the sacrifice of it in an ecstasy of joy. But before I part with it I must thank you, my parents, who gave it to me. I stretch out my arms to you, and thank you from my heart for all the sacrifices you have made for my sake. My country calls me. *Mamma, mia adorata*, be filled with happiness. And you, *padre mio*, be proud in the thought that I shall bring honour to your name. I beseech you, my adored parents, to be calm and resigned." ("Corriere della Sera," June 12th, 1915.)

Another soldier, Renato Mazzucehelli, wrote to his family at Turin : "I am going on to the battlefield, where the life of nations is moulded and tempered by fire and sword, where there is no such thing as death—because only cowards and traitors die. He who falls on the battlefield acquires an immortal glory. His friends and the circle of his acquaintances will speak of him to their children and say : 'Behold the name of a hero who fell in the fight for his country.' To you, my country, *Italia bella*, to you, my mother, beloved and holy, I give the heart of my hearts, all my prayers, and my eternal thoughts." ("Tribuna," July 2nd, 1915.)

These letters are typical specimens of the hundreds which were published in the Press. And they express not only the spirit of the soldiers, but also the spirit of the people at home. I was in Italy at that time, and I remember what a thrilling experience it was to live in the midst of such an all-consuming fire. In the railway trains everyone talked of the war, not in fear or with a sense of awe, but as if it were an act of sacrificial worship for which the soul of the nation thirsted. The rich villa owners rushed in crowds to the military authorities and offered their homes as hostels for the convalescent soldiers. Along the shores of Lakes Como and Maggiore there was scarcely a villa that did not unfurl the Red

became a sacred crusade for the rescue of the holy things and holy places of Latin civilisation from the hands of the barbarians.

There is no other explanation of that wonderful spirit which transfigured the nation and its soldiers. Each one felt as if revenge for all were fixed in him alone. The soldiers showed an almost fanatical disregard of danger and death. In the letters they sent to their parents, —sometimes crude epistles badly and ungrammatically written—there was a loftiness of thought and diction which

Cross banner. As the trains filled with wounded soldiers made their way through the Venetian plain, crowds met them at the stations, eager to help in relieving the pain of the sufferers. At Maestre on one occasion I saw the people leave the first and second class carriages of the mail train for Bologna and ask that some of the wounded in a Red Cross train which stood by should be given places in the express, so that they might reach their destination more quickly. It was a wonderful spirit, transfusing every fibre of the nation's being from one end of the country to the other.

So far, the democratic origin of the war was an immense source of strength. But it was also a source of weakness. From the military point of view—at least, as far as concerned the Italian campaign exclusively—it might have been better had the war started a month later, because the Alpine rivers are generally in flood up to the middle of June. But from the political point of view the decision came if anything too soon. Sufficient time had not been allowed for a full exchange of views between Italy and her intended Allies. Not until the Triple Alliance had been denounced did proper opportunity present itself for negotiating with the allied diplomatists.

The result was that Italy entered the conflict without having come to an absolutely unequivocal understanding with her new friends. In the allied countries her aims and claims were still vaguely understood. People talked picturesquely about *Italia Irredenta*, without any precise knowledge of what the phrase meant. In these circumstances clever pro-German agitators, seizing the opportunity, strove to make it appear in the countries of the

considerations were dealt with exclusively, and all others carefully left out of count. But, as a matter of fact, the necessity of an Italian footing on the eastern shore of the Adriatic is a doctrine as old as the Roman Republic. It is founded not merely on the rights of a nation to gather within her fold the scattered children of her race, but primarily and essentially it is founded on strategic necessity. For the Italian coast can be defended only on the eastern shore of the Adriatic.

Italy grievously misrepresented

Italians could not understand why so just a claim was misunderstood and misconstrued among their friends. And they did not seriously set about explaining it. The result was that a feeling of uneasiness arose both on the one side and on the other. The failure to come to Serbia's aid was exploited as proof of sinister ambitions on Italy's part. Furthermore, and worse than all else, Italy had not declared war against Germany. Why? Many answers were given, the best of which were only half truths, while the worst were malicious misconstructions. It was surprising how many sensible people believed some of the more curious explanations. For instance, it was widely circulated and believed that Italy had not declared open hostilities against Germany because she hoped to have a voice on both sides during the discussion of the peace terms; and it was added that Germany, fearing ultimate defeat, agreed to the arrangement in the hope of having a friend in the enemy's camp!

The explanation of Italy's hesitation to make open war against Germany, and of Germany's reluctance to make war against Italy, must be attributed to causes that have been in operation for well-nigh a quarter of a century. The story of how Italy was peacefully penetrated in every fibre of her political, industrial

Alliance that Italy was out for herself. She was described as Imperialistic, anxious for the expansion of her territory and her commerce, to the detriment of her neighbours, especially the Balkan nations. Her claims on the eastern shore of the Adriatic, which were neither understood nor discussed in the Entente, were painted as preposterous. Taking advantage of the artificial immigration of Slavonians and Croatians into Dalmatia and Istria —which had been engineered by Austria in order that her blind tools might get control of the old Italian municipalities—pamphlet after pamphlet was written to prove the almost negligible character of the Italian minority. Census figures, specially manufactured by Austria, were quoted as gospel. The ethnic

INTERCHANGE OF VISITS BETWEEN LEADING MEN OF THE ALLIED POWERS. M. Briand, French Premier (accompanied by Signor Salandra, Italian Premier, and Baron Sonnino, Italian Minister for Foreign Affairs), leaving the Villa Borghese after the banquet given in his honour by the Governor of Rome. Above: General Cadorna, Italian Commander-in-Chief, starting for the British Headquarters in France.

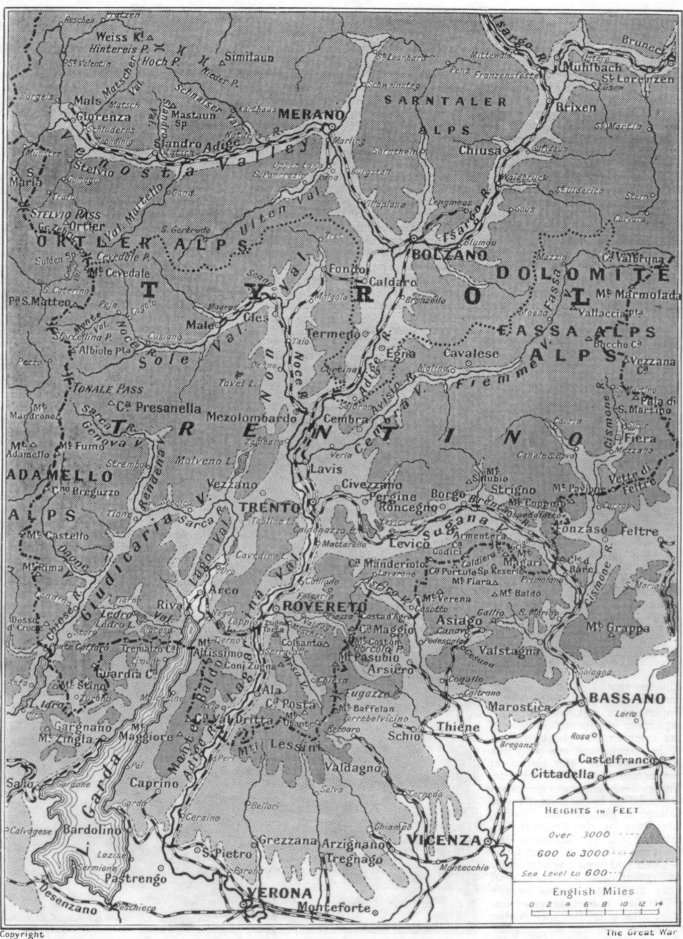

The Great War

AREA OF THE OPERATIONS IN THE TRENTINO, THE HIGH MOUNTAIN SECTOR OF THE ITALIAN BATTLE-FRONT.

Without waiting for complete mobilisation, General Cadorna rushed the Alpini to the strategic positions which Austria had prepared in the Trentino, and at the end of July, 1915, Italy had gained control of every opening into her territory.

DRAMATIC PICTURE OF AN ITALIAN MUNITION WORKS IN FULL BLAST.

A fascinating, Dantesque vision of European war-time industrialism. Huge projectiles were being wrought here by men of herculean strength and iron nerve, wearing asbestos clothes and face masks. When Mr. Asquith paid his visit to Italy in the spring of 1916 Signor Salandra promised the Allies the fullest co-ordinated co-operation of his country in the field of industry as well as in that of war.

and commercial being reads like a tale of mystery and imagination. The aims of the German crusade were colossal, its projects daring, and absolutely blind to any moral considerations in the carrying out of its operations. The plodding patience and scientific swindling which succeeded in overcoming or circumventing every obstacle that lay in its path, the undermining of every main and tributary channel connected with the politico-economic life of the nation, the manner in which, like some poisonous microbe, it worked its way even into the Government itself, possessing an initial capital of only £800,000, but devoid of every scruple and conscious of the power of a great Empire at its back—all this makes up a tale which is one of the most astounding in modern history.

German commercial intrigue

Twenty years ago the Banca Commerciale was founded in Milan. Though it had a high-sounding Italian name it was simply the headquarters of a great German campaign for the capture of every industrial and commercial position in Italy. It started by lending money to trading companies on attractive terms, claiming in return for its patronage a representation on the directorates of the companies it had helped. For a little while it played gently with those who had swallowed the bait. Then it gathered them in wholesale. They were induced to lodge their funds in the bank and transact their business through it. Thus the bank received from the companies far more money than it had originally given. Take the Navigazione Generale Italiana—which is the largest shipping concern in Italy—as an instance. The company borrowed £38,000 from the bank and then lodged with it a block of its shares worth £1,800,000. Thus the bank gained control of a most important section of Italian shipping trade. Having actually secured £1,600,000 of the reserve fund of the Navigazione Generale, and arranged that every penny of its intake should be deposited as part of a current account, the bank was enabled to control two other shipping concerns—La Veloce and L'Italia—which were practically subsidiary companies of the Navigazione Generale.

Its action in securing control of the Loyd Italiano was characterised by still more dastardly methods. Senator Piaggio, the proprietor of the Loyd Italiano, was approached. He was induced to exchange a certain bulk of his shares for a corresponding bulk of those of the Navigazione Generale, with the understanding and explicit promise that he would be made president of the amalgamated companies. Once the bank had the transaction secured, it politely told Senator Piaggio that he might whistle for the promised presidency. Later on it bought out his full interest and became sole ruler of the concern. In like manner other shipping companies were roped in until at the outbreak of the war, the German bank largely controlled the destinies of the Italian mercantile marine.

Another important branch of native industry which readily fell into the clutches of the German bank were the electro-mechanical institutions of Northern Italy. At the opening of the year 1916 there were in Italy one hundred and fifty-one companies which manufactured every class of machinery connected with the electro-mechanical industry and controlled electric railroads and electric-lighting systems. Of these thirty-two were in German hands. Not a large proportion, one might say, but the total capital represented by the one hundred and fifty-one companies amounted to £24,000,000, of which £13,080,000 was in German hands. From this it will be seen that the thirty-two German-controlled companies, possessing the overwhelming majority of the capital invested, were well on the way towards swamping all the smaller ones. I might go on *ad infinitum*, dealing with each branch of Italian industry or commerce, and showing how Germany had spread her tentacles everywhere. The effect which the whole system had in controlling the general trade of Italy is clearly shown by comparing statistics of the trade returns between Italy and France on the one hand, and Italy and Germany on the other, for an average year preceding 1890 with those for an average year following the German crusade. Before 1890 Italian exportations

German bank's machinations

into France were valued at £16,200,000 annually, and her importations from France at £13,800,000. After the German crusade was started the importation from France fell to £4,600,000 and the exportation to £6,800,000. Naturally, Germany reaped the benefit.

It must be remembered that the whole process of grabbing Italian commerce and industry, and deflecting Italian trade from France and Britain to Germany, was carried out with very small expenditure on Germany's part. She never invested large sums of money in Italy, but she used her technical skill and daring unscrupulously in securing control of Italian wealth. It is an amazing fact, but none the less eloquent, that though the Banca Commerciale was the centre of all this German financial control, the German capital sunk in the concern amounted to only five per cent. of the whole stock.

All these facts are of value here in so far as they throw light upon the condition of affairs in Italy during her first year of conflict. A declaration of war against Germany at the same time as she declared it against Austria would have created an upheaval and thrown the economic life of the country into chaos. **Germany's technical skill and daring** Large sums of money had already been taken away to Germany, so that the German bank could not meet the demands of its Italian depositors. So enormous were the interests involved that the only hope of carrying on the commercial activity of the country was some arrangement whereby financial relations with Germany might still remain unbroken. On the other hand, Germany was also anxious to arrive at some such agreement, for the obvious reason that she did not wish to abandon for ever her Italian interests.

Accordingly, Baron Sonnino and Prince von Bülow signed a compact whereby each nation agreed to safeguard the rights of private property held by the citizens of the other. As a confirmation of the deed, a meeting was held in Switzerland between representatives of both nations, to devise ways and means of putting its contents into operation. And a few weeks afterwards the Prussian Minister of Commerce officially announced that German merchants might freely export and import goods to and from Italy.

Seeing no other way out of the pressing difficulty, Baron Sonnino, who has a genuine talent for careful economic management, bowed to the **Italian patriotism at white heat** iron necessity of the circumstances. But herein lay the danger of cleavage between Italy and her partners in the new Alliance. Financial intercourse with Germany, no matter how carefully supervised on the part of one member of the Alliance, was bound to have a disintegrating effect. It kept German agents still in touch with the course of events in Italy and gave them a certain amount of influence over the public mind of the country.

During the first months of the campaign the metal of Italian patriotism, glowing at white heat, cast off every atom of German influence, but the glow of the metal died down somewhat with the course of time. The war had reached a point where it seemed about to become stalemate, and failed to keep alive the same enthusiasm which it had kindled during the first victorious onslaught. Besides, it was being waged in the enemy's territory, a circumstance which naturally led the people at home to take things easier.

INTERIOR OF A COLOSSAL ITALIAN MUNITION FACTORY.

Nearly a year elapsed between the outbreak of the European War and the Italian intervention on behalf of the Allies. Thus Italy was able to study modern conditions of warfare and amass a store of high-explosive shells. Judging by this illustration, which shows the interior of one of our Mediterranean ally's large munition factories, these institutions became no less active than those of a kindred character in the countries of her Allies.

"FAITHFUL COMMONS" OF KING VICTOR: A SITTING OF THE CHAMBER OF DEPUTIES.
There are two Chambers in the Italian Parliament, the Senate and the Chamber of Deputies. Members of the Chamber of Deputies are salaried, receiving £160 a year in direct payment and £80 in the form of a current account with the railways and Post Office for defraying travelling and postal expenses up to that amount.

All this was no more than natural, for the first fervour could not have been expected to last. At heart the nation remained sound and as ardent as ever in its devotion to the cause for which it had unsheathed the sword. But certain new factors were introduced which had a disturbing influence on the people. Though Italy had signed the London pact in November, whereby she agreed not to make a separate peace, her Allies did not seem to treat her with a very generous share of consideration. In view of the newly-cemented friendship, it seemed strange to the ordinary Italian that he was called upon to pay six or eight pounds a ton for English coal, whereas he might have got six or eight times that amount from Germany for the same sum. Inquiries were made, and ship-owners were partially blamed and partially exonerated. But eight pounds per ton was an exorbitant price to pay for coal. Not un-naturally the Italian began to wonder whether he was being bled by his friends. He needed coal for the forging of muni-tions which were to be used in fighting on the side of his Allies, for his railroads and steam-ships which were being mainly used for military

BETWEEN TWO FLAGS.
The Austro-Italian frontier in the Isonzo zone of operations. Pontebba (on the right) was an Italian, Pontafel (on the left) an Austrian village, and only a little stream separated the two flags at the beginning of the war.

purposes, for the camp and hospital; yet he had to buy it from his friends at an exorbitant price. Furthermore, he had to pay thirty-two francs for the English pound sterling, whereas a Frenchman could buy it for twenty-eight francs. That showed how Italian credit in England lacked the backing which might have been expected in view of the newly-formed Alliance.

These anomalies had their explanation and justification, but here we are simply concerned with the historical fact of their influence on the Italian mind. And that fact is of the highest interest, because in matters of national moment the state of the public mind in Italy was of more im-portance than the plans and projects of states-men.

Those of us who had an opportunity of coming into close contact with Italian life during the early months of 1916, not only throughout the country but also amid the soldiers' camps in the war zone, could not fail to notice a certain change that had come over the public mind. It was not a profound change, and that is per-haps the reason why it was all the more notice-able. It did not make a very prominent

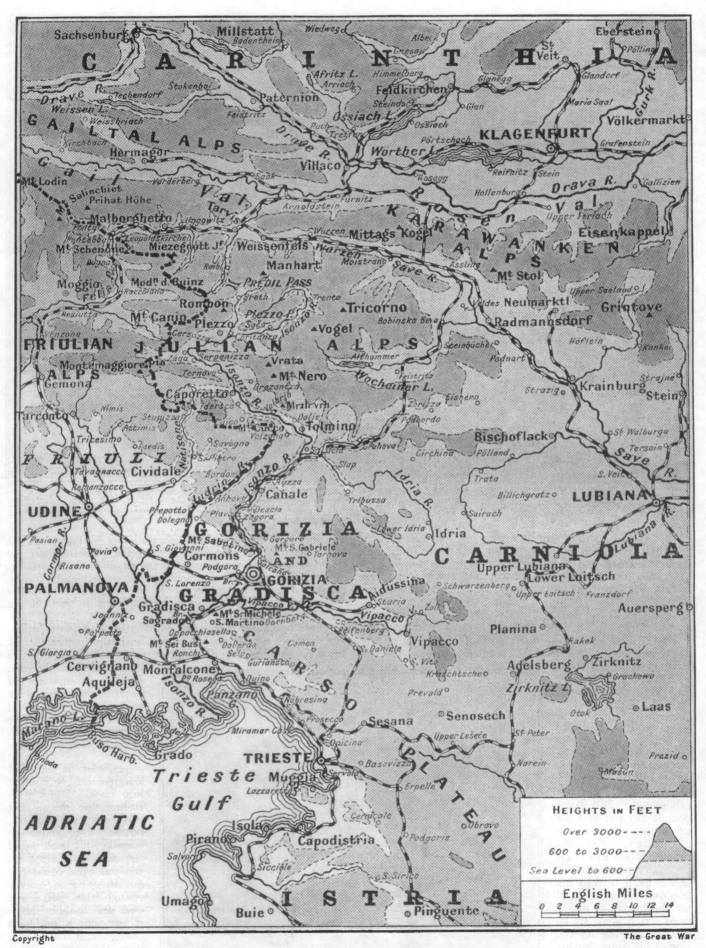

MAP SHOWING THE AREA OF GENERAL CADORNA'S ADVANCE ON THE ISONZO.

It was on the Isonzo front that Austria drew up her main line of defence, and the initial objective of the Italians was to destroy that defence and so open a way into the interior of Austrian territory.

appearance in the Press, but it filled one with an uncomfortable fear that what the people were saying to-day official circles and the Press might be saying to-morrow. It was hard to discover its causes or acquire a definite idea of its character and extent; but it was there all the same, and all the more dangerous because it was alive and throbbing and unable to express itself in definite form.

The Anglo-Italian union of hearts The people of Italy, with every desire to think well of us, were finding it difficult to understand our relations with them, for the Anglo-Italian union of hearts was far older and deeper than the Alliance with Germany. Though Italy had been bound up with Germany in matters political and financial, the union was merely an outer tie. It did not deeply affect the spirit of the nation, which breathed more freely once the Triple Alliance had been denounced. There could be no chance, therefore, of effectively preventing the country from forming a firm Alliance with Britain, founded not merely on political

walls of her own home hordes of Teutons who had an indisputable right to remain where they were. Furthermore, many of them had adopted Italian wives, so that the family infiltration had become almost as formidable and ubiquitous as the commercial and political penetration. Here you had what Italians picturesquely called the "Trojan Horse"—the cloven hoof of the German influence in Italy. It was responsible for the attitude of criticism assumed by an important section of the Press. To poison many of the springs from which the Press drew its material was not a task of insurmountable difficulty, for there was a very large number of journalists in Italy who received rather poor returns from their profession. It was impossible to tamper with the more representative journals, but a host of smaller papers and periodicals published news items and literary articles which they had received from sources that were not entirely above suspicion. Foreign correspondents innocently took stock of rumours that had been manufactured specially for their

MODERN RED CROSS KNIGHTS TAKING THE OATH OF FEALTY.
Popular feeling in Italy ran high in favour of the war. Large numbers of men not otherwise required for combatant service were enrolled as Red Cross soldiers, and joined the Army to swell the ranks of the Army Medical Corps.

and commercial interests, but on fundamental ideals and principles that are the common heritage of both races.

But it was possible to delay the formation of that Alliance. In Italy there existed an important pro-German element which could not be eliminated from the country's public life. In 1913 Germany had passed a law which permitted her citizens who were resident abroad to adopt the citizenship of the country wherein they dwelt, while still retaining the rights and privileges of German subjects. To give effect to that extraordinary measure—which, by the way, throws a rather telling light on the attitude of the German official mind towards the coming war—the consuls in France, Italy, and Russia were ordered to facilitate by every means the naturalisation of German subjects resident in the respective countries. In Italy the behest was carried out more thoroughly and more readily than elsewhere, thanks to the control in political affairs already secured by the agents of the German bank. The result of the whole manœuvre was that, on the rupture of diplomatic relations with Germany, Italy found within the

benefit. The diplomatists of the cafés and salons expounded theories to one another which had a rather sinister bearing on the mutual good faith of the allied Powers.

As a case in point, let me mention the following instance A few mornings after Mr. Asquith's visit to the Vatican I was stopped by a very well-known journalist in the street in the frontier town where the Italian Headquarters was established and asked if I knew what was the meaning of Mr. Asquith's visit to the Pope. I answered that it was merely a matter of courtesy. Then my friend said: "Ah, no! It had a much **Mr. Asquith and** more important purpose. At their con- **the Pope** ference in Paris the Allies were of the opinion that they could not beat the German armies, therefore they decided to form a firm and abiding Alliance for commercial purposes. There are other than military ways of conquering a nation. A well-managed trade war on the part of the Allies would isolate Germany in an economic sense and render her powerless to threaten the liberties of Europe once again. Germany is ready to offer terms of peace which, though not all the Allies desire, are not too favourable to Teuton ambitions. If the Pope would treat with the Germans and lay their case before the Alliance, the Alliance is ready to consider it."

He repeated the whole tale in good faith, without having for a moment suspected its origin, though it was manifestly attributable to that all-pervading system which was ever ready with its constructions and explanations of every incident that afforded material for the indirect pro-German propaganda. Though exceedingly shrewd, the Italians are a very unsuspecting people. In their cafés and salons and family gatherings they are for ever discussing the affairs of the world, and eager for every item of news that comes to hand. The German agent was astute enough to discard direct methods in his plan of campaign; he worked by suggestion and innuendo, suiting his case to the temper of his audience. In other countries political gossip is of little account, but in Italy it does much towards the formation of public opinion, and consequently is an important factor in directing the policy of the nation.

During March and April, 1916, affairs took a decided turn for the better. The visit of M. Briand to Rome, that of General Cadorna to Paris and London, and that of Signor Salandra and Baron Sonnino to Paris in April, together with the many conferences held by the Allies, opened the way for Italy to become an intimate partner in the Alliance. She felt that her counsels were at last being taken and that her position was being understood. Members of the Serbian Royal Family and Government had already visited Rome and discussed affairs with the Italian authorities. The result was that an interchange of views smoothed out all the old difficulties, and did much to bring about a union of purpose among friends who were fighting for a common cause. The pity of it was that such conferences had not taken place a year earlier.

Old difficulties smoothed out

Soon the effect of the whole movement became evident in Italian life. A vigorous campaign was set on foot for the Italianisation of the Banca Commerciale, championing ways and means whereby German interests and control might be rooted out and replaced by Franco-British and American interests. Signor Corradini, of the "Idea Nazionale," carried on the campaign day after day, backed up by many writers of ability and courage, such as Professor

Maffeo Pantaleoni, Signor Ezio Grey, Signor G. Preziosi, and the Hon. G. H. di Cesaro. Their war-cry was very eloquently voiced by Professor Pantaleoni—in his preface to Signor Preziosi's book, "La Germania alla Conquista dell' Italia"—when he said "Our unredeemed land is not merely in Trentino and Istria and on the Dalmatian coast, it is also here in our own house. That territory will not figure explicitly in the treaty of peace; but, nevertheless, our war cannot be considered a success unless it be crowned by decisive victory on our internal front." On the eve of the first birthday of the Quadruple Alliance the war for the rescue of Italian finance was still being vigorously waged. Though it had not yet routed the forces entrenched in the German bank, other banks in Italy had profited by the impetus given to the financial orientation of Italy towards the Powers of the Alliance. In some cases British finance had come to the rescue and helped the banks to cast off their Teuton shackles.

" La vittoria e secura ! "

The visit of Mr. Asquith to Italy was hailed as though it were a triumphal procession. To the Italian mind it was the symbol of the Alliance for which the Italian soul had yearned so long. The old friendship burst out in new fire and faith and hope.

I was staying at Italian Headquarters when Mr. Asquith paid his visit there. The little frontier town was decked out as for a national festa. In the early morning crowds had gathered in the piazza to greet the British Premier. Over the entrance to the Town Hall the allied flags were unfurled, so as to form a sort of triumphal arch. The flaming red of Britain's furnaces was floating there, the buoyant Tricolour of France, the trailing blue of Russia—which reminds one of her vast unconquerable spaces—the yellow of Belgium's cornfields, with the black of her mourning and the red of her still bleeding wounds, the flashing rays of Japan's morning sun, the green of Italy's plains and the purple of her vineyards, bearing between them the cross of Savoy. The throngs who had gathered in the square looked upon the mass of colour and spoke of it as symbolic. As the procession passed, a chorus of "evvivas" rent the air. Then the people dispersed, and one heard them say to one another in accents of proud confidence, "La vittoria e secura! La vittoria e secura!"

INVOKING THE BLESSING OF THE CHURCH UPON THE NATIONAL FLAG.
Standard-bearers marching across the Piazza Venetia, Rome, on their way to the ceremony of blessing the colours.

CHAPTER CXX.

STRATEGY AND TACTICS OF THE GREAT WAR.
By Major G. W. Redway.

An Attempt to Appraise the Events Already Recorded in these Volumes is Now Possible—Some Theory Needed by which Facts can be Explained—Mechanism of Armies and Principles of War—Task of the Government when a Nation Declares War—Functions of the War Office and Admiralty—War Office Chiefs and their Relations to Commanders in the Field—Forces at a Commander's Disposal—Organisation in Various Countries—Adoption of the Offensive or Defensive The First Problem of War—The Importance of this as a Strategic Question Explained—German Strategy in 1914—Penetration, Frontal Attack, and Envelopment in Strategy Illustrated from German Plans on the Eastern Front—Strategy Defined—The Army as a Piece of Mechanism—How Orders are Passed Down—Supply and Organisation—Lines of Communication—Tactics Includes all the Ramifications of the Art of War—Organisation the Key to Tactics—Analysis of Divisions and Corps—How the Fighting Troops Fulfil their Respective Duties—Infantry, Gunners, Cavalry, Engineers, Aircraft—The Lower Organisations of the Fighting Troops—Harmonious Co-operation of all his Instruments the Task of a General—General Barrett's Order of March in Mesopotamia—Opposing Principles of Penetration and Envelopment—General Barrett's Plan of Action used to Illustrate the Scope of Higher Tactics —The Power of the Rifle—Tactical Principles Involved in the Question of Formations—The Crux of Infantry Tactics—General Monro's Solution—The Advance to the Battle of Barjisiyah—Problem of the " Mass " Formation—Infantry in Defence and the Power of Defensive Tactics—Lessons of Recent Wars, 1862-1912—Curtain Fire—Artillery Work—A Lesson from Verdun—The Training of Cavalry—The Mounted Attack or " Charge "—Collapse of Shock Action at Mons—Different Versions of Tactical Action—Tactical Operations in Alsace-Lorraine—Cause of Defeat of French Armies of the North—General Joffre's New Dispositions and the German Retreat—Why the Battle of the Marne was Inconclusive—The Mutual Attempt at Outflanking—The Battle of Flanders—End of the War of Masses—The Decisive Battle a Chimera—Military Situation in the West not Defined —Modification in the Roles of all Arms—The Conditions Obtaining along the Allied Western Front—Underground Warfare— The Military Importance of Verdun Recognised on Both Sides—The Task of the French and the Time for a Counter-Invasion.

WE have now reached a stage of the war at which it is possible with some degree of historic insight to appraise the events already recorded in these volumes and place them in perspective. But we need some clue or theory by which the facts can be explained and connected, and in seeking it we shall have to investigate the mechanism of armies and the various military doctrines and principles of war. For, of course, the character of the operations must reflect and express the views and opinions which generals have formed in peace time on the basis of history, as modified by actual contact with new forces representing the modern spirit or "the unexpected " in war.

When a nation has resolved to unsheathe the sword, it entrusts to the Government of the day the task of assembling and putting in motion the whole of the national forces with the object of compelling the enemy to submit to its will. The Government acts mainly through those departments of State known as the War Office and the Admiralty, whose functions in peace are to prepare for war, and the immediate result is the formation of a field army and a fleet and the appointment of commanders.

These commanders are furnished with instructions which disclose the policy of the Government in regard to allies and neutrals and, incidentally, prescribe a theatre of operations. For instance, the British Government in August, 1914, ordered Sir John French to take our Expeditionary Force to the aid of General Joffre while our main Fleet kept open the Channel passage by detaining the German Navy in the North Sea. Policy later on ordained subsidiary operations

"FLAG-WAGGERS" ON THE BALKAN FRONT.
Men of the Signal Corps with the British forces in the Balkans watching the activity of the enemy.

for which fresh armies and fleets were called into being and despatched to the Dardanelles and Salonika.

It is the business of the War Office and the Admiralty not only to furnish such armies and fleets, but to make good the current wastage in men, horses, and material, apprising the Government if and when the means begin to fail. The respective responsibilities of the Government of the day and the permanent executive departments arise from the circumstance that the former, having legislative power, can raise men and money, while the latter possesses the machinery by which these resources can be utilised for the purposes of the war. If the Government should hesitate to tax or borrow or secure personal service, vessels, railway transport, etc., the work of the Admiralty and War Office

ATTENDING TO THE "NERVOUS SYSTEM" OF THE ALLIES IN THE BALKANS.
French field telegraphists laying telegraph and telephone wires connecting a field station with the advanced firing-line on the Balkan front.

must come to a standstill; but since two members of the Cabinet, called the First Lord of the Admiralty and the Secretary of State for War, are in charge of these departments, their failure from any cause must ultimately recoil on the Government itself; for it is the Government that is responsible for the conduct of the war as a whole, and is seised of authority to co-ordinate the operations by sea and land in the various theatres with or without the aid of allies.

The restatement of these facts, which are more or less known, will clear the way for a consideration of the duties and responsibilities of commanders, who are directly accountable to the War Office and the Admiralty with this reservation—our army in India is controlled by the Indian Government, and the forces in Canada,

Work of the War Office Australia, New Zealand, and South Africa are at the final disposition of the self-governing Dominions. Thus, Sir John Nixon in Mesopotamia, General Botha in South-West Africa, and Colonel Logan in German Samoa reported to their respective Governments and not to the War Office in London. The work of the Navy in war is to police the seas in which hostile craft may do us damage, convey or escort troops from shore to shore, give assistance to the Army in landings and embarkations, as well as interrupt the enemy's overseas commerce. But in this chapter we are concerned only with the land operations.

The War Office, for the purpose of the field armies, consists of three sections, controlled respectively by the Chief

of the Imperial General Staff, the Adjutant-General, and the Quartermaster-General. The first submits military advice and information, both to the Government and the commanders in the field, and trains the new levies. The second superintends recruiting and the medical service : and the third supplies the troops with food, clothing, weapons, means of transport, and equipment of all kinds. **General's task in the field** Representatives of each section accompany a commander into the field as his Staff in order to facilitate the provision of all these commodities.

Let us now imagine the situation of a general who has been appointed to conduct a campaign in a certain region. Subject to instructions as to policy—such as required Sir John French to subordinate his action to that of General Joffre, in the Dardanelles placed the French forces under Sir Ian Hamilton, and in Salonika suspended the rule as to avoidance of neutral territory— he is left to work out his own salvation as a commander-in-chief with the help of his Staff and the forces placed at his disposal.

These forces will consist of (1) the field army, (2) fortress and garrison troops, (3) ancillary troops. The field army is primarily organised in divisions. A typical division consists of three brigades (12 battalions) of infantry, 13 batteries of artillery, and a cavalry squadron, besides engineer and signal companies, field-ambulances, ammunition and supply columns, and the baggage train. The

SPINNING A WIRE THREAD IN THE WEB OF WAR.
As the British forces advanced through the desert towards beleaguered Kut-el-Amara they erected telegraph-posts in the sand and spun a wire behind them to link them with the base.

personnel would for certain purposes be classified as fighting troops, administrative troops, signallers, and Staff. In every such division every day 18,073 men and 5,592 horses must be fed. The food, ammunition, and other consumable stores would be conveyed in 876 carts and waggons. Rapid transport for the Staff is provided by motor-cars, while the signallers and orderlies have in use 284 bicycles and motor-cycles. A British division would occupy about fifteen miles of road space on the march, and if assembled in Hyde Park would take five hours to pass out by one gate.

Most Continental armies adopt a " corps " organisation, consisting of two divisions and some additional troops —mainly artillery. The German corps thus includes 25 battalions, 8 squadrons, and 24 batteries—about 36,000 personnel and 9,000 horses—as fighting troops, to which we must add the columns and train. This migratory population of 41,000 men and 14,000 horses is accompanied by 2,400 vehicles. A French corps is practically of the same numerical strength, though it has 24 fewer guns.

German and French corps organisation The British corps in France is an improvised unit of indeterminate strength, our normal unit—like that of the Japanese—being the division.

The French constitute an " army " of two or three corps and one or two cavalry divisions, with groups of heavy artillery, air squadrons, and a vast assemblage of parks and convoys carrying food and ammunition, bridging material, tools, and explosives, telegraphic equipment, hospitals, etc., supplementary to the material carried by each division and corps. There is reason to believe that a German " army " includes four or five corps. Sir John French followed the fashion in 1915, and formed three " armies " after his force had been largely increased and our front was prolonged southwards to the Somme. Brigades, divisions, corps, and armies are all commanded by generals of various grades, but supreme power within the territory they occupy is vested in the senior, whose entourage is known as General or Main Headquarters.

From the moment a campaign opens the mobilised strength of units begins to dwindle from sickness, wounds, and death. The field-ambulances and hospital trains make their way to the rear every day, while the consumption of food, forage, petrol, and the other necessaries of military life calls for the forward movement of supply columns. The marching area of the troops thus becomes filled with military traffic, and the " corps " transport alone of the original German Army (25 corps and 10 cavalry divisions)

FLASHING NEWS FROM THE HILLS.
Official photograph issued by the Press Bureau showing signallers heliographing news to the command from the hills above Salonika.

OTHER APPLIANCES FOR THROWING LIGHT UPON THE SITUATION.
British troops loading telegraph-poles on lorries for conveyance to the French front. Above : A searchlight found in Fort Kara Baroun, dominating the entrance to the Gulf of Salonika, occupied by the Allies.

included 62,000 vehicles and 403,000 horses. The care and management of this host is centralised at Main Headquarters, and its employment for the purposes of the campaign is the peculiar function of the Chief of the General Staff.

The first problem of a generalissimo in war is whether to adopt an aggressive or defensive attitude at the outset of the campaign. The advantage of exploiting the mobility of a well-equipped army for the purpose of invasion is that in crossing the frontier the home territory is covered, the enemy's

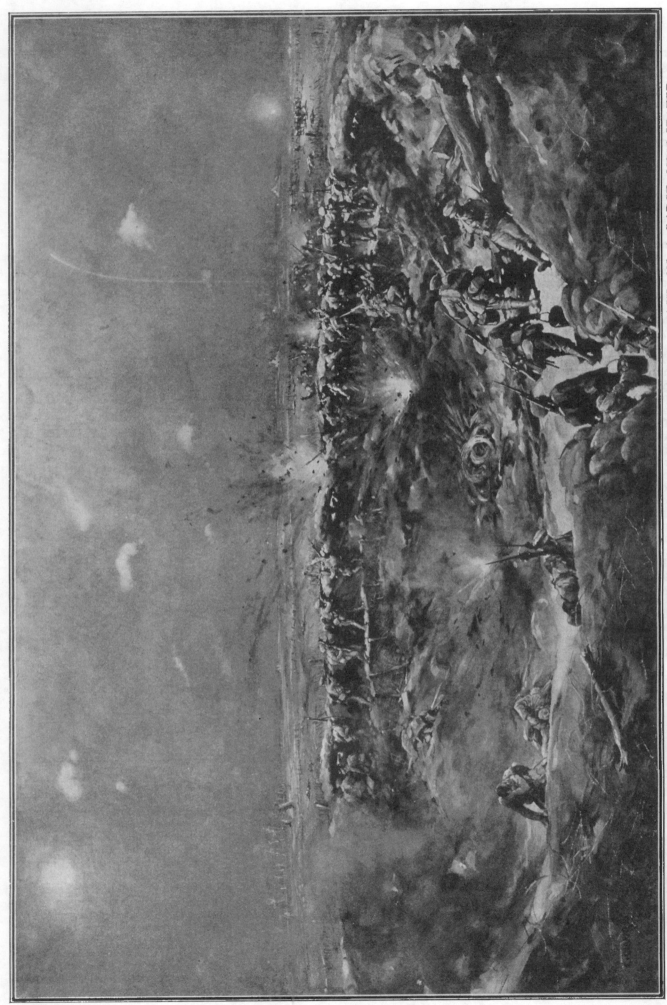

FIGHT FOR A "MOUTH OF HELL": BRITISH REPELLING THE GERMAN COUNTER-ATTACK ON A LARGE MINE-CRATER.

Mining in trench warfare was a method of which abundant use was made throughout the war. Directly a mine exploded the position was rushed while the men who had held the trench were still dazed by the shock. The crater formed was hurriedly converted into a crude fortification, with parapets against the counter-attack which inevitably followed. This dramatic picture, by Christopher Clark, shows the British repelling, almost hand to hand, the enemy's counter-attack on a crater which the British had formed and stormed in German trenches on the western front.

provinces are occupied, and his population compelled to furnish food and money—results that cannot fail to impress both friends and foes. It was the German ideal in 1866, 1870, and in 1914—in Austria, France, and Belgium—thus to make war at the enemy's expense.

On the other hand, by allowing the enemy to take the initiative a commander resorting to the defensive gains time for preparation, conserves the strength of his army, and so is enabled to bring into play the detaining power of fortresses. In defence of hearth and home we win the sympathy of neutrals who may become our allies; and popular resentment against the invader is a stimulus to patriotism and draws forth the resources of the country. Finally, by a waiting attitude we compel the enemy to show his hand, to weaken his force in proportion to the length of his marches, and so smooth the way for our counter-stroke.

Thus the German invasion of France between Paris and Verdun carried the war into French territory, but afforded General Joffre an early opportunity to retaliate at the Battle of the Marne. The Austrian invasion of

Offensive or Defensive? Serbia in December, 1914, resulted in the complete expulsion of the intruders. The attempts of the Turks to cross the Suez Canal in 1915 proved abortive. The invaders of the Gallipoli Peninsula also miscalculated their staying powers and ultimately evacuated the ground they had won at terrible cost. Our expedition to Mesopotamia was always in grave difficulties from similar causes.

The question "Offensive or Defensive?" is called a strategic question—that is to say, it has no necessary connection with fighting on a large scale. We have seen, for instance, the Austro-German armies overrun Serbia almost without opposition, yet in military language we say that the invaders were engaged in a "strategic attack" and the Serbians in "strategic defence." Strategy has been defined as "a power which differs from the mere ability to fight." The combinations of a strategist may be so overwhelming that the enemy can have no thought but how to evade fighting. The "strategic attack" may thus become simply a triumphal march through the enemy's country.

When the Serbian and Montenegrin armies, in the autumn of 1915, fled to the mountains and thence to the Adriatic coast, actually quitting their country in order to avoid a

decisive battle, they proved General Mackensen's ability as a strategist in having thus conquered a country with hardly more fighting than is associated with the contact of advanced and rear guards. The Austrian General Potiorek had met with a very different reception in Serbia, and to say that one army was stronger than the other is not to disparage the one or excuse the other general, for it is the business of strategy to ensure superiority of force and to count the cost of a campaign before undertaking it. The British expedition to Gallipoli will remain a monument of error in this respect. The campaigns of General Botha and General Dobell in South-West Africa and Cameroon are examples of strategic attacks where the means were calculated to a nicety and the end was gained with a minimum of fighting.

The commander who has decided to take the offensive, to deliver the strategic attack, must at once select the routes of invasion, called his lines of operation. These will be likely to follow the main roads and railways, which are carried over such obstacles as rivers by means of bridges, and so promise an easy path for army transport—an important consideration, since even a single division must drag after it 1,028 carts, waggons, and gun-carriages. But the enemy will most likely have constructed fortresses in order to bar these routes, and it may therefore be more expedient to choose second-class roads which are not thus defended. Moreover, these routes must embrace an extent of territory to be measured laterally by the size of the expedition. The marching columns must have elbow-room. Each division needs its share of camping grounds and billets in towns and villages;

ALLIES STUDYING THE THEORIES OF STRATEGY AND TACTICS FOR IMMEDIATE PRACTICAL EXPERIMENT.
Japanese military attachés of war experience were attached to most of the French commands. One is shown here discussing the dispositions in an important sector. Above: Official photograph issued by the Photographic Service of the French Armies showing a French general studying a Headquarters Staff map.

MMM

FRENCH PRESIDENT WITH MILITARY LEADERS AT THE FRONT.
M. Poincaré visited the front as frequently as his many heavy duties would permit. When this photograph was taken he was watching the effect of the French artillery fire in company with General Dubail and General Humbert.

it also requires space in which to deploy for battle. When General von Kluck was marching from Brussels on Mons the Crown Prince was marching from Luxemburg on Verdun, and the space between them—over a hundred miles—was divided among three other armies. The Allies were distributed on an equally broad front.

In the case of the Germans, strategy was made easy in 1914 by a most unusual concession on the part of policy. Of course, the task of strategy was to select a line of operations between Thionville and Mulhouse for the invasion of France through Alsace and Lorraine. But when the choice lies between attacking fortresses like Verdun and Toul or toiling over inhospitable moun-

Geographical and other factors tains like the Vosges, the Staff of the invading army will look round for an alternative, and then occurs the temptation to violate the neutrality of some weak nation. So it was when the German Staff won the consent of its Government to enter Luxemburg and Belgium in order to invade France from the north.

The geographical factor is, however, only one of many that enter into this problem. For instance, the invading army must not be exposed to "alarums and excursions" while on the march, and since even a corps stretches out for thirty miles along a road, how would the German army have fared in taking a southerly course over the Ardennes if the Belgian and British armies had been allowed to concentrate at Brussels and move eastward? The Germans foresaw this danger, and after a rapid mobilisation they swiftly demolished the Meuse fortresses, drove the Belgian army towards Antwerp, and occupied Brussels before the British army could reach the scene. Seated at Brussels, the Germans secured railway communication with Aix-la-Chapelle on the one hand and Metz on the other. Their right wing was thus ready for the invasion of France, while their left wing was holding Alsace-Lorraine against General Castelnau's attempts to raid the country between Metz and Strassburg.

Another consideration is the distribution of the enemy's forces. The explorations of air scouts would inform the German Staff that General Joffre had no more than fifteen corps and five British divisions in the field to oppose the five German armies of Kluck, Bülow, Hausen, the Duke of Würtemberg, and the German Crown Prince, and that the Allies were deployed échelon-wise in four masses.

No doubt German hopes ran high that the French Generalissimo would accept battle and stake his all for the defence of the northern frontier. But the independent will of the enemy is apt to upset the best-laid plans, and the retreat of the Allies to the Seine drew the five invading armies one hundred and fifty miles to the line Paris - Châlons-Verdun. Then occurred a situation all too common in war—the offensive is arrested from sheer exhaustion of its initial energy at the moment when the defending general has accumulated the power necessary for a counter-stroke.

The precise form of strategic attack designed by the German Staff will doubtless be the subject of hot dispute in years to come. Knowing as we do that the Allies' three principal masses were separated by the valleys of the Sambre and the Meuse, it may be suggested that the German plan was to destroy them piecemeal after driving the Belgian army towards the Dutch frontier. This form of strategic attack is called penetration, or breaking the front. But since the Belgian army afterwards escaped from Antwerp and General Joffre succeeded in keeping the British and French armies together during the retreat, it may be made to appear that nothing more was intended by the German Staff than a straightforward expression of superior strength by a direct advance on parallel lines in order to bring on a decisive battle. This is called the strategic frontal attack, a form adopted only when it is believed that no artifice is needed to ensure a complete victory if the enemy will stand and fight.

In favour of the theory of penetration, however, it may be said that General Joffre did not until September 5th, 1914, overcome the fear of seeing his left wing cut off by a manœuvre which is peculiar to this form of strategic attack; and, further, that the German army on that date found itself so nearly embedded between the French detachment on the Verdun- **Forms of strategic** Nancy line and the detachment of General **attack** Maunoury north of Paris, while the main army of the Allies still faced it south of the Marne, that the German Staff took the only way out of a difficulty inherent to a frustrated penetration by a rapid withdrawal to the right bank of the Aisne.

Another form of strategic attack, and one which the Germans—taught by Moltke—have made specially their own, is called envelopment. We should understand by this term rather the envelopment of territory than of troops, and among the geographical conditions which favour envelopment is a salient frontier like that of Poland, within which the enemy has somewhere concentrated his main army, leaving hostile territory on his flanks. This hostile territory in the case of the Russian army was East Prussia on the right (north) and Galicia on the left (south). In such a theatre of operations the German Staff was perfectly at home, and

German plans against Russia

as soon as the campaign in France began to languish at the end of 1914, the converging movements so familiar to students of the 1866 and 1870 campaigns were planned for the undoing of Russia. The Grand Duke Nicholas —after tentative advances which at the end of August, 1914, seemed to threaten Königsberg, and in the middle of November menaced Posen and Cracow—had now entrenched the line of the Vistula in such a fashion that to force him from his works in front of Warsaw seemed impossible.

But the spring campaign had been designed on the grand scale in Berlin, and just when we thought the Russian greatness was "a-ripening"—the Army of Galicia in April was attempting the passage of the Carpathians—there came the "killing frost" of strategic envelopment to blight our hopes. A German army under General Hindenburg was to operate from East Prussia towards the line Warsaw-Vilna, while an Austro-German army under General Mackensen was to clear Galicia, recover Przemysl and Lemberg, and then operate towards the line Warsaw-Lutzk. These movements were to be synchronised so that the two armies would unite in the region Brest-Litovsk-Bielostok-Grodno. Meanwhile, the Russian main army was to be detained in front of Warsaw by a show of activity on the part of the German central force. A complete realisation of this plan would have enclosed the Russian army of the Vistula, cut it off from its resources and communications with the interior, and so placed it in a position which is usually the prelude to surrender.

Military plans, however, seldom mature in every detail, and strategists always provide a factor of safety to allow for the fortune of war; but in working to a comprehensive scheme an ideal is kept in view, and if the results are not all that were possible, they at least exceed what could have been expected if the operations had been of a haphazard character. And so it proved in this case. The Grand Duke, on the anniversary of the declaration of war, realised that the enemy's combinations were about to fructify, and if he would avoid being hemmed in on all sides he must decamp at once. Accordingly, he gave up a position which was impregnable against assault from the west and made haste to escape before his lines of communication with Petrograd were severed. This he barely succeeded in doing by yielding up a dozen important fortresses with much of their valuable stores of munitions.

In the course of these operations, which lasted six months, scores of skirmishes, combats, battles, and sieges took place as the invaders from the north and south forced their way towards their respective objectives with the design of combining against the Grand Duke in an attack

Austro-German tactical reverses

from the east while he was assailed from the west by the central force. The Russian armies of the north and south, however, fought stoutly, and the Austro-Germans experienced tactical reverses that often seemed to warrant the abandonment of their enterprise, but Main Headquarters repaired all losses, the generals who were incapable or unlucky received their congé, and the task was recommenced with fresh troops. A confident reliance

IRONSIDES OF REPUBLICAN FRANCE: HORSEMEN IN THE INCREDIBLE BATTLE OF VERDUN.
A French outpost riding through a village in the neighbourhood of Verdun. With their helmets and heavy equipment, their powerful, long-tailed horses, and their grim strength of face and figure, these troopers suggested Cromwell's Ironsides come to strike another blow for freedom.

AT THE CROSS-ROADS—"SOMEWHERE IN FRANCE."
Two British non-commissioned officers halting where the road divided to study the map. Finer specimens of keen intelligence and concentrated attention to the duty in hand never posed unconsciously before a camera.

on sound strategy sustained the Austro-Germans in the most desperate situations, and finally their ardour and tenacity were rewarded by the acquisition of Poland and a large slice of West Russia.

Immediately this campaign against Russia closed in the autumn of 1915 another one was opened against Serbia, and General Mackensen was appointed to conduct it. He saw that the geographical conditions again favoured strategic envelopment, and three armies were assembled— one in Bulgaria, another in Bosnia, and a third in Hungary. These moving forward, each on a line of operations covering its base, were to effect a junction in Serbia, and it was soon apparent that the Serbian Army must either evade an unequal contest by flight or stand to fight on three fronts. King Peter's Army, in alliance with the Army of King Nicholas of Montenegro, escaped the worst consequences of

The campaign against Serbia Mackensen's strategy by retreat into Albania and subsequent embarkation in the ships of their western allies; but, of course, at the price of surrendering the whole of their territories to the invaders. The strategic envelopment by Marshal von der Goltz of General Townshend's division ended, after a siege of one hundred and forty-three days, in surrender at Kut in April, 1916. Although the gain was small in a material sense the moral effect was considerable, and the method employed to obtain it exhibited the highest aim of strategy—namely, to destroy the enemy completely by capture, bag and baggage, with the minimum of actual fighting. Hamley calls this procedure "interception."

Turning now to consider the main forms of defensive strategy, we shall notice that geographical conditions are paramount. Defensive war is always most successful in

semi-civilised continents like Asia and Africa, where the frontier is usually defined by a belt of desert, an unbridged river, trackless mountains, or a bush country, while the interior can only be reached by toilsome marches. The defence of Egypt, of East Africa, of Cameroon, and of Mesopotamia are cases in point. It was a sorry army of Turks that in January, 1915, after crossing the desert, reached the obstacle presented by the Suez Canal, and, destitute of tactical power, ultimately melted away under cover of a sandstorm which prevented our pursuit. The defence of Mesopotamia against Indian expeditions is based on the geographical fact that the only route of invasion is a river, which at certain seasons can be flooded, at others is unnavigable through drought, and at all times affords a precarious line of communication with the coast, whence all the invader's supplies and reinforcements are derived and to which his sick and wounded must be transported. In Cameroon a small body of German colonists held at bay for eighteen months considerable contingents of British, French, and Belgian troops whose operations were sustained by the presence and aid of warships.

In such countries defensive strategy can almost make good to-day the boast of the Scythians, as reported by Herodotus, that "no invader of their country shall ever escape out of it, or shall ever be able to find out and overtake them unless they themselves choose." It is far different in Western Europe, where it is only possible to stem invasion on the frontier by substituting for Nature's obstacles the artificial barriers called fortresses, while retreat into the interior involves the surrender of much of the national resources. The heart of England, for instance, is within the quadrilateral **Forms of defensive** Leeds — Liverpool — Nottingham — Bir- **strategy** mingham, and a hostile landing at Hull, three hundred and eighty-two miles from Hamburg, would expose us to the fate of France and Belgium, whose industrial regions proved an El Dorado to the Germans during the period of occupation. Even the fortresses on the Vistula availed not to prevent the sack of Poland.

Whether the defences of France, natural and artificial, between Luxemburg and Switzerland—that is, the Vosges and the chain of forts from Belfort to Verdun—would really withstand a determined attack, or whether the Metz-Strassburg fortresses across the frontier would yield to French prowess, were problems still unsolved in the spring of 1916. But to that date strategic defence in Europe had only proved effective in three instances, and in two of them Nature had provided the main bulwark. On the Austro-Italian frontier the rocky heights of the Alps defied the utmost efforts of Italian infantry, artillery, and engineers to break through. On the Gallipoli Peninsula the Turks, similarly aided by geographical conditions, defended the frontier of Turkey in covering the rear of the Dardanelles forts; for, of course, if the navy of the Allies had been able to steam through the Strait the fate of Constantinople had been sealed, and the forts were impervious to attack in front.

The strategic situation was, however, more normal when the Austrian General Potiorek, in November, 1914, invaded Serbia in two columns from Bosnia and Hungary. The frontier was an open one; the passage of the Rivers Danube, Save, and Drina was hardly disputed, and the Serbian commander abandoned Belgrade. The Austrians seized the Nish railway and occupied Valievo with little resistance, and then, confident of his power to crush any opposition, Potiorek detached two corps for the Carpathians. Meanwhile, the Serbian Crown Prince and Marshal Putnik had prepared the counter-stroke, and early in December they fell upon the invaders and routed six Austrian corps in a three days' battle, took 40,000 prisoners, expelled the remnants of Potiorek's force from the country and re-entered Belgrade on December 15th. So was aggression swiftly punished at the minimum of cost and suffering to the inhabitants, and this model defensive campaign is peculiarly interesting

Lieut.-Gen. Sir Francis J. Davies, K.C.B., K.C.M.G., Military Secretary to War Minister.

Down to the pool : French dragoons, some of the finest cavalry of France, close to the front near the Meuse.

Watering the horses : The dragoons, steel helmeted, carrying lance, sword, and carbine in case of encounter with enemy patrols.

General Joffre investing General Balfourier with the Star of the Legion of Honour.

to study, since even so good a judge as Sir John French, when fresh from the Flanders front, was tempted to declare that "war has become revolutionised."

It would seem then that strategy is no more than a general's initial plan of campaign based on the task that policy has set him and upon the means placed at his disposal. In framing his plans he has first to consider the geographical conditions and then to seek inspiration from history, the teachings of which are popularly known as "the art of war." He will thus learn that an immediate success may be gained by seeking out the enemy's main army and bringing it to battle in Napoleonic fashion, but as an alternative course he may prefer what Wellington called "the sure game," and leave to climate, season, natural obstacles, and spectral Want the disintegration of the enemy's forces. In any case the plan will include the preservation of whatever will facilitate his own operations and the destruction of everything that will give aid and comfort to the enemy. Martial law abrogates all private rights, local interests, and patriotic obligations on the part of the population ; the will of the conqueror alone prevails in occupied territory.

Clausewitz and "the art of war"

Strategy is the intellectual side of the art of war —an exercise carried on out of sight or hearing of the troops. The army becomes its instrument, but fighting takes place only as a means of overcoming opposition to the commander's designs. To discover the enemy's vital points and menace them is the surest way of inducing him to fight at full strength with the utmost determination. Such a battle is called "decisive" because it involves in theory the destruction of one of the belligerent armies and the end of the campaign, and it is in this sense only that the maxim of Clausewitz is to be understood—"the thing of the highest importance in war will always be the art of conquering the enemy in battle."

In speaking of strategy we are bound to generalise and regard the army as an integer, as a piece of mechanism set in motion and brought to rest at the will of Main Headquarters, whose orders are issued in the name of the generalissimo by the Chief of the Staff to commanders of corps, fortresses. and garrisons, to directors of signals, of

responsible for any item of supply or transport, or for any other duty in connection with the well-being of the army, has been set his appointed task.

The orders for the fighting troops are restricted to the hours of marching and the places of halting, but the administrative instructions embrace a thousand details, except when battle is imminent—then the situation is reversed, the corps, divisions, and brigades being the subject of minute directions necessary to produce a certain arrangement of units for attack or defence, while the system of ravitaillement is in abeyance, the troops living on their regimental supplies. And here we enter the domain of tactics. But

MILITARY SKETCH-MAP OF FRANCE.

before leaving the subject of strategy it may be well to notice that the humane method of waging war has a considerable influence upon the organisation of armies.

When a Government seeks power to raise and maintain a million men the public is apt to suppose that fifty divisions are about to be put in the field. But that is far from being the case, for it is ordained that only soldiers shall wait on soldiers, and consequently one-fourth of the number enlisted would be taken for ancillary duties, and we should be lucky to get even forty divisions out of a million quasi-soldiers. Some idea may be formed of the extreme elaboration of what the French call the rearward services from the "graphic" of the lines of communication of an army taken from the German Field Service Regulations and given on this page.

The domain of tactics

Similar arrangements are made by all belligerents, though a different terminology is used, as may be seen from the sketch-map of France given above, showing that the "zone de l'arrière" connects the "area of operations" with the "home territory," which remains under the authority of the Minister of War.

In approaching the subject of tactics, we are confronted with all the ramifications of the art of war which proceed from the diverse mental processes of subordinate commanders, the varieties of ground on which fighting is possible, the different classes of troops employed, their drill and organisation, and the resources of modern arsenals. On almost every tactical proposition a whole literature exists. Every army and every branch of the service has its own training manuals. Yet there is hardly a private soldier

"GRAPHIC" OF THE LINES OF COMMUNICATION OF AN ARMY IN MODERN WARFARE.

supply and transport, medical services, etc., to the inspector of communications, and to officers holding special appointments. These orders are passed on by the staffs of corps, etc., in greater detail to the next order of subordinates, who in turn dilute them for local application until every person in charge of a body of troops, or

who could not give some useful advice on how to win a battle. It is difficult, indeed, to see the wood for the trees. Let us, to begin with, examine more closely the fighting unit which is common to all armies—the division ; for only if we can gauge its power for attack and defence can we usefully consider what use a general should make of it in battle. The organisation of a unit is the key to its tactics. The typical division contains twelve battalions of infantry, grouped in brigades; but these brigades are differently constituted in the British and Continental armies. We have no "infantry regiment," and therefore we form our brigades of four battalions. The French and Germans group two "infantry regiments," each of three battalions, in a brigade, and so have only two brigades in a division. The Continental colonel therefore stands for our brigadier-general with fewer troops at his disposal—these, however, are associated by a sort of family tie. The two regiments grouped in brigade become a half division under a brigadier. Of cavalry the French and British divisions

Organisation of fighting units   contain only one squadron; the German division has a cavalry regiment (four squadrons). All divisions dispose of twenty-four machine-guns.

Of artillery the German and British divisions have twelve batteries each of six guns or howitzers; the French division has nine batteries, each of four guns; the British division has also a battery of four heavy guns (60-pounders). Thus the British division is strongest and the French weakest in artillery.

The following table exhibits some peculiarities of the corps organisation on the Continent:

DIVISIONS.

			Battalions.	Squadrons.	Guns.
Italy	..	..	12	None	30
Austria	..	..	15	3	36
Russia	..	..	16	?	48

ARMY CORPS.

Italy	..	..	39	5	126
Austria	..	..	45	9	115
Russia	..	..	32	14	108

AT THE END OF THE LINE.
Looking, but for their helmets, like peaceful artists, these Frenchmen were on dangerous vigil at the end of the French line, in the Bois le Pretre.

SNIPING ON FLEMISH MARSHES.
French snipers, with eyes as keen as their bayonets, waiting invisible behind the hedgerow for a shot and a kill.

We may notice that although the Italian division is far weaker than the Austrian or Russian division, the Italian corps is numerically stronger than that of Russia in infantry, and has more guns than either the Russian or Austrian corps. The Austrian corps preponderates in infantry and the Russian corps in cavalry.

The cavalry division is a far smaller body than the infantry division, but is similarly constituted. The British have twelve regiments (thirty-six squadrons) in four brigades, and twenty-four machine-guns—a pair per regiment—with four batteries of horse-artillery (twenty-four guns). The German cavalry division has six regiments (twenty-four squadrons) in three brigades, a machine-gun battery, and three batteries of horse-artillery (eighteen guns). The French also have three brigades, each of two regiments, but give a pair of machine-   **Control of orders** guns to each regiment, and reduce   **and reports** their artillery to two batteries (eight guns). Every cavalry division has engineers, signallers, and ambulances, equipped for rapid movement.

For the issue of orders and the reception of reports the divisional commander utilises his signal company, which provides telegraph and telephone cable lines—cavalry has wireless—heliographs, flags, and lamps, and connects him with the headquarters of brigades, etc. His engineers lay pontoon bridges or demolish steel bridges, organise the water supply and supervise the construction of entrenchments. The ambulances establish field-hospitals and attend to sanitary matters. A British divisional commander would issue orders to eleven sub-units—namely: (1) Divisional cavalry, (2) field-artillery, (3) heavy battery, (4) ammunition column, (5) engineer companies, (6) signal company, (7) field-ambulances, (8) train, (9-11) infantry brigades, Nos. 1, 2, 3.

GETTING OUT OF THE "RAIN."
View of a French trench during bombardment. The men retired into their dug-outs and philosophically waited for the hail of shell to cease.

For tactical or fighting purposes the question fines down to guns and rifles, machine-guns and grenades; and here a woeful disparity occurs between the ration strength and fighting strength of a division. The commander who has to feed in an infantry division 18,073, and in a cavalry division 9,269 persons, will find that when all deductions are made of those who supervise and assist in various ways to keep the unit in fighting trim, including men who serve the guns, he can muster on the day of battle, as a maximum at mobilised strength only 9,024 infantry and 3,744 cavalry privates. Sir Ian Hamilton tells us that for the attack on Ismail Oglu Tepe and the Anafarta spur, in August, 1915, he could muster only 30,000 rifles out of eleven brigades, "owing to casualties"; but, in fact, a brigade on mobilisation includes no more than 3,008 infantry "privates." And as the Hon. Sidney Peel remarks in his delightful book, "Trooper 8008":

Ration and fighting strength

You must have privates. Even in the Haytian army, in which they used to have two generals besides other officers to each man, there were, at any rate, some privates, and I know from my own experience that, when an order was given, no matter where it started, and through however many grades of officers, commissioned and non-commissioned, it was passed down, it was always the private who had to turn out and do something in the end. Collectively, indeed, privates are of the utmost importance!

No doubt all modern armies suffer from this shrinkage of fighting strength and accumulation of what the Navy calls "idlers"; but it may be doubted whether any fighting force demands so many followers as the British Army. It has been calculated that for every "Tommy" who actually reaches the firing-line another man and a horse must be maintained in order to keep him effective. Unfortunately, too, this horde of non-combatants is even more highly paid than the soldier who

goes into action, and this is a serious handicap to us financially, as service in Continental armies is practically gratuitous as well as compulsory.

We must now inquire how the fighting troops fulfil their respective duties in war; and first we have to realise that each "arm" has its special characteristics. Infantry is slow in its movements, but is capable of getting over almost any ground by day or night in all weathers. The foot soldier offers but a small target to the enemy and can find cover easily; he can employ either fire action or shock action and hit at a distance or at close quarters. Mounted on bicycles or carried in motor transport, infantry can move on roads faster than cavalry.

The gunners of a division can deliver destructive fire up to 6,500 yards; their heavy gun range is 10,000 yards; they use shrapnel and high-explosive shells. Shrapnel is the man-killing projectile; high-explosive shells break down the enemy's entrenchments, destroy his guns and waggons, and affect the nerves of hostile infantry, who dislike "Jack Johnsons" and "Coal-boxes" more than any other missile. The howitzer is a piece of ordnance that combines lightness and mobility with great shell power, and as it always fires at a high angle its shells fall almost perpendicularly, so that no form of overhead cover affords protection against howitzer fire. "Horse" artillery consists of lighter guns, which can keep pace with cavalry. Mountain guns can be carried on pack mules where guns on wheels cannot be moved.

Characteristics of each "arm"

Cavalry may be regarded to-day as infantry who can also fight on horseback with sabre or lance; it is, therefore, the most mobile force that can be employed. But a mounted soldier affords too good a target to the enemy. Machine-

OBSERVATION-POST IN THE FRENCH FIRST-LINE.
Observation work was particularly dangerous, and in the most advanced trench lines the observation-posts were elaborately armoured and fortified.

TWO BRILLIANT OFFICERS OF THE FRENCH HIGH
COMMAND.

General Franchet d'Espérey and General de Castelnau. The latter had
the particularly distressing experience of seeing one of his sons killed
before his eyes. (Official photograph issued by the French War Office.)

guns of various types which can deliver a stream of bullets from positions in which it is difficult to locate them are attached to both infantry and cavalry units as a " reserve" of fire. Aircraft also may take part in tactical operations by the use of machine-guns and bombs. The field engineers accompany infantry and cavalry to assist them in entrenching, to create obstacles for the enemy, and to open up routes for attacking troops. Battalions of pioneers are employed who contrive "a double debt to pay," combining the work of infantry and engineers.

The lower organisations of the fighting troops may now be glanced at. Four platoons of infantry under-subalterns form a company under a major, and four companies together with a pair of machine-guns form the battalion under a lieutenant-colonel. The cavalry regiment is similarly composed of a machine-gun section and three squadrons ; the squadron is subdivided into four troops, each commanded by a subaltern. The brigade of artillery, under a lieutenant-colonel, consists of three batteries, each of three sections, together with an ammunition column which carries cartridges for infantry as well as shells for guns. The section is the subaltern's unit. Field

Our great tactical maxim engineers form four sections into a field company. Captains nowadays assist and deputise for the major in command of a company, squadron, or battery. Our great tactical maxim is this : "The full power of an army can be exerted only when all its parts act in close combination," and therefore it is incumbent on each " arm " to have a general knowledge of the organisation and characteristics of the other " arm."

Like the leader of an orchestra, the general officer ensures the harmonious co-operation of all his instruments and appliances. His first care in war, however, is to prevent the disaster that nowadays will overtake any body of troops that allows itself to be surprised by the enemy, and

so he will neither march nor camp in one mass ; he always provides detachments called, according to circumstances, advanced, rear, or flank guards on the march and outposts when at rest. When the enemy is watched closely he cannot very well spring upon us suddenly, and aircraft—the new " arm "—is most useful for observation purposes as, weather permitting, it saves fatigue to the cavalry. It will be remembered that our army first used the aeroplane for reconnaissance in August, 1914, when Sir John French by this means confirmed the news he had received of the retreat of General Lanrezac's French army on his right and the advance of the German army of General von Kluck on his front, ill-tidings which determined his retreat to Jenlain-Maubeuge on August 24th. **" How fields are won "**

General Sir A. A. Barrett, in marching to a new camp in Mesopotamia, detailed as advanced guard a squadron, a mountain battery, a company of engineers—called sappers and miners in the Indian Army—and two battalions. He also threw out two flank guards—three companies on the right and one company on the left—and closed his column with a rearguard of one company. These were his protecting detachments. It was the advanced guard that on November 17th, 1914, first encountered the Turks and located their position at Zain, giving General Barrett time to prepare for battle. He was experienced in frontier warfare, having taken part in Lord Roberts' great march from Kabul to Kandahar in 1880 and served in four later expeditions, and as might be expected he delivered a very pretty attack, the details of which may be profitably followed by those who would know " how fields are won."

First of all he reinforced his advanced guard with one battalion as soon as the enemy's guns opened fire. Then he moved his artillery on the right of the advanced guard, and farther still to the right he sent three battalions and an engineer company. He retained two battalions as a general reserve to meet contingencies. Meanwhile, the cavalry had been placed on the extreme left of his force, consisting of a division on the Indian scale, which now deployed for action. The enemy was, of course, entrenched and Bimbashi Adie Bey commanded about four battalions with three machine-guns, eight mountain guns and four field-guns of 3·25 in. calibre. He was assisted by about 1,000 Arabs.

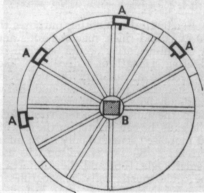

DIAGRAM OF MODES OF ATTACK.

The attacking force was, therefore, none too strong for the task of clearing away this obstacle to its advance by what is called an encounter battle. General Barrett, while his troops were moving into position, had to concert some plan of attack, and his choice lay between the two forms we have already discussed from the strategic point of view, and to which we must again refer.

The opposing principles of penetration and envelopment may be best explained by the accompanying figure of a sector of a cartwheel, if we imagine the rim to represent an army " A," fractioned against another army " B " which is concentrated at the hub, while the spokes represent the routes of advance common to both. It is evident that the approach of the divided force " A " will tend to envelop or surround the concentrated force " B." On the other hand, " B " on the inside track is at liberty to manœuvre in any direction, and with small forces entrenched may detain two or three of the fractions of " A " while massing the remainder against one or two

CROSSING A BOURNE FROM WHICH THEY MIGHT RETURN.
With every sense on the alert, and with bombs and rifles ready, an advance party of Italians began to ford a stream.

DEATH ESCORTED THROUGH STREAM AND THICKET.
Next, two men bore the tube, followed by an expert bomb-thrower. Circle : Across the stream, they crept through the thicket, covered by rifles.

DARING CROWNED BY TRIUMPH: AN AUSTRIAN TRENCH BLOWN UP IN FLAME AND THUNDER.
In the Isonzo region the Italians devised a method of mining enemy trenches by means of long tubes of explosives which they carried right up to their objective. These pictures show successive stages of one of these most dangerous adventures.

of them. " A " is said to operate on outer lines, " B " on inner lines ; the attack of the former is convergent, that of the latter is divergent. " B " is liable to be surrounded en bloc, while " A " having divided his forces is exposed to defeat in detail.

Accidents of ground, the mobility of the higher organisations and generalship in deceiving the enemy as to the plan of action and lines of approach, will determine the issue so far as tactics is concerned, assuming proportionate numbers and equal resolution in the troops. In strategy, as we have seen, the principles of attack are employed in reference to frontiers ; in tactics they are employed against troops. In strategy the plan may be conceived in peace time or during mobilisation and the initial movements of troops by rail be made to conform—as when Prussia, in 1866, formed three armies in Silesia, Saxony, and Brandenburg respectively, while the Austrians concentrated in Bohemia—

but in tactics the decision cannot be taken until the enemy is within striking distance. In strategy the choice is irrevocable, for you cannot toss armies with all their impedimenta to and fro from day to day ; but in tactics it is possible and proper to modify the original plan if the changing situation demands it, and for this purpose the commander retains under his immediate control a body of troops known as the general reserve.

Now General Barrett on this occasion had resolved to envelop one flank of the enemy—his right—while demonstrating in his front, but in the course of the engagement it was discovered that this flank had been thrown far back into some broken ground and palm-groves. To seek it there would have involved the separation of our forces. A change of plan, therefore, seemed advisable, and so the general **British tactics in** directed the 18th Brigade—his original **Mesopotamia** advanced guard—to engage the enemy's centre and right while our 16th Brigade turned the left flank and captured a fort which formed the key of the position. For this task he strengthened the 16th Brigade with a battalion from the reserve. The enemy, however, now remembered the proverb that " he who fights and runs away, may live to fight another day," and, early in the afternoon, quitting his entrenchments, he fled rapidly towards his right into the broken ground, where palm-trees, mud walls, and long earthen embankments formed a rallying-point, and then decamped under cover of a rearguard. The fortune of war also served the Turks, for a heavy downpour of rain had converted the ground into a

WHERE MEN MIGHT NOT SLUMBER OR SLEEP: THE CEASELESS VIGIL OF THE TRENCHES.
French artillery observers at work in bleak conditions.   In oval : A trench in the Meurthe et Moselle sector carried down to the edge of a lake.   Two Frenchmen grimly watched the German lines, ready to fire on sight of the first enemy head.

their training as inculcated in peace time being carried out automatically." Let us now see what this peace training aims at, and what minor tactics are employed by the different arms in order to inflict the greatest possible loss upon their opponents, while avoiding unnecessary damage to themselves.

The foot soldier's essential weapon is his rifle, which is now capable of being loaded a dozen times a minute. The bullet is sped on its way at the rate of eight hundred yards a second, and this high velocity not only carries the missile 2,800 yards, but ensures a flat trajectory so that the curve of flight shall at ranges up to six hundred yards not exceed the height of a man. Consequently, an entrenched force can cover its front for a third of a mile with a hail of bullets which on open ground no attackers can stand up against, and which even at a range of a mile would force attackers to seek shelter from un- **The crux of** aimed fire or adopt such formations as **infantry tactics** shallow columns on narrow fronts in order to reduce the size of the target. The controversy on infantry formations for attack has only been exceeded in length and bitterness by the disputes on guns versus armour, to which of course it is akin, since the rifle bullet will penetrate a bank of earth forty inches thick, five feet of soft wood like fir, a nine-inch brick wall with cement mortar, or an ordinary mild steel plate three-quarters of an inch thick.

This question of formations involves many tactical principles. For instance, to scatter men under fire is to reduce losses ; but a wide extension of front carries troops out of the control of their leaders—a disadvantage which may be put up with as long as there is no need to open fire.

quagmire, ankle deep, over which our guns and cavalry in attempting pursuit could only move at a walk. The enemy, therefore, escaped with a loss of two mountain guns and about 1,500 casualties. Barrett's force bivouacked on the banks of the river below Basra, covered by outposts, while the ambulances were busy far into the night bringing in the wounded, including Turks and Arabs, who were placed on the vessels which formed our field hospitals.

This little affair illustrates perfectly the scope of the higher tactics—namely, measures for protection on the march, reconnaissance, the selection of a plan of action, its modification as the situation develops through the interference of the enemy, change of terrain, and even change of

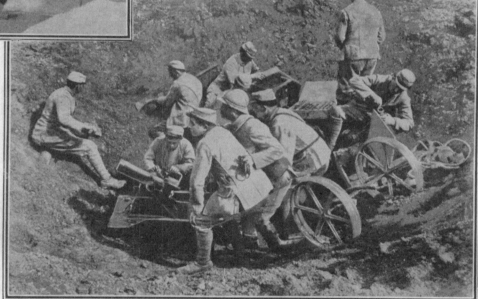

TRENCH-MORTARS BUSY IN FRANCE AND AT SALONIKA.
This French mortar team had just rushed a mine crater and begun to bombard the enemy. Above : Official photograph issued by the Press Bureau showing British at Salonika firing bombs from a small trench-howitzer.

weather. While a crowning victory and the complete destruction of the enemy's fighting power are the ideals to strive for, universal experience shows that generals have usually to be content with a half measure of success. The Great War would have been over in a twelvemonth if even a tithe of the reported " decisive " battles had had any foundation in fact.

Space forbids our showing what part was played in this battle by the tactical units who bore the burden and heat of the day, but we are told that General Barrett's troops, British and Indian, in this their first battle " behaved as steadily as if at an ordinary field day, all the details of

But infantry will not advance far under heavy fire without replying to it, and then the difficulty is that in a dispersed formation on every hundred yards of front you would have only twenty-five men answering the fire of one hundred entrenched riflemen. Yet if the men are closed in to the same extent as the defenders, the serried ranks, unprotected by earthworks, offer the enemy a remunerative target and will suffer undue loss.

Here is a dilemma from which platoon leaders endeavour in vain to escape, for in attempting to combine movement with fire effect and cover with control we are evidently at cross purposes ; it is the crux of infantry tactics. A

IN A VERY WARM CORNER: TRENCH GUNS IN ACTION ON THE WESTERN FRONT.

French soldiers firing "taupias," small trench guns made of shell-casing, set on movable stands for range-finding purposes and fired through a touch-hole; at short range these were very effective. The squat, wide-mouthed "crapouillot" (seen in the foreground) flung a larger projectile with a deafening report and was highly destructive.

solution that was offered some years ago by General Monro—namely, to organise long-range covering fire by supporting infantry—is only practicable with highly-trained units, and his plan to attach to all officers, and even to section commanders, "specially trained observers" would further deplete the firing-line by the abstraction of actual fighting men. But the tactical conditions vary so widely, not only in different theatres but from battle to battle in each theatre and even in parts of the same scene of action, that the text-books dare not prescribe any fixed order of proceedings. Their principles have to be applied according to the stage of the attack, the range, the nature of the enemy's fire and the changing character of the ground —hilly here, flat elsewhere, and at another point obstructed by crops, buildings, streams, and hedges. Only highly-trained troops after years of practice acquire that sort of instinct which enables them to avoid extremes of density or dispersion in passing over the danger zone.

At the Battle of Barjisiyah, April 14th, 1915, our troops under Sir John Nixon had to advance over a plain devoid of cover in order to reach a superior force of the enemy, who was skilfully entrenched and concealed on a front of over three miles, and in the last four hundred yards our advance was down a glacis-like slope. It was in surmounting the crest of this slope that our principal losses occurred. Our infantry consisted of seven battalions, of which only two —the Norfolks and Dorsets—were British, and if we assume eight hundred effectives in each unit, it is apparent that on an average we had only one man per yard of frontage— sufficient, as it proved, to turn out of his position an enemy who had no stomach for a close encounter, but a totally inadequate force to carry a position of similar extent in Europe, as the following story of the Mons battle shows :

A story of Mons

As the Germans came into view in the open, in front of our hastily dug trenches, our men opened on them with a steady fire that never once went wide, and we could see clean-cut gaps in the tightly-packed ranks as the hail of lead tore its jagged way through them. They were a game lot, however, and kept closing up the gaps in their ranks as though they were so many marionettes. Flesh and blood cannot stand this sort of thing for ever, and after a while they began to come along with less confident step. Then they halted for a few minutes, gazed about them in a dazed sort of way, and ran like hares. Their place was taken by another bluish-grey mass behind them, and this body came on in much the same way until they, too, had had as much as they could stand, and then there was another bolt for the rear. This advancing and retreating went on for hours, each retirement unmasking a fresh body of men, and by the time they were close enough to hurl themselves on our trenches. *it was an entirely fresh mass of men, who had suffered little from our fire.*

This is the rationale of the so-called "mass" formation, and it involves a problem that besets all generals—namely, the strength, disposition, and use of reserves. On the one hand, it is alleged that only the possession of powerful reserves will enable a leader to storm a position or change the course of a battle, to launch a pursuit or cover a retreat ; on the other side, we have painful experiences of battles lost, as at Loos in September, 1915,

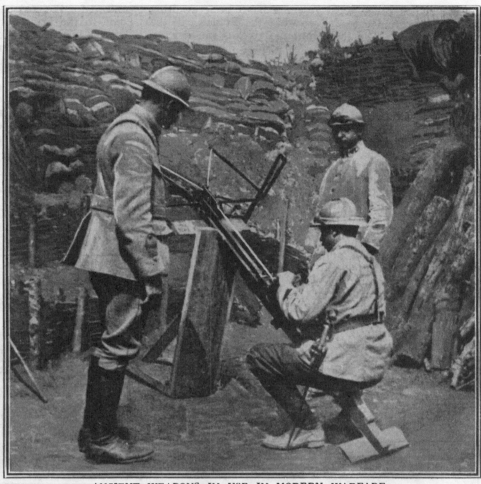

ANCIENT WEAPONS IN USE IN MODERN WARFARE.
With the progress of the war came the reintroduction of some very early weapons. To project bombs these Frenchmen were using an adaptation of the old Roman ballista, a huge iron cross-bow that flung a heavy "quarrel" (or bolt) by means of a cord of sinew worked by levers.

for want of the troops standing idle in reserve at some distant point out of harm's way. At the end of April, 1915, on the Vilna front, when General von Eichhorn's Tenth Army attacked the Russians, each side asserted of the other's attack or counter-attack that it was "in close formation." The Germans were successful, and we may assume that they put in the largest number of troops to the yard.

The Germans at Gravelotte in 1870 had attacked with as many as ten men to the yard on a front of eleven and a half miles, and it is now certain that against European troops wave after wave of infantry must flow upon an entrenched position until the defenders are overwhelmed, unless the factor of surprise can be introduced into the problem. Such a factor was present on April 22nd, 1915, when the Germans ejected a French Algerian division from its position in front of Ypres by a deluge of asphyxiating gas. Into the four-mile gap in our line thus created we expected the enemy to pour division after division and corps after corps to win their way to St. Omer and Calais ; and when the Germans seemed content with such enterprises as could be checked by our Canadian division, it was evident that the higher tactics were in abeyance ; and so it is that **Higher tactics in abeyance** the practice of war is often an object-lesson in bad generalship, an illustration of the results of violating a principle of war.

Infantry in defence have a comparatively easy task, for, ensconced behind parapets of earth affording loopholes for rifles, they shoot from a rest at ranges already marked at a target of running men. Abundance of ammunition is handy. When a man falls his place is taken by a fresh man from the support, and the shooting is kept up even though the enemy swarm over the trenches, for certain formed bodies called local reserves have been awaiting such an opportunity to deliver what the French call the offensive-return. The thing that most vexes the defence is the enemy's shell fire, and this scourge must be borne unless the guns of the defence are sufficiently powerful to silence the attacking artillery as well as stop the progress of his infantry, which is always the point of first importance.

An awakening in regard to the power of defensive tactics was expected after the American Civil War; but neither the Austrians in 1866 nor the French in 1870 heeded the moral conveyed by the fighting at the Wilderness and Cold Harbour, and so they were beaten in every battle by the Prussians. Then came Plevna with the same lesson in 1877, but we are slow to learn, and the later teachings of Manchuria in 1904 and of the Balkans in 1912 were unheeded. It remained, therefore, for the Germans to convince us, after recrossing the Aisne, that our penchant for the tactical offensive was ill-timed, and that only an uplifting strategic attack, like that of Hindenburg in Poland in 1915, could deliver us from the grip of passive defence, a mode of action which current text-books had utterly condemned, declaring that "the action of a force which is content with warding off the enemy's blows is not considered as an aspect in the battle."

Gunners, too, have their tactical squabbles. There is a school that is unable to rid itself of a deep concern for the cost of bringing shells from the arsenal at home to the firing battery overseas, that holds the belief that the business of gunners is "to hit," that eschews a seemingly fruitless bombardment; but another class of expert demands that guns shall keep in action throughout a battle if only to hearten up their own infantry and, at any rate, alarm the enemy by their racket; and in 1916 we heard of the doctrine of "curtain" fire.

The object of the so-called *tir de barrage* is to keep a belt of ground smothered in shells, so that the enemy's troops shall pay a heavy toll in passing it, and it is this method—obviously effective but a very cormorant for ammunition—that gave rise to the shell question. Formerly it was supposed that if a gun fired five hundred rounds in one day, thereby using up its share of the ammunition carried

WORMING THEIR WAY THROUGH THE WIRES.
French scouts cutting and creeping through enemy entanglements, perhaps the most laborious and dangerous task that fell to their lot.

by the division to which it belongs, the maximum of effort had been reached; but then we heard of a French battery discharging shells at the rate of twenty a minute per gun and expending three thousand one hundred rounds in forty-five minutes. After firing 30,000 shells the gun was in need of repair, and therefore the gun factory and a light railway became almost an appanage of the artillery of a French army corps.

Another great change in artillery practice arose from the mechanical facility possessed for shooting at targets not visible to the gunners. This "indirect" fire is controlled by an individual who is stationed in some eyrie whence the burst of the shells can be observed, and who is connected with the battery by telephone to correct the errors in shooting after the target has been indicated by aircraft. In Europe, where batteries and targets remain stationary as in siege operations, the most elaborate arrangements for observation are feasible; but in such encounters as that of Barjisiyah, we find an officer going into the infantry firing-line for the better observation of fire, and an infantry adjutant signalling by flag the gunner's message to his battery commander.

The effective range of field-artillery is about two miles, but distant range is 6,500 yards. The targets vary and so do the methods of dealing with them. Against aircraft and troops in the open field-guns use shrapnel with time-fuse; against walls and buildings the same shell with a percussion fuse is effective. High-explosive shells are intended to destroy whatever material is being used as cover by hostile infantry, and when this cover is "overhead" the howitzer is brought into service. From distant ranges the heavy guns will aid by oblique or enfilade fire.

FIRE-SCREENS IN THE SNOW.
Hungarian cutting barbed-wire on the eastern front, protected by a screen from the fire he might draw at any moment.

A "TUBE" STATION ON THE JOURNEY FROM PARIS TO BERLIN.
Trench architecture became increasingly elaborate during the prolonged stationary period of the war. This photograph from the western front shows one form of bomb-proof shelter which had even an artistic façade. It was called the "Tube" by our men and the equivalent "Metro" by the French soldiers.

from Verdun by the Paris correspondent of the "Times."

Hill 304, the new objective of the Germans, is a C-shaped ridge to the south-west of Mort Homme. The ground rises rapidly from a fringe of thin woods to a bare ridge about two and a half miles long and a few hundred yards wide. On the west and north-west small woods bound the position. The whole of this position and the roads leading to it were subjected to a bombardment of overwhelming weight on Wednesday night (May 3rd, 1916), heavy artillery only being employed. In addition to high explosive, gas shells of unwonted calibre were flung all over the French positions. Trenches disappeared completely, no shelter or dug-out could withstand the deluge. By two o'clock on Friday morning the destruction was complete, so the French withdrew their troops from the first line, which had ceased to exist for defensive purposes, and established them slightly to the rear. The Germans then launched a fresh division, taken from another part of the front, to assault the ridge. The French *barrage* fire was unable, as has frequently been the case, to nip the assault in the bud. The attacking infantry streamed through the fire zone in apparently unending waves, and finally managed to instal themselves on the slopes of the ridge.

Thus the attackers' artillery supports its infantry by deluging with high-explosive shells the enemy's entrenchments, blinding the riflemen with dust and dirt, and so forcing them to cease fire and take cover under the parapets. That is the opportunity for the attacking infantry to rush forward. Thus gaining ground hour by hour or day by day at last the moment arrives for the assault ; and then we shall hear of a bayonet charge, though, in fact, it is seldom that bayonets are crossed, for when infantry in defence can no longer shoot they are too demoralised to engage in single combat. They quit their trenches and run to escape capture, lucky if they can find a rallying-point far behind their rearguard. Thus by means of guns and rifles the attackers shoot their way into the enemy's position, and if the general form of attack is converging, as in a case of envelopment, great facilities are offered for the more destructive kinds of fire called oblique, reverse, and enfilade fire, which the figure given on p. 532 explains.

Oblique, reverse, and enfilade fire

Artillery in defence, like infantry, have the advantage of shooting at marked ranges from concealed positions, and as each 18-pounder shrapnel shell contains three hundred and seventy-five bullets, which fall upon an area fifty to one hundred yards deep by twenty-five yards wide, the attacking infantry are sore smitten before they come within range of the defenders' rifle fire. But in opening fire the guns often reveal their positions by the flashes, and then the attackers' guns—we have always to assume that the force attacking is far superior in strength to the force defending—will endeavour to silence them, and in this way support its own infantry.

As an illustration of the co-operation of artillery and infantry in attack, and incidentally of the effect of such co-operation upon the defenders of an entrenched position, we may quote a story

The cavalry soldier's disdain of infantry before the Great War was proverbial, and his attitude to a class of troops known as mounted infantry one of contempt when the war began. His training had taught him to regard the troop horse as his chief weapon in battle ; his mode of action was to be always aggressive; his attack formation was that of a line of centaurs, knee to knee. Cavalry was to strike terror into infantry after their nerves had been shaken by the other arms, using its mobility as a means of surprise. Cavalry, preserving cohesion through all stages of the mounted attack at the trot and the gallop, within fifty yards of the enemy was to charge, or in other words ride the enemy down by sheer weight and momentum. Alas! for these ideals. Our regiments, magnificently trained

MAXIMUM INSURANCE AGAINST BOMBS AND SHELLS.
Even greater care was taken to minimise the danger of enemy shell fire in the trenches occupied by the artillery in the Champagne district. In this picture a French artillery commander is seen at his quarters near the front.

and led by tried commanders, found their occupation gone, at least upon French battlefields.

On August 24th, 1914, General de Lisle thought he saw a good opportunity " to paralyse the further advance of the German infantry by making a mounted attack on their flank " with the 2nd Cavalry Brigade. Sir John French says that the brigade formed up and advanced for this purpose but was " held up " by wire about five hundred yards from its objective, and that the 9th Lancers and the 18th Hussars " suffered severely " before the brigade could withdraw. A French corps of cavalry under General Sordet was unable to render the British divisions any assistance at a critical moment because their horses were " too tired to move."

Against the German cavalry on August 28th, we are told, our 3rd and 5th Cavalry Brigades

DIRECTIONS OF RIFLE FIRE.
(See p. 531.)

gave a good account of themselves under Generals Gough and Chetwode, but we were given no particulars of their tactics on the occasion. Lord Kitchener's statement, published August 31st, 1914, told us of the unsuccessful charge of the German Guard Cavalry Division upon our 12th Infantry Brigade, an incident not referred to in Sir John French's despatch. But when our 6th and 7th Cavalry Brigades (Byng's 3rd Division) arrived at Ostend in October they found themselves within a fortnight acting as infantry in the fire-trenches in front of Ypres, where the

only part of their previous training that was of any value —the use of the rifle and the spade—was that which had been reluctantly introduced by Lord Roberts after the South African War.

That the masses of cavalry which the French and Germans put into the field in 1914 as covering troops should have been able to avoid such encounters as we saw in 1870 between Metz and Sedan is indeed astonishing. General von Bernhardi, although an advocate of dismounted action, could not ignore the purpose of equipping mounted troops with sword and lance, and says: " We may yet be certain **Status of Cavalry** next time of having to deal with a **in 1916** numerous and determined cavalry who will quite conceivably endeavour to meet us in shock action with the *arme blanche.*" But after nearly two years of the war the great cavalry battle was still to come.

Tedious as many of these details may be, they are nevertheless indispensable to an understanding of the mental and moral atmosphere of an army and of its tactics, which is of all arts the one most difficult to grasp in its essentials or to view comprehensively. Long periods go by without any exhibition on the part of its professors, and when a battle occurs rarely is anybody present to observe and report in a spirit of cool impartiality. " Eye-witness " accounts of fighting are necessarily one-sided ; views are coloured by prepossessions or distorted by the angle of vision ; the picture presented is out of perspective. The general sees one thing, the regimental officer sees another, and the private soldier " sees red." To take for instance the case of the 2nd Cavalry Brigade above mentioned, on comparing the official despatch with " The First Seven Divisions " (page 27) we find two very different versions of the story.

GERMAN AIR-BOMBS BURSTING OVER BOTHA'S TROOPS.
This remarkable photograph shows German air-bombs bursting over General Botha's troops during their advance across the desert to conquer German South-West Africa. Airmen flew out to meet the advancing Union forces. This striking impression was taken from a German aeroplane.

HOW MARSEILLES WELCOMED A BRITISH CONTINGENT TO THE SOIL OF FRANCE.
Intimation having been given that a British contingent would land at Marseilles early in May, 1916, a fervent public welcome was
prepared. The troops were passed in review by the Prefecture, and then, decked with flowers, marched through the town, being greeted
everywhere with enthusiastic cheering.

In one account the 18th Hussars took part in the mounted attack; in the other this regiment was detached in order to act dismounted; and further, according to Lord Ernest Hamilton, the two regiments detailed to stop the German advance realised the impossibility of mounted action as soon as the wire fence came in view, and wheeling to the right took cover behind some big slag heaps, where they dismounted and opened fire, thus checking the enemy for four hours in co-operation with two batteries. But Sir John French says the whole brigade retired after being held up by wire.

Similar discrepancies will be found by the score as fresh reports become available, and only historians know that the touchstone of truth is evolved from a consideration of military principles and the trend of peace training modified by the personal equation—the latter providing those almost incredible instances of valour mentioned in the "Gazettes," in which the seemingly impossible was achieved. Armed with such an *apparatus criticus* our readers may fearlessly test any military proposition or statement, no matter from what quarter or what authority it comes.

Military training aims ultimately at procuring the utmost from individual effort by subtle appeals to the dormant instinct in man to combat, while

"THE HERO OF BELGRADE."
Major Djoukitch watching his rearguard action against the
Austrians on Mount Kosmai, which changed hands eight times
before the invaders swept over Serbia at the end of 1915.

suppressing any tendency to strive for personal glorification. The individual is sunk in the unit; the smaller units are absorbed in the life of the larger one to which they are affiliated; not even a general can play for his own hand; altruism is the bedrock of army discipline. In firm reliance on the skill and endurance of his troops the commander in due season offers or accepts battle, and so permits or orders units to engage with the enemy. Each unit will fight its immediate opponent in its own way as it has been taught, upon some theory or principle adopted by its own leader, and it is the combination of all these separate engagements that constitutes a modern battle.

This battle has presumably been designed by the generalissimo, who has placed the units in certain topographical relations to each other and to the enemy before signifying that fire may be opened. He preserves this framework of the battle and sustains his theory of the combat through all its phases, restraining excess of zeal in one direction and supporting and urging in another case where necessary. When all goes smoothly his office is to all appearance a light one; but when checks occur and reverses are reported it is his onerous function to apply suitable remedies on the spot. General Joffre's reputation was made by his handling of a critical

HONOURING INDIA AT
MARSEILLES.

Indian cavalry were in the British
contingent that landed at Marseilles
on May 8th, 1916, and showed
grave pleasure at the enthusiastic
welcome given them.

situation in August-September, 1914, a situation in which strategy and tactics overlapped, as they are apt to do since time and space have become factors in the manipulation of groups of armies.

Sir John French regarded his own operations on August 23rd-26th, 1914, as a "four days' battle," and his despatch dated September 7th of that year shows how he handled his few divisions of infantry and cavalry in retreating from Mons to Guise with some aid from the French on both flanks. The author of "The First Seven Divisions" gives a detailed account of the fighting of the units on the principles we have here described.

General Joffre's stupendous task   But General Joffre's task was stupendous by comparison. Between the Sambre and the Seine from north to south, from Paris to Nancy from west to east, he controlled eight armies which encountered an enemy who was believed to have thirty-four corps and ten cavalry divisions in the field.

On August 14th the French right wing (First and Second Armies) had crossed the frontiers in Alsace-Lorraine to meet the enemy, and for a week with varying success it engaged certain German forces, which drove it back but did not press their advantage on August 24th. Meanwhile, the French centre (Third and Fourth Armies) and the French left (Fifth Army) on August 21st had entered Belgium to attack the enemy in the north. Separated by the Meuse River both met with serious reverses between Charleroi and Spincourt. The French Fifth Army abandoned the line of the Sambre on August 24th, falling back to Beaumont-Givet on the right (east) of the British army. The defeat of the central mass of ten corps—comprising 1,200 guns, 480 machine-guns, 10 cavalry regiments, and 240 battalions of infantry—was officially ascribed to individual and collective failures, imprudences committed under

the fire of the enemy, divisions ill-engaged, rash deployments, and precipitate retreats, a premature waste of men, and finally the inadequacy of certain of our troops and their leaders, both as regards the use of infantry and artillery.

The French centre recrossed the Meuse on August 26th and retreated in line with the Fifth Army which aided the British at St. Quentin and Guise on August 29th. The retreat was continued with daily fighting between the covering detachments until the Seine Valley was reached.

During this period General Joffre, leaving tactical details to his subordinates, had been busy removing inept generals, constituting new armies (Sixth and Seventh), and preparing railway transport for a concentration under General Maunoury against the German right flank, north of Paris. He had also fixed the point at which the retreat of his centre should be stayed. On September 6th Maunoury's flanking movement from the Ourcq with the Sixth Army arrested the German advance. For General von Kluck **His splendid counter-stroke** withdrew troops from the front to strengthen his right, and thus enabled the British on September 9th to combine with Maunoury's attack on the German right wing. On September 10th D'Espérey's Fifth, reinforced by Foch's Seventh Army, threw back the German centre, while the armies of De Cary and Sarrail attacked the German left west of the Argonne. The advance was methodically conducted.

Each army gained ground step by step, opening the road to its neighbour, and at the same time, supported by it, taking in flank the adversary which the day before it had attacked in front. The efforts of one coincided closely with those of the other, a perfect unity of intention and method animating the supreme command.

General Joffre thus retorted with a fine counter-stroke, meeting penetration

SCOTLAND AND AUSTRALIA CAPTURE FRANCE.

The Australians in the contingent were loaded with flowers, and the Scotsmen (in circle) delighted the French crowd by swinging along to the skirl of their pipes.

RUSSIANS IN FRANCE.
Falling-in on the quayside at Marseilles for the grand parade through the town.

REAL WARRIORS, NOT CREATURES OF FOND IMAGINATION.
A contingent of Russian troops landed at Marseilles on April 20th, 1916, and had the cordial welcome due from France to her faithful ally. Immediately after debarkation Senegalese soldiers distributed rifles to them.

with envelopment *secundum artem*. The French called this a seven days' battle.

The Germans, in fear of envelopment on both flanks, retreated and entrenched between the Oise and the Meuse. The Allies in pursuit recrossed the Rivers Marne and Aisne. On September 12th Maunoury's Sixth Army on the Oise was reinforced to meet an extension of the German right wing, while the British and the armies of D'Espérey, Foch, De Cary, and Sarrail for some weeks were engaged in testing the strength of the German defences from the Oise to the Meuse and thence eastward to the Moselle. Our share of this enterprise is known as the Battle of the Aisne, in which our six divisions lost 561 officers and 12,980 men.

The salient feature of these long-drawn-out battles is the utilisation of strategic reserves—that is, forces which
Utilisation of strategic reserves were in course of training or concentration when the battle began. There is time also to close down secondary operations in other theatres and bring the troops by rail or motor-lorries to the principal scene of action. Thus the strength of the belligerents is constantly changing, apart from losses in battle. The victory of to-day may be followed by defeat to-morrow through the arrival of reinforcements to the enemy. But the manipulation of these vast forces makes prodigious demands upon the energy of the Staff. General Joffre's bold bid to envelop his enemy led to an entirely fresh distribution of troops during the retreat to the Seine and the Battle of the Marne.

Part of his original centre went to strengthen his right wing; a new army restored the balance in the centre; he prolonged his original left by creating the army of Maunoury to operate north of Paris.

Yet the so-called Battle of the Marne was inconclusive. The enemy evaded the toils in September just as General Joffre had done in August. The colossal responsibility involved in the care of a vast army had not yet become so familiar a burden that any commander was disposed to add to it by accepting the onus of a fight to a finish. General Joffre would not accept a decisive battle astride the Meuse, nor would the Kaiser stake the fortunes of his army between the Aisne and the Marne. The latter resorted to the tactics which the Russians had exploited in Manchuria, and so brought the Allies up against modern earthworks. Between the Oise and the Upper Meuse began the kind of siege tactics of which we shall have more to say presently.

At this period, however, both sides played the legitimate game in one respect ; they resorted to passive defence in order to economise numbers and so retain their mobility in other quarters. The Germans moved troops to their outer flank and began to form a new front facing westward, and continually extending this new front they at length reached the coast of the North Sea.

Both sides resort to passive defence The French followed suit and brought into play forces that had hitherto been employed in the defence of Antwerp.

The Belgian army quitted Antwerp on October 9th, 1914, and took up a position behind the Yser, and upon their right in front of Ypres stood the British army from the Aisne, reinforced by the 7th Division from Ostend and presently to be joined by other divisions from India. But the Belgians were strengthened by the formation of a French army under General d'Urbal, consisting of about six corps and five cavalry divisions, and on the right (south) of the British army stood the two new French armies—all under General Foch, whose headquarters were at Doullens. One of these armies had been formed on September 17th when General Joffre, after reinforcing Maunoury's army with one corps, ordered " a mass to be constituted on the left wing of our disposition capable of coping with the outflanking movement of the enemy." This French army was given the task of " acting against the German right wing in order to disengage its neighbour, while preserving a flanking direction in its march in

operate in front of St. Omer, with its right on Lille and its left on Cassel, to contend against eight German cavalry divisions with very strong infantry supports, until the British army arrived. By the middle of October both belligerents rested their outer flanks on the sea, and in this position they remained.

The angular front thus created had its apex at Noyon on the Oise. From the North Sea at Nieuport to Noyon is one hundred and ten miles as the crow flies ; the same distance separates Noyon from Verdun ; and it is perhaps fifty miles from Verdun to Nancy. A general assault upon the whole of this front was manifestly impossible, for with twelve battalions of infantry to the mile (only five men per yard) two hundred and sixty-seven divisions would be engaged, or a total of five million combatants a side. The tactical plans, therefore, never went further than to organise an attack upon a section of the front and to

OBSERVATION-POSTS TO DETECT OBSERVERS.
It was practically impossible for enemy aircraft to approach the Allies' lines unobserved. Ceaseless watch was kept for them through powerful telescopes in close touch with the air scouts and anti-aircraft guns.

relation to any fresh units that the enemy might put into line " ; and in fact, from September 21st to September 26th General Castelnau was engaged in a fierce struggle with the Prince of Bavaria's Sixth German Army between the Oise and the Somme, on the line Lassigny-Roye-Peronne, both armies having been transferred from the Lorraine region

Early in October the enemy gained the plateau of Thiepval, south-west of Bapaume, and thence slipped forces farther and farther north, so that General Joffre had to create a fresh army under General Maud'huy to

limit this venture to a certain proportion of the available forces. Thus the Germans devoted fifteen corps to the attack of the northern section between the River Lys and the sea, and this three weeks' encounter is generally known as the Battle of Flanders. On this front of thirty miles thirty German divisions were arrayed, and from October 22nd to November 15th the Duke of Würtemberg and the Prince of Bavaria strove to break through the defences of the Allies. They took Dixmude and then concentrated against Ypres ; they gained some ground at frightful cost ; then they abandoned the enterprise.

Similar battles punctuated the continuous strife along many miles of front for a year and a half, but the tactics employed were such as naturally grow out of a stationary warfare. The original armies trained and equipped for fighting **The immortal 7th Division** in the open had practically vanished within six months. The fate of our 1st Brigade, which mobilised 4,500 strong and on November 12th, 1914, after its fight with the Prussian Guard was reduced to something like the skeleton of its original strength, was not much more lamentable than that of other brigades—less so, indeed, than that of the 7th Division, which, in the course of one month's campaigning in Belgium, endured the most devastating losses of officers and men. Of course a similar story could be told of the original French and German armies.

It is naturally more difficult to assess the enemy losses than those of the Allies; but we know they cannot have been less and were most likely vastly greater. In the war of masses the decisive battle had nevertheless proved a chimera, and the winter of 1914-15 saw a renewal of the struggle under other conditions with fresh troops equipped for siege tactics.

It is remarkable that neither of the belligerents in the west attempted to define, at least for the benefit of the public, its conception of the military situation between the North Sea and Switzerland. The tactics were those of siege warfare. But who were the besiegers, and which the besieged garrison? Formerly it was deemed an essential condition of siege operations that the garrison, like General Townshend's division at Kut, should be isolated and dependent on a relieving force, and that in default of its arrival the attackers, whose numerical strength does not diminish at the same rate, must prevail. In these circumstances we expect the sorties of the garrison to become weaker and weaker with the flux of time, while the attackers are at liberty to bring up heavier guns and larger bodies of infantry. But who in the west would have admitted being the worse off in this respect? *Prima facie*, the Germans, having possessed themselves of a large portion of Belgium and France in 1914, were defending their ill-gotten gains. But, then, why did they attack at Verdun in 1916? By parity of reasoning the Allies should have attacked in order to recover

FRUITS OF VICTORY.
German aeroplane and guns which were exhibited at the Invalides to crowds of interested Parisians.

the stolen property, but on the whole they acted defensively.

These mysteries will, perhaps, be unravelled by and by, and meanwhile we may note that both sides had their communications open, so there could be no question of "investment," and that neither side possessed the force to justify an "active attack." We may, therefore, describe the operations generally as those of "masking" a fortress—that is to say, keeping the enemy under close observation and entrenching troops in positions which must be attacked by the enemy if he seeks to advance in any direction. These tactics are governed by two salient facts—the troops are stationary and time is no factor in the problem from which it follows that the leisurely art of the engineer can supplement the work of infantry and artillery.

But the roles of all arms undergo some modification; the infantry no longer march, and the artillery therefore bring forward the heavy guns which cannot accompany a mobile force; the engineers take to sapping and mining; the cavalry act dismounted. The expenditure of ammunition ceases to preoccupy the higher commanders, since light railways can be laid down in rear of the batteries and arsenals can be established in the vicinity of the troops. Experiments of all kinds with new weapons are feasible; the enemy's methods can be copied or neutralised; and above all a type of soldier can be utilised in siege warfare that would otherwise be unserviceable. Long-forgotten devices are resuscitated, like sharpshooting and grenade throwing; the catapult of the Greeks and Romans, the ancient "coehorn," the hand-mortar, and the armour of the Crusaders are adapted to modern requirements; and but for such inventions as steel and high-explosive

TROPHIES FOR NAPOLEON'S TOMB.
Enemy rifles and trench-mortars taken during the French advance in Champagne in September, 1915. Each piece was labelled with particulars of its capture.

we might find in the tactics of the seventeenth century an exact parallel to those of the twentieth.

Throughout the British front of ninety miles and the French front of three hundred miles a constant watch, day and night, was maintained by about one-fourth of the troops while the remainder rested in billets; the line of resistance was strengthened in every way, while bomb-proof shelter was constructed with obstacles of wire and underground approaches. An officer's kit now includes a periscope and wire-cutters, electric torch and wading boots. The men are provided with "smoke and tube" helmets in readiness for a gas attack. Knapsack-sprayers precede troops who enter poison-infected trenches. The field telephone gives warning of the passage of Zeppelins.

Periodical local assaults

On the principle that "the offensive is the soul of defence," local assaults were delivered periodically. The area affected by a sortie of this kind is extremely circumscribed, but the arrangements are perfected to the last detail. Elaborate orders are issued which prescribe the exact position and function of even the smallest fractions of the attacking force. The enemy's defences have been minutely surveyed

UNIQUE TYPE OF MACHINE-GUN.
Large calibre machine-gun in possession of the Germans at Lille. The weapon was fitted with a "revolver" mechanism, and was said to have been of French design.

by aircraft and officers' patrols; his trenches are known by letters or numbers; and in many respects the affair may be likened to the forcible entry of the house of an opposite neighbour in broad daylight after artillery has broken down whatever contraptions may have been set up to prevent trespass.

Perhaps a division will undertake an enterprise of this nature with its field engineers and one-half of its infantry while the other half holds three miles of front. The attacking force would form two distinct columns, each of two battalions and two sections of engineers, and retain two battalions in reserve. Each battalion would also keep a company in reserve. From the enemy point of view each "column" would appear as a line of six companies on a front of two hundred or two hundred and fifty yards with about seven men to the yard. Each company has its four platoons side by side; each platoon has its four sections one behind the other, with parties of engineers interspersed. The distance to advance may be three hundred or four hundred yards; and as each man wears his heavy pack and carries three hundred rounds, his entrenching implement and sand-bag, and perhaps an extra pick

or shovel, the pace of the "charge" is not that which the artist's fancy depicts; and certainly the trench garrisons do not usually take part in the attack as so many people believe. There is an instinctive dislike of quitting cover on the part of riflemen defending trenches, and therefore assaults need to be carried out by fresh troops who have not recently been under fire, and who pass over the trenches by light bridges or gangways carried by the leading men. The enemy's trenches are often captured without a shot being fired by the assaulting troops, and without any use of the bayonet. The real difficulty is to hold the trenches when gained.

Sometimes the intruders will be summarily ejected by shells; sometimes the enemy's infantry which had retired momentarily into the support trenches and bomb-proof shelters will emerge armed with hand-grenades; or a counter-attack may be delivered by the enemy's local reserves while the attackers' supports are held back by "curtain fire"; and in all cases the penalty of breaking through a line of defence is that a salient is produced which is susceptible to enfilade fire.

But the lust of combat is easily aroused, and when 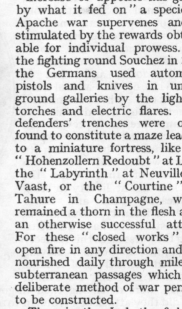 "increase of appetite has grown by what it fed on" a species of Apache war supervenes and is stimulated by the rewards obtainable for individual prowess. In the fighting round Souchez in 1915 the Germans used automatic pistols and knives in underground galleries by the light of torches and electric flares. The defenders' trenches were often found to constitute a maze leading to a miniature fortress, like the "Hohenzollern Redoubt" at Loos, the "Labyrinth" at Neuville St. Vaast, or the "Courtine" at Tahure in Champagne, which remained a thorn in the flesh after an otherwise successful attack. For these "closed works" can open fire in any direction and are nourished daily through miles of subterranean passages which the deliberate method of war permits to be constructed.

There in the dark the fighting nearly always begins with the throwing of hand-grenades, which fill the trench or the gallery with their fumes and noise, and ends in desperate hand-to-hand encounters. Yet there may be quite another mode of fighting going on beside it. "A bombardment preceded the order to advance across a plain in skirmishing formation. Within an hour the objective is reached, three lines of German trenches are captured and many prisoners. Then a rest is taken and a further advance is ordered, again in skirmishing order over perfectly open ground, to within two hundred yards of a machine-gun, which compels the attackers to lie down and there remain from 11.30 in the morning until seven o'clock at night, when a retirement is effected under cover of darkness." In the Souchez region, **A species of Apache war** where General d'Urbal's Tenth French Army operated in July, 1915, on the right of the British First Army, the Germans had trench block-houses with armoured cupolas, armoured dug-outs, and batteries of machine-guns protected by regular works. They had dug to an almost incredible depth—in some sections fifty or sixty feet below the surface—and the Labyrinth included a system of tunnelled underground ways and communication "bowels," as the French call them.

British bomber wearing a carrier full of hand-grenades in the trenches at Salonika. (*Official photograph. Crown copyright reserved.*)

French soldiers in the trenches before Verdun throwing hand-grenades across the neutral zone to the enemy position.

Vitriolic warfare on the Isonzo front. Hungarian soldiers using a mechanical spray which projected acid into the Italian trenches.

Austrian soldiers throwing grenades into the Italian lines. Some of these missiles were made with bully-beef tins filled with explosives.

WEAPONS OF SIEGE WAR: GRENADES AND ACID ON THREE FRONTS.

Defences of this nature, which cannot be stormed by infantry nor destroyed by artillery, must be attacked by military mines; so the British added to their engineering resources bodies of men accustomed to work underground, forming them into tunnelling companies, with the result that reports from General Headquarters in June, 1916, often contained such references as : " Mining activity near Beaumont, Havel, and Fricourt, both sides blowing camouflets." A camouflet is a sap for a mine which is to blow in a counter-mine. What were originally fire-trenches became siege parallels, and a subterranean warfare was waged which was quite without precedent.

Attack by military mines As we have already shown, in a siege the " front of attack " is restricted, and the besiegers are cheered by the knowledge that an enemy's resources both in personnel and matériel are constantly failing; his counter-mines, like his reply to bombardments, cause a diminution of his explosives, whereas the besiegers with their communications open are able to renew their stores of all kinds. But in France in 1915-16 no such conditions were present, both belligerents being equally free to draw upon their arsenals in the home territory, and it is therefore difficult to see what object was intended by either of them. We are again reminded of the wisdom of Clausewitz, who said, " A defensive without any positive principle is a contradiction in strategy as well as in tactics." From the sea to the Somme the belligerents won or lost ground by the square yard at a cost which was indicated by the Roll of Honour issued daily in London. History only will tell us—for naturally generals are silent during operations—the reason why on the British front in France we did not see in June, 1916, either an attack such as was being delivered round Verdun or an advance by leaps and bounds like that which was proceeding on the borders of Galicia, where the Austrian Army experienced the might of a Russian counter-stroke. The motive and plan in both these operations were plain to participants in the struggle, as they were to observers at a distance.

The Verdun position is the northernmost and the strongest of the French fortresses forming a breakwater against invasion from the east. Upon Verdun was lavished all the art of the French engineer. It was a magnet that attracted the flower of the French Army in its defence, and to win it was a worthy object on the part of any enemy of France. Remembering the penchant of the German Staff for envelopment, it was obvious that the distribution of force astride the Meuse from Fort Vaux in the east to the Avocourt Wood in the west portended an attempt to crush both flanks; and it is not likely that the strategic importance of the French left flank escaped notice, for here are the roads and railways leading to Paris and the heart of France, the seizure of which would effect what was intended at the outset in August, 1914. The Verdun position, which on June 30th, 1916, was substantially intact after one hundred and thirty-two days of assault, had become the pivot of the war in the west. The fighting embodied all that had been learnt of modern tactics during the war. In one section there was wood fighting; in another the attack and defence of villages was exhibited; here the extended formations of open country were in vogue, there we saw columns in close order employed for the storming of forts. The casualties on both sides were prodigious.

Unfortunately, little was heard of the tactical encounters of the Austrians and Russians south of the Pripet, but the reported capture by the Russians of 121,720 prisoners between June 5th and June 14th, 1916, and the length of their marches showed that during this period the Austrians made no serious stand. The contrast between the operations east of the line Berlin-Trieste and those west of it in 1914-16 must always **Contrasts between** strike the student of the Great War, **East and West** and it will be a point of military interest to determine whether armament alone, or whether generalship and terrain, played the principal part in producing this phenomenon.

At Verdun, each division engaged had its special objective and unceasingly strove to attain it in co-operation with its neighbours, so that on each sector a distinct battle raged, and it was known that on the aggregate of successes and failures the fate of the fortress depended.

In this situation the French Army was gaining fresh experience of defensive war, and its leaders could thereby estimate the strength required to attack in turn.

SOLDIERS OF THE GLORIOUS REPUBLIC ONE AND INDIVISIBLE.
Dramatic photograph of French veterans passing through a village behind the lines on their way to the zone of operations. Women of the village came to their doors and young children stood at the street corners to watch the men of France pass on their way to the battle-front.

CHAPTER CXXI.

BRITAIN IN WAR TIME: A BRIEF SURVEY.

By John Foster Fraser.

Although every aspect of the Great War finds itself reflected in this chronicle of the events which marked its progress in every clime, and home affairs as well as the clash of arms on the many fighting fronts have engaged the pens of our contributors, it has seemed desirable to the Editors that a chapter especially devoted to a survey of the many and various changes in the political and social life of our own country should be given. Mr. Foster Fraser, the well-known traveller and author, who as a Parliamentary journalist of wide experience, and also as a lecturer visiting all parts of Great Britain, is peculiarly qualified to deal with this phase of our history, here describes the remarkable changes which were effected in the life of Great Britain by the needs of the war. It has been well said that in one respect, at least, the Germans had succeeded in conquering us; the strength of their pre-war organisation and the ingenuity of their methods for pressing on with their hostilities had the effect of developing in Great Britain schemes of national service which had previously been essentially characteristic of German organisation and quite foreign to British institutions. In a word, " Kultur " had imposed itself upon us in making us take some leaves out of its book, the better to fight it. To what extent this transformation of Great Britain will leave a permanent mark upon the life and character of our country is matter for the future historian, but the importance of the change we have witnessed is of real concern for us to-day, and hence this chapter.

I F we would survey, even cursorily, the strange and moving spectacle of Britain transforming herself under pressure of the Great War, we must go back to the frontal blow dealt by Germany at Belgium, for that was the day when every Briton knew the hour had sounded—the dread hour in the coming of which so few had believed. That crime against Belgium consolidated the British Empire, and no people ever went into war so single-minded as did Great Britain in answer to Germany's deliberate defiance of the law of nations.

It was then that the great transformation began. Though the dominant party in Parliament insisted on putting the Home Rule Bill on the statute book—the assent of the King in the House of Lords being received with loud Nationalist cheers—it was done on the understanding that no movement should be made towards its realisation till after the war. All the old political controversies were dropped and, to an extent, forgotten. The official Opposition ceased criticism of the Government and granted it unquestioned support. Hundreds of millions of money were speedily voted for the prosecution of the war. Emergency

legislation, rendered necessary as the consequence of the war, was passed at an unprecedented rate through Parliament, bringing about changes which the majority of politicians did not fully realise at the time, imposing obligations, curtailing liberty, but all conceded at the wish of the administration. The Defence of the Realm Act practically annulled the rights of the individual citizen. The freedom of the Press was fettered, rather crudely and often without wisdom, for it was hindered from stimulating the patriotism of the people by keeping them informed of what was actually happening on the high seas and in the mighty struggles which our soldiers, hurried to France, had to face before the superior forces of the Kaiser's Army.

A wave of enthusiasm swept over the land. Nightly, streets were crowded with cheering crowds eager to learn the progress of our arms. Lord Kitchener joined the Cabinet as Minister for War, not as a politician but as a soldier. We wanted more soldiers. In a fortnight 50,000 volunteers were enrolled, and in a little over a month the number was well over 100,000. Succeeding, however, the terrible push-back the British Army had at Mons, the cheerfulness of the nation waned; but the nation itself strengthened

REGIMENTAL MASCOT ON A RECRUITING MARCH.
This bulldog mascot of the 2/6th West Riding Regiment completed a recruiting march of three hundred miles, heading the column throughout the whole distance.

OFF TO THE FLEET.
Journalists aboard a destroyer approaching the Grand Fleet. (*Official photograph issued by the Press Bureau.*)

in stubborn determination. The magic of Lord Kitchener's personality was used to raise a new force, which went by the name of Kitchener's Army. A great recruiting campaign, engineered in common by the Liberal, Unionist, and Labour parties, was conducted in every county. The response of Britain's young manhood was spontaneous and magnificent, and soon more than a million men were in khaki and eagerly undergoing training as a preliminary to being sent on active service. The Territorial regiments in the field proved as worthy of their race as the regular Army. Each new story of heroism that came home was like a tocsin quickening the blood of Britons. Thousands more of our lads jumped to the Colours.

There were men, however, who began to see that the stream of voluntary recruits was losing its impetus. The best of valorous young Britons had already joined the Army. Many men, married and with heavy professional and commercial responsibilities, sacrificed their careers, sought commissions in Kitchener's Army, or were content to serve as privates. The slouching, lounging sons of well-to-do people, the "nuts" of the fashionable seaside resorts, whose main ambition had been to lower their golf handicap, affected and rather useless youths whose chatter was

Sacrifices by professional men

irritating, proved that below their superciliousness was real British grit. The "nut" as a feature in English social life, completely disappeared. The promenades at watering-places and the golf-links knew him no more He joined the Army, became keen, and gave a worthy account of himself in battle.

The working classes of Britain came forward bravely. The wealthy, the leisured, the county classes answered the call not less, but even more, quickly. The British aristocracy gave its sons. They played the great game well. There was not one great family which had not cause to mourn the loss of a relative. Peerages were threatened with extinction because the heirs were killed. Fifty were slain. For long years there had been a widening social gulf between various classes. The spread of democracy did not soften the distinctions, but accentuated them. Much recent legislation had been directed toward despoiling the "upper circles" of their privileges. The aristocracy had been fighting a rearguard action for a generation in the field of politics, and much of their old authority was sapped. But the war put an end to this class antagonism. The inherent spirit of justice in the British composition aroused genuine appreciation of what others were doing. Silently, almost as if by the working

Class antagonism disappears

NAVAL OBSERVATION BALLOON OVER A SHIP AT SEA.
Peaceful scene which met the eyes of the party of journalists invited to inspect the Grand Fleet shortly before the Battle off Jutland on the last day of May, 1916. (*Official photograph issued by the Press Bureau.*)

of a miracle, captious criticism of class by class ceased. Very little of the old social distrust remained. A gentler, kindlier feeling began to show itself throughout all sections of the population, to be revealed later on in a myriad ways.

Still there was a growing consciousness that the voluntary system of recruiting would not produce all the fighting men needed, first to make good the wastage of war, and then to produce enough soldiers so that a phalanx could be hurled against the foe. The Germans drove our men south to near Paris, and then our men, rallying, drove the Germans north of the Marne and farther. The two armies seemed to get in a locked grip. Though there were turns in fortune in the mighty struggle in the trenches, the tide of battle on the British-German front seemed to cease

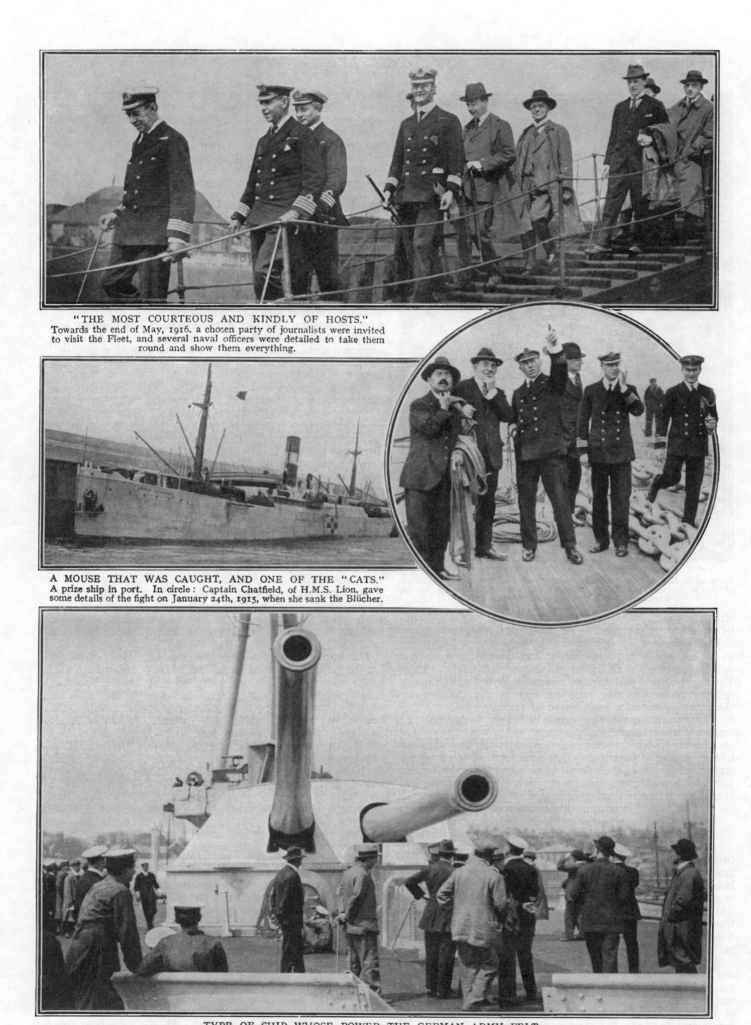

"THE MOST COURTEOUS AND KINDLY OF HOSTS."
Towards the end of May, 1916, a chosen party of journalists were invited to visit the Fleet, and several naval officers were detailed to take them round and show them everything.

A MOUSE THAT WAS CAUGHT, AND ONE OF THE "CATS."
A prize ship in port. In circle: Captain Chatfield, of H.M.S. Lion, gave some details of the fight on January 24th, 1915, when she sank the Blücher.

TYPE OF SHIP WHOSE POWER THE GERMAN ARMY FELT.
Monitors proved very interesting. Three ships of this type, the Severn, Humber, and Mersey, shelled the German right flank in the Belgian coast battles in October, 1914. (*Official photographs issued by the Press Bureau.*)

QUALIFIED TO GIVE AN OPINION.
Party of Indian officers on leave visiting the Natural History Museum at South Kensington. They appeared particularly interested in the elephants' heads that adorned the staircase.

either to ebb or flow. So the agitation that soldiers should be obtained by the exercise of conscription began to grow.

The news that our operations in the war were hampered by a shortage of big guns, rifles, and munitions caused a painful surprise. Effective measures had to be taken. The Government had already assumed control of the many railway systems in the kingdom and placed them under the management of a joint board of railway officials. The first consideration was the transit of troops, the second the conveyance of munitions, the third the regular supply of commodities necessary for commerce and the maintenance of the civilian population. The consideration of passenger traffic came last. The result was some disorganisation, but soon an adequate though restricted train service was arranged. The situation of our railways was aggravated by hundreds of thousands of railway workers joining the Colours; indeed, so many went that a restraining hand had to be placed upon them, or there would have been a breakdown. As it was, the use of restaurant cars was gradually abolished. Women were employed to act as booking-clerks, ticket examiners and collectors, cleaners of engines and carriages, and in many places even as porters. This change was the first indication Britain got of the part that women were about to play in the war—a change which the nation soon came to realise would have a permanent effect on industrial life.

Women fill the gaps

When the war broke out there was apprehension that our overseas trade would be crippled and, as a consequence, great masses of our artisans would be thrown out of employment, and that we would have to face a vast amount of distress. This expectation had the effect of sending many artisans into the Army, not only single men but,

what seemed strange, a greater number of married men. But suddenly it was realised that attention to our overseas trade was of secondary importance. What was of prime importance was the reorganisation of our industries to prosecute the war. Great engineering firms were invited to adapt themselves to the manufacture of war material. They did. Mr. Lloyd George laid aside his robes as Chancellor of the Exchequer and became Minister of Munitions. All over the country Munitions Committees were established with lesser bodies in sub-areas, and these, supplied with information from the War Office about military requirements, gave out orders to the great establishments, and were able to show lesser firms the suitable war work they could do. So, before long, engineering shops throughout the land, construction departments of railroads, huge electrical establishments, motor works and bicycle works, factories of agricultural machinery, were all busy turning out war material. The clothing and equipment of the New Army, the feeding of it, the making of waggons, ambulances, and a hundred and one "side lines," all filled a place in the mighty, complicated machine of war.

Engineers on war service

Instead of facing distress the industrial districts of Great Britain became frenzied with energy. The cry was "Work, work, work! Turn out shells! The man in the munition factory is doing his part in the war as well as the lad in the trenches!" The response was splendid. Hundreds of thousands of our skilled artisans worked long hours, seven days in the week, until so many collapsed from nervous breakdown that it had to be arranged that the men should have a Saturday afternoon and a full Sunday off every three weeks. Here and there, as was inevitable, there were wastrels who soon got tired, began drinking, and not only failed to do their own work but were often the cause of holding up other men whose labour depended upon the work of those "on the spree." It was a black spot on our reputation. The evil, however, was represented as being worse than it actually was, for some of our statesmen and most of our newspapers made a great commotion about the sluggishness of these sots, who were, after all, but a mere handful compared with the millions of men who were steadily and strenuously doing their duty.

The strong arm of a new law was exercised. Workers had to do their allotted task, and if they absented themselves without cause they were brought before Munition Courts and severely dealt with. To prevent men dodging work by leaving one firm and having an interval of drinking before they sought another job—scarcity of labour made jobs easily obtainable—they had to be in possession of a certificate from their late employer before they could be engaged by another employer. Some protests were made that the working classes were being made serfs. It was feared that some employers would deliberately refuse a certificate in order to retain a man and prevent him from securing a better post and improving his position. There was the possibility; but in practice the thing did not happen, because there was always a court to which an aggrieved workman might apply.

But that something in the nature of martial law had been established was a great transformation in the industrial life of Britain, where freedom of the individual had been almost a religion. Other changes were made, startling in their nature, amounting almost to revolution, which would have plunged the whole country into wildest agitation if it had not been that somewhere at the back of the public mind was the common-sense conviction that all predilections, all principles, all prejudices, must give way before the supreme needs of the nation. Personal liberty disappeared. Dissemination of gossip likely to cause alarm became a crime. Secret trial was established. Arrest and imprisonment without any trial at all, merely on the instruction of the Home Secretary, was

Framework of Zeppelin shot down in the Vardar Marshes, near Salonika.

After the fall of Erzerum : Grand Duke Nicholas reviews the ser

ranks of Caucasian and Siberian troops from his field automobile.

Austrian soldiers charging down on an Italian patrol.

Italian gun about to fire on Austrian position across an Alpine valley.

permitted. Newspapers were muzzled. The time came when even Parliament itself sat in secret session, and it was high misdemeanour to give currency to what took place during the debates.

The Government, having taken control of the railroads, proceeded to commandeer much of the shipping. Hundreds of works became "controlled establishments" under the Ministry of Munitions, increasing until ultimately there were well over a thousand. In a word, the Government was laying a grip on the industries and liberties of Great Britain. Often there was resentment, but it was the outcome of suspicion rather than objection on principle.

The trade union bodies, which through prolonged years of struggle had built up protective associations, were called upon to make huge sacrifices. Their federated members were incapable of coping with all the work which the necessities of the war demanded. It was known that with the perfection of machinery there were many operations, hitherto done by skilled workers, which under comparatively slight tuition could be done by an unskilled worker, and even by a woman or girl. The trade unions were asked to relax their rules, which, in many cases forbade their members working alongside non-union hands. They hesitated. Regarding employers as their natural enemies, they had an idea that if they conceded their hard-won principles, if they allowed a return to the old condition of free and unfederated labour, a time would come when employers would continue to employ non-union hands and, in

Pledge to the Trade Unions the competition of post-war days, smash the unions and so force down wages. A solemn Parliamentary promise was, however, given that if they made the concession the power and the authority of the trade unions should be recognised after the war. On that they gave way. Then one of the most wonderful transformations took place— the dilution of skilled labour. Crowds of men and women, following other occupations, forsook those and went to work in munition factories. Peers, titled ladies, clergymen, ministers of all denominations, stockbrokers and lawyers, as well as people of the artisan class, turned to war work. No doubt many young fellows started war work in the belief that, so engaged, they would escape being called upon to serve in the Army, for the need of compulsion to secure a big enough Army was beginning to be recognised. At great modern universities munition classes were started. Lads at public schools devoted their spare time to the turning of shells. Young women with private incomes sought employment. Most of these amateurs were of better social standing than the regular workers, and it was remarked that with their superior intelligence and greater enthusiasm for their new employment many of them were as capable within six weeks of doing unskilled or semi-skilled work as men who had spent years at the task. Considerable bodies of professional men, following their ordinary avocations, were unable to give their whole time. But multitudes of them gave certain evenings of the week, or their week ends, to the production of war material.

CHAMPION GOLF ON BEHALF OF THE WOUNDED.

A golf match between Edward Ray (ex-champion), J. P. Batley (International), James G. Sherlock, (winner of the World Tournament), and F. G. Steele was played at Rochford in May, 1916, on behalf of three Red Cross hospitals at Southend. The proceeds were nearly £100. An auction for clubs realised £35, one presented by J. B. Batley, and signed by him, realising £10. This photograph shows the four players standing in the doorway.

The adaptability of the women was a revelation. The withdrawal of so many men for the Army had, of course, left a vast number of trades and occupations short-handed. I have already referred to women's services on the railroads. But in the munition factories, too, women displayed keenness and alacrity not only in doing delicate work, such as the adjustment of electrical appliances, but in the heavier work of shell-making. It became an ordinary thing for a woman to make munitions or to take the place of a man who was serving his country. So women were drafted into banks as clerks; they took to the driving of motor-cars; they became omnibus and tramcar conductors; they went into many businesses which formerly had been closed to them. They went on to farms as labourers. Thousands upon thousands took to nursing and charitable work generally. Awkward, slow, and unimaginative though the majority of the British people are supposed to be, there was a noble answer to the call.

The war found us unprepared and unorganised. The first excitement produced chaos, but out of the confusion **Aid to our Allies** there was evolved a machine of productiveness unexampled in British history. We started in the fight severely handicapped. The doggedness of our race won through. Being the richest of the Allies, we had to find hundreds of millions to finance France, Russia, Belgium and Serbia. Then we proceeded to supply them with boots and clothing. Not only did we make up our own shortage of munitions; we were able to have a surplus and to send quantities to our friends.

All this was being done at a heavy cost. With almost reckless prodigality the Government poured forth a stream of gold. The war was costing Great Britain £5,000,000 a day. The national credit was staked within the first year to something like £20,000,000,000. Government contractors, especially at the opening of hostilities,

ELEPHANTS AT THE PLOUGH.
In Surrey there was such a shortage of horses due to military requirements that farmers took to using elephants instead.

IN UNFAMILIAR SURROUNDINGS.
Camels also were requisitioned for farm work, and teams of these creatures of the desert drew furrows across English fields.

themselves better ; they bought better furniture. Nor did they disregard luxuries. Fur-coat shops did well ; piano dealers never did better ; there was something of a boom in jewellery. While theatres generally patronised by the wealthier and middle classes were adversely affected, the " popular " houses which produce melodrama, especially in the great industrial areas, were crowded. Music-halls were packed twice a night, and cinema shows did thriving business. And to all charitable objects associated with the war the working classes were constant givers. Britain saw very little of the privation amongst the civilian population which is supposed to stalk alongside war. But there were always people who saw the shadow behind the glare. What,

got extravagant prices. The work-people began to clamour that they should " have their bit," and they got it. The cost of living began to increase, and at every rise there was a demand for more wages to meet the higher price of provisions. The middle, salaried, and professional classes were hit hard by the war ; those who were dependent on income from investments were harshly pinched not only by a fall of revenue, for the concern in which they were interested might have nothing to do with the war, but by the heavier taxation that accompanied reduction of incomes.

The main industries of the country, however, blazed with prosperity. Immense fortunes were made. The working classes, as a whole, were never better off. Seeing a strained time ahead, the authorities started a national savings campaign. So far as those for whom it was mainly intended were concerned, it was futile. Appeals were issued for decreased consumption. In fact, our national consumption was never greater. Wages increased abnormally, especially in industries that supplied necessities, and there was a drift of labour from the less well paid trades and occupations. Domestic servants found they could make more money elsewhere ; so they discarded the housemaid's apron and donned the uniform of the ticket-collector. Many sensible artisans, knowing that the financial sunshine would not always be so radiant, put some of their earnings in the bank for the cloudy days. But the mass of people made no provision whatever. Receiving wages two, three, and four times as great as formerly, they proceeded to have a good time, justifying themselves with the argument that in the past they had had plenty of bad times and that the future could look after itself. So they lived well ; they clothed

War-time prodigality

they asked, would be the position of the industrial classes when war work ceased and the population tried to readjust itself to normal conditions ? And what would happen when the abnormal wages disappeared and maybe, with a slump in trade, there was very little wages at all ?

Other important changes swiftly progressed. Though the ostensible reason was to stop drunkenness amongst munition workers, while the real reason was to prevent people wasting their money, restrictions were imposed on opportunities to consume alcohol. They began with a gentle limitation of the hours ; but as the public acquiesced in this without demur, the restrictions soon became severe. Power was granted to local authorities to close public-houses altogether in the neighbourhood of munition works. Instead of public-houses being open from early morning till ten or eleven o'clock at night in the provinces, and half-past twelve in London, the rule was applied that spirituous refreshment could be obtained only during two and a half hours at midday and three hours in the earlier part of the evening. Friendly treating was prohibited. The carrying away of small quantities was not allowed, for this would undoubtedly have been the plan adopted by those who had a weakness towards drink. Large quantities for home consumption had to be paid for at the time of purchase. In munition areas no spirits for home use could be purchased between Friday midday and Monday midday. It might have been expected that interference with the working man's right to enjoy himself would have led to trouble. There were individual and unorganised protests, complaints that people were being treated as children, and that the restrictions implied that Britain had been sottish, which was not true. But the murmuring was really infinitesimal. Britain accepted the change, and will never go back to the old state of things.

Change was piled on change. There was the exploitation of necessities. Merchants of many kinds held up commodities beyond need in order to extort higher

Profiteers exploit the situation prices. This was markedly so at the start of the war, when the public, somewhat alarmed, played into the hands of these people by wanting to buy superabundant food, and were disposed to give famine prices before there was even a vestige of famine. The Government, through the Board of Trade, secretly bought up most of the available sugar in the world, and by letting it drain into the market as occasion required, did much to steady the price to the consumer. In other articles of food, shopkeepers, under the plea that wholesale prices had leapt up, enhanced charges for old stock, to the gathering discontent of the people. Pleas were advanced in Parliament that the Government should regulate prices. This the Government did not see its way to do ; but at repeated intervals it issued statements of what ought to be, all things considered, the legitimate retail price. Thus the whole country knew what was the proper charge, and the moral effect on tradesmen who might have been disposed to squeeze an extra profit out of the customer was undoubted.

Perhaps it would have been well if the Government had acted more boldly in putting a restraining hand on imports. But by gradual action alarm was stilled and the public got used to changed conditions which, if imposed suddenly, would probably have caused an outcry. As far as was feasible supplies were regulated, and the Board of Trade exercised an increasing authority in regulating the supplies of necessaries which were sent into England.

With war charges rising colossally, the Government not only mortgaged the future but proceeded to impose heavy taxation. Every available source of income was squeezed for the benefit of the Exchequer. Many of the ordinary taxes were doubled and trebled. It being considered unfair that people should grow inordinately wealthy

EXAMPLE OF THE WAR-TIME WORK OF BRITISH WOMANHOOD.
Female manual labour at Coventry gasworks—women loading coke into barrows. To cope with the shortage of navvies at the municipal gasworks fifty women were engaged in filling barrows with coke or breeze, and wheeling them along planks to trucks.

FROM ANZAC TO WESTMINSTER.
General Sir William and Lady Birdwood arriving at Westminster Abbey on the occasion of the Anzac Day celebration, April 25th, 1916.

in time of war—especially as there were so many men offering everything, even to the sacrifice of their lives, for their country—a great innovation was introduced in the shape of special taxation of profits. In regard to " controlled establishments," the arrangement was that the companies which managed them should have their profits fixed on an average of the previous three years, with the addition of something like six per cent. on the annual revenue which it was assumed would probably have been the normal expansion in time of peace. But in the case of non-controlled establishments, all businesses, outside the professional classes, whether the increase was due to the war or quite independent from it, were compelled to yield as much as sixty-three per cent. of their surplus profits to the State. Gold coinage was withdrawn from circulation and Treasury notes substituted.

Ban on foreign luxuries To keep much of the wealth of the country at home to meet war charges, instead of allowing it to go abroad, strong endeavours were made to induce the public to buy British articles, and not goods—particularly luxuries—from foreign lands. This was not very successful. The Government moved towards prohibition by putting heavy import duties on certain luxuries, which gave rise to animated discussions in Parliament whether the Ministry was justified in time of war in abandoning the old principles of Free Trade on which our commerce had so long rested. The answer was that in time of war, apart from the maintenance of principles, every act beneficial to the nation is justifiable. Then the Government, on the same plea, began to restrict and prohibit importations. The importation of paper pulp was reduced by fully a third, so that newspapers had to be curtailed in size, stationery became scarce, and some articles of paper manufacture disappeared altogether.

But behind the argument for retaining wealth within the country was the important matter of shipping facilities. The Government had exercised its power in securing to itself an immense proportion of British ships, not only for the transporting of troops, but for conveying commissariat and performing particular functions round our coasts. Thus there was a shortage of carrying capacity. Freights rose three, four, and six fold, and this of course had a striking effect on prices at home. Shippers were compelled to charter the vessels of neutral countries, and, as there was always the danger of these falling victims to German submarines, the foreigners' charges, with big insurance imposed, were high, to say the least of it—and payment for these neutral ships meant the exportation of vast quantities of gold out of the country. The object, therefore, of restricting imports was to have vessels used as little as possible for carrying anything that had not directly to do with the war.

All things considered, though the prices of foodstuffs went up considerably, they rose to nothing like the extent expected, and were much lower than in any other belligerent country. And as **The doom of sport** wages in the main were particularly good, the Government looked round for fresh objects of taxation. Now, when the war came, there had been a sudden check to the outdoor pleasures of Englishmen. Cricket, the national pastime, disappeared as though by a wave of the hand ; the institution of county matches ceased to be. Golf-courses were deserted except for a few " old boys." Ever self-conscious, the average Briton did not like to be seen carrying a golf-bag, which indicated that he was off to enjoy himself while crowds of his friends were risking their life in France, Flanders, and elsewhere. Horse-racing became unpopular ; most of the famous " weeks " were abandoned, except at places like Newmarket, where, in the interests of horse-breeding, some meetings continued to be held. Hunting slackened because all the best huntsmen were in khaki and soldiering. Yachting, the exclusive and expensive enjoyment of the wealthy, was never spoken about. But professional football continued, although there was an outcry raised against the slackers who hung round ropes, cheering rival teams, instead of going into the Army and fighting for their country. The criticism was not quite fair, because the Saturday afternoon crowds were generally composed of artisans who had been working on munitions long hours through the week, and watching a football match for an hour and a half on Saturday afternoon was their relaxation, just as going to theatres and concerts, even Wagner concerts, at the end of a strenuous day, was the relaxation of some of their critics. Accordingly, the taxation of amusements, a novel device in Britain for raising revenue, aroused no valid objection. Whether to theatres, concerts, races, football matches, or cinema shows the public went, they were called upon to pay a tax fixed in proportion to the price of the ticket. Big extra duties were clapped on the owners of motor-cars, and everything was done to put a stop to the use of motor-cars for pleasure. Matches were taxed ; mineral waters were taxed. It became bad form to be garish or sprightly in costume. To wear old clothes was regarded as a sign of patriotism. The giving of dinner-parties was taboo. To live simply and without any extravagance was the right thing. Daylight saving was effected by advancing the clock one hour in the summer months. Of course, there were some, ostentatiously wealthy, who restrained themselves in nothing, and by their extravagant expenditure undid much of the good attempted by advice given the working classes that they should save a portion of their earnings. Nevertheless, there was a striking change in the social habits of the people.

The war struck more deeply into the conscience of the British nation than the people themselves realised. Too ready to profess the easy faith that whatever is British is right, and that neither Germany nor any other land had

General Sir William Birdwood (centre figure) with General Sir Newton Moore (on his right) proceeding to Westminster Abbey, to take part in the anniversary celebration of the Anzac attack on Gallipoli.

On April 25th, 1916, Londoners, for the first time since the outbreak of war, had the opportunity of welcoming the Anzacs who fought in Gallipoli. Several thousand Australians and New Zealanders took part in the anniversary celebration of the landing at Anzac, and an impressive service was held in Westminster Abbey. This illustration shows some of the Anzacs marching down the Strand between crowds of admiring Londoners.

ONE YEAR AFTER THE LANDING AT ANZAC: ANNIVERSARY CELEBRATION IN LONDON.

any chance of inflicting serious injury upon the Island Kingdom, the early boastfulness was soon modified into a grim understanding that the Empire was really engaged in a life-or-death struggle. Things were not going well in the conduct of the war, in the administration of things at home, and in the obtaining of recruits. There was much grumbling but no depression. Whatever happened adversely was received with glum resignation, with explanations that in the long account it would not really matter ; but while there was a natural tendency to belittle events which told against us

"Taking pleasures sadly" there was often also a natural tendency to exaggerate minor points in our favour to lofty importance. The general nonchalance of the Briton, half inbred, half affected, remained, but only as a veneer. On the surface the general life of the country seemed to be running on in its usual way. Sheeting our cities with blackness, so that enemy aircraft cruising over England would have difficulty in finding them, had some effect in keeping people indoors at night, and the better-class theatres suffered ; but another cause, particularly in the metropolis, was that so many taxi-drivers had joined the Army that the supply of vehicles had shrunk, and those remaining, being in demand, were disposed to be arrogant and extortionate. Undoubtedly there was a certain amount of gloom, but it was all external ; it did not touch the nation itself, except in homes where tragedy sat dumb when the news came that a father or a son had fallen on the field of honour.

The war burst in the middle of the summer holidays of 1914, and scattered holiday-makers stampeded for home. Popular tourist centres began to groan as they felt they were tottering toward the bankruptcy court. The recovery, however, came quickly, except along the East Coast, upon which the German cruisers had fired and which was always exposed to the devastating visits of Zeppelins. Inland health resorts and watering-places on the South and West Coasts not only survived the first shock, but within a few months were basking in the sunshine of a new prosperity. The rich were debarred from taking their annual cures abroad ; they were compelled to try British cures, and were rather surprised to find that their own country could provide them with practically all obtained at fashionable German spas, except the gaiety. The ordinary holiday-maker was shy of the East Coast and tried the South and the West. Considerable numbers of families migrated from places open to Zeppelin attack to holiday resorts elsewhere. Among the general population the old spirit of seeking distraction revived. Thus many towns dependent on tourists, which saw ruin before them, did better than in all their previous career. At times of popular holiday in 1915—

Christmas, Easter, Whitsuntide, and August Bank Holiday —the rush from the cities was greater than in pre-war times. Yet there was a more sober strain running through the pleasures of the people than formerly. This was partly evidenced in the reading habits of the people. Not so much flimsy fiction was consumed. There was a demand for books which provided information about the lives and aspirations of our Allies, and there was a constant appetite for volumes which revealed the " soul " of Germany.

The student endeavouring to appraise the real condition of Britain was constantly encountering contradictions and paradoxes. The nation had to be regarded as a whole, but while one part was making sacrifices there were spots which told of greed and callous indifference. The evening newspapers would provide their tale of the hardships and the bravery of the men in the front of the fighting " over there," and then a visit to the huge dining caravansaries of London would present the spectacle of thousands of people enjoying themselves, amid the uproar of loud talk, dishes clattering, bottles popping, and the crash of a big band. But it was wrong to draw general conclusions from these instances. The domestic trouble with servants sent crowds to restaurants for their meals. People working hard all day found relief in the glitter and noise. And troops of lads home on short leave or freshly released from hospital were brought to these places to find jollity before they returned to their work as soldiers in France or elsewhere.

Yet, amidst the medley of life, the confusions and the distrust, the heart of the British folk was beating sound. In the pursuit of kindly work social distinctions began to lapse. Those who could not fight could do many other things. A whole volume could be written about the heart of Britain during the war. The first thought was for the dependents—the wives and children and aged parents of the men on service. The Government did something, but the purses of the wealthy were opened wide, and literally millions of pounds were **Looking after the** provided, until it almost became a joke **soldiers' homes** that the wives of soldiers were " having the time of their lives," for more money was coming into the home than in the old days. Samaritan associations sprang into existence in every town and hamlet. Generosity gushed forth in something of a torrent. The War Office had military hospitals erected in favourable districts. But towns set aside parts of their infirmaries for the wounded, and in some cases built hospitals and handed them over fully equipped to the military authorities. Many wealthy people converted their residences into hospitals and bore the sole charge. Others handed their

TRIALS OF AN INSPECTOR.
Army automobile inspector endures a shower-bath while watching trials of cars to be used with the British transport in France.

beautiful country houses over to the Red Cross Societies to be used as hospitals or places of convalescence. Everywhere, doors were flung wide open to receive destitute Belgian refugees who, harried by the invading Germans, had been obliged to flee from Belgium to the protection of Britain. "Flag days" took possession of the land. There were days when everybody had to buy a miniature Russian flag and so contribute to a fund for destitute Poles ; or a Serbian flag to help the stricken Serbs, or a French flag, or a Belgian flag. There were flag days for British regiments, for hospitals, for the Red Cross, for tobacco funds to send cigarettes to the soldiers. The Prince of Wales started a fund to relieve destitution at home; speedily it amounted to more than £5,000,000, and then it was closed as adequate to all needs. There were

PRIVILEGE TO THE ATTESTED.
In response to an advertisement issued by the War Office for a thousand married men between the ages of thirty-six and forty to be employed as munition workers, such crowds turned up at the Inquiry Office, Great Scotland Yard, that the officials were quite unable to cope with each individual applicant.

WOULD-BE MUNITION WORKERS.
Another impression of the crowd of men who responded to a War Office advertisement for one thousand physically fit war workers for home service. These men, classified in Groups 42 to 46, presented themselves at Scotland Yard.

funds started to send ambulances to Russia and to France. There were funds set going to furnish hospital ships.

From London away to the most distant hamlet in the North of Scotland there were constant big theatrical displays or little sing-songs in order to raise money for some excellent purpose. If there were mean people about who failed to be responsive they must have been few, for the grand totals were represented by tens of millions. People were not only cheerful givers, they were lavishly munificent. It was a saturnalia of generosity.

As far as could be judged, every woman in the land, from the Queen down to the wife of the humblest labourer, was engaged in some needlework guild to provide shirts for

soldiers, socks for the men in the trenches, mufflers for the sailors keeping watch on the North Sea. There was scarcely a thing likely to be needed for the fighting men that was not made by the million by the women of Britain. A call came for sand-bags, and they were made till notice was issued that there was a surplus. Respirators were called for to guard the men from the poison gas when first used by Germans, and in a day there was a sufficiency. Thousands of women gave their time in huge depôts in preparing bandages for the wounded. All over the land the good work went on.

So came the great change in the social life of the people. Classes which previously were rarely in contact were now brought together, and were quick to appreciate each other's merits. There was no display of this friendliness ; it was only by recalling the state of things before the war that one was conscious of it. In true British fashion the nation continued to quarrel, to bicker, and grumble, but underneath it there lay a genuine strain of sympathy, a deep-sunk realisation that in the hours of stress the people were all brothers and sisters with common interests.

Unity in spite of grumbles

While all this was taking place in the social life of the people something like a miracle was being worked in the political life of the nation. The Liberals were in office when the war broke out, and a fortnight before the first shot was fired the whole energy of the Unionist Opposition was bent to overthrow Mr. Asquith and his Government. With the burst of war, party politics were put on one side as though locked in an iron safe. The first fortune of war, however, did not run to the advantage of Britain. We had been unprepared, and in the confusion of the first months there were very black days. The inadequacy of our armaments was not known to the outside public. But it was known to the leaders of the Unionist party. Had they cared to speak out they would have been able to hurl the Asquith Ministry from power. That, however, would have exposed the weak spots in Britain's armour at a time when the disclosure would have been of advantage to the enemy. Then facts began to leak out, sinister and damaging. Unionists remained dumb for, although there were things open to public discussion, they felt that if they made the attack there would be many of the public who would ascribe it to a revival of party spirit, a desire to do an injury to the political foe. No such charge, however,

The Coalition Ministry could be levelled against Liberals, whose faith was unimpeachable, but who felt it their duty, on patriotic grounds, to take the Government to task for remissness. The war had been in progress for nearly six months before this criticism found expression; but once it started it grew alarmingly, until scarcely a day passed when Ministers were not heckled about the conduct of the war by a sturdy and unappeasable band of Liberals. Then the Government did a bold thing. It invited the Unionist leaders to join in forming a Coalition Ministry. Unionists were aware

that if they held their hand there must be an upheaval which would mean the resignation of the Liberal Government. Unionists, knowing the state of things, were by no means eager to assume the responsibility for the war. To join the Liberals in a Coalition Ministry was distasteful. They would have to share the responsibility, at any rate, and later on they would be out of court if they desired to remind the Liberals that they had rejected advice which in pre-war days had been offered by the Opposition in **Liberals and Unionists** the interests of national defence. To **join hands** have held back, however, would have produced a political cataclysm, and that would have been a tragedy for Britain at such a time.

So a Coalition Government was formed. The Unionists went in because they felt it to be a duty and not because they had any appetite for it. There had to be a wholesale rearrangement of offices. Some of the former Ministers were given their congé in order to make a Government equally balanced of Liberals and Unionists, with Mr. Asquith remaining Prime Minister and Mr. Bonar Law second in command. Mr. Churchill who, rightly or wrongly, had been held responsible as First Lord of the Admiralty for the premature attempt to force a way through the Dardanelles, was allowed to withdraw, and Mr. Balfour, emerging from his retirement, took his place—but it was not long before Mr. Churchill, wearying of what he called "well-paid inactivity," in an office with no duties, resigned from the Government and went off for a period to fight in France. But here was a spectacle

A BEAUTIFUL ENGLISH RETREAT FOR MEN BROKEN IN FLANDERS.
Wounded soldiers and nurses taking the air in the gardens of Longleat, the beautiful, historic country seat of the Marquis and Marchioness of Bath, which was converted into a Red Cross hospital. This charming photograph shows the fountain before one of the entrances to Longleat.

which no one before had even dreamt of ever seeing—Mr. Asquith, Mr. Bonar Law, Mr. Lloyd George, Mr. Chamberlain, Mr. Arthur Henderson—for the Labour Party was also brought into the Coalition, though the Nationalists refused to enter—Lord Lansdowne, Mr. McKenna, Lord Curzon, Mr. Runciman, all members of the same Ministry. If it did not prove to be a strong Government it was unquestionably a representative Government—bearing in mind that the chiefs of the national administration are politicians.

In some quarters it was anticipated that the Coalition would secure the unabated confidence of every group of politicians. The old hatchets were buried, the truce was respected, and an arrangement was made that in Parliamentary vacancies somebody of the same **Criticism from** political views as the previous member **the Liberals** should be elected without any objection taken by the other party. For a time—but a very short time—Parliament was dazed by the existence of a Coalition. But the band of criticising Liberals still continued their criticism.

Back-bench Unionists, now that their own chiefs were sitting on the Treasury bench, were freed from the suspicion that they were actuated by party ties, and felt they need no longer be dumb. They brought to light grievances and pressed the Government on patriotic grounds. There was an unacknowledged compact between a group of Liberals and a group of Unionists to work in common, urging the Ministry to prosecute the war with much more energy than was apparently being done. The main body of the House of Commons gave the Government sturdy and loyal support ; but there were groups that kept up

A FALLING FIR.
Members of the famous Canadian Foresters Battalion who were employed in felling Scotch firs in Windsor Great Park. This timber was principally used for consolidating trenches in Flanders.

CONSCRIPTION OF LOGS.
Many splendid fir-trees from the Royal estate at Windsor were requisitioned for service at the front. The comprehensive system of trenches which developed throughout the long months of siege warfare exacted a heavy toll of timber. This photograph shows one of the officers in charge of the soldier-lumbermen.

guerilla attack on the administration until there was a very real though unorganised Opposition.

Now and then there were occasions when the Unionist party as a whole seemed to be in antagonism to the Ministry. Mr. Bonar Law was compelled to say quite openly that he entered the Coalition as the representative of the Unionist party, but that the day he recognised he was a member of a Government that had not the support of the Unionist party he would leave the Government. Innumerable were the points, generally indicating slackness and lack of foresight, that were made against the Ministry. But gradually one grew in importance, until it overshadowed all the rest—the failure of the voluntary system and the necessity to adopt conscription in order to get a sufficiency of recruits for the Army.

There had long been a party in Britain, chiefly amongst Unionists, favourable to national military service in case we were ever threatened with invasion. It may be said that as a whole the Liberal, Labour, and Nationalist parties were strenuously opposed to what they believed was the thin end of the wedge for the establishment in Britain of the Continental system of military conscription.

Imperative circumstances now compelled many Liberals to abandon their former attitude. So the country was divided into two camps—those who saw that the only solution of the recruiting problem was the adoption of compulsion, and those who clung to **Voluntaryism** the belief that all the men necessary **on trial** could be obtained by appeal and who contended that we could not allow an unlimited number of men to go into the Army because, as finance played so important a part in modern war, we must keep our industries going and our overseas commerce maintained. Our Allies could afford men better than we could, for we were doing our full share in securing the freedom of the seas, in finding money for the Allies and providing them with war material. To save a rupture every opportunity was given to allow the voluntary system to justify itself. News of big battles was always an incentive to recruiting. But

ROYAL HOSPITALITY FOR SOLDIERS.
The Royal Riding School building at Buckingham Palace was utilised as a Rest for Soldiers arriving at Victoria from the front.

COMFORTS OF CIVILISATION.
Soldiers from the front availing themselves of a welcome refresher after the long journey from Trench Town.

when something like 3,000,000 men had been secured—a truly wonderful record in itself—it was felt that the best of Britain's manhood had answered the call.

It was obvious that millions of other men lagged behind for a multitude of reasons into which it is now needless to inquire too deeply. There was anger in the public mind when it came out that thousands of lads were going into munition factories and into trades which must be continued whatever happened, such as coal-mining, with the expectation that if compulsion did come they at any rate would escape military service. There was even a "boom" in marriage, for it was reckoned that, whoever **Modified compulsion** was press-ganged, married men would **adopted** be allowed to go free. To back up the "voluntary" system some not very creditable methods were adopted. A register was taken of the manhood of the country, so that some official calculation could be made of national resources in men of military age. All kinds of pressure were exerted to induce young men, without responsibilities, to enter the Army. There were parades to stimulate imagination. There were patriotic meetings. A variety of illustrated posters, many in bad taste, were plastered on the hoardings to shame the sluggards.

The result of all this propaganda was not satisfactory. Reluctantly the Government was obliged to adopt modified compulsion. With few exceptions it was accepted by the country as the right course, though the Labour party was suspicious that it might be the forerunner of compulsion in regard to labour, to which they were vehemently opposed. The strictest pledges were extracted from the Prime Minister and others that it would not be so. Upon this an appeal was made to the younger married men of the country to attest their willingness to serve after the supply of available single men had been exhausted, and there was a truly magnificent response.

But when calculations began to be made of the number of unmarried men in the country and of those who could be called upon to join the Army a startling discrepancy revealed itself. The explanation was that there existed an extraordinary number of "reserved occupations," **Grievance of the married** trades which Ministers, who had nothing directly to do with the war, decided must not be touched and into which literally thousands of men had gone to avoid military service. Indignation began to show itself. It burst furiously when attested married men were called upon to report themselves. They were willing to fight for their country, but they had been promised deliberately and in set terms that unmarried men should go first. These married men, commanded to throw up their trades and businesses and respond to their undertaking, felt they had been tricked when thousands upon thousands of the others, with no

A LABOUR OF LOVE.
Headguards for their soldier brothers. Women in a steel-helmet factory about to pack some of the shrapnel-proof casques.

LAMPS FOR THE NAVY.
Helping to keep up naval supremacy. Girl workers finishing signal lamps for use in the Grand Fleet.

responsibilities, were allowed to remain behind and make "good money."

On the whole the Government acted tenderly to the young men in Great Britain, providing all kinds of exemptions. What surprised many people was the total exemption of young men who reached eighteen years of age after August, 1915, thus turning the tap against what would have been a constant stream of sturdy young recruits. An agitation swept through the land which the Government could not ignore. So strenuous was the objection to what was believed to be the Government's unfairness that the Ministry had to yield, considerably reduce the number of "reserved occupations," and proceed with vigour to "comb out" the lads who had taken shelter in munition works when their places could be taken without detriment by older men or by women. So the attested men, though not appeased, were reconciled.

Even then, all likely recruits counted, the War Office said there were not enough to meet increasing military requirements. So another agitation was started, represented in the current phrase "equality of sacri-**"Equality of** fice." Why should married men with **sacrifice"** heavy claims, possibly several children, be sent to fight, even if they had volunteered, while other married men, possibly with few claims, were permitted to stay at home? The movement for general all round compulsion grew apace. The hard fact of shortage of men converted the Government. It was not clear, however, that Parliament would be converted without the information which the Cabinet possessed and which could not in the national interest be made public.

So Parliament had two secret sittings, and members of both Houses, sworn not to divulge what they were told, had the facts presented. But it soon leaked out there was nothing in the facts which well-informed persons had not known before. The Government introduced another bit of piecemeal compulsion, securing all lads as they reached eighteen years and compelling time-expired soldiers to remain with the Colours—a flagrant piece of injustice, for they had done their contracted **Injustice to time-** "bit" and were called upon to do more **expired men** while thousands of their countrymen had done nothing. Still another endeavour was made to whip up married volunteers, so that there should be a regular supply of soldiers. The endeavour failed. General compulsion had to come, applicable to all men married or unmarried of military age—a compulsion which did not mean that all such men should join the Army, but which gave the military authorities the right to call up all those who were not able to prove they were engaged in some service necessary to the State during war time. Great Britain became a conscript nation.

This was by no means the end of the astonishing transformations brought about during the first two years of the war. The negation of political controversy opened the way for what was nothing short of topsy-turvydom. No sooner had the people got used to living under a political party truce than the question began to be asked: Why should the United Kingdom be managed by professional politicians? The nagging, querulous debates in Parliament, constant talk without very much to show for it, disgusted a considerable section of the population.

BRITISH SOLDIERS BLINDED IN THE WAR LISTENING TO A CONCERT AT ST. DUNSTAN'S HOME, REGENT'S PARK.

OFFICIAL RECOGNITION OF THE NATIONAL VOLUNTEER RESERVE.
Following upon their official recognition, Lord French reviewed ten thousand men of the National Volunteer Reserve in Hyde Park on June 17th, 1916. In circle: Lord French with General Sir Moore O'Creagh.

differences of opinion, squabbling and inertia in dealing with national matters, there was unquestionably a zealous desire to press on. In order to meet the huge cost of the war, the heaviest taxation was imposed upon the nation and borne without a whimper. Old political principles, by which men had held as firmly as by the tenets of their religious faith, were thrown into the melting-pot. Many men saw a number of their most precious articles of political belief swept ruthlessly away by the sea of necessity. For three generations Britain had been a Free Trade country. Liberals had fought fiercely for ten years against the arguments of Unionists that we should adopt a tariff policy. But it was a Liberal Free Trade Chancellor of the Exchequer who proceeded to put heavy tariffs on a variety of imported articles, non-essential and mainly associated with pleasure, partly to raise revenue, but chiefly to keep them out of Britain, so that the money might be kept here and the ships be employed in carrying more useful freights. The Board of Trade put an embargo on a number of goods that could not be counted as essentials. Some men in the House of Commons were aghast at this departure from Britain's traditional policy; indeed, the accusation was made that Liberal Ministers had sold the Free Trade fort to Unionist Ministers.

The answer was a repudiation, with the argument added that this was not the time to talk of principles, but of doing whatever was considered requisite to win the war. Throughout the commercial community there gradually spread conviction that following the war there would be a trade war, with Germany again as the enemy.

Complacent and old dry bones were shaken, and there came a determination to shackle German trade, so that it should be unable to injure British commerce in the future. Though how this was to be made operative was vague, there was a growing consensus of opinion that with peace British ports would no longer be open for the free ingress of German goods, but that the heaviest toll should be imposed, even if they were not prohibited altogether. Thus under war conditions marvellous changes were taking place in the political and social life of the country. Landmarks in policy were uprooted. Everybody knew we would never be able to return to the old conditions of life even were it desirable. Germany had done much harm; but she had been beneficial in directions she had never contemplated. The war had consolidated the British Empire. Germany provided the nations within the Empire with a better understanding of the relationship in which they must stand to each other. The war stirred national sentiment; it broke down social barriers; it revealed weak spots in our character which had to be repaired, and it produced a stern patriotism that remained firm despite obstacles. It transformed Great Britain. The war cleared away the mists that had been gathering round the Empire, and brought forward the vision of a strenuous, democratic Imperialism.

Parliament sank low in popular esteem. It was quite usual to hear old party men declare they had done with party politics for ever. And as the Government, while well supported, was not giving general satisfaction, a spirit of antagonism began to display itself. The various political parties, though under a truce not to resist each other in having M.P.'s of the same complexion returned at by-elections, could not debar outsiders from challenging the return of what was called the National Government candidate, were he Liberal or Unionist.

Independent Parliamentary candidates
So when by-elections occurred, independents, voicing the feeling of discontent, jumped into the field and forced contests. These revealed a gathering tide of dissatisfaction, especially with British inadequacy in air defence, with the result that in one particular constituency an "air candidate" was returned by a striking majority over the candidate who had been supported by the full force of the Coalition.

From all this it must not be assumed that Parliament was not doing good work. It did an immense amount of service in the organisation of the country to meet the exigencies of war conditions. At the back of all the